THE CRB COMMODITY YEARBOOK 2000

BRIDGE Information Systems, Inc.

John Wiley & Sons, Inc.
New York • Chichester • Weinheim • Brisbane • Singapore • Toronto

Published by John Wiley & Sons, Inc.

ISBN 0-471-38260-4

Printed in the United States of America
10 9 8 7 6 5 4 3 2 1

Bridge Commodity Research Bureau
30 South Wacker Drive, Suite 1810
Chicago IL 60606
312-454-1801
800-621-5271
http://www.crbindex.com
E-mail: crbinfo@bridge.com

TABLE OF CONTENTS

The first Commodity Year Book was published in 1939 by a then five year old company known as Commodity Research Bureau, Inc. To mark the passing of the 20th Century, we have reproduced here the Introduction that appeared in Commodity Year Book 1939.

INTRODUCTION

This book was designed to fill a definite need for a comprehensive, up-to-date reference work on commodities. Although the Bureau is primarily a private and independent service organization which analyzes commodities and their price movements for client subscribers, in recent years it has had an added status, namely, as a semi-public clearinghouse for commodity information. Thousands of requests for specific information have been received from commodity brokers, merchants, banks, advertising agencies, financial experts, industrial purchasing agents, universities, etc. While answering these questions, the staff of the Bureau was in an excellent position to note exactly what information was needed.

The great volume of questions indicated clearly that there existed a pressing need for some adequate reference material on commodities. The editors analyzed all available sources of information. There were many publications covering one or two commodities and in some cases publications covered one or two groups. Nowhere was there an all-inclusive compilation. The solution was then obvious – a year book to cover all the important commodities on which information was so sorely needed, i.e., farm products, metals, tropical products, etc.

The commodities covered were chosen only after much deliberation and consultation as to the needs of the majority of business men. As far as possible, contents are confined to factual data from official and semi-official sources. To obtain the high degree of accuracy necessary in such a compilation, all material was carefully checked and re-checked by experts in the various fields.

We have drawn heavily on the statistical series of many competent sources, particularly from governmental agencies. The editors acknowledge and are grateful for the valuable contributions these organizations have made toward the successful completion of this volume. Without their cooperation this work would have been impossible.

While this is the first Commodity Year Book, our plan is to publish a new book annually. Accordingly, Commodity Year Book-1940 will come off the press early in 1940. It will contain many special features, in addition to having complete up-to-date statistics. All suggestions in regard to additional commodity listings or proposed subjects for research will be highly appreciated for guidance in preparing the 1940 edition.

Commodity Research Bureau, Inc.

ACKNOWLEDGEMENTS

The editors wish to thank the following for source material:

Agricultural Marketing Service (AMS)
Agricultural Research Service (ARS)
American Bureau of Metal Statistics, Inc. (ABMS)
American Forest & Paper Association (AF & PA)
The American Gas Association (AGA)
American Iron and Steel Institute (AISI)
American Metal Market (AMM)
Bureau of the Census
Bureau of Economic Analysis (BEA)
Bureau of Labor Statistics (BLS)
Chicago Board of Trade (CBT)
Chicago Mercantile Exchange (CME / IMM / IOM)
Coffee, Sugar & Cocoa Exchange (CSCE)
Commodity Credit Corporation (CCC)
Commodity Futures Trading Commision (CFTC)
The Conference Board
Economic Research Service (ERS)
Edison Electric Institute (EEI)
E D & F Man Cocoa Ltd
Farm Service Agency (FSA)
Federal Reserve Bank of St. Louis
Fiber Economics Bureau, Inc.
Florida Department of Citrus
Food and Agriculture Organization of the United Nations (FAO)
Foreign Agricultural Service (FAS)
Futures Industry Association (FIA)
International Cotton Advisory Committee (ICAC)
International Rubber Study Group (IRSG)
Johnson Matthey
Kansas City Board of Trade (KCBT)
Leather Industries of America
MidAmerica Commodity Exchange (MidAm)
Minneapolis Grain Exchange (MGE)
National Agricultural Statistics Service (NASS)
National Coffee Association of U.S.A., Inc. (NCA)
New York Cotton Exchange (NYCE / NYFE / FINEX)
New York Mercantile Exchange (NYMEX) Commodity Exchange, Inc. (COMEX)
Oil World
The Organisation for Economic Co-Operation and Development (OECD)
Random Lengths
The Silver Institute
The Society of the Plastics Industry, Inc. (SPI)
United Nations (UN)
United States Department of Agriculture (USDA)
United States Geological Survey (USGS)
Wall Street Journal (WSJ)
Winnipeg Commodity Exchange (WCE)

THE COMMODITY PRICE TREND

In 1999, the Bridge Commodity Research Bureau's Futures Price Index snapped a streak of three consecutive losing years and posted the first annual increase since 1995. The December 31, 1999 closing value of 205.14 was 13.92 points higher, or 7.28 percent, above the December 31, 1998 closing level of 191.22. While the Index was able to post a gain for the year, the closing level was still among the lowest closes registered in the last 25 years. Commodity prices, in general, remained at very depressed levels at yearend with the exception of the energy group which rose sharply in 1999.

For the year, four of the six Bridge/CRB Futures Price Subindices posted gains. The energy group advanced the most rising over 82 percent for the year. The soft group displayed the weakest performance of the six, falling over 18 percent year-on-year.

Energy

The Energy subindex rose 82.88 percent in 1999, led by a 112 percent gain in the price of crude oil from $12.05 per barrel at the end of 1998, to $25.60 per barrel at the end of 1999. Heating oil rose 101.37 percent on the year and natural gas prices posted a 19.74 percent year-on-year increase. Interestingly, the energy group had turned in the weakest performance among all subindex groups in 1998.

Crude oil and heating oil both trended consistently higher throughout 1999, setting their lows in February and their highs in November. Natural gas prices followed a similar path, although a steep decline during November cut its price nearly in half.

Crude oil prices responded to a production cutback agreement reached by members of the Organization of Petroleum Exporting Countries (OPEC) late in 1998. Unlike previous production cutting agreements OPEC nations had drafted in recent years, the 1998 accord drew the participation of all members and succeeded in withdrawing excess supplies from the market. The decline in available supplies occurred simultaneously with rising demand from those countries affected by the 1997 global currency crisis and forced prices sharply higher throughout the year.

Grains

The Grains subindex ended 1999 with yet another loss, its fourth consecutive losing year. The 9.11 percent decline left the index at 157.09, the lowest yearly closing value since 1972. All three component commodities lost ground on the year, with soybeans registering the largest decline of 14.13 percent. Wheat lost 10.05 percent and corn was down 4.22 percent for the year.

Global demand for grain continued slack in 1999, continuing the trend that began in late 1997 when Pacific Rim economies were rocked by currency crisis. The burdensome supplies that resulted from the crisis did begin to shrink in 1999, but it will be another year or two before they fall to pre-crisis levels.

Industrials

The Industrial subindex managed a small 4.09 percent gain in 1999, snapping a two-year losing streak. Strength in copper, which rose 28.42 percent in 1999, was balanced by a 15.94 percent decline in cotton, the group's other component.

Copper prices rebounded from the 11-year lows reached in 1998 due to increased demand from Pacific Rim nations and cutbacks in production from leading producers. Cotton prices continued weak on slack demand in spite of back-to-back below average U.S. crops.

Livestock

The Livestock subindex rose 28.34 percent in 1999, reversing a sharp 21.59 percent decline the prior year. Lean hog prices rebounded from thirty-year lows at the end of 1998 and registered a 66.92 percent increase for the year. Live cattle, the other livestock index component, gained 15 percent in 1999.

U.S. consumers, confident in both the economy and their own prosperity, consumed larger amounts pork and beef in 1999. A reemergence of "Steak Houses" combined with fast-food restaurants featuring bacon on their sandwiches to put upward pressure on meat and livestock prices.

Precious Metals

The Precious Metals subindex rose 7.52 percent in 1999. Platinum was the strongest component gaining 18.02 percent, silver rose 8.63 percent while gold rose just 0.14 percent.

Irregular and reduced exports of palladium from Russia sparked sharp gains in both palladium and platinum prices and influenced silver higher as well.

Softs

The Softs subindex fell by 18.85 percent in 1999, the weakest among the CRB family of sub-indices. Three of the four components declined. Cocoa fell 39.30 percent, sugar fell 22.14 percent and orange juice fell 12.62 percent. Coffee prices bucked the downward movement by rising 6.92 percent for the year.

Large supplies resulting from the slack global demand for commodities in late 1997 and 1998 contributed to the weakness in cocoa, sugar and orange juice prices. Coffee prices moved higher in late 1999 as dry weather in Brazil during the critical flowering stage for the 2000-01 crop caused widespread damage.

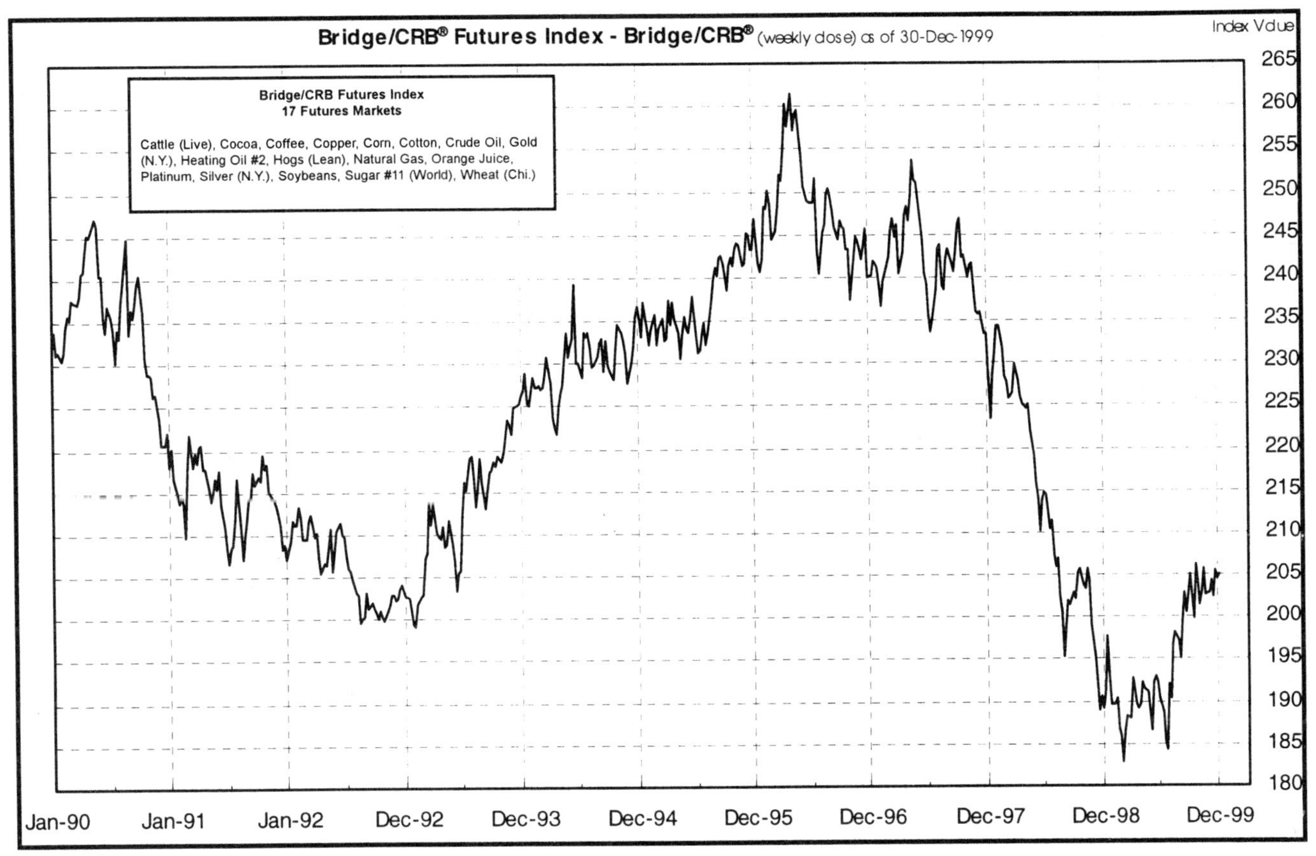

Monthly Bridge/CRB Futures Index High, Low and Close (1967=100)

Year		Jan.	Feb.	Mar.	Apr.	May	June	Jule	Aug.	Sept.	Oct.	Nov.	Dec.	Range
1989	High	251.6	243.3	248.1	244.6	242.8	235.4	237.0	225.5	226.8	228.1	231.7	229.9	251.6
	Low	241.1	236.6	241.7	237.7	229.4	227.9	221.2	221.5	222.9	223.0	226.0	225.6	221.2
	Close	242.4	243.2	242.1	238.0	229.4	234.4	221.2	225.5	226.8	225.7	228.8	229.9	------
1990	High	235.1	236.3	239.0	245.8	247.8	241.2	240.0	244.7	239.8	242.0	231.1	223.8	247.8
	Low	228.8	229.9	234.2	238.4	241.5	233.8	230.3	233.1	234.9	228.6	223.2	220.1	220.1
	Close	229.9	234.6	238.2	245.8	241.5	236.9	235.0	233.7	239.2	229.8	223.3	222.6	------
1991	High	222.8	215.6	221.8	222.2	217.0	217.7	214.1	216.5	217.6	219.8	218.6	213.9	222.8
	Low	214.1	209.7	217.3	216.2	214.1	208.4	205.9	204.7	211.9	216.2	213.3	207.2	204.7
	Close	214.1	215.6	218.5	216.2	215.4	208.4	214.1	211.8	215.6	218.2	213.3	208.1	------
1992	High	212.2	215.3	212.9	210.3	211.7	212.9	209.1	204.9	203.5	202.9	203.6	204.3	215.3
	Low	206.9	207.2	208.6	204.5	204.9	208.0	203.0	198.2	199.3	199.1	199.2	201.2	198.2
	Close	211.2	209.6	209.8	204.8	208.0	209.3	203.1	201.0	200.4	199.9	203.1	202.8	------
1993	High	203.2	204.9	214.3	213.9	211.8	210.0	219.7	223.5	217.8	220.6	223.8	226.8	226.8
	Low	199.3	198.4	203.4	207.8	207.4	202.6	207.2	212.1	211.9	216.6	217.4	218.4	198.4
	Close	199.5	202.9	212.5	210.9	208.7	207.1	219.3	217.2	216.1	218.4	218.0	226.3	------
1994	High	229.8	229.2	231.0	227.8	239.2	239.7	234.7	235.4	234.4	235.2	234.7	237.2	239.7
	Low	226.2	225.7	227.4	227.8	225.2	235.9	230.4	228.0	228.6	227.0	228.8	227.0	225.2
	Close	225.6	227.6	227.7	225.0	235.5	230.4	233.7	231.9	229.9	233.3	229.2	236.6	------
1995	High	238.0	236.2	236.9	237.7	237.1	238.0	235.9	240.3	245.8	242.7	244.5	246.5	246.5
	Low	232.6	231.0	231.1	233.2	229.6	232.2	229.3	231.7	239.4	238.3	240.9	240.9	229.3
	Close	232.8	234.3	232.9	235.3	232.7	233.4	233.2	240.0	241.7	242.2	241.8	243.2	------
1996	High	247.6	251.2	253.5	263.8	261.2	252.9	251.9	252.0	250.4	249.6	247.1	246.9	263.8
	Low	238.6	245.6	242.7	250.2	251.8	246.6	240.1	242.8	243.1	237.8	236.0	238.1	236.0
	Close	247.5	248.8	251.4	256.1	254.1	248.7	242.0	249.5	245.6	237.8	243.4	239.6	------
1997	High	244.3	243.9	248.0	249.0	254.8	250.0	243.4	245.3	244.5	247.6	243.5	238.4	254.8
	Low	238.9	236.1	241.6	237.6	245.5	238.5	232.0	236.7	240.0	238.3	235.3	228.8	228.8
	Close	239.0	242.4	245.2	248.3	251.0	239.4	242.8	242.0	243.1	240.0	235.9	229.1	------
1998	High	235.4	236.1	231.7	229.1	226.7	216.8	216.8	207.5	205.0	206.6	206.7	197.3	236.1
	Low	221.6	224.0	223.0	223.4	214.0	208.4	206.0	195.2	196.3	201.3	195.2	187.9	187.9
	Close	234.3	227.7	228.9	224.0	215.9	214.6	206.0	195.7	203.3	203.3	195.4	191.2	------

Source: Bridge/Commodity Research Bureau (CRB)

Bridge/CRB Indices

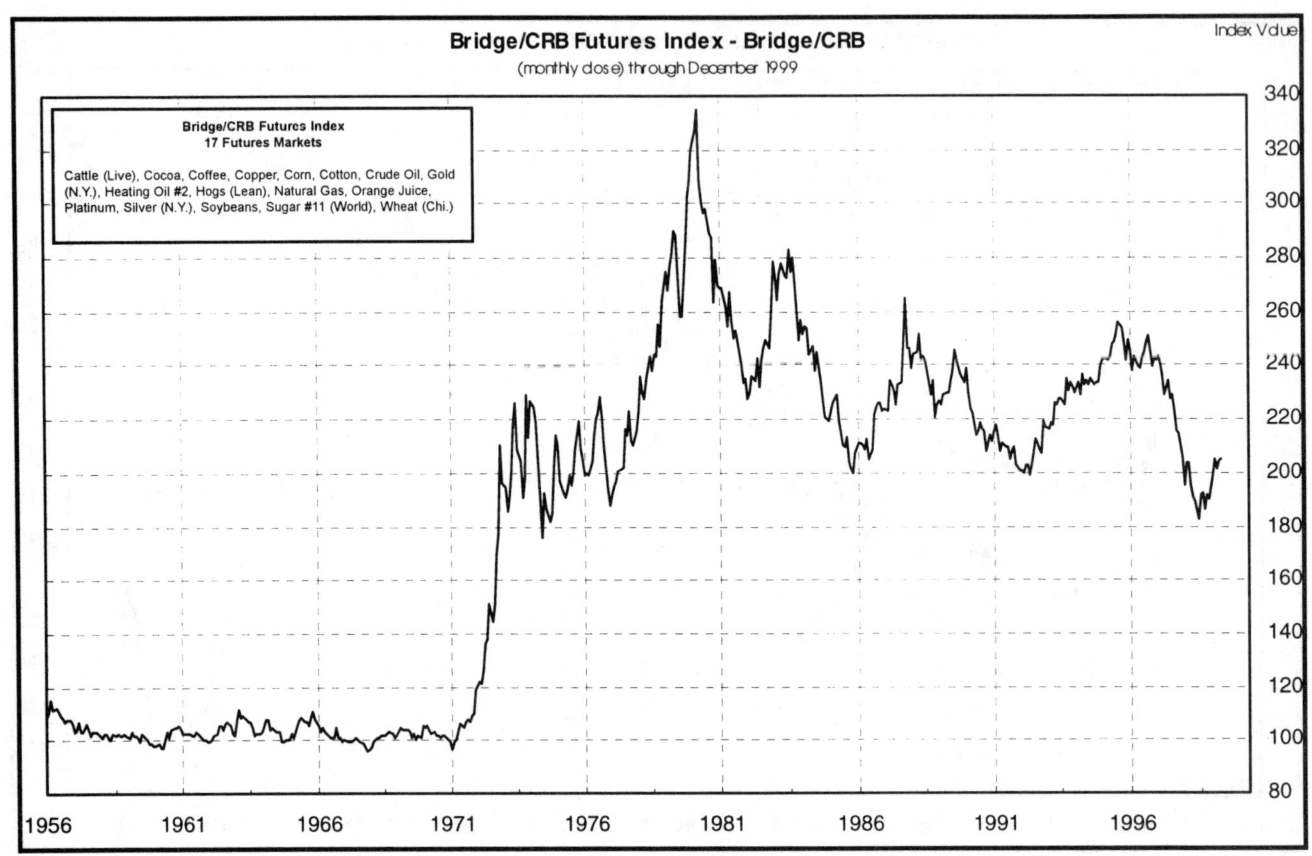

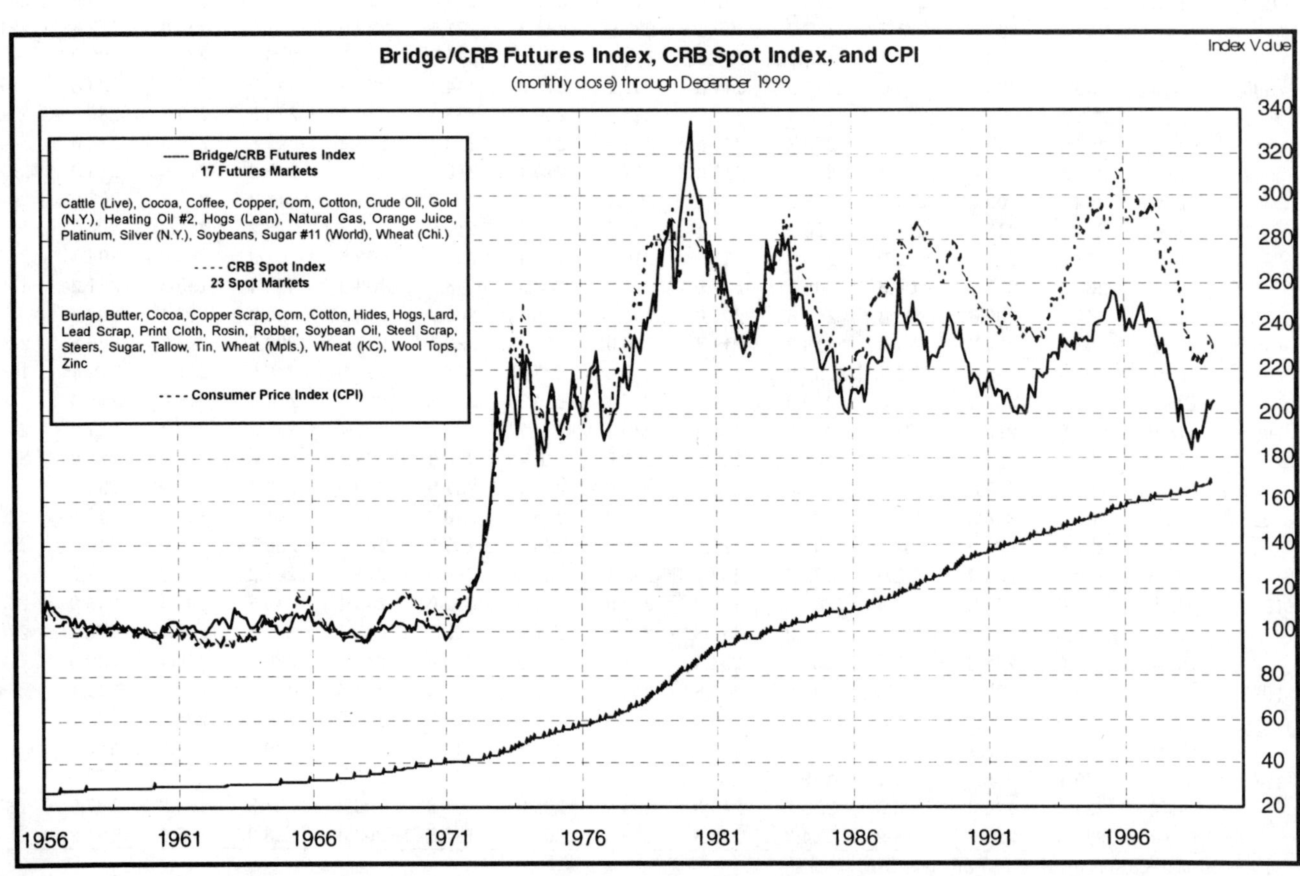

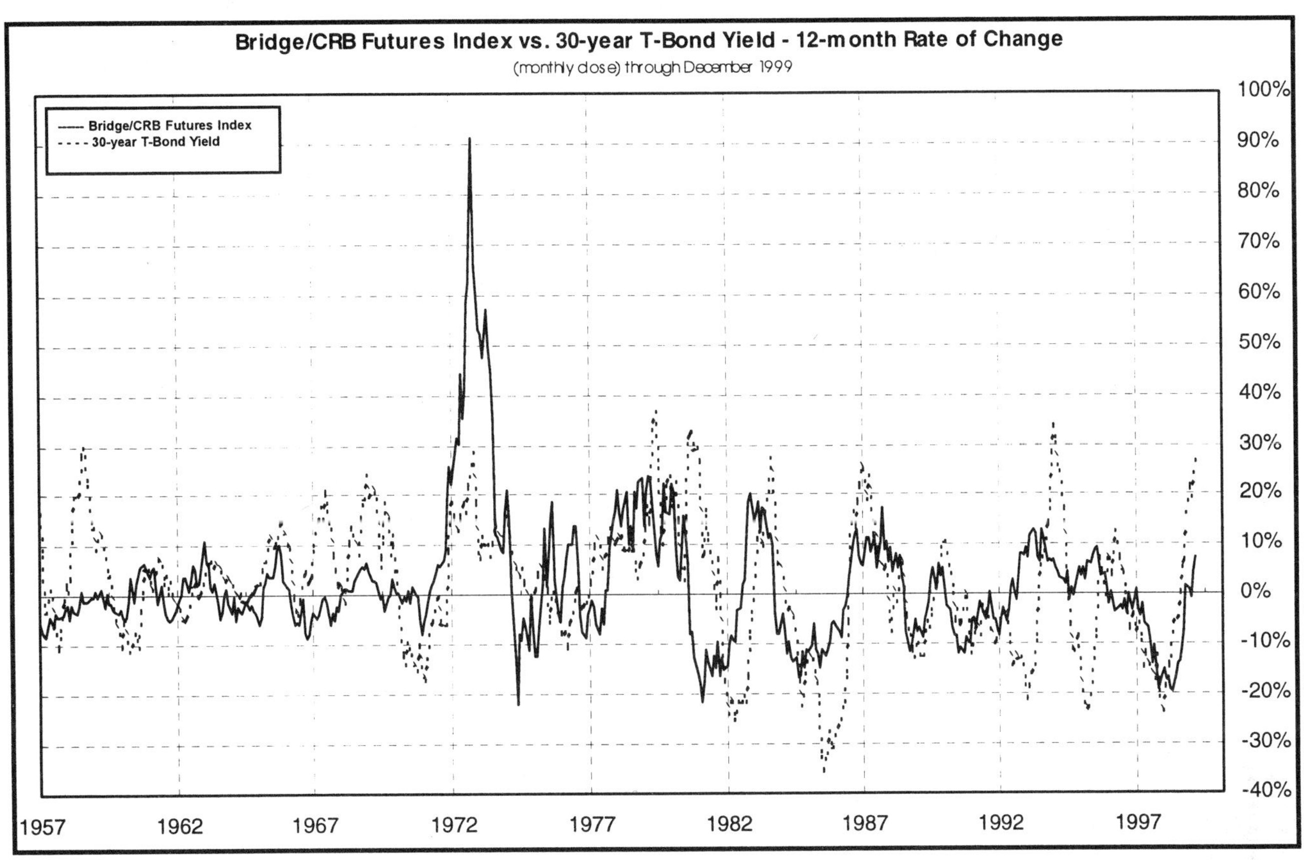
Bridge/CRB Futures Index vs. 30-year T-Bond Yield - 12-month Rate of Change
(monthly close) through December 1999
Bridge/CRB Futures Index
30-year T-Bond Yield
100%
90%
80%
70%
60%
50%
40%
30%
20%
10%
0%
-10%
-20%
-30%
-40%
1957
1962
1967
1972
1977
1982
1987
1992
1997

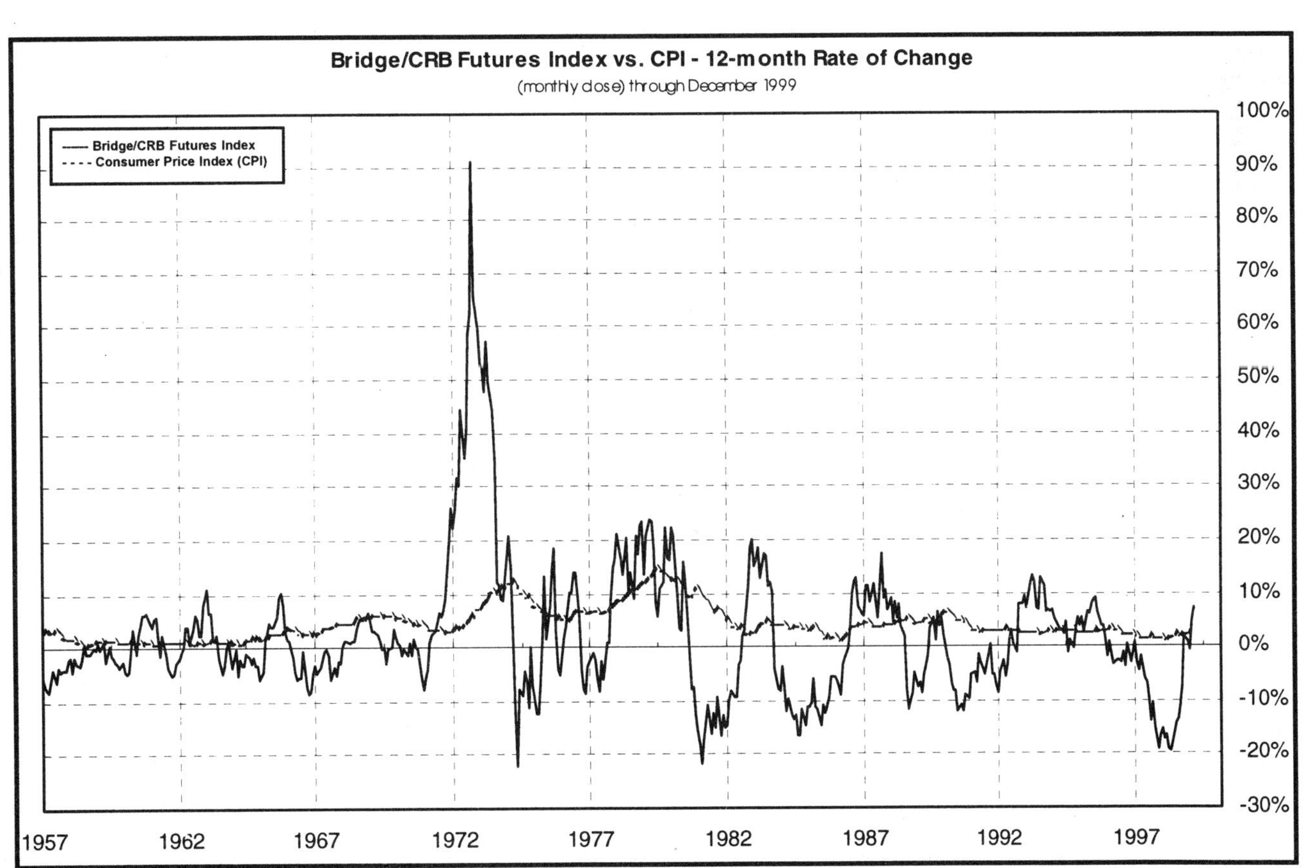
Bridge/CRB Futures Index vs. CPI - 12-month Rate of Change
(monthly close) through December 1999
Bridge/CRB Futures Index
Consumer Price Index (CPI)
100%
90%
80%
70%
60%
50%
40%
30%
20%
10%
0%
-10%
-20%
-30%
1957
1962
1967
1972
1977
1982
1987
1992
1997

Bridge/CRB® Total Return Index (weekly close) as of 30-Dec-1999
Index Value
240
230
220
210
200
190
180
170
160
150
140
Jan-90
Jan-91
Jan-92
Dec-92
Dec-93
Dec-94
Dec-95
Dec-96
Dec-97
Dec-98
Dec-99

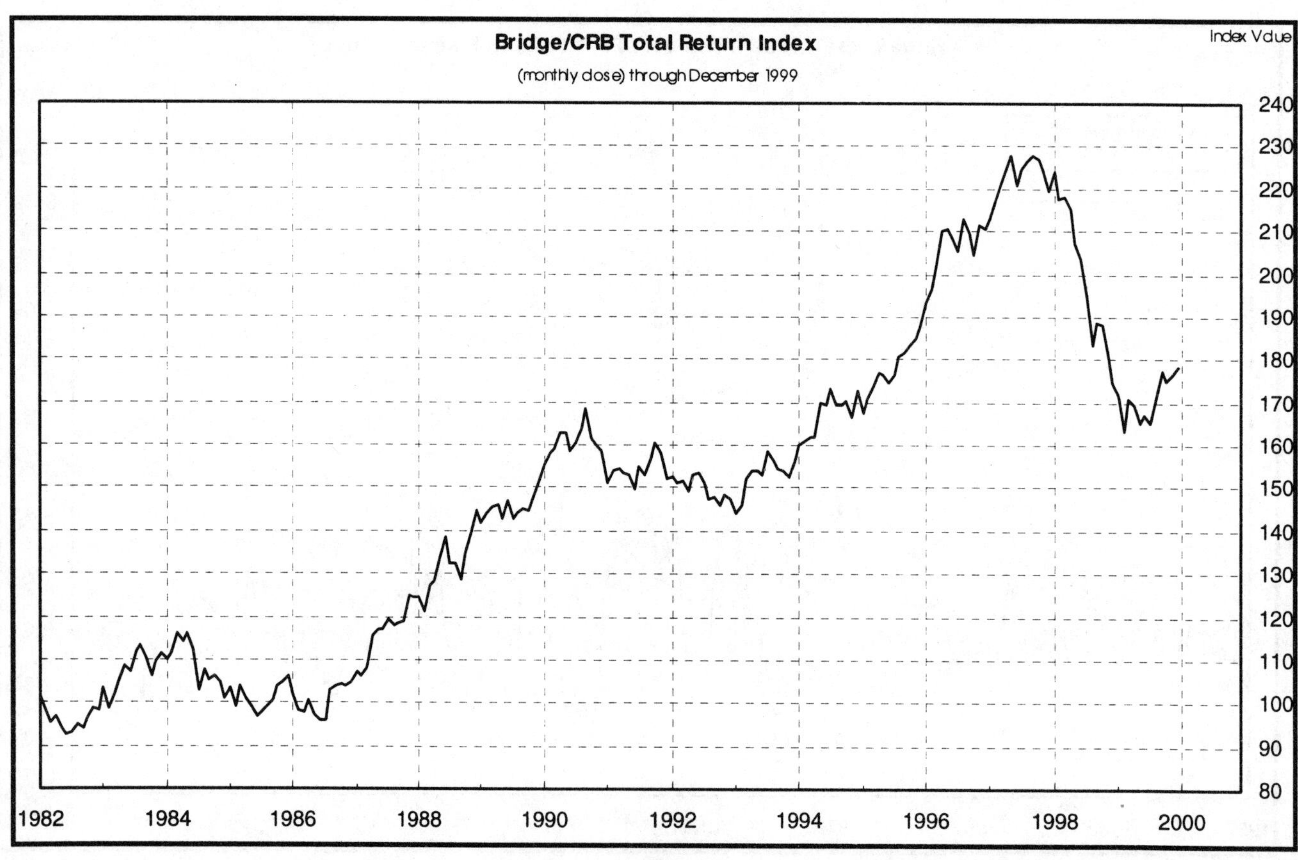
Bridge/CRB Total Return Index
(monthly close) through December 1999
Index Value
240
230
220
210
200
190
180
170
160
150
140
130
120
110
100
90
80
1982
1984
1986
1988
1990
1992
1994
1996
1998
2000

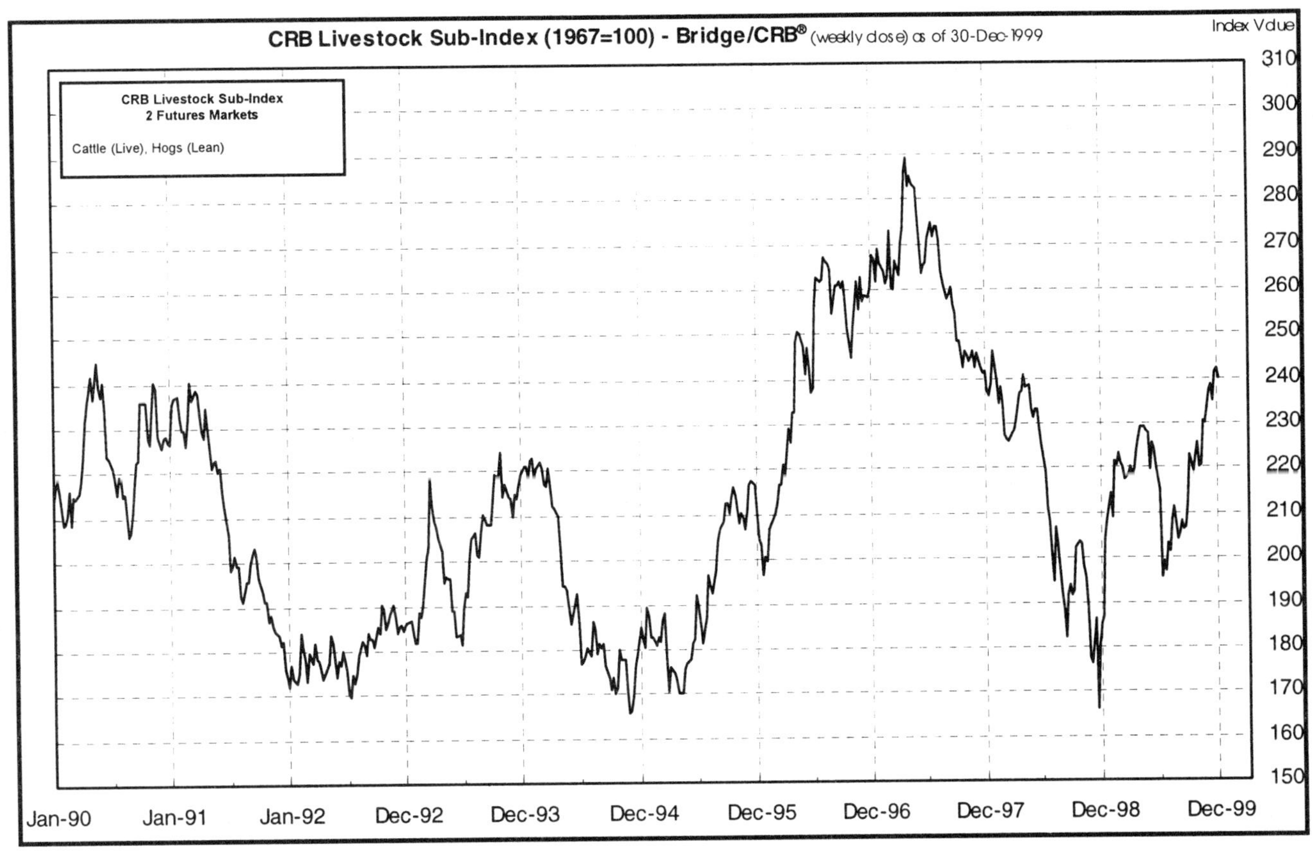
CRB Livestock Sub-Index (1967=100) - Bridge/CRB® (weekly close) as of 30-Dec-1999
Index Value
CRB Livestock Sub-Index
2 Futures Markets
Cattle (Live), Hogs (Lean)
310
300
290
280
270
260
250
240
230
220
210
200
190
180
170
160
150
Jan-90
Jan-91
Jan-92
Dec-92
Dec-93
Dec-94
Dec-95
Dec-96
Dec-97
Dec-98
Dec-99

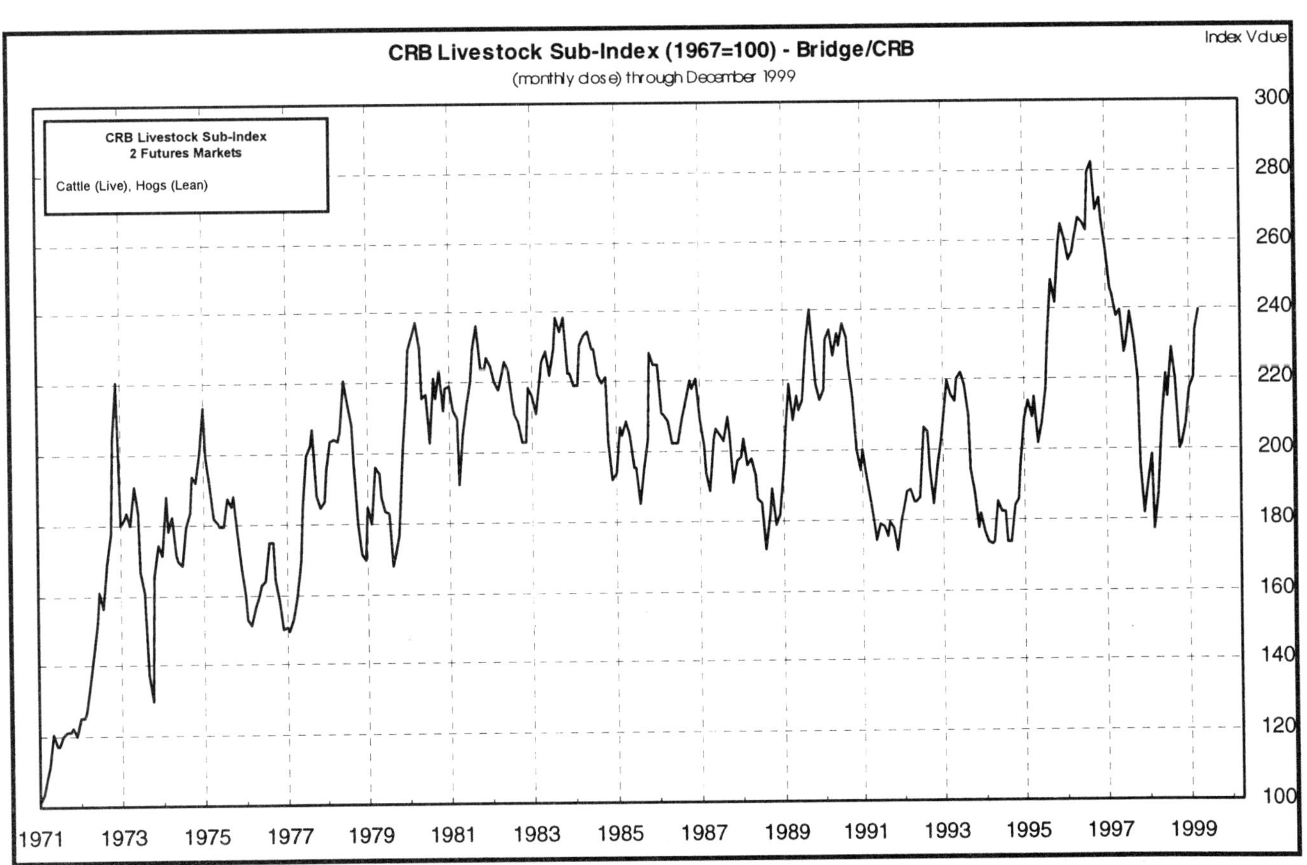
CRB Livestock Sub-Index (1967=100) - Bridge/CRB
(monthly close) through December 1999
Index Value
CRB Livestock Sub-Index
2 Futures Markets
Cattle (Live), Hogs (Lean)
300
280
260
240
220
200
180
160
140
120
100
1971
1973
1975
1977
1979
1981
1983
1985
1987
1989
1991
1993
1995
1997
1999

CRB Grains and Oilseeds Sub-Index (1967=100) - Bridge/CRB® (weekly close) as of 30-Dec-1999
Index Value
CRB Grains and Oilseeds Sub-Index
3 Futures Markets
Corn, Soybeans, Wheat (Chi.)
340
320
300
280
260
240
220
200
180
160
140
120
Jan-90
Jan-91
Jan-92
Dec-92
Dec-93
Dec-94
Dec-95
Dec-96
Dec-97
Dec-98
Dec-99

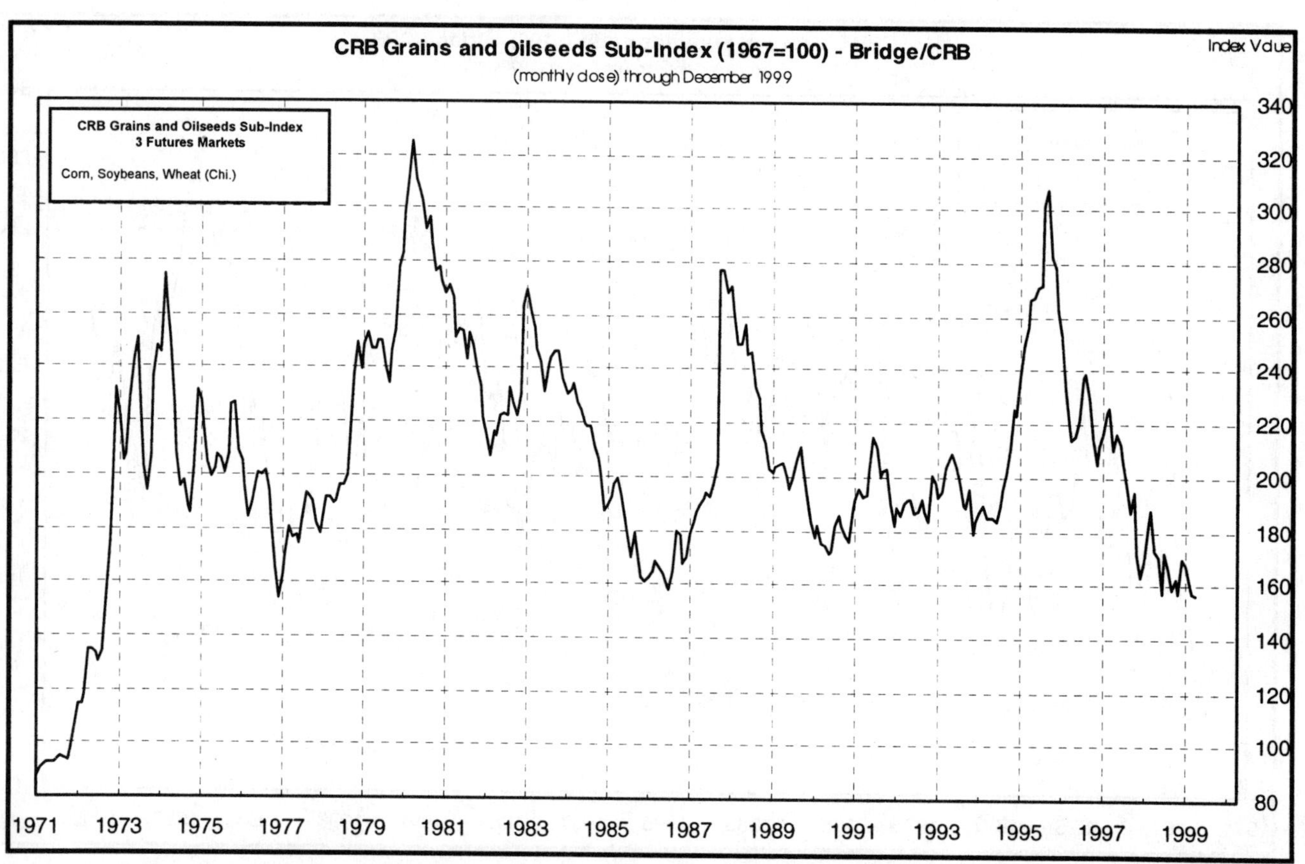
CRB Grains and Oilseeds Sub-Index (1967=100) - Bridge/CRB
(monthly close) through December 1999
Index Value
CRB Grains and Oilseeds Sub-Index
3 Futures Markets
Corn, Soybeans, Wheat (Chi.)
340
320
300
280
260
240
220
200
180
160
140
120
100
80
1971
1973
1975
1977
1979
1981
1983
1985
1987
1989
1991
1993
1995
1997
1999

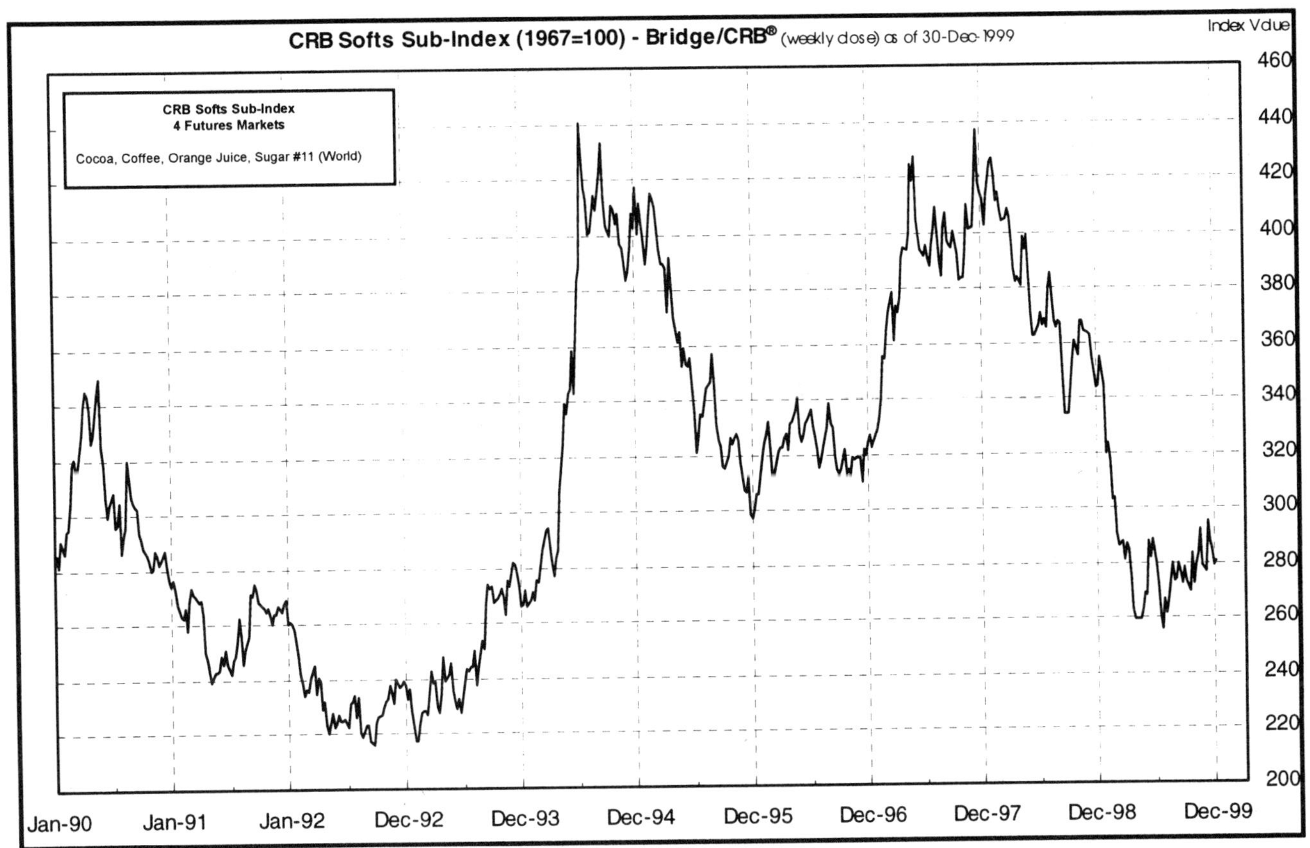
CRB Softs Sub-Index (1967=100) - Bridge/CRB® (weekly close) as of 30-Dec-1999
Index Value
CRB Softs Sub-Index
4 Futures Markets
Cocoa, Coffee, Orange Juice, Sugar #11 (World)
460
440
420
400
380
360
340
320
300
280
260
240
220
200
Jan-90
Jan-91
Jan-92
Dec-92
Dec-93
Dec-94
Dec-95
Dec-96
Dec-97
Dec-98
Dec-99

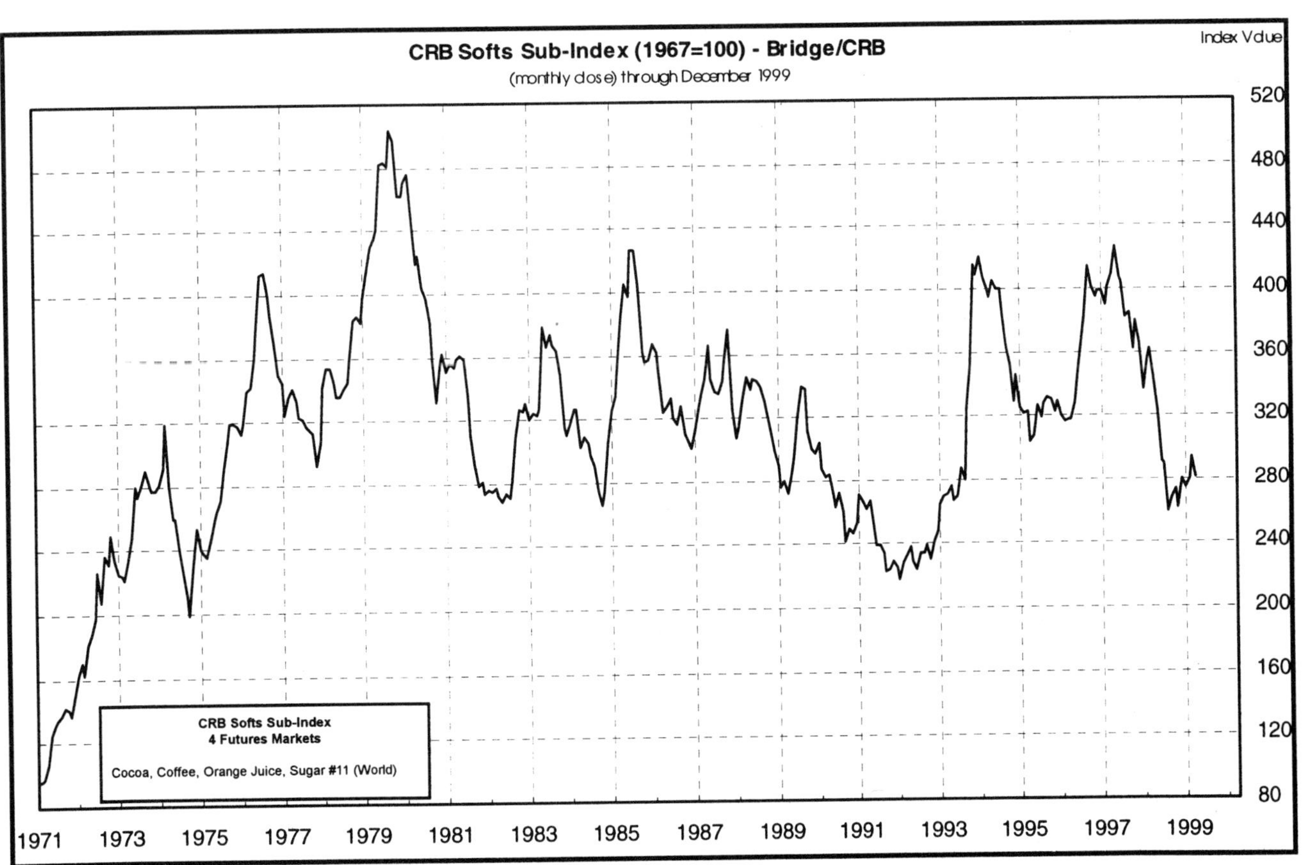
CRB Softs Sub-Index (1967=100) - Bridge/CRB
(monthly close) through December 1999
Index Value
520
480
440
400
360
320
280
240
200
160
120
80
CRB Softs Sub-Index
4 Futures Markets
Cocoa, Coffee, Orange Juice, Sugar #11 (World)
1971
1973
1975
1977
1979
1981
1983
1985
1987
1989
1991
1993
1995
1997
1999

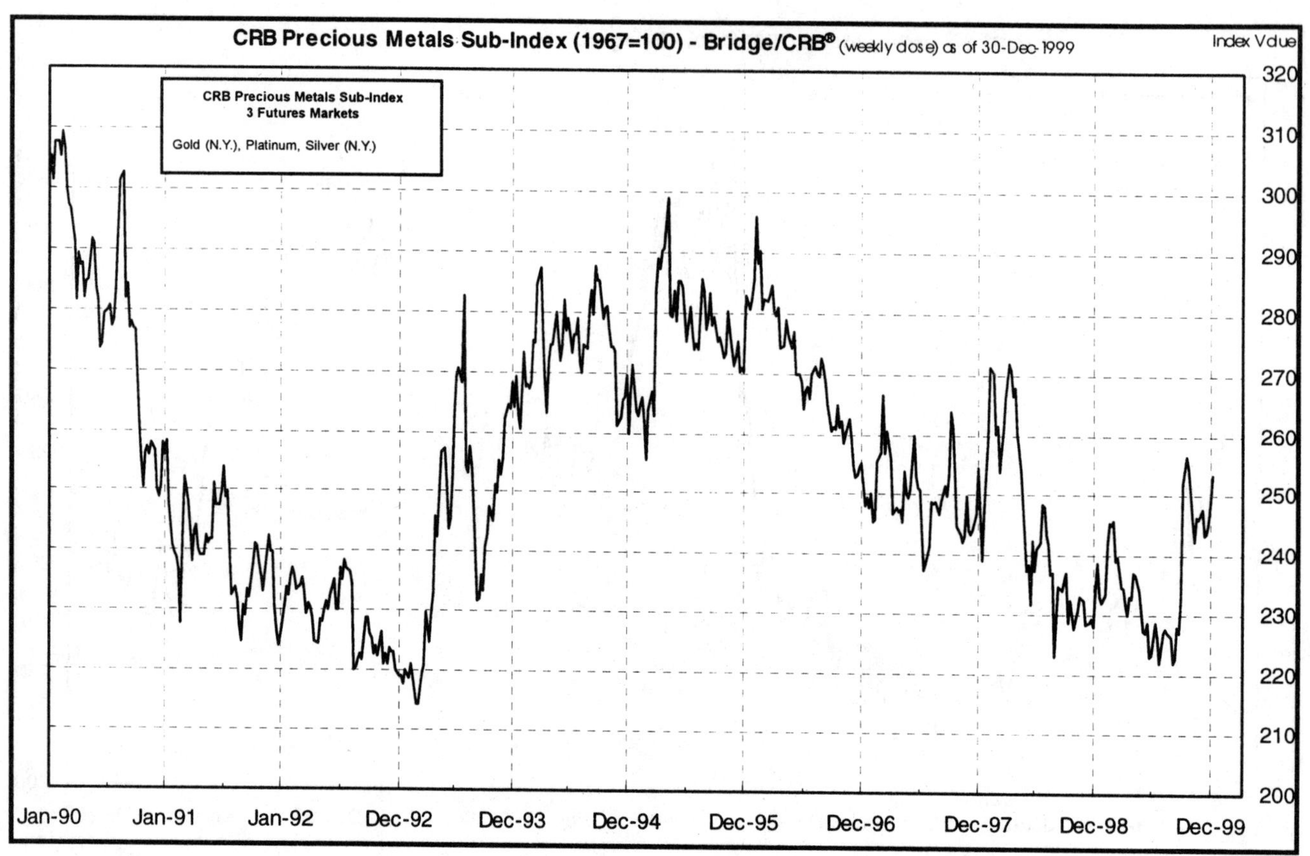

CRB Precious Metals Sub-Index (1967=100) - Bridge/CRB® (weekly close) as of 30-Dec-1999
Index Value
CRB Precious Metals Sub-Index
3 Futures Markets
Gold (N.Y.), Platinum, Silver (N.Y.)
320
310
300
290
280
270
260
250
240
230
220
210
200
Jan-90
Jan-91
Jan-92
Dec-92
Dec-93
Dec-94
Dec-95
Dec-96
Dec-97
Dec-98
Dec-99

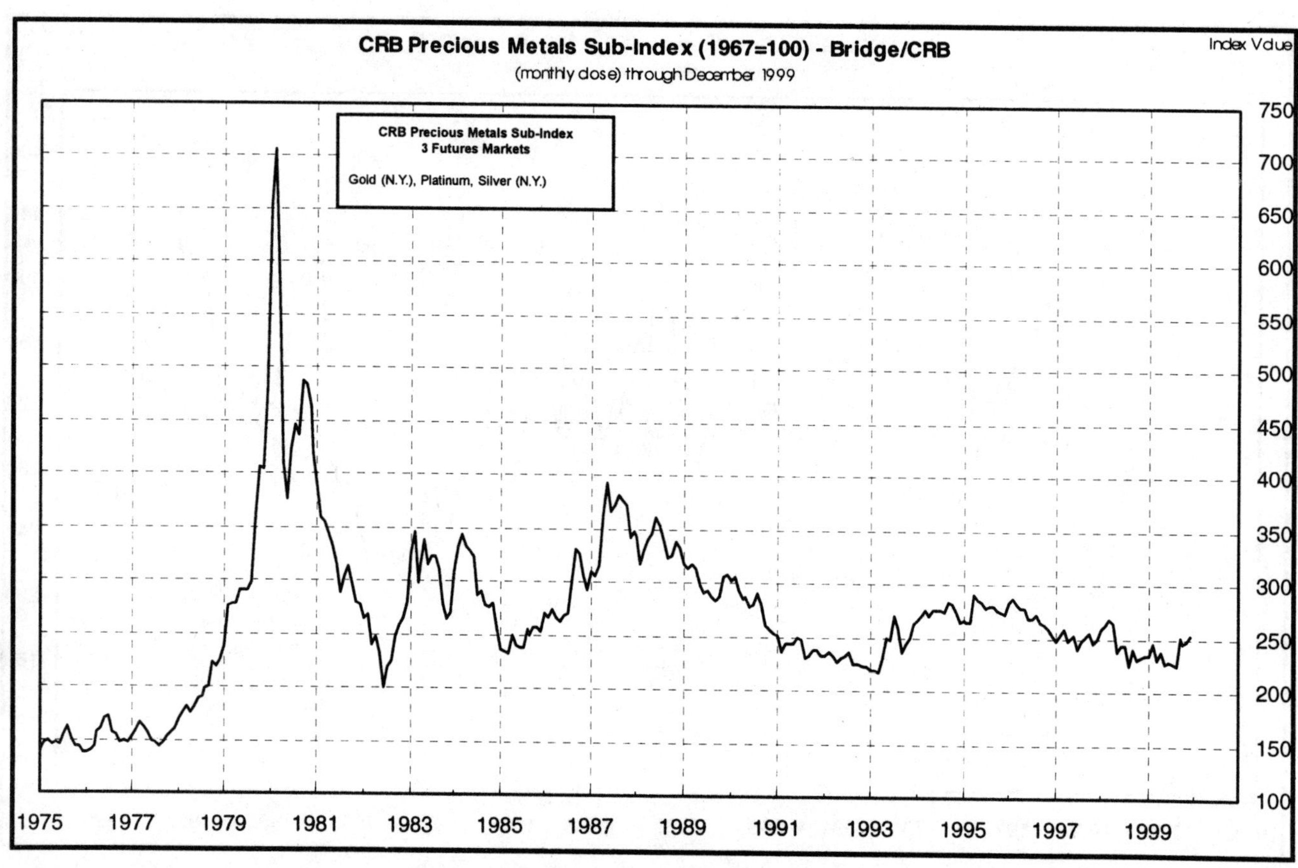

CRB Precious Metals Sub-Index (1967=100) - Bridge/CRB
(monthly close) through December 1999
Index Value
CRB Precious Metals Sub-Index
3 Futures Markets
Gold (N.Y.), Platinum, Silver (N.Y.)
750
700
650
600
550
500
450
400
350
300
250
200
150
100
1975
1977
1979
1981
1983
1985
1987
1989
1991
1993
1995
1997
1999

CRB Industrials Sub-Index (1967=100) - Bridge/CRB® (weekly close) as of 30-Dec-1999
Index Value
290
280
270
260
250
240
230
220
210
200
190
180
170
160
CRB Industrials Sub-Index
2 Futures Markets
Copper, Cotton
Jan-90
Jan-91
Jan-92
Dec-92
Dec-93
Dec-94
Dec-95
Dec-96
Dec-97
Dec-98
Dec-99

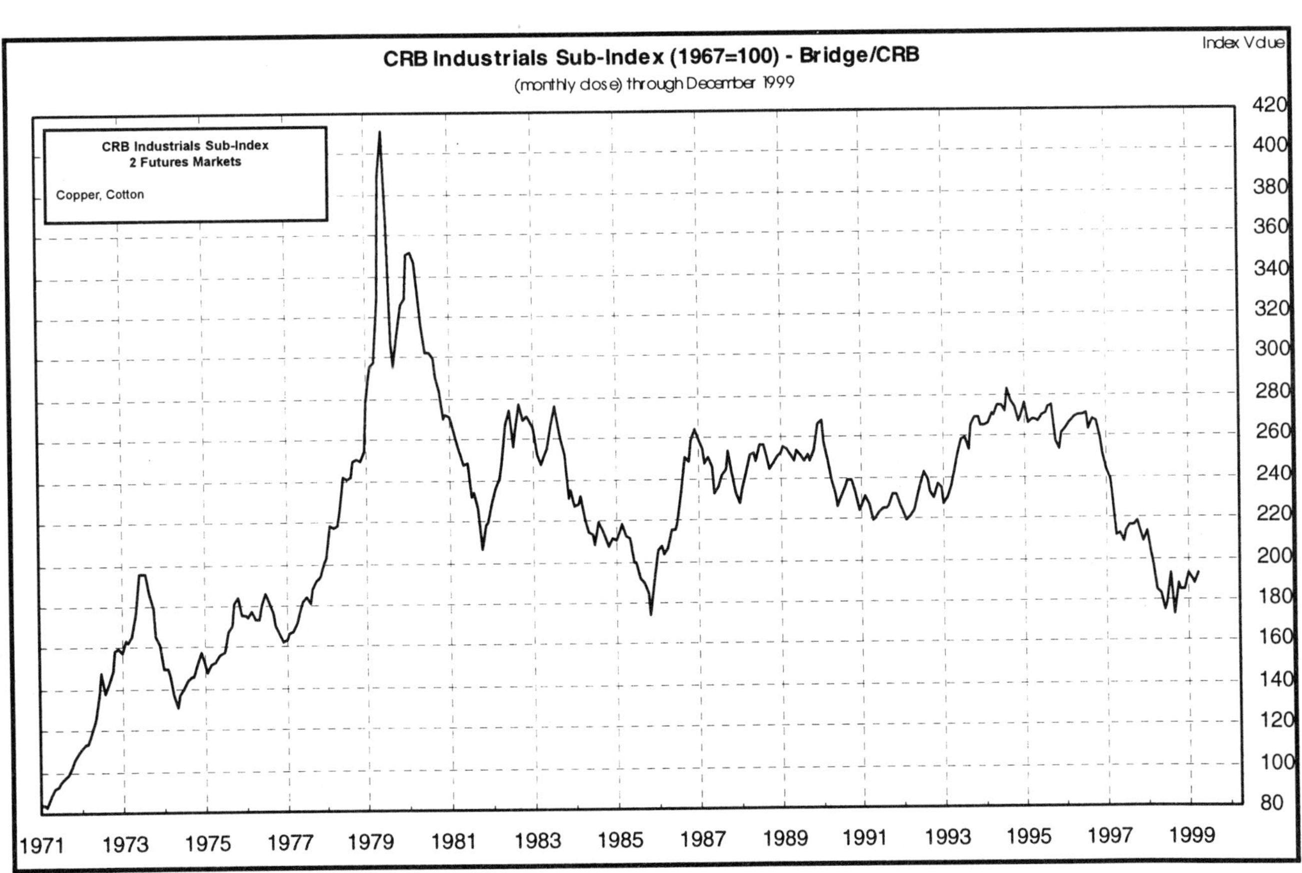
CRB Industrials Sub-Index (1967=100) - Bridge/CRB
(monthly close) through December 1999
Index Value
420
400
380
360
340
320
300
280
260
240
220
200
180
160
140
120
100
80
CRB Industrials Sub-Index
2 Futures Markets
Copper, Cotton
1971
1973
1975
1977
1979
1981
1983
1985
1987
1989
1991
1993
1995
1997
1999

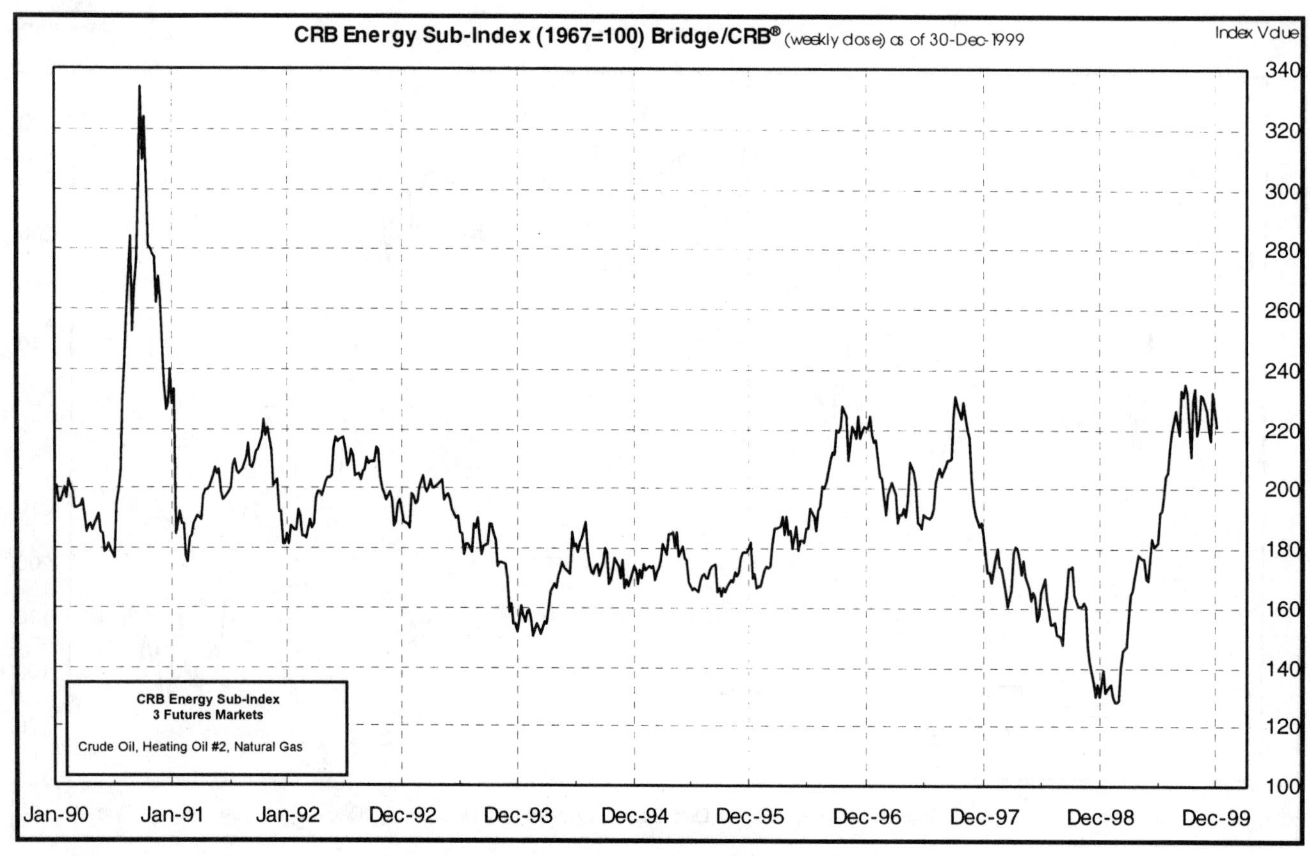
CRB Energy Sub-Index (1967=100) Bridge/CRB® (weekly close) as of 30-Dec-1999
Index Value
340
320
300
280
260
240
220
200
180
160
140
120
100
CRB Energy Sub-Index
3 Futures Markets
Crude Oil, Heating Oil #2, Natural Gas
Jan-90
Jan-91
Jan-92
Dec-92
Dec-93
Dec-94
Dec-95
Dec-96
Dec-97
Dec-98
Dec-99

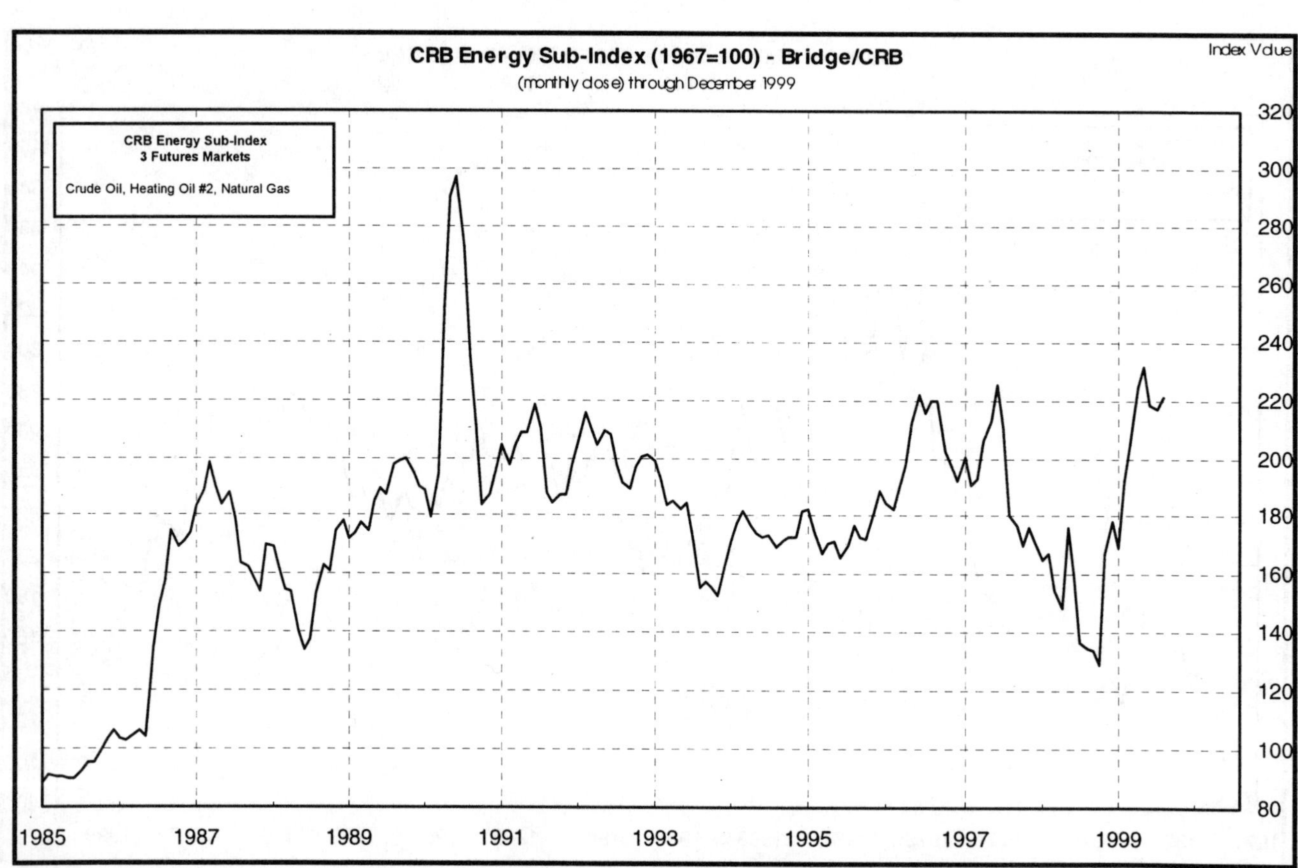
CRB Energy Sub-Index (1967=100) - Bridge/CRB
(monthly close) through December 1999
Index Value
320
300
280
260
240
220
200
180
160
140
120
100
80
CRB Energy Sub-Index
3 Futures Markets
Crude Oil, Heating Oil #2, Natural Gas
1985
1987
1989
1991
1993
1995
1997
1999

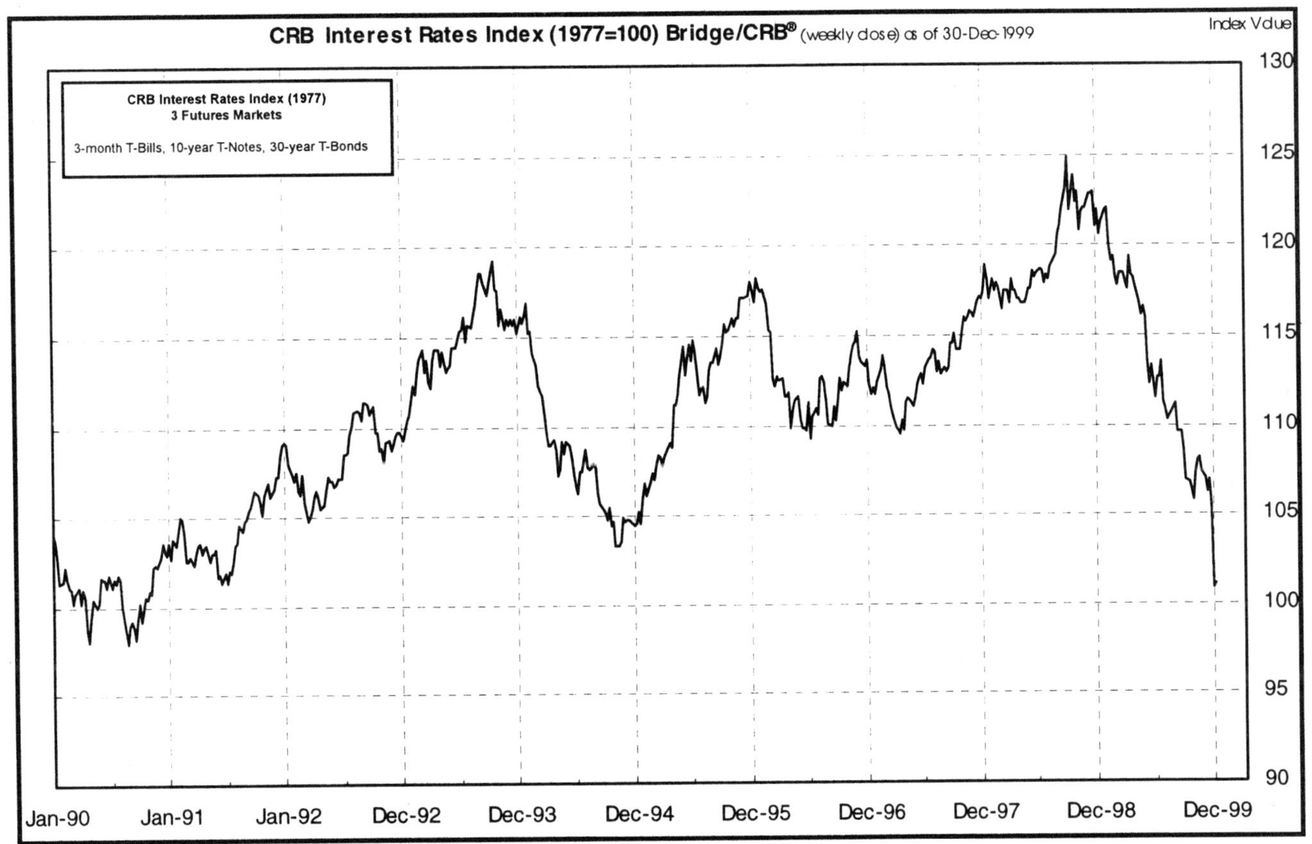
CRB Interest Rates Index (1977=100) Bridge/CRB® (weekly close) as of 30-Dec-1999
Index Value
CRB Interest Rates Index (1977)
3 Futures Markets
3-month T-Bills, 10-year T-Notes, 30-year T-Bonds
130
125
120
115
110
105
100
95
90
Jan-90
Jan-91
Jan-92
Dec-92
Dec-93
Dec-94
Dec-95
Dec-96
Dec-97
Dec-98
Dec-99

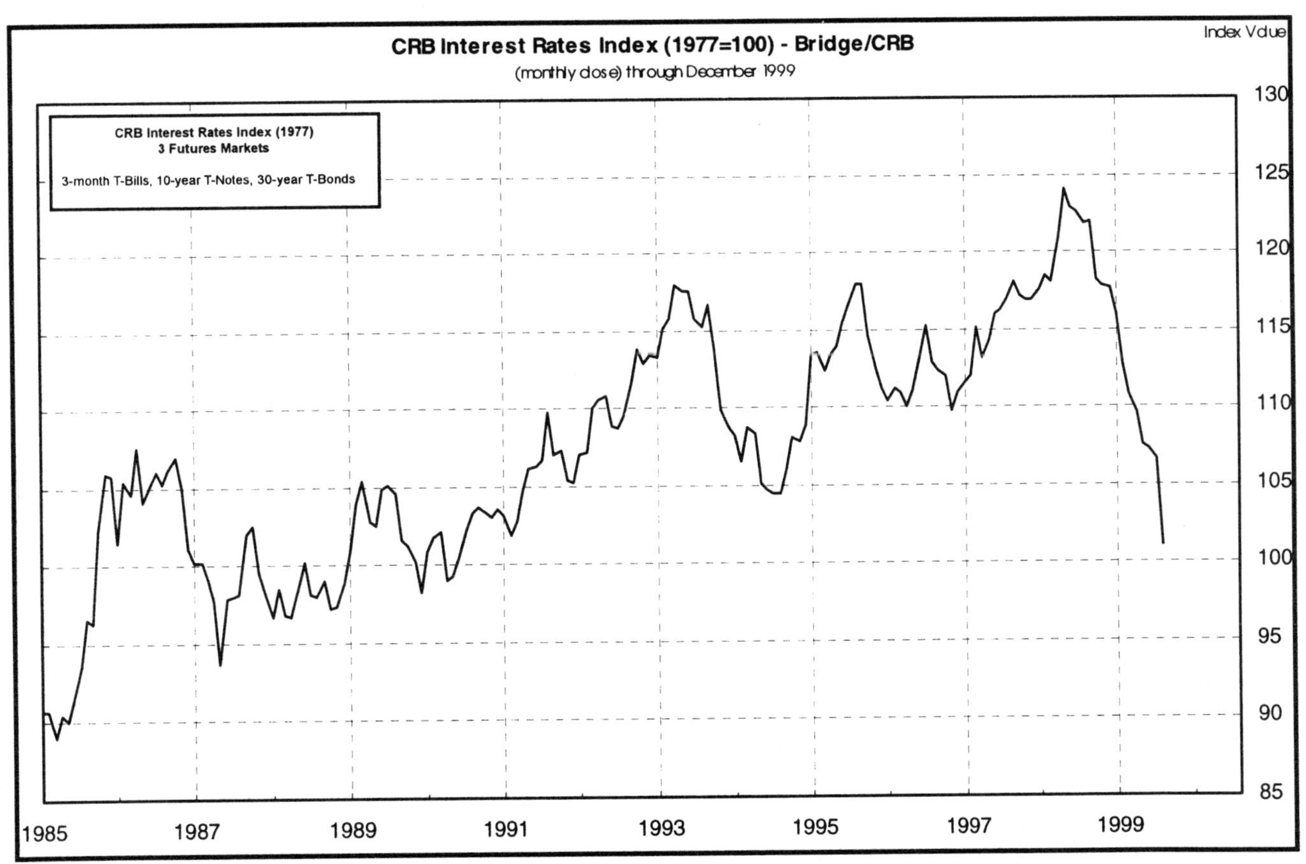
CRB Interest Rates Index (1977=100) - Bridge/CRB
(monthly close) through December 1999
Index Value
CRB Interest Rates Index (1977)
3 Futures Markets
3-month T-Bills, 10-year T-Notes, 30-year T-Bonds
130
125
120
115
110
105
100
95
90
85
1985
1987
1989
1991
1993
1995
1997
1999

CRB Metals Sub-Index (1967=100) - Bridge/CRB® (weekly close) as of 30-Dec-1999
Index Value
CRB Spot Index
5 Spot Markets
Copper Scrap, Lead Scrap, Steel Scrap, Tin, Zinc
340
330
320
310
300
290
280
270
260
250
240
230
220
210
200
Jan-90
Jan-91
Jan-92
Dec-92
Dec-93
Dec-94
Dec-95
Dec-96
Dec-97
Dec-98
Dec-99

CRB Metals Sub-Index (1967=100) - Bridge/CRB
(monthly close) through December 1999
Index Value
CRB Spot Index
5 Spot Markets
Copper Scrap, Lead Scrap, Steel Scrap, Tin, Zinc
380
360
340
320
300
280
260
240
220
200
180
160
140
120
100
80
60
1947
1952
1957
1962
1967
1972
1977
1982
1987
1992
1997

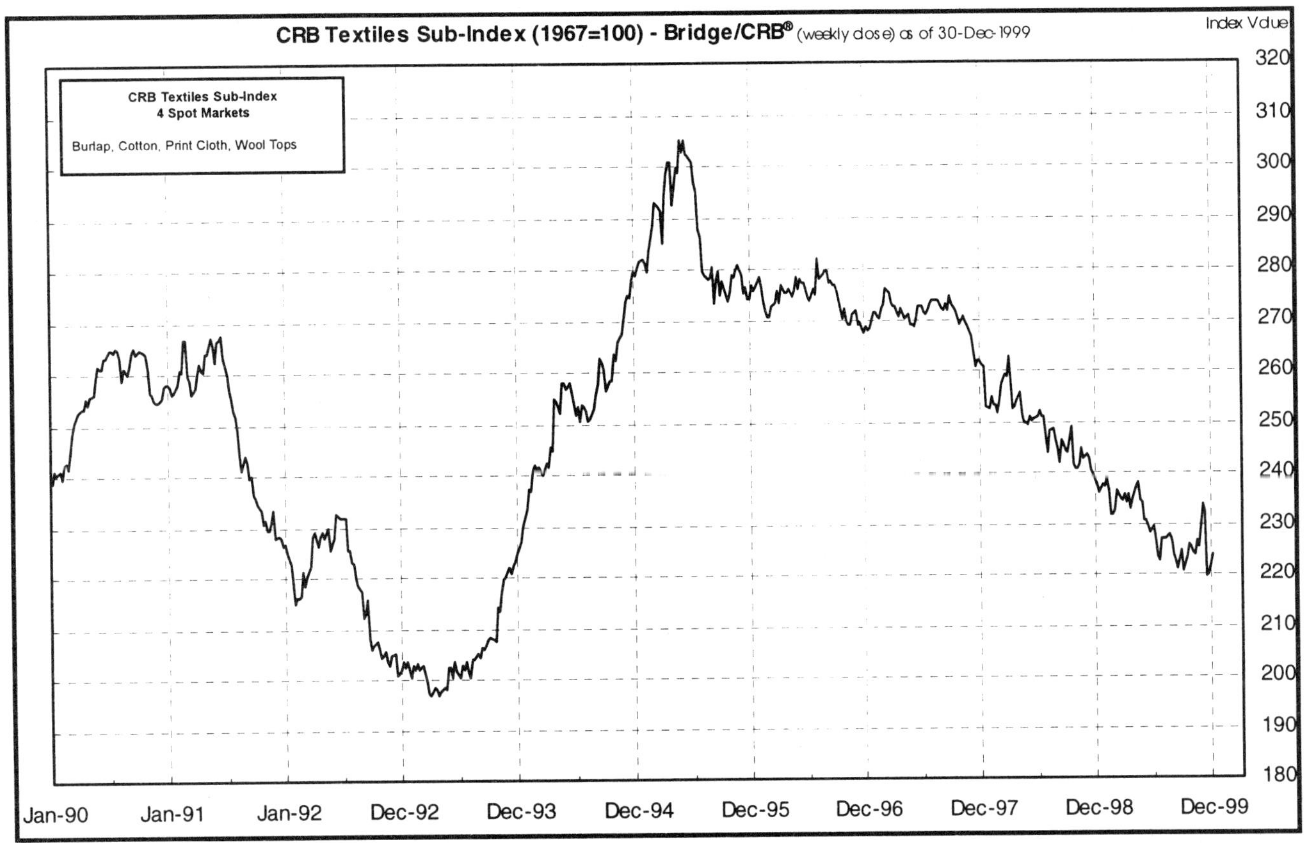
CRB Textiles Sub-Index (1967=100) - Bridge/CRB® (weekly close) as of 30-Dec-1999
Index Value
CRB Textiles Sub-Index
4 Spot Markets
Burlap, Cotton, Print Cloth, Wool Tops
320
310
300
290
280
270
260
250
240
230
220
210
200
190
180
Jan-90
Jan-91
Jan-92
Dec-92
Dec-93
Dec-94
Dec-95
Dec-96
Dec-97
Dec-98
Dec-99

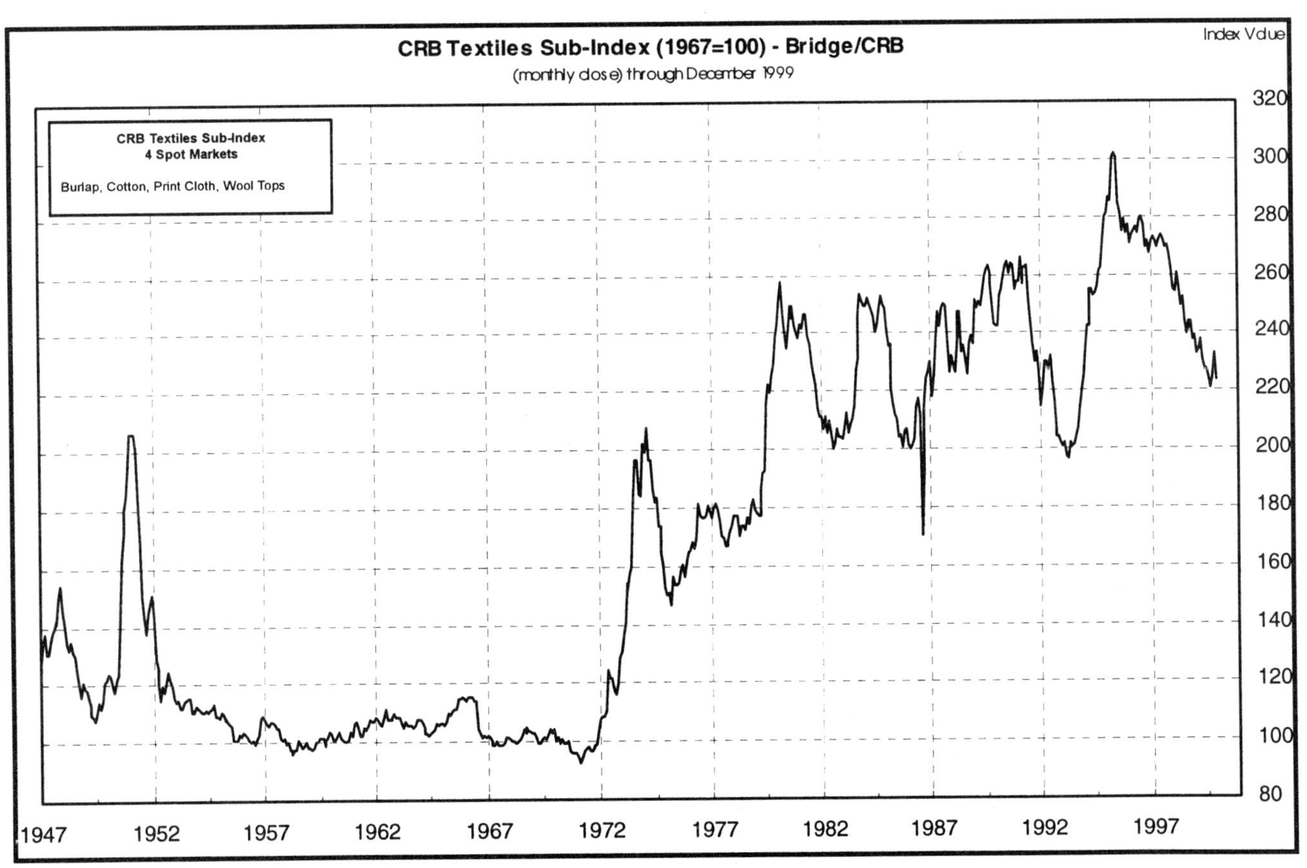
CRB Textiles Sub-Index (1967=100) - Bridge/CRB
(monthly close) through December 1999
Index Value
CRB Textiles Sub-Index
4 Spot Markets
Burlap, Cotton, Print Cloth, Wool Tops
320
300
280
260
240
220
200
180
160
140
120
100
80
1947
1952
1957
1962
1967
1972
1977
1982
1987
1992
1997

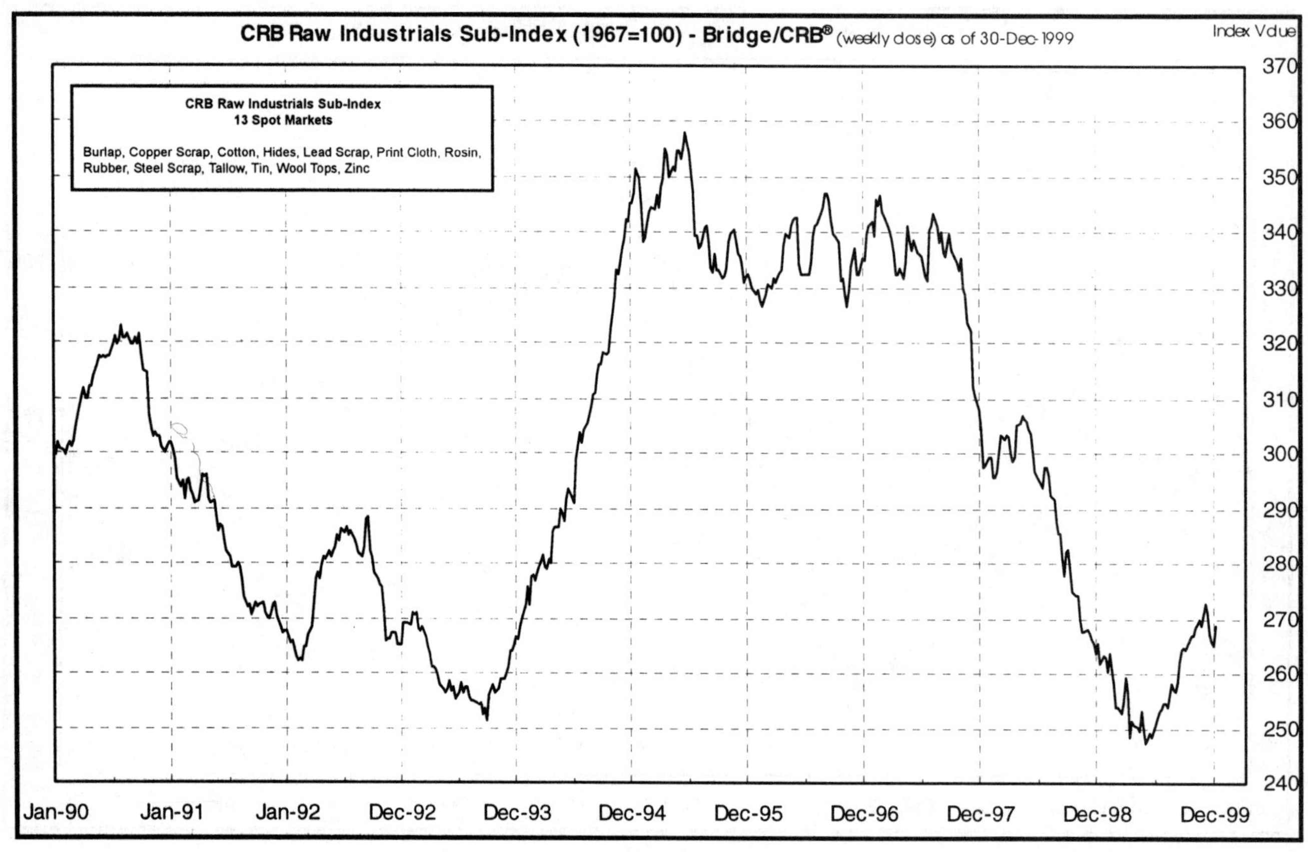
CRB Raw Industrials Sub-Index (1967=100) - Bridge/CRB® (weekly close) as of 30-Dec-1999
Index Value
CRB Raw Industrials Sub-Index
13 Spot Markets
Burlap, Copper Scrap, Cotton, Hides, Lead Scrap, Print Cloth, Rosin, Rubber, Steel Scrap, Tallow, Tin, Wool Tops, Zinc
370
360
350
340
330
320
310
300
290
280
270
260
250
240
Jan-90
Jan-91
Jan-92
Dec-92
Dec-93
Dec-94
Dec-95
Dec-96
Dec-97
Dec-98
Dec-99

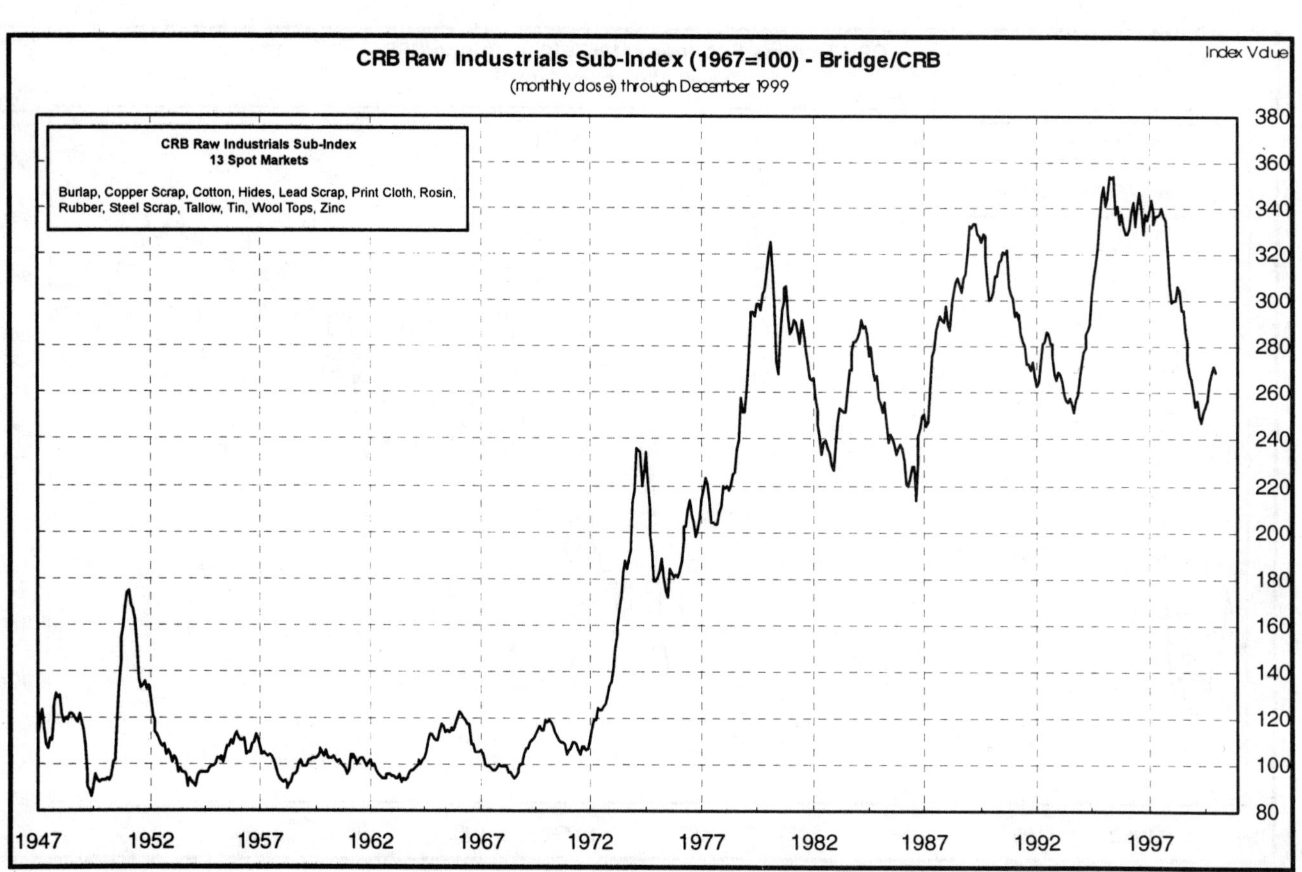
CRB Raw Industrials Sub-Index (1967=100) - Bridge/CRB
(monthly close) through December 1999
Index Value
CRB Raw Industrials Sub-Index
13 Spot Markets
Burlap, Copper Scrap, Cotton, Hides, Lead Scrap, Print Cloth, Rosin, Rubber, Steel Scrap, Tallow, Tin, Wool Tops, Zinc
380
360
340
320
300
280
260
240
220
200
180
160
140
120
100
80
1947
1952
1957
1962
1967
1972
1977
1982
1987
1992
1997

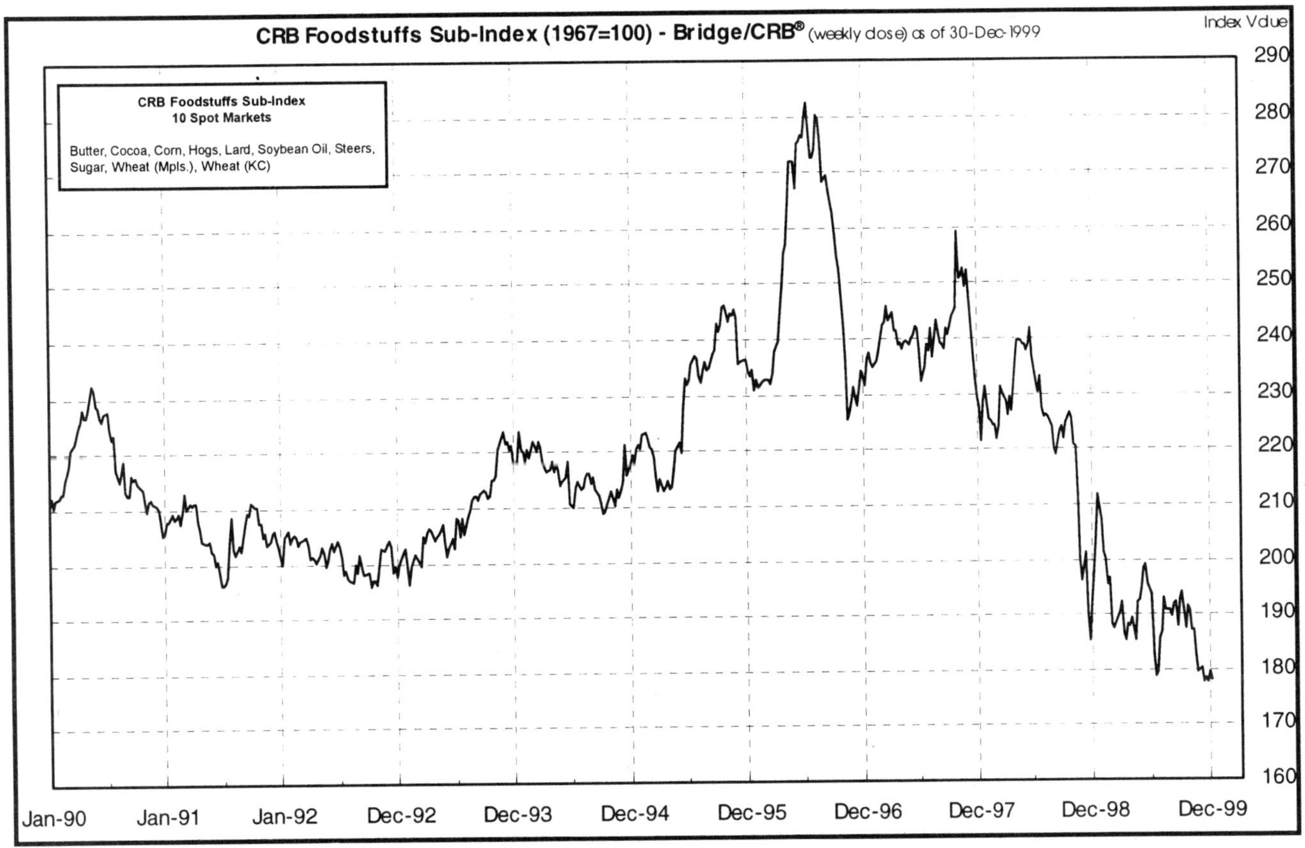
CRB Foodstuffs Sub-Index (1967=100) - Bridge/CRB® (weekly close) as of 30-Dec-1999
Index Value
CRB Foodstuffs Sub-Index
10 Spot Markets
Butter, Cocoa, Corn, Hogs, Lard, Soybean Oil, Steers, Sugar, Wheat (Mpls.), Wheat (KC)
290
280
270
260
250
240
230
220
210
200
190
180
170
160
Jan-90
Jan-91
Jan-92
Dec-92
Dec-93
Dec-94
Dec-95
Dec-96
Dec-97
Dec-98
Dec-99

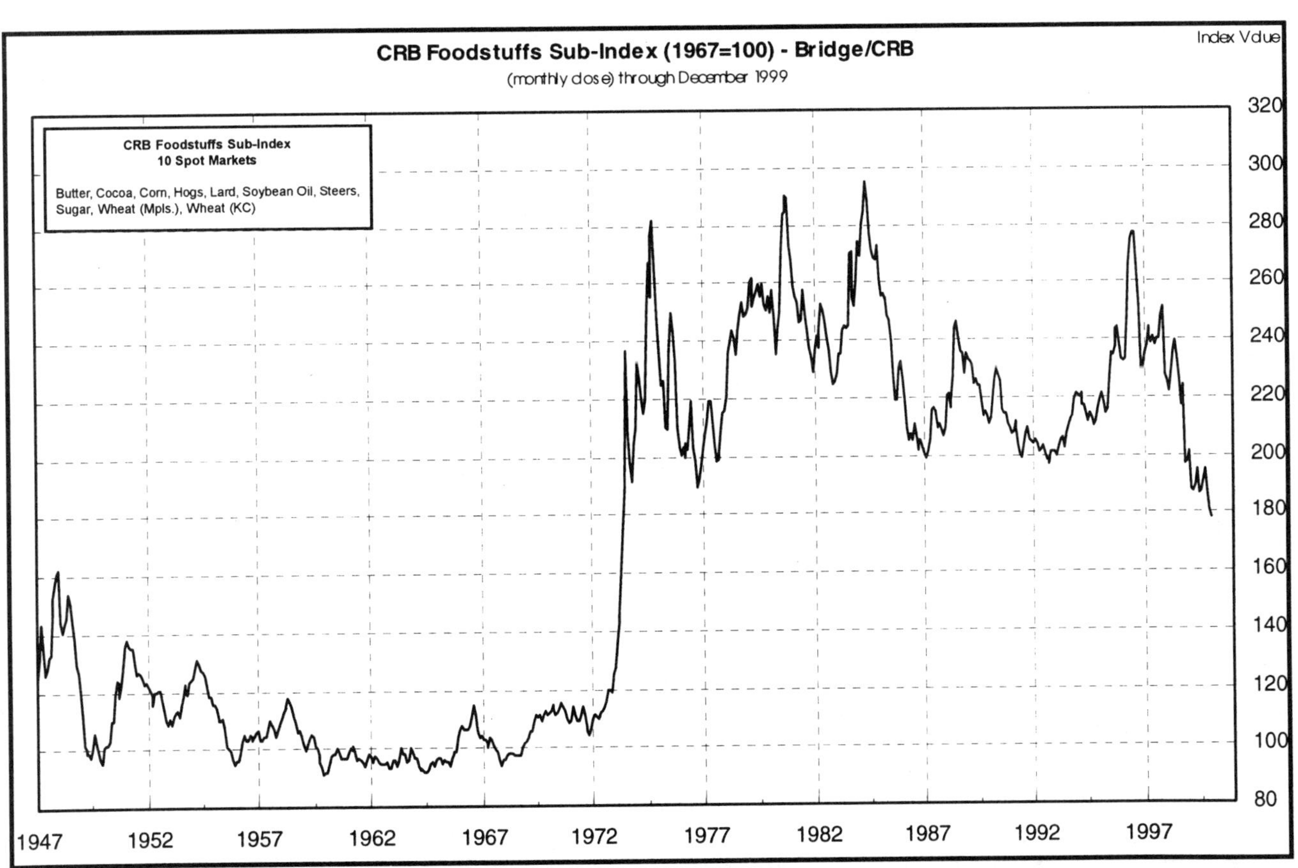
CRB Foodstuffs Sub-Index (1967=100) - Bridge/CRB
(monthly close) through December 1999
Index Value
CRB Foodstuffs Sub-Index
10 Spot Markets
Butter, Cocoa, Corn, Hogs, Lard, Soybean Oil, Steers, Sugar, Wheat (Mpls.), Wheat (KC)
320
300
280
260
240
220
200
180
160
140
120
100
80
1947
1952
1957
1962
1967
1972
1977
1982
1987
1992
1997

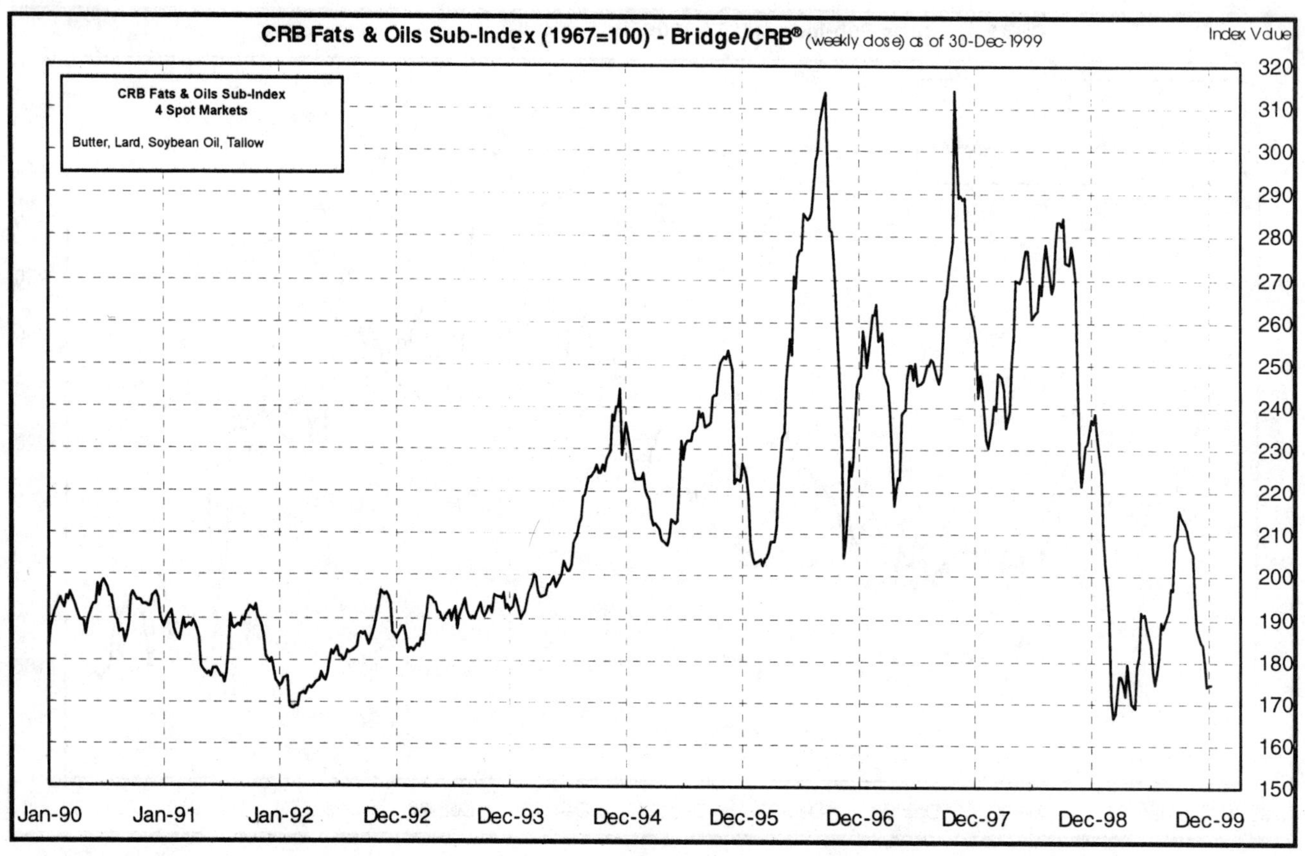
CRB Fats & Oils Sub-Index (1967=100) - Bridge/CRB® (weekly close) as of 30-Dec-1999
Index Value
CRB Fats & Oils Sub-Index
4 Spot Markets
Butter, Lard, Soybean Oil, Tallow
320
310
300
290
280
270
260
250
240
230
220
210
200
190
180
170
160
150
Jan-90
Jan-91
Jan-92
Dec-92
Dec-93
Dec-94
Dec-95
Dec-96
Dec-97
Dec-98
Dec-99

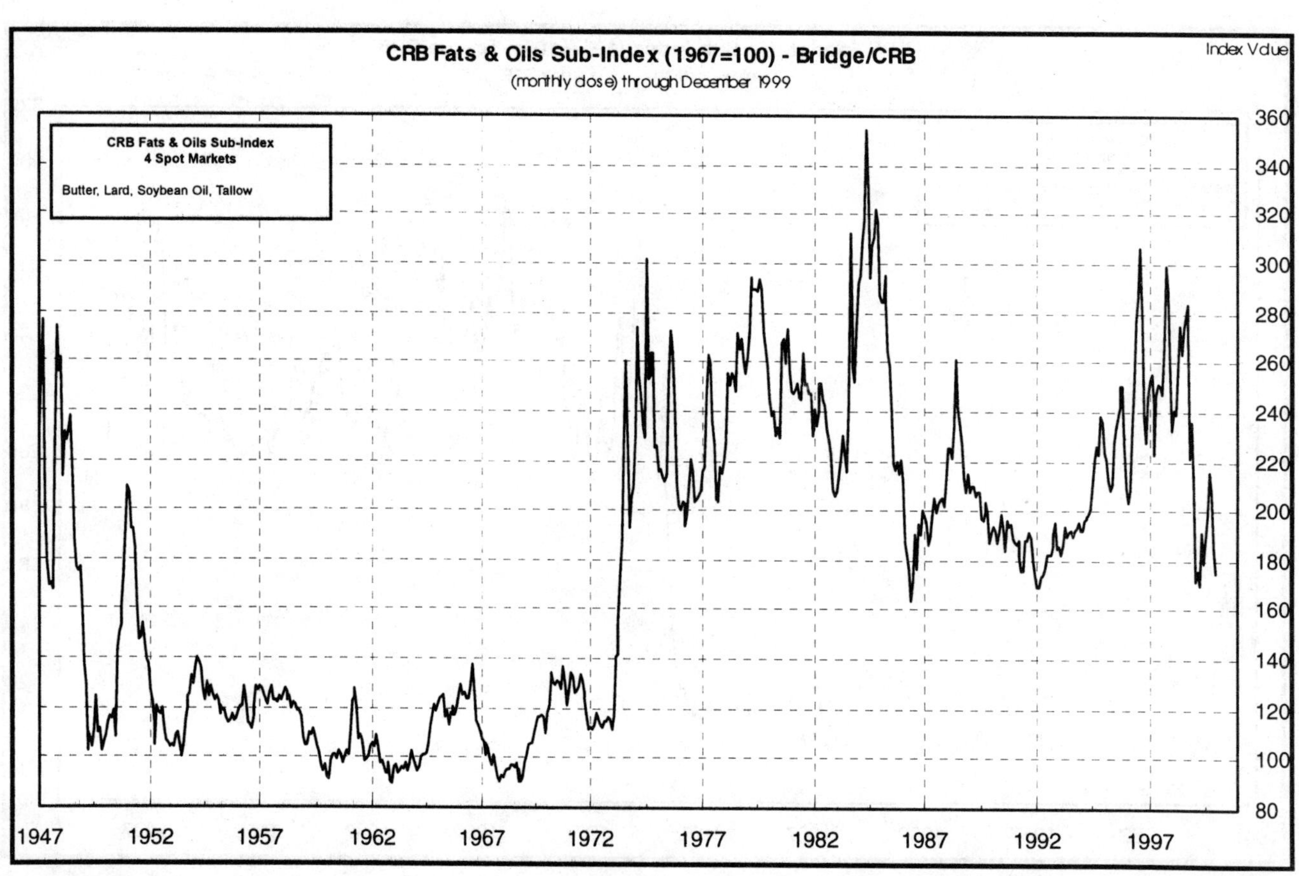
CRB Fats & Oils Sub-Index (1967=100) - Bridge/CRB
(monthly close) through December 1999
Index Value
CRB Fats & Oils Sub-Index
4 Spot Markets
Butter, Lard, Soybean Oil, Tallow
360
340
320
300
280
260
240
220
200
180
160
140
120
100
80
1947
1952
1957
1962
1967
1972
1977
1982
1987
1992
1997

CRB Livestock Sub-Index (1967=100) - Bridge/CRB® (weekly close) as of 30-Dec-1999
Index Value
CRB Livestock Sub-Index
5 Spot Markets
Hides, Hogs, Lard, Steers, Tallow
420
400
380
360
340
320
300
280
260
240
220
200
180
Jan-90
Jan-91
Jan-92
Dec-92
Dec-93
Dec-94
Dec-95
Dec-96
Dec-97
Dec-98
Dec-99

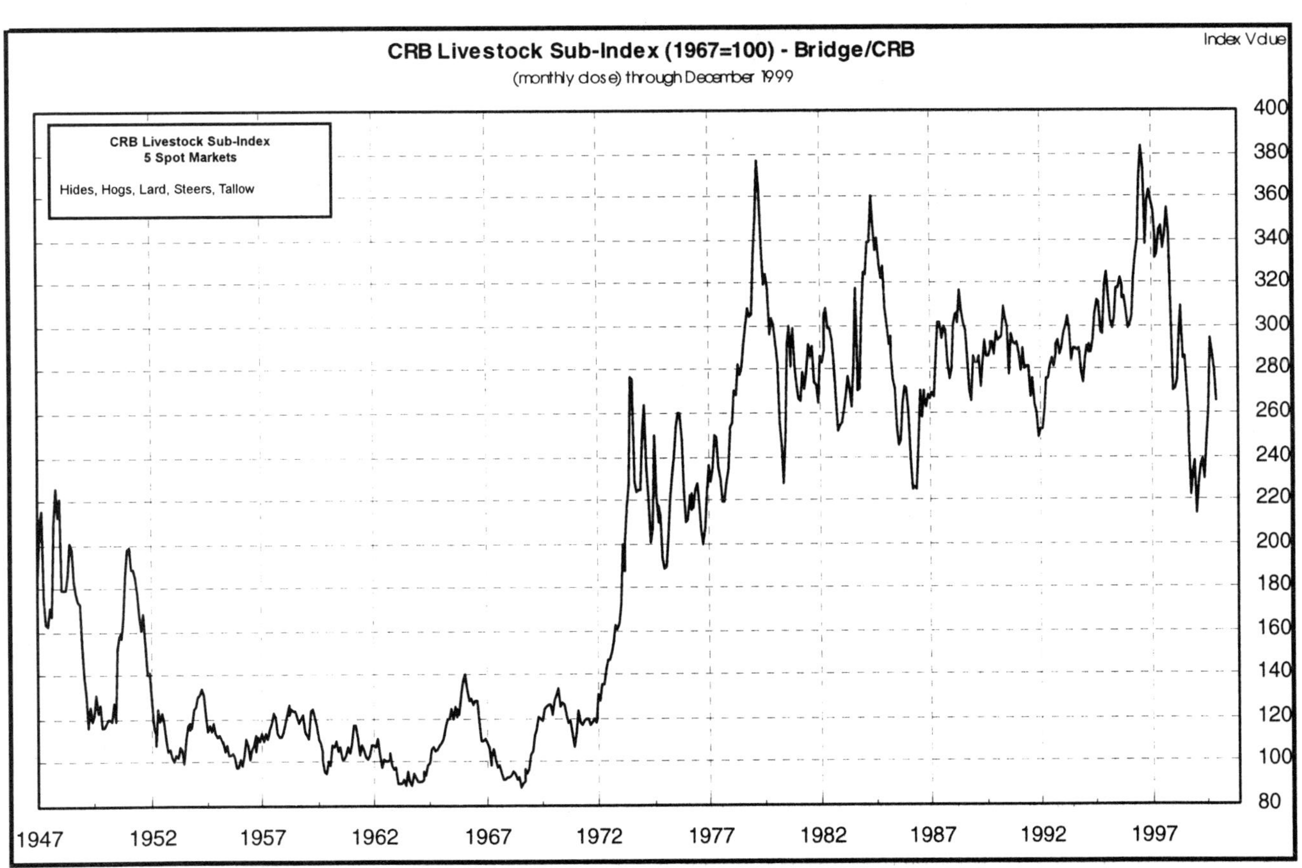
CRB Livestock Sub-Index (1967=100) - Bridge/CRB
(monthly close) through December 1999
Index Value
CRB Livestock Sub-Index
5 Spot Markets
Hides, Hogs, Lard, Steers, Tallow
400
380
360
340
320
300
280
260
240
220
200
180
160
140
120
100
80
1947
1952
1957
1962
1967
1972
1977
1982
1987
1992
1997

Bridge/CRB Indices

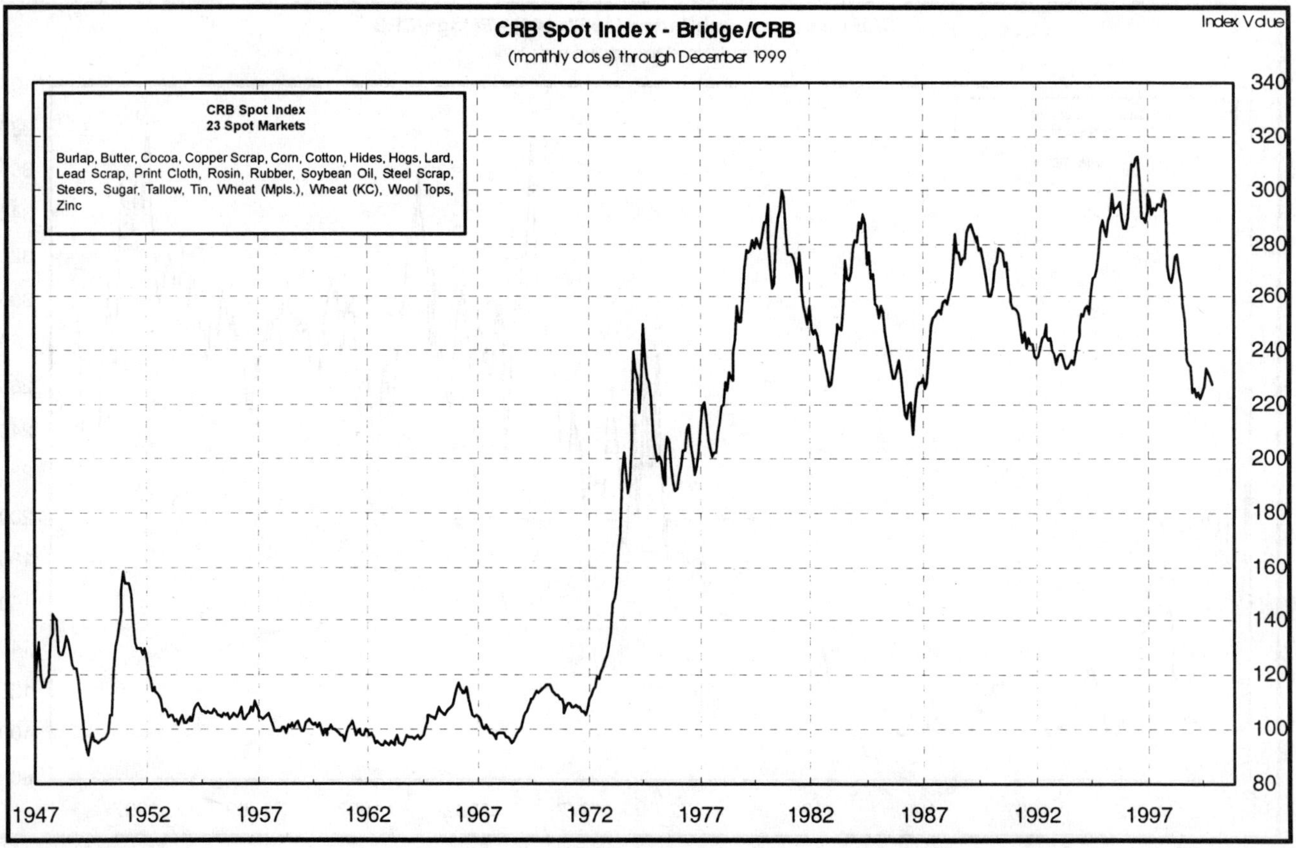

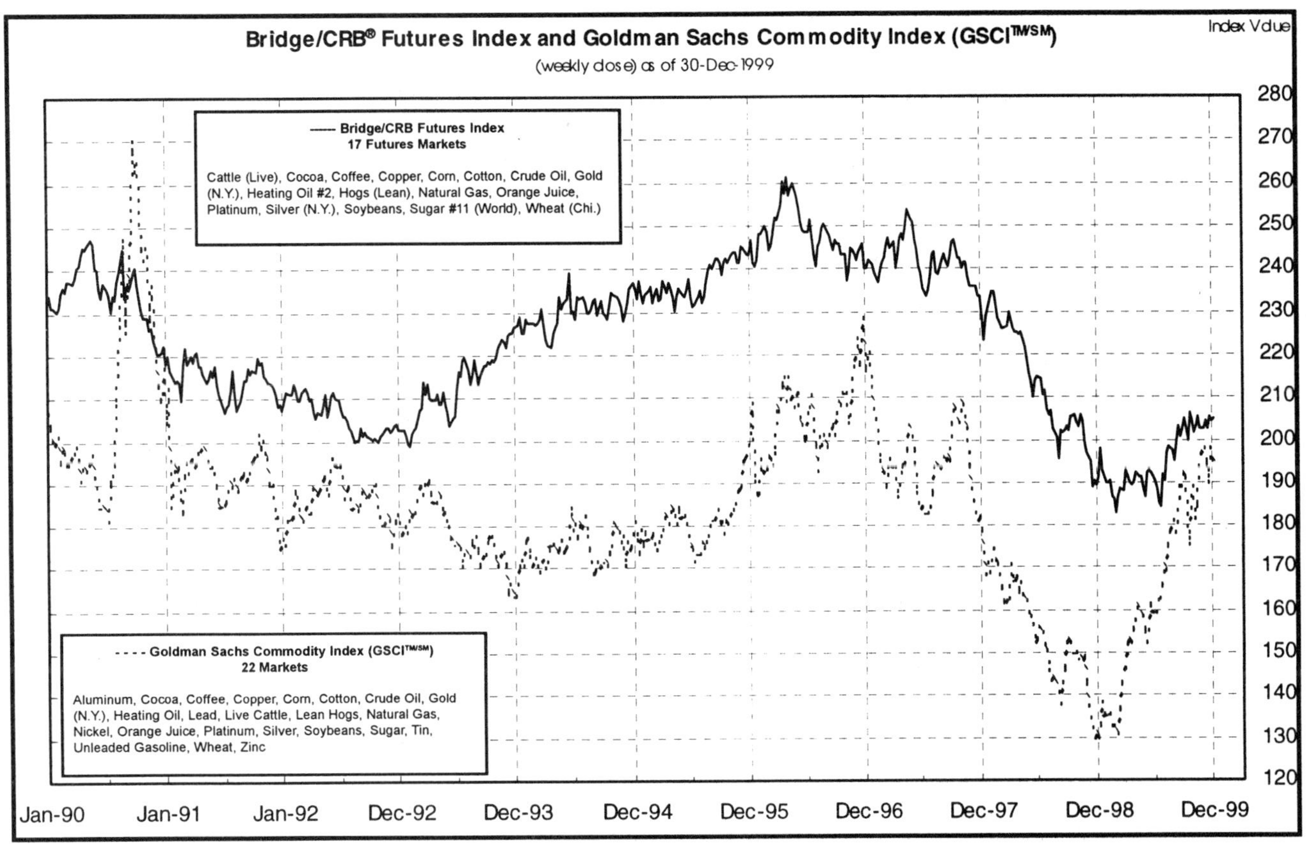
Bridge/CRB® Futures Index and Goldman Sachs Commodity Index (GSCI™/SM)
(weekly close) as of 30-Dec-1999
Index Value
—— Bridge/CRB Futures Index
17 Futures Markets
Cattle (Live), Cocoa, Coffee, Copper, Corn, Cotton, Crude Oil, Gold (N.Y.), Heating Oil #2, Hogs (Lean), Natural Gas, Orange Juice, Platinum, Silver (N.Y.), Soybeans, Sugar #11 (World), Wheat (Chi.)
- - - - Goldman Sachs Commodity Index (GSCI™/SM)
22 Markets
Aluminum, Cocoa, Coffee, Copper, Corn, Cotton, Crude Oil, Gold (N.Y.), Heating Oil, Lead, Live Cattle, Lean Hogs, Natural Gas, Nickel, Orange Juice, Platinum, Silver, Soybeans, Sugar, Tin, Unleaded Gasoline, Wheat, Zinc
280
270
260
250
240
230
220
210
200
190
180
170
160
150
140
130
120
Jan-90
Jan-91
Jan-92
Dec-92
Dec-93
Dec-94
Dec-95
Dec-96
Dec-97
Dec-98
Dec-99

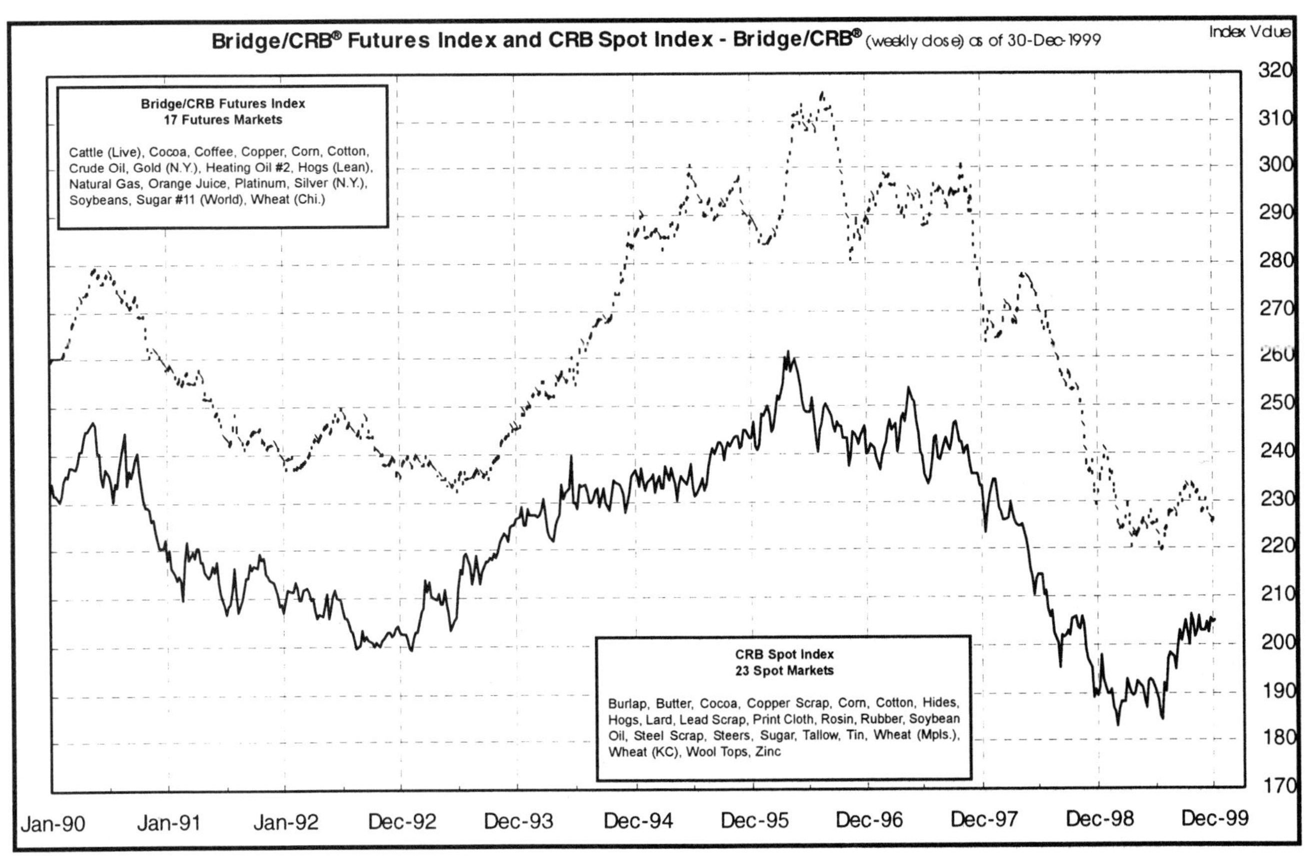
Bridge/CRB® Futures Index and CRB Spot Index - Bridge/CRB® (weekly close) as of 30-Dec-1999
Index Value
Bridge/CRB Futures Index
17 Futures Markets
Cattle (Live), Cocoa, Coffee, Copper, Corn, Cotton, Crude Oil, Gold (N.Y.), Heating Oil #2, Hogs (Lean), Natural Gas, Orange Juice, Platinum, Silver (N.Y.), Soybeans, Sugar #11 (World), Wheat (Chi.)
CRB Spot Index
23 Spot Markets
Burlap, Butter, Cocoa, Copper Scrap, Corn, Cotton, Hides, Hogs, Lard, Lead Scrap, Print Cloth, Rosin, Rubber, Soybean Oil, Steel Scrap, Steers, Sugar, Tallow, Tin, Wheat (Mpls.), Wheat (KC), Wool Tops, Zinc
320
310
300
290
280
270
260
250
240
230
220
210
200
190
180
170
Jan-90
Jan-91
Jan-92
Dec-92
Dec-93
Dec-94
Dec-95
Dec-96
Dec-97
Dec-98
Dec-99

UNDERSTANDING ONLINE FUTURES TRADING

by Joseph H. Zoller

Online Trading: A Step Closer to the Customer

"Please enter your user name;" "What is your pass word?" Those are familiar phrases to any of the millions of traders who are joining the Internet revolution for online trading.

Since early 1999, the evolution of electronic trading has shifted from developments in exchange systems to a new emphasis on the technological developments by Futures Commission Merchants (FCM's), Introducing Brokers (IB's), and brokers as they attempt to retain their individual customers.

This change in emphasis is due to consumer demand, fueled in large part by exposure to online shopping, banking, and information gathering. Today, the emphasis is on speed, control, and cost savings, with most individuals seeking instantaneous execution and confirmation.

In many cases this is an illusion that is easily satisfied by the brokerage and FCM software designed to allow the individual to trade online. Most often it is a result of the broker establishing a web site as the "front-end" of a system that is connected to its back room operations software and the Applications Program Interface (API) offered by the exchanges.

Although the e-mini contracts at the Chicago Mercantile Exchange are still the only true straight-through electronic trading available, many brokers still promote their online trading systems without detailing the necessary human intervention to complete most trades. Since both execution and confirmation are usually very quick, the individual trader is quite satisfied. Only in extremely fast markets, when the open outcry method falls behind in its paperwork, does the individual become aware of the human involvement in the "online" trade.

Development of Online Trading in Equities

The momentum for online trading among individuals began with the heavy promotion by online brokers that offered discount pricing, accuracy, and speed. Online trading began as an alternative to "calling the broker." Charles Schwab and a few other brokers were in the forefront, ready to respond to consumer's inclination to use their own computers to transact trades.

Initially, using the computer was a logical adjunct to the quotes, research, charts, brokerage reports, and recommendations that were becoming readily available online. The growth of chat rooms and newsgroups devoted to various aspects of investing also fed the demand, in both equities and derivatives, for the ability to place buy and sell orders online.

Soon, additional brokerages began to offer online communications to their customers and it wasn't long before brokerages were formed that were primarily online operations. E*Trade, Ameritrade, and others began heavy promotion and were quick to meet the desires of individual traders. It was hardly surprising that their growth was meteoric. According to 1998 census data, computer penetration had reached 80 percent in households with annual incomes over $75,000. If those with Internet access at their place of business are included, as well as those who have acquired computers during the past two years, there is almost universal reach among the target audience for brokerage services. Online trading access has become as available as telephone access.

Growth of Futures Trading

It was the growth in online trading of equities that made individual investors and traders aware of online futures brokerage services.

Futures brokerages utilized electronic networks and systems for several years. Until 2000, U.S. futures exchanges were developing systems that would speed order flow into the pits for transaction by open outcry. Although there were some technical problems with these electronic networks in 1997 and 1998, most were resolved by the end of 1999. Today, brokers generally give the exchanges' systems high marks for reliability.

In addition to the e-mini contracts on the Chicago Mercantile Exchange, which are true electronically traded products, other developments that will be launched in 2000 include an expanded Globex2, the Chicago Board of Trade's (CBOT) API, the CME FIX API, as well as the long anticipated Eurex/CBOT system.

The development of these systems, as well as the consumer exposure to online equities trading, created the impetus for futures brokers to offer comparable systems.

Currently the CME, with its Globex2, permits the individual trader to direct and execute trades almost around the clock with exchanges in Paris, London, Sao Paulo, Singapore, and of course, Chicago. Additionally, the CME's Financial Industry eXchange (FIX) API will allow brokers to link their front-end systems directly with the exchanges' systems, giving qualified customers the ability to trade 24 hours a day from their home computers.

The Role of FCMs and Brokers in Online Trading

In spite of the progress of electronic systems and automatic order entry via the Internet, the FCM is still the responsible party for all trades. For example:

1. FCM's and individual brokers must still screen traders for suitability and determine equity and margin requirements.

2. FCM risk management systems must determine the customer's equity position and the status of their margin account without impeding the flow of the order execution. The customer's credit worthiness must be evaluated before each submitted trade.

3. FCM's and brokers must provide market knowledge in a timely manner at the time of the trade and after it is executed. In addition, it is the FCM's responsibility to insure that the trade is executed and cleared properly, and all required accounting and paperwork are generated.

4. The FCM must provide documentation of each trade to the clearing houses in a timely manner.

5. FCM's, IB's, and brokers must provide customers with a timely status report of account activity, open orders, and equity levels.

Many proprietary systems, as well as third-party backroom systems, already provide these functions. Third party vendors include Rolfe & Nolan, SunGard, Linleigh, and ATSM.

Trading Systems

Currently, there are two basic systems by which an individual can trade futures and options electronically. One utilizes uniquely designed software that will allow the trader to connect with the broker or FCM's own system. The customer may be connected via a dial-up system driven by specific broker software or a hard-wired system that is a dedicated line between the trader and the broker's system. Because of the expense involved, hard-wired systems have been used primarily by professional traders, such as institutional trading desks, CTA's, and CPO's.

It was the recent growth of the World Wide Web, and browser software such as Internet Explorer and Netscape Communicator, that democratized electronic trading systems. For a relatively low price, the Internet-savvy customer can access market data, research, commentary, charts, and news. Price information is available at no charge with a 15-minute delay, and in real-time with a subscription from a data vendor. Additionally, the individual can open an account and download the broker's specific software from the broker's web site.

Risk management is handled in a variety of ways. The newer proprietary systems evaluate each customer's order as it is entered, according to predetermined margin requirements that are set based upon the customer's financial situation. If the order meets all these requirements, it will automatically pass through the system to be executed. If a problem exists, a message will advise the trader.

Access Between the Individual and the Broker

As previously noted, the first electronic systems were based on direct connections between the individual and the broker. These initial systems were software-based and designed to interact exclusively with the broker's or FCM's computers.

The development of secure sites and improved encryption methods have ensured that confidential information traveling over the Internet is not compromised. Most brokers have very secure systems, although there is always the threat of rogue computer hackers. Even during the highly publicized February 2000 events, the biggest problem was the inability to access popular sites, not the breaching of confidentiality.

An individual or institutional trading desk can trade futures or options online in several ways. First, one must establish an account with a broker who has electronic trading capability and a web site. There are different levels of sophistication offered by different brokers. Some use the web site merely as a conduit to enter their orders online and send them electronically to the broker's office. From there, the order is handled in the same manner as if came in by telephone. Basically, this approach allows the customer to review his instructions before transmitting the order, thereby reducing errors that may develop from verbal misunderstandings. While some IB's still do not offer electronic trading to their customers, they do transmit orders from their office to the clearing FCM electronically.

Other systems include one pioneered by Timber Hill, which is now being offered to other brokers through their Interactive Traders Group. In this system, the order is directly transmitted by wireless transmission to Timber Hill's floor traders, each of whom holds a small computer. The order appears on the trader's screen, and is executed and confirmed on the wireless computer immediately. Similar systems are being developed by other trading groups who use Personal Data Assistants (PDA's) that can receive and transmit data. Some of these systems are based on the Palm PDA operating system, others use devices operating on the Windows CE operating system.

Until recently, most online systems were built around off-the-shelf products offered by third parties who handled executions, clearing, and back-office operations electronically. Vendors such as Rolfe & Nolan, AudiTrack, and SunGard were able to seamlessly tie their order entry systems into their back office operations.

AudiTrack's AudiTrade program, for virtual paper trading, received the CME's endorsement and is offered through the CME's web site. Others offered systems that quickly and easily allowed brokers to establish their own web sites capable of electronic trading.

A Look at Some Third Party Systems

Theodore: Linleigh Management systems

Theodore is used primarily by brokers, IB's, order desks, and customers at work stations. The system speeds orders from the work station to the floor, and then reports fills and a record of trades to bookkeeping and clearing houses electronically. Theodore has been improved and now offers better quality and speed of information for execution, confirmation, management reporting, and risk control. It also provides an audit trail with required time stamps.

RANOrder: Rolfe & Nolan

Rolfe & Nolan's Internet order routing system is RANOrder. This turnkey operation allows Internet based order entry, account data access, and electronic routing of orders. By mid-1999, R&N announced that ten futures and options firms had selected RANOrder as their system, although many have coined their own unique name for marketing and promotional purposes.

SunGard Futures Systems

SunGard, which merged with GMI systems in 1997, specializes in exchange traded derivatives, back office software, and turnkey online trading systems. SunGard/GMI was an early innovator among vendors offering these systems.

ATSM

ATSM offers a series of different products, but the principal one for the futures industry is UBIX. This is a comprehensive management system for exchange-traded futures and options on all major exchanges. The system can be easily connected to an FCM's front-end system, such as a web-based trading platform.

AudiTrack: AudiTrack, Inc.

AudiTrack is a simulated brokerage operation that offers customers all the benefits of live market trading without the capital risk. AudiTrade is offered by the CME and many FCM's to their customers as a practice or paper trading exercise.

Futures brokers began concentrating on the development of their own proprietary systems after work on meeting Y2K requirements was complete. Many of the newer systems allow for straight-through trading by customers to the trading pit where the order is executed via open outcry. Given the speed of most trades via open outcry, these electronic systems shorten the interval between the order entry and confirmation on the customer's screen. In addition, FCM's take advantage of electronic matching in the CME's e-mini contracts and anticipate participating in the CBOT/Eurex system.

Representative Survey of Online FCMs and Brokers

With the introduction of electronic trading by Charles Schwab, DLJ, and others, it was not long before several firms based their primary business on electronic trading. E*Trade, Ameritrade, and Daytek were among the most notable firms promoting online trading as their principal method of customer order entry. As these firms increased their market share, they also began to include traditional brokerage services such as assisted trading, recommendations, and telephone access. The development of futures brokerages electronic trading offerings followed the trends in the equities markets.

What follows is a survey of futures brokers that are participants in the "online revolution." It is not intended to be a comprehensive list, and inclusion should not be considered a recommendation or endorsement of any firm.

ZAP Futures

ZAP Futures is one of the oldest online trading firms in the futures industry, providing brokerage services to individuals and institutional customers since 1994. Originally, ZAP offered a simple trading program in conjunction with LFG, its parent. LFG introduced LeoWeb, a browser-based system, that after entry of a user name and password accesses a virtual trading ticket where customers select the contract name, trading month, quantity, and order type.

Recently, ZAP introduced a new proprietary program: ZAP 2000 ("Hands-Free Trading" system). This software provides an interface that can be manually filled-in by the customer, but it also allows customers to contract for real-time data, analytical software, or online newsletters that automatically generate orders based on the trader's preset parameters. These orders appear on the screen for a final review by the customer and can be transmitted with a click of the mouse. ZAP 2000 imports the files from trend-based systems such as Essex Trading or from newsletters. Day-trading programs that follow contracts such as the S&P 500 or NASDAQ e-minis can send orders instantaneously via signals that are compatible with the TOPS system. The total elapsed time from origination of the trading signal to confirmation of an executed order is 3 to 4 seconds. Since speed and accuracy are ZAP's primary goal, its new system includes a very fast, software-based risk management system that requires no human intervention for order approval.

Alaron Trading Corporation

Alaron is one of the fastest growing brokerages due primarily to their orientation and extensive promotion. Alaron estimates that over 70 percent of their clients use their online trading system, Alaronline. Although some customers simply use the system to check account positions and balances, Alaron estimates that over three-quarters of their accounts use Alaronline to input orders.

Until Spring 2000, Alaronline utilized the Rolfe and Nolan system for online trading. This system was replaced by Alaron's proprietary system based on its own source code. In addition to their direct customers, Alaron also offers the system to their IB's with unique overlays on the pages that show the IB's own logo and identification.

Lind-Waldock

Lind-Waldock is recognized as one of the largest futures discount brokerage firms with both individuals and institutions as clients. Customers of all Lind-Waldock services, whether LindPlus (broker assisted) programs, LindSystems (system traded accounts), or self-directed accounts can access their account information at anytime from the Lind-Waldock web site. Customers can determine their account status, fills, working orders, and current account balances.

In addition, the firm offers LindConnect as its online trading system. Using a series of simple, easy-to-understand templates, it allows for order entry, review, parking, charts, and the ability to get real-time quotes. Fills are communicated automatically via a "pop-up" screen on the customer's computer. Lind-Waldock also offers Lind P.R.O.F.I.T., which is its version of AudiTrack's AudiTrade.

Iowa Grain Company

After searching unsuccessfully for a third-party system that met its needs, Iowa Grain finally developed its own in-house system for exchange-traded derivatives which has several unique features. The Iowa Grain OAK system was one of the first to utilize Microsoft's COM (Component Object Model) where each component works independently of the other. The browser-based front-end uses either Internet Explorer or Netscape Communicator software to access the OAK order entry module.

Iowa Grain claims that the business logic and risk analysis middleware is OAK's most competitive feature. Each OAK account can have different margining or permissioning set-ups and margin call parameters. Customers also have the ability to filter orders, fills, etc., by their own specific criteria. Oak connects with the CBOT floor API, CBOT Order API, and CME Order API. In addition, it routes via Globex2 to the e-mini contracts.

Three-quarters of Iowa Grain's customers are IB's who have the ability to link directly into OAK utilizing their own web site links. Commercial traders, who constitute the remainder of the clients, can access OAK directly, without requiring an Internet front-end.

Iowa Grain offers other features including preset give-ups and trade allocations that make their system appropriate for CTA's and commercial traders. The firm is currently offering to license OAK to other FCM's.

Cargill Investor Services (CIS)

The CIS customer base is oriented more toward institutional traders than many other online brokerages. In fact, many of their customers are connected to the firm's order entry system from proprietary trading terminals with hard-wired connections as well as the Internet.

Many customers are European based and are heavy users of Eurex. Because of security concerns and Internet connection costs, European traders are more inclined to have hard-wired connections than their U.S. counterparts who readily use the Internet because of cost efficiency.

CIS believes there will be an inevitable shift to electronic trading at all levels since volume will follow liquidity. As a result, the firm is converting all its systems to be compatible with the CBOT and CME API's, and is already connected with Globex2 and the Eurex systems.

ABN AMRO

ABN AMRO, Incorporated, is a subsidiary of the Dutch banking giant, ABN AMRO Bank N.V. The firm concentrates on institutional and commercial clients located in the U.S., Europe, and the Asia/Pacific region.

Recently the firm created a FIX-compliant global order entry system on a Windows NT platform. The system utilizes touch-screen technology to speed up trade interaction with the exchange floors.

ABN AMRO Systems are designed primarily to meet the trading needs of banks, institutional clients, grain groups, and others that have either a global operation or global orientation. With most of its clients professional traders, ABN AMRO's system allows the client to enter an order by touch, have it routed to the appropriate exchange, and confirmed automatically. This is very important in 24-hour trading and for transferring the book around the world. The system enables credit and risk controls to remain in place over the entire trading period and across multiple exchanges, while also facilitating order flow from 24-hour trading desks.

The Role of the Exchanges

As brokerage firms improve their technology, and specifically their order entry systems, the exchanges must continually provide systems that meet the needs of FCM's, brokers, and individuals.

One system used by all major U.S. exchanges is the Trade Order Processing System (TOPS) route. This electronic link between broker firms and the floor booths was developed jointly by the CBOT and the CME. It is the standard order entry and fill reporting system. TOPS electronically sends information directly from the FCM to the trading floor compiling all of the relevant information to maintain an order book, advise the clearing house, and confirm the execution of the order to the customers. This entire process can be accomplished within minutes or less. Both the CBOT and CME are developing successor systems to increase the speed and accuracy of order flow.

The CME has an updated version of its CME Universal Broker Station (CUBS). CUBS2 automates the filling broker's order deck. It enables brokers to electronically fill and report orders to the originator, thereby providing a direct link between the FCM's order desk and the filling broker. The system captures endorsement information for filled orders and provides on-line inquiry. Individual customers benefit from expedient order fill reporting, improved audit trails, as well as reduced paper flow, transcription errors, and out-trades.

The Chicago Board of Trade has developed The Electronic Outcry Market. Essentially, this system is a paperless trading floor environment that enables FCM's to electronically manage customer business from both off-floor and on-floor locations. The principal component is the customer electronic order ticket (e-ticket) that is created during the order initiation phase. This can be accomplished by a customer using an Internet order entry system, an off-floor FCM using an order entry system, or an FCM's floor staff using an order entry device. New information is simply added to the original order during the trade execution and trade processing phases. The CBOT facilitates the FCM's ability to connect into this system with the OrderDirect API.

Firms have additional means of shortening the trading process. An Internet interface with a database incorporating customer information such as credit worthiness and available margin can be connected directly to the TOPS route, or one of the other systems, without the need to have intervention by anyone in the FCM's office. Both the CBOT and CME have developed API's to assist the member firms in connecting with their trading operations. Depending on the contract and timing, the order can transmitted directly to the exchange order matching system, CUBS2/ GLOBEX2, or the Electronic Open Outcry Market.

A Look to the Future

Some of the latest technological advances are in the field of individual communications. Laptop computers, PDA's such as the Palm VII, and even cell phones can read and transmit information over the Internet. The growth of these instruments, coupled with the electronic devices that communicate with floor traders, will make individual customers and their brokers even more accessible to each other.

These trends should accelerate growth in the number of futures traders and their ability to trade, regardless of their geographic location or personal time commitments.

Since many brokerage systems and methods were initially developed for equities trading, the current trends in those markets give us insight as to what can be expected in the futures industry.

One of the most innovative features has been the development of Electronic Communication Networks (ECN's). These include such firms as Instinet, Archipelago, Island, and others. Many brokers have affiliated with or purchased one of these entities, which to many resemble exchanges in and of themselves. Originally, ECN's were just as the name implies: high speed electronic networks to transmit orders to the various exchanges. Quickly, however, ECN's began to match their electronic orders for execution before passing them on to either the New York Stock Exchange or NASDAQ.

Currently, eleven firms qualify as ECN's. Recently, the ECN's joined together to offer after-hours trading in equities, strictly among their own networks. As they interconnect with each other, they generate more depth and liquidity on most major equity issues.

A futures equivalent of the ECN's is a real possibility unless U.S. futures exchanges maintain a leadership role in transmitting, executing, and confirming trades. The U.S. exchanges remain behind their European counterparts in embracing electronic trading, placing their existance at risk in today's world of technology.

---

* * *

Joseph H. Zoller, is president of The Zoller Organization, a marketing/communications firm specializing in marketing, creative, and communications services for the futures and financial services industry since 1981. Mr. Zoller's clients have included major futures and options exchanges, as well as leading FCM's, IB's, and CTA's. The Zoller Organization offers clients a broad range of communication services, including sales materials, advertising, trade show management, and editorial assistance. Additionally, Zoller consults with management of various firms regarding marketing and communications situations. Mr. Zoller can be contacted at The Zoller Organization, 1861 Old Briar Road, Highland Park, Illinois 60035, 847-831-4788, (FAX, 847-831-9082), or at joezoller@worldnet.att.net.

COMMODITY INVESTMENT AS AN ALTERNATIVE ASSET CLASS

by Raymond T. Murphy

Commodities as an Asset Class

As the world markets continue their evolution toward one global marketplace, the advent of financial futures trading has contributed much to that unification. The popularity of financial futures has removed some of the stigmas and fears that were associated with the perception of the rough and tumble world of commodities. Previously, investors who sought the stability associated with a traditional diversified portfolio often considered commodity futures too risky. Recently, with money managers searching the globe for additional investment opportunities, commodities have moved into the spotlight. The advantages of asset diversification have illuminated the value of commodity futures and options markets as the newest tools for investors to mitigate their long-term exposure to the price swings inherent in today's markets. By allocating some of their investment dollars to commodities, investors improve their ability to obtain desirable long-term results and, at the same time, lower the overall volatility of their portfolio.

Diversification into commodities gives the portfolio a more balanced inventory of assets. Whether or not high levels of inflation resurface, the allocation of a percentage of investable funds into an asset that will successfully lower the overall volatility of a portfolio and improve the annual performance is every investors goal. The counter-cyclic nature of commodities to financial assets makes commodities an ideal asset class to incorporate into a portfolio and thereby achieve a more desirable return scenario. Should inflation remain under control, the commodity portion of a properly allocated portfolio may lag other asset classes, but that lag normally indicates that the other non-commodity assets performed well. This is historically true because low to moderate inflationary periods allow for the stable environment in which traditional financial assets have performed well. In such a case, the commodity allocation would have served its purpose as a counter-cyclic asset to the rest of the portfolio. Commodity futures and options also provide a hedge against political instability and natural disasters that may adversely affect existing supply/demand alliances.

The Bridge/Commodity Research Bureau Futures Price Index (Bridge/CRB) and the Goldman Sachs Commodity Index (GSCI) are currently the only two commodity indexes that have exchange-listed futures contracts. Bridge/CRB, in conjunction with RTM Management, have created a continuous contract (CRB-CC) and total return (CRB-TR) calculation based upon the widely followed Bridge/CRB Futures Price Index. All three calculations are directly related to the New York Futures Exchange listed Bridge/CRB Futures Price Index futures contract.

Description of the Bridge/CRB

The Bridge/CRB Futures Price Index (Bridge/CRB), developed in 1956, is the best-known indicator of overall commodity prices in the world. At its 1956 origin, the Index was composed of 28 component markets, 26 exchange listed futures contracts and 2 cash markets. Its original design had weighted the index heavily towards agricultural commodities but over the past ten years changes have been made so that the Bridge/CRB today is more equally representative of a broad range of commodity prices.

The index is geometrically weighted evenly among 17 arithmetically averaged component commodities. Bridge/CRB futures and options contracts have been traded on the New York Futures Exchange (a division of the New York Board of Trade) since June, 1986. The Bridge/CRB futures contract has 6 expiration months per year (Jan-Feb-Apr-Jun-Aug-Nov). All futures and options expire to cash on the same date. One Bridge/CRB contract is worth $500 times the price of the index.

Bridge/CRB Futures Price Index components:

Grains:	Corn, Soybeans, Wheat
Livestock:	Live Cattle, Lean Hogs
Softs:	Cocoa, Coffee, Orange Juice, Sugar #11
Metals:	Gold, Platinum, Silver
Industrial:	Cotton, High Grade Copper
Energy:	Crude Oil, Heating Oil, Natural Gas

The Bridge/CRB Index is based on the average price of individual commodity futures contracts over a six-month period of time. When a futures contract expires or becomes eligible for delivery, whichever comes first, it is removed from the index. Distant contracts are added when their expiration date is on or before the end of the sixth calendar month from the current date. There are always a minimum of two contract months used, and a maximum of five, even if the contracts fall outside of the six month time window. When component contracts are added or deleted the Index may move significantly from the closing price to the next day's opening price before any of the components have opened for trading. This "adjustment" is the result of the addition or deletion of component futures contracts to the index and the price differences between them.

The Bridge/CRB Index is widely viewed as a broad measure of overall commodity price trends because of the diverse nature of the 17 commodities of which it is comprised. As a broad measure of commodity price trends it serves as an excellent price measure for macro-economic analysis. This reflects the fact that a more diverse index contains more information and, thus, can be used to better analyze economy-wide market forces.

Equal weighting is used for both arithmetic averaging of individual commodity contract months, and for geometric averaging of these 17 commodity averages. From a pricing point of view, equal weighting is attractive because no single month or single commodity has an undue impact on the Index. This makes it harder to manipulate the Index and means that the Index is less subject to the discontinuities associated with temporary supply and demand imbalances in any one contract month or in a single commodity.

It properly reflects price levels for its component commodities and is therefore useful in gauging commodity price strength or weakness against historical periods. It does not show, however, the *returns* that would have been achieved by a passively held investment using the CRB as a benchmark. By calculating this return characteristic, investment professionals can now accurately assess the usability of commodities in their overall investment program. A total return index allows commodities to be examined on an even playing field with other traditional asset classes.

Description of the GSCI

The GSCI is a production weighted, arithmetically averaged index. The weightings for the included component commodities are based on "Total World Production Dollar Value." Because of this method of weighting the component commodities, the GSCI is very heavily weighted toward the energy sector.

Historically the energy markets have traded in "backwardation," a term that describes those commodities that are priced with a premium in the nearest contract months, and successively lower prices for the deferred contracts. Goldman Sachs promotes the returns realized over time by capturing the backwardation historically present in the energy futures markets, particularly in Crude Oil, 28.5% of the Index; Brent Crude, 12% of the Index; Heating Oil, 7.2% of the Index; and Unleaded Gasoline, 5.7% of the Index.

GSCI future and option contracts have been traded on the Chicago Mercantile Exchange since July, 1992. The GSCI futures contract has serial (monthly) expirations. All futures and options expire to cash on the same date. The GSCI has the same cash and total return characteristics as the Bridge/CRB.

GSCI Sector and Component Weightings

ENERGY - 58.38%	
Crude Oil	24.88%
Brent Crude	11.29
Natural Gas	7.77
Heating Oil	6.68
Unleaded Gas	4.98
Gas Oil	2.78
AGRICULTURE - 20.63%	
Corn	5.11%
Wheat	4.71
Soybeans	2.45
Cotton	2.30
Sugar	1.88
Red Wheat	1.64
Coffee	1.33
Orange Juice	0.92
Cocoa	0.29
LIVESTOCK - 10.05%	
Live Cattle	7.19%
Lean Hogs	2.86
INDUSTRIAL METALS - 8.48%	
Aluminum	4.22%
Copper	2.20
Zinc	0.98
Nickel	0.65
Lead	0.31
Tin	0.12
PRECIOUS METALS - 2.46%	
Gold	2.02%
Silver	0.27
Platinum	0.17

Total Rate of Return

The nature of commodity futures makes it difficult to determine the actual long-term returns associated with a passive position over long periods of time. A passive long position in futures contracts needs to be continually rolled in order to avoid delivery and/or expiring contracts. The total return, by definition, measures the actual dollar return on an entire investment. Generally, futures contracts require only a 5 percent "performance bond" as a margin requirement so the vast majority of a fully collateralized investment in futures can be held in interest bearing certificates, normally three-month Treasury bills. Therefore, a total return calculation on a passive investment in futures must incorporate the interest earned from these certificates.

The total rate of return for both the Bridge/CRB and the GSCI is determined by three factors: spot yield, roll level, and the collateral yield.

1. The *spot yield* is the return associated with the price performance of the index.

2. The *roll yield* is the return associated with the continuous rolling of near-term commodity contracts to more deferred ones. The levels of these rolls will either involve rolling into a lower priced contract (backwardation) or a more expensive one (contango). The roll yield may be either positive or negative, depending on the prices present during the roll period. The combination of the spot yield and the roll yield make up the *continuous contract* (GSCI literature refers to this calculation as the *"excess return"*). The continuous contract is a measurement of the realized return of a passive investment in any commodity based on price movement alone. Adjustments are made to account for the rolling of contracts to more deferred contract months without affecting the actual dollar return of the instrument.

3. The *collateral yield* is the interest rate component derived from an unleveraged commodity investment. The total return index for both the Bridge/CRB and GSCI is determined by the continuous contract plus interest earned from the uncollateralized position. Each index uses 90-day T-Bill rates for this component of their respective total return results.

Using Listed Futures Contracts to Obtain the Total Return Benchmark

Both the Bridge/CRB and GSCI have a measurable benchmark associated with them. The investor must now decide which one to use or, more probably, what combination of the two should be used. In determining a benchmark for a commodity allocation, it is important to understand how each of these commodity indices function in regard to the arbitrage strategies involved with them. Arbitrage on the Bridge/CRB and GSCI represents, like all arbitrages, the ability to capture a mispricing in the futures market versus the underlying cash index. By selling/buying the index futures contract when it is at a premium/discount to its fair value, a trader can capture the differential between the two. This is a critical factor when deciding the best way to allocate commodity exposure because a total return benchmark is only useful if it can be achieved. It is important, therefore, to examine how the Bridge/CRB and the GSCI futures contracts work in real life.

The GSCI is an arithmetically weighted index. The only way an arbitrageur can make a profit is by selling the futures above their fair value or buying them at a discount to their fair value. The futures generally trade at a *premium* because of the significant passive long interest in the product. The roll period for the GSCI takes place on the five days preceding each month's expiration. It is during this period that a passive long investor must roll one fifth of his position into the next contract month. This process is repeated 12 times a year. By paying a premium to the fair value of the index (fair value being the number used for total return calculations), a passive long investor who uses the GSCI as a diversifying asset pays a premium to keep the position and therefore under-performs the GSCI total return benchmark. It also is weighted at 250 times the index (the CRB is 500 times the index). This means it takes roughly two times as many GSCI contracts as Bridge/CRB contracts on a dollar-weighted scale to achieve an investor's required allocation.

The Bridge/CRB, on the other hand, is a geometrically weighted index and normally trades at a *discount* to its fair value. The discount exists because the arbitrageurs that trade the Bridge/CRB can sell the index futures at a discount and then proceed to profit from the volatility of the underlying components. By capturing this discount and rolling it at each expiration (six times a year), the passive long investor can outperform a Bridge/CRB total return benchmark.

It is also useful to examine the arithmetic/geometric argument that inevitably comes up whenever discussing these two indices. While a geometric average will under-perform a similar arithmetic average, a passive long investor must consider a number of other factors. If an investor can buy a geometrically averaged index at a discount versus buying an arithmetically averaged index at a premium, a good portion of the geometric underperformance argument can be excused (if not occasionally exploited).

A second argument concerns volatility of returns. Because the GSCI is heavily weighted in energy, it is much more volatile than the Bridge/CRB. Contributing to this volatility is the fact that when a component commodity of the GSCI rises or falls significantly, an investor holds the same fixed number of equivalent futures contracts. For example, a 100 lot GSCI futures position has the equivalent of about 30 crude oil futures contracts. During the rise in crude oil from $11 per barrel to $30 per barrel, an investor's crude oil component position would go from a value of $330,000 to $900,000. The owner of Bridge/CRB futures contracts would have a decreasing number of equivalent crude oil contracts since the index constantly rebalances itself. The equal weighting scheme of the Bridge/CRB requires that all of its components be constantly readjusted as their prices move up or down. It is this feature which keeps the volatility of the index lower than the GSCI and also allows investors to purchase Bridge/CRB futures contracts at a discount.

The individual investor must develop a commodity exposure that best suits his or her needs. By combining the energy weighted GSCI and the more equally weighted, broad-based Bridge/CRB, an investor will be able to tap into this often overlooked asset class.

---

* * *

Raymond T. Murphy is president of RTM Management, Inc. (RTMM), a commodity trading advisory company. RTMM specializes in developing commodity allocation strategies for investment professionals. Office phone: 203-792-1100; Email address: raytmet@aol.com.

A HISTORY OF THE COMMODITY RESEARCH BUREAU

It was 1933, the country was in the depth of the Depression, and the United States had just gone off the gold standard. At a value of $0.59 compared to the pre-devalued dollar, capital began flowing back into the country and trading activity in stocks, bonds, and commodity futures was beginning to show some life. Nevertheless, traders and those interested in commodities found very few sources of comprehensive information were available to them.

At this time, Milton Jiler, a young reporter for the New York American, was covering commodity exchanges and doing freelance public relations work for some of the exchanges to supplement his income. Gregarious by nature, Jiler soon became known among the exchanges' commodity traders. He was quick to realize that unless one was actually on the floor of the exchanges, price and volume information was difficult to come by. Although The Wall Street Journal covered the stock market quite thoroughly, there was little if any price information available for commodity futures.

Milton Jiler had a simple idea. If no one was providing information about the commodities markets, trading was limited to those people with direct access to the floor. Increased use of the telephone made communications between customers and their brokers easier, but there was no source of closing prices that could be used to establish trends and trading strategies. This was particularly important to brokers, advisors, and commercial users of the various commodities as well as the speculators who made the markets.

As a journalist, Jiler firmly believed that, "No publication should be started unless it is needed." What he saw was the need for a medium that would bring information about the futures markets to interested parties on a timely basis. With that in mind he founded the Commodity Research Bureau, with the Futures Market Service as its first publication.

Starting with virtually no capital, Jiler had to convince potential customers and suppliers of the viability of his new idea. He first found a printer willing to produce one issue of the Futures Market Service on credit; an unheard of arrangement in light of the economic times. Additionally, he located a paper supplier willing to provide stock on the same terms.

He then approached several of the people he knew would benefit from his idea. His first calls were placed to some of the leading brokerage houses of the day: Ed Pierce, president of E.A. Pierce and Company, and Harold Bache, president of Bache & Company, were early supporters. They agreed to purchase several hundred copies of the new publication on a trial basis and distribute them to their brokers and key clients. When it finally appeared that the concept would become a reality, Milton convinced his brother, Harry Jiler, to join him as president of the fledgling firm. A Certified Public Accountant and an economist, Harry's experience and insight would prove to be extremely valuable to the new company.

According to Milton Jiler, "Getting that first issue out required 'chutzpah.'" But on February 3, 1934, the CRB Futures Market Service made its debut. The report consisted of seven legal-size pages, with typewritten text, divided into multiple sections. The lead article was an overall analysis of the markets headed, "The Outlook for Commodity Prices." This feature set the tone for the publication and remains as the front page story to this day.

Following the lead report was an analysis of the individual commodities, grouped according to letter grades. In retrospect, this grouping provided an insight to governmental policies as well as general economic conditions of the day. Group A-1 commodities included "those contracts entitled to further price improvement on the basis of actual or indicated statistical improvement." Group B-1 included "commodities dependent on new governmental aid or international restriction for further price increase." Group C-1 was classified as "these commodities should join in the general advance. This group has evidently discounted special factors."

These groupings of commodities remained in effect until World War II, when each wartime issue contained the following statement:

> "Our regular readers will note that we have dropped our rating system for the various commodities which, under the present national emergency, might be confused by some as catering to the uninformed speculator."

The Commodity Research Bureau Futures Market Service became profitable within its first year of existence, allowing the company to pay all its early creditors. Its success was due in large part to its ability to provide information that was not readily available to traders. CRB built a network of more than a dozen sources to provide the current fundamental information for each exchange-traded commodity.

In 1939, CRB published its first Commodity Year Book. Priced at $10.00, this volume incorporated comprehensive statistical information on all of the exchange-traded commodities. Long considered the "Bible of the Industry," it has been published annually ever since then, with just a brief hiatus during World War II.

Wartime restrictions reduced commodities trading volume as well as trader interest in the Commodity Research Bureau. During the War, shortages, allocations, rationing, price controls and fixed price ceilings on exchange-traded commodities precluded a free market and, for all practical purposes, halted trading on the futures exchanges.

During the conflict, Milton served in the Pacific Theatre as a United States Army Officer, leaving Harry, who was beyond draft age, to run the company in his brother's absence. In order to keep the company alive during the war years, Harry started a new publishing division, Employees Relations Productions. He authored and published booklets to be sold en masse to corporations who would distribute them to their employees. Employees Relations Productions' biggest seller was a book Harry wrote on Social Security which was approved by the Social Security Administration. Hundreds of thousands were sold. Later on, books on Income Tax and Veterans Benefits were added. This new enterprise kept CRB alive and financially healthy throughout and immediately after the War years.

By May, 1945, the Futures Market Service (now referred to as the Blue Sheet because of the color of its paper stock) reactivated the staff and resumed publishing on a full scale. Following V-E Day, the Blue Sheet concluded that the country was heading for a temporary economic slowdown and lower commodity prices.

On May 14, 1945, the CRB predicted:

> "...industrial activity will decline. A slight decline has been under way since 1943, owing to labor and material shortages, but it will be accelerated as reconversion proceeds. The trend in industrial activity is likely to be lower for the next few months and probably won't level out until the fall. This means a substantial reduction in the production of war materials."
>
> "But it does not spell an immediate expansion in the production of civilian goods. The output of civilian goods will be delayed by preparations for reconversion. Hence, on a supply and demand basis, there is little reason to anticipate any weakening of the finished goods price level."
>
> "...In summarizing, we doubt whether V-E Day is going to influence any protracted price declines in the commodity level...Hence, we doubt whether commodity prices will be faced with a crisis until V-J Day."

By August 13, 1945, the CRB issued this prescient message:

> "...Hence, we believe that the greatest threat of inflation will occur during the immediate post-war reconstruction period because production will not be fully geared to meet all demands. Once production catches up with demand, the inflationary threat will vanish. However, we believe that more favorable buying opportunities will occur before the post-war recovery gets under way."

As the CRB regained its peacetime footing, the first post-war edition of the Commodity Year Book was published in 1947. Similarly, the Blue Sheet was expanding its reach to new heights. In 1950, the Jiler's recruited their youngest brother, William, to work on a project during the summer following the completion of his graduate degree in corporate finance. Not anticipating a career in the commodity industry, Bill had previously earned a degree in chemistry and had worked for almost three years as a research chemist for the pharmaceutical company, E.J. Squibb. In the summer of 1950, Bill was on a leave of absence to complete a business degree, a prerequisite for entrance into the Squibb Executive Training Program. The excitement of the financial markets and hands-on exposure to running a business had great appeal to Bill. At summer's end he stayed on at CRB and never looked back.

Bill immersed himself in the study of economics. He took night classes at New York University and The New School For Social Research for several years in subjects ranging from economics to futures markets, securities markets, and original writing courses. As an aerial navigator on a B-29 during World War II, he had a lot of experience with maps and charts. Bill found that price charts were indespensable in following the futures markets. This led to the creation of CRB Commodity Chart Service, a weekly publication of updated charts for all of the futures markets.

Price charts had long been a feature of the Commodity Year Book, so it was fitting that the staff publish these charts on a more frequent basis. On March 2, 1956, the inaugural issue of Commodity Chart Service was published. Charts were meticulously hand-drawn and updated on a daily basis. Whenever a market made a large price move, the entire chart would need to be redrawn from the beginning to fit a larger price scale. CRB ultimately required a staff of six full-time employees just for drawing and updating the daily charts.

There is no doubt that CRB's Commodity Chart Service was one of the first products to popularize technical analysis and make charts available to ordinary investors outside of the profession. Although most of the narrative of the Futures Market Service was, and still is, based on fundamentals, the text accompanying the set of weekly and monthly charts was the "Technical Comment," as interpreted by the CRB staff.

This was stated in the first issue:

> "The technical views which will be expressed in this column are the opinions of the chartists on the staff of the Commodity Research Bureau. They are not based on any specific traditional charting system, although they may contain elements of a number of previously established methods. Comments in this section will be confined to interesting chart situations either from the technical aspect, unusual interest, or possibly profitable trading opportunities."

After introducing the Commodity Chart Service, Bill Jiler later started the Trendline Chart Service, which covered the equity markets. Trendline Chart Service was the first service to publicize the 200-day moving average and apply it to equity prices as a technical analysis tool. Now, some 40 years later, the 200-day moving average is arguably the most important long-term technical indicator of stock price trends. Approximately five years later, Trendline Chart Service was sold to the Standard & Poor's Corporation and Bill Jiler assumed the title of President of Trendline Corp.

Yet another CRB achievement attributed to Bill Jiler was the development of the CRB Index. According to Jiler, he felt that the industry needed something that better reflected the overall price activity in the commodity markets then the antiquated Dow Jones Futures Index. The CRB Futures Price Index was created in late 1956, and quickly took hold among established futures traders, soon becoming the dominant index of futures activity. Today, 44 years later, the CRB Futures Price Index remains the global benchmark for measuring commodity price movement.

This Redemption Notice appeared in the New York Herald Tribune on April 2, 1964:

> ## S & P Acquires Trendline
>
> Standard & Poor's Corporation announces that it has acquired two chart publishing companies, effective April 1, 1964. The major acquisition is Trendline Corp. purchased for cash and S & P stock from Messrs. Harry, Milton and William Jiler, owners and founders of Trendline.
>
> In a seperate transaction OTC Publications, Inc. was also acquired on the basis of an exchange of S & P stock for 100% of the stock of OTC Publications. The S & P stock involved in both acquisitions was Treasury stock, previously purchased in the open market.
>
> The acquired companies will continue to operate at 82 Beaver Street, New York, with no change in management or personnel. William L. Jiler will be President of Trendline Corp.
>
> The acquired companies publish a series of widely used chart services know as Trendline's Daily Basis Stock Charts, Trendline's Current Market Perspectives and the OTC Chart Manual, as well as the book "How Charts Can Help You in the Stock Market." These publications will help to round out the services provided by S & P to the investment field, since S & P does not publish any chart services.
>
> STANDARD & POOR'S CORPORATION
> **345 Hudson Street, New York, NY 10014**

REDEMPTION NOTICE

The CRB Index was originally designed to provide a dynamic representation of broad trends in commodity prices and was more reflective of the overall price of exchange-traded commodities than was the Spot Commodity Index, then compiled by the Bureau of Labor Statistics. Although the BLS index was interesting, it covered only cash transactions and was not as timely as the one compiled by the Commodity Research Bureau. Eventually the government turned over the BLS Spot Commodity Index to CRB to calculate.

In order to maintain the usefulness of the CRB Futures Price Index it has been periodically adjusted to reflect changes in market structure and activity. There have been nine modifications to the Index calculation and component commodities since its inception in 1956, the last change occuring in 1995.

The talents of each of the Jiler's meshed very well in their role as the management team of the Commodity Research Bureau. According to outside observers and long-time staff members, Milton was the "idea" man. Developing the company and its initial products, and with his many contacts within the industry, he was responsible for marketing and promotion. The older brother, Harry, knew how to implement Milton's ideas and run the operation on a business-like basis. Bill, the youngest brother, was considered the innovator and developer of new products. He recognized the value of developing companion products and services, most of which became successful in their own right. CRB began to publish text books, such as *Guide To Commodity Price Forecasting*, *Techniques of a Professional Commodity Chart Analyst*, and *Economics of Futures Trading* to name a just a few.

Bridge/CRB Futures Price Index Components

CRB Index Components, 1956	CRB Index Components, 2000
Barley	Cocoa
Cocoa	Coffee "C"
Coffee "B"	Copper
Copper	Corn
Corn	Cotton
Cotton	Crude Oil
Cottonseed Oil	Gold
Eggs	Heating Oil
Flaxseed	Lean Hogs
Grease Wool	Live Cattle
Hides	Natural Gas
Lard	Orange Juice
Lead	Platinum
Minneapolis Wheat (cash)	Silver
New Orleans Cotton (cash)	Soybeans
Oats	Sugar "11"
Onions	Wheat
Potatoes	
Rubber	
Rye	
Soybean Meal	
Soybean Oil	
Soybeans	
Sugar "4"	
Sugar "6"	
Wheat	
Wool Tops	
Zinc	

In 1979, Harry Jiler passed away. Public participation in the futures markets was the highest it had ever been since the founding of CRB due to rampant inflation and highly publicized bull markets in precious metals, strategic metals, and grains. Speculators were rushing headfirst into any type of "real asset," and shunning any investment that was debt or equity related.

In the early 1980's, the two surviving Jiler brothers received several offers for the company and its publications. At first they resisted, but with Milton in his seventies, and commodity prices and public participation already declining from their 1980 peaks, they finally agreed to an offer from Knight-Ridder Financial Publishing (KRFP). On December 1, 1984, KRFP acquired the Commodity Research Bureau including its products, subscriber base, and the classic CRB books that were still being published. William Jiler remained with the company for a time until he retired in late 1986.

Knight-Ridder Financial Publishing initiated a switch from hand-drawn to computer-generated charts. The company already owned Commodity Perspective, a Chicago-based futures market charting service it had purchased in the early 1980's, so after acquiring CRB the company published both Commodity Perspective and Commodity Price Charts until the two services were merged into one in 1996. The newly merged publication was named CRB Futures Perspective and it continues to be published every Friday afternoon, immediately after the markets close.

Computers and electronic databases were becoming more and more common as a business tool at the time Knight-Ridder Financial Publishing acquired CRB. Shortly after the acquisition, the staff of KRFP began the arduous process of copying into an electronic database the entire commodity price history CRB had collected and cataloged on paper since 1934. Price data from exchanges, cash markets, and third party sources, some going back into the 1800's, was painstakingly hand-transferred to the new computerized database. After the project was finally completed, KRFP released a new product they named InfoTech. The InfoTech product was a CD-ROM that contained the entire CRB historical database, both historical prices and the supply and demand information that had appeared in every CRB Commodity Yearbook since 1965. At that time, CD-ROMs were so new that KRFP included a CD-ROM player with every InfoTech order because very few computers had one. Daily price data updates were delivered to the new computerized customers by direct modem connection to KRFP-maintained servers in New York, Chicago, London, Singapore, and Hong Kong.

The acquisition of CRB by Knight-Ridder Financial Publishing presented a logistical challenge as well, operating a publishing business from two different cities, Jersey City and Chicago. KRFP began by moving CRB from Jersey City back into New York's financial district. By 1990, KRFP had consolidated all of the CRB operations into one location at the Knight-Ridder Financial corporate headquarters at 75 Wall Street. In 1993, the Commodity Research Bureau was moved to Chicago, home of the world's largest futures community, and incorporated into the Knight-Ridder Financial Publishing organization there, where it continues its operations today.

A futures contract on the CRB Futures Price Index was introduced on the New York Futures Exchange

(NYFE) in 1986, and quickly became the most watched contract on the exchange. Bill Jiler worked with the NYFE in creating the contract that ultimately generated considerable additional exposure for the Index. The contract continues to actively trade today on the NYFE division of the New York Board of Trade (NYBOT).

In 1997, Bridge Information Systems Inc., a growing global financial information provider, purchased Knight-Ridder Financial, including KRFP and the Commodity Research Bureau. The organization that had been known as KRFP took on the new name Bridge Commodity Research Bureau (Bridge/CRB). Today, Bridge/CRB continues to publish the Futures Market Service and distributes it in both hard copy and via e-mail. CRB Futures Perspective remains a weekly publication and is printed and mailed every Friday afternoon. The CRB Commodity Yearbook, in both hard cover and CD-ROM format, is published annually every May. Additionally, Electronic Futures Trend Analyzer (EFTA), a pioneer computerized trading system CRB developed in the early 1970's, is available online. Subscribers can also obtain Final Markets end-of-day price data, daily Futures Market Service commentary, EFTA, and daily news summaries via the online Bridge/CRB DataCenter. Additionally, CRB/MarketCenter, Bridge/CRB's newest product, provides subscribers with real-time information including quotes, news, charts, and analytics delivered without resident software via the Internet.

Milton Jiler still lives in New York City with his wife, Daisy. Although acknowledging that although he didn't anticipate the growth of electronic data and automated trading systems, he still believes that a publication, whether on paper, on the Internet, or as digital data, must provide a need to justify its existence. Harry Jiler passed away in 1979, when CRB was still a family owned business. William Jiler and his wife, Jan, reside in Florida. Bill remains an active follower of the markets, when he is not playing golf or enjoying the sun.

Volume U.S.

U.S. FUTURES VOLUME HIGHLIGHTS

1999 in Comparison with 1998

1999 Rank	Top 50 Contracts Traded in 1999	1999 Contracts	1999 %	1998 Contracts	1998 %	1998 Rank
1	Eurodollar, CME	93,418,498	19.55%	109,742,507	21.76%	2
2	T-Bonds, CBT	90,042,282	18.84%	112,224,081	22.30%	1
3	Crude Oil, NYMEX	37,860,064	7.92%	30,495,647	6.06%	5
4	T-Notes (10 Year), CBT	34,045,758	7.12%	32,482,576	6.46%	3
5	S&P 500 Index, CME	27,003,387	5.65%	31,430,523	6.25%	4
6	Natural Gas, NYMEX	19,165,096	4.01%	15,978,286	3.18%	7
7	T-Notes (5 Year), CBT	16,983,812	3.55%	18,060,048	3.59%	6
8	Corn, CBT	15,724,845	3.29%	15,795,493	3.14%	8
9	Soybeans, CBT	12,481,947	2.61%	12,431,156	2.47%	9
10	E Mini S&P, CME	10,953,551	2.29%	4,466,032	0.89%	19
11	Gold (100 oz.), COMEX Div. of NYMEX	9,575,788	2.00%	8,990,094	1.79%	10
12	#2 Heating Oil, NYMEX	9,200,703	1.93%	8,863,764	1.76%	11
13	Unleaded Regular Gas, NYMEX	8,701,216	1.82%	7,992,269	1.59%	12
14	Wheat, CBT	6,570,025	1.37%	5,681,569	1.13%	17
15	Soybean Meal, CBT	6,326,897	1.32%	6,553,846	1.30%	15
16	Japanese Yen, CME	5,935,843	1.24%	7,065,266	1.40%	13
17	Sugar #11, NYBOT	5,911,299	1.24%	5,524,111	1.10%	18
18	Soybean Oil, CBT	5,663,895	1.19%	6,498,263	1.29%	16
19	Silver (5,000 oz), COMEX Div. of NYMEX	4,157,500	0.87%	4,094,616	0.81%	21
20	Swiss Franc, CME	4,114,824	0.86%	3,974,163	0.79%	22
21	Dow Jones Industrial Index, CBOT	3,896,086	0.82%	3,567,512	0.71%	23
22	Live Cattle, CME	3,839,548	0.80%	4,216,506	0.84%	20
23	Euro FX	3,002,453	0.63%			
24	High Grade Copper, COMEX Div. of NYMEX	2,852,962	0.60%	2,483,610	0.49%	26
25	British Pound, CME	2,738,600	0.57%	2,645,017	0.53%	25
26	Coffee "C", NYBOT	2,659,233	0.56%	2,095,030	0.42%	29
27	Canadian Dollar, CME	2,573,762	0.54%	2,396,300	0.48%	27
28	Cotton, NYBOT	2,448,087	0.51%	3,200,830	0.64%	24
29	NASDAQ 100, CME	2,360,938	0.49%	1,063,328	0.21%	37
30	Lean Hogs, CME	2,358,096	0.49%	2,136,282	0.42%	28
31	Wheat, KCBT	2,321,059	0.49%	2,006,779	0.40%	30
32	Cocoa, NYBOT	1,868,036	0.39%	1,810,580	0.36%	31
33	Deutsche Mark, CME	1,497,389	0.31%	6,884,026	1.37%	14
34	Mexican Peso, CME	1,143,641	0.24%	1,353,867	0.27%	33
35	Wheat, MGE	1,119,812	0.23%	1,092,964	0.22%	36
36	T-Bonds, MIDAM	1,058,816	0.22%	1,537,286	0.31%	32
37	T-Notes (2 Year), CBT	1,047,348	0.22%	1,347,575	0.27%	34
38	30 Day Federal Funds, CBT	1,023,716	0.21%	844,408	0.17%	42
39	Euroyen, CME	945,419	0.20%	962,574	0.19%	39
40	Goldman Sachs Commodity Index, CME	926,933	0.19%	854,264	0.17%	41
41	Australian Dollar, CME	861,023	0.18%	664,563	0.13%	45
42	One Month LIBOR, CME	843,054	0.18%	1,108,454	0.22%	35
43	Municipal Bond Index, CBT	798,597	0.17%	1,002,075	0.20%	38
44	Orange Juice (Frozen Conc.), NYCE	793,882	0.17%	914,614	0.18%	40
45	E-Mini NASDAQ 100, CME	682,059	0.14%			
46	Soybeans, MIDAM	651,268	0.14%	767,858	0.15%	43
47	Feeder Cattle, CME	650,071	0.14%	738,567	0.15%	44
48	Platinum, NYMEX	567,268	0.12%	528,269	0.10%	47
49	Nikkei, CME	513,848	0.11%	479,248	0.10%	49
50	Oats, CBT	371,406	0.08%			
	Top 50 Contracts	47,251,640		496,776,696 *		
	Contracts Below the Top 50	5,667,668	1.19%	6,424,749	1.28%	
	TOTAL	**477,919,308**	**100.00%**	**503,201,445**	**100.00%**	

* For 1998 Top 50 contracts totaled 498,317,566 including 3 contracts that are not among 1999's Top 5

U.S. FUTURES VOLUME HIGHLIGHTS

1999 in Comparison with 1998

1999 RANK	EXCHANGE	1999 CONTRACTS	1999 %	1998 CONTRACTS	1998 %	1998 RANK
1	Chicago Board of Trade (CBT	195,147,279	40.83%	217,138,928	43.15%	1
2	Chicago Mercantile Exchange (CME	168,013,357	35.16%	183,627,443	36.49%	2
3	New York Mercantile Exchange (NYMEX)	92,415,006	19.34%	80,011,517	15.90%	3
4	New York Board of Trade (NYBOT) *	15,958,237	3.34%	16,049,651	3.19%	4
5	MidAmerica Commodity Exchang	2,433,894	0.51%	3,081,181	0.61%	6
6	Kansas City Board of Trade (KCBT	2,378,271	0.50%	2,164,959	0.43%	7
7	Minneapolis Grain Exchange (MGE	1,134,945	0.24%	1,125,194	0.22%	8
8	Cantor Exchange (CE	438,068	0.09%			
9	Philadelphia Board of Trade (PBOT	251	0.00%	2,572	0.00%	9
	TOTAL	**477,919,308**	**100.00%**	**397,402,153**	**100.00%**	

* Includes Comex Division

** Includes the New York Futures Exchange, New York Cotton Exchange and Coffee, Sugar and Cocoa Exchan

U.S. FUTURES VOLUME 1995 - 1999

CANTOR EXCHANGE (CE)

FUTURE	CONTRACT UNIT	1999	1998	1997	1996	1995
8% U.S. Treasury Bonds (30-year)	100,000 USD	299,094				
8% U.S. Treasury Notes (5-year)	100,000 USD	30,439				
8% U.S. Treasury Notes (10-year)	100,000 USD	101,510				
6% U.S. Treasury Bonds (30-year)	100,000 USD	5,135				
6% U.S. Treasury Notes (5-year)	100,000 USD	85				
6% U.S. Treasury Notes (10-year)	100,000 USD	1,805				
Total		**438,068**				

CHICAGO BOARD OF TRADE (CBT)

FUTURE	CONTRACT UNIT	1999	1998	1997	1996	1995
Wheat	5,000 bu	6,570,025	5,681,569	5,058,645	5,385,967	4,955,067
Corn	5,000 bu	15,724,845	15,795,493	16,984,951	19,620,188	15,105,147
Oats	5,000 bu	371,406	397,332	397,332	501,858	475,538
Soybeans	5,000 bu	12,481,947	12,431,156	14,539,766	14,236,295	10,611,534
Soybean Oil	60,000 lbs	5,663,895	6,498,263	5,284,994	4,980,277	4,611,336
Soybean Meal	100 tons	6,326,897	6,553,846	6,424,945	5,955,977	5,601,242
Rice	200,000 lbs	139,592	157,764	171,973	119,900	121,914
Crop Yield	Crop yield est. X 10	115	337	1,472	1,343	3,123
Diammonium Phosphate	100 tons			144	3,935	6,755
Anhydrous Ammonia	100 tons			19	351	1,060
Edible Oil Index	100 tons					21
Structural Panel Index	100,000 sq. ft.					885
National Catastrophe Insurance	Loss/EP x 25,000 USD					
Com Ed Hub Electricity	1,680 Mwh		88			
TVA Hub Electricity	1,680 Mwh	22	184			
Silver	5,000 oz	125	7	61	110	8,617
Silver	1,000 oz	20,560	35,505	30,771	41,575	76,667
Gold	100 oz	4	204	138	335	647
Gold	Kilo	10,247	13,363	13,620	17,687	20,245
U.S. Treasury Bonds (30-year)	100,000 USD	90,042,282	112,224,081	99,827,659	84,725,128	86,375,916
U.S. Treasury Notes (10-year)	100,000 USD	34,045,758	32,482,576	23,961,819	21,939,725	22,445,356
U.S. Treasury Notes (5-year)	100,000 USD	16,983,812	18,060,048	13,488,725	11,463,640	12,637,054
U.S. Treasury Notes (2-year)	200,000 USD	1,047,348	1,347,575	1,018,545	643,845	744,866
30-Day Federal Funds	5,000,000 USD	1,023,716	844,408	910,474	608,308	643,717
German Bund	250,000			200,588		
Municipal Bond Index	1,000 USD x Index	798,597	1,002,075	983,877	883,901	1,169,470
Treasury Note Inflation Indices	100,000 USD			22		
Dow Jones Industrial Index	10 USD x Index	3,896,086	3,567,512	755,476		
Brady Bond Index	1,000 USD x Index				69	
Yield Curve Spread	25,000 USD x 100YC			271	3,771	
Total		**195,147,279**	**142,241,377**	**190,056,287**	**171,134,185**	**165,616,177**

Volume U.S.

CHICAGO MERCANTILE EXCHANGE (CME)

FUTURE	CONTRACT UNIT	1999	1998	1997	1996	1995
Live Hogs	40,000 lbs				1,784,564	1,669,680
Lean Hogs	40,000 lbs	2,358,096	2,136,282	2,100,909	311,347	984
Pork Bellies, Frozen	40,000 lbs	368,309	481,252	595,319	612,649	561,913
Pork Bellies, Fresh	40,000 lbs	195	4,922			
Boneless Beef	200,000 lbs 90% lean	105	3,433	4,245		
Boneless Beef Trimmings	200,000 lbs 50% lean		1,239	4,876		
Butter	40,000 lbs	3,354	667	2,805	273	
Cheddar Cheese	40,000 lbs	8	1,540	533		
Fluid MIlk	50,000 lbs	45,753	30,734	4,188	2,336	
Live Cattle	40,000 lbs	3,839,548	4,216,506	3,919,642	3,926,192	3,257,105
Stocker Cattle	25,000 lbs	906	411			
Feeder Cattle	44,000 lbs	650,071	738,567	837,165	772,222	511,895
Pork Cutout	40,000 lbs	847				
Lumber	160,000 bd ft				26,293	179,538
Orient Strand Board Lumber	100,000 bd ft	535	505	1,115	235	
Random Lumber	80,000 bd ft	287,856	249,847	260,318	277,781	3,148
U.S. Trreasury Bills (90-day)	1,000,000 USD	41,260	104,180	199,084	251,353	620,223
Eurodollars (3-month)	1,000,000 USD	93,418,498	109,472,507	99,770,237	88,883,119	95,730,019
Euroyen	1,000,000,000 Yen	945,419	962,574	1,119,827	503,104	
Federal Funds Rate	3,000,000 USD			2,790	47,495	52,412
Federal Funds Turn	45,000,000 USD	373	370			
One Month LIBOR	3,000,000 USD	843,054	1,108,454	1,504,230	1,190,652	1,707,062
Argentine FRB Bond	1,000 USD X Bond		5	1,553	9,610	
Brazilian C Bond	500 USD x Bond			2,995	10,198	
Brazilian EL Bond	500 USD x Bond	822	3,150		253	
Japanese Government Bond	50,000,000 Yen	73				
Mexican PAR Bond	500 USD x Bond			366	1,926	
Mexican CETES	2,000,000	1	343	8,598		
Mexican TIIE	6,000,000	2		1,897		
BP/DM Crossrate	125,000 GBP		109	127		
JY/DM Crossrate	250,000 DEM		3	180		
DM/JY Cross (New)	125,000 x dm/jy X					106
British Pound	62,500	2,738,600	2,645,017	2,664,401	2,961,782	2,610,510
Brazilian Real	100,000	59,104	79,509	49,092	87,323	20,364
Canadian Dollar	100,000	2,573,762	2,396,300	2,542,102	1,932,729	1,756,569
Deutsche Mark	125,000	1,497,389	6,884,026	7,044,783	5,979,464	7,186,476
Euro Canada	1,000,000	50	12,311			
Japanese Yen	12,500,000	5,935,843	7,065,266	6,034,565	5,101,819	5,630,053
Mexican Peso	500,000	1,143,641	1,353,867	1,707,706	850,040	133,791
Swiss Franc	125,000	4,114,824	3,974,163	4,222,268	3,929,225	4,399,932
Australian Dollar	100,000	861,023	664,563	595,573	461,084	346,823
French Franc	250,000	6,745	72,562	112,520	67,835	48,621
New Zealand Dollar	100,000	42,646	16,580	3,506		
South African Rand	500,000	51,762	12,766	6,287		
Russian Ruble	500,000	43	21,766			
Euro FX (ECU)	125,000	3,002,453	17			
E-mini Euro FX	62,500	1,775				
E-Mini Japanese Yen	6,250,000	1,072				
Euro / British Pound	125,000 x Euro	3,332				
Euro / Japanese Yen	125,000 x Euro	2,018				
Euro / Swiss Franc	125,000 x Euro	398				
EuroYen LIBOR	100,000,000 Yen	3,869				
Deutsche Mark Forward	250,000 USD					38,582
Japanese Yen Forward	250,000 USD					16,898
Japanese Yen Rolling Spot	250,000 USD					15,310
Deutschemark Rolling Spot	250,000 USD					44,013
Nikkei 225	5 USD x Index	513,848	479,248	417,541	502,072	609,720
Mexican IPC Index	25 USD x Index			88	4,481	
E-Mini S&P	50 USD x Index	10,953,551	4,466,032	885,825		
S&P 500 Index	500 USD x Index	27,003,387	31,430,523	21,294,584	19,899,999	18,852,149
S&P 500 Barra Growth Index	500 USD x Index	11,015	9,816	6,196	3,400	1,240
S&P 500 Barra Value Index	500 USD x Index	26,698	21,245	11,203	7,531	1,478
S&P MidCap 400 Index	500 USD x Index	326,117	310,008	262,017	289,989	253,741
Major Market	500 USD x Index		4	732	4,592	58,048
NASDAQ 100 Index	500 USD x Index	2,360,938	1,063,328	807,604	380,963	
E-Mini NASDAQ 100 Index	20 USD x Index	682,059				
Dow Jones Taiwan Stock Index	250 USD x Index			8,558		
Russell 2000	500 USD x Index	363,041	276,662	182,717	78,353	43,857
Goldman Sachs Commodity Index	250 USD x Index	926,933	854,264	773,088	446,186	270,504
Atlanta HDD	100 x HDD	197				
Chicago HDD	100 x HDD	20				
Cincinnati HDD	100 x HDD	70				
New York HDD	100 x HDD	49				
Total		168,013,357	183,627,443	159,975,955	141,600,469	146,662,764

KANSAS CITY BOARD OF TRADE (KCBT)

FUTURE	CONTRACT UNIT	1999	1998	1997	1996	1995
Wheat	5,000 bu	2,321,059	2,006,779	1,937,140	1,830,276	1,560,538
Western Natural Gas	10,000 MMBtu	18,382	77,350	86,723	89,706	77,595
Western Natural Gas Index	10,000 MMBtu	3				
Value Line Index	500 USD x Index	1,264	4,485	14,047	28,663	35,185
Mini Value Line	100 USD x Index	31,377	76,345	154,784	135,848	74,346
ISDEX	100 USD x Index	6,186				
Total		**2,378,271**	**2,164,959**	**2,192,694**	**2,084,493**	**1,747,664**

MIDAMERICA COMMODITY EXCHANGE (MidAm)

FUTURE	CONTRACT UNIT	1999	1998	1997	1996	1995
Wheat	1,000 bu	132,392	133,200	130,968	151,755	137,573
Corn	1,000 bu	291,186	314,815	432,461	462,318	305,347
Oats	1,000 bu	3,509	5,451	4,916	8,449	5,846
Soybeans	1,000 bu	651,268	767,858	1,026,830	976,134	868,577
Soybean Meal New	20 tons	15,914	18,371	23,773	11,638	4,060
Soybean Oil	30,000 lbs	23,955	27,923	37,962	14,248	6,658
Live Cattle	20,000 lbs	16,285	18,883	16,316	20,983	18,811
Lean Hogs	20,000 lbs	31,027	18,507	1,312		
Live Hogs	20,000 lbs		1,354	4,152	21,118	24,059
New York Silver	1,000 oz	23,493	14,999	8,928	8,398	13,320
New York Gold	33.2 oz	23,662	14,060	15,161	15,876	18,964
Platinum	25 oz	1,162	1,582	4,248	6,949	3,055
U.S. Treasury Bonds (30-year)	50,000 USD	1,058,816	1,537,286	1,513,925	1,281,967	1,341,877
U.S. Treasury Bills (3-month)	500,000 USD	117	315	461	753	754
U.S. Treasury Notes (10-year)	50,000 USD	33,364	39,458	49,700	41,849	38,494
U.S. Treasury Notes (5-year)	50,000 USD	29	96	479	383	37
Eurodollars	500,000 USD	5,745	5,347	5,997	8,893	23,550
Australian Dollar	50,000	846	1,205	585	266	221
British Pound	12,500	17,871	23,929	28,094	21,424	23,620
Swiss Franc	62,500	29,039	33,599	47,504	48,027	50,201
Deutschemark	62,500	17,764	36,674	84,344	79,093	95,775
Japanese Yen	6,250,000	41,167	47,821	48,585	42,085	55,213
Canadian Dollar	50,000	13,865	18,358	14,090	7,104	11,970
Euro Currency	62,500	618				
Total		**2,433,894**	**3,081,181**	**3,500,791**	**3,229,710**	**3,047,982**

MINNEAPOLIS GRAIN EXCHANGE (MGE)

FUTURE	CONTRACT UNIT	1999	1998	1997	1996	1995
Wheat	5,000 bu	1,119,812	1,092,964	1,024,523	996,780	914,882
White Wheat	5,000 bu	4,786	15,209	14,284	14,602	20,411
Durum Wheat	5,000 bu	9,818	15,997			
Barley	180,000 lbs			452	631	
White Shrimp	5,000 lbs	164	679	737	56	336
Black Tiger Shrimp	5,000 lbs	115	291	598	529	387
Twin Cities Electricity - On Peak	736 Mhw	250	54			
Total		**1,134,945**	**1,125,194**	**1,040,594**	**1,012,598**	**936,016**

NEW YORK BOARD OF TRADE (NYBOT)*

FUTURE	CONTRACT UNIT	1999	1998	1997	1996	1995
Coffee "C"	37,500 lbs	2,659,233	2,095,030	2,294,181	2,039,576	2,003,014
Sugar #11	112,000 lbs	5,911,299	5,524,111	5,284,971	4,751,852	4,711,082
Sugar #14	112,000 lbs	138,661	157,987	158,431	182,393	119,508
White Sugar	50 metric tons			10	333	
Cocoa	10 metric tons	1,868,036	1,810,580	2,274,509	2,121,576	2,090,098
Cheddar Cheese	40,000 lbs		4	289	980	977
Non Fat Dry Milk	44,000 lbs		7	559	282	90
Butter	10,000 lbs			1,482	93	
BFP Milk		5,385	6,222	7,084		
BFP Milk Large Lot		3,156				
Milk	50,000 lbs		3	911	4,944	436
Cotton #2	50,000 lbs	2,448,087	3,200,830	2,837,280	2,373,855	2,525,434
Potato	85,000 lbs		70	540	744	
Orange Juice Frozen Concentrate	15,000 lbs	793,882	914,614	1,029,861	654,937	688,932
Orange Juice Frozen Concentrate - 2	15,000 lbs	82				
Orange Juice Frozen Concentrate - Diff		886				
Deutsche Mark / British Pound	125,000 GBP	7,399	123,043	86,166	87,757	32,804
Deutsche Mark / Spanish Peseta	250,000 DEM		11,869	754		
Deutsche Mark / French Franc	500,000 DEM		71,290	158,740	77,263	36,649
Deutsche Mark / Japanese Yen	125,000 DEM	12,568	301,555	172,612	167,093	66,405
Deutsche Mark / Italian Lira	250,000 DEM	207	119,667	137,077	74,997	31,604
Deutsche Mark / Swiss Franc	125,000 DEM	4,980	220,117	121,303	37,566	1,209
Deutsche Mark / Swedish Krona	125,000 DEM	864	121,203	63,685	8,378	
British Pound / Swiss Franc	125,000 GBP	28,789	29,902	5,699		
British Pound / Japanese Yen	125,000 GBP	69,207	46,584	9,629		
Swiss Franc / Japanese Yen	200,000 CHF	20,988	6			

Volume U.S.

NEW YORK BOARD OF TRADE (NYBOT)* (continued)

FUTURE	CONTRACT UNIT	1999	1998	1997	1996	1995
U.S. Dollar / Deutsche Mark	125,000 USD	200	43,331	33,917	32,441	29,441
U.S. Dollar / Canadian Dollar	200,000 USD	3,406	3,726	830		
U.S. Dollar / Swiss Franc	200,000 USD	25,523	18,224	4,282	4,098	1,586
U.S. Dollar / Japanese Yen	200,000 USD	41,632	23,828	9,060	9,037	4,943
U.S. Dollar / British Pound	125,000 GBP	16,571	7,795	6,375	2,290	3,021
U.S. Dollar / South African Rand	100,000 USD	10,859	3,165	4,683		
Australian Dollar / New Zealand Dollar	200,000 AUD	26,088				
U.S. Dollar / Australian Dollar	200,000 AUD	40,711	7,310	5,393		
Australian Dollar / Japanese Yen		18,538				
U.S. Dollar / New Zealand Dollar	200,000 NZD	70,717	30,622	9,499		
U.S. Dollar / Indian Rupiah	500,000,000 RUD			2		
U.S. Dollar / Malaysian Ringgit	500,000 RIN		70	228		
U.S. Dollar / Thai Baht	5,000,000 BAH			2		
ECU			1,574			
Euro		85,211	1,325			
Euro, Small		2,337				
Euro / Japanese Yen	100,000 EUR	192,987	356			
Euro / Swedish Krona	100,000 EUR	101,605	89			
Euro / Norwegian	100,000 EUR	10,452				
Euro / British Pound	100,000 EUR	200,560	50			
Euro / Swiss Franc	100,000 EUR	147,650	199			
U.S. Dollar Index	1,000 USD x Index	356,544	469,291	485,481	509,067	456,859
Emerging Markets Debt Index	1,000 USD x Index			261	341	732
U.S. Treasury Notes (5 Year)	100,000 USD	8,503	13,088	18,040	45,064	44,959
U.S. Treasury Notes (2 Year)	200,000 USD		830	1,790	1,147	11,072
NYSE Composite Index	500 USD x Index	334,222	590,327	916,716	791,325	685,922
Russell 1000 Index	500 USD x Index	161,114				
PSE Tech 100 Index	500 USD x Index	40,402	9,814	9,848	8,663	
PSE Tech 100 Index, Small	100 USD x Index		10,950			
Commodity Research Bureau Index	500 USD x Index	88,696	58,993	71,482	81,113	81,413
Total*		**15,958,237**	**16,049,651**	**16,223,662**	**14,069,205**	**13,628,190**

NEW YORK MERCANTILE EXCHANGE (NYMEX)**

COMEX DIVISION

FUTURE	CONTRACT UNIT	1999	1998	1997	1996	1995
High Grade Copper	25,000 lbs	2,852,962	2,483,610	2,356,170	2,311,919	2,519,414
Silver	5,000 oz	4,157,500	4,094,616	4,893,520	4,870,808	5,183,236
Gold	100 oz	9,575,788	8,990,094	9,541,904	8,902,179	7,781,596
Eurotop 100 Index	100 USD x Index	25,181	50,619	47,427	38,925	49,328
Eurotop 300 Index	200 USD x Index	6,279				
Aluminum	44,000 lbs	27,978				
Total		**16,645,688**	**15,618,939**	**16,839,021**	**16,123,831**	**15,533,574**

NYMEX DIVISION

FUTURE	CONTRACT UNIT	1999	1998	1997	1996	1995
Palladium	100 oz	75,394	131,250	238,716	205,610	166,713
Platinum	50 oz	567,268	528,269	698,597	802,468	846,693
No. 2 Heating Oil, NY	1,000 bbl	9,200,703	8,863,764	8,370,964	8,341,877	8,266,783
Unleaded Gasoline, NY	1,000 bbl	8,701,216	7,992,269	7,475,145	6,312,339	7,071,787
Natural Gas	10,000 MMBTU	19,165,096	15,978,286	11,923,628	8,813,867	8,086,718
Gulf Coast Unleaded Gas	42,000 gal					252
Alberta Natural Gas	10,000 MMBTU			110	2,876	
Palo Verde Electricity	736 Mwh	51,852	139,738	155,977	17,548	
California Oregon Border Electricity	736 Mwh	52,032	128,423	120,896	52,340	
Cinergy Electricity	736 Mwh	34,367	48,483			
Entergy Electricity	736 Mwh	20,528	42,580			
PJM Electricity	736 Mwh	3,254				
Permian Basin Natural Gas	10,000 MMBTU			15	8,811	
Propane	42,000 gal	37,544	43,868	40,255	53,903	49,532
Sour Crude Oil	1,000 bbl		1			
Crude Oil	1,000 bbl	37,860,064	30,495,647	24,771,375	23,487,821	23,613,994
Total		**75,769,618**	**64,392,578**	**53,795,678**	**48,099,460**	**48,102,472**
Total**		**92,415,006**	**80,011,517**	**70,634,699**	**64,223,291**	**63,636,046**

PHILADELPHIA BOARD OF TRADE (PBOT)

FUTURE	CONTRACT UNIT	1999	1998	1997	1996	1995
Australian Dollar	100,000	20	148	1,270	2,532	1,716
British Pound	62,500	92	235	2,543	1,761	4,147
Canadian Dollar	100,000	27		80	91	208
ECU	125,000	28		158	616	
Deutschemark	125,000		909	12,510	23,904	17,121
Swiss Franc	125,000	39	445	3,913	4,723	3,915
French Franc	500,000		101	3,489	3,704	4,162
Japanese Yen	12,500,000	45	734	5,112	10,871	7,372
Total		251	2,572	29,075	48,202	38,641

	1999	1998	1997	1996	1995
TOTAL FUTURES	477,919,308	503,201,445	443,653,757	397,402,153	395,313,480
PERCENT CHANGE	-5.02%	13.42%	11.64%	0.53%	-7.27%

* Includes the New York Futures Exchange, New York Cotton Exchange and Coffee, Sugar and Cocoa Exchange.
** In August 1994, the Commodity Exchange and the New York Mercantile Exchange merged and is now listed as one exchange.

OPTIONS TRADED ON U.S. FUTURES EXCHANGES VOLUME HIGHLIGHTS

1999 in Comparison with 1998

1999 RANK	EXCHANGE	1999 CONTRACTS	1999 %	1998 CONTRACTS	1998 %	1998 RANK
1	Chicago Board of Trade (CBT)	59,413,936	51.66%	64,050,508	50.24%	1
2	Chicago Mercantile Exchange (CME)	32,723,766	28.46%	42,991,388	33.72%	2
3	New York Mercantile Exchange (NYMEX) *	17,123,825	14.89%	15,007,168	11.77%	6
4	New York Board of Trade (NYBOT) **	5,519,619	4.80%	5,252,288	4.12%	4
5	Kansas City Board of Trade (KCBT)	146,105	0.13%	114,542	0.09%	5
6	Minneapolis Grain Exchange (MGE)	53,870	0.05%	44,339	0.03%	6
7	MidAmerica Commodity Exchange (MidAm)	18,969	0.02%	25,728	0.02%	7
	TOTAL	115,000,090	100.00%	127,485,961	100.00%	

* Includes Comex Division.
** Includes the New York Futures Exchange, New York Cotton Exchange and Coffee, Sugar and Cocoa Exchange.

OPTIONS VOLUME ON U.S. FUTURES EXCHANGES 1995 - 1999

CHICAGO BOARD OF TRADE (CBT)

OPTION	CONTRACT UNIT	1999	1998	1997	1996	1995
Corn	5000 bu	4,205,325	4,267,274	4,963,603	6,602,010	3,783,446
Soybeans	5000 bu	4,792,245	3,845,804	5,339,936	5,135,124	3,149,635
Oats	5000 bu	56,418	51,852	21,654	45,037	35,250
Wheat	5000 bu	1,516,037	1,346,272	1,698,969	1,886,909	1,243,567
Soybean Oil	60,000 lbs	801,367	752,627	381,193	285,274	232,635
Soybean Meal	100 tons	709,194	889,462	716,079	593,165	304,835
Rice	200,000 lbs	48,515	33,602	37,769	14,658	14,336
Diammonium Phosphate	100 tons				50	
Crop Yield	Crop yield est. X 10	25	841	165	1,001	3,510
Silver	1,000 oz	38	154	68	515	1,476
Eastern Catastrophe Insurance	Loss/EP x 25,000 USD				66	3,274
Midwest Catastrophe Insurance	Loss/EP x 25,000 USD					50
PCS Castastrophe Insurance		561	7,753	15,706	14,688	1,064
U.S. Treasury Bonds (30-year)	100,000 USD	34,680,068	39,941,672	30,805,885	25,930,661	25,639,950
U.S. Treasury Notes (10 Year)	100,000 USD	9,738,808	9,296,742	6,032,088	7,907,650	6,887,102
U.S. Treasury Notes (5 Year)	100,000 USD	2,537,044	3,184,609	2,105,792	2,723,525	3,619,462
U.S. Treasury Notes (2 Year)	200,000 USD	1,780	2,780	4,268	2,806	13,189
German Bund	250,000 USD			15,620		
Muni Bonds	1,000 USD x Index	33,754	100,739	210,990	43,219	13,018
Brady Bond Index	1,000 USD x Index				440	
Yield Curve Spread	25,000 USD x 100 YCS			360	3,284	
Flexible U.S. T-Bonds		54,454	68,043	118,895	94,453	59,804
Flexible T-Notes (10 Year)		6,150	10,520	15,910	12,735	36,425
Flexible T-Notes (5 Year)		2,593	4,364	1,350	6,990	14,730
Flexible T-Notes (2 Year)				200		100
Dow Jones Industrial Index	10 USD x Index	229,560	245,398	156,132		
Total		59,413,936	64,050,508	52,642,632	51,304,320	45,056,867

Volume U.S.

CHICAGO MERCANTILE EXCHANGE (CME)

OPTION	CONTRACT UNIT	1999	1998	1997	1996	1995
Live Hogs	40,000 lbs				169,214	137,435
Lean Hogs	40,000 lbs	231,273	206,014	210,429	35,831	
Live Cattle	40,000 lbs	545,709	685,606	540,804	539,523	463,455
Stocker Cattle	25,000 lbs	41				
Fluid Milk	40,000 lbs				307	
Boneless Beef	20,000 lbs 90% lean		425	997		
Boneless Beef Trimmings	20,000 lbs 50% lean		134	1,054		
Butter	50,000 lbs	752	595	479	92	
Cheddar Cheese	40,000 lbs		168	54		
Fluid Milk	200,000 lbs	12,604	16,680	4,078		
Mini BFP Milk	50,000 lbs	607	304			
Mini BFP Milk	100,000 lbs	387				
Pork Bellies, Frozen	40,000 lbs	16,780	21,545	29,324	52,040	21,156
Pork Bellies, Fresh	40,000 lbs		19			
Feeder Cattle	44,000 lbs	130,410	170,857	161,100	174,518	109,096
Lumber	160,000 bd ft				1,753	14,433
Orient Strand Board	100,000 bd ft		40	489	86	
Random Lumber	80,000 bd ft	24,745	18,928	19,826	26,922	491
One Month LIBOR	3,000,000 USD	1,916	5,541	28,809	16,031	54,219
Brazilian C Bond	500 USD x Index				30	
Mexican PAR Bond	500 USD x Index				130	
Mexican TIIE	6,000,000		35	110		
Eurodollar (3-month)	1,000,000 USD	24,884,494	33,147,148	29,595,246	22,234,888	22,363,853
Eurodollar 5-year Bundle			64			
Euroyen	100,000,000 JPY	41,073	38,208	41,577		
T-Bill (90-day)	1,000,000 USD				80	3,594
British Pound	62,500	208,921	241,720	986,950	2,886,041	1,668,624
Brazilian Real	100,000		14,397	114,464	74,106	3,700
Deutschemark	125,000	140,522	734,678	1,411,110	1,822,649	2,642,904
Euro Canada	1,000,000		2,109			
Mexican Peso	500,000	8,133	25,948	186,594	13,466	1,114
Swiss Franc	125,000	178,433	281,354	591,509	753,418	630,016
Japanese Yen	12,500,000	1,100,130	1,942,417	1,661,417	1,734,186	2,141,043
Canadian Dollar	100,000	121,933	278,730	253,075	197,741	259,857
New Zealand Dollar	100,000		46	32		
Australian Dollar	100,000	9,509	9,133	25,465	5,785	9,892
French Franc	250,000		38	1,884	2,149	4,935
Euro FX	125,000 x EUR	167,078				
Deutsche Mark / Japanese Yen	250,000 DEM	58				
Euro / British Pound	125,000 x EUR	200				
Nikkei 225	5 USD x Index	6,007	7,725	7,834	5,722	8,986
Mexican IPC Index	25 USD x Index				75	
S&P 500 Index	500 USD x Index	4,603,946	4,986,687	4,734,950	4,636,236	4,568,232
E-Mini S&P	50 USD x Index	54,480	20,629	8,661		
S&P 500 Barra Value Index	500 USD x Index		40	1,791	4,765	30
S&P 500 Barra Growth Index	500 USD x Index		82	962	2,960	
S&P MidCap 400 Index	500 USD x Index	3,841	1,899	3,272	2,201	5,435
Major Market	500 USD x Index			20	729	289
NASDAQ 100 Index	500 USD x Index	225,981	127,532	108,922	23,992	
Dow Jones Taiwan Index	250 USD x Index			146		
Russell 2000	500 USD x Index	1,230	2,656	2,849	2,089	1,532
Goldman Sachs Commodity Index	250 USD x GSCI	2,573	1,257	2,190	1,971	28,028
Total		**32,723,766**	**42,991,388**	**40,738,473**	**35,421,726**	**35,142,349**

KANSAS CITY BOARD OF TRADE (KCBT)

OPTION	CONTRACT UNIT	1999	1998	1997	1996	1995
Wheat	5,000 bu	143,974	112,825	99,092	65,190	75,849
Western Natural Gas	10,000 MMBtu		55	240	1,850	2,546
Mini Value Line	100 USD x Index	2,094	1,662	4,547	1,439	3,014
ISDEX	100 USD x Index	37				
Total		**146,105**	**114,542**	**103,879**	**68,479**	**81,409**

MIDAMERICA COMMODITY EXCHANGE (MidAm)

OPTION	CONTRACT UNIT	1999	1998	1997	1996	1995
Soybeans	1,000 bu	10,705	44,603	19,594	13,689	11,908
Soybean Oil	30,000 lbs	6	7	3		5
Soft Red Winter Wheat	5,000 bu	1,813	3,121	4,491	3,422	2,425
Corn	1,000 bu	4,325	8,348	8,904	9,753	7,296
T-Bonds	50,000 USD	2,095	2,646	1,282	530	721
Gold	33.2 oz	25	3	63	137	772
Total		**18,969**	**25,728**	**34,337**	**27,531**	**23,127**

MINNEAPOLIS GRAIN EXCHANGE (MGE)

OPTION	CONTRACT UNIT	1999	1998	1997	1996	1995
American Spring Wheat	5,000 bu	53,246	41,702	40,383	21,126	26,893
European Spring Wheat	5,000 bu		153	88	44	184
White Wheat	5,000 bu	205	1,772	6,320	5,175	5,333
Durum Wheat	5,000 bu	154	97			
Barley	180,000 lbs				8	
White Shrimp	5,000 lbs	118	337	180	7	118
Black Tiger Shrimp	5,000 lbs	147	278	739	531	138
Total		**53,870**	**44,339**	**47,710**	**26,891**	**32,666**

NEW YORK BOARD OF TRADE (NYBOT)**

OPTION	CONTRACT UNIT	1999	1998	1997	1996	1995
Sugar #11	112,000 lbs	2,275,704	2,113,369	1,369,465	1,094,879	1,203,779
Flexible Sugar		5,200	9,930	155		
Coffee	37,500 lbs	1,369,021	974,690	1,272,767	856,710	867,303
Cocoa	10 metric tons	364,450	326,221	399,408	335,173	319,513
Cheddar Cheese	40,000 lbs				4	76
Non Fat Dry Milk	44,000 lbs				21	
BFP Milk		13,177	12,193	1,364		
BFP Milk, Large		2,682				
Butter	10,000 lbs			77		
Milk	50,000 lbs			379	963	103
Cotton	50,000 lbs	706,589	1,127,326	648,154	816,550	1,416,054
Orange Juice Frozen Concentrate	15,000 lbs	351,763	464,773	457,143	316,469	171,209
Potato	85,000 lbs			14	26	
U.S. Dollar Index	500 USD x Index	11,654	21,575	22,539	50,461	23,987
Deutsche Mark / British Pound	125,000 GBP		10,687	3,484	9,247	116
Deutsche Mark / French Franc	500,000 DEM			105	1,473	570
Deutsche Mark / Japanese Yen	125,000 DEM	50	884	458	2,010	160
Deutsche Mark / Swiss Franc	125,000 DEM	4,278	6,926	675	7,313	33
Deutsche Mark / Swedish Krona	125,000 DEM		37			
Deutsche Mark / Italian Lira	250,000 DEM		3,500	1,637	367	354
British Pound / Swiss Franc	125,000 GBP	361				
British Pound / Japanese Yen	125,000 GBP	291	20			
New Zealand Dollar / U.S. Dollar	200,000 NZD		2			
Swiss Franc / Japanese Yen	200,000 CHF	321				
Euro		7,137				
Euro / Bristish Pound	100,000 EUR	2,228				
Euro / Japanese Yen	100,000 EUR	5,200				
U.S. Dollar / Deutsche Mark	125,000 DEM		3,974	912	266	
U.S. Dollar / British Pound	125,000 GBP	280	6	32	22	
U.S. Dollar / South African Rand	100,000 USD	910	11			
U.S. Dollar / Swiss Franc	200,000 USD	300				
U.S. Dollar / Japanese Yen	12,500,000 JPY	2,431	1,811	1,225	1,209	
NYSE Composite Index	500 USD x Index	112,052	93,343	81,038	48,714	26,457
Russell 1000 Index	500 USD x Index	69,990				
PSE Tech 100 Index	500 USD x Index	204,682	37,339	8,801	2,211	
PSE Tech 100 Index	100 USD x index		37,827			
Bridge/CRB Futures Index	500 USD x Index	8,868	5,844	5,835	4,771	6,384
Total**		**5,519,619**	**5,252,288**	**4,275,667**	**3,548,859**	**4,036,098**

NEW YORK MERCANTILE EXCHANGE (NYMEX)*

COMEX DIVISION

OPTION	CONTRACT UNIT	1999	1998	1997	1996	1995
Gold	100 oz	2,815,831	1,945,366	2,064,883	2,079,663	2,006,695
5 Day Gold	100 oz				150	688
Silver	5,000 oz	722,885	818,053	842,923	949,239	1,146,513
5 Day Silver	5,000 oz				96	221
High Grade Copper	25,000 lbs	160,857	153,332	133,603	150,339	134,212
5 Day Copper	25,000 lbs					34
Aluminum	44,000 lbs	642				
Total		**3,703,215**	**2,916,751**	**3,041,409**	**3,179,487**	**3,288,363**

Volume U.S.

NYMEX DIVISION

OPTION	CONTRACT UNIT	1999	1998	1997	1996	1995
No. 2 Heating Oil	42,000 gal	695,558	669,725	1,147,034	1,108,935	703,388
Crude Oil	1,000 bbl	8,161,976	7,448,095	5,790,333	5,271,456	3,975,611
Unleaded Gasoline	1,000 bbl	600,009	730,421	1,033,778	655,965	766,557
Natural Gas	10,000 MMBTU	3,849,454	3,115,765	2,079,607	1,234,691	921,520
Alberta Natural Gas	10,000 MMBTU				15	
Gas-Crude Oil Spread	1,000 bbl	46,281	22,575	41,867	31,743	64,285
Heating Oil-Crude Oil Spread	1,000 bbl	46,482	36,615	18,657	45,920	72,969
Palo Verde Electricity	736 Mwh	4,419	28,597	19,328	3,964	
California Oregon Border Electricity	736 Mwh	3,761	19,989	13,495	7,650	
Cintergy Electricity	736 Mwh	1,419	2,597			
Entergy Electricity	736 Mwh	105	1,855			
Platinum	50 oz	11,146	14,183	31,139	36,175	43,601
Total		**13,420,610**	**12,090,417**	**10,175,238**	**8,396,514**	**6,547,931**
Total*		**17,123,825**	**15,007,168**	**13,216,647**	**11,576,001**	**9,836,294**
TOTAL OPTIONS		**115,000,090**	**127,485,961**	**111,059,345**	**101,973,807**	**94,208,810**
PERCENT CHANGE		**-9.79%**	**14.79%**	**8.91%**	**8.24%**	**-6.61%**

* In August 1994, the Commodity Exchange and the New York Mercantile Exchange merged and is now listed as one exchange.
** Includes the New York Futures Exchange, New York Cotton Exchange and Coffee, Sugar and Cocoa Exchange.

Volume Worldwide

Agricultural Futures Markets (AFM), Netherlands

	1999	1998	1997	1996	1995
Live Hogs	43,051	45,705	57,069	49,986	30,877
Piglets	1,172	2,531	2,610	2,529	1,047
Potatoes	67,663	114,601	76,646	75,046	165,313
Potatoes Options	10,967	16,394			
Total	**122,853**	**179,231**	**136,325**	**128,097**	**197,237**

Amsterdam Exchanges (AEX), Netherlands

(formerly European Options Exchange (EOE))	1999	1998	1997	1996	1995
AEX Stock Index (FTI)	2,925,385	3,484,558	2,554,776	2,426,699	1,004,005
Light AEX Stock Index (FTIL)	12,445				
Dutch Top 5 Index (FT5)	101	14,412	58,891	70,873	63,751
Amsterdam Information Technology Index (FIA)	25				
Amsterdam Financial Sector Index (FFA)	1,345				
Amsterdam MidCap Index (FTM)	263				
FTSE sStars (FTES)	32				
FTSE Eurotop 100 Index (FETI)	292				
Eurotop 100 Index		2,026	249	31	233
Old U.S. Dollar/Guilder (OFUS)		1,818	16,604	7,955	14,663
Euro / U.S. Dollar (FED)	167				
US Dollar / Euro (FDE)	1,241	4,411	2,987		
Guilder Bond (FTO)		211	6,052	21,368	8,051
Gold Options	35,627	29,562	59,871	89,779	45,283
Silver Options	2,640	4,435	4,320	7,799	5,704
US Dollar/Guilder (FUS) Options		4,511	408,820	539,799	552,452
Euro / U.S. Dollar (EDX)	17,398				
US Dollar / Euro (FDE) Options	87,249	273,455	270,088		
Dutch Government Bond Options	77,619	208,994	286,808	474,525	406,500
AEX Stock Index Options	5,527,137	7,864,884	8,232,719	6,039,984	3,681,781
Light AEX Stock Index (AEXL) Options	38,872				
Eurotop 100 Options	19,763	33,586	12,127	5,090	5,204
FTSE sStars (STAR) Options	1,137				
FTSE Eurotop 100 Index (ETI) Options	11,017				
Amsterdam Information Technology Index (AIS) Optior	514				
Amsterdam Financial Sector Index (AFS) Options	16,069				
Amsterdam MidCap Index (MID) Options	743				
Eurotop Bank Sector Index (EBS) Options	35				
Eurotop Information Technology Sector Index Options	57				
O100 Index Options		2,520			
Dutch Top 5 Index Options	446	86,454	414,956	861,025	561,611
All Options on Individual Equities	40,653,520	52,741,082	36,340,078	18,754,623	
Total	**46,489,843**	**61,249,483**	**48,669,669**	**29,299,550**	**6,349,238**

Wiener Borse - Derivatives Market of Vienna, Austria

(formerly the Austrian Futures & Options Exchange)	1999	1998	1997	1996	1995
Austrian Government Bond	180	35,865	107,421	151,633	176,527
ATX Index	598,981	618,358	566,459	412,047	498,234
CeCe (5 Eastern European Indices)	203,421	472,077	464,480		
ATX Index Options	395,323	557,463	572,644	960,513	1,748,567
ATX LEOs (Long-term Equity Options)	7,971	11,421	4,693	43,990	71,555
CeCe (5 Eastern European Indices) Options	24,157	75,709	43,424		
All Options on Individual Equities	802,924	1,201,197	1,346,990	1,266,960	
Total	**2,032,957**	**2,972,090**	**3,111,523**	**2,841,978**	**2,494,883**

Belgian Futures and Options Exchange (BELFOX), Belgium

	1999	1998	1997	1996	1995
Belgian Government Bonds		5,169	200,413	390,013	507,254
Belgian Medium Term Government Bond (BMB)		20	7,887		
Euribor 3-Month (ERF)	98				
BIBOR 3-Months		45,841	230,714	157,909	175,082
Mini Bel 20 Index (MBEL)	4,888,140				
Bel 20 Index	823,244	664,360	551,044	326,542	187,686
Bel 20 Index Options	1,151,862	978,341	954,238	1,170,948	862,492
USO (Dollar/Belgian Franc)	9,684	81,806	119,251	128,548	108,471
Gold Index Options	8,793	34,611	61,269	82,442	81,897
All Options on Individual Equities	530,389	364,885	402,547	378,034	
Total	**7,412,210**	**2,175,033**	**2,527,665**	**2,635,945**	**1,927,386**

Bolsa Brasileira de Futuros (BBF), Brazil

(Merged with BM&F)	1999	1998	1997	1996	1995
R$/US$ Exchange Rate			5,225	41,130	22,948
U.S. Denominated Arabica Coffee			570	7,308	6,733
Stock Price Future Return Index			335,908	189,773	
Average Interest Rate on Interbank Deposits			7,140	58,325	78,662
R$ (Brazilian Real)/US$ Exchange Rate Options			178,000	1,819,120	89,700
Average Interest Rate on Interbank Deposits Options			502,820	48,213,690	127,924,464
Total			**1,029,663**	**50,047,438**	**128,734,681**

Volume Worldwide

Beijing Commodity Exchange (BCE), China

	1999	1998	1997	1996	1995
Greenbean	Suspended	549,679	9,275,688	81,081,235	141,662,184
Total		**549,679**	**9,275,688**	**81,100,110**	**141,664,141**

Bolsa de Mercadorias & Futuros (BM&F), Brazil

	1999	1998	1997	1996	1995
Arabica Coffee	317,722	198,547	114,521	116,071	76,206
Live Cattle	123,442	88,054	109,261	117,395	39,174
Sugar Crystal	33,764	30,080	8,330	6,212	4,301
Cotton	5,115	17,007	13,689	2,339	
Corn	10,432	15,949	18,907	3,696	
Soybean Futures	13,424	13,489	16,082	20,274	3,750
Gold Futures		108,942	195,310	219,567	607,288
Gold Forward	25	10			
Gold Spot	155,947	132,747	173,752	278,476	
Bovespa Stock Index Futures	5,551,918	9,926,890	14,914,692	15,122,751	15,304,666
Interest Rate	22,235,992	35,150,416	36,466,961	49,541,598	35,152,630
Interest Rate Swap	8,224,534	8,562,215	11,660,972	6,313,852	3,592,277
Interest Rate x Stock Basket Swap	18,586				
Interest Rate x Exchange Rate Swap	2,440,318	2,499,084	3,504,600	2,069,329	1,500,685
Interest Rate x Reference Rate Swap	80,140	83,256	139,929	161,159	127,796
Interest Rate x Inflation Index Swap (formerly Inflation)	17,163	4,496	10,324	6,486	7,601
Interest Rate x Basic Financial Rate Swap	18,985	16,187			
Interest Rate x Ibovespa Swap	42	4,113		1	
ID x U.S. Dollar Spread Futures	2,126,164	3,013,081	52,587	99,631	
C-Bond	646	6,581	296,758	608,798	
El-Bond	2,074	703	4,060	1,850	
U.S. Dollar	11,420,923	18,573,100	40,387,111	45,132,135	74,241,367
Mini U.S. Dollar	110				
Exchange Rate Swap		6,333	71,713	58,885	174,177
Price Index x Exchange Rate		9	773	564	
Gold Options on Actuals	283,221	88,932	141,880	363,089	1,882,502
Gold Options Exercise	35,634	41,928	81,542	150,144	1,124,792
U.S. $ Denominated Arabica Coffee Options	42,918	17,921	3,210	14,767	2,810,322
U.S. $ Denominated Arabica Coffee Options Exercise	4,856	1,103	1,256	29,249	1,375,756
Corn Options	10	122			
Corn Exercise Options	26				
Soybean Options	22	82			
Soybean Exercise Options	3				
Live Cattle Options		308	392	5,882	34,240
Bovespa Stock Options	26,020	103,860	359,846	201,757	74,469
Bovespa Stock Options Exercise	210	2,810	31,971	15,722	1,765
Interest Rate Options Exercise	22,461	57,015	57,390	30,550	
Interbank Deposit Rate Index Options	908,004	1,605,106	348,990		
Fexible Bovespa Stock Index Options	257,870	333,582	618,424	167,918	
U.S. Dollar Options on Actuals	694,483	3,405,413	7,211,258	5,180,578	3,338,020
U.S. Dollar Options Exercise	50,741	86,963	974,381	142,710	403,456
Flexible Currency Options	807,153	2,818,616	3,809,659	7,662,050	6,097,019
Total	**55,931,098**	**87,015,050**	**122,179,393**	**134,609,876**	**148,055,778**

Budapest Commodity Exchange (BCE), Hungary

	1999	1998	1997	1996	1995
Milling Wheat	3,785	35,164	108,431	65,454	18,065
Corn	48,918	37,941	77,992	44,253	16,954
Euro Wheat	747	17,254	2,263		
Feed Wheat	48	858	13,693	6,179	1,790
Feed Barley	2,518	2,139	10,330	5,982	767
Wheat	65,823	2,011			
Black Seed	7,351	9,623	4,448	2,580	2,933
Rapeseed	121				
Soybean	19				
TAX	2				
Europe I Live Hogs	198	198	249	191	150
Europe II Live Hogs	194	40	101	322	358
Deutsche Mark	200,027	5,823,625	2,731,592	751,130	697,200
U.S. Dollar	470,550	1,730,165	1,097,502	871,174	357,610
Japanese Yen	101,884	183,118	852,629	916,857	269,826
EUR	596,258				
British Pound	17,103	42,454	201,974	304,872	
Swiss Franc	72,500	389,118	849,185	419,885	
Czech Crown	1				
Italian Lira		550	83,692	710,455	
3 Month BUBOR		178,684	405,726	22,333	
Corn Options	1,665	290			
Milling Wheat Options	250	360			
Black Seed Options	270				
Wheat Options	3,464	525			
Euro Wheat Options		5			
Total	**1,593,696**	**8,454,122**	**6,439,807**	**4,121,667**	**1,365,653**

Budapest Stock Exchange (BSE), Hungary

	1999	1998	1997	1996	1995
3-Month Hungarian T-Bills		10	3,409	30,933	6,333
1-Year Hungarian T-Bills		14,097	8,126		
3-Year Hungarian Government Bond	12,230				
1-Month BUBOR		97	101	4,585	
3-Month BUBOR		18,031	3,679	161	
Budapest Stock Index (BUX) Futures	1,555,939	1,993,353	1,208,388	136,920	3,207
DEM/HUF	5,975	503,539	183,470	25,429	1,407
EURO/HUF	33,527	1			
CHF/HUF	120	1,004			
GBP/HUF	150	1,602			
USD/HUF	25,106	144,368	55,116	20,439	940
ECU/HUF		25,561	2,339	24,299	494
All Futures on Individual Equities	181,031	71,158			
Total	**1,814,078**	**2,772,821**	**1,464,628**	**242,766**	**12,381**

EUREX, Frankfurt, Germany

(formerly Deutsche Terminborse (DTB))	1999	1998	1997	1996	1995
DAX	12,876,982	6,937,139	6,623,287	5,452,505	4,788,661
MDAX	4,040	58,013	180,668	47,865	
VOLAX		14,737			
FOX	741				
DJ Nordic STOXX 30	1				
DJ Euro STOXX 50	5,341,864	366,435			
DJ STOXX 50	326,136	94,771			
BUND	22,846,162	89,877,840	31,337,633	16,496,809	12,525,264
Euro BUND	121,311,878	2			
Medium Term Notional Bond (BOBL)	6,473,320	31,683,256	24,299,906	18,269,169	7,351,783
Euro-BOBL	45,481,843				
1-Month Euribor	64,019	10,418			
3-Month Euribor	3,031,138	378,420			
1-Month Euro-Libor		1			
3-Month Euro-Libor		400			
1-Month Euromark		36,811	166,936	85,519	
3-Month Euromark	6,236	400,168	964,096		
Jumbo-Pfandbrief		177,057			
Euro-BUXL	226	625			
Euro-SCHATZ	17,748,784				
SCHATZ	1,898,555	10,043,087	4,805,755		
Rollover BUND Mar / FGBL Jun	105,682				
Rollover BOBL Mar / FGBM Jun	50,005				
Rollover SHAZ Mar / FGBS Jun	12,761				
FEU3-LIB3 Rollover Facility	98				
SHAZ-FGBS Rollover Facility	1,970				
BOBL-FGBM Rollover Facility	857				
BUND-FGBL Rollover Facility	10,660				
DAX Odd Lot*	68,670				
MDAX Odd Lot*	37				
DAX Options	32,613,783	29,948,503	31,521,286	26,042,463	24,299,078
FOX Options	652				
DJ Euro STOXX 50	3,791,738	122,951			
DJ STOXX 50	80,254	73,779			
BUND Options	1,799,617	6,827,203	702,882	205,520	194,036
Euro-BUND Options	24,940,113	5,000			
SCHATZ Options	35,546	378,448			
Euro-SCHATZ Options	450,836				
3-Month Euribor Options	2,966	900			
3-Month Euromark Options		169,029			
Euro-BOBL Options	1,787,840				
Medium Term Notional Bond (BOBL) Options	94,638	1,077,939	1,640,211	663,502	123,019
US$/DM Options		14,267	250,783		
All Options on Individual NEMAX Equities	111,332				
All Options on Individual DAX Equities	36,123,317	30,853,782	9,667,248	10,024,170	
DAX Odd Lot Options*	319,632				
Total	**339,426,590**	**209,550,981**	**112,164,106**	**77,314,480**	**49,407,307**

* Odd lots are a result of the Euro conversion and are not included in the total volume figures

EUREX, Zurich, Switzerland

(formerly SOFFEX)	1999	1998	1997	1996	1995
Swiss Market Index	6,515,036	4,445,396	1,810,698	1,720,053	1,457,108
Swiss Government Bond (CONF)	577,030	722,066	638,638	913,466	955,895
Medium Term Swiss Government Bond (COMI)	80	1,534	20,055	42,007	
Swiss Market Index Options	3,669,386	3,394,098	8,632,768	8,018,333	6,027,308
Swiss Government Bond Options	1,650	3,423	5,289	26,446	35,695
All Options on Individual Equities*	28,570,528	30,095,937	33,334,251	28,802,225	
Total	**39,333,710**	**38,662,454**	**40,125,315**	**39,522,530**	**8,476,006**

* 1998 data reflects different contract size introduced in July. Not comparable with 1997 data

Volume Worldwide

Helsinki Exchanges, Finland

(formerly the Finnish Options Market Exchange(FOM))

	1999	1998	1997	1996	1995
Finnish Government Bond	7,234	156,455	374,214	291,658	125,298
FRA Interest Rate		634,735	1,827,730	1,167,155	4,375
STOX Stock Future	820,574	811,834	640,268	275,172	
FOX Index	273,808	236,220	246,907	203,138	181,428
FOX Index Options	270,133	267,959	684,704	404,161	521,008
All Options on Individual Equities (STOX)	1,263,363	693,310	1,699,591	1,143,787	
Total	**2,635,112**	**2,814,089**	**5,513,479**	**3,491,471**	**841,778**

FUTOP Clearing Centre, Denmark

	1999	1998	1997	1996	1995
Danish Government Bonds 8% 2003	658	9,042	422		
Danish Government Bonds 7% 2004	5,563				
Danish Government Bonds 7% 2007	7,435	68,535	49,768		
6% 2009 Mortgage Bonds	24,036				
6% 2026 Mortgage Bonds		38,234	44,395	58,590	54,885
6% 2029 Mortgage Bonds	25,641	15,722			
KFX Stock Index	1,298,360	289,424	252,571	303,856	263,537
Danish Government Bonds 6% 2009 Options	8,852				
Danish Government Bonds 7% 2007 Options	4,484	23,170	7,859		
KFX Stock Index Options	21,617	4,073	31,638	42,586	51,053
All Options on Individual Equities	3,307	4,152	34,306	44,810	
Total	**1,399,953**	**454,019**	**681,466**	**747,723**	**653,078**

International Petroleum Exchange (IPE), United Kingdom

	1999	1998	1997	1996	1995
Brent Crude Oil	12,177,333	13,674,664	10,301,918	10,675,389	9,773,146
Gasoil	4,610,450	4,974,171	4,031,608	4,361,062	4,491,463
Fuel Oil	1,935				
Natural Gas BOM	7,270				
Natural Gas Daily (NBP)	11,300	3,160			
Natural Gas Monthly (NBP)	207,490	328,350	81,445		
Brent Crude Oil Options	360,347	337,999	250,176	374,233	571,308
Gasoil Options	88,813	104,523	68,195	110,226	116,424
Total	**17,464,938**	**19,422,867**	**14,733,342**	**15,520,910**	**14,955,371**

Italian Derivatives Market of the Italian Stock Exchange, Italy

	1999	1998	1997	1996	1995
MIB 30 Index	5,094,312	5,896,238	4,463,034	2,675,238	1,140,636
MIDEX	5,144	30,072			
MIB 30 Index Options	2,236,241	1,616,635	1,159,059	476,138	12,464
All Options on Individual Equities	1,947,931	1,296,791	2,444,424		
Total	**9,283,628**	**8,839,736**	**8,066,517**	**3,151,376**	**1,153,100**

Korea Stock Exchange (KSE), Korea

	1999	1998	1997	1996	1995
KOPSI 200	17,200,349	17,893,592	3,252,060	715,621	
KOPSI 200 Options	79,936,658	32,310,812	4,528,424		
Total	**97,137,007**	**50,204,404**	**7,780,484**	**715,621**	

Commodity and Monetary Exchange of Malaysia, Malaysia

(formerly the Kuala Lumpur Commodity Exchange)

	1999	1998	1997	1996	1995
Crude Palm Oil	388,105	353,545	935,595	498,118	524,665
3-Month KLIBOR	28,670				
Total	**416,775**	**353,545**	**935,595**	**498,118**	**524,665**

Kuala Lumpur Options & Financial Futures Exchange, Malaysia

	1999	1998	1997	1996	1995
KLSE Composite Index	436,678	771,244	382,974	71,278	
Total	**436,678**	**771,244**	**382,974**	**71,278**	

London Metal Exchange (LME), United Kingdom

	1999	1998	1997	1996	1995
High Grade Primary Aluminum	22,211,729	20,091,765	22,484,144	14,552,878	14,060,243
Aluminum Alloy	740,955	498,839	389,558	292,429	210,787
Copper - Grade A	16,789,674	15,699,702	15,099,842	18,484,367	17,530,263
Standard Lead	3,310,109	2,420,777	2,352,731	2,202,864	1,758,742
Primary Nickel	5,396,342	4,676,526	4,627,929	3,104,514	3,319,697
Special High Grade Zinc	7,341,620	5,742,948	7,390,436	4,852,942	5,241,931
Silver	1,773				
Tin	1,770,807	1,429,115	1,119,776	1,121,836	1,275,718
High Grade Primary Aluminum Options	1,502,276	909,526	1,659,879	1,030,703	1,241,596
Aluminum Alloy Options	1,037	1,031	535	242	96
Copper - Grade A Options	1,156,929	1,052,239	1,732,509	1,623,575	2,212,821
Standard Lead Options	114,498	36,862	34,531	30,992	22,262
Primary Nickel Options	250,823	119,406	60,645	54,646	83,637
Special High Grade Zinc Options	520,942	204,479	285,453	126,094	177,005
Tin Options	147,615	61,132	13,005	8,925	15,532
Primary Aluminum TAPOS	299,167	115,626	47,447		
Copper TAPOS	41,261	15,108	74,080		
Total	**61,597,557**	**53,075,081**	**57,372,500**	**47,487,007**	**47,150,330**

London International Financial Futures Exchange (LIFFE), United Kingdom

(LCE merged with LIFFE in 1996)	1999	1998	1997	1996	1995
3-Month Short Sterling	27,272,559	33,750,746	20,370,846	15,793,775	15,314,576
3-Month Euromark	3,785,667	54,559,028	43,326,030	36,231,178	25,737,379
1-Month Euromark		8,908	113,408	48,644	
3-Month Eurolira	70,207	15,592,396	14,894,163	6,936,873	4,005,125
3-Month Euroswiss	5,956,797	7,381,809	4,746,234	3,299,058	1,749,774
3-Month ECU	739,667	262,997	534,457	602,518	693,526
3-Month Euribor	35,657,690	1,269			
3-Month Euroyen TIBOR	27,006	39,240	162,686	242,413	
3-Month Euroyen LIBOR	15				
10-Year Euro EFB	3,897	14,190			
5-Year Euro EFB	1,487	8,185			
Long Gilt	8,421,533	16,185,316	19,651,565	15,408,010	13,796,555
5-Year Gilt	78	113,372			
German Government Bund		14,548,537	44,984,029	39,801,928	32,231,210
Medium Term German Government Bond (BOBL)		90,222	731,865		
Euro BTP	1,180,170				
Euro Bund	1				
Italian Government Bond	574,034	8,213,552	15,260,072	12,603,754	9,612,899
Japanese Government Bond	465,727	692,404	813,241	816,059	845,329
FTSE 100 Index	8,704,574	6,955,090	3,098,308	3,027,044	3,373,250
FTSE Eurotop 100 Index	139,552	42,058			
FTSE Eurotop 300 Index	1,780				
FTSE Eurotop 300 Index ex. UK	15,070				
FTSE Estars Index	1,862				
FTSE Eurobloc 100 Index	1,750				
MSCI Euro Index	41,746				
MSCI Pan-Euro Index	22,171				
FTSE Mid 250 Index	47,663	65,219	68,280	34,068	35,068
Barley	6,526	11,142	15,325	17,892	18,088
BIFFEX (Baltic Freight Index)	16,085	23,595	45,059	60,577	74,696
Cocoa	1,862,119	1,786,090	1,857,065	1,688,921	1,653,790
U.S. Dollar Coffee	1,565,708	1,290,049	1,544,193	1,182,528	1,062,744
Potatoes in Bulk	15,850	24,697	22,933	21,330	27,268
Wheat	100,127	98,501	128,411	115,869	101,025
White Sugar	990,595	945,896	686,302	579,463	575,734
3-Month Short Sterling Options	6,451,680	7,348,877	2,662,716	2,213,494	3,348,945
3-Month Sterling Mid-curve Options	112,735	35,480			
3-Month Euro Options		4			
3-Month Euromark Options	656,429	5,878,551	4,225,874	4,888,942	3,427,376
3-Month Euromark Mid-curve Options		70,123			
3-Month Euroswiss Options	89,777	154,477	31,390	45,568	33,781
3-Month Euribor Options	4,819,366				
3-Month Euribor Mid Curve Options	3,200				
3-Month Euro LIBOR Options	338,037				
3-Month Eurolira Options		2,632,896	2,402,371	953,558	100,129
3-Month Eurolira Mid-curve Options		100			
Long Gilt Options	159,713	1,644,323	1,799,660	1,361,344	1,756,533
German Government Bond Options		5,186,402	10,082,217	8,462,806	6,988,655
Medium Term German Gov't Bond (BOBL) Options		29,507	196,128		
Italian Government Bond Options		564,504	2,544,870	2,456,177	1,130,762
FTSE 100 Index Options (ESX)	4,858,373	3,512,173	7,188,349	6,738,955	4,434,086
FTSE 100 Index Options (SEI)	843,100	1,001,428			
FTSE Estars Index Options	1				
MSCI Pan-Euro Index Options	51				
FTSE 100 Index FLEX Options	58,878	27,855	32,985	65,701	60,699
Barley Options	280	40	206	22	103
BIFFEX (Baltic Freight Index) Options	862	1,350	149	728	447
Cocoa Options	22,758	25,317	27,838	57,094	48,196
U.S. Dollar Coffee Options	186,155	159,557	184,975	129,844	169,130
Potatoes Options	171	35	5	35	
Wheat Options	41,436	10,784	9,326	8,758	12,907
White Sugar Options	105,932	97,949	21,062	13,268	23,016
All Options on Individual Equities	3,601,383	3,307,913	4,295,877	4,298,010	
Total	**120,040,031**	**194,394,159**	**209,425,578**	**170,805,206**	**128,678,388**

Volume Worldwide

Marche a Terme International de France (MATIF), France

	1999	1998	1997	1996	1995
ECU Bond		62,327	357,094	579,493	657,152
Notional Bond	6,130,969	23,284,475	33,752,483	35,321,843	33,610,221
Euro 5-Year	114,946	2,825,479	2,100,683		
Euro 2-Year	3,968				
30-Year Eurobond	754	3,932			
Long Gilt		1,637			
3-Month Euribor	2,968,774	5,305,778	14,417,310	14,133,278	15,488,076
Sugar 45	4,614	86,762	144,849	193,024	305,598
Sugar 100		1,695	7,086		
Wheat		573	13,673	7,236	
Wheat #2	43,193	41,091			
Corn	7,158				
European Rapeseed Meal	132				
Rapeseed	137,244	102,897	74,387	60,148	51,135
Euro Notional Bond Options	135,742	3,302,799	8,376,474	8,894,196	9,517,932
3-Month Euribor Options	31,990	484,057	2,788,126	3,107,113	4,615,434
Euro 5-Year Options	5,950	91,936	70,416		
Rapeseed Options	3,332				
Total	**9,588,766**	**35,595,438**	**62,102,581**	**62,296,331**	**64,245,548**

Marche des Options Negociables de Paris (MONEP), France

	1999	1998	1997	1996	1995
CAC 40 Index*		16,443,276	6,461,308	5,853,172	6,549,953
ECU Bond	4,201,673				
Notional Bond	20,973,911				
5-Year Bond	437,447				
30-Year Eurobond	103,160				
Long Gilt	1,131				
3-Month Pibor & Euribor	501,809				
CAC 40 Index (Short Term) Options	7,728,661	5,108,041	6,250,090	2,465,497	2,425,363
CAC 40 Index (Long Term) Options	75,652,724	2,752,536	3,285,383	2,126,001	3,013,926
DJ STOXX 50 Options	4,031	14,536			
DJ STOXX Sector Indices Options	215				
Euro STOXX 50 Options	131,106	106,457			
All Options on Individual Equities*	68,095,743	28,953,142	5,565,057	3,980,856	
CAC 40 Index (Short Term) Options Odd Lot*	186,197				
CAC 40 Index (Long Term) Options Odd Lot*	477,598				
Total	**177,329,802**	**53,377,988**	**21,561,838**	**14,425,526**	**11,989,242**

* 1998 data reflects different contract size introduced in July. Not comparable with 1997 data

MEFF RENTA FIJA (RF), Spain

	1999	1998	1997	1996	1995
90 Day MIBOR Plus	12,980	1,886,299	2,462,893	1,275,222	302,681
360 Day MIBOR Plus	464	32,523	80,555	61,702	15,403
Euribor	11,321				
German Diff		4,489	17,446	123,311	
3-Year Notional Bond		1,561	4,930	212,933	456
5-Year Notional Bond	37	44,893	9,731		
10-Year Notional Bond	3,614,750	15,662,560	21,046,078	18,535,566	13,035,805
30-Year Notional Bond	96	55,047			
10 Year Notional Bond Options	1,106	1,078,904	2,563,370	3,372,235	1,888,547
5-Year Notional Bond Options		200			
90 Day MIBOR Plus Options	2,400	150,683	400,311	249,806	58,297
Total	**3,643,154**	**18,917,159**	**26,585,419**	**23,931,008**	**19,082,575**

MEFF RENTA VARIABLE (RV), Spain

	1999	1998	1997	1996	1995
IBEX 35 Plus	5,101,588	8,627,374	6,053,283		
IBEX 35 Plus Options	861,255	1,681,205	1,411,101		
All Options on Individual Equities	8,091,728	2,695,206	1,485,074	951,271	
Total	**14,054,571**	**13,003,785**	**8,949,458**	**4,739,599**	**3,627,630**

MERCADO A TERMINO DE BUENOS AIRES, Argentina

	1999	1998	1997	1996	1995
Wheat	54,271	48,558	49,492		
Corn	39,475	42,486	42,125		
Sunflowerseed	34,080	23,576	19,312		
Soybean	43,882	29,069	26,934		
Wheat Options	26,930	20,567	24,490		
Corn Options	9,787	15,045	20,679		
Sunflowerseed Options	6,104	9,957	9,805		
Soybean Options	17,736	10,920	9,905		
Total	**232,265**	**200,178**	**202,742**		

Mercato Italiano Futures (MIF), Italy

	1999	1998	1997	1996	1995
10-Year BTP	188,650	1,293,408	2,851,585	2,240,085	2,636,161
30-Year BTP	70				
5-Year BTP		146	28,585	68,697	166,002
Euribor	20,890				
RIBOR		101,839	135,414		
10-Year BTP Options		45,150	140,597	130,307	113,665
Total	**209,610**	**1,440,543**	**3,156,181**	**2,439,089**	**2,915,828**

Montreal Exchange (ME), Canada

	1999	1998	1997	1996	1995
3-Month Bankers Acceptance	6,047,542	6,803,028	4,139,777	2,415,563	2,326,709
10-Year Canadian Government Bond	1,598,463	1,836,937	1,272,970	1,072,111	1,026,854
5-Year Canadian Government Bond	23,768	45,113	50,944	35,649	63,842
S&P Canada 60 Index	262,058				
5-Year Canadian Government Bond Options	2,667	2,797	933	703	2,191
3-Month Bankers Acceptance Options	168,903	210,850	155,308	75,224	51,855
10-Year Canadian Government Bond Options	9,190	18,533	23,175	30,159	40,147
S&P Canada 60 Index Options	40,650				
All Options on Individual Equities	1,439,476	1,375,274	1,016,945	660,962	
Total	**9,592,717**	**10,292,532**	**6,660,052**	**4,200,686**	**3,618,823**

New Zealand Futures Exchange (NZFOE), New Zealand

	1999	1998	1997	1996	1995
3-Year Government Stock	2,356	18,240	43,967	15,046	26,912
10-Year Government Stock	2,853	9,948	17,265	8,565	8,456
90 Day Bank Bill	816,931	1,236,944	1,019,686	655,270	478,806
Trade Weighted Index		220	40		
NZSE-10 Captial Share Price Index	1,842	2,138	3,037	5,686	2,971
New Zealand Electricity	1,564	3,092	4,596		
90-Day Bank Bill Options	11,600	410	1,811	8,845	16,321
10-Year Government Stock Options		20			
NZSE-10 Captial Share Price Index Options		33	7	23	24
All Options on Individual Equities	24,621	71,847	117,669	144,207	
Total	**861,767**	**1,342,892**	**1,208,079**	**837,672**	**539,839**

OM Stockholm (OMS), Sweden

	1999	1998	1997	1996	1995
Interest Rate	8,002,707	9,356,221	12,704,397	15,642,920	10,949,860
OMX Index	11,931,352	9,265,510	2,163,560	1,625,391	1,593,408
NOX Index	234				
All Futures on Individual Equities	1,129,453	533,508	288,841	272,514	
Interest Rate Options	100	2,727	5,846	32,825	42,783
OMX Index Options	5,733,106	4,947,486	3,545,967	5,399,227	6,067,268
NOX Index Options	1,554				
All Options on Individual Equities	26,824,117	20,589,273	19,485,816	12,920,145	
Total	**53,622,623**	**44,694,725**	**38,194,473**	**35,896,860**	**18,653,319**

Oslo Stock Exchange (OSE), Norway

	1999	1998	1997	1996	1995
OBr10	21,116	36,423	58,518	55,376	52,001
OBr2		1,000			
OBr5	8,224	31,332	33,422	50,673	49,187
Forwards	170,950	57,938	1,630		
OBX	675,240	354,602	135,284	36,366	18,615
OBX Options	978,014	828,445	926,646	512,460	481,865
All Options on Individual Equities	2,580,178	883,045	1,086,171	815,396	
Total	**4,433,722**	**2,192,785**	**2,241,671**	**1,470,271**	**613,768**

SHANGAI METAL EXCHANGE (SME), China

	1999	1998	1997	1996	1995
Copper	2,559,687	2,772,124	1,299,520		
Aluminum	256,485	60,656	73,077		
Rubber	318,096	391,009			
Nickel		8	74		
Total	**3,134,268**	**3,223,797**	**1,372,671**		

Volume Worldwide

Singapore International Monetary Exchange (SIMEX), Singapore

	1999	1998	1997	1996	1995
Eurodollar	8,999,879	9,837,115	7,400,058	8,184,887	8,394,933
Singapore Dollar Interest Rate	18,725				
Deferred Spot US$/JY		3,324	61,468	86,833	58,922
Deferred Spot US$/DM		2,682	49,264	70,651	109,181
Nikkei 225 Index	5,429,843	5,537,558	4,844,495	4,887,912	6,456,984
Nikkei 300 Index	34,273	95,255	129,695	156,482	174,234
Dow Jones Thailand Index	1,347	721			
MSCI Hong Kong Index	2,597	6,124			
MSCI Singapore Index	291,527	27,727			
MSCI Taiwan Index	2,362,385	1,842,977	677,295		
Brent Crude	18,853	32,600	33,067	63,535	73,445
Euroyen TIBOR	6,777,548	8,757,516	9,624,680	8,162,548	6,549,295
Euroyen LIBOR	374,198				
Japanese Government Bond	168,829	194,373	132,104	138,471	297,426
Eurodollar Options		559	7,825	3,319	5,247
Euroyen Options	234,630	661,008	481,138	208,363	128,944
Japanese Government Bond Options	1,962	2,211	11,658	18,709	35,071
MSCI Taiwan Index Options	8,828	20,521	7,550		
Nikkei 225 Index Options	1,137,716	838,891	628,222	58,660	1,943,096
Total	**25,863,140**	**27,861,162**	**24,090,285**	**22,568,545**	**24,251,339**

South African Futures Exchange (SAFEX), Africa

	1999	1998	1997	1996	1995
All Share Index	6,037,573	4,620,298	2,599,489	1,943,973	1,816,846
Industrial Index	2,838,168	2,609,146	1,960,260	1,493,987	1,030,714
Financial Index (FNDI)		850	3,710	10,080	4,290
Financial Index (FINI)	80,497	80,229			
Mining Index	1,260	3,010			
RESI	14,120				
Gold Index		53,033	491,351	603,205	656,696
3-Month Bank Bill	1,029	92	106	1,360	5,154
Johannesburg Interbank Rate (JBAR)	6,092				
R 150	1,723	8,375	8,489	37,982	30,472
R 153	1,026	8,394	5,924	101	
R 157		2			
R 162		300			
All Share Index Options	8,511,293	7,915,791	4,873,560	3,759,424	2,932,564
Industrial Index Options	973,633	713,337	1,282,555	913,342	481,053
Financial Index (FNDI) Options		400	3,533	11,168	
Financial Index (FINI) Options	123,585	56,924			
Mining Index Options	3,200				
RESI Options	4,000				
Gold Index Options		31,978	248,765	1,015,065	195,720
R 150 Options	955	5,294	10,467	26,682	29,683
R 153 Options	2,720	5,957	20,085	2,060	
All Options on Individual Equities	82,576	152,960	75,360		
Total	**18,683,450**	**16,266,370**	**11,583,654**	**9,822,581**	**7,218,914**

Taiwan Futures Exchange, Taiwan

	1999	1998	1997	1996	1995
TAIEX Index	951,578	277,909			
Taiwan Stock Exchange Electronic Sector Index	87,156				
Taiwan Stock Exchange Bank & Insurance Sector Inde	18,938				
Total	**1,077,672**	**277,909**			

Sydney Futures Exchange (SFE), Australia

	1999	1998	1997	1996	1995
All Ordinaries Share Price Index	3,819,800	3,678,151	3,204,266	2,675,754	2,476,331
DJ AP/ELS Australian Index	68				
90 Day Bank Bills	7,184,423	7,735,231	5,918,447	4,977,945	6,172,512
3 Year Treasury Bonds	10,787,444	10,485,750	10,378,357	9,209,228	8,820,651
10 Year Treasury Bonds	53,745,640	5,640,716	5,819,677	5,315,845	5,740,870
NSW Electricity	4,670	6,797	1,191		
NSW Peak Period Electricity	846				
VIC Electricity	2,130	4,615	1,129		
VIC Peak Period Electricity	557				
Wheat	8,017	9,692	7,937	6,482	
Fine Wool	4,106	2,041			
Broad Wool	699	496			
Greasy Wool	16,108	11,507	10,127	7,554	4,799
All Futures on Individual Equities	8,658	9,026	29,157	54,463	
All Ordinaries Share Price Index Options	1,237,294	847,375	896,340	896,880	652,607
90 Day Bank Bills Options	453,048	770,229	984,363	911,005	712,834
3-Year Treasury Bond Options	289,196	223,842	418,081	457,808	426,836
Overnight 3 Year Treasury Bond Options	217,959	64,394	43,540	42,461	7,443
10-Year Treasury Bonds Options	242,732	354,311	545,359	845,571	580,091
Overnight 10 Year Treasury Bond Options	169,347	90,015	149,817	128,426	24,419
Wheat Options	561	2,040	1,740	788	
Greasy Wool Options	30	47	11	41	
Total	**29,793,333**	**29,936,275**	**28,409,539**	**25,530,251**	**25,620,614**

Toronto Futures Exchange (TFE), Canada

	1999	1998	1997	1996	1995
TSE 35 Index	374,525	440,851	317,408	155,652	110,011
TSE 100 Index	7,624	16,900	19,317	8,135	2,963
TSE 35 Options	250,960	388,273	431,623	254,199	337,764
Total	**633,109**	**846,024**	**768,399**	**418,831**	**459,218**

Winnipeg Commodity Exchange (WCE), Canada

	1999	1998	1997	1996	1995
Wheat	106,378	146,713	197,619	206,120	155,699
Oats	375	3,970	3,205	3,496	32,761
Flaxseed	78,433	115,552	140,756	99,889	132,525
Canola (Rapeseed)	1,685,756	1,557,358	1,387,675	1,345,952	1,075,683
Feed Peas	70	3,286	14,247	17,979	7,802
Field Peas	4,520				
Western Barley	211,377	238,994	284,614	334,809	172,733
Wheat Options	115	537	250	355	734
Flaxseed Options	3,295	1,093	66	466	1,567
Western Barley Options	1,648	553	959	3,166	274
Canola Options	61,476	23,310	31,810	61,233	71,197
Total	**2,153,443**	**2,091,366**	**2,061,201**	**2,073,465**	**1,670,037**

Hong Kong Futures Exchange (HKFE), Hong Kong

	1999	1998	1997	1996	1995
Hang Seng Index	5,132,332	6,969,708	6,446,696	4,656,084	4,546,613
Hang Seng 100 Index	66,822	15,450			
Hang Seng Properties Sub-Index	341				
HKFE Taiwan Index		71			
Red-Chip Index	30,753	170,385	143,078		
Rolling Forex	9,042	17,146	251,226	195,355	21,321
1-Month HIBOR	9,726	4,405			
3-Month HIBOR	308,646	502,982	87,819		
All Futures on Individual Equities	5,696	4,082	4,453		
Hang Seng Index Options	714,309	798,712	1,147,374	1,093,871	645,538
Hang Seng 100 Index Options	51,393	4,610			
Hang Seng Properties Sub-Index Options	2,330				
HKFE Taiwan Index Options		56			
Red-Chip Index Options	10	2,035	1,234		
Total	**6,331,400**	**8,489,642**	**8,081,880**	**5,945,310**	**5,213,472**

Kanmon Commodity Exchange (KCE), Japan

	1999	1998	1997	1996	1995
Red Beans	92,622	200,215	95,982	118,438	237,745
Imported Soybeans	498,795	572,570	1,382,063	496,376	130,520
Refined Sugar	1,421	1,433	1,421	1,438	1,449
Corn	2,897,402	2,951,184	5,069,142	4,346,586	2,890,258
Total	**4,693,896**	**3,725,402**	**6,548,608**	**4,962,838**	**3,259,972**

Kansai Agricultural Commodities Exchange (KANEX), Japan

	1999	1998	1997	1996	1995
Red Beans	177,039	450,610	483,330	877,474	1,723,230
Imported Soybeans	1,245,358	1,513,589	4,022,023	2,656,174	1,695,414
Refined Sugar	2,842	2,866	2,842	2,876	2,886
Raw Sugar	462,427	558,075	643,742	577,641	730,582
Raw Silk (formerly at Kobe Raw Silk Exchange)	178,114	231,376	327,009	458,243	591,922
Kansai International Grain Index	376,660	60,008			
Raw Sugar Options	30,363	70,561	47,189	71,145	79,365
Total	**2,472,803**	**2,887,085**	**5,526,135**	**4,643,553**	**4,823,399**

Chubu Commodity Exchange (CCE), Japan

(formerly NGSE, NTE, and TDCE)	1999	1998	1997	1996	1995
Red Beans	147,511	188,937	241,008	287,220	502,369
Sweet Potato Starch		35	48	48	48
Imported Soybeans	348,567	505,345	1,010,201	620,703	307,451
Refined Sugar	1,421	1,433	1,421	1,438	1,449
Dried Cocoon	240,841	277,944	684,141	1,202,536	488,709
Cotton Yarn (40S)	183,945	114,877	126,684	296,455	755,844
Staple Fiber Yarn (Dull)	1,913	9,194	9,948	10,001	9,967
Wool Yarn	12,351	33,973	35,315	27,277	53,811
Hen Egg	390,475				
Total	**1,327,024**	**1,131,738**	**2,108,766**	**2,445,678**	**2,119,648**

Volume Worldwide

Osaka Securities Exchange(OSE), Japan

	1999	1998	1997	1996	1995
Nikkei 225 Index	9,067,883	8,191,130	7,484,182	7,043,977	7,220,900
Nikkei 300 Index	1,470,954	1,531,004	1,526,538	1,872,983	2,318,652
High-Tech Index	457	3,794			
Financial Index	471	3,576			
Consumer Index	459	2,626			
Nikkei 225 Index Options	5,753,760	5,230,046	4,910,359	3,924,543	5,174,571
Nikkei 300 Index Options	652	2,577	7,798	44,254	122,084
High-Tech Index Options		57			
Financial Index Options	1	86			
Consumer Index Options		5			
All Options on Individual Equities	683,778	363,901	222,094		
Total	**16,978,415**	**15,328,802**	**14,150,971**	**12,885,757**	**14,836,207**

Osaka Mercantile Exchange (OME), Japan

(formerly KRE and OTE)	1999	1998	1997	1996	1995
Staple Fiber Yarn (Dull)	705	4,338	4,952	2,928	2,940
Wool Yarn	8,062	15,677	22,589	18,624	64,073
Cotton Yarn (20S)	189,240	583,851	1,245,452	1,109,607	2,151,580
Cotton Yarn (40S)	34,378	42,993	147,444	254,828	659,110
Rubber (RSS3)	1,546,297	2,835,126	1,200,850	2,232,827	3,810,938
Rubber Index	1,355,731	672,582	382,913	373,879	173,409
Aluminum	2,218,159	1,107,266	160,060		
Total	**5,352,572**	**5,261,833**	**3,164,947**	**3,995,802**	**6,866,178**

Tokyo Commodity Exchange (TOCOM), Japan

	1999	1998	1997	1996	1995
Gold	16,011,962	9,373,909	8,871,965	9,510,941	10,945,134
Silver	966,838	1,679,647	792,844	752,995	1,440,297
Platinum	13,277,043	16,944,343	10,839,577	6,895,464	5,975,872
Palladium	5,832,649	5,194,391	3,817,892	434,163	629,034
Aluminum	710,782	305,436	567,175		
Gasoline	3,973,668				
Kerosene	1,441,163				
Rubber	6,193,292	9,975,520	4,758,390	9,085,709	14,287,783
Cotton Yarn	33,986	110,645	524,717	874,052	1,838,448
Woolen Yarn	778	5,832	5,789	6,830	8,859
Total	**48,442,161**	**43,589,723**	**30,178,349**	**27,560,154**	**35,125,427**

Tokyo Grain Exchange (TGE), Japan

	1999	1998	1997	1996	1995
American Soybeans	3,279,175	3,820,850	9,966,257	7,120,741	2,699,926
Arabica Coffee	3,508,798	831,163			
Red Beans	1,378,169	1,953,638	2,542,760	2,847,511	3,384,267
Corn	8,107,879	7,267,045	13,840,721	16,034,716	6,899,593
Refined Sugar	2,842	2,866	2,842	2,876	2,898
Robusta Coffee	699,153	305,160			
Raw Sugar	1,042,427	189,778	1,279,550	1,045,438	1,291,441
American Soybean Options	79,955	97,599	263,990	275,269	206,993
Corn Options	141,578	201,269	44,220		
Raw Sugar Options	153,285	143,434	186,698	182,724	158,044
Total	**18,393,261**	**15,412,802**	**28,127,038**	**27,509,275**	**14,643,162**

Tokyo International Financial Futures Exchange (TIFFE), Japan

	1999	1998	1997	1996	1995
3-Month Euroyen TIBOR	14,572,255	21,162,012	25,523,583	29,334,830	36,329,959
3-Month Euroyen LIBOR	57,479				
U.S. Dollar / Japanese Yen	28,681	46,949	63,755	44,194	5,037
Euroyen Options	271,487	500,002	535,895	567,793	361,920
Total	**14,929,902**	**21,708,963**	**26,123,233**	**29,970,017**	**36,722,216**

Tokyo Stock Exchange (TSE), Japan

	1999	1998	1997	1996	1995
5-Year Government Yen Bond	111,975	195,207	118,447	220,955	
10-Year Government Yen Bond	9,727,855	10,784,966	11,873,549	12,450,925	14,010,374
20-Year Government Yen Bond		123	2,167	2,242	2,734
TOPIX Stock Index	3,157,441	2,727,070	3,035,724	2,857,272	2,745,614
Electric Appliance Index	182	2,671			
Transportation Equipment Index	239	429			
Bank Index	25,719	1,127			
30-Year U.S. T-Bond		2,060	30,650	31,030	102,340
TOPIX Options	2,030	583	9,356	13,444	16,742
10-Year Government Yen Bond Options	1,137,319	1,848,851	2,002,357	1,975,274	2,017,031
Total	**14,162,760**	**15,563,087**	**17,072,250**	**17,551,142**	**16,877,804**

Yokohama Commodity Exchange, Japan

(formerly Maebashi Dried Cocoon & Yokohama Raw Silk Ex.)	1999	1998	1997	1996	1995
Raw Silk	704,657	371,732	658,176	1,083,386	1,256,094
Dried Cocoon	191,048	520,698	565,423	864,703	443,411
Total	**895,705**	**892,430**	**1,223,599**	**1,948,089**	**1,699,505**

	1999	1998	1997	1996	1995
TOTAL FUTURES	775,569,595	798,107,856	750,548,594	703,482,637	783,168,145
PERCENT CHANGE	-2.82%	6.29%	7.54%	-1.68%	0.35%
TOTAL OPTIONS	520,827,726	344,862,103	275,602,274	271,860,316	265,921,807
PERCENT CHANGE	51.02%	25.14%	-1.22%	-26.70%	87.30%
TOTAL	1,296,397,321	1,142,969,959	1,026,150,868	975,342,953	1,049,089,952
PERCENT CHANGE	13.42%	11.35%	5.10%	-8.03%	16.18%

Conversion Factors

Commonly Used Agricultural Weights and Measurements

Bushel Weights:
wheat and soybeans = 60 lbs.
corn, sorghum and rye = 56 lbs.
barley grain = 48 lbs.
barley malt = 34 lbs.
oats = 32 lbs.

Bushels to tonnes:
wheat and soybeans = bushels X 0.027216
barley grain = bushels X 0.021772
corn, sorghum and rye = bushels X 0.0254
oats = bushels X 0.014515

1 tonne (metric ton) equals:
2204.622 lbs.
1,000 kilograms
22.046 hundredweight
10 quintals

1 tonne (metric ton) equals:
36.7437 bushels of wheat or soybeans
39.3679 bushels of corn, sorghum or rye
45.9296 bushels of barley grain
68.8944 bushels of oats
4.5929 cotton bales (the statistical bale used by the USDA and ICAC contains a net weight of 480 pounds of lint)

Area Measurements:
1 acre = 43,560 square feet = 0.040694 hectare
1 hectare = 2.4710 acres = 10,000 square meters
640 acres = 1 square mile = 259 hectares

Yields:
wheat: bushels per acre X 0.6725 = quintals per hectare
rye, corn: bushels per acre X 0.6277 = quintals per hectare
barley grain: bushels per acre X 0.538 = quintals per hectare
oats: bushels per acre X 0.3587 = quintals per hectare

Commonly Used Weights

The troy, avoirdupois and apothecaries' grains are identical in U.S. and British weight systems, equal to 0.0648 gram in the metric system. One avoirdupois ounce equals 437.5 grains. The troy and apothecaries' ounces equal 480 grains, and their pounds contain 12 ounces.

Troy weights and conversions: 100 kilograms = 1 quintal
24 grains = 1 pennyweight
20 pennyweights = 1 ounce
12 ounces = 1 pound
1 troy ounce = 31.103 grams
1 troy ounce = 0.0311033 kilogram
1 troy pound = 0.37224 kilogram
1 kilogram = 32.1507 troy ounces
1 tonne = 32,151 troy ounces

Avoirdupois weights and conversions:
27 11/32 grains = 1 dram
16 drams = 1 ounce
16 ounces = 1 lb.
1 lb. = 7,000 grains
14 lbs. = 1 stone (British)
100 lbs. = 1 hundredweight (U.S.)
112 lbs. = 8 stone = 1 hundredweight (British)
2,000 lbs. = 1 short ton (U.S. ton)
2,240 lbs. = 1 long ton (British ton)
160 stone = 1 long ton
20 hundredweight = 1 ton
1 lb. = 0.4536 kilogram
1 hundredweight (cwt.) = 45.359 kilograms
1 short ton = 907.18 kilograms
1 long ton = 1,016.05 kilograms

Metric weights and conversions:
1,000 grams = 1 kilogram

1 tonne = 1,000 kilograms = 10 quintals
1 kilogram = 2.204622 lbs.
1 quintal = 220.462 lbs.
1 tonne = 2204.6 lbs.
1 tonne = 1.102 short tons
1 tonne = 0.9842 long ton

U.S. dry volumes and conversions:
1 pint = 33.6 cubic inches = 0.5506 liter
2 pints = 1 quart = 1.1012 liters
8 quarts = 1 peck = 8.8098 liters
4 pecks = 1 bushel = 35.2391 liters
1 cubic foot = 28.3169 liters

U.S. liquid volumes and conversions:
1 ounce = 1.8047 cubic inches = 29.6 milliliters
1 cup = 8 ounces = 0.24 liter = 237 milliliters
1 pint = 16 ounces = 0.48 liter = 473 milliliters
1 quart = 2 pints = 0.946 liter = 946 milliliters
1 gallon = 4 quarts = 231 cubic inches = 3.785 liters
1 milliliter = 0.033815 fluid ounce
1 liter = 1.0567 quarts = 1,000 milliliters
1 liter = 33.815 fluid ounces
1 imperial gallon = 277.42 cubic inches = 1.2 U.S. gallons = 4.546 liters

ENERGY CONVERSION FACTORS

U.S. Crude Oil (average gravity)
1 U.S. barrel = 42 U.S. gallons
1 short ton = 6.65 barrels
1 tonne = 7.33 barrels

Barrels per tonne for various origins

Abu Dhabi	7.624
Algeria	7.661
Angola	7.206
Australia	7.775
Bahrain	7.335
Brunei	7.334
Canada	7.428
Dubai	7.295
Ecuador	7.58
Gabon	7.245
Indonesia	7.348
Iran	7.37
Iraq	7.453
Kuwait	7.261
Libya	7.615
Mexico	7.104
Neutral Zone	6.825
Nigeria	7.41
Norway	7.444
Oman	7.39
Qatar	7.573
Romania	7.453
Saudi Arabia	7.338
Trinidad	6.989
Tunisia	7.709
United Arab Emirates	7.522
United Kingdom	7.279
United States	7.418
Former Soviet Union	7.35
Venezuela	7.005
Zaire	7.206

Barrels per tonne of refined products:

aviation gasoline	8.9
motor gasoline	8.5
kerosene	7.75
jet fuel	8
distillate, including diesel	7.46
residual fuel oil	6.45
lubricating oil	7
grease	6.3
white spirits	8.5
paraffin oil	7.14
paraffin wax	7.87
petrolatum	7.87
asphalt and road oil	6.06
petroleum coke	5.5
bitumen	6.06
LPG	11.6

(continued above)

Approximate heat content of refined products:
(Million Btu per barrel, 1 British thermal unit is the amount of heat required to raise the temperature of 1 pound of water 1 degree F.)

Petroleum Product	**Heat Content**
asphalt	6.636
aviation gasoline	5.048
butane	4.326
distillate fuel oil	5.825
ethane	3.082
isobutane	3.974
jet fuel, kerosene	5.67
jet fuel, naptha	5.355
kerosene	5.67
lubricants	6.065
motor gasoline	5.253
natural gasoline	4.62
pentanes plus	4.62

Petrochemical feedstocks:

naptha less than 401*F	5.248
other oils equal to or greater than 401*F	5.825
still gas	6
petroleum coke	6.024
plant condensate	5.418
propane	3.836
residual fuel oil	6.287
special napthas	5.248
unfinished oils	5.825
unfractionated steam	5.418
waxes	5.537

Source: U.S. Department of Energy

Natural Gas Conversions

Although there are approximately 1,031 Btu in a cubic foot of gas, for most applications, the following conversions are sufficient:

Cubic Feet					**MMBtu**
1,000	(one thousand cubic feet)	=	1 Mcf	=	1
1,000,000	(one million cubic feet)	=	1 MMcf	=	1,000
10,000,000	(ten million cubic feet)	=	10 MMcf	=	10,000
1,000,000,000	(one billion cubic feet)	=	1 Bcf	=	1,000,000
1,000,000,000,000	(one trillion cubic feet)	=	1 Tcf	=	1,000,000,000

Aluminum

World smelter production of aluminum in 1998 was estimated at 22.2 million metric tonnes. This represented an increase of almost 4 percent from 1997. In terms of smelter production of aluminum, the U.S. remains the largest producer with 1998 production of 3.7 million metric tonnes, an increase of almost 3 percent from the previous year. The next largest producer was Russia with 1998 production estimated at 2.96 million tonnes, an increase of almost 2 percent from the previous year. Other large producers include Canada, China, Australia and Brazil.

Despite the economic problems seen in Asia, aluminum demand in the U.S. and Western Europe remained strong. Production increased as idled capacity was brought back on stream. World aluminum smelter capacity in 1998 was estimated at 24.8 million tonnes, up almost 3 percent from 1997. The U.S. has the most capacity which for 1998 was estimated at 4.2 million tonnes. Russia's capacity was 2.97 million tonnes. Other countries with large capacity include China, Canada, Australia and Brazil.

The U.S. Geological Survey reported that domestic primary production of aluminum in August 1999 was 324,000 tonnes, up almost 2 percent from July. For the first eight months of 1999, primary aluminum production was 2.5 million tonnes. That was up almost 2 percent from the same period in 1998. For all of 1998, primary production of aluminum was 3.71 million tonnes.

There is also substantial recovery of aluminum from secondary sources. In August 1999, secondary recovery of aluminum totaled 296,000 tonnes. For the January-August 1999 period, aluminum recovered from secondary sources totaled 2.31 million tonnes, an increase of almost 6 percent from a year ago. Of the recovered aluminum, 60 percent came from new manufacturing scrap with the rest from old scrap. In the first eight months of 1999, secondary recovery of aluminum from new sources was 1.38 million tonnes while old sources provided 927,000 tonnes. For all of 1998, secondary recovery totaled 3.44 million tonnes with 1.95 million tonnes from new sources and 1.5 million tonnes from old sources.

U.S. imports for consumption of aluminum crude metals and alloys in July 1999 were 213,000 tonnes, down 17 percent from the previous month. For all of 1998, imports of crude metals and alloys were 2.4 million tonnes. Imports of aluminum plates, sheets and bars in July were 62,000 tonnes, down 2 percent from the previous month. For all of 1998, imports were 649,000 tonnes.

The total new supply of aluminum (including primary production, secondary recovery and imports for consumption) in July 1999 was 881,000 tonnes, down 5 percent from the previous month. U.S. stocks of aluminum, including scrap, at the end of July 1999 were 1.95 million tonnes, up 8 percent from the previous month. At the end of 1998, stocks were 1.93 million tonnes.

U.S. imports for consumption of aluminum (including scrap) in July 1999 were 334,000 tonnes. For the January-July 1999 period imports were 2.48 million tonnes. The major suppliers were Canada, Russia and Venezuela. U.S. exports of aluminum in July 1999 were 125,000 tonnes with the January-July total being 918,000 tonnes. Most exports are in the form of plates, sheets and bars. The largest export market is Canada followed by Mexico.

Futures Markets

Aluminum futures and options are listed on the London Metals Exchange (LME). A new Pig Ingot contract began trading on the COMEX division of the New York Mercantile Exchange in 1999.

World Production of Primary Aluminum In Thousands of Metric Tons

Year	Australia	Brazil	Canada	China	France	Germany	Norway	Russia[3]	Spain	United Kingdom	United States	Vene-zuela	World Total
1990	1,230	931	1,570	850	326	740	845	3,523	353	294	4,050	590	19,300
1991	1,228	1,140	1,822	963	286	690	833	3,251	355	294	4,121	601	19,700
1992	1,236	1,193	1,972	1,100	418	603	838	2,700	359	244	4,042	561	19,500
1993	1,381	1,172	2,308	1,220	426	552	887	2,820	364	239	3,695	568	19,800
1994	1,317	1,185	2,255	1,450	437	505	857	2,670	338	231	3,299	585	19,200
1995	1,297	1,188	2,172	1,680	372	575	847	2,724	361	238	3,375	630	19,700
1996	1,372	1,195	2,283	1,770	380	576	863	2,874	362	240	3,577	629	20,800
1997[1]	1,495	1,200	2,327	1,960	399	572	919	2,906	360	248	3,603	634	21,500
1998[2]	1,627	1,200	2,374	2,100	400	572	996	3,005	362	260	3,713	580	22,100

[1] Preliminary. [2] Estimate. [3] Formerly part of the U.S.S.R.; data not reported separately until 1992. *Source: U.S. Geological Survey (USGS)*

Production of Primary Aluminum (Domestic and Foreign Ores) in the U.S. In Thousands of Metric Tons

Year	Jan.	Feb.	Mar.	Apr.	May	June	July	Aug.	Sept.	Oct.	Nov.	Dec.	Total
1990	345	311	345	331	342	330	340	341	332	347	337	347	4,048
1991	349	317	352	340	353	343	354	350	336	347	337	343	4,121
1992	344	320	343	330	342	330	339	340	330	343	335	347	4,043
1993	335	292	323	313	325	315	316	302	291	303	287	294	3,696
1994	292	261	286	269	277	268	275	274	267	277	270	280	3,296
1995	281	253	280	272	285	277	288	286	280	289	285	299	3,375
1996	301	283	303	293	303	293	301	302	292	304	295	305	3,577
1997	305	277	307	295	304	296	305	304	294	307	298	310	3,603
1998	309	280	312	305	316	307	319	318	309	315	307	317	3,713
1999[1]	315	287	320	309	319	310	319	324	310	323	316		3,766

[1] Preliminary. *Source: U.S. Geological Survey (USGS)*

ALUMINUM

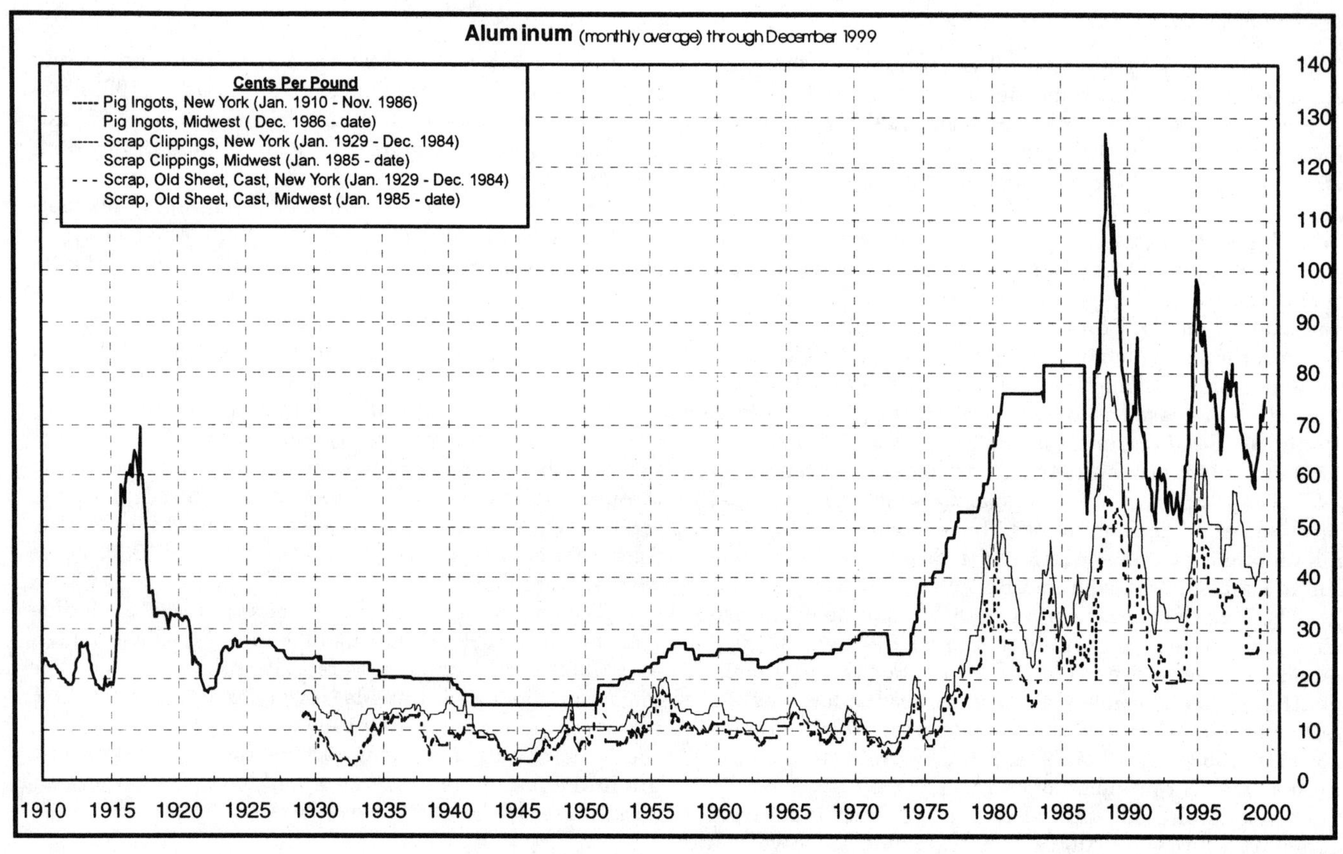

Salient Statistics of Aluminum in the United States   In Thousands of Metric Tons

								Net Shipments[5] by Producers								
								Wrought Products				Castings				
Year	Net Import Reliance as a % of Apparent Consumption	Production Primary	Production Second-ary	Primary Ship-ments	Recovery from Scrap OLd	Recovery from Scrap New	Apparent Con-sumption	Plate, Sheet, Foil	Rolled Structural Shapes[3]	Ex-truded Shapes[4]	All	Perma-nent Mold	Die	Sand	All	Total All Net Ship-ments
1989	E	4,030	2,054	6,751	1,011	1,043	4,957	3,900	339	1,280	5,633	210	740	110	1,096	6,728
1990	E	4,048	2,390	6,590	1,360	1,030	5,260	3,799	301	1,211	5,425	208	620	103	968	6,393
1991	E	4,121	2,290	6,400	1,320	969	5,040	3,787	311	1,096	5,300	168	575	97	864	6,156
1992	1	4,042	2,760	6,810	1,610	1,140	5,730	4,097	303	1,186	5,691	198	595	99	804	6,609
1993	19	3,695	2,940	7,300	1,630	1,310	6,600	4,030	297	1,300	5,770	225	645	103	994	6,770
1994	30	3,299	3,090	8,160	1,500	1,580	6,880	4,810	296	1,420	6,690	247	551	208	1,050	7,740
1995	23	3,375	3,190	8,260	1,510	1,680	6,300	4,900	526	1,540	7,130	442	627	207	1,440	8,580
1996	22	3,577	3,310	8,330	1,570	1,730	6,610	4,430	350	1,540	6,480	473	612	180	1,390	7,860
1997	23	3,603	3,550	8,880	1,530	2,020	6,720	4,710	315	1,610	6,800	468	670	153	1,410	8,210
1998[1]	25	3,713	3,440	9,270	1,500	1,950	7,090	4,720	330	1,710	6,930	NA	NA	NA	NA	NA

[1] Preliminary. [2] To domestic industry. [3] Also rod, bar & wire. [4] Also rod, bar, tube, blooms & tubing. [5] Consists of total shipments less shipments to other mills for further fabrication. NA = Not available. E = Net exporter. *Source: U.S. Geological Survey (USGS)*

Supply and Distribution of Aluminum in the United States   In Thousands of Metric Tons

Year	Apparent Consump-tion	Production Primary	Production From Old Scrap	Imports	Exports	Inventories December 31 Private	Inventories December 31 Govern-ment[2]	Year	Apparent Consump-tion	Production Primary	Production From Old Scrap	Imports	Exports	Inventories December 31 Private	Inventories December 31 Govern-ment[2]
1987	5,469	3,343	852	1,850	917	2,000	2	1993	6,600	3,695	1,630	2,540	1,210	1,980	57
1988	5,373	3,944	1,045	1,620	1,247	1,883	2	1994	6,880	3,299	1,500	3,380	1,370	2,070	57
1989	4,957	4,030	1,011	1,470	1,615	1,822	2	1995	6,300	3,375	1,510	2,980	1,610	2,000	57
1990	5,260	4,048	1,360	1,514	1,659	1,820	2	1996	6,610	3,577	1,570	2,810	1,500	1,860	57
1991	5,040	4,121	1,320	1,490	1,762	1,780	2	1997[1]	6,720	3,603	1,530	3,080	1,570	1,860	[4]
1992	5,730	4,042	1,610	1,725	1,453	1,880	57	1998[2]	7,090	3,713	1,500	3,550	1,590	1,930	[4]

[1] Preliminary. [2] Estimate. [3] National Defense Stockpile. [4] Less than 1/2 unit. Source: U.S. Geological Survey (USGS)

Aluminum Products Distribution of End-Use Shipments in the United States In Thousands of Metric Tons

Year	Building & Construction	Consumer Durables	Containers & Packaging	Electrical	Exports	Machinery & Equipment	Trans-portaion	Other	Total
1989	1,294	544	2,112	663	1,060	436	1,448	264	7,821
1990	1,208	509	2,157	594	1,131	452	1,388	261	7,700
1991	1,052	472	2,210	579	1,357	426	1,414	241	7,752
1992	1,144	523	2,259	587	1,236	448	1,591	256	8,045
1993	1,240	563	2,180	609	1,090	477	1,970	259	8,390
1994	1,400	647	2,270	682	1,200	572	2,310	276	9,360
1995	1,220	621	2,310	657	1,310	570	2,610	279	9,570
1996	1,330	655	2,180	671	1,290	569	2,640	291	9,610
1997	1,320	694	2,220	708	1,360	626	2,990	318	10,200
1998[1]	1,390	725	2,270	714	1,260	629	3,250	286	10,500

[1] Preliminary. *Source: U.S. Geological Survey (USGS)*

World Consumption of Primary Aluminum In Thousands of Metric Tons

Year	Brazil	Canada	China	France	Germany	India	Italy	Japan	Rep. of Korea	Russia	United Kingdom	United States	World Total
1989	420.1	450.2	920.0	685.5	1,289.1	420.0	607.0	2,211.6	287.6	2,700.0	454.7	4,381.4	19,281.1
1990	341.2	387.2	861.0	723.0	1,295.4	433.3	652.0	2,414.3	368.9	2,790.0	453.7	4,330.4	19,275.4
1991	354.2	408.2	938.0	725.9	1,360.9	430.2	670.0	2,431.6	383.5	2,409.0	412.4	4,137.2	18,778.2
1992	377.1	420.4	1,253.8	730.5	1,457.1	414.3	660.0	2,271.6	397.0	1,242.0	550.0	4,616.9	18,529.5
1993	378.9	492.5	1,339.9	667.2	1,150.7	475.3	554.0	2,138.3	524.8	657.0	540.0	4,877.1	18,122.6
1994	414.1	559.0	1,500.1	736.3	1,370.3	475.0	660.0	2,344.8	603.9	470.0	570.0	5,407.1	19,670.8
1995	500.6	611.9	1,941.6	743.8	1,503.9	581.0	665.4	2,335.6	675.4	476.0	620.0	5,054.8	20,490.4
1996	497.0	619.9	2,135.3	671.7	1,355.0	584.8	585.1	2,392.6	674.3	443.8	600.0	5,348.0	20,702.8
1997	478.6	642.4	2,260.3	723.6	1,567.5	555.7	653.4	2,434.3	666.3	469.7	619.1	5,390.0	21,777.6
1998[1]	421.2	550.1	2,473.4	689.4	1,766.8	555.0	744.2	2,040.4	462.0	400.0	678.5	5,813.6	21,712.1

[1] Preliminary. *Source: American Metal Market (AMM)*

Salient Statistics of Recycling Aluminum in the United States

Year	Percent Recycled	New Scrap[1]	Old Scrap[2]	Recycled Metal[3]	Apparent Supply	New Scrap[1]	Old Scrap[2]	Recycled Metal[3]	Apparent Supply
		In Thousands of Metric Tons				Value in Millions of Dollars			
1989	34	1,043	1,011	2,054	6,000	2,020	1,958	3,978	11,620
1990	38	1,034	1,359	2,393	6,298	1,688	2,218	3,906	10,280
1991	38	969	1,320	2,290	6,010	1,270	1,730	3,000	7,880
1992	40	1,140	1,610	2,760	6,870	1,450	2,040	3,500	8,710
1993	37	1,310	1,630	2,940	7,920	1,540	1,920	3,460	9,300
1994	36	1,580	1,500	3,090	8,460	2,480	2,360	4,840	13,300
1995	40	1,680	1,510	3,190	7,980	3,190	2,850	6,040	15,100
1996	40	1,730	1,570	3,310	8,340	2,730	2,480	5,200	13,100
1997	41	2,020	1,530	3,550	8,740	3,430	2,590	6,020	14,800
1998	38	1,950	1,500	3,440	9,040	2,810	2,160	4,970	13,100

[1] Scrap that results from the manufacturing process. [2] Scrap that results from consumer products. [3] Metal recovered from new plus old scrap.
Source: U.S. Geological Survey (USGS)

Producer Prices for Aluminum Used Beverage Can Scrap In Cents Per Pound

Year	Jan.	Feb.	Mar.	Apr.	May	June	July	Aug.	Sept.	Oct.	Nov.	Dec.	Average
1989	72.64	73.76	73.15	69.50	71.55	66.59	57.92	55.50	54.68	55.50	54.30	51.50	63.05
1990	48.50	45.50	47.55	50.50	50.77	50.50	49.71	51.13	57.53	52.15	48.00	44.67	49.71
1991	49.00	49.11	48.67	42.09	37.86	37.00	39.79	37.50	37.50	35.76	35.18	34.50	40.33
1992	35.38	38.32	40.73	43.91	44.40	41.50	41.50	41.69	39.93	38.07	38.00	38.68	40.18
1993	41.00	41.00	38.04	36.63	35.00	35.00	37.52	37.59	36.50	34.19	33.60	34.78	36.74
1994	38.45	43.08	42.50	46.60	45.50	48.98	56.40	56.00	56.00	62.64	70.40	71.00	53.13
1995	74.85	72.24	65.00	65.00	65.00	65.00	65.00	67.98	64.80	58.45	57.00	58.50	64.91
1996	57.73	56.00	56.24	58.90	59.00	49.70	47.50	49.25	50.20	48.50	49.03	53.50	52.96
1997	56.98	59.00	59.00	58.27	58.05	58.05	58.32	59.60	59.50	59.13	59.00	57.12	58.50
1998	54.53	57.00	57.00	52.95	49.85	47.09	45.50	44.50	46.21	44.50	44.50	46.14	49.15

Source: American Metal Market (AMM)

ALUMINUM

Average Price of Cast Aluminum Scrap (Crank Cases) in Chicago In Cents Per Pound

Year	Jan.	Feb.	Mar.	Apr.	May	June	July	Aug.	Sept.	Oct.	Nov.	Dec.	Average
1990	34.68	30.50	30.77	32.50	32.50	32.50	35.93	37.50	41.97	42.50	40.58	39.00	35.91
1991	33.50	32.00	32.00	30.64	28.45	22.40	21.50	21.50	21.13	19.00	18.11	18.00	24.85
1992	18.71	23.00	26.91	27.00	24.45	24.00	24.00	24.00	21.21	19.50	19.50	19.50	22.65
1993	19.50	19.50	19.50	19.50	19.50	19.50	20.79	21.00	20.62	20.00	20.00	20.00	19.95
1994	20.00	25.79	28.33	32.50	32.50	33.18	35.90	36.50	41.07	44.45	50.50	53.50	36.19
1995	53.53	54.08	49.02	48.50	44.41	42.50	43.76	45.80	45.05	39.27	37.50	37.50	45.08
1996	37.50	37.50	37.50	37.50	37.50	37.50	37.50	36.50	35.40	33.80	33.50	33.50	36.27
1997	36.09	36.50	36.50	36.50	36.50	36.50	36.50	39.36	38.60	38.50	38.50	38.07	37.34
1998	37.50	37.50	37.50	35.95	35.50	31.59	25.50	25.50	25.50	25.50	25.50	25.50	30.71
1999	25.50	25.50	25.50	25.50	26.45	29.23	36.83	37.50	37.50	37.50	37.50	37.50	31.83

Source: American Metal Market (AMM)

Aluminum Exports of Crude Metal and Alloys from the United States In Thousands of Metric Tons

Year	Jan.	Feb.	Mar.	Apr.	May	June	July	Aug.	Sept.	Oct.	Nov.	Dec.	Total
1990	79.0	65.1	55.3	61.4	41.4	48.6	41.5	39.0	53.6	59.6	62.2	76.0	679.8
1991	61.1	54.8	46.7	82.8	56.4	71.3	69.0	80.1	54.6	68.0	80.7	67.3	792.8
1992	50.8	43.8	49.7	38.6	33.6	39.8	50.0	50.3	40.4	82.1	50.5	73.5	603.1
1993	54.8	38.6	41.7	26.3	38.6	30.7	33.9	24.5	27.9	31.7	24.1	27.6	400.4
1994	22.1	18.3	28.3	17.9	37.5	30.5	30.6	38.3	40.3	24.8	26.1	24.1	338.9
1995	26.1	32.7	25.4	31.1	31.4	20.7	26.6	39.2	38.9	33.0	30.4	33.6	369.1
1996	23.1	27.9	31.2	34.3	46.2	54.3	36.3	33.7	30.2	40.3	33.2	26.2	416.9
1997	31.0	25.5	22.5	33.0	24.1	34.9	23.9	33.2	34.4	26.5	33.0	30.0	352.0
1998	21.2	21.4	21.8	17.4	22.6	21.8	20.9	21.5	28.0	23.9	20.4	24.7	265.6
1999[1]	18.6	26.7	23.9	22.7	25.2	27.7	23.7	27.5	26.1	31.4			304.2

[1] Preliminary. *Source: U.S. Geological Survey (USGS)*

Aluminum General Imports of Crude Metal and Alloys into the United States In Thousands of Metric Tons

Year	Jan.	Feb.	Mar.	Apr.	May	June	July	Aug.	Sept.	Oct.	Nov.	Dec.	Total
1990	84.4	73.4	85.4	85.1	90.4	94.0	102.6	82.1	76.4	66.8	58.7	60.6	959.6
1991	79.5	79.4	84.3	88.2	85.1	75.9	97.3	89.0	86.6	90.4	81.0	88.0	1,024.7
1992	100.7	93.1	97.1	94.6	96.3	87.8	82.4	103.4	94.3	108.4	100.5	96.8	1,155.4
1993	120.8	123.9	165.8	172.0	152.1	152.6	125.1	162.7	173.5	149.4	182.9	155.6	1,836.4
1994	200.2	157.8	282.0	206.9	251.9	179.3	202.8	198.3	160.0	183.4	240.1	222.2	2,484.9
1995	214.0	168.0	204.0	195.0	184.0	172.0	136.0	134.0	117.0	137.0	139.0	133.0	1,933.0
1996	158.0	150.0	148.0	188.0	176.0	169.0	139.0	149.0	136.0	170.0	147.0	180.0	1,910.0
1997	145.0	147.0	209.0	196.0	198.0	167.0	157.0	152.0	150.0	175.0	146.0	222.0	2,060.0
1998	220.0	204.0	202.0	200.0	189.0	243.0	170.0	204.0	198.0	198.0	189.0	177.0	2,394.0
1999[1]	191.0	200.0	240.0	311.0	281.0	258.0	213.0	219.0	178.0	202.0			2,751.6

[1] Preliminary. *Source: U.S. Geological Survey (USGS)*

Average Open Interest of Aluminum Futures in New York In Contracts

Year	Jan.	Feb.	Mar.	Apr.	May	June	July	Aug.	Sept.	Oct.	Nov.	Dec.	Total
1999	-----	-----	-----	-----	1,032	1,461	1,875	1,983	1,767	1,244	625	616	15,298

Source: New York Mercantile Exchange (NYMEX), COMEX Division

Volume of Trading of Aluminum Futures in New York In Contracts

Year	Jan.	Feb.	Mar.	Apr.	May	June	July	Aug.	Sept.	Oct.	Nov.	Dec.	Total
1999	-----	-----	-----	-----	6,179	5,875	5,275	3,373	3,114	2,801	639	722	27,978

Source: New York Mercantile Exchange (NYMEX), COMEX Division

Antimony

Antimony is primarily a by-product of the mining, smelting and refining of three metals, mainly lead and silver-copper ores. It is used in the production of flame retardants, ceramics, glass, ammunition and chemicals. Most antimony in the U.S. is found in Idaho, Nevada, Alaska and Montana.

The U.S. Geological Survey reported that world mine production of antimony in 1998 was 140,000 metric tonnes, a decline of 6 percent from 1997. By far the largest producer of antimony is China with 1998 production estimated at 110,000 tonnes, down from 120,000 tonnes in 1997. Other producers of antimony include Bolivia, Russia and South Africa. World antimony reserves were estimated at 2.1 million tonnes. Most reserves are in China with other significant amounts in Russia, Bolivia and South Africa.

U.S. production of primary smelter antimony in second quarter 1998 was 6,190 tonnes (antimony content), virtually unchanged from the first quarter 1999. For all of 1998, primary smelter production of antimony was 23,700 tonnes. Secondary production of antimony in the second quarter of 1999 was 702 tonnes, a decline of 27 percent from the first quarter. For all of 1998, secondary production of antimony was 4,750 tonnes.

U.S. imports for consumption of antimony in the first quarter of 1999 were 7,630 tonnes. For 1998, imports for consumption were 34,600 tonnes. Metal antimony imports in the first quarter 1999 were 3,500 tonnes while for all of 1998 they were 13,500 tonnes. In first quarter 1999 they were 4,010 tonnes while for all of 1998 they were 19,100 tonnes.

Exports of antimony products in the April-May 1999 period were 598 tonnes while in the first quarter 1999 they were 1,210 tonnes. Exports in 1998 were 4,830 tonnes. Metal, alloy and scrap exports in April-May 1999 were 64 tonnes. For all of 1998, exports were 898 tonnes. Antimony oxide exports in April-May 1999 were 534 tonnes while for all of 1998 they were 3,930 tonnes. Consumption of primary antimony in second quarter 1999 totaled 3,280 tonnes. This was down 8 percent from the first quarter. For all of 1998, consumption was 13,300 tonnes.

Producer and consumer stocks of antimony at the end of second quarter 1999 were 13,400 tonnes. Metal stocks were 4,310 tonnes, oxide stocks 6,250 tonnes and other antimony material stocks which included ore were 2,880 tonnes.

World Mine Production of Antimony (Content of Ore) In Metric Tons

Year	Australia	Bolivia	Canada	China[3]	Guatemala	Kyrgyzstan[4]	Mexico[5]	Peru[6]	Russia[4]	South Africa	Thailand	Turkey	World Total
1995	900	6,426	684	125,000	665	1,500	1,783	460	6,000	5,537	230	416	151,000
1996	1,800	6,488	1,716	129,000	880	1,200	983	460	6,000	5,137	70	285	155,000
1997[1]	1,900	5,999	529	131,000	880	1,200	1,909	460	6,000	3,415	60	250	155,000
1998[2]	1,300	6,000	554	120,000	880	100	1,301	460	4,000	3,500	55	250	140,000

[1] Preliminary. [2] Estimate. [3] Formerly part of Czechoslovakia, data not reported separately until 1993. [4] Formerly part of the USSR; data not reported separately until 1992. [5] Includes antimony content of miscellaneous smelter products. [6] Recoverable. W = Withheld proprietary data ; not included in total. *Source: U.S. Geological Survey (USGS)*

Salient Statistics of Antimony in the United States In Metric Tons

		Production[3]			Imports for Consumption				Industry Stocks, December 31[3]				
		Primary[2]			Ore								
Year	Avg. Price cents/lb. CIF U.S. Ports	Mine	Smelter	Secondary (Alloys)[2]	Gross Weight	Antimony Content	Oxide (Gross Weight)	Exports (Oxide)	Metallic	Oxide	Sulfide	Other	Total[4]
1995	227.8	262	23,500	10,500	6,140	4,260	18,600	6,950	2,450	4,450	W	3,680	10,600
1996	146.5	242	25,600	7,780	1,610	1,000	22,100	3,990	3,520	4,420	W	3,060	11,000
1997[1]	97.8	356	26,400	7,550	1,530	1,300	27,900	3,230	3,070	4,530	W	3,240	10,800
1998[2]	71.8	242	23,700	7,710	2,640	1,880	23,000	3,270	2,920	4,570	W	3,060	10,600

[1] Preliminary. [2] Estimate. [3] Antimony content. [4] Including primary antimony residues & slag. W = Withheld proprietary data.
Source: U.S. Geological Survey (USGS)

Industrial Consumption of Primary Antimony in the United States In Metric Tons (Antimony Content)

	Metal Products						Flame Retardents		Non-Metal Products				
Year	Ammunition	Antimonial Lead	Sheet & Pipe	Bearing Metal & Bearings	Solder	Total All Metal Products	Plastics	Total	Ceramics & Glass	Pigments	Plastics	Total	Grand Total
1995	W	2,230	W	53	192	3,760	6,690	7,800	1,080	492	1,090	2,770	14,300
1996	W	1,760	W	44	256	3,110	6,850	7,770	1,030	450	1,080	2,690	13,600
1997	W	1,180	W	45	226	2,600	6,610	7,560	1,080	824	1,230	3,310	13,500
1998[1]	W	1,130	W	33	153	2,580	5,490	6,220	1,660	881	1,590	4,460	13,300

[1] Preliminary. [2] Estimated coverage based on 77% of the industry. W=Withheld proprietary data. *Source: U.S. Geological Survey (USGS)*

Average Price of Antimony in the United States In Cents Per Pound

Year	Jan.	Feb.	Mar.	Apr.	May	June	July	Aug.	Sept.	Oct.	Nov.	Dec.	Average
1996	153.00	152.50	152.50	150.12	142.50	142.50	132.50	127.50	127.50	127.50	127.50	127.50	138.59
1997	127.50	127.50	115.95	106.50	106.50	106.50	105.27	93.00	94.90	98.00	98.00	86.00	105.47
1998	80.00	80.00	80.00	80.00	74.38	71.25	66.25	61.50	62.50	65.00	65.00	65.00	70.91
1999	65.00	65.00	65.00	65.55	66.50	66.50	66.50	66.50	66.50	66.50	66.50	66.50	66.05

[1] Prices are for antimony metal (99.65%) merchants, minimum 18-ton containers, c.i.f. U.S. Ports. *Source: American Metal Market (AMM)*

Apples

The U.S. Department of Agriculture forecasts the 1999 U.S. apple crop at 10.6 billion pounds, down 7 percent from 1998 and some 3 percent lower than the average crop over the last five years. Lower apple production in the western states will not be offset by an expected increase in production in the central and eastern states. Washington is by far the largest producer of fresh and processed apples with 1999 production expected to be 5.2 billion pounds, a decline of 19 percent from the 1998 crop of 6.4 billion pounds. The second largest producer of apples in the west is California with an expected 1999 crop of 825 million pounds, an increase of 1 percent from the 1998 crop of 815 million pounds.

In the central states, 1999 production is forecast at 1.48 billion pounds, an increase of 12 percent from 1998. The largest producing state is Michigan where the crop is forecast at 1.05 billion pounds, an increase of 8 percent from 1998. In the eastern states, 1999 production is forecast at 2.75 billion pounds, an increase of 18 percent from last year. The largest producing state is New York with a 1999 crop forecast of 1.21 billion pounds, up 13 percent from 1998.

The U.S.D.A. reported that U.S. apple juice and cider exports in 1998-99 (August-June) fell 15 percent from the same period in 1997-98. They totaled 8.2 million gallons. Exports to Japan increased while exports to Canada fell.

World Production of Apples[3], Fresh (Dessert & Cooking) In Thousands of Metric Tons

Year	Argentina	Canada	France	Germany	Hungary	Italy	Japan	Netherlands	South Africa	Spain	Turkey	United States	World Total
1988-9	1,030	501	1,935	2,467	1,131	2,443	1,042	383	534	845	1,950	4,140	22,662
1989-90	1,050	538	1,818	1,727	959	2,162	1,045	417	557	747	1,850	4,519	21,654
1990-1	950	540	1,895	2,222	945	2,102	1,053	431	542	635	1,900	4,398	21,224
1991-2	1,043	513	1,236	1,165	859	1,869	760	223	605	517	1,900	4,413	18,250
1992-3	947	564	2,398	3,228	666	2,394	1,039	640	633	1,095	2,100	4,798	35,443
1993-4	1,006	488	2,079	1,719	819	2,145	1,011	670	638	891	2,080	4,847	36,505
1994-5	1,146	554	2,166	2,080	610	2,153	989	590	577	739	2,095	5,217	37,712
1995-6	1,254	608	2,089	1,373	353	1,889	963	595	703	843	2,100	4,801	36,443
1996-7[1]	1,300	513	2,047	1,878	552	2,025	899	490	639	894	2,200	4,714	40,825
1997-8[2]	1,417	503	2,027	1,465	560	2,014	993	470	660	880	2,550	4,711	40,697

[1] Preliminary. [2] Estimate. [3] Commercial crop. *Source: Foreign Agricultural Service, U.S. Department of Agriculture (FAS-USDA)*

Salient Statistics of Apples[2] in the United States

	Production		Growers Prices		Utilization of Quantities Sold: Processed[5]								Foreign Trade[4]: Domestic			
Year	Total	Utilized	Fresh cents/lb.	Processing $/ton	Fresh	Canned	Dried	Frozen	Juice & Cider	Other[3]	Avg. Farm Price cents /lb.	Farm Value Million $	Exports Fresh	Dried[5]	Imports Fresh & Dried[5]	Fresh Per Capita Consumption Lbs.
	Millions of Pounds												Metric Tons			
1989	9,917	9,871	13.9	107.0	5,822	1,320	282	322	2,068	57	10.4	1,024.6	357.4	23.7	119.7	21.2
1990	9,657	9,618	20.9	144.0	5,515	1,378	270	304	2,077	74	15.1	1,447.7	371.3	55.5	122.0	19.6
1991	9,707	9,637	25.1	171.0	5,447	1,311	299	286	2,194	100	17.9	1,727.0	530.1	44.2	143.9	18.2
1992	10,569	10,463	19.5	130.0	5,767	1,498	324	247	2,472	155	13.6	1,428.0	487.8	22.1	139.3	19.3
1993	10,685	10,574	18.4	107.0	6,124	1,335	366	282	2,382	85	12.9	1,363.8	662.9	19.2	130.9	19.2
1994	11,501	11,333	18.6	114.0	6,366	1,406	415	304	2,707	133	12.9	1,466.9	663.1	25.1	171.7	19.6
1995	10,578	10,384	24.0	159.0	5,840	1,292	334	305	2,538	78	17.0	1,767.0	565.0	24.6	202.9	18.9
1996	10,382	10,330	20.8	171.0	6,207	1,294	317	268	2,185	61	15.9	1,641.5	689.7	20.4	187.5	19.0
1997	10,324	10,254	22.1	130.0	5,815	1,499	267	349	2,145	180	15.4	1,575.4	559.1		158.7	18.4
1998[1]	11,387	10,500	17.1	98.0	6,361	1,186	316	423	2,124	90	12.3	1,226.4				19.2

[1] Preliminary. [2] Commercial crop. [3] Mostly crushed for vinegar, jam, etc. [4] Year beginning July. [5] Fresh weight basis.
Source: Economic Research Service, U.S. Department of Agriculture (ERS-USDA)

Price of Apples Received by Growers (for Fresh Use) in the United States In Cents Per Pound

Year	Jan.	Feb.	Mar.	Apr.	May	June	July	Aug.	Sept.	Oct.	Nov.	Dec.	Average
1990	12.2	12.4	12.3	12.0	12.6	13.7	20.3	22.3	22.2	19.3	19.6	20.9	16.7
1991	20.1	20.5	20.3	20.2	22.5	23.2	24.6	23.2	26.4	23.8	25.1	25.7	23.0
1992	24.6	24.8	24.3	24.1	25.0	25.2	28.6	33.3	27.1	21.2	19.4	19.9	24.8
1993	18.3	16.7	14.5	14.3	14.9	16.1	17.8	24.4	24.1	21.1	19.3	18.6	18.3
1994	18.7	17.8	16.6	15.5	14.3	13.5	19.4	29.0	20.8	19.2	16.4	19.2	18.4
1995	19.5	18.3	18.2	16.6	15.4	15.6	17.5	24.5	26.0	25.1	23.5	24.0	20.4
1996	25.4	24.2	25.1	22.6	21.9	21.9	23.3	25.2	30.2	24.6	23.2	22.6	24.2
1997	22.5	20.3	17.6	15.6	14.3	13.7	14.6	19.2	25.9	25.3	23.0	23.3	19.6
1998	21.9	20.8	20.5	19.4	17.8	16.3	12.7	13.8	22.6	22.1	17.5	14.9	18.4
1999[1]	15.8	15.0	15.3	14.1	13.3	12.7	12.4	18.4	23.2	23.5	23.3	23.7	17.6

[1] Preliminary. Source: Economic Research Service, U.S. Department of Agriculture (ERS-USDA)

Arsenic

The U.S. Geological Survey reported that there was no arsenic recovered from domestic ores. All arsenic metals and compounds used in the U.S. are imported. More than 95 percent of the arsenic consumed is in compound form, mostly as arsenic trioxide which is in turn converted to arsenic acid. Production of chromated copper arsenate, a wood preservative, accounts for over 90 percent of the domestic consumption of arsenic trioxide. Chromated copper arsenate in manufactured by three companies in the U.S., while another company uses arsenic acid to produce arsenical herbicides. Arsenic metal is used in the production of nonferrous alloys, primarily in lead-acid batteries.

The largest market for arsenic in the U.S. is in the production of arsenical wood preservatives. Demand for arsenic is closely related to the home construction industry. Continued robust economic growth along with relatively low interest rates should mean that demand for arsenic remains strong. Wooden decks on homes use arsenical preservatives. Due to the toxic nature of arsenic there will always be questions about its future in the construction industry.

One area where arsenic does seem to have a future is in the semiconductor industry. Very high-purity arsenic is used in the production of gallium arsenide. High speed and high frequency integrated circuits that use gallium arsenide have better signal reception and lower power consumption. It is estimated that about 15 tonnes per year of high-purity arsenic is used in the production of semiconductor materials.

World production of arsenic trioxide in 1998 was estimated at 42,000 metric tonnes, up 2 percent from 1997. By far the largest producer of arsenic trioxide is China with 1998 production estimated at 15,000 tonnes. Other large producers include Chile, Ghana, Mexico and France.

U.S. imports of arsenic metal in 1998 were 997 tonnes, an increase of almost 10 percent from the previous year. Imports of arsenic compounds in 1998 were 29,300 tonnes, an increase of nearly 29 percent from 1997. The total U.S. supplies in 1998 were 30,300 tonnes, an increase of 28 percent from the previous year. U.S. exports of arsenic metal in 1998 were 177 tonnes, up substantially from the 61 tonnes exported in 1997. U.S. apparent demand for arsenic compounds in 1998 was estimated at 30,100 tonnes, an increase of 27 percent from 1997.

Of the 30,100 tonnes of arsenic compounds demanded, some 27,000 tonnes went for wood preservatives, an increase of 35 percent from the previous year. Agricultural chemicals accounted for 1,600 tonnes of the total, or some 14 percent more than in 1997. Glass manufacturing used some 700 tonnes, the same as in 1997, while nonferrous alloys and electronics took 1,000 tonnes, some 11 percent more than the year before.

U.S. imports of arsenic trioxide in 1998 were 38,600 tonnes, an increase of 29 percent from the previous year. The major suppliers of arsenic trioxide were China, Chile, Hong Kong, Mexico and France. There were very minor imports of arsenic acid in 1998, though in 1997 imports were 117 tonnes. China has been a major supplier of arsenic acid. China is also the largest supplier of arsenic metal to the U.S.

World Production of White Arsenic (Arsenic Trioxide) In Metric Tons

Year	Belgium	Bolivia	Canada[4]	Chile	China	France	Germany	Mexico	Namibia[3]	Peru	Phillip-pines	Russia[5]	World Total
1991	2,500	463	236	6,820	10,000	2,000	300	4,920	1,800	661	5,000	7,000	46,000
1992	2,000	633	250	6,020	15,000	2,000	300	4,293	2,456	644	5,000	2,500	45,800
1993	2,000	663	250	6,200	14,000	3,000	300	4,447	2,290	391	2,000	2,000	42,100
1994	2,000	341	250	4,050	18,000	6,000	300	4,400	3,047	286	-----	1,500	46,800
1995	2,000	362	250	4,076	21,000	5,000	250	3,620	1,661	285	-----	1,500	47,000
1996	2,000	255	250	8,000	15,000	3,000	250	2,942	1,559	285	-----	1,500	43,000
1997[1]	2,000	282	250	8,350	15,000	2,500	250	2,999	1,232	285	-----	1,500	41,700
1998[2]	1,500	290	250	8,400	15,500	2,000	250	3,000	300	285	-----	1,500	40,800

[1] Preliminary. [2] Estimate. [3] Output of Tsumeb Corp. Ltd. only. [4] Includes low grade dusts that were exported to the U.S. for further refining. [5] Formerly part of the U.S.S.R.; not reported separately until 1992. *Source: U.S. Geological Survey (USGS)*

Salient Statistics of Arsenic in the United States In Metric Tons (Arsenic Content)

	Supply					Distribution	Estimated Demand Pattern						Average Price			
	Imports												Trioxide	Metal		
Year	Metal	Compounds	Industry Stocks Jan. 1	Total	Apparent Demand	Industry Stocks Dec.31	Agricultural Chemicals	Glass	Wood Preservatives	Non-Ferrous Alloys & Electric	Other	Total	Mexican (Cents/Pound)	Chinese (Cents/Pound)	Imports Trioxide[3]	Exports
1991	1,010	20,700	100	21,810	21,600	-----	5,000	900	14,300	1,000	400	21,600	25	68	27,142	233
1992	740	23,300	-----	24,040	23,900	-----	3,900	900	17,900	800	400	23,900	29	56	30,671	94
1993	767	20,900	-----	21,667	21,300	-----	3,000	900	16,200	800	400	21,300	33	44	27,500	364
1994	1,330	20,300	-----	21,630	21,500	-----	1,200	700	18,000	1,300	300	21,500	32	40	26,800	79
1995	557	22,100	-----	22,657	22,300	-----	1,000	700	19,600	600	400	22,300	33	66	29,000	430
1996	252	21,200	-----	21,452	21,400	-----	950	700	19,200	250	300	21,400	33	40	28,000	36
1997[1]	909	22,800	-----	23,709	23,700	-----	1,400	700	20,000	900	300	23,700	31	32	30,000	61
1998[2]	997	29,300	-----	30,297	30,100	-----	1,600	700	27,000	1,000	300	30,100	30	40	38,600	177

[1] Preliminary. [2] Estimate. [3] For Consumption. Source: U.S. Geological Survey (USGS)

Barley

World barley production nose-dived in the past two years, totaling only 128 million metric tons in 1999/2000 vs. 137 million in 1998/99 and 155 million in 1997/98. Production in the early 1990's averaged about 165 million tons. The decline largely reflects less acreage.

Collectively, the E.U. is the largest producing area with 49 million tons forecast for 1999/00 vs. 52 million in 1998/99. Germany is both the largest producer within the EU and the world's largest producer with 13.3 million tons forecast for 1999/00. Russia continues to see a steady drop in production, falling from 20.8 million tons in 1997/98, to 10 million in 1998/99 and 11.5 million in 1999/00. Canada's 1999/00 crop of 12.7 million tons is unchanged from 1998/99. In the U.S., barley is the third largest produced feed grain, but on a worldwide basis U.S. production accounts for only 5% of the total.

World barley usage totaled 127 million tons in 1999/00 vs. 133 million in 1998/99. Ending 1999/00 world carryover of 23.6 million tons compares with 28.9 million the previous year.

The U.S. barley crop year begins June 1. Production peaked in the 1980's and has since declined sharply as producers found returns more favorable on wheat and sunflower crops. Barley production in 1999/00 of a record low 284 million bushels compares with the 1998/99 crop of 352 million. Planted acreage for the 1999 crop totaled 5.2 million acres vs. an annual average of 8 million in the early 1990's. North Dakota and Montana are the largest producing states.

U.S. disappearance in 1999/00 of a record low 327 million bushels compares to the previous year's 360 million. Feed and residual use are estimated at only 125 million bushels. Industrial use, mostly for beer and alcohol, is forecast at 172 million bushels, about unchanged from 1998/99.

Estimated exports of 30 million bushels are also unchanged; while imports of 35 million bushels compare to 30 million the previous year, mostly of malting quality barley from Canada. Carryover stocks on May 31, 2000, of 134 million bushels, compare with 142 million a year earlier.

World barley trade is forecast at 16.1 million tons in 1999/00 vs. 16.5 million in 1998/99. The European Union exports at least half of the total, with Canada and Australia accounting for most of the balance. Importing countries are more numerous.

Barley prices paid to U.S. farmers are forecast to average between $1.80-2.20 per bushel in 1999/00 vs. $1.98 in 1998/99.

Futures Markets

Barley futures and options are traded on the Winnipeg Commodity Exchange (WCE) and are quoted in Canadian dollars per ton. Futures are traded on the London International Financial Futures and Options Exchange (LIFFE) and on the Budapest Commodity Exchange.

World Barley Supply and Demand In Thousands of Metric Tons

	Exports						Imports			Utilization			Ending Stocks		
Year	Australia	Canada	EC-12	Total Non-US	U.S.	Total Exports	Saudi Arabia	Unaccounted	Total Imports	Russia	U.S.	Total Utilization	Canada	U.S.	Total Stocks
1990-1	2,683	4,460	7,053	17,016	1,507	18,523	4,342	742	18,523	29,156	8,283	174,898	2,646	2,948	32,317
1991-2	1,951	3,379	9,459	16,929	2,090	19,019	6,873	77	19,019	25,635	8,735	165,833	2,615	2,800	32,471
1992-3	2,600	2,859	5,816	15,084	1,611	16,695	3,917	807	16,695	28,368	7,916	166,065	3,271	3,292	31,923
1993-4	4,232	3,789	6,793	16,986	1,553	18,539	4,497	384	18,539	27,041	9,053	170,104	3,376	3,023	33,349
1994-5	1,356	2,556	5,061	14,197	1,355	15,552	4,303	99	15,552	24,488	8,726	166,107	1,820	2,451	28,498
1995-6	3,375	2,596	2,480	12,006	1,181	13,187	3,876	214	13,187	17,556	7,635	150,854	1,749	2,168	19,353
1996-7	3,967	3,442	6,183	16,684	1,213	17,897	6,212	519	17,897	16,435	8,459	149,253	2,919	2,383	23,607
1997-8	2,838	1,897	2,856	11,710	1,066	12,776	4,061	598	12,776	16,494	6,879	145,967	2,459	2,596	32,234
1998-9[1]	4,267	1,185	7,800	16,439	600	17,039	4,900	515	17,039	13,000	7,208	140,870	2,687	3,084	28,544
1999-00[2]	2,800	1,800	9,000	16,170	600	16,770	4,800	400	16,770	12,150	6,467	135,282	2,557	2,645	24,441

[1] Preliminary. [2] Estimate. *Source: Foreign Agricutural Service, U.S. Department of Agriculture (FAS-USDA)*

World Production of Barley In Thousands of Metric Tons

Year	Australia	Canada	China	Denmark	France	Germany	India	Kazakhstan	Spain	Turkey	United Kingdom	United States	World Total
1990-1	4,184	13,441	3,930	4,990	10,150	13,990	1,490	8,500	9,410	6,600	7,900	9,192	178,056
1991-2	4,606	11,617	3,928	5,041	10,789	14,494	1,640	3,085	9,140	6,800	7,700	10,110	169,136
1992-3	5,460	11,032	4,000	2,974	10,580	12,196	1,700	8,511	6,105	6,500	7,350	9,908	165,767
1993-4	6,956	12,972	4,327	3,369	8,981	11,000	1,510	7,149	9,520	7,300	6,040	8,666	170,241
1994-5	2,913	11,690	4,411	3,450	7,650	10,900	1,310	5,100	7,600	6,500	5,950	8,162	161,246
1995-6	5,823	13,035	4,089	3,860	7,740	11,890	1,730	2,178	5,200	6,900	6,830	7,824	142,147
1996-7	6,696	15,562	4,000	3,950	9,540	12,070	1,510	2,700	9,600	7,200	7,780	8,544	153,507
1997-8	6,482	13,527	4,000	3,890	10,180	13,400	1,460	2,670	8,600	7,300	7,830	7,835	154,594
1998-9[1]	5,680	12,709	3,500	3,570	10,740	12,520	1,670	1,100	10,900	7,600	6,630	7,667	137,180
1999-00[2]	4,700	13,196	3,000	3,500	9,700	13,300	1,500	2,500	7,450	7,000	6,800	6,137	131,179

[1] Preliminary. [2] Estimate. *Source: Foreign Agricutural Service, U.S. Department of Agriculture (FAS-USDA)*

Barley Acreage and Prices in the United States

Year Beginning June 1	Acreage (1,000 Acres) Planted	Acreage (1,000 Acres) Harvested for Grain	Yield Per Harvested Acre (Bushels)	Seasonal Prices: Received by Farmers[3] All	Received by Farmers[3] Feed[4]	Received by Farmers[3] Malting[4]	Portland No. 2 Western	Government Price Support Operations: National Average Loan Rate	Target Price	Put Under Support (mil. Bu.)	% of Production
				Dollars per Bushel							
1991-2	8,941	8,413	55.2	2.10	2.17	2.38	2.66	1.32	2.36	38.0	8.2
1992-3	7,762	7,285	62.5	2.04	2.11	2.37	2.57	1.40	2.36	42.9	9.4
1993-4	7,786	6,753	58.9	1.99	2.05	2.48	2.40	1.40	2.36	37.7	9.5
1994-5	7,159	6,667	56.2	2.03	2.02	2.75	2.51	1.54	2.36	28.2	7.5
1995-6	6,689	6,279	57.3	2.89	2.67	3.69	3.51	1.54	2.36	14.9	4.1
1996-7	7,094	6,707	58.5	2.74	2.29	3.18	3.07	1.55	NA	28.7	NA
1997-8[1]	6,706	6,198	58.1	2.38	1.91	2.50	2.49	1.57	NA	32.8	NA
1998-9[2]	6,340	5,867	60.1	1.98	1.55	2.31	NA	1.56	NA	NA	NA

[1] Preliminary. [2] Estimate. [3] Excludes support payments. [4] Duluth through May 1998. *Source: Economic Research Service, U.S. Department of Agriculture (ERS-USDA)*

Salient Statistics of Barley in the United States In Millions of Bushels

Year Beginning June 1	Supply: Beginning Stocks	Production	Imports	Total Supply	Disappearance: Domestic Use: Food & Acohol Beverages	Seed	Feed & Residual	Total	Exports	Total Disappearance	Ending Stocks: Gov't Owned	Privately Owned[3]	Total Stocks
1992-3	128.6	455.1	11.4	595.1	158.4	12.9	190.9	363.6	80.3	443.9	5.4	145.8	151.2
1993-4	151.2	398.0	71.5	620.7	162.9	11.9	243.7	415.8	66.1	481.8	5.2	133.7	138.9
1994-5	138.9	374.9	65.9	579.6	163.8	11.1	228.1	400.8	66.2	467.0	5.0	107.6	112.6
1995-6	112.6	359.4	40.7	512.7	160.1	11.7	178.9	350.7	62.4	413.1	4.2	95.4	99.6
1996-7	99.6	392.4	36.8	528.8	160.9	11.1	216.5	388.5	30.8	419.3	0	109.5	109.5
1997-8	109.0	360.0	40.0	510.0	161.6	10.4	144.0	316.0	74.4	390.3	0	119.2	119.2
1998-9[1]	119.0	352.0	30.0	501.0	161.3	8.7	161.0	331.0	28.0	360.0	1.0	142.0	143.0
1999-00[2]	142.0	282.0	25.0	449.0	162.0	10.0	125.0	297.0	30.0	327.0	0	122.0	122.0

[1] Preliminary. [2] Estimate. [3] Uncommitted inventory. [4] Includes quantity under loan & farmer-owned reserve. *Source: Economic Research Service, U.S. Department of Agriculture (ERS-USDA)*

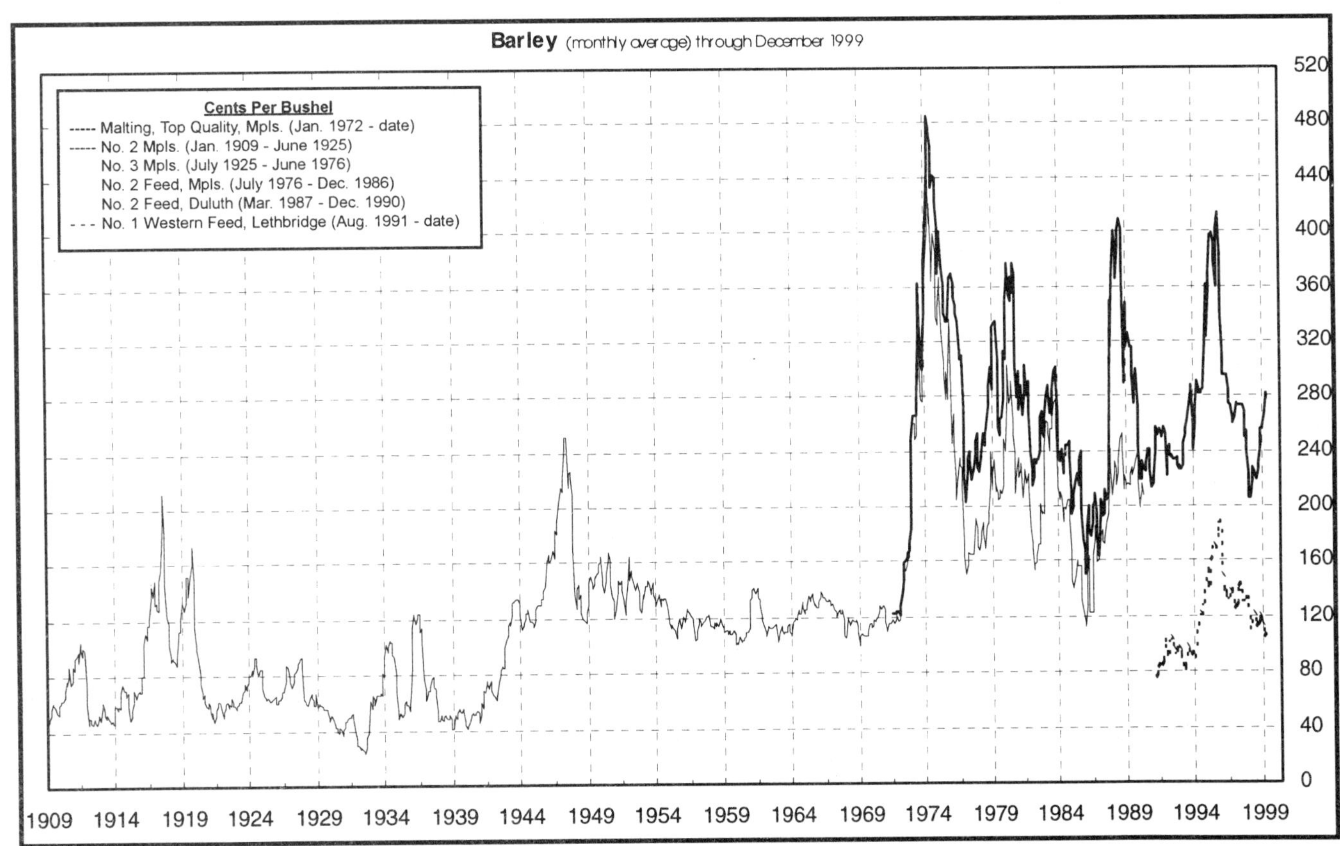

BARLEY

Average Price Received by Farmers for Feed[2] Barley in the United States In Cents Per Bushel

Year	June	July	Aug.	Sept.	Oct.	Nov.	Dec.	Jan.	Feb.	Mar.	Apr.	May	Average
1992-3	230	215	203	212	211	208	206	206	208	210	212	205	211
1993-4	199	196	189	189	201	216	214	215	216	207	208	211	205
1994-5	205	202	199	204	195	204	200	202	206	202	197	211	202
1995-6	222	225	209	206	258	298	292	294	300	286	299	320	267
1996-7	322	279	260	234	210	190	196	195	201	222	233	245	232
1997-8	231	204	210	229	205	198	166	158	156	151	142	NQ	186
1998-9	182	162	149	140	146	147	155	158	158	148	155	161	155
1999-00[1]	155	148	151	164	161	163	164	176					160

[1] Preliminary. [2] Duluth No. 2 through May 1998. NQ = No quote. *Source: Economic Research Service, U.S. Department of Agriculture (ERS-USDA)*

Average Price Received by Farmers for All Barley in the United States In Cents Per Bushel

Year	June	July	Aug.	Sept.	Oct.	Nov.	Dec.	Jan.	Feb.	Mar.	Apr.	May	Average
1992-3	209	226	216	184	192	205	195	207	200	200	209	197	203
1993-4	195	190	202	187	182	201	202	215	207	201	202	206	199
1994-5	191	192	207	193	193	209	199	205	213	213	215	221	204
1995-6	225	241	262	257	288	309	315	315	328	324	324	345	294
1996-7	355	318	299	278	269	265	267	252	245	237	229	231	270
1997-8	226	227	235	238	244	261	243	242	240	213	216	213	233
1998-9	193	201	207	201	191	205	203	189	177	192	177	181	193
1999-00[1]	170	204	237	203	196	215	224	219					209

[1] Preliminary. *Source: National Agricultural Statistical Service, U.S. Department of Agriculture (NASS-USDA)*

Average Open Interest of Western Feed Barley Futures in Winnipeg In Contracts

Year	Jan.	Feb.	Mar.	Apr.	May	June	July	Aug.	Sept.	Oct.	Nov.	Dec.
1994	7,600	8,164	7,650	8,212	8,153	9,019	8,511	8,558	9,633	12,340	10,802	9,457
1995	8,900	9,295	9,965	8,657	7,279	8,731	9,297	9,770	10,704	12,043	10,324	12,089
1996	13,803	12,979	15,746	18,022	19,045	18,502	15,504	14,190	16,647	20,143	21,233	24,590
1997	22,718	19,290	15,080	14,620	14,385	12,291	10,023	13,641	12,909	13,147	14,473	13,576
1998	15,789	17,337	18,039	14,706	12,666	10,847	9,915	10,384	11,420	11,460	11,338	8,622
1999	8,231	10,635	10,579	9,713	8,333	8,993	10,347	11,959	13,206	15,012	15,662	14,991

Source: Winnipeg Commodity Exchange (WCE)

Bauxite

Bauxite is a naturally occurring, heterogeneous material composed primarily of one or more aluminum hydroxide minerals, plus various mixtures of silica, iron oxide, titania, aluminosilicates and other impurities in trace amounts.

Bauxite is the only raw material used in the production of alumina on a commercial scale in the United States. Bauxites are typically classified according to their intended commercial applications: abrasive, cement, chemical, metallurgical, refractory and others. Of all the bauxite mined, approximately 85 percent is converted to alumina for the production of aluminum metal. Another 10 percent goes to nonmetal uses as various form of specialty alumina with the remaining 5 percent used in non-metallurgical bauxite applications.

A U.S. Geological Survey study indicated that 24 countries are involved in bauxite mine production. World production of bauxite has been increasing. Between 1988 and 1997, world production increased 19 percent or just over 2 percent per year on average. The largest producer of bauxite is Australia with a market share of about 35 percent. The next largest producer is Guinea, followed by Brazil and Jamaica. Other large producers include China, Russia and Suriname.

U.S. imports for consumption of crude and dried bauxite in second quarter 1999 were 2.21 million tonnes. That represented a decline of 21 percent from the first quarter 1999. Total imports in the first half of 1999 were 5.01 million tonnes. For all of 1998, imports were 11 million tonnes. The major suppliers of crude and dried bauxite to the U.S. were Jamaica, Guinea, Brazil and Guyana. U.S. exports of crude and dried bauxite in the first half of 1999 were 55,200 tonnes compared to 83,000 tonnes for all of 1998. The major markets were Canada and Mexico.

U.S. imports of alumina (calcined equivalent) in the second quarter of 1999 were 967,000 tonnes. Imports in the first quarter were 970,000 tonnes. Total imports in the first half of 1999 were 1.94 million tonnes. For all of 1998, imports of alumina were 4.05 million tonnes. By far the largest supplier was Australia. Other large suppliers included Suriname, Jamaica, India, Canada and Trinidad. U.S. exports of alumina in second quarter 1999 were 308,000 tonnes, up 11 percent from first quarter 1999. In the first half of 1999, exports totaled 585,000 tonnes, while for all of 1998 they were 1.28 million tonnes. The major destinations were Canada and Mexico.

U.S. imports of calcined bauxite in second quarter 1999 were 180,300 tonnes. Imports in first quarter 1999 were 73,500 tonnes. For all of 1998, imports were 393,000 tonnes. The major suppliers of calcined bauxite were Brazil, China and Guyana. U.S. exports of calcined bauxite in the first half of 1999 were 19,990 tonnes. For all of 1998 they were 16,250 tonnes. The major market was Japan.

World Production of Bauxite In Thousands of Metric Tons

Year	Australia	Brazil	China	Greece	Guinea	Guyana[2]	Hungary	India	Jamaica[3]	Russia[34]	Sierra Leone	Suriname	World Total
1989	38,584	8,665	2,388	2,550	15,792	1,321	2,644	4,471	9,601	5,500	1,548	3,530	103,722
1990	41,391	9,678	2,400	2,496	15,772	1,424	2,559	4,852	10,921	5,500	1,430	3,283	113,000
1991	40,510	10,365	2,600	2,133	15,466	2,204	2,037	4,735	11,552	5,000	1,288	3,198	111,000
1992	39,746	9,366	2,700	2,078	13,800	2,376	1,721	4,898	11,302	4,578	1,250	3,250	105,000
1993	41,320	10,001	3,500	2,205	15,300	2,125	1,561	5,277	11,307	4,260	1,165	3,421	110,000
1994	41,733	8,673	3,700	2,196	13,300	1,732	836	4,809	11,564	3,000	735	3,772	106,000
1995	42,655	10,214	5,000	2,200	15,800	2,028	1,015	5,240	10,857	3,100	-----	3,530	112,000
1996	43,063	10,998	6,200	2,452	16,500	2,485	1,044	5,757	11,863	3,300	-----	3,695	118,000
1997[1]	44,465	11,671	8,000	1,877	17,100	2,502	743	5,800	11,987	3,350	-----	3,877	123,000
1998[2]	44,553	11,700	8,200	2,000	15,000	2,600	750	5,700	12,646	3,450	-----	4,000	122,000

[1] Preliminary. [2] Estimate. [3] Dry Bauxite equivalent of ore processed. [4] Formerly part of the U.S.S.R.; data not reported separately until 1992.

Source: U.S. Geological Survey (USGS)

Salient Statistics of Bauxite in the United States In Thousands of Metric Tons

Year	Net Import Reliance as a % of Apparent Consumption	Average Price FOB Mine $ per Ton	Consumption by Industry: Total	Alumina	Abrasive	Chemical	Refractory	Dry Equivalent: Imports[3] (for Consumption)	Exports[3]	Consumption	Stocks, December 31: Producers & Consumers	Government	Total
1989	96	15-20	11,810	10,782	275	223	407	10,893	44	11,810	2,891	18,474	21,365
1990	98	15-20	12,042	11,064	276	212	387	12,144	74	12,042	2,318	18,477	20,795
1991	100	15-18	12,204	11,383	204	218	328	11,871	51	12,204	2,620	18,477	21,097
1992	100	15-18	11,873	11,066	223	190	334	10,939	63	11,873	2,319	17,805	20,124
1993	100	15-24	11,917	11,002	203	225	429	11,621	90	12,200	1,590	16,938	18,500
1994	99	15-24	11,200	10,400	197	192	350	10,700	129	11,200	1,560	17,200	18,800
1995	99	15-18	10,900	10,100	133	201	394	10,100	108	10,900	1,730	16,300	18,100
1996	100	15-18	11,000	10,300	117	W	380	10,200	132	11,000	1,930	15,700	17,600
1997[1]	100	15-18	11,500	10,700	98	W	466	10,700	85	11,500	2,260	14,300	16,500
1998[2]	100		12,700	12,000	135	W	332	11,000	99	12,700	1,860	11,000	12,800

[1] Preliminary. [2] Estimate. [3] Including concentrates. W = Withheld to avoid disclosing company proprietary data.

Source: U.S. Geological Survey (USGS)

Bismuth

Bismuth finds a wide variety of uses ranging from pharmaceutical compounds, to glass ceramics, to chemicals and pigments. Bismuth is found in household pharmaceuticals and is used to treat stomach ulcers. There has been interest in using bismuth as a nontoxic substitute for lead in such applications as plumbing fixtures and ammunitions. Bismuth is substituted for lead in ceramic glass for china. Bismuth has the advantage of being as durable as lead without being as hazardous.

The U.S. Geological Survey has reported that the U.S. no longer is a primary bismuth producer with the recent closure of the last refinery. In 1998 the last U.S. stocks of bismuth in the National Defense Stockpile were sold putting the U.S. in the position of being totally dependent on foreign suppliers.

The largest producers of mine produced bismuth are Mexico, Peru and China. Other producers include Canada and Japan. The major producers of refined bismuth are Mexico, Peru, China and Belgium. Other large producers include Japan and Kazakhastan. Recent developments internationally have seen a possible reduction in Mexican production in an effort to reduce pollution. In Peru, bismuth production has declined as there has been a switch from high bismuth-containing concentrates to high silver and gold-containing concentrates which are higher value by-products in the production of copper. Both of these countries are important suppliers of bismuth to the U.S.

U.S. consumption of bismuth in second quarter 1999 was 483,000 kilograms. This was a decline of 4 percent from the first quarter of 1999. For all of 1998, consumption of bismuth was 1.99 million kilograms. Stocks of bismuth held by consumers at the end of second quarter 1999 were 192,000 kilograms. This was some 37 percent higher than stocks at the end of first quarter 1999. Bismuth stocks held by consumers at the end of 1998 were 175,0000 kilograms.

Bismuth metal consumed in the U.S. in the second quarter of 1999 was 483,000 kilograms. Of this total, 185,000 kilograms were industrial and laboratory chemicals, cosmetics and pharmaceuticals. This represented a decline of 13 percent from the first quarter of 1999. In all of 1998, this category of consumption was 884,000 kilograms. Bismuth alloys consumed in the second quarter 1999 were 207,000 kilograms, an increase of 8 percent from first quarter 1999. For all of 1998, bismuth alloys consumed were 741,000 kilograms. Metallurgical additives consumed in second quarter 1999 were 83,000 kilograms, down 10 percent from the first quarter. For all of 1998, consumption was 335,000 kilograms. Consumption of other bismuth metal products in second quarter 1999 were 7,000 kilograms, down 12 percent from first quarter 1999. In 1998 consumption was 32,000 kilograms.

U.S. imports for consumption of bismuth metal in May 1999 were 133,000 kilograms. This was down 29 percent from April 1999. In the first five months of 1999, imports totaled 793,000 kilograms. For all of 1998 they totaled 2.72 million kilograms. The major suppliers were Mexico, Belgium, China, Canada and Peru.

World Production of Bismuth   In Metric Tons (Mine Output=Metal Content)

	Mine Output, Metal Content						Refined Metal						
Year	Canada	China	Japan	Mexico	Peru	Total	Belgium	China	Kazak-hastan[3]	Japan	Mexico	Peru	Total
1989	205	850	150	883	687	3,750	800	850	85	502	597	646	3,970
1990	87	1,060	133	733	555	3,440	1,000	1,060	80	442	549	521	4,190
1991	65	1,040	138	651	610	3,230	800	1,260	70	461	500	377	3,820
1992	224	820	159	807	550	2,870	800	1,060	170	530	550	419	3,710
1993	144	740	149	908	1,300	3,550	950	1,050	180	497	650	937	4,390
1994	129	610	152	1,047	1,210	3,410	900	850	85	505	836	877	4,180
1995	187	740	177	995	900	3,440	800	800	33	591	924	581	3,840
1996	150	610	169	1,070	1,000	3,610	800	750	50	562	957	939	4,180
1997[1]	183	550	165	1,642	1,000	4,480	800	760	50	550	990	774	4,070
1998[2]	180	600	150	1,204	1,000	4,020	700	750	50	500	900	744	3,780

[1] Preliminary. [2] Estimate. [3] Formerly part of the U.S.S.R.; data not reported separately until 1992. *Source U.S. Geological Survey (USGS)*

Salient Statistics of Bismuth in the United States   In Metric Tons

	Bismuth Consumed, By Uses							Imports from Metallic Bismuth from				
Year	Metal-lurgical Additives	Other Alloys & Uses	Fusible Alloys	Chem-icals[3]	Total Con-sumption	Consumer Stocks Dec. 31	Exports of Metal & Alloys	Belgium	Mexico	Peru	Total	Dealer Price $ Per Pound
1989	396	25	272	659	1,352	440	122	835.7	390.8	271.4	1,880	5.76
1990	424	24	249	577	1,274	331	122	668.1	404.8	262.7	1,612	3.56
1991	341	26	271	789	1,427	247	75	345.1	535.0	169.8	1,411	3.00
1992	381	33	278	758	1,450	272	90	467.4	550.5	75.7	1,621	2.66
1993	232	59	256	750	1,300	323	70	275.1	479.1	117.2	1,330	2.50
1994	306	26	276	841	1,450	402	160	512.0	665.0	114.9	1,660	3.25
1995	257	27	544	1,320	2,150	390	261	636.0	444.0	10.9	1,450	3.85
1996	231	35	401	855	1,520	122	151	584.0	453.0	19.5	1,490	3.65
1997[1]	252	31	593	655	1,530	213	206	691.0	601.0	163.0	2,170	3.50
1998[2]	335	32	741	884	1,990	175	245	739.0	807.0	68.8	2,720	3.60

[1] Preliminary. [2] Estimate. [3] Includes pharmaceuticals. *Source: U.S. Geological Survey (USGS)*

Broilers

Federally inspected U.S. broiler production is expected to reach 29.7 billion pounds in 1999 vs. the record high of 27.9 billion in 1998. In the early 1990's, production averaged about 20 billion pounds. Initial forecasts place production in the year 2000 at 31.2 billion pounds. Production of ready-to-cook (RTC) broiler meat in the second half of 1999 of 14.8 billion pounds compares with 14 billion a year earlier and forecasts of 15.7 billion in the first half of 2000.

Hot summer weather in 1999 may have contributed to lower broiler weights, but the broiler hatchery supply in mid-1999 was still larger than a year ago. Producer net returns were quite strong as lower feeding costs offset lower bird prices. The 12-city average wholesale whole broiler price in mid-1999 of about 57.5 cents per pound compares with about 60 cents a year earlier. Retail prices in mid-1998 neared $1.00 per pound, but topped $1.00 in mid-1999.

U.S. per capita broiler consumption in 1999 of a record high 77.8 pounds, retail weight, compares with the previous year's 72.6 pounds. A sharper gain is forecast for 2000 with usage expected to reach 81.9 pounds, suggesting that the persistent publicity directed towards the need for proper cooking of poultry meat, notably at fast-food outlets, has not dampened consumption.

A key factor for the steady gains in U.S. broiler production is strong foreign demand, notably for leg quarters. Exports in the first half of 1999 of 2.2 billion pounds compares with 2.1 billion a year earlier, but for the year the total of 4.6 billion may lag slightly behind 1998's pace. Exports in 2000 are forecast at a record high 4.7 billion pounds. The major importers are Russia, Hong Kong, Japan and Mexico. Percentagewise, the strongest gain in U.S. exports during 1999 emanated from Latvia.

Broiler Supply and Prices in the United States

	Federally Inspected Slaughter				Total	Per Capita	Prices	
Year & Quarters	Number (Millions)	Average Weight (Pounds)	Liveweight Pounds (Mil. Lbs.)	Certified RTC Weight (Mil. Lbs.)	Production RTC[3] (Mil. Lbs.)	Consumption RTC Basis (Mil. Lbs.)	Farm (Cents per Pound)	Geogia Dock[4] (Cents per Pound)
1994	7,270	4.64	33,595	23,846	23,666	79.4	35.06	54.40
1995	7,371	4.66	34,348	25,021	24,827	79.2	34.68	54.73
1996	7,546	4.78	36,034	36,336	26,124	81.4	38.67	61.09
1997	7,714	4.81	39,098	27,271	27,271	71.9	37.35	59.96
1998[1]	7,825	4.86	38,016	27,832	27,863	72.6	39.81	59.81
1999[2]	2,012	4.99	10,035	7,377	29,674	77.5	36.49	58.75
I	1,974	5.01	9,889	7,243	7,295	19.3	36.27	59.92
II	2,049	5.02	10,281	7,547	7,594	19.8	36.87	58.20
III	2,064	4.89	10,094	7,430	7,486	19.4	36.93	59.41
IV	1,962	5.03	9,877	7,288	7,300	19.0	35.90	57.47

[1] Preliminary. [2] Estimate. [3] Total production equals federal inspected slaughter plus other slaughter minus cut-up & further processing condemnation. [4] Ready-to-cook basis. *Source: Economic Research Service, U.S. Department of Agriculture (ERS-USDA)*

Salient Statistics of Broilers in the United States

	Commercial Production		Average			Total Chickens[3] Supply and Distribution							
						Production			Storage			Consumption	
Year	Number (Mil. Lbs.)	Liveweight (Mil. Lbs.)	Liveweight Per Bird (Pounds)	Average Price (Cents/Lb.)	Value of Production (Mil. $)	Federally Inspected (In Millions of Pounds)	Other Chickens (In Millions of Pounds)	Total (In Millions of Pounds)	Stocks January 1 (In Millions of Pounds)	Exports (In Millions of Pounds)	Broiler Feed Ratio (Pounds)	Total (Mil. Lbs.)	Per Capita[4] (Pounds)
1993	6,694	30,618	4.56	34.0	10,417	22,178	36	22,015	368	1,966	5.3	20,059	68.50
1994	7,018	32,529	4.64	35.0	11,372	23,846	38	23,666	358	2,876	5.2	20,690	69.50
1995	7,326	34,222	4.66	34.4	11,762	25,021	39	24,827	458	3,894	5.1	20,832	68.80
1996	7,598	36,483	4.80	38.1	13,903	26,336	38	26,124	560	4,420	4.4	21,626	70.40
1997	7,764	37,541	4.84	37.7	14,159	27,271	35	27,041	641	4,664	4.7	22,416	71.90
1998[1]	6,906	33,818	4.90	39.4	15,145	27,863	26	27,612	607	4,673	NA	22,841	72.60
1999[2]						29,446	27	29,175	711	4,512	NA	24,629	77.60

[1] Preliminary. [2] Estimate. [3] Ready-to-cook. [4] Retail weight basis. *Source: Economic Research Service, U.S. Department of Agriculture (ERS-USDA)*

Average Wholesale Broiler[1] Prices RTC (Ready-to-Cook) (In Cents Per Pound)

Year	Jan.	Feb.	Mar.	Apr.	May	June	July	Aug.	Sept.	Oct.	Nov.	Dec.	Average
1993	52.14	53.01	54.02	54.66	57.86	55.04	55.36	57.77	57.59	55.72	55.82	53.17	55.18
1994	52.67	55.22	57.56	57.80	61.39	60.71	57.36	54.65	55.80	54.02	50.50	50.87	55.71
1995	51.14	51.73	52.32	51.51	52.94	55.88	58.76	61.74	61.48	58.79	61.08	58.87	56.35
1996	59.00	55.31	54.31	56.01	61.71	65.52	64.58	64.07	64.01	62.64	64.37	63.50	61.25
1997	61.99	59.53	58.41	59.77	58.53	59.05	63.04	63.25	59.86	55.39	54.62	52.25	58.81
1998	54.66	56.40	58.10	58.52	60.08	64.26	68.53	72.13	70.53	68.04	64.13	60.45	62.99
1999[2]	59.33	58.23	56.79	55.08	60.02	60.33	59.46	57.65	57.15	54.87	59.52	58.50	58.08

[1] 12-city composite wholesale price. [2] Preliminary. *Source: Economic Research Service, U.S. Department of Agriculture (ERS-USDA)*

Butter

U.S. butter production in 1998 slipped to 491,000 metric tonnes following a period in the mid-1990's when it appeared annual production was stabilizing at about 575,000 tonnes. However, production is forecast to rebound to 515,000 tonnes in 1999, the first increase in seven years. Most of the increase is due to the surge in milk supplies available for butter production. Record high butter production of 619,000 tonnes was realized in 1992. Despite the expected increase in butter output, strong demand in 1999 has had the effect of keeping prices over a $1.00/pound.

U.S. annual butter consumption fell during much of the 1990's, totaling only 505,000 tonnes in 1997, down from 570,000 tonnes in 1994. A marginal increase to 510,000 was noted in 1998, and another for 1999 to 515,000 tonnes. With the exception of 1998, annual domestic production has exceeded consumption. There is definite production seasonality: January is the highest producing month and August the lowest.

U.S. butter stocks, once mostly government owned, dropped sharply in the 1990's; from a high at year-end 1991 of 249,000 tonnes to 12,000 at year-end 1998. Annual U.S. per capita butter use in 1997-99 of 1.88 kilograms compares with more than 2.0/kg. in the mid-1990's.

Butter production is derived directly from milk production. Butter manufacture is the third largest use of milk production, the first being milk as a fluid and then its conversion into cheese. California and Wisconsin vied for largest producing state in 1999.

World butter production in 1999 of 5.4 million tonnes compares with 5.3 million in 1998. The U.S. is the world's largest producer followed by France and Germany, the three countries combined accounting for about a third of global production. India's 1999 output of a record large 1.8 million tonnes compares with 1.6 million in 1998, but their product is mostly Ghee, a butter-like substance that is consumed almost entirely in India.

World consumption lagged production during the 1990's with 1999 usage forecast at 5.1 million tonnes vs. 4.9 million in 1998, and ending 1999 carryover of 514,000 tonnes comparing with 504,000 a year earlier. Outside of India, the world's largest consumer in 1999 was Germany with 565,000 tonnes, followed by France. Russia, once the largest consumer, now ranks fourth.

Global trade in butter is small. Exports were forecast at 693,000 tonnes in 1999, about unchanged from 1998, almost two-thirds of which come from New Zealand and Australia. U.S. exports and imports are insignificant. In recent years, the E.U. relied heavily on Russia to absorb its surplus butterfat, but Russia's economic crisis has cut deeply into their butter imports, the effect of which buoyed world stocks and pressured world prices; a scenario that's expected to persist if the Russian economy fails to improve. Russia's per capita butter consumption in 1999 of 2.76 kilograms compares with 3.80 in 1995; for the Ukraine per capita use of 1.02 kg. compares with 4.65 kg., respectively.

1998 U.S. wholesale butter prices, basis grade AA-Chicago, averaged $1.772/lb. vs. $1.162 in 1997, but towards the end of 1998 and into 1999 prices were averaging over $2.50/lb. World butter prices at the start of 1998 were over $2000 per metric tonne but had fallen under $1900 by yearend; mid-1999 prices were averaging about $1300/tonne, basis Northern Europe.

Supply and Distribution of Butter in the United States In Millions of Pounds

	Supply				Distribution							93 Score AA Wholesale Price	
					Domestic Disappearance			Department of Agriculture					
Year	Production	Cold Storage Stocks[3] Jan. 1[5]	Imports	Total Supply	Total	Per Capita (Pounds)	Exports	Jan. 1 Stocks[4]	Dec. 31 Stocks[4]	Removed by USDA Programs	Total Use	California ($ per Pound)	Chicago ($ per Pound)
1989	1,295	215	4.621	1,515	1,240	4.4	112	173	223	413.4	1,243	1.5660	1.2951
1990	1,302	256	4.798	1,582	1,165	4.4	126	223	373	400.3	1,167	1.3050	1.0346
1991	1,336	416	4.740	1,759	1,209	4.4	26	373	511	442.8	1,208	1.2856	1.0182
1992	1,365	550	4.153	1,919	1,464	4.4	142	511	430	439.5	1,466	1.1386	.8427
1993	1,315	454	4.374	1,774	1,530	4.7	204	430	229	288.8	1,532	1.0612	.7693
1994	1,296	244	3.340	1,543	1,463	4.8	101	229	67	204.3	1,464	.9581	.7068
1995	1,264	80	1.536	1,340	1,329	4.5	141	67	-----	78.5	-----	-----	.8188
1996	1,174	19	10.544	1,175	1,180	4.3	42	-----	-----	0	-----	-----	1.0824
1997[1]	1,152	14	24.153	1,151	1,109	4.2	40	-----	-----	1	-----	-----	1.1625
1998[2]	1,082	21	66.138	1,082	1,137	4.2	20	-----	-----	-----	-----	-----	1.7760

[1] Preliminary. [2] Estimates. [3] Includes butter-equivalent. [4] Includes butteroil. [5] *Includes stocks held by USDA.*
Source: Economic Research Service, U.S. Department of Agriculture (ERS-USDA)

Commercial Disappearance of Creamery Butter in the United States In Millions of Pounds

Year	First Quarter	Second Quarter	Third Quarter	Fourth Quarter	Total	Year	First Quarter	Second Quarter	Third Quarter	Fourth Quarter	Total
1988	194.5	221.6	219.7	274.0	909.8	1994	261.7	254.9	285.0	298.3	1,097.3
1989	188.3	145.6	228.8	291.3	854.1	1995	335.7	269.0	261.2	304.9	1,186.0
1990	197.5	218.1	218.1	281.8	915.2	1996	325.6	301.8	237.5	310.3	1,180.0
1991	186.8	184.0	255.6	276.5	903.5	1997	302.7	250.7	265.8	287.6	1,109.0
1992	214.6	216.6	236.8	276.2	944.3	1998	289.0	276.3	255.3	308.6	1,137.0
1993	224.6	231.5	271.9	312.7	1,040.6	1999[1]	273.6	293.4	284.5	303.0	1,154.5

[1] Preliminary. *Source: Economic Research Service, U.S. Department of Agriculture (ERS-USDA)*

World (Total) Butter[3] Production In Thousands of Metric Tons

Year	Australia	France	Germany	India	Ireland	Netherlands	New Zealand	Poland	Russia	Ukraine	United Kingdom	United States	World Total
1990	111	514	640	970	159	209	276	300	833	444	138	591	6,090
1991	111	496	555	1,020	146	196	269	220	729	376	132	606	5,667
1992	116	454	474	1,060	142	191	268	180	762	303	127	619	5,470
1993	131	444	480	1,110	135	184	276	180	732	312	152	596	5,493
1994	147	444	461	1,200	136	159	297	160	488	254	154	588	5,221
1995	138	453	486	1,300	150	132	280	163	419	219	130	573	5,173
1996	153	462	480	1,400	150	122	309	160	290	163	129	533	5,094
1997	147	466	442	1,470	145	134	307	178	280	109	139	522	5,073
1998[1]	154	463	427	1,600	145	149	343	183	270	113	137	491	5,216
1999[2]	173	464	415	1,750	145	141	310	181	245	105	147	530	5,361

[1] Preliminary. [2] Forecast. [3] Factory (including creameries and dairies) & farm. *Source: Foreign Agricultural Service, U.S. Department of Agriculture (FAS-USDA)*

Production of Creamery Butter in Factories in the United States In Millions of Pounds

Year	Jan.	Feb.	Mar.	Apr.	May	June	July	Aug.	Sept.	Oct.	Nov.	Dec.	Total
1990	134.0	127.3	136.2	125.6	118.6	96.7	84.6	84.2	83.4	106.7	110.1	112.2	1,319.6
1991	142.1	126.3	131.6	133.7	126.0	98.3	88.9	85.0	84.7	105.2	108.5	130.1	1,360.4
1992	156.0	132.0	129.9	119.7	118.2	103.0	97.8	86.7	96.6	101.6	98.3	119.8	1,365.2
1993	147.3	127.2	131.6	121.8	116.4	102.3	86.2	80.7	86.3	97.8	97.3	120.3	1,315.2
1994	135.3	118.4	118.0	119.4	118.2	99.2	84.2	88.2	91.2	101.8	100.7	121.4	1,295.9
1995	135.6	121.7	127.3	120.6	119.4	98.4	85.0	76.0	80.2	93.5	90.5	112.4	1,260.7
1996	132.4	114.7	111.9	109.3	100.9	72.7	75.2	73.2	80.7	96.6	95.3	111.3	1,174.5
1997	127.6	108.6	105.4	118.3	102.7	82.0	80.0	68.8	79.3	83.3	89.1	106.0	1,151.3
1998[1]	117.8	105.7	106.7	107.1	92.6	69.9	63.8	64.3	68.2	88.5	91.1	106.3	1,081.9
1999[2]	123.3	111.5	113.7	106.4	104.7	86.0	75.8	66.1	78.8	93.0	90.4	107.8	1,157.4

[1] Preliminary. [2] Estimate. *Source: Economic Research Service, U.S. Department of Agriculture (ERS-USDA)*

Cold Storage Holdings of Creamery Butter on First of Month in the United States In Millions of Pounds

Year	Jan.	Feb.	Mar.	Apr.	May	June	July	Aug.	Sept.	Oct.	Nov.	Dec.
1990	256.2	269.7	293.8	335.4	358.8	399.6	420.0	420.8	427.9	412.3	413.6	407.6
1991	416.1	470.8	524.8	555.9	620.5	646.7	662.7	659.8	629.4	597.2	567.1	539.4
1992	539.4	565.4	624.8	645.3	678.7	712.6	747.0	755.8	705.7	608.1	541.7	487.6
1993	447.7	489.1	492.5	515.6	552.7	559.0	569.0	516.4	473.3	395.4	341.1	276.3
1994	234.7	251.0	243.2	253.5	265.7	281.4	275.1	245.9	206.6	163.4	124.6	84.5
1995	79.5	89.9	88.3	74.8	79.1	81.3	79.2	68.3	50.2	32.8	23.6	15.7
1996	18.6	25.5	33.7	48.7	39.8	34.0	29.7	31.7	27.3	21.4	20.5	17.6
1997	13.7	23.2	36.0	50.3	86.8	104.2	93.7	85.6	69.5	43.9	26.6	15.4
1998	20.8	34.2	44.2	55.9	67.4	72.7	60.6	51.0	41.1	34.1	31.2	28.7
1999[1]	25.9	60.8	95.0	108.9	126.4	136.6	121.3	123.6	95.2	71.5	64.4	30.2

[1] Preliminary. *Source: Agricultural Statistics Board, U.S. Department of Agriculture (ASB-USDA)*

Wholesale Price of 92 Score Creamery (Grade A) Butter, Central States[1] In Cents Per Pound

Year	Jan.	Feb.	Mar.	Apr.	May	June	July	Aug.	Sept.	Oct.	Nov.	Dec.	Average
1990	110.9	108.3	108.3	106.9	99.0	98.4	100.3	98.9	98.9	98.9	98.9	98.0	102.1
1991	97.3	97.3	97.3	97.3	97.3	98.6	98.9	98.9	100.7	106.3	104.6	98.4	99.3
1992	94.9	86.3	86.3	86.3	83.8	76.6	76.6	76.6	81.7	82.2	80.7	78.6	82.5
1993	75.3	75.3	75.3	75.3	75.3	76.2	73.5	74.6	74.3	74.2	73.6	69.7	74.4
1994	64.0	64.0	65.5	65.5	64.5	65.1	66.9	71.5	71.5	71.5	71.5	67.0	67.4
1995	64.0	65.5	66.5	66.5	66.5	69.9	74.5	79.5	80.9	95.4	103.5	74.4	75.6
1996	75.4	66.4	65.5	69.0	87.8	129.3	145.3	145.5	145.5	128.6	74.1	71.9	100.4
1997	81.9	98.4	106.3	95.6	86.1	105.5	102.7	102.5	101.6	135.3	148.8	120.1	107.1
1998	109.2	139.8	134.1	136.4	153.2	186.7	203.1	216.6	273.1	242.3	187.9	140.8	176.9
1999	144.4	133.1	130.3	103.9	111.0	147.7	134.7	141.4	135.8	113.8	109.6		127.8

[1] Data prior to June 1998 are for Grade AA in Chicago. *Source: Economic Research Service, U.S. Department of Agriculture (ERS-USDA)*

Cadmium

Cadmium is a rare chemical element that is the by-product of the smelting and refining of zinc ores. It is used primarily in the plating of iron and steel to protect them from corrosion. Due to the cost of waste disposal and problems with toxicity, the use of electroplating has decreased. Cadmium is highly toxic and its disposal remains a problem for users.

The U.S. Geological Survey reported that world production of cadmium in 1998 was estimated at 19,900 metric tonnes, nearly the same as in 1997. The largest producer of cadmium in 1998 was Japan with 2,400 tonnes, down 2 percent from 1997. Japan is the largest producer and also the largest net importer of refined cadmium metal. The next largest producer is Canada with 1998 estimated production of 2,300 tonnes, down 3 percent from 1997. Other large producers include the U.S., China, Belgium, Mexico and Australia. The world reserve base of cadmium is estimated to be 1.2 million tonnes. Australia has the largest reserves of cadmium followed by the U.S. and Canada. U.S. reserves of cadmium are located in zinc-bearing coals in the central part of the country.

U.S. production of cadmium metal in 1998 was estimated to be 1,880 tonnes, down 9 percent from the previous year although on a longer term cadmium production has been increasing. In 1994, U.S. production was 1,010 tonnes.

Most of the cadmium consumed by Western countries goes into the manufacture of batteries. Most of the cadmium used in batteries is used to make cellular phones and cordless electronic equipment. Other uses for cadmium are in emergency power supplies for telephone exchanges and hospital operating rooms. Because of the concerns about the toxicity of cadmium and damage to the environment, some nickel-cadmium batteries used in electronic equipment are being replaced with lithium-ion batteries. One area of expanded cadmium use is in electric automotive vehicles. If that market develops, it is likely to require larger amounts of cadmium metal. U.S. apparent consumption of cadmium metal in 1998 was estimated at 2,220 tonnes, down 12 percent from the previous year.

U.S. imports for consumption of cadmium metal in 1998 were 620,000 kilograms, down 22 percent from 1997. The major supplier of cadmium metal to the U.S. was Canada, followed by Australia and Mexico. U.S. imports of cadmium sulfide in 1998 were 9,460 kilograms, a decline of 76 percent from 1997. The major supplier of cadmium sulfide was the United Kingdom, followed by Japan.

U.S. exports of cadmium metal in 1998 were 606,000 kilograms, an increase of 9 percent from 1997. The major market for cadmium metal was the Netherlands, followed by India and the United Kingdom. U.S. exports of cadmium sulfide in 1998 were 28,900 kilograms, down substantially from the 399,000 kilograms exported in 1997. The major markets were Germany, Taiwan and South Korea. Industry stocks of cadmium metal at the end of 1998 were 763 tonnes.

World Refinery Production of Cadmium In Metric Tons

Year	Australia	Belgium	Canada	China	Finland	Germany	Italy	Japan	Kazakhstan[4]	Mexico	United Kingdom	United States[3]	World Total
1989	696	1,764	1,620	800	612	1,234	776	2,694	3,000	976	395	1,550	20,873
1990	638	1,960	1,470	1,100	569	990	691	2,450	2,800	882	438	1,680	20,200
1991	1,076	1,807	1,829	1,200	593	1,048	658	2,889	2,500	688	449	1,680	20,900
1992	1,001	1,549	1,963	1,150	590	961	742	2,986	1,000	602	383	1,620	19,800
1993	951	1,573	1,944	1,160	785	1,056	517	2,832	800	797	458	1,090	18,400
1994	910	1,556	2,173	1,280	548	1,145	475	2,629	1,097	646	469	1,010	18,200
1995	838	1,710	2,349	1,450	539	1,150	308	2,652	794	689	549	1,270	20,100
1996	639	1,579	2,537	1,570	648	1,150	296	2,344	800	784	541	1,530	19,000
1997[1]	632	1,420	1,272	1,980	540	1,145	287	2,473	800	1,223	455	2,060	19,200
1998[2]	600	1,318	2,310	2,000	550	1,150	328	2,336	900	1,100	440	1,880	19,600

[1] Preliminary. [2] Estimate. [3] Primary and secondary metal. [4] Formerly part of the U.S.S.R.; data not reported separately until 1992.
Source: U.S. Geological Survey (USGS)

Salient Statistics of Cadmium in the United States In Metric Tons of Contained Cadmium

Year	Net Import Reliance as a % of Apparent Consumption	Production (Metal)	Producer Shipments	Cadmium Sulfide Production	Production Other Compounds	Imports of Cadmium Metal[3]	Exports[4]	Apparent Consumption	Industry Stocks Dec. 31[5]	New York Dealer Price $ per Pound
1989	62	1,550	2,015	267	1,451	2,787	369	4,096	726	6.28
1990	46	1,680	1,860	228	1,144	1,740	385	2,800	653	3.38
1991	50	1,680	1,740	263	1,089	2,040	448	3,080	835	2.01
1992	50	1,620	2,080	270	1,073	1,960	213	3,330	868	.91
1993	64	1,090	1,320	303	731	1,420	38	2,940	579	.45
1994	3	1,010	1,290	170	898	1,110	1,450	1,040	423	1.13
1995	E	1,270	1,280	105	936	848	1,050	1,160	990	1.84
1996	32	1,530	1,310	119	720	843	201	2,250	1,140	1.24
1997[1]	16	2,060	1,370	113	607	790	554	2,510	1,090	.51
1998[2]	21	1,880	1,230	125	638	620	606	2,220	763	.28

[1] Preliminary. [2] Estimate. [3] For consumption. [4] Cadmium metal, alloys, dross, flue dust. [5] Metallic, Compounds, Distributors (including in compounds from 1985) [6] Sticks & Balls in 1 to 5 short ton lots. E = Net exporter. *Source: U.S. Geological Survey (USGS)*

Canola (Rapeseed)

World canola (or rapeseed, the terms are interchangeable) production in the 1990's increased about 40 percent, and canola is now the second largest oilseed in crop size. However, production is only about 25 percent that of soybeans. In 1999/2000, world production was forecast to be a record large 42.2 million metric tonnes vs. 36.6 million in 1998/99, and about 25.0 million in 1990.

On a protein meal basis rapeseed has been the world's second largest crop for some time. Production totaled a record large 22.8 million tonnes in 1999/00 vs. 19.6 million in 1998/99. On a vegetable oil basis rapeseed ranks third (after soybean and palm), with production of a record 13.9 million tonnes in 1999/00 vs. 12.1 million in 1998/99. For the seed and products 1999/00 production exceeded initial estimates.

World rapeseed supplies in 1999/00 of 43.6 million tonnes compares with 37.4 million in 1998/99, which includes relatively small carryover stocks for both crop years. The world 1999/00 (July/June) crush of a record 37.9 million tonnes compares with the previous year's record of 32.5 million tonnes.

Collectively, the European Union (E.U.) is the largest producer with about 11 million tonnes in 1999/00 vs. 9.4 million in 1998/99, with Germany the largest producer within the E.U. China is the largest single producer: production in 1999/00 of 9.8 million tonnes compares with 8.3 million in 1998/99; Canada then follows with 8.3 million and 7.6 million, respectively. Although China continues to increase rapeseed acreage, average yield has failed to show much improvement and is at least 50 percent less than the yields realized in Western Europe.

In terms of protein meal consumption, the European Union's 1999/00 meal consumption of 5.6 million tonnes is about one-fifth that of soybean meal. However, E.U. estimated rapeseed oil usage in 1999/00 of 3.1 million tonnes is nearly twice that of soybean oil. For both products, 1999/00 usage is forecast at record highs.

Foreign trade in rapeseed is second only to soybeans: exports of 8.1 million tonnes in 1999/00 compare with a record 8.3 million in 1998/99.

U.S. production of canola seed is small in absolute terms, but percentagewise it is increasing rather quickly. The crop is grown mostly in the Northern Plains states. Production in 1999/00 (June/May) of 1.6 billion pounds was marginally below the record crop of 1998/99, but compares with crops of less than a 100 million pounds in the 1980's.

Acreage is also growing, almost doubling from year to year during the 1990's. Contributing to the gains in U.S. production include: (1) government incentives to increase acreage; (2) development of better varieties that can be grown in the U.S.; and (3) the wider acceptance of canola oil in cooking due to its lower content of saturated fats. Canola oil is said to be 94 percent saturated fat free, the lowest of any leading oil. Demand for canola meal has also grown sharply as a livestock feed.

U.S. canola oil production in 1999/00 (October/September) of a record large 669 million pounds compares with 556 million in 1998/99. The U.S. imports even more oil, 1.1 billion pounds in 1999/00. Domestic usage in 1999/00 of a record 1.4 billion pounds compares with 1.3 billion a year earlier, and about a half billion pounds at the start of the 1990's. The U.S. is expected to export about 347 million pounds in 1999/00 vs. 295 in 1998/99 million, and virtually no yearly exports in the late 1980's.

U.S. canola meal production in 1999/00 of 528,000 short tons compares with 438,000 in 1998/99; imports totaled 1.4 millions tons vs. 1.3 million tons, respectively. Domestic usage of a record large 1.9 million tons compares with 1.7 million the year before. U.S. exports of canola meal are minimal, as are carryover stocks.

The average price received by farmers for canola seed in 1999/00 was forecast to range between $8.10-8.90/cwt. vs. $9.10 a year earlier. Canola oil's price was forecast at 18.75-21.25 cents per pound vs. 21.9 cents, respectively, while meal's price of $100.00-125.00 per short ton in 1999/00 compares with $98.00 in 1998/99.

Futures Markets

Canola futures and options are traded on the Winnipeg Commodity Exchange (WCE) and quoted in Canadian dollars per ton. Rapeseed futures are traded on the Marche a Terme International de France (MATIF).

World Production of Canola (Rapeseed) In Thousands of Metric Tons

Year	Austrlia	Canada	China	Czecho-slovakia	France	Germany	India	Pakistan	Poland	Sweden	United Kingdom	Former USSR	World Total
1988-9	58	4,218	5,044	380	2,303	1,642	4,377	249	1,199	250	1,040	420	22,646
1989-90	78	3,209	5,436	387	1,748	1,908	4,125	233	1,586	370	976	424	22,096
1990-1	98	3,266	6,958	380	1,926	2,155	5,152	228	1,206	367	1,258	506	25,321
1991-2	170	4,224	7,436	446	2,270	3,030	5,863	219	1,043	252	1,308	409	28,489
1992-3	179	3,872	7,653	430	1,810	2,617	4,872	207	758	247	1,159	388	25,588
1993-4	294	5,480	6,939	466	1,550	2,848	5,390	215	594	313	1,256	325	27,039
1994-5	309	7,228	7,492	452	1,800	2,896	5,884	312	756	214	1,254	363	30,626
1995-6	584	6,436	9,777	662	2,782	3,103	6,071	385	1,377	216	1,235	415	34,919
1996-7	641	5,062	9,201	531	2,902	2,190	6,300	286	449	143	1,415	214	31,015
1997-8[1]	861	6,393	9,578	561	3,496	2,867	4,650	280	595	132	1,527	221	33,065
1998-9[2]	1,761	7,643	8,301	680	3,736	3,388	5,000	300	1,099	129	1,575	300	36,079
1999-00[3]	2,103	8,798	9,750	956	4,483	4,212	5,450		1,124	152	1,679	390	42,133

[1] Preliminary. [2] Estimate. [3] Forecast. *Source: The Oil World*

CANOLA

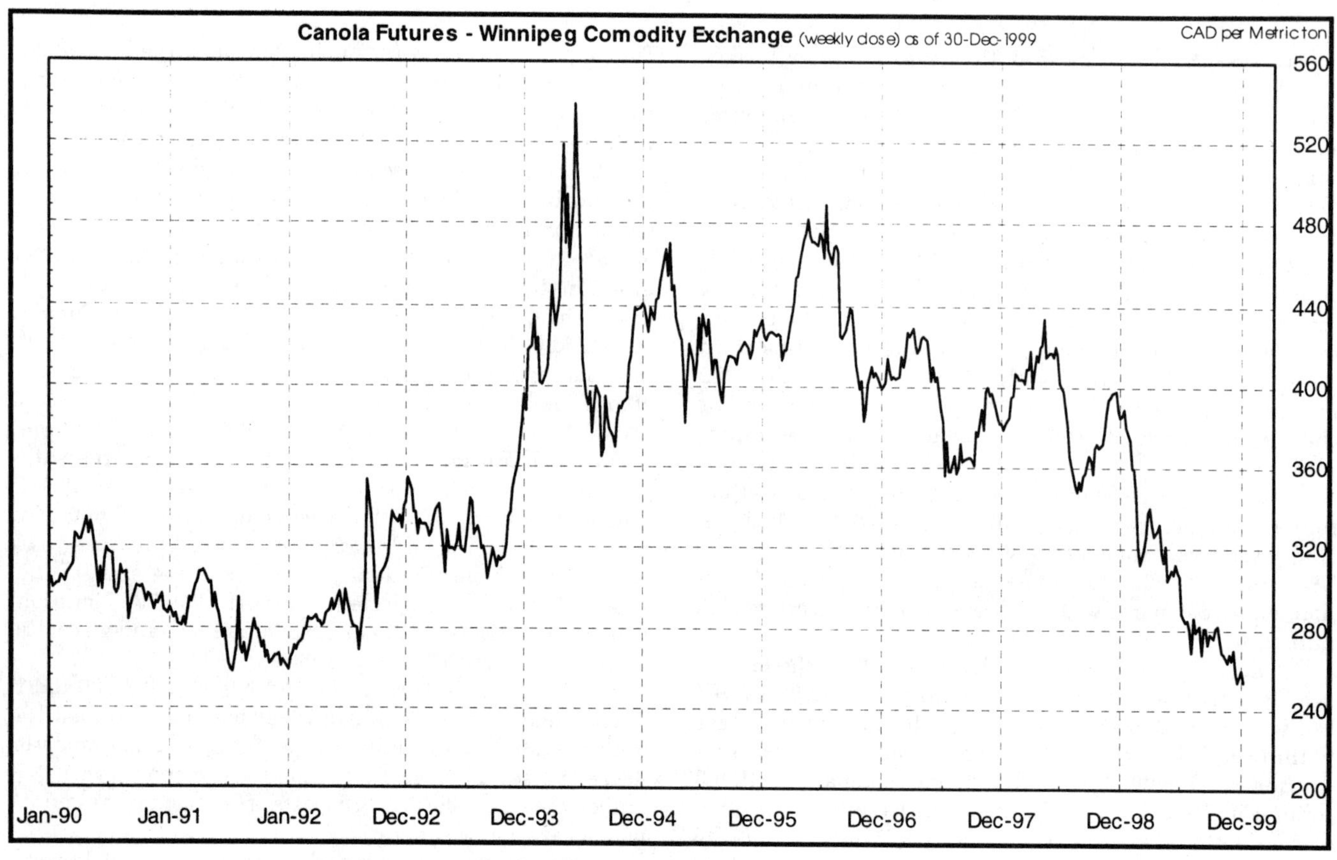

Volume of Trading of Canola Futures in Winnipeg In Contracts

Year	Jan.	Feb.	Mar.	Apr.	May	June	July	Aug.	Sept.	Oct.	Nov.	Dec.	Total
1990	52,473	66,423	52,720	55,158	82,685	53,085	51,270	61,642	56,933	57,302	49,450	58,994	698,135
1991	67,489	59,380	64,193	67,572	68,849	59,270	90,575	65,541	76,966	75,457	53,660	66,421	815,373
1992	57,429	54,546	57,174	38,674	87,638	75,018	50,157	72,971	79,034	93,692	99,577	73,805	839,715
1993	73,411	74,362	63,737	73,358	61,996	70,117	94,286	77,325	56,377	73,953	107,485	112,377	938,784
1994	119,691	103,517	85,125	100,923	111,962	79,307	83,903	95,712	54,893	87,350	101,727	96,797	1,120,907
1995	75,068	87,113	86,340	67,937	95,447	85,126	94,576	70,904	94,794	126,210	84,991	107,177	1,075,683
1996	99,542	95,034	76,704	128,169	148,189	103,892	135,652	87,896	108,490	161,894	90,105	110,453	1,346,020
1997	121,433	133,056	131,473	148,647	117,219	116,117	80,867	72,602	93,967	150,065	97,984	124,245	1,387,675
1998	100,926	144,309	110,708	140,789	130,551	121,829	107,816	89,457	121,573	181,002	127,120	181,278	1,557,358
1999	100,926	144,309	110,708	143,282	102,838	134,179	94,256	113,913	130,505	184,973	157,428	179,798	1,685,756

Source: Winnipeg Commodity Exchange (WCE)

Volume of Trading of Canola Futures in Winnipeg In Contracts

Year	Jan.	Feb.	Mar.	Apr.	May	June	July	Aug.	Sept.	Oct.	Nov.	Dec.	Total
1990	52,473	66,423	52,720	55,158	82,685	53,085	51,270	61,642	56,933	57,302	49,450	58,994	698,135
1991	67,489	59,380	64,193	67,572	68,849	59,270	90,575	65,541	76,966	75,457	53,660	66,421	815,373
1992	57,429	54,546	57,174	38,674	87,638	75,018	50,157	72,971	79,034	93,692	99,577	73,805	839,715
1993	73,411	74,362	63,737	73,358	61,996	70,117	94,286	77,325	56,377	73,953	107,485	112,377	938,784
1994	119,691	103,517	85,125	100,923	111,962	79,307	83,903	95,712	54,893	87,350	101,727	96,797	1,120,907
1995	75,068	87,113	86,340	67,937	95,447	85,126	94,576	70,904	94,794	126,210	84,991	107,177	1,075,683
1996	99,542	95,034	76,704	128,169	148,189	103,892	135,652	87,896	108,490	161,894	90,105	110,453	1,346,020
1997	121,433	133,056	131,473	148,647	117,219	116,117	80,867	72,602	93,967	150,065	97,984	124,245	1,387,675
1998	100,926	144,309	110,708	140,789	130,551	121,829	107,816	89,457	121,573	181,002	127,120	181,278	1,557,358
1999	100,926	144,309	110,708	143,282	102,838	134,179	94,256	113,913	130,505	184,973	157,428	179,798	1,685,756

Source: Winnipeg Commodity Exchange (WCE)

Production of Creamery Butter in Factories in the United States In Millions of Pounds

Year	Jan.	Feb.	Mar.	Apr.	May	June	July	Aug.	Sept.	Oct.	Nov.	Dec.	Total
1990	134.0	127.3	136.2	125.6	118.6	96.7	84.6	84.2	83.4	106.7	110.1	112.2	1,319.6
1991	142.1	126.3	131.6	133.7	126.0	98.3	88.9	85.0	84.7	105.2	108.5	130.1	1,360.4
1992	156.0	132.0	129.9	119.7	118.2	103.0	97.8	86.7	96.6	101.6	98.3	119.8	1,365.2
1993	147.3	127.2	131.6	121.8	116.4	102.3	86.2	80.7	86.3	97.8	97.3	120.3	1,315.2
1994	135.3	118.4	118.0	119.4	118.2	99.2	84.2	88.2	91.2	101.8	100.7	121.4	1,295.9
1995	135.6	121.7	127.3	120.6	119.4	98.4	85.0	76.0	80.2	93.5	90.5	112.4	1,260.7
1996	132.4	114.7	111.9	109.3	100.9	72.7	75.2	73.2	80.7	96.6	95.3	111.3	1,174.5
1997	127.6	108.6	105.4	118.3	102.7	82.0	80.0	68.8	79.3	83.3	89.1	106.0	1,151.3
1998[1]	117.8	105.7	106.7	107.1	92.6	69.9	63.8	64.3	68.2	88.5	91.1	106.3	1,081.9
1999[2]	123.3	111.5	113.7	106.4	104.7	86.0	75.8	66.1	78.8	93.0	90.4	107.8	1,157.4

[1] Preliminary. [2] Estimate. *Source: Economic Research Service, U.S. Department of Agriculture (ERS-USDA)*

Salient Statistics of Canola and Canola Oil in the United States In Millions of Pounds

	Canola							Canola Oil						
	Supply				Disappearance			Supply				Disappearance		
Year	Stocks June 1	Production	Imports	Total	Crush	Exports	Total[3]	Stocks June 1	Production	Imports	Total	Domestic	Exports	Total
1990-1	21	97	141	259	195	32	227	24	18	583	625	577	7	584
1991-2	32	191	2	225	109	97	212	41	32	815	888	801	15	816
1992-3	13	144	27	184	59	104	174	71	49	861	981	898	16	914
1993-4	10	252	773	1,036	850	78	941	67	406	902	1,375	1,162	76	1,238
1994-5	95	447	630	1,173	899	227	1,139	137	299	938	1,374	1,167	153	1,320
1995-6	34	548	558	1,140	899	138	1,052	54	356	1,086	1,497	1,273	147	1,420
1996-7	88	481	570	1,139	868	173	1,059	77	342	1,075	1,494	1,136	293	1,429
1997-8	80	781	782	1,642	1,298	277	1,600	65	451	1,088	1,604	1,143	349	1,492
1998-9[1]	42	1,558	684	2,284	1,533	543	2,115	112	548	1,068	1,728	1,264	295	1,559
1999-00[2]	169	1,364	683	2,216	1,544	496	2,073	169	614	1,173	1,956	1,466	318	1,784

[1] Preliminary. [2] Forecast. *Source: Economic Research Service, U.S. Department of Agriculture (ERS-USDA)*

Wholesale Price of Canola Oil, Refined (Denatured), in Tanks in New York In Cents Per Pound

Year	Jan.	Feb.	Mar.	Apr.	May	June	July	Aug.	Sept.	Oct.	Nov.	Dec.	Average
1989	70.00	70.00	80.25	80.25	80.25	80.75	80.25	80.25	80.25	80.25	80.25	80.25	78.60
1990	81.75	82.25	82.23	82.25	82.25	82.25	82.25	82.25	79.25	77.25	77.25	81.00	81.00
1991	82.25	82.25	82.25	82.25	82.25	82.25	82.25	82.25	82.25	82.25	82.25	82.25	82.30
1992	82.25	82.25	82.25	82.25	82.25	82.25	82.25	82.25	67.25	62.25	62.25	62.25	76.00
1993	62.25	62.25	62.25	62.25	55.88	53.75	53.25	53.00	53.00	52.00	52.50	50.00	56.00
1994	53.75	53.75	53.75	53.75	53.75	53.75	53.75	53.75	53.75	53.75	53.75	53.75	53.75
1995	53.75	53.75	53.75	53.75	53.15	50.75	50.75	50.75	50.75	50.75	50.75	50.75	51.95
1996	50.75	50.75	50.75	50.75	50.75	50.75	50.75	50.75	50.75	60.56	90.00	90.00	58.11
1997	90.00	90.00	90.00	90.00	90.00	90.00	90.00	90.00	90.00	82.00	82.00	82.00	88.00
1998[1]	90.00	90.00	90.00	90.00	90.00	90.00	90.00	90.00	90.00				90.00

[1] Preliminary. *Source: Economic Research Service, U.S. Department of Agriculture (ERS-USDA)*

Average Price of Canola in Vancouver In Canadian Dollars Per Tonne

Year	Jan.	Feb.	Mar.	Apr.	May	June	July	Aug.	Sept.	Oct.	Nov.	Dec.	Average
1990	300.01	301.45	311.00	318.78	322.24	303.89	300.83	299.43	292.74	295.23	290.08	290.01	302.14
1991	285.01	280.36	291.50	298.57	293.83	277.25	258.12	269.40	275.00	270.30	262.90	261.60	276.99
1992	264.15	273.35	282.70	276.85	288.08	292.35	272.20	282.26	320.62	302.10	327.22	331.57	292.79
1993	344.22	329.26	328.67	325.06	318.85	319.23	331.29	322.85	311.29	311.66	331.44	366.37	328.35
1994	408.60	413.10	422.23	454.90	481.44	484.95	388.63	382.54	381.70	379.99	401.38	432.35	419.32
1995	431.85	440.41	456.13	425.40	404.27	414.31	426.49	405.94	405.89	413.29	416.03	423.77	421.98
1996	424.07	422.60	417.55	443.94	473.04	469.28	470.38	453.86	453.53	444.01	432.30	439.79	445.36
1997	441.96	441.68	457.95	448.09	446.00	428.47	395.58	400.68	390.38	398.81	419.12	410.21	423.24
1998	416.48	428.88	434.68	441.44	450.56	443.11	404.86	387.05	389.34	400.40	412.17	417.41	418.87
1999	402.74	368.17	363.24	362.16	353.21	356.53	317.36	305.73	302.93	302.68	297.76	287.62	335.01

Source: Winnipeg Commodity Exchange (WCE)

Cassava

Cassava, or tapioca root, is used primarily as an animal feed and as a foodstuff in tropical countries. Cassava has been viewed as a food that could be the solution to the hunger problems that exist in less developed countries. Technological advances have promised that there could be substantial increases in yields. New strains of cassava root are being developed in Africa that could eventually be used in the fight against world hunger.

Cassava is grown in countries with mostly tropical climates. It is a popular crop to produce since it is resistant to drought and relatively easy to grow. Cassava is a diet staple in many countries. In some countries, the prices of other imported foodstuffs have increased leading to more demand for locally produced foods like cassava.

For 1997, the Food and Agricultural Organization of the United Nations reported that world production of cassava was 164.8 million metric tonnes, down 1 percent from the previous year. World production of cassava between 1991 and 1997 averaged 161.3 million tonnes.

The world's largest producer of cassava in 1997 was Nigeria with production of 30.4 million tonnes, some 18 percent of the world total. Nigerian production in 1997 was 3 percent less than in 1996. In Nigeria, root crops like cassava and yams are diet staples.

The next largest producer of cassava (tapioca root) was Brazil. 1997 production was 24.4 million tonnes, a decline of 1 percent from the previous year. Between 1991 and 1997, Brazilian cassava production averaged 23.9 million tonnes.

Another large producer of cassava is Thailand with 1997 output of 18 million tonnes, about the same level as the previous year. Thailand's production of cassava has been trending lower. In 1991 production was over 20.3 million tonnes. Between 1991 and 1997, Thailand's production of cassava fell by 12 percent.

Indonesia's cassava production in 1997 was estimated at 16.1 million tonnes, down 5 percent from the previous season. Other large producers of cassava are the Congo, Ghana and India.

The world's largest exporter of cassava is Thailand with 1997 exports of 4.2 million tonnes or 93 percent of the world total. Most exports go to European countries.

World Cassava Production In Thousands of Metric Tons

Year	Brazil	China	Ghana	India	Indo-nesia	Mozam-bique	Nigeria	Para-guay	Tan-zania	Thailand	Uganda	Zaire	World Total
1991	24,538	3,310	3,600	5,416	15,954	3,690	20,000	2,585	7,460	20,356	3,229	19,500	153,562
1992	21,919	3,357	4,000	5,469	16,516	3,239	21,320	2,591	7,112	20,356	2,896	20,210	153,058
1993	21,837	3,403	4,500	5,413	16,799	3,511	29,900	2,656	6,833	20,203	3,139	20,835	163,002
1994	24,464	3,501	6,025	5,784	15,729	3,352	31,005	2,518	7,209	19,091	2,080	18,051	163,514
1995	25,423	3,501	6,612	5,929	15,442	4,178	31,404	3,054	5,969	17,388	2,224	17,500	165,436
1996	24,584	3,501	7,111	5,979	17,003	4,734	31,418	2,649	5,992	18,084	2,245	18,000	165,650
1997[1]	24,354	3,501	6,800	5,979	16,103	5,337	30,409	3,155	6,444	18,000	2,291	-----	164,751

[1] Estimate. *Source: Food and Agriculture Organization of the United Nations (FAO-UN)*

Prices of Tapioca, Hard Pellets, F.O.B. Rotterdam U.S. Dollars Per Tonne

Year	Jan.	Feb.	Mar.	Apr.	May	June	July	Aug.	Sept.	Oct.	Nov.	Dec.	Average
1992	197	184	179	177	179	181	184	192	195	187	172	170	183
1993	160	150	140	149	145	133	130	131	136	127	120	125	137
1994	122	123	128	133	138	141	147	154	158	161	161	161	144
1995	164	170	180	178	174	176	183	176	178	184	182	178	177
1996	167	160	155	158	163	154	149	154	146	139	140	133	152
1997	133	118	112	108	114	110	100	97	100	102	102	100	108
1998	96	100	98	104	106	104	105	106	112	122	124	109	107
1999	104	102	101	102	108	104	99	102	100	99	100	97	102

Source: The Oil World

World Trade in Tapioca In Thousands of Metric Tons

	Exports					Imports						
Year	China	Indonesia	Thailand	Viet Nam	Total World Exports	China	EC-12[2]	Japan	Rep. of Korea	United States	Former USSR	Total World Imports
1992	316	873	8,045	32	9,422	230	6,128	181	876	217	22	8,951
1993	269	936	6,707	29	8,090	149	6,449	151	658	60	8	8,376
1994	77	686	4,703	28	5,645	92	5,441	94	132	18	-----	6,076
1995	10	481	3,297	1	3,860	362	2,924	16	140	-----	-----	3,590
1996	11	389	3,607	1	4,052	75	3,321	22	554	-----	-----	4,174
1997	11	247	4,155	26	4,477	242	3,413	15	455	-----	-----	4,475
1998[1]	10	221	3,199	-----	3,468	250	2,620	19	347	-----	-----	3,440

[1] Estimate. [2] Intra-EU trade is excluded. *Source: The Oil World*

Castor Beans

World production of castorseed beans in the 1998/99 season was estimated by the U.S.D.A. at 1.24 million metric tonnes, up over 4 percent from the previous season. Over the last seven seasons, world production has averaged 1.18 million tonnes.

India is by far the largest producer of castor beans which are used in the production of castor oil. Production in 1998/99 was estimated at 900,000 tonnes, up 13 percent from the previous season. Most of India's castor beans are produced in the western state of Gujarat. The 1999/00 crop was impacted by a dry spell in August-September 1999 which was expected to have an adverse impact on the final size of the crop. Gujarat accounts for about three-fourths of India's castorseed production. The drought in India was not expected to have a major impact on prices because there are ample stocks from the previous season. India is the largest exporter of castor oil.

The next largest producer of castor beans is China with the 1998-99 crop estimated at 210,000 tonnes, up 17 percent from the previous year. The third largest producer of castorseeds is Brazil with 1998-99 production estimated at 45,000 tonnes. Other producers of smaller amounts include Thailand, Paraguay, the Philippines and Pakistan.

The U.S. is a major importer and user of castor oil. U.S. castor oil (in inedible products like plastics and resins) consumption between 1992-93 and 1998-99 averaged 52.9 million pounds per year. Consumption has been trending lower. U.S. stocks of castor oil at the beginning of the 1998-99 season were 40 million pounds, an increase of 59 percent from the beginning of the 1997-98 season.

World Production of Castorseed Beans In Thousands of Metric Tons

Crop Year	Brazil	China	Ecuador	India	Mexico	Paraguay	Pakistan	Philippines	Sudan	Tanzania	Thailand	Former U.S.S.R.	World Total
1993-4	45	280	13	700	1	15	7	7	6	3	22	4	1,135
1994-5	53	230	7	850	1	10	5	7	4	3	15	8	1,226
1995-6	33	165	5	930	1	9	9	7	2	3	16	3	1,214
1996-7	43	220	4	770	1	15	5	4	1	2	15	3	1,117
1997-8[1]	125	180	4	800	1	16	6	4	1	3	14	3	1,191
1998-9[2]	40	190	4	810	1	19	7	4	1	3	12	3	1,127
1999-00[3]	45	210		680		18	7	4			8	3	1,018

[1] Preliminary. [2] Estimate. [3] Forecast. *Sources: Foreign Agricultural Service, U.S.Department of Agriculture (FAS-USDA); The Oil World*

Castor Oil Consumption[2] in the United States In Thousands of Pounds

Year	Oct.	Nov.	Dec.	Jan.	Feb.	Mar.	Apr.	May	June	July	Aug.	Sept.	Total
1993-4	5,046	5,649	5,092	5,510	4,982	5,766	4,548	6,335	5,258	4,603	4,929	4,543	62,261
1994-5	5,032	4,204	5,092	6,001	5,179	4,911	4,722	3,740	5,067	4,891	6,452	4,834	60,125
1995-6	5,228	5,463	6,232	5,794	6,979	5,545	3,369	5,864	5,469	5,439	4,332	3,818	63,532
1996-7	3,921	4,460	4,555	3,738	4,679	4,256	4,476	4,006	3,851	3,855	3,763	5,050	50,610
1997-8	3,276	4,353	4,367	4,409	3,035	4,389	4,218	3,645	4,651	4,350	3,489	4,210	48,392
1998-9	2,348	3,579	3,740	3,323	4,197	5,004	5,218	4,639	4,396	4,471	4,465	4,494	49,874
1999-00[1]	4,281	3,917	4,682										51,520

[1] Preliminary. [2] In inedible products (Resins, Plastics, etc.). *Source: Bureau of the Census, U.S. Department of Commerce*

Castor Oil Stocks in the United States, on First of Month In Thousands of Pounds

Year	Oct.	Nov.	Dec.	Jan.	Feb.	Mar.	Apr.	May	June	July	Aug.	Sept.
1993-4	22,981	21,275	23,482	21,132	29,871	9,946	18,394	25,249	22,550	21,795	27,911	20,950
1994-5	21,066	23,484	23,357	21,132	29,245	20,986	10,387	5,492	22,765	33,557	37,542	42,516
1995-6	27,143	35,329	43,189	51,713	45,746	37,210	29,718	36,829	55,687	43,954	37,802	25,535
1996-7	23,831	38,785	41,016	31,755	23,630	15,157	7,200	24,164	14,166	27,754	17,426	20,656
1997-8	25,098	24,188	25,425	17,543	12,736	7,138	2,804	18,897	15,386	24,682	16,586	29,862
1998-9	40,018	46,809	36,881	35,668	31,961	22,252	13,771	11,950	5,568	13,952	34,956	25,944
1999-00[1]	44,427	34,180	31,191	44,315								

[1] Preliminary. *Source: Bureau of the Census, U.S. Department of Commerce*

Average Wholesale Price of Castor Oil No. 1, Brazilian Tanks in New York In Cents Per Pound

Year	Jan.	Feb.	Mar.	Apr.	May	June	July	Aug.	Sept.	Oct.	Nov.	Dec.	Average
1993	34.00	32.00	32.00	32.00	37.00	37.00	37.00	37.00	38.50	41.50	44.00	44.00	37.17
1994	44.00	41.75	41.00	41.00	46.00	45.00	45.00	45.00	45.00	45.00	45.00	45.00	44.06
1995	45.00	45.00	45.00	45.00	45.00	45.00	45.00	45.00	45.00	45.00	45.00	45.00	45.00
1996	43.50	41.50	41.50	41.50	41.50	41.50	41.50	41.50	41.50	41.50	41.50	41.50	41.67
1997	41.50	41.50	41.50	41.50	41.50	41.50	41.50	41.50	41.50	41.50	41.50	41.50	41.50
1998	41.50	41.50	41.50	41.50	41.50	48.00	48.00	48.00	48.00	48.00	48.00	48.00	45.29
1999	48.00	48.00	48.00	48.00	48.00	48.00	48.00	48.00	48.00				48.00

Source: Foreign Agricultural Service, U.S.Department of Agriculture (FAS-USDA)

Cattle and Calves

The world cattle inventory showed a marginal slippage during the last half of the 1990's; the January 1, 1999 total of 1,026,000 head, the low for the decade, compares with 1,027,000 a year earlier and the mid-1990's high of 1,059,000 head. However, some large changes have occurred in selected areas, notably the decline in cattle numbers in the former U.S.S.R. and the increase in numbers in China. Russia's and the Ukraine's cattle inventory in early 1999 was estimated at only 45 million head vs. 50 million in 1998 and 71 million in 1995. In contrast, China's January 1, 1999 inventory of a near record high 123 million head compares with 117 million a year earlier and around 100 million early in the 1990's. India, which held about 25 percent of the world's total cattle inventory at the start of 1999, 307 million head, appears to be slowly increasing its inventory following little expansion in the first half of the decade. Brazil had the second largest inventory in 1999 with about 143 million head vs. 145 million in 1998.

The U.S. cattle inventory apparently peaked in the 1980's at around 110 million head, then sliding to 96 million by early 1990. A moderate cyclical expansion followed that carried the inventory to 103 million head by early 1996; a cyclical downturn then followed that does not yet appear to have run its course. The January 1, 1999 inventory of 98.5 million head compares with 99.7 million a year earlier. Moreover, the mid-1999 inventory was down 1 percent from a year earlier.

Cow-calf operators have lost money since 1995 and were apt to see only modest improvement in 1999, suggesting that producers are not going to start breeding more replacement heifers until at least 2000. The earliest the calf crop is likely to rise is forecast to be 2001. However, the cyclical liquidation of the beef cow inventory apparently ended in 1999 although heifer slaughter was at near record levels. The three largest cattle inventory states are generally Texas, Kansas and Nebraska.

World beef use in 1999 proved relatively routine; consumption was estimated at 47.5 million metric tonnes vs. 47.8 million in 1997. European Union use in 1999 of 7.1 million tonnes was about unchanged from 1998 and compares with 6.9 million tonnes in 1996 when usage was adversely affected by the mad cow disease outbreak. Minimal latent fears of mad cow disease are still noted in some countries during 1999. China beef consumption in 1999 of a record high 4.7 million tonnes compares with 4.4 million in 1998. In the former U.S.S.R., consumption fell to 3.6 million tonnes from 3.8 million in 1998.

U.S. commercial cattle slaughter in 1999 (through October) of 30.3 million head compares with 29.8 million in the like 1998 period. Dressed slaughter weights in late 1999 averaged near a record large 740 pounds. U.S. beef production in 1999 is forecast at 26.2 billion pounds vs. 25.7 billion in 1998. U.S. per capita beef consumption has shown little growth in recent years as consumers opt for less red meat in their diet; per capita use in 1999 of 68.7 pounds (retail weight) compares with 68.1 pounds in 1998 and a 2000 estimate of 65.4. However, a subtle positive shift in the consumer attitude towards beef seemed to take hold in 1999 reflecting (1) the strong U.S. economy and greater disposable income and (2) a change in the industry's advertising that stressed beef's high protein nutritional value; factors that could help buoy demand for beef in 2000 over initial forecasts.

U.S. beef (and veal) exports in 1999 of 2.4 billion pounds compare with 2.2 billion in 1998 and forecasts of 2.3 billion in 1999. Typically, Japan has been the largest market for U.S. beef, but Mexico has been a rapidly growing market recently. U.S. beef imports in 1999 of 2.8 billion pounds compare with 2.6 billion in 1998 and 2.9 billion estimated for 2000. Australia, New Zealand and Canada are the largest beef suppliers to the U.S. In addition, live cattle are imported from Canada and Mexico.

Choice steer prices, basis Nebraska, in 1999 averaged about $64.91 per cwt. vs. $61.48 in 1998. Prices are forecast between $66.00-$72.00/cwt. in 2000. On the retail level, choice beef prices in mid-1999 averaged around $2.86/lb., about 15 cents above a year earlier.

Futures Markets

Live cattle futures and options on futures are traded on the Chicago Mercantile Exchange (CME), the Bolsa de Mercadorias & Futures (BM&F), and the Midamerica Commodity Exchange (MidAm). Feeder cattle futures are traded on the CME and the BM&F, and feeder cattle options are traded on the CME.

World Cattle and Buffalo Numbers as of January 1 In Thousands of Head

Year	Argentina	Australia	Brazil	China	Colombia	France	Germany	India	Mexico	Russia	Ukraine	United States	World Total (Mil. Head)
1990	56,482	24,673	140,400	100,752	16,835	21,394	20,287	270,070	31,747	58,800	25,195	95,816	1,035
1991	56,982	25,026	142,900	102,884	16,225	21,446	19,488	272,300	29,847	57,000	24,623	96,393	1,036
1992	55,229	25,857	141,800	104,592	16,008	20,970	17,134	271,200	30,232	54,677	23,728	97,556	1,032
1993	55,577	25,182	149,000	107,840	16,391	20,383	16,207	271,255	30,649	52,226	22,457	99,176	1,031
1994	54,875	25,758	149,100	113,157	16,614	20,112	15,897	291,973	30,702	48,914	21,607	100,974	1,053
1995	54,207	25,736	149,315	123,317	16,725	20,524	15,962	293,922	30,191	43,296	19,624	102,785	1,057
1996	53,569	26,500	149,228	104,000	16,768	20,662	15,890	296,462	28,140	39,700	17,558	103,548	1,034
1997	51,696	26,780	146,110	110,318	18,455	20,557	15,760	299,802	26,822	35,800	15,313	101,656	1,031
1998	49,238	26,710	144,670	116,847	18,631	20,154	15,227	303,030	25,628	31,700	12,579	99,744	1,024
1999[1]	49,437	25,833	143,893	124,000	18,849	20,097	14,943	306,967	24,498	28,600	11,696	98,522	1,025
2000[2]	49,342	25,900	144,153	133,000	19,111	19,800	14,574	312,572	23,223	26,600	11,000	96,595	1,032

[1] Preliminary. [2] Forecast. *Source: Foreign Agricultural Service, U.S. Department of Agriculture (FAS-USDA)*

Cattle Supply and Distribution in the United States In Thousands of Head

Year	Cattle & Calves on Farms January 1	Imports	Calves Born	Total Supply	Livestock Slaughter - Cattle and Calves: Commercial: Federally Inspected	Other[3]	All Commercial	Farm	Total Slaughter	Deaths on Farms	Exports	Total Disap-pearance
1990	95,816	2,135	38,613	139,546	34,133	800	35,032	245	35,277	4,327	120	39,724
1991	96,393	1,939	38,583	139,861	33,285	841	34,126	242	34,368	4,247	311	38,927
1992	97,556	2,255	38,933	141,104	33,428	817	34,245	244	34,489	4,366	322	39,177
1993	99,176	2,499	39,369	142,750	33,752	767	34,519	227	34,746	4,630	153	39,529
1994	100,974	2,083	40,105	143,799	34,719	745	25,464	227	35,691	4,254	231	40,176
1995	102,755	2,694	40,264	145,713	36,272	798	37,069	225	37,294	4,382	88	41,764
1996	103,548	1,965	39,823	145,336	37,435	917	38,351	224	38,575	4,577	174	43,326
1997	101,656	2,046	38,961	142,663	37,101	792	37,893	218	38,111	4,684	282	43,077
1998[1]	99,744	2,034	38,582	140,360	34,787	677	35,464	215	37,138	4,600	285	42,023
1999[2]	98,522	1,788			35,486	674	36,160				286	

[1] Preliminary. [2] Estimate. [3] Wholesale and retail. *Source: Economic Research Service, U.S. Department of Agriculture (ERS-USDA)*

Beef Supply and Utilization in the United States

Year/ Quarter	Beginning Stocks	Production: Commercial	Production: Total	Imports	Total Supply	Exports	Ending Stocks	Total Disap-pearance	Per Capita Disappearance: Carcass Weight	Per Capita Disappearance: Retail Weight
	Million Pounds								Pounds	
1995	548	25,115	25,222	2,104	27,874	1,821	519	25,534	97.0	67.4
I	548	5,888	5,925	572	7,045	368	514	6,163	23.5	16.3
II	514	6,325	6,341	540	7,395	452	471	6,472	24.6	17.1
III	471	6,625	6,641	539	7,651	499	464	6,688	25.4	17.6
IV	464	6,277	6,315	453	7,232	502	519	6,211	23.5	16.4
1996	519	25,419	25,525	2,073	28,117	1,877	377	25,863	97.4	67.7
I	519	6,303	6,340	508	7,367	452	461	6,454	24.4	17.0
II	461	6,642	6,658	526	7,645	544	406	6,695	25.2	17.5
III	406	6,390	6,406	555	7,367	436	414	6,517	24.5	17.0
IV	414	6,084	6,121	484	7,019	445	377	6,197	23.2	16.2
1997	377	25,384	25,490	2,343	28,210	2,136	465	25,609	96.7	67.2
I	377	6,112	6,149	536	7,062	455	387	6,220	23.3	16.2
II	387	6,419	6,435	716	7,538	513	425	6,600	24.7	17.1
III	425	6,603	6,636	576	7,741	600	430	6,811	25.4	17.6
IV	430	6,258	6,187	515	7,152	568	400	6,302	23.4	16.3
1998[1]	465	25,666	27,145	2,611	29,756	2,158	465	25,536	94.5	68.1
I	465	6,215	6,680	644	7,324	500	375	6,317	23.4	16.7
II	375	6,463	6,838	682	7,520	537	316	6,451	23.9	17.2
III	316	6,638	6,954	685	7,639	563	323			17.5
IV	323	6,350	6,673	600	7,273	558	465			16.7
1999[2]	296	26,315	27,508	2,790	30,298	2,340	302			67.4
I	296	6,397	6,693	700	7,393	595	309			16.7
II	309	6,627	6,936	760	7,696	610	293			17.7
III	293	6,841	7,134	725	7,859	565	294			17.2
IV	294	6,450	6,744	605	7,349	570	302			15.8

[1] Preliminary. [2] Forecast. *Source: Economic Research Service, U.S. Department of Agriculture (ERS-USDA)*

United States Cattle on Feed in 13 States In Thousands of Head

Year/ Quarter	Number on Feed[3]	Placed on Feed	Marketings	Other Disappearance	Year/ Quarter	Number on Feed[3]	Placed on Feed	Marketings	Other Disappearance
1996	10,346	23,210	22,085	913	1998[1]	11,155	19,476	18,878	712
I	10,346	5,210	5,531	213	I	11,155	4,931	5,706	262
II	9,812	4,226	5,937	261	II	10,118	1,563	2,033	72
III	7,840	6,664	5,481	182	III	9,161	6,606	5,857	163
IV	8,841	7,050	5,076	257	IV	9,747	6,376	5,282	215
1997	10,558	24,271	22,774	930	1999[2]	10,667	25,147	23,465	894
I	10,558	5,605	5,563	239	I	10,667	5,742	5,819	206
II	10,391	4,856	6,014	275	II	10,384	5,501	6,064	266
III	8,958	7,135	5,975	155	III	9,555	6,994	6,114	169
IV	9,963	6,675	5,222	261	IV	10,266	6,910	5,468	253

[1] Preliminary. [2] Estimate. [3] Beginning of period. *Source: Economic Research Service, U.S. Department of Agriculture (ERS-USDA)*

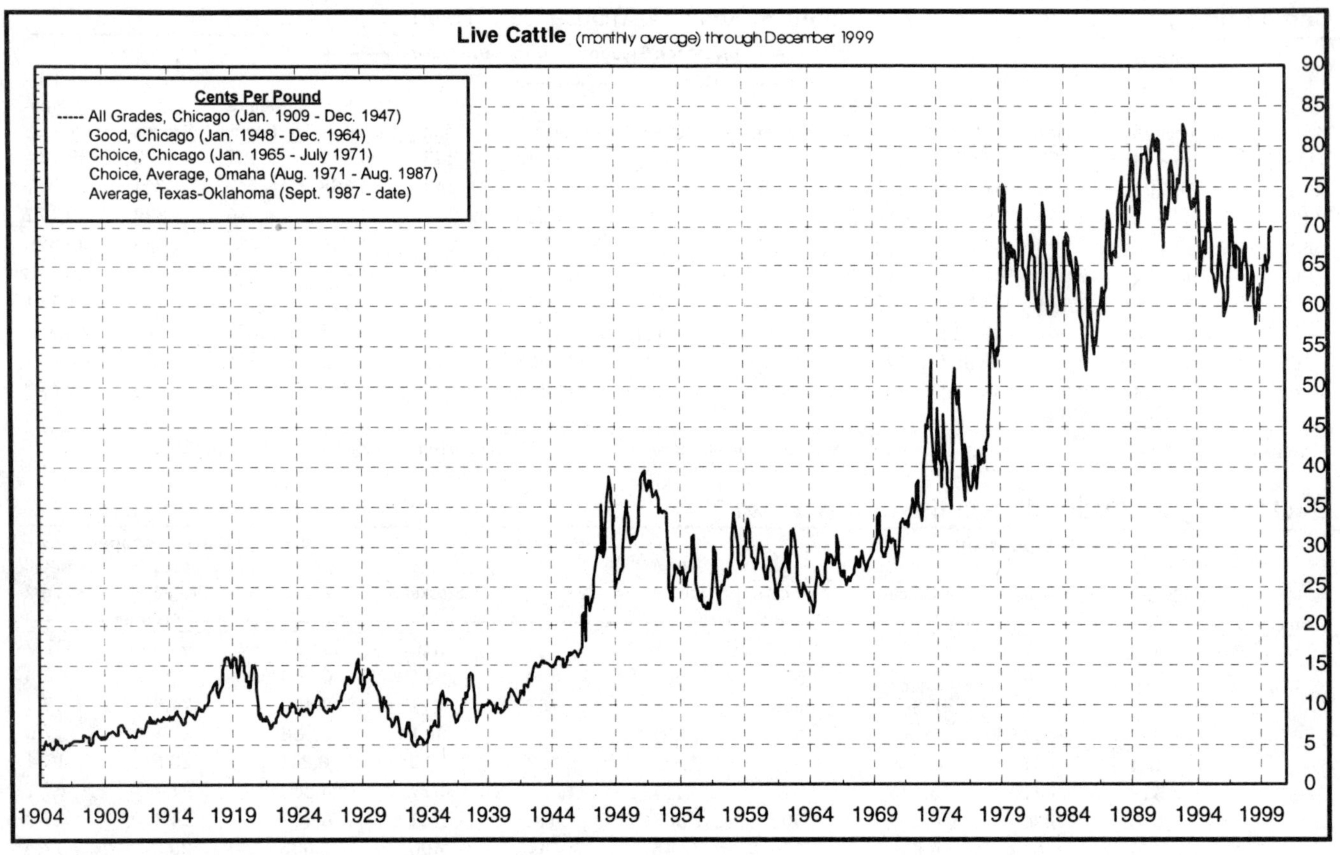

United States Cattle on Feed in 7 States, on First of Month In Thousands of Head

Year	Jan.	Feb.	Mar.	Apr.	May	June	July	Aug.	Sept.	Oct.	Nov.	Dec.
1990	8,378	8,526	8,319	8,483	8,181	7,867	7,310	6,998	6,975	7,635	8,669	9,039
1991	8,992	8,963	8,874	8,941	8,590	8,570	7,877	7,388	7,064	7,216	8,013	8,477
1992	8,397	8,223	8,195	8,058	7,868	7,876	7,377	7,050	7,018	7,565	8,704	8,984
1993	9,163	9,140	8,851	8,781	8,409	8,393	7,973	7,703	7,794	8,224	8,219	8,418
1994	8,256	8,139	7,981	7,960	7,772	7,511	6,910	6,841	6,949	7,295	7,988	8,198
1995	8,031	8,119	8,227	8,328	8,233	8,182	7,734	7,391	7,189	7,722	8,420	8,685
1996	8,667	8,304	8,152	8,286	7,758	7,253	6,578	6,337	6,612	7,486	8,534	9,003
1997	8,943	8,813	8,769	8,904	8,484	8,231	7,679	7,536	7,850	8,558	9,390	9,718
1998	9,455	9,180	8,835	8,607	8,295	8,289	7,825	7,706	7,750	8,376	9,195	9,409
1999[1]	9,021	8,907	8,868	8,889	8,573	8,537	8,173	7,879	8,175	8,783	9,769	10,000

[1] Preliminary. *Source: Economic Research Service, U.S. Department of Agriculture (ERS-USDA)*

United States Cattle Placed on Feedlots in 7 States In Thousands of Head

Year	Jan.	Feb.	Mar.	Apr.	May	June	July	Aug.	Sept.	Oct.	Nov.	Dec.	Total
1990	1,881	1,383	1,862	1,362	1,597	1,325	1,530	1,745	2,199	2,726	1,987	1,433	21,030
1991	1,721	1,455	1,703	1,427	1,772	1,102	1,327	1,459	1,826	2,539	1,917	1,456	19,704
1992	1,565	1,502	1,516	1,425	1,724	1,319	1,432	1,641	2,189	2,688	1,813	1,694	20,508
1993	1,641	1,262	1,626	1,326	1,801	1,430	1,513	1,865	2,148	2,494	1,610	1,215	19,931
1994	1,416	1,256	1,518	1,310	1,359	1,113	1,520	1,761	1,915	2,244	1,642	1,345	18,863
1995	1,631	1,532	1,681	1,403	1,673	1,356	1,404	1,653	2,173	2,278	1,804	1,446	20,353
1996	1,312	1,441	1,666	1,150	1,242	1,068	1,483	1,965	2,267	2,536	1,953	1,423	19,506
1997	1,663	1,552	1,694	1,296	1,612	1,224	1,751	2,111	2,278	2,454	1,826	1,304	20,765
1998	1,492	1,290	1,421	1,358	1,740	1,314	1,677	1,773	2,254	2,396	1,725	1,235	19,675
1999[1]	1,671	1,553	1,731	1,433	1,723	1,505	1,565	2,080	2,345	2,609	1,823	1,408	21,446

[1] Preliminary. *Source: Economic Research Service, U.S. Department of Agriculture (ERS-USDA)*

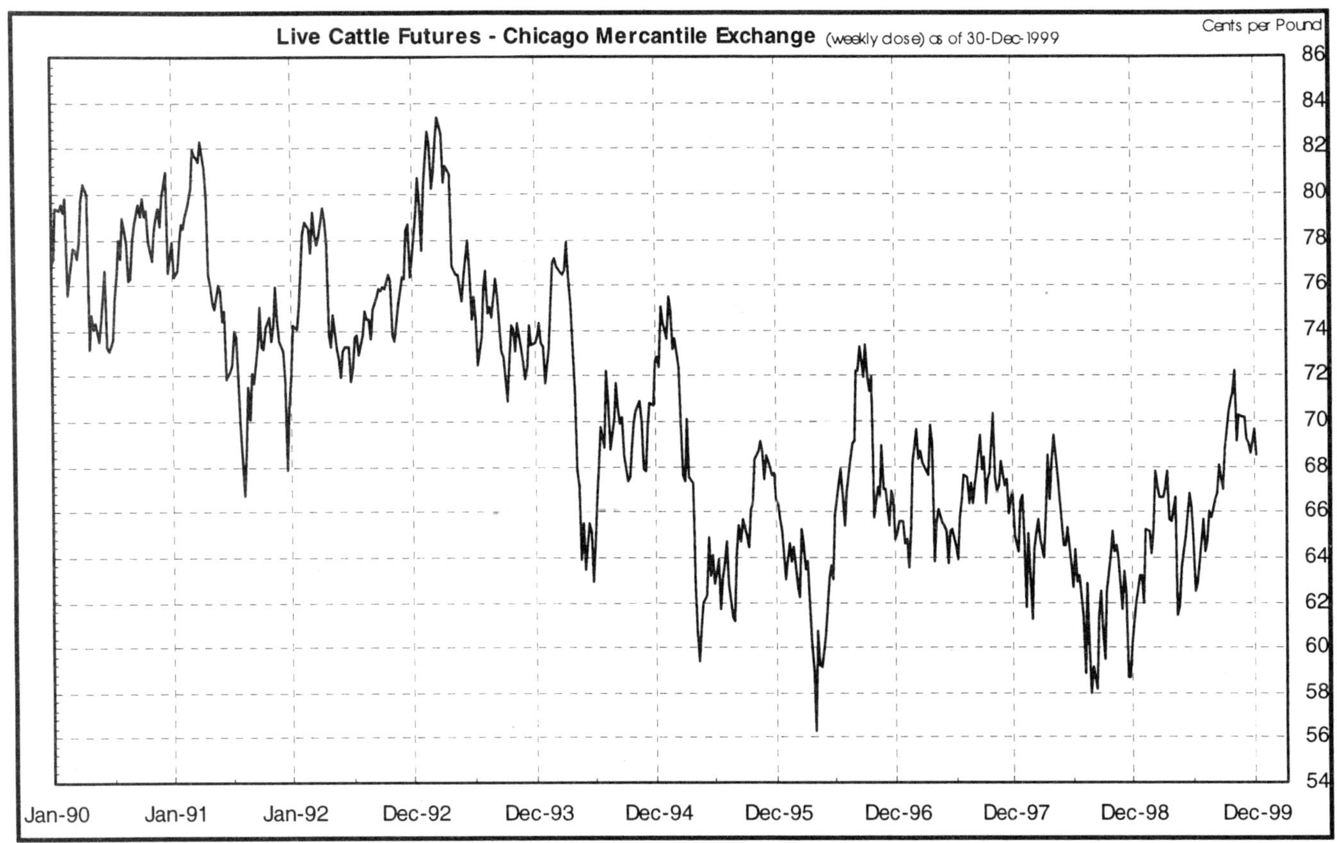

United States Cattle Marketings in 7 States In Thousands of Head

Year	Jan.	Feb.	Mar.	Apr.	May	June	July	Aug.	Sept.	Oct.	Nov.	Dec.	Total
1990	1,619	1,495	1,578	1,539	1,761	1,809	1,765	1,686	1,460	1,605	1,522	1,359	19,198
1991	1,632	1,431	1,499	1,650	1,651	1,681	1,724	1,716	1,598	1,665	1,376	1,443	19,066
1992	1,640	1,410	1,536	1,490	1,594	1,702	1,674	1,592	1,581	1,473	1,442	1,414	18,548
1993	1,534	1,441	1,585	1,572	1,681	1,743	1,702	1,692	1,652	1,546	1,322	1,305	18,775
1994	1,481	1,357	1,467	1,430	1,542	1,632	1,550	1,602	1,525	1,504	1,370	1,432	18,317
1995	1,484	1,372	1,513	1,437	1,667	1,754	1,698	1,815	1,594	1,529	1,478	1,412	19,038
1996	1,626	1,541	1,476	1,613	1,747	1,696	1,678	1,653	1,342	1,431	1,418	1,415	18,636
1997	1,728	1,554	1,497	1,648	1,785	1,732	1,852	1,755	1,528	1,545	1,429	1,499	19,552
1998	1,689	1,579	1,580	1,609	1,681	1,727	1,755	1,687	1,577	1,537	1,448	1,554	19,423
1999[1]	1,738	1,550	1,658	1,671	1,686	1,825	1,816	1,742	1,682	1,560	1,530	1,601	20,059

[1] Preliminary. *Source: Economic Research Service, U.S. Department of Agriculture (ERS-USDA)*

Quarterly Trade of Live Cattle in the United States In Head

	Imports					Exports				
Year	First Quarter	Second Quarter	Third Quarter	Fourth Quarter	Annual	First Quarter	Second Quarter	Third Quarter	Fourth Quarter	Annual
1990	566,516	577,328	301,668	689,488	2,135,000	33,929	28,384	23,335	34,266	119,914
1991	599,398	551,390	225,710	562,556	1,939,054	49,497	62,134	103,866	95,465	310,962
1992	599,255	505,568	389,417	801,025	2,255,265	97,683	100,282	74,827	48,998	321,790
1993	672,447	635,341	469,439	721,819	2,499,046	50,733	33,286	22,049	47,348	153,416
1994	569,466	540,845	386,596	585,597	2,082,504	51,803	43,115	62,729	73,144	230,791
1995	868,694	804,686	488,515	624,350	2,786,245	26,597	18,441	19,794	29,716	94,548
1996	605,648	467,059	391,633	501,108	1,965,448	33,906	42,796	42,757	54,848	174,307
1997	494,637	500,052	423,838	627,825	2,046,352	63,217	58,153	81,095	79,879	282,344
1998	538,018	503,547	373,451	618,993	2,034,009	69,824	63,459	53,145	98,781	285,209
1999[1]	549,847	424,182	313,211	608,385	1,895,625	51,830	59,195	47,049	240,798	398,872

[1] Preliminary. *Source: Economic Research Service, U.S. Department of Agriculture (ERS-USDA)*

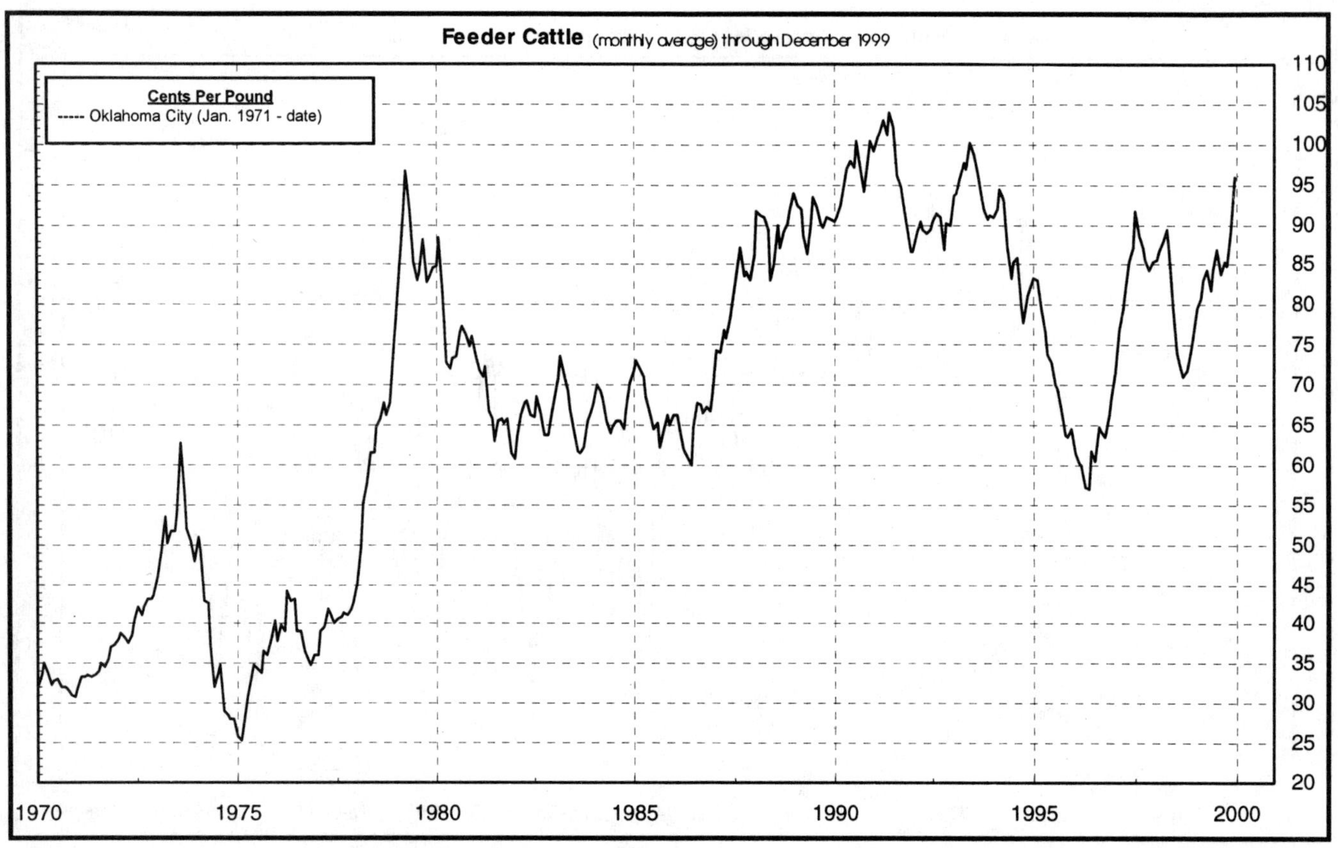

Average Slaughter Steer Price, Choice 2-4, Texas, 1100-1300 Lb. In Dollars Per 100 Pounds

Year	Jan.	Feb.	Mar.	Apr.	May	June	July	Aug.	Sept.	Oct.	Nov.	Dec.	Average
1993	80.05	80.91	82.66	81.78	80.84	77.31	74.32	75.09	73.46	72.13	73.23	72.42	77.02
1994	72.88	73.03	75.41	75.48	68.12	63.60	66.58	68.04	66.79	66.51	69.43	69.35	69.60
1995	73.60	73.79	70.64	67.54	64.27	63.08	61.81	61.95	63.80	64.89	67.94	66.14	66.62
1996	64.63	63.00	61.77	59.85	59.78	61.37	64.07	67.15	71.12	70.95	70.70	66.25	65.05
1997	65.07	65.35	67.44	67.66	67.36	63.53	63.80	65.19	66.04	66.93	67.66	65.91	66.00
1998	64.57	60.77	64.52	65.00	64.52	63.85	60.28	60.00	57.93	61.54	62.23	59.97	62.10
1999	61.46	63.17	64.75	65.34	65.00	66.15	64.51	65.29	66.05	69.63	70.28	69.00	65.89

Source: Economic Research Service, U.S. Department of Agriculture (ERS-USDA)

Average Price of Steers (Feeder) in Oklahoma City In Dollars Per 100 Pounds

Year	Jan.	Feb.	Mar.	Apr.	May	June	July	Aug.	Sept.	Oct.	Nov.	Dec.	Average
1993	93.59	93.80	95.82	97.65	96.85	100.09	98.58	96.48	94.78	91.82	90.57	91.04	95.09
1994	90.90	91.88	94.34	93.18	87.21	83.45	85.48	85.97	79.77	77.88	80.99	82.58	86.14
1995	83.41	83.05	79.50	76.62	73.69	72.89	70.09	69.62	66.71	68.60	63.45	64.44	72.67
1996	61.38	60.16	60.03	57.20	57.06	61.66	60.56	64.79	64.33	63.45	66.33	68.26	62.10
1997	71.52	76.77	79.66	81.60	85.43	87.04	91.67	88.69	87.23	85.66	84.37	85.25	83.74
1998	85.58	86.53	87.87	89.46	86.84	79.54	74.13	72.72	71.13	71.85	74.24	75.71	79.63
1999	79.49	80.92	83.21	84.44	81.80	84.37	86.80	83.84	85.24	84.75	89.13	95.92	84.99

Source: The Wall Street Journal

Federally Inspected Slaughter of Cattle in the United States In Thousands of Head

Year	Jan.	Feb.	Mar.	Apr.	May	June	July	Aug.	Sept.	Oct.	Nov.	Dec.	Total
1993	2,601	2,411	2,712	2,623	2,720	2,957	2,811	2,883	2,810	2,729	2,632	2,706	32,593
1994	2,679	2,501	2,799	2,656	2,780	2,984	2,770	3,001	2,885	2,878	2,744	2,806	33,483
1995	2,802	2,524	2,890	2,591	3,064	3,187	2,878	3,160	3,019	2,982	2,897	2,741	34,735
1996	3,046	2,855	2,834	3,039	3,257	3,078	3,080	3,148	2,693	3,074	2,801	2,800	35,721
1997	3,169	2,726	2,795	2,998	3,125	3,003	3,127	3,050	2,909	3,156	2,698	2,811	35,567
1998	2,977	2,691	2,838	2,872	2,906	3,050	2,987	2,987	2,938	2,991	2,717	2,834	34,787
1999[1]	2,904	2,665	2,990	2,916	2,947	3,154	3,037	3,099	3,045	3,033	2,882	2,814	35,486

[1] Preliminary. *Source: National Agricultural Statistics Board, U.S. Department of Agriculture (NASS-USDA)*

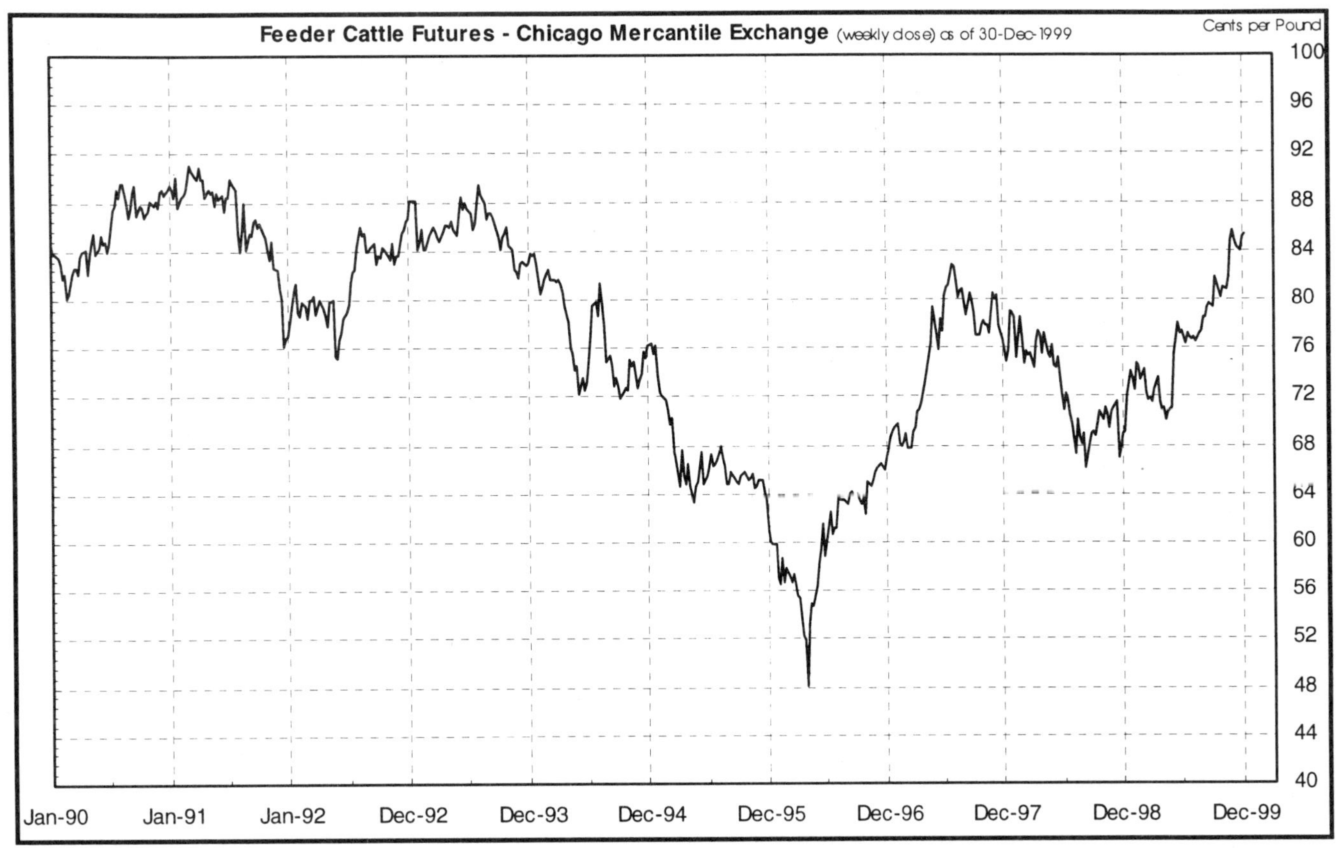

Average Open Interest of Live Cattle Futures in Chicago In Contracts

Year	Jan.	Feb.	Mar.	Apr.	May	June	July	Aug.	Sept.	Oct.	Nov.	Dec.
1990	95,515	108,149	104,647	95,709	86,875	76,130	70,462	68,375	69,611	67,122	70,576	69,647
1991	74,392	79,695	84,574	83,322	78,284	70,107	67,868	68,359	74,483	70,395	75,788	74,687
1992	79,638	97,500	97,222	90,823	83,112	68,135	67,828	62,656	61,783	60,761	63,945	67,125
1993	78,481	79,256	88,113	78,144	72,183	68,287	66,617	66,560	70,275	70,559	73,571	76,042
1994	87,923	87,578	83,949	70,287	72,851	75,470	76,663	72,988	73,391	67,924	74,152	68,600
1995	80,306	78,793	76,821	64,763	61,460	56,783	58,077	55,511	58,319	62,222	69,495	69,065
1996	72,870	83,064	91,348	97,315	97,911	96,320	96,547	93,557	92,804	88,467	88,062	87,305
1997	97,014	103,437	108,157	98,354	99,640	96,279	99,042	98,590	94,137	93,579	100,368	102,741
1998	105,559	102,036	101,264	88,257	88,167	87,493	86,776	86,874	95,013	102,636	108,263	106,156
1999	115,254	115,283	115,410	104,482	103,290	101,078	96,842	101,858	122,501	123,466	126,040	120,204

Source: Chicago Mercantile Exchange (CME)

Volume of Trading of Live Cattle Futures Chicago In Thousands of Contracts

Year	Jan.	Feb.	Mar.	Apr.	May	June	July	Aug.	Sept.	Oct.	Nov.	Dec.	Total
1990	400.5	350.0	354.1	327.6	372.2	263.9	298.5	327.7	273.3	320.3	268.4	240.8	3,797.4
1991	344.2	252.1	288.9	300.4	247.2	254.8	311.2	406.1	321.2	386.3	327.7	352.8	3,792.9
1992	375.6	322.5	353.8	319.1	275.9	263.9	268.9	231.0	196.0	227.9	203.8	246.7	3,319.6
1993	328.8	294.2	363.4	263.5	199.7	255.4	269.3	226.0	269.5	297.6	248.4	291.1	3,307.0
1994	280.8	291.8	262.4	264.2	372.9	363.9	318.2	317.1	270.0	308.9	275.9	254.6	3,580.9
1995	289.7	259.2	391.7	287.2	285.7	290.2	245.3	266.8	233.4	220.1	246.7	241.1	3,257.1
1996	312.0	275.4	333.2	457.5	385.9	303.1	319.8	299.5	278.1	339.4	312.6	309.7	3,926.2
1997	361.6	352.2	312.1	331.9	285.9	303.4	387.5	324.9	316.8	374.6	238.0	330.6	3,919.6
1998	355.7	400.2	327.2	400.6	296.7	321.4	334.4	369.6	370.3	373.2	318.2	349.1	4,216.5
1999	298.8	342.6	338.1	320.5	296.5	342.9	287.6	266.5	371.7	345.3	376.0	253.2	3,839.5

Source: Chicago Mercantile Exchange (CME)

CATTLE AND CALVES

Beef Steer-Corn Price Ratio in the United States

Year	Jan.	Feb.	Mar.	Apr.	May	June	July	Aug.	Sept.	Oct.	Nov.	Dec.	Average
1992	30.3	31.0	30.7	30.8	30.2	29.8	31.7	34.7	35.0	37.3	38.2	38.7	33.2
1993	38.8	39.8	38.8	37.8	37.8	37.1	33.8	33.4	33.7	31.8	29.8	27.0	35.0
1994	27.1	26.3	27.5	28.5	26.8	24.0	28.4	31.6	30.2	32.1	34.4	31.9	29.1
1995	32.6	32.4	30.5	28.4	26.3	25.2	23.5	23.5	23.0	22.3	22.7	21.1	26.0
1996	20.3	18.1	17.2	15.1	13.9	14.2	14.0	15.0	19.1	23.6	25.8	24.9	18.4
1997	24.2	24.6	24.3	24.3	25.4	25.4	27.0	26.6	25.2	26.5	27.1	26.5	25.6
1998	25.8	24.8	25.2	27.5	28.3	28.3	27.9	31.6	32.2	32.1	32.3	30.2	28.9
1999[2]	30.2	31.0	31.8	32.2	32.6	33.9	37.5	37.8	38.3	41.5	41.7	38.9	35.6

[1] Bushels of corn equal in value to 100 pounds of steers and heifers. [2] Preliminary. *Source: Economic Research Service, U.S. Department of Agriculture*

Farm Value, Income and Wholesale Prices of Cattle and Calves in the United States

	January 1		Gross Income From C & C[2]	At Ohama[3] Steers[3]		At Ohama[3] Heifers		Feeder Heifers at Oklahoma City[5]	Cows, Boning Utility Sioux Falls[6]	Cows, Commercial Sioux Falls	Wholesale Prices, Central U.S.		
Year	Per Head Dollars	Total Million $	Million $	Choice	Select	Select	Choice	Dollars per 100 Pounds			Choice 700-850 lb.	Select 700-850 lb.	Cow[6], Canner[7]
1992	630	61,451	37,680	75.17	73.65	72.88	74.95	78.41	44.84	51.22	116.02	111.66	93.85
1993	649	64,436	39,750	76.23	74.09	73.77	76.01	82.79	47.52	56.47	117.71	113.53	95.43
1994	659	66,513	36,744	67.60	66.33	66.14	67.93	74.55	42.51	48.28	106.73	102.08	84.39
1995	615	63,185	34,310	65.64	63.94	63.69	65.46	64.43	35.58	39.03	106.09	98.45	68.67
1996	503	52,056	31,377	74.50	61.83	61.22	64.18	57.21	30.45	33.70	102.01	95.70	58.16
1997	525	53,383	36,414	65.92	63.85	63.36	65.66	70.48	35.00	37.13	102.38	96.96	65.39
1998[1]	603	60,193	NA	60.07	56.17	55.17	59.23	NA	NA	NA	NA	NA	NA

[1] Preliminary. [2] Excludes interfarm sales & Gov't. payments. Cash receipts from farm marketings + value of farm home consumption. [3] 1,000 to 1,100 lb. [4] 1,000 to 1,200 lb. [5] 1992 to date are 700 to 750 lb., 1987 thru 1991 are 600 to 700 lb. [6] All weights. [7] & Cutter.
Source: Economic Research Service, U.S. Department of Agriculture (NASS-USDA)

Average Price Received by Farmers for Beef Cattle in the United States   In Dollars Per 100 Pounds

Year	Jan.	Feb.	Mar.	Apr.	May	June	July	Aug.	Sept.	Oct.	Nov.	Dec.	Average
1992	68.90	72.50	72.80	72.60	71.90	70.20	70.60	71.80	71.80	71.80	70.20	70.80	71.30
1993	75.10	75.80	77.20	77.30	77.10	74.50	72.50	72.70	71.40	69.10	69.30	68.50	73.40
1994	69.90	70.10	72.30	72.00	67.20	62.70	62.90	65.90	63.50	62.90	64.40	64.40	66.50
1995	67.50	68.70	66.90	63.80	60.80	60.90	59.50	59.40	59.10	58.80	60.70	60.60	62.20
1996	59.10	57.90	56.80	54.90	54.70	56.40	59.10	61.30	63.80	63.30	63.40	61.00	59.30
1997	61.40	61.90	64.80	64.80	65.10	62.30	62.80	63.90	63.60	63.30	63.30	62.90	63.30
1998	62.50	60.40	61.30	63.00	63.00	61.80	58.40	57.40	56.10	58.00	58.10	56.80	59.70
1999[1]	59.00	60.60	62.40	62.70	62.10	63.70	62.60	63.50	63.80	66.20	66.20	66.60	63.28

[1] Preliminary. *Source: National Agricultural Statistics Service, U.S. Department of Agriculture (NASS-USDA)*

Average Price Received by Farmers for Calves in the United States   In Dollars Per 100 Pounds

Year	Jan.	Feb.	Mar.	Apr.	May	June	July	Aug.	Sept.	Oct.	Nov.	Dec.	Average
1992	88.30	92.80	94.10	92.00	89.60	88.50	90.10	90.40	87.40	86.00	86.50	87.00	89.40
1993	94.70	96.00	98.60	99.60	99.20	99.10	96.90	95.10	93.50	93.90	91.60	92.80	95.90
1994	93.90	94.90	97.60	95.80	89.40	84.80	83.80	84.40	80.00	78.20	81.00	81.90	87.10
1995	85.00	86.90	84.40	81.80	77.00	76.90	72.00	70.90	68.50	66.20	64.00	63.30	74.70
1996	61.80	60.20	59.40	55.10	54.40	55.10	56.80	59.30	61.00	60.10	61.20	61.80	58.90
1997	68.10	74.90	80.00	82.20	84.30	85.40	86.90	88.00	86.90	84.30	82.90	83.30	82.30
1998	86.60	88.70	89.80	90.80	88.90	81.70	76.60	76.90	74.10	75.70	77.50	80.20	82.30
1999[1]	83.20	86.90	87.30	88.20	87.60	89.00	89.20	89.60	90.90	91.90	93.00	98.60	89.62

[1] Preliminary. *Source: National Agricultural Statistics Board, U.S. Department of Agriculture (NASS-USDA)*

Federally Inspected Slaughter of Calves and Vealers in the United States   In Thousands of Head

Year	Jan.	Feb.	Mar.	Apr.	May	June	July	Aug.	Sept.	Oct.	Nov.	Dec.	Total
1992	128	111	120	108	103	105	106	107	107	111	109	121	1,328
1993	101	97	116	96	82	91	90	95	94	94	101	103	1,159
1994	99	94	112	92	90	98	93	106	106	112	114	121	1,237
1995	121	104	118	96	114	115	111	121	119	124	125	125	1,393
1996	140	140	141	128	133	131	156	153	146	159	139	149	1,715
1997	143	122	128	126	114	115	131	123	133	137	121	142	1,534
1998	125	111	125	107	99	115	131	122	132	121	109	127	1,422
1999[1]	103	98	115	95	87	102	109	115	117	102	100	110	1,252

[1] Preliminary. *Source: Crop Reporting Board, U.S. Department of Agriculture (CRB-USDA)*

Cement

The U.S. Geological Survey reported that 1998 world production of cement was estimated at 1.5 billion tonnes. That was down slightly from the 1997 output of 1.52 billion tonnes.

By far the largest producer of cement is China with 1998 production estimated at 495 million metric tonnes, up very slightly from 1997. The next largest producer was Japan with cement production of 91 million tonnes, down 1 percent from the previous year. The third largest producer was the U.S. with output of 87.2 million tonnes, an increase of 3 percent from 1997. India is another large cement producer with 1998 production estimated at 85 million tonnes, an increase of 6 percent from 1997. Other large producers include South Korea, Germany, Turkey, Thailand and Italy.

World clinker cement production capacity at the end of 1998 was estimated at 1.5 billion tonnes. Clinker is the main intermediate product in cement manufacture. One trend in the cement market is the increasing use worldwide of natural and synthetic pozzolans as partial or complete replacements for Portland cement. Pozzolans are materials which, in the presence of free lime, have properties similar to hydraulic cement. Pozzolan materials include certain volcanic rocks and industrial by-products like fly ash. Pozzolans have seen increased use because they are less energy-intensive to produce than clinker.

The use of cement in the U.S. is largely related to developments in the construction industry. The 1998 construction market in the U.S. was strong leading to record consumption levels for cement. With transportation spending expected to increase, the outlook for still higher levels of cement use is bright.

U.S. shipments of Portland and blended cement in July 1999 were 10.2 million tonnes. In the January-July 1999 period, shipments were 59.2 million tonnes. Shipments of prepared masonry cement in July 1999 were 392,358 tonnes, with the total shipments over the first seven months of 1999 being 2.5 million tonnes. U.S. shipments of finished Portland cement in July 1999 were 9.97 million tonnes and the January-July total was 58.6 million tonnes.

Clinker production in July 1999 was 6.55 million tonnes. In January-July 1999, total clinker production was 43.3 million tonnes. U.S. imports of clinker in June 1999 were 542,474 tonnes. In the first half of 1999, clinker imports were 2.03 million tonnes. The major supplier of clinker to the U.S. was Thailand followed by Canada, Australia and Greece.

World Production of Hydraulic Cement In Thousands of Short Tons

Year	Brazil	China	France	Germany	India	Italy	Japan	Rep. of Korea	Russia	Spain	Turkey	United States	World Total
1992	23,903	308,220	21,165	37,529	50,000	41,347	88,253	44,444	61,700	24,615	28,607	70,883	1,239,683
1993	24,843	367,880	20,464	36,649	53,812	33,771	88,046	47,313	49,900	22,878	31,241	75,117	1,290,905
1994	25,230	421,180	21,296	36,130	57,000	32,713	91,624	50,730	37,200	25,150	29,493	79,353	1,370,000
1995	28,256	475,910	19,692	33,302	62,000	33,715	90,474	55,130	36,500	26,423	33,153	78,320	1,444,000
1996	34,597	491,190	19,514	31,533	75,000	33,327	94,492	58,434	27,800	25,157	35,214	80,818	1,493,000
1997[1]	38,069	511,730	19,780	35,945	80,000	33,721	91,938	60,317	26,700	27,632	36,035	84,255	1,540,000
1998[2]	43,000	513,500	19,500	36,610	85,000	35,000	81,328	46,791	26,000	27,943	38,200	85,522	1,519,000

[1] Preliminary. [2] Estimate. *Source: U.S. Geological Survey (USGS)*

Salient Statistics of Cement in the United States

Year	Net Import Reliance as a % of Apparent Consumption	Production: Portland	Production: Others[3]	Production: Total	Capacity Used at (Portland Mills) %	Shipments From Mills: Total Mil. Tons	Shipments From Mills: Value[4] Mil. $	Average Value (F.O.B. Mill) $ per ton	Stocks at Mills Dec. 31	Exports	Apparent Consumption	Imports for Consumption[5] by Country: Canada	Japan	Mexico	Spain	Total
		Thousand Tons							Million Tons			Thousands of Short Tons				
1992	6	66,841	2,744	69,585	76.0	69,203	3,779	54.61	5,272	746	74,158	2,997	278	825	446	6,166
1993	7	70,845	2,962	73,807	79.1	72,770	4,175	55.65	4,788	625	79,198	3,629	43	783	597	7,060
1994	10	74,335	3,613	77,948	82.3	79,087	4,845	61.26	4,701	633	86,476	4,268	14	640	1,342	11,303
1995	11	73,303	3,603	76,906	81.2	78,518	5,329	67.87	5,814	759	86,003	4,886	[6]	850	1,501	13,848
1996	12	75,797	3,469	79,266	83.4	83,963	5,952	71.19	5,488	803	90,355	5,351	[6]	1,272	1,595	14,154
1997[1]	14	78,948	3,634	82,582	84.7	90,490	6,622	73.49	5,784	791	96,018	5,350	-----	995	1,845	17,596
1998[2]	17	79,942	3,989	83,931	84.9	96,857	7,404	76.46	5,393	743	103,457	5,957	-----	1,280	2,204	24,085

[1] Preliminary. [2] Estimate. [3] Masonry, natural & pozzolan (slag-line). [4] Value received F.O.B. mill, excluding cost of containers. [5] Hydraulic & clinker cement for consumption. [6] Less than 1/2 unit. *Source: U.S. Geological Survey (USGS)*

Shipments of Finished Portland Cement from Mills in the United States In Thousands of Metric Tons

Year	Jan.	Feb.	Mar.	Apr.	May	June	July	Aug.	Sept.	Oct.	Nov.	Dec.	Total
1994	3,406.1	3,790.2	5,884.3	6,227.3	7,320.8	7,689.9	6,877.4	7,938.1	7,461.9	7,237.8	6,203.5	5,093.2	75,130.4
1995	3,685.2	3,959.7	5,556.6	5,668.6	6,720.6	7,336.8	6,748.1	7,660.9	7,177.0	7,736.3	6,238.3	4,667.7	73,155.6
1996	3,913.3	4,312.7	5,234.1	6,801.6	7,621.3	7,395.1	7,749.4	8,193.4	7,178.3	8,276.7	6,011.4	4,763.3	77,550.0
1997	4,111.3	4,487.1	5,739.1	7,009.5	7,489.3	7,733.7	8,132.4	7,909.2	8,186.1	8,678.9	6,108.6	5,471.9	81,064.3
1998	4,560.0	4,567.0	5,878.5	7,019.7	7,430.5	8,108.6	8,309.6	7,963.3	8,089.5	8,404.6	6,640.5	6,057.6	82,955.0
1999[1]	4,519.8	5,164.2	6,423.0	7,151.7	7,450.2	8,138.3	7,825.4	8,232.1	7,738.3	8,254.0	7,491.5		85,514.8

[1] Preliminary. *Source: U.S. Geological Survey (USGS)*

Cheese

World cheese production in 1999 reached a record high 12.4 million metric tonnes vs. 12.2 million in 1998 with U.S. production accounting for about 3.57 million and 3.40 million, respectively. France produces half the U.S. total to rank in second place globally.

World consumption of a record large 12 million tonnes in 1999 compares with 11.9 million in 1998, with the U.S. totals at 3.69 million and 3.35 million, respectively. France consumed about 2.3 million tons in both years.

Worldwide, the supply and demand for cheese has set new highs in each year of the 1990's. Most of the world's cheese is consumed where produced. However, record per capita cheese consumption in the U.S. of 13.4 kilograms in 1999 pales relative to Europe where usage tops 20.0 kg. in some countries, notably France and Greece.

World foreign trade of cheese is biased towards exports, nearly one million tonnes in 1999, marginally higher than in 1998. New Zealand was the single largest exporter in 1999 with 245,000 tonnes. Collectively, the European Union exported about half of the world total. U.S. exports are small, averaging 36,000 tonnes in 1997-99.

Total world imports hovered around 740,000 metric tonnes in both 1999 and 1998. Japan is the world's largest importer taking 185,000 metric tonnes in 1999. The U.S. runs a close second with 155,000 tonnes in 1999.

Ending 1999 world stocks of 1.86 million tonnes compares with 1.90 million a year earlier. Italy, as is typical, accounted for about 40 percent of the world total with 785,000 tonnes while the U.S. holds about 15 percent at 235,000 tonnes.

Cheese is a $10 billion plus a year industry in the U.S. and American cheese, mostly cheddar, accounts for the largest individual variety of U.S. production and consumption. However, in recent years, other varieties, mostly Italian, have had a combined production that exceeds American cheese. Per capita consumption of American cheese slipped during the 1990's to about 12 pounds while other cheese use has climbed to over 10 pounds. Mozzarella makes up the bulk of Italian cheese use.

Wholesale American cheese prices (40-pound blocks, Wisconsin) averaged about $1.58 per pound in 1998 with the highest prices seen near yearend and carrying into 1999, with new record highs reached in mid-1999.

Futures Markets

Cheddar cheese futures and options are traded on both the Coffee, Sugar & Cocoa Exchange, Inc. (CSCE) and the Chicago Mercantile Exchange (CME).

World Production of Cheese In Thousands of Metric Tons

Year	Argentina	Australia	Brazil	Canada	Denmark	France	Germany	Italy	Netherlands	New Zealand	United Kingdom	United States	World Total
1991	290	178	290	262	285	1,500	777	885	610	125	303	2,747	10,366
1992	310	197	296	262	290	1,489	783	890	634	142	324	2,943	10,931
1993	350	211	310	271	321	1,509	821	885	637	145	331	2,961	10,895
1994	385	234	330	282	286	1,541	855	913	648	192	326	3,054	11,194
1995	370	241	360	277	311	1,579	875	942	680	197	354	3,138	11,345
1996	390	268	385	289	298	1,594	947	950	688	230	364	3,274	11,702
1997	415	285	405	329	290	1,645	990	985	693	240	368	3,324	12,043
1998	407	305	421	330	289	1,648	1,008	1,003	638	266	357	3,403	12,225
1999[1]	425	312	434	333	288	1,665	1,015	1,005	630	245	370	3,595	12,465
2000[2]	425	335	445	336	290	1,650	1,015	1,005	625	285	370	3,690	12,630

[1] Preliminary. [2] Estimate. *Source: Foreign Agricultural Service, U.S. Department of Agriculture (FAS-USDA)*

Supply and Distribution of All Cheese in the United States In Millions of Pounds

	Supply					Cheese	Distribution						
	Production										Domestic Disappearance		
Year	Whole Milk[2]	All Cheese[3]	January 1 Commercial Stocks	Imports[4]	Total Supply	40-lb. Blocks Wisconsin Assembly Points cents/lb.	Exports & Shipments[6]	Gov't Dec. 31 Stocks	American Cheese Removed by USDA Programs	Total Disappearance	American Cheese Donated	Total	Per Capita
1989	2,674	5,615	398	279	6,255	138.79	74	6.6	37.4	5,959	67	5,885	23.81
1990	2,894	6,059	329	302	6,685	136.69	75	8.2	21.5	6,231	21	6,156	24.64
1991	2,769	6,055	458	301	6,806	124.41	72	23.1	76.9	6,393	60	6,321	25.01
1992	2,937	6,488	416	286	7,167	131.91	78	16.5	14.4	6,720	0	6,642	26.01
1993	2,957	6,528	470	321	7,303	131.52	87	2.2	8.3	6,853	0	6,766	26.24
1994	2,974	6,735	466	345	7,546	131.45	55	.9	6.9	7,094	0	6,994	26.82
1995	3,131	6,917	437	337	7,691	132.77	65	-----	6.1	7,279	0	7,174	27.30
1996	3,281	7,218	412	338	7,968	149.14	71	-----	4.6	7,478	0	7,364	27.70
1997	3,286	7,330	487	312	8,129	132.40	84	-----	11.3	7,646	0	7,510	28.00
1998[1]	3,326	7,502	480	344	8,326	158.10	82	-----			0	7,562	28.30

[1] Preliminary. [2] Whole milk American cheddar. [3] All types of cheese except cottage, pot and baker's cheese. [4] Imports for consumption. [5] Commercial. *Source: Economic Research Service, U.S. Department of Agriculture (ERS-USDA)*

Production of Cheese in the United States In Millions of Pounds

	American			Swiss,				Cream &				Total	Cottage Cheese		
Year	Whole Milk	Part Skim	Total	Including Block	Munster	Brick	Lim-burger	Neufchatel Cheese	Italian Varieties	Blue Mond	All Other Varieties	of All Cheese[2]	Lowfat	Curd[3]	Creamed[4]
1989	2,674	0.8	2,675	231.2	91.1	17.5	.9	401.0	2,042.9	34.6	121.2	5,615	300.9	526.9	572.3
1990	2,894	0.8	2,895	261.1	100.2	17.3	.8	430.8	2,207.0	36.4	110.7	6,059	301.8	493.5	530.6
1991	2,769	0.8	2,770	234.5	106.4	15.3	.7	446.7	2,328.6	34.3	118.5	6,055	321.1	490.9	497.9
1992	2,937	1.2	2,938	237.3	116.4	15.5	1.0	516.7	2,508.6	33.3	121.9	6,488	329.5	502.4	457.3
1993	2,957	3.7	2,961	231.4	117.5	12.5	.9	539.9	2,494.5	33.3	137.2	6,528	317.0	471.4	430.5
1994	2,974	24.7	2,999	221.2	113.6	12.2	.8	573.4	2,625.7	36.5	152.1	6,735	321.1	463.3	410.0
1995	3,131	24.0	3,155	221.7	109.1	10.4	.9	543.8	2,674.4	36.6	164.6	6,917	325.9	458.9	384.9
1996	3,281	NA	3,281	219.0	106.8	10.6	.7	574.7	2,812.4	38.3	106.7	7,218	329.9	448.3	360.4
1997	3,286	NA	3,286	207.6	100.2	8.5	.7	614.9	2,881.4	42.8	119.8	7,330	346.7	458.5	359.5
1998[1]	3,326	NA	3,326	206.4	94.6	7.6	.9	623.5	3,001.1	43.9	122.0	7,502	361.9	464.9	366.8

[1] Preliminary. [2] Excludes full-skim cheddar and cottage cheese. [3] Includes cottage, pot, and baker's cheese with a butterfat content of less than 4%. [4] Includes cheese with a butterfat content of 4 to 19 %. *Source: Economic Research Service, U.S. Department of Agriculture ERS-USDA)*

Wholesale Price of Cheese, 40-lb. Blocks, Wisconsin Assembly Points[2] In Cents Per Pound

Year	Jan.	Feb.	Mar.	Apr.	May	June	July	Aug.	Sept.	Oct.	Nov.	Dec.	Average
1990	152.3	131.6	130.7	140.5	145.8	149.5	151.0	150.3	142.6	114.9	112.0	112.7	136.2
1991	111.4	111.5	111.5	111.7	115.0	121.4	128.4	136.1	139.7	140.2	135.8	130.2	124.4
1992	125.4	119.0	119.8	131.9	140.0	141.3	141.8	142.0	136.9	132.4	129.4	123.2	131.9
1993	119.3	118.6	124.3	140.8	141.8	133.7	126.3	124.8	137.4	138.9	138.7	133.7	131.5
1994	132.2	134.2	140.0	143.3	125.7	120.2	129.1	132.2	135.6	135.4	127.9	121.3	131.5
1995	124.5	130.4	131.1	122.8	122.1	126.9	126.7	132.2	141.3	145.0	145.8	144.6	132.8
1996	139.3	139.3	140.9	145.1	151.8	151.5	158.2	167.6	145.5	162.3	133.9	126.0	146.8
1997	127.9	132.3	134.0	125.6	116.5	117.9	123.3	137.6	141.4	142.4	143.8	146.1	132.4
1998	144.5	144.7	138.8	129.7	123.0	151.3	162.6	166.9	171.0	183.5	188.7	192.5	158.1
1999[1]	162.4	131.5	134.0	133.6	124.8	138.1	159.7	189.0	167.3	134.0	117.3		144.7

[1] Preliminary. *Source: Economic Research Service, U.S. Department of Agriculture (ERS-USDA)*

Production[2] of Cheese in the United States In Millions of Pounds

Year	Jan.	Feb.	Mar.	Apr.	May	June	July	Aug.	Sept.	Oct.	Nov.	Dec.	Total
1990	483.7	471.9	531.7	521.1	542.8	522.8	502.2	495.0	472.6	505.9	495.5	522.1	6,061
1991	501.7	458.0	530.1	515.4	532.3	509.0	499.5	498.2	485.0	521.0	502.3	533.7	6,061
1992	514.1	497.1	542.7	534.7	550.9	549.8	541.8	534.6	528.3	558.2	547.5	571.6	6,488
1993	517.3	492.5	563.2	561.4	576.9	563.2	537.9	525.8	531.1	560.0	540.1	558.9	6,528
1994	538.3	505.8	591.8	554.3	590.4	558.7	550.7	562.4	565.5	574.5	559.3	578.3	6,730
1995	559.3	523.3	596.0	559.6	595.3	579.2	556.5	550.8	571.3	588.6	584.7	618.4	6,883
1996	590.0	576.0	625.4	606.0	636.5	595.8	582.2	589.5	584.5	612.2	595.5	623.9	7,218
1997	598.1	577.1	638.0	598.5	642.0	623.4	613.2	596.5	604.3	615.5	594.5	627.9	7,329
1998	617.4	574.1	646.6	639.1	652.6	642.1	610.1	598.6	584.1	632.1	636.6	668.5	7,502
1999[1]	638.7	600.2	691.7	673.0	676.2	672.8	653.0	651.3	638.4	673.8	679.6	698.2	7,947

[1] Preliminary. [2] Excludes cottage cheese. *Source: National Agricultural Statistics Service, U.S. Department of Agriculture (NASS-USDA)*

Cold Storage Holdings of All Varieties of Cheese in the United States, on First of Month Millions of Pounds

Year	Jan.	Feb.	Mar.	Apr.	May	June	July	Aug.	Sept.	Oct.	Nov.	Dec.
1990	328.0	358.4	374.9	395.8	413.4	441.6	465.0	484.6	475.7	459.9	445.4	437.3
1991	457.8	483.9	475.1	492.4	510.3	512.1	521.5	511.5	494.1	477.9	429.3	409.0
1992	415.4	440.9	445.9	449.0	449.7	455.9	465.2	496.2	487.3	449.7	441.1	462.0
1993	462.0	476.1	454.4	460.0	453.6	480.5	541.2	533.3	517.7	500.1	471.9	462.4
1994	465.2	495.2	473.6	473.3	487.9	513.4	521.4	506.3	474.7	453.0	448.3	434.2
1995	436.9	449.7	448.7	458.8	466.1	465.8	473.6	482.4	458.1	428.5	418.7	393.6
1996	412.1	441.3	466.4	490.9	525.5	541.8	542.8	536.6	506.9	495.8	494.6	480.2
1997	487.0	501.5	494.6	517.0	555.4	584.3	604.8	604.9	582.3	543.7	505.0	474.4
1998	480.4	509.3	521.5	533.1	557.6	568.5	583.7	595.8	576.8	553.0	522.7	494.5
1999[1]	517.2	499.7	543.8	552.1	623.5	676.7	734.9	750.3	697.6	652.7	621.0	591.7

Quantities are given in net weight. [1] Preliminary. *Source: National Agricultural Statistics Service, U.S. Department of Agriculture (NASS-USDA)*

Chromium

Chromite is the ore mineral of chromium. Chromium has a wide variety of uses in metals, chemicals and refractories. Chromium enhances hardenability, and resistance to corrosion and oxidation in iron, steel and nonferrous alloys. Two of its applications are the production of stainless steel and nonferrous alloys. It is also used in alloy steel, plating of metals, pigments, leather processing, surface treatments, catalysts and refractories.

According to the U.S. Geological Survey, the U.S. consumes about 13 percent of world chromite ore production in various forms of imported materials (chromite ore, chromium ferroalloys, chromium metal and chromium chemicals). In the U.S., imported chromite was consumed by two chemical firms, one metallurgical firm and four refractory firms. It was also used in the production of chromium chemicals, chromium ferroalloys and chromite-containing refractories. Consumption of chromium ferroalloys and metal by end uses was: stainless and heat-resisting steel, 76 percent; full-alloy steel, 8 percent; superalloys, 2 percent; and others, 14 percent.

World mine production of chromium in 1998 was estimated at 12.6 million metric tonnes (contained chromium), an increase of 100,000 tonnes from 1997. The world's largest producer of chromium was South Africa with 6 million tonnes, an increase of 4 percent from 1997. The next largest producer was Turkey with 1.7 million tonnes, down 3 percent from 1997. Other large producers include India, Kazakhstan and Zimbabwe. World reserves of chromium are estimated at 3.7 billion tonnes. South African reserves represent 81 percent of this total.

U.S. stainless steel production in the January-July 1999 period was 539,000 tonnes. For all of 1998, production was 1.98 million tonnes. U.S. stainless steel scrap receipts in the January-July 1999 period were 413,000 tonnes compared to 612,000 tonnes for all of 1998. Stainless steel scrap consumption in the same period of 1999 was 685,000 tonnes while for all of 1998 it was 1.04 million tonnes. U.S. imports for consumption of chromite ore in the first seven months of 1999 were 162,000 tonnes. Imports of high-carbon ferrochromium were 368,000 tonnes. Medium-carbon ferrochromium imports were 3,000 tonnes while low-carbon ferrochromium imports were 25,600 tonnes. Ferrochromium silicon imports were 18,400 tonnes. Total ferroalloy imports in the first seven months of 1999 were 415,000 tonnes. For all of 1998 they were 441,000 tonnes.

Imports of chromium metal over the first seven months of 1999 were 5,550 tonnes. Imports of stainless steel were 516,000 tonnes in the same period while stainless steel scrap imports were 23,000 tonnes. Consumption of ferroalloys and metal were 238,000 tonnes. For all of 1998 they were 434,000 tonnes.

The U.S. Government stockpile of chromite ore in August 1999 was 851,000 tonnes, the same as in July. The stockpile of chromium ferroalloys was 973,000 tonnes while the stockpile of chromium metal was 7,720 tonnes.

World Mine Production of Chromite In Thousands of Metric Tons (Gross Weight)

Year	Albania	Brazil	Cuba	Finland	India	Iran	Kazakhstan[3]	Madagascar	Philippines	South Africa	Turkey	Zimbabwe	World Total
1989	900	476	51	513	1,003	73	3,800	63	217	4,951	1,077	627	14,006
1990	950	263	50	504	1,050	77	3,800	151	183	4,620	836	573	13,200
1991	587	340	50	473	940	90	3,800	149	191	5,100	940	564	13,300
1992	322	449	50	499	1,082	130	3,500	161	66	3,363	759	522	11,100
1993	115	308	15	511	1,000	124	2,900	144	62	2,838	767	252	9,300
1994	118	360	20	573	909	354	2,020	90	76	3,599	1,270	517	10,200
1995	160	448	31	598	1,536	371	2,871	106	111	5,085	2,080	707	14,500
1996	143	408	37	574	1,363	250	1,190	137	78	4,971	1,279	697	11,500
1997[1]	106	330	44	611	1,363	200	1,000	140	88	5,779	1,750	680	12,500
1998[2]	NA	300	NA	600	1,400	200	1,000	NA	NA	6,000	1,700	670	12,600

[1] Preliminary. [2] Estimate. [3] Formerly part of the U.S.S.R.; data not reported separately unitl 1992. *Source: U.S. Geological Survey (USGS)*

Salient Statistics of Chromite in the United States In Thousands of Metric Tons (Gross Weight)

Year	Net Import Reliance as a % of Apparent Consumption	Production of Ferrochromium	Exports	Imports for Consumption	Reexports	Consumption by - Primary Conumer Groups - Total	Metallurgical & Chemical	Refractory	-- Consumer Stocks, Dec. 31 -- Metallurgical & Chemical	Refractory	Total Stocks	- $ per Metric Ton - South Africa[3]	Turkish[4]
1989	78	147	40	525	2	561	517	44	368	24	392	65	185
1990	79	109	6	347	4	405	361	44	333	21	355	55	135
1991	73	68	9	310	-----	375	339	36	310	11	321	50	130
1992	73	61	7	324	-----	362	335	27	308	13	321	60	110
1993	81	63	10	329	2	337	314	23	259	16	275	60	110
1994	75	67	33	273	-----	322	302	20	250	17	266	60	110
1995	80	73	27	416	-----	W	W	W	194	11	205	80	230
1996	79	37	51	362	-----	W	W	W	165	8	173	80	230
1997[1]	75	61	30	303	-----	W	W	W	167	8	175	75	150
1998[2]	79	W	57	358	-----	W	W	W	W	W	159	68	145

[1] Preliminary. [2] Estimate. [3] Cr_2O_3, 44% (Transvaal). [4] 48% Cr_2O_3. W = Withheld. *Source: U.S. Geological Survey (USGS)*

Coal

U.S. production of coal in the January-March 1999 period was 282.2 million short tons. For all of 1998, production was 1.12 billion tons. In the first quarter of 1999, coal production east of the Mississippi River was 140.8 million tons, while production west of the Mississippi River was 141.5 million tons. In the first quarter of 1999, the largest producing state was Wyoming with 83.6 million tons. The next largest producing state was West Virginia with 42.7 million tons. Production in Kentucky was 36.8 million tons with Pennsylvania producing 20.1 million tons.

U.S. exports of coal in the first quarter of 1999 were 13 million tons, down 30 percent from a year ago. The major market for U.S. coal is Canada with exports in the January-March 1999 period of 1.88 million tons, down 19 percent from a year ago. Exports to Japan were 1.39 million tons, down 44 percent from a year ago. Shipments to the Netherlands were 1.32 million tons, up 13 percent from the previous year. Other markets for U.S. coal were the United Kingdom, Brazil, Italy and Spain.

U.S. imports of coal in the first quarter 1999 were 2.25 million tons, up 22 percent from a year ago. The major supplier of coal to the U.S. was Colombia with 1.2 million tons. The next largest supplier was Venezuela with 514,409 tons.

U.S. coal consumption in first quarter 1999 was 243.4 million tons. Electric utilities used 217.2 million tons, coke plants took almost 7 million tons, other industrial plants used 17.5 million tons while residential and commercial users took 1.9 million tons.

World Production)[3] of Coal (Monthly Average) In Thousands of Metric Tons

Year	Australia	Canada	China	Czech-Rep.[4]	Germany	India	Indonesia	Kazakhstan[5]	Poland	Russia[5]	Ukraine[5]	United Kingdom	United States
1990	13,236	3,139	90,000	1,842	6,363	16,819	611	-----	12,306	39,300	-----	7,442	71,137
1991	13,720	3,326	88,212	1,623	6,063	18,905	1,143	-----	11,698	33,769	-----	8,028	68,755
1992	14,594	2,693	91,278	1,532	6,013	19,490	1,760	10,546	10,960	16,123	-----	7,273	75,413
1993	14,746	2,943	96,177	1,532	5,347	20,503	2,300	9,323	10,873	16,200	9,545	5,683	71,473
1994	14,721	3,664	100,508	1,451	4,802	20,974	2,603	8,298	11,136	14,730	7,650	3,976	78,102
1995	15,921	3,215	107,624	1,432	4,905	22,131	3,460	6,626	11,347	14,743	6,717	4,282	86,081
1996	16,154	3,359	116,117	1,377	4,428	23,782	3,945	6,086	11,425	13,875	5,852	4,109	88,574
1997	20,200	3,435	113,523	1,339	4,267	24,688	4,352	6,268	11,496	13,317	6,412	4,041	82,398
1998[1]	20,677	3,274	94,806	1,343	3,776	24,805	5,027	5,672	9,698	12,779	6,431	3,439	83,897
1999[2]	24,486	NA	74,776	NA	3,678	24,506	4,044	4,175	9,340	13,784	6,737	3,214	83,429

[1] Preliminary. [2] Estimate. [3] All grades of anthracite and bituminous coal, but excludes recovered slurries, lignite and brown coal. [4] Formerly part of Czechoslovakia; data not reported separately until 1993. [5] Formerly part of the U.S.S.R.; data not reported separately until 1992. NA = Not avaliable. *Source: United Nations*

Production of Bituminous & Lignite Coal in the United States In Thousands of Short Tons

Year	Alabama	Colorado	Illinois	Indiana	Kentucky	Montana	Ohio	Pennsylvania	Texas	Virginia	West Virginia	Wyoming	Total
1990	29,030	18,910	60,393	35,907	128,396	37,616	35,252	67,008	55,755	46,917	169,205	184,249	1,029,076
1991	27,269	17,834	60,258	31,468	158,980	38,237	30,569	61,936	53,825	41,954	167,352	193,854	995,984
1992	25,796	19,226	59,857	30,466	161,068	38,889	30,403	65,498	55,071	43,024	162,164	190,172	997,545
1993	24,768	21,886	41,098	29,295	156,299	35,917	28,816	55,394	54,567	39,317	130,525	210,129	945,424
1994	23,266	25,304	52,797	30,927	161,642	41,640	29,897	62,237	52,346	37,129	161,776	237,092	1,033,504
1995	24,640	25,710	48,180	26,007	153,739	39,451	26,118	61,576	52,684	34,099	162,997	263,822	1,032,974
1996	24,637	24,886	46,656	29,670	152,425	37,891	28,572	67,942	55,164	35,590	170,433	278,440	1,063,856
1997	24,468	27,449	41,159	35,497	155,853	41,005	29,154	76,198	53,328	35,837	173,743	281,881	1,089,932
1998[1]	23,224	30,025	38,182	36,297	145,609	42,092	28,600	76,519	53,578	34,059	175,794	313,983	1,109,768
1999[2]	19,777	28,596	39,907	35,257	141,112	40,573	23,456	77,009	52,917	32,297	159,372	334,756	1,099,120

[1] Preliminary. [2] Estimate. *Source: Energy Information Administration, U.S. Department of Energy (EIA-DOE)*

Production[2] of Bituminous Coal in the United States In Thousands of Short Tons

Year	Jan.	Feb.	Mar.	Apr.	May	June	July	Aug.	Sept.	Oct.	Nov.	Dec.	Total
1990	90,304	81,796	91,357	83,350	86,615	84,720	79,585	91,558	83,107	93,418	86,772	75,676	1,028,258
1991	85,810	82,592	85,012	79,324	79,917	76,896	79,745	88,851	81,533	90,307	81,730	79,383	991,100
1992	87,979	82,102	85,835	82,364	80,197	79,968	80,768	84,401	83,555	86,265	80,240	83,021	996,695
1993	80,508	76,341	84,782	79,329	73,759	80,949	70,771	76,209	79,705	80,628	79,404	79,905	942,290
1994	76,578	81,569	95,969	87,534	82,105	86,223	77,421	93,881	88,346	85,085	86,317	87,856	1,028,884
1995	88,351	83,893	93,020	80,092	83,291	84,210	79,511	88,035	89,052	90,573	86,779	81,292	1,032,974
1996	83,013	83,671	90,392	88,158	88,562	83,824	88,331	94,664	87,388	94,195	86,400	86,493	1,059,104
1997	92,425	88,028	92,265	87,909	94,296	86,382	88,666	89,319	92,298	94,562	83,344	94,913	1,085,254
1998	97,012	86,167	95,091	91,735	90,397	92,099	90,497	91,212	95,442	96,723	90,544	94,567	1,106,128
1999[1]	90,928	92,015	98,223	88,424	84,240	89,518	87,486	92,283	91,926	91,930	93,525	93,997	1,094,495

[1] Preliminary. [2] Includes small amount of lignite. *Source: Energy Information Administration, U.S. Department of Energy (EIA-DOE)*

Production[2] of Pennsylvania Anthracite Coal — In Thousands of Short Tons

Year	Jan.	Feb.	Mar.	Apr.	May	June	July	Aug.	Sept.	Oct.	Nov.	Dec.	Total
1990	237	221	259	297	329	327	225	280	323	354	310	183	3,345
1991	248	243	259	230	224	235	253	313	285	346	299	238	3,173
1992	247	257	279	296	274	287	305	337	311	322	321	306	3,542
1993	272	266	290	175	305	358	222	277	351	603	315	271	3,705
1994	318	335	415	380	375	379	346	457	412	453	452	395	4,717
1995	304	304	372	332	335	353	307	396	428	445	388	347	4,682
1996	302	349	367	371	361	335	367	418	385	557	505	434	4,751
1997	351	366	492	374	351	390	407	423	415	448	384	415	4,678
1998	306	305	309	405	384	388	525	454	452	533	167	167	4,612
1999[1]	355	369	392	335	435	381	340	431	475	374	368	373	4,642

[1] Preliminary. [2] Represents production in Pennsylvania only. *Source: Energy Information Administration, U.S. Department of Energy (EIA-DOE)*

Salient Statistics of Coal in the United States — In Thousands of Short Tons

				Exports						
Year	Production	Imports	Consumption	Brazil	Canada	Europe	Asia	Total	Total Ending Stocks[2]	Losses & Unaccounted For[3]
1990	1,029,076	2,699	895,480	5,847	15,511	58,382	22,725	105,804	201,629	3,949
1991	995,984	3,390	887,621	7,052	11,178	65,520	21,788	108,969	200,682	3,731
1992	997,545	3,803	907,655	6,370	15,140	57,255	20,540	102,516	197,685	-5,826
1993	945,424	7,309	944,081	5,197	8,889	37,575	19,500	74,519	120,458	-13,924
1994	1,033,504	7,584	951,461	5,482	9,193	35,825	17,957	71,359	136,139	-5,348
1995	1,032,974	7,201	962,039	6,351	9,427	48,620	19,095	88,547	134,639	-10,136
1996	1,063,856	7,126	1,005,573	6,540	12,029	47,193	17,980	90,473	122,979	-7,608
1997	1,089,932	7,487	1,030,453	7,455	14,975	41,331	14,498	83,545	106,401	-4,101
1998	3,354,399	26,172	3,044,001	6,475	19,901	33,773	12,311	77,295	128,089	-17,798
1999[1]	3,273,690	26,076	2,897,892	4,438	15,376	24,761	7,751	54,820	149,005	-24,567

[1] Preliminary. [2] Producer & distributor and consumer stocks, excludes stocks held by retail dealers for consumption by the residential and commercial sector. [3] Equals production plus imports minus the change in producer & distributor and consumer stocks minus consumption minus exports.
Source: Energy Information Administraion, U.S. Department of Energy (EIA-DOE)

Consumption and Stocks of Coal in the United States — In Thousands of Short Tons

	Consumtion								Stocks, Dec. 31[3]			
	Electric Utilities				Industrial		Residential		Consumer			Producers
Year	Anthracite	Bituminous	Lignite	Total	Coke Plants	Other Industrial[2]	and Commercial	Total	Electric Utilities	Coke Plants	Other Industrials	and Distributors
1990	1,031	694,317	78,201	773,549	38,877	76,330	6,724	895,480	156,166	3,329	8,716	33,418
1991	994	691,275	79,999	772,268	33,854	75,405	6,094	887,621	157,876	2,773	7,061	32,971
1992	986	698,626	80,248	779,860	32,366	74,042	6,153	892,421	154,130	2,597	6,965	33,993
1993	951	732,736	79,821	813,508	31,323	74,892	6,221	925,944	111,341	2,401	6,716	25,284
1994	1,123	737,102	79,045	817,270	31,740	75,179	6,013	930,201	126,897	2,657	6,585	33,219
1995	978	749,951	78,078	829,007	33,011	73,055	5,807	940,880	126,304	2,632	5,702	34,444
1996	1,009	795,252	78,421	874,681	31,706	70,941	6,006	983,334	114,623	2,667	5,688	28,648
1997	1,014	821,823	77,524	900,361	30,203	70,599	6,463	1,007,626	98,826	1,978	5,597	33,973
1998	867	832,094	77,906	910,867	28,189	69,240	6,372	1,014,667	120,501	2,026	5,561	36,144
1999[1]	571	824,953	76,686	902,213	27,895	66,449	5,546	1,002,102	132,954	1,639	5,046	34,830

[1] Preliminary. [2] Including transportation. [3] Excludes stocks held at retail dealers for consumption by the residential and commercial sector.
Source: Energy Information Administration, U.S. Department of Energy (EIA-DOE)

Average Prices of Coal in the United States — In Dollars Per Short Ton

	End-Use-Sector				Exports				End-Use-Sector				Exports		
Year	Electric Utilities	Coke Plants	Other Industrial[3]	Imports[4]	Steam	Metal-lurgical	Total Average[4]	Year	Electric Utilities	Coke Plants	Other Industrial[3]	Imports[4]	Steam	Metal-lurgical	Total Average[4]
1990	30.45	47.73	33.59	34.45	36.81	46.51	42.63	1995	27.01	47.34	32.42	34.13	34.51	44.30	40.27
1991	30.02	48.88	33.54	33.12	36.91	46.15	42.39	1996	26.45	47.33	32.32	33.45	34.09	45.49	40.76
1992	29.36	47.92	32.78	33.46	35.73	45.41	41.34	1997	26.16	47.36	32.40	34.32	32.45	45.47	40.59
1993	28.58	47.44	32.23	29.89	36.03	44.11	41.41	1998	25.64	46.06	32.26	32.29	30.27	44.53	38.92
1994	28.03	46.56	32.55	30.21	34.34	42.77	39.93	1999[1]	25.15	46.47	31.79	30.46	31.11	43.42	38.63

[1] Preliminary. [2] Estimate. [3] Manufacturing plants only. [4] Based on the free alongside ship (F.A.S.) value. NA = Not available.
Source: Energy Information Administration, U.S. Department of Energy (EIA-DOE)

Trends in Bituminous Coal, Lignite and Pennsylvania Anthracite in the U.S. In Thousands of Short Tons

	Bituminous Coal and Lignite							Pennsylvania Anthracite					
	Production				Labor Productivity								All Mines
Year	Undergound	Surface	Total	Miners[1] Employed	Underground	Surface	Average	Underground	Surface	Total	Miners[1] Employed	Labor Product. Short Tons Miner/Hr.	Labor Product. Short Tons Miner/Hr.
					Short Tons Per Miner Per Hour								
1985	350,073	528,856	878,930	167,009	1.78	4.24	2.74	727	3,982	4,708	2,272	1.05	2.74
1986	359,800	526,223	886,023	152,668	2.00	4.60	3.01	638	3,654	4,292	1,977	1.03	3.01
1987	372,238	542,963	915,202	141,065	2.20	4.98	3.30	636	2,925	3,560	1,602	1.13	3.30
1988	381,546	565,164	946,710	133,913	2.38	5.32	3.55	610	2,945	3,555	1,453	1.21	3.55
1989	393,322	584,058	977,381	130,103	2.46	5.61	3.70	513	2,835	3,348	1,394	1.12	3.70
1990	424,119	601,449	1,025,570	129,619	2.54	5.94	3.83	427	3,080	3,506	1,687	1.03	3.83
1991	406,901	585,638	992,539	119,441	2.69	6.38	4.09	324	3,121	3,445	1,161	1.39	4.09
1992	406,815	587,248	994,062	108,979	2.93	6.59	4.36	424	3,058	3,483	1,217	1.33	4.36
1993	350,637	590,482	941,119	100,099	2.95	7.23	4.70	416	3,889	4,306	1,124	1.85	4.70
1994	399,100	634,400	1,033,500	-----	3.19	7.67	4.98	-----	-----	-----	-----	-----	-----
1995	396,200	636,700	1,032,900	-----	3.39	8.48	5.38	-----	-----	-----	-----	-----	-----
1996	409,800	654,000	1,063,800	-----	3.57	9.05	5.69	-----	-----	-----	-----	-----	-----
1997	420,700	669,300	1,090,000	-----	3.83	9.46	6.04	-----	-----	-----	-----	-----	-----
1998	431,800	686,900	1,118,700	-----	-----	-----	-----	-----	-----	-----	-----	-----	-----

[1] Excludes miners employed at mines producing less than 10,000 tons. *Source: Energy Information Administration, U.S. Department of Energy (EIA-DOE)*

Average Mine Prices of Coal in the United States In Dollars Per Short Ton

	Average Mine Price by Method			Average Mine Prices by Rank						All Coal
Year	Underground	Surface	Total	Lignite	Subbituminous	Bituminous	Anthracite[1]	Bituminous & Lignite FOB Mines[2]	Anthracite FOB Mines[2]	CIF[3] Electric Utility Plants
1985	32.91	20.13	25.20	10.68	12.57	30.78	45.80	25.10	45.80	34.53
1986	30.33	19.34	23.79	10.64	12.26	28.84	44.12	23.70	44.12	33.30
1987	29.63	18.58	23.07	10.85	11.32	28.19	43.65	23.00	43.65	31.83
1988	28.97	17.43	22.07	10.06	10.45	27.66	44.16	22.00	44.16	30.64
1989	28.44	17.38	21.82	9.91	10.16	27.40	42.93	21.76	42.93	30.15
1990	28.58	16.98	21.76	10.13	9.70	27.43	39.40	21.71	39.40	30.45
1991	28.56	16.60	21.49	10.89	9.68	27.49	36.34	21.45	36.34	30.02
1992	27.83	16.34	21.03	10.81	9.68	26.78	34.24	20.98	34.24	29.36
1993	26.92	15.67	19.85	11.11	9.33	26.15	32.94	20.56	37.80	28.64
1994	-----	-----	-----	10.77	8.37	25.68	36.07	-----	-----	-----
1995	-----	-----	-----	10.83	8.10	25.56	39.78	-----	-----	-----
1996	-----	-----	-----	10.92	7.87	25.17	36.78	-----	-----	-----
1997	-----	-----	-----	10.91	7.42	24.64	35.12	-----	-----	-----
1998	-----	-----	-----	10.90	6.97	24.11	33.46	-----	-----	-----

[1] Produced in Pennsylvania. [2] FOB = free on board. [3] *CIF = cost, insurance and freight. W = Withheld data.*
Source: Energy Information Adminstration, U.S. Department of Energy (EIA-DOE)

Cobalt

Cobalt is a strategic and critical metal with a variety of uses in industrial and military applications. It is found in the ores of iron and copper. Cobalt's largest usage is in superalloys that are used in the manufacture of gas turbine aircraft engines. It is also used to make magnets; cemented carbides and diamond tools; catalysts for the petroleum and chemical industries; drying agents for paints; ground coats for porcelain enamels; pigments; battery electrodes; steel-belted radial tires; and magnetic recording media.

The U.S. Geological Survey reported that world cobalt production was expected to increase during the next five years as new nickel-cobalt, copper-cobalt and primary cobalt mines open. There are also new projects to recover cobalt from stockpiled tailings, slags and concentrates. Demand for cobalt in any given year is largely dependent on world economic conditions. A number of industry sectors are expected to increase their consumption of cobalt including the superalloy industry and the battery industry.

World mine production of cobalt in 1998 was estimated at 30,300 metric tonnes, up 12 percent from 1997. The world's largest producer of cobalt is Zambia with 1998 production estimated at 7,500 tonnes. Other large producers include Canada, the Congo, Australia, Russia and Cuba.

The world reserve base of cobalt is estimated at 9.5 million tonnes. The largest reserves are in the Congo followed by Cuba. The cobalt resources of the U.S. are estimated to be about 1.3 million tonnes and are held in Minnesota, Alaska, California, Idaho and Missouri. There are also cobalt resources on the ocean floor.

U.S. reported consumption of cobalt materials in July 1999 was 766 tonnes (contained cobalt). In the January-July 1999 period, consumption was 5,240 tonnes. For all of 1998, consumption of cobalt materials was 9,180 tonnes. Consumption of cobalt metal in July 1999 was 324 tonnes while for the first seven months of 1999 it was 2,240 tonnes. For 1998, consumption of cobalt metal was 4,240 tonnes. Consumption of cobalt oxide and other chemical compounds in July 1999 was 186 tonnes while in January-July 1999 it was 1,240 tonnes. For 1998, consumption was 1,860 tonnes. Consumption of cobalt scrap in July 1999 was 257 tonnes and in the first seven months of 1999 it was 1,760 tonnes. In 1998, scrap consumption was 3,080 tonnes.

U.S. reported stocks of cobalt metal in July 1999 were 343 tonnes. At the end of 1998 they were 356 tonnes. Stocks of cobalt oxide and other chemical compounds in July 1999 were 214 tonnes compared to 306 tonnes at the end of 1998. Stocks of cobalt scrap were 132 tonnes in July 1999 and 89 tonnes at the end of 1998. U.S. Government stocks of cobalt metal in July 1999 were 13,600 tonnes. At the end of 1998 they were 14,700 tonnes. The U.S. Department of Defense National Stockpile Center announced that in late August it had sold 87 metric tonnes of cobalt granules and rondelles. There were no sales in late September, and for the year of 1999 a total of 1,960 tonnes of cobalt were sold.

World Mine Production of Cobalt In Metric Tons (Cobalt Content)

Year	Australia	Botswana	Canada	Cuba	Finland (Refinery)	France (Refinery)	Japan (Refinery)	New Caledonia	Norway (Refinery)	Russia[3]	Congo[4]	Zambia	World Total
1989	1,100	215	6,167	1,825	1,295	165	99	800	1,946	5,700	18,400	7,255	42,873
1990	1,200	205	5,470	1,460	1,300	150	199	800	1,830	5,500	19,000	7,000	42,300
1991	1,400	208	5,274	1,100	1,503	123	185	800	1,983	5,800	9,900	6,994	33,300
1992	1,600	208	5,102	1,150	2,100	150	105	800	2,293	4,000	5,700	6,910	27,800
1993	1,900	205	5,108	1,061	2,200	144	191	800	2,414	3,500	2,459	4,840	21,900
1994	2,300	225	4,265	972	3,000	146	161	1,000	2,823	3,000	826	3,600	18,000
1995	2,500	271	5,339	1,591	3,610	161	227	1,100	2,804	3,500	1,647	5,908	24,400
1996	2,800	408	5,714	2,011	4,160	174	258	1,100	3,098	3,300	2,000	6,959	26,200
1997[1]	3,000	334	5,709	2,082	5,000	159	264	1,000	3,417	3,300	3,500	6,043	27,100
1998[2]	3,300	335	6,039	2,200	10,600	300	480	1,000	4,500	3,200	1,500	7,000	26,300

[1] Preliminary. [2] Estimate. [3] Formerly part of the U.S.S.R.; data not reported separately until 1992. [4] Formerly Zaire.

Source: U.S. Geological Survey (USGS)

Salient Statistics of Cobalt in the United States In Metric Tons (Cobalt Content)

					Consumption by End Uses											
Year	Net Import Reliance as a % of Apparent Consumption	Cobalt Secondary Production	Processors and Consumer Stocks Dec. 31	Imports for Consumption	Ground Coat Frit	Stainless & Heat Resisting	Catalysts	Superalloys	Tool Steel	Magnetic Alloys	Pigments	Drier in Paints, etc.[3]	Cutting & Wear-Resistant Material	Welding Materials	Total Apparent Uses	Price $ Per Pound[4]
1989	83	1,184	1,456	5,793	366	74	819	2,860	219	870	319	718	538	136	7,172	7.64
1990	84	1,225	1,853	6,530	357	41	W	3,345	123	710	W	751	541	180	7,512	10.09
1991	80	1,578	1,622	6,920	W	51	W	3,066	W	713	W	781	525	135	7,240	16.92
1992	76	1,613	840	5,760	257	26	949	2,697	47	670	197	745	522	128	6,590	22.93
1993	79	1,566	819	5,950	W	41	935	2,530	59	569	193	732	569	171	7,350	13.79
1994	81	1,570	914	6,780	W	41	871	2,810	84	698	198	809	723	312	8,730	24.66
1995	81	1,540	818	6,440	196	38	732	2,940	146	757	172	770	748	287	8,970	29.21
1996	78	2,000	770	6,710	391	38	652	3,360	95	719	191	733	722	347	9,380	25.50
1997[1]	77	2,530	763	8,430	490	38	734	4,170	112	879	201	556	789	342	11,200	23.34
1998[2]	77	2,500	750	7,670	W	38	W	4,110	96	771	W	W	844	421	11,500	21.43

[1] Preliminary. [2] Estimate. [3] Or related usage. [4] Annual spot for cathodes. W = Withheld proprietary data.

Source: U.S. Geological Survey (USGS)

Cocoa

Cocoa is a tropical crop found mostly in a zone that extends approximately 15 degrees north and 15 degrees south of the equator. Cocoa trees can attain a height of 35 feet and produce fruits known as pods. A mature cocoa pod is six to ten inches long and can contain 20-50 seeds or beans. In the course of a season, the cocoa tree produces thousands of flowers but only a very small number of pods. Flowers and pods are present on the tree throughout the year but at certain times are in greater numbers. Typically a large main crop is harvested to be followed by a smaller mid crop. After planting it takes about 5-6 years for the tree to become productive and peak productivity is reached in the tenth to eleventh year. Cocoa trees can remain productive for 50 years.

The major production area for cocoa is West Africa where about 60 percent of the world's cocoa is grown. The four major West African producers are the Ivory Coast, Ghana, Nigeria and Cameroon. The Ivory Coast is by far the world's largest producer with a market share of 40 percent. Ghana is the next largest producer with about 15 percent market share. Outside of West Africa, other major producers of cocoa are Indonesia, Malaysia, Brazil, the Dominican Republic and Ecuador. A number of countries have been increasing their output. Brazil was a major producer and exporter of cocoa but disease has damaged their trees. In the 1999/2000 season, several countries whose prior crops had been damaged by El Nino have now recovered. As a result, world production in 1999/00 should increase.

The U.S.D.A. forecast world cocoa production in 1999/00 (October-September) at 2.89 million tonnes, up just over 1 percent from the previous season. If realized, this would be the largest crop since the 1995/96 crop of 2.94 million tonnes. The Ivory Coast is by far the most important producer and exporter of cocoa. The U.S.D.A. forecast the Ivory Coast 1999/00 crop at 1.2 million tonnes, down 10,000 tonnes from a year ago and some 2 percent less than the record output of 1995/96. While the season is just getting underway in terms of harvesting, it has already been a tumultuous year. The Ivory Coast cocoa industry has been liberalized in that government control and influence has been removed. In the face of lower cocoa prices from a large crop, producers have banded together to protest the low prices by reducing the amount of cocoa that they would sell. This strike action was followed by a military coup which removed the government from office. There was no indication that there would be any changes in the cocoa industry. Prices responded to the developments by moving higher but then fell back. The U.S.D.A. forecast Ivory Coast exports at 1.03 million tonnes. One trend in the cocoa market has been for the producing countries to process more of their own crop and export value-added products.

The U.S.D.A. forecast Ghana's crop at 450,000 tonnes, up 5 percent from the previous season. This will be a large crop though it is well below the record 1964/65 crop of 566,053 tonnes. The larger crop this year is due to timely rains which can make a great deal of difference in determining the size of the crop. Ghana cocoa is considered to be high quality and the government takes steps to ensure that quality is maintained. The U.S.D.A. forecast that Ghana would export 400,000 tonnes of cocoa.

The U.S.D.A. forecast Indonesia's 1999/00 crop at 350,000 tonnes, up 4 percent from the previous year. The larger crop was due to favorable weather as well as new trees coming into production. Despite the recent economic crisis in Indonesia, the cocoa industry appears to be strong. The U.S.D.A. forecast exports at 280,000 tonnes, up 4 percent from the previous season.

One country that has seen a steady decline in production is Brazil. The U.S.D.A. forecast the 1999/00 crop at 125,290 tonnes, down 21 percent from 1998/99. Because of damage from Witch's Broom disease, production has been on the decline and shows no sign of recovering. Brazil, which had been a net exporter of cocoa for many years, is now a net importer. The U.S.D.A. forecast that Brazil's imports of cocoa in 1999/00 would be 75,000 tonnes.

World consumption or grind of cocoa for the 1999/00 season was estimated by E.D.&F. Man at 2.8 million tonnes, up less than 1 percent from the previous season. While cocoa consumption has been trending higher in recent years, recent data form the major consuming countries shows it has been close to flat. With world production of cocoa expected to exceed consumption, global cocoa stocks should increase by the end of 1999/00.

Futures Markets

Cocoa futures and options are traded on the CSCE Division of the New York Board of Trade (NYBOT) and on the London International Financial Futures and Options Exchange (LIFFE).

World Supply and Demand Cocoa In Thousands of Metric Tons

Crop Year Beginning October	Stocks Oct. 1	Net World Production	Total Availability	Seasonal Grindings	Closing Stocks	Stock Change	Crop Year Beginning October	Stocks Oct. 1	Net World Production	Total Availability	Seasonal Grindings	Closing Stocks	Stock Change
1984-5	474	1,939	2,393	1,862	531	58	1992-3	1,439	2,360	3,775	2,441	1,334	-105
1985-6	531	1,962	2,474	1,877	597	65	1993-4	1,334	2,502	3,811	2,485	1,326	-8
1986-7	597	1,988	2,565	1,896	669	72	1994-5	1,326	2,386	3,688	2,507	1,181	-145
1987-8	669	2,194	2,841	2,003	838	169	1995-6	1,181	2,907	4,059	2,650	1,409	228
1988-9	838	2,460	3,273	2,118	1,155	317	1996-7	1,409	2,693	4,075	2,753	1,321	-87
1989-90	1,155	2,425	3,556	2,212	1,343	188	1997-8[1]	1,321	2,644	3,939	2,802	1,137	-185
1990-1	1,343	2,510	3,828	2,351	1,476	133	1998-9[2]	1,137	2,777	3,886	2,774	1,112	-24
1991-2	1,476	2,269	3,723	2,284	1,439	-38	1999-00[3]	1,112	2,953	4,036	2,851	1,185	73

[1] Preliminary. [2] Estimate. [3] Forecast. [4] Obtained by adjusting the Gross World Crop for one percent loss in weight.

Source: E D & F Man Cocoa Ltd.

COCOA

World Production of Cocoa Beans In Thousands of Metric Tons

Crop Year Beginning October	Brazil	Came-roon	Colom-bia	Domin-ican Republic	Ecuador	Ghana	Indo-nesia	Ivory Coast	Mal-aysia	Mexico	Nigeria	Papua New Guinea	World Total
1990-1	380	107	52	42	104	293	147	804	224	43	170	33	2,510
1991-2	310	108	47	48	83	243	169	748	217	51	110	41	2,269
1992-3	305	99	54	52	70	312	234	697	219	51	130	39	2,360
1993-4	280	97	49	58	79	255	251	917	204	39	142	31	2,502
1994-5	230	109	48	52	83	310	238	886	120	43	144	29	2,386
1995-6	235	117	45	52	103	404	284	1,224	116	30	163	35	2,907
1996-7	170	121	45	45	101	323	327	1,133	102	35	157	28	2,693
1997-8[1]	168	115	46	57	28	404	331	1,110	57	34	165	29	2,644
1998-9[2]	130	124	45	23	72	380	393	1,163	79	33	202	32	2,777
1999-00[3]	116	125	45	40	95	410	420	1,300	85	30	155	35	2,953

[1] Preliminary. [2] Estimate. [3] Forecast. *Source: Foreign Agricultural Service, U.S. Department of Agriculture (FAS-USDA)*

World Consumption of Cocoa[4] In Thousands of Metric Tons

Year													
1990-1	45	275	115	70	295	56	77	268	52	145	272	83	2,351
1991-2	46	216	108	67	306	62	87	294	51	153	307	25	2,284
1992-3	47	218	100	80	330	58	99	309	47	169	326	95	2,441
1993-4	50	220	110	95	315	65	103	331	52	170	317	90	2,485
1994-5	53	189	108	108	290	69	101	350	52	154	331	80	2,507
1995-6	54	183	135	111	275	73	96	385	56	191	345	80	2,650
1996-7	55	180	150	106	265	71	103	402	57	172	394	85	2,753
1997-8[1]	55	188	205	107	240	72	94	425	60	174	399	75	2,802
1998-9[2]	55	200	221	120	210	72	109	415	60	166	406	45	2,774
1999-00[3]	55	200	245	125	200	72	110	420	60	170	425	50	2,851

[1] Preliminary. [2] Estimate. [3] Forecast. [4] Figures represent the grindings of cocoa beans in each country. *Source: Foreign Agricultural Service, U.S. Department of Agriculture (FAS-USDA)*

Raw Cocoa Grindings in Selected Countries In Metric Tons

Year	Total	First Quarter	Second Quarter	Third Quarter	Fourth Quarter	Total	First Quarter	Second Quarter	Third Quarter	Fourth Quarter
	Germany[2]					Netherlands				
1990	281,855	69,125	64,613	70,994	77,123	247,590	62,243	58,817	58,702	67,828
1991	290,703	73,172	72,396	70,934	73,661	274,741	64,299	71,643	63,973	74,826
1992	319,251	78,661	73,797	80,111	86,682	293,157	77,954	71,537	69,871	73,795
1993	298,681	74,119	69,805	74,010	80,747	320,060	78,338	75,548	81,183	84,991
1994	296,219	80,242	68,033	67,706	80,238	334,384	83,963	78,055	84,249	88,117
1995	258,817	69,441	56,478	61,523	71,375	355,492	91,314	85,248	85,311	93,619
1996	251,070	69,520	59,471	65,824	56,255	388,412	100,866	90,724	99,549	97,273
1997	245,244	61,379	57,402	65,233	61,230	407,340	102,338	100,132	101,817	103,053
1998	217,442	62,154	47,565	55,267	52,456	427,393	104,936	108,101	108,580	105,776
1999[1]	194,182	48,486	48,605			411,933	107,189	102,933	98,828	
	United Kingdom					United States[3]				
1990	124,791	32,116	29,322	29,419	33,934	216,740	51,559	51,683	58,278	55,220
1991	148,191	32,902	36,016	41,863	37,410	255,781	51,191	64,365	66,544	73,681
1992	159,284	39,831	37,903	37,120	44,430	313,921	70,335	74,515	84,109	84,962
1993	171,343	44,575	41,975	37,496	47,297	321,905	78,968	77,720	84,593	80,624
1994	163,170	44,131	39,063	39,591	40,385	322,629	71,398	78,805	86,247	86,179
1995	159,877	43,410	35,348	34,431	46,688	338,401	78,835	78,886	87,360	93,320
1996	189,037	50,500	44,535	48,855	45,147	351,042	79,044	82,713	93,933	95,352
1997	173,522	44,059	42,702	41,180	45,581	397,895	95,435	97,223	105,984	99,253
1998	171,773	45,787	42,338	40,047	43,601	397,389	99,189	96,341	104,359	97,500
1999[1]	163,404	42,557	39,758	40,238		401,412	98,218	102,488		

[1] Preliminary. [2] Beginning October 1990, includes former East Germany. [3] Data incomplete January 1984-March 1991, excludes one major processor. *Source: Foreign Agricultural Service, U.S. Department of Agriculture (FAS-USDA)*

Imports of Cocoa Butter in Selected Countries In Metric Tons

Year	Australia	Austria	Belgium	Canada	France	Germany	Italy	Japan	Nether-Lands	Seden	Switzer-land	United Kingdom	United States
1989	10,291	4,599	17,748	8,224	26,597	41,765	5,932	15,280	22,924	5,735	16,276	35,045	64,353
1990	10,025	6,047	22,125	8,830	28,539	49,999	6,187	15,686	34,529	5,855	16,306	34,604	92,165
1991	11,218	5,171	24,795	8,682	28,628	54,452	7,813	15,245	29,729	6,299	16,544	26,876	90,004
1992	10,697	5,249	31,836	10,706	28,560	44,906	8,431	15,835	29,999	5,885	17,422	26,300	99,509
1993	13,129	5,417	28,989	10,225	30,611	37,269	9,851	16,422	51,559	6,390	16,711	25,941	85,400
1994	13,030	5,410	34,061	11,551	36,698	59,170	9,173	15,937	43,192	7,079	17,242	35,453	54,550
1995	12,150	7,425	26,185	11,146	40,245	69,928	12,027	12,898	38,300	7,078	17,835	30,654	57,210
1996	14,316	7,124	23,771	12,166	47,349	69,298	11,178	16,096	39,193	5,698	18,690	32,781	68,761
1997	14,896	6,922	34,222	16,782	46,516	71,094	9,706	16,609	29,023	6,937	19,058	37,021	87,687
1998[1]	16,305	5,984	25,722	16,941	43,610	76,057	8,957	15,363	28,523	7,403	19,857	32,951	65,306

[1] Preliminary. [2] Formerly part of the U.S.S.R.; data not reported separately until 1992. NA = Not available.

Sources: E D & F Man Cocoa Limited; Food and Agricultural Organization of the United Nations (FAO-UN)

Imports of Cocoa Liquor and Cocoa Powder in Selected Countries In Metric Tons

	Cocoa Liqour						Cocoa Powder						
Year	France	Germany	Nether-lands	Japan	United Kingdom	United States	Denmark	France	Germany	Italy	Japan	Nether-lands	United States
1989	29,257	1,040	9,315	3,451	2,524	27,556	2,810	10,920	18,470	10,233	6,033	5,862	53,736
1990	35,146	1,860	9,875	3,123	1,713	25,047	3,014	12,244	21,294	11,418	6,284	6,446	58,280
1991	40,251	3,242	7,443	2,057	1,918	25,320	3,583	12,215	25,315	12,189	6,557	6,239	55,636
1992	45,056	2,540	7,130	2,246	3,611	24,255	3,291	14,896	27,745	14,469	6,067	9,412	56,089
1993	41,999	1,694	15,543	2,468	1,490	31,641	3,402	16,773	25,732	13,221	5,771	5,626	66,533
1994	42,392	2,682	14,913	2,312	4,443	26,846	3,625	19,215	28,806	12,884	6,461	10,078	67,207
1995	46,570	5,083	6,822	1,832	5,030	19,192	3,229	17,081	32,247	15,265	6,310	10,048	66,075
1996	62,938	7,437	9,926	2,133	5,069	15,357	3,711	18,398	36,211	15,006	13,069	6,678	68,658
1997	61,148	10,299	8,401	1,393	5,860	17,850	4,189	19,555	35,069	15,872	8,941	4,424	71,024
1998[1]	70,883	9,121	12,534	1,144	3,813	21,894	3,865	19,533	32,479	17,122	8,779	3,746	84,211

[1] Preliminary. NA = Not available. *Source: E D & F Man Cocoa Limited*

Imports of Cocoa and Products in the United States In Thousands of Metric Tons

Year	Jan.	Feb.	Mar.	Apr.	May	June	July	Aug.	Sept.	Oct.	Nov.	Dec.	Total
1990	72	53	70	110	83	60	NA	61	41	NA	72	49	716
1991	70	53	51	74	62	66	65	59	53	NA	NA	73	761
1992	83	66	62	55	50	60	52	60	67	67	64	69	755
1993	67	57	56	61	58	61	77	58	59	71	71	98	801
1994	67	68	56	61	49	51	49	58	58	61	45	48	672
1995	68	54	44	48	47	48	48	51	53	49	54	79	643
1996	90	87	90	80	55	49	62	53	53	60	60	86	821
1997	80	47	77	71	64	54	59	47	64	61	56	88	768
1998	86	105	90	71	55	65	65	62	72	63	54	77	865
1999[1]	100	79	81	93	51	60	77	62	68	67			886

[1] Preliminary. NA = Not available. *Source: Foreign Agricultural Service, U.S. Department of Agriculture (FAS-USDA)*

Visible Stocks of Cocoa in Port of Hampton Road Warehouses[1], at End of Month In Thousands of Bags

Year	Jan.	Feb.	Mar.	Apr.	May	June	July	Aug.	Sept.	Oct.	Nov.	Dec.
1990	403.6	445.9	583.2	674.3	807.4	1,064.7	917.2	67.2	1,046.5	19.0	996.5	958.2
1991	946.5	953.3	910.1	946.0	906.1	1,036.6	1,174.5	1,291.2	1,386.2	1,429.0	1,426.0	1,502.9
1992	1,588.3	1,892.1	2,233.1	2,236.2	2,236.9	2,204.8	2,150.8	2,087.4	1,982.4	2,018.6	2,043.9	2,188.5
1993	2,209.9	2,497.3	2,443.9	2,676.8	2,771.8	2,689.7	2,920.0	2,708.6	2,740.1	2,418.7	2,328.3	2,356.9
1994	2,329.6	2,441.1	2,443.9	2,522.9	2,533.1	2,460.2	2,445.4	2,335.0	2,308.4	2,360.2	2,306.9	2,253.7
1995	2,152.7	2,098.6	2,195.7	2,212.3	2,120.2	2,016.0	1,919.8	1,786.6	1,713.1	1,598.2	1,463.9	1,470.3
1996	1,439.8	1,492.8	1,458.0	1,549.6	1,561.7	1,493.9	1,412.3	1,315.4	1,239.6	1,338.9	1,108.1	1,116.2
1997	1,128.3	1,132.1	1,133.0	1,094.0	1,010.5	970.2	872.4	840.1	727.3	763.9	695.7	704.8
1998	726.5	693.4	841.9	842.5	811.6	764.7	714.3	712.3	795.4	801.9	705.9	673.0
1999	661.6	693.2	642.5	579.7	536.9	500.7	489.0	472.7	473.4	451.8	438.9	421.2

[1] Licensed and unlicensed warehouses approved by the CSCE. *Source: New York Board of Trade (NYBOT)*

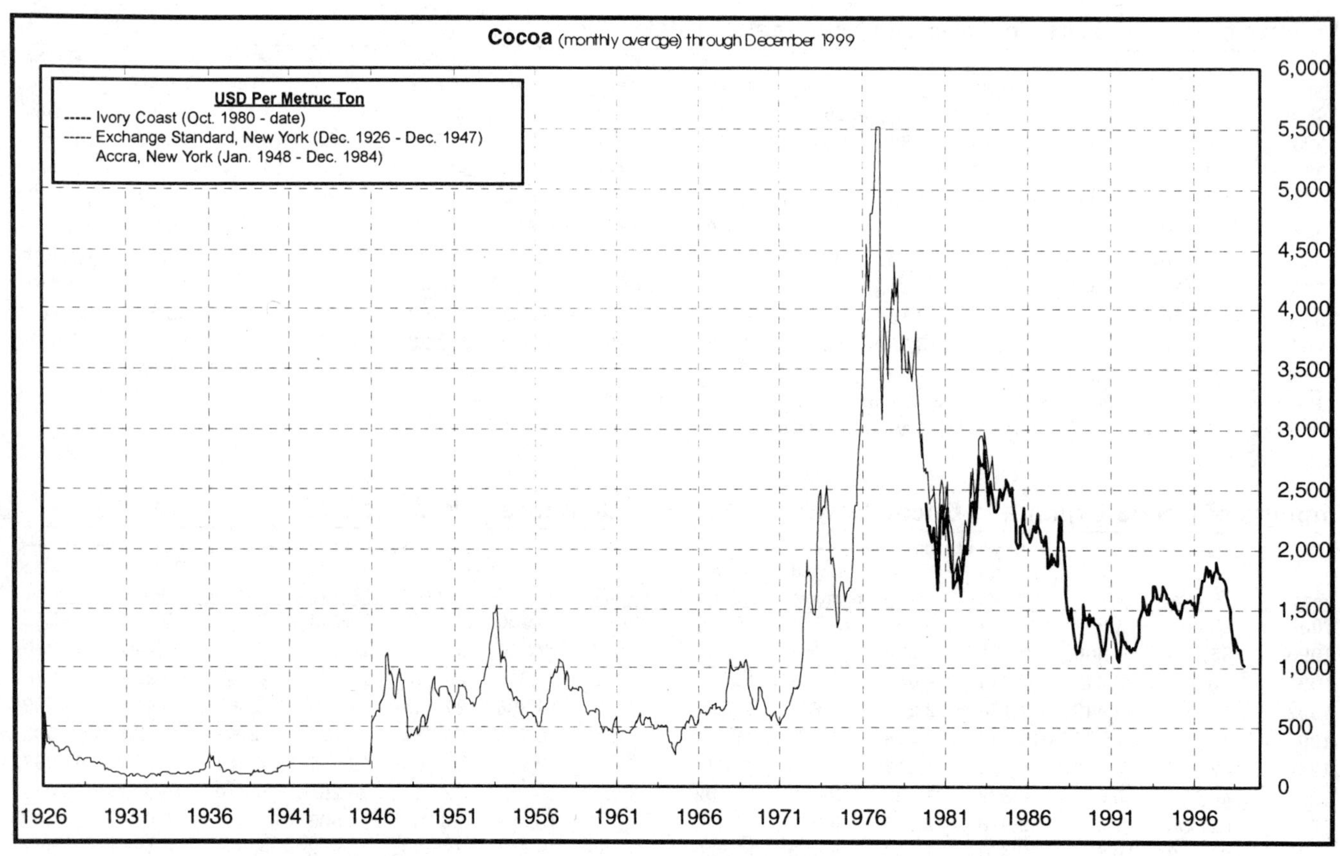

Visible Stocks of Cocoa in Philadelphia (Del. River) Warehouses[1], at End of Month   In Thousands of Bags

Year	Jan.	Feb.	Mar.	Apr.	May	June	July	Aug.	Sept.	Oct.	Nov.	Dec.
1990	35.1	61.1	87.5	107.9	120.5	204.4	297.1	231.2	185.9	193.0	195.3	215.1
1991	216.2	226.9	249.3	254.9	309.2	376.8	382.8	376.8	375.5	355.1	280.5	282.7
1992	344.6	345.5	412.1	547.6	576.7	632.0	637.7	654.0	616.4	606.0	565.8	612.4
1993	562.2	589.8	603.9	606.0	653.1	678.0	665.7	648.9	600.6	611.5	685.2	781.8
1994	831.5	937.7	1,004.2	1,010.9	1,055.4	1,095.2	1,076.0	1,029.8	968.5	857.1	843.9	818.9
1995	807.5	1,034.3	1,038.9	1,020.2	963.7	924.3	860.7	759.2	852.2	727.0	666.0	735.6
1996	960.2	1,005.2	1,205.6	1,658.8	1,871.3	1,851.7	1,969.1	1,816.2	1,851.1	1,705.1	1,671.7	1,696.5
1997	1,753.0	1,634.4	1,579.6	1,641.0	1,578.7	1,625.9	1,696.2	1,637.6	1,530.9	1,491.8	1,414.2	1,394.0
1998	1,420.3	1,435.7	1,592.6	1,555.3	1,398.5	1,287.8	1,279.8	1,376.9	1,373.7	1,260.6	1,406.7	1,637.1
1999	1,763.0	1,832.8	1,982.7	2,217.8	2,019.4	1,999.6	2,084.6	2,133.4	2,144.1	2,015.5	1,774.4	1,608.5

[1] Licensed and unlicensed warehouses approved by the CSCE.   *Source: New York Board of Trade (NYBOT)*

Visible Stocks of Cocoa in New York Warehouses[1], at End of Month   In Thousands of Bags

Year	Jan.	Feb.	Mar.	Apr.	May	June	July	Aug.	Sept.	Oct.	Nov.	Dec.
1990	288.4	267.5	311.9	335.3	294.8	359.2	431.3	409.0	442.2	406.3	413.4	397.2
1991	355.6	219.6	295.9	294.1	250.4	292.6	313.3	317.1	271.5	253.9	292.9	282.4
1992	321.2	303.7	278.7	302.6	273.4	287.8	329.7	301.5	280.5	252.3	212.7	183.3
1993	150.9	144.1	122.0	125.0	119.8	119.8	119.8	119.8	119.8	118.6	132.4	187.7
1994	271.0	275.0	280.8	296.6	358.6	394.1	447.5	447.5	467.3	427.3	407.2	556.1
1995	560.5	634.5	559.2	539.4	510.4	561.1	579.3	595.4	459.9	598.7	679.7	598.7
1996	667.6	646.1	632.7	627.2	656.1	633.5	1,191.7	1,154.2	1,121.4	973.2	950.1	919.0
1997	984.7	981.3	945.0	1,250.0	1,574.4	1,524.7	1,512.8	1,348.0	1,217.3	1,073.7	1,020.0	980.4
1998	973.9	1,342.7	1,271.3	1,675.7	1,552.3	1,516.7	1,404.6	1,293.1	1,300.1	1,126.4	989.2	1,031.6
1999	1,085.0	1,089.3	1,083.1	1,134.1	1,139.4	1,114.3	1,093.5	974.5	941.9	821.7	847.5	1,573.1

[1] Licensed and unlicensed warehouses approved by the CSCE.   *Source: New York Board of Trade (NYBOT)*

Spot Cocoa Prices[1] for Selected Origins of Cocoa Beans and Products in the U.S. Dollars Per Metric Ton

Crop Year Beginning October	Cocoa Beans: Brazil	Cocoa Beans: Cote d'Ivoire	Cocoa Beans: Dominican Republic	Cocoa Beans: Ecuador	Cocoa Beans: Malaysia	Chocolate Liqour: Brazil	Chocolate Liqour: Ecuador	Cocoa Butter: African	Cocoa Butter: Other	Cocoa Cake 10-12% Fat
1988-9	1,669	1,773	1,442	1,466	1,364	2,136	1,912	3,543	3,515	945
1989-90	1,259	1,307	1,142	1,250	1,162	1,775	1,640	3,176	3,151	666
1990-1	1,222	1,289	1,091	1,168	1,131	1,704	1,646	3,232	3,199	394
1991-2	1,234	1,262	1,051	1,136	1,111	1,656	1,540	2,763	2,815	393
1992-3	1,109	1,199	969	1,123	1,020	1,571	1,513	2,517	2,572	539
1993-4	1,378	1,560	1,277	1,393	1,326	2,076	2,028	3,348	3,393	649
1994-5	1,547	1,596	1,347	1,436	1,434	2,202	2,105	3,730	3,737	560
1995-6	1,539	1,522	1,387	1,390	1,449	2,167	2,023	3,780	3,795	519
1996-7	1,641	1,631	1,498	1,511	1,539	2,305	2,163	4,022	4,021	553
1997-8[2]	1,806	1,792	1,671	1,789	1,676	2,558	2,496	4,248	4,248	636

[1] All prices are nominal and are net ex-dock or ex-warehouse, U.S. eastern seaboard north of Hatteras, for merchandise physically available in interstate commerce, in truckload and regular commercial quantities. [2] Preliminary. NA = Not available. *Source: Foreign Agricultural Service, U.S. Department of Agriculture (FAS-USDA)*

Average Open Interest of Cocoa Futures in New York In Contracts

Year	Jan.	Feb.	Mar.	Apr.	May	June	July	Aug.	Sept.	Oct.	Nov.	Dec.
1990	52,094	52,599	55,796	51,299	51,076	50,385	49,603	49,083	47,332	50,084	44,944	41,955
1991	42,446	38,205	40,198	45,250	47,764	49,111	53,153	53,886	53,974	54,854	53,390	53,412
1992	54,464	54,797	52,110	49,904	48,076	47,690	49,924	50,532	51,706	56,101	57,426	60,521
1993	64,886	68,307	69,464	68,533	71,802	71,792	87,011	83,057	88,000	94,844	96,507	91,573
1994	89,174	87,349	91,715	82,500	82,970	72,288	72,249	69,614	73,436	74,163	72,232	75,995
1995	78,873	80,786	82,299	78,435	80,547	75,496	74,975	65,794	68,547	72,758	76,680	79,844
1996	90,478	93,533	98,049	95,390	96,346	88,232	80,873	77,134	77,942	79,572	77,139	78,592
1997	86,960	90,589	96,771	96,956	94,651	97,385	101,815	101,138	106,487	108,263	99,544	97,009
1998	90,574	82,205	78,022	73,237	79,294	74,347	74,295	73,975	71,978	74,139	74,127	73,480
1999	77,067	72,324	69,221	65,856	71,990	75,195	70,787	69,939	74,571	79,770	89,035	92,609

Source: New York Board of Trade (NYBOT)

Volume of Trading of Cocoa Futures in New York In Contracts

Year	Jan.	Feb.	Mar.	Apr.	May	June	July	Aug.	Sept.	Oct.	Nov.	Dec.	Total
1990	121,610	128,357	166,277	191,007	194,759	181,377	126,596	143,323	75,757	120,689	116,175	69,990	1,635,917
1991	94,609	92,450	104,973	99,176	76,435	104,327	96,840	146,379	104,136	135,677	106,888	72,629	1,234,519
1992	122,576	119,375	94,131	116,804	66,185	135,373	104,660	145,815	113,589	109,888	137,815	95,024	1,397,235
1993	145,378	139,932	111,751	149,771	82,961	189,474	225,901	215,044	240,371	217,697	229,752	183,352	2,128,384
1994	178,303	190,804	205,623	188,004	267,188	251,300	193,883	241,340	142,589	183,975	210,635	164,917	2,417,006
1995	197,032	183,784	191,328	208,707	169,061	199,211	140,789	205,169	120,433	149,810	211,171	113,603	2,090,098
1996	177,720	226,701	213,189	242,988	164,749	183,544	159,070	164,719	107,634	167,227	185,226	128,809	2,121,576
1997	180,669	172,510	219,896	235,020	130,041	251,471	186,280	200,707	168,981	204,394	180,805	143,735	2,274,509
1998	175,844	145,311	171,333	192,120	143,602	183,719	131,642	156,737	115,066	125,320	155,280	114,606	1,810,580
1999	136,109	155,090	141,090	180,837	130,019	230,925	125,360	144,290	147,124	143,335	209,608	124,249	1,868,036

Source: New York Board of Trade (NYBOT)

Coconut Oil and Copra

World copra production is small at only about 2 percent of total world oilseed production and crop size showed relatively little, if any, growth during the 1990's. Copra, dried coconut meat, is crushed or processed to yield coconut oil and copra meal. Coconut oil, an important ingredient in cosmetics and soap, is also used as a food ingredient. As an edible oil, however, feedstock use is shrinking, especially in the U.S., as the oil contains 92 percent saturated fat, a very high level for today's health conscious consumers. U.S. coconut oil imports are primarily processed into inedible products.

Nearly the entire world copra crop is crushed and processed into coconut oil. The 1999/2000 total copra crop of 5.4 million metric tonnes compares with 4.7 million in 1998/99. From those totals coconut oil comprised 3.4 million tonnes and 2.9 million tonnes, respectively. Copra meal output at 1.84 million tons compares with 1.60 million in 1998/99. Coconut oil accounts for about 3 percent of the world's vegetable and marine oil usage while coconut meal accounts for an even smaller percentage of total world meal usage.

The Philippines and Indonesia account for about two-thirds of world copra output; production of which is not only dependent on the weather, but the crop is believed to have a well entrenched biological cycle that triggers relatively sharp swings in output. Indonesia's output has remained fairly constant in the 1990's at about 1.1 million metric tonnes. Philippine output, however, has slipped to less than 2 million tonnes late in the 1990's from a high of 2.5 million in 1995. Conversely, India's production is slowly rising, from less than a half million tonnes in the first half of the 1990's to over 700,000 tonnes in the second half.

Foreign trade in copra products is small: coconut oil exports in 1999/00 of 1.7 million tonnes compares with 1.4 million in 1998/99; meal exports were a shade under a million tonnes in both years. World carryover stocks of both products are also minimal: ending 1999/00 oil carryover of at 150,000 tonnes compares with 130,000 tons a year earlier, while meal totals are about 125,000 tonnes for both years.

US coconut oil prices through August 1999, 12-month average, of $786 per metric tonne compare with $660 per tonne a year earlier. US processors, however, are not adverse to switching to palm oil should coconut oil's premium to palm oil widen too far which may have been the case into mid-1999.

World copra meal prices, basis Rotterdam, in 1998/99 of $108 per metric tonne compare with $105 per tonne in 1997/88, and the 1987/88-1996/97 average of $128 per tonne. Rotterdam oil prices in 1997/98 averaged $748 per metric tonne vs. $625 per tonne a year earlier and the ten-year average of $484 per tonne. Average copra seed prices of $468 per tonne in 1998/99 compare with $398 per tonne in 1997/98.

World Production of Copra In Thousands of Metric Tons

Year	India	Indonesia	Ivory Coast	Malaysia	Mexico	Mozambique	New Guinea	Philippines	Sri Lanka	Thailand	Vanuatu	Vietnam	World Total
1991	440	1,110	79	82	175	72	110	1,845	70	65	27	220	4,612
1992	440	1,110	65	82	200	72	117	1,845	70	65	24	220	4,624
1993	515	1,100	60	65	173	73	120	1,980	50	60	28	225	4,776
1994	592	1,270	65	60	216	74	104	1,930	104	100	27	210	5,072
1995	655	1,080	72	66	217	74	125	2,500	113	103	30	208	5,544
1996	720	1,155	75	60	204	75	178	1,725	75	61	33	210	4,880
1997	720	1,300	45	60	215	76	159	2,210	67	62	34	96	5,363
1998[1]	735	970	43	52	200	76	150	2,270	95	90	37	123	5,147
1999[2]	710	900	42	52	195	73	135	1,280	90	87	35	120	4,017
2000[3]	740	1,300	45	55	200	73	160	2,000	95	90		133	5,250

[1] Preliminary. [2] Estimate. [3] Forecast. *Source: The Oil World*

World Supply and Distribution of Coconut Oil In Thousands of Metric Tons

	Production							Consumption						Ending Stocks		
Year	India	Indonesia	Malaysia	Philippines	Total	Exports	Imports	European Union	India	Indonesia	Philippines	United States	Total	Philippines	United States	Total
1990-1	272	843	34	1,283	3,192	1,450	1,490	664	279	682	279	402	3,332	51	127	473
1991-2	274	701	33	1,110	2,848	1,343	1,321	513	285	380	257	409	2,880	115	85	420
1992-3	299	691	29	1,294	3,035	1,667	1,583	516	312	441	249	491	3,007	38	114	364
1993-4	343	704	32	1,242	3,009	1,361	1,437	547	346	337	294	483	2,962	181	74	457
1994-5	383	638	36	1,564	3,312	1,775	1,760	660	384	492	309	491	3,325	99	74	430
1995-6	397	612	35	1,206	2,912	1,374	1,405	606	396	373	306	427	3,005	100	38	368
1996-7	421	756	35	1,257	3,152	1,751	1,695	692	429	213	315	504	3,081	92	68	382
1997-8[1]	439	652	40	1,628	3,451	2,122	2,117	777	437	185	302	540	3,230	32	178	598
1998-9[2]	430	479	43	780	2,419	1,050	1,107	548	440	134	294	470	2,794	56	56	280
1999-00[3]	439	768	39	1,199	3,179	1,657	1,648	600	445	168	320	500	3,000	80	67	450

[1] Preliminary. [2] Estimate. [3] Forecast. *Source: The Oil World*

Supply and Distribution of Coconut Oil in the United States In Millions of Pounds

	----- Rotterdam -----						--------- Disappearance ---------			-------- Production of Coconut Oil (Refined) --------				
Year	Copra Tonne -------- $ U.S. --------	Coconut Oil, CIF	Imports For Consumption	Stocks Oct. 1	Total Supply	Exports	Total Domestic	Edible Products	Inedible Products	Total	Oct.-Dec.	Jan.-Mar.	April-June	July-Sept.
1989-90	251	371	1,038	152	1,190	44	866	161	705	703.1	195.4	163.8	187.3	156.6
1990-1	247	364	946	279	1,225	51	897	169	742	754.6	196.8	150.8	141.8	265.2
1991-2	397	605	838	277	1,115	22	906	164	699	733.9	145.3	158.8	159.3	270.5
1992-3	292	446	1,162	187	1,349	15	1,082	202	692	650.5	156.0	158.8	166.6	169.1
1993-4	388	564	999	251	1,250	20	1,067	234	716	536.2	155.6	129.0	131.8	119.8
1994-5	432	656	1,100	163	1,263	18	1,082	247	694	546.8	137.5	142.7	144.3	122.3
1995-6	487	746	873	163	1,036	11	941	221	453	445.0	127.5	118.4	132.8	66.4
1996-7	452	693	1,188	83	1,271	11	1,111	120	471	324.2	77.0	61.5	101.5	84.2
1997-8[1]	391	587	1,440	149	1,589	7	1,190	141	472	397.8	113.4	103.6	100.4	80.4
1998-9[2]	473	766	820	392	1,212	7	1,140	144	380	363.2	89.6	82.9	99.3	91.4

[1] Preliminary. *Source: Bureau of Census, U.S. Department of Commerce*

Consumption of Coconut Oil in End Products (Edible and Inedible) in the U.S. In Millions of Pounds

Year	Jan.	Feb.	Mar.	Apr.	May	June	July	Aug.	Sept.	Oct.	Nov.	Dec.	Total
1990	45.4	44.9	44.3	44.6	43.2	39.4	39.8	39.5	39.2	49.7	41.0	43.9	514.9
1991	-----	137.6	-----	-----	150.6	-----	-----	134.4	-----	-----	122.1	-----	544.7
1992	72.5	70.6	76.5	70.7	78.7	74.8	65.2	70.6	77.4	75.8	76.2	66.4	875.4
1993	74.4	75.9	81.3	77.6	72.1	71.0	73.6	78.2	72.6	85.9	90.9	84.6	938.1
1994	74.4	77.4	77.5	80.4	86.6	88.8	76.0	88.4	65.1	74.6	85.1	95.0	969.3
1995	78.2	79.5	86.5	81.0	79.7	82.0	76.5	71.4	61.6	62.1	59.8	59.9	878.0
1996	47.0	54.3	60.1	60.2	68.6	54.6	55.1	47.9	44.9	49.6	50.3	47.9	640.7
1997	44.1	44.8	52.8	46.1	41.9	49.4	49.9	48.3	66.9	53.4	43.9	48.0	589.5
1998	51.5	48.1	59.4	54.3	54.5	47.0	49.3	50.3	53.7	49.4	50.0	42.1	609.6
1999[1]	39.9	44.7	50.8	43.0	41.4	45.4	36.9	33.3	46.2	41.5	43.6	38.8	505.5

[1] Preliminary. *Source: Bureau of Census, U.S. Department of Commerce*

Stocks of Coconut Oil (Crude and Refined) in the U.S., on First of Month In Millions of Pounds

Year	Jan.	Feb.	Mar.	Apr.	May	June	July	Aug.	Sept.	Oct.	Nov.	Dec.
1990	297.3	304.4	307.0	348.0	305.6	306.6	292.2	264.3	315.4	281.1	309.3	304.6
1991	NA	NA	359.0	NA	NA	364.3	NA	NA	279.3	NA	NA	298.0
1992	NA	266.3	274.2	239.7	211.2	173.7	178.3	141.1	187.1	187.7	225.1	278.8
1993	355.7	406.7	418.9	348.7	338.3	305.2	257.2	233.8	321.4	250.8	335.0	299.1
1994	291.7	316.5	284.5	251.5	237.6	199.9	151.4	163.7	156.0	164.1	166.2	152.9
1995	155.6	173.6	168.1	163.7	148.5	183.5	163.8	136.9	124.1	162.9	199.7	187.7
1996	164.7	229.1	200.4	217.7	173.6	175.9	171.5	116.7	113.8	84.0	78.6	65.0
1997	125.9	147.4	141.1	204.5	174.5	161.3	143.8	143.4	154.3	149.6	162.1	194.2
1998	274.2	332.4	344.5	337.4	318.8	300.6	366.3	424.6	434.4	392.6	431.8	447.3
1999[1]	401.7	446.5	387.5	366.3	309.8	240.5	134.7	197.5	191.8	152.0	106.4	142.2

[1] Preliminary. NA = Not available. *Source: Bureau of Census, U.S. Department of Commerce*

Average Price of Coconut Oil (Crude) Tank Cars in New York In Cents Per Pound

Year	Jan.	Feb.	Mar.	Apr.	May	June	July	Aug.	Sept.	Oct.	Nov.	Dec.	Average
1990	24.31	23.69	22.10	21.63	21.15	20.31	19.16	18.58	18.26	18.18	20.45	20.13	20.66
1991	20.22	20.31	20.50	19.38	19.69	21.69	26.19	25.63	25.63	28.50	31.50	32.38	24.30
1992	39.33	36.00	34.57	34.63	33.56	32.13	29.63	27.31	27.88	26.95	27.00	25.50	31.21
1993	24.94	24.37	23.65	23.13	24.13	24.95	25.35	25.61	24.44	23.88	26.69	34.25	25.45
1994	30.30	29.69	27.31	28.19	29.45	30.25	29.56	30.35	30.63	30.60	34.19	33.69	30.35
1995	32.50	32.00	31.13	31.00	30.50	35.00	37.90	35.63	35.00	36.00	37.88	33.69	34.02
1996	35.80	36.63	36.75	38.75	39.50	42.25	41.80	42.80	47.20	48.00	49.50	50.00	42.42
1997	44.20	44.00	42.88	42.50	42.50	35.00	36.50	36.50	37.00	37.25	37.25	37.25	39.40
1998	37.25	37.25	37.25	37.25	37.25	37.00	36.50	35.50	36.50	39.00	37.50	38.50	37.23
1999[1]	35.38	35.00	34.00	34.06	38.25	42.13	39.83	36.08	46.00	35.02	40.73	41.43	38.16

[1] Preliminary. NA = Not available. *Source: Economic Research Service, U.S. Department of Agriculture (ERS-USDA)*

Coffee

Coffee prices moved higher in late 1999 as dry weather in Brazil during the critical flowering stage for the 2000/2001 crop caused widespread damage. There was a great deal of uncertainty in the market as to what would likely happen. Following the harvest of the 1999/00 crop in September, the September-November 1999 period in Brazil was very dry. Normally, humid air moves south from the Amazon Basin meeting cooler air moving north from Argentina. The result is rain which is normally heavy, widespread and timely. These rains initiate the flowering of the trees which in turn leads to the development of the crop. This season the rains were inconsistent and light, and they often fell in only one part of the extensive coffee growing region. Early on, the rains were predominantly in the northern parts of the coffee region. The southern and central regions were dry for the most part. The light rains touched off flowering only to be followed by a dry stretch which caused the flowers to fall off the trees. It was particularly dry in the important growing region of Minas Gerais. As a result of the poor initial growing conditions, the production potential for the new crop was reduced leading to higher prices.

Brazil is by far the world's largest producer and exporter of coffee. Production in Brazil follows a biennial cycle. Large crops are followed by small crops which, in turn, are followed by large crops. Based on U.S.D.A. estimates, the 1995/96 (July-June) crop was 16.8 million bags, followed by the 1996/97 crop of 28 million bags, which was followed by the 1997/98 crop of 23.5 million bags. The 1998/99 crop was a cyclically large one at 35.6 million bags and that resulted in record coffee exports. That crop, in turn, was followed by the 1999/00 crop which was harvested between May and September 1999. That crop was 26.5 million bags. Based on the two year production cycle, the 2000/01 crop had been expected to be about 40 million bags. Because of the dry weather, the 2000/01 crop forecast was reduced to 30 million bags or less. This means that Brazilian exporters will have potentially less coffee to export in the 2000/01 season. There remains a great deal of uncertainty about the size of the crop which may not be known until the harvest.

In addition to the important questions about the next Brazilian crop, there are also questions about the 1999/00 (October-September) Colombian coffee crop. Colombia is the second largest producer and exporter of coffee in the world. The U.S.D.A. in its December report forecast the crop at 12 million bags, some 10 percent larger than the previous season. That crop was damaged by a combination of heavy La Nina related rains and insect infestation. In Colombia, the National Coffee Growers Federation has reported that the 1999/00 crop could in fact turn out to be much smaller than expected, perhaps less than 10 million bags. The National Coffee Growers Federation reported that for the first three months of the 1999/00 season, production was just over 3 million bags or some 15 percent less than in 1998-99.

The next largest producer of arabica coffee is Mexico. The U.S.D.A. forecast Mexico's 1999/00 crop at 5.2 million bags, up 12 percent from the small 1998/99 crop of 4.65 million bags. Mexico is a major exporter of coffee to the U.S. and the larger crop in 1999/00 should permit a substantial increase in exports. The U.S.D.A. forecast Guatemala's 1999/00 coffee crop at 4.9 million bags, the same as in 1998/99. It was interesting that Guatemala was a country affected in 1998 by Hurricane Mitch. In the final assessment, conditions following the hurricane were very favorable and yields were better than expected.

A number of countries outside North and South America are increasing the amount of coffee they produce. The most notable of these is Vietnam which has been increasing production at a very fast rate. Vietnam has overtaken Indonesia to become the largest producer of robusta coffee. The U.S.D.A. forecast the 1999/00 crop at a record 7.5 million bags, up 12 percent from the year before. In 1994/95, Vietnam produced 3.5 million bags so output has more than doubled in the last five years. Indonesia, which had been the largest producer of robustas, has fallen behind Vietnam. The U.S.D.A. forecast the 1999/00 (April-March) crop at 7.2 million bags, up almost 4 percent from the previous year. Another country in Asia that has expanded production is India which grows both arabica and robusta coffee. The U.S.D.A. forecast the 1999/00 crop at 4.7 million bags, up 6 percent from 1998/99. In 1994/95, India's coffee crop was 3.1 million bags.

In Africa, the Ivory Coast is the largest robusta coffee producer. A military coup in late 1999 changed the government but there was no indication of any change in the coffee industry as a result of this. The U.S.D.A. estimated the 1999/00 Ivory Coast crop at 5.3 million bags, some 150 percent higher than the 1998/99 crop which was damaged by drought related to El Nino. Uganda's 1999/00 coffee crop was forecast at 4 million bags, up 11 percent from the previous year.

Overall, world coffee production in 1999/00 is forecast to be 107.2 million bags, down less than 1 percent from 1998/99. What is most interesting is how the 2000/01 crop will turn out. That crop will include the Brazilian coffee crop that has been damaged by drought.

Futures Markets

Coffee futures are traded on the Bolsa de Mercadorias & Futuros (BM&F), the Tokyo Grain Exchange (TGE), the Singapore Commodity Exchange (SCE), the London International Financial Futures and Options Exchange (LIFFE), and the CSCE Division of the New York Board of Trade (NYBOT). Options are traded on the BM&F, the LIFFE and the CSCE.

World Supply and Distribution of Coffee In Thousands of 60 Kilogram Bags (132.276 Lbs. Per Bag)

Crop Year	Beginning Stocks	Production	Imports	Supply	Total Exports	Bean Exports	Rst/Grn Exports	Soluble Exports	Domestic Use	Ending Stocks
1990-1	43,012	100,181	331	143,524	76,163	73,278	83	2,802	22,265	45,096
1991-2	45,096	104,064	291	149,451	80,887	77,844	53	2,990	22,266	46,298
1992-3	46,298	92,959	713	139,970	77,869	73,881	117	3,871	21,579	40,522
1993-4	40,522	92,406	585	133,513	76,284	71,779	108	4,397	22,928	34,301
1994-5	34,301	97,024	1,070	132,395	68,654	64,414	230	4,010	22,529	41,212
1995-6	41,212	88,873	1,081	131,166	74,049	68,968	231	4,850	23,999	33,118
1996-7	33,118	103,763	1,091	137,972	84,490	79,900	195	4,395	24,297	29,185
1997-8[1]	29,185	96,827	1,211	127,223	77,538	72,855	193	4,490	25,185	24,500
1998-9[2]	24,500	107,742	1,241	133,483	83,891	80,033	207	3,651	26,141	23,451
1999-00[3]	23,451	107,215	1,124	131,790	84,979	80,659	198	4,122	26,772	20,039

[1] Preliminary. [2] Estimate. [3] Forecast. *Source: Foreign Agricultural Service, U.S. Department of Agriculture (FAS-USDA)*

World Production of Green Coffee In Thousands of 60 Kilogram Bags (132.276 Lbs. Per Bag)

Crop Year	Brazil	Cameroon	Colombia	Costa Rica	El Salvador	Ethiopia	Guatemala	India	Indonesia	Ivory Coast	Mexico	Uganda	World Total
1990-1	31,000	1,450	14,500	2,565	2,603	3,500	3,282	2,970	7,480	3,300	4,550	2,700	100,417
1991-2	28,500	1,920	17,980	2,530	2,357	3,000	3,549	3,200	7,100	3,967	4,620	2,900	103,731
1992-3	24,000	837	14,950	2,620	2,894	3,500	3,584	2,700	7,350	2,500	4,180	2,800	92,894
1993-4	28,500	676	11,400	2,475	2,361	3,700	3,078	3,465	7,400	2,700	4,200	2,700	92,319
1994-5	28,000	401	13,000	2,492	2,314	3,800	3,500	3,060	6,400	3,733	4,030	3,100	97,024
1995-6	16,800	518	12,939	2,595	2,325	3,800	3,827	3,717	5,800	2,900	5,400	4,200	88,873
1996-7	28,000	1,432	10,779	2,376	2,498	3,800	4,141	3,417	7,900	5,333	5,300	4,297	103,763
1997-8[1]	23,500	889	11,932	2,455	2,040	3,500	4,200	3,805	7,000	4,080	4,950	3,032	96,827
1998-9[2]	35,600	1,333	10,868	2,459	1,860	3,867	4,900	4,415	6,950	2,123	4,650	3,600	107,742
1999-00[3]	26,500	1,300	12,000	2,550	2,221	3,500	4,900	4,700	7,200	5,300	5,200	4,000	107,215

[1] Preliminary. [2] Estimate. [3] Forecast. *Source: Foreign Agricultural Service, U.S. Department of Agriculture (FAS-USDA)*

World Exportable[4] Production of Green Coffee In Thousands of 60 Kilogram Bags (132.276 Lbs. Per Bag)

Crop Year	Brazil	Cameroon	Colombia	Costa Rica	El Salvador	Ethiopia	Guatemala	Indonesia	Ivory Coast	Kenya	Mexico	Uganda	Worl Total
1990-1	21,500	1,420	12,885	2,305	2,423	1,800	2,972	6,185	3,264	1,433	3,150	2,650	78,271
1991-2	19,500	1,895	16,580	2,270	2,173	1,400	3,239	5,550	3,929	1,483	3,170	2,845	81,729
1992-3	15,500	812	13,647	2,365	2,677	2,000	3,274	5,570	2,461	1,195	2,880	2,745	71,726
1993-4	19,100	611	9,700	2,225	2,131	2,200	2,777	5,535	2,661	1,208	2,900	2,640	69,678
1994-5	18,300	371	11,564	2,252	2,079	2,300	3,220	4,440	3,687	1,562	3,030	3,040	74,957
1995-6	6,300	453	11,439	2,360	2,055	2,300	3,527	3,750	2,852	1,788	4,340	4,140	65,373
1996-7	17,000	1,332	9,279	2,130	2,268	2,300	3,856	5,820	5,282	1,115	4,450	4,217	79,822
1997-8[1]	12,000	789	10,372	2,150	1,805	1,900	3,850	5,360	4,025	859	3,955	2,952	72,108
1998-9[2]	23,100	1,233	9,268	2,144	1,633	2,217	4,500	5,350	2,065	1,077	3,650	3,540	82,127
1999-00[3]	13,700	1,200	10,360	2,225	1,994	1,825	4,470	5,520	5,240	1,307	4,200	3,920	80,963

[1] Preliminary. [2] Estimate. [3] Forecast. [4] Marketing year begins in October in some countries and April or July in others. Exportable production represents total harvested production minus estimated domestic consumption. *Source: Foreign Agricultural Service, U.S. Department of Agriculture*

Green Coffee Imports in the United States In Thousands of 60 Kilogram Bags (132.276 Lbs. Per Bag)

Year	Brazil	Colombia	Costa Rica	Dominican Republic	Ecuador	El Salvador	Ethiopia	Guatemala	Indonesia	Mexico	Peru	Venezuela	Grand Total
1989	4,155	2,413	393	402	1,137	790	432	1,404	635	3,937	673	87	19,377
1990	3,633	2,771	403	445	876	843	234	1,871	830	3,305	473	222	19,566
1991	5,335	3,048	603	343	785	868	31	1,489	536	2,993	610	108	18,849
1992	4,253	4,852	662	254	753	1,344	23	1,812	581	3,042	526	104	21,673
1993	3,376	2,957	437	213	671	1,274	192	1,815	542	2,947	158	444	18,023
1994	2,850	2,372	325	207	969	376	215	1,403	558	2,516	249	295	14,913
1995	2,302	2,485	388	266	745	284	109	1,637	513	2,887	621	89	15,886
1996	1,852	3,011	482	255	665	401	137	1,748	1,246	3,734	441	445	17,947
1997	2,331	3,179	608	150	431	500	308	1,921	1,325	2,935	652	65	18,848
1998[1]	2,688	3,410	771	164	347	501	183	1,563	1,273	2,471	771	146	18,998

[1] Preliminary. *Source: Bureau of Census, U.S. Department of Commerce*

COFFEE

Monthly Green Coffee Imports in the United States In Thousands of 60 Kilogram Bags[2]

Year	Jan.	Feb.	Mar.	Apr.	May	June	July	Aug.	Sept.	Oct.	Nov.	Dec.	Total
1990	1,950	1,989	2,358	1,783	1,658	1,548	1,451	1,261	1,229	1,611	1,140	1,591	19,566
1991	2,106	1,946	1,590	1,748	1,556	984	1,056	1,335	1,424	1,368	1,616	2,122	18,849
1992	2,262	1,944	2,125	1,698	1,534	1,795	1,806	1,692	1,644	1,615	1,508	2,050	21,673
1993	1,782	1,663	2,012	1,481	1,631	1,253	1,442	1,344	1,374	1,464	1,018	1,561	18,023
1994	1,538	1,152	1,409	1,077	1,082	1,151	1,195	1,560	1,266	1,127	1,103	1,213	14,872
1995	1,469	1,253	1,702	1,221	1,190	1,240	1,117	1,094	1,220	1,326	1,492	1,563	15,886
1996	1,824	1,657	1,753	1,395	1,444	1,236	1,329	1,341	1,364	1,279	1,485	1,828	17,936
1997	1,582	1,837	1,966	1,792	1,738	1,583	1,783	1,391	1,147	1,215	1,184	1,629	18,848
1998	1,747	1,893	1,827	1,587	1,540	1,412	1,386	1,478	1,369	1,499	1,423	1,837	18,998
1999[1]	1,742	1,866	2,243	1,787	1,602	1,691	1,488	1,639					14,058

[1] Preliminary. [2] 132.276 pounds per bag. *Source: Bureau of the Census, U.S. Department of Commerce*

Average Price of Brazilian[1] Coffee in New York In Cents Per Pound

Year	Jan.	Feb.	Mar.	Apr.	May	June	July	Aug.	Sept.	Oct.	Nov.	Dec.	Average
1990	70.36	77.59	86.17	87.45	86.31	82.94	78.94	90.25	92.20	85.78	77.46	80.17	82.97
1991	75.59	79.39	83.83	81.58	75.56	72.44	69.24	68.15	75.08	65.91	66.03	62.14	72.91
1992	62.03	58.05	59.60	54.94	51.11	49.08	48.53	46.40	49.43	59.64	64.64	74.39	56.49
1993	67.13	66.34	62.60	54.92	57.26	55.70	65.76	73.25	75.58	71.65	74.20	74.51	66.58
1994	71.42	80.14	84.72	87.14	118.37	136.43	211.81	192.38	212.73	191.21	172.83	159.73	143.24
1995	162.81	161.07	171.48	166.54	161.72	145.22	139.68	149.54	130.26	127.23	125.33	110.46	145.95
1996	127.54	144.05	140.99	132.92	134.76	125.44	106.93	108.28	103.10	105.77	103.76	103.71	119.77
1997	127.28	160.21	179.75	183.73	209.62	184.21	158.52	158.25	167.77	152.12	149.07	171.12	166.80
1998	179.83	177.78	154.84	141.11	124.89	104.09	96.04	101.92	92.76	91.32	96.67	100.28	121.81
1999	99.43	91.72	88.90	86.14	96.29	91.69	78.13	76.67	70.43	78.74	98.41		86.96

[1] And other Arabicas. NA = Not Avaliable. *Source: Foreign Agricultural Service, U.S. Department of Agriculture (FAS-USDA)*

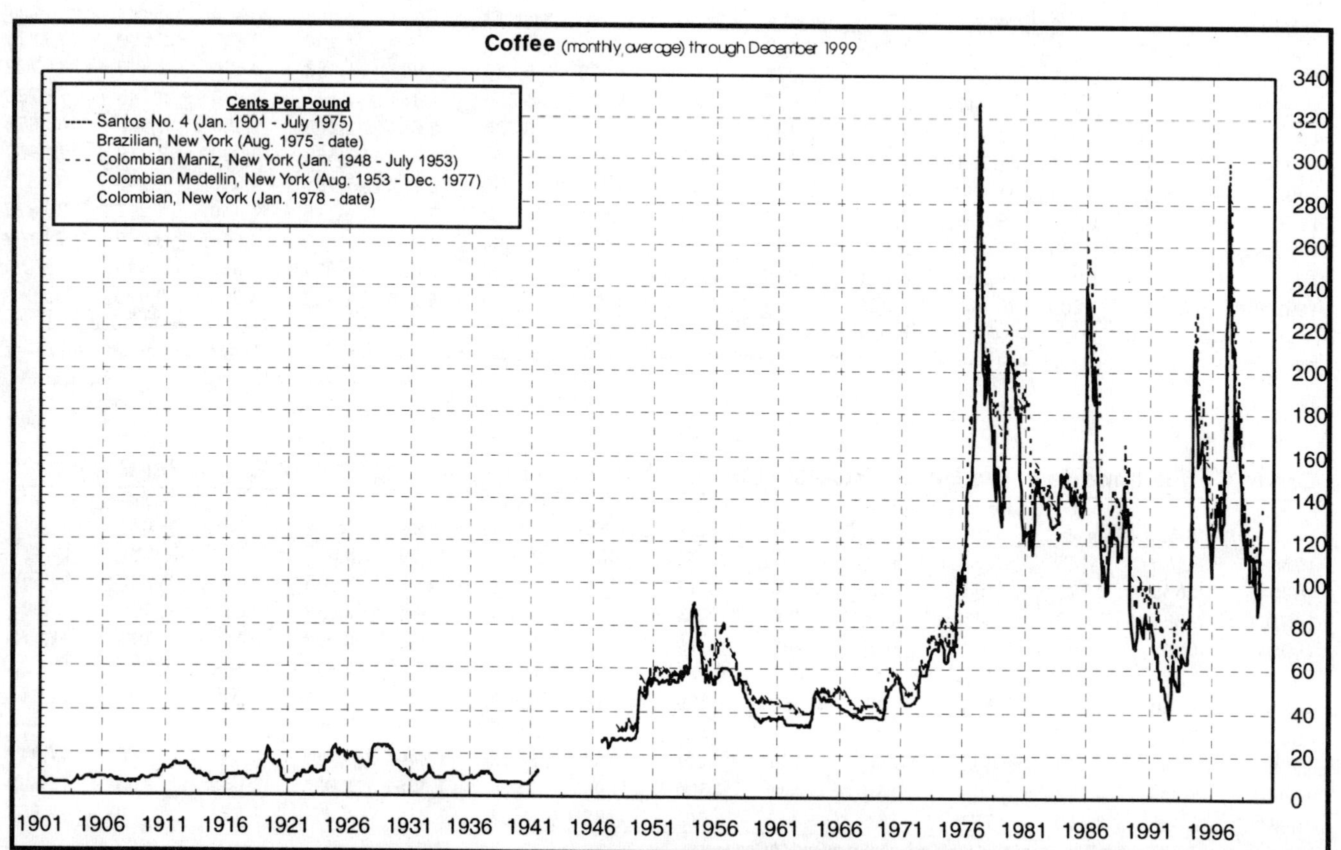

Average Monthly Retail [1] Price of Coffee in the United States In Cents Per Pound

Year	Jan.	Feb.	Mar.	Apr.	May	June	July	Aug.	Sept.	Oct.	Nov.	Dec.	Average
1992	266.8	268.8	263.1	261.2	266.0	262.5	265.2	261.3	253.7	249.2	239.1	236.4	257.8
1993	235.2	245.2	246.2	247.7	251.4	253.3	254.8	250.0	249.3	241.5	243.3	248.0	247.2
1994	253.0	252.9	251.5	251.6	253.5	259.8	334.1	448.0	445.8	445.0	448.2	438.2	340.1
1995	439.8	423.4	410.8	408.4	406.7	405.9	402.7	405.1	399.6	386.5	381.4	375.2	401.8
1996	357.7	359.0	355.0	352.7	344.4	343.8	338.0	339.0	333.3	334.4	328.3	330.7	343.0
1997	330.0	331.6	351.2	389.4	410.9	442.8	462.8	466.9	461.7	439.2	430.3	416.1	411.1
1998	402.5	397.3	403.3	395.9	387.8	378.6	377.1	370.4	362.0	350.3	348.2	344.6	376.5
1999	343.5	342.8	347.6	346.6	349.5	342.1	342.0	342.8	339.3	348.2	333.7		343.5

[1] Roasted in 13.1 to 20 ounce cans. *Source: Foreign Agricultural Service, U.S. Department of Agriculture (FAS-USDA)*

Average Price of Colombian Mild Arabicas[1] in the United States In Cents Per Pound

Year	Jan.	Feb.	Mar.	Apr.	May	June	July	Aug.	Sept.	Oct.	Nov.	Dec.	Average
1992	78.40	71.75	73.67	69.55	64.93	64.10	62.50	56.49	56.18	64.77	71.72	81.52	67.97
1993	71.61	72.45	67.07	59.77	67.35	68.13	76.40	84.18	86.58	83.02	85.56	87.33	75.79
1994	85.85	93.04	93.23	97.53	133.90	151.85	222.75	210.57	231.52	206.07	186.96	173.94	157.27
1995	177.23	175.07	185.75	180.30	177.18	170.87	157.22	163.21	141.49	132.08	129.09	110.47	158.33
1996	119.08	134.94	160.60	134.31	142.56	133.25	135.39	137.68	123.30	127.77	129.41	126.41	133.73
1997	146.18	188.62	212.96	199.22	318.50	227.15	190.57	193.46	196.29	169.40	161.38	183.32	198.92
1998	184.21	190.59	166.07	158.17	146.33	135.83	125.03	129.45	117.56	115.01	121.74	123.96	142.83
1999	123.07	116.92	117.05	114.02	123.95	121.45	107.05	105.28	97.77	103.69	126.76		114.27

[1] ICO monthly and composite indicator prices on the New York Market, 1979 ICA Agreement basis. *Source: Foreign Agricultural Service, U.S. Department of Agriculture (FAS-USDA)*

Average Price of Other Mild Arabicas[1] in the United States In Cents Per Pound

Year	Jan.	Feb.	Mar.	Apr.	May	June	July	Aug.	Sept.	Oct.	Nov.	Dec.	Awwerage
1992	72.99	67.88	69.96	65.23	60.14	58.38	57.68	52.42	52.73	61.40	67.36	77.46	63.64
1993	68.66	67.46	62.77	56.88	61.48	61.61	71.46	76.56	79.87	75.05	77.07	80.00	69.91
1994	77.21	82.69	85.57	89.23	121.97	142.57	217.67	198.07	220.10	199.06	180.76	167.47	148.53
1995	171.74	168.71	178.22	172.81	168.63	151.56	143.83	151.41	131.87	125.38	123.23	103.99	149.28
1996	109.38	122.71	119.05	122.01	128.56	124.46	120.47	122.49	114.05	120.62	119.90	115.01	119.89
1997	131.83	167.20	193.82	204.43	264.50	212.55	186.52	185.17	184.38	161.45	154.15	174.25	185.02
1998	175.04	175.87	154.82	147.08	134.35	121.56	113.86	119.89	108.07	107.07	113.84	115.54	132.25
1999	110.99	103.24	103.23	99.69	109.10	104.21	90.85	87.64	81.06	92.22	112.74		99.54

[1] ICO monthly and composite indicator prices on the New York Market, 1979 ICA Agreement basis. *Source: Foreign Agricultural Service, U.S. Department of Agriculture (FAS-USDA)*

Average Price of Robustas 1976[1] in the United States In Cents Per Pound

Year	Jan.	Feb.	Mar.	Apr.	May	June	July	Aug.	Sept.	Oct.	Nov.	Dec.	Average
1992	49.44	43.22	43.08	42.32	38.79	38.07	39.60	39.92	42.39	45.50	49.08	52.09	43.63
1993	48.13	48.25	46.86	45.51	46.91	47.65	50.39	59.29	63.44	60.05	62.53	62.90	53.49
1994	60.91	62.25	66.46	72.64	96.05	113.31	164.65	162.68	182.95	170.09	154.19	130.48	119.72
1995	132.26	135.22	146.83	145.47	141.89	129.53	120.89	131.28	116.41	114.15	112.79	94.72	126.79
1996	91.99	98.99	91.99	91.45	92.10	86.46	78.14	80.16	74.83	72.97	70.51	63.08	82.72
1997	67.66	76.65	81.31	78.48	95.74	91.94	82.52	76.92	77.43	76.90	78.20	84.65	80.70
1998	86.03	85.79	84.67	90.60	92.64	84.55	78.40	79.98	80.88	80.36	80.40	82.82	83.93
1999	81.65	77.68	72.70	68.89	68.28	66.20	62.28	63.80	60.44	59.25	64.10		67.75

[1] ICO monthly and composite indicator prices on the New York Market, 1979 ICA Agreement basis. *Source: Foreign Agricultural Service, U.S. Department of Agriculture (FAS-USDA)*

Average Price of Composite 1979[1] in the United States In Cents Per Pound

Year	Jan.	Feb.	Mar.	Apr.	May	June	July	Aug.	Sept.	Oct.	Nov.	Dec.	Average
1992	61.12	55.51	56.48	53.64	49.27	48.13	48.70	45.89	47.11	52.88	57.49	64.00	53.35
1993	58.14	57.32	54.76	51.38	54.18	54.54	60.61	67.69	71.64	67.78	70.03	71.53	61.63
1994	69.17	72.37	76.11	81.19	108.42	127.91	191.44	181.53	202.39	185.64	168.12	149.14	134.45
1995	152.08	152.24	162.73	159.59	155.96	141.66	132.71	141.70	124.75	120.02	117.99	99.57	138.42
1996	100.33	110.50	105.89	107.09	110.24	105.79	99.97	102.73	96.52	98.56	97.14	90.04	102.07
1997	100.03	121.89	137.47	142.20	180.44	155.38	135.04	132.63	132.51	121.09	118.16	130.02	133.91
1998	130.61	130.78	119.93	119.66	114.23	103.84	97.32	101.25	95.82	95.01	98.26	100.73	108.95
1999	97.63	92.36	89.41	85.72	89.51	85.41	78.21	77.22	71.94	76.36	88.22		84.73

[1] ICO monthly and composite indicator prices on the New York Market, 1979 ICA Agreement basis. *Source: Foreign Agricultural Service, U.S. Department of Agriculture (FAS-USDA)*

Average Open Interest of Coffee 'C' Futures in New York In Contracts

Year	Jan.	Feb.	Mar.	Apr.	May	June	July	Aug.	Sept.	Oct.	Nov.	Dec.
1990	37,352	43,516	46,187	43,978	41,756	40,464	39,856	41,428	39,278	39,523	43,750	41,365
1991	42,320	41,326	39,948	39,410	41,726	43,717	42,037	40,661	42,126	43,940	41,819	40,628
1992	47,042	51,183	48,961	51,979	59,275	58,304	59,096	58,401	56,446	59,808	57,527	58,257
1993	59,193	54,249	53,618	55,578	51,797	50,918	53,871	48,541	47,649	49,809	46,901	48,812
1994	54,796	50,230	53,713	57,226	58,574	54,589	43,056	35,052	35,800	34,258	31,046	31,134
1995	34,455	35,391	36,925	34,387	34,615	34,462	30,156	27,448	27,800	28,408	24,505	26,412
1996	28,430	28,224	28,127	28,793	28,394	25,096	26,188	25,799	23,929	26,202	27,599	27,201
1997	38,516	42,888	39,092	32,644	30,324	22,552	21,497	19,818	22,788	25,109	23,636	28,577
1998	30,042	30,539	30,211	32,617	36,345	36,651	37,531	30,074	30,429	32,940	31,677	32,816
1999	36,194	36,693	41,294	43,846	45,947	45,674	45,410	46,725	46,255	47,955	46,270	46,764

Source: New York Board of Trade (NYBOT)

Volume of Trading of Coffee 'C' Futures in New York In Contracts

Year	Jan.	Feb.	Mar.	Apr.	May	June	July	Aug.	Sept.	Oct.	Nov.	Dec.	Total
1990	130,223	174,115	211,105	144,641	128,121	147,605	127,767	172,947	119,088	113,569	175,067	119,802	1,774,050
1991	138,642	174,688	188,842	153,436	103,344	135,887	107,058	170,113	180,017	148,640	159,099	112,882	1,772,648
1992	153,332	199,420	174,662	188,232	156,944	164,586	177,493	182,741	163,214	108,707	211,678	199,374	2,152,383
1993	290,120	214,771	183,354	209,607	176,559	197,761	193,002	233,479	202,363	187,763	217,947	182,486	2,489,223
1994	188,508	219,455	208,113	284,734	380,119	304,542	210,479	196,685	159,574	177,424	184,172	142,713	2,658,073
1995	169,250	191,352	213,326	156,191	163,248	186,550	162,562	161,076	165,337	152,959	157,240	123,923	2,003,014
1996	203,369	186,526	152,797	197,442	137,454	158,929	171,800	196,991	136,054	196,696	135,305	166,213	2,039,576
1997	242,719	280,014	267,369	223,330	219,214	186,227	135,664	136,807	142,610	151,171	145,610	163,446	2,294,181
1998	155,774	194,435	186,712	194,732	157,935	189,768	165,868	189,047	156,556	172,956	197,776	133,471	2,095,030
1999	216,810	201,670	252,841	243,630	237,968	243,164	187,019	232,817	151,724	270,013	244,258	177,309	2,659,223

Source: New York Board of Trade (NYBOT)

Coke

U.S. production of coke in the January-March 1999 period was 4.79 million short tons, about the same as in the like period of 1998. For all of 1998, coke production was 20 million tons. Stocks of coke at coke plants at the end of March 1999 were 1.02 million tons. A year earlier stocks were 952,000 tons. Consumption of coke in the January-March 1999 period was 5.29 million tons.

U.S. coke exports in the first quarter of 1999 were 194,836 tons, down 1 percent compared to the first quarter of 1998. Virtually all of the coke exported goes to North American markets. In first quarter 1999, exports to Canada were 141,797 tons, up 19 percent from the year before. Exports to Mexico were 49,529 tons, down 32 percent from the previous.

Imports of coke in first quarter 1999 were 781,220 tons, up 2 percent from a year ago. Imports from Japan were 469,300 tons while imports from China were 305,657 tons.

Salient Statistics of Coke in the United States In Thousands of Short Tons

	Production at Coke Plants						Exports			Producer & Distributor	Avg. Price of Coal
Year	Merchant Coke Plants	Furnace Coke Plants	Total Coke	Breeze	Imports	Consumption[2]	Total	Canada	Mexico	Ending Stocks	Receipts at Coke Plants
1993	3,209	19,973	23,182	3,424	1,534	24,303	835	417	92	1,461	47.44
1994	3,244	19,443	22,686	1,392	1,612	24,163	660	371	94	986	46.56
1995	3,239	20,509	23,749	1,463	1,816	24,500	750	579	60	1,302	47.34
1996	3,105	19,971	23,075	1,402	1,111	23,043	1,121	491	143	1,323	47.33
1997[1]	2,903	19,212	22,120	1,233	1,570	22,880	830	498	251	1,320	47.36
1998[2]	2,604	18,268	20,210	1,196	1,720	21,710	620	548	238	1,110	45.65

[1] Preliminary. [2] Estimate. [3] Equal to production plus imports minus the change in producer and distributor stocks minus exports.
Source: Energy Information Administration, U.S. Department of Energy (EIA-DOE)

Production of Petroleum Coke in the United States In Thousands of Barrels[2]

Year	Jan.	Feb.	Mar.	Apr.	May	June	July	Aug.	Sept.	Oct.	Nov.	Dec.	Total
1993	18,551	17,289	19,226	18,200	18,587	18,715	20,196	19,319	18,547	18,695	18,954	19,737	226,016
1994	19,170	16,873	18,695	18,454	19,748	19,325	20,008	19,473	17,868	18,753	18,995	19,697	227,059
1995	19,079	17,117	18,556	18,519	19,774	19,949	19,527	19,722	19,184	19,292	19,349	19,887	229,955
1996	19,536	18,706	21,015	20,663	20,426	19,927	19,836	20,328	20,124	20,558	20,447	21,389	242,955
1997	19,798	17,594	20,603	21,274	22,210	21,052	21,619	22,229	21,630	21,782	20,313	21,827	251,931
1998	20,929	18,968	21,998	21,834	21,790	20,856	21,790	22,469	21,526	21,234	20,837	22,258	256,489
1999[1]	22,312	20,084	22,148	21,444	21,410	20,943	21,741	22,180	21,249	22,166			258,812

[1] Preliminary. *Source: Energy Information Administration, U.S. Department of Energy (EIA-DOE)*

Coal Receipts and Carbonization at Coke Plants in the United States In Thousands of Short Tons

	Coal Receipts at Coke Plants							Coal Carbonized at Coke Plants						
	By State					By Plant Type		By State					By Plant Type	
Year	Alabama	Indiana	Ohio	Pennsylvania	Total	Merchant Coke Plants	Furnace Coke Plants	Alabama	Indiana	Ohio	Pennsylvania	Total	Merchant Coke Plants	Furnace Coke Plants
1993	3,184	6,515	2,853	10,424	31,104	4,184	26,921	3,206	6,591	2,892	10,333	31,323	4,267	27,056
1994	3,242	5,023	3,064	10,776	31,719	4,205	27,514	3,253	4,841	3,092	10,849	31,740	4,218	27,522
1995	3,183	5,731	2,758	10,959	33,036	4,189	28,848	3,257	5,883	2,777	10,858	33,011	4,248	28,763
1996	3,213	5,884	1,770	10,562	31,672	4,135	27,537	3,247	5,823	1,842	10,689	31,706	4,135	27,570
1997[1]	2,966	5,676	1,823	10,272	30,138	3,800	26,338	2,956	5,715	1,848	10,334	29,443	3,826	25,618
1998[2]	2,548	5,260	1,752	9,140	27,360	3,556	23,808	2,420	5,432	1,816	9,436	27,752	3,408	24,344

[1] Preliminary. [2] Estimate. *Source: Energy Information Administration, U.S. Department of Energy (EIA-DOE)*

Coke Distribution and Stocks in the United States In Thousands of Short Tons

	Distribution							Coke Plant Stocks, Dec. 31			
	By Plant Type		By Consumer Category						By Plant Type		
Year	Merchant Coke Plants	Furnace Coke Plants	Blast Furnace	Foundries	Other Industrial	Total Coke	Breeze	Total Coke	Merchant Coke Plants	Furnace Coke Plants	Breeze
1993	3,226	27,009	28,295	1,373	567	30,235	3,563	1,461	272	1,189	486
1994	3,400	25,949	27,248	1,480	621	29,349	1,735	986	122	864	105
1995	3,284	25,103	26,346	1,401	639	28,386	1,638	1,302	112	1,189	136
1996	-----	-----	-----	-----	-----	-----	-----	1,323	160	1,163	161
1997	-----	-----	-----	-----	-----	-----	-----	1,326	79	1,247	141
1998[1]	-----	-----	-----	-----	-----	-----	-----	933	-----	-----	144

[1] Preliminary. *Source: Energy Information Administration, U.S. Department of Energy (EIA-DOE)*

Copper

Copper metals and copper alloys have considerable commercial importance due to their electrical, mechanical and physical properties. Copper for commercial purposes is obtained by the reduction of copper compounds in ores and by electrolytic refining. Copper is used in alloys such as brass which is composed of copper and zinc.

The U.S. Geological Survey reported that world production of copper in 1998 was 11.9 million metric tonnes, up 4 percent from 1997. The world's largest producer of copper is Chile with 1998 production estimated at 3.66 million tonnes, up 8 percent from the previous year. The U.S. is the second largest copper producer in the world. Indonesia's 1998 production was estimated at 750,000 tonnes, up 42 percent from the previous year. Canada's copper production was estimated at 710,000 tonnes, up 8 percent from the previous year.

U.S. mine production of recoverable copper in July 1999 was 132,000 tonnes, down 1,000 tonnes from June. In the January-June 1999 period, U.S. mine production was 1.01 million tonnes. For all of 1998, production was 1.86 million tonnes. U.S. smelter production of copper in July 1999 was 85,800 tonnes vs. 77,100 tonnes in June. In the January-July 1999 period, smelter production of copper was 708,000 tonnes while for all of 1998 it was 1.49 million tonnes. Total refinery production of copper in July 1999 was 140,000 tonnes, down from 155,000 tonnes in June. In the first seven months of 1999, refinery production was 1.15 million tonnes while for all of 1998 it was 2.12 million tonnes. Copper is also produced by secondary recovery. In the January-July 1999 period, secondary refinery production was 137,000 tonnes. Ingot makers production was 76,800 tonnes while brass and wire-rod mills produced 486,000 tonnes.

U.S. apparent consumption of copper in June 1999 was 248,000 tonnes. For all of 1998, apparent copper consumption in the U.S. was 3.01 million tonnes. Copper and copper alloy products were consumed as follows: building construction, 42 percent; electric and electronic products, 25 percent; industrial machinery and equipment, 11 percent; transportation equipment, 13 percent; and consumer and general products, 9 percent. Refined consumption of copper in July 1999 was 240,000 tonnes. In the January-July 1999 period, consumption was 1.74 million tonnes while for 1998 it was 2.88 million tonnes. Purchased copper-base scrap in July 1999 was 146,000 tonnes. In the first seven months of 1999 it was 1.07 million tonnes while for 1998 it was 1.72 million tonnes.

U.S. stocks of refined copper at the end of July 1999 were 631,000 tonnes compared to 637,000 tonnes at the end of June 1999. At the end of 1998, refined copper stocks were 531,000 tonnes. Blister stocks at the end of July 1999 were 136,000 tonnes compared to 135,000 tonnes at the end of June and 160,000 tonnes at the end of 1998.

U.S. imports of copper ores and concentrates in June 1999 were 60,500 tonnes while for all of 1998 they were 217,000 tonnes. Imports of refined copper in June 1999 were 63,800 tonnes and for all of 1998 they were 683,000 tonnes.

Futures Markets

Copper futures and options are traded on the London Metals Exchange (LME) and the New York Mercantile Exchange, COMEX division. Copper futures are traded on the Shanghai Futures Exchange (SHFE).

World Mine Production of Copper (Content of Ore) In Thousands of Metric Tons

Year	Australia	Canada[3]	Chile	China	Indonesia	Mexico	Peru	Poland	Russia[4]	South Africa	United States[3]	Zambia	World Total
1989	296.0	723.1	1,609.3	276	144.0	264.2	387.9	384.0	1,000	181.9	1,507	466.3	9,058
1990	330.0	793.7	1,588.4	285	164.1	293.9	339.3	330.0	950	178.7	1,588	421.0	8,950
1991	320.0	811.1	1,814.3	304	211.7	292.1	357.2	320.0	900	184.6	1,531	390.6	9,090
1992	378.0	768.6	1,932.7	334	280.8	279.0	345.6	331.9	699	176.1	1,760	429.5	9,470
1993	402.0	732.6	2,055.4	345	298.6	301.2	355.0	382.6	584	166.3	1,800	396.2	9,430
1994	415.6	616.8	2,219.9	396	322.2	294.7	346.5	378.0	573	160.1	1,850	373.2	9,520
1995	419.9	726.3	2,488.6	445	443.6	333.6	440.4	384.2	525	161.6	1,850	323.7	10,100
1996	524.8	688.4	3,115.8	439	507.5	340.7	486.5	421.9	520	152.6	1,920	333.8	11,000
1997[1]	545.0	657.4	3,392.0	414	529.1	390.5	491.0	414.0	505	186.0	1,940	353.0	11,400
1998[2]	600.0	710.0	3,660.0	440	750.0	400.0	450.0	420.0	450	NA	1,850	280.0	11,900

[1] Preliminary. [2] Estimate. [3] Recoverable. [4] Formerly part of the U.S.S.R.; data not reported separately until 1992.
Source: U.S. Geological Survey (USGS)

Commodity Exchange Inc. Warehouse Stocks of Copper, on First of Month In Thousands of Short Tons

Year	Jan.	Feb.	Mar.	Apr.	May	June	July	Aug.	Sept.	Oct.	Nov.	Dec.
1990	16.3	7.2	4.1	4.5	6.0	14.7	18.1	11.5	8.9	6.7	8.3	9.3
1991	20.2	14.7	16.4	30.2	30.9	25.0	25.1	35.9	33.6	24.4	26.8	29.3
1992	33.7	34.8	29.5	28.2	30.3	32.4	31.8	36.0	40.4	51.7	70.1	73.8
1993	105.9	124.0	114.8	107.6	110.8	108.3	105.5	113.8	100.1	94.1	96.6	80.5
1994	74.0	56.7	49.8	37.2	31.6	30.4	36.0	37.4	28.5	17.9	20.3	21.5
1995	26.7	18.7	17.7	9.0	11.5	7.0	13.1	16.7	16.5	11.2	6.0	5.0
1996	23.7	12.1	12.4	13.9	20.7	13.2	7.6	17.7	22.1	21.7	30.8	36.2
1997	29.3	18.4	24.8	43.3	48.9	42.6	44.7	30.0	46.5	61.5	68.0	82.3
1998	91.9	101.8	113.7	112.6	106.5	83.0	62.5	55.7	56.1	67.7	70.7	75.8
1999	93.9	102.0	114.2	123.4	132.6	131.7	133.7	119.5	108.1	97.5	90.9	90.9

Source: New York Mercantile Exchange (NYMEX), COMEX division

Salient Statistics of Copper in the United States In Thousands of Metric Tons

	New Copper Produced						Imports[3]		Exports		Stocks, Dec 31			Apparent Consumption	
	From Domestic Ores														
Year	Mines	Smelters	Refineries	From Foreign Ores[3]	Total New	Secondary Recovered[4]	Unmanufactured	Refined	Ore, Concentrate[6]	Refined[7]	COMEX	Primary Producers (Refined)	Blister & Material in Solution	Refined Copper (Reported)	Primary & Old Copper[8]
1988	1,417	1,043	1,043	124	1,406	518	513	332	211	58	12	97	121	2,210	2,214
1989	1,498	1,120	1,120	125	1,477	548	515	300	267	130	15	107	132	2,203	2,185
1990	1,590	1,160	1,110	75	1,577	537	512	262	258	211	18	101	119	2,150	2,168
1991	1,630	1,120	1,060	77	1,577	518	512	289	253	263	31	132	135	2,048	2,105
1992	1,760	1,180	1,110	96	1,710	555	593	289	266	177	96	205	166	2,178	2,311
1993	1,800	1,270	1,210	89	1,790	543	637	343	227	217	67	153	146	2,360	2,510
1994	1,850	1,310	1,280	64	1,840	500	763	470	261	157	24	119	171	2,680	2,690
1995	1,850	1,250	1,300	91	1,930	442	825	429	239	217	22	163	174	2,530	2,540
1996[1]	1,920	1,300	1,290	147	2,010	428	961	543	195	169	27	146	173	2,610	2,830
1997[2]	1,940	1,440	1,370	113	2,060	496	978	647	127	93	83	314	180	2,790	2,950

[1] Preliminary. [2] Estimate. [3] Also from matte, etc., refinery reports. [4] From old scrap only. [5] For consumption. [6] Blister (copper content). [7] Ingots, bars, etc. [8] Old scrap only. *Source: U.S. Geological Survey (USGS)*

Consumption of Refined Copper[3] in the United States In Thousands of Metric Tons

	By-Products						By Class of Consumer						Total
Year	Cathodes	Wire Bars	Ingots & Ingot Bars	Cakes & Slabs	Billets	Other[4]	Wire Rod Mills	Brass Mills	Chemiacl Plants	Ingot Makers	Foundries	Miscellaneous[5]	Consumption
1988	1,967.4	14.0	54.2	63.0	99.0	12.7	1,667.2	493.2	1.0	2.6	14.5	31.9	2,210.4
1989	1,981.6	6.1	34.4	64.9	104.9	11.2	1,698.4	461.0	0.9	1.3	14.9	26.5	2,203.1
1990	1,922.4	6.6	50.5	57.9	W	113.0	1,653.5	445.2	1.1	4.5	14.6	31.6	2,150.4
1991	1,854.9	W	24.7	33.3	W	135.4	1,591.8	458.5	0.9	3.4	12.7	25.3	2,048.3
1992	1,974.9	W	20.0	43.7	W	139.6	1,675.0	458.5	0.9	3.0	15.0	25.8	2,178.2
1993	2,130.0	W	37.7	55.5	W	136.0	1,819.1	503.0	0.9	2.2	10.2	27.6	2,360.0
1994	2,410.0	W	37.3	73.2	W	164.0	2,060.0	568.0	1.1	4.5	11.1	30.4	2,680.0
1995	2,250.0	W	31.3	75.9	W	181.0	1,950.0	533.0	1.1	7.7	15.6	31.4	2,530.0
1996[1]	2,320.0	W	26.8	80.8	W	181.0	1,980.0	588.0	1.1	3.6	15.8	28.6	2,610.0
1997[2]	2,490.0	W	29.5	81.1	W	194.0	2,140.0	597.0	1.0	4.2	16.6	29.9	2,790.0

[1] Preliminary. [2] Estimate. [3] Primary & secondary. [4] 1991 to date include Wirebars and Billets. [5] Includes iron and steel plants, primary smelters producing alloys other than copper, consumers of copper powder and copper shot, and other manufacturers. W - Withheld proprietary data.
Source: U.S. Geological Survey (USGS)

London Metals Exchange Warehouse Stocks of Copper, at End of Month In Thousands of Metric Tons

Year	Jan.	Feb.	Mar.	Apr.	May	June	July	Aug.	Sept.	Oct.	Nov.	Dec.
1990	121.5	106.8	71.9	67.0	92.8	67.7	126.8	161.1	227.1	221.1	199.9	220.6
1991	189.0	202.8	213.9	237.9	275.0	264.9	266.5	307.1	308.4	291.7	308.3	332.3
1992	308.6	302.7	296.4	279.7	265.4	259.1	246.8	275.2	299.7	317.8	327.0	315.8
1993	313.5	333.1	365.8	403.5	429.1	446.9	464.3	521.7	600.7	612.3	590.9	599.5
1994	597.6	554.5	504.3	446.4	379.0	350.9	338.9	367.8	359.3	333.1	318.4	302.2
1995	309.9	280.9	239.9	204.9	197.9	166.5	151.5	163.1	178.2	193.6	222.2	364.8
1996	355.1	348.4	322.3	303.9	309.7	263.0	227.6	275.5	240.7	122.1	96.1	110.6
1997	194.2	216.2	177.2	145.8	133.0	128.3	234.9	278.7	332.8	344.6	338.8	337.8
1998	365.7	376.0	339.5	262.3	261.8	249.3	260.9	307.7	414.2	460.6	511.9	590.1
1999[1]	646.9	695.9	722.2	748.2	776.6	754.8	769.6	789.0	774.0	793.8	779.7	790.5

[1] Preliminary. *Source: American Bureau of Metal Statistics (ABMS)*

Copper Refined from Scrap in the United States In Thousands of Metric Tons

Year	Jan.	Feb.	Mar.	Apr.	May	June	July	Aug.	Sept.	Oct.	Nov.	Dec.	Total
1990	37.3	35.2	37.1	38.5	39.3	38.1	34.6	39.2	29.9	34.3	31.9	32.0	440.8
1991	35.4	32.8	40.5	39.6	38.2	35.7	32.6	33.0	28.5	37.3	32.1	32.6	417.7
1992	27.8	34.1	39.8	34.8	36.7	39.4	27.8	35.4	39.8	40.0	34.3	35.8	433.2
1993	38.1	45.9	38.9	37.8	36.4	41.1	35.0	37.6	37.4	43.0	35.4	32.2	459.8
1994	33.3	28.3	37.9	30.7	37.1	28.7	26.9	33.0	38.7	27.0	34.3	37.3	391.7
1995	30.9	30.6	36.0	32.7	33.7	28.2	18.7	25.1	25.4	25.0	26.2	24.4	319.0
1996	25.0	23.7	25.5	22.5	26.8	30.9	24.4	25.0	26.8	30.6	25.9	26.3	333.0
1997	35.9	30.0	36.4	32.6	35.4	30.8	26.4	28.4	34.3	36.5	24.6	29.3	383.0
1998	25.9	28.6	23.7	31.0	17.8	21.4	24.2	23.9	23.8	31.8	23.2	26.3	336.0
1999[1]	20.1	21.8	23.7	17.6	16.2	17.5	21.2	18.2	20.2				235.3

[1] Preliminary. *Source: U.S. Geological Survey (USGS)*

COPPER

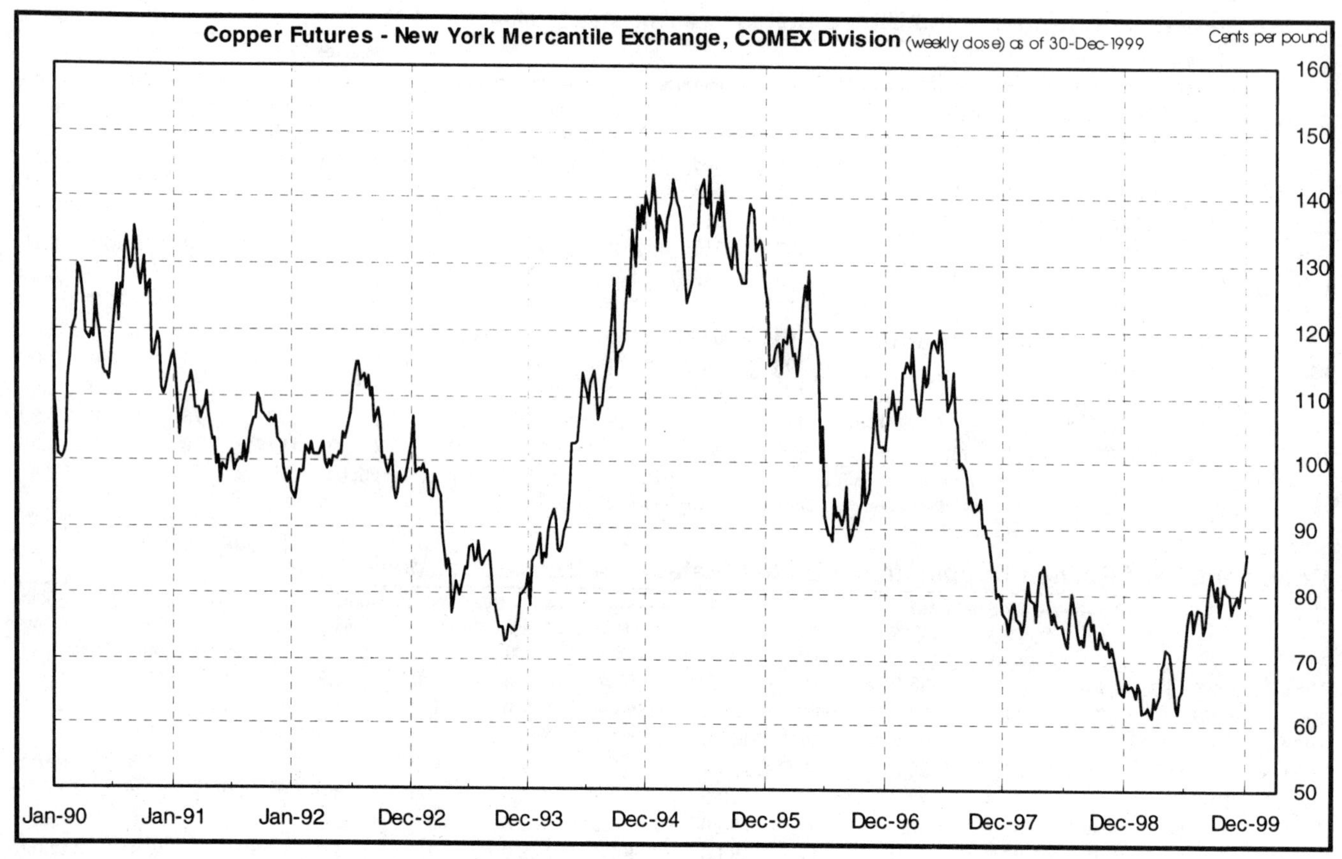

Average Open Interest of Copper Futures[1] in New York In Contracts

Year	Jan.	Feb.	Mar.	Apr.	May	June	July	Aug.	Sept.	Oct.	Nov.	Dec.
1990	31,466	33,908	34,654	34,405	31,552	30,113	32,780	31,515	32,578	36,145	35,088	30,128
1991	34,927	35,978	35,026	34,096	44,153	39,879	33,100	33,333	40,347	42,028	41,618	44,283
1992	47,109	47,929	48,700	45,114	39,986	48,129	47,065	38,397	37,041	41,658	44,927	45,541
1993	47,433	48,707	48,220	51,217	52,762	56,856	54,861	54,571	54,929	57,406	63,632	69,311
1994	65,518	65,446	66,177	59,346	63,825	60,383	51,616	46,855	56,344	59,060	59,158	51,078
1995	52,632	50,770	47,267	47,793	50,089	48,200	40,968	37,744	33,709	36,476	38,475	35,996
1996	47,771	45,706	42,732	46,771	47,284	52,558	56,564	56,549	55,408	58,124	61,031	55,807
1997	54,468	56,022	58,205	50,574	56,740	56,774	47,767	44,632	49,612	54,912	67,026	67,502
1998	69,607	72,302	67,154	68,670	65,033	66,002	63,271	61,116	60,520	62,944	67,984	76,846
1999	76,861	73,109	75,318	70,534	76,341	70,842	75,640	70,084	80,188	72,239	69,179	69,819

[1] Through December 1989 includes Old Copper and New High Grade Copper contracts. *Source: New York Mercantile Exchange (NYMEX), COMEX division*

Volume of Trading of Copper Futures[1] in New York In Contracts

Year	Jan.	Feb.	Mar.	Apr.	May	June	July	Aug.	Sept.	Oct.	Nov.	Dec.	Total
1990	152,156	148,766	179,445	181,726	164,489	163,372	141,602	154,383	156,924	161,814	133,718	114,790	1,853,185
1991	159,621	131,044	108,191	150,390	148,777	139,207	110,025	149,702	132,354	125,757	153,910	135,132	1,643,310
1992	145,245	168,015	105,003	157,473	77,722	182,091	138,225	177,581	137,423	121,392	146,062	117,931	1,674,163
1993	152,387	148,388	132,705	212,086	160,751	181,427	165,727	169,428	222,099	133,364	203,729	182,538	2,064,629
1994	197,959	233,016	231,239	207,963	247,143	297,393	188,644	242,393	219,788	208,957	290,585	178,887	2,737,967
1995	242,760	267,883	232,229	242,302	195,554	274,587	167,836	213,110	169,689	181,945	185,141	146,378	2,519,414
1996	184,431	173,689	157,553	210,836	200,469	255,172	150,445	174,351	166,537	250,420	227,800	160,216	2,311,919
1997	193,543	221,504	190,000	218,607	164,728	238,918	191,609	198,156	197,746	202,615	203,376	135,368	2,356,170
1998	172,133	223,117	197,652	264,061	175,956	217,316	202,596	213,541	196,355	195,255	250,986	174,642	2,483,610
1999	159,147	288,394	230,716	296,162	224,221	319,157	244,567	267,325	267,325	220,958	231,399	161,434	2,910,805

[1] Through December 1989 include Old Copper and New High Grade Copper contracts *Source: New York Mercantile Exchange (NYMEX), COMEX division*

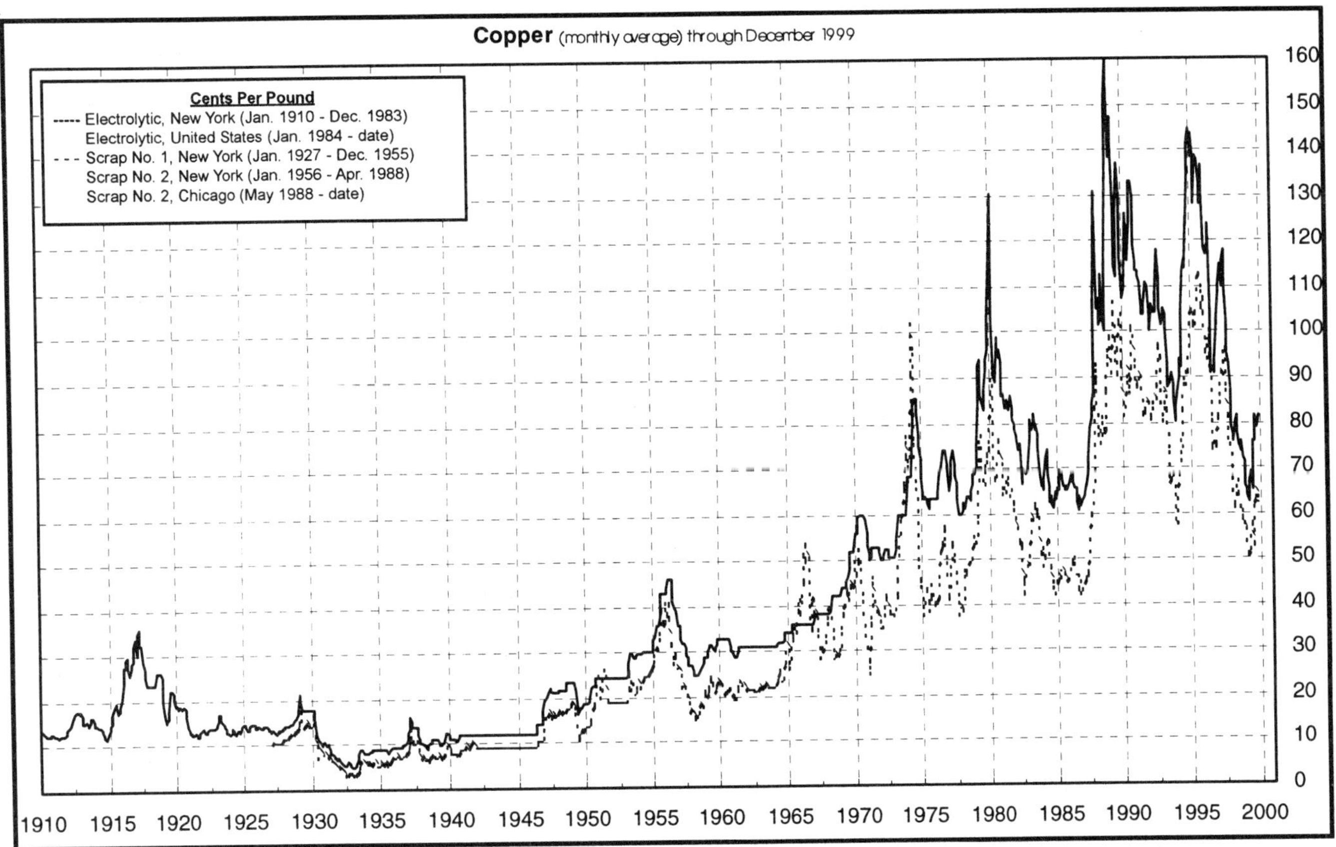

Producers' Price of Electrolytic (Wirebar) Copper, Delivered to U.S. Destinations In Cents Per Pound

Year	Jan.	Feb.	Mar.	Apr.	May	June	July	Aug.	Sept.	Oct.	Nov.	Dec.	Average
1990	116.36	119.35	136.22	134.38	132.32	124.93	133.91	142.53	142.45	138.41	127.76	124.39	131.08
1991	122.59	122.73	121.24	120.35	133.11	111.72	111.90	113.48	118.92	118.90	117.26	110.33	118.54
1992	108.16	112.52	113.56	112.35	112.56	116.74	125.66	124.30	119.39	112.09	108.23	111.13	114.72
1993	112.57	110.26	107.80	99.03	92.35	94.98	93.41	97.06	92.36	81.69	86.07	91.08	96.56
1994	95.65	99.13	101.76	99.87	112.30	120.58	123.68	121.38	132.53	130.91	141.92	148.86	119.05
1995	152.02	146.00	151.14	146.03	139.80	149.51	150.00	149.77	144.14	140.00	148.48	143.78	146.72
1996	130.09	128.75	130.20	131.29	135.33	116.33	102.68	104.14	102.51	105.46	112.78	114.78	117.86
1997	120.29	122.22	126.80	121.70	127.25	129.57	121.94	114.11	107.14	105.08	99.53	95.65	115.94
1998	88.88	87.52	91.69	93.54	90.02	86.90	87.37	85.30	87.62	84.26	83.51	78.30	87.08
1999	77.07	75.96	74.50	78.79	81.07	77.23	88.02	90.63	92.89	91.26	91.10	93.35	84.32

Source: American Metal Market (AMM)

Dealers' Buying Price of No. 2 Heavy Copper Scrap in Chicago[1] In Cents Per Pound

Year	Jan.	Feb.	Mar.	Apr.	May	June	July	Aug.	Sept.	Oct.	Nov.	Dec.	Average
1990	78.27	71.00	78.73	88.00	88.00	84.38	84.00	85.50	91.84	89.50	86.48	83.00	84.06
1991	83.00	79.50	82.21	82.50	78.66	72.40	71.00	71.00	72.05	75.39	75.08	74.50	76.44
1992	73.21	73.37	75.23	75.16	74.00	74.27	77.18	78.38	75.38	70.27	69.00	67.18	73.55
1993	67.95	67.00	67.00	62.95	55.12	53.59	56.33	54.18	52.67	49.10	47.00	48.00	56.74
1994	50.80	56.11	59.61	62.00	64.86	72.32	76.40	74.30	75.69	76.45	78.10	82.95	69.13
1995	89.48	90.79	89.39	91.75	85.91	88.73	92.32	92.65	92.70	90.64	92.00	92.00	90.70
1996	87.17	82.90	83.24	83.29	82.95	71.48	61.43	62.00	62.00	63.00	64.84	66.00	72.53
1997	68.73	71.63	77.50	79.18	77.33	78.19	72.64	70.24	65.67	63.74	61.31	58.43	70.38
1998	53.26	52.58	53.09	54.00	52.60	49.64	48.00	47.71	46.00	44.00	40.00	40.00	48.41
1999	36.32	36.00	36.00	36.00	39.60	41.77	41.00	45.09	46.19	48.00	48.00	48.67	41.89

Source: American Metal Market (AMM)

COPPER

Imports of Refined Copper into the United States   In Thousands of Metric Tons

Year	Jan.	Feb.	Mar.	Apr.	May	June	July	Aug.	Sept.	Oct.	Nov.	Dec.	Total
1990	24.7	15.8	26.5	25.3	31.3	24.0	20.6	18.0	21.4	18.4	20.8	16.7	263.6
1991	22.7	27.1	21.7	30.9	17.5	23.6	23.7	17.4	22.9	36.3	26.8	18.0	288.6
1992	22.6	24.5	31.9	25.2	25.3	26.1	24.7	25.3	24.0	19.6	20.3	20.8	289.1
1993	21.8	25.6	28.2	35.9	29.5	26.9	30.6	28.3	22.5	31.6	32.2	30.5	343.4
1994	28.7	33.6	49.8	36.8	36.1	46.8	35.6	34.4	34.7	62.4	35.9	36.2	470.0
1995	34.9	30.0	37.1	36.9	36.5	37.9	31.5	31.8	28.7	38.7	44.4	40.3	429.0
1996	43.1	41.2	48.2	49.6	56.8	44.6	53.8	64.8	62.3	46.1	61.8	47.2	543.0
1997	55.4	48.0	43.6	43.6	61.0	42.0	53.1	73.3	53.8	55.0	53.4	42.0	632.0
1998	62.8	49.6	59.9	64.7	57.6	52.8	45.0	51.7	71.1	52.7	62.0	63.4	683.0
1999[1]	64.7	53.2	68.1	59.9	62.3	63.8	73.0	84.5					794.3

[1] Preliminary.   *Source: U.S. Geological Survey (USGS)*

Exports of Refined Copper from the United States   In Thousands of Metric Tons

Year	Jan.	Feb.	Mar.	Apr.	May	June	July	Aug.	Sept.	Oct.	Nov.	Dec.	Total
1990	18.1	20.8	12.2	7.6	15.6	12.2	23.9	20.1	22.4	21.5	17.2	19.8	211.3
1991	33.6	21.4	37.4	16.8	31.5	23.9	20.6	20.9	17.9	13.4	15.4	17.9	270.7
1992	21.7	18.4	10.8	12.3	11.7	12.0	9.3	13.0	13.6	24.1	14.1	16.1	176.9
1993	14.0	24.9	23.6	16.3	15.4	13.1	10.7	10.1	19.5	19.5	14.9	14.5	216.7
1994	13.0	10.2	10.7	6.8	14.8	9.1	15.6	10.9	15.4	15.9	13.1	21.1	157.0
1995	11.1	24.0	25.6	18.2	23.4	38.9	16.3	16.6	12.1	9.0	12.5	9.5	217.0
1996	13.7	16.5	12.7	12.3	10.8	10.7	15.7	17.7	14.5	16.4	12.8	16.0	170.0
1997	11.1	9.8	6.5	6.5	71.9	8.2	6.9	7.5	6.3	7.4	8.2	8.5	93.3
1998	6.2	12.1	12.2	7.5	7.8	6.4	7.5	6.4	5.8	5.0	3.6	6.2	86.2
1999[1]	2.4	1.1	1.8	1.3	1.6	4.2	1.6	1.5					23.4

[1] Preliminary.   *Source: U.S. Geological Survey (USGS)*

Stocks of Refined Copper in the United States[2], on First of Month   In Thousands of Short Tons

Year	Jan.	Feb.	Mar.	Apr.	May	June	July	Aug.	Sept.	Oct.	Nov.	Dec.
1990	72.7	42.4	38.6	45.2	55.9	60.2	67.5	67.2	67.6	27.4	27.9	45.4
1991	72.3	72.8	53.2	68.6	63.2	52.8	52.4	71.4	64.4	48.5	48.3	63.1
1992	75.3	76.3	67.2	69.7	75.9	65.0	62.2	71.2	87.1	99.5	110.3	107.1
1993	135.4	152.7	144.3	132.3	146.0	153.6	137.1	151.0	128.4	117.2	124.6	107.1
1994	103.0	87.7	83.6	72.8	70.7	70.4	73.3	81.1	74.6	66.5	52.7	53.6
1995	55.8	39.6	37.0	22.6	33.1	30.8	27.0	50.0	60.6	71.1	69.4	73.4
1996	120.0	131.4	125.5	123.1	126.3	107.9	102.8	106.2	104.7	68.0	76.0	77.5
1997	88.2	98.8	104.4	116.0	117.9	121.7	122.9	148.8	177.1	197.9	227.6	253.3
1998	281.5	282.2	312.7	315.7	304.5	308.6	306.2	319.0	334.1	367.4	407.2	444.6
1999[1]	562.6	593.1	614.6	653.5	676.6	687.8	668.4	657.2	639.7	611.2	626.5	608.2

Recoverable copper content.   [1] Preliminary.   [2] New reporting method beginning January 1995, includes Comex, London Metal Exchange, and Refiners. Beginning January 1999, includes Consumers.   *Source: American Bureau of Metal Statistics (ABMS)*

Stocks of Refined Copper Outside the United States[2], on First of Month   In Thousands of Short Tons

Year	Jan.	Feb.	Mar.	Apr.	May	June	July	Aug.	Sept.	Oct.	Nov.	Dec.
1990	362.3	382.0	335.6	320.0	332.6	356.3	291.8	370.9	417.9	484.6	483.0	447.6
1991	439.5	464.2	447.1	501.1	559.5	595.4	593.1	605.4	664.7	653.5	644.9	676.9
1992	640.4	718.1	704.2	715.7	714.9	723.2	726.4	737.9	816.5	822.5	873.8	896.1
1993	757.1	765.9	789.6	817.2	885.1	912.2	910.4	943.8	1,040.3	1,124.3	1,133.9	1,106.1
1994	1,075.0	1,095.5	1,046.8	984.9	913.7	859.5	843.7	839.7	874.6	870.7	835.1	818.4
1995	611.6	655.8	622.2	577.9	537.0	525.6	494.9	464.7	465.7	467.7	481.4	503.5
1996	560.2	566.0	552.5	517.5	498.7	563.9	507.9	476.6	544.4	499.5	391.8	362.0
1997	405.4	469.5	476.3	445.7	413.5	402.4	408.3	489.6	550.9	607.7	574.5	553.3
1998	580.8	512.4	487.3	438.1	371.1	368.0	335.7	324.0	387.2	468.0	506.9	509.0
1999[1]	922.6	944.3	960.3	963.0	990.5	1,008.3	993.3	990.0	1,017.0	992.6	988.9	977.4

Recoverable copper content.   [1] Preliminary.   [2] New reporting method beginning January 1995, includes London Metal Exchange and Refiners. Beginning January 1999, also includes Shanghai Metal Exchange, Consumers and Other.   *Source: American Bureau of Metal Statistics (ABMS)*

Production of Refined Copper in North America[2] In Thousands of Short Tons

Year	Jan.	Feb.	Mar.	Apr.	May	June	July	Aug.	Sept.	Oct.	Nov.	Dec.	Total
1990	136.0	122.0	150.4	140.1	147.5	136.1	125.5	132.5	130.1	141.6	141.0	125.5	1,628
1991	129.0	127.7	134.9	119.7	137.1	124.8	136.8	142.7	135.6	153.1	141.0	149.7	1,632
1992	139.9	135.6	150.6	142.8	123.0	138.5	140.3	150.1	146.9	155.3	156.8	153.7	1,734
1993	153.9	153.8	173.2	166.0	160.3	177.0	151.4	153.7	160.2	157.3	157.2	166.2	1,930
1994	160.9	150.0	167.8	157.2	165.5	160.4	148.9	165.6	162.1	157.3	153.3	159.8	1,909
1995	202.7	185.5	204.8	194.6	210.0	198.3	193.8	208.8	199.0	206.5	211.3	208.1	2,423
1996	210.8	197.6	209.7	212.4	213.5	193.4	206.1	199.5	198.8	223.1	199.3	212.0	2,476
1997	220.7	200.7	216.7	216.3	205.9	196.5	222.1	213.5	226.2	241.2	229.3	230.6	2,624
1998	193.3	201.4	200.7	202.7	185.5	204.8	194.6	210.0	198.3	193.8	208.8	199.0	2,393
1999[1]	292.9	285.3	334.2	313.1	302.2	282.3	256.8	254.0	278.9	280.2	270.7	274.0	3,425

Recoverable copper content. [1] Preliminary. [2] New reporting method beginning January 1995. Data through December 1998 are in the United States.
Source: American Bureau of Metal Statistics (ABMS)

Production of Refined Copper Outside North America[2] In Thousands of Short Tons

Year	Jan.	Feb.	Mar.	Apr.	May	June	July	Aug.	Sept.	Oct.	Nov.	Dec.	Total
1990	423.7	396.7	424.6	412.8	414.1	395.6	372.6	407.1	404.6	422.6	417.4	411.0	4,902
1991	416.5	381.1	427.7	405.5	425.3	404.5	375.1	378.7	411.4	411.8	409.2	424.5	4,871
1992	441.2	412.6	447.0	418.0	438.7	449.5	418.5	425.8	418.7	438.9	431.3	426.1	5,166
1993	429.2	405.6	475.1	426.2	440.9	447.5	421.6	449.4	448.0	425.9	447.2	436.5	5,253
1994	432.5	390.8	432.7	400.6	432.9	421.1	387.8	413.8	421.5	416.3	437.4	428.8	5,016
1995	817.5	797.6	868.4	858.2	859.4	844.8	849.7	825.7	819.8	865.2	833.8	872.2	10,112
1996	903.2	869.3	929.3	922.2	916.3	918.3	908.3	931.1	938.2	972.9	935.8	992.4	11,137
1997	962.5	936.0	981.1	1,007.9	1,032.8	1,021.5	1,024.0	1,008.2	990.0	1,023.4	1,011.7	1,028.3	12,053
1998	1,073.1	1,012.8	1,066.3	1,039.4	1,057.2	1,027.6	1,027.9	1,031.9	1,069.7	1,072.8	1,050.1	1,139.1	12,668
1999[1]	1,192.3	1,252.1	1,240.7	1,303.4	1,364.9	1,413.8	1,404.9	1,393.2	1,377.8	1,323.6	1,344.7	1,311.6	15,923

Recoverable copper content. [1] Preliminary. [2] New reporting method beginning January 1995, includes crude production. Data through December 1998 are Outside the United States. NA = Not avaliable. *Source: American Bureau of Metal Statistics (ABMS)*

Deliveries of Refined Copper to Fabricators in the United States In Thousands of Short Tons

Year	Jan.	Feb.	Mar.	Apr.	May	June	July	Aug.	Sept.	Oct.	Nov.	Dec.	Total
1990	167.4	132.8	163.3	156.6	153.3	144.5	129.5	132.5	130.1	140.9	130.7	108.6	1,733
1991	128.4	153.3	125.3	126.7	152.7	115.0	125.4	152.8	135.6	167.7	130.4	132.9	1,684
1992	144.9	159.0	165.9	155.5	149.4	161.4	145.8	144.1	146.9	150.4	166.2	130.0	1,813
1993	142.9	165.3	201.6	170.4	162.5	209.6	144.8	191.4	178.9	164.3	194.8	182.7	2,109
1994	193.3	168.6	204.6	178.3	187.8	171.9	154.3	194.6	188.2	188.7	167.5	175.1	2,173
1995[2]	233.8	209.2	239.1	200.9	230.0	210.5	187.1	208.8	202.9	224.7	222.4	175.5	2,545
1996	221.6	227.2	240.0	242.2	270.7	222.1	233.8	246.8	277.5	239.7	240.6	231.9	2,896
1997	246.3	234.5	240.6	247.4	254.9	228.1	241.1	258.2	252.3	259.2	256.0	236.6	2,959
1998	284.5	248.4	288.1	289.2	278.7	258.0	252.4	242.1	260.7	232.0	251.9	220.0	3,106
1999[1]	199.6	202.8	235.0	221.4	206.3	201.9	188.0	186.8	193.7	182.3	182.4	175.2	2,375

Recoverable copper content. [1] Preliminary. [2] New reporting method beginning January 1995, includes crude copper deliveries.
Source: American Bureau of Metal Statistics (ABMS)

Deliveries of Refined Copper to Fabricators Outside the United States In Thousands of Short Tons

Year	Jan.	Feb.	Mar.	Apr.	May	June	July	Aug.	Sept.	Oct.	Nov.	Dec.	Total
1989	426.0	369.9	411.8	360.9	459.0	398.0	386.8	464.2	393.2	456.9	423.0	399.1	4,949
1990	419.9	466.3	436.7	392.9	408.3	466.7	303.7	373.5	370.8	448.9	469.1	420.7	4,972
1991	405.0	404.4	391.5	361.2	406.3	433.5	368.5	323.4	420.7	499.1	391.4	483.4	4,807
1992	453.7	408.9	441.8	416.4	413.4	432.4	410.4	364.7	432.6	403.5	406.1	461.3	5,045
1993	427.9	392.9	452.3	361.7	422.2	442.6	384.4	347.9	387.5	414.8	463.4	458.5	4,956
1994	399.8	429.5	481.2	466.5	468.9	428.1	387.9	369.2	423.5	448.9	457.1	436.0	5,197
1995[2]	758.5	810.1	892.8	882.2	853.0	867.3	863.7	814.1	803.4	835.1	796.6	726.2	9,903
1996	875.2	859.4	934.3	907.2	816.7	950.7	908.3	817.4	911.5	1,056.0	922.7	918.3	10,878
1997	862.2	889.7	977.9	1,007.1	991.1	982.7	897.8	873.9	886.2	1,009.0	980.4	966.6	11,349
1998	1,091.7	973.8	1,062.0	1,055.5	995.7	1,014.8	986.8	924.8	913.3	987.9	982.1	1,025.6	12,014

Recoverable copper content. [1] Preliminary. [2] New reporting method beginning January 1995, includes crude copper deliveries.
Source: American Bureau of Metal Statistics (ABMS)

Corn

U.S. corn prices, basis nearby Chicago futures, drifted within the $2.00-$2.25 range during the first half of 1999, but midsummer witnessed price spikes in both directions; first a break to under $2.00/bushel followed by a short-lived recovery to over $2.25. Futures then lapsed into another drifting mode in the closing months of 1999, but with a bearish bias. In some respects the price action was similar to 1998 during which corn fell to a 10-year low. In both years the market was largely reacting to world production exceeding usage and the resulting increase in carryover stocks.

The U.S. 1999/2000 crop was estimated at 9.47 billion bushels (240.5 million metric tonnes), the third highest on record and comparing with 9.76 billion in 1998/99. The record high 10.1 billion bushel crop was realized in 1994/95. Both harvested acreage and average yield decreased in 1999; acreage of 70.9 million compares with 72.6 million in 1998, while average yield of 133.5 bushels per acre was down from 134.4 bushels, respectively. Two states, Iowa and Illinois, generally account for about a third of U.S. production.

The large crop, combined with the expected decline in 1999/00 exports, will lift carryover stocks as of August 31, 2000, to almost 2 billion bushels, a record high, and comparing with the year earlier 1.8 billion bushel carryover. The stock-to-use ratio in 1999/00 was forecast at 21 percent vs. the previous season's 19 percent and the very low 5 percent ratio of 1995/96: typically, the higher the ratio, the greater the pressure on prices. In 1999/00 the average price received by farmers was forecast to range between $1.65-2.05 per bushel vs. the 1998/99 average of $1.95, and the 1995/96 record high of $3.24. If a less than $2.00 per bushel average is realized in 1999/00 it would be the lowest of the past decade.

Corn is by far the leading U.S. feed grain with sorghum a very distant second. The crop year (marketing) encompasses September/August, but the international trade year is October/September. Animal feed usage in 1999/00 of 5.5 billion bushels is marginally higher than in 1998/99. Food, seed, and industrial use (FSI) was estimated at a record high 1.88 billion bushel in 1999/00 vs. 1.82 billion in 1998/99. The increases in FSI use during the past few years is not surprising considering the rising industrial demand for corn as a sweetener; High Fructose Corn Syrup (HFCS) usage continues to gain, up another 3 percent during 1998/99 from 1997/98. Corn used to make ethanol was also up, 9 percent from the prior year, and forecast to rise 5 percent during 1999/00.

The U.S. is the world's largest corn exporter, with Argentina a distant second. Importers are numerous but the leaders are generally in Asia paced by Japan, South Korea and Taiwan. U.S. exports in 1999/00 of 1.9 billion bushels (47.5 million tonnes) compare with 2 billion in 1998/99 and the record large 2.2 billion in 1995/96. U.S. corn imports are minimal, on average about 12 million bushels.

World foreign trade in corn in 1999/00 of 66.8 million metric tonnes is higher than initially forecast and compares with the record large 69.3 million tonnes in 1998/99. The U.S. accounted for about two-thirds of total trade volume in both years but the amounts are down from the mid-1990's when the U.S. supplied about 80 percent of world exports. Argentina now exports about 15 percent of the world total vs. less than 10 percent in the mid-1990's.

Japan is the world's largest importer taking around 16 million tonnes in recent years. South Korea tends to be the second largest importer with 8.3 million tonnes in 1999/00 vs. 7.7 million in 1998/99. China imports small amounts of corn; estimated at one million tonnes in 1999/00 vs. 1.2 million in 1998/99.

The near record large world corn production in 1999/00 of 599 million tonnes exceeded initial forecasts by 7 million tonnes with China and the U.S. accounting for most of the increase. This compares with the record world corn production of 605 million tonnes in 1998/99. China, second in world production since 1987/88, produced 128 million tonnes in 1999/00 vs. a record large 133 million in 1998/99. China's corn output has increased sharply from the 1980's when annual production averaged less than 100 million tons. The U.S. and China are forecast to produce about 61 percent of the world's corn in 1999/00; Brazil and Mexico combined produce about 9 percent. The gains seen in China's production in the 1990's reflects increases in per capita income and meat consumption, and the need for more corn as a livestock feed.

Global usage in 1999/00 of a record large 594 million tonnes compares with 583 million in 1998/99. China will use 120 million tonnes this year, compared to 117 million in 1998/99, and is the fifth consecutive year in which China's usage has topped 100 million tonnes. The U.S. is the largest consumer using almost a third of the world total, 187 million tonnes in 1999/00. Brazil is in third place with about 34 million tonnes. World corn stocks are forecast to increase in 1999/00 to 113 million tonnes from 108 million a year earlier.

U.S. #2 yellow corn prices vary with the location. Typically, Gulf Port prices are about 30¢ per bushel higher than prices in Central Illinois, while quotes at St. Louis run about 10¢-12¢ higher than Illinois prices. In midsummer 1999, #2 yellow corn in Central Illinois averaged around $1.84 per bushel vs. $1.86 a year earlier; for the Gulf ports the average was $2.20 per bushel vs. $2.24, respectively.

Futures Markets

Corn futures are traded on the Beijing Commodity Exchange (BCE), the Budapest Commodity Exchange, the Tokyo Grain Exchange (TGE), the Chicago Board of Trade (CBOT), and the Mid-American Commodity Exchange (MidAm). Corn options are traded on the CBOT and the MidAm. The CBOT also trades Iowa Corn Yield Insurance futures and options and U.S. corn yield insurance futures and options.

World Production of Corn or Maize In Thousands of Metric Tons

Crop Year	Argentina	Brazil	Canada	China	France	India	Italy	Mexico	Romania	South Africa	United States	Yugo-slavia	World Total
1990-1	7,600	24,330	7,067	96,820	9,500	8,962	5,864	14,100	6,800	8,300	201,534	6,724	477,855
1991-2	10,600	30,800	7,413	98,770	12,930	8,060	6,240	14,689	10,500	3,125	189,868	11,500	487,307
1992-3	10,200	29,200	4,883	95,380	14,870	9,992	7,410	18,631	6,829	9,990	240,719	6,650	538,552
1993-4	10,000	32,934	6,501	102,700	14,840	9,600	8,030	19,141	8,000	13,275	160,954	5,912	475,386
1994-5	11,360	37,440	7,043	99,280	12,640	9,120	7,480	17,005	8,500	4,845	255,295	7,500	560,277
1995-6	11,100	32,480	7,271	112,000	12,390	9,530	8,450	17,780	9,923	10,200	187,970	8,375	517,120
1996-7	15,500	35,700	7,380	127,470	14,430	10,612	9,550	18,922	9,610	10,136	234,518	8,100	592,040
1997-8[1]	19,360	30,520	7,180	104,300	16,750	10,852	10,010	16,934	12,680	7,544	233,864	9,700	575,313
1998-9[2]	13,500	32,200	8,952	132,954	15,200	10,780	8,600	17,600	8,500	7,100	247,882	8,200	605,083
1999-00[3]	15,500	32,000	9,096	128,000	15,500	10,500	10,000	19,000	10,000	8,500	239,719	7,000	597,986

[1] Preliminary. [2] Estimate. [3] Forecast. *Source: Foreign Agricultural Service, U.S. Department of Agriculture (FAS-USDA)*

World Supply and Demand of Course Grains In Millions of Metric Tons/Hectares

Crop Year Beginning Oct.1	Area Harvested	Yield	Pro-duction	World Trade	Total Con-sumption	Ending Stocks	Stocks as % of Con-sumption
1990-1	316.4	2.62	828.8	88.8	817.2	134.8	16.5
1991-2	321.9	2.52	810.4	95.6	809.7	135.6	16.7
1992-3	323.5	2.69	871.5	92.2	843.7	163.2	19.3
1993-4	316.8	2.52	798.8	85.0	838.7	123.4	14.7
1994-5	322.3	2.70	871.2	97.8	857.4	137.2	16.0
1995-6	313.3	2.56	802.9	87.3	842.3	97.8	11.6
1996-7	321.9	2.82	908.3	94.7	877.3	128.7	14.7
1997-8	311.0	2.84	883.3	85.5	875.5	136.4	15.6
1998-9[1]	308.8	2.88	890.5	95.9	873.2	153.7	17.6
1999-00[2]	303.7	2.88	873.7	96.1	878.5	149.0	17.0

[1] Preliminary. [2] Estimate. [3] Represents the ratio of marketing year ending stocks to total consumption. [4] Thru 1975-6; crop year beginning July 1.
Source: Foreign Agricultural Service, U.S. Department of Agriculture (FAS-USDA)

Acreage and Supply of Corn in the United States In Millions of Bushels

Crop Year Beginning Sept. 1[3]	Planted	Harvested: For Grain	Harvested: For Silage	Yield Per Harvested Acre Bushels	Carry-over, Sept. 1: On Farms	Carry-over, Sept. 1: Off Farms	Supply: Beginning Stocks	Supply: Pro-duction	Supply: Imports	Supply: Total Supply
	In Thousands of Acres									
1990-1	74,166	66,952	6,124	118.5	754.8	589.7	1,344	7,934	3	9,282
1991-2	75,957	68,822	6,101	108.6	691.2	830.0	1,521	7,475	20	9,016
1992-3	79,311	72,077	6,069	131.5	605.0	494.8	1,100	9,477	7	10,584
1993-4	73,235	62,921	6,831	100.7	1,070.7	1,042.0	2,113	6,338	21	8,472
1994-5	79,175	72,887	5,601	138.6	395.4	454.7	850	10,051	10	10,910
1995-6	71,245	64,995	5,295	113.5	740.9	816.9	1,558	7,400	16	8,974
1996-7	79,229	72,644	5,607	127.1	196.6	229.3	426	9,233	13	9,672
1997-8	79,537	72,671	6,054	126.7	475.0	408.2	883	9,207	9	10,099
1998-9[1]	80,165	72,589	5,913	134.4	640.0	667.8	1,308	9,761	19	11,088
1999-00[2]	77,431	70,537	6,062	133.8	797.0	990.0	1,787	9,437	15	11,239

[1] Preliminary. 2 Estimate. *Source: Economic Research Service, U.S. Department of Agriculture (ERS-USDA)*

Production of Corn (For Grain) in the United States, by State In Million of Bushels

Year	Illinois	Indiana	Iowa	Kansas	Mich-igan	Minn-esota	Missouri	Nebraska	Ohio	South Dakota	Texas	Wis-consin	Total
1990	1,320.8	703.1	1,562.4	188.5	238.1	762.6	205.8	934.4	417.5	234.0	130.5	354.0	7,934.0
1991	1,177.0	510.6	1,427.4	206.3	253.0	720.0	213.4	999.6	326.4	240.5	165.0	380.8	7,475.5
1992	1,646.5	877.6	1,903.7	259.5	241.5	741.0	324.0	1,066.5	507.7	277.2	202.5	306.8	9,476.7
1993	1,300.0	712.8	880.0	216.0	225.5	322.0	166.5	785.2	360.8	160.7	212.8	216.2	6,336.5
1994	1,786.2	858.2	1,930.4	304.6	260.9	915.9	273.7	1,153.7	486.5	367.2	238.7	437.1	10,102.7
1995	1,130.0	598.9	1,402.2	244.3	249.6	731.9	149.9	854.7	375.1	193.6	216.6	347.7	7,373.9
1996	1,468.8	670.4	1,711.2	357.2	211.5	868.8	340.4	1,179.8	310.8	365.0	198.2	333.0	9,232.6
1997	1,425.5	701.5	1,642.2	371.8	255.1	851.4	299.0	1,135.2	475.7	326.4	241.5	402.6	9,206.8
1998	1,473.5	760.4	1,769.0	419.0	227.6	1,032.8	285.0	1,239.8	470.9	429.6	185.0	404.2	9,761.1
1999[1]	1,491.0	736.0	1,781.8	397.6	241.3	951.4	247.0	1,138.5	387.5	341.3	233.6	400.4	9,380.9

[1] Preliminary. *Source: National Agricultural Statistics Service, U.S. Department of Agriculture (NASS-USDA)*

CORN

Supply and Disappearance of Corn in the United States In Millions of Bushels

Crop Year Beginning Sept. 1	Supply: Beginning Stocks	Supply: Production	Supply: Imports	Supply: Total Supply	Disappearance – Domestic Use: Food, Alcohol & Industrial	Disappearance – Domestic Use: Seed	Disappearance – Domestic Use: Feed & Residual	Disappearance – Domestic Use: Total	Disappearance: Exports	Total Disappearance	Ending Inventory: Gov't Owned[3]	Ending Inventory: Privately Owned	Ending Inventory: Total
1995-6	1,558	7,400	16.5	8,948	1,592	20.2	4,682	6,294	2,228	8,522	30	396	426
Sept.-Nov.	1,558	7,400	3.6	8,935	413	0	1,756	2,169	660	2,830	42	6,064	6,106
Dec.-Feb.	6,106	-----	5.0	6,111	401	0	1,348	1,749	562	2,311	42	3,758	3,800
Mar.-May	3,800	-----	5.0	3,805	411	17.6	1,048	1,477	610	2,087	41	1,677	1,718
June-Aug.	1,718	-----	2.9	1,721	367	2.6	530	899	396	1,295	30	396	426
1996-7	426	9,233	13.3	9,672	1,672	20.3	5,299	6,991	1,797	8,789	2	881	883
Sept.-Nov.	426	9,233	3.4	9,662	383	0	1,890	2,272	487	2,759	30	6,873	6,903
Dec.-Feb.	6,903	-----	2.4	6,905	394	0	1,492	1,887	525	2,411	30	4,464	4,494
Mar.-May	4,494	-----	3.7	4,498	445	19.7	1,103	1,568	433	2,001	10	2,486	2,497
June-Aug.	2,497	-----	3.8	2,500	449	.6	814	1,264	353	1,617	2	881	883
1997-8	883	9,207	8.8	10,099	1,761	20.4	5,505	7,287	1,504	8,791	4	1,304	1,308
Sept.-Nov.	883	9,207	2.2	10,092	429	0	2,036	2,465	380	2,845	2	7,245	7,247
Dec.-Feb.	7,247	-----	1.0	7,248	418	0	1,510	1,928	380	2,308	2	4,938	4,940
Mar.-May	4,940	-----	3.6	4,944	445	19.7	1,089	1,553	350	1,904	2	3,038	3,040
June-Aug.	3,040	-----	2.0	3,042	469	.7	870	1,340	394	1,734	4	1,304	1,308
1998-9[1]	1,308	9,761	19.0	11,088	1,822		5,498	7,320	1,981	9,301			1,787
Sept.-Nov.	1,308	9,761	4.0	11,073	444		2,127	2,571	450	3,021			8,052
Dec.-Feb.	8,052	-----	6.0	8,058	427		1,467	1,894	465	2,359			5,698
Mar.-May	5,698	-----	7.0	5,706	489		1,103	1,592	497	2,089			3,616
June-Aug.	3,616	-----	2.0	3,618	462		801	1,263	568	1,831			1,787
1999-00[2]	1,787	9,437	15.0	11,239	1,900		5,650	7,550	1,975	9,525			1,714
Sept.-Nov.	1,787	9,437	3.0	11,227	453		2,224	2,677	530	3,207			8,020

[1] Preliminary. [2] Estimate. [3] Uncommitted inventory. [4] Includes quantity under loan and farmer-owned reserve.
Source: Economic Research Service, U.S. Department of Agriculture (ERS-USDA)

Corn Production Estimates and Cash Price in the United States

Year	Corn for Grain Production Estimates (In Thousands of Bushels): Aug. 1	Sept. 1	Oct. 1	Nov. 1	Final	St. Louis No. 2 Yellow (Dollars Per Bushel)	Omaha No. 2 Yellow	Gulf Ports No. 2 Yellow	Kansas City No. 2 White	Chicago No. 2 Yellow	Average Farm Price	Value of Production (Million Dollars)
1991-2	7,474,480	7,295,071	7,479,421	7,485,901	7,475,480	2.53	2.36	2.74	3.06	2.52	2.37	17,864
1992-3	8,762,060	7,873,436	8,592,821	9,328,850	9,476,698	2.25	2.10	2.46	2.49	2.22	2.07	19,723
1993-4	7,423,142	7,229,427	6,961,902	6,503,237	6,336,470	2.67	2.56	2.85	2.78	2.68	2.50	16,032
1994-5	9,214,420	9,257,170	9,602,340	10,010,310	10,102,735	2.51	2.33	2.78	2.91	2.43	2.26	22,992
1995-6	8,121,520	7,832,140	7,541,400	7,373,700	7,373,876	4.06	3.87	4.30	4.14	3.97	3.24	24,118
1996-7	8,694,628	8,803,928	9,012,148	9,265,288	9,293,435	2.90	2.70	3.07	3.09	2.84	2.71	25,149
1997-8	9,275,870	9,267,655	9,311,705	9,359,485	9,206,832	2.63	2.36	2.78	2.49	2.56	2.43	22,352
1998-9	9,592,089	9,737,949	9,743,399	9,836,069	9,758,685	2.19	1.90	2.40	2.03	2.10	1.95	19,093
1999-00[1]	9,560,919	9,380,947	9,466,977	9,537,137	9,437,337	-----	-----	-----	-----	-----	1.60-2.00	

[1] Preliminary. [2] Season-average price based on monthly prices weigthed by monthly marketings. *Source: Economic Research Service, U..S. Department of Agriculture (ERS-USDA)*

Distribution of Corn in the United States In Millions of Bushels

Crop Year Beginning Sept. 1	Food, Seed and Industrial Use: HFCS	Glucose & Dextrose	Starch	Alcohol: Fuel	Alcohol: Beverage[3]	Seed	Cereal & Other Products	Total	Livestock Feed[4]	Exports (Including Grain Equiv. of Products)	Domestic Disappearance	Total Utilization
1990-1	379	200	232	349	80	19	114	1,373	4,611	1,725	6,036	7,761
1991-2	392	210	237	398	81	20	116	1,454	4,798	1,584	6,331	7,915
1992-3	414	214	238	426	83	19	117	1,493	5,252	1,663	6,808	8,471
1993-4	444	223	223	458	106	20	118	1,571	4,684	1,328	6,293	7,621
1994-5	465	231	226	533	100	18	132	1,686	5,470	2,178	7,175	9,352
1995-6	482	237	219	396	125	20	133	1,592	2,708	2,228	6,321	8,548
1996-7	504	246	229	429	130	20	135	1,672	5,299	1,797	6,991	8,789
1997-8[1]	530	250	235	480	133	20	137	1,765	5,505	1,504	7,287	8,791
1998-9[2]	550	255	240	510	135	20	139	1,829	5,625	1,800	7,485	9,285

[1] Preliminary. [2] Estimate. [3] Also includes nonfuel industrial alcohol. [4] Feed and waste (residual, mostly feed). *Source: Economic Research Service, U.S. Department of Agriculture (ERS-USDA)*

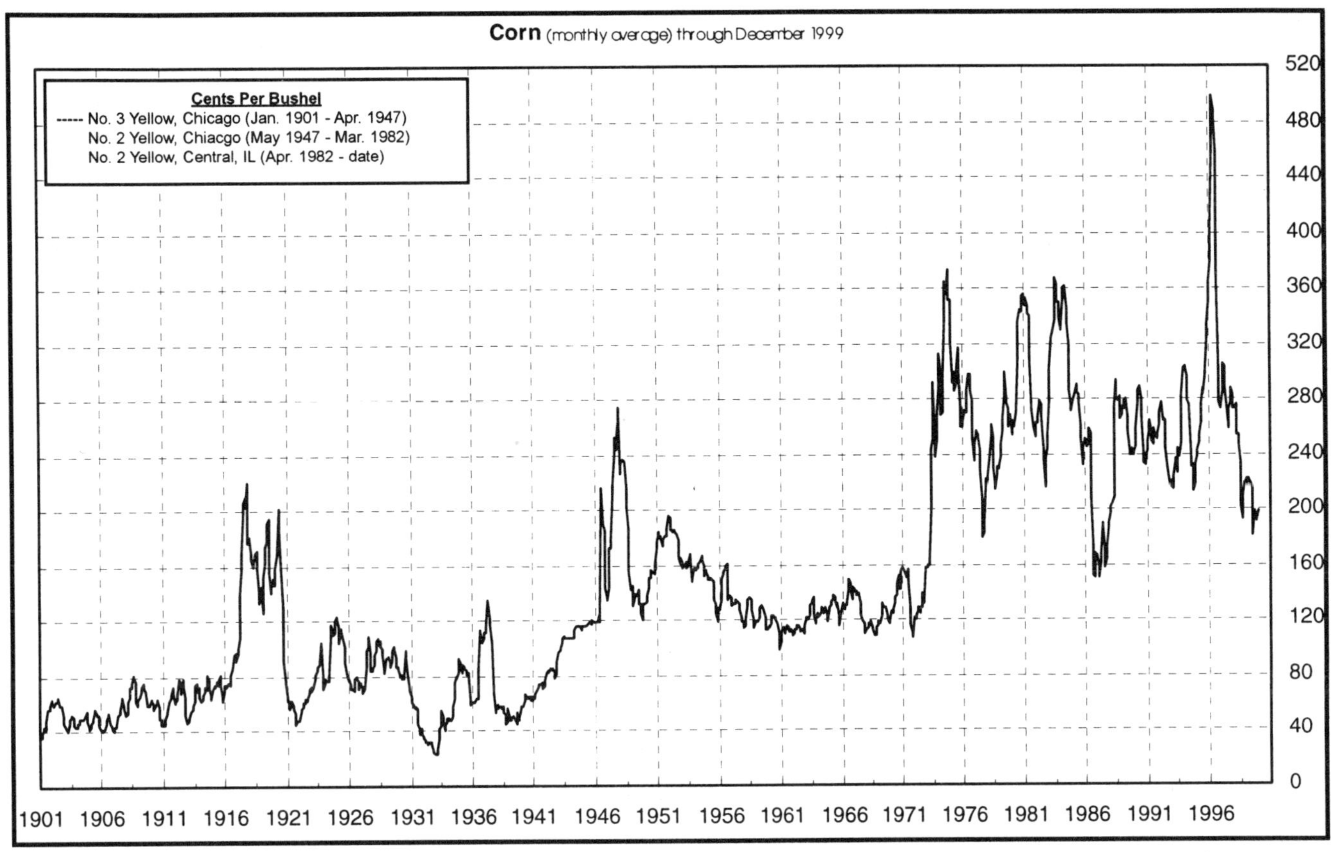

Average Cash Price of Corn, No. 2 Yellow in Central Illinois   In Dollars Per Bushel

Year	Sept.	Oct.	Nov.	Dec.	Jan.	Feb.	Mar.	Apr.	May	June	July	Aug.	Average
1990-1	2.25	2.18	2.20	2.27	2.31	2.36	2.45	2.50	2.41	2.34	2.34	2.45	2.34
1991-2	2.39	2.41	2.41	2.42	2.49	2.58	2.64	2.50	2.51	2.51	2.31	2.17	2.45
1992-3	2.13	1.97	1.99	2.05	2.07	2.05	2.16	2.23	2.20	2.09	2.25	2.27	2.12
1993-4	2.22	2.27	2.63	2.81	2.89	2.83	2.76	2.61	2.58	2.61	2.19	2.13	2.54
1994-5	2.08	1.92	2.03	2.16	2.22	2.27	2.36	2.41	2.50	2.65	2.79	2.68	2.34
1995-6	2.83	3.12	3.22	3.36	3.53	3.71	3.92	4.47	4.86	4.74	4.70	4.48	3.91
1996-7	3.39	2.81	2.63	2.62	2.62	2.71	2.90	2.87	2.74	2.59	2.44	2.60	2.74
1997-8	2.61	2.66	2.70	2.60	2.60	2.58	2.59	2.41	2.37	2.29	2.16	1.86	2.45
1998-9	1.78	1.94	2.09	2.08	2.07	2.05	2.09	2.05	2.03	1.99	1.67	1.84	1.97
1999-00[1]	1.81	1.72	1.82										1.78

[1] Preliminary. *Source: Economic Research Service, U.S. Department of Agriculture (ERS-USDA)*

Average Cash Price of Corn, No. 2 Yellow at Gulf Ports[2]   In Dollars Per Bushel

Year	Sept.	Oct.	Nov.	Dec.	Jan.	Feb.	Mar.	Apr.	May	June	July	Aug.	Average
1990-1	2.59	2.55	2.54	2.60	2.68	2.70	2.77	2.80	2.69	2.65	2.67	2.79	2.67
1991-2	2.76	2.76	2.72	2.71	2.70	2.89	2.96	2.77	2.77	2.80	2.61	2.48	2.74
1992-3	2.50	2.40	2.42	2.39	2.39	2.40	2.48	2.55	2.50	2.36	2.59	2.55	2.46
1993-4	2.57	2.68	2.94	3.08	3.22	3.14	3.05	2.88	2.81	2.85	2.51	2.44	2.85
1994-5	2.48	2.44	2.43	2.61	2.72	2.72	2.79	2.79	2.84	3.04	3.23	3.21	2.78
1995-6	3.32	3.57	3.63	3.76	4.00	4.18	4.34	4.80	5.17	4.99	5.07	4.73	4.30
1996-7	3.69	3.27	2.97	2.97	3.02	3.08	3.25	3.17	3.01	2.86	2.69	2.86	3.07
1997-8	2.88	3.05	2.98	2.89	2.90	2.88	2.89	2.71	2.69	2.64	2.55	2.24	2.78
1998-9	2.18	2.43	2.47	2.42	2.48	2.40	2.45	2.39	2.35	2.36	2.12	2.20	2.35
1999-00[1]	2.21	2.17	2.17										2.18

[1] Preliminary. [2] Barge delivered to Louisiana Gulf. *Source: Economic Research Service, U.S. Department of Agriculture (ERS-USDA)*

CORN

Weekly Outstanding Export Sales and Cumulative Exports of U.S. Corn In Thousands of Metric Tons

Marketing Year 1997/98 Week Ending	1997/98 Outstanding Sales	1997/98 Cumulative Exports	Marketing Year 1998/99 Week Ending	1998/99 Outstanding Sales	1998/99 Cumulative Exports	Marketing Year 1999/00 Week Ending	1999/00 Outstanding Sales	1999/00 Cumulative Exports
Sept. 4, 1997	7,730	207	Sept. 3, 1998	7,776	208	Sept. 2, 1999	8,647	475
11	7,761	793	10	7,783	601	9	8,841	1,333
18	7,750	2,097	17	7,831	1,630	16	8,558	2,508
25	7,693	2,914	24	8,168	2,230	23	8,224	3,543
Oct. 2	7,487	3,602	Oct. 1	7,907	3,097	30	8,037	4,398
9	7,279	4,445	8	7,649	3,882	Oct. 7	7,682	5,355
16	7,126	5,118	15	7,796	4,840	14	7,769	6,322
23	7,121	5,593	22	8,252	5,654	21	8,270	7,455
30	7,299	6,207	29	8,202	6,536	28	8,418	8,627
Nov. 6	7,606	6,829	Nov. 5	8,206	7,312	Nov. 4	8,508	9,266
13	7,810	7,776	12	8,713	8,315	11	8,756	10,254
20	7,673	8,329	19	9,014	9,281	18	8,836	11,180
27	7,565	9,138	26	8,675	10,263	25	8,387	12,191
Dec. 4	7,459	9,919	Dec. 3	8,699	11,108	Dec. 2	8,356	13,225
11	6,921	10,830	10	8,472	12,570	9	8,351	14,278
18	6,701	11,617	17	8,515	13,690	16	8,645	15,227
25	6,634	12,031	24	8,193	14,673	23	8,220	16,191
Jan. 1, 1998	6,481	12,764	31	7,779	15,501	30	7,894	17,010
8	6,318	13,280	Jan. 7, 1999	7,870	16,080	Jan. 6, 2000	7,360	17,826
15	6,469	14,007	14	7,813	16,920	13	7,487	18,825
22	6,276	14,771	21	8,070	17,562	20	7,737	19,709
29	6,531	15,492	28	8,433	18,441	27	7,579	20,689
Feb. 5	6,632	16,276	Feb. 4	8,485	19,411	Feb. 3		
12	6,567	17,189	11	8,500	20,266	10		
19	6,634	17,755	18	8,415	21,168	17		
26	6,759	18,685	25	8,539	22,175	24		
Mar. 5	6,771	19,374	Mar. 4	8,151	23,320	Mar. 2		
12	6,821	19,970	11	7,759	24,514	9		
19	6,686	20,540	18	7,275	25,468	16		
26	6,550	21,240	25	7,078	26,310	23		
Apr. 2	6,005	22,216	Apr. 1	7,142	27,073	30		
9	5,414	23,035	8	7,129	28,194	Apr. 6		
16	5,383	23,666	15	7,367	29,040	13		
23	5,426	24,138	22	7,408	30,029	20		
30	5,412	24,599	29	7,565	31,145	27		
May 7	5,256	25,268	May 6	8,246	31,807	May 4		
14	5,520	25,837	13	8,236	32,560	11		
21	5,532	26,248	20	7,534	33,825	18		
28	5,541	27,031	27	7,972	34,755	25		
June 4	5,612	27,814	June 3	8,373	35,737	June 1		
11	5,831	28,294	10	8,086	36,874	8		
18	5,244	29,187	17	7,668	38,119	15		
25	4,825	29,928	24	7,335	39,126	22		
July 2	4,786	30,546	July 1	6,956	40,286	29		
9	4,497	31,299	8	7,148	41,070	July 6		
16	4,317	32,008	15	7,104	42,207	13		
23	4,141	32,637	22	6,850	43,096	20		
30	3,540	33,373	29	6,145	44,348	27		
Aug. 6	3,399	34,114	Aug. 5	5,651	45,500	Aug. 3		
13	3,190	35,034	12	4,833	46,606	10		
20	2,346	35,807	19	3,625	47,536	17		
27	1,878	36,494	26	2,435	48,832	24		

Source: Foreign Agricultural Service, U.S. Department of Agriculture (FAS-USDA)

U.S. Exports[1] of Corn (Including Seed), By Country of Destination In Thousands of Metric Tons

Year Beginning Oct. 1	Algeria	Canada	Egypt	Irael	Japan	Mexico	Rep. of Korea	Russia[3]	Saudi Arabia	Spain	Taiwan	Vene-zuela	Total
1988-9	973	896	1,014	304	13,016	3,113	4,591	15,573	616	1,280	3,625	0	50,676
1989-90	1,146	637	1,135	250	13,885	4,585	5,680	16,371	707	1,712	5,009	593	59,854
1990-1	1,328	302	1,756	299	13,639	1,901	1,982	9,077	725	1,434	5,086	321	44,497
1991-2	827	314	1,058	369	13,481	1,041	1,508	6,533	602	1,273	4,998	552	40,693
1992-3	1,224	1,189	1,543	539	14,235	396	1,021	3,380	787	1,075	5,450	777	41,766
1993-4	1,182	640	1,437	268	12,032	1,678	631	2,337	851	1,116	4,955	751	33,057
1994-5	846	1,135	2,608	671	16,107	3,166	8,921	9	864	2,497	6,210	886	58,645
1995-6	567	751	2,106	625	14,900	6,268	7,426	58	844	1,156	5,600	479	52,681
1996-7	929	879	2,364	556	15,482	3,141	5,452	88	1,025	1,080	5,609	730	46,638
1997-8[2]	829	1,397	1,951	-----	13,994	4,373	3,364	-----	928	-----	3,488	651	37,697

[1] Excludes exports of corn by-products. [2] Preliminary. [3] Formerly part of the U.S.S.R.; data not reported separately until 1992. *Source: Economic Research Service, U.S. Department of Agriculture (ERS-USDA)*

Stocks of Corn (Shelled and Ear) in the United States In Millions of Bushels

	On Farms				Off Farms				Total Stocks			
Year	Mar. 1	June 1	Sept. 1	Dec. 1	Mar. 1	June 1	Sept. 1	Dec. 1	Mar. 1	June 1	Sept. 1	Dec. 1
1990	2,910.5	1,623.5	754.8	4,874.0	1,901.9	1,219.7	589.7	2,066.3	4,812.4	2,843.2	1,344.5	6,940.3
1991	3,064.5	1,755.0	691.2	4,294.5	1,724.5	1,237.0	830.0	2,246.6	4,789.0	2,992.0	1,521.2	6,541.1
1992	2,610.2	1,517.5	605.5	5,736.9	1,950.8	1,221.1	494.8	2,169.5	4,561.0	2,738.6	1,100.3	7,906.4
1993	3,630.0	2,216.5	1,070.7	3,803.0	2,048.2	1,492.9	1,042.3	2,133.5	5,678.2	3,709.4	2,113.0	5,936.5
1994	2,210.0	1,203.0	395.4	5,417.5	1,785.5	1,156.9	454.7	2,663.0	3,995.7	2,359.9	850.1	8,080.5
1995	3,502.0	2,072.0	740.9	3,960.0	2,089.7	1,342.9	816.9	2,145.8	5,591.7	3,414.9	1,557.8	6,105.8
1996	2,000.2	780.1	196.6	4,800.0	1,799.3	937.8	229.3	2,103.7	3,799.5	1,717.9	425.9	6,903.7
1997	2,870.0	1,501.0	475.0	4,822.0	1,624.1	995.6	408.2	2,424.8	4,494.1	2,496.6	883.2	7,246.8
1998	2,975.0	1,830.0	640.0	5,320.0	1,964.9	1,209.8	667.8	2,731.8	4,939.9	3,039.8	1,307.8	8,051.8
1999[1]	3,570.0	2,257.0	797.0	5,180.0	2,128.4	1,359.2	990.0	2,839.9	5,698.4	3,616.2	1,787.0	8,019.9

[1] Preliminary. *Source: National Agricultural Statistics Service, U.S. Department of Agriculture (NASS-USDA)*

CORN

Volume of Trading of Corn Futures in Chicago In Thousands of Contracts

Year	Jan.	Feb.	Mar.	Apr.	May	June	July	Aug.	Sept.	Oct.	Nov.	Dec.	Total
1990	649.6	798.2	924.6	1,148.4	1,429.2	1,353.4	1,101.8	908.2	605.6	787.8	1,136.4	579.8	11,422.8
1991	846.8	696.8	932.6	1,041.0	845.4	1,012.8	1,253.6	1,097.2	692.4	884.0	907.8	632.2	10,852.8
1992	901.2	1,002.6	952.2	868.6	938.2	1,015.2	865.6	795.0	688.6	688.4	996.2	644.4	10,356.6
1993	517.6	636.4	774.0	894.8	688.0	1,047.4	1,395.6	1,014.2	896.0	1,036.0	1,574.4	988.2	10,539.4
1994	1,251.4	1,035.6	1,045.6	1,108.8	1,079.2	1,455.0	747.6	601.8	615.0	703.0	1,025.4	861.4	11,529.8
1995	787.2	832.4	973.7	987.7	1,213.7	1,759.5	1,293.7	1,318.6	1,220.2	1,613.2	1,743.1	1,356.0	15,105.1
1996	1,992.2	1,819.6	1,607.6	2,655.2	2,085.2	1,545.1	1,590.5	1,144.6	1,183.4	1,435.7	1,514.7	1,046.3	19,620.2
1997	1,160.6	1,483.0	1,693.3	1,780.1	1,291.7	1,347.5	1,527.7	1,318.3	1,060.2	1,700.2	1,434.4	1,188.0	16,985.0
1998	1,250.2	1,276.5	1,432.8	1,620.3	1,148.5	1,771.0	1,415.3	1,231.4	1,126.3	1,319.3	1,217.2	986.6	15,795.5
1999	955.1	1,374.2	1,440.1	1,420.6	975.1	1,597.4	1,708.0	1,669.8	1,131.9	1,096.2	1,500.9	855.6	15,724.8

Source: Chicago Board of Trade (CBT)

Average Open Interest of Corn Futures in Chicago In Contracts

Year	Jan.	Feb.	Mar.	Apr.	May	June	July	Aug.	Sept.	Oct.	Nov.	Dec.
1990	178,094	202,845	229,946	252,155	250,020	242,462	212,749	207,951	206,603	211,222	230,333	203,881
1991	210,006	219,236	229,010	229,404	204,828	202,100	198,527	219,700	215,527	242,466	257,065	228,347
1992	254,195	294,957	285,429	260,527	230,359	232,189	211,221	219,796	208,613	239,888	262,345	244,803
1993	256,113	260,986	248,638	250,000	229,016	232,590	265,672	264,938	243,892	275,792	332,445	327,226
1994	346,077	336,342	327,539	305,722	262,621	246,308	215,081	208,990	212,983	243,678	262,849	250,646
1995	292,090	311,372	336,433	355,443	368,381	427,744	413,839	418,450	439,170	473,698	490,970	487,977
1996	500,837	508,496	469,697	453,707	403,118	350,066	304,265	298,894	302,170	326,373	332,809	306,256
1997	305,779	347,392	382,261	351,852	290,649	274,760	267,531	281,194	307,415	378,453	379,045	331,386
1998	328,020	341,444	358,221	366,657	337,703	327,237	297,894	318,162	321,992	332,337	342,868	322,157
1999	357,682	363,153	357,126	343,624	338,467	323,657	329,459	315,858	316,247	410,955	461,036	389,187

Source: Chicago Board of Trade (CBT)

Corn Price Support Data in the United States

Crop Year Beginning Sept. 1	National Average Loan Rate[3]	Target Price	Placed Under Loan	% of Production	Acquired by CCC	Owned by CCC Aug. 31	CCC Inventory As of Dec. 31: CCC Owned	Under CCC Loan	Quantity Pledged (Thousands of Bushels)	Face Amount (Thousands of Dollars)
	Dollars Per Bushel		Millions of Bushels							
1989-90	1.65	2.84	920	12.2	361	233	676	1,110	920,068	1,487,026
1990-1	1.57	2.75	1,071	13.5	285	371	214	1,071	1,071,040	1,616,948
1991-2	1.62	2.75	1,006	13.5	291	113	265	678	26,636	45,609
1992-3	1.72	2.75	1,646	17.4	0	56	125	1,021	15,245	28,947
1993-4	1.72	2.75	618	9.7	0	45	54	812	13,697	26,052
1994-5	1.89	2.75	2,002	19.8	0	-----	44	1,598	26,318	53,474
1995-6	1.89	2.75	970	9.2	0	-----	42	579	677,115	1,232,669
1996-7	1.89	-----	561	-----	0	-----	30	756	-----	-----
1997-8[1]	1.89	-----	1,132	-----	19	-----	2	81	-----	-----
1998-9[2]	1.89	-----	823	-----	0	-----	-----	-----	-----	-----

[1] Preliminary. [2] Estimate. [3] Findley or announced loan rate. *Source: National Agricultural Statistics Service, U.S. Department of Agriculture (NASS-USDA)*

Average Price Received by Farmers for Corn in the United States In Dollars Per Bushel

Year	Sept.	Oct.	Nov.	Dec.	Jan.	Feb.	Mar.	Apr.	May	June	July	Aug.	Average
1990-1	2.32	2.19	2.16	2.22	2.27	2.32	2.39	2.42	2.38	2.31	2.27	2.33	2.28
1991-2	2.33	2.31	2.29	2.33	2.40	2.46	2.49	2.48	2.49	2.47	2.33	2.15	2.37
1992-3	2.16	2.05	1.98	1.97	2.03	2.00	2.10	2.16	2.14	2.09	2.22	2.25	2.07
1993-4	2.21	2.28	2.45	2.67	2.70	2.79	2.74	2.65	2.60	2.61	2.29	2.16	2.50
1994-5	2.19	2.06	1.99	2.13	2.19	2.23	2.30	2.36	2.41	2.51	2.63	2.63	2.26
1995-6	2.69	2.79	2.87	3.07	3.09	3.37	3.51	3.85	4.14	4.20	4.43	4.30	3.53
1996-7	3.55	2.89	2.66	2.63	2.69	2.65	2.79	2.80	2.69	2.56	2.42	2.50	2.74
1997-8	2.52	2.54	2.51	2.52	2.56	2.55	2.54	2.41	2.34	2.28	2.19	1.89	2.40
1998-9	1.83	1.91	1.93	2.00	2.06	2.05	2.06	2.05	2.00	1.97	1.74	1.75	1.95
1999-00[1]	1.75	1.69	1.70	1.82	1.90								1.77

[1] Preliminary. *Source: Economic Research Service, U.S. Department of Agriculture (ERS-USDA)*

Corn Oil

The steady year-to-year uptrend in U.S. corn oil production carried to a record high 2.4 billion pounds in 1998/99 (October/September) vs. the previous record of 2.34 billion in 1997/98. Production in the early 1990's averaged about 1.9 billion pounds. Seasonally, production tends to peak around March and reaches a low in either November or July. On a total usage basis the gain in domestic usage pales against the decade's growth in export demand.

Total 1998/99 disappearance of nearly 2.5 billion pounds compares with almost 2.4 billion in 1997/98. Domestic usage of a record high 1.4 billion pounds in 1998/99 compares with 1.27 billion in 1997/98. Corn oil is cholesterol free which has enhanced its appeal among health conscious consumers. However, the real growth in usage has been in exports which totaled nearly 1.1 billion pounds in 1998/99, marginally under the 1997/98 record pace but still well above the early 1990's when exports averaged about 600 million pounds. The European Union is a major importer of U.S. corn oil. U.S. imports are minimal. Carryover stocks show considerable variation: from a low of 44 million pounds at the end of 1989/90 to a high of 241 million five years later. Estimated ending 1998/99 stocks are 92 million pounds vs. 122 million a year earlier.

Crude corn oil prices, basis wet/dry-milled Central Illinois, averaged 29.87 cents a pound in 1998 (vs. a marketing year average of 28.94 cents). Calendar 1999 prices through September averaged near 23 cents a pound vs. a marketing year average 25.30 cents.

Supply and Disappearance of Corn Oil in the United States In Millions of Pounds

Crop Year Beginning Oct. 1	Supply: Stocks Oct. 1	Supply: Production	Supply: Imports	Supply: Total Supply	Disappearance: Baking and Frying Fats	Disappearance: Salad and Cooking Oil	Disappearance: Margarine	Disappearance: Total Edible Products	Disappearance: Domestic Disappearance	Disappearance: Exports	Disappearance: Total Disappearance
1993-4	150	1,906	7.0	2,062	86	413	W	649	1,228	717	1,944
1994-5	118	2,227	10.0	2,356	100	446	W	636	1,250	865	2,115
1995-6	241	2,139	11.0	2,391	82	434	79	595	1,298	977	2,275
1996-7	116	2,230	14.0	2,361	73	386	68	527	1,244	988	2,232
1997-8	129	2,335	28.0	2,492	42	339	39	446	1,271	1,118	2,390
1998-9[1]	102	2,374	42.0	2,519	73	386	68	527	1,394	989	2,383
1999-00[2]	135	2,417	27.0	2,579					1,366	1,085	2,451

[1] Preliminary. [2] Estimate. W = Withheld proprietary data. *Source: Economic Research Service, U.S. Department of Agriculture (ERS-USDA)*

Production[2] of Crude Corn Oil in the United States In Millions of Pounds

Year	Oct.	Nov.	Dec.	Jan.	Feb.	Mar.	Apr.	May	June	July	Aug.	Sept.	Total
1993-4	160.8	153.4	162.5	140.6	138.6	166.9	155.3	164.2	171.8	164.8	162.3	165.1	1,906
1994-5	175.5	165.3	180.9	163.2	161.8	232.7	188.4	191.2	193.6	193.5	180.3	188.5	2,215
1995-6	179.5	173.8	184.5	180.6	160.4	192.9	192.1	175.9	178.4	147.1	162.2	171.2	2,099
1996-7	183.8	182.3	208.2	172.5	170.9	209.9	188.3	182.5	184.3	174.0	180.6	182.2	2,220
1997-8	199.2	207.5	202.0	171.4	162.7	201.0	203.9	201.2	201.4	192.8	202.8	188.9	2,335
1998-9	209.2	199.4	189.2	182.9	177.0	201.0	201.1	205.3	205.7	194.8	212.5	196.3	2,374
1999-00[1]	204.3	212.3	218.6										2,541

[1] Preliminary. [2] Not seasonally adjusted. *Source: Bureau of the Census, U.S. Department of Commerce*

Consumption Corn Oil, in Refining, in the United States In Millions of Pounds

Year	Oct.	Nov.	Dec.	Jan.	Feb.	Mar.	Apr.	May	June	July	Aug.	Sept.	Total
1993-4	106.7	101.7	114.3	71.8	76.5	92.6	79.4	91.5	91.7	90.6	106.4	109.1	1,132
1994-5	103.5	107.2	116.9	100.7	92.3	109.9	97.3	95.6	108.9	97.2	78.2	95.5	1,203
1995-6	82.9	97.9	102.0	78.6	91.6	100.0	84.8	90.0	90.5	74.5	66.5	90.2	1,049
1996-7	82.0	83.0	84.7	69.7	71.0	79.5	71.4	76.1	80.4	86.9	90.8	58.5	934
1997-8	87.5	83.8	100.6	83.0	89.2	100.5	92.5	100.5	104.2	90.6	101.7	94.6	1,129
1998-9	106.6	104.4	105.0	82.0	W	102.0	94.6	101.7	104.3	90.1	97.0	103.5	1,190
1999-00[1]	96.2	97.1	114.7										1,232

[1] Preliminary. W = Withheld proprietary data. *Source: Bureau of Census, U.S. Department of Commerce*

Average Corn Oil Price, Wet Mill in Chicago In Cents Per Pound

Year	Oct.	Nov.	Dec.	Jan.	Feb.	Mar.	Apr.	May	June	July	Aug.	Sept.	Average
1993-4	22.25	23.06	26.93	28.00	29.89	30.30	29.63	29.48	29.43	27.20	25.02	24.87	27.17
1994-5	24.73	24.75	24.75	28.01	27.26	28.17	27.30	26.42	26.61	27.38	26.35	25.93	26.47
1995-6	26.05	25.54	24.99	24.52	24.30	24.34	25.60	27.98	25.66	25.46	24.33	24.14	25.24
1996-7	22.67	21.96	22.27	23.39	23.97	24.38	24.60	24.66	24.82	25.34	25.36	25.15	24.05
1997-8	25.20	26.25	26.28	26.04	27.31	28.50	30.93	33.20	32.82	31.52	29.93	29.25	28.94
1998-9	29.46	29.65	29.88	29.15	26.58	23.01	23.08	22.96	22.95	22.43	22.41	22.08	25.30
1999-00[1]	21.97	21.96	21.68										21.87

[1] Preliminary. *Source: Economic Research Service, U.S. Department of Agriculture (ERS-USDA)*

Cotton

U.S. cotton production in the 1999/2000 (August-July) season was forecast by the U.S.D.A. at 16.88 million bales. This was some 2.96 million bales more than the previous season. At the start of the 1999/00 season, it had appeared that the crop could potentially be as large as 20 million bales but poor growing conditions reduced the crop's potential. Drought adversely affected the crop in some states. Most notable was a late season hurricane in North Carolina which did an extensive amount of damage. The North Carolina crop was 780,000 bales compared to 1.03 million bales in 1998/99.

Cotton growers planted 14.6 million acres to the natural fiber, up 1.21 million acres from the previous season. Due to poor conditions in many regions, the amount of acreage that was harvested was some 8 percent less than that planted. The average rate of cotton acreage abandonment is about 6 percent. In 1998/99, 20 percent of the planted acreage was abandoned. For 1999/00, acreage harvested was 13.41 million. Some 1.19 million acres were abandoned. The national average cotton yield was 604 pounds per acre compared to 625 pounds a year earlier.

Texas was the largest producing state with 1999/00 production of 5.15 million bales. That was up 41 percent from last season. The Texas yield was 492 pounds per acre which was down 6 percent from last season. Texas harvested 5.03 million acres. California's crop was estimated at 2.15 million bales, up 43 percent from the season before. The yield was 899 pounds or some 7 percent more than the previous season. The Mississippi crop was 1.74 million bales, up 21 percent from 1998/99. The Georgia crop was 1.55 million bales, up 1 percent from the previous year. The Arkansas crop was 1.43 million bales, up 18 percent from the previous season.

At the beginning of the 1999/00 season, U.S. cotton stocks were 3.94 million bales, some 1 percent more than the previous season. Stocks amounted to about 4 months worth of use. Imports of cotton in 1999/00 were forecast to be 80,000 bales, well below the 440,000 bales imported in 1998/99. The total supply of cotton is equal to the sum of beginning stocks and production and imports. For the 1999/00 season, the total supply of cotton was 20.89 million bales, up 14 percent from a year ago.

Domestic use of cotton was forecast by the U.S.D.A. to be 10.2 million bales. That would be some 2 percent or 200,000 bales less than in 1998/99. How much cotton is consumed by U.S. textile mills is dependent on a number of factors including the direction and strength of the U.S. economy as well as consumer tastes. In a period of declining interest rates leading to an expanding housing sector, the use of cotton will increase. In late 1999, interest rates were rising and it was likely that at some point the housing sector would slow leading to a decline in cotton use. An important consideration in determining how much cotton will be used by domestic mills is the amount of cotton textiles imported into the U.S. relative to the amount exported. The North American Free Trade Agreement has increased the cotton textile trade over the last five years. The U.S. imports more cotton textiles than it exports leading to a trade deficit that is increasing. This, in turn, reduces the amount of cotton that textile mills need to use. The National Cotton Council reported that in the month of November 1999, the seasonally adjusted annual rate of cotton use was 10.13 million bales which was down from the October estimate of 10.22 million bales. Because of the growing trade deficit in cotton textiles, it is possible that domestic textile mills will use less than 10.2 million bales.

The other source of cotton use is exports. Cotton exports from season to season tend to vary more than domestic use. In the past, U.S. cotton prices have been higher than foreign prices putting U.S. exporters at a competitive disadvantage. To counter this the U.S.D.A. enacted a new Step 2 cotton user payment program. This program in effect reimburses to exporters the difference between higher priced domestic cotton and lower priced foreign cotton allowing export sales to be made. The U.S.D.A. forecasts that exports of U.S. cotton in the 1999/00 season will be 6.2 million bales. If that result comes about, it would represent an increase of almost 43 percent from the previous year. The U.S.D.A. reported in its Export Sales report for the week of December 9, 1999, that since the start of the 1999/00 season, cumulative exports of cotton were some 38 percent less than the year before. Total use of cotton in 1999/00 was estimated at 16.4 million bales, up 11 percent from the previous season. Projected ending stocks of cotton were 4.5 million bales, up 14 percent from a year ago.

World production of cotton was forecast by U.S.D.A. to be 87.38 million bales, up 3 percent from 1998/99. Production of cotton outside the U.S. was forecast to be 70.51 million bales. The largest producer of cotton is China with the 1999/00 crop estimated at 19 million bales. China has been reducing its cotton production because of a buildup in stocks. China has also been exporting some of its excess cotton. For the 1999/00 season, the U.S.D.A. forecast China's net exports at over a million bales. China's stocks of cotton have been estimated to be about 15 million bales.

India's cotton crop was estimated to be 13 million bales, up 2 percent from 1998-99. Pakistan's crop was estimated at 7.8 million bales, some 24 percent higher than in 1998/99. Production in the Central Asian countries (Uzbekistan and Turkmenistan) was forecast to be 6.5 million bales or some 16 percent more than a year ago. The South American crops were damaged by drought. Brazil's crop of 1.9 million bales was down 10 percent from a year ago. Argentina's crop of 600,000 bales was down 33 percent from the previous year. Australia's crop was forecast at 3.1 million bales, down 6 percent from a year ago.

Futures Markets

Cotton futures and options are traded on the New York Cotton Exchange (NYCE). Cotton futures are traded on the Bolsa de Mercadorias & Futuros (BM&F). Cotton yarn futures are traded on the Chuba Commodity Exchange (C-COM), the Osaka Mercantile Exchange (OME), and the Tokyo Commodity Exchange (ToCom).

Supply and Distribution of All Cotton in the United States   In Thousands of 480-Pound Bales

Crop Year Beginning Aug. 1	Acre: Planted (1,000 Acres)	Acre: Harvested (1,000 Acres)	Acre: Yield (Lbs./acre)	Supply: Beginning Stocks[3]	Supply: Production[4]	Supply: Imports	Supply: Total	Disappearance: Mill Use	Disappearance: Exports	Disappearance: Total	Unaccounted	Ending Stocks	Farm Price[5] (Cents per Lb.)	"A" Index Price[6] (Cents per Lb.)	Value of Production (Million $)
1990-1	12,348	11,732	634	3,000	1,505	4	18,509	8,657	7,793	16,450	285	2,344	67.1	82.87	5,075.8
1991-2	14,052	12,960	652	2,344	17,614	13	19,971	9,613	6,646	16,259	-8	3,704	58.1	62.90	4,913.2
1992-3	13,240	11,143	699	3,704	16,219	1	19,923	10,250	5,201	15,451	190	4,662	54.9	56.87	4,273.9
1993-4	13,438	12,783	606	4,662	16,134	6	20,802	10,418	6,862	17,280	8	3,530	58.4	70.75	4,520.9
1994-5	13,720	13,322	708	3,530	19,662	20	23,212	11,198	9,402	20,600	38	2,650	72.0	92.66	6,796.7
1995-6	16,931	16,007	537	2,650	17,900	408	20,958	10,604	7,675	18,322	-27	2,609	76.5	85.61	6,574.6
1996-7	14,653	12,888	705	2,609	18,942	403	21,954	11,126	6,865	17,991	8	3,971	70.5	78.66	6,408.1
1997-8	13,898	13,406	673	3,971	18,793	13	22,777	11,349	7,500	18,849	-41	3,887	66.2	72.11	5,975.6
1998-9[1]	13,393	10,684	625	3,887	13,918	443	18,248	10,401	4,344	14,745	436	3,939	61.2	58.97	4,321.6
1999-00[2]	14,601	13,405	592	3,939	16,531	75	20,545	10,200	5,700	15,900	-45	4,600			3,836.5

[1] Preliminary. [2] Estimate. [3] Excludes preseason ginnings (adjusted to 480-lb. bale net weight basis). [4] Includes preseason ginnings. [5] Marketing year average price. [6] Average of 5 cheapest types of SLM 1 3/32 staple length cotton *offered on the European market.*
Source: Economic Research Service, U.S. Department of Agriculture (ERS-USDA)

World Production of All Cotton   In Thousands of 480-Pound Bales

Crop Year Beginning Aug. 1	Argentina	Brazil	China	Egypt	India	Iran	Mexico	Pakistan	Sudan	Turkey	United States	Uzbekistan	World Total
1990-1	1,355	3,215	20,700	1,378	9,135	553	813	7,522	380	3,007	15,505	7,317	86,980
1991-2	1,148	3,445	26,100	1,338	9,291	543	831	10,000	386	2,578	17,614	6,628	95,992
1992-3	666	2,113	20,700	1,620	10,775	465	138	7,073	276	2,635	16,218	5,851	82,709
1993-4	1,075	1,860	17,200	1,882	9,487	310	110	6,282	250	2,666	16,134	6,067	76,049
1994-5	1,608	2,526	19,900	1,225	10,814	762	458	6,250	400	2,886	19,662	5,778	85,610
1995-6	1,930	1,791	21,900	1,088	12,649	800	860	8,200	490	3,911	17,900	5,740	92,174
1996-7	1,493	1,300	19,300	1,568	13,781	825	1,077	7,300	460	3,600	18,942	4,750	89,179
1997-8	1,350	1,750	21,100	1,550	12,258	-----	984	7,175	400	3,700	18,793	5,300	91,595
1998-9[1]	900	2,100	20,700	1,050	12,727	638	1,000	6,300	250	3,850	13,918	4,600	84,535
1999-00[2]	550	1,900	17,600	1,075	13,000	600	600	8,000	375	3,950	16,953	5,300	86,358

[1] Preliminary. [2] Estimate. *Source: Foreign Agricultural Service, U.S. Department of Agriculture (FAS-USDA)*

World Supply and Demand of Cotton   In Thousands of 480-Pound Bales

Crop Year Beginning Aug. 1	Beginning Stocks: United States	Beginning Stocks: Uzbekistan	Beginning Stocks: China	Beginning Stocks: World Total	Production: United States	Production: Uzbekistan	Production: China	Production: World Total	Consumption: United States	Consumption: Russia	Consumption: China	Consumption: World Total	Exports: United States	Exports: Uzbekistan	Exports: China	Exports: World Total
1990-1	3,000	460	4,379	25,771	15,505	7,317	20,700	86,968	8,657	5,469	20,000	85,677	7,793	5,393	928	29,656
1991-2	2,344	1,555	5,956	27,073	17,614	6,628	26,100	95,659	9,613	4,539	20,500	86,045	6,646	5,200	602	28,196
1992-3	3,704	2,295	12,284	37,403	16,218	5,851	20,700	82,445	10,250	2,200	21,500	85,765	5,201	5,500	684	25,583
1993-4	4,662	1,845	10,442	35,121	16,134	6,067	17,200	76,697	10,418	2,200	21,300	85,353	6,862	5,800	749	26,731
1994-5	3,530	737	6,101	26,507	19,662	5,778	19,900	85,534	11,198	1,263	20,200	84,688	9,402	5,006	183	28,476
1995-6	2,650	956	9,678	28,977	17,900	5,740	21,900	92,174	10,647	1,150	19,500	85,444	7,675	4,500	21	27,359
1996-7	2,609	1,304	13,202	33,813	18,942	4,750	19,300	89,179	11,126	1,100	21,000	88,626	6,865	4,550	10	26,494
1997-8	3,971	822	14,755	38,160	18,793	5,300	21,100	91,595	11,349	1,200	20,800	88,402	7,500	4,400	34	26,590
1998-9[1]	3,887	635	16,855	40,772	13,918	4,600	20,700	84,535	10,401	900	19,800	85,216	4,344	3,800	681	23,645
1999-00[2]	3,939	615	17,433	41,743	16,953	5,300	17,600	86,358	10,200	1,000	20,500	88,193	6,400	4,100	1,200	26,479

[1] Preliminary. [2] Estimate. *Source: Foreign Agricultural Service, U.S. Department of Agriculture (FAS-USDA)*

World Consumption of All Cottons in Specified Countries   In Thousands of 480-Pound Bales

Year	Brazil	China	Egypt	France	Germany	India	Italy	Japan	Mexico	Pakistan	United States	Uzbekistan[3]	World Total
1989-90	3,445	20,000	1,352	600	1,435	8,667	1,450	3,229	725	4,801	8,759	9,200	86,579
1990-1	3,215	20,000	1,457	530	955	9,018	1,470	3,027	712	5,648	8,657	8,700	85,677
1991-2	3,215	19,000	1,465	484	830	8,674	1,447	2,783	772	6,482	9,613	860	86,136
1992-3	3,445	21,500	1,640	470	680	9,761	1,400	2,301	740	6,634	10,250	950	85,770
1993-4	3,675	20,900	1,530	500	750	9,950	1,375	2,060	825	6,500	10,418	925	85,325
1994-5	4,000	20,200	1,350	500	660	10,334	1,525	1,800	800	6,750	11,198	750	84,574
1995-6	3,904	19,500	1,010	450	610	12,282	1,470	1,529	1,000	7,000	10,647	875	85,444
1996-7	3,900	21,000	900	440	600	13,000	1,560	1,400	1,550	7,000	11,126	800	88,626
1997-8[1]	3,400	20,800	950	550	650	12,675	1,600	1,400	2,050	7,100	11,349	750	88,402
1998-9[2]	3,250	20,000	1,000	500	575	12,000	1,500	1,300	2,200	7,000	10,500	700	84,786

[1] Preliminary. [2] Estimate. [3] Formerly part of the U.S.S.R.; data not reported separately until 1991. *Source: Foreign Agricultural Service, U.S. Department of Agriculture (FAS-USDA)*

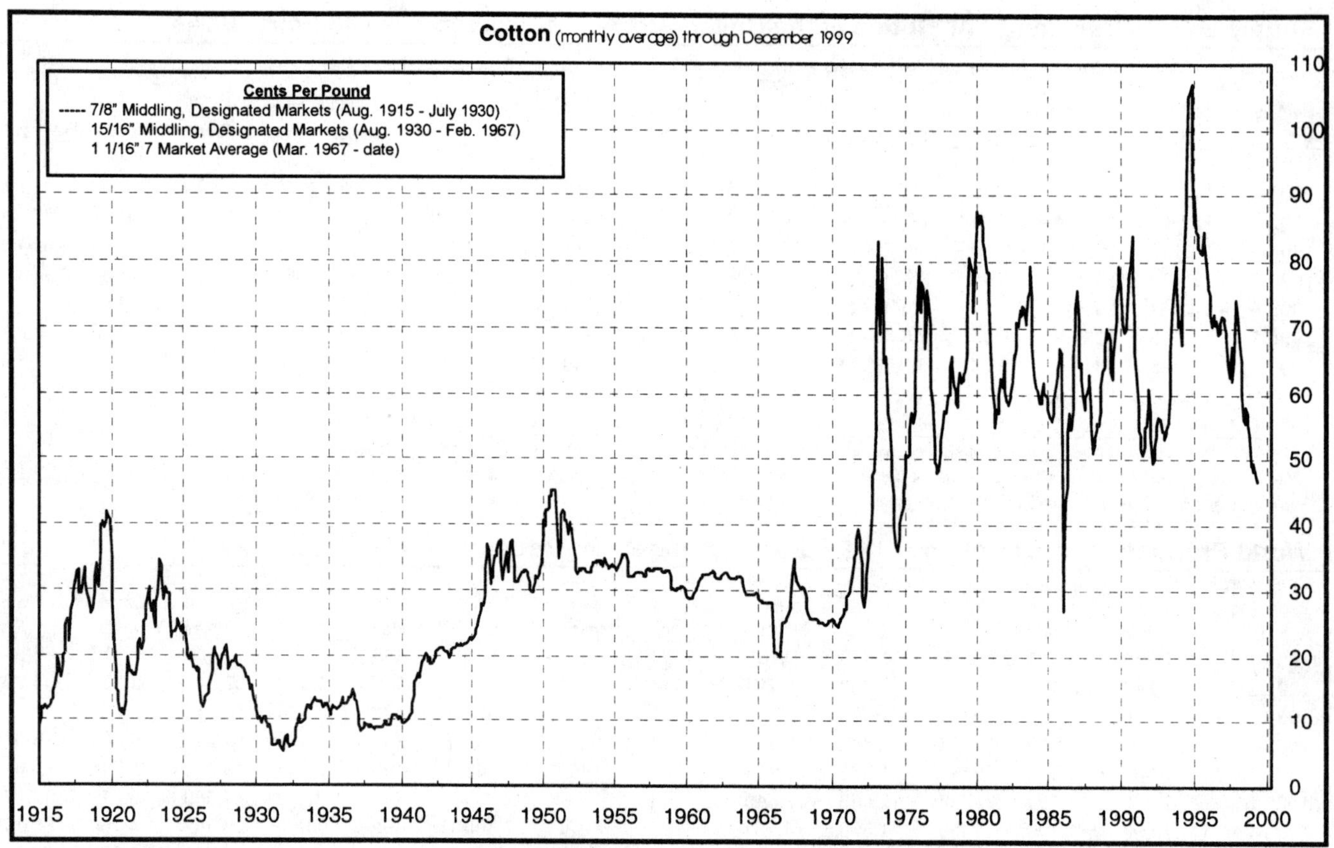

Average Spot Cotton Prices[2], C.I.F. Northern Europe   In U.S. Cents Per Pound

Crop Year Beginning Aug. 1	Argentina "C"[3] 1 1/16"	Australia M 1 3/32"	Cotlook Index A	Cotlook Index B	Egypt Giza[4] 81	Greece M 1 3/32"	Mexico[5] M 1 3/32"	Pakistan Sind/ Punjab[6]	Tanzania AR[7] Type 3	Turkey Izmir[8] 1 3/32"	U.S. Calif. ACALA SJV[9]	U.S. Memphis Terr.[10] M 1 3/32"	U.S. Orleans/ Texas [11] M 1 1/32"
1989-90	77.05	84.16	82.40	77.40	189.54	83.76	82.50	76.75	86.68	90.49	88.59	83.90	78.93
1990-1	77.06	85.58	82.90	77.80	177.43	84.24	84.46	77.19	89.62	81.32	92.84	88.13	80.35
1991-2	55.08	65.97	63.05	58.50	128.10	65.90	68.19	58.14	68.90	74.66	74.47	66.35	63.41
1992-3	64.31	64.01	57.70	53.70	99.24	56.92	-----	52.66	62.24	-----	68.37	63.08	58.89
1993-4	80.20	72.81	70.60	67.30	88.35	58.81	-----	54.42	69.83	59.80	77.55	72.80	69.78
1994-5	101.88	81.05	92.75	92.40	93.70	88.64	82.65	73.75	-----	-----	106.40	98.67	95.70
1995-6	82.98	93.75	85.61	81.06	-----	84.95	94.94	81.86	96.20	90.38	103.49	94.71	90.37
1996-7	79.71	83.24	78.59	74.80	-----	75.85	79.60	73.37	79.22	-----	89.55	82.81	79.77
1997-8	69.96	77.49	72.19	70.69	-----	72.03	81.70	72.93	84.04	-----	85.11	78.12	74.74
1998-9[1]	57.19	66.48	58.91	54.26	-----	58.66	65.78	-----	72.70	-----	78.57	73.65	70.95

[1] Preliminary. [2] Generally for prompt shipment. [3] 1 1/32 prior to January 20, 1984; 1 1/16 since. [4] Dendera until 1969/70; Giza 67 1969/70 until December 1983; Giza 69/75/81 until November 1990; Giza 81 since. [5] S. Brazil Type 5, 1 1/32 prior to 1968-69; 1 1/16 until 1987/88; Brazilian Type 5/6, 1 1/16 since. [6] Punjab until 1979/80; Sind SG until June 1984; Sind/Punjab SG until January 1985; Afzal 1 until January 1986; Afzal 1 1/32 since. [7] No. 1 until 1978/79; No. 1/2 until February 1986; AR' Mwanza No. 3 until January 1992; AR' Type 3 since. [8] Izmir ST 1 White 1 1/16 RG prior to 1981/82; 1 3/32 from 1981/82 until January 1987; Izmir/Antalya ST 1 White -3/32 RG since. [9] SM 1 3/32 prior to 1975/76; SM 1 1/8 since. [10] SM 1 1/16 prior to 1981/82; Middling 1 3/32 since. [11] Middling 1 prior to 1988/89; Middling 1 1/32 since. *Source: International Cotton Advisory Committee*

Average Producer Price Index of Gray Cotton Broadwovens   Index 1982 = 100

Year	Jan.	Feb.	Mar.	Apr.	May	June	July	Aug.	Sept.	Oct.	Nov.	Dec.	Average
1990	113.7	113.8	113.8	114.0	114.1	109.9	115.1	115.1	112.3	112.5	116.1	116.4	113.8
1991	113.3	113.6	114.1	114.5	114.9	115.2	115.3	115.3	115.3	115.4	115.7	115.6	114.9
1992	116.9	116.8	116.7	116.7	116.8	117.5	117.3	117.3	117.2	116.9	117.1	117.2	117.0
1993	117.0	116.8	115.9	116.3	115.7	115.7	115.2	115.2	112.5	114.1	114.1	114.9	115.3
1994	109.9	110.8	115.4	115.7	114.9	114.9	115.0	117.5	117.6	118.9	117.2	118.0	116.2
1995	117.8	120.2	120.7	121.6	123.4	123.6	124.1	125.4	125.3	123.7	123.7	123.8	122.6
1996	123.6	123.7	122.0	122.0	121.1	120.7	120.7	119.9	119.7	120.4	120.0	120.4	121.2
1997	120.3	120.8	120.7	120.8	121.2	120.6	121.4	121.6	121.4	120.8	121.6	121.2	121.0
1998	122.8	122.0	122.1	121.5	121.8	120.8	120.0	119.1	118.8	118.1	117.3	117.8	120.2
1999[1]	117.1	117.3	118.8	116.5	116.4	116.1	116.5	112.9	112.9	113.1	112.6	108.2	114.9

[1] Preliminary. *Source: Bureau of Labor Statistics (0337-01), U.S. Department of Commerce*

Average Price of Strict Low Midd. 11/16,Cotton at Designated U.S. Mkts In Cents Per Pound (Net Weight)

Year	Aug.	Sept.	Oct.	Nov.	Dec.	Jan.	Feb.	Mar.	Apr.	May	June	July	Average
1990-1	76.27	71.01	70.54	69.48	69.92	70.50	77.69	77.92	79.94	83.94	79.05	71.33	74.80
1991-2	66.44	62.39	58.28	54.70	53.89	51.54	50.76	52.01	54.97	55.45	58.82	60.93	56.68
1992-3	57.56	53.49	49.47	49.98	51.85	53.72	55.38	56.45	56.17	56.37	54.38	54.35	54.10
1993-4	53.04	54.01	54.58	55.61	60.29	66.53	72.69	72.74	76.12	79.30	76.85	71.71	66.12
1994-5	70.32	71.10	67.58	72.00	81.92	88.11	91.89	104.20	104.94	105.38	106.96	93.26	88.14
1995-6	85.90	90.00	84.65	84.16	82.18	81.81	81.56	81.13	84.69	83.22	80.23	76.84	83.03
1996-7	76.15	75.24	72.21	70.12	71.98	70.53	70.53	71.12	69.09	69.30	71.03	71.83	71.59
1997-8	71.61	70.75	69.46	68.90	64.57	62.75	63.66	67.04	61.88	65.21	73.50	74.18	67.79
1998-9	71.87	71.75	67.61	64.95	59.88	56.20	55.46	58.17	57.01	55.54	53.74	49.23	60.12
1999-00[1]	49.72	48.39	49.46	48.12	46.65	51.92							49.04

[1] Preliminary. [2] Grade 41, leaf 4, staple 34, mike 35-36 and 43-49 , strength 23.5-26.4. *Source: Agricultural Marketing Service, U.S. Department of Agriculture (AMS-USDA)*

Average Spot Cotton, 1 3/32 , Price (SLM) at Designated U.S. Markets In Cents Per Pound (Net Weight)

Year	Aug.	Sept.	Oct.	Nov.	Dec.	Jan.	Feb.	Mar.	Apr.	May	June	July	Average
1990-1	78.06	72.87	72.19	70.97	71.61	72.14	79.38	79.86	81.99	85.94	81.02	73.28	76.61
1991-2	68.24	64.18	59.74	55.57	54.62	52.39	51.84	53.11	56.30	56.90	60.26	62.35	57.96
1992-3	59.08	54.99	50.96	51.41	53.37	55.24	56.86	58.30	58.03	58.23	56.24	56.22	55.74
1993-4	54.89	55.90	56.46	57.34	61.76	67.97	73.99	74.15	77.55	80.42	78.01	72.97	67.62
1994-5	71.46	72.42	68.82	73.38	83.41	89.92	94.25	106.66	107.50	107.93	109.52	96.31	90.13
1995-6	88.31	92.71	87.06	86.43	84.25	84.32	84.04	83.65	87.25	85.90	82.71	78.86	85.46
1996-7	77.97	76.92	73.90	71.74	75.75	72.53	72.86	73.60	71.23	71.38	73.25	74.04	73.76
1997-8	73.69	72.64	71.13	70.35	66.30	64.55	65.78	69.25	64.31	67.66	76.02	76.63	69.86
1998-9	73.93	73.75	69.90	67.18	62.18	58.56	58.27	61.34	60.33	58.89	56.85	52.61	62.82
1999-00[2]	52.90	51.27	52.43	51.51	49.73								51.57

[1] Preliminary. *Source: Agricultural Marketing Service, U.S. Department of Agriculture (AMS-USDA)*

Average Spot Prices of U.S. Cotton[1], Base QualityÑ(SLM) at Designated Markets In Cents Per Pound

Crop Year Beginning Aug. 1	Dallas (East Tex.-Okl.)	Fresno (San Joaquin Valley)	Greenville (South-east)	Greenwood (South Delta)	Lubbock (West Texas)	Memphis (North Delta)	Phoenix Desert (South-west)	Average
1989-90	67.11	73.47	70.64	69.50	67.06	69.51	71.19	69.78
1990-1	71.40	78.30	75.90	75.53	71.09	75.49	75.90	74.80
1991-2	55.63	57.50	57.70	56.21	55.79	56.18	57.77	56.68
1992-3	53.78	52.84	56.73	55.03	53.53	55.03	51.61	54.10
1993-4[2]	66.22	65.04	67.46	67.04	65.92	67.04	64.16	66.12
1994-5	86.96	93.73	87.17	87.25	86.66	87.25	87.96	88.14
1995-6	80.89	87.40	83.86	83.76	80.64	83.76	80.90	83.03
1996-7	70.29	74.47	72.06	71.84	69.98	72.11	69.88	71.59
1997-8	65.93	71.79	68.60	68.36	65.88	68.36	66.79	67.79
1998-9[3]	59.92	66.78	63.91	63.75	60.08	63.75	58.61	62.35

[1] Prices are for mixed lots, net weight, uncompressed in warehouse. [2] 1993 prices are for mixed lots, net weight, compressed, FOB car/truck.
[3] Preliminary. *Source: Agricultural Marketing Service, U.S. Department of Agriculture (AMS-USDA)*

Average Price[1] Received by Farmers for Upland Cotton in the United States In Cents Per Pound

Year	Aug.	Sept.	Oct.	Nov.	Dec.	Jan.	Feb.	Mar.	Apr.	May	June	July	Average
1990-1	64.6	65.1	67.7	68.4	67.1	64.9	67.9	68.9	69.5	70.1	67.5	66.3	67.1
1991-2	66.3	64.9	62.9	61.2	55.7	51.7	49.8	50.3	53.1	53.2	58.0	56.3	56.8
1992-3	52.7	52.8	53.9	52.7	54.3	53.0	53.8	56.3	55.1	54.4	53.6	53.7	53.7
1993-4	52.4	51.4	52.4	53.3	56.5	62.7	65.7	66.6	67.5	69.0	63.3	58.7	58.1
1994-5	66.8	65.9	66.2	68.5	73.3	78.7	80.2	82.6	77.6	76.2	86.5	80.1	72.0
1995-6	72.2	74.8	74.2	75.0	75.7	76.4	75.7	76.8	78.9	76.7	76.9	73.6	75.4
1996-7	71.9	71.6	71.5	69.7	69.3	67.9	68.1	69.3	67.6	68.3	67.1	67.5	69.3
1997-8	67.0	69.6	69.4	67.9	63.8	61.1	62.5	63.9	63.6	63.5	69.7	68.0	65.2
1998-9	66.0	66.2	65.9	64.6	60.6	58.1	55.6	55.1	55.6	55.0	54.6	53.8	60.2
1999-00[2]	53.0	46.2	45.9	44.7	43.0	44.4							46.2

[1] Weighted average by sales. [2] Preliminary. *Source: Agricultural Marketing Service, U.S. Department of Agriculture (AMS-USDA)*

Purchases Reported by Exchanges in Designated U.S. Spot Markets[1] In Running Bales

Crop Year Beginning Aug. 1	Aug.	Sept.	Oct.	Nov.	Dec.	Jan.	Feb.	Mar.	Apr.	May	June	July	Market Total
1990-1	36,735	53,948	154,499	376,790	600,752	516,421	180,949	66,869	138,503	101,180	45,731	40,551	2,312,928
1991-2	50,469	55,637	179,671	347,393	776,233	1,043,190	1,063,959	699,026	302,102	110,764	134,500	105,795	4,868,739
1992-3	81,778	233,424	325,600	853,846	1,049,780	1,321,861	317,451	330,381	224,874	208,962	189,401	231,390	5,368,748
1993-4	143,237	173,896	321,119	1,071,518	1,213,655	500,246	602,766	318,008	234,331	318,244	83,083	40,699	5,020,802
1994-5	92,401	98,251	426,371	1,075,829	1,491,429	608,701	233,159	149,762	49,192	44,228	43,821	13,244	4,326,388
1995-6	60,442	38,855	73,857	209,279	381,943	765,502	153,758	241,197	225,797	73,459	59,042	31,324	2,314,455
1996-7	62,884	73,925	148,337	477,331	613,430	696,494	412,095	242,606	72,234	130,163	201,557	93,205	3,224,261
1997-8	48,504	106,503	323,400	367,010	617,470	655,432	482,625	396,946	92,072	210,906	105,139	39,647	3,445,654
1998-9	27,193	52,066	114,998	229,743	498,082	414,832	191,872	236,762	71,993	63,335	62,192	64,092	2,027,160
1999-00	83,564	95,241	195,370	320,434	517,579	744,400							3,913,176

[1] commencing September 1, 1988, spot transactions are for seven markets. *Source: Agricultural Marketing* Service, *U.S. Department of Agriculture (AMS-USDA)*

Production of Cotton (Upland and American-Pima) in the U.S. In Thousands of 480-Pound Bales

	Upland												Total
Year	Alabama	Arizona	Arkansas	California	Georgia	Louisiana	Mississippi	Missouri	North Carolina	South Carolina	Tennessee	Texas	American-Pima
1990	375	811	1,081	2,734	405	1,177	1,850	314	263	145	495	4,965	358.5
1991	553	898	1,576	2,548	722	1,414	2,275	429	640	344	701	4,710	398.4
1992	621	725	1,681	2,817	744	1,299	2,131	541	468	226	834	3,265	508.3
1993	469	790	1,094	2,918	733	1,105	1,550	376	429	204	545	5,095	369.3
1994	726	862	1,772	2,902	1,537	1,512	2,132	615	829	393	885	4,968	337.7
1995	492	793	1,468	2,312	1,941	1,375	1,841	513	798	376	724	4,460	367.6
1996	789	778	1,636	2,390	2,079	1,286	1,876	591	1,002	455	675	4,345	528.5
1997	550	847	1,683	2,191	1,919	986	1,821	565	930	410	662	5,140	548.0
1998[1]	553	608	1,209	1,146	1,542	641	1,444	350	1,026	350	546	3,600	442.3
1999[2]	640	680	1,430	1,575	1,570	900	1,740	465	810	275	590	5,050	695.5

[1] Preliminary. [2] Forecasted. *Source: Agricultural Statistics Board, U.S. Department of Agriculture (ASB-USDA)*

Cotton Production and Yield Estimates

	Forecast of Production (1,000 Bales of 480 Lbs.[1])						Actual	Forecasts of Yield (Lbs. Per Harvested Acre)						Actual
Year	Aug. 1	Sept. 1	Oct. 1	Nov. 1	Dec. 1	Jan. 1	Crop	Aug. 1	Sept. 1	Oct. 1	Nov. 1	Dec. 1	Jan. 1	Crop
1990	14,864	14,722	14,540	14,905	15,399	15,617	15,499	622	616	609	622	640	640	634
1991	17,648	17,868	17,614	13,429	14,052	17,542	17,614	630	638	620	635	630	656	652
1992	16,533	16,943	15,885	16,204	16,259	16,260	16,219	696	685	694	698	696	700	699
1993	18,545	17,867	17,014	16,297	16,284	16,176	16,134	668	645	614	594	597	607	606
1994	19,195	19,025	19,303	19,453	19,573	19,728	19,662	690	690	690	695	699	710	708
1995	21,811	20,266	18,771	18,838	18,236	17,971	17,900	663	615	574	567	551	540	537
1996	18,577	17,900	18,189	18,594	18,738	18,951	18,942	686	661	673	698	704	709	705
1997	17,783	18,418	18,410	18,848	18,819	18,977	18,793	637	658	665	673	672	686	673
1998	14,263	13,563	13,288	13,231	13,452	-----	13,918	640	614	616	612	621	-----	625
1999	18,304	17,535	16,430	16,531	16,875	-----		649	621	588	592	604	-----	

[1] Net weight bales. *Source: Agricultural Statistics Board, U.S. Department of Agriculture (ASB-USDA)*

Supply and Distribution of Upland Cotton in the United States In Thousands of 480-Pound Bales

Crop Year Beginning Aug. 1	Area: Planted	Area: Harvested	Yield	Supply: Beginning Stocks[3]	Supply: Production[4]	Supply: Imports	Supply: Total	Disappearance: Mill Use	Disappearance: Exports	Disappearance: Total	Ending Stocks	Farm Price[5]
	1,000 Acres	1,000 Acres	Lbs./Acre									Cents/Lb.
1990-1	12,117	11,505	632	2,798	15,147	4	17,949	8,592	7,378	15,970	2,262	67.1
1991-2	13,802	12,716	650	2,262	17,216	13	19,491	9,548	6,348	15,896	3,583	56.8
1992-3	12,977	10,863	694	3,583	15,710	1	19,294	10,190	4,869	15,059	4,456	53.7
1993-4	13,248	12,594	601	4,456	15,764	6	20,226	10,346	6,555	16,901	3,303	58.4
1994-5	13,552	13,156	705	3,303	19,324	18	22,645	11,109	8,978	20,087	2,588	72.0
1995-6	16,717	15,796	533	2,588	17,532	400	20,520	10,538	7,375	17,913	2,543	75.4
1996-7	14,376	12,612	701	2,543	18,413	403	21,359	11,020	6,399	17,419	3,920	69.3
1997-8	13,648	13,157	666	3,920	18,245	13	22,178	11,234	7,060	18,294	3,822	65.2
1998-9[1]	13,064	10,449	619	3,822	13,476	431	17,729	10,250	4,056	14,310	3,836	60.2
1999-00[2]	14,283	13,096	581	3,836	15,846	65	19,747	10,040	5,300	15,340	4,352	

[1] Preliminary. [2] Estimate. [3] Excludes preseason ginnings (adjusted to 480-lb. bale net weight basis). [4] Includes preseason ginnings. [5] Marketing year average price. [6] Average of 5 cheapest types of SLM 1 3/32 staple length cotton offered on the European market. *Source: Economic Research Service, U.S. Department of Agriculture (ERS-USDA)*

Average Open Interest of No. 2 Cotton Futures in New York In Contracts

Year	Jan.	Feb.	Mar.	Apr.	May	June	July	Aug.	Sept.	Oct.	Nov.	Dec.
1990	40,237	36,291	36,073	37,829	37,908	38,556	36,083	34,042	35,250	40,431	43,997	40,241
1991	43,003	46,793	44,001	43,957	50,086	46,637	40,924	39,616	38,252	39,772	39,295	36,066
1992	38,097	40,095	38,592	36,228	37,839	36,861	35,891	42,241	46,168	46,577	40,425	38,487
1993	41,946	38,657	38,576	33,641	33,012	34,057	32,118	33,872	37,393	36,479	38,567	45,975
1994	54,424	55,558	53,724	54,670	52,830	51,001	52,357	50,597	50,955	51,561	53,563	59,065
1995	71,353	75,100	79,090	71,488	71,714	68,159	65,656	69,653	69,528	65,768	38,475	35,996
1996	58,001	60,231	57,542	61,795	64,555	62,342	61,921	60,182	58,168	58,415	57,397	47,652
1997	59,909	65,392	72,130	76,779	73,464	70,296	73,893	79,309	87,134	92,430	89,150	87,120
1998	89,358	86,739	81,236	85,505	84,562	90,178	81,652	78,571	85,378	88,970	88,917	77,873
1999	79,598	75,794	62,857	60,384	61,470	66,789	68,975	65,689	63,976	60,369	63,746	61,474

Source: New York Board of Trade (NYBOT)

Volume of Trading of No. 2 Cotton Futures in New York In Contracts

Year	Jan.	Feb.	Mar.	Apr.	May	June	July	Aug.	Sept.	Oct.	Nov.	Dec.	Total
1990	135,260	116,806	126,820	121,203	139,489	135,040	132,329	129,081	103,936	142,670	150,958	98,895	1,534,611
1991	133,415	179,656	148,918	156,978	174,690	122,242	116,458	115,175	107,742	125,558	150,545	82,867	1,614,244
1992	134,531	134,184	149,711	167,778	173,128	153,194	105,534	142,323	144,844	129,680	161,194	105,157	1,701,258
1993	171,180	135,400	136,965	135,300	105,920	128,985	130,886	122,280	110,989	107,571	178,350	139,344	1,603,027
1994	210,011	207,421	210,363	252,614	179,591	208,945	161,688	128,879	140,574	179,604	205,936	203,021	2,289,998
1995	223,073	290,600	286,098	219,187	214,052	185,276	183,171	199,050	191,534	196,676	195,601	141,116	2,525,434
1996	215,882	196,225	147,393	251,786	236,684	264,047	131,183	177,430	166,629	229,305	229,281	128,010	2,373,855
1997	201,610	253,475	302,609	258,851	175,227	314,406	234,718	202,008	212,966	216,771	266,800	197,839	2,837,280
1998	221,308	289,222	310,075	362,688	218,595	407,922	226,138	230,752	195,690	303,849	272,775	161,816	3,200,830
1999	179,049	244,300	209,127	250,622	157,552	260,649	187,631	178,236	175,282	193,552	298,531	120,120	2,454,651

Source: New York Board of Trade (NYBOT)

Daily Rate of Upland Cotton Mill Consumption[2] on Cotton-System Spinning Spindles in the U.S.
In Thousands of Running Bales

Crop Year Beginning Aug. 1	Aug.	Sept.	Oct.	Nov.	Dec.	Jan.	Feb.	Mar.	Apr.	May	June	July	Average
1990-1	33.8	41.4	33.2	30.2	29.7	-----	32.3	-----	-----	34.0	-----	-----	33.5
1991-2	33.6	-----	-----	33.1	-----	34.6	36.3	35.7	35.6	37.3	35.2	33.9	35.0
1992-3	38.5	37.8	39.7	37.6	31.5	39.1	39.5	38.8	38.7	39.4	37.8	34.5	37.8
1993-4	39.8	38.4	39.4	36.4	31.4	36.9	37.9	39.0	39.3	39.5	40.4	40.3	38.2
1994-5	41.0	41.4	41.1	41.8	41.7	42.6	42.1	42.4	41.1	40.2	39.2	37.2	41.0
1995-6	38.8	39.4	37.6	38.1	37.9	37.5	38.1	39.5	39.4	39.6	40.5	39.8	38.9
1996-7	40.5	40.7	40.5	41.5	41.1	41.3	40.4	39.4	41.0	41.0	40.9	42.5	40.9
1997-8	40.7	42.4	42.0	42.4	43.9	41.8	41.7	41.1	40.5	40.8	40.0	41.5	41.6
1998-9	39.3	38.7	39.9	37.4	37.5	38.4	38.2	37.9	37.8	37.4	37.7	36.7	38.1
1999-00[1]	36.0	36.3	37.4	37.3	37.7								37.0

[1] Preliminary. [2] Not seasonally adjusted. *Source: Bureau of the Census: U.S. Department of Commerce*

Consumption of American and Foreign Cotton in the United States
In Thousands of Running Bales

Year	Aug.	Sept.	Oct.	Nov.	Dec.	Jan.	Feb.	Mar.	Apr.	May	June	July	Total
1990-1	680	835	671	610	601	-----	2,068	-----	-----	2,212	-----	-----	8,367
1991-2	2,215	-----	-----	2,199	-----	870	730	898	718	752	885	682	9,949
1992-3	776	950	799	756	792	788	796	976	778	792	951	694	9,846
1993-4	801	965	792	731	790	743	785	999	806	830	1,032	744	10,019
1994-5	870	1,070	873	838	897	858	878	1,097	847	842	999	681	10,750
1995-6	829	1,020	798	761	801	744	787	1,029	810	824	1,040	731	10,216
1996-7	847	1,028	829	816	858	810	819	1,014	834	840	1,044	781	10,519
1997-8	868	1,100	872	855	951	848	861	1,068	839	854	1,017	770	10,902
1998-9	835	1,013	834	758	796	979	795	983	777	793	970	678	10,210
1999-00[1]	762	949	793	757	797								9,740

[1] Preliminary. *Source: Bureau of the Census, U.S. Department of Commerce*

Exports of All Cotton[2] from the United States
In Thousands of Running Bales

Year	Aug.	Sept.	Oct.	Nov.	Dec.	Jan.	Feb.	Mar.	Apr.	May	June	July	Total
1990-1	480	355	433	591	639	1,112	950	804	960	488	404	273	7,489
1991-2	219	126	239	396	674	961	725	791	787	535	430	466	6,349
1992-3	252	263	277	342	528	501	502	533	639	401	317	395	4,950
1993-4	287	248	345	405	571	738	512	743	761	854	770	626	6,860
1994-5	531	333	341	710	1,098	1,115	1,383	1,392	1,104	684	410	300	9,402
1995-6	315	245	452	733	1,230	1,262	1,295	777	576	343	263	183	7,675
1996-7	257	171	277	573	899	666	728	848	711	631	604	501	6,866
1997-8	458	299	400	581	774	734	777	888	669	477	574	571	7,202
1998-9	402	280	265	795	1,027	156	182	221	169	256	261	330	4,344
1999-00[1]	254	146	167										2,268

[1] Preliminary. *Source: Foreign Agricultural Service, U.S. Department of Agriculture (FAS-USDA)*

U.S. Exports of American Cotton to Countries of Destination
In Thousands of 480-Pound Bales

Crop Year Beginning Aug. 1	Canada	China	Hong Kong	Indo-nesia	Italy	Japan	Rep. of Korea	Mexico	Philip-pines	Taiwan	Thai-land	United Kingdom	Total
1989-90	197	670	244	499	431	1,594	1,365	117	134	320	375	74	7,694
1990-1	191	1,233	306	561	425	1,437	1,168	202	132	358	317	36	7,793
1991-2	181	792	335	739	240	1,107	1,024	213	181	380	368	60	6,646
1992-3	154	1	100	429	144	839	1,031	557	117	279	150	65	5,201
1993-4	165	1,183	314	653	96	790	976	653	168	356	277	65	6,862
1994-5	253	2,257	347	925	83	1,061	951	558	173	352	441	89	9,402
1995-6	294	1,847	223	794	115	940	769	618	144	255	331	85	7,675
1996-7	253	1,756	129	594	46	630	568	733	84	255	197	66	6,865
1997-8[1]	288	737	151	464	85	637	712	1,447	53	376	220	13	7,202
1998-9[2]	281	71	245	241	29	421	382	1,355	60	251	82	6	4,344

[1] Preliminary. [2] Estimate. *Source: Foreign Agricultural Service, U.S. Department of Agriculture (FAS-USDA)*

Cotton[1] Government Loan Program in the United States

Crop Year Beginning Aug. 1	Support Price (Cents Per Lb.)	Target Price (Cents Per Lb.)	Put Under Support (Ths Bales)	% of Production	Acquired (Ths. Bales)	Owned July 31 (Ths. Bales)
1989-90	50.00	73.4	3,732	32.4	2	27
1990-1	50.27	72.9	3,205	21.1	1	4
1991-2	50.77	72.9	6,312	36.6	8	[3]
1992-3	52.35	72.9	8,302	52.9	10	8
1993-4	52.35	72.9	7,721	49.0	3	14
1994-5	50.00	72.9	4,716	24.4	[3]	[3]
1995-6	51.92	72.9	3,478	19.8	0	0
1996-7	51.92	NA	3,340	18.1	0	0
1997-8	51.92	NA	4,281	23.5	0	0
1998-9	51.92	NA	NA	NA	0	0

[1] Upland. [2] Preliminary. [3] Less than 500 bales. NA = Not applicable. *Source: Economic Research Service, U.S. Department of Agriculture (ERS-USDA)*

Production of Cotton Cloth[1] in the United States In Millions of Square Yards

Year	First Quarter	Second Quarter	Third Quarter	Fourth Quarter	Total Year
1990	1,202	1,127	1,087	1,048	4,463
1991	1,081	1,148	1,082	1,093	4,404
1992	1,154	1,172	1,130	1,144	4,600
1993	1,150	1,144	1,071	1,039	4,403
1994	1,073	1,125	1,131	1,143	4,473
1995	1,169	1,137	1,090	1,093	4,488
1996	1,182	1,230	1,198	1,187	4,796
1997	1,211	1,276	1,283	1,309	5,078
1998	1,226	1,167	1,218	1,142	4,753
1999[2]	1,166	1,161	1,081		4,544

[1] Cotton broadwoven goods over 12 inches in width. [2] Preliminary. *Source: Bureau of Census, U.S. Department of Commerce*

Cotton Ginnings[1] in the United States To: In Thousands of Running Bales

Crop Year	Aug. 1	Sept. 1	Sept. 15	Oct. 1	Oct. 15	Nov. 1	Nov. 15	Dec. 1	Dec. 15	Jan. 1	Jan. 15	Feb. 1	Total Crop
1990-1	120	583	1,090	2,616	4,739	7,955	10,207	12,428	13,863	14,516	14,809	14,963	15,082
1991-2	NA	699	983	2,467	4,955	8,351	10,752	13,260	15,067	15,888	16,402	16,765	17,146
1992-3	14	446	740	1,664	4,046	7,584	10,296	12,597	14,083	14,944	15,311	15,527	15,786
1993-4	9	435	748	1,846	4,471	7,975	10,952	13,244	14,695	15,321	15,517	15,590	15,675
1994-5	113	680	943	2,324	5,002	8,878	12,479	15,587	17,465	18,438	18,842	19,028	19,127
1995-6	17	433	898	2,455	4,795	8,430	11,262	14,199	16,101	17,011	17,292	17,416	17,469
1996-7	48	342	637	2,146	4,780	8,876	11,906	14,623	16,528	17,681	18,101	18,308	18,439
1997-8	2	359	683	1,210	3,752	7,930	11,601	14,735	16,662	17,613	18,013	18,170	18,301
1998-9	146	523	739	2,056	4,265	7,359	9,366	11,272	12,558	13,067	13,366	13,464	13,534
1999-00[2]	81	561	1,018	2,708	4,943	8,238	11,012	13,587	14,928	15,899	16,224		

[1] Excluding linters. [2] Preliminary. *Source: National Agricultural Statistics Service, U.S. Department of Agriculture (NASS-USDA)*

Fiber Prices in the United States In Cents Per Pound

Year	Cotton[1] Actual	Cotton[1] Raw[5] Equivalent	Rayon[2] Actual	Rayon[2] Raw[5] Equivalent	Polyester[3] Actual	Polyester[3] Raw[5] Equivalent	Price Ratios[4] in Percent Cotton/Rayon	Price Ratios[4] in Percent Cotton/Polyester
1991	79.05	87.83	122.00	127.08	73.50	76.56	.69	1.15
1992	61.92	68.80	114.08	118.84	73.50	76.56	.58	.90
1993	62.43	69.37	111.42	116.06	72.50	75.52	.60	.92
1994	78.69	87.43	103.00	107.29	74.92	78.04	.82	1.12
1995	100.76	111.95	118.67	123.61	88.83	92.53	.91	1.21
1996	86.24	95.83	118.00	122.92	81.10	84.48	.78	1.14
1997	76.29	84.77	115.00	119.79	69.50	72.40	.71	1.17
1998	74.21	82.45	110.25	114.84	62.50	65.11	.72	1.29
1999[6]	61.45	68.28	98.92	103.04	51.67	53.82	.66	1.27
Jan.	64.47	71.63	101.00	105.21	51.00	53.13	.68	1.35
Feb.	63.39	70.43	101.00	105.21	51.00	53.13	.67	1.33
Mar.	66.31	73.68	101.00	105.21	51.00	53.13	.70	1.39
Apr.	64.69	71.88	101.00	105.21	50.00	52.08	.68	1.38
May	63.17	70.19	100.00	104.17	50.00	52.08	.67	1.35
June	60.87	67.63	98.00	102.08	51.00	53.13	.66	1.27
July	56.24	62.49	95.00	98.96	52.00	54.17	.63	1.15
Aug.	57.14	63.49	98.00	102.08	52.00	54.17	.64	1.17
Sept.	55.98	62.20	97.00	101.04	53.00	55.21	.62	1.13
Oct.	57.79	64.21	97.00	101.04	53.00	55.21	.64	1.16
Nov.	55.88	62.09	97.00	101.04	53.00	55.21	.61	1.13
Dec.	71.48	79.42	101.00	105.21	53.00	55.21	.76	1.44

[1] SLM-1 1/16 at group B Mill points, net weight. [2] 1.5 and 3.0 denier, regular rayon staples. [3] Reported average market price for 1.5 denier polyester staple for cotton blending. [4] Raw fiber equivalent. [5] Actual prices converted to estimated raw fiber equivalent as follows: cotton, divided by 0.90, rayon and polyester, divided by 0.96. [6] Preliminary. *Source: Economic Research Service, U.S. Department of Agriculture (ERS-USDA)*

Cottonseed and Products

Cottonseed production is directly related to the amount of cotton produced. Cottonseed is crushed to produce cottonseed meal and cottonseed oil. The meal is used as a feed ingredient for livestock while the oil is used in cooking. For the U.S., the 1999/2000 season was an interesting one. The cotton crop was initially expected to be a large one, possibly as much as 20 million bales. There were 14.6 million acres planted, an increase of about 9 percent from the previous year. The weather during the growing season was less than optimal and the crop was 16.9 million bales, according to USDA estimates. The national average cotton yield was 604 pounds per acre, down 3 percent from the previous season.

With the larger cotton crop, cottonseed production increased. The USDA forecast that U.S. cottonseed production in the 1999-00 season would be 5.8 million metric tonnes. This represented an increase of 19 percent from the 1998-99 season when output was 4.87 million tonnes.

The U.S.D.A. forecast world cottonseed production in 1999/00 to be 33.77 million tonnes, an increase of 3 percent from the year before. The world's largest producer was forecast to be China. Their production in 1999/00, with a cotton crop of 19 million bales, was 7.45 million tonnes, down 8 percent from the year before. China has been reducing cotton production because of excessive stocks.

After the U.S., the next largest producer was India with output of 5.5 million tonnes or some 2 percent more than in 1998/99. Pakistan's cottonseed production in 1999/00 was forecast to be 3.4 million tonnes, some 24 percent more than the year before. Another important cotton production region is central Asia where Uzbekistan and Turkmenistan together were forecast to produce 2.78 million tonnes of cottonseed, an increase of 360,000 tonnes or 15 percent from 1998/99. Other large cottonseed producers include Turkey, Australia and Brazil.

World Production of Cottonseed In Thousands of Metric Ton

Crop Year	Argentina	Australia	Brazil	China	Egypt	Greece	India	Mexico	Pakistan	Turkey	United States	Former USSR	World Total
1991-2	435	724	1,313	10,499	491	355	4,090	307	4,352	878	6,283	4,283	37,691
1992-3	275	528	800	8,024	571	410	4,740	50	3,080	905	5,652	3,557	31,914
1993-4	392	466	910	6,655	649	454	4,183	42	2,735	900	5,754	3,600	29,850
1994-5	638	474	980	7,727	411	574	4,709	187	2,959	930	6,898	3,380	33,129
1995-6	748	595	690	8,487	384	725	5,339	344	3,604	1,288	6,213	3,150	35,290
1996-7	564	859	568	7,481	560	540	5,890	421	3,230	1,259	6,480	2,561	34,490
1997-8	542	941	763	8,193	563	590	5,150	329	3,180	1,310	6,291	2,785	34,843
1998-9[1]	337	990	916	8,012	365	650	5,420	363	2,900	1,370	4,867	2,580	32,842
1999-00[2]	280	961	900	7,300		670	5,600	240	3,400	1,340	5,674	3,100	34,046

[1] Preliminary. [2] Estimate. *Source: The Oil World*

Salient Statistics of Cottonseed in the United States In Thousands of Short Tons

Crop Year Beginning Aug. 1	Supply: Stocks	Supply: Production	Supply: Total Supply	Disappearance: Crush	Disappearance: Exports	Disappearance: Other	Disappearance: Total Disappearance	Farm Price $/Ton	Value of Production Mil. $	Products Produced: Oil Million Lbs.	Products Produced: Meal Thousand Sh. Tons
	In Thousands of Short Tons										
1991-2	651	6,926	7,579	3,981	161	2,977	7,119	71	492.3	1,279	1,765
1992-3	460	6,230	6,690	3,629	192	2,504	6,325	98	608.4	1,137	1,533
1993-4	365	6,343	6,708	3,470	157	2,649	6,276	113	714.4	1,119	1,563
1994-5	432	7,604	8,036	3,947	232	3,306	7,485	101	771.3	1,312	1,830
1995-6	551	6,849	7,399	3,882	114	2,886	6,882	106	731.0	1,229	1,748
1996-7	517	7,144	7,681	3,860	116	3,182	7,158	126	914.6	1,310	1,807
1997-8	523	6,935	7,553	3,885	149	2,957	6,990	121	835.4	1,224	1,769
1998-9[1]	563	5,365	6,135	2,719	68	2,955	5,742	123	661.9	832	1,232
1999-00[2]	393	6,422	6,916	3,200	70	3,171	6,441	-----	562.5	1,025	1,440

[1] Preliminary. [2] Estimate. *Source: Economic Research Service, U.S. Department of Agriculture (ERS-USDA)*

Average Wholesale Price of Cottonseed Meal (41% Solvent)[2] in Memphis In Dollars Per Short Ton

Year	Jan.	Feb.	Mar.	Apr.	May	June	July	Aug.	Sept.	Oct.	Nov.	Dec.	Average
1991	125.00	118.10	125.00	122.50	118.10	117.20	127.50	130.90	133.10	131.00	144.40	162.00	129.57
1992	156.25	140.10	124.25	121.25	127.50	132.50	133.75	146.90	163.00	154.40	157.50	174.50	144.33
1993	164.40	149.40	153.50	149.00	143.10	153.00	170.30	178.50	193.75	173.10	181.00	180.00	165.75
1994	170.30	173.10	174.00	166.25	157.75	154.10	152.50	144.50	145.00	134.40	120.50	114.20	150.55
1995	106.75	97.50	100.30	98.10	92.75	108.75	116.90	116.50	137.60	153.25	165.00	185.80	123.27
1996	208.80	202.80	195.60	220.00	191.25	192.20	201.56	193.10	193.10	183.25	196.60	224.50	200.23
1997	207.20	183.75	189.10	189.10	193.75	190.30	170.75	176.25	192.00	189.10	189.10	190.50	188.41
1998	153.10	139.10	128.70	116.25	105.00	129.40	146.65	130.30	115.60	106.50	107.90	119.75	124.85
1999[1]	110.60	101.25	106.90	110.90	108.75	114.50	115.00	100.65	111.92	111.83	112.00	124.17	110.71

[1] Preliminary. *Source: Economic Research Service, U.S. Department of Agriculture (ERS-USDA)*

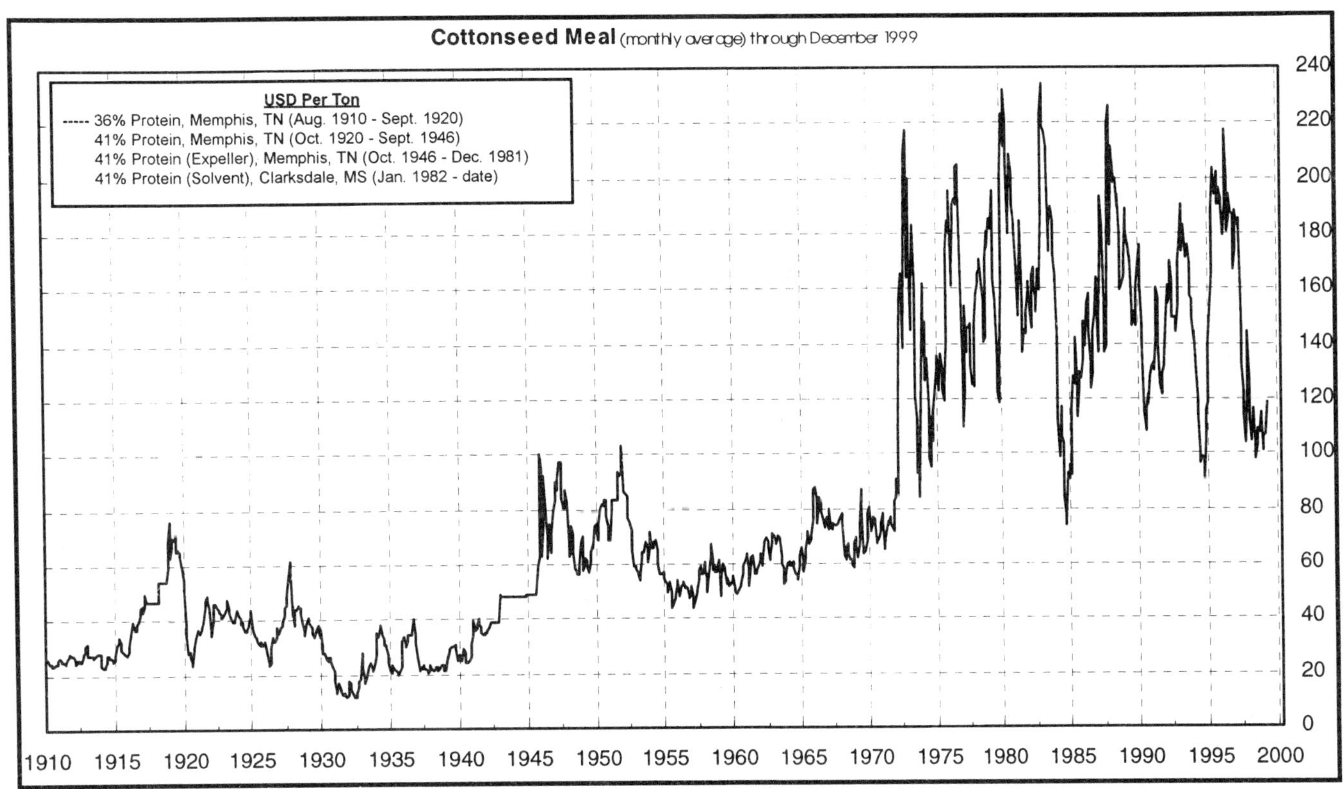

Supply and Distribution of Cottonseed Oil in the United States In Millions of Pounds

Crop Year Beginning Oct. 1	Supply: Stocks	Supply: Production	Supply: Imports	Supply: Total Supply	Disappearance: Domestic	Disappearance: Exports	Disappearance: Total	Per Capita Cunsump. of Salad & Cook Oils - In Lbs. -	Utilization Food Uses: Shortening	Utilization Food Uses: Salad & Cooking Oils	Utilization Food Uses: Total	Prices U.S.[3] (Crude) $/Met. Ton	Prices Rott[4] (Cif) $/Met. Ton
1993-4	81	1,119	26.0	1,226	873	248	1,121	27	217	289	558	684	750
1994-5	106	1,312	0	1,417	1,006	329	1,335	26	217	262	532	683	671
1995-6	82	1,229	.3	1,311	996	221	1,217	27	218	235	497	575	613
1996-7	94	1,216	.3	1,310	1,012	232	1,244	26	271	265	556	564	590
1997-8	66	1,224	.1	1,291	1,004	208	1,212	29	187	171	379	663	693
1998-9[1]	79	832	37.0	948	760	112	872	28	271	265	556	633	632
1999-00[2]	76	1,010	7.5	1,094	909	110	1,019					460	486

[1] Preliminary. [2] Estimate. [3] Valley Points FOB; Tank Cars. [4] Rotterdam; US, PBSY, fob gulf. *Source: Economic Research Service, U.S. Department of Agriculture (ERS-USDA)*

Consumption of Crude Cottonseed Oil in Refining in the United States In Millions of Pound

Year	Oct.	Nov.	Dec.	Jan.	Feb.	Mar.	Apr.	May	June	July	Aug.	Sept.	Total
1993-4	82.7	113.0	103.8	110.8	96.7	111.5	69.6	74.8	73.2	74.6	88.4	64.2	1,063.3
1994-5	81.9	97.2	109.8	107.7	87.1	96.2	87.2	72.8	73.4	76.0	83.3	71.6	1,044.4
1995-6	76.1	91.8	89.7	94.5	87.2	92.2	83.4	77.3	55.5	56.2	64.3	54.4	922.5
1996-7	67.2	85.1	85.1	88.7	83.3	80.8	77.4	79.2	58.4	55.3	59.0	39.2	858.7
1997-8	73.1	73.1	77.2	85.0	75.7	70.2	72.1	57.1	51.9	54.9	57.5	30.1	778.1
1998-9	52.9	49.6	50.2	46.6	48.9	50.7	36.4	28.3	28.4	30.5	46.2	43.5	512.3
1999-00[1]	51.9	57.3	61.5										682.5

[1] Preliminary. *Source: U.S. Bureau of Census, U.S. Department of Commerce*

Exports of Cottonseed Oil (Crude and Refined) from the United States In Thousands of Pounds

Year	Jan.	Feb.	Mar.	Apr.	May	June	July	Aug.	Sept.	Oct.	Nov.	Dec.	Total
1993	23,904	14,238	6,294	27,370	25,849	17,685	5,066	7,065	19,246	7,079	15,103	14,075	182,974
1994	32,011	11,093	21,156	26,595	34,921	11,583	24,303	24,644	25,265	17,487	33,385	36,613	299,056
1995	18,808	43,454	48,471	34,500	28,775	22,692	18,490	11,973	-----	9,896	30,268	13,223	306,055
1996	26,407	8,103	38,597	24,628	16,052	14,135	7,827	21,197	10,903	12,526	10,345	13,145	203,865
1997	25,722	26,835	22,647	22,230	30,319	9,535	25,207	24,717	8,919	15,351	24,217	8,164	243,863
1998	24,003	15,077	16,150	22,874	20,791	22,994	15,348	14,392	8,818	11,056	7,610	11,447	190,560
1999[1]	11,548	10,235	7,780	11,387	6,328	7,161	8,725	8,111	8,818	11,023			109,339

[1] Preliminary. *Source: Economic Research Service, U.S. Department of Agriculture (ERS-USDA)*

COTTONSEED AND PRODUCTS

Cottonseed Crushed (Consumption) in the United States   In Thousands of Short Tons

Year	Aug.	Sept.	Oct.	Nov.	Dec.	Jan.	Feb.	Mar.	Apr.	May	June	July	Total
1991-2	813.6	ÑÑ	ÑÑ	1,145.2	ÑÑ	420.6	378.3	381.3	297.8	245.4	292.1	270.2	4,245
1992-3	245.7	162.9	323.2	353.3	372.1	413.3	334.6	324.1	323.8	296.4	242.7	237.2	3,629
1993-4	182.9	162.6	300.4	391.4	375.0	391.0	335.2	358.6	265.7	257.7	239.4	210.2	3,470
1994-5	192.1	195.5	343.9	386.2	397.5	404.6	360.5	391.0	345.4	304.0	316.5	310.0	3,947
1995-6	264.4	245.5	337.1	386.7	362.4	402.3	373.5	381.4	349.6	325.2	223.7	209.2	3,861
1996-7	229.2	225.0	331.7	355.1	352.6	381.0	362.8	362.2	334.4	351.3	280.8	294.0	3,860
1997-8	244.4	178.6	329.7	374.5	371.3	428.4	352.3	370.8	359.1	309.1	278.8	277.6	3,875
1998-9	246.0	174.9	272.7	254.3	262.7	282.2	259.5	280.2	205.5	172.0	159.9	149.2	2,719
1999-00[1]	166.8	230.7	281.6	302.5	296.4								3,067

[1] Preliminary. *Source: Economic Research Service, U.S. Department of Agriculture* (ERS-USDA)

Production of Cottonseed Cake and Meal in the United States   In Thousands of Short Tons

Year	Aug.	Sept.	Oct.	Nov.	Dec.	Jan.	Feb.	Mar.	Apr.	May	June	July	Total
1991-2	388.6	-----	-----	533.9	-----	192.6	170.5	173.5	138.2	111.7	129.9	127.8	1,967
1992-3	111.2	76.0	143.7	150.2	160.5	176.2	146.6	136.4	140.9	126.1	103.0	101.0	1,572
1993-4	76.7	71.5	130.1	172.2	166.6	161.8	151.8	164.0	119.6	116.1	106.9	93.4	1,531
1994-5	90.6	89.4	154.2	171.5	176.9	184.1	162.2	174.3	154.2	137.4	143.9	137.2	1,776
1995-6	120.1	113.6	159.9	178.2	161.0	183.8	169.8	168.3	158.7	147.1	102.4	102.7	1,766
1996-7	100.9	99.1	146.1	161.5	158.2	174.5	164.6	162.1	152.2	160.7	128.6	123.2	1,732
1997-8	128.2	92.1	147.8	168.7	178.2	194.4	158.5	170.4	162.3	141.8	128.8	124.0	1,795
1998-9	114.7	77.1	118.7	115.9	122.5	130.2	114.8	127.2	90.6	75.6	75.6	71.0	1,234
1999-00[1]	82.1	107.5	132.1	140.8	138.3								1,442

[1] Preliminary. *Source: Bureau of Census, U.S. Department of Commerce*

Production of Crude Cottonseed Oil[2] in the United States   In Millions of Pounds

Year	Aug.	Sept.	Oct.	Nov.	Dec.	Jan.	Feb.	Mar.	Apr.	May	June	July	Total
1991-2	263.7	-----	-----	398.9	-----	137.4	127.2	121.5	97.5	79.3	91.8	91.3	1,409
1992-3	77.8	56.8	99.5	110.2	117.6	134.7	107.2	104.9	101.7	96.1	77.7	76.5	1,161
1993-4	59.1	51.7	93.5	122.2	117.5	124.7	99.9	119.6	85.3	85.2	78.4	69.8	1,107
1994-5	61.7	61.0	109.8	122.6	125.6	133.4	115.6	125.2	110.4	97.7	102.4	96.6	1,262
1995-6	87.8	84.3	105.2	121.6	111.6	130.9	121.4	125.6	110.4	101.9	73.3	76.7	1,251
1996-7	70.3	69.4	98.9	114.8	115.9	123.9	114.8	114.7	103.7	109.8	86.9	85.9	1,209
1997-8	80.6	66.0	97.8	120.3	119.6	136.4	111.1	115.5	112.7	96.1	87.3	88.8	1,232
1998-9	77.8	59.6	78.3	80.0	80.6	84.0	80.2	86.7	64.4	53.4	52.4	45.9	843
1999-00[1]	56.1	69.6	88.3	95.4	94.2								969

[1] Preliminary. [2] Not seasonally adjusted. *Source: Bureau of Census, U.S. Department of Commerce*

Production of Refined Cottonseed Oil in the United States   In Millions of Pounds

Year	Aug.	Sept.	Oct.	Nov.	Dec.	Jan.	Feb.	Mar.	Apr.	May	June	July	Total
1991-2	209.3	-----	-----	205.0	-----	103.2	105.6	97.9	85.6	73.4	82.1	81.1	1,043
1992-3	69.3	46.3	72.6	90.2	91.9	103.1	82.0	74.5	88.8	75.6	70.8	62.4	928
1993-4	65.1	54.6	79.4	109.1	100.6	107.2	93.4	107.8	66.9	71.6	70.0	72.2	998
1994-5	86.3	62.9	80.0	94.4	106.2	104.2	94.4	92.6	84.2	70.1	70.7	72.6	1,019
1995-6	80.5	69.0	74.0	89.5	86.9	91.7	84.6	89.8	81.7	75.0	53.8	54.5	931
1996-7	62.4	53.0	64.9	82.8	82.2	85.9	80.7	78.1	75.2	76.9	56.4	53.6	852
1997-8	57.4	38.1	48.3	71.0	74.8	82.2	73.1	68.2	69.8	55.2	50.3	53.0	741
1998-9	55.8	29.1	51.1	47.9	48.5	45.4	47.3	49.0	35.2	27.4	27.5	29.7	494
1999-00[1]	44.8	42.4	50.4	55.6	59.4								606

[1] Preliminary. *Source: Bureau of the Census, U.S. Department of Commerce*

Stocks of Cottonseed Oil (Crude and Refined) in the U.S., at End of Month   In Millions of Pounds

Year	Aug.	Sept.	Oct.	Nov.	Dec.	Jan.	Feb.	Mar.	Apr.	May	June	July
1991-2	136.3	-----	-----	163.3	-----	193.1	183.6	180.3	171.5	154.0	139.9	119.8
1992-3	94.3	81.0	93.1	101.7	123.2	148.4	152.6	167.1	157.0	159.2	144.8	143.8
1993-4	85.8	54.6	79.4	109.1	100.6	107.2	93.4	107.8	66.9	71.6	70.0	72.1
1994-5	112.4	105.6	103.5	117.0	114.7	122.2	150.5	129.9	120.8	95.7	96.9	92.2
1995-6	87.8	82.1	82.6	89.3	94.8	118.2	147.2	151.2	155.6	143.3	128.1	125.4
1996-7	101.2	94.1	97.5	102.5	106.0	120.9	133.7	137.5	131.7	116.1	103.4	85.9
1997-8	78.0	66.4	68.6	86.4	105.3	133.8	141.2	140.7	159.8	150.4	130.9	118.8
1998-9	97.3	78.6	89.1	110.0	85.5	109.5	113.3	125.3	126.0	112.0	100.7	83.7
1999-00[1]	107.8	76.0	81.1	88.7	83.4							

[1] Preliminary. *Source: Bureau of Census, U.S. Department of Commerce*

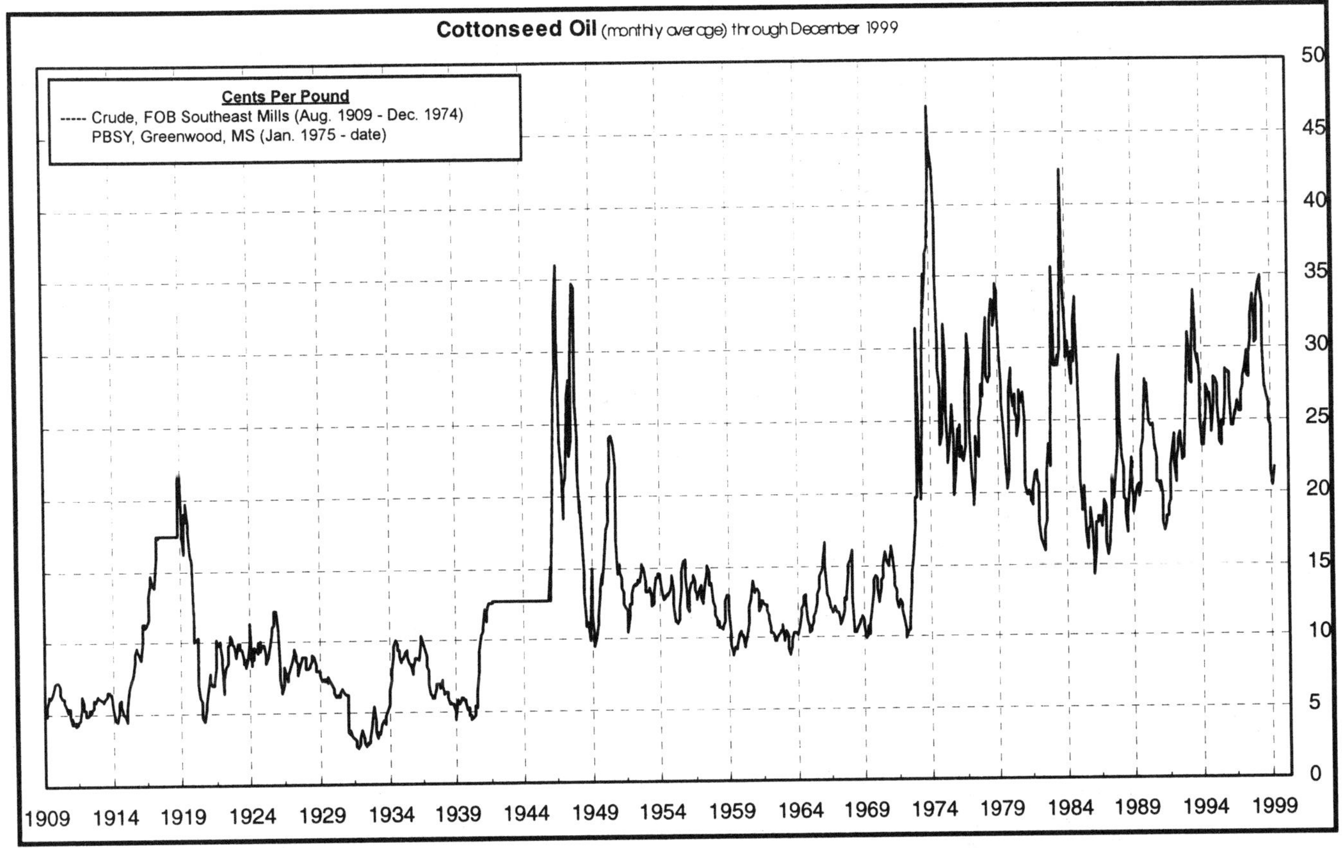

Average Price of Crude Cottonseed Oil, PBSY, Greenwood, MS.[1] in Tank Cars In Cents Per Pound

Year	Jan.	Feb.	Mar.	Apr.	May	June	July	Aug.	Sept.	Oct.	Nov.	Dec.	Average
1990	19.95	20.19	22.88	22.83	26.90	26.94	26.00	24.60	24.88	24.80	24.19	24.75	24.08
1991	23.75	22.88	23.00	22.13	20.67	20.31	20.50	21.00	19.88	17.98	17.41	18.07	20.63
1992	18.50	18.13	19.25	19.38	21.38	22.58	24.45	21.86	21.04	22.17	22.96	23.91	21.30
1993	24.09	22.03	22.24	22.55	22.70	26.76	30.74	30.45	28.98	24.79	26.69	30.39	26.03
1994	33.16	29.96	29.60	29.06	29.66	27.55	24.20	23.71	24.51	23.64	24.85	25.50	27.12
1995	28.70	29.95	27.14	27.61	27.51	30.04	30.63	30.26	28.61	27.61	26.27	26.10	26.36
1996	24.45	24.35	24.25	26.77	28.46	27.94	28.25	27.81	26.13	24.55	24.28	24.29	25.96
1997	25.21	25.44	26.18	25.10	25.19	25.01	26.53	27.11	28.03	28.47	29.11	26.78	26.51
1998	27.69	29.37	30.46	32.47	33.13	30.22	29.40	30.11	33.26	33.99	34.16	33.40	31.47
1999	31.72	28.21	26.27	24.39	24.25	25.19	24.70	21.39	20.22	20.15	19.69	21.25	23.95

[1] Data prior to 1995 are F.O.B. Valley Points, Southeastern mills. *Source: Economic Research Service, U.S. Department of Agriculture (ERS-USDA)*

Exports of Cottonseed Oil to Important Countries from the United States In Thousands of Metric Tons

Year	Canada	Dominican Republic	Egypt	Guate-mala	Japan	Mexico	Nether-lands	Salvador	South Korea	Turkey	Vene-zuela	Total
1989	6.6	5.1	39.4	6.0	34.3	3.2	3.4	30.5	21.0	2.0	53.7	209.4
1990	6.8	6.0	14.7	.4	36.7	1.4	2.9	21.0	36.0	-----	9.2	136.3
1991	7.8	2.1	14.7	-----	24.1	4.8	3.4	13.0	13.0	5.5	4.2	97.0
1992	11.3	1.0	8.2	3.2	15.3	8.5	17.4	26.5	10.9	7.0	3.7	123.3
1993	10.9	-----	-----	.5	17.6	5.8	.2	30.8	6.6	.5	1.5	83.1
1994	10.8	-----	7.5	12.3	29.8	10.3	1.9	26.1	16.9	-----	4.5	135.7
1995	12.0	-----	10.3	1.9	17.9	5.7	1.5	37.8	19.2	-----	2.8	133.7
1996	23.2	-----	-----	1.7	15.8	3.3	-----	20.6	8.1	2.0	-----	100.0
1997	28.1	-----	-----	.4	11.3	2.5	4.2	25.3	1.9	2.5	-----	110.6
1998[1]	37.6	-----	-----	-----	6.0	6.1	-----	16.1	1.5	-----	-----	86.3

[1] Preliminary. *Source: The Oil World*

Bridge/CRB Futures Index

The Bridge Commodity Research Bureau Futures Price Index was first calculated by Commodity Research Bureau, Inc. in 1957 and made its inaugural appearance in the 1958 CRB Commodity Year Book.

The Index was originally comprised of two cash markets and 26 futures markets, which were traded on exchanges in the U.S. and Canada. It included barley and flaxseed from the Winnipeg exchange; cocoa, coffee "B", copper, cotton, cottonseed oil, grease wool, hides, lead, potatoes, rubber, sugar #4, sugar #6, wool tops and zinc from New York exchanges; and corn, oats, wheat, rye, soybeans, soybean oil, soybean meal, lard, onions, and eggs from Chicago exchanges. In addition to those 26, the Index also included the spot New Orleans cotton and Minneapolis wheat markets.

Like the Bureau of Labor Statistics spot index, the Bridge/CRB Futures Price Index is calculated to produce an unweighted geometric mean of the individual commodity price relatives. In other words, a ratio of the current price to the base year average price. Currently, 1967 is the base year the Index is calculated against (1967 = 100).

The formula considers all future delivery contracts that expire on or before the end of the sixth calendar month from the current date, using up to a maximum of five contracts per commodity. However, a minimum of two contracts must be used to calculate the current price, even if the second contract is outside the six-month window. Contracts are excluded from the calculation when in their delivery period.

The 1999 closing value of 205.14 was 7.28 percent higher than the 1998 close of 191.22. The 1999 advance was also the first increase in the Index since 1995, breaking a string of three consecutive losing years. 10 of the 17 component commodities finished higher for the year.

Futures Markets

Futures and options on the CRB Futures Price Index are traded on the NYFE Division of the New York Board of Trade (NYBOT).

Bridge/CRB Futures Index Component Commodities by Group

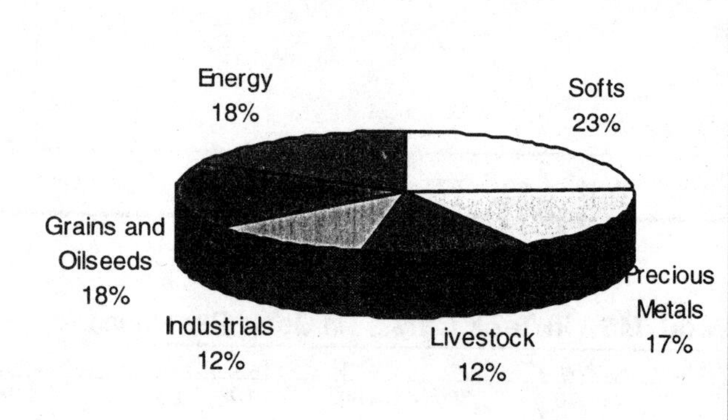

Groups:	*Components*
Energy:	Crude Oil, Heating Oil, Natural Gas
Grains and Oilseeds:	Corn, Soybeans, Wheat
Industrials:	Copper, Cotton
Livestock:	Live Cattle, Live Hogs
Precious Metals:	Gold, Platinum, Silver
Softs:	Cocoa, Coffee, Orange Juice, Sugar #11

The Bridge/CRB Futures Index is computed using a three-step process:

1) Each of the Index's 17 component commodities is arithmetically average using the prices for all of the designated contract months which expire on or before the end of the sixth calendar month from the current date, except that: a) no contract shall be included in the calculation whie in delivery; b) there shall be a minimum of two contract months for each component commodity (adding contracts beyond the six month window if necessary); c) there shall be a maximum of five contract months for each commodity (dropping the most deferred contracts to remain at five, if necessary). The result is that the Index extends six to seven months into the futures depending on where one is in the current month. For example, live cattle's average price on October 30, 1995 would be computed as follows:

$$\text{Cattle Average} = \frac{\text{Dec. '96} + \text{Feb. '97}}{2}$$

2) These 17 component averages are then geometrically average by multiplying all of teh number together and taking the 17th root.

$$\text{Geometric Average} = 17 \sqrt{\text{Crude Avg.} * \text{Heating Oil Avg.} * \text{Sugar Avg....}}$$

3) The resulting average is divided by 30.7766, the 1967 base-year average for these 17 commodities. That result is then multiplied by an adjustment factor of .8486. This adjustment factor is necessitated by the nine revisions to the Index since its inception in 1957. Finally, that result is multiplied by 100 in order to convert the Index into percentage terms:

$$\text{Bridge/CRB Futures Index} = \frac{\text{Current Geometric Average}}{\text{1967 Geometric Avg. (30.7766)}} * .8486 * 100$$

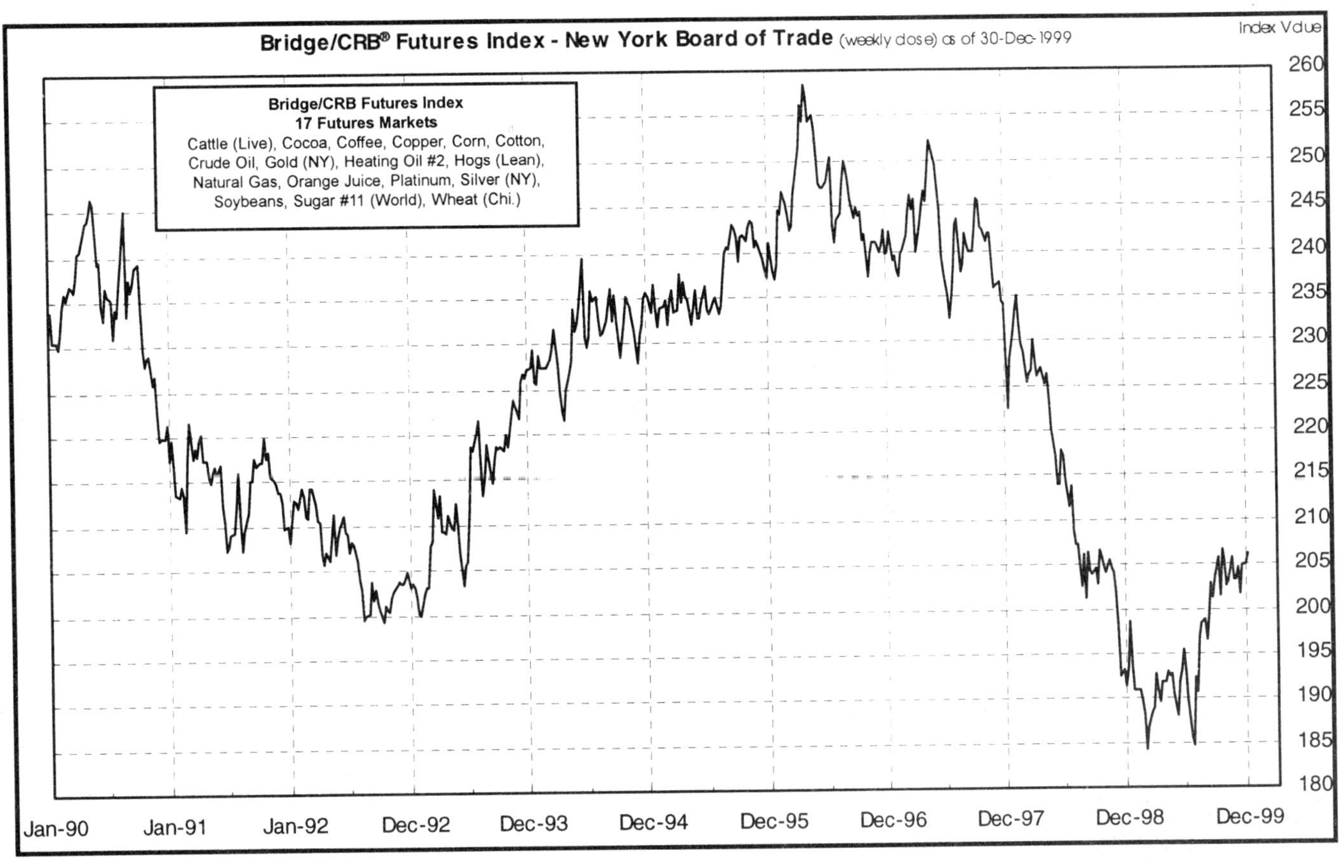

Average Open Interest of Bridge/CRB Futures Index in New York In Contracts

Year	Jan.	Feb.	Mar.	Apr.	May	June	July	Aug.	Sept.	Oct.	Nov.	Dec.
1990	1,889	1,229	1,476	1,858	1,499	1,459	1,289	1,286	1,181	1,247	1,505	1,530
1991	1,443	1,593	1,524	1,620	1,511	1,524	1,168	1,071	1,045	1,172	1,357	1,383
1992	1,435	1,472	1,185	1,347	1,311	1,087	951	1,179	1,075	1,226	1,283	1,406
1993	1,969	1,984	1,842	2,201	2,564	2,947	2,616	2,409	2,128	2,383	2,432	2,351
1994	2,607	3,146	2,680	2,691	2,339	2,698	3,838	5,146	4,562	4,942	4,535	2,800
1995	2,144	2,164	2,147	2,370	2,016	2,144	2,053	2,070	2,062	1,942	2,003	1,640
1996	1,934	1,826	1,753	2,355	1,881	1,890	1,562	1,345	1,596	1,853	1,861	1,866
1997	1,944	2,128	2,090	2,245	2,192	1,817	1,957	1,741	1,656	1,843	1,789	1,752
1998	1,679	1,557	1,626	1,509	1,641	1,895	1,832	1,719	1,839	2,162	2,639	2,787
1999	2,863	3,027	3,153	3,041	3,785	3,387	3,300	3,443	4,230	4,851	4,579	4,086

Source: New York Board of Trade (NYBOT)

Volume of Trading of Bridge/CRB Futures Index in New York In Contracts

Year	Jan.	Feb.	Mar.	Apr.	May	June	July	Aug.	Sept.	Oct.	Nov.	Dec.	Total
1990	6,505	5,829	7,042	6,670	7,191	6,687	6,477	6,415	4,096	4,744	4,409	3,842	69,907
1991	5,835	5,391	6,715	6,432	3,671	5,557	4,853	5,876	4,414	3,766	4,132	4,543	61,185
1992	4,895	6,031	4,136	5,697	5,496	4,487	4,162	4,617	3,874	3,183	5,277	4,400	56,255
1993	3,620	5,720	8,050	7,340	8,680	10,722	12,418	8,590	6,192	4,350	8,535	6,954	91,171
1994	6,956	7,473	10,085	10,274	11,298	14,652	10,560	8,967	7,445	6,575	10,186	5,515	109,986
1995	6,151	5,545	5,763	7,955	7,877	7,573	6,875	10,094	7,376	5,030	5,865	5,309	81,413
1996	7,490	6,041	6,428	10,784	9,526	5,543	7,476	5,816	6,311	6,527	5,990	3,181	81,113
1997	6,645	4,942	5,245	8,600	8,156	7,776	6,248	7,685	4,537	4,588	3,468	3,592	71,482
1998	7,659	4,623	3,953	3,890	2,933	5,634	3,394	4,578	5,101	4,013	8,814	4,401	58,993
1999	7,606	7,766	7,556	7,808	4,986	8,404	4,378	12,053	6,660	8,063	9,497	3,932	88,709

Source: New York Board of Trade (NYBOT)

Currencies

Two major, but opposing, forces pivoting off the U.S. dollar developed in the FOREX markets during 1999: the Japanese yen's strength against the dollar, and the weakness of the new Euro currency against the dollar and yen. Of the two, the Euro's slide may be the more important. Europe's single 11-nation basket currency, which began trading in January 1999 with a value of about $1.17 to the dollar, fell steadily during the first half of the year but was able to establish a footing, albeit short lived, at just above parity with the dollar. The root cause of the slide was the remarkable strength of the U.S. economy which showed an annualized third-quarter growth rate of 5.5 percent vs. 2 percent growth among the Euro-zone nations. In economic terms, the Euro's decline could prove to have little short term effect, however, the psychological impact could have longer term implications because it implied shaky confidence in either the Euro or Europe's ability to achieve sustained growth. Moreover, should the Euro's weakness persist deep into 2000 it might (1) stroke inflationary fears and cause the European Central bank to tighten monetary policy which could slow some European economies, and (2) politically, it might harden the resistance of countries who have so far refused to adopt the Euro, including the United Kingdom. The European Union forecasts annualized growth of 3 percent in the next few years which is above their estimates for U.S. economic growth.

Trading in the world's currencies expanded rapidly during the 1990's, reaching by decade's end almost $2 trillion per day. Most of the trading is via electronic transfers for central banks and commercial banks, but a small portion of the trading is on organized exchanges where intraday price swings often have speculative based roots that can exaggerate short-term movements. However, the U.S. dollar is the fulcrum from which the long-term market value of many currencies is determined. The U.S. economy's strength, and benign inflation, was a magnet for foreign capital, especially during the second half of the 1990's, notwithstanding the fact that in 1999 the Asian and Latin American economic problems lost some of the uncertainties that had triggered a flight to the dollar in 1998.

In mid-1999 the yen was trading around 120 yen to the U.S. dollar, towards yearend it was near 100 yen per dollar, a level not seen since 1995. Despite the yen's rise, Japan's economic problems still run deep. The success of 1999's new government monetary and fiscal policies remains uncertain. The Japanese economy stagnated during much of the 1990's, and at the decade's end Japanese bank officials still appeared in limbo about setting policy in an era of deflation. It was rumored that the Bank of Japan would print more yen in 1999 to help pull the nation out of its slump and check the yen's rise, but it apparently never happened. The yen's strength would suggest a tight monetary policy, but at yearend 1999 Japan's key interest rates were still within an eyelash of zero. However, the yen's rise partially reflected prospects of higher interest rates because of heavy borrowing the government must take to stimulate growth. The flip side is that a strong yen may dampen exports and possibly reverse the economy's recovery by 2001.

The Canadian dollar also firmed against the U.S. dollar in 1999, trading at yearend near $0.68 vs. $0.64 a year earlier. The rise partially reflected a perception that the currency was severely undervalued following the Asian economic crisis in 1997 that cut deeply into Canada's exports. In 1999, with the crisis largely gone, both Canada's exports and currency did indeed improve.

The British pound strengthened against the U.S. dollar midyear, with the move carrying from about $1.55 to over $1.65 by October, before some of the gain was pared towards yearend. A rise in key short-term interest rates, the first in more than a year, helped kick the pound's value higher.

The Finex U.S. Dollar Index moved higher during the first half of 1999, nearly reaching 105.00 vs. the January level of 94.00. Towards yearend the index was trading near 102.00. The dollar's outlook for 2000 looks promising. The U.S. economy's strong growth rate is apt to slow but still prove at least on a par with most of the world's key economies, even if the Federal Reserve continues to raise interest rates as they did in 1999.

Futures Markets

The Chicago Mercantile's International Monetary Market (IMM) trades futures and options on the British pound, Duetsche mark, Swiss franc, Japanese yen, the Canadian, Australian and New Zealand dollars, Mexican Peso, French franc, Brazilian real, South African Rand, the Euro FX and the Russian Ruble. Chicago's MidAmerica Exchange (MidAm) trades smaller futures contracts on many of the IMM's currencies. The FINEX division of the New York Cotton Exchange (NYCE) trades futures and options on a composite dollar index and also offers crossrate contracts: D-mark/J-yen, D-mark/French Franc and D-Mark/B-pound.

CRB Currency Futures Index 1977 = 100

Year	Jan.	Feb.	Mar.	Apr.	May	June	July	Aug.	Sept.	Oct.	Nov.	Dec.	Average
1990	126.68	127.50	124.71	125.11	127.77	127.85	131.67	136.42	137.52	141.69	143.64	140.48	132.59
1991	140.91	142.85	134.41	130.85	130.02	126.44	126.33	128.27	130.86	131.57	134.66	136.78	132.83
1992	136.15	133.37	129.33	129.78	132.13	135.42	139.83	142.26	140.65	136.30	129.70	129.91	134.57
1993	127.91	126.74	127.99	132.20	132.73	131.17	129.44	130.64	132.87	131.38	129.31	129.14	130.13
1994	128.54	129.57	130.89	130.57	132.23	134.18	137.60	137.51	139.78	141.94	140.29	137.85	135.08
1995	139.31	140.54	147.85	152.52	150.20	150.85	150.58	145.41	143.89	146.33	145.21	143.83	146.38
1996	141.69	141.01	141.12	139.61	138.11	138.37	139.53	140.52	139.51	138.74	139.92	137.47	139.63
1997	134.61	130.36	129.56	128.71	130.83	131.75	130.14	126.84	128.02	129.07	129.58	126.93	129.70
1998	125.06	126.10	125.65	124.96	124.33	122.86	121.89	120.65	126.18	130.98	128.86	130.69	125.68
1999	130.77	128.20	126.07	125.37	124.99	124.08	123.49	126.14	128.07	129.80	127.44	126.96	126.78

Average. *Source: Bridge Commodity Research Bureau (CRB)*

British Pound Futures - International Monetary Market (weekly close) as of 30-Dec-1999
USD/GBP
2.05
2.00
1.95
1.90
1.85
1.80
1.75
1.70
1.65
1.60
1.55
1.50
1.45
1.40
1.35
Jan-90
Jan-91
Jan-92
Dec-92
Dec-93
Dec-94
Dec-95
Dec-96
Dec-97
Dec-98
Dec-99

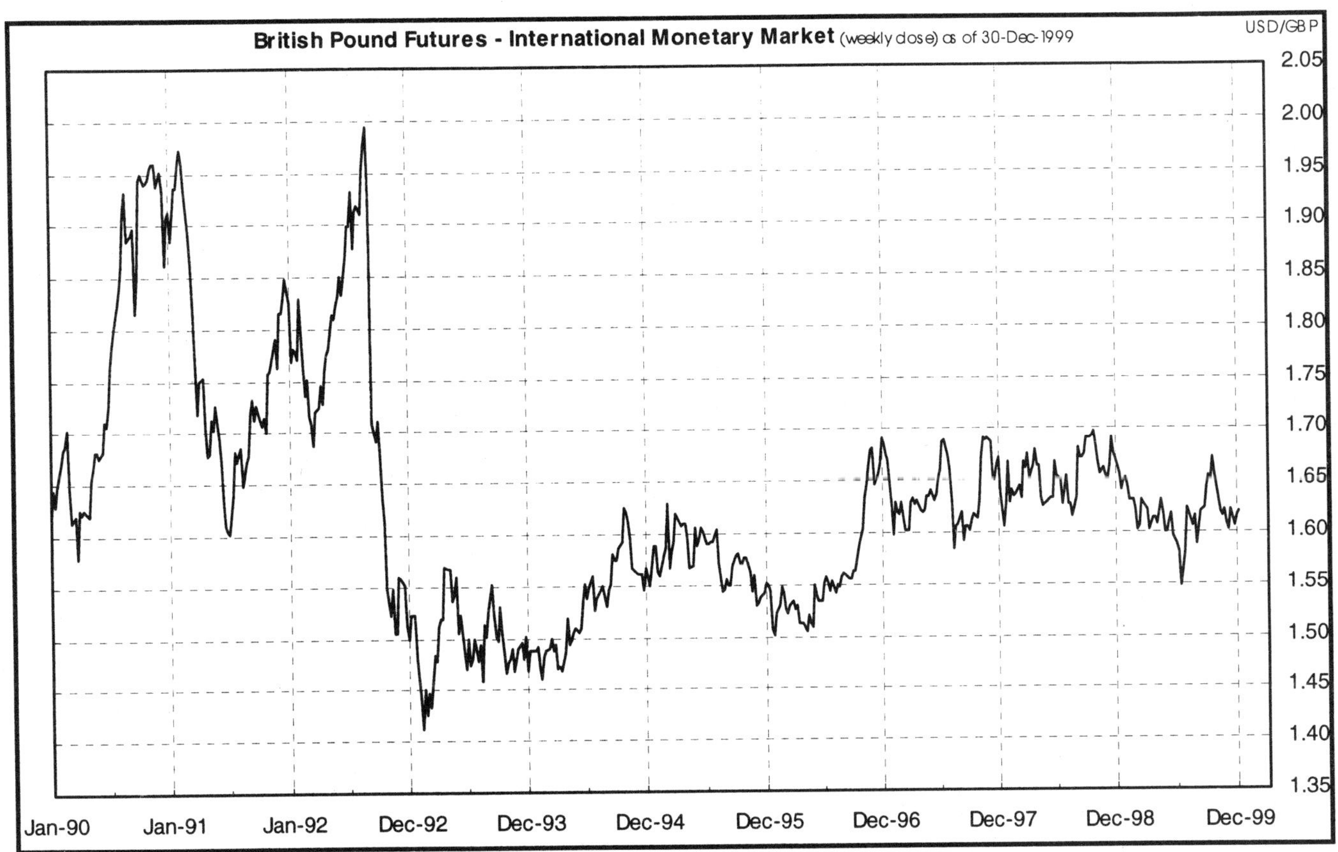

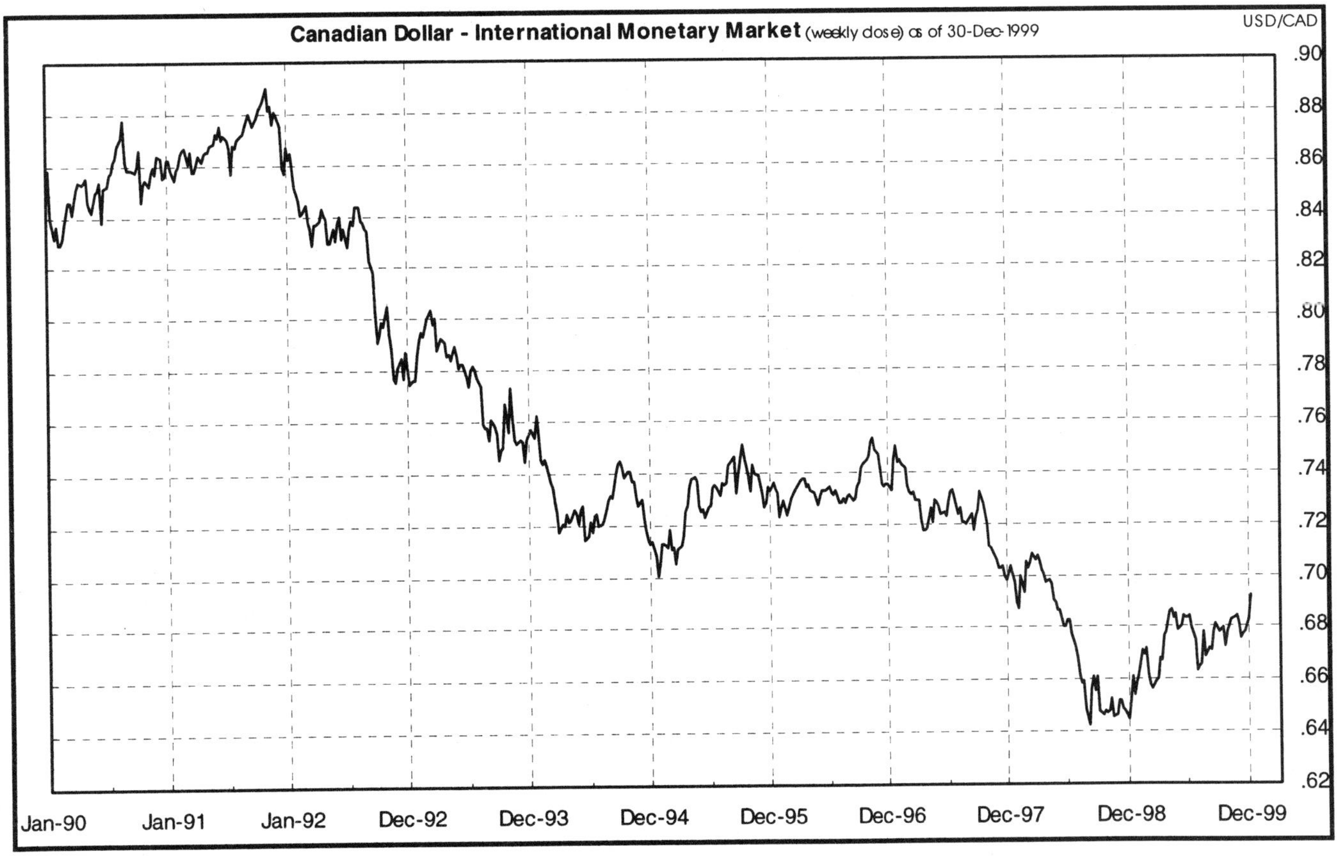

Canadian Dollar - International Monetary Market (weekly close) as of 30-Dec-1999
USD/CAD
.90
.88
.86
.84
.82
.80
.78
.76
.74
.72
.70
.68
.66
.64
.62
Jan-90
Jan-91
Jan-92
Dec-92
Dec-93
Dec-94
Dec-95
Dec-96
Dec-97
Dec-98
Dec-99

Euro FX Futures - International Monetary Market (weekly close) as of 30-Dec-1999

USD/EUR

1.40
1.35
1.30
1.25
1.20
1.15
1.10
1.05
1.00
.95

Jan-90 Jan-91 Jan-92 Dec-92 Dec-93 Dec-94 Dec-95 Dec-96 Dec-97 Dec-98 Dec-99

Japanese Yen Futures - International Monetary Market (weekly close) as of 30-Dec-1999

USD/JPY

1.25
1.20
1.15
1.10
1.05
1.00
.95
.90
.85
.80
.75
.70
.65
.60

Jan-90 Jan-91 Jan-92 Dec-92 Dec-93 Dec-94 Dec-95 Dec-96 Dec-97 Dec-98 Dec-99

Swiss Franc Futures - International Monetary Market (weekly close) as of 30-Dec-1999
USD/CHF
.90
.88
.86
.84
.82
.80
.78
.76
.74
.72
.70
.68
.66
.64
.62
.60
Jan-90
Jan-91
Jan-92
Dec-92
Dec-93
Dec-94
Dec-95
Dec-96
Dec-97
Dec-98
Dec-99

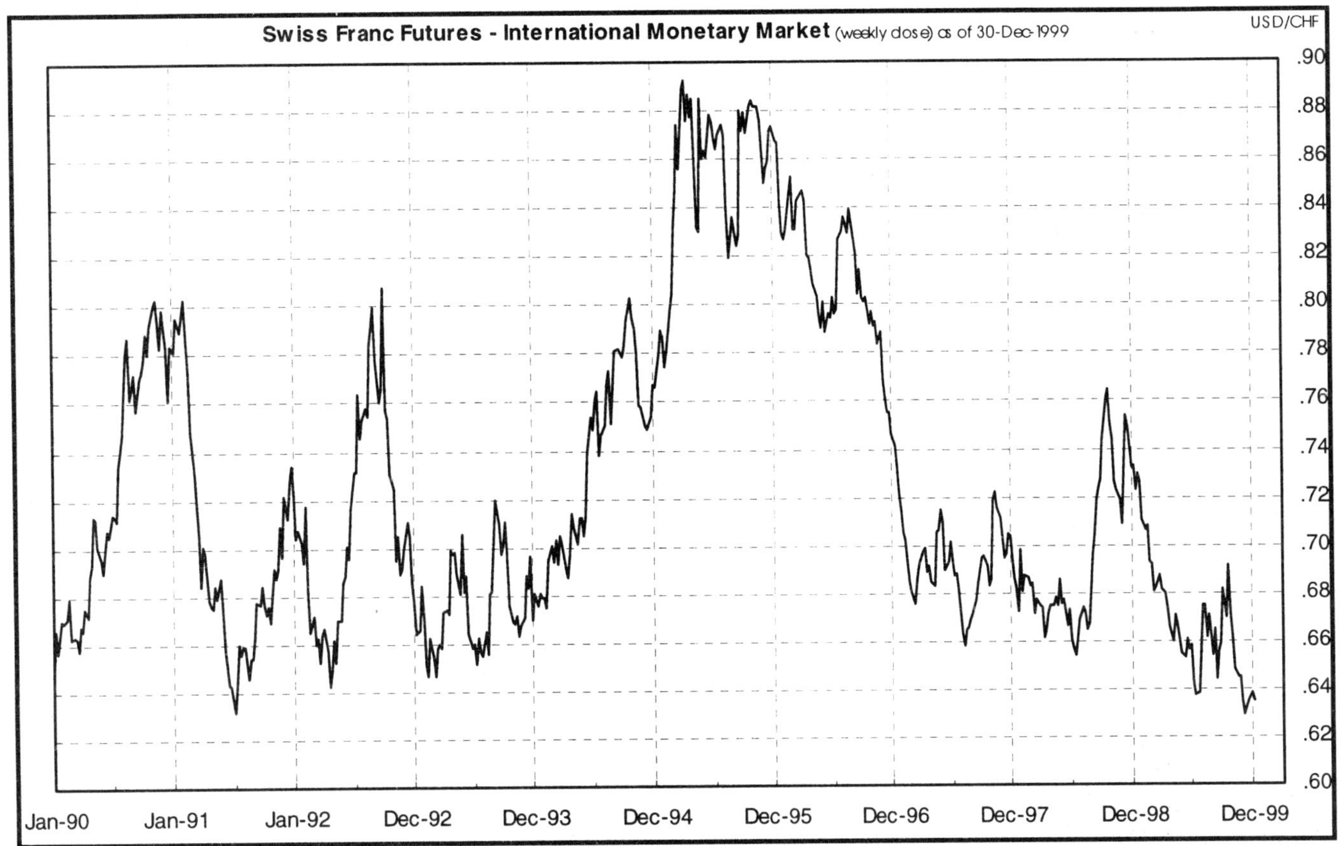

CRB Currency Index (1977=100) (weekly close) as of 30-Dec-1999
Index Value
CRB Currency Index (1977 = 100)
5 Futures Markets
British Pound, Canadian Dollar, Deutsche Mark,
Japanese Yen, Swiss Franc
154
152
150
148
146
144
142
140
138
136
134
132
130
128
126
124
122
120
118
Jan-90
Jan-91
Jan-92
Dec-92
Dec-93
Dec-94
Dec-95
Dec-96
Dec-97
Dec-98
Dec-99

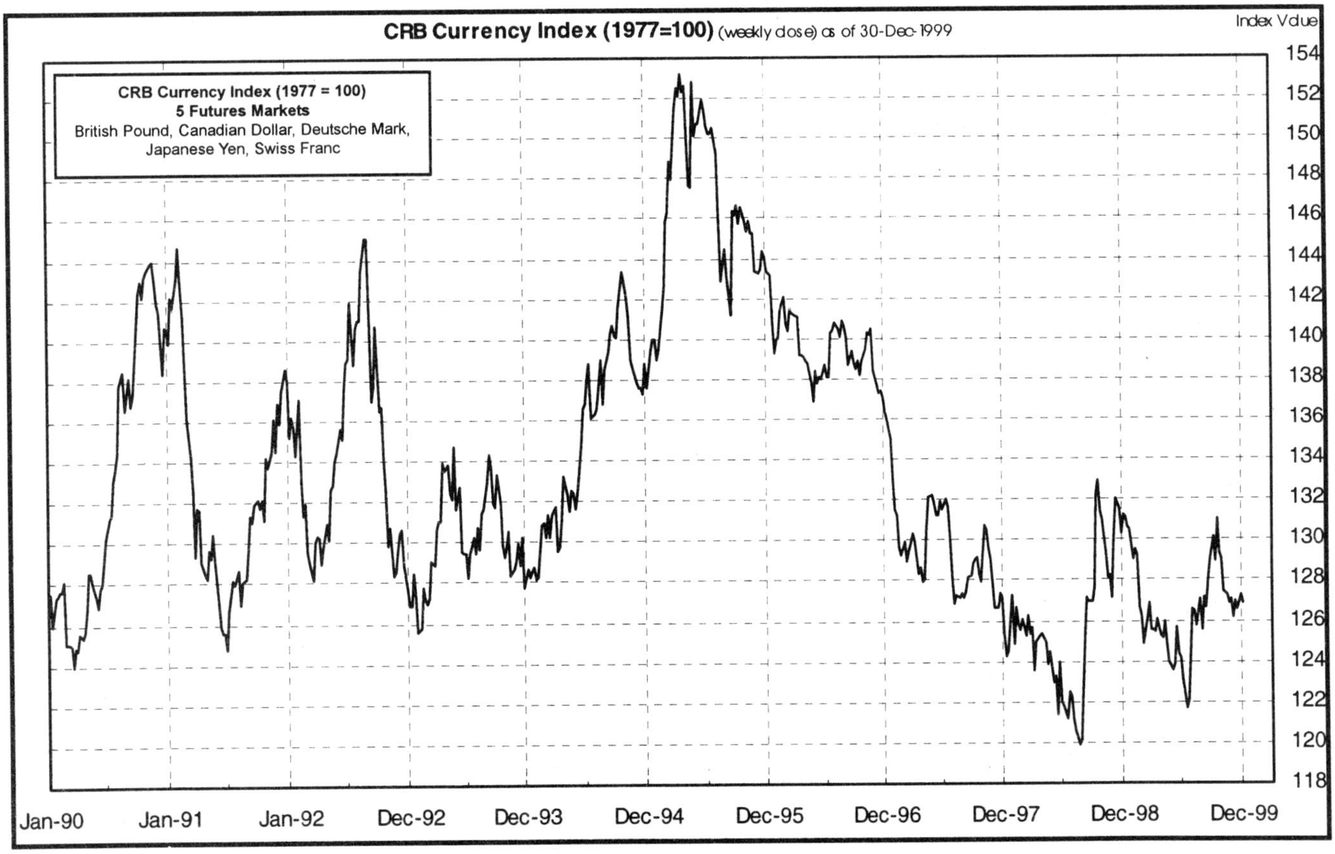

CURRENCIES

Canadian Dollars per U.S. Dollar

Year	Jan.	Feb.	Mar.	Apr.	May	June	July	Aug.	Sept.	Oct.	Nov.	Dec.	Average
1991	1.1563	1.1545	1.1572	1.1535	1.1497	1.1438	1.1493	1.1451	1.1372	1.1281	1.1310	1.1474	1.1461
1992	1.1569	1.1827	1.1923	1.1871	1.1990	1.1955	1.1916	1.1906	1.2208	1.2440	1.2683	1.2711	1.2083
1993	1.2774	1.2595	1.2467	1.2616	1.2686	1.2788	1.2817	1.3078	1.3210	1.3253	1.3166	1.3307	1.2896
1994	1.3175	1.3419	1.3645	1.3821	1.3805	1.3831	1.3818	1.3777	1.3536	1.3495	1.3649	1.3896	1.3656
1995	1.4120	1.3995	1.4065	1.3749	1.3607	1.3772	1.3609	1.3550	1.3495	1.3449	1.3525	1.3685	1.3718
1996	1.3664	1.3753	1.3651	1.3591	1.3690	1.3649	1.3687	1.3717	1.3691	1.3501	1.3382	1.3621	1.3633
1997	1.3484	1.3555	1.3727	1.3947	1.3793	1.3844	1.3769	1.3894	1.3865	1.3863	1.4127	1.4272	1.3845
1998	1.4407	1.4335	1.4159	1.4294	1.4449	1.4647	1.4865	1.5344	1.5212	1.5430	1.5400	1.5429	1.4831
1999	1.5189	1.4971	1.5174	1.4868	1.4614	1.4691	1.4877	1.4921	1.4772	1.4767	1.4671	1.4713	1.4852

Average. *Source: Bridge Information Systems, Inc.*

Euro per U.S. Dollar

Year	Jan.	Feb.	Mar.	Apr.	May	June	July	Aug.	Sept.	Oct.	Nov.	Dec.	Average
1991	1.3587	1.3842	1.2747	1.2122	1.1987	1.1537	1.1477	1.1773	1.2101	1.2115	1.2578	1.3047	1.2409
1992	1.2903	1.2634	1.2319	1.2433	1.2671	1.3029	1.3717	1.4064	1.3836	1.3205	1.2385	1.2383	1.2965
1993	1.2130	1.1856	1.1779	1.2214	1.2171	1.1828	1.1379	1.1253	1.1720	1.1587	1.1292	1.1285	1.1708
1994	1.1138	1.1183	1.1412	1.1390	1.1636	1.1819	1.2167	1.2182	1.2314	1.2559	1.2357	1.2129	1.1857
1995	1.2380	1.2536	1.3030	1.3292	1.3085	1.3196	1.3340	1.2939	1.2782	1.2987	1.2947	1.2757	1.2939
1996	1.2629	1.2543	1.2544	1.2430	1.2278	1.2386	1.2554	1.2686	1.2587	1.2532	1.2695	1.2416	1.2523
1997	1.2088	1.1592	1.1460	1.1396	1.1441	1.1309	1.0999	1.0694	1.0976	1.1190	1.1418	1.1114	1.1306
1998	1.0859	1.0896	1.0854	1.0931	1.1099	1.1015	1.0991	1.1041	1.1566	1.2015	1.1680	1.1746	1.1224
1999	1.1584	1.1202	1.0882	1.0700	1.0622	1.0385	1.0366	1.0603	1.0501	1.0705	1.0327	1.0117	1.0666

Average. *Source: Bridge Information Systems, Inc.*

Japanese Yen per U.S. Dollar

Year	Jan.	Feb.	Mar.	Apr.	May	June	July	Aug.	Sept.	Oct.	Nov.	Dec.	Average
1991	133.67	130.58	137.48	137.05	138.12	139.66	137.97	136.87	134.41	130.78	129.74	127.93	134.52
1992	125.24	127.65	132.79	133.51	130.61	126.72	125.69	126.10	222.58	121.23	123.80	123.94	134.99
1993	124.94	120.77	116.99	112.22	110.10	107.29	107.57	103.74	105.41	107.00	107.78	109.89	111.14
1994	111.33	106.22	105.00	103.36	103.76	102.37	98.65	99.88	98.78	98.36	98.08	100.08	102.16
1995	99.67	98.14	90.40	83.59	84.96	84.55	87.22	94.72	100.49	100.76	101.93	101.84	94.02
1996	105.66	105.57	105.90	107.23	106.42	108.91	109.21	107.84	109.87	112.40	112.35	114.01	108.78
1997	117.93	122.90	122.72	125.66	118.93	114.25	115.30	117.90	120.85	121.06	125.35	129.62	121.04
1998	129.39	125.71	129.04	131.79	135.01	140.40	140.75	144.51	134.45	120.49	120.41	117.01	130.75
1999	113.23	116.62	119.49	119.73	121.88	120.69	119.38	113.16	107.00	105.94	104.62	102.64	113.70

Average. *Source: Bridge Information Systems, Inc.*

Swiss Francs per U.S. Dollar

Year	Jan.	Feb.	Mar.	Apr.	May	June	July	Aug.	Sept.	Oct.	Nov.	Dec.	Average
1991	1.2712	1.2690	1.3891	1.4382	1.4557	1.5304	1.5507	1.5204	1.4819	1.4797	1.4357	1.3825	1.4337
1992	1.4045	1.4567	1.5072	1.5179	1.4895	1.4234	1.3322	1.2948	1.2763	1.3193	1.4276	1.4231	1.4060
1993	1.4775	1.5197	1.5199	1.4572	1.4471	1.4767	1.5138	1.4947	1.4158	1.4421	1.4966	1.4629	1.4770
1994	1.4707	1.4558	1.4295	1.4363	1.4120	1.3723	1.3256	1.3176	1.2895	1.2636	1.2974	1.3275	1.3665
1995	1.2865	1.2694	1.1691	1.1362	1.1678	1.1564	1.1542	1.1958	1.1868	1.1444	1.1440	1.1624	1.1811
1996	1.1810	1.1942	1.1945	1.2194	1.2546	1.2574	1.2324	1.2022	1.2333	1.2583	1.2757	1.3296	1.2361
1997	1.3925	1.4543	1.4622	1.4614	1.4298	1.4419	1.4810	1.5123	1.4702	1.4507	1.4057	1.4393	1.4501
1998	1.4756	1.4616	1.4896	1.5050	1.4782	1.4951	1.5126	1.4927	1.4002	1.3376	1.3856	1.3600	1.4495
1999	1.3856	1.4273	1.4656	1.4972	1.5078	1.5359	1.5472	1.5092	1.5251	1.4891	1.5541	1.5827	1.5022

Average. *Source: Bridge Information Systems, Inc.*

U.S. Dollars per British Pound

Year	Jan.	Feb.	Mar.	Apr.	May	June	July	Aug.	Sept.	Oct.	Nov.	Dec.	Average
1991	1.9347	1.9641	1.8214	1.7514	1.7259	1.6491	1.6482	1.6839	1.7253	1.7214	1.7780	1.8311	1.7695
1992	1.8083	1.7776	1.7251	1.7562	1.8101	1.8555	1.9193	1.9445	1.8510	1.6547	1.5269	1.5497	1.7649
1993	1.5330	1.4383	1.4621	1.5465	1.5492	1.5090	1.4973	1.4928	1.5251	1.5027	1.4808	1.4904	1.5023
1994	1.4933	1.4787	1.4921	1.4832	1.5038	1.5261	1.5446	1.5421	1.5647	1.6073	1.5864	1.5582	1.5317
1995	1.5742	1.5727	1.6004	1.6087	1.5886	1.5960	1.5955	1.5668	1.5595	1.5782	1.5612	1.5411	1.5786
1996	1.5289	1.5376	1.5278	1.5159	1.5154	1.5417	1.5538	1.5501	1.5595	1.5863	1.6629	1.6660	1.5622
1997	1.6590	1.6258	1.6095	1.6285	1.6325	1.6457	1.6717	1.6044	1.6020	1.6331	1.6887	1.6606	1.6385
1998	1.6347	1.6402	1.6615	1.6720	1.6370	1.6509	1.6429	1.6355	1.6814	1.6933	1.6613	1.6713	1.6568
1999	1.6495	1.6269	1.6213	1.6085	1.6147	1.5957	1.5754	1.6051	1.6237	1.6570	1.6206	1.6131	1.6176

Average. *Source: Bridge Information Systems, Inc.*

Average Open Interest of Canadian Dollar Futures in Chicago In Contracts

Year	Jan.	Feb.	Mar.	Apr.	May	June	July	Aug.	Sept.	Oct.	Nov.	Dec.
1990	26,426	29,204	23,848	24,048	33,823	30,809	39,843	42,092	34,998	29,434	31,250	25,272
1991	29,072	28,214	25,550	24,894	29,310	33,136	25,113	25,310	30,909	28,805	27,453	22,311
1992	19,724	24,020	24,118	21,354	24,020	22,860	24,773	27,665	28,221	27,827	28,025	24,923
1993	20,410	24,376	25,877	23,639	27,438	29,784	29,385	45,397	40,639	43,476	32,469	28,879
1994	28,277	38,157	48,411	42,730	44,363	42,845	35,370	39,582	49,312	40,706	42,353	59,763
1995	55,863	44,677	33,706	45,394	47,832	36,677	44,930	42,629	49,526	43,032	40,047	40,592
1996	31,028	37,674	38,551	41,411	46,470	37,141	37,522	42,063	44,014	68,674	82,817	72,586
1997	55,949	56,600	72,803	82,732	73,747	57,243	43,937	59,112	56,387	59,265	75,027	74,221
1998	63,300	67,862	61,528	58,938	64,859	74,027	71,313	75,193	60,863	51,967	61,318	50,271
1999	50,061	71,819	63,782	73,773	84,885	71,922	65,877	71,457	61,993	58,748	59,860	51,967

Source: International Monetary Market (IMM), division of the Chicago Mercantile Exchange (CME)

Average Open Interest of Deutschemark Futures in Chicago In Contracts

Year	Jan.	Feb.	Mar.	Apr.	May	June	July	Aug.	Sept.	Oct.	Nov.	Dec.
1998	-----	-----	-----	-----	1	1	1	1	1	0	7	7
1999	8,261	30,546	37,837	37,881	46,446	50,614	46,776	55,858	49,351	57,379	58,846	65,346

Source: International Monetary Market (IMM), division of the Chicago Mercantile Exchange (CME)

Average Open Interest of Japanese Yen Futures in Chicago In Contracts

Year	Jan.	Feb.	Mar.	Apr.	May	June	July	Aug.	Sept.	Oct.	Nov.	Dec.
1990	60,012	67,723	82,783	71,709	79,850	62,252	62,760	65,050	77,686	74,890	77,115	65,365
1991	43,552	64,694	57,115	49,060	52,964	55,727	53,045	56,496	66,174	74,353	74,585	64,219
1992	63,856	67,714	71,702	63,938	63,079	64,596	56,465	58,353	53,462	44,488	45,941	46,887
1993	50,066	70,195	81,979	76,696	82,028	81,103	72,186	80,780	73,002	83,097	84,812	95,817
1994	101,792	94,470	73,286	57,281	65,835	70,759	73,734	72,798	63,419	63,091	80,053	92,834
1995	86,569	86,852	77,649	63,379	67,644	56,285	48,680	63,463	73,830	67,336	73,335	70,268
1996	80,645	78,915	71,643	76,655	73,832	85,398	77,941	73,535	86,723	76,620	72,130	67,301
1997	73,391	82,542	78,466	81,117	85,984	73,322	62,488	82,369	96,468	90,080	130,606	121,001
1998	95,338	101,448	97,183	97,389	106,139	132,732	113,084	145,241	108,808	88,991	89,108	79,262
1999	78,767	81,859	96,271	87,829	118,819	120,681	118,329	136,825	115,884	82,644	87,694	87,594

Source: International Monetary Market (IMM), division of the Chicago Mercantile Exchange (CME)

Average Open Interest of Swiss Franc Futures in Chicago In Contracts

Year	Jan.	Feb.	Mar.	Apr.	May	June	July	Aug.	Sept.	Oct.	Nov.	Dec.
1990	36,339	42,435	34,953	32,853	45,464	42,862	39,769	48,544	40,269	37,216	44,166	37,220
1991	31,489	36,483	49,061	40,026	38,601	43,476	36,031	35,881	29,833	24,949	32,342	32,439
1992	24,653	33,640	42,825	36,230	38,269	36,668	30,159	33,707	33,167	34,767	45,428	44,901
1993	52,713	49,472	48,002	43,514	47,832	42,343	40,703	44,329	60,446	49,320	58,406	49,670
1994	41,914	46,280	44,134	37,450	42,071	49,162	45,223	43,746	44,495	39,587	51,539	55,424
1995	39,726	44,364	39,358	30,270	30,586	26,766	23,121	30,267	34,228	34,889	38,033	44,741
1996	42,280	42,902	36,924	39,233	46,810	44,848	38,300	40,298	43,695	47,613	53,581	59,405
1997	51,652	54,114	51,121	45,725	48,651	42,530	55,279	58,098	49,296	43,585	51,822	48,560
1998	57,740	46,160	67,722	67,303	63,477	77,564	85,984	70,569	81,465	57,413	44,810	43,436
1999	39,434	58,279	66,250	66,530	73,322	75,322	66,602	71,060	60,213	65,020	67,817	64,506

Source: International Monetary Market (IMM), division of the Chicago Mercantile Exchange (CME)

Average Open Interest of British Pound Futures in Chicago In Contracts

Year	Jan.	Feb.	Mar.	Apr.	May	June	July	Aug.	Sept.	Oct.	Nov.	Dec.
1990	23,272	30,729	26,219	23,909	33,355	35,528	37,898	41,820	33,458	32,213	39,623	32,790
1991	23,686	34,680	33,558	29,900	30,697	33,792	26,443	21,578	28,215	22,882	31,792	26,443
1992	21,578	28,215	22,882	31,595	36,426	35,529	27,160	28,041	30,137	30,330	33,121	27,935
1993	26,614	41,752	40,238	38,544	39,654	34,953	26,056	32,446	33,560	29,733	37,246	33,606
1994	39,223	43,878	35,554	44,725	46,577	41,801	37,633	34,988	40,751	42,648	49,684	65,834
1995	47,740	44,935	36,805	23,161	26,571	28,402	22,662	34,932	38,900	34,485	43,634	49,804
1996	40,315	50,106	52,349	54,954	52,573	61,461	55,080	50,862	53,868	51,934	62,128	47,652
1997	40,479	38,370	43,742	37,701	40,956	48,890	60,592	50,829	41,801	35,752	56,825	44,667
1998	33,616	31,282	38,712	41,256	47,303	55,511	39,156	49,645	63,756	53,458	54,004	53,578
1999	51,519	59,705	66,913	64,937	58,744	60,413	65,205	54,373	50,948	65,037	49,468	34,191

Source: International Monetary Market (IMM), division of the Chicago Mercantile Exchange (CME)

United States Merchandise Trade Balance In Millions of Dollars

Year	Jan.	Feb.	Mar.	Apr.	May	June	July	Aug.	Sept.	Oct.	Nov.	Dec.	Total
1990	-9,640	-6,150	-6,369	-6,527	-7,308	-6,476	-10,759	-10,509	-9,157	-12,805	-10,529	-6,211	-109,030
1991	-7,079	-4,201	-1,889	-3,411	-4,158	-3,948	-7,894	-7,450	-7,111	-8,735	-4,942	-5,908	-74,068
1992	-5,470	-2,178	-3,527	-5,772	-5,409	-6,718	-9,893	-10,218	-9,693	-9,706	-8,644	-7,276	-96,106
1993	-6,113	-5,905	-8,886	-8,428	-6,542	-11,749	-12,609	-11,949	-12,516	-12,638	-11,521	-9,115	-132,609
1994	-11,999	-13,573	-11,477	-13,405	-14,079	-14,009	-15,831	-14,232	-14,566	-14,926	-15,292	-13,272	-166,192
1995	-15,746	-14,221	-14,487	-16,051	-16,010	-15,862	-15,887	-13,415	-13,243	-13,108	-12,324	-12,600	-173,729
1996	-15,623	-12,911	-14,574	-15,897	-16,826	-14,839	-17,757	-16,759	-17,976	-15,320	-15,176	-17,695	-191,270
1997	-18,167	-16,780	-14,896	-16,505	-16,982	-15,610	-15,864	-16,909	-16,524	-16,270	-16,605	-16,962	-196,652
1998	-17,187	-18,331	-20,615	-20,860	-22,236	-20,404	-21,066	-22,291	-21,611	-20,990	-21,539	-21,059	-246,932
1999[2]	-23,350	-25,173	-25,681	-25,334	-27,899	-31,179	-31,422	-30,132	30,211	31,996			-189,556

[1] Not seasonally adjusted. [2] Preliminary. *Source: Bureau of Economic Analysis, U.S. Department of Commerce (BEA)*

Index of Real Trade-Weighted Dollar Exchange Rates for Total Agriculture[2] 1990 = 100[3]

Year		Jan.	Feb.	Mar.	Apr.	May	June	July	Aug.	Sept.	Oct.	Nov.	Dec.
1992	U.S. Markets	75.5	76.4	80.9	78.2	76.5	76.0	74.7	74.2	74.2	75.2	77.6	77.3
	U.S. Competitors	76.2	76.8	81.1	76.6	77.4	76.6	75.6	75.1	77.2	75.7	77.7	77.4
1993	U.S. Markets	78.2	78.4	78.3	77.0	77.3	76.0	77.1	76.8	76.0	76.6	77.4	77.9
	U.S. Competitors	78.3	78.6	79.1	78.4	78.9	77.7	78.5	78.7	78.0	78.3	78.6	78.1
1994	U.S. Markets	77.0	77.0	97.1	97.4	97.0	96.9	95.3	95.2	94.3	93.8	94.2	96.7
	U.S. Competitors	78.3	78.3	107.3	107.6	105.7	104.5	101.5	101.2	100.1	98.4	99.1	100.5
1995	U.S. Markets	99.2	98.6	96.7	92.5	92.0	92.0	92.2	94.8	96.6	96.7	98.3	98.0
	U.S. Competitors	98.9	98.0	95.3	93.9	94.5	93.8	92.7	94.5	95.6	94.4	94.4	94.8
1996	U.S. Markets	99.4	99.2	99.4	99.4	99.4	100.1	100.4	99.4	100.1	101.1	100.8	101.5
	U.S. Competitors	96.0	96.0	96.3	97.0	97.9	97.5	96.7	96.2	96.8	97.4	96.5	97.8
1997	U.S. Markets	103.0	105.3	107.0	110.2	104.3	107.8	107.6	109.3	106.9	106.9	112.8	114.0
	U.S. Competitors	99.8	102.8	105.9	107.3	103.9	106.8	110.5	113.3	110.6	110.6	110.7	113.1
1998	U.S. Markets	115.9	114.6	117.1	115.2	115.1	117.6	117.5	119.8	118.5	113.8	113.1	111.9
	U.S. Competitors	117.2	115.6	115.5	114.2	114.8	116.3	117.1	116.3	112.3	109.0	110.4	110.7
1999[1]	U.S. Markets	110.4	110.9	111.7	111.1	111.0	110.6	110.4					
	U.S. Competitors	111.4	111.7	111.1	110.4	109.7	109.4	109.1					

[1] Preliminary. [2] Real indexes adjust nominal exchange rates for differences in rates of inflation, to avoid the distortion caused by high-inflation countries. A higher value means the dollar has appreciated. Federal Reserve Board Index of trade-weighted value of the U.S. dollar against 10 major currencies. Weights are based on relative importance in world financial markets. [3] Thru 1984; 1971 = 100, 1985 thru 1987; 1980 = 100, 1988 thru February 1994; 1985 = 100; March 1994 to date; 1990 = 100. *Source: Economic Research Service, U.S. Department of Agriculture (ERS-USDA)*

United States Balance on Current Account[1] In Millions of Dollars

Year	First Quarter	Second Quarter	Third Quarter	Fourth Quarter	Annual
1990	-15,895	-17,957	-29,312	-16,169	-79,332
1991	17,838	4,653	-11,036	-7,171	4,284
1992	467	-10,809	-19,777	-20,509	-50,629
1993	-7,248	-19,867	-28,745	-29,425	-85,286
1994	-17,355	-27,813	-39,199	-37,313	-121,680
1995	-22,940	-32,213	-35,454	-22,959	-113,566
1996	-26,744	-31,456	-38,327	-32,774	-129,295
1997	-34,898	-31,471	-35,615	-41,478	-143,465
1998	-33,690	-51,346	-73,892	-61,634	-220,562
1999[2]	-59,568	-80,251	-100,155		-319,965

[1] Not seasonally adjusted. [2] Preliminary. *Source: Bureau of Economic Analysis, U.S. Department of Commerce (BEA)*

Merchandise Trade and Current Account Balances In Billions of Dollars

	Merchandise Trade Balance					Current Account Balance				
Year	Canada	Germany	Japan	Switzerland	U.K.	Canada	Germany	Japan	Switzerland	U.K.
1991	6.1	19.5	96.1	-5.9	-18.0	-22.4	-17.1	68.2	10.6	-14.8
1992	7.4	28.2	124.5	-1.0	-22.9	-21.1	-13.3	112.4	15.1	-17.7
1993	10.2	41.2	139.3	1.7	-20.0	-21.7	-8.9	131.9	19.5	-15.9
1994	14.8	50.9	144.1	1.6	-17.0	-13.0	-22.9	130.5	17.5	-2.2
1995	25.8	65.1	131.2	.9	-18.5	-4.4	-19.0	110.4	21.3	-5.9
1996	30.8	71.3	83.6	.9	-20.4	3.3	-5.6	65.8	22.0	-.9
1997	17.1	72.0	101.7	-.3	-19.5	-10.3	-1.7	94.5	22.8	10.1
1998	12.7	79.2	122.1	-1.9	-34.4	-11.1	-4.2	120.6	21.4	.2
1999[1]	21.0	79.7	130.1	-1.8	-48.8	-1.6	-1.1	119.7	20.9	-22.0
2000[2]	22.2	86.6	140.1	-4.1	-52.7	-.7	2.6	134.7	19.9	-22.4

[1] Estimate. [2] Projections. *Source: Organization for Economic Cooperation and Development (OECD)*

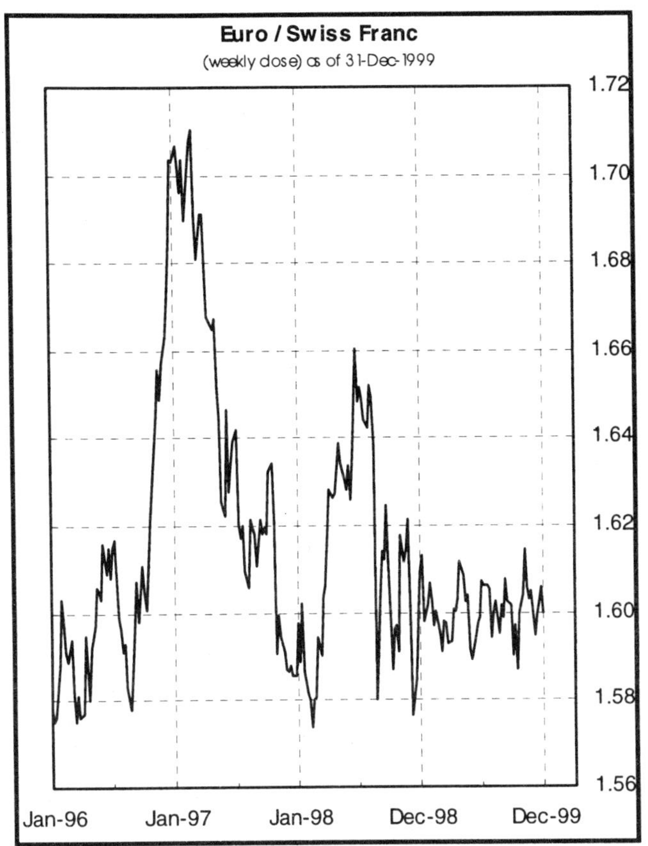
Euro / Swiss Franc
(weekly close) as of 31-Dec-1999
1.72
1.70
1.68
1.66
1.64
1.62
1.60
1.58
1.56
Jan-96
Jan-97
Jan-98
Dec-98
Dec-99

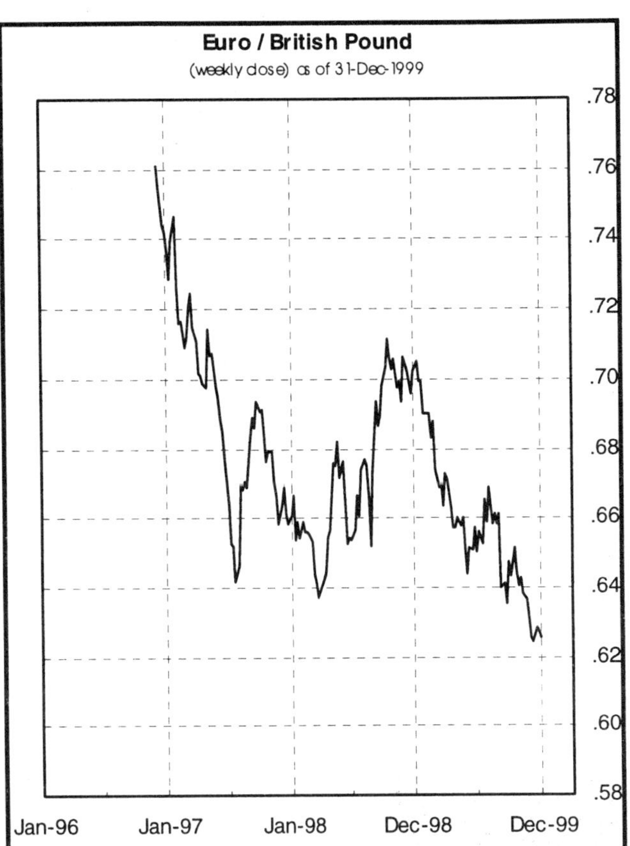
Euro / British Pound
(weekly close) as of 31-Dec-1999
.78
.76
.74
.72
.70
.68
.66
.64
.62
.60
.58
Jan-96
Jan-97
Jan-98
Dec-98
Dec-99

Japanese Yen / British Pound
(weekly close) as of 31-Dec-1999
250
240
230
220
210
200
190
180
170
160
150
Jan-96
Jan-97
Jan-98
Dec-98
Dec-99

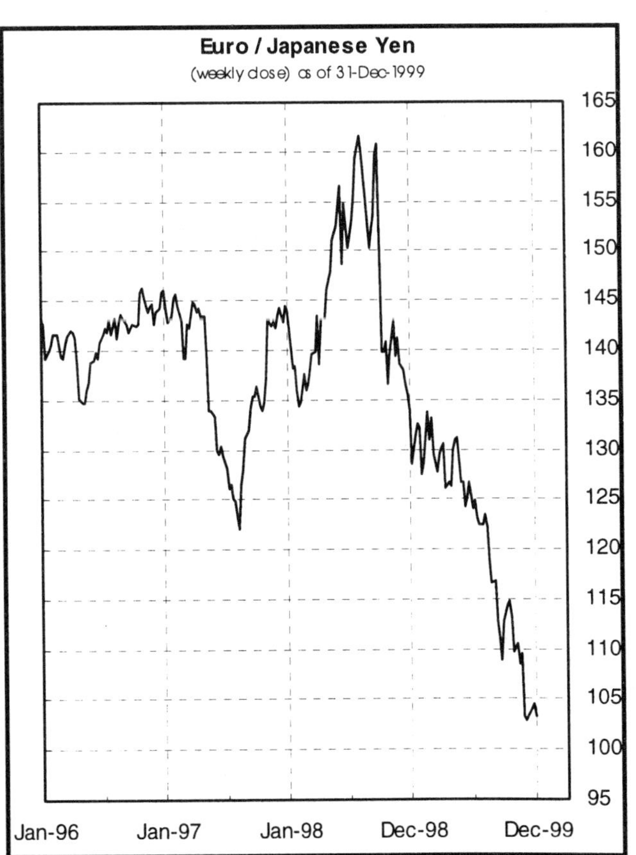
Euro / Japanese Yen
(weekly close) as of 31-Dec-1999
165
160
155
150
145
140
135
130
125
120
115
110
105
100
95
Jan-96
Jan-97
Jan-98
Dec-98
Dec-99

Diamonds

Diamonds have unique properties that give them value not only as gemstones but as industrial materials. Diamonds are the strongest and hardest material known and as such are used in grinding, drilling, cutting and polishing applications. Industrial diamonds, that do not meet gem-quality standards, are used as abrasives despite their higher costs. Diamonds prove to be cost effective because they cut faster and last longer than competing materials.

World production of natural diamonds in 1998 was estimated by the U.S. Geological Survey at 115 million carats, down 5 percent from 1997. Production of diamond gemstones in 1998 was estimated at 55 million carats, down 2 percent from 1997. The major producer of diamond gemstones is Australia with 1998 production estimated at 18.4 million carats. The nest largest producer is Botswana with 1998 production of 13.5 million carats.

World production of industrial diamonds in 1998 was estimated at 59.9 million carats, down 7 percent from 1997. The largest producer of industrial diamonds was Australia with output of 22.5 million carats. Other large producers include the Congo, Russia, South Africa and Botswana.

World Production of Natural Gem Diamonds In Thousands of Carats

Year	Angola	Australia	Botswana	Brazil	Central African Republic	China	Congo[3]	Ghana	Namibia	Russia	Sierra Leone	South Africa	World Total
1993	130	18,800	10,300	1,000	370	230	2,010	106	1,120	8,000	90	4,600	47,400
1994	270	19,500	10,550	300	401	230	4,000	118	1,312	10,000	155	5,050	52,900
1995	2,600	18,300	11,500	676	400	230	4,000	126	1,382	10,500	113	5,070	55,700
1996	2,250	18,897	12,400	200	350	230	3,600	142	1,400	10,500	162	4,280	55,400
1997[1]	1,110	18,100	15,100	300	400	230	3,300	664	1,420	10,500	64	4,380	56,600
1998[2]	2,400	18,400	13,500	300	330	230	13,000	640	1,600	10,500	50	4,100	66,000

[1] Preliminary. [2] Estimate. [3] Formerly Zaire. *Source: U.S. Geological Survey (USGS)*

World Production of Natural Industrial Diamonds[4] In Thousands of Carats

Year	Angola	Australia	Botswana	Brazil	Central African Republic	China	Congo[3]	Ghana	Russia	Sierra Leone	South Africa	Venezuela	World Total
1993	15	23,000	4,420	600	125	850	13,600	484	8,000	68	5,700	144	57,300
1994	30	23,800	5,000	600	131	850	13,000	473	10,000	100	5,800	203	60,300
1995	300	22,400	5,300	600	130	900	13,000	505	10,500	101	5,880	66	60,100
1996	250	23,096	5,000	600	120	900	17,000	573	10,500	108	5,670	73	64,400
1997[1]	124	22,100	5,000	600	100	900	18,900	166	10,500	40	5,790	90	64,700
1998[2]	364	22,500	5,000	600	200	900	2,000	160	10,500	30	6,200	150	48,900

[1] Preliminary. [2] Estimate. [3] Formerly Zaire. *Source: U.S. Geological Survey (USGS)*

World Production of Synthetic Diamonds In Thousands of Carats

Year	Belarus	China	Czech Republic	France	Greece	Ireland	Japan	Russia	South Africa	Sweden	Ukraine	United States	World Total
1993	30,000	15,500	5,000	3,500	1,000	65,000	32,000	80,000	60,000	25,000	10,000	103,000	440,000
1994	25,000	15,500	5,000	3,500	1,000	65,000	32,000	80,000	60,000	25,000	8,000	104,000	434,000
1995	25,000	15,500	5,000	3,000	1,000	60,000	32,000	80,000	60,000	25,000	8,000	115,000	440,000
1996	25,000	15,500	5,000	3,000	750	60,000	32,000	80,000	60,000	25,000	8,000	114,000	439,000
1997[1]	25,000	16,000	5,000	3,500	750	60,000	32,000	80,000	60,000	25,000	8,000	125,000	451,000
1998[2]	25,000	16,500	5,000	3,000	750	60,000	32,000	80,000	60,000	25,000	8,000	140,000	463,000

[1] Preliminary. [2] Estimate. W = Withheld proprietary data. *Source: U.S. Geological Survey (USGS)*

Salient Statistics of Industrial Diamonds in the United States In Millions of Carats

	Bort, Grit & Powder & Dust — Natural and Synthetic								Stones (Natural)						
	Production														
Year	Manufactured Diamond	Secondary	Imports for Consumption	Exports & Reexports	In Manufactured Products	Gov't Sales	Apparent Consumption	Price Value of Imports $ Per Carat	Secondary Production	Imports for Consumption	Exports & Reexports	Gov't Sales	Apparent Consumption	Price Value of Imports $ Per Carat	Net Import Reliance % of Consumption
1993	105.0	15.9	133.0	107.0	.6	-----	146.0	.61	.1	5.2	3.4	1.3	1.9	6.85	95
1994	104.0	16.0	174.0	150.0	.4	2.0	146.0	.51	.1	2.8	.5	3.1	5.5	9.41	98
1995	115.0	26.1	188.0	98.0	-----	.2	231.0	.43	.3	4.1	.5	.3	4.2	6.62	86
1996	114.0	20.0	218.0	105.0	-----	1.0	248.0	.46	.4	2.9	.5	.5	3.3	7.54	88
1997[1]	125.0	10.0	254.0	126.0	-----	.7	264.0	.43	.5	2.8	.6	1.2	3.9	7.69	87
1998[2]	130.0	10.0	250.0	102.0	-----	-----	288.0	.42	.5	3.8	.9	.4	3.8	5.32	87

[1] Preliminary. [2] Estimate. NA = Not avaliable. W = Withheld proprietary data. *Source: U.S. Geological Survey (USGS)*

Eggs

World production in 1999 of a record large 777 billion eggs (64 billion dozen) compares with 748 billion in 1998. China is the world's largest producer and consumer of eggs with about half the world's total. China's production has about doubled since the early 1990's, reaching 380 billion in 1999 vs. 364 billion in 1998. The U.S. is the second largest producer with 1999 production placed at 82 billion vs. 80 billion in 1998.

However, a major difference persists between the two nations in respect to usage. Much of China's production is directly consumed as fresh brown eggs, whereas in the U.S. about a third of production is processed and white eggs are favored for table use. China's egg consumption in 1999 of 372 billion compares with 355 billion in 1998, while U.S. consumption of 68 billion compares with the 1994-98 average of about 64 billion. U.S. per capita egg consumption (including egg products) in 1999 was forecast at a record large 254 vs. 245 in 1998 with an increase to 255 eggs expected in 2000. U.S. consumer preference shows signs of shifting to egg products relative to table eggs although per capita use is still biased towards the latter. Per capita use is much higher abroad: Taiwan is first with 370 eggs in 1999, followed by Japan with 347 and then China at 301. On balance, European per capita usage tends to run below U.S. levels.

Foreign egg trade is small and skewed towards exports. The E.U. generally accounts for about a third of world exports—2.8 billion in 1999 vs. the world total of 8.1 billion. Asia, paced by Japan and Hong Kong, import 60 percent of the world total—3.3 billion in 1999 out of 5.1 billion. U.S. shell egg exports totaled 102 million dozen in 1998 with Canada the primary destination. Exports in the first eight months of 1999 were running less than the 1998 pace, but with larger shipments to Canada.

There are definitive seasonal swings in U.S. egg production and table consumption. The table egg flocks typically reach a low in midsummer, when heat stress is greatest on the birds and reduces the size of eggs produced by hens from large to medium. Larger egg production increases as the weather cools, reaching its average monthly high in the winter. However, table egg consumption tends to be highest in the summer when consumers have more time for leisurely meals. Thirty states account for most of U.S. production with Ohio, Iowa and California the largest producers in 1999. The bulk of total production is table eggs with the balance hatching eggs.

The New York wholesale market price in 1999 averaged 68.60 cents per dozen vs. 75.80 cents in 1998. Prices are forecast to range between 63.00-68.00 cents in 2000. Wholesale prices can change quickly: New York large egg prices had fallen to 46 cents a dozen in late June 1999, by mid-July were at 84 cents, and then fell back to 65 cents in mid-August as more moderate summer weather helped to increase the supply of large eggs. Late summer 1999 retail prices averaged around $0.98 per dozen, basis grade A large, marginally lower than a year earlier.

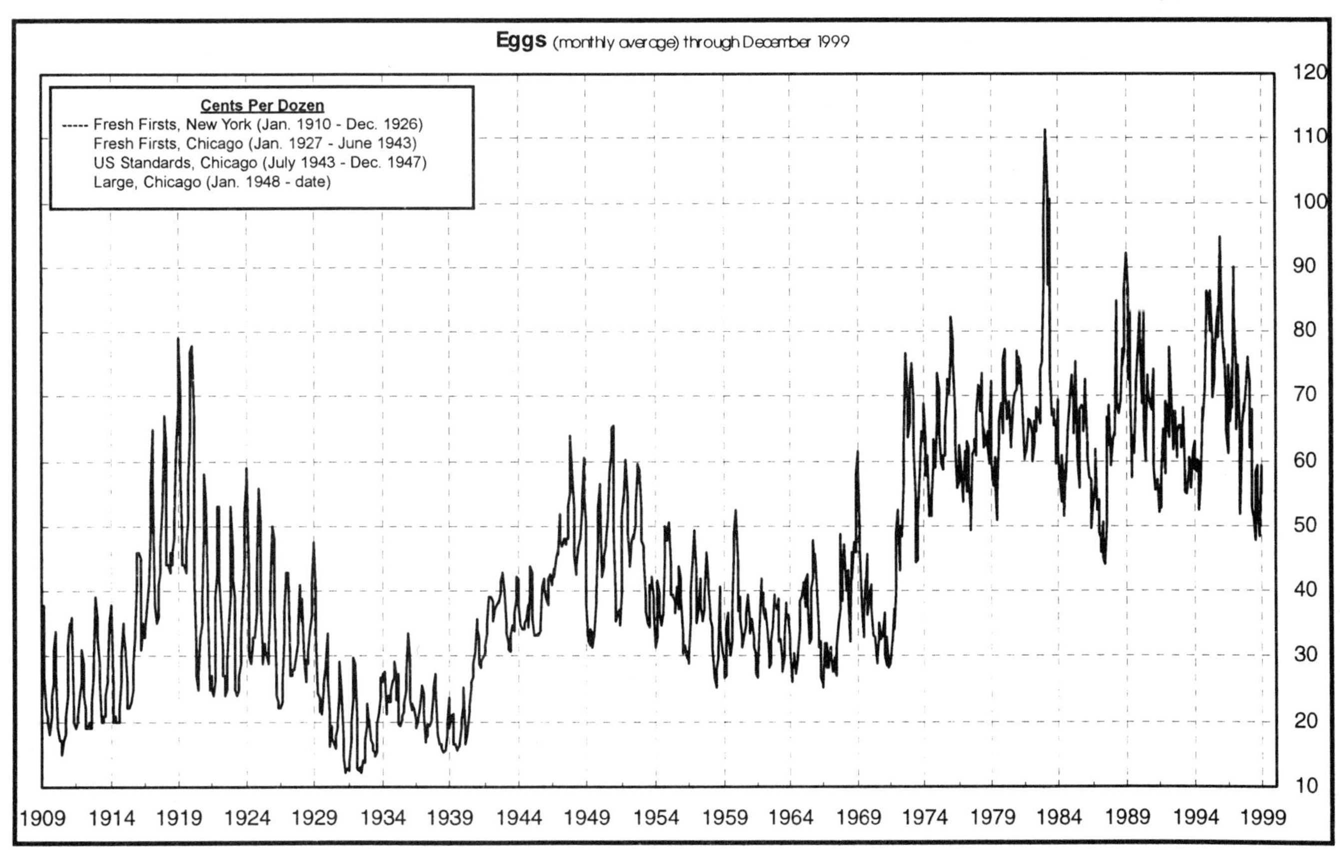

EGGS

World Production of Eggs   In Millions of Eggs

Year	Brazil	China	France	Germany	Italy	Japan	Mexico	Russia	Spain	Ukraine	United Kingdom	United States	World Total[3]
1991	13,655	184,400	15,300	15,525	11,568	41,638	19,840	46,900	10,184	15,188	12,485	69,612	529,075
1992	14,190	230,980	15,375	15,165	11,454	42,911	19,650	42,900	8,675	13,445	10,699	70,860	541,859
1993	12,700	235,960	15,355	13,678	11,502	43,252	21,471	40,300	8,454	11,766	10,645	72,072	593,734
1994	13,460	281,010	16,370	13,960	11,599	43,047	25,896	37,400	9,670	10,145	10,620	74,136	643,045
1995	16,065	301,860	16,911	13,838	12,017	42,167	25,760	33,720	9,983	9,404	10,644	74,592	670,211
1996	15,932	312,640	16,500	13,922	11,923	42,786	26,045	31,500	8,952	8,763	10,668	76,452	685,206
1997	12,596	340,064	16,084	14,025	12,298	42,588	28,170	31,900	9,450	8,242	10,752	77,676	718,762
1998	13,636	363,870	16,900	14,164	12,433	42,117	29,898	33,000	9,084	8,269	10,812	79,908	745,642
1999[1]	14,692	382,065	17,400	14,200	12,000	42,000	30,436	31,500	9,400	8,300	10,400	82,608	768,380
2000[2]	15,426	400,000	17,200	14,250	12,400	41,800	30,984	31,000	9,200	8,000	10,100	84,360	793,673

[1] Preliminary. [2] Forecast. [3] Selected countries. *Source: Foreign Agricultural Service, U.S. Department of Agriculture (FAS-USDA)*

Salient Statistics of Eggs in the United States

	-- Hens & Pullets --		Rate	-------- Eggs --------							---- Consumption ----	
Year	On Farm Dec. 1[3]	Average Number During Year	of Lay Per Layer During Year[4]	Total Produced	Price in Cents Per Dozen	Value of Production[5]	Total Egg Production	Imports[6]	Exports[6]	Used for Hatching	Total	Per Capita Eggs[6]
	----- Thousands -----		(Number)	------ Millions ------		Million Dollars	------ Million Dozen ------					(Number)
1990	271,963	270,946	251	68,134	70.8	4,021	5,666	9.1	100.8	678.5	4,916	236.0
1991	279,325	275,451	252	69,465	67.6	3,915	5,779	2.3	154.5	708.6	4,938	234.6
1992	282,034	278,824	254	70,749	57.6	3,397	5,885	4.3	157.0	732.0	5,020	235.9
1993	290,626	284,770	253	71,936	63.4	3,800	5,960	4.7	158.9	769.6	5,082	236.2
1994	298,509	291,018	254	73,911	61.4	3,780	6,177	3.7	187.6	803.0	5,186	238.7
1995	298,753	293,854	253	74,591	62.4	3,880	6,216	4.1	208.9	847.2	5,167	235.7
1996	303,754	297,958	256	76,281	74.9	4,762	6,378	5.4	253.1	863.8	5,269	238.0
1997	312,137	304,230	255	77,532	70.3	4,540	6,473	6.9	227.8	894.7	5,359	240.0
1998[1]	321,718	312,035	255	79,690	65.5	4,350	6,659	5.8	218.8	921.8	5,523	245.2
1999[2]	329,305	322,322	257	82,707			6,831	4.6	187.8	963.5	5,688	250.3

[1] Preliminary. [2] Forecast. [3] All layers of laying age. [4] Number of eggs produced during the year divided by the average number of all layers of laying age on hand during the year. [5] Value of sales plus value of eggs consumed in households of producers. [6] Shell-egg equivalent of eggs and egg products. *Source: National Agricultural Statistics Service, U.S. Department of Agriculture (NASS-USDA)*

Average Wholesale Price of Shell Eggs (Large) Delivered, Chicago   In Cents Per Dozen

Year	Jan.	Feb.	Mar.	Apr.	May	June	July	Aug.	Sept.	Oct.	Nov.	Dec.	Average
1990	86.50	72.63	83.14	72.35	57.41	63.90	61.19	70.91	72.37	77.09	77.00	83.00	73.12
1991	80.19	69.00	83.10	64.59	59.93	63.35	73.07	71.30	68.80	67.96	68.50	74.12	70.33
1992	59.16	55.68	55.73	57.17	52.00	56.05	52.82	57.86	64.83	58.14	69.30	68.05	58.90
1993	65.65	63.61	77.50	71.07	61.90	67.64	62.79	67.59	60.64	64.21	65.55	65.55	66.14
1994	62.07	64.89	68.28	58.34	55.12	55.05	58.75	60.63	59.21	55.93	61.50	62.88	60.22
1995	58.55	58.24	60.22	59.87	52.50	56.84	68.10	65.93	71.10	71.34	83.93	86.35	66.08
1996	85.25	80.00	86.12	78.88	69.77	73.00	74.73	80.59	83.80	79.13	93.68	94.60	81.63
1997	79.77	75.18	77.25	68.55	64.40	61.02	74.66	66.07	74.26	68.39	89.87	82.68	73.51
1998	75.20	64.92	74.68	63.64	51.91	61.86	65.00	68.76	67.76	71.45	75.85	75.27	68.03
1999	72.34	62.13	67.85	52.74	51.35	47.86	58.40	59.30	52.86	48.38	59.26	55.07	57.30

Source: The Wall Street Journal

Total Egg Production in the United States   In Millions of Eggs

Year	Jan.	Feb.	Mar.	Apr.	May	June	July	Aug.	Sept.	Oct.	Nov.	Dec.	Total
1990	5,708	5,172	5,838	5,655	5,769	5,533	5,703	5,718	5,533	5,783	5,695	5,910	68,244
1991	5,865	5,316	5,935	5,666	5,796	5,643	5,840	5,855	5,675	5,915	5,807	6,052	69,607
1992	5,951	5,558	6,042	5,832	5,918	5,693	5,908	5,919	5,753	6,019	5,920	6,163	70,860
1993	6,030	5,432	6,067	5,861	6,009	5,816	5,992	6,015	5,876	6,144	6,085	6,264	72,037
1994	6,186	5,598	6,320	6,073	6,189	5,992	6,205	6,272	6,125	6,377	6,265	6,516	74,121
1995	6,369	5,714	6,448	6,177	6,251	6,010	6,145	6,146	5,990	6,260	6,232	6,523	74,265
1996	6,398	5,954	6,495	6,243	6,340	6,169	6,440	6,447	6,235	6,495	6,409	6,696	76,321
1997	6,577	5,909	6,625	6,355	6,519	6,292	6,457	6,500	6,366	6,664	6,572	6,841	77,677
1998[1]	6,766	6,109	6,869	6,603	6,665	6,456	6,720	6,694	6,480	6,791	6,723	7,047	79,923
1999[2]	6,979	6,281	7,052	6,784	6,941	6,742	6,903	6,971	6,860	7,131	7,016	7,274	82,934

[1] Preliminary. [2] Estimate. *Source: National Agricultural Statistics Service, U.S. Department of Agriculture (NASS-USDA)*

Per Capita Disappearance of Eggs[4] in the United States   In Number of Eggs

Year	First Quarter	Second Quarter	Third Quarter	Fourth Quarter	Total	Total Consumption (Million Dozen)	Year	First Quarter	Second Quarter	Third Quarter	Fourth Quarter	Total	Total Consumption (Million Dozen)
1989	49.2	47.2	47.5	49.0	192.2	3,978	1995	44.0	43.1	42.7	45.0	174.9	3,834
1990	47.0	46.3	46.0	47.7	186.8	3,891	1996	44.5	42.1	43.4	45.0	175.0	3,893
1991	46.7	43.8	45.1	47.0	182.6	3,844	1997	59.0	59.3	59.7	62.1	240.1	3,894
1992	45.1	44.1	44.4	46.7	180.3	3,838	1998[1]	60.5	60.5	61.1	63.2	245.3	3,993
1993	46.1	44.0	43.8	46.0	179.7	3,825	1999[2]	62.7	62.7	63.9	65.6	254.9	4,070
1994	45.0	43.0	43.9	46.0	177.9	3,864	2000[3]	63.5	62.9	63.4		253.1	4,124

[1] Preliminary. [2] Estimate. [3] Forecast *Source: Economic Research Service, U.S. Department of Agriculture (ERS-USDA)*

Egg-Feed Ratio[1] in the United States

Year	Jan.	Feb.	Mar.	Apr.	May	June	July	Aug.	Sept.	Oct.	Nov.	Dec.	Average
1990	14.3	11.5	13.0	11.0	8.5	9.0	7.9	9.9	10.9	12.1	12.4	12.3	11.1
1991	13.2	11.1	12.6	10.0	8.6	8.8	10.4	9.8	9.4	9.7	9.9	11.2	10.4
1992	8.4	7.8	7.4	7.6	6.7	7.0	7.3	8.1	9.6	9.3	11.2	11.1	8.5
1993	10.5	10.3	11.7	10.6	9.2	9.8	8.2	8.9	8.1	8.8	8.8	8.3	9.4
1994	7.9	8.0	8.6	7.9	7.2	7.1	7.9	9.0	9.2	9.0	10.3	10.2	8.5
1995	9.7	9.6	9.2	9.2	7.8	7.8	8.0	8.7	9.2	8.9	10.4	10.6	9.1
1996	10.1	8.9	9.3	8.1	6.6	6.7	6.3	6.9	8.1	9.3	11.3	12.5	8.7
1997	10.0	9.9	8.6	7.4	7.1	6.6	8.2	7.8	9.3	8.7	11.4	11.0	8.8
1998	10.1	8.3	9.4	8.5	6.7	8.0	7.9	10.8	10.7	11.3	12.6	12.8	9.8
1999[2]	11.7	10.6	11.3	9.2	7.7	8.4	9.8	10.1	9.3	7.8	11.9	10.1	9.8

[1] Pounds of laying feed equivalent in value to one dozen eggs. [2] Preliminary. *Source: Economic Research Service, U.S. Department of Agriculture (ERS-USDA)*

Total Eggs -- Supply and Distribution in the United States   In Millions of Dozen

	Supply				Utilization			Consumption	
Year & Quarters	Beginning Stocks	Production	Imports[4]	Total Supply	Exports[4]	Eggs Used for Hatching	Ending Stocks	Total	Per Capita (Number)
1994 I	10.7	1,509	1.0	1,520	40.2	195.3	12.1	1,273	58.8
II	12.1	1,521	1.1	1,535	45.5	205.3	11.9	1,272	58.6
III	11.9	1,550	1.0	1,563	49.3	202.8	13.8	1,297	59.6
IV	13.8	1,597	.6	1,611	52.6	199.6	14.9	1,344	61.6
1995 I	14.9	1,549	1.1	1,565	45.5	207.1	14.9	1,297	59.4
II	14.9	1,545	1.2	1,561	50.1	214.1	17.9	1,279	58.4
III	17.9	1,533	1.0	1,552	47.0	213.0	13.0	1,279	58.3
IV	13.0	1,589	.8	1,602	66.4	212.9	11.2	1,312	59.6
1996 I	11.2	1,571	1.5	1,583	59.3	217.4	9.8	1,297	58.8
II	9.8	1,563	1.6	1,574	65.6	217.2	9.6	1,282	58.0
III	9.6	1,594	1.2	1,604	66.0	215.8	11.9	1,311	59.1
IV	11.9	1,632	1.0	1,645	62.2	214.3	8.5	1,360	61.2
1997 I	8.5	1,593	1.9	1,603	61.7	221.1	6.5	1,314	59.0
II	6.5	1,597	1.5	1,605	50.3	227.2	6.3	1,321	59.3
III	6.3	1,610	1.6	1,618	51.6	225.1	8.2	1,333	59.7
IV	8.2	1,673	1.9	1,683	64.2	221.3	7.4	1,390	62.1
1998[1] I	7.4	1,645	1.7	1,654	61.7	226.5	7.9	1,358	60.5
II	7.9	1,644	1.2	1,653	51.5	233.3	7.7	1,360	60.5
III	7.7	1,658	1.2	1,667	53.3	230.6	6.3	1,377	61.1
IV	6.3	1,712	1.8	1,720	52.3	231.4	8.4	1,428	63.2
1999[2] I	8.4	1,691	1.6	1,701	39.8	233.5	7.0	1,421	62.7
II	7.0	1,702	2.3	1,712	37.3	241.2	8.6	1,425	62.8
III	8.6	1,727	1.9	1,737	39.8	236.5	6.4	1,455	64.2
IV	6.4	1,765	1.8	1,773	42.0	235.0	5.0	1,491	65.8
2000[3] I	5.0	1,735	1.0	1,741	40.0	245.0	5.0	1,451	63.5
II	5.0	1,735	1.0	1,741	40.0	255.0	5.0	1,441	62.9
III	5.0	1,755	1.0	1,761	44.0	255.0	5.0	1,457	63.4
IV	5.0	1,805	1.0	1,811	46.0	250.0	5.0	1,510	65.6

[1] Preliminary. [2] Estimate. [3] Forecast. [4] Shell-egg equivalent of eggs and egg products. *Source: Economic Research Service, U.S. Department of Agriculture (ERS-USDA)*

EGGS

Hens and Pullets of Laying Age (Layers) in the United States, on First of Month   In Thousands

Year	Jan.	Feb.	Mar.	Apr.	May	June	July	Aug.	Sept.	Oct.	Nov.	Dec.
1990	271,164	272,826	271,921	272,813	270,664	269,040	265,647	266,767	267,004	268,835	270,274	271,963
1991	273,917	275,533	274,446	272,541	272,150	272,944	272,779	272,998	274,277	276,187	278,433	279,325
1992	280,697	279,274	279,117	279,009	276,757	275,645	275,179	275,091	274,010	279,233	280,183	282,034
1993	281,639	282,933	282,005	282,480	281,468	280,795	280,517	282,201	282,341	284,771	285,298	290,626
1994	290,413	289,625	290,416	290,979	289,125	288,398	287,454	288,484	292,116	294,576	295,719	298,509
1995	300,331	298,202	297,689	296,290	294,697	290,806	289,018	286,519	289,595	290,889	294,486	298,293
1996	299,261	298,320	298,348	298,029	295,123	293,740	294,044	296,612	296,911	298,433	299,910	303,754
1997	305,011	303,449	304,276	303,997	302,766	300,692	299,007	298,844	300,138	305,664	307,146	312,137
1998	311,593	312,111	314,322	313,833	309,945	309,235	309,049	308,747	309,706	312,807	316,840	321,718
1999[1]	322,137	322,100	323,357	321,632	320,149	319,510	320,632	319,101	321,375	323,365	327,169	329,305

[1] Preliminary. *Source: National Agricultural Statistics Service, U.S. Department of Agriculture (NASS-USDA)*

Eggs Laid Per Hundred Layers in the United States   In Number of Eggs

Year	Jan.	Feb.	Mar.	Apr.	May	June	July	Aug.	Sept.	Oct.	Nov.	Dec.	Average
1990	2,149	1,940	2,185	2,120	2,171	2,105	2,179	2,181	2,104	2,189	2,140	2,208	2,139
1991	2,186	1,977	2,217	2,124	2,168	2,108	2,186	2,190	2,106	2,175	2,124	2,208	2,147
1992	2,176	2,036	2,216	2,148	2,186	2,110	2,196	2,204	2,125	2,200	2,140	2,226	2,164
1993	2,192	1,970	2,209	2,132	2,182	2,112	2,175	2,183	2,124	2,209	2,167	2,237	2,158
1994	2,199	1,987	2,246	2,160	2,204	2,142	2,222	2,230	2,152	2,227	2,180	2,176	2,177
1995	2,130	1,919	2,173	2,092	2,137	2,075	2,137	2,135	2,065	2,140	2,108	2,183	2,108
1996	2,141	1,996	2,178	2,105	2,153	2,099	2,180	2,172	2,094	2,171	2,124	2,199	2,134
1997	2,161	1,943	2,176	2,093	2,156	2,093	2,155	2,165	2,096	2,172	2,122	2,193	2,127
1998	2,169	1,950	2,187	2,117	2,153	2,088	2,175	2,165	2,082	2,157	2,109	2,190	2,129
1999[1]	2,164	1,946	2,184	2,109	2,165	2,104	2,159	2,177	2,128	2,193	2,137	2,213	2,140

[1] Preliminary. *Source: National Agricultural Statistics Service, U.S. Department of Agriculture (NASS-USDA)*

Egg-Type Chicks Hatched by Commercial Hatcheries in the United States   In Thousands

Year	Jan.	Feb.	Mar.	Apr.	May	June	July	Aug.	Sept.	Oct.	Nov.	Dec.	Total
1990	32,004	32,107	36,509	36,915	37,895	34,471	31,582	32,949	31,219	32,926	29,809	31,046	398,432
1991	34,487	34,837	37,041	39,775	38,404	36,227	33,696	33,656	34,007	34,307	30,400	32,717	419,554
1992	32,496	31,950	36,490	35,755	38,513	34,568	32,265	28,349	28,760	32,843	27,718	31,612	391,319
1993	34,885	34,009	38,264	37,163	36,742	35,587	33,980	31,455	31,775	31,634	30,074	30,448	405,986
1994	33,236	31,086	33,489	35,657	35,322	31,985	29,613	31,295	31,587	32,066	26,075	30,166	381,577
1995	32,374	32,743	36,019	35,078	37,540	34,996	29,572	31,442	33,586	33,383	29,129	30,639	396,501
1996	31,580	34,608	36,890	35,740	38,028	33,017	31,920	31,782	31,930	32,319	30,947	32,879	401,640
1997	33,752	35,655	37,347	38,842	39,020	36,796	33,772	33,061	37,118	35,262	28,122	35,796	424,543
1998	37,159	34,593	40,590	39,043	39,192	39,302	35,558	33,380	37,943	34,649	31,251	35,733	438,393
1999[1]	35,653	35,648	41,325	42,043	40,590	40,569	34,269	35,453	38,841	38,559	33,078	32,730	448,758

[1] Preliminary. *Source: National Agricultural Statistics Service, U.S. Department of Agriculture (NASS-USDA)*

Cold Storage Holdings of Frozen Eggs in the United States, on First of Month   In Millions of Pounds[1]

Year	Jan.	Feb.	Mar.	Apr.	May	June	July	Aug.	Sept.	Oct.	Nov.	Dec.
1990	13.6	14.2	15.2	16.8	19.7	16.8	18.1	17.1	17.1	16.6	16.8	17.2
1991	14.7	14.8	14.0	14.1	13.0	13.5	14.2	18.1	16.3	16.5	17.0	15.1
1992	16.0	20.0	19.2	19.7	18.8	18.9	21.1	19.5	20.2	20.0	21.7	18.7
1993	17.2	16.7	16.9	15.1	14.3	15.5	15.1	17.6	18.1	14.4	14.0	13.5
1994	13.7	14.8	15.8	15.6	16.3	15.2	15.4	19.0	19.7	17.8	20.0	19.1
1995	19.5	19.5	18.3	18.5	17.3	18.1	22.9	20.6	18.0	16.2	14.4	12.5
1996	13.8	15.6	16.2	12.4	11.5	11.4	11.7	13.5	15.0	14.9	12.6	10.4
1997	10.2	11.0	11.5	8.5	8.5	8.3	8.6	8.9	11.1	10.8	10.9	10.3
1998	9.7	12.0	12.3	10.4	9.2	12.9	10.2	11.8	9.0	8.2	9.0	9.3
1999[2]	11.0	11.0	10.8	9.2	9.4	9.7	11.3	11.1	8.8	9.5	9.0	8.5

[1] Converted on basis 39.5 pounds frozen eggs equals 1 case. [2] Preliminary. *Source: National Agricultural Statistics Service, U.S. Department of Agriculture (NASS-USDA)*

Electric Power

U.S. net generation of electric power in the January-June 1999 period was 1.55 trillion kilowatt-hours. That was about the same level of electric power generation as the year before. In the same period of 1998, electric power generation was 1.55 trillion kilowatt-hours while in the like period of 1997 it was 1.49 trillion kilowatt-hours. For all of 1998, U.S. electric power generation was 3.21 trillion kilowatt-hours. In 1997, electric generation was 3.12 trillion kilowatt-hours. For the first half of 1999, coal powered utilities provided 55 percent of the electricity generated. Nuclear powered plants provided 10 percent. Gas powered plants provided 9 percent of the electricity generated. Other sources of electricity generation included petroleum, geothermal, biomass, wind, photovoltaic and solar thermal.

In June 1999, U.S. generation of electric power was 282 billion kilowatt-hours, up 10 percent from May 1999. It was a decline of 3 percent from a year earlier. Electric power generation tends to be highest in the months of July and August. Of the June total, 152 billion kilowatt-hours were provided by coal powered electric utilities. Another 8.3 billion kilowatt-hours were provided by petroleum powered electric utilities. Gas powered utilities generated 30.9 billion kilowatt-hours. Nuclear powered electric utilities provided 62 billion kilowatt-hours while hydroelectric utilities generated 28.1 billion kilowatt-hours. Smaller amounts of electricity were generated by geothermal, biomass, wind, photovoltaic and solar thermal energy sources.

Electric utility consumption of coal in June 1999 was 76.8 million short tons. That was up 8 percent from the previous month but down 3 percent from a year ago. For the January-June 1999 period, consumption of coal by electric utilities was 432 million tons. Petroleum consumption by electric utilities in June 1999 was 14.2 million barrels, an increase of 18 percent from the previous month but 29 percent less than the year before. For the January-June 1999 period, petroleum consumption by utilities was 81.6 million barrels, up 3 percent from the same period of 1998. Electric utility consumption of gas in June 1999 was 323.7 million cubic feet, an increase of 19 percent from the previous month but some 15 percent less than the year before. In the first half of 1999, gas consumption by electric utilities was 1.39 billion cubic feet, up 2 percent from the same period in 1998.

Electric utility stocks of coal at the end of June 1999 were 142.2 million short tons, down 1 percent from the previous month. Stocks of coal a year earlier were 117.8 million tons. Almost all of the coal is bituminous. Utility stocks of petroleum in June 1999 were 51.1 million barrels, up almost 2 percent from the previous month. Stocks of light petroleum were 16.9 million barrels while stocks of heavy petroleum were 51.1 million barrels. Stocks of petroleum coke in June 1999 were 690,000 tons.

World Electricity Production (Monthly Average) In Millions of Kilowatt Hours

Year	Australia	Canada	China	Germany	India	Italy	Japan	Rep. of Korea	Russia[3]	South Africa	Ukraine[3]	United Kingdom	United States
1990	12,923	40,169	51,500	37,433	22,025	18,074	71,439	8,972	139,455	13,782	-----	26,581	250,979
1991	13,071	42,326	55,918	44,949	23,893	18,503	74,007	9,885	136,156	14,026	-----	26,900	254,818
1992	13,313	41,803	61,562	44,761	25,081	18,854	74,611	10,914	84,038	14,008	21,044	27,240	256,209
1993	13,646	42,591	67,723	37,722	26,961	18,566	75,559	12,036	79,716	14,548	19,159	26,834	262,158
1994	13,929	44,502	75,312	37,786	29,250	19,292	80,361	13,754	72,993	15,650	17,425	27,637	272,354
1995	14,450	44,868	81,979	38,207	31,675	20,093	82,490	15,388	71,669	15,752	16,167	27,870	278,776
1996	14,777	45,747	88,275	45,586	32,808	21,227	84,345	17,124	70,600	16,679	15,086	28,989	288,256
1997	14,404	46,151	91,277	45,133	35,105	22,329	75,439	18,704	69,511	17,525	14,834	27,470	260,210
1998[1]	14,737	45,259	94,011	45,860	37,326	21,499	75,774	17,942	68,930	17,119	14,402	26,925	267,681
1999[2]	15,052	46,402	99,328	48,244	39,280		69,896	19,548	74,665	16,942	13,681	26,663	254,454

[1] Preliminary. [2] Estimate. [3] Formerly part of the U.S.S.R.; data not reported separately until 1992. *Source: United Nations*

Installed Capacity, Capability & Peak Load of the U.S. Electric Utility Industry In Millions of Kilowatt Hours

	Installed Generating Capacity on December 31															
		Type of Prime Mover				Type of Ownership										
Year	Total Electric Utility Industry	Hydro	Gas, Turbine & Steam	Nuclear Power	Internal Combustion	Investor Owned	Cooperative	Subtotal Gov't	Municipal Utilities	Federal	Power Districts, State Projects	Capability at Winter Peak Load	Non-Coincident Winter Peak Load	Capacity Margin Non-Coincident Peak Load (%)	Total Electric Utility Industry Generation	Annual Peak Load Factor (%)
1989	730.9	87.5	529.1	106.7	7.5	562.1	26.4	142.4	40.7	67.2	34.5	685.2	496.4	22.3	2,784.3	62.2
1990	735.1	87.2	531.1	108.0	8.7	568.8	26.3	139.9	40.1	65.4	34.4	696.8	484.0	20.4	2,808.2	60.4
1991	740.0	88.7	534.1	108.4	8.8	573.0	26.5	140.5	40.4	65.6	34.5	703.2	485.4	20.2	2,825.0	60.9
1992	741.7	89.7	534.5	107.9	9.6	572.9	26.0	142.7	41.6	66.1	35.0	707.8	493.0	21.1	2,797.2	61.1
1993	744.7	90.2	536.9	107.8	9.8	575.2	26.1	143.4	41.8	66.1	35.5	712.0	521.7	17.1	2,882.5	61.0
1994	746.0	90.3	537.9	107.9	9.9	574.8	26.4	144.7	42.0	66.3	36.4	715.1	518.3	16.7	2,910.7	61.2
1995	750.5	91.1	541.6	107.9	9.9	578.7	27.1	144.8	42.2	65.9	36.6	727.7	544.7	13.2	2,994.5	59.8
1996	756.5	91.0	546.6	109.0	9.9	582.2	27.2	147.1	43.0	67.2	36.9	740.5	545.1	14.9	3,073.1	61.0
1997	759.9	92.5	549.7	107.6	10.0	582.5	28.0	149.4	43.8	68.9	36.7	743.8	560.2	13.4	3,119.1	61.3
1998[1]	728.8	91.2	522.6	104.8	10.2	542.9	29.9	164.4	52.1	66.5	37.3	742.4	573.1	10.8	3,212.2	60.9

[1] Preliminary. *Source: Edison Electric Institute (EEI)*

Available Electricity and Energy Sales in the United States In Billions of Kilowatt Hours

	Net Generation									Sales to Ultimate Customers							
	Electric Utility Industry																
Year	Total[2]	Hydro	Natural Gas	Coal	Fuel Oil	Nuclear	Other Source[3]	Total	Total Million $	Total	Residential	Inter-departmental	Commercial	Industrial	Street & Highway Lighting	Other Public Auth.	Rail ways & Railroads
1985	2,470	281.1	291.9	1,402	100.2	383.7	10.7	2,568	149,188	2,311	793	5.3	605.9	820	14.6	62.2	4.7
1986	2,487	290.8	248.5	1,386	136.6	414.0	11.5	2,599	152,481	2,360	820	5.2	629.0	819	15.0	61.9	4.7
1987	2,572	249.7	272.6	1,464	118.5	455.3	12.3	2,719	155,734	2,441	846	4.5	658.4	844	14.4	63.0	4.9
1988	2,704	222.9	252.8	1,541	148.9	527.0	12.0	2,879	162,449	2,561	886	4.2	697.8	882	14.6	64.6	5.1
1989	2,784	265.1	266.6	1,554	158.3	529.4	11.3	2,985	169,903	2,636	899	4.3	715.9	913	14.6	69.3	5.3
1990	2,808	279.9	264.1	1,560	117.0	576.9	10.7	3,041	176,929	2,705	916	4.2	738.9	932	15.2	72.8	5.3
1991	1,825	275.5	264.2	1,551	111.5	612.6	10.1	3,100	185,220	2,745	949	2.6	753.3	935	15.6	76.1	5.3
1992	2,797	239.6	263.9	1,576	88.9	618.8	10.2	3,107	187,399	2,744	929	2.6	755.7	949	15.8	77.2	5.2
1993	2,883	265.1	258.9	1,639	99.5	610.3	9.6	3,210	197,992	2,860	994	2.7	803.1	957	18.1	69.7	5.4
1994	2,911	243.7	291.1	1,635	91.0	640.4	8.9	3,283	202,597	2,936	1,008	3.0	833.5	990	18.5	70.6	5.8
1995	2,995	293.7	307.3	1,653	60.8	673.4	6.4	3,395	207,652	3,017	1,042	2.1	863.5	1,006	17.9	69.9	5.5
1996	3,073	324.5	262.3	1,737	67.0	674.7	7.2	3,473	212,390	3,103	1,082	2.5	887.1	1,028	18.0	70.3	5.3
1997	3,119	333.5	283.1	1,789	77.1	629.4	7.5	3,536	215,264	3,154	1,079	2.6	929.0	1,028	19.7	75.6	5.3
1998[1]	3,212	304.4	309.2	1,807	110.2	673.7	7.2	3,726	218,491	3,256	1,128	NA	968.6	1,040	16.3	87.2	NA

[1] Preliminary. [2] Includes internal combustion. [3] Includes electricity produced from geothermal, wood, waste, wind, solar, etc. NA = Not available.
Source: Edison Electric Institute (EEI)

Electric Power Production by Electric Utilities in the United States In Millions of Kilowatt Hours

Year	Jan.	Feb.	Mar.	Apr.	May	June	July	Aug.	Sept.	Oct.	Nov.	Dec.	Total
1985	227,856	198,242	194,970	184,877	196,790	205,363	226,722	226,050	202,499	194,789	192,427	219,255	2,469,841
1986	217,470	192,336	196,834	186,074	197,315	215,015	242,672	225,166	206,692	197,754	196,432	213,551	2,487,310
1987	222,749	194,034	201,849	189,496	206,074	225,589	247,915	247,645	213,008	203,009	200,258	220,500	2,572,127
1988	237,897	216,937	214,013	196,000	208,371	232,747	257,461	267,693	220,179	210,608	209,593	232,752	2,704,250
1989	232,747	219,826	226,742	208,042	220,124	235,689	257,050	258,687	227,150	219,910	219,300	259,038	2,784,304
1990	237,289	212,880	226,034	211,070	222,908	249,175	266,375	268,527	237,017	224,694	213,748	237,434	2,808,151
1991	248,455	210,821	221,400	209,004	234,373	248,427	271,976	268,115	233,885	223,430	221,377	233,760	2,825,023
1992	243,970	217,761	224,665	210,837	220,355	236,842	266,148	255,203	234,760	221,289	221,263	244,126	2,797,219
1993	245,782	224,617	234,801	211,374	222,396	249,633	282,292	279,132	236,603	223,629	225,855	246,412	2,882,525
1994	261,697	225,011	231,544	214,817	227,703	263,859	278,149	274,645	237,663	227,972	224,745	242,906	2,910,712
1995	253,077	228,127	233,675	217,381	236,381	256,083	292,827	304,709	245,574	234,409	234,117	258,170	2,994,529
1996	268,713	245,388	247,989	226,423	251,570	268,644	289,329	290,458	250,672	240,674	241,077	258,138	3,077,442
1997	273,410	233,907	244,659	230,512	243,143	266,588	304,628	294,557	266,649	253,267	243,726	267,477	3,122,522
1998	265,435	235,340	256,575	232,457	265,077	291,029	317,521	312,538	279,198	251,380	239,089	266,532	3,212,171
1999[1]	276,404	240,756	259,590	239,764	256,002	281,944	319,529	308,467	261,904				3,259,147

[1] Preliminary. *Source: Energy Information Administration, U.S. Department of Energy (EIA-DOE)*

Use of Fuels for Electric Generation in the United States

	Consumption of Fuell									
Year	Coal (Thousand Short Tons)	Fuel Oil (Thousand Barels)[2]	Gas (Million Cubic Feet)	Total Fuel in Coal Equivalent[3] (Thousand Short Tons)	Net Generation by Fuels4 (Million Kilowatthour)	Pounds of Coal Per Kilowatthour (Pounds)	Cost of Fossil-fuel at Elec. Util. Cents/MBTU	Average Cost of Fuel Per Kiliowatthour (Cents)	Heat Rate BTU Per kilowatthour	Cost Per Million BTU Consumed (Cents)
1985	693,841	173,414	3,044,083	926,793	1,794,276	.990	209.4	2.27	10,429	217.7
1986	685,056	230,482	2,602,370	907,720	1,770,925	.989	175.0	1.92	10,423	184.5
1987	717,894	199,378	2,844,051	944,420	1,854,895	.981	170.6	1.84	10,354	177.7
1988	758,372	248,096	2,635,613	984,969	1,942,353	.984	164.3	1.76	10,328	170.7
1989	766,888	267,451	2,787,012	1,004,964	1,978,577	.987	167.5	1.79	10,312	174.0
1990	773,549	196,054	2,787,332	988,300	1,940,712	.997	168.9	1.80	10,366	174.1
1991	772,268	184,886	2,789,014	987,469	1,926,801	.996	160.3	1.75	10,322	169.6
1992	779,860	147,335	2,765,608	983,484	1,928,683	.990	159.0	1.72	10,340	166.6
1993	813,508	162,454	2,682,440	1,017,086	1,997,605	.993	159.5	1.72	10,351	166.6
1994	817,270	151,004	2,987,146	1,033,575	2,017,646	.999	152.6	1.59	10,425	152.6
1995	829,007	102,150	3,196,507	1,039,174	2,021,064	1.003	145.3	1.48	10,173	145.2
1996	874,616	112,565	2,727,173	1,063,755	2,066,666	1.007	151.9	1.55	10,176	151.9
1997	898,332	124,739	2,955,694	1,103,037	2,148,756	1.005	152.2	1.53	10,081	152.2
1998[1]	910,867	178,614	3,258,054	1,147,317	2,226,860	.960	143.8	1.49	10,360	143.8

[1] Preliminary. [2] 42-gallon barrels. [3] Coal equivalents are calculated on the basis of Btu instead of generation data. [4] Excludes wood & waste fuels.
Source: Edison Electric Institute (EEI)

Fertilizer

The three primary fertilizer chemicals used in the United States are nitrogen, phosphorus and potassium. They provide basic nutrients to plants. The basic nitrogen fertilizer is ammonia which is comprised of nitrogen and natural gas. Nitrogen is required for proper nutrition and maturation of the plant. Phosphorus is also important in plant nutrition. Phosphorus is produced from phosphate rock minerals. Potash denotes a variety of mined and manufactured salts, all containing the element potassium in water soluble form. Potassium activates plant enzymes, aids photosynthesis in the leaves and increases disease resistance.

The U.S. Geological Survey reported that in 1998 production of nitrogen was 13 million metric tonnes, down from 13.2 million in 1997. U.S. imports for consumption in 1998 were 3.6 million tonnes, up from 3.53 million tonnes the year before. Import sources for the U.S. include Trinidad and Tobago, Canada, Mexico and Venezuela. Exports of nitrogen in 1998 were estimated at 400,000 tonnes. U.S. apparent consumption of nitrogen in 1998 was 16.1 million tonnes, up from 15.8 million tonnes in 1997. U.S. consumption of nitrogen was for fertilizer use, urea, ammonium nitrates, ammonium phosphates and other nitrogen compounds. Nitrogen was also used in the production of plastics, synthetic fibers, resins, explosives and in other chemical compounds. U.S. stocks of nitrogen at the end of 1998 were 16 million tonnes.

U.S. production of marketable phosphate rock in the 1998/99 (July-June) season was 42.6 million tonnes, down 2 percent from the year before. Marketable phosphate rock sold or used, including exports, was 43.3 million tonnes in 1998-99, up 2 percent from 1997-98. Stocks of phosphate rock in the Florida-North Carolina region fell by 14 percent while in the Idaho-Utah region they increased 13 percent. Exports of phosphate rock in 1998-99 increased by 332,000 tonnes, an increase of 41 percent from the previous season. Imports of phosphate rock were 2.13 million tonnes, up 24 percent from 1997-98. The manufacturing of fertilizers and animal feed supplements accounted for 93 percent of phosphate rock consumption. The remainder is used to produce elemental phosphorus. Estimated domestic consumption increased 2 percent to 45.1 million tonnes.

U.S. production of marketable potash in 1998 was estimated at 1.3 million tonnes, down 7 percent from 1997. U.S. imports of potash in 1998 were 4.5 million tonnes, down 18 percent from the previous year. Imports originated from Canada, Russia and Belarus. U.S. exports of potash were 450,000 tonnes, down 3 percent from a year ago. U.S. apparent consumption of potash in 1998 was 5.3 million tonnes, down 18 percent from the previous year. The fertilizer industry used about 90 percent of U.S. potash sales while the chemical industry used 10 percent. More than 50 percent of the potash was produced as potassium chloride. Other forms included potassium sulfate and potassium magnesium sulfate. Producer stocks of potash at the end of 1998 were 300,000 tonnes.

World Production of Ammonia In Thousands of Metric Tons of Contained Nitrogen

Year	Canada	China	France	Germany	India	Indo-nesia	Japan	Mexico	Nether-lands	Poland	Russia[3]	United States	World Total
1990	3,054	17,500	1,586	2,690	7,010	2,789	1,531	2,164	3,188	1,962	18,200	12,680	97,160
1991	3,016	18,000	1,604	2,123	7,132	2,706	1,553	2,221	3,033	1,531	17,100	12,803	93,800
1992	3,104	18,000	1,848	2,113	7,452	2,688	1,545	2,203	2,588	1,222	8,786	13,400	93,400
1993	3,410	19,000	1,871	2,100	7,176	2,888	1,471	1,758	2,472	1,163	8,138	12,600	91,600
1994	3,470	20,100	1,480	2,170	7,503	3,012	1,483	2,030	2,479	1,230	7,300	13,300	93,600
1995	3,773	22,600	1,470	2,518	8,287	3,336	1,584	1,992	2,580	1,726	7,900	13,000	100,000
1996	3,840	23,000	1,570	2,485	8,549	3,647	1,567	2,054	2,652	1,713	7,900	13,400	103,000
1997[1]	4,081	25,000	1,757	2,470	9,298	3,770	1,589	1,448	2,480	1,824	7,150	13,300	104,000
1998[2]	3,900	26,500	1,570	2,512	10,037	3,600	1,580	1,449	2,350	1,683	6,500	14,700	106,000

[1] Preliminary. [2] Estimate. [3] Formerly part of the U.S.S.R.; data not reported separately until 1992. *Source: U.S. Geological Survey (USGS)*

Salient Statistics of Nitrogen[3] (Ammonia) in the United States In Thousands of Metric Tons

Year	Net Import Reliance as a % of Apparent Consumption	--- Production[3] (Fixed) --- Fertilizer	Non-fertilizer	Total	Imports[4] (Fixed)	Exports	Nitrogen[5] --- Compounds --- Produced	Consumption	- Stocks, Dec. 31- Ammonia	Fixed Nitrogen Compounds	Ammonia Consumption (Apparent)	-- Average Price ($ Per Tonne) -- ------- Urea ------- FOB Gulf[6] Coast	Urea FOB Corn Belt	Ammonium Nitrate: FOB Corn Belt	Ammonia FOB Gulf Coast
1991	14	11,559	1,244	12,803	2,742	580	9,770	9,815	936	1,607	14,826	142-143	146-160	108-130	117
1992	14	12,000	1,349	13,349	2,690	354	10,404	10,448	1,059	1,789	15,600	142-146	149-160	138-149	106
1993	17	11,300	1,320	12,620	2,657	378	10,000	10,100	852	1,600	15,100	139-141	141-165	138-149	121
1994	19	11,600	1,750	13,350	3,450	215	10,000	11,700	956	1,650	16,500	219-226	204-215	165-176	211
1995	15	11,600	1,410	13,010	2,630	319	10,400	10,700	959	1,580	15,300	217-222	220-235	162-170	191
1996	19	11,500	1,720	13,220	3,390	435	11,502	11,100	881	1,390	16,400	188-190	197-210	160-170	190
1997[1]	16	11,400	1,900	13,300	3,530	395	11,441	11,300	1,530	2,220	15,800	102-103	125-135	122-125	173
1998[2]	19	12,500	2,230	14,700	3,460	614	11,510	11,200	1,050	1,270	18,100	82-85	110-125	110-115	121

[1] Preliminary. [2] Estimate. [3] Anhydrous ammonia, synthetic. [4] For consumption. [5] Major downstream nitrogen compounds. [6] *Granular.*
E = Net exporter. *Source: U.S. Geological Survey (USGS)*

World Production of Phosphate Rock, Basic Slag & Guano In Thousands of Metric Tons (Gross Weight)

Year	Brazil	China	Egypt	Israel	Jordan	Morocco	Russia[3]	Senegal	Syria	Togo	Tunisia	United States	World Total
1989	3,655	20,000	1,355	3,922	6,900	18,067	37,500	2,273	2,256	3,355	6,610	49,817	167,342
1990	2,968	21,550	1,151	3,516	6,082	21,396	36,800	2,147	1,633	2,314	6,258	46,343	162,783
1991	3,280	22,000	1,652	3,370	4,433	17,900	28,400	1,741	1,359	2,965	6,352	48,096	150,731
1992	2,825	21,400	2,000	3,595	4,296	19,145	11,500	2,284	1,266	2,083	6,400	46,965	139,000
1993	3,419	21,200	1,585	3,680	4,129	18,193	9,400	1,667	931	1,794	5,500	35,494	119,000
1994	3,937	24,100	632	3,961	4,217	19,764	8,000	1,587	1,203	2,149	5,699	41,100	127,000
1995	3,888	19,300	765	4,063	4,984	20,200	9,000	1,500	1,551	2,570	7,241	43,500	130,000
1996	3,823	21,000	808	3,839	5,355	20,855	8,500	1,340	2,189	2,731	7,167	45,400	135,000
1997[1]	4,270	24,500	900	4,047	5,896	23,367	9,900	1,300	2,392	2,200	7,068	45,900	144,000
1998[2]	4,270	25,000	950	4,100	5,900	24,000	9,800	1,300	2,500	2,200	7,950	44,200	145,000

[1] Preliminary. [2] Estimate. [3] Formerly part of the U.S.S.R.; data not reported separately until 1992. *Source: U.S. Geological Survey (USGS)*

Salient Statistics of Phosphate Rock in the United States In Thousands of Metric Tons

Year	Mine Production	Marketable Production	Value Million Dollars	Imports For Consumption	Exports	Apparent Consumption	Stocks, Dec. 31 (Producer)	Price - $ Avg. Per Metric Ton (FOB Mine)	Avg. Price of Florida & N. Carolina - $/Tonne - FOB Mine (-60% to +74%) - Domestic	Export	Average
1989	170,268	49,817	1,084	705	7,842	42,143	11,027	21.76	20.65	28.67	21.76
1990	151,277	46,343	1,075	451	6,238	43,967	8,912	23.20	22.44	30.43	23.55
1991	154,485	48,096	1,109	552	5,082	40,177	10,168	23.06	22.67	31.69	23.69
1992	155,000	47,000	1,060	1,530	3,720	42,900	12,600	22.53	22.47	32.29	23.32
1993	107,000	35,500	759	534	3,200	38,300	9,220	21.38	21.26	28.51	21.89
1994	157,000	41,100	869	1,800	2,800	42,900	5,980	21.14	21.79	25.60	22.08
1995	165,000	43,500	947	1,800	2,760	42,700	5,710	21.75	21.29	28.35	21.75
1996	179,000	45,400	1,060	1,800	1,570	43,700	6,390	23.40	22.90	35.82	23.40
1997[1]	166,000	45,900	1,080	1,830	335	43,600	7,910	24.50	24.40	34.80	24.50
1998[2]	170,000	44,200	1,110	1,760	378	45,000	7,920	25.59	25.46	42.70	25.59

[1] Preliminary. [2] Estimate. *Source: U.S. Geological Survey (USGS)*

World Production of Marketable Potash In Thousands of Metric Tons (K_2O Equivalent)

Year	Belarus[3]	Brazil	Canada	China	France	Germany	Israel	Jordan	Russia[3]	Spain	United Kingdom	United States	World Total
1989	ÑÑ-	97	7,333	42	1,195	5,388	1,273	792	10,200	741	462	1,595	29,276
1990	ÑÑ-	66	6,989	29	1,292	4,960	1,311	841	9,000	686	488	1,713	27,493
1991	ÑÑ-	101	7,406	32	1,129	3,855	1,320	818	8,560	585	495	1,749	26,136
1992	3,311	85	7,270	21	1,141	3,461	1,296	794	3,470	594	529	1,710	23,900
1993	1,947	168	3,836	25	890	2,861	1,309	822	2,628	661	555	1,510	20,400
1994	3,021	234	8,037	74	870	3,286	1,259	930	2,498	684	580	1,400	23,100
1995	3,211	215	8,855	80	799	3,278	1,330	1,112	2,800	760	582	1,480	24,600
1996	2,720	243	8,120	110	751	3,332	1,500	1,060	2,620	680	618	1,390	23,200
1997[1]	3,250	243	9,235	115	725	3,423	1,488	849	3,400	640	565	1,400	25,500
1998[2]	3,400	243	9,000	120	656	3,200	1,500	850	3,500	635	575	1,300	25,100

[1] Preliminary. [2] Estimate. [3] Formerly part of the U.S.S.R.; data not reported separately until 1992. *Source: U.S. Geological Survey (USGS)*

Salient Statistics of Potash in the United States In Thousands of Metric Tons (K_2O Equivalent)

Year	Net Import Reliance as a % of Consumption	Production	Sales by Producers	Value Million Dollars	Imports For Consumption	Exports	Apparent Consumption	Producer Stocks Dec. 31	---- $ Per Ton ---- Avg. Value Per Ton of Product ($)	Avg. Value of K_2O Equiv.	Avg. Price[3] $ Per Tonne
1989	66	1,595	1,536	271.5	3,410	446	4,500	307	90.28	176.74	126.50
1990	68	1,713	1,716	303.3	4,164	470	5,410	303	89.46	176.80	130.00
1991	67	1,749	1,709	304.5	4,158	624	5,243	343	91.52	178.20	131.00
1992	68	1,710	1,770	334.0	4,250	663	5,350	283	96.45	189.36	134.00
1993	72	1,510	1,480	286.0	4,360	415	5,430	305	94.36	192.72	130.74
1994	76	1,400	1,470	284.0	4,800	464	5,810	234	95.93	193.50	125.34
1995	75	1,480	1,400	284.0	4,820	409	5,820	312	98.58	202.43	137.99
1996	77	1,390	1,430	299.0	4,940	481	5,890	265	101.08	208.57	134.07
1997[1]	80	1,400	1,400	320.0	5,490	466	6,500	200	110.00	230.00	138.00
1998[2]	80	1,300	1,300	320.0	4,780	480	5,700	300	115.00	250.00	145.00

[1] Preliminary. [2] Estimate. [3] Unit of K_2O, standard 60% muriate F.O.B. mine. *Source: U.S. Geological Survey (USGS)*

Fish

The U.S.D.A. reported that sales of catfish by growers to processors in 1999 were expected to be between 585 million and 595 million pounds. This would be 3 percent to 5 percent more than a year earlier. In the January-August 1999 period, catfish sales totaled 397 million pounds, up almost 4 percent from a year earlier. Depending on the size of grower inventories reported at the beginning of July 1999, grower sales of catfish are expected to show modest growth in late 1999 and into 2000. Declining prices for corn and soybeans in the last few seasons has resulted in a decline in feed costs for catfish farmers. Farm prices for catfish have been stable so the declining feed prices have resulted in an improved economic position. This, in turn, has allowed for an expansion of pond acreage and increased inventories of catfish. Grain prices could be reaching their lows and if they increase in 2000 that could lead to a reduced expansion in production.

Catfish growers indicated that their stocks of broodfish, foodsize fish, stockers and fingerlings were all higher than in 1998. A report as of July 1, 1999, indicated that in the largest states of Mississippi, Alabama, Arkansas and Louisiana, foodsize fish and fingerling holdings have increased. As of July 1, 1999, the number of foodsize fish in inventory was 302 million, up 16 percent from a year ago. The report showed that the number of stockers increased 24 percent from the previous year. The number of fingerlings was up 8 percent. The inventory of stockers and fingerlings represents those fish that will be available for processing in late 1999 and in the first half of 2000. Because of the favorable conditions in the industry due to low prices for feed, pond acreage has increased. In the July 1 report, growers indicated that some 172,200 acres of ponds would be in use between July 1 and December 31, 1999. That is up 5 percent from a year ago.

In the first half of 1999, U.S. imports of shrimp were 299 million pounds, down 2 percent from 1998. Most of the decline was due to fewer imports from Mexico and Ecuador. Part of the decline was attributed to effects from El Nino which adversely impacted the shrimp industry along the west coast of South America. These declines were partially offset by an increase in imports from Asian countries. U.S. imports of shrimp in 1999 are expected to be less than in the record year of 1998. For 1999, shrimp imports are expected to be between 675 million and 685 million pounds. Shrimp is the most commonly consumed seafood product in the United States. In 1998, per capita shrimp consumption was a record 2.8 pounds on an edible meat weight basis.

Fishery Products -- Supply in the United States In Millions of Pounds[2]

					Domestic Catch					Imports				
	Grand	For Human Food		For Industrial		% of Grand	For Human Food		For Industrial		% of Grand	For Human Food		For Industrial
Year	Total	Finfish	Shellfish[3]	Use[4]	Total	Total	Finfish	Shellfish[3]	Use[4]	Total	Total	Finfish	Shellfish[3]	Use[4]
1988	14,628	7,786	2,719	4,123	7,192	49.2	3,306	1,282	2,604	7,436	50.8	4,480	1,437	1,519
1989	15,485	9,735	2,533	3,217	8,463	54.7	4,897	1,307	2,259	7,022	45.3	4,838	1,226	958
1990	16,349	10,120	2,542	3,687	9,404	57.5	5,747	1,294	2,363	6,945	42.5	4,373	1,248	1,324
1991	16,364	10,186	2,834	3,344	9,484	58.0	5,564	1,467	2,453	6,879	42.0	4,622	1,367	890
1992	16,106	10,297	2,945	2,864	9,637	59.8	6,182	1,436	2,019	6,469	40.2	4,115	1,509	845
1993	20,334	10,796	3,025	6,513	10,467	51.5	6,770	1,444	2,253	9,867	48.5	4,026	1,581	4,260
1994	19,309	10,719	2,995	5,595	10,461	54.2	6,612	1,324	2,525	8,848	45.8	4,107	1,671	3,070
1995	16,484	10,692	2,891	2,900	9,788	59.4	6,414	1,252	2,121	6,696	40.6	4,278	1,639	779
1996	16,474	10,699	2,927	2,848	9,565	58.1	6,205	1,271	2,089	6,909	41.9	4,494	1,656	759
1997[1]	17,131	10,577	3,162	3,392	9,845	57.5	5,969	1,279	2,597	7,286	42.5	4,608	1,883	759

[1] Preliminary. [2] Live weight, except percent. [3] For univalue and bivalues mollusks (conchs, clams, oysters, scallops, etc.) the weight of meats, excluding the shell is reported. [4] Fish meal and sea herring. *Source: Fisheries Statistics Division, U.S. Department of Commerce*

Fisheries -- Landings of Principal Species in the United States In Millions of Pounds

	Fish									Shelfish					
Year	Cod, Atlantic	Flounder	Halibut	Herring, Sea	Man-haden	Pollock	Salmon, Pacific	Tuna	Whiting	Clams (Meats)	Crabs	Lobsters (American)	Oysters (Meats)	Scallops (Meats)	Shrimp
1988	76	229	82	222	2,086	1,290	606	111	36	132	456	49	32	43	331
1989	78	202	75	209	1,989	2,385	786	89	39	138	458	53	30	41	352
1990	96	255	70	221	1,962	3,129	733	62	44	139	499	61	29	42	346
1991	93	405	66	230	1,977	2,873	783	36	37	134	650	63	32	40	320
1992	62	646	67	282	1,644	2,952	716	57	36	142	624	56	36	34	338
1993	51	599	63	216	1,983	3,258	888	55	36	148	604	57	34	19	293
1994	39	427	58	214	2,324	3,133	901	72	36	131	447	66	38	25	283
1995	30	423	45	265	1,847	2,853	1,137	14	34	134	364	66	40	20	307
1996	31	460	49	318	1,755	2,630	877	85	35	123	392	71	38	18	317
1997[1]	27	566	70	348	2,028	2,522	568	83	34	114	430	84	40	15	290

[1] Preliminary. *Source: National Marine Fisheries Service, U.S. Department of Commerce*

FISH

U.S. Fisheries: Quantity & Value of Domestic Catch & Consumption & World Fish Oil Production

Year	Disposition: Fresh & Frozen	Canned	Cured	For Meal, Oil, Etc.	Total	For Human Food	For Industrial Products	Ex-vessel Value[3]	Average Price	Fish Per Capita Cunsumption	World[2] Fish Oil Production
	Millions of Pounds							- Million $ -	- Cents/Lb. -	- Pounds -	- 1,000 Tons -
1991	6,541	674	119	2,150	9,484	7,031	2,453	3,308	34.9	14.8	1,105
1992	7,288	543	110	1,696	9,637	7,618	2,019	3,678	38.2	14.7	1,038
1993	7,744	649	115	1,959	10,467	8,214	2,253	3,471	33.2	14.9	1,184
1994	7,475	622	95	2,269	10,461	7,936	2,525	3,807	36.8	NA	1,470
1995	7,099	769	90	1,830	9,788	7,667	2,121	3,770	38.5	NA	1,302
1996	7,054	678	93	1,740	9,565	7,475	2,090	3,487	36.5	NA	1,337
1997[1]	6,877	648	108	2,213	9,846	7,248	2,598	3,467	35.2	NA	1,214

[1] Preliminary. [2] Crop years on a marketing year basis. [3] At the Dock Prices. *Source: Fisheries Statistics Division, U.S. Department of Commerce*

Imports of Seafood Products into the United States In Thousands of Pounds

Year	Fresh: Atlantic Salmon	Fresh: Pacific Salmon	Fresh: Shrimp	Frozen: Trout	Frozen: Atlantic Salmon	Frozen: Pacific Salmon	Frozen: Shrimp	Oysters[2]	Mussels[3]	Clams[4]	Canned Salmon	Prepared Shrimp[5]
1994	68,254	31,952	-----	3,878	7,851	11,210	580,010	15,415	11,032	8,265	3,190	47,912
1995	95,739	33,371	-----	4,076	9,982	8,849	539,630	14,866	15,483	5,930	3,582	57,577
1996	116,606	43,962	-----	4,552	10,752	8,514	507,823	14,222	21,241	6,596	4,182	74,648
1997	150,135	38,999	-----	5,403	14,956	25,662	572,111	14,531	26,903	5,703	3,675	76,213
1998	190,131	38,486	-----	5,670	19,092	17,134	599,466	18,049	34,099	6,541	3,430	95,942
1999[1]	217,948	26,467	-----	5,259	24,222	16,596	617,089	18,325	34,969	7,537	5,627	114,191

[1] Preliminary. [2] Oysters fresh or prepared. [3] Mussels fresh or prepared. [4] Clams, fresh or prepared. [5] Shrimp, canned, breaded or prepared.
NA = Not available. *Source: Bureau of the Census, U.S. Department of Commerce*

Exports of Seafood Products into the United States In Thousands of Pounds

Year	Fresh: Atlantic Salmon	Fresh: Pacific Salmon	Fresh: Shrimp	Frozen: Trout	Frozen: Atlantic Salmon	Frozen: Pacific Salmon	Frozen: Shrimp	Oysters[2]	Mussels[3]	Clams[4]	Canned Salmon	Prepared Shrimp[5]
1994	1,184	22,483	-----	1,958	384	260,469	13,622	2,634	1,935	3,785	90,393	15,778
1995	6,823	26,142	-----	1,545	231	266,706	14,795	2,531	1,896	3,968	95,611	14,837
1996	7,280	42,999	-----	1,867	322	223,346	11,180	2,097	1,603	5,126	94,842	17,665
1997	7,504	25,529	-----	1,709	322	152,516	11,967	2,890	1,157	4,916	81,407	14,826
1998	7,978	34,645	-----	1,453	243	105,869	11,323	2,496	1,347	5,375	77,201	13,882
1999[1]	10,717	40,683	-----	1,697	182	157,278	13,607	2,727	1,861	5,240	113,556	13,153

[1] Preliminary. [2] Oysters fresh or prepared. [3] Mussels fresh or prepared. [4] Clams, fresh or prepared. [5] Shrimp, canned, breaded or prepared.
NA = Not available. *Source: Bureau of the Census, U.S. Department of Commerce*

World Production of Fish Meal In Thousands of Metric Tons

Year	Chile	Spain	Denmark	EU-12	FSU-12	Iceland	Japan	Norway	Peru	South Africa	Thailand	United States	World Total
1991-2	1,322.1	122.1	351.7	602.5	465.1	158.9	509.6	239.9	1,095.6	150.3	313.4	312.2	5,948.5
1992-3	1,091.2	97.9	300.1	544.0	355.0	197.7	395.0	250.8	1,767.3	128.3	352.8	352.5	6,258.6
1993-4	1,526.1	65.1	352.7	558.6	295.0	190.5	343.0	216.8	2,254.4	92.9	373.2	447.8	7,216.7
1994-5	1,549.7	70.1	363.4	573.1	280.0	173.8	239.0	225.0	2,052.6	95.8	383.9	338.3	6,920.8
1995-6	1,387.6	76.4	322.9	532.1	260.0	271.0	197.0	233.8	1,702.7	49.6	380.0	331.1	6,385.4
1996-7[1]	1,209.9	75.0	334.6	538.7	260.0	272.5	184.0	259.7	2,150.5	52.6	385.0	345.0	6,670.3
1997-8[2]	708.5	77.0	317.2	526.4	250.0	223.1	180.0	296.7	697.2	89.3	409.0	341.0	4,710.0
1998-9[3]	900.0	76.0	340.0	548.8	240.0	248.0	190.0	287.0	1,380.0	89.0	400.0	345.0	5,652.0

[1] Preliminary. [2] Estimate. [3] Forecast. *Source: The Oil World*

World Production of Fish Oil In Thousands of Metric Tons

Year	Canada	Chile	China	Denmark	Iceland	Japan	Norway	Peru	South Africa	FSU-12	United States	World Total	Fish Oil CIF[4]
1991-2	11.0	155.9	8.7	114.5	63.0	186.1	92.9	102.1	16.1	104.2	84.4	1,042.1	361
1992-3	11.8	165.3	9.4	90.3	86.0	107.4	112.3	250.9	17.0	71.6	119.0	1,150.4	375
1993-4	9.9	280.0	9.4	112.0	96.5	93.3	122.7	426.5	8.5	52.7	141.2	1,473.5	332
1994-5	10.1	323.1	9.9	118.3	85.0	57.7	94.1	388.1	7.5	48.5	109.6	1,371.6	405
1995-6	10.6	280.2	12.0	120.0	120.5	45.8	93.7	410.0	3.7	43.0	110.4	1,363.4	461
1996-7[1]	10.5	192.6	12.0	129.5	134.6	51.2	86.4	407.1	4.1	41.0	110.0	1,293.8	502
1997-8[2]	10.5	91.4	12.6	106.4	107.0	54.0	89.0	74.0	7.8	39.5	116.0	826.2	722
1998-9[3]	10.2	155.0	12.7	118.0	120.0	52.5	100.0	255.0	8.1	38.8	115.0	1,103.3	445

[1] Preliminary. [2] Estimate. [3] Forecast. [4] Any origin, N.W. Europe. NA = Not available. *Source: The Oil World*

Monthly Production of Catfish--Round Weight Processed, in the US In Thousands of Pounds (Live Weight)

Year	Jan.	Feb.	Mar.	Apr.	May	June	July	Aug.	Sept.	Oct.	Nov.	Dec.	Total
1990	33,066	31,884	33,120	30,980	31,542	28,967	29,540	31,108	27,566	29,211	27,913	25,538	360,435
1991	32,206	33,036	35,951	31,205	31,322	31,588	32,720	32,912	33,244	35,400	31,114	30,172	390,870
1992	36,200	39,228	45,048	41,177	39,111	36,813	36,128	37,958	37,857	39,212	35,073	33,562	457,367
1993	40,327	40,277	43,521	39,920	37,030	35,496	37,086	37,706	37,072	39,472	36,557	34,549	459,013
1994	36,714	35,035	40,446	34,494	34,163	34,595	35,901	39,813	38,716	39,072	36,054	34,266	439,269
1995	38,807	38,515	42,200	36,588	37,030	36,047	35,800	38,827	37,634	39,456	34,119	31,863	446,886
1996	38,475	38,004	46,376	38,557	39,583	36,810	39,025	40,463	38,807	42,070	37,210	36,874	472,254
1997	42,409	45,067	48,431	45,721	43,409	42,282	43,376	44,154	43,472	46,275	40,137	40,216	524,949
1998	46,723	47,606	53,761	49,393	45,218	46,244	46,383	47,739	46,579	47,904	43,224	43,581	564,355
1999[1]	48,723	48,891	56,310	46,830	47,703	48,445	50,074	50,372	50,414	52,407	48,118	48,341	596,628

[1] Preliminary. *Source: Economic Research Service, U.S. Department of Agriculture ERS-USDA)*

Average Price Paid to Producers for Farm-Raised Catfish in the US In Cents Per Pound (Live Weight)

Year	Jan.	Feb.	Mar.	Apr.	May	June	July	Aug	Sept.	Oct.	Nov.	Dec.	Average
1990	72.0	74.0	78.0	78.0	78.0	78.0	76.0	76.0	76.0	76.0	75.0	72.0	75.8
1991	69.0	69.0	69.0	69.0	66.0	65.0	63.0	60.0	59.0	58.0	57.0	53.0	63.1
1992	53.0	56.0	60.0	63.0	63.0	61.0	59.0	58.0	59.0	61.0	62.0	63.0	59.8
1993	63.0	67.0	70.0	71.0	72.0	72.0	72.0	73.0	73.0	73.0	73.0	73.0	71.0
1994	74.0	77.0	79.0	80.0	80.0	80.0	80.0	80.0	80.0	77.0	77.0	77.0	78.4
1995	78.0	79.0	79.0	79.0	79.0	79.0	79.0	79.0	78.0	78.0	78.0	78.0	78.6
1996	77.0	78.0	78.0	78.0	79.0	79.0	79.0	78.0	77.0	76.0	75.0	73.0	77.3
1997	73.0	73.0	73.0	73.0	73.0	72.0	71.0	70.0	69.0	69.0	69.0	69.0	71.2
1998	69.0	73.0	78.0	79.0	79.0	78.0	76.0	74.0	73.0	71.0	70.0	70.0	74.2
1999[1]	70.3	71.4	73.2	75.6	77.7	77.5	76.8	74.3	72.8	71.6	71.3	71.6	73.7

[1] Preliminary. *Source: Economic Research Service, U.S. Department of Agriculture (ERS-USDA)*

Sales and Prices of Fresh Catfish in the United States In Thousands of Pounds

Year	Jan.	Feb.	Mar.	Apr.	May	June	July	Aug.	Sept.	Oct.	Nov.	Dec.	Total/Average
						In Thousands of Pounds							
SALES -- Whole													
1996	3,673	3,593	4,168	3,508	3,230	2,868	3,001	3,107	3,215	3,324	2,763	2,925	39,375
1997	3,402	3,632	4,133	3,770	3,456	3,447	3,481	3,284	3,370	3,598	3,002	3,051	41,626
1998	3,700	4,049	4,308	3,856	3,421	3,340	3,342	3,270	3,332	3,431	3,152	3,254	42,455
1999[1]	3,650	3,957	4,467	3,459	3,492	3,380	3,471	3,271	3,583	3,561	3,209	3,313	42,813
Fillets[2]													
1996	3,439	3,866	4,366	3,883	3,824	3,374	3,556	3,615	3,645	3,758	3,254	3,222	43,802
1997	3,627	4,272	4,531	4,084	4,126	3,894	4,033	4,135	4,009	4,464	3,623	3,543	48,341
1998	4,292	4,784	5,130	4,634	4,371	4,220	4,542	4,622	4,626	4,588	4,092	3,975	53,876
1999[1]	4,581	5,030	5,768	4,897	4,918	4,707	4,846	5,002	4,550	4,811	4,171	4,142	57,423
Other[3]													
1996	1,097	1,263	1,438	1,154	1,124	937	1,045	1,128	1,081	1,228	1,063	982	13,540
1997	1,287	1,497	1,562	1,530	1,430	1,307	1,385	1,332	1,358	1,498	1,212	1,147	16,545
1998	1,499	1,712	1,721	1,509	1,395	1,453	1,246	1,360	1,314	1,345	1,117	1,081	16,761
1999[1]	1,243	1,614	1,724	1,153	1,227	1,126	1,305	1,495	1,354	1,676	1,299	1,227	16,443
						In Dollars Per pound							
PRICE -- Whole													
1996	1.63	1.64	1.68	1.68	1.73	1.77	1.73	1.71	1.67	1.65	1.64	1.60	1.68
1997	1.59	1.60	1.58	1.56	1.56	1.52	1.51	1.53	1.54	1.52	1.54	1.50	1.55
1998	1.52	1.57	1.63	1.61	1.65	1.60	1.60	1.63	1.59	1.59	1.56	1.52	1.59
1999[1]	1.54	1.55	1.57	1.59	1.63	1.60	1.59	1.63	1.61	1.63	1.59	1.57	1.59
Fillets[2]													
1996	2.88	2.85	2.86	2.87	2.88	2.92	2.91	2.88	2.85	2.83	2.84	2.81	2.87
1997	2.80	2.79	2.80	2.78	2.78	2.77	2.75	2.74	2.73	2.69	2.67	2.71	2.75
1998	2.71	2.75	2.85	2.86	2.86	2.85	2.84	2.82	2.78	2.78	2.75	2.73	2.80
1999[1]	2.73	2.71	2.76	2.75	2.84	2.86	2.86	2.85	2.85	2.83	2.84	2.83	2.81
Other[3]													
1996	1.77	1.75	1.77	1.84	1.87	1.90	1.86	1.81	1.77	1.74	1.75	1.73	1.80
1997	1.72	1.67	1.68	1.64	1.68	1.68	1.70	1.69	1.65	1.60	1.66	1.64	1.67
1998	1.61	1.65	1.72	1.78	1.78	1.76	1.79	1.71	1.72	1.69	1.73	1.69	1.72
1999[1]	1.61	1.55	1.59	1.70	1.74	1.76	1.66	1.62	1.66	1.57	1.65	1.66	1.65

[1] Preliminary. [2] Includes regular, shank and strip fillets; excludes breaded products. [3] Includes steaks, nuggets and all other products not reported.
Source: Economic Research Service, U.S. Department of Agriculture (ERS-USDA)

Flaxseed and Linseed Oil

In the U.S., the area planted to flaxseed increased in the past few years following a protracted steady decline. Still, flaxseed (from which linseed oil is derived) is considered a minor U.S. oilseed with recent yearly production under 6 million bushels, about equal to the quantity imported. Planted acreage in 1999/2000 of 341,000 acres compares with 336,000 in 1998/99, but during much of the 1980's planted acreage often exceeded 500,000 acres.

Flaxseed production in 1999/00 (June/May) of 5.7 million bushels compares with 6.7 million the previous year which was the high for the 1990's. The decade's low was 1.6 million bushels in 1996/97. The U.S. crop is produced mostly in the Northern Plains states. Imports of flaxseed, mostly from Canada, the world's largest producer with about a third of global production, were forecast at 5.7 million bushels in 1999/00 vs. 5.6 million in 1998/99, and a record large 9.6 million in 1997/98. The U.S. has been a net importer of flaxseed since 1978.

Total 1999/00 supplies of 13.6 million bushels were marginally above 1998/99 and include a carry-in of 2.2 million bushels. Disappearance in 1999/00 was forecast at 11.6 million bushels vs. 11.4 million in 1998/99, which if realized would suggest an ending carryover of more than 4 million bushels, the highest since 1980/81.

1999/00 U.S. domestic demand for linseed oil of 151 million pounds is about unchanged from the previous two seasons and compares with annual averages of 200 million pounds in the mid-1980's. Exports were put at a near record 66 million pounds, marginally higher than in 1998/99. The 1999/00 production of 212 million pounds is the highest since the late 1980's and compares with 210 million in 1998/99.

Linseed oil is used as a drying agent in paint, but domestic use has fallen due to the acceptance of water based latex paints. Carryover stocks as of June 1, 1999, of 44 million pounds is slightly larger than a year earlier and are expected to total the same at the season's end.

Linseed meal production in 1999/00 of 196,000 short tons is marginally above 1998/99. Meal usage in 1999/00 should about equal the total supply with carryover holding near 5,000 tons, as it has for much of the 1990's.

The average price received by U.S. farmers for flaxseed in 1999/00 is estimated at $3.65-$4.45 per bushel vs. $5.10 in 1998/99. Linseed oil prices were projected at 26.0-29.0 cents per pound vs. 37.75 cents in 1998/99, basis Minneapolis. Linseed meal prices, basis Minneapolis, 34 percent protein, were forecast at $57.50-77.50 per short ton in 1999/00 vs. $62.00/ton in 1998/99.

Futures Markets

Flaxseed futures are traded on the Winnipeg Commodity Exchange (WCE). Prices are quoted in Canadian dollars per metric ton.

World Production of Flaxseed In Thousands of Metric Tons

Year	Argentina	Australia	Bangladesh	Canada	China	Egypt	France	Hungary	India	Romania	United States	Former USSR	World Total
1989-90	526	2	47	498	400	21	31	11	326	49	31	227	2,352
1990-1	458	4	48	889	535	28	34	10	339	53	97	197	2,923
1991-2	341	5	55	635	410	24	26	13	292	23	158	140	2,458
1992-3	177	5	49	334	430	21	29	10	268	18	84	130	1,966
1993-4	112	8	49	627	410	22	27	4	330	28	88	120	2,191
1994-5	152	6	48	960	511	18	44	4	325	7	74	110	2,474
1995-6	149	15	49	1,105	420	16	27	4	308	5	56	113	2,518
1996-7[1]	72	7	46	851	480	17	29	4	319	5	41	86	2,300
1997-8[2]	75	6	50	1,038	400	18	25	4	310	5	62	84	2,437
1998-9[3]	85	8	46	1,170	435	18	25	4	300	5	170	87	2,773

[1] Preliminary. [2] Estimate. [3] Forecast. *Source: The Oil World*

Supply and Distribution of Flaxseed in the United States In Thousands of Bushels

Crop Year Beginning June 1	Planted	Harvested	Yield Per Acre (Bushels)	Supply: Beginning Stocks	Supply: Production	Supply: Imports	Supply: Total Supply	Distribution: Seed	Distribution: Crush	Distribution: Exports	Distribution: Residual	Distribution: Total Distribution
	1,000 Acres											
1990-1	260	253	15.1	244	3,812	6,715	10,771	288	8,800	549	163	9,800
1991-2	356	342	18.1	971	6,200	4,371	11,542	139	9,050	541	256	9,986
1992-3	171	165	19.9	1,556	3,288	6,035	10,879	167	8,600	230	337	9,334
1993-4	206	191	18.2	1,545	3,480	5,118	10,143	144	8,650	126	69	8,989
1994-5	178	171	17.1	1,155	2,922	6,005	10,082	134	8,550	72	156	8,912
1995-6	165	147	15.0	1,170	2,212	7,248	10,681	78	9,000	119	203	9,399
1996-7	96	92	17.4	1,230	1,602	8,390	11,222	122	10,000	144	503	10,769
1997-8[1]	151	146	16.6	453	2,420	9,636	12,509	272	10,500	174	382	11,328
1998-9[2]	336	329	20.4	1,181	6,708	5,992	13,881	276	10,600	476	371	11,723
1999-00[3]	341	334	17.0	2,158	5,680	5,816	13,654	284	10,700	500	170	11,654

[1] Preliminary. [2] Estimate. [3] Forecast. *Source: Economic Research Service, U.S. Department of Agriculture*

Production of Flaxseed in the United States, by States In Thousands of Bushels

Crop Year	Minne-sota	North Dakota	South Dakota	Other States	Total	Crop Year	Minne-sota	North Dakota	South Dakota	Other States	Total
1990	238	3,118	456	-----	3,812	1995	171	1,725	260	55	2,211
1991	640	4,860	578	122	6,200	1996	60	1,386	126	30	1,602
1992	220	2,730	322	16	3,288	1997	96	1,997	252	75	2,420
1993	170	2,886	323	101	3,480	1998	432	5,817	294	165	6,708
1994	126	2,450	304	42	2,922	1999[1]	300	6,867	357	356	7,880

[1] Preliminary. *Source: National Agricultural Statistics Service, U.S. Department of Agriculture (NASS-USDA)*

Factory Shipments of Paints, Varnish and Lacquer in the United States In Millions of Dollars

Year	First Quarter	Second Quarter	Third Quarter	Fourth Quarter	Total	Year	First Quarter	Second Quarter	Third Quarter	Fourth Quarter	Total
1990	2,754.7	3,188.6	3,080.1	2,632.6	11,762	1995	3,330.3	3,838.0	3,814.5	3,423.4	14,406
1991	2,498.4	3,158.7	3,123.0	2,611.2	11,707	1996	3,438.6	4,161.9	3,954.9	3,428.9	14,984
1992	2,852.3	3,464.1	3,308.7	2,816.4	12,441	1997	3,515.2	4,023.4	3,924.1	3,323.0	14,786
1993	2,894.1	3,600.5	3,448.9	2,993.7	12,937	1998	3,519.7	4,152.8	3,993.8	3,705.9	15,372
1994	3,039.8	3,783.0	3,736.2	3,240.8	13,800	1999[1]	3,876.6	4,395.6	4,157.6		16,573

[1] Preliminary. *Source: Bureau of the Census, U.S. Department of Commerce*

Factory Shipments of Paints, Varnish and Lacquer in the United States In Millions of Dollars

Year	First Quarter	Second Quarter	Third Quarter	Fourth Quarter	Total	Year	First Quarter	Second Quarter	Third Quarter	Fourth Quarter	Total
1990	2,754.7	3,188.6	3,080.1	2,632.6	11,762	1995	3,330.3	3,838.0	3,814.5	3,423.4	14,406
1991	2,498.4	3,158.7	3,123.0	2,611.2	11,707	1996	3,438.6	4,161.9	3,954.9	3,428.9	14,984
1992	2,852.3	3,464.1	3,308.7	2,816.4	12,441	1997	3,515.2	4,023.4	3,924.1	3,323.0	14,786
1993	2,894.1	3,600.5	3,448.9	2,993.7	12,937	1998	3,519.7	4,152.8	3,993.8	3,705.9	15,372
1994	3,039.8	3,783.0	3,736.2	3,240.8	13,800	1999[1]	3,876.6	4,395.6	4,157.6		16,573

[1] Preliminary. *Source: Bureau of the Census, U.S. Department of Commerce*

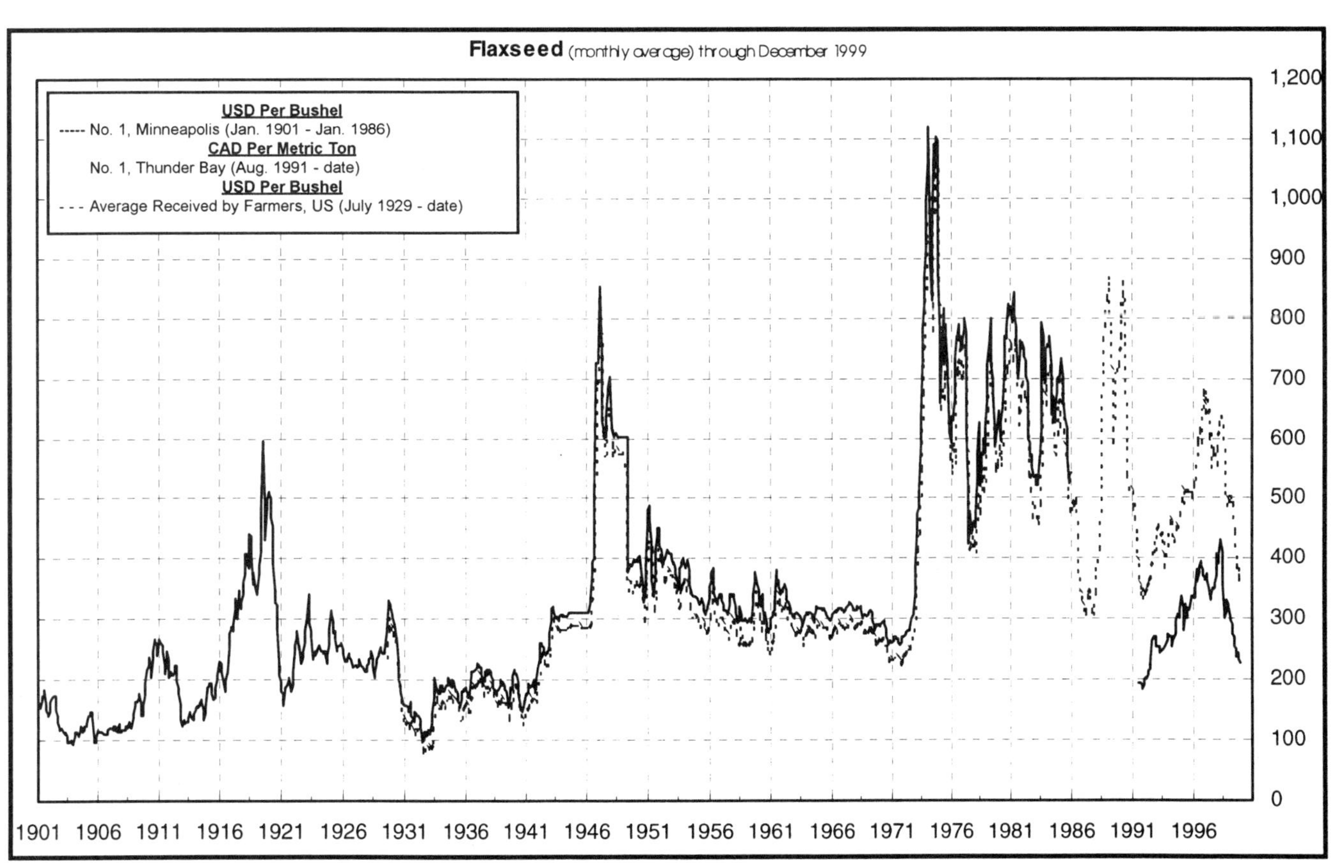

FLAXSEED AND LINSEED OIL

Supply and Distribution of Linseed Oil in the United States In Millions of Pounds

Crop Year Beginning June 1	Supply: Stocks June 1	Supply: Production	Supply: Total	Disappearance: Exports	Disappearance: Domestic	Disappearance: Total Disappearance	Average Price at Minneapolis Cents/Lb.
1990-1	37	176	213	6	167	173	38.0
1991-2	40	182	222	12	170	182	32.0
1992-3	40	172	212	8	150	158	31.5
1993-4	54	174	228	7	162	165	31.8
1994-5	63	171	237	24	168	192	33.7
1995-6	45	180	228	23	155	178	36.5
1996-7	50	200	256	66	155	221	36.0
1997-8	35	210	252	58	152	210	36.3
1998-9[1]	42	212	266	63	155	218	37.8
1999-00[2]	48	214	268	65	156	221	-----

[1] Preliminary. [2] Forecast. *Source: Economic Research Service, U.S. Department of Agriculture (ERS-USDA)*

World Production and Price of Linseed Oil In Thousands of Metric Tons

Year	Argentina	Bangladesh	Belgium	China	Egypt	Germany	India	Japan	United Kingdom	United States	Former USSR	World Total	Rotterdam Ex-Tank $/Tonne
1989-90	158.8	11.6	12.9	104.1	11.7	44.9	92.9	31.4	11.4	76.1	11.5	646.6	756
1990-1	141.5	12.0	12.2	126.9	12.3	57.5	94.2	34.7	16.8	84.0	10.1	685.8	502
1991-2	114.0	13.5	14.7	111.0	11.3	56.1	83.8	31.9	27.0	87.9	9.1	637.9	377
1992-3	62.3	12.6	25.5	117.0	8.1	56.8	78.0	28.4	27.2	80.0	9.6	570.0	450
1993-4	32.2	12.7	28.8	121.8	8.6	77.2	90.7	30.7	35.2	78.7	11.2	617.9	476
1994-5	46.8	13.0	35.2	127.8	8.2	104.0	91.4	29.2	41.4	81.7	10.6	698.1	657
1995-6	47.5	13.0	44.3	117.3	8.0	72.0	88.1	30.0	28.9	80.0	12.7	663.9	579
1996-7	17.1	12.5	52.1	129.0	9.6	52.2	88.8	31.0	34.1	97.9	9.6	656.9	560
1997-8[1]	24.1	13.4	54.7	112.5	10.9	66.9	87.5	31.3	35.1	106.4	9.9	682.2	686
1998-9[2]	24.0	13.1	59.2	126.0	10.9	74.8	84.7	29.8	39.9	107.9	10.9	725.8	612

[1] Preliminary. [2] Forecast. *Source: The Oil World*

Average Price Received by Farmers for Flaxseed in the United States In Dollars Per Bushel

Year	July	Aug.	Sept.	Oct.	Nov.	Dec.	Jan.	Feb.	Mar.	Apr.	May	June	Average
1990-1	7.56	5.86	5.36	5.15	5.16	5.15	5.12	4.82	4.90	4.66	4.33	3.98	5.17
1991-2	3.92	3.69	3.55	3.39	3.31	3.46	3.39	3.43	3.51	3.53	3.61	3.66	3.54
1992-3	3.70	3.68	4.12	4.09	4.08	4.24	4.11	4.46	4.52	4.40	4.42	4.45	4.19
1993-4	4.29	3.79	4.24	4.09	4.05	4.18	4.38	4.61	4.64	4.60	4.43	4.25	4.30
1994-5	4.28	4.52	4.54	4.49	4.51	4.71	4.76	4.94	5.13	5.10	4.91	5.03	4.74
1995-6	5.11	5.21	5.11	5.11	5.17	5.03	5.26	5.21	5.28	5.31	6.13	5.90	5.32
1996-7	6.19	6.15	5.89	6.49	6.38	6.77	6.43	6.74	6.66	6.43	6.45	5.99	6.38
1997-8	6.07	5.53	5.72	5.81	5.71	5.72	5.82	6.27	6.26	6.23	6.33	6.17	5.97
1998-9	6.17	5.45	5.09	4.86	4.97	5.00	5.05	5.05	4.95	4.94	4.87	4.37	5.06
1999-00[1]	4.40	3.86	4.00	3.76	3.66	3.61	3.55						3.83

[1] Preliminary. *Source: National Agricultural Statistics Service, U.S. Department of Agriculture (NASS-USDA)*

Stocks of Linseed Oil (Crude and Refined) at Factories and Warehouses in the US In Millions of Pounds

Year	July 1	Aug. 1	Sept. 1	Oct. 1	Nov. 1	Dec. 1	Jan. 1	Feb. 1	Mar. 1	Apr. 1	May 1	June 1
1990-1	28.2	21.9	17.2	41.8	41.4	47.5	-----	61.7	-----	-----	75.4	-----
1991-2	-----	60.6	-----	-----	64.2	-----	73.1	51.2	62.3	45.6	45.7	41.4
1992-3	34.6	35.5	29.7	41.3	49.1	47.7	39.9	44.2	45.1	49.1	42.8	43.1
1993-4	45.2	39.0	42.1	47.0	27.9	19.3	22.5	38.0	42.0	49.4	52.0	62.6
1994-5	60.3	56.5	49.4	60.6	48.1	39.3	38.6	38.9	31.0	35.7	37.9	44.8
1995-6	39.5	44.6	37.4	46.0	48.0	44.5	45.3	58.9	64.0	62.0	60.6	47.2
1996-7	51.3	50.9	59.0	46.1	38.8	41.8	49.2	48.1	53.9	50.5	44.5	45.6
1997-8	39.9	35.2	40.3	33.3	38.6	40.3	46.9	60.8	55.8	63.1	54.6	49.4
1998-9	49.6	45.3	38.5	55.4	35.7	44.5	53.2	68.2	54.6	68.2	65.3	76.2
1999-00[1]	68.7	65.5	68.9	74.0	92.4	69.6	72.0					

[1] Preliminary. *Source: Bureau of the Census, U.S. Department of Commerce*

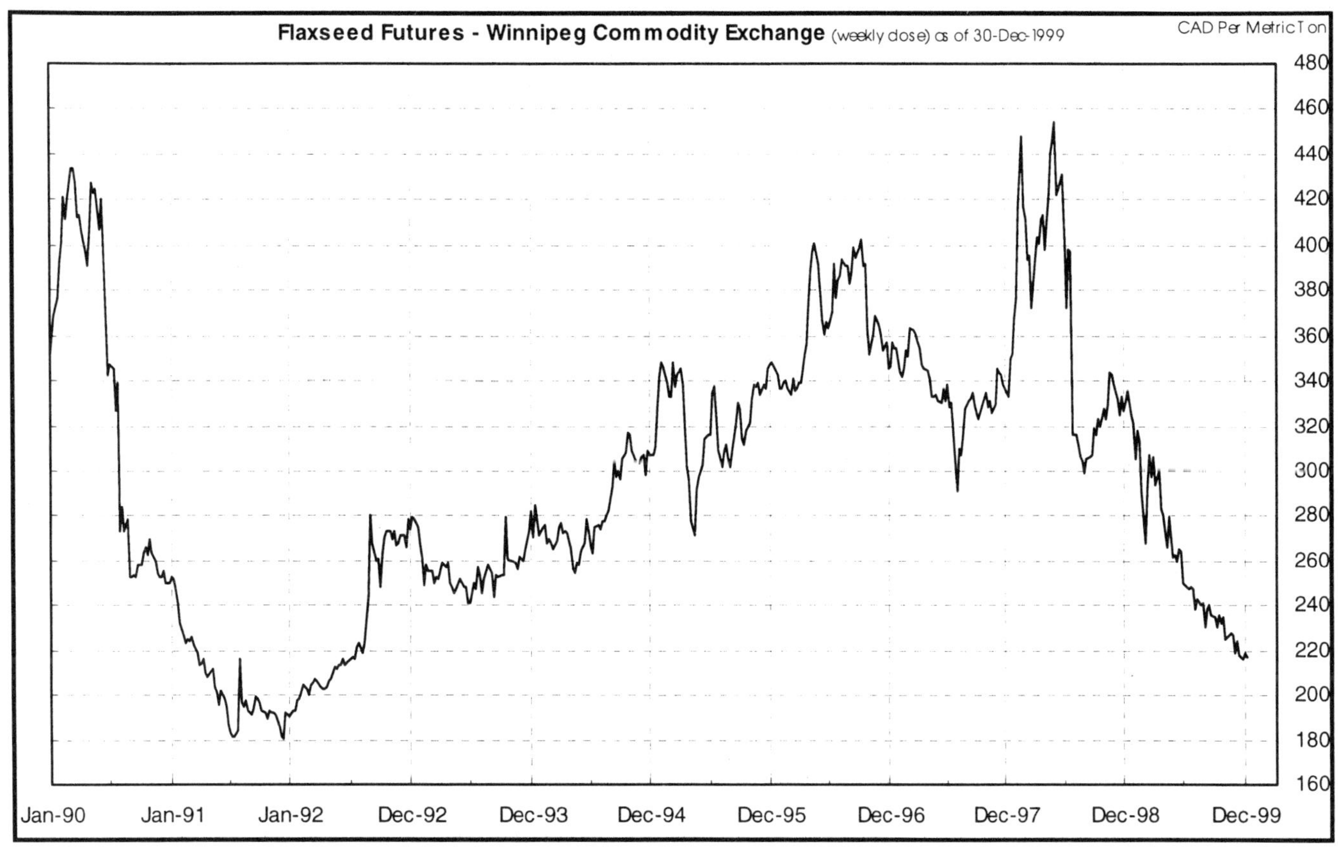

Wholesale Price of Raw Linseed Oil at Minneapolis in Tank Cars In Cents Per Pound

Year	July	Aug.	Sept.	Oct.	Nov.	Dec.	Jan.	Feb.	Mar.	Apr.	May	June	Average
1990-1	44.00	40.40	39.75	36.80	36.00	36.00	36.00	36.00	36.00	36.00	36.50	36.00	37.45
1991-2	36.00	36.00	36.00	30.00	30.00	30.00	30.00	30.00	30.00	30.00	30.00	30.00	31.50
1992-3	30.00	30.00	32.00	32.00	32.00	32.00	32.00	32.00	32.00	32.00	32.00	28.50	31.38
1993-4	32.00	32.00	32.00	32.00	32.00	32.00	32.00	32.00	32.00	32.00	32.00	32.00	32.00
1994-5	30.31	32.00	32.00	33.50	35.00	35.00	35.00	35.00	35.00	35.00	35.00	35.00	33.98
1995-6	35.00	35.50	37.00	37.00	37.00	37.00	37.00	37.00	37.00	37.00	37.00	37.00	36.71
1996-7	37.00	37.20	37.50	37.00	33.75	32.12	36.00	36.00	36.00	36.00	36.00	36.00	35.88
1997-8	36.00	36.00	36.00	37.00	37.00	37.00	36.00	36.00	36.00	36.00	37.00	37.00	36.42
1998-9	37.00	37.00	37.00	37.00	37.00	37.00	36.00	36.00	36.00	36.00	36.00	36.00	36.50
1999-00[1]	36.00	36.00	36.00										36.00

[1] Preliminary. *Source: Economic Research Service, U.S. Department of Agriculture (ERS-USDA)*

Average Open Interest of Flaxseed Futures in Winnipeg In Contracts

Year	Jan.	Feb.	Mar.	Apr.	May	June	July	Aug.	Sept.	Oct.	Nov.	Dec.
1990	3,812	5,165	5,701	5,790	4,839	4,985	4,950	4,908	4,651	4,477	5,079	4,502
1991	4,033	4,140	4,175	4,861	4,137	4,642	5,317	6,106	6,173	5,733	5,669	5,333
1992	5,620	6,772	7,864	7,984	7,786	7,321	6,299	6,553	5,623	4,860	6,734	5,979
1993	7,810	8,052	6,203	5,672	5,505	5,321	4,246	5,777	5,923	3,568	3,763	3,922
1994	6,118	6,201	5,946	5,519	4,683	3,945	4,301	4,654	4,997	3,077	4,888	5,251
1995	6,242	8,731	7,505	7,121	8,107	7,212	6,436	5,557	6,230	5,245	5,937	4,414
1996	6,059	6,056	4,402	5,192	6,970	4,435	3,102	2,989	3,257	3,438	4,326	5,119
1997	5,420	5,356	5,591	5,151	4,923	4,075	3,891	4,031	7,131	8,284	7,255	7,955
1998	10,059	10,190	9,707	8,540	6,480	6,874	6,030	6,767	7,421	7,221	7,564	5,828
1999	4,372	4,552	4,533	4,238	3,719	2,456	2,145	2,758	3,725	4,210	4,492	4,279

Source: Winnipeg Commodity Exchange (WCE)

Fruits

The U.S.D.A. forecast 1999 U.S. apple production at 10.6 billion pounds, down 7 percent from 1998. A decline in apple production in the Western States will not be offset by increased production in the Eastern and Central States. Washington state is by far the largest producer of fresh and processed apples. Apple orchards in Washington bloomed variably and there was a relatively cool spring. Some frost damage and a reduction in acreage reduced the size of the crop. The Central States are forecast to have 1999 production of 1.48 billion pounds, up 12 percent from 1998. Michigan is the largest producer with an expected crop of 1.05 billion pounds, up 8 percent from 1998. Production in the Eastern States for 1999 was forecast at 2.75 billion pounds, up 18 percent from last year.

U.S. pear production for 1999 is forecast at 1.9 billion pounds, 1 percent below 1998. Bartlett pear production was forecast at 1.03 billion pounds, up 6 percent from 1998. The major producer of Bartlett pears is California with 1999 production of 570 million pounds, 3 percent above 1998. Washington state production of Bartlett pears in 1999 was 330 million pounds, an increase of 14 percent from the previous year. Oregon production was forecast at 132 million pounds. Production of other-than-Bartlett pears in 1999 was forecast at 854 million pounds, down 9 percent from 1998.

The U.S. peach crop in 1999 was forecast at 2.5 billion pounds, an increase of 3 percent from 1998. California is by far the largest producer of peaches. California Clingstone peach production in 1999 was forecast at 1.1 billion pounds, a 5 percent increase from last season. The Clingstone crop is used mostly for canning. Californian Freestone peach production was forecast to decline 3 percent to 690 million pounds. The next largest peach producer is South Carolina with a forecast crop of 160 million pounds, 14 percent more than in 1998.

Commercial strawberry production in the six largest producing states, California, Florida, Oregon, Washington, Michigan and New Jersey, was forecast to increase 5 percent to 1.73 billion pounds. California, the largest producer, had increased acreage and higher yields. The crop was forecast at 1.48 billion pounds, up 6 percent from 1998. The Florida crop was forecast at 179.8 million pounds, an increase of 12 percent from 1998. Production in the other major producing states declined 14 percent.

U.S. production of apricots in 1999 was forecast at 260 million pounds, an increase of 10 percent from the previous year. California produces virtually all of the nation's apricots with the 1999 crop forecast at 250 million pounds.

Commerical Production for Selected Fruits in the United States — In Thousands of Short Tons

Year	Apples	Cherries[2]	Cranberries	Grapes	Grapefruit	Lemons	Nectarines	Oranges	Peaches	Pears	Pineapples	Prunes & Plums	Strawberries	Tangelos	Tangerines	Total All Fruits
1993	5,342	339	196	6,023	2,791	942	205	10,992	1,330	948	370	588	724	137	247	31,741
1994	5,750	359	234	5,874	2,661	984	242	10,329	1,257	1,046	365	879	825	150	318	31,869
1995	5,293	363	210	5,922	2,912	897	176	11,432	1,151	948	345	744	804	142	287	32,140
1996	5,191	290	234	5,554	2,718	992	247	11,426	1,052	821	347	952	813	110	349	30,904
1997	5,162	373	275	7,291	2,885	962	264	12,692	1,312	1,043	324	899	814	178	425	35,480
1998[1]	5,694	384	269	5,903	2,593	897	230	13,670	1,215	955	332	542	844	128	360	34,539

[1] Preliminary. [2] Sweet and tart. [3] Utilized production. *Source: Economic Research Service, U.S. Department of Agriculture (ERS-USDA)*

Utilized Production for Selected Fruits in the United States — In Thousands of Short Tons

	Utilized Production (In Thousands of Short Tons)			Value of Production (In Thousands of Dollars)		
Year	Citrus[1]	Noncitrus[2]	Total	Citrus[1]	Noncitrus[2]	Total
1993	15,274	16,563	31,837	2,151,173	6,135,411	8,286,584
1994	14,561	17,341	31,902	2,268,330	6,269,879	8,542,929
1995	15,799	16,358	32,178	2,328,915	6,818,439	9,144,877
1996	15,712	16,103	31,815	2,517,394	7,265,788	9,783,182
1997	17,271	18,382	35,653	2,582,767	8,136,431	10,719,198
1998[3]	17,770	16,484	34,254	2,600,066	7,237,709	9,837,775

[1] Year harvest was completed. [2] Includes bushberries (beginning 1992), cranberries and strawberries. [3] Preliminary.
Source: Economic Research Service, U.S. Department of Agriculture (ERS-USDA)

Annual Average Retail Prices for Selected Fruits in the United States — In Dollars Per Pound

							Oranges	
Year	Red Delicious Apples	Bananas	Anjou Pears	Thompson Seedless Grapes	Lemons	Grapefruit	Navel	Valencias
1993	.834	.439	.846	1.465	1.084	.529	.557	.654
1994	.803	.462	.802	1.642	1.090	.513	.545	.587
1995	.835	.490	.774	1.551	1.136	.548	.625	.648
1996	.930	.490	.916	1.685	1.114	.574	.707	.703
1997	.907	.487	.985	1.712	1.154	.520	.592	.682
1998[1]	.943	.494	1.089	1.589	1.198	.599	.565	.657

[1] Estimate. *Source: Economic Research Service, U.S. Department of Agriculture (ERS-USDA)*

Utilization of Noncitrus Fruit Production, and Value in the U.S. 1,000 Short Tons (Fresh Equivalent)

Year	Utilized Production	Fresh	Canned	Dried	Juice	Frozen	Wine	Other	Value of utilized Production $1,000
			Processed						
1989	16,345	6,104	2,266	2,857	1,580	479	2,869	190	5,279,382
1990	15,640	6,093	2,244	2,440	1,448	506	2,717	192	5,525,279
1991	15,740	6,215	2,119	2,417	1,583	501	2,739	167	6,021,210
1992	17,124	6,317	2,386	2,369	1,743	584	3,256	261	6,036,615
1993	16,554	6,391	2,042	2,339	1,749	627	3,029	181	6,130,119
1994	17,339	6,710	2,090	2,816	1,886	665	2,711	228	6,268,176
1995	16,348	6,285	1,753	2,400	1,857	647	2,992	205	6,815,962
1996	16,103	6,313	1,873	2,275	1,582	604	3,043	180	7,265,788
1997	18,363	6,643	2,130	2,660	1,675	699	4,035	247	8,136,431
1998[1]	16,484	6,503	1,836	1,984	1,607	766	3,315	204	7,237,708

[1] Preliminary. *Source: Economic Research Service, U.S. Department of Agriculture (ERS-USDA)*

Average Price Indexes for Fruits in the United States

Year	Index of all Fruit and Nut Prices Received by Growers (1990-92=100)	Producer Price Index: Fresh Fruit	Producer Price Index: Dried Fruit	Producer Price Index: Canned Fruits and Juices	Producer Price Index: Frozen Fruits and Juices	Consumer Price Index: Fresh Fruit	Consumer Price Index: Processed Fruit
		1982 = 100				1982-84 = 100	
1989	99	113.2	103.1	122.6	124.5	152.4	125.9
1990	97	118.1	107.0	126.9	138.9	170.9	136.6
1991	112	129.9	111.5	128.6	115.1	193.9	131.8
1992	99	84.0	114.3	134.6	125.7	184.2	137.7
1993	93	84.5	117.6	126.1	110.9	188.8	132.3
1994	90	82.7	120.9	126.0	111.9	201.2	133.1
1995	99	85.8	121.0	129.4	115.8	219.0	137.2
1996	118	100.8	124.2	137.5	123.9	234.4	145.2
1997	108	101.3	124.9	137.5	117.3	236.3	148.8
1998[1]	110	90.5	124.4	138.6	-----	246.5	101.9

[1] Estimate. *Source: Economic Research Service, U.S. Department of Agriculture (ERS-USDA)*

Fresh Fruit: Per Capita Consumption[1] in the United States In Pounds

Year	Oranges	Tangerines and Tangelos	Lemons	Grapefruit	Total	Apples	Apricots	Avacados	Bananas	Cherries	Cranberries
	Citrus Fruit					Noncitrus Fruit					
1989	12.17	1.71	2.39	6.60	23.56	21.22	.10	1.54	24.71	.62	.07
1990	12.38	1.31	2.60	4.43	21.37	19.60	.16	1.07	24.36	.39	.05
1991	8.46	1.38	2.60	5.87	19.07	18.18	.13	1.41	25.12	.40	.07
1992	12.91	1.94	2.54	5.95	24.36	19.25	.15	1.43	27.26	.53	.08
1993	14.24	1.87	2.65	6.23	25.97	19.17	.13	2.17	26.80	.43	.07
1994	13.06	2.11	2.68	6.12	24.96	19.58	.15	1.34	28.06	.53	.08
1995	11.97	2.01	2.87	6.07	24.12	18.94	.10	1.37	27.42	.29	.08
1996	12.77	2.19	2.90	5.93	24.95	18.97	.09	1.60	28.02	.41	.08
1997	14.16	2.57	2.80	6.28	26.98	18.42	.15	1.61	27.64	.61	.08
1998[2]	14.90	2.21	2.51	6.05	27.10	19.19	.12	1.76	28.57	.58	.07

[1] All data on calendar-year basis except for citrus fruits; apples, August; grapes and pears, July; grapefruit, September; lemons, August of prior year; all other citrus, November. [2] Preliminary. *Source: Economic Research Service, U.S. Department of Agriculture (ERS-USDA)*

Fresh Fruit: Per Capita Consumption[1] in the United States In Pounds

Year	Grapes	Kiwifruit	Mangos	Nectarines & Peaches	Pears	Pineapples	Papaya	Plums & Prunes	Strawberries	Total Noncitrus	Total Fruit
	Noncitrus Fruit Continued										
1990	7.92	.49	.54	5.54	3.22	2.05	.18	1.55	3.24	70.35	91.72
1991	7.27	.45	.85	6.43	3.15	1.92	.17	1.42	3.58	70.55	89.62
1992	7.19	.39	.68	6.03	3.14	2.00	.24	1.78	3.61	73.75	98.11
1993	7.05	.60	.90	5.89	3.38	2.05	.28	1.28	3.64	73.84	99.81
1994	7.32	.57	.98	5.47	3.48	2.04	.30	1.62	4.09	75.62	100.59
1995	7.52	.56	1.13	5.39	3.40	1.93	.37	.94	4.16	73.59	97.72
1996	6.93	.55	1.36	4.44	3.10	1.92	.55	1.45	4.38	73.85	98.80
1997	8.04	.49	1.46	5.61	3.45	2.38	.48	1.54	4.17	76.13	103.11
1998[2]	7.29	.56	1.52	4.84	3.36	2.81	.48	1.20	4.11	76.46	103.56

[1] All data on calendar-year basis except for citrus fruits; apples, August; grapes and pears, July; grapefruit, September; lemons, August of prior year; all other citrus, November. [2] Preliminary. *Source: Economic Research Service, U.S. Department of Agriculture (ERS-USDA)*

Gas

Energy prices increased substantially in 1999 as the nations participating on the Organization of Oil Exporting Countries (OPEC) agreed to production cuts. As those production cuts moved closer to targeted values, prices for all energy products increased.

The U.S. Energy Information Agency reported that in September 1999 dry natural gas production in the U.S. was 1.55 trillion cubic feet. That was down 3 percent from the previous month but about the same as a year ago. In the January-September 1999 period, dry natural gas production was 14 trillion cubic feet, down 1 percent from the same period in 1998. For all of 1998, dry natural gas production was 18.9 trillion cubic feet. Net imports of dry natural gas in September 1999 were 281 billion cubic feet, down 2 percent from the previous month but 12 percent more than a year earlier. In the January-September 1999 period, net imports were 2.47 trillion cubic feet, up 11 percent from a year earlier. For all of 1998, net imports were 2.99 trillion cubic feet. U.S. consumption of dry natural gas in September 1999 was 1.45 trillion cubic feet, down 7 percent from August 1999 and 2 percent less than a year earlier. For the first nine months of 1999, dry natural gas consumption was 16.1 trillion cubic feet while for all of 1998 it was 21.3 trillion cubic feet.

Gross withdrawals of natural gas in July 1999 were 2 billion cubic feet, up 1 percent from the previous month and 1 percent less than the year before. For all of 1998, gross withdrawals of natural gas were 24.3 trillion cubic feet. Natural gas repressuring in July 1999 was 286 billion cubic feet, down 1 percent from the previous month and down 3 percent from the year before. For all of 1998, natural gas repressuring was 3.68 trillion cubic feet.

Nonhydrocarbon gases removed in July 1999 were 44 billion cubic feet, down 2 percent from the year before. For all of 1998, nonhydrocarbon gases removed totaled 531 billion cubic feet. Vented and flared natural gas in July 1999 totaled 22 billion cubic feet, down 4 percent from the previous year. For all of 1998, vented and flared natural gas was 261 billion cubic feet.

Marketed production of natural gas in September 1999 was 1.63 trillion cubic feet, down 3 percent from the previous month. In the first nine months of 1999, marketed production of natural gas was 14.69 trillion cubic feet, down 1 percent from the same period in 1998. For all of 1998, marketed production was 19.82 trillion cubic feet.

U.S. imports of natural gas in July 1999 were 288 billion cubic feet. In the January-July 1999 period, imports were 2 trillion cubic feet while for all of 1998 they were 3.15 trillion cubic feet. The largest supplier of natural gas to the U.S. is Canada.

Futures Markets

Natural gas futures and options are traded on the New York Mercantile Exchange (NYMEX) and the Kansas City Board of Trade (KCBT). Futures are traded on the International Petroleum Exchange (IPE).

World Production of Natural Gas (Monthly Average Marketed Production[3]) (In Terajoule[4])

Year	Australia	Canada	China	Germany	Indonesia	India	Italy	Mexico	Netherlands	Romania	Rissia[5]	United Knigdom	Uinted States
1990	66,445	342,826	49,380	44,162	195,448	36,795	54,389	79,594	211,717	79,931	2,311,092	158,628	1,614,310
1991	62,194	362,029	49,955	52,460	158,214	43,284	53,037	79,009	239,349	68,977	2,286,626	176,344	1,609,083
1992	67,696	397,229	50,052	51,911	165,761	43,297	57,117	95,688	240,043	61,470	1,743,167	176,661	1,614,941
1993	72,848	437,922	52,297	47,904	171,828	44,475	60,792	93,646	244,205	58,499	1,708,083	196,792	1,667,401
1994	87,356	438,335	55,230	50,535	190,775	47,219	64,142	97,285	207,317	52,697	1,525,232	203,875	1,700,081
1995	78,460	607,608	55,872	55,451	203,633	53,422	64,467	100,488	209,229	51,375	1,891,583	213,987	1,683,692
1996	90,912	625,469	63,792	60,310	248,574	59,452	63,864	112,850	236,803	49,264	1,846,065	360,395	1,727,420
1997	93,006	521,791	78,195	59,984	291,502	61,246	62,852	170,284	201,193	42,852	1,608,012	270,136	1,711,216
1998[1]	87,257	538,236	72,074	59,072	275,065	64,262	59,514	182,615	198,554	32,932	1,665,726	334,060	1,709,949
1999[2]	91,972	546,742	77,287	64,518	280,373	61,241	NA	183,929	219,900	36,329	1,756,529	NA	1,689,994

[1] Preliminary. [2] Estimate. [3] Compares all gas collected & utilized as fuel or as a chemical industry raw material, including gas used in oilfields and/or gasfields as a fuel by producers. [4] Terajoule = 10 to the 12th power Joule = approximately 10 to the 9th power BTU. [5] Formerly part os U.S.S.R., data not reported seperately until 1992. NA = Not available. *Source: United Nations*

Marketed Production of Natural Gas in the United States, by States (In Million Cubic Feet)

Year	Alaska	California	Colorado	Kansas	Louisiana	Michigan	MIssissippi	New Mexico	Oklahoma	Texas	Wyoming	Total
1989	393,729	362,860	216,737	601,196	5,078,125	155,988	102,645	854,615	2,237,037	6,241,425	665,699	18,095,147
1990	402,907	362,748	242,997	573,603	5,241,989	172,151	94,616	965,104	2,258,471	6,343,146	735,728	18,593,792
1991	437,822	378,384	285,961	628,459	5,034,361	195,749	108,031	1,038,284	2,153,852	6,280,654	776,528	18,532,439
1992	443,597	365,632	323,041	658,007	4,914,300	194,815	91,697	1,268,863	2,017,356	6,145,862	842,576	18,711,808
1993	430,350	315,851	400,985	686,347	4,991,138	204,635	80,695	1,409,429	2,049,942	6,249,624	634,957	18,981,915
1994	555,402	309,427	453,207	712,730	5,169,705	222,657	63,448	1,557,689	1,934,864	6,353,844	696,018	19,709,525
1995	469,550	279,555	523,084	721,436	5,108,366	238,203	95,533	1,625,837	1,811,734	6,330,048	673,775	19,506,474
1996	480,828	286,494	572,071	712,796	5,240,747	245,740	103,263	1,554,087	1,734,887	6,449,022	666,036	19,750,793
1997	468,311	285,690	637,375	687,215	5,229,821	305,950	107,300	1,558,633	1,703,888	6,453,873	738,368	19,866,093
1998[1]	467,688	314,240	668,014	573,520	5,473,067	298,560	108,069	1,669,951	1,654,824	6,355,996	754,206	19,823,742

[1] Preliminary. *Source: Energy Information Administration, U.S. Department of Energy (EIA-DOE)*

World Production of Natural Gas Plant Liquids (Thousand Barrels per Day)

Year		Algeria	Canada	Mexico	Saudi Arabia	Former USSR	United States	Persian Gulf[2]	OAPEC[3]	OPEC[4]	World
1990	Average	130	426	428	620	425	1,559	930	1,107	1,281	4,632
1991	Average	140	431	457	680	420	1,659	931	1,113	1,299	4,827
1992	Average	140	460	454	713	230	1,697	1,003	1,185	1,364	4,974
1993	Average	145	506	459	704	220	1,736	1,040	1,238	1,435	5,180
1994	Average	140	529	461	698	200	1,727	1,071	1,267	1,465	5,292
1995	Average	145	581	447	701	180	1,762	1,106	1,301	1,506	5,485
1996	Average	150	596	423	697	185	1,830	1,082	1,295	1,501	5,580
1997	Average	160	636	388	712	195	1,817	1,158	1,390	1,614	5,750
1998	Average	155	651	424	711	230	1,759	1,161	1,395	1,608	5,783
1999[1]	Average	155	646	442	666	206	1,805	1,116	1,350	1,563	5,723

[1] Preliminary. [2] Bahrain, Iran, Iraq, Kuwait, Qatar, Saudi Arabia and the United Arab Emirates. [3] Organization of Arab Petroleum Exporting Countries. [4] Organization of Pertroleum Exporting Countries. [5] Through 1991; Former USSR. *Source: Energy Information Administration, U.S. Department of Energy (EIA-DOE)*

Recoverable Reserves and Deliveries of Natural Gas in the United States (in Billions of Cubic Feet)

		Recoverable	Deliveries						Consumption		Heating
Year	Gross Withdrawals	Reserves of Natural Gas Dec. 31[2]	Residential	Commercial	Electric Utility Plants[3]	Industrial	Total Deliveries	Lease & Plant Fuel	Used as Pipeline Fuel	Value BTU per Cubic Foot
1989	21,074	167,116	4,781	2,718	2,787	6,816	17,102	1,070	629	1,031
1990	21,523	169,346	4,391	2,623	2,786	7,018	16,819	1,236	660	1,031
1991	21,750	167,062	4,556	2,729	2,789	7,231	17,305	1,129	601	1,030
1992	22,132	165,015	4,690	2,803	2,766	7,527	17,786	1,171	588	1,030
1993	22,726	162,415	4,956	2,863	2,682	7,981	18,483	1,172	624	1,027
1994	23,581	163,837	4,848	2,895	2,987	8,167	18,899	1,124	685	1,028
1995	23,744	165,146	4,850	3,031	3,197	8,580	19,660	1,220	700	1,027
1996	24,114	166,474	5,241	3,158	2,732	8,870	20,006	1,250	711	1,027
1997	24,213	167,223	4,984	3,215	2,968	8,832	20,004	1,203	751	1,026
1998[1]	23,924	NA	4,520	2,999	3,258	8,686	19,469	1,157	635	1,031

[1] Preliminary. [2] Estimated proved recoverable reserves of dry natural gas. [3] Figures include gas other than natural (impossible to segregate); therefore, shown separately from other consumption. *Source: Energy Information Administration, U.S. Department of Energy (EIA-DOE)*

Gas Utility Sales in the United States by Types and Class of Service (In Trillions of BTUs)

	Total	Number of	Class by Service					Revenue - Million $ From Sales to Customers					
Year	Utility Sales	Customers (Millions)	Residential	Commercial	Industrial	Electric Generation	Other	Total	Residential	Commercial	industrial	Electric Generation	Other
1990	9,842	54.3	4,468	2,192	1,890	1,120	171	45,153	25,000	10,604	6,034	2,962	553
1991	9,601	55.2	4,546	2,198	1,743	888	226	44,647	25,729	10,669	5,326	2,250	674
1992	9,907	56.1	4,694	2,209	1,959	813	231	46,178	26,702	10,865	5,837	2,077	698
1993	10,151	57.0	5,054	2,397	2,009	524	168	50,137	29,787	12,076	6,162	1,480	632
1994	9,248	57.9	4,845	2,253	1,690	420	159	49,852	30,552	12,276	5,529	1,170	597
1995	9,221	58.7	4,803	2,281	1,591	328	218	46,436	28,742	11,573	4,816	836	549
1996	9,532	59.8	5,198	2,395	1,519	271	148	51,115	32,021	12,726	5,039	783	545
1997[1]	8,880	59.8	5,013	2,234	1,279	245	123	51,531	33,175	12,632	4,518	766	488
1998[2]	8,341	60.4	4,693	2,043	1,153	336	116	46,924	30,671	11,189	3,779	899	387

[1] Preliminary. [2] Estimate. *Source: American Gas Association (AGA)*

Salient Statistics of Natural Gas in the United States

	Supply						Disposition				Average Price Delivered to Consumers						
Year	Marketed Production	Extraction Loss	Dry Production	Storage Withdrawals	Imports (Consumed)	Total Supply	Consumption	Exports	Added to Storage	Total Disposition	Wellhead Price	Imports	Exports	Residential	Commercial	Industrial	Electric Utilities
	In Billions of Cubic Feet										USD Per Thousand Cubic Feet						
1989	18,095	785	17,311	2,804	1,382	21,435	18,801	107	2,491	21,074	1.69	1.82	2.51	5.64	4.74	2.96	2.43
1990	18,594	784	17,810	1,934	1,532	21,302	18,716	86	2,433	21,523	1.71	1.94	3.10	5.80	4.83	2.93	2.38
1991	18,532	835	17,698	2,689	1,773	21,836	19,035	129	2,608	21,750	1.64	1.82	2.59	5.82	4.81	2.69	2.18
1992	18,712	872	17,840	2,724	2,138	22,360	19,544	216	2,555	22,132	1.74	1.85	2.25	5.89	4.88	2.84	2.36
1993	18,982	886	18,095	2,717	2,350	23,578	20,279	140	2,760	23,578	2.04	2.03	2.59	6.16	5.22	3.07	2.61
1994	19,710	889	18,821	2,508	2,624	24,207	20,708	162	2,796	24,207	1.85	1.87	2.50	6.41	5.44	3.05	2.28
1995	19,506	908	18,599	2,974	2,841	24,837	21,581	154	2,566	24,837	1.55	1.49	2.39	6.06	5.05	2.71	2.02
1996	19,751	958	18,854	2,911	2,937	25,635	21,967	153	2,906	25,635	2.17	1.97	2.97	6.34	5.40	3.42	2.69
1997[1]	19,866	964	18,902	2,824	2,994	25,502	21,959	157	2,800	25,502	2.32	2.17	3.02	6.94	5.80	3.59	2.78
1998[2]	19,824	938	18,708	2,377	3,152	24,842	21,262	159	2,904	24,842	1.94	1.97	2.45	6.82	5.48	3.14	2.40

[1] Preliminary. [2] Estimate. *Source: Energy Information Administration, U.S. Department of Energy (EIA-DOE)*

Average Open Interest of Natural Gas Futures in New York In Contracts

Year	Jan.	Feb.	Mar.	Apr.	May	June	July	Aug.	Sept.	Oct.	Nov.	Dec.
1990	-----	-----	-----	1,320	2,699	4,268	6,130	8,760	11,077	12,998	13,813	10,814
1991	10,523	13,825	13,125	13,225	16,782	18,502	19,235	21,460	23,853	24,003	21,692	19,065
1992	24,718	28,661	29,851	33,626	41,456	49,642	49,829	57,346	68,306	77,034	80,349	74,569
1993	69,499	77,053	91,132	116,366	136,074	132,667	124,038	126,443	129,940	130,619	124,627	129,963
1994	127,254	128,336	118,480	119,908	120,894	120,956	111,044	135,652	156,238	145,766	139,471	139,054
1995	148,448	151,882	157,097	150,101	148,797	144,402	143,942	140,297	135,226	133,969	140,301	166,227
1996	155,024	150,521	149,809	159,132	147,616	156,959	151,913	135,191	138,657	144,944	147,854	151,498
1997	156,231	162,567	171,467	181,745	206,685	197,637	199,296	213,640	235,509	242,184	231,556	210,259
1998	192,652	198,853	203,402	251,344	255,837	264,517	255,878	273,350	275,868	252,827	236,292	240,832
1999	244,472	268,649	284,312	315,336	332,398	330,725	315,617	353,766	336,621	316,156	309,130	292,160

Source: New York Mercantile Exchange (NYMEX)

Volume of Trading of Natural Gas Futures in New York (In Thousands of Contracts)

Year	Jan.	Feb.	Mar.	Apr.	May	June	July	Aug.	Sept.	Oct.	Nov.	Dec.	Total
1990	-----	-----	-----	4.1	6.4	10.5	14.3	17.3	15.2	25.3	15.9	22.3	131.4
1991	29.2	14.9	22.8	20.3	28.7	51.2	37.0	33.1	42.3	46.6	49.0	50.2	425.3
1992	89.0	45.4	77.9	98.9	137.5	116.4	156.0	192.2	268.7	300.0	213.5	227.6	1,923.2
1993	194.3	274.4	318.8	443.0	471.5	365.9	335.6	353.3	459.6	417.1	449.7	613.9	4,697.1
1994	667.6	470.9	373.5	344.7	411.1	465.8	438.8	724.2	578.7	594.2	621.9	721.8	6,413.2
1995	733.0	557.8	676.1	524.5	621.3	622.5	641.8	745.6	548.3	664.4	763.0	988.5	8,086.7
1996	887.2	655.7	694.6	620.0	590.7	681.3	829.0	628.8	679.1	924.4	802.8	820.4	8,813.9
1997	922.8	693.6	664.7	836.3	945.4	803.7	812.9	1,313.8	1,377.1	1,394.0	1,104.8	1,054.6	11,923.6
1998	1,005.6	1,089.1	1,193.5	1,625.9	1,245.2	1,568.8	1,310.4	1,237.0	1,656.3	1,339.5	1,243.1	1,464.0	15,978.3
1999	1,296.7	1,158.6	1,788.5	1,655.8	1,465.3	1,474.2	1,865.8	1,892.1	1,978.6	1,676.5	1,552.3	1,360.7	19,165.1

Source: New York Mercantile Exchange (NYMEX)

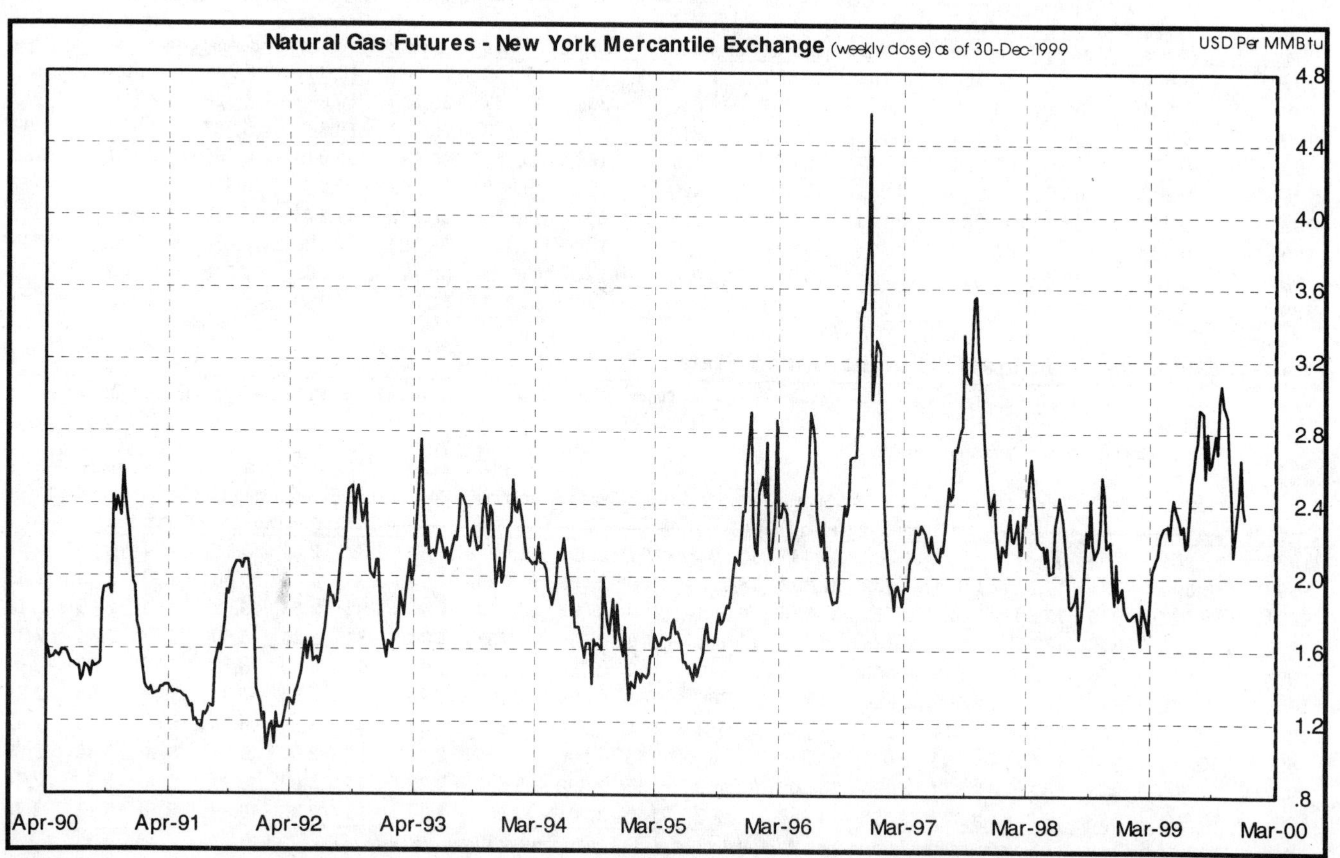

Gasoline

Unleaded gasoline prices moved sharply higher in 1999 as the Organization of Oil Exporting Countries (OPEC) agreed to and then adhered to production cuts. Smaller supplies of petroleum will in time mean that there will be smaller supplies of finished motor gasoline. Additionally, the continued strength of the U.S. economy implied that demand for energy products was more likely to increase.

Production of gasoline follows a seasonal pattern. Going into the peak driving season of June-September, petroleum refineries increase production of gasoline to build inventories. At the end of the summer driving season, refineries switch to the production of heating oil for the winter heating season. Another feature of the energy market is that the U.S. is becoming more and more dependent on imports of various energy products to meet growing demand. This, in turn, makes the U.S. subject to changes in export policies by the countries that export energy products.

U.S. production of finished motor gasoline in August 1999 was 8.3 million barrels per day. That represented a decline of almost 2 percent from the previous month. In August 1998, gasoline production was 8.2 million barrels per day. Over the January-August 1999 period, production of finished motor gasoline averaged 8 million barrels per day. This was slightly below the average of the same period in 1998, but 3 percent more than in 1997. For all of 1998, gasoline production averaged 8.1 million barrels per day. In 1990, production averaged 7 million barrels per day while in 1985 it averaged 6.4 million barrels per day.

U.S. imports of finished gasoline in August 1999 averaged 356,000 barrels per day, a decline of 18 percent from the previous month. In August 1998, imports averaged 331,000 barrels per month. In the January-August 1999 period, imports of gasoline averaged 380,000 barrels per day, an increase of 23 percent from the same period of 1998 and some 15 percent more that in the same period of 1997. For all of 1998, imports averaged 311,000 barrels per day. In 1990, imports averaged 342,000 barrels per day while in 1985 they averaged 381,000 barrels.

U.S. exports of motor gasoline in August 1999 averaged 120,000 barrels per day, an increase of 35 percent from the previous month. In August 1998, exports averaged 141,000 barrels per day. In the January-August 1999 period, exports averaged 98,000 barrels per day, down 20 percent from the same period in 1998 and 19 percent less than the like period in 1997. For all of 1998, exports averaged 125,000 barrels per day. In 1990, exports of gasoline averaged 55,000 barrels per day while in 1985 they averaged 10,000 barrels.

Ending stocks of finished gasoline at the end of August 1999 were 157 million barrels, down 4 percent from the previous month. In August 1998, ending stocks were 167 million barrels. Ending stocks of gasoline, along with blending components, at the end of August 1999 were 199 million barrels, down 2 percent from the previous month. Ending stocks of oxygenates at the end of July 1999 were 13 million barrels.

Futures markets

Unleaded gasoline futures and options are traded on the New York Mercantile Exchange (NYMEX).

Average Spot Price of Unleaded Gasoline in New York In Cents Per Gallon

Year	Jan.	Feb.	Mar.	Apr.	May	June	July	Aug.	Sept.	Oct.	Nov.	Dec.	Average
1990	64.20	59.59	56.15	61.86	64.24	64.55	65.25	89.61	99.85	95.68	88.10	68.07	73.10
1991	68.88	65.82	74.25	72.07	70.28	63.59	65.23	69.90	62.17	64.41	65.10	55.55	66.44
1992	53.04	55.14	54.10	59.75	63.48	64.51	59.94	62.06	61.63	60.81	58.22	53.24	58.83
1993	52.96	52.54	54.33	59.35	59.37	54.78	51.80	53.13	48.61	50.22	44.30	37.68	51.59
1994	42.40	43.75	44.04	48.98	50.62	52.84	54.52	55.61	46.53	51.14	52.32	46.87	49.14
1995	50.99	51.43	50.74	61.01	64.76	59.47	51.45	53.45	56.10	48.89	51.15	53.44	54.41
1996	50.70	53.26	58.56	69.17	65.10	58.03	61.65	61.17	62.43	65.52	69.23	68.58	61.95
1997	67.64	62.49	61.28	58.59	62.08	55.17	58.58	70.42	62.17	58.35	55.60	51.75	60.34
1998	47.85	45.14	44.13	46.98	48.26	43.95	42.29	40.14	42.70	43.71	36.78	30.92	42.74
1999	34.24	31.81	42.33	50.11	48.86	48.65	58.35	63.89	69.37	62.63	69.57	70.55	54.20

Source: *The Wall Street Journal*

Average Open Interest of Unleaded Regular Gasoline Futures in New York In Contracts

Year	Jan.	Feb.	Mar.	Apr.	May	June	July	Aug.	Sept.	Oct.	Nov.	Dec.
1990	77,580	80,425	75,368	71,132	62,121	72,105	68,826	59,528	60,558	61,253	56,332	56,569
1991	54,807	75,337	81,393	74,801	71,900	73,633	74,503	87,073	90,680	100,606	111,745	125,578
1992	124,896	117,155	108,388	89,775	79,680	80,394	81,110	76,741	71,264	68,059	71,110	77,508
1993	80,610	93,630	100,657	96,607	88,311	94,926	104,260	103,371	100,921	107,339	126,649	150,359
1994	135,366	120,204	118,977	122,092	96,525	89,854	86,401	76,213	67,881	70,258	71,245	63,679
1995	61,015	67,631	65,201	76,323	76,269	69,676	64,379	58,426	62,089	58,782	57,902	70,098
1996	64,561	64,990	70,100	71,895	66,172	52,882	55,394	55,618	57,119	59,993	58,416	62,760
1997	68,188	84,693	92,520	97,619	90,407	78,492	83,082	103,538	103,250	94,602	92,852	103,497
1998	106,353	102,656	108,667	117,521	107,235	100,792	89,846	86,902	85,188	81,991	87,306	103,079
1999	105,532	113,683	111,449	110,531	107,644	102,926	113,619	120,468	120,328	111,758	109,428	96,651

Source: *New York Mercantile Exchange (NYMEX)*

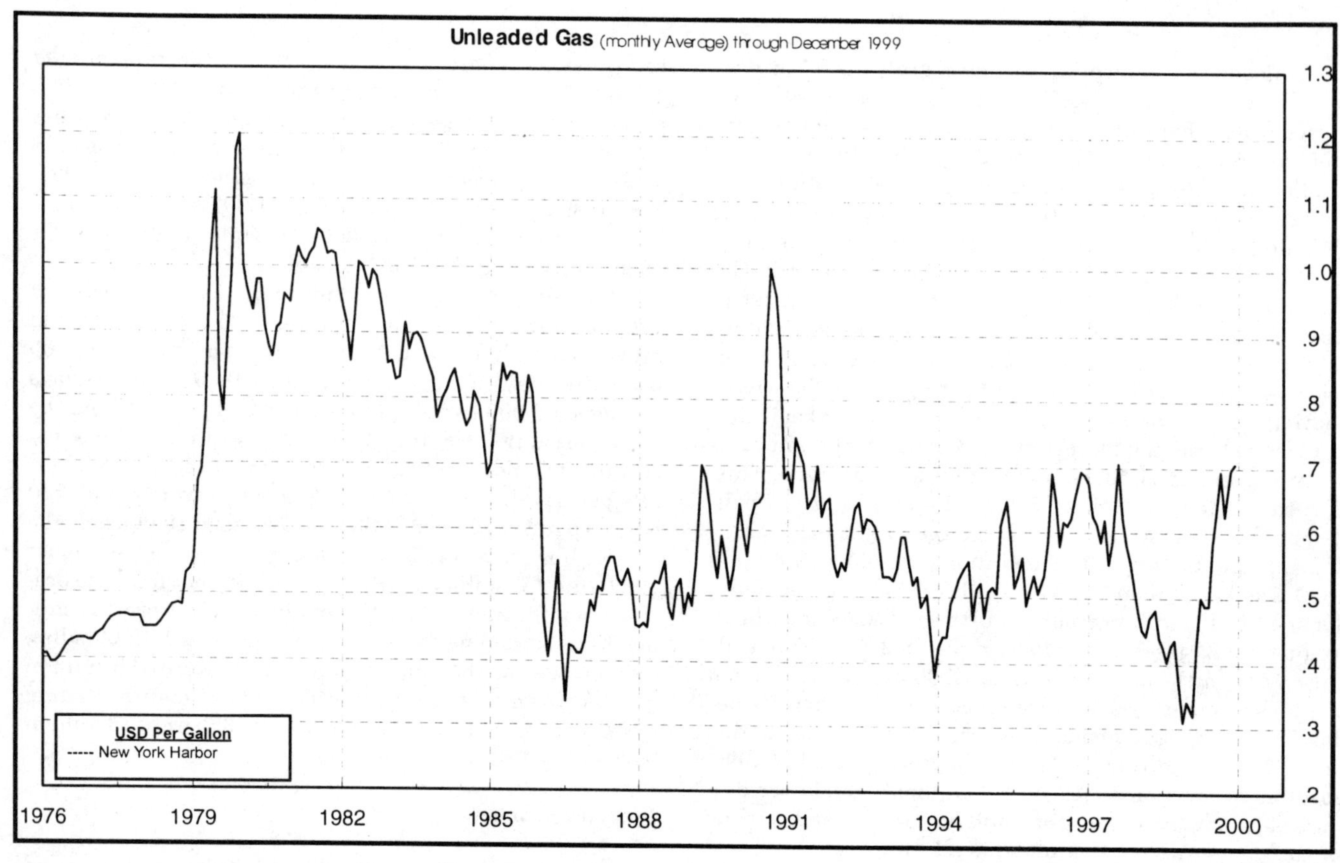

Volume of Trading of Unleaded Regular Gasoline Futures in New York In Contracts

Year	Jan.	Feb.	Mar.	Apr.	May	June	July	Aug.	Sept.	Oct.	Nov.	Dec.	Total
1990	540,633	349,439	461,438	481,665	527,637	472,377	456,342	549,702	373,102	386,472	314,051	248,137	5,160,995
1991	366,772	351,188	525,432	541,073	482,943	446,350	396,429	562,085	386,421	477,111	537,834	529,940	5,603,578
1992	565,922	558,476	604,678	668,490	580,088	620,114	600,897	545,520	469,844	563,856	435,847	461,025	6,674,757
1993	531,780	558,770	584,899	539,785	571,860	611,951	594,740	721,852	642,959	629,733	674,814	729,717	7,392,860
1994	634,027	526,505	615,594	677,891	636,990	673,034	601,980	748,415	569,384	684,670	582,359	519,987	7,470,836
1995	592,329	506,640	736,704	663,743	780,568	680,792	565,655	556,589	573,551	473,014	480,507	461,695	7,071,787
1996	543,818	449,537	570,341	676,193	623,347	467,953	533,793	463,830	469,036	527,553	487,624	499,314	6,312,339
1997	590,066	563,180	605,121	623,169	618,312	555,543	721,386	795,404	664,906	613,557	509,893	614,608	7,475,145
1998	613,643	612,266	766,430	789,293	681,052	753,120	680,551	591,985	654,247	670,159	577,799	601,724	7,992,269
1999	561,493	619,704	876,350	741,511	721,122	737,690	821,991	800,399	751,305	705,144	748,839	615,668	8,701,216

Source: New York Mercantile Exchange (NYMEX)

Production of Finished Motor Gasoline in the United States In Thousand Barrels per Day

Year	Jan.	Feb.	Mar.	Apr.	May	June	July	Aug.	Sept.	Oct.	Nov.	Dec.	Average
1990	6,879	6,989	6,613	6,775	6,610	7,101	7,238	7,326	7,274	6,880	6,940	6,887	6,959
1991	6,629	6,573	6,643	6,742	7,063	7,351	7,274	7,247	7,030	6,749	7,018	7,354	6,975
1992	7,013	6,726	6,683	6,954	7,092	7,198	7,195	6,817	7,071	7,198	7,323	7,411	7,058
1993	7,228	7,144	6,904	7,126	7,446	7,442	7,337	7,335	7,573	7,394	7,652	7,725	7,360
1994	7,097	6,790	6,760	7,195	7,348	7,455	7,380	7,432	7,385	7,151	7,849	7,867	7,312
1995	7,303	7,243	7,168	7,529	7,678	7,843	7,747	7,642	7,785	7,544	7,739	7,821	7,588
1996	7,333	7,303	7,242	7,475	7,724	7,820	7,811	7,696	7,585	7,496	7,835	7,784	7,593
1997	7,308	7,315	7,322	7,822	8,056	8,180	7,947	8,048	8,147	8,039	7,984	8,143	7,862
1998	7,749	7,485	7,591	8,029	8,057	8,372	8,287	8,200	8,029	7,995	8,263	8,395	8,041
1999[1]	7,896	7,608	7,492	8,061	8,129	8,295	8,157	8,198	8,165	8,270	8,142	8,329	8,064

[1] Preliminary. *Source: Energy Information Administration, U.S. Department of Energy (EIA-DOE)*

Disposition of Finished Motor Gasoline, Total Product Supplied in the U.S. In Thousand Barrels per Day

Year	Jan.	Feb.	Mar.	Apr.	May	June	July	Aug.	Sept.	Oct.	Nov.	Dec.	Average
1990	6,643	7,179	7,338	7,121	7,358	7,519	7,496	7,796	6,914	7,226	7,241	6,978	7,235
1991	6,645	6,838	7,017	7,137	7,437	7,456	7,561	7,528	7,083	7,281	7,008	7,224	7,188
1992	6,869	6,963	7,137	7,238	7,328	7,460	7,639	7,380	7,344	7,338	7,102	7,396	7,268
1993	6,639	7,112	7,389	7,435	7,585	7,700	7,785	7,864	7,607	7,382	7,533	7,661	7,476
1994	6,980	7,275	7,395	7,564	7,644	7,922	7,884	7,975	7,615	7,548	7,464	7,924	7,601
1995	7,163	7,481	7,788	7,651	7,894	8,220	7,888	8,187	7,786	7,781	7,866	7,742	7,789
1996	7,254	7,552	7,729	7,869	7,998	8,089	8,135	8,216	7,641	8,038	7,875	7,775	7,849
1997	7,312	7,651	7,808	8,067	8,128	8,260	8,471	8,195	8,004	8,166	7,955	8,093	8,007
1998	7,590	7,755	7,956	8,137	8,070	8,437	8,659	8,500	8,308	8,405	8,136	8,401	8,199
1999[1]	7,630	8,091	8,081	8,389	8,233	8,752	8,783	8,583	8,350	8,528	8,249	8,571	8,354

[1] Preliminary. *Source: Energy Information Administration, U.S. Department of Energy (EIA-DOE)*

Stocks of Finished Gasoline[2] on Hand in the United States, at End of Month In Millions of Barrels

Year	Jan.	Feb.	Mar.	Apr.	May	June	July	Aug.	Sept.	Oct.	Nov.	Dec.
1990	197.6	203.3	187.9	186.3	180.3	177.7	182.0	175.4	190.5	181.9	178.7	182.4
1991	189.1	182.7	174.4	171.9	173.7	178.5	173.5	172.8	179.1	168.3	173.3	183.3
1992	192.8	191.4	182.9	185.0	187.4	189.5	182.0	168.2	170.0	168.7	178.2	179.1
1993	197.8	201.9	189.0	184.0	186.8	184.2	176.8	166.7	171.2	175.6	182.6	187.1
1994	194.1	186.2	175.6	176.4	179.0	176.9	172.9	167.6	169.2	161.7	176.6	175.9
1995	182.7	180.0	167.8	167.1	167.1	163.5	166.0	154.6	158.9	155.6	155.6	161.3
1996	168.7	168.4	158.3	159.8	161.8	163.8	163.7	154.9	161.3	149.1	150.7	157.0
1997	164.9	161.3	153.8	152.0	157.8	163.9	150.6	149.6	158.1	158.0	161.1	166.1
1998	175.3	172.8	166.4	168.3	174.9	177.7	172.5	168.8	164.7	160.0	167.5	172.0
1999[1]	185.2	178.4	167.8	168.9	176.5	172.3	163.6	158.6	159.2	158.8		

[1] Preliminary. [2] Includes oxygenated and other finished. *Source: Energy Information Administration, U.S. Department of Energy (EIA-DOE)*

Average Refiner Price of Finished Motor Gasoline to End Users[1] in the U.S. In Cents Per Gallon

Year	Jan.	Feb.	Mar.	Apr.	May	June	July	Aug.	Sept.	Oct.	Nov.	Dec.	Average
1990	78.8	76.5	75.1	77.9	80.2	81.5	80.8	92.4	101.2	108.7	107.2	98.4	88.3
1991	88.8	79.5	74.0	77.0	82.0	81.9	78.9	81.1	80.2	77.9	79.1	76.0	79.7
1992	71.2	70.2	71.0	74.6	80.3	84.0	83.5	82.3	82.3	81.3	81.4	78.5	78.4
1993	76.9	76.1	75.7	77.8	80.1	79.8	77.6	76.2	74.9	75.3	72.5	68.0	75.9
1994	66.8	67.6	67.3	69.5	71.1	74.1	77.0	81.5	79.6	76.9	77.5	75.1	73.8
1995	74.5	73.3	73.1	77.3	83.4	83.9	80.0	76.9	75.8	73.6	71.8	73.0	76.5
1996	74.6	74.8	79.8	88.1	92.7	90.3	87.5	84.9	84.4	84.4	86.7	85.9	84.7
1997	86.6	86.1	84.3	83.9	84.5	83.3	81.5	86.8	87.2	84.3	81.6	77.8	83.9
1998	73.3	69.0	65.6	67.4	71.0	70.4	69.4	66.7	65.4	66.4	64.0	60.0	67.3
1999[2]	59.2	56.8	65.1	79.0	78.2	75.6	80.6	86.5	88.8	87.2			75.7

[1] Excludes aviation and taxes. [2] Preliminary. *Source: Energy Information Administration, U.S. Department of Energy (EIA-DOE)*

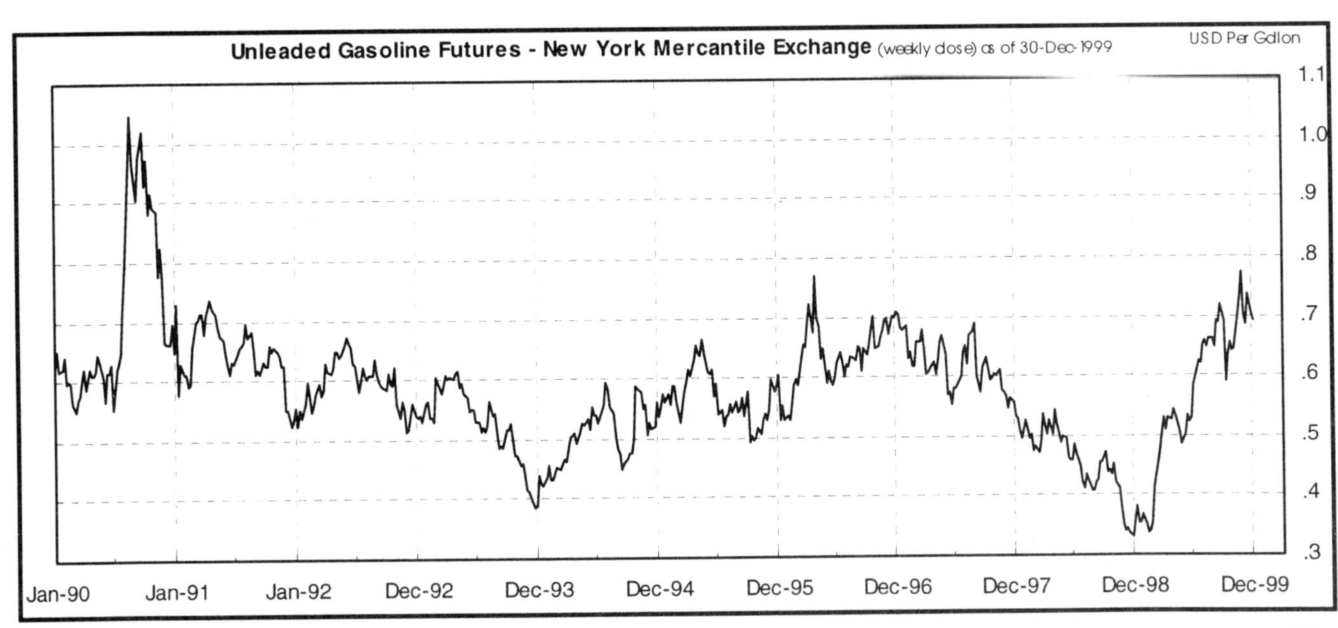

GASOLINE

Average Retail Price of Unleaded Premium Motor Gasoline[2] in the United States In Cents per Gallon

Year	Jan.	Feb.	Mar.	Apr.	May	June	July	Aug.	Sept.	Oct.	Nov.	Dec.	Average
1990	123.0	122.7	121.8	123.3	124.8	127.1	127.2	136.9	146.7	155.4	155.9	153.7	134.9
1991	143.1	132.1	126.4	128.1	133.1	133.8	131.3	131.8	132.4	130.7	131.8	130.9	132.1
1992	126.7	124.8	125.0	126.8	131.7	135.9	136.3	134.8	134.6	134.5	135.1	133.0	131.6
1993	131.3	130.1	129.4	130.4	131.9	132.1	130.5	129.4	128.2	132.3	130.5	126.8	130.2
1994	124.0	124.5	124.3	126.0	127.4	130.0	132.7	136.7	136.4	134.5	135.4	133.7	130.5
1995	132.4	131.6	130.6	132.5	138.3	141.1	138.4	135.2	133.2	131.5	129.2	129.0	133.6
1996	131.7	131.1	134.8	143.1	150.7	148.1	145.3	142.1	141.7	140.8	142.8	143.8	141.3
1997	144.1	143.4	141.5	141.3	140.9	141.1	138.8	143.3	145.8	142.6	139.7	136.3	141.6
1998	131.9	127.1	122.9	123.7	127.5	127.9	126.8	124.4	123.0	123.6	122.5	118.7	125.0
1999[1]	117.1	115.5	118.6	136.7	137.0	133.9	137.8	144.1	146.8	146.4	145.4		134.5

[1] Preliminary. [2] Including taxes. *Source: Energy Information Administration, U.S. Department of Energy (EIA-DOE)*

Average Retail Price of Unleaded Regular Motor Gasoline[2] in the United States In Cents per Gallon

Year	Jan.	Feb.	Mar.	Apr.	May	June	July	Aug.	Sept.	Oct.	Nov.	Dec.	Average
1990	104.2	103.7	102.3	104.4	106.1	108.8	108.4	119.0	129.4	137.8	137.7	135.4	116.4
1991	124.7	114.3	108.2	110.4	115.6	116.0	112.7	114.0	114.3	112.2	113.4	112.3	114.0
1992	107.3	105.4	105.8	107.9	113.6	117.9	117.5	115.8	115.8	115.4	115.9	113.6	112.7
1993	111.7	110.8	109.8	111.2	112.9	113.0	110.9	109.7	108.5	112.7	111.3	107.0	110.8
1994	104.3	105.1	104.5	106.4	108.0	110.6	113.6	118.2	117.7	115.2	116.3	114.3	111.2
1995	112.9	112.0	111.5	114.0	120.0	122.6	119.5	116.4	114.8	112.7	110.1	110.1	114.7
1996	112.9	112.4	116.2	125.1	132.3	129.9	127.2	124.0	123.4	122.7	125.0	126.0	123.1
1997	126.1	125.5	123.5	123.1	122.6	122.9	120.5	125.3	127.7	124.2	121.3	117.7	123.4
1998	113.1	108.2	104.1	105.2	109.2	109.4	107.9	105.2	103.3	104.2	102.8	98.6	105.9
1999[1]	97.2	95.5	99.1	117.7	117.8	114.8	118.9	125.5	128.0	127.4	126.4		115.3

[1] Preliminary. [2] Including taxes. *Source: Energy Information Administration, U.S. Department of Energy (EIA-DOE)*

Average Retail Price of All-Types[2] Motor Gasoline[3] in the United States In Cents per Gallon

Year	Jan.	Feb.	Mar.	Apr.	May	June	July	Aug.	Sept.	Oct.	Nov.	Dec.	Average
1990	109.0	108.6	107.6	109.6	111.4	114.0	113.9	124.6	134.7	143.1	143.2	141.0	121.7
1991	130.4	119.8	113.8	115.9	120.9	121.4	118.5	119.6	119.9	118.0	119.3	118.2	119.6
1992	113.5	111.7	112.2	114.3	119.7	123.9	123.8	122.1	122.2	121.9	122.3	120.1	119.0
1993	118.2	117.2	116.3	117.5	119.3	119.4	117.4	116.3	115.1	119.3	117.8	113.6	117.3
1994	110.9	111.4	110.9	112.8	114.3	116.7	119.9	124.3	123.7	121.2	122.2	120.3	117.4
1995	119.0	118.1	117.3	119.7	125.6	128.1	125.2	122.2	120.6	118.5	116.1	116.0	120.5
1996	118.6	118.1	121.9	130.5	137.8	135.4	132.8	129.8	129.3	128.7	130.8	131.8	128.8
1997	131.8	131.2	129.3	128.8	128.4	128.6	126.3	131.0	133.4	130.0	127.1	123.6	129.1
1998	118.6	113.7	109.7	110.6	114.6	114.8	113.4	110.8	109.1	109.9	108.6	104.6	111.5
1999[1]	103.1	101.4	104.8	123.2	123.3	120.4	124.4	130.9	133.4	132.9	131.9		120.9

[1] Preliminary. [2] Also includes types of motor oil not shown separately. [3] Including taxes. *Source: Energy Information Administration, U.S. Department of Energy (EIA-DOE)*

Average Refiner Price of Finished Aviation Gasoline to End Users[2] in the U.S. In Cents per Gallon

Year	Jan.	Feb.	Mar.	Apr.	May	June	July	Aug.	Sept.	Oct.	Nov.	Dec.	Average
1990	102.0	102.4	100.9	101.4	103.6	104.2	103.9	112.8	125.6	134.4	131.7	122.5	112.0
1991	112.1	106.4	101.3	101.2	105.3	105.2	103.6	105.8	105.7	104.6	104.3	102.0	104.7
1992	98.5	98.5	98.0	99.1	102.4	106.4	106.8	105.7	104.9	104.3	103.4	101.3	102.7
1993	100.3	99.9	99.4	100.7	102.2	102.5	99.7	98.8	98.2	98.0	95.7	91.2	99.0
1994	88.6	88.4	89.0	91.3	92.3	95.6	95.9	101.7	101.1	100.0	100.0	99.2	95.6
1995	99.6	99.8	99.0	101.3	105.8	106.4	101.8	99.2	101.3	96.8	95.4	96.0	100.5
1996	97.6	100.6	105.0	111.2	114.4	113.5	113.7	114.4	114.3	115.0	115.1	115.3	111.6
1997	113.7	114.9	113.8	114.7	115.7	114.6	112.5	114.6	115.6	113.9	113.0	107.7	113.8
1998	104.3	101.1	98.2	98.6	99.9	99.0	98.4	95.9	94.1	95.1	93.2	88.5	97.2
1999[1]	87.0	85.0	89.7	101.3	103.5	103.3	110.0	114.8	117.7	118.4			103.1

[1] Preliminary. [2] Excluding taxes. *Source: Energy Information Administration, U.S. Department Energy (EIA-DOE)*

Gold

After moving in a sideways pattern for most of the year, gold prices staged a spectacular rally in September 1999, moving from under $260 per ounce to over $320 per ounce. There were a number of developments in the gold market involving the sale of gold stocks by central banks. In May, the Bank of England indicated that it would sell over 400 metric tonnes of its gold stocks in a series of 25 tonne auctions. That news forced gold prices lower and lower until late September when several European central banks indicated that they would limit gold sales. Some fifteen central banks, plus the United Kingdom, Switzerland and Sweden, reported that they would limit gold sales to 400 tonnes per year for a five-year period. This was considered very positive news in the gold market and led to the strong rally. In effect, the agreement limits gold sales by the banks to an aggregate total of 2,000 tonnes. The high prices were quickly retraced on announcements by central banks of intentions to make some gold sales, with the Netherlands indicating it would sell a total of 300 tonnes over the next five years. Switzerland was to sell 1,300 tonnes of excess gold reserves. As the year 2000 began, the gold market appeared to be concerned about sales of gold reserves while at the same time it looked like demand for gold was starting to exceed the supply of gold.

The U.S. Geological Survey reported that U.S. production of gold in June 1999 was 31,900 kilograms, up 2 percent from the previous month and 4 percent less than a year ago. In the January-June period, U.S. production of gold was 176,000 kilograms. In 1998, U.S. gold production was 366,000 kilograms. Gold is produced in about 70 major lode mines, a dozen or more large placer mines and numerous smaller placer mines. Many of the placer mines are in Alaska and the Western States. Some gold in the U.S. is produced as a by-product of processing base metals such as copper. Some thirty mines yielded about 90 percent of the gold produced in the United States. Production of gold in Nevada in June 1999 was 22,200 kilograms, up 2 percent from the previous month but down 13 percent from the year before. In the January-June 1999 period, gold production in Nevada was 127,000 kilograms while for all of 1998 it was 273,000 kilograms. California gold production in June 1999 was 1,510 kilograms, up 4 percent from the previous month but down 24 percent from a year ago. In the January-June 1999 period, California gold production was 8,350 kilograms while for all of 1998 it was 18,700 kilograms. Other states, including Alaska, Colorado, Idaho and Montana, produced 8,160 kilograms in June 1999 compared to 8,030 kilograms in May 1999. In June 1998, other states production was 5,530 kilograms. In the first half of 1999, other gold producing states had production of 39,800 kilograms and for all of 1998 production was 72,700 kilograms.

U.S. exports of gold in May 1999 were 16,800 kilograms. This was some 45 percent less than the previous month. Exports of refined bullion in May 1999 were 8,870 kilograms. The major markets for gold were Switzerland, the United Kingdom and Mexico. In the first five months of 1999, U.S. exports of gold were 104,000 kilograms while for all of 1998 they were 522,000 kilograms. In addition to bullion, the U.S. exports other gold products like waste and scrap and gold metal powder.

U.S. imports of gold in May 1999 were 16,700 kilograms, up 34 percent from the previous month. The major suppliers of gold to the U.S. were Canada, Brazil, Peru, Mexico and Nicaragua. In the January-May 1999 period, U.S. imports of gold were 87,700 kilograms while for all of 1998 they were 278,000 kilograms. In the first five months of 1999, imports of gold waste and scrap were 8,960 kilograms. Imports of gold metal powder in the same period were 2,730 kilograms.

Futures Markets

Gold futures are traded on the Bolsa de Mercadorias & Futuros (BM&F), the Tokyo Commodity Exchange (ToCom), the Chicago Board of Trade (CBOT), the MidAmerica Commodity Exchange (MidAm) and the COMEX division of the New York Mercantile Exchange. Gold options are traded on the BM&F, The Amsterdam Exchanges (AEX-Optiebeurs), the MidAm, and the COMEX.

World Mine Production of Gold In Kilograms (1 Kilogram = 32.1507 Troy Ounces)

Year	Australia	Brazil	Canada	Chile	China	Ghana	Indonesia	Papua N. Guinea	Russia[3]	South Africa	United States	Uzbekistan[3]	World Total
1989	203,563	52,527	159,527	22,559	90,000	13,358	6,155	27,538	304,000	607,460	265,731	-----	2,013,913
1990	244,137	101,913	169,412	27,503	100,000	16,840	11,158	31,938	302,000	605,100	294,189	-----	2,180,000
1991	234,218	89,578	176,552	28,879	120,000	26,311	16,879	60,780	260,000	601,110	294,062	-----	2,190,000
1992	243,400	85,862	161,402	33,774	125,000	31,032	37,983	71,190	146,000	614,071	330,212	70,000	2,260,000
1993	247,196	69,894	152,929	33,638	130,000	38,911	42,097	61,671	149,500	619,201	331,000	70,000	2,280,000
1994	256,188	72,397	146,428	38,786	132,000	43,478	42,600	59,286	146,600	580,201	327,000	65,000	2,250,000
1995	253,504	64,424	152,032	44,585	140,000	53,087	62,909	53,405	132,170	523,809	317,000	65,000	2,210,000
1996	289,530	60,011	166,378	53,174	145,000	49,211	69,000	51,119	123,000	496,846	326,000	72,000	2,260,000
1997[1]	314,500	58,488	171,479	49,459	175,000	54,446	73,000	49,900	115,000	491,680	362,000	81,700	2,400,000
1998[2]	312,000	58,500	166,089	44,980	178,000	73,300	105,000	58,500	103,700	473,771	366,000	80,000	2,460,000

[1] Preliminary. [2] Estimate. [3] Formerly part of the U.S.S.R.; data not reported separately until 1992. *Source: U.S. Geological Survey (USGS)*

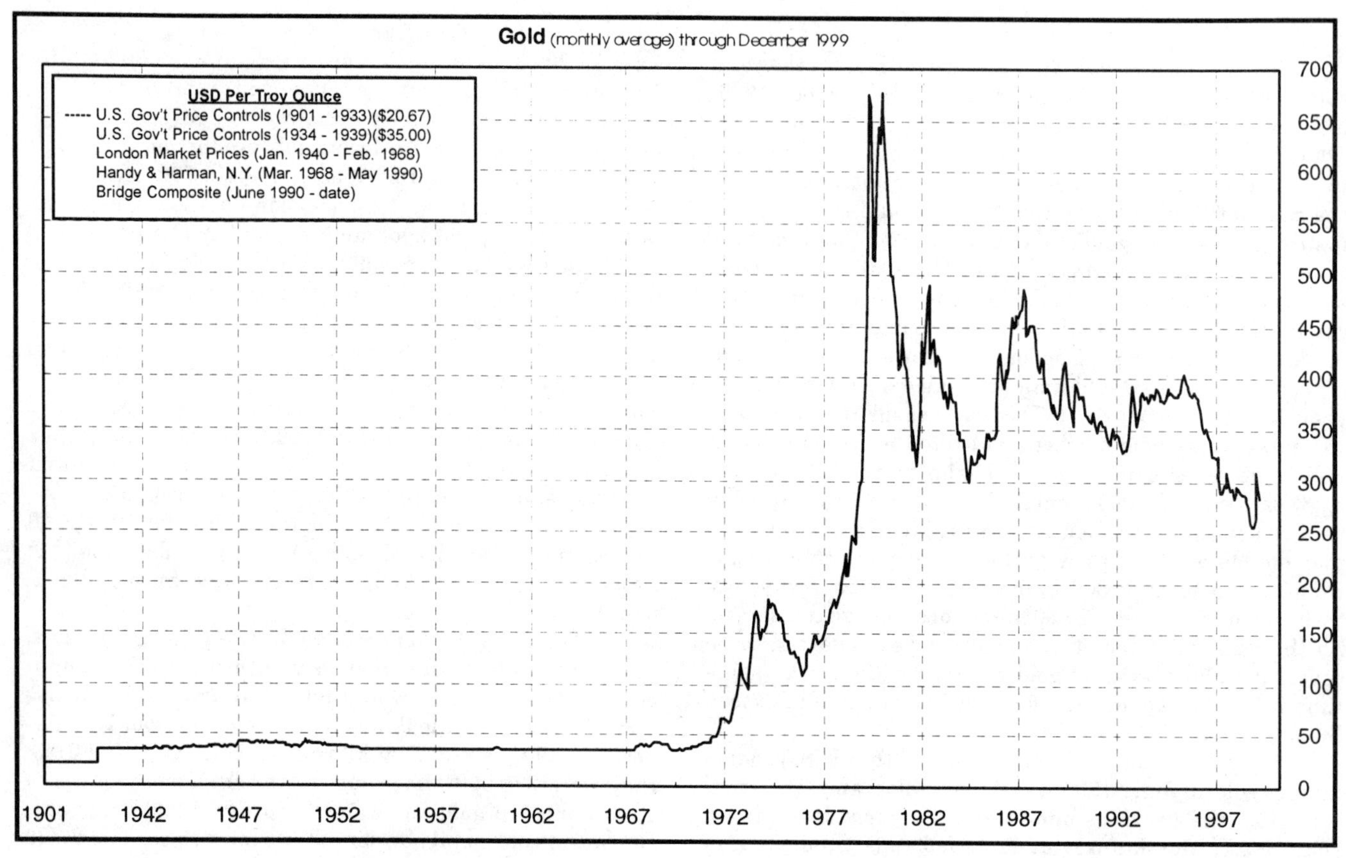

Salient Statistics of Gold in the United States In Kilograms (1 Kilogram = 32.1507 Troy Ounces)

			Refinery Production				---------- Stocks, Dec. 31 ---------				-------------- Consumption --------------			
Year	Mine Production	Value Million $	Domestic & Foreign Ores	Secondary (Old Scrap)	Exports (Excluding Coinage)	Imports for Consumption	Treasury Department[3]	Futures Exchange	Industry	Official World Reserves[4]	Dental	Industrial[5]	Jewelry & Arts	Total
1989	265,731	3,268.6	183,685	51,943	211,091	152,504	8,147,169	69,727	30,462	35,603	7,927	37,621	69,524	115,078
1990	294,189	3,640.8	225,183	43,980	296,397	97,519	8,146,432	50,881	37,065	35,572	8,700	30,996	78,514	118,216
1991	294,062	3,434.7	224,675	48,088	284,127	178,749	8,145,696	49,893	39,411	35,501	8,485	21,793	84,096	114,375
1992	330,212	3,662.4	283,951	53,396	368,851	174,341	8,145,000	46,453	36,713	35,100	6,543	20,360	83,508	110,410
1993	331,013	3,840.0	243,000	152,000	792,680	169,305	8,143,000	78,514	34,400	34,900	6,173	19,663	65,600	91,400
1994	327,000	4,050.0	241,000	148,000	471,000	114,000	8,142,000	49,100	32,700	34,800	5,430	17,013	53,700	76,100
1995	317,000	3,950.0	NA	NA	347,000	126,000	8,140,000	45,400	NA	34,600	NA	NA	NA	NA
1996	326,000	4,090.0	NA	NA	471,000	159,000	8,140,000	20,700	NA	34,400	NA	NA	NA	NA
1997[1]	362,000	3,870.0	270,000	100,000	476,000	209,000	8,140,000	15,200	NA	34,000	NA	NA	NA	NA
1998[2]	366,000	3,480.0	277,000	163,000	522,000	278,000	8,130,000	25,200	NA	33,600	NA	NA	NA	NA

[1] Preliminary. [2] Estimate. [3] Includes gold in Exchange Stabilization Fund. [4] Held by market economy country central banks and governments andinternational monetary orgainzations. [5] Including space and defense. *Source: U.S. Geological Survey (USGS)*

Monthly Average Gold Price (Handy & Harman) in New York In Dollars Per Troy Ounce

Year	Jan.	Feb.	Mar.	Apr.	May	June	July	Aug.	Sept.	Oct.	Nov.	Dec.	Average
1990	410.10	416.80	393.10	374.30	369.20	352.30	362.50	395.00	389.50	380.70	381.70	378.20	383.61
1991	383.60	363.80	363.40	358.40	356.80	366.70	367.50	356.20	348.80	358.70	359.50	361.10	362.18
1992	354.50	353.90	344.30	338.50	337.20	340.80	353.00	343.00	345.40	344.40	335.10	334.70	343.74
1993	329.00	329.40	330.10	341.90	366.70	371.90	392.40	378.50	354.90	364.20	373.50	383.70	359.67
1994	387.02	382.01	384.13	378.20	381.21	385.64	385.44	380.43	391.80	389.77	349.43	379.60	384.14
1995	378.55	376.51	382.12	391.11	385.46	387.56	386.40	383.63	382.22	383.14	385.53	387.42	384.22
1996	399.59	404.73	396.21	392.96	391.98	385.58	383.69	387.43	382.97	381.07	378.46	369.02	387.81
1997	355.10	346.71	351.67	344.47	343.75	340.75	324.08	324.03	322.74	324.87	307.10	288.65	331.16
1998	289.18	297.49	295.90	308.40	299.39	292.31	292.79	283.76	289.01	295.92	293.89	291.29	294.12
1999[1]	287.05	287.22	285.96	282.45	276.94	261.31	255.81	256.56	265.23	310.72	292.74		278.36

[1] Preliminary. *Source: U.S. Geological Survey (USGS)*

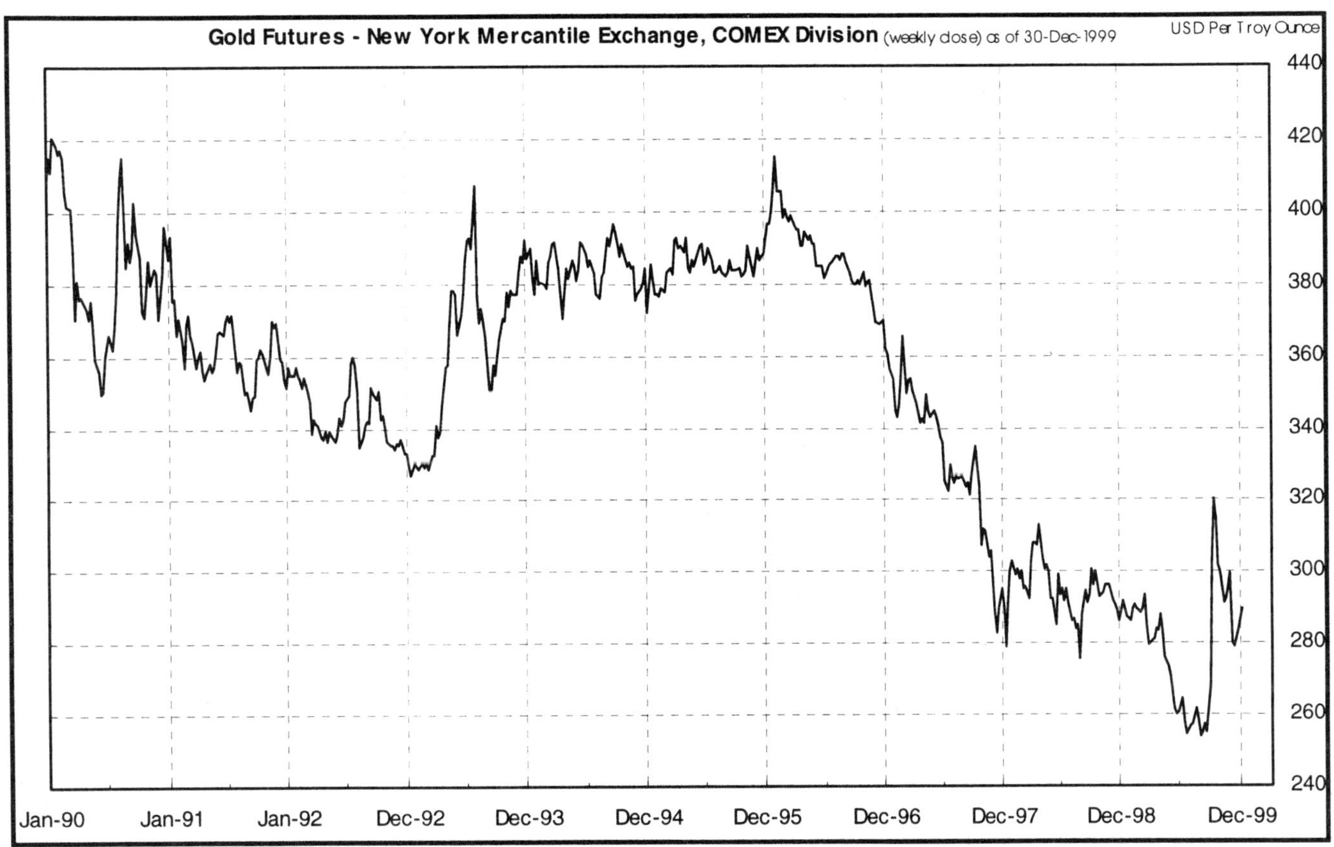

Average Open Interest of Gold in New York (NYMEX) In Thousands of Contracts

Year	Jan.	Feb.	Mar.	Apr.	May	June	July	Aug.	Sept.	Oct.	Nov.	Dec.
1990	147,884	132,400	126,890	118,750	117,707	113,958	105,496	120,579	116,331	113,873	111,638	110,343
1991	104,666	98,000	98,429	101,266	100,341	88,961	94,467	99,790	105,053	96,302	109,030	109,004
1992	106,110	103,319	109,796	106,485	109,947	98,127	111,039	102,239	102,376	102,232	109,965	100,328
1993	112,420	109,093	115,505	142,208	172,491	170,829	200,168	180,509	166,201	152,531	152,853	154,730
1994	156,045	139,354	146,269	144,386	147,738	146,255	148,915	155,641	167,981	166,041	166,536	178,998
1995	184,549	170,972	168,651	191,667	173,805	174,075	175,727	176,135	185,128	185,854	170,674	141,751
1996	210,695	226,160	203,968	201,826	203,056	192,423	185,374	159,435	185,907	192,606	187,145	185,994
1997	199,710	190,524	167,595	157,176	160,512	170,640	207,352	198,099	201,267	188,365	212,757	188,558
1998	180,994	171,507	183,358	180,267	158,157	172,250	169,180	192,623	183,351	186,680	164,304	153,063
1999	179,726	185,345	178,456	198,202	193,978	207,121	205,686	193,022	206,186	216,034	189,432	156,753

Source: New York Mercantile Exchange (NYMEX), COMEX division

Volume of Trading of Gold Futures in New York (NYMEX) In Thousands of Contracts

Year	Jan.	Feb.	Mar.	Apr.	May	June	July	Aug.	Sept.	Oct.	Nov.	Dec.	Total
1990	1,327.1	885.1	975.6	472.4	745.2	541.0	747.4	1,191.5	729.4	879.9	705.3	530.1	9,730.0
1991	957.3	497.8	617.7	446.1	584.4	520.0	551.4	457.2	429.1	551.0	677.3	510.6	6,799.9
1992	729.8	388.4	607.3	425.4	485.4	427.2	734.6	500.2	465.3	414.1	504.1	320.1	6,001.9
1993	506.0	446.2	661.4	640.4	1,140.7	809.6	1,171.7	808.8	728.9	565.2	892.3	533.2	8,904.4
1994	981.8	584.0	889.5	589.2	922.6	740.2	723.8	626.0	645.6	651.2	687.8	461.5	8,503.2
1995	881.9	420.0	1,087.5	613.0	777.0	588.1	669.9	500.5	495.5	387.7	982.5	378.1	7,781.6
1996	1,384.7	987.5	943.6	647.1	858.5	582.1	749.8	541.9	541.9	528.5	795.2	458.8	8,694.5
1997	1,102.8	830.2	899.4	508.5	762.1	522.7	1,147.5	667.8	715.8	988.0	808.8	588.1	9,541.9
1998	1,078.2	534.2	877.2	698.1	845.2	718.7	712.4	680.0	851.7	769.6	705.6	519.0	8,990.1
1999	860.8	517.4	1,147.6	561.1	1,069.6	573.6	964.3	709.6	1,067.3	993.8	674.7	436.1	9,575.8

Source: New York Mercantile Exchange (NYMEX), COMEX division

Commodity Exchange, Inc. (COMEX) Depository Warehouse Stocks of Gold In Thousands of Troy Ounces

Year	Jan. 1	Feb. 1	Mar. 1	Apr. 1	May 1	June 1	July 1	Aug. 1	Sept. 1	Oct. 1	Nov. 1	Dec. 1
1990	2,241	2,225	2,245	2,220	2,048	1,809	1,582	1,530	1,539	1,564	1,585	1,347
1991	1,636	1,686	1,540	1,298	1,458	1,711	1,772	1,875	1,220	1,342	1,302	1,479
1992	1,605	1,362	1,435	1,411	1,591	1,618	1,605	1,733	1,688	1,947	1,766	1,524
1993	1,507	1,340	1,365	1,426	1,383	2,231	2,247	2,448	2,437	2,425	2,349	2,552
1994	2,524	2,955	2,958	2,862	2,802	2,434	2,665	2,574	2,030	1,904	1,843	1,867
1995	1,577	1,498	1,386	1,360	1,391	1,488	1,505	1,608	1,448	1,745	1,395	1,315
1996	1,460	1,869	1,412	1,429	1,335	1,711	1,263	1,273	1,402	1,283	1,060	1,104
1997	666	837	583	1,000	946	878	850	914	733	894	615	761
1998	488	446	481	720	658	1,077	1,055	1,092	911	958	827	819
1999	809	809	731	1,032	896	876	818	936	1,198	928	874	1,195

Source: New York Mercantile Exchange (NYMEX), COMEX division

Central Gold Bank Reserves In Millions of Troy Ounces

	Industrial Countries															
Year	Belgium	Canada	France	Germany	Italy	Japan	Netherlands	Switzerland	United Kingdom	United States	Industrial Total	Developing Oil	Developing Non-Oil	IMF[2]	Bank for Int'l Settlements	World Total
1989	30.2	16.1	81.9	95.2	66.7	24.2	43.9	83.3	19.0	261.9	891.5	42.1	101.2	103.4	6.6	1,144.8
1990	30.2	14.8	81.9	95.2	66.7	24.2	43.9	83.3	18.9	261.9	889.4	41.5	101.7	103.4	7.8	1,143.8
1991	30.2	13.0	81.9	95.2	66.7	24.2	43.9	83.3	18.9	261.9	887.3	42.0	102.4	103.4	6.6	1,141.6
1992	25.0	9.9	81.9	95.2	66.7	24.2	43.9	83.3	18.6	261.8	877.4	42.0	100.3	103.4	6.8	1,129.9
1993	25.0	6.1	81.9	95.2	66.7	24.2	35.1	83.3	18.5	261.8	860.4	42.4	108.1	103.4	8.6	1,123.0
1994	25.0	3.9	81.9	95.2	66.7	24.2	34.8	83.3	18.4	261.7	856.9	42.4	106.6	103.4	7.0	1,116.2
1995	20.5	3.4	81.9	95.2	66.7	24.2	34.8	83.3	18.4	261.7	848.7	41.9	111.9	103.4	7.3	1,113.2
1996	15.3	3.1	81.9	95.2	66.7	24.2	34.8	83.3	18.4	261.7	840.1	42.5	115.5	103.4	6.6	1,108.2
1997	15.3	3.1	81.9	95.2	66.7	24.2	27.1	83.3	18.4	261.6	821.9	42.3	115.8	103.4	6.2	1,089.7
1998[1]	7.6	2.6	81.9	95.2	66.7	24.2	27.1	83.3	18.4	261.6	811.3	40.6	116.4	103.4	6.4	1,078.2

[1] Preliminary. [2] International Monetary Fund. *Source: American Metal Market (AMM)*

Mine Production of Recoverable Gold in the United States In Kilograms

Year	Arizona	California	Idaho	Montana	Nevada	Alaska	Colorado	South Dakota	New Mexico	Utah	Other States	Total
1989	2,768	29,804	3,057	12,434	153,995	5,756	3,448	16,123	1,076	W	37,270	265,731
1990	5,000	29,607	W	13,012	179,078	3,232	2,357	17,870	888	W	43,145	294,189
1991	6,195	30,404	3,348	13,715	178,488	3,200	3,181	16,371	W	W	41,055	295,957
1992	6,656	33,335	4,037	13,994	203,393	5,003	3,763	18,681	W	W	40,262	329,124
1993	2,710	35,800	4,324	14,300	211,000	2,780	W	19,200	995	W	39,891	331,000
1994	2,050	30,100	3,610	12,600	214,000	5,660	4,420	W	W	W	33,560	306,000
1995	1,920	25,600	8,850	12,400	210,000	4,410	W	W	W	W	53,820	317,000
1996	1,740	23,800	7,410	9,110	213,000	5,020	W	W	W	W	57,920	318,000
1997	2,140	24,200	7,490	10,200	243,000	18,400	W	16,400	W	W	40,170	362,000
1998[1]	1,840	18,700	W	8,200	273,000	18,300	W	12,100	W	W	33,860	366,000

[1] Preliminary. W = Withheld proprietary data, included in Other States. *Source: U.S. Geological Survey (USGS)*

Consumption of Gold, By End-Use in the United States In Kilograms

	Jewelry and the Arts				Industrial					
Year	Gold-Filled & Other	Electro-plating	Karat Gold	Total	Dental	Gold-Filled & Other	Electro-plating	Karat Gold	Total	Grand Total
1989	7,364	1,283	60,877	69,524	7,927	15,723	20,684	1,215	37,621	115,078
1990	8,132	429	69,952	78,514	8,700	12,725	17,251	1,020	30,996	118,216
1991	3,848	373	79,875	84,096	8,485	8,102	12,624	1,068	21,793	114,375
1992	3,546	581	79,381	83,508	6,543	8,802	10,476	1,082	20,360	110,410
1993	3,530	373	61,700	65,600	6,170	9,470	9,090	1,100	19,700	91,400
1994	3,650	369	49,700	53,700	5,430	7,450	9,470	96	17,000	76,100
1995	NA	NA	NA	NA	NA	NA	NA	NA	NA	NA
1996	NA	NA	NA	NA	NA	NA	NA	NA	NA	NA
1997	NA	NA	NA	NA	NA	NA	NA	NA	NA	NA
1998[1]	NA	NA	NA	NA	NA	NA	NA	NA	NA	NA

[1] Preliminary. **Source: U.S. Geological Survey (USGS)**

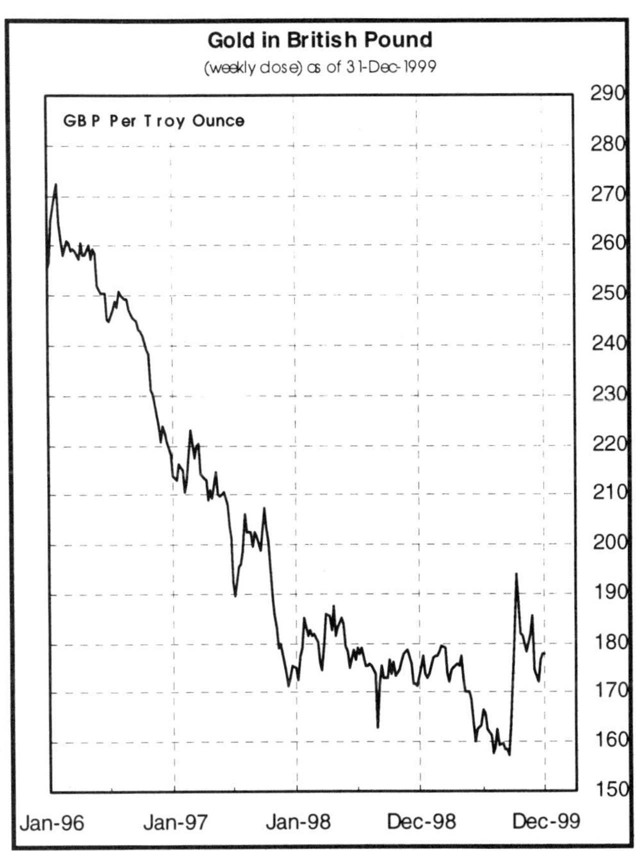
Gold in British Pound
(weekly close) as of 31-Dec-1999
GBP Per Troy Ounce
290
280
270
260
250
240
230
220
210
200
190
180
170
160
150
Jan-96
Jan-97
Jan-98
Dec-98
Dec-99

Gold in Euro
(weekly close) as of 31-Dec-1999
EUR Per Troy Ounce
330
320
310
300
290
280
270
260
250
240
230
Jan-96
Jan-97
Jan-98
Dec-98
Dec-99

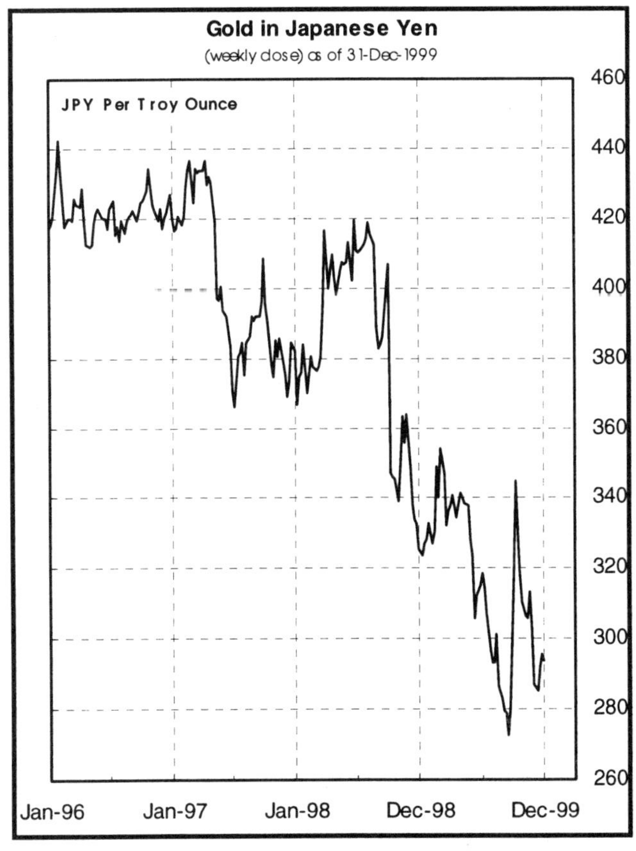
Gold in Japanese Yen
(weekly close) as of 31-Dec-1999
JPY Per Troy Ounce
460
440
420
400
380
360
340
320
300
280
260
Jan-96
Jan-97
Jan-98
Dec-98
Dec-99

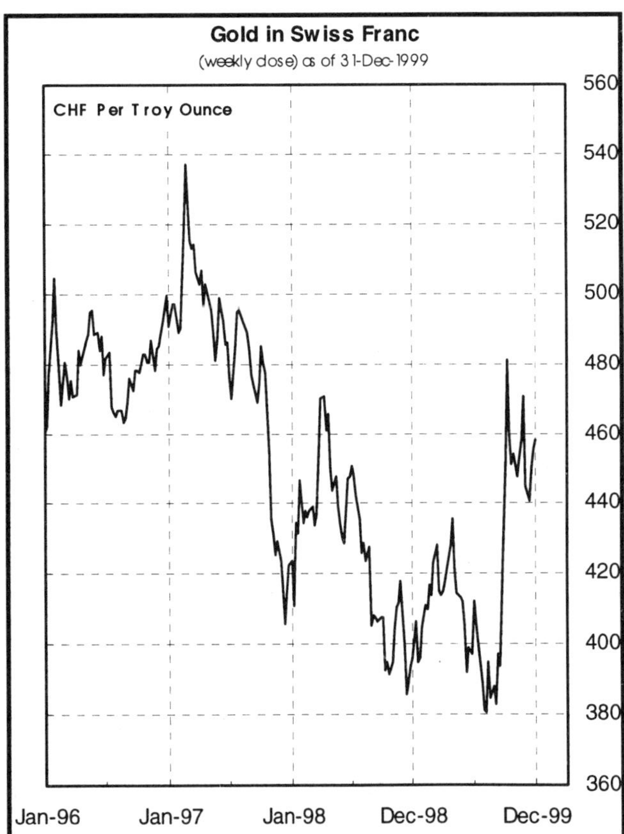
Gold in Swiss Franc
(weekly close) as of 31-Dec-1999
CHF Per Troy Ounce
560
540
520
500
480
460
440
420
400
380
360
Jan-96
Jan-97
Jan-98
Dec-98
Dec-99

Grain Sorghum

The U.S. is the world's largest producer of grain sorghum (milo) with India a distant second. World production in 1999/2000 of 60 million metric tonnes is marginally below the 1998/99 crop. The U.S. produced nearly a quarter of the total with 14.7 million tonnes, but on balance U.S. production and its share of the world total has trended irregularly lower during the 1990's. However, unlike most of the world's sorghum producing nations who consume their production domestically, the U.S. generally consumes about two-thirds and exports the balance.

India's estimated 1999/00 crop of 8 million tonnes was about 1 million tonnes less than expected and compares with 1998/99 production of 8.5 million and 11 plus million in 1996/97. Significantly, India's sorghum acreage of 10.4 million hectares in 1999/00 accounts for about a quarter of the world's sorghum acreage, but India's average yield is consistently among the world's lowest, 0.77 metric tonne per hectare vs. a world average of 1.45 and the U.S. average of 4.29 mt/hectare. In contrast, China's 1999/00 average yield was one of the highest at 4.09 mt/hectare, on acreage of only 1.1 million hectare, yielding a crop of 4.5 million tonnes.

World sorghum trade is small; 6.4 million tonnes in 1999/00 vs. 6.1 million in 1998/99 and an early 1990's average of 9 million. The U.S. accounts for most of the exports, 5.2 million tonnes in 1999/00, mostly to Japan and Mexico who are generally the two largest importers. Argentina is the second largest exporter with 800,000 tonnes in 1999/00. The world 1999/00 carryover is forecast at 5.7 million tonnes vs. 5.9 million a year earlier, almost a third of which will be in the U.S.

The U.S. sorghum crop year begins September 1. The three major producing states are usually Kansas, Texas and Nebraska. Texas acreage is among the highest, but the state's yield is typically under 50 bushels per acre vs. the Kansas average of almost 80 bushels. Total U.S. supplies in 1999/00 of 645 million bushels includes a carry-in of 65 million bushels vs. production of 569 million bushels in 1998/99, plus a carry-in of 49 million bushels. No sorghum is imported into the U.S. Total disappearance in 1999/00 of 580 million bushels includes exports of 200 million, feed and residual usage of 325 million, and other usage of 55 million which, if realized, will leave the season's ending carryover unchanged.

Sorghum prices received by farmers during 1999/00 are forecast between $1.40-$1.80 per bushel vs. the 1998/99 average of $1.70 and the 1990's high of $3.19 in 1995/96.

World Supply and Demand Grain Sorghum In Thousands of Metric Tons

	Exports				Imports				Total	Utilization				Ending Stocks		
Year	Argen-tina	Non-U.S.	U.S.	Total	Japan	Mexico	Unac-counted	Total	Pro-duction	China	Mexico	U.S.	Total	Non-U.S.	U.S.	Total
1994-5	192	756	5,653	6,409	2,334	2,544	118	6,409	57,964	6,355	5,644	10,223	57,932	2,294	1,819	4,113
1995-6	812	1,703	4,757	6,460	2,542	1,764	267	6,460	55,241	4,935	6,900	7,977	56,689	2,245	467	2,712
1996-7	617	944	5,207	6,151	2,774	2,091	194	6,151	69,471	5,389	8,500	14,246	67,589	3,388	1,206	4,594
1997-8[1]	1,370	1,664	5,164	6,828	2,769	3,340	112	6,828	58,834	3,650	8,940	10,670	58,829	3,357	1,242	4,599
1998-9[2]	600	1,325	5,150	6,475	2,453	3,150	42	6,475	60,017	4,600	9,700	7,804	58,963	3,999	1,654	5,653
1999-00[3]	800	1,200	5,200	6,400	2,200	3,300	125	6,400	60,983	4,450	10,200	9,653	60,757	3,819	2,060	5,879

[1] Preliminary. [2] Estimate. [3] Forecast. *Source: Foreign Agricultural Service, U.S. Department of Agriculture (FAS-USDA)*

Salient Statistics of Grain Sorghum in the United States

	Acreage Planted[4] for All Purposes	Acreage Harvested	For Grain					For Silage			Sorghum Grain Stocks			
											Dec. 1		June 1	
Year	1,000 Acres		Pro-duction 1,000 Bushels	Yield Per Harvested Acre Bushels	Price in Cents Per Bushel	Value of Pro-duction Million $		Acreage Harvested 1,000 Acres	Pro-duction 1,000 Tons	Yield Per Harvested Acre	On Farms	Off Farms	On Farms	Off Farms
											1,000 Bushels			
1994-5	9,827	8,917	649,206	72.8	213	1,323.8		329	3,932	12.0	126,650	295,809	44,570	114,212
1995-6	9,454	8,278	460,373	55.6	319	1,395.4		368	3,652	9.9	79,090	222,186	13,955	56,433
1996-7	13,097	11,811	795,274	67.3	234	1,986.3		423	4,976	11.8	144,590	322,767	38,815	80,329
1997-8[1]	10,052	9,158	633,545	69.2	221	1,408.9		412	5,385	13.1	96,625	274,244	27,200	68,907
1998-9[2]	9,626	7,723	519,933	67.3	166	905.5		308	3,526	11.4	95,900	239,416	27,400	88,691
1999-00[3]	9,288	8,544	595,166	69.7	145-185	971.0		320	3,716	11.6	89,300	259,264		

[1] Preliminary. [2] Estimate. [3] Forecast. NA = Not available. *Source: Economic Research Service, U.S. Department of Agriculture (ERS-USDA)*

Production of All Sorghum for Grain in the United States, by States In Thousands of Bushels

Year	Arkansas	Colorado	Illinois	Kansas	Louisiana	Miss-issippi	Missouri	Nebraska	New Mexico	Oklahoma	South Dakota	Texas	Total
1994	18,375	7,140	17,820	231,000	8,364	5,250	49,500	117,600	7,410	14,000	11,375	153,400	649,206
1995	13,135	4,620	11,730	173,600	5,880	2,665	35,770	56,840	3,380	12,800	4,800	129,600	460,373
1996	16,280	13,260	12,600	354,200	11,628	5,040	50,960	97,850	7,425	28,910	7,975	182,400	795,274
1997	11,100	6,000	10,465	265,200	6,600	2,475	36,800	60,750	9,988	22,500	11,360	185,850	633,545
1998	6,890	10,545	7,918	264,000	7,500	2,340	26,560	56,400	2,925	15,300	9,940	105,800	519,933
1999[1]	9,750	8,610	9,215	258,400	19,270	4,872	22,010	42,770	7,425	18,000	4,640	185,850	595,166

[1] Preliminary. *Source: National Agricultural Statistics Service, U.S. Department of Agriculture (NASS-USDA)*

Grain Sorghum Quarterly Supply and Disappearance in the United States In Millions of Bushels

Crop Year Beginning Sept. 1	Supply: Beginning Stocks	Supply: Production	Supply: Imports	Supply: Total Supply	Disappearance – Domestic Use: Food Alcohol & Industrial	Domestic Use: Seed	Domestic Use: Feed & Residual	Domestic Use: Total	Disappearance: Export	Disappearance: Total	Ending Stocks: Gov't Owned[3]	Ending Stocks: Privately Owned[4]	Ending Stocks: Total Stocks
1996-7	18.4	795.3	0	813.7	43.7	1.2	515.9	560.8	205.4	766.2	0	47.5	47.5
Sept.-Nov.	18.4	795.3	0	813.6	14.5	0	275.5	290.1	56.2	346.3	0	467.4	467.4
Dec.-Feb.	467.4	-----	0	467.4	15.0	0	119.1	134.1	59.0	193.1	0	274.4	274.4
Mar.-May	274.4	-----	0	274.4	8.9	.7	84.6	94.2	61.0	155.2	0	119.1	119.1
June-Aug.	119.1	-----	0	119.1	5.2	.5	36.7	42.4	29.2	71.6	0	47.5	47.5
1997-8	47.5	633.5	0	681.0	53.9	1.2	364.9	420.0	212.1	632.1	.2	48.7	48.9
Sept.-Nov.	47.5	633.5	0	681.0	18.4	0	239.3	257.7	49.4	307.1	0	373.9	373.9
Dec.-Feb.	373.9	-----	0	373.9	18.5	0	37.5	56.0	83.2	139.2	0	234.7	234.7
Mar.-May	234.7	-----	0	234.7	11.3	.8	71.3	83.4	55.1	138.5	0	96.1	96.1
June-Aug.	96.1	-----	0	96.1	5.7	.4	16.8	22.9	24.3	47.2	.2	48.7	48.9
1998-9[1]	49.0	520.0	0	569.0	45.0	1.1	262.0	504.0	197.0	701.0	0	63.8	65.0
Sept.-Nov.	49.0	520.0	0	569.0	15.0	0	178.0	234.0	41.0	275.0	.7	334.6	335.0
Dec.-Feb.	335.0	-----	0	335.0	15.0	0	34.0	113.0	64.0	177.0	3.3	223.1	222.0
Mar.-May	222.0	-----	0	222.0	10.0	0	45.0	106.0	51.0	157.0			116.0
June-Aug.	116.0	-----	0	116.0	6.0	0	5.0	51.0	41.0	92.0			65.0
1999-00[2]	65.0	595.0	0	660.0	55.0	0	340.0	605.0	210.0	815.0			55.0
Sept.-Nov.	65.0	595.0	0	660.0	18.0	0	234.0	312.0	60.0	372.0			349.0

[1] Preliminary. [2] Forecast. [3] Uncommitted inventory. [4] Includes quantity under loan & farmer-owned reserve. *Source: Economic Research Service, U.S. Department of Agriculture (ERS-USDA)*

Average Price of Sorghum Grain, No. 2, Yellow in Kansas City In Dollars Per Hundred Pounds (Cwt.)

Year	Sept.	Oct.	Nov.	Dec.	Jan.	Feb.	Mar.	Apr.	May	June	July	Aug.	Average
1992-3	3.76	3.60	3.61	3.70	3.70	3.66	3.70	3.72	3.82	3.58	3.99	4.01	3.74
1993-4	3.89	4.03	4.60	4.91	4.93	4.81	4.64	4.33	4.38	4.43	3.79	3.73	4.37
1994-5	3.72	3.55	3.60	3.81	3.92	3.90	4.01	4.08	4.27	4.50	4.93	4.85	4.10
1995-6	5.08	5.45	5.68	6.19	6.39	6.58	6.81	7.79	8.17	7.79	7.24	6.74	6.66
1996-7	5.29	4.64	4.31	4.22	4.24	4.46	4.88	4.83	4.63	4.48	4.18	4.28	4.54
1997-8	4.13	4.36	4.30	4.26	4.33	4.36	4.40	4.10	4.09	4.03	3.74	3.27	4.11
1998-9	2.98	3.17	3.45	3.41	3.41	3.43	3.48	3.37	3.35	3.32	2.92	3.24	3.29
1999-00[1]	2.97												2.97

[1] Preliminary. *Source: Economic Research Service, U.S. Department of Agriculture (ERS-USDA)*

Exports of Grain Sorghum, by Country of Destination from the United States In Metric Tons

Year Beginning Oct. 1	Canada	Ecuador	Ethiopia	Israel	Japan	Jordon	Mexico	South Africa	Spain	Sudan	Turkey	World Total
1991-2	1,613	36,000	42,150	104,952	1,738,075	120,001	4,956,607	19,031	174,758	122,183	99,394	7,454,616
1992-3	1,795	9,501	0	217,110	1,933,012	0	3,970,069	56,186	188,893	4,287	132,182	6,651,528
1993-4	1,699	0	86,697	66,264	1,681,976	0	3,118,139	0	169,454	48,042	0	5,245,524
1994-5	3,713	0	0	214,073	1,987,738	0	2,543,696	0	398,339	12,304	0	5,652,585
1995-6	5,734	0	25,700	356,868	1,616,384	0	1,665,541	332	431,578	0	0	4,757,055
1996-7[1]	3,347	0	10,020	456,271	2,203,669	0	2,189,598	0	125,827	8,000	138,590	5,206,964
1997-8[2]					1,650,000		3,222,000					5,334,000

[1] Preliminary. [2] Estimate. *Source: Economic Research Service, U.S. Department of Agriculture (ERS-USDA)*

Grain Sorghum Price Support Program and Market Prices in the United States

Year	Price Support Operations – Price Support: Quantity (Million Cwt.)	Price Support: % of Production	Aquired by CCC (Million Cwt.)	Owned by CCC at Year End (Million Cwt.)	Basic Loan Rate ($ Per Bushel)	Target Price ($ Per Bushel)	Findley Loan Rate ($ Per Bushel)	Effective Base[3] Million Acres	Participation Rate[4] % of Base	No. 2 Yellow ($ Per Cwt.): Kansas City	Texas High Plains	Los Angeles	Gulf Ports
1991-2	9.5	2.9	5.4	4.5	1.80	2.61	1.54	13.5	77.1	4.36	4.78	5.69	4.86
1992-3	27.2	5.5	0	2.2	1.91	2.61	1.63	13.6	78.6	3.74	4.06	5.11	4.27
1993-4	8.2	2.6	0	1.4	1.89	2.61	1.63	13.5	81.6	4.37	4.95	-----	4.90
1994-5	25.2	6.9	0	.4	1.89	2.61	1.80	13.5	81.1	4.10	4.75	-----	4.62
1995-6	4.0	1.6	0	0	1.84	2.61	1.80	13.3	76.9	6.66	7.30	-----	7.19
1996-7[1]	11.4	2.5	0	0	-----	[5]	1.81	13.2	98.8	4.54	5.02	-----	5.03
1997-8[2]	9.8	2.7	.1	.1	-----	[5]	1.76	-----	-----	-----	-----	-----	-----

[1] Preliminary. [2] Estimate. [3] National effective crop acreage base as determined by ASCS. [4] Percentage of effective base acres enrolled in acreage reduction programs. [5] Beginning with the 1996-7 marketing year, target prices are no longer applicable. Source: Economic Research Service, U.S. Department of Agriculture (ERS-USDA)

Hay

Total U.S. hay production in 1999 (marketing year, May 1 to April 30) of a record high 161 million short tons was up 10 million tons from 1998. The all-hay yield of a record 2.6 tons per acre was up 3 percent: the acreage harvested of all-hay of 62 million acres was also 3 percent above 1998. Alfalfa production of 85.5 million short tons was 4 percent over 1998 with average yield at a record high 3.57 tons per acre. Among the top ten producing states, Iowa and Minnesota showed the largest increases in yield. Other hay production was put at a record high 76 million tons, up 9 percent from 1998. The two largest producing states are Texas with 12 million tons in 1999 and California with 8.4 million tons. Hay is produced in virtually of the lower 48 states.

Roughage consuming animal units (RCAUs) in 1999/2000 are estimated as virtually unchanged from 1998/99. With hay production and carry-in stocks up, hay supplies in 1999/00 per RCAU of 2.51 tons compares with 2.34 tons in 1998/99.

Hay prices have been weaker in 1999/00, reflecting larger supplies. Prices received by farmers for all hay averaged $80.72 per ton in May-September 1999 vs. $91.08 in 1998. Alfalfa hay prices in May-September averaged $84.30 per ton, down from $94.84 in 1998. Prices received by farmers for hay other than alfalfa and alfalfa mixtures averaged $65.94 in the aforementioned 1999 period vs. $75.34 a year earlier.

Salient Statistics of All Hay in the United States

Crop Year Beginning May 1	Acres Harvested 1,000 Acres	Yield Per Acre Tons	Production (Millions of Tons)	Carryover May 1 (Millions of Tons)	Disappearance (Millions of Tons)	Supply Per Animal Unit (In Tons)	Disappearance Per Animal Unit (In Tons)	Animal Units Fed[3] Millions	Farm Price $ Per Ton	Farm Production Value Million $	Alfalfa (Certified)	Timothy	Red Clover	Sudan-Grass
											Retail Price Paid by Farmers for Seed, April 15 — Dollars Per Cwt.			
1994-5	58,735	2.55	150.1	22.1	151.4	2.21	1.94	77.9	86.7	11,114	266.00	76.00	148.00	47.90
1995-6	59,629	2.59	154.2	20.8	154.2	2.25	1.98	77.9	82.2	11,042	274.00	71.00	134.00	51.80
1996-7	61,169	2.45	149.8	20.8	152.8	2.24	2.01	76.1	95.8	12,727	277.00	76.00	172.00	51.90
1997-8	61,084	2.50	152.5	17.4	148.1	2.28	2.00	74.4	100.0	13,250	282.00	73.00	153.00	51.40
1998-9[1]	60,076	2.53	151.8	21.8	NA	2.36	NA	73.4	84.6	11,607	288.00	71.20	152.00	53.70
1999-00[2]	63,160	2.52	159.1						77.0	10,890	288.00	71.20	152.00	53.70

[1] Preliminary. [2] Estimate. [3] Roughage-consuming animal units fed annually. NA = Not available. *Source: Economic Research Service, U.S. Department of Agriculture (ERS-USDA)*

Production of All Hay in the United States, by States In Thousands of Tons

Year	California	Idaho	Iowa	Minnesota	Missouri	New York	North Dakota	Ohio	Oklahoma	South Dakota	Texas	Wisconsin	Total
1994	8,210	4,438	5,775	7,530	6,770	7,415	4,510	4,384	4,198	7,330	8,455	6,550	150,060
1995	8,341	5,080	5,665	6,943	6,818	6,975	5,095	4,035	4,174	9,050	8,136	6,820	154,166
1996	8,008	4,760	5,310	5,998	7,270	7,455	4,825	3,400	4,940	8,200	7,815	6,050	149,779
1997	8,408	4,730	5,190	6,398	7,340	6,790	4,375	3,850	5,108	7,810	10,955	6,353	152,536
1998	8,554	5,549	5,332	7,110	7,703	7,680	4,190	3,875	3,380	8,160	6,870	6,370	151,780
1999[1]	8,462	5,132	5,970	7,130	7,225	7,610	5,511	3,060	5,000	9,440	13,135	7,510	159,077

[1] Preliminary. *Source: Agricultural Statistics Board, U.S. Department of Agriculture (ASB-USDA)*

Hay Production and Farm Stocks in the United States In Thousands of Short Tons

Year	Production: Alfalfa & Mixtures	Production: All Others	Production: All Hay	Production: Corn for Silage[1]	Production: Sorghum Silage[1]	Farm Stocks: May 1	Farm Stocks: Dec. 1
1994	81,336	68,724	150,060	88,588	3,932	22,096	105,296
1995	84,515	69,651	154,166	77,867	3,652	20,775	109,438
1996	79,139	70,640	149,779	86,581	4,976	20,739	105,179
1997	78,535	74,001	152,536	97,192	5,385	17,424	103,044
1998	82,310	69,470	151,780	95,479	3,526	21,827	111,839
1999[2]	83,924	75,153	159,077	96,169	3,716	24,795	108,668

[1] Not included in all tame hay. [2] Preliminary. *Source: Agricultural Statistics Board, U.S. Department of Agriculture (ASB-USDA)*

Mid-Month Price Received by Farmers for All Hay (Baled) in the United States In Dollars Per Ton

Year	May	June	July	Aug.	Sept.	Oct.	Nov.	Dec.	Jan.	Feb.	Mar.	Apr.	Average[2]
1994-5	100.0	88.7	82.5	83.1	82.4	86.8	86.6	85.5	84.8	85.0	86.7	90.3	86.7
1995-6	90.4	83.9	80.6	81.1	80.3	83.0	81.0	80.3	81.7	81.2	83.4	90.3	82.2
1996-7	97.1	92.3	89.6	92.9	90.1	93.0	92.0	90.8	97.9	105.0	108.0	117.0	95.8
1997-8	118.0	108.0	98.4	99.0	103.0	103.0	101.0	97.7	98.1	97.2	97.5	101.0	100.0
1998-9	103.0	91.8	88.6	88.5	86.5	85.2	81.4	77.5	78.5	79.0	78.5	81.9	85.0
1999-00[1]	91.6	81.7	78.4	77.4	74.5	73.7	74.0	71.1	71.8				77.1

[1] Preliminary. [2] Marketing year average. *Source: Economic Research Service, U.S. Department of Agriculture (ERS-USDA)*

Heating Oil

Heating oil prices moved higher in 1999, as the Organization of Oil Exporting Countries (OPEC) agreed to implement production cuts. When the market recognized that these cuts were being adhered to by the O.P.E.C. countries, prices for all energy products increased. Smaller supplies of petroleum will, in time, translate into smaller supplies of heating oil.

Continued strength in the U.S. economy implied that demand for energy products was more likely to increase than to decline. Early in February 1999, No. 2 fuel oil in New York was trading below 30 cents per gallon. By September 1999, the price had exceeded 60 cents per gallon. There is some seasonality in fuel oil production. Petroleum refineries increase production in the summer months, ahead of the winter heating season, to build inventories. One factor that affects the use of heating oil is the weather. Most of the heating oil used in the U.S. is consumed in the northeastern states. The last two years have seen mild winters, greatly reducing the amount of heating oil used by residential customers. The winter of 1999/2000 began mild as well, though by January 2000 more winterlike temperatures had engulfed the region.

U.S. distillate fuel oil production in August 1999 was 3.46 million barrels per day. The Energy Information Agency reported that this was some 2 percent less than the previous month. In August 1998, production averaged 3.48 million barrels per day. In the January-August 1999 period, production of distillate fuel oil averaged 3.36 million barrels per day. This was some 3 percent less than in the same period in 1998, and 1 percent more than the like period of 1997. For all of 1998, production averaged 3.42 million barrels per day. In 1990, production averaged 2.93 million barrels while in 1985 it averaged 2.69 million barrels.

U.S. imports of distillate fuel oil in August 1999 averaged 172,000 barrels per day. This was 1 percent less than the previous month. In August 1998, imports averaged 181,000 barrels per day. In the January-August 1999 period, imports averaged 214,000 barrels per day, an increase of almost 4 percent from the same period of 1998 and 10 percent less than in the like period of 1997.

U.S. exports of distillate fuel oil in August 1999 averaged 166,000 barrels per day. This was some 35 percent more than the previous month. In August 1998, fuel oil exports averaged 150,000 barrels per day. In the first eight months of 1999, heating oil exports averaged 155,000 barrels per day. This was up 12 percent from the same period in 1998, and was 4 percent higher than the like period of 1997. For all of 1998, exports averaged 149,00 barrels per day. In 1990, exports averaged 109,000 barrels per day while in 1985 they averaged 67,000 barrels per day.

Product supplied in August 1999 averaged 3.32 million barrels per day, down 3 percent from the previous month. In the first eight months of 1999, product supplied averaged 3.48 million barrels per day. This was about unchanged from the same period in 1998 and almost 3 percent more than the like period of 1997. For all of 1998, product supplied average 3.46 million barrels per day. In 1990, the average was 3.02 million barrels per day while in 1985 it was 2.87 million barrels.

U.S. ending stocks of distillate fuel oil at the end of August 1999 were 141 million barrels, up 2 percent from the end of July. At the end of 1998, fuel oil stocks were 156 million barrels. Stocks of low sulfur fuel oil (less than .05 percent) at the end of August 1999 were 68 million barrels. Stocks of high sulfur (greater than .05 percent) fuel oil were 73 million barrels.

U.S. production of residual fuel oil in August 1999 averaged 741,000 barrels per day, up 1 percent from the previous month. In the January-August 1999 period, residual fuel oil production averaged 724,000 barrels per day. This was down 6 percent from the same month period in 1998 and 6 percent higher than the like period of 1997. For all of 1998, residual fuel oil production averaged 762,000 barrels per day. In 1990, residual fuel oil production averaged 950,000 barrels per day while in 1985 it averaged 882,000 barrels per day.

U.S. imports in August 1999 averaged 219,000 barrels per day. In the January-August 1999 period they averaged 236,000 barrels per day. This was some 15 percent less than in the same period of 1998, but 14 percent more than in the like period of 1997.

Futures Markets

Heating oil futures and options are traded on the New York Mercantile Exchange (NYMEX). In London, gasoil futures and options are listed on the International Petroleum Exchange (IPE).

Average Price of No. 2 Heating Oil In Cents Per Gallon

Year	Jan.	Feb.	Mar.	Apr.	May	June	July	Aug.	Sept.	Oct.	Nov.	Dec.	Average
1990	73.26	57.48	57.93	58.51	53.99	48.22	53.14	75.23	88.82	93.95	87.51	79.73	68.98
1991	74.96	70.80	61.92	56.36	55.04	53.67	57.74	60.48	61.54	66.58	64.33	53.35	61.31
1992	51.72	53.39	52.49	56.22	57.38	61.26	60.24	58.29	61.90	62.72	56.52	54.98	57.25
1993	53.14	56.02	58.13	55.49	54.53	52.62	49.74	50.70	51.96	54.00	50.30	43.47	52.51
1994	49.93	55.81	49.18	48.01	47.98	49.37	49.93	49.51	47.90	48.23	49.62	48.41	49.49
1995	47.98	47.64	45.95	49.40	50.31	47.75	46.65	49.14	50.21	48.89	51.89	57.76	49.46
1996	55.64	61.24	65.19	67.90	57.59	51.56	55.58	60.42	67.61	72.34	70.13	72.13	63.11
1997	69.90	61.15	54.83	57.74	56.31	52.32	53.11	54.02	53.19	57.24	56.23	51.09	56.43
1998	46.59	44.26	42.12	42.97	41.07	37.88	36.24	34.48	40.15	38.29	35.59	31.38	39.25
1999	33.41	30.48	38.74	43.07	41.68	43.36	50.02	54.81	60.27	58.34	64.89	67.36	48.87

Source: The Wall Street Journal

Average Open Interest of No. 2 Heating Oil Futures in New York In Contracts

Year	Jan.	Feb.	Mar.	Apr.	May	June	July	Aug.	Sept.	Oct.	Nov.	Dec.
1990	83,020	68,065	67,389	76,954	85,349	112,506	116,108	103,280	97,589	93,631	92,399	81,864
1991	74,216	81,742	81,103	82,419	89,482	102,887	115,896	125,463	135,804	144,026	128,330	117,182
1992	108,337	96,543	91,508	90,816	87,459	101,185	98,623	109,787	119,595	129,951	140,952	135,380
1993	130,536	125,603	130,438	107,363	102,708	113,898	131,816	142,054	166,253	172,940	175,781	199,299
1994	196,390	185,607	186,539	164,417	140,658	129,005	124,764	149,571	172,071	165,475	152,570	148,298
1995	128,664	112,508	118,700	121,974	115,501	122,163	136,722	140,214	149,934	152,244	139,232	138,596
1996	114,324	95,745	90,080	94,161	98,038	97,699	109,524	119,366	138,513	141,217	127,512	108,558
1997	100,333	105,223	122,149	139,981	135,523	141,864	151,403	149,243	151,407	141,008	126,528	145,153
1998	171,177	163,114	177,158	174,587	176,663	196,903	205,071	198,527	188,096	188,019	192,835	184,100
1999	167,686	160,388	166,472	172,127	170,842	168,307	182,382	188,726	192,882	179,040	165,333	146,996

Source: New York Mercantile Exchange (NYMEX)

Volume of Trading of No. 2 Heating Oil Futures in New York In Thousands of Contracts

Year	Jan.	Feb.	Mar.	Apr.	May	June	July	Aug.	Sept.	Oct.	Nov.	Dec.	Total
1990	754.9	415.4	462.5	451.7	517.0	463.3	519.0	723.2	505.8	612.3	522.0	429.8	6,376.9
1991	603.7	523.9	392.5	387.2	399.9	425.1	507.8	595.9	538.2	689.1	781.3	835.6	6,680.2
1992	815.2	574.0	550.1	592.1	586.7	601.1	645.0	663.7	625.7	709.5	808.2	807.1	8,005.5
1993	829.0	660.5	747.3	537.5	482.0	543.4	632.2	721.9	833.8	761.8	886.6	988.9	8,625.1
1994	1,085.7	875.7	766.8	631.7	629.3	723.7	612.3	783.2	706.8	721.4	652.3	798.1	8,986.8
1995	779.8	608.7	716.0	622.8	729.8	618.8	612.7	563.6	714.2	650.8	659.5	990.1	8,266.8
1996	977.2	768.1	666.2	586.5	530.9	402.0	530.2	624.4	766.5	1,014.2	725.0	750.7	8,341.9
1997	794.4	719.0	588.6	710.1	592.0	679.4	679.6	694.7	828.3	742.7	619.3	722.9	8,371.0
1998	793.6	641.8	776.4	578.4	688.5	904.9	720.2	683.0	748.2	768.2	766.5	793.9	8,863.8
1999	738.9	662.3	973.3	706.3	768.1	802.7	770.4	707.9	720.1	819.6	818.6	712.7	9,200.7

Source: New York Mercantile Exchange (NYMEX)

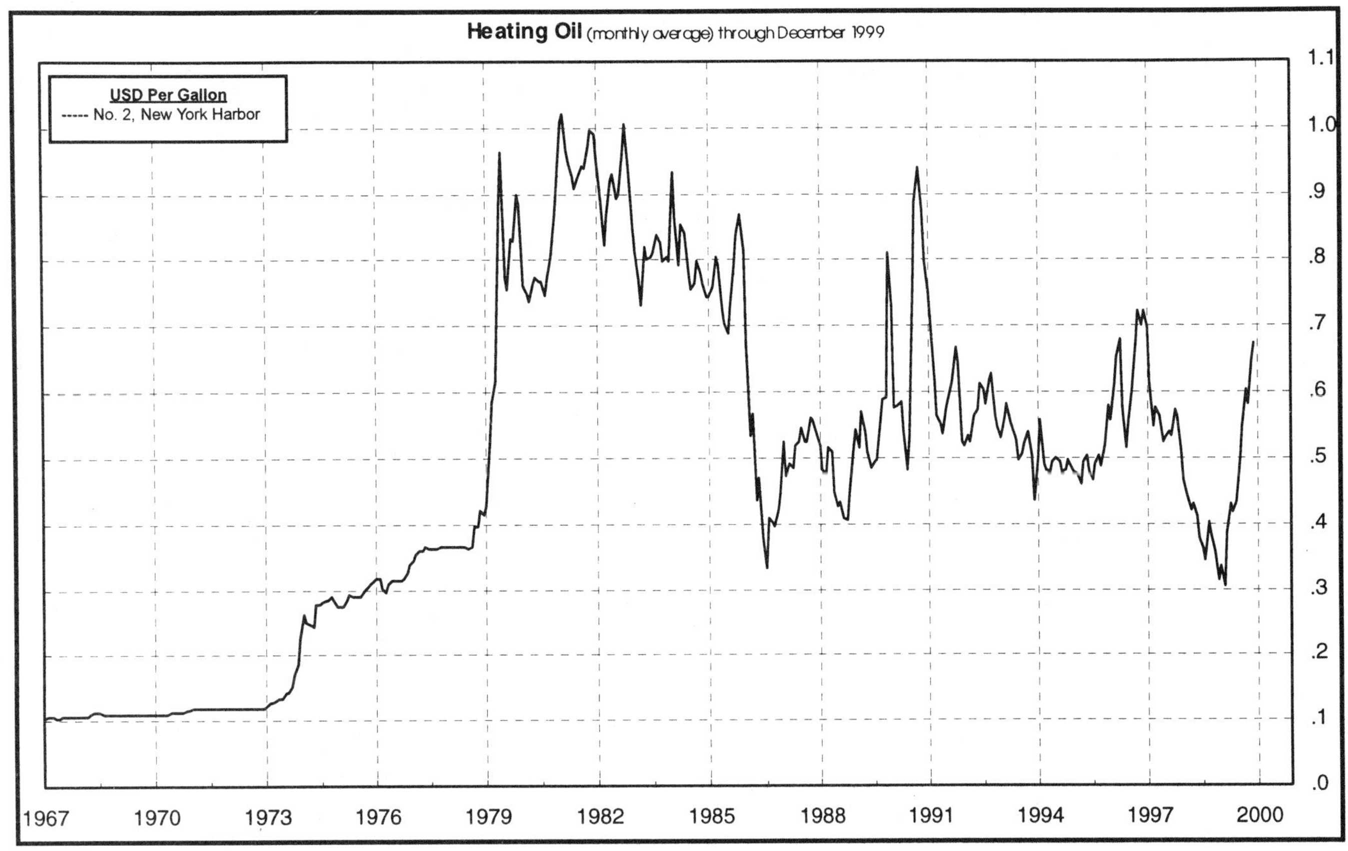

Stocks of Distillate and Residual Fuel in the United States, on First of Month In Millions of Barrels

												Residual Fuel ----- Oil Stocks -----	
Year	Jan.	Feb.	Mar.	Apr.	May	June	July	Aug.	Sept.	Oct.	Nov.	Dec.	Jan. 1	July 1
1990	105.7	118.0	112.2	99.7	99.5	102.8	109.4	125.2	136.0	136.3	132.4	132.2	43.8	46.8
1991	112.1	111.7	101.6	98.2	102.9	106.9	113.7	124.7	131.4	140.1	138.3	144.5	47.6	43.7
1992	143.5	126.7	108.8	97.7	92.1	96.4	104.5	114.6	122.8	127.8	136.8	146.3	49.9	40.9
1993	140.6	130.7	110.4	97.3	99.5	102.8	110.0	120.7	128.2	131.3	145.3	149.2	42.6	45.7
1994	140.9	117.5	102.9	99.4	102.6	112.4	119.5	134.2	138.6	144.7	146.0	147.3	44.2	39.4
1995	145.2	140.2	122.1	115.4	114.6	118.3	114.7	125.0	130.9	131.7	131.4	135.4	41.9	36.0
1996	130.2	113.8	97.3	89.7	90.1	95.7	101.6	106.8	110.3	115.0	114.7	121.8	36.8	34.8
1997	126.7	111.3	105.9	101.8	97.5	108.4	118.2	123.0	132.9	138.9	136.2	140.5	45.9	39.2
1998	139.0	133.1	127.9	124.4	125.7	136.8	139.1	148.8	150.5	152.5	147.5	154.6	40.4	39.8
1999[1]	156.2	147.9	142.3	125.7	125.3	134.8	133.2	138.1	142.0	145.2	137.6		44.9	42.5

[1] Preliminary. *Source: Energy Information Administration; U.S. Department of Energy (EIA-DOE)*

Production of Distillate Fuel Oil in the United States In Thousand Barrels per Day

Year	Jan.	Feb.	Mar.	Apr.	May	June	July	Aug.	Sept.	Oct.	Nov.	Dec.	Average
1990	3,130	2,753	2,657	2,803	2,874	2,996	3,008	3,131	2,968	2,928	2,915	2,917	2,925
1991	2,845	2,870	2,865	2,819	2,929	2,941	2,998	2,961	3,055	3,040	3,103	3,107	2,962
1992	2,818	2,661	2,749	2,930	2,933	2,995	3,067	2,865	2,983	3,251	3,240	3,179	2,974
1993	2,914	2,815	2,919	3,047	2,994	3,093	3,186	3,100	3,205	3,432	3,474	3,382	3,132
1994	3,114	3,018	3,096	3,249	3,317	3,285	3,191	3,187	3,285	3,203	3,270	3,232	3,205
1995	3,054	2,954	3,157	3,126	3,111	3,109	3,056	3,145	3,287	3,169	3,341	3,344	3,155
1996	3,110	3,145	3,110	3,305	3,258	3,291	3,139	3,295	3,403	3,626	3,665	3,558	3,325
1997	3,119	3,089	3,258	3,291	3,525	3,517	3,362	3,427	3,452	3,488	3,543	3,578	3,389
1998	3,321	3,297	3,385	3,447	3,521	3,526	3,583	3,472	3,399	3,223	3,439	3,431	3,421
1999[1]	3,200	3,276	3,196	3,394	3,457	3,388	3,526	3,427	3,487	3,511	3,614	3,424	3,409

[1] Preliminary. *Source: Energy Information Administration, U.S. Department of Energy (EIA-DOE)*

HEATING OIL

Imports of Distillate Fuel Oil in the United States In Thousand Barrels per Day

Year	Jan.	Feb.	Mar.	Apr.	May	June	July	Aug.	Sept.	Oct.	Nov.	Dec.	Average
1990	505	357	281	308	209	257	236	293	226	190	238	239	278
1991	192	139	206	258	186	209	155	168	237	207	249	252	205
1992	232	217	238	202	179	157	172	229	237	263	236	229	216
1993	182	224	235	209	153	168	130	159	137	242	214	160	184
1994	161	276	318	226	202	182	164	211	193	159	166	187	203
1995	313	289	188	125	109	176	157	171	142	162	262	235	193
1996	243	271	253	258	215	185	194	195	187	246	192	253	224
1997	293	246	245	256	220	219	223	202	210	213	161	232	227
1998	187	183	220	189	178	193	212	173	194	226	152	225	195
1999[1]	286	265	248	195	190	190	173	212	181	207	230	202	215

[1] Preliminary. *Source: Energy Information Administration, U.S. Department of Energy (EIA-DOE)*

Disposition of Distillate Fuel Oil, Total Product Supplied in the U.S. In Thousand Barrels per Day

Year	Jan.	Feb.	Mar.	Apr.	May	June	July	Aug.	Sept.	Oct.	Nov.	Dec.	Average
1990	3,185	3,260	3,277	3,043	2,900	2,923	2,726	3,218	2,864	2,960	3,094	2,816	3,021
1991	3,367	2,976	2,984	2,839	2,765	2,775	2,648	2,770	2,865	3,047	2,921	3,087	2,921
1992	3,231	3,219	3,207	3,039	2,753	2,679	2,710	2,705	2,908	3,056	2,929	3,316	2,979
1993	3,128	3,465	3,420	2,943	2,685	2,863	2,674	2,820	2,973	2,983	3,218	3,357	3,041
1994	3,698	3,581	3,307	3,116	2,912	3,062	2,663	3,063	3,133	3,066	3,180	3,203	3,162
1995	3,389	3,675	3,344	3,106	2,899	3,267	2,732	3,044	3,285	3,104	3,233	3,449	3,207
1996	3,681	3,722	3,453	3,385	3,118	3,194	3,046	3,184	3,178	3,575	3,460	3,434	3,368
1997	3,780	3,422	3,515	3,523	3,240	3,235	3,279	3,124	3,302	3,659	3,411	3,665	3,430
1998	3,566	3,585	3,589	3,408	3,219	3,492	3,322	3,442	3,417	3,537	3,300	3,458	3,444
1999[1]	3,637	3,624	3,820	3,412	3,154	3,450	3,419	3,383	3,402	3,770	3,574	3,909	3,546

[1] Preliminary. *Source: Energy Information Administration, U.S. Department of Energy (EIA-DOE)*

Production of Residual Fuel Oil in the United States In Thousands Barrels per Day

Year	Jan.	Feb.	Mar.	Apr.	May	June	July	Aug.	Sept.	Oct.	Nov.	Dec.	Average
1990	1,163	1,060	976	882	884	926	987	944	909	799	846	1,021	950
1991	1,001	1,050	995	916	929	933	871	925	838	814	896	1,051	934
1992	965	957	990	900	964	894	838	815	810	818	895	862	892
1993	820	840	818	896	908	795	762	752	822	841	899	869	835
1994	809	852	859	846	860	779	807	838	800	755	835	871	826
1995	903	776	778	789	748	746	797	801	811	724	705	874	788
1996	774	776	701	671	732	731	646	732	713	693	712	753	719
1997	800	789	639	617	618	727	645	643	688	711	786	810	705
1998	766	673	789	852	773	749	782	778	749	668	741	810	762
1999[1]	778	746	684	679	724	711	732	701	702	660	596	643	696

[1] Preliminary. *Source: Energy Information Administration U.S. Department of Energy (EIA-DOE)*

Supply and Disposition of Residual Fuel Oil in the United States

	Supply		Disposition			Ending	Average
	Total Production	Imports	Stock Change	Exports	Product Supplied	Stocks Million	Sales to End Users[3]
Year	Thousand Barrels Per Day					Barrels	Cents per Gallon
1990	950	504	13	211	1,229	49	44.4
1991	934	453	4	226	1,158	50	34.0
1992	892	375	-20	193	1,094	43	33.6
1993	835	373	4	123	1,080	44	33.7
1994	826	314	-6	125	1,021	42	35.2
1995	788	187	-13	136	852	37	39.2
1996	726	248	24	102	848	46	45.5
1997	708	194	-15	120	797	40	42.3
1998	762	275	12	138	887	45	30.5
1999[1]	696	235	-21	128	824	35	

[1] Preliminary. [2] Less than +500 barrels per day and greater than -500 barrels per day. [3] Refiner price excluding taxes.
Source: Energy Information Administration, U.S. Department of Energy (EIA-DOE)

Hides and Leather

The major producers of bovine hides and skins are the U.S., Brazil, Argentina and Russia. The U.S. has about 25 percent of the world market in terms of production. U.S. production of hides and skins in 1999 was forecast by the U.S. Department of Agriculture to be 910,000 metric tonnes, down 8 percent from the previous year. U.S. production appears to be trending slightly lower. In 1990 production was 1.06 million tonnes. Production in Brazil appears to be trending higher. The U.S.D.A. forecast 1999 production at 605,000 tonnes, up almost 2 percent from the previous year. Argentina was the third largest producer in 1999, with hide and skin production forecast to be 260,000 tonnes, up 2 percent from 1998. Production in Russia has been declining with a 1999 forecast of 215,000 tonnes, down 9 percent from the previous year. In 1990, Russian production of bovine hides and skins was 503,000 tonnes.

The U.S.D.A. reported that for the week ended December 9, 1999, net new export sales of cattle hides in pieces were 406,400. South Korea purchased 151,600 pieces, Mexico 60,800, Taiwan 35,400, Japan 34,800, Italy 28,000 and Turkey 25,400. Actual export shipments for the week were 498,000 pieces. In the 1999 marketing year (January-December), cumulative exports of whole cattle hides were 19.44 million pieces. The largest market was South Korea which took 8 million pieces. The next largest market was Taiwan with 2.84 million pieces, followed by Mexico with 2.56 million pieces. Japan took 2.26 million pieces.

Most U.S. leather is used in the shoe industry. U.S. production of nonrubber footwear and slippers in the second quarter of 1999 was 26.3 million pair. That represented a decline of 1 percent from the first quarter. In terms of the type of footwear, in the second quarter of 1999, production of men's shoes was 7.18 million pair (except athletic). Of the total, work shoe production was 3.79 million pairs and shoes and boots (except work and athletic) were 3.39 million pair. Men's shoe production in the second quarter of 1999 was down 8 percent from the first quarter of 1999. Work shoe production was up almost 2 percent while shoe and boot production was down 8 percent.

Women's shoes and boots production (except athletic) in the second quarter of 1999 were 7.83 million pair, up 5 percent from the first quarter of 1999. Nonrubber children's shoe production, all types (except athletic) in the second quarter of 1999 was 187,000 pair, down 33 percent from the first quarter. Infant's and babies' shoe production in second quarter 1999 was 1.1 million pair, up 16 percent from the first quarter. Slipper production was 9.45 million pair in the second quarter, about unchanged from the first quarter.

World Production of Bovine Hides and Skins In Thousands of Metric Tons

Year	Argentina	Australia	Brazil	Canada	Colombia	France	Germany	Italy	Mexico	Russia	United Kingdom	United States	World Total
1991	308	153	448	75	104	182	251	95	155	502	93	1,061	4,076
1992	298	162	442	77	88	180	205	98	160	466	88	1,073	3,983
1993	303	154	565	73	79	160	175	95	161	460	77	1,078	4,418
1994	305	152	573	74	77	151	158	93	166	350	81	942	4,073
1995	301	145	608	75	84	154	156	93	170	310	85	976	4,177
1996	306	145	615	81	88	158	164	92	160	280	90	994	4,179
1997	330	166	590	83	92	158	164	92	160	270	84	985	4,144
1998	285	170	622	83	93	148	152	90	160	235	87	987	4,093
1999[1]	300	160	637	88	92	145	150	90	157	210	84	999	4,088
2000[2]	295	158	667	85	92	148	149	90	159	200	84	950	4,065

[1] Preliminary. [2] Forecast. *Source: Foreign Agricultural Service, U.S. Department of Agriculture (FAS-USDA)*

Salient Statistics of Hides and Leather in the United States In Thousands of Equivalent Hides

Year	New Supply of Cattle Hides: Domestic Slaughter: Federally Inspected	Uninspected[4]	Total Production	Net Exports	Wholesale Prices (Cents Per Pound): Heavy Native Cows[2]	Heavy Native Steers[3]	Wholesale Leather Production (In 1,000 Equiv. Hides): All U.S. Tanning	Cattlehide	Value of Leather Exports ($1,000)	Indexes, Upper (1982 = 100): Men	Women	Footwear (Million Pairs): Production[5]	Exports
1989	33,010	907	33,917	22,500	83.16	89.4	12,932	11,242	624,925	126.5	114.8	221,790	14,358
1990	32,391	851	33,242	20,920	92.58	92.0	14,820	13,018	750,836	132.8	118.8	184,568	15,174
1991	31,887	803	32,690	18,636	76.92	78.9	14,800	13,021	680,348	136.9	120.7	167,386	18,109
1992	32,094	780	32,874	17,810	81.71	75.9	15,900	14,474	705,038	140.5	124.2	168,451	21,401
1993	32,593	731	33,324	17,117	82.16	78.9	18,057	16,931	764,120	142.8	126.9	171,733	20,700
1994	33,483	713	34,196	16,259	94.99	87.3	18,842	18,117	811,951	144.7	127.2	163,000	22,505
1995	34,879	760	35,639	18,336	93.89	87.6	18,092	17,480	870,247	150.1	129.0	147,550	20,571
1996	36,583	177	36,760	18,626	92.15	86.4	18,769	18,135	950,510	152.4	132.1	127,315	23,726
1997	35,567	925	36,492	17,562	90.99	86.1	19,592	18,930	1,145,664	156.4	132.2	123,739	28,300
1998[1]	34,787	850	35,637	15,937	75.45	69.5	20,297	19,706	1,289,547	158.0	132.4	122,247	28,175

[1] Preliminary. [2] Central U.S., heifers. [3] F.O.B. Chicago. [4] Includes farm slaughter; diseased & condemned animals & hides taken off fallen animals. [5] Other than rubber. *Sources: Leather Industries of America (LIA); Bureau of Labor Statistics, U.S. Department of Commerce (BLS)*

Production of All Footwear (Shoes, Sandals, Slippers, Athletic, Etc.) in the U.S. In Millions of Pairs

Year	First Quarter	Second Quarter	Third Quarter	Fourth Quarter	Total	Year	First Quarter	Second Quarter	Third Quarter	Fourth Quarter	Total
1990	53.5	52.3	49.6	46.2	184.6	1995	37.2	38.3	34.8	36.7	147.0
1991	48.1	37.8	41.8	41.2	169.0	1996	33.2	31.8	29.7	33.2	128.0
1992	41.1	40.8	43.6	39.3	164.8	1997	31.4	33.1	28.6	30.6	123.7
1993	43.3	44.6	42.8	41.0	171.7	1998	32.8	31.8	29.3	28.6	122.5
1994	42.5	40.8	40.1	39.5	163.0	1999[1]	26.7	26.1	24.5		103.1

[1] Preliminary. *Source: Bureau of the Census, U.S. Department of Commerce*

Average Factory Price[2] of Footwear in the United States In Dollars Per Pair

Year	First Quarter	Second Quarter	Third Quarter	Fourth Quarter	Total	Year	First Quarter	Second Quarter	Third Quarter	Fourth Quarter	Total
1990	18.04	18.65	19.91	20.72	19.37	1995	19.61	21.46	25.37	21.26	21.79
1991	22.14	20.40	19.74	18.52	20.14	1996	23.65	22.78	22.14	20.38	22.07
1992	20.19	22.21	21.15	20.46	20.96	1997	21.99	21.15	21.79	21.82	21.69
1993	21.62	21.67	21.37	21.79	21.61	1998	24.00	23.82	19.95	19.46	21.81
1994	25.77	23.60	21.49	22.44	23.22	1999[1]	23.33	22.70	19.90		21.98

[1] Preliminary. [2] Average value of factory shipments per pair. *Source: Bureau of the Census, U.S. Department of Commerce*

Imports and Exports of All Cattle Hides in the United States In Thousands of Hides

	-------- Imports --------		---------- U.S. Exports - by Country of Destination ----------										
Year	Total	From Canada	Total	Canada	Italy	Japan	Rep. of Korea	Mexico	Portugal	Romania	Spain	Taiwan	Thailand
1989	901	1,043	23,401	614	343	6,268	10,322	1,284	46	1,154	64	1,886	70
1990	661	678	21,582	674	136	6,802	9,839	1,438	29	253	175	1,476	91
1991	1,549	1,088	20,185	561	138	4,662	9,300	2,702	7	-----	39	2,058	123
1992	1,536	1,457	19,347	684	107	4,647	8,589	2,729	100	4	30	1,823	160
1993	1,660	1,597	18,777	965	354	4,167	7,919	2,217	79	1	60	1,950	386
1994	1,731	-----	17,990	995	309	3,133	7,472	1,553	168	72	141	2,491	332
1995	1,759	-----	20,095	952	332	3,246	8,283	899	111	63	215	3,017	781
1996	1,702	-----	20,328	1,149	522	2,372	7,956	2,123	64	171	189	2,871	455
1997	1,633	-----	19,195	1,320	469	1,802	7,470	2,501	55	-----	148	2,866	323
1998[1]	1,930	-----	17,867	1,126	1,164	1,407	4,897	2,846	91	-----	440	2,701	336

[1] Preliminary. *Source: Leather Industries of America*

Imports of Bovine Hides and Skins by Selected Countries In Metric Tons

Year	Brazil	Canada	Hong Kong	Italy	Japan	Mexico	Portugal	Rep. of Korea	Spain	Taiwan	Turkey	United States	World Total
1992	11	17	80	131	188	71	32	385	26	91	28	65	1,266
1993	21	26	81	141	188	71	39	372	35	94	37	57	1,426
1994	16	28	95	243	139	60	56	356	29	112	17	49	1,556
1995	33	35	100	250	152	30	43	342	42	112	43	57	1,618
1996	20	34	79	263	123	71	42	341	33	124	50	60	1,586
1997	13	39	64	254	114	96	37	323	44	140	68	60	1,860
1998	10	42	71	249	96	110	39	229	44	139	45	59	1,760
1999[1]	8	38	74	245	105	115	42	240	40	142	55	57	1,787
2000[2]	8	39	76	245	105	115	43	245	40	142	60	57	1,815

[1] Preliminary. [2] Forecast. *Source: Foreign Agricultural Service, U.S. Department of Agriculture (FAS-USDA)*

Exports of Bovine Hides and Skins by Selected Countries In Metric Tons

Year	Australia	Brazil	Canada	Germany	Hong Kong	Italy	Nether-lands	New Zealand	Poland	Russia	United Kingdom	United States	World Total
1992	144	71	74	38	75	9	66	31	17	28	19	610	1,261
1993	142	76	87	40	76	7	35	21	5	150	25	581	1,374
1994	96	84	79	24	93	10	37	22	2	216	22	455	1,271
1995	85	148	90	34	100	10	47	22	2	195	22	510	1,351
1996	93	174	97	33	72	20	47	28	3	212	24	506	1,423
1997	115	216	97	35	60	16	48	27	3	210	25	473	1,475
1998	111	220	90	31	69	24	32	28	6	202	18	443	1,412
1999[1]	115	230	85	28	74	26	30	28	8	190	19	436	1,411
2000[2]	112	250	85	31	76	26	25	28	6	170	19	387	1,365

[1] Preliminary. [2] Forecast. *Source: Foreign Agricultural Service, U.S. Department of Agriculture (FAS-USDA)*

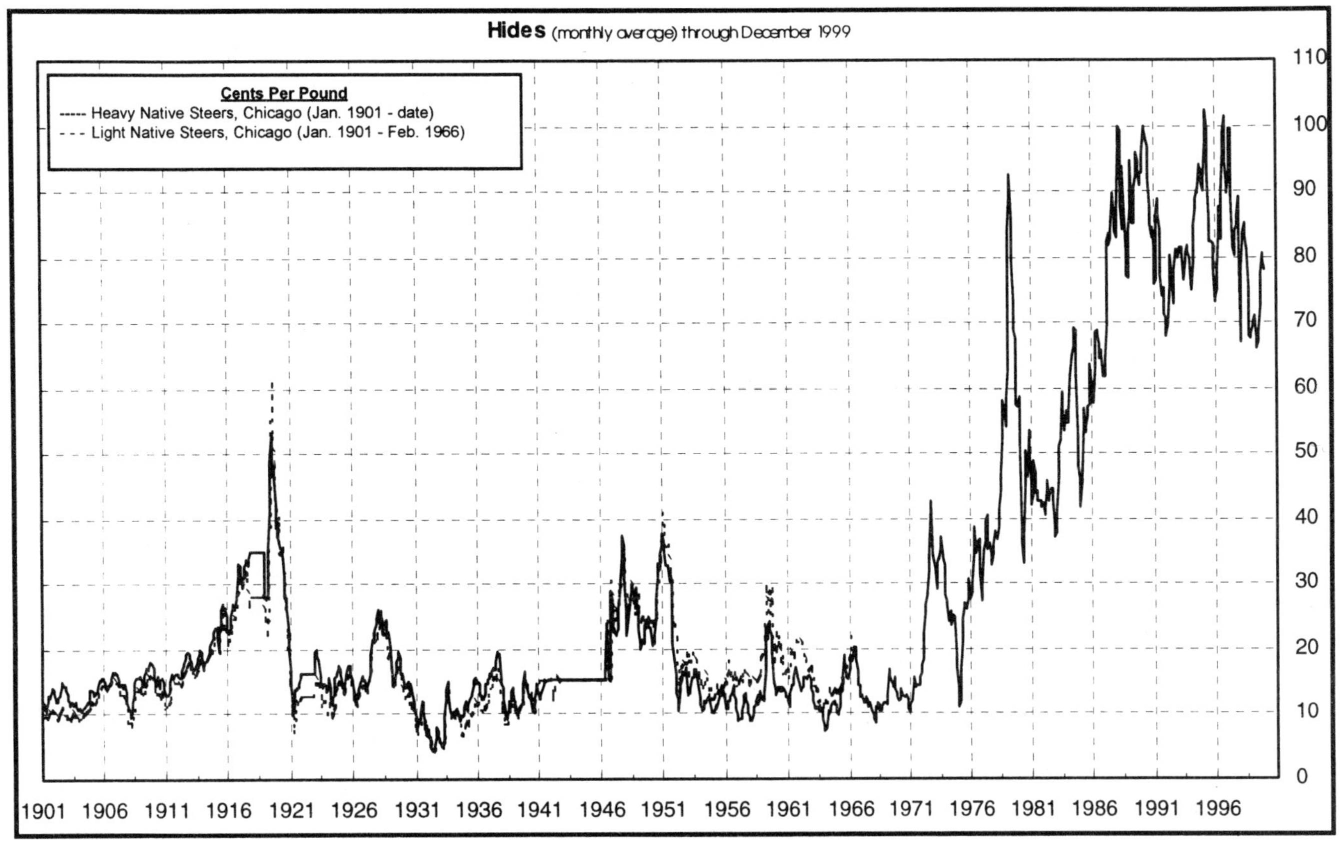

Utilization of Bovine Hides and Skins by Selected Countries In Metric Tons

Year	Argentina	Brazil	Colombia	Germany	Italy	Japan	Mexico	Rep. of Korea	Spain	Taiwan	Turkey	United States	World Total
1991	308	396	98	143	435	253	225	400	119	101	78	491	4,009
1992	298	382	97	129	435	229	231	400	98	91	90	528	3,977
1993	302	510	94	100	435	226	232	385	98	94	95	554	4,322
1994	304	505	96	83	550	200	226	374	94	112	85	536	4,282
1995	300	493	89	79	570	191	200	355	98	112	100	523	4,398
1996	308	461	91	80	615	165	230	353	95	124	110	548	4,329
1997	332	387	89	101	570	150	251	347	106	140	120	572	4,508
1998	285	412	91	100	540	135	265	265	108	139	100	603	4,448
1999[1]	300	415	89	102	530	135	267	266	110	142	110	620	4,466
2000[2]	285	425	89	103	520	137	269	270	112	142	120	620	4,508

[1] Preliminary. [2] Forecast. *Source: Foreign Agricultural Service, U.S. Department of Agriculture (FAS-USDA)*

Wholesale Price of Hides (Packer Heavy Native Steers) F.O.B. Chicago In Cents Per Pound

Year	Jan.	Feb.	Mar.	Apr.	May	June	July	Aug.	Sept.	Oct.	Nov.	Dec.	Average
1990	92.68	92.76	95.50	99.95	99.57	97.90	96.69	91.74	87.51	84.70	82.90	84.40	82.19
1991	81.64	75.84	76.50	86.32	88.77	86.60	84.05	77.18	74.05	75.30	75.30	71.29	79.40
1992	70.55	67.84	69.68	75.95	80.05	76.77	76.50	72.76	77.62	81.18	80.05	81.00	75.83
1993	79.82	81.05	81.48	81.44	80.35	76.95	76.62	79.27	80.52	81.76	80.81	79.83	79.99
1994	75.07	75.08	79.00	84.75	87.33	88.77	90.38	89.76	93.90	93.67	93.19	91.13	86.84
1995	90.10	91.42	97.99	102.32	99.64	92.45	85.74	82.46	82.45	82.16	78.02	73.02	88.15
1996	73.67	75.11	77.96	84.58	87.56	82.51	89.45	96.06	98.91	101.51	94.60	90.65	87.71
1997	89.77	93.47	99.44	99.40	89.44	81.45	80.20	83.92	84.86	86.35	89.20	82.61	88.34
1998	66.88	77.33	82.61	83.72	85.05	83.13	81.17	81.11	75.23	67.95	67.53	68.26	76.66
1999	69.42	69.97	70.84	67.36	65.96	66.89	68.17	72.41	77.52	80.43	79.67	78.00	72.22

Source: The Wall Street Journal

Hogs

1999 U.S. hog prices, basis nearby Chicago futures, tripled in the first half of 1999 to about $60.00 per hundredweight from the late 1998 near historic low of $20.00/cwt. An early summer break carried prices down to about $40.00/cwt. which was reversed when Hurricane Floyd ripped through North Carolina, the country's second largest hog producing state, leaving in its wake substantial damage to that state's hog industry. Towards late 1999, nearby futures were again trading in the mid $50.00/cwt. area. Due to the hurricane damage it is possible, at least in states prone to severe weather, that the industry's push into concentrated corporate based finishing and marketing operations may be reviewed, if for no other reason than the environmental concerns that the storm triggered.

The world's hog inventory in early 1999 of 734 million head compares with 723 million in 1998. World pork consumption set a new high in 1999 at 76.8 million metric tonnes vs. 75.3 million in 1998, but on a per capita basis the 1999 estimate of 18.6 kilograms per person trails the 1995 record of 19.4 kg.

China is the world's largest hog producer with more than half the total with the U.S. a distant second. China's 1999 inventory of 395 million head compares with 389 million in 1998. In the U.S., the 1999 total of 62.2 million head was unchanged from 1998. Germany's inventory, the largest in the European Union, of 25.7 million head compares with 24.8 million in 1998. The protracted slide in Russia's and the Ukraine's inventory persisted into 1999, as their combined total of 26.4 million head compares with 26.6 million in 1998 and over 50 million head as recently as 1992.

The September 1, 1999 U.S. inventory of 60.7 million head compares with 63.5 million a year earlier. Of the total, 6.3 million head were kept for breeding vs. 6.9 million in 1998, with the balance to be marketed. The decrease in the 1999 inventory was expected given the depressed 1998 hog prices. Farrowing intentions during the closing months of 1999 and into the first quarter of 2000 were forecast at 3 percent below the year earlier periods. Although the U.S. hog inventory is only about 8 percent of the world total, slaughter runs about 10 percent and pork production somewhat higher. U.S. per capita pork usage in 1999 of 53.5 pounds compares with 52.6 pounds in 1998 and a forecast of 51.6 pounds in 2000.

More than half the inventory share of U.S. hog marketings now come from contract hog operations. In a contractual agreement, the contractor provides the hogs, feed, medication and supplies, while the contractee provides the housing, utilities and labor. Most hog production still occurs in Corn Belt states with Iowa the leading producing state. Southern states have seen dramatic growth in contractual operations in recent years. Still, most U.S. producers continue to raise hogs in farrow-to-finish operations. As of September 1, 1999, the total number of hogs under contract, owned by operations with over 5,000 head total inventory but raised by contractees, accounted for 31 percent of the total U.S. inventory.

Commercial U.S. hog slaughter in the January-October 1999 period of 83.8 million head compares with 82.8 million in the like 1998 period, with an average dressed weight of about 190 pounds in both years. Pork production in 1999 was estimated at 19.2 billion pounds vs. 19.0 billion in 1998. Based upon fall 1999 hog inventory and breeding intentions, pork production in 2000 is forecast at 18.6 billion pounds.

The U.S. is among the world's largest pork exporters moving 606,000 metric tonnes in 1999 vs. 557,000 in 1998, and the world total of 2.8 million tonnes in both years. Japan, Russia, Canada and Mexico are generally the largest importers of U.S. pork. The U.S. imports pork products, mostly from Canada and Denmark with 318,000 tonnes in both 1998 and 1999. The U.S. imports live hogs from Canada.

Midwest wholesale barrow and gilt hog prices during 1999 averaged about $32.42 per cwt. vs. $34.72 in 1998 and forecasts of $34.00 to $37.00 in 2000.

Futures Markets

Lean hog futures and options are traded on the Chicago Mercantile Exchange (CME) where futures settle against the CME Lean Hog Index(TM). Their proprietary Index tracks the value of lean pork at select U.S. packing plants.

Live hog futures are traded on the Mid-America Commodity Exchange (MidAm) and the Budapest Commodity Exchange.

Salient Statistics of Pigs and Hogs in the United States

	Pig Crop						Value of Hogs on Farms, Dec. 1					Hogs Slaughtered in Thousand Head				
	Spring[3]			Fall[4]								Commercial				
Year	Sows Farrowed --- 1,000 Head	Pig Crop --- 1,000 Head	Pigs Per Litter	Sows Farrowed --- 1,000 Head	Pig Crop --- 1,000 Head	Pigs Per Litter	$ Per Head	Total Million $	Hog Marketings Thousand Head	Quantity Produced (Live Wt.) Mill. Lbs.	Value of Production Mil. $	Federally Inspected	Other	Total	Farm	Total
1989	6,028	47,141	7.82	5,767	44,779	7.76	79.1	4,253	92,432	21,907	9,281	86,328	2,364	88,692	315	89,007
1990	5,732	45,223	7.89	5,709	44,877	7.86	85.4	4,648	89,240	21,287	11,346	82,901	2,235	85,136	296	85,431
1991	5,988	47,413	7.92	6,071	47,902	7.89	68.8	3,966	92,220	22,727	11,067	85,952	2,217	88,169	276	88,445
1992	6,260	50,466	8.06	6,012	48,676	8.10	71.2	4,147	98,589	23,947	9,854	92,611	2,278	94,889	268	95,157
1993	6,034	49,084	8.14	5,976	48,216	8.07	74.9	4,338	98,351	23,693	10,628	90,933	2,135	93,068	229	93,296
1994	6,257	51,217	8.18	6,139	50,262	8.19	53.2	3,192	100,747	24,437	9,692	93,435	2,261	95,696	208	95,905
1995	6,046	50,077	8.28	5,843	48,739	8.35	70.7	4,120	102,684	24,426	9,829	94,203	2,123	96,325	210	96,535
1996	5,648	47,888	8.46	5,449	46,571	8.55	94.0	5,284	101,852	23,267	12,013	90,534	1,860	92,394	175	92,569
1997[1]	5,595	48,394	8.65	5,884	51,190	8.70	81.0	4,880	104,301	23,979	12,552	90,228	1,733	91,960	165	92,125
1998[2]	6,014	52,469	8.73	6,044	52,511	8.69			117,275	25,766	8,640	99,285	1,745	101,029	165	101,194

[1] Preliminary. [2] Estimate. [3] December-May. [4] June-November. *Source: Economic Research Service, U.S. Department of Agriculture (ERS-USDA)*

World Hog Numbers in Specified Countries as of January 1 In Thousands of Head

Year	Brazil	Canada	China	Denmark	France	Germany	Philip-pines	Poland	Russia	Spain	Ukraine	United States	World Total
1991	32,550	10,468	362,408	9,282	12,013	30,818	8,007	19,739	38,500	16,001	19,427	54,416	760,788
1992	33,050	10,498	369,646	9,767	12,067	26,063	8,022	20,725	35,384	17,209	17,839	57,469	728,789
1993	31,050	10,577	384,210	10,345	13,015	26,514	7,954	21,059	31,520	18,260	16,175	58,202	740,758
1994	31,200	10,534	393,000	10,870	14,791	26,075	8,227	17,422	28,600	18,234	15,298	57,940	743,930
1995	31,338	11,291	414,619	10,864	14,593	24,698	8,941	19,138	24,859	18,295	13,946	59,738	758,461
1996	32,068	11,588	345,848	10,709	14,523	23,737	9,023	20,343	22,630	18,600	13,144	58,201	686,581
1997	31,369	11,480	362,836	11,081	14,968	24,283	9,750	17,697	19,500	18,651	11,236	56,124	695,133
1998	31,427	11,985	388,965	11,442	15,443	24,845	10,210	18,498	16,579	18,970	9,479	61,158	720,412
1999[1]	30,997	12,402	396,000	11,891	15,764	26,299	10,398	19,275	16,400	21,715	9,909	62,206	734,049
2000[2]	29,810	13,164	397,000	12,147	15,550	27,049	10,550	18,300	16,000	22,328	10,000	59,600	732,030

[1] Preliminary. [2] Forecast. *Source: Foreign Agricultural Service, U.S. Department of Agriculture (FAS-USDA)*

Hogs and Pigs on Farms in the United States on December 1 In Thousands of Head

Year	Geargia	Illinois	Indiana	Iowa	Kansas	Minne-sota	Missouri	Nebraska	North Carolina	Ohio	South Dakota	Wis-consin	Total
1990	1,100	5,700	4,400	13,800	1,500	4,500	2,800	4,300	2,800	2,000	1,770	1,200	54,477
1991	1,130	5,900	4,600	15,000	1,430	4,900	2,700	4,500	3,650	1,925	1,950	1,180	57,684
1992	1,100	5,900	4,600	16,400	1,440	4,700	2,850	4,650	4,500	1,800	1,830	1,210	59,815
1993	1,000	5,450	4,300	15,000	1,350	4,750	3,000	4,300	5,400	1,630	1,750	1,170	57,904
1994	1,020	5,350	4,500	14,500	1,310	4,850	3,500	4,350	7,000	1,800	1,740	1,040	59,990
1995	900	4,800	4,000	13,400	1,230	4,950	1,100	4,050	8,200	1,800	1,450	900	58,264
1996	800	4,400	3,750	12,200	1,450	4,850	3,450	3,600	9,300	1,500	1,200	800	56,171
1997	520	4,700	3,950	14,600	1,530	5,700	3,550	3,500	9,600	1,700	1,400	740	61,158
1998	480	4,850	4,050	15,300	1,590	5,700	3,300	3,400	9,700	1,700	1,400	690	62,206
1999[1]	480	4,100	3,250	15,400	1,460	5,500	3,150	3,000	9,500	1,500	12,601	570	59,407

[1] Preliminary. *Source: National Agricultural Statistics Service, U.S. Department of Agriculture (NASS-USDA)*

Hog-Corn Price Ratio[1] in the United States

Year	Jan.	Feb.	Mar.	Apr.	May	June	July	Aug.	Sept.	Oct.	Nov.	Dec.	Average
1990	20.5	20.8	21.6	21.4	23.4	22.9	23.2	23.3	22.3	23.3	25.9	21.5	22.5
1991	22.0	22.5	21.5	21.0	22.7	23.7	23.9	22.0	19.9	18.9	16.6	16.6	20.9
1992	15.3	16.3	15.7	16.5	18.1	18.9	19.1	20.5	19.5	20.5	20.8	21.2	18.5
1993	20.3	22.0	22.1	21.0	21.9	23.0	20.6	21.0	21.6	20.6	17.3	15.2	20.6
1994	16.1	17.2	16.2	16.1	16.4	16.3	18.6	19.4	16.2	15.4	14.1	14.5	16.4
1995	16.8	17.5	16.4	15.1	15.4	16.8	17.6	18.5	18.0	16.4	13.9	14.2	16.4
1996	13.7	13.8	13.9	12.9	13.7	13.4	13.2	13.9	15.4	19.2	20.5	21.1	15.4
1997	20.0	19.9	17.7	19.2	21.6	22.6	24.3	22.1	20.0	18.6	18.0	16.5	20.0
1998	14.1	14.1	13.7	14.8	18.1	18.6	16.8	18.6	16.1	14.6	9.7	7.4	14.7
1999[2]	12.8	13.5	13.5	14.7	18.2	17.4	17.9	20.7	19.3	20.1	19.6	19.6	17.3

[1] Bushels of corn equal in value to 100 pounds of hog, live weight. [2] Preliminary. *Source: Economic Research Service, U.S. Department of Agriculture (ERS-USDA)*

Cold Storage Holdings of Frozen Pork[1] in the United States, on First of Month In Millions of Pounds

Year	Jan.	Feb.	Mar.	Apr.	May	June	July	Aug.	Sept.	Oct.	Nov.	Dec.
1990	255.8	272.5	303.9	294.6	320.3	320.3	292.6	256.4	224.7	225.8	231.9	221.5
1991	233.6	247.0	281.2	289.0	340.0	333.3	312.3	277.9	282.4	280.5	299.7	308.0
1992	311.1	341.2	364.0	372.2	362.6	344.9	319.0	307.0	266.7	297.3	306.8	316.7
1993	314.5	329.5	344.4	330.4	378.5	371.6	351.3	342.5	308.9	311.2	324.8	313.0
1994	299.2	348.8	356.9	393.1	429.7	437.6	410.8	393.7	364.0	352.7	385.4	383.2
1995	365.3	389.6	395.1	416.8	422.3	434.9	431.1	408.3	354.0	332.6	321.6	347.1
1996	334.8	382.2	385.5	352.9	385.5	381.3	351.8	322.7	322.9	340.3	333.3	316.4
1997	313.8	342.2	383.9	404.7	440.2	413.4	406.2	388.7	371.8	346.6	354.2	334.1
1998	346.4	446.1	464.5	458.8	487.0	477.4	426.8	414.6	392.6	388.9	411.9	443.4
1999[2]	503.5	517.6	545.4	559.9	595.2	585.6	532.1	500.0	438.1	430.6	438.1	422.5

[1] Excludes lard. [2] Preliminary. *Source: Economic Research Service, U.S. Department of Agriculture (ERS-USDA)*

HOGS

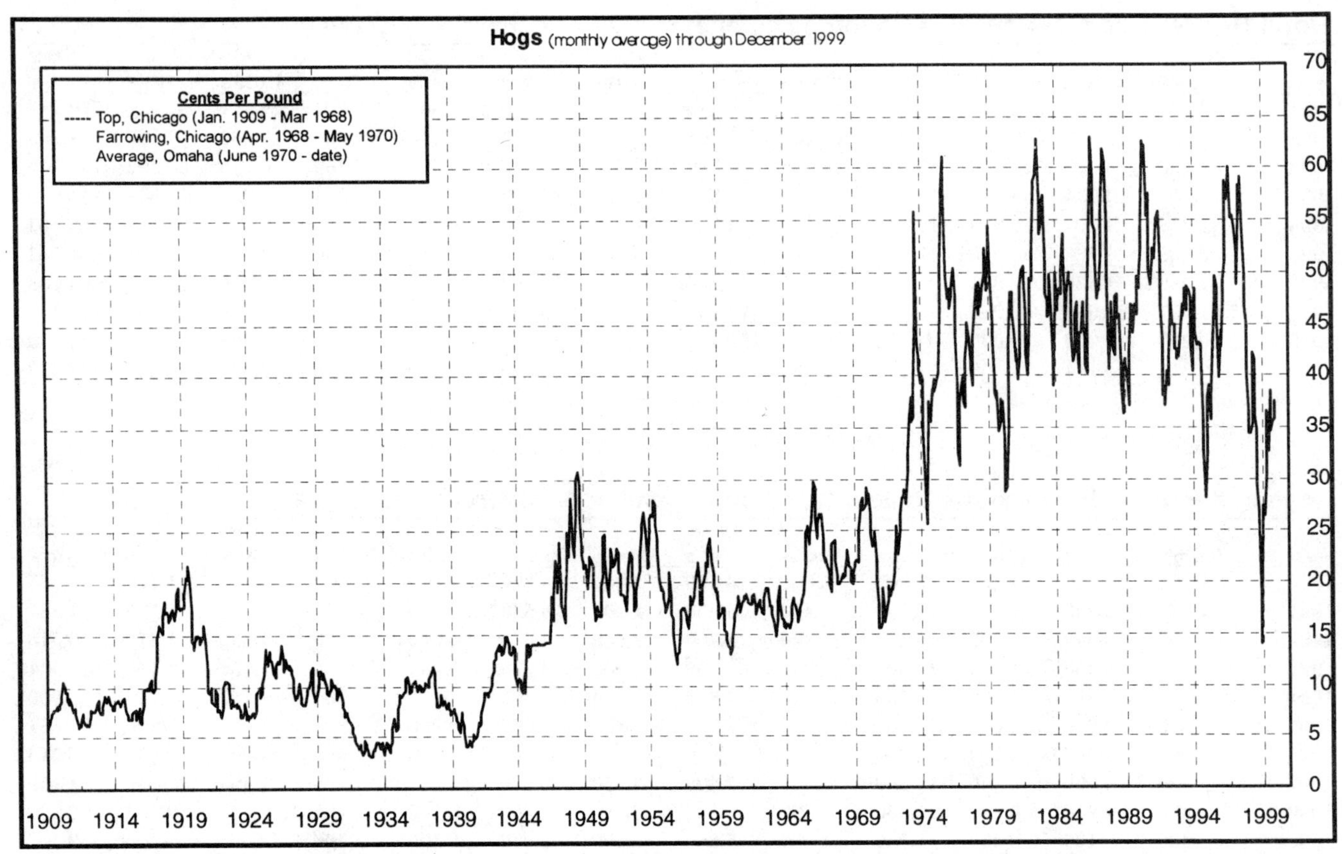

Average Wholesale Price of Hogs, Average (All Weights) in Sioux City In Dollars Per Hundred Pounds (Cwt.)

Year	Jan.	Feb.	Mar.	Apr.	May	June	July	Aug.	Sept.	Oct.	Nov.	Dec.	Average
1988	44.59	47.45	43.19	42.28	47.75	48.26	45.60	45.98	41.28	38.92	36.52	40.58	43.53
1989	41.64	41.11	39.88	37.22	42.40	46.24	47.26	47.04	44.58	47.49	47.21	49.65	44.31
1990	48.41	49.48	52.56	54.63	62.80	61.34	62.54	56.37	55.64	58.02	50.17	48.96	55.08
1991	51.32	52.31	51.92	51.42	54.83	54.79	55.74	51.11	46.76	43.51	38.29	38.93	49.24
1992	37.15	40.45	39.09	42.01	45.90	47.59	44.98	44.88	42.50	42.57	41.98	42.12	42.60
1993	41.66	44.57	46.76	45.46	47.10	48.52	46.38	48.67	48.40	47.27	42.76	40.38	45.66
1994	43.99	48.12	44.30	42.72	42.27	42.76	42.62	42.37	35.49	32.56	28.25	31.59	39.75
1995	37.82	39.09	37.94	35.88	37.35	43.03	47.18	49.46	48.67	45.42	40.02	43.80	42.14
1996	42.39	46.93	49.06	50.88	58.29	56.45	59.47	60.49	54.60	55.41	54.42	55.47	53.66
1997[1]	52.96	51.36	48.52	54.41	57.84	57.43	58.89	54.17	49.45	46.12	44.86	40.33	51.36

[1] Preliminary. *Source: Economic Research Service, U.S. Department of Agriculture (ERS-USDA)*

Average Price Received by Farmers for Hogs in the United States In Cents Per Pound

Year	Jan.	Feb.	Mar.	Apr.	May	June	July	Aug.	Sept.	Oct.	Nov.	Dec.	Average
1990	47.30	48.20	51.30	53.80	61.20	60.30	60.80	55.90	54.30	56.80	50.20	47.80	53.99
1991	50.00	52.20	51.50	50.90	54.10	54.70	54.20	51.20	46.40	43.60	38.00	38.60	48.78
1992	36.80	40.20	39.10	41.00	45.10	46.70	44.60	44.10	42.10	42.00	41.10	41.70	42.04
1993	41.20	44.00	46.50	45.40	46.90	48.10	45.70	47.30	47.80	46.90	42.50	40.40	45.23
1994	43.50	47.90	44.40	42.70	42.70	42.70	42.20	41.80	35.40	31.80	28.00	30.80	39.49
1995	36.90	39.10	37.80	35.70	37.20	42.30	46.30	48.60	48.40	45.70	39.90	43.50	41.78
1996	42.30	46.50	48.70	49.70	56.80	56.40	58.60	59.70	54.70	55.60	54.40	55.60	53.25
1997	53.80	52.80	49.40	53.80	58.20	57.80	58.90	55.30	50.40	47.30	45.10	41.60	52.03
1998	36.00	35.90	34.90	35.60	42.30	42.40	36.90	35.20	29.50	27.80	18.80	14.70	32.50
1999[1]	26.30	27.60	27.80	30.20	36.40	34.20	31.20	36.20	33.70	34.00	33.40	35.60	32.22

[1] Preliminary. *Source: Economic Research Service, U.S. Department of Agriculture (ERS-USDA)*

Quarterly Hogs and Pigs Report in the United States, 10 States In Thousands of Head

Year[2]	Inventory[3]	Breeding[3]	Market[3]	Farrowings	Pig Crop	Year[2]	Inventory[3]	Breeding[3]	Market[3]	Farrowings	Pig Crop
1990	42,200	5,275	36,925	8,960	70,589	1995	59,990	7,060	52,930	11,847	98,516
I	42,200	5,275	36,925	2,013	15,748	I	59,990	7,060	52,930	2,886	23,851
II	40,190	5,245	34,945	2,458	19,576	II	58,465	6,998	51,467	3,170	26,373
III	42,630	5,405	37,225	2,236	17,684	III	59,560	7,180	52,380	2,976	24,813
IV	44,120	5,300	38,820	2,238	17,459	IV	60,540	6,898	53,642	2,815	23,479
1991	42,900	5,257	37,643	9,516	75,330	1996	58,264	6,839	51,425	11,114	94,458
I	42,900	5,257	37,643	2,129	16,700	I	58,264	6,839	51,425	2,735	23,054
II	41,990	5,450	36,540	2,577	20,555	II	55,741	6,701	49,040	2,930	24,833
III	44,520	5,700	38,820	2,413	19,260	III	56,038	6,682	49,356	2,718	23,244
IV	46,950	5,685	41,265	2,433	18,551	IV	56,961	6,577	50,384	2,731	23,327
1992	45,735	5,610	40,125	10,202	82,497	1997	56,124	6,578	49,546	11,480	99,583
I	45,735	5,610	40,125	2,296	18,532	I	56,141	6,667	49,474	2,684	23,164
II	44,800	5,555	39,245	2,663	21,570	II	55,049	6,637	48,412	2,911	25,229
III	47,255	5,845	41,410	2,501	20,395	III	57,366	6,789	50,577	2,946	25,696
IV	49,175	5,840	43,335	2,398	19,351	IV	60,456	6,858	53,598	2,939	25,494
1993	58,202	7,109	51,093	11,982	97,050	1998	61,158	6,957	54,200	12,062	104,981
I	58,202	7,109	51,093	3,665	29,739	I	61,158	6,957	54,200	2,929	25,480
II	47,145	5,735	41,410	2,363	19,267	II	60,163	6,942	53,220	3,086	26,989
III	58,395	7,320	51,075	2,972	24,041	III	62,213	6,958	55,254	3,054	26,634
IV	59,030	7,130	51,900	2,982	24,003	IV	63,488	6,875	56,612	2,993	25,878
1994	57,904	7,130	50,739	12,376	101,400	1999[1]	62,206	6,682	55,523	11,666	102,569
I	57,904	7,130	50,739	2,885	23,368	I	62,206	6,682	55,523	2,891	25,247
II	57,350	7,210	50,140	3,390	27,984	II	60,191	6,527	53,663	2,986	26,270
III	60,715	7,565	53,150	3,107	25,547	III	60,686	6,515	54,170	2,920	25,860
IV	62,320	7,415	54,905	2,997	24,517	IV	60,736	6,291	54,444	2,869	25,192

[1] Preliminary. [2] Quarters are Dec. preceding year-Feb.(I), Mar.-May(II), June-Aug.(III) and Sept.-Nov.(IV). [3] Beginning of period.
Source: National Agricultural Statistics Service, U.S. Department of Agriculture (NASS-USDA)

Federally Inspected Hog Slaughter in the United States In Thousands of Head

Year	Jan.	Feb.	Mar.	Apr.	May	June	July	Aug.	Sept.	Oct.	Nov.	Dec.	Total
1990	7,407	6,643	7,279	6,785	6,799	6,152	5,938	7,110	6,716	7,546	7,334	7,140	82,901
1991	7,461	6,469	7,044	7,320	6,948	6,296	6,557	7,098	7,177	8,292	7,744	7,708	85,951
1992	8,144	7,153	7,934	7,610	6,897	7,166	7,461	7,494	8,217	8,599	7,796	8,142	92,613
1993	7,649	6,921	7,958	7,840	6,988	7,338	7,010	7,473	7,763	7,857	7,952	8,184	90,993
1994	7,285	6,783	8,148	7,609	7,383	7,452	6,941	7,997	8,192	8,585	8,516	8,547	93,435
1995	7,882	7,157	8,628	7,379	8,012	7,731	6,918	8,083	7,752	8,358	8,424	7,881	94,203
1996	8,129	7,506	7,549	7,886	7,485	6,395	7,187	7,509	7,541	8,423	7,469	7,455	90,534
1997	7,610	6,836	7,437	7,590	6,971	6,859	7,169	7,197	7,872	8,625	7,601	8,461	90,228
1998	8,454	7,590	8,335	8,198	7,443	7,596	8,130	8,024	8,443	9,192	8,650	9,231	99,285
1999[1]	8,373	7,746	8,945	8,386	7,303	8,176	7,778	8,256	8,501	8,806	8,750	8,719	99,739

[1] Preliminary. *Source: National Agricultural Statistics Service, U.S. Department of Agriculture (NASS-USDA)*

Average Live Weight of all Hogs Slaughtered Under Federal Inspection In Pounds Per Head

Year	Jan.	Feb.	Mar.	Apr.	May	June	July	Aug.	Sept.	Oct.	Nov.	Dec.	Average
1990	249	248	248	250	251	252	249	249	248	250	253	252	250
1991	251	250	250	252	254	253	251	250	251	253	256	255	252
1992	255	253	252	253	254	254	251	250	252	252	255	255	253
1993	254	253	253	254	254	256	254	252	252	254	257	258	254
1994	254	254	254	256	255	256	252	252	255	259	261	260	256
1995	258	256	257	258	258	258	256	253	252	255	259	258	257
1996	257	254	255	255	255	256	251	250	250	255	258	257	254
1997	257	256	256	256	256	257	253	252	255	257	261	260	256
1998	259	258	257	257	256	255	252	252	253	257	262	261	257
1999[1]	259	259	259	260	260	260	257	254	256	259	262	262	259

[1] Preliminary. *Source: Economic Research Service, U.S. Department of Agriculture (ERS-USDA)*

Average Open Interest of Lean Hog[1] Futures in Chicago In Contracts

Year	Jan.	Feb.	Mar.	Apr.	May	June	July	Aug.	Sept.	Oct.	Nov.	Dec.
1990	30,335	31,018	37,789	39,257	47,291	43,631	32,942	29,964	26,982	25,691	27,648	25,757
1991	22,742	24,798	24,449	22,400	25,871	21,275	18,154	16,771	17,281	18,462	21,572	19,167
1992	23,854	31,545	32,441	32,430	30,947	26,362	24,935	24,535	27,535	32,555	32,738	30,468
1993	27,210	25,620	28,264	24,139	22,581	19,840	19,026	20,761	20,544	20,051	21,167	24,096
1994	31,899	32,123	31,012	31,713	30,889	27,327	26,414	25,335	28,957	32,077	36,304	33,516
1995	36,705	30,958	30,736	28,035	28,294	28,729	29,959	31,599	34,183	31,312	31,519	35,127
1996	35,253	34,823	38,730	42,900	41,916	36,620	35,616	32,541	32,591	34,329	33,148	32,163
1997	33,105	33,953	31,289	34,071	41,978	37,398	36,141	33,712	31,483	36,928	39,363	39,394
1998	45,908	42,241	38,965	33,610	34,257	32,456	32,085	31,199	34,165	34,051	42,224	45,241
1999	46,003	44,211	43,803	48,277	55,951	52,398	54,723	49,915	53,055	54,089	54,432	50,690

[1] Data thru October 1995 are Live Hogs, November 1995 thru December 1996 are Live Hogs and Lean Hogs.
Source: Chicago Mercantile Exchange (CME)

Volume of Trading of Lean Hog[1] Futures in Chicago In Contracts

Year	Jan.	Feb.	Mar.	Apr.	May	June	July	Aug.	Sept.	Oct.	Nov.	Dec.	Total[2]
1990	181,034	119,902	189,666	188,789	278,259	276,933	212,451	169,924	146,953	160,314	186,110	130,429	2,241.3
1991	177,858	150,267	147,953	156,966	155,739	120,815	131,142	120,855	102,890	118,445	104,470	94,834	1,582.2
1992	135,226	136,997	140,411	138,248	116,738	131,209	148,754	102,165	116,565	149,458	117,023	123,298	1,556.1
1993	131,475	96,320	159,973	137,528	120,200	121,096	112,493	91,496	109,402	102,722	116,081	102,968	1,401.8
1994	144,701	96,736	146,934	93,105	127,381	144,373	116,181	122,058	110,697	128,980	150,744	172,132	1,554.0
1995	155,766	115,800	181,919	116,767	145,350	155,295	139,013	144,590	135,262	132,122	142,460	136,191	1,700.7
1996	177,299	138,002	150,117	216,476	208,696	177,359	185,872	157,540	158,077	203,789	170,586	152,098	2,095.9
1997	180,241	159,600	200,118	212,810	222,759	188,615	181,637	146,297	149,950	175,135	152,876	130,871	2,100.9
1998	180,241	182,698	174,752	132,952	155,737	167,767	185,427	157,973	164,964	173,163	218,950	241,767	2,136.3
1999	218,608	171,108	196,825	189,773	214,852	237,240	239,096	167,787	190,238	187,794	205,505	139,270	2,358.1

[1] Data thru October 1995 are Live Hogs, November 1995 thru December 1996 are Live Hogs and Lean Hogs. [2] In thousands of contracts.
Source: Chicago Mercantile Exchange (CME)

Honey

World honey production has been declining steadily, from over 700,000 metric tonnes in 1990 to less than 400,000 tonnes at the end of the 1990's. The long-term decline largely reflects a contraction in the number of beekeepers and producing bee colonies. Also, the steady expansion of the more aggressive Africanized bees has virtually erased honey production in some countries. On a shorter-term basis, weather can have a decisive impact on honey production if its effect harms the flowering plants the bees need to make honey.

China is the world's largest producer with average annual production in the second half of the 1990's at about 160,000 tonnes, more than a third of global output. U.S. production is a distant second with 90,000 tonnes annually, followed by Argentina and Mexico with about 60,000 tonnes each. The latter two nations, during the past ten years, have increased output whereas China's production has declined by almost a third during the period.

U.S. honey production in 1998, from producers with five or more colonies, totaled 220 million pounds, up 12 percent from 1997's 197 million pounds. There were 2.63 million producing colonies in 1998, about unchanged from 1997. Yield per colony averaged 83.7 pounds, up 9 pounds from 1997. Producer honey stocks of 80.8 million pounds as of December 15, 1998, compares with 70.7 million a year earlier. Honey is produced is almost every state, but California is the leading producer with 37.4 million pounds in 1998 vs. 31.5 million in 1997. Other leading producing states include North and South Dakota, Florida and Minnesota.

The U.S. also imports honey, 132 million pounds in 1998 vs. a record high 167 million pounds in 1997. Imports seem to have a pattern of totals in excess of 100 million pounds for a few consecutive years, and protracted periods with annual averages of less than 80 million pounds as seen during 1987-91. Argentina is the largest exporter of honey to the U.S. with almost 70 million pounds in 1998 vs. 107 million in 1997; China was second with 30.5 million pounds and 25.3 million, respectively. U.S. honey exports are small: 10.4 million pounds in 1998 vs. 8.9 million in 1997 and a ten-year high of 12.4 million in 1990.

U.S. prices for the 1998 crop averaged 65.5 cents per pound, down 13 percent from the 75.2 cents in 1997. In the early 1990's prices averaged 53.0 cents per pound. Prices are based on retail sales by producers and sales to private processors and co-ops. At the state level, prices reflect the portions of honey sold retail, coop and private. At the U.S. level, prices for each color—ranging from white to amber—are derived by weighting quantities sold for each marketing channel.

World Production of Honey In Metric Tons

Year	Argentina	Australia	Brazil	Canada	China	Germany	Japan	Mexico	Russia	United States	Total[2]
1990	47,000	27,561	30,000	32,115	193,000	23,000	4,854	51,000	236,219	89,717	732,466
1991	54,000	20,604	32,300	31,606	206,000	25,000	4,202	58,770	240,000	99,414	714,790
1992	61,000	18,948	18,841	30,339	178,000	24,677	3,800	48,852	47,000	100,055	531,512
1993	59,000	22,556	18,367	30,758	176,000	24,648	3,800	48,000	52,700	104,620	540,449
1994	64,000	24,000	19,000	32,920	177,000	22,233	3,500	41,500	43,900	98,500	526,553
1995	70,000	24,000	19,200	30,575	178,000	36,685	3,500	49,228	44,000	95,490	550,678
1996	57,000	-----	-----	24,895	184,000	14,674	-----	47,997	-----	89,850	418,416
1997	70,000	-----	-----	30,021	207,000	15,069	-----	53,681	-----	89,148	464,919
1998	75,000	-----	-----	42,456	155,000	16,306	-----	56,061	-----	99,932	444,755
1999[1]	85,000	-----	-----	34,000	180,000	13,000	-----	57,500	-----	90,000	459,500

[1] Preliminary. [2] Only for countries listed. *Source: Foreign Agricultural Service, U.S. Department of Agriculture (FAS-USDA)*

Salient Statistics of Honey in the United States In Millions of Pounds

									Program Activity					
Year	Number of Colonies (1,000)	Yield Per Colony Pounds	Stocks Jan. 1	Total U.S. Production	Imports for Consumption	Domestic Disappearance	Exports	Total Supply	Placed Under Loan	CCC Take Over	Net Gov't Expenditure[3] Mil. $	Domestic Avg. Price All Honey - Cents Per Pound -	National Avg. Price Support - Cents Per Pound -	Per Capita Consumption Pounds
1989	3,443	51.4	192.4	177.0	77.3	292.0	10.0	446.7	161.7	2.8	41.7	49.8	56.4	1.0
1990	3,210	61.6	144.7	197.8	77.0	303.4	12.4	419.5	183.5	1.1	46.7	53.7	53.8	1.0
1991	3,181	68.9	103.7	219.2	92.2	303.4	9.6	415.1	112.9	3.2	18.6	55.6	53.8	1.0
1992	3,045	72.8	109.3	221.7	114.6	330.5	10.4	444.5	122.7	4.1	16.6	55.0	53.8	1.0
1993	2,875	80.2	103.5	230.6	133.6	342.0	8.5	467.8	136.8	16.4	22.1	53.9	53.8	1.0
1994	2,783	78.4	117.3	218.2	123.2	355.2	8.3	457.7	73.4	0	-.2	52.8	50.0	1.0
1995	2,655	79.5	94.1	211.1	88.6	341.6	9.3	393.2	64.4	0	-9.3	68.5	50.0	1.0
1996	2,581	77.3	42.2	199.5	150.6	334.1	9.9	390.9	-----	-----	-----	88.8	-----	-----
1997[1]	2,631	74.7	47.0	196.5	167.4	328.8	8.9	406.8	-----	-----	-----	75.2	-----	-----
1998[2]	2,633	83.7	69.1	220.3	132.3	332.9	9.9	397.5	-----	-----	-----	65.5	-----	-----

[1] Preliminary. [2] Forecast. [3] Fiscal year. *Source: Economic Research Service, U.S. Department of Agriculture (ERS-USDA)*

Interest Rates, U.S.

Federal Reserve policy during 1999 was virtually the opposite of 1998 when the Fed lowered short-term rates three times; in 1999 rates were raised three times, 25 basis points each time. The rational for the Fed's reversal was the stronger than expected U.S. economy and the fear that inflationary pressures would resurface. By yearend, however, the economy's strength showed little sign of tiring and inflation remained benign, suggesting perhaps that the Fed's tightening was possibly premature and/or unnecessary.

The U.S. economy's performance in 1999 seemed to defy traditional economic thinking, specifically that tight U.S. labor force and strong consumer buying would historically trigger a cost push and/or demand pull inflation; neither of which happened. Moreover, the surging equity markets sharply increased the public's net worth which, in turn, led to further consumer buying of durable goods and buoyed housing demand and prices.

The U.S. economy experienced a metamorphosis during the second half of the 1990's as a burgeoning high-tech economy increased labor productivity and new product development while holding labor costs in check. Inasmuch as the nation is adjusting to the economic changes the Fed's tightening attitude during 1999 seemed to be: let's not take any chances with a possible inflation.

Long-term rates fell to a generational low below 5 percent in October 1998, but by yearend 1999 the benchmark 30-year T-bond yield was 6.48 percent compared with 5.09 a year earlier; 3 month T-bills were 5.16 percent vs. 4.45; and fed funds were at 5.75 percent vs. 4.07, respectively. The prime rate was unchanged at 8.50 percent, while the discount rate of 5.00 percent was up from 4.50 during much of 1999.

An influencing variable in fed policy that may have been modified in 1999 is what the Fed is willing to accept for the nation's annualized growth rate—gross domestic product—which in the past was thought to be 2 - 2 1/2 percent, but is now thought to lie between 3 - 3 1/2 percent due to the sharp gains in worker productivity. The implications of the latter suggests that the Fed has more breathing room before any dramatic tightening becomes necessary.

Initial forecasts for 2000 suggest a slowing in the nation's torrid pace, which during the third quarter of 1999 was running at a G.D.P. annualized rate of 5.7 percent. Without a significant slowdown in U.S. economic growth the Fed is likely to raise interest rates once or twice during the first half of 2000, policy moves that could be constrained if key foreign interest rates are not raised to protect currency stability.

Equally likely to influence Fed policy in 2000 are the equity markets. Should they continue to surge ahead and further boost consumer confidence the Fed may elect to either overtly tighten monetary policy and/or attempt to curb equity market speculation by suggesting higher interest rates lie ahead. Either way, it is likely that key long and short-term interest rates, during the first half of 2000, will be higher than ending 1999 levels.

Futures Markets

A futures (and options) contract exists for almost every maturity on the yield curve, as well as for municipal and commercial credit risks. Major U.S. contracts include Eurodollars on Chicago's International Monetary Market (IMM), and T-bonds, 10-year T-notes, 5-year T-notes and 2-year T-notes on the Chicago Board of Trade (CBOT). Futures are also traded in Chicago on municipal bonds, 30 day fed funds, one month LIBOR, and yield curve spreads. Smaller size contracts on some interest rate instruments are listed at the MidAmerica Commodity Exchange (MidAm).

U.S. Producer Price Index[2] (Wholesale, All Commodities) 1982 = 100

Year	Jan.	Feb.	Mar.	Apr.	May	June	July	Aug.	Sept.	Oct.	Nov.	Dec.	Average
1991	119.0	117.2	116.2	116.0	116.5	116.4	116.1	116.2	116.1	116.4	116.4	115.9	116.5
1992	115.6	116.0	116.1	116.3	117.2	118.0	117.9	117.7	118.0	118.1	117.8	117.6	117.2
1993	118.0	118.4	118.7	119.3	119.7	119.5	119.2	118.7	118.7	119.1	119.0	118.6	118.9
1994	119.1	119.3	119.7	119.7	119.9	120.5	120.7	121.2	120.9	120.9	121.5	121.9	120.4
1995	122.9	123.5	123.9	124.6	124.9	125.3	125.3	125.1	125.2	125.3	125.4	125.7	124.8
1996	126.3	126.2	126.4	127.4	128.1	128.0	128.0	128.3	128.2	128.0	128.2	129.1	127.7
1997	129.7	128.5	127.3	127.0	127.4	127.2	126.9	127.2	127.5	127.8	127.9	126.8	127.6
1998	125.4	125.0	124.7	124.9	125.1	124.8	124.9	124.2	123.8	124.0	123.6	122.8	124.4
1999[1]	122.9	122.3	122.6	123.6	124.7	125.2	125.7	126.9	128.0	127.9	128.4	128.0	125.5

[1] Preliminary. [2] Not seasonally adjusted. *Source: Bureau of Labor Statistics, U.S. Department of Commerce (BLS)*

U.S. Consumer Price Index[2] (Retail Price Index for All Items: Urban Consumers) 1982-84 = 100

Year	Jan.	Feb.	Mar.	Apr.	May	June	July	Aug.	Sept.	Oct.	Nov.	Dec.	Average
1991	134.6	134.8	135.0	135.2	135.6	136.0	136.2	136.6	137.2	137.4	137.8	137.9	136.2
1992	138.1	138.6	139.3	139.5	139.7	140.2	140.5	140.9	141.3	141.8	142.0	141.9	140.3
1993	142.6	143.1	143.6	144.0	144.2	144.4	144.4	144.8	145.1	145.7	145.8	145.8	144.5
1994	146.2	146.7	147.2	147.4	147.5	148.0	148.4	149.0	149.4	149.5	149.7	149.7	148.2
1995	150.3	150.9	151.4	151.9	152.2	152.5	152.5	152.9	153.2	153.7	153.6	153.5	152.4
1996	154.4	154.9	155.7	156.3	156.6	156.7	157.0	157.3	157.8	158.3	158.6	158.6	157.0
1997	159.1	159.6	159.8	160.0	160.1	160.4	160.6	160.9	161.3	161.6	161.8	161.9	160.6
1998	161.9	162.0	162.0	162.4	162.8	163.0	163.2	163.4	163.6	163.9	164.2	164.4	163.1
1999[1]	164.6	164.7	165.0	166.2	166.2	166.2	166.7	167.2	167.9	168.2	168.4	168.8	166.7

[1] Preliminary. [2] Not seasonally adjusted. *Source: Bureau of Labor Statistics, U.S. Department of Commerce (BLS)*

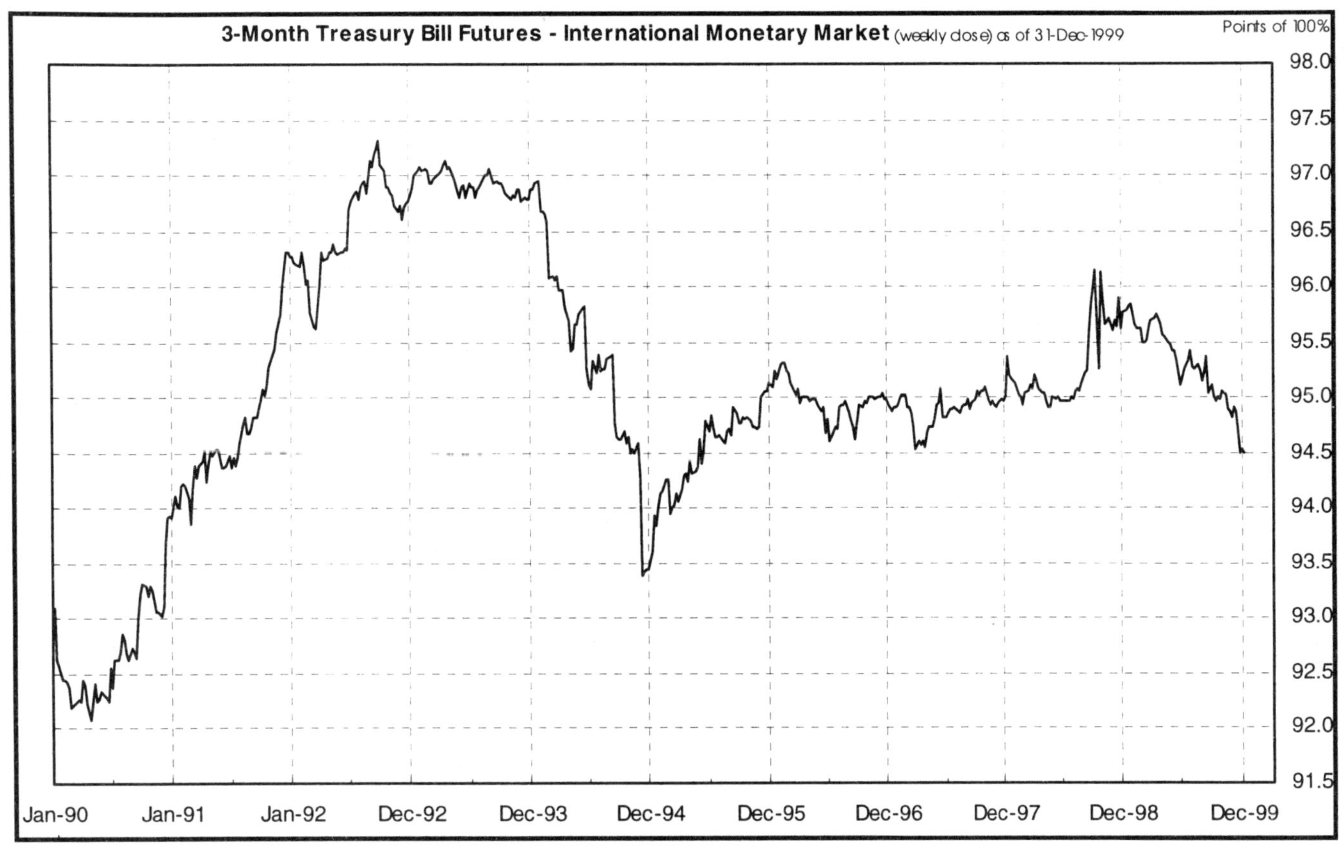

Average Open Interest of 13 Week[1] Treasury Bill Futures in Chicago In Thousands of Contracts

Year	Jan.	Feb.	Mar.	Apr.	May	June	July	Aug.	Sept.	Oct.	Nov.	Dec.
1990	39,168	38,358	27,668	31,274	25,128	21,171	26,524	37,903	35,723	46,974	53,284	50,146
1991	55,371	53,484	38,259	43,538	53,941	51,178	55,514	55,999	47,509	50,865	57,680	51,750
1992	51,312	45,902	35,539	44,757	47,734	41,091	38,399	35,638	29,781	32,556	35,379	29,566
1993	32,544	35,756	32,556	39,115	40,724	34,614	30,895	34,177	28,983	30,121	33,800	30,996
1994	36,456	41,150	43,243	51,485	41,164	34,580	32,572	29,559	24,522	32,325	30,077	22,322
1995	21,065	26,289	33,420	35,873	34,608	25,930	20,534	19,195	18,929	16,781	16,384	11,279
1996	14,769	16,906	14,161	14,460	15,709	10,285	8,973	9,770	6,536	6,906	7,516	7,002
1997	8,114	9,793	9,968	10,390	10,048	8,949	8,425	9,760	7,899	9,497	11,223	10,679
1998	10,295	11,647	7,903	4,993	3,818	4,123	4,330	4,407	2,840	1,929	2,123	2,264
1999	2,179	2,998	2,720	1,523	2,367	1,585	690	909	471	475	1,033	2,321

[1] 90-day U.S. Treasury Bill. *Source: International Monetary Market (IOM), division of the Chicago Mercantile Exchange (CME)*

Volume of Trading of 13 Week[1] Treasury Bill Futures in Chicago In Thousands of Contracts

Year	Jan.	Feb.	Mar.	Apr.	May	June	July	Aug.	Sept.	Oct.	Nov.	Dec.	Total
1990	169.3	153.6	118.5	120.3	102.4	96.7	138.1	206.6	168.9	178.5	223.7	193.1	1,869.6
1991	252.9	197.9	166.8	164.0	188.2	173.3	141.7	223.2	111.0	110.8	140.8	141.6	1,912.2
1992	143.8	137.9	145.0	115.9	106.5	106.1	85.8	76.2	103.0	127.0	106.5	83.4	1,337.1
1993	86.1	100.4	97.0	65.6	103.2	106.0	71.7	75.7	89.3	69.1	87.4	66.0	1,071.3
1994	59.8	137.0	115.9	104.4	99.4	89.4	53.7	60.9	77.6	57.4	81.2	83.8	1,020.5
1995	72.2	80.0	90.3	37.4	58.7	49.9	28.1	41.5	44.4	36.9	46.6	34.2	620.2
1996	32.0	36.0	36.5	17.9	16.6	25.2	12.0	19.4	19.8	10.8	10.4	14.3	250.9
1997	10.6	19.4	20.6	11.6	16.6	14.9	11.5	15.4	19.0	20.4	16.8	22.1	199.1
1998	18.5	14.3	14.4	9.5	9.4	7.6	3.4	7.6	5.2	4.8	3.9	5.7	104.2
1999	4.8	6.1	6.5	2.9	3.6	3.2	1.9	2.0	0.6	0.8	2.1	6.8	41.3

[1] 90-day U.S. Treasury Bill. *Source: International Monetary Market (IOM), division of the Chicago Mercantile Exchange (CME)*

Average Open Interest of 30-year U.S. Treasury Bond Futures in Chicago In Contracts

Year	Jan.	Feb.	Mar.	Apr.	May	June	July	Aug.	Sept.	Oct.	Nov.	Dec.
1990	315,671	324,954	294,968	280,745	303,544	278,889	285,934	317,197	297,075	286,291	288,581	254,775
1991	257,229	279,378	250,028	283,473	279,443	254,983	273,774	325,303	310,110	304,198	317,445	301,604
1992	343,156	353,782	318,737	313,742	346,542	347,293	370,850	427,723	385,645	364,250	362,231	321,706
1993	336,327	375,435	361,675	362,404	370,485	349,285	361,393	396,411	388,188	360,859	359,739	337,575
1994	380,057	422,902	454,539	500,790	497,296	421,286	441,884	451,462	447,924	436,684	449,642	397,554
1995	384,356	389,908	369,989	367,964	399,500	421,234	438,267	381,237	361,394	395,346	447,409	426,384
1996	382,001	403,403	395,338	381,926	413,944	443,644	464,145	471,203	420,622	409,950	463,731	479,086
1997	497,539	545,775	509,573	493,511	554,418	480,669	530,011	608,474	624,231	723,321	719,186	737,703
1998	744,894	764,309	766,233	806,559	888,215	1,040,659	1,084,889	1,061,223	837,986	769,932	782,677	662,025
1999	657,180	801,115	664,131	618,453	717,453	674,224	672,983	748,974	647,816	621,815	637,656	561,919

Source: Chicago Board of Trade (CBT)

Volume of Trading of 30-year U.S. Treasury Bond Futures in Chicago In Thousands of Contracts

Year	Jan.	Feb.	Mar.	Apr.	May	June	July	Aug.	Sept.	Oct.	Nov.	Dec.	Total
1990	7,215.0	7,438.0	7,175.0	5,653.0	6,189.0	5,279.0	4,895.0	8,855.0	4,939.0	6,659.0	6,570.0	4,691.0	75,559.0
1991	5,804.0	5,717.0	5,658.0	5,957.0	6,186.0	5,582.0	4,293.0	6,592.0	4,765.0	6,450.0	6,239.0	4,643.0	67,886.0
1992	7,523.4	6,270.1	6,793.4	4,810.1	5,417.7	4,828.8	6,081.0	6,085.5	5,953.3	6,870.7	5,287.8	4,083.0	70,004.8
1993	5,577.4	6,482.7	7,902.9	6,156.1	6,799.8	5,817.2	6,218.4	6,914.5	7,443.9	6,537.4	8,193.5	5,384.5	79,428.5
1994	7,287.8	8,430.2	10,836.7	9,557.4	9,999.0	9,804.0	6,987.0	7,910.0	7,913.0	7,004.0	8,533.0	5,699.0	99,960.0
1995	7,058.0	7,714.0	9,623.8	5,835.4	8,721.5	8,446.7	5,790.2	7,083.7	7,317.1	6,927.2	6,626.3	5,232.1	86,375.9
1996	7,528.6	8,781.4	7,199.3	6,010.6	7,932.3	6,520.6	6,422.1	6,625.8	6,926.1	6,772.4	7,297.7	6,708.4	84,725.1
1997	8,104.7	7,522.8	7,493.3	7,519.9	8,339.1	7,400.2	7,679.8	10,228.1	8,356.2	12,467.6	7,735.5	6,980.4	99,827.7
1998	9,595.3	9,368.1	9,763.9	8,516.7	9,054.1	10,208.6	8,070.9	12,024.8	11,159.2	10,698.1	8,155.0	5,609.2	112,224.1
1999	8,075.2	10,031.5	8,667.5	7,196.9	9,555.8	8,072.1	6,415.1	7,995.2	6,559.6	6,301.1	6,909.0	4,263.5	90,042.3

Source: Chicago Board of Trade (CBT)

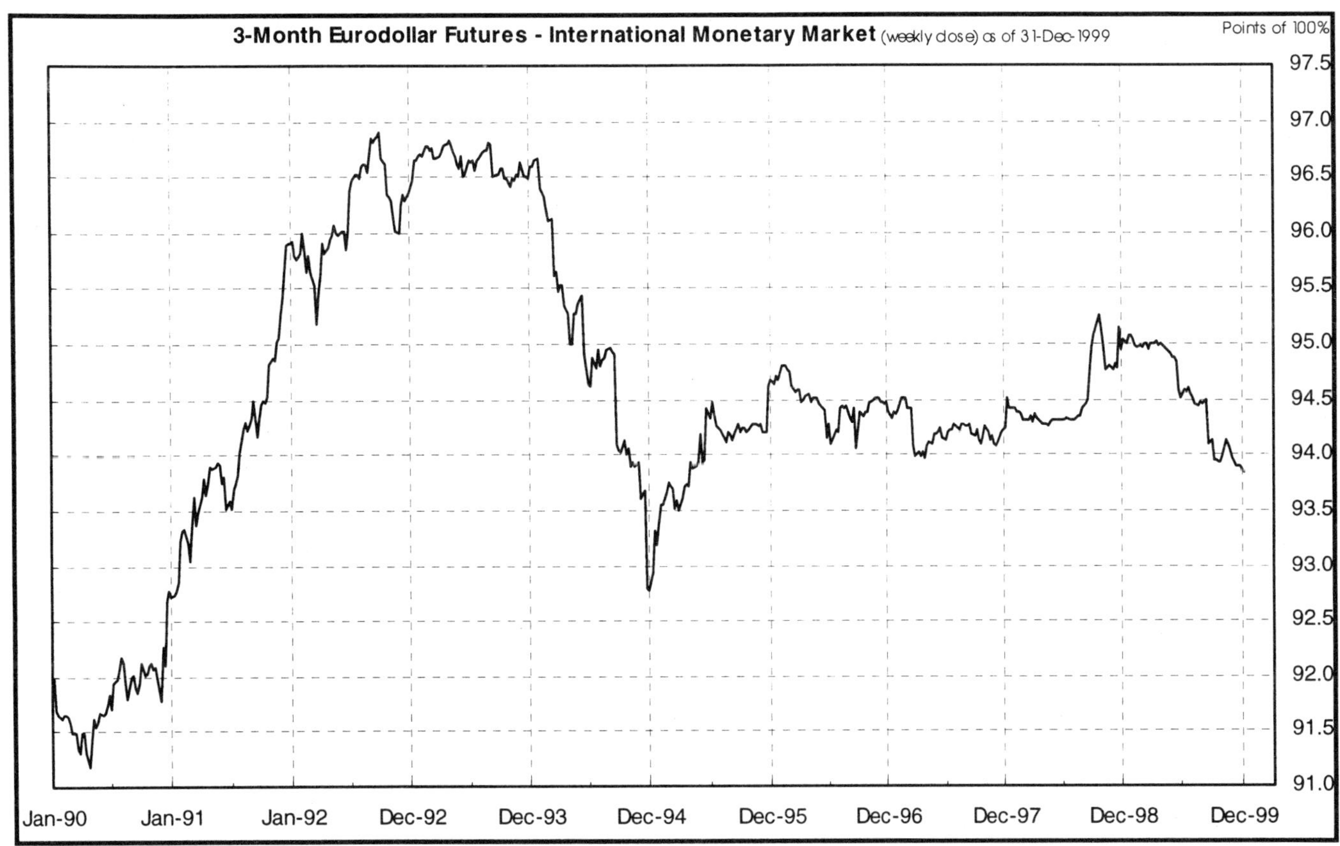

Average Open Interest of 3-month Eurodollar Futures in Chicago In Thousands of Contracts

Year	Jan.	Feb.	Mar.	Apr.	May	June	July	Aug.	Sept.	Oct.	Nov.	Dec.
1990	638.5	662.9	653.2	616.9	662.8	676.3	690.6	740.0	697.8	678.2	728.4	664.1
1991	630.9	722.7	741.1	767.6	857.4	835.2	797.9	883.1	916.7	949.5	1,054.7	1,067.2
1992	1,129.8	1,213.7	1,244.6	1,269.1	1,377.2	1,382.7	1,434.1	1,549.9	1,537.0	1,537.6	1,547.0	1,418.7
1993	1,429.4	1,586.7	1,643.3	1,653.4	1,782.8	1,739.1	1,777.7	1,918.4	1,940.7	2,026.5	2,149.0	2,150.2
1994	2,300.5	2,529.5	2,568.1	2,627.3	2,734.3	2,565.2	2,599.1	2,703.8	2,699.6	2,561.2	2,660.3	2,606.3
1995	2,443.6	2,535.4	2,463.9	2,447.4	2,503.3	2,390.8	2,279.5	2,374.6	2,347.2	2,290.3	2,405.5	2,480.5
1996	2,519.4	2,638.6	2,511.4	2,483.5	2,571.8	2,590.1	2,504.4	2,485.5	2,392.4	2,349.7	2,378.2	2,225.7
1997	2,190.8	2,333.2	2,423.1	2,523.1	2,671.3	2,706.5	2,699.2	2,788.0	2,769.3	2,815.1	2,799.5	2,661.6
1998	2,713.4	2,821.5	2,797.9	2,892.6	3,089.0	3,093.9	3,027.7	3,223.0	3,359.9	3,303.4	3,297.4	3,000.1
1999	2,917.9	3,039.5	2,973.5	2,894.7	3,183.2	3,208.8	3,064.4	3,115.6	2,904.0	2,918.2	2,879.7	2,859.4

Source: International Monetary Market (IOM), division of the Chicago Mercantile Exchange (CME)

Volume of Trading of 3-month Eurodollar Futures in Chicago In Thousands of Contracts

Year	Jan.	Feb.	Mar.	Apr.	May	June	July	Aug.	Sept.	Oct.	Nov.	Dec.	Total
1990	3,244.0	2,459.0	2,727.0	2,566.0	3,132.0	2,473.0	2,947.0	3,857.0	2,730.0	2,898.0	2,982.0	2,680.0	34,696.0
1991	2,859.0	2,635.0	3,445.0	3,208.0	2,458.0	2,972.0	2,629.0	4,035.0	3,000.0	3,505.0	3,301.0	3,196.0	37,243.0
1992	5,365.7	4,418.5	5,582.8	4,942.2	4,819.0	4,602.6	5,357.8	4,016.3	4,705.2	6,691.6	5,461.3	4,568.1	60,531.1
1993	5,556.8	5,003.8	6,013.8	4,059.4	5,977.8	5,672.9	5,656.7	4,494.2	6,340.6	4,888.4	6,269.8	4,477.3	64,411.4
1994	6,074.8	8,745.3	9,468.9	9,639.2	11,494.0	9,348.0	7,810.0	7,128.0	7,641.0	7,992.0	9,715.0	9,766.0	104,823.0
1995	10,341.1	10,429.3	9,549.0	6,069.2	9,897.1	10,104.7	6,669.9	7,013.5	7,171.1	6,477.9	6,055.2	5,952.1	95,730.0
1996	7,485.7	9,267.2	9,526.3	6,872.4	7,413.7	7,415.0	8,323.2	6,967.5	8,232.5	7,014.5	5,056.9	5,308.1	88,883.1
1997	7,903.4	6,918.0	8,936.4	9,351.7	8,447.4	8,049.7	7,291.6	9,295.4	7,634.7	12,569.7	6,314.1	7,058.2	99,770.2
1998	10,908.0	7,861.4	8,842.1	9,488.4	7,202.4	8,349.5	5,452.3	9,811.3	13,593.9	11,756.9	9,627.8	6,578.5	109,472.5
1999	7,470.9	7,674.5	8,718.6	7,346.5	8,957.0	9,649.8	7,746.3	8,898.0	7,629.1	7,500.6	6,223.2	5,604.0	93,418.5

Source: International Monetary Market (IOM), division of the Chicago Mercantile Exchange (CME)

Average Open Interest of 10-year U.S. Treasury Note Futures in Chicago In Contracts

Year	Jan.	Feb.	Mar.	Apr.	May	June	July	Aug.	Sept.	Oct.	Nov.	Dec.
1990	73,155	82,211	76,939	76,030	82,174	78,498	71,413	75,644	72,900	67,309	73,744	76,697
1991	72,621	79,355	79,413	71,451	84,203	81,884	85,527	94,379	96,836	93,187	95,450	87,063
1992	119,739	114,521	106,497	102,862	112,666	126,228	143,924	158,831	179,045	191,725	199,990	195,705
1993	190,018	206,852	198,653	209,221	229,378	217,521	233,458	238,189	237,243	237,877	273,336	262,831
1994	264,848	258,643	300,080	328,821	294,091	254,612	232,373	253,233	273,564	277,313	301,000	271,992
1995	282,978	285,187	265,747	263,816	273,945	289,052	306,046	323,078	277,011	278,832	270,527	249,073
1996	260,374	297,850	285,501	319,234	331,032	293,416	302,330	326,391	291,208	284,581	313,298	303,702
1997	332,285	343,661	323,982	348,683	350,814	336,927	363,744	407,147	387,284	398,645	404,980	374,448
1998	430,335	507,986	474,916	494,417	533,214	513,369	512,173	604,862	555,268	482,928	508,299	503,533
1999	528,538	549,518	515,404	510,091	541,057	574,514	588,272	623,805	607,304	653,079	582,002	487,888

Source: Chicago Board of Trade (CBT)

Volume of Trading of 10-year U.S. Treasury Note Futures in Chicago In Thousands of Contracts

Year	Jan.	Feb.	Mar.	Apr.	May	June	July	Aug.	Sept.	Oct.	Nov.	Dec.	Total
1990	491.3	650.5	480.9	381.1	638.7	427.4	415.0	703.0	399.3	449.6	574.3	442.6	6,053.7
1991	507.7	519.6	508.3	466.5	566.9	456.6	318.9	705.9	467.2	573.2	661.3	591.4	6,342.0
1992	929.6	866.4	824.9	531.2	758.9	683.3	859.4	1,047.7	1,138.5	1,300.2	1,225.8	1,052.1	11,218.0
1993	1,134.6	1,286.3	1,763.1	1,089.5	1,341.4	1,390.6	1,147.0	1,390.7	1,523.7	1,279.5	1,926.6	1,328.2	16,601.2
1994	1,484.3	1,935.7	2,572.4	2,213.5	2,399.4	2,250.2	1,621.8	2,028.7	1,932.9	1,635.1	2,253.6	1,750.2	24,078.0
1995	1,752.6	1,978.8	2,458.7	1,368.2	2,236.5	2,495.8	1,588.9	2,028.7	1,859.0	1,459.7	1,730.8	1,487.6	22,445.4
1996	1,649.1	2,313.1	2,075.8	1,632.1	2,211.3	1,715.6	1,556.3	1,865.7	1,810.4	1,494.7	1,904.5	1,711.2	21,939.7
1997	1,780.5	1,939.9	2,051.8	1,703.2	2,025.6	1,942.3	1,509.6	2,535.9	2,062.5	2,593.7	1,825.6	1,991.2	23,961.8
1998	2,393.5	2,748.7	2,817.5	2,342.1	2,695.9	2,681.9	1,704.1	3,632.2	3,560.3	2,882.7	2,912.2	2,111.5	32,482.6
1999	2,269.1	3,562.1	2,993.8	2,145.3	3,519.3	3,153.0	2,438.5	3,735.6	2,508.7	2,470.9	3,201.5	2,048.0	34,045.8

Source: Chicago Board of Trade (CBT)

Average Open Interest of 5-Year U.S. Treasury Note Futures in Chicago In Contracts

Year	Jan.	Feb.	Mar.	Apr.	May	June	July	Aug.	Sept.	Oct.	Nov.	Dec.
1990	81,705	74,568	74,999	60,841	59,417	56,485	54,004	64,100	75,955	78,370	82,981	93,549
1991	80,059	82,666	83,109	74,612	75,799	65,543	72,197	86,981	85,794	91,096	102,890	99,291
1992	116,322	121,667	125,155	130,826	135,111	144,386	143,928	143,203	127,418	122,113	129,548	127,690
1993	139,207	150,443	152,711	158,607	169,234	152,262	152,403	160,258	159,754	154,501	181,492	206,914
1994	200,812	213,037	200,626	185,083	192,659	186,026	189,828	182,027	181,518	181,578	176,322	205,150
1995	206,539	210,192	199,357	200,087	213,531	189,332	176,329	173,897	163,419	162,121	177,915	171,023
1996	163,026	184,523	200,253	191,690	179,951	177,370	174,484	179,599	154,764	138,246	155,820	154,764
1997	176,691	208,928	219,540	235,543	227,882	225,691	226,306	225,792	234,309	233,480	248,377	257,886
1998	257,094	270,048	282,327	277,540	274,145	257,193	264,756	389,118	382,855	383,809	353,399	326,860
1999	290,373	268,561	247,526	246,916	311,106	348,626	325,347	341,494	298,861	328,580	272,628	288,522

Source: Chicago Board of Trade (CBT)

Volume of Trading of 5-Year U.S. Treasury Note Futures in Chicago In Thousands of Contracts

Year	Jan.	Feb.	Mar.	Apr.	May	June	July	Aug.	Sept.	Oct.	Nov.	Dec.	Total
1990	184.5	277.5	164.9	107.6	266.6	140.8	131.6	320.4	189.0	197.9	305.7	40.8	544.4
1991	220.5	318.5	252.3	181.4	307.6	232.4	179.7	385.4	243.9	291.5	419.9	353.1	1,064.5
1992	498.6	543.8	560.0	322.2	590.1	551.5	484.2	565.7	582.1	539.0	640.8	563.2	1,743.0
1993	539.5	673.1	886.0	447.6	755.9	753.8	506.4	711.3	753.8	472.6	908.0	715.8	2,096.4
1994	695.9	1,235.1	1,295.4	917.1	1,202.0	1,154.9	834.8	944.9	1,107.3	840.6	1,156.7	1,078.0	12,463.0
1995	988.5	1,296.2	1,386.9	783.4	1,291.1	1,402.9	828.6	1,100.5	1,008.7	769.6	996.0	784.7	12,637.1
1996	837.3	1,312.0	1,084.6	815.7	1,135.5	878.3	881.7	1,061.8	979.0	689.5	831.1	957.1	11,463.4
1997	927.5	1,156.7	1,271.1	984.4	1,190.6	1,143.8	761.4	1,244.6	1,243.7	1,314.1	1,068.1	1,182.8	13,488.7
1998	1,451.9	1,482.0	1,390.7	1,154.7	1,281.1	1,376.9	944.0	2,480.5	1,913.5	1,583.1	1,722.7	1,279.1	18,060.0
1999	1,119.7	1,553.6	1,336.6	1,115.0	1,906.4	1,543.9	1,166.4	2,163.6	1,034.1	1,245.2	1,606.6	1,192.8	16,983.8

Source: Chicago Board of Trade (CBT)

U.S. Federal Funds Rate In Percent

Year	Jan.	Feb.	Mar.	Apr.	May	June	July	Aug.	Sept.	Oct.	Nov.	Dec.	Average
1990	8.23	8.24	8.28	8.26	8.18	8.29	8.15	8.13	8.20	8.11	7.81	7.31	8.10
1991	6.91	6.25	6.12	5.91	5.78	5.90	5.82	5.66	5.45	5.21	4.81	4.43	5.69
1992	4.03	4.06	3.98	3.73	3.82	3.76	3.25	3.30	3.22	3.10	3.09	2.92	3.52
1993	3.02	3.03	3.07	2.96	3.00	3.04	3.06	3.03	3.09	2.99	3.02	2.96	3.02
1994	3.05	3.25	3.34	3.56	4.01	4.25	4.26	4.47	4.73	4.76	5.29	5.45	4.20
1995	5.53	5.92	5.98	6.05	6.01	6.00	5.85	5.74	5.80	5.76	5.80	5.60	5.84
1996	5.56	5.22	5.31	5.22	5.56	5.27	5.40	5.22	5.30	5.24	5.31	5.29	5.30
1997	5.25	5.19	5.39	5.51	5.50	5.56	5.52	5.54	5.54	5.50	5.52	5.50	5.46
1998	5.56	5.51	5.49	5.45	5.49	5.56	5.54	5.55	5.51	5.07	4.83	4.68	5.35
1999	4.63	4.76	4.81	4.74	4.74	4.76	4.99	5.07	5.22	5.20			4.89

Source: Bureau of Economic Analysis, U.S. Department of Commerce (BEA)

U.S. Municipal Bond Yield[1] In Percent

Year	Jan.	Feb.	Mar.	Apr.	May	June	July	Aug.	Sept.	Oct.	Nov.	Dec.	Average
1990	7.10	7.22	7.29	7.39	7.35	7.24	7.19	7.32	7.53	7.49	7.18	7.09	7.28
1991	7.08	6.91	7.10	7.02	6.95	7.13	7.05	6.90	6.80	6.68	6.73	6.69	6.92
1992	6.54	6.74	6.76	6.67	6.57	6.49	6.13	6.16	6.25	6.41	6.36	6.22	6.44
1993	6.16	5.86	5.85	5.76	5.73	5.63	5.57	5.45	5.29	5.25	5.47	5.35	5.61
1994	5.31	5.40	5.91	6.23	6.19	6.11	6.23	6.21	6.28	6.52	6.97	6.80	6.18
1995	6.53	6.22	6.10	6.02	5.95	5.84	5.92	6.06	5.91	5.80	5.64	5.45	5.95
1996	5.43	5.43	5.79	5.94	5.98	6.02	5.92	5.76	5.87	5.72	5.59	5.64	5.76
1997	5.72	5.63	5.76	5.88	5.70	5.53	5.35	5.41	5.39	5.38	5.33	5.19	5.52
1998	5.06	5.10	5.21	5.23	5.20	5.12	5.14	5.10	4.99	4.93	5.03	4.98	5.09
1999	5.02	5.03	5.10	5.08	5.18	5.37	5.36	5.58	5.69	5.92			5.33

[1] 20-bond average. *Source: Bureau of Economic Analysis, U.S. Department of Commerce (BEA)*

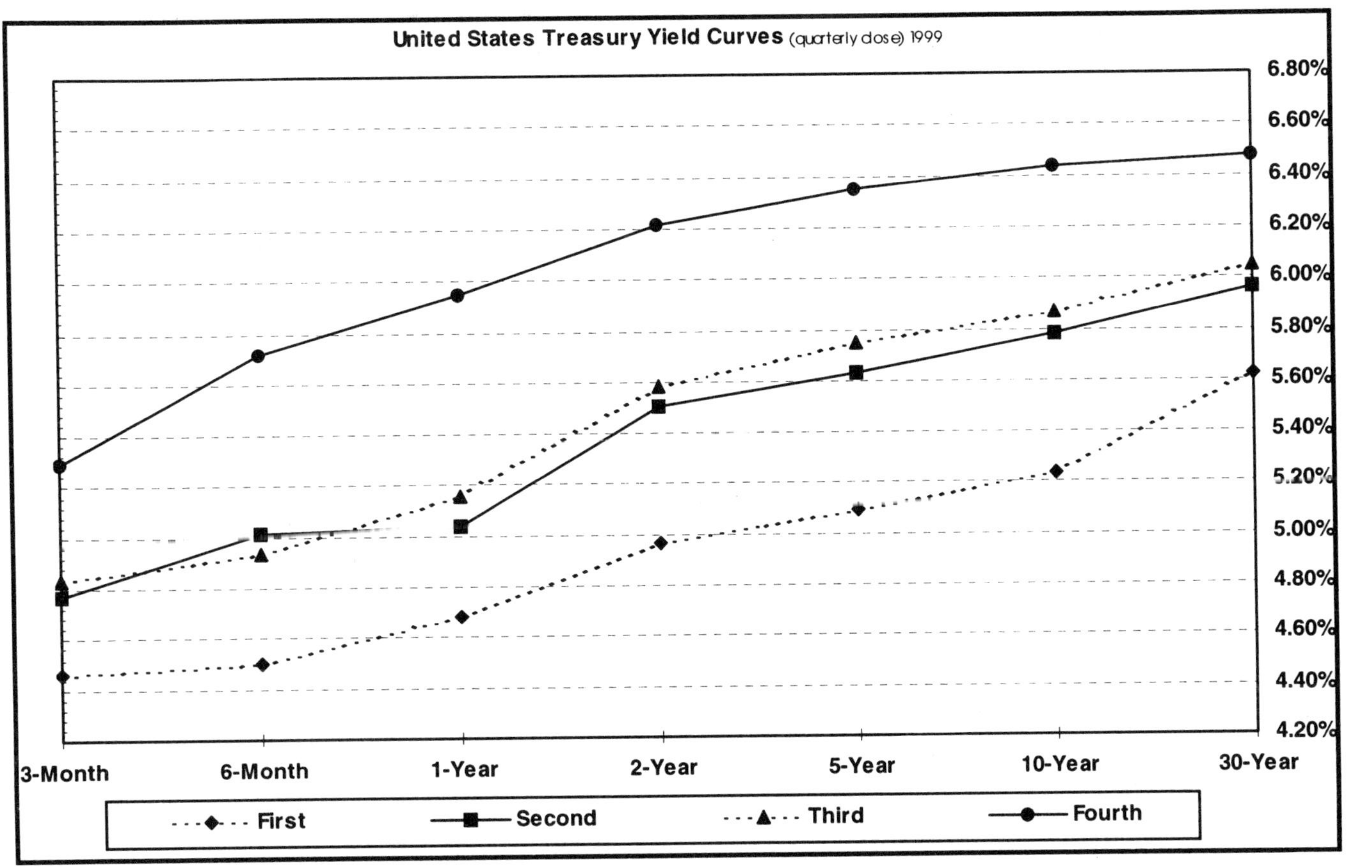

U.S. Industrial Production Index[1] 1992 = 100

Year	Jan.	Feb.	Mar.	Apr.	May	June	July	Aug.	Sept.	Oct.	Nov.	Dec.	Average
1990	98.5	99.0	99.4	98.9	99.3	99.3	99.2	99.4	99.5	99.0	97.7	97.1	98.9
1991	96.7	95.9	95.0	95.3	96.0	97.2	97.2	97.4	98.3	98.2	98.1	97.4	96.9
1992	97.5	98.1	98.9	99.6	100.0	99.7	100.4	100.1	100.5	101.3	101.9	101.9	100.0
1993	102.3	102.8	102.8	103.2	102.6	102.8	103.1	102.8	103.9	104.1	104.6	105.4	103.4
1994	105.7	106.2	107.0	107.4	108.1	108.6	109.1	109.2	109.3	109.9	110.6	111.6	108.6
1995	111.9	111.6	111.7	111.4	111.5	111.7	111.7	112.6	113.0	112.5	112.7	112.8	114.5
1996	112.4	113.8	113.2	114.3	114.8	115.5	115.5	115.8	116.0	116.2	120.6	120.9	119.5
1997	121.3	122.1	122.5	123.1	123.3	123.5	124.5	125.2	125.6	129.3	129.9	130.3	127.0
1998	130.3	130.2	130.7	131.3	131.9	130.6	130.5	132.4	131.9	134.1	133.8	133.8	132.4
1999[2]	134.1	134.5	135.1	135.5	136.2	136.6	137.4	137.6	137.6	138.5			136.3

[1] Total Index of the Federal Reserve Index of Quantity Output, seasonally adjusted. [2] Preliminary. *Source: Bureau of Economic Analysis, U.S. Department of Commerce (BEA)*

U.S. Gross National Product, National Income, and Personal Income In Billions of Constant Dollars[1]

	Gross Domestic Product					National Income					Personal Income				
Year	First Quarter	Second Quarter	Third Quarter	Fourth Quarter	Annual Average	First Quarter	Second Quarter	Third Quarter	Fourth Quarter	Annual Average	First Quarter	Second Quarter	Third Quarter	Fourth Quarter	Annual Average
1990	6,154	6,174	6,145	6,081	6,139	4,396	4,461	4,475	4,507	4,460	4,689	4,772	4,838	4,868	4,792
1991	6,048	6,074	6,089	6,104	6,079	4,493	4,529	4,555	4,599	4,720	4,885	4,951	4,979	5,059	4,969
1992	6,175	6,214	6,261	6,327	6,244	4,889	4,941	4,912	5,103	4,990	5,161	5,236	5,233	5,429	5,277
1993	6,326	6,357	6,393	6,469	6,386	5,160	5,237	5,282	5,389	5,267	5,369	5,504	5,544	5,659	5,519
1994	6,509	6,588	6,645	7,096	6,947	5,423	5,556	5,636	5,747	5,591	5,616	5,767	5,838	5,911	5,758
1995	7,171	7,211	7,305	7,392	7,270	5,816	5,873	5,965	6,040	5,924	5,980	6,030	6,094	6,185	6,072
1996	7,495	7,629	7,703	7,818	7,662	6,120	6,227	6,304	6,374	6,256	6,284	6,390	6,477	6,550	6,425
1997	7,955	8,063	8,171	8,255	8,301	6,509	6,605	6,705	6,768	6,635	6,667	6,744	6,821	6,905	6,951
1998	8,384	8,684	8,798	8,948	8,760	6,875	6,978	7,087	7,194	7,036	7,004	7,296	7,414	7,531	7,359
1999[2]	9,073	9,146	9,298		9,172	7,335	7,423	7,522		7,427	7,630	7,733	7,831		7,731

[1] Seasonally adjusted at annual rates. [2] Preliminary. *Source: Bureau of Economic Analysis, U.S. Department of Commerce (BEA)*

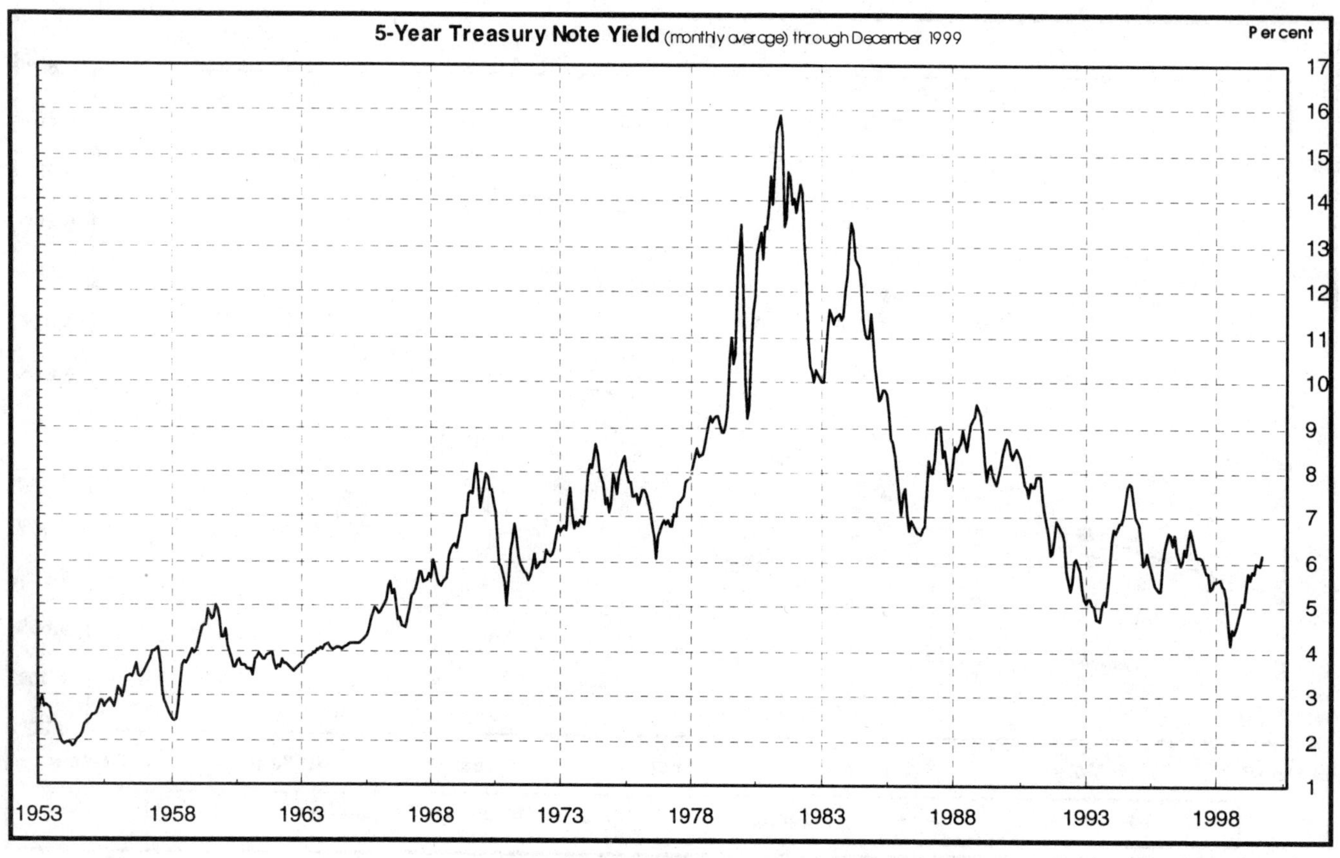

U.S. Money Supply M1[2] In Billions of Dollars

Year	Jan.	Feb.	Mar.	Apr.	May	June	July	Aug.	Sept.	Oct.	Nov.	Dec.	Average
1990	795.3	798.2	801.7	806.3	804.6	810.3	810.4	816.0	821.6	819.8	822.0	825.8	811.0
1991	826.7	832.8	839.8	842.5	849.1	858.6	861.3	867.2	870.6	877.5	888.6	897.3	859.3
1992	910.0	926.2	936.8	944.3	952.4	954.2	963.2	975.4	988.2	1,003.9	1,016.7	1,025.0	966.4
1993	1,032.0	1,034.0	1,038.4	1,047.8	1,067.5	1,075.4	1,084.7	1,094.5	1,104.2	1,114.3	1,123.6	1,129.8	1,078.9
1994	1,132.8	1,137.3	1,140.1	1,142.4	1,143.5	1,144.7	1,150.9	1,149.7	1,150.8	1,150.4	1,150.4	1,150.7	1,145.3
1995	1,150.3	1,148.4	1,147.1	1,150.4	1,145.1	1,142.7	1,145.0	1,144.0	1,141.6	1,135.7	1,133.1	1,129.0	1,142.7
1996	1,122.2	1,119.8	1,126.2	1,123.5	1,117.1	1,115.5	1,108.8	1,099.8	1,093.3	1,080.3	1,080.1	1,081.1	1,106.1
1997	1,080.8	1,078.8	1,075.0	1,068.3	1,064.3	1,065.4	1,065.6	1,071.1	1,063.5	1,061.9	1,069.2	1,076.0	1,069.6
1998	1,073.8	1,076.0	1,080.6	1,082.1	1,078.2	1,077.8	1,075.4	1,072.2	1,074.7	1,080.4	1,089.0	1,093.4	1,079.5
1999[1]	1,091.0	1,092.6	1,102.0	1,108.4	1,104.8	1,101.1	1,099.5	1,102.4	1,093.4	1,098.4			1,099.4

[1] Preliminary. [2] M1 -- This measure is currency, travelers checks, plus deposits at commercial banks and interest-earning checkable deposits at all depository institutions. *Source: Bureau of Economic Analysis, U.S. Department of Commerce (BEA)*

U.S. Money Supply M2[2] In Billions of Dollars

Year	Jan.	Feb.	Mar.	Apr.	May	June	July	Aug.	Sept.	Oct.	Nov.	Dec.	Average
1990	3,173.1	3,185.3	3,196.9	3,209.3	3,207.0	3,221.0	3,230.2	3,248.4	3,262.3	3,265.3	3,269.6	3,279.5	3,229.0
1991	3,293.4	3,311.1	3,329.4	3,337.9	3,348.0	3,359.1	3,361.0	3,360.5	3,360.0	3,363.9	3,372.5	3,379.6	3,348.0
1992	3,387.7	3,407.1	3,410.5	3,408.8	3,407.4	3,401.3	3,402.2	3,408.9	3,418.2	3,432.0	3,435.3	3,434.0	3,412.8
1993	3,431.3	3,424.0	3,420.4	3,423.6	3,447.6	3,452.9	3,452.7	3,456.8	3,463.6	3,469.7	3,480.2	3,486.6	3,450.8
1994	3,490.8	3,491.7	3,494.3	3,503.0	3,504.0	3,493.7	3,502.1	3,498.2	3,498.4	3,499.4	3,500.9	3,502.1	3,498.2
1995	3,506.3	3,506.1	3,506.7	3,519.1	3,534.9	3,562.9	3,583.1	3,604.4	3,620.1	3,629.8	3,639.3	3,655.0	3,572.3
1996	3,669.9	3,685.0	3,713.9	3,724.5	3,725.6	3,741.9	3,750.0	3,762.7	3,775.3	3,788.1	3,798.3	3,821.8	3,745.6
1997	3,840.7	3,853.3	3,868.9	3,890.0	3,892.5	3,908.0	3,922.5	3,954.8	3,979.3	3,999.3	4,023.6	4,046.4	3,931.5
1998	4,071.4	4,100.9	4,126.2	4,155.2	4,174.8	4,198.6	4,216.1	4,241.7	4,284.2	4,325.5	4,364.0	4,401.0	4,221.1
1999[1]	4,425.0	4,445.6	4,455.5	4,488.3	4,505.9	4,522.2	4,543.1	4,564.5	4,583.1	4,602.4			4,513.6

[1] Preliminary. [2] M2 -- This measure adds to M1 overnight repurchase agreements (RPs) issued by commercial banks and certain overnight Eurodollars (those issued by Caribbean branches of member banks) held by U.S. nonbank residents, general purpose and broker/dealer money market mutual funds shares (MMMF), and savings and small-denomination time deposits. *Source: Bureau of Economic Analysis, U.S. Department of Commerce (BEA)*

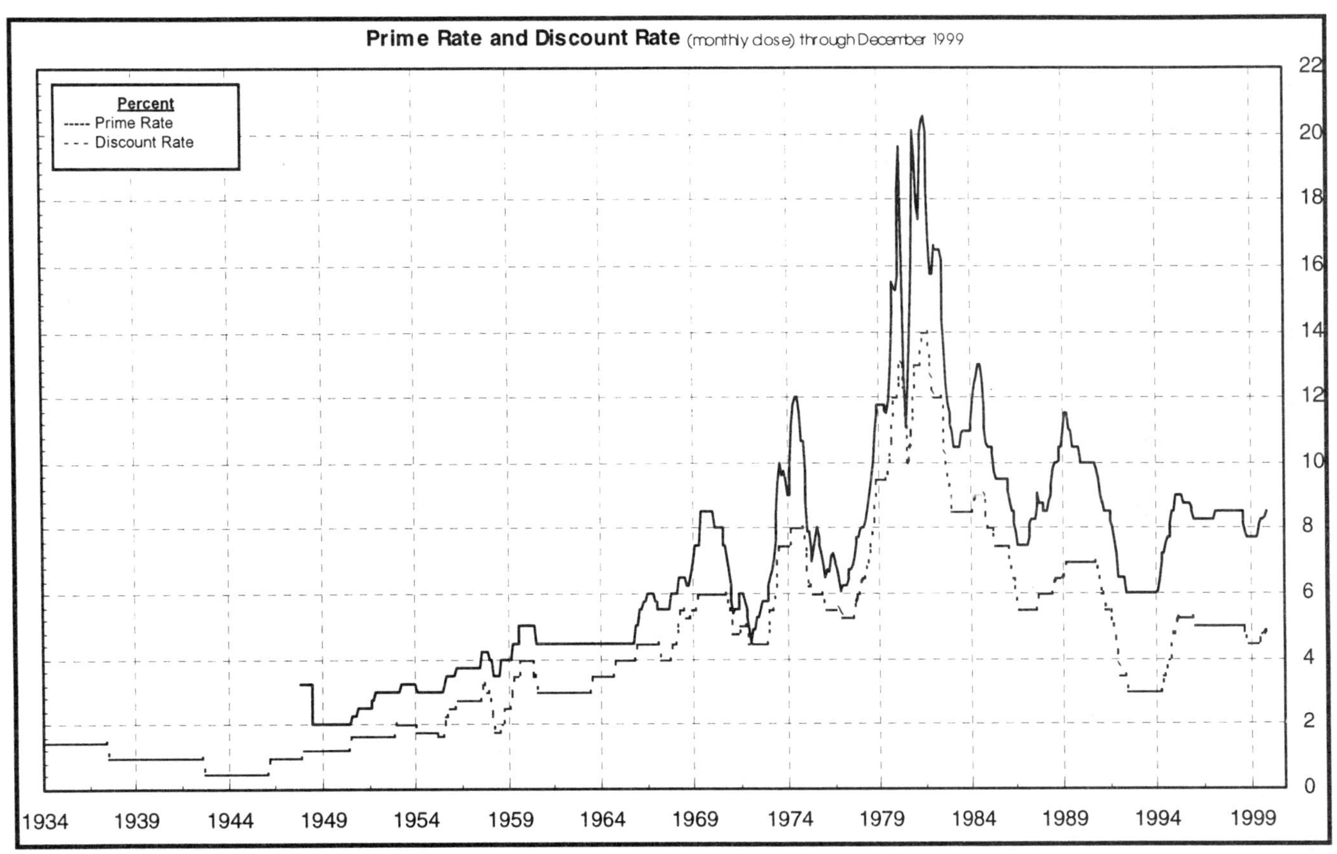
Prime Rate and Discount Rate (monthly close) through December 1999
Percent
----- Prime Rate
- - - Discount Rate
0
2
4
6
8
10
12
14
16
18
20
22
1934
1939
1944
1949
1954
1959
1964
1969
1974
1979
1984
1989
1994
1999

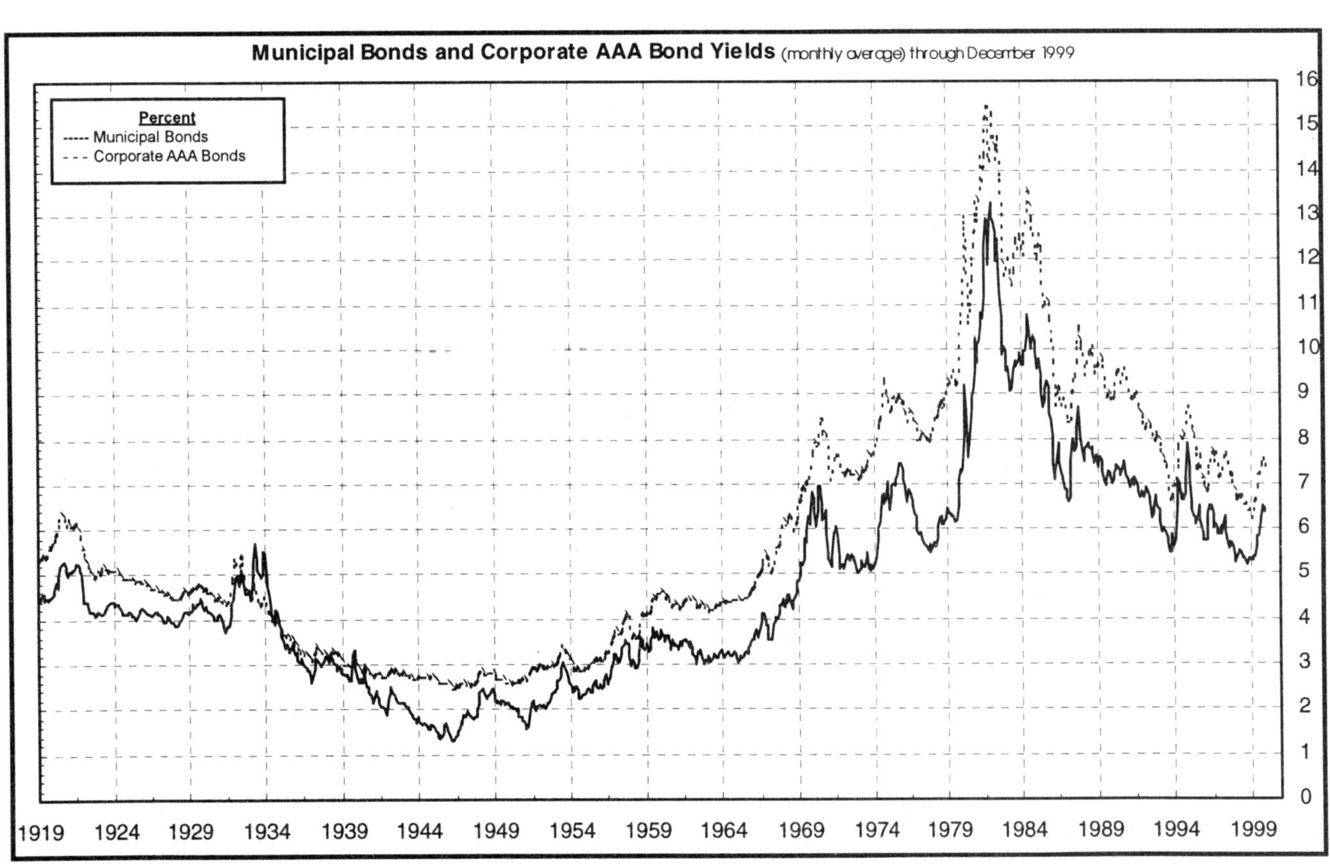
Municipal Bonds and Corporate AAA Bond Yields (monthly average) through December 1999
Percent
----- Municipal Bonds
- - - Corporate AAA Bonds
0
1
2
3
4
5
6
7
8
9
10
11
12
13
14
15
16
1919
1924
1929
1934
1939
1944
1949
1954
1959
1964
1969
1974
1979
1984
1989
1994
1999

Key Interest Rates (weekly close) as of 31-Dec-1999
Percent
----- Prime Rate
- - - 30-Year Bond
- - - Discount Rate
----- 3-Month Treasury Bill
Jan-90
Jan-91
Jan-92
Dec-92
Dec-93
Dec-94
Dec-95
Dec-96
Dec-97
Dec-98
Dec-99
11
10
9
8
7
6
5
4
3
2

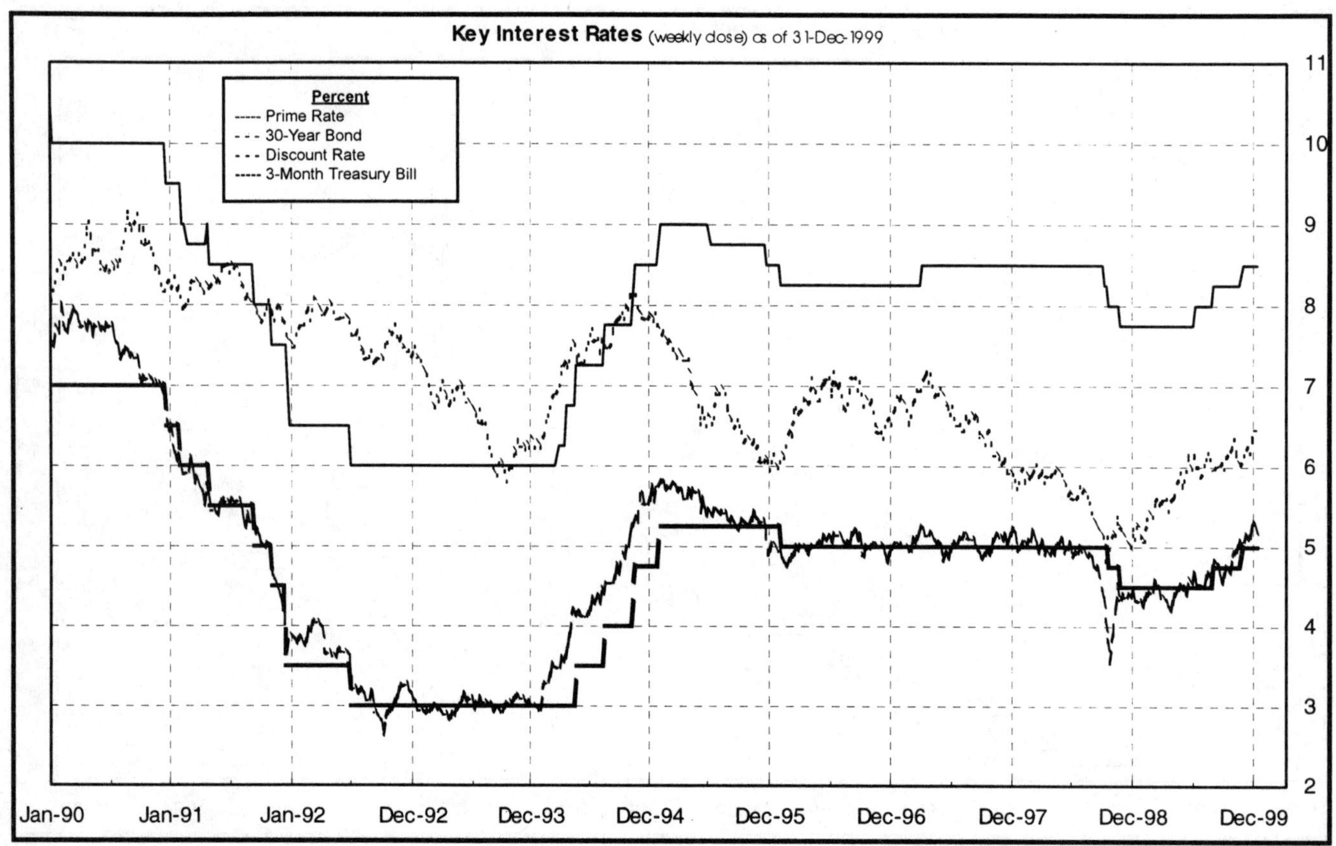

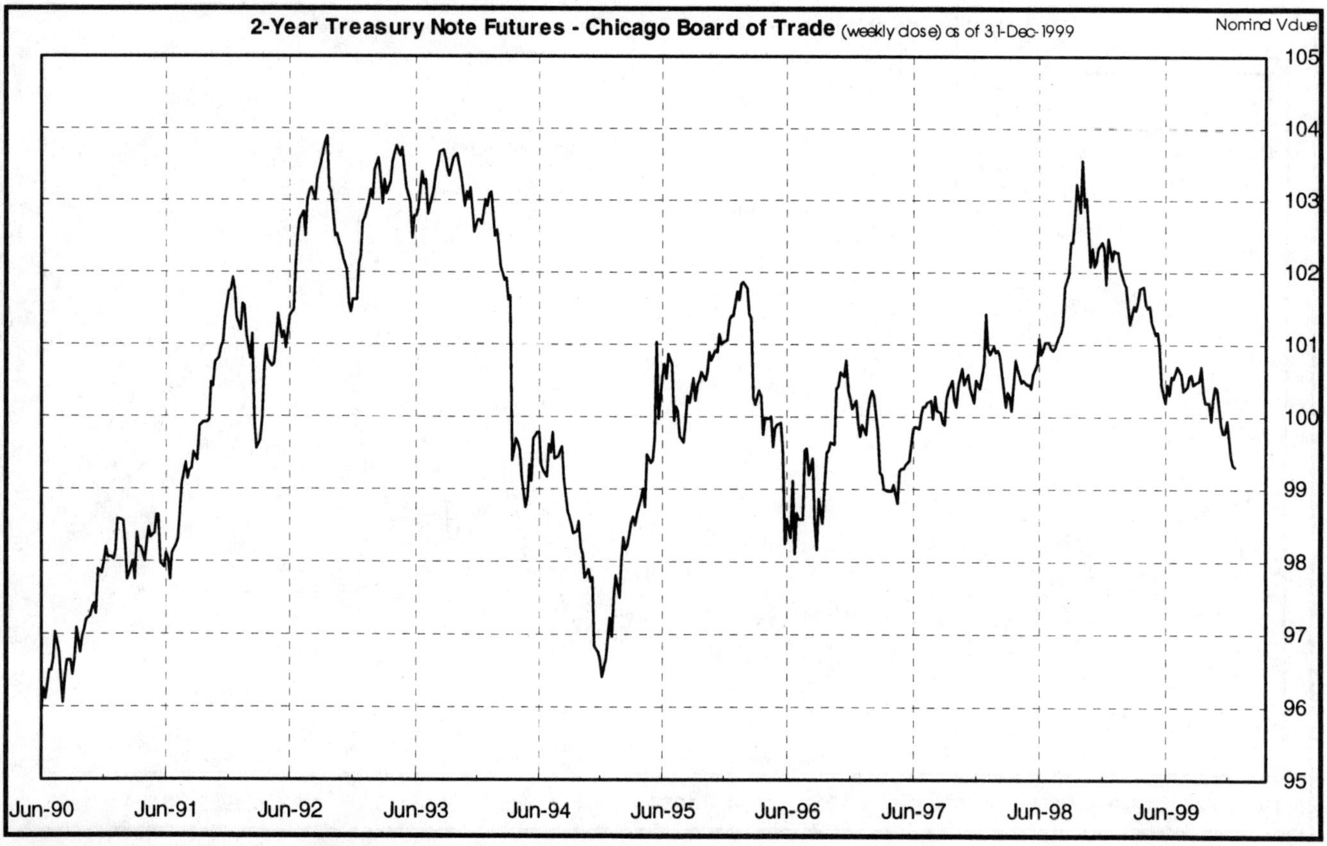

2-Year Treasury Note Futures - Chicago Board of Trade (weekly close) as of 31-Dec-1999
Nominal Value
105
104
103
102
101
100
99
98
97
96
95
Jun-90
Jun-91
Jun-92
Jun-93
Jun-94
Jun-95
Jun-96
Jun-97
Jun-98
Jun-99

Interest Rates, Worldwide

The world's major central banks tightened monetary policy in 1999, albeit moderately, but enough to generally erase the easier policies implemented in 1998. The rationale for the tightenings were the faster, stronger than expected improvements in the major economies, but significantly without any strong inflationary pressures. Thus, the central bank actions were largely preemptive and designed to slow the economies and, in turn, check inflation before it took hold. The concern was especially evident in the U.S., but at yearend 1999 the jury was still out as to whether the Federal Reserve, and other major central banks, were being overly cautious. What has yet to be determined is whether the emergence of high-tech economies and attending improvements in worker productivity can absorb tight labor markets without triggering either cost-push and/or demand-pull inflation. From a historical economic stance it shouldn't happen. However, it does appear that subtle changes are taking root in the global economies which may yet give central banks more flexibility towards monetary policy.

As the new century unfolds, the role of the central bank is likely to prove a major issue. A century ago there were only 18 central banks, 16 of them in Europe. Now there are 172 central banks with more and more of them claiming some degree of independence from their national governments. The European Central Bank (E.C.B.) represents eleven nations with a new degree of independence since no one government appoints all its members. The claim for such independence rests largely on the success of tight monetary policies in quelling inflation in the 1980's.

In early November 1999, the E.C.B. raised the benchmark refinancing rate to 3.0 percent from 2.5, the bank's first increase in its then short history. The move was not unexpected and was in response to a better than expected economic setting for Western Europe. Earlier in the year, the E.C.B. had lowered rates to 2 1/2 percent in an effort to prevent an economic downturn and possible deflationary pressures. Whether the rate decrease buoyed Europe's economies in midyear is uncertain, but it did help the equity markets and the wealth created, on paper and/or realized, obviously had an impact on consumer spending. Still, the European Union benchmark rate of 3 percent in late 1999 was still under the U.S. and U.K., by at least 2 percent, but well above Japan's 1/2 percent.

In September, Britain's central bank raised the short term securities repurchase rate 25 basis points to 5.25 percent, the first increase in more than a year and breaking a series of seven moderate rate cuts. The Bank's action was unexpected since U.K. inflation was below its target of 2.5 percent, but the economy's growth was accelerating and traders apparently surmised that the 1/4 point increase would have little dampening impact, the implication of which suggested additional increases would soon come and in November another 25 basis point increase lifted the repurchase rate to 5.50 percent.

However, the economic situation in the U.K. in late 1999 was still considerably better than across much of Continental Europe. Growth in France was good with the G.D.P. growing at more than 2.5 percent. Growth was seen as torrid in Ireland and Holland. In Germany, which accounts for about one-third of the Euro zone's economic output, growth was modest at best. Germany's G.D.P. in 1999 was put at +1.5 percent and was forecast at +2.5 percent in 2000.

The U.S. economy continues to dominate the world and its robust growth in 1999, annualized at over 5 percent, prompted the federal reserve to raise short-term rates three times, effectively erasing the three rate cuts in 1998. The Fed's rational for the increases was that the economy was too strong for its own good. Unemployment was at a thirty year low and skilled workers were lacking in a number of industries. However, the flip side of the economic equation was that productivity per worker was the best in years which effectively restrained labor costs. Thus, inflation, either producer or consumer, which the Fed fears as the most damaging economic variable, showed little sign of surfacing in 1999. Still, the strong equity markets buoyed consumer spending, and if the scenario carries into 2000 additional rate hikes are apt to be seen by midyear. A major restraint on any aggressive Fed tightening may be the fear higher rates would have on strengthening the U.S. dollar, but the Fed has always stressed that its primary concern is containing inflation, not the dollar's value.

In Japan, short-term interest rates stayed within an eyelash of zero during 1999. The nation's monetary policy was viewed my many as dangerously passive. Until 1998, the Bank of Japan basically took its orders on monetary policy from the Ministry of Finance, but now it is independent and perhaps overly protective of its new responsibility, as evidenced in 1999 when the bank refused to print more yen, as requested by the Finance Ministry, to help bring down the yen's soaring value against the U.S. dollar. Although Japan slowly pulled itself out of its economic malaise during 1999, the change has been largely due to fiscal policy rather than monetary.

In early 1999, global deflation and rising unemployment were the primary economic fears, by yearend those fears had largely dissipated. The question for the year 2000 is how strongly the central banks will react to strengthening economies and inflation fears, real or perceived. The odds appear to favor some further credit tightening, especially in the U.S., if the wealth generating equity markets continue to move higher.

Futures Markets

A number of actively traded interest rate futures markets are traded worldwide. The London International Financial Futures Exchange (LIFFE) trades contracts on 3-month Sterling prices and British long Gilts. LIFFE also offers futures on Euroswiss and Italian government bonds. The all-electronic Eurex exchange in Frankfurt trades a variety of Swiss and German government bonds as well as Euribors. Canadian Bankers Acceptances are traded on the Montreal Exchange (ME). 3-year Australian Commonwealth T-bonds are traded on the Sydney Futures Exchange. Notional bond and PIBOR futures are traded on the Paris MATIF. Euroyen futures and Japanese yen government bonds are traded in Tokyo. Libor and eurodollars are traded on Chicago's Mercantile Exchange, with the latter also on the Mid-America Exchange. A Brady Bond Index futures is traded on the CBOT.

Long Gilt Futures - London International Financial Futures Exchange (weekly close) as of 31-Dec-1999
Nominal Value
128
124
120
116
112
108
104
100
96
92
88
84
80
76
9% through March 1998 contract
7% June 1998 contract to date
Jan-90
Jan-91
Jan-92
Dec-92
Dec-93
Dec-94
Dec-95
Dec-96
Dec-97
Dec-98
Dec-99

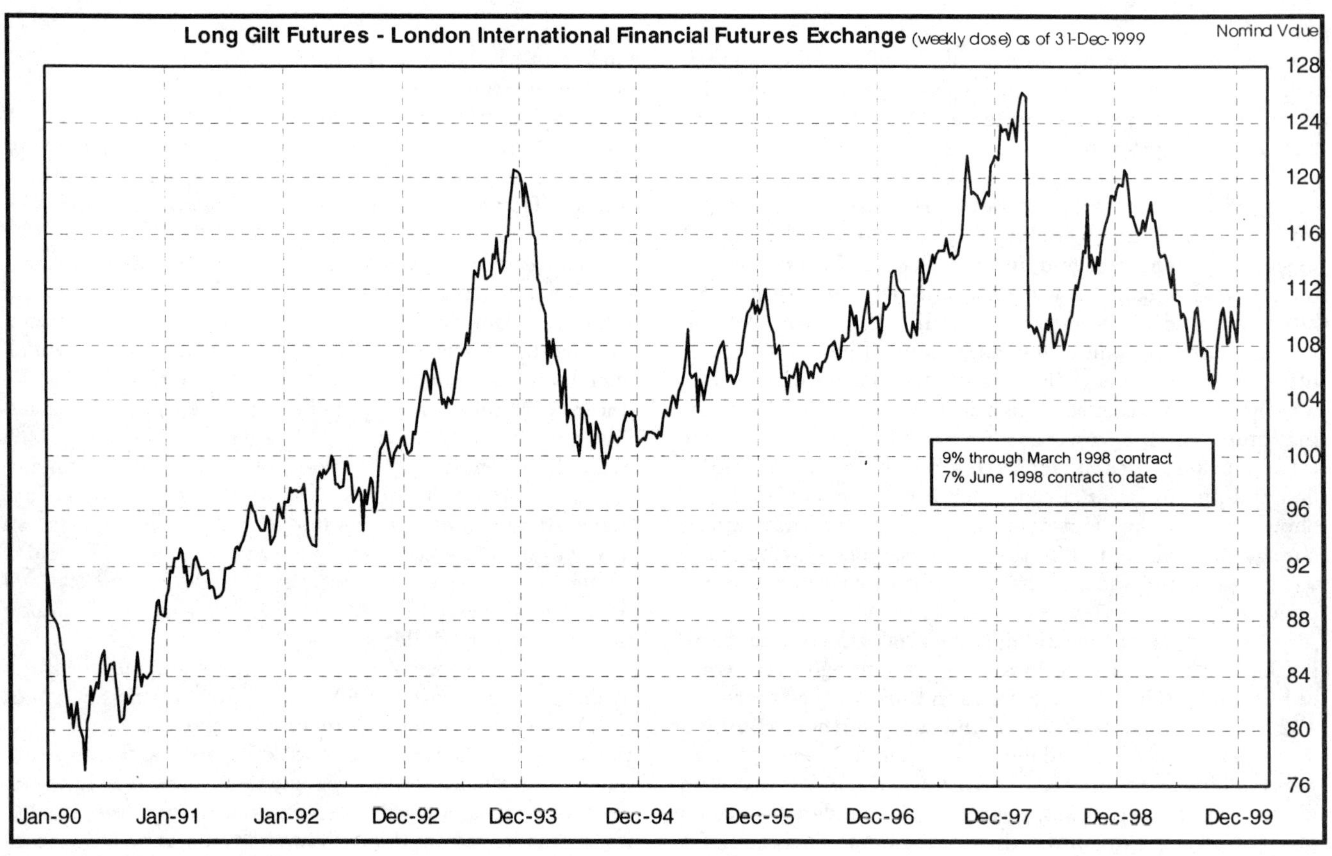

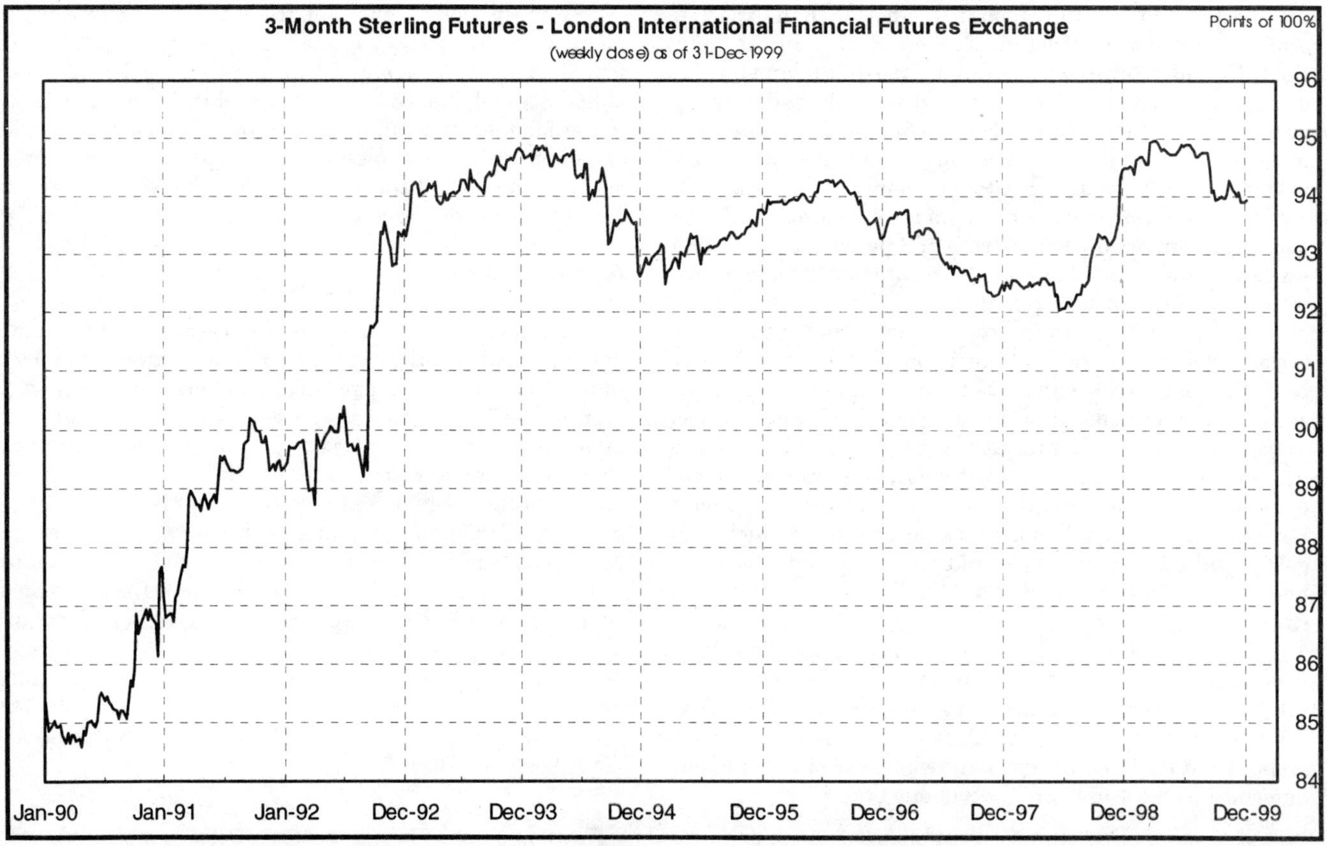

3-Month Sterling Futures - London International Financial Futures Exchange
(weekly close) as of 31-Dec-1999
Points of 100%
96
95
94
93
92
91
90
89
88
87
86
85
84
Jan-90
Jan-91
Jan-92
Dec-92
Dec-93
Dec-94
Dec-95
Dec-96
Dec-97
Dec-98
Dec-99

10-Year Japanese Government Bond Futures - Tokyo Stock Exchange
(weekly close) as 31-Dec-1999
Nominal Value
145
140
135
130
125
120
115
110
105
100
95
90
85
Jan-90
Jan-91
Jan-92
Dec-92
Dec-93
Dec-94
Dec-95
Dec-96
Dec-97
Dec-98
Dec-99

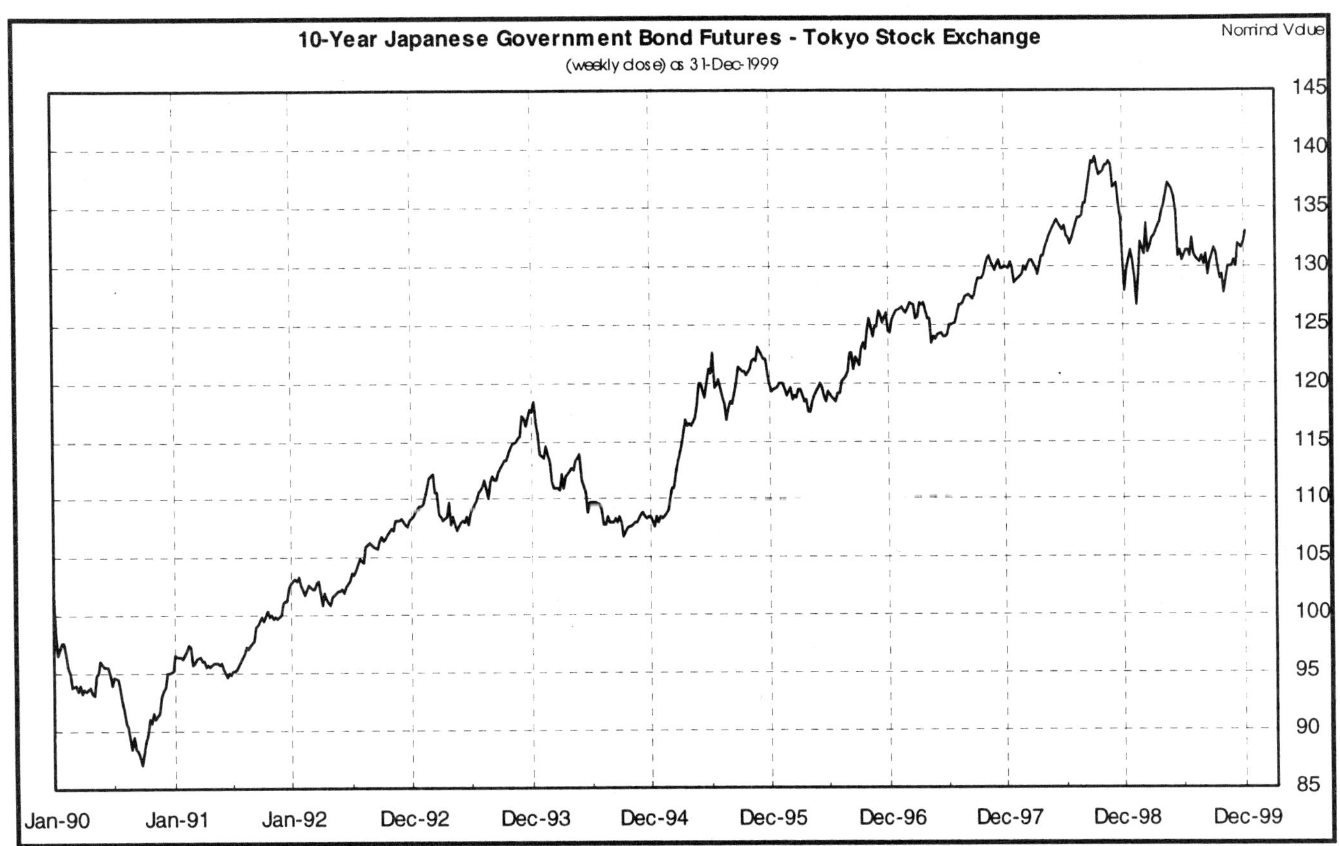

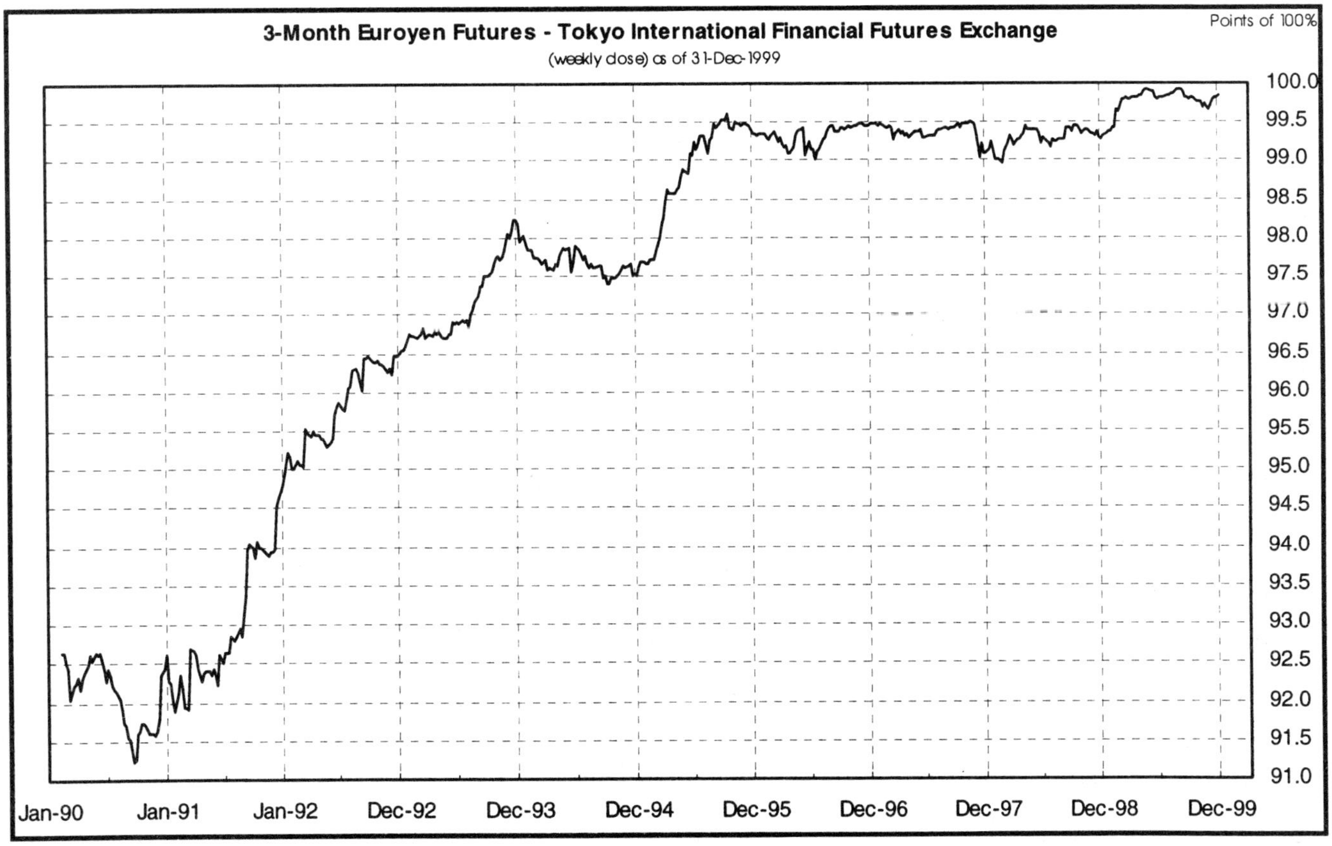

3-Month Euroyen Futures - Tokyo International Financial Futures Exchange
(weekly close) as of 31-Dec-1999
Points of 100%
100.0
99.5
99.0
98.5
98.0
97.5
97.0
96.5
96.0
95.5
95.0
94.5
94.0
93.5
93.0
92.5
92.0
91.5
91.0
Jan-90
Jan-91
Jan-92
Dec-92
Dec-93
Dec-94
Dec-95
Dec-96
Dec-97
Dec-98
Dec-99

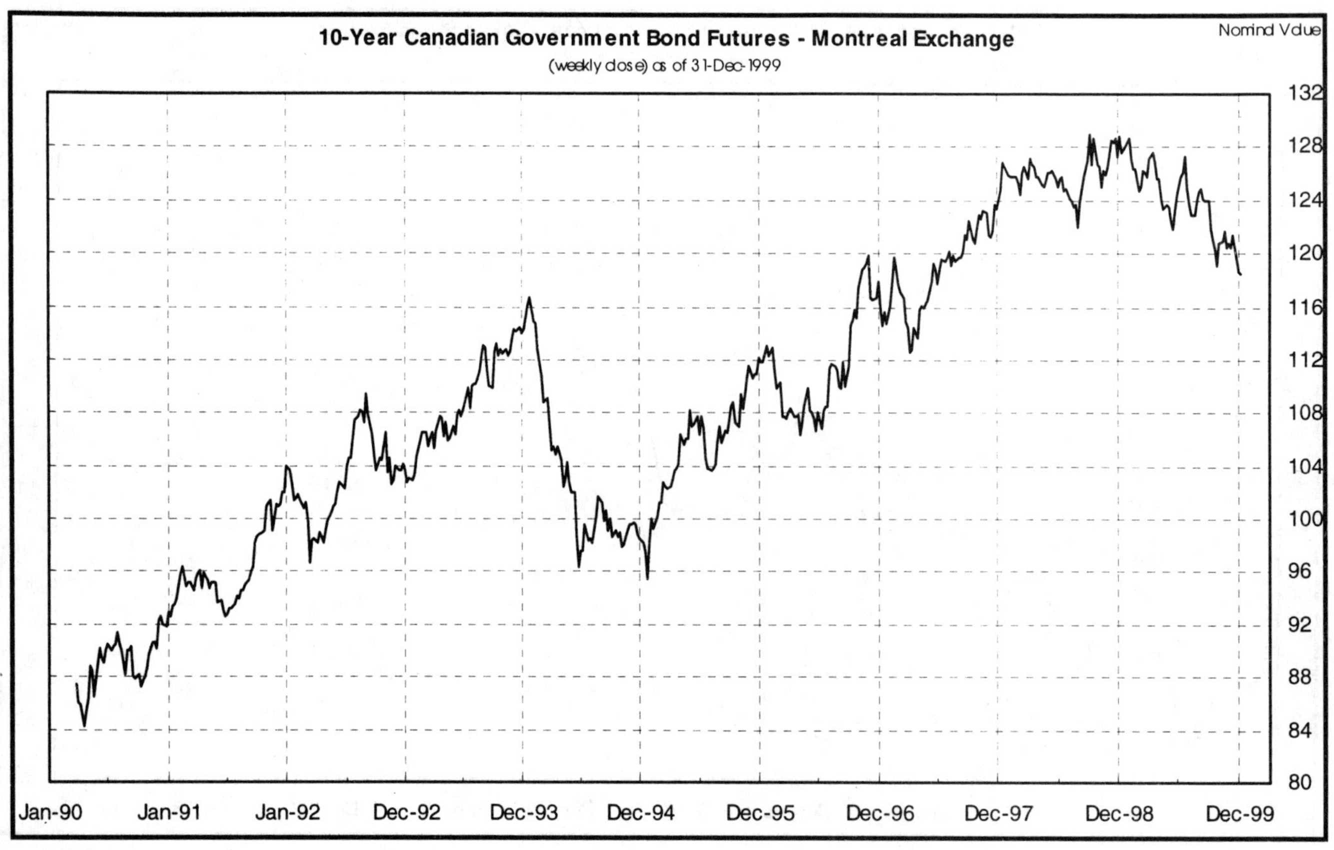
10-Year Canadian Government Bond Futures - Montreal Exchange
(weekly close) as of 31-Dec-1999
Nominal Value
132
128
124
120
116
112
108
104
100
96
92
88
84
80
Jan-90
Jan-91
Jan-92
Dec-92
Dec-93
Dec-94
Dec-95
Dec-96
Dec-97
Dec-98
Dec-99

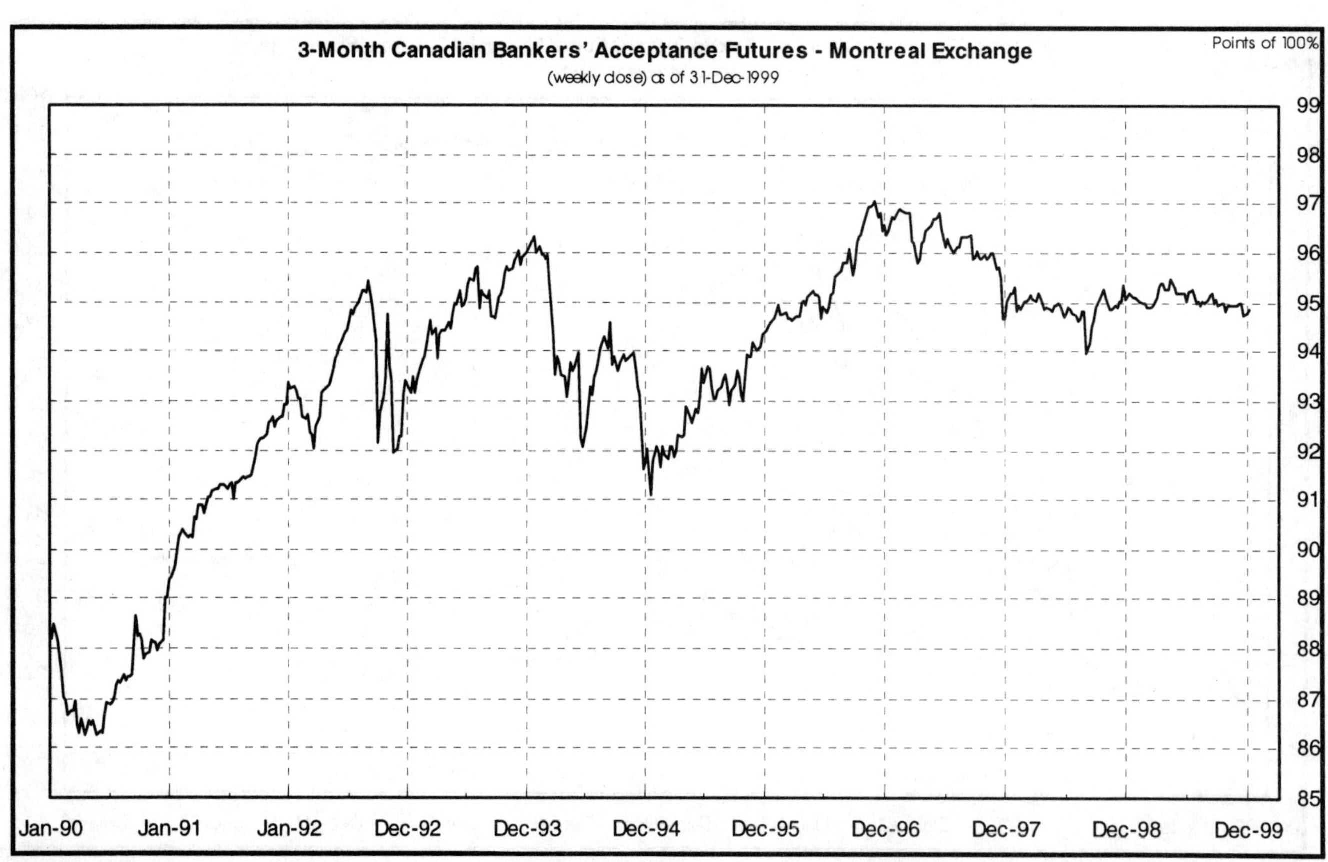
3-Month Canadian Bankers' Acceptance Futures - Montreal Exchange
(weekly close) as of 31-Dec-1999
Points of 100%
99
98
97
96
95
94
93
92
91
90
89
88
87
86
85
Jan-90
Jan-91
Jan-92
Dec-92
Dec-93
Dec-94
Dec-95
Dec-96
Dec-97
Dec-98
Dec-99

Australia -- Economic Statistics Percentage Change from Previous Period

Year	Real GDP	Nominal GDP	Real Private Consump-tion	Real Public Consump-tion	Grossed Fixed Invest-ment	Real Total Domestic Demand	Real Exports of Goods & Services	Real Imports of Goods & Services	Consumer Prices[1]	Unem-ployment Rate
1992	2.6	4.1	2.7	1.0	2.8	3.0	5.4	7.1	1.0	10.7
1993	3.8	5.3	1.8	.5	4.8	3.1	8.0	4.2	1.8	10.9
1994	5.0	5.9	4.0	3.9	12.3	5.4	9.0	14.1	1.9	9.7
1995	4.4	5.9	5.1	3.6	2.8	4.7	5.1	8.1	4.6	8.5
1996	4.0	6.1	3.3	2.3	5.0	3.3	10.6	8.2	2.6	8.4
1997	3.9	5.3	3.9	1.9	11.6	3.6	11.5	10.3	.3	8.5
1998	5.1	5.4	4.3	2.7	6.2	6.2	-.4	5.9	.9	8.0
1999[2]	3.9	5.3	4.8	4.2	3.4	4.8	2.0	6.5		7.3
2000[3]	3.0	5.7	3.8	2.2	1.6	2.5	7.8	4.0		6.9

[1] National accounts inplicit private consumption deflator. [2] Estimate. [3] Projection. *Source: Organization for Economic Co-opertation and Development (OECD)*

Canada -- Economic Statistics Percentage Change from Previous Period

Year	Real GDP	Nominal GDP	Real Private Consump-tion	Real Public Consump-tion	Grossed Fixed Invest-ment	Real Total Domestic Demand	Real Exports of Goods & Services	Real Imports of Goods & Services	Consumer Prices[1]	Unem-ployment Rate
1992	.9	2.2	1.8	1.0	-1.3	.9	7.9	6.2	1.5	11.3
1993	2.3	3.8	1.8	.1	-2.7	1.4	10.9	7.4	1.9	11.2
1994	4.7	5.9	3.1	-1.2	7.4	3.2	13.1	8.3	.2	10.4
1995	2.8	5.2	2.1	-.5	-1.9	1.7	9.0	6.2	2.2	9.5
1996	1.7	3.3	2.5	-1.1	6.5	1.6	5.8	5.8	1.6	9.7
1997	4.0	4.8	4.2	-.5	13.9	5.7	8.5	14.6	1.6	9.2
1998	3.1	2.5	2.8	1.7	3.6	2.2	8.2	5.8	1.0	8.4
1999[2]	3.7	5.2	2.4	1.4	8.8	3.3	9.1	7.8		8.1
2000[3]	3.0	5.1	2.3	1.5	6.3	3.0	6.4	6.6		8.0

[1] National accounts inplicit private consumption deflator. [2] Estimate. [3] Projection. *Source: Organization for Economic Co-opertation and Development (OECD)*

France -- Economic Statistics Percentage Change from Previous Period

Year	Real GDP	Nominal GDP	Real Private Consump-tion	Real Public Consump-tion	Grossed Fixed Invest-ment	Real Total Domestic Demand	Real Exports of Goods & Services	Real Imports of Goods & Services	Consumer Prices[1]	Unem-ployment Rate
1992	1.4	3.4	.8	3.6	-1.7	.7	5.0	1.7	2.4	10.4
1993	-1.0	1.5	-.3	4.3	-6.6	-1.7	.2	-3.7	2.1	11.7
1994	1.8	3.7	.8	.5	1.6	1.8	7.9	8.6	1.7	12.2
1995	1.8	3.5	1.4		2.1	1.7	7.8	7.9	1.7	11.6
1996	1.2	2.6	1.4	2.2		.7	3.1	1.3	2.0	12.3
1997	2.0	3.4	.2	1.6	.5	.9	10.6	6.4	1.2	12.4
1998	3.4	4.3	3.6	1.1	6.1	3.9	6.9	9.4	.8	11.8
1999[2]	2.4	3.1	2.3	1.5	6.5	2.5	1.8	2.2		11.2
2000[3]	3.0	4.1	2.7	1.3	5.2	2.7	6.3	5.5		10.6

[1] National accounts inplicit private consumption deflator. [2] Estimate. [3] Projection. *Source: Organization for Economic Co-opertation and Development (OECD)*

Germany[2] -- Economic Statistics Percentage Change from Previous Period

Year	Real GDP	Nominal GDP	Real Private Consump-tion	Real Public Consump-tion	Grossed Fixed Invest-ment	Real Total Domestic Demand	Real Exports of Goods & Services	Real Imports of Goods & Services	Consumer Prices[1]	Unem-ployment Rate
1992	2.2	7.4	2.8	5.0	4.5	2.8	-.8	1.5	5.1	7.7
1993	-1.1	2.5	.2	.1	-4.5	-1.0	-5.5	-5.4	4.4	8.8
1994	2.3	4.9	1.0	2.4	4.0	2.2	7.6	7.3	2.8	9.6
1995	1.7	3.8	2.1	1.5	-.7	1.7	5.7	5.6	1.7	9.4
1996	.8	1.8	.8	2.1	-1.1	.3	5.1	3.2	1.4	10.3
1997	1.5	2.2	.7	-1.1	.5	.7	10.9	8.3	1.9	11.4
1998	2.2	3.2	2.3	.5	1.4	2.5	7.0	8.5	.9	11.2
1999[3]	1.3	2.5	1.7	.7	3.2	1.7	1.7	3.1		10.8
2000[4]	2.3	3.6	2.2	.5	2.8	1.9	6.1	4.9		10.3

[1] National accounts inplicit private consumption deflator. [2] Data are for Western Germany only, except for foreign trade statistics. [3] Estimate. [4] Projection. *Source: Organization for Economic Co-operation and Development (OECD)*

Italy -- Economic Statistics Percentage Change from Previous Period

Year	Real GDP	Nominal GDP	Real Private Consumption	Real Public Consumption	Grossed Fixed Investment	Real Total Domestic Demand	Real Exports of Goods & Services	Real Imports of Goods & Services	Consumer Prices[1]	Unemployment Rate
1992	.8	5.3	1.9	.6	-1.4	.9	7.3	7.4	5.3	8.8
1993	-.9	3.0	-3.7	-.2	-10.9	-5.1	9.0	-10.9	4.6	10.2
1994	2.2	5.8	1.5	-.9	.1	1.7	9.8	8.1	4.1	11.3
1995	2.9	8.1	1.7	-2.2	6.0	2.0	12.6	9.7	5.2	12.0
1996	.9	6.1	.9	1.4	2.3	.4	.9	-.8	4.0	12.1
1997	1.5	4.1	2.5	-.5	.9	2.5	5.2	10.1	2.0	12.3
1998	1.3	4.2	1.8	1.2	3.5	2.6	1.1	6.0	2.0	12.2
1999[2]	1.0	2.6	1.4	2.4	2.9	2.3	-1.2	3.3		12.1
2000[3]	2.4	4.1	2.0	1.1	4.0	2.2	5.3	4.5		11.9

[1] National accounts inplicit private consumption deflator. [2] Estimate. [3] Projection. *Source: Organization for Economic Co-opertation and Development (OECD)*

Japan -- Economic Statistics Percentage Change from Previous Period

Year	Real GDP	Nominal GDP	Real Private Consumption	Real Public Consumption	Grossed Fixed Investment	Real Total Domestic Demand	Real Exports of Goods & Services	Real Imports of Goods & Services	Consumer Prices[1]	Unemployment Rate
1992	1.0	2.8	2.1	2.0	-1.5	.4	4.9	-.7	1.7	2.2
1993	.3	.9	1.2	2.4	-2.0	.1	1.3	-.3	1.2	2.5
1994	.6	.8	1.9	2.4	-.8	1.0	4.6	8.9	.7	2.9
1995	1.5	.8	2.1	3.3	1.7	2.3	5.4	14.2	-.1	3.1
1996	5.1	3.5	2.9	1.9	11.1	5.7	6.3	11.9	.1	3.4
1997	1.4	1.5	1.0	1.5	-1.9	.1	11.6	.5	1.7	3.4
1998	-2.8	-2.5	-1.1	.7	-8.8	-3.5	-2.3	-7.5	.6	4.2
1999[2]	1.4	.7	1.7	.7	1.2	1.5	.3	1.1		4.6
2000[3]	1.4	.9	1.6	.8	-.2	1.2	4.6	3.3		4.9

[1] National accounts inplicit private consumption deflator. [2] Estimate. [3] Projection. *Source: Organization for Economic Co-opertation and Development (OECD)*

Switzerland -- Economic Statistics Percentage Change from Previous Period

Year	Real GDP	Nominal GDP	Real Private Consumption	Real Public Consumption	Grossed Fixed Investment	Real Total Domestic Demand	Real Exports of Goods & Services	Real Imports of Goods & Services	Consumer Prices[1]	Unemployment Rate
1992	-.1	2.6	.1	.7	-6.6	-2.7	3.0	-4.2	4.0	2.5
1993	-.5	2.2	-.9	-.1	-2.7	-1.0	1.5	.1	3.3	4.5
1994	.5	2.2	1.0	2.0	6.5	2.7	1.8	7.9	.9	4.7
1995	.5	1.6	.6	-.1	1.8	1.8	1.6	5.1	1.8	4.2
1996	.3	.7	.7	2.0	-2.4	.4	2.5	2.7	.8	4.7
1997	1.7	1.6	1.3	.6	1.5	1.3	9.0	8.1	.5	5.2
1998	2.1	2.3	2.3	-.2	4.4	4.1	4.6	9.4	.0	4.0
1999[2]	1.4	1.8	1.9	.2	4.7	2.2	3.0	4.8		3.4
2000[3]	1.8	2.4	2.0	.3	4.0	2.5	4.5	6.0		3.0

[1] National accounts inplicit private consumption deflator. [2] Estimate. [3] Projection. *Source: Organization for Economic Co-opertation and Development (OECD)*

United Kingdom -- Economic Statistics Percentage Change from Previous Period

Year	Real GDP	Nominal GDP	Real Private Consumption	Real Public Consumption	Grossed Fixed Investment	Real Total Domestic Demand	Real Exports of Goods & Services	Real Imports of Goods & Services	Consumer Prices[1]	Unemployment Rate
1992	.1	4.1	.4	.5	-.7	.8	4.1	6.8	3.7	10.2
1993	2.3	5.1	2.9	-.8	.8	2.2	3.9	3.2	1.6	10.3
1994	4.4	6.0	2.9	1.4	3.6	3.5	9.2	5.4	2.5	9.4
1995	2.8	5.4	1.7	1.6	2.9	1.8	9.5	5.5	3.4	8.6
1996	2.6	5.9	3.6	1.7	4.9	3.0	7.5	9.1	2.4	8.0
1997	3.5	6.5	3.9	-1.4	7.5	3.8	8.6	9.2	3.1	6.9
1998	2.2	5.0	3.4	1.0	9.9	4.1	2.0	8.4	3.4	6.5
1999[2]	1.7	3.8	3.9	3.7	4.9	3.4	-.1	5.0		7.4
2000[3]	2.7	5.4	2.6	2.6	3.0	2.9	4.0	4.3		8.0

[1] National accounts inplicit private consumption deflator. [2] Estimate. [3] Projection. *Source: Organization for Economic Co-opertation and Development (OECD)*

Iron and Steel

Iron ore is used to make steel. In the U.S., about 97 percent of the iron ore consumed is used in steelmaking. Iron ore production and consumption is concentrated in a few countries. The U.S. Geological Survey estimated that world mine production of iron ore in 1998 was 1.02 billion metric tonnes, down 2 percent from 1997. The largest producer was China with estimated production of 240 million tonnes. The next largest producer was Brazil with mine output of 180 million tonnes. Other large producers include Australia, Russia and India. The world crude iron ore reserve base was estimated at 300 billion tonnes with an iron ore content of 160 billion tonnes.

U.S. production of iron ore in August 1999 was 3.87 million tonnes, down 26 percent from the month before. In the January-August 1999 period, U.S. iron ore production was 39.1 million tonnes. For all of 1998, production was 62.6 million tonnes. Shipments of iron ore in August 1999 were 5.57 million tonnes, down 6 percent from the previous month. Shipment for the first eight months of 1999 were 35.5 million tonnes while for all of 1998 they were 61.4 million tonnes.

U.S. consumption of iron ore in July 1999 was 5.54 million tonnes. In the January-July 1999 period consumption of iron ore was 38.5 million tonnes, down 9 percent from the same period a year ago. Of the total iron ore consumed in 1999, 85 percent was comprised of U.S. ores, 8 percent was made up of Canadian ores and the remainder foreign. Of the total, 91 percent of the ore is used in blast furnaces. Consumer stocks of iron ore and agglomerates on July 31, 1999 were 17.55 million tonnes.

U.S. exports of iron ore in July 1999 were 401,000 tonnes compared to 737,000 tonnes in June. Virtually all of the exports went to Canada. U.S. imports for consumption of iron ore in July 1999 were 1.1 million tonnes. In the January-July 1999 period, imports were 6.25 million tonnes, down 36 percent from the same period in 1998. The major suppliers of iron ore to the U.S. are Canada and Brazil with smaller amounts supplied by Australia, Sweden and Venezuela.

World production of raw steel in 1998 was estimated to be 781 million tonnes, down 3 percent from 1997. The largest producer of raw steel was China with 1998 output of 114 million tonnes. Another large producer is Japan with 1998 output of nearly 94 million tonnes. U.S. production of raw steel in 1998 was estimated at 98.6 million tonnes, about unchanged from 1997. World production of pig iron in 1998 was estimated at 541 million tonnes, down 2 percent from the previous year.

U.S. production of iron and steel scrap in 1998 was estimated at 76 million tonnes, down 4 percent from the previous year. U.S. reported consumption of iron and steel scrap in 1998 was 69 million tonnes, down 5 percent from 1997.

World Production of Raw Steel (Ingots and Castings) In Thousands of Metric Tons

Year	Brazil	Canada	China	France	Germany	Italy	Japan	Rep. of Korea	Russia[3]	Ukraine[3]	United Kingdom	United States	World Total
1989	25,055	15,458	61,587	19,340	41,073	25,213	107,908	21,873	160,096	-----	18,740	88,852	785,973
1990	20,567	12,281	66,349	19,016	38,434	25,467	110,339	23,125	154,414	-----	17,841	89,726	770,458
1991	22,617	12,987	71,000	18,434	42,169	25,112	109,649	26,001	77,093	45,002	16,474	79,738	733,592
1992	23,934	13,933	80,935	17,972	39,711	24,835	98,132	28,055	67,029	41,759	16,212	84,322	719,679
1993	25,207	14,387	89,539	17,106	37,625	25,720	99,623	33,026	58,346	32,609	16,625	88,793	727,548
1994	25,747	13,897	92,613	18,031	40,837	26,151	98,295	33,745	48,812	24,081	17,286	91,244	725,207
1995	25,076	14,415	95,360	18,100	42,051	27,766	101,640	36,772	51,589	22,309	17,604	95,191	752,356
1996	25,237	14,735	101,237	17,633	39,793	23,910	98,801	38,903	49,253	22,332	17,992	95,535	750,127
1997[1]	26,153	15,554	108,911	19,767	45,007	25,842	104,545	42,554	48,502	25,629	18,489	98,486	798,969
1998[2]	25,760	15,930	114,347	20,126	44,046	25,714	93,548	39,896	43,822	24,445	17,319	97,653	776,280

[1] Preliminary. [2] Estimate. [3] Formerly part of the U.S.S.R.; data not reported separately until 1992. *Source: U.S. Geological Survey (USGS)*

Average Wholesale Prices of Iron and Steel in the United States

	No. 1 Heavy Melting Steel Scrap		Pittsburg Prices								
			Hot Rolled	Sheet Bars		Hot Rolled	Carbon Steel	Cold Rolled	Galvanized	Railroad Steel	Used Steel
	Pittsburg	Chicago	Sheet[2]	Hot Rolled	Cold Finished	Strip	Plates	Strip	Sheets	Scrap[3]	Cans[4]
Year	$ Per Gross Ton		Cents Per Pound							$ Per Gross Ton	
1989	106.80	108.33	22.21	19.60	25.21	22.10	23.50	37.24	32.48	145.23	60.18
1990	106.61	108.62	22.25	20.43	25.37	22.10	23.75	37.24	33.55	131.59	77.16
1991	95.18	95.19	22.88	20.60	25.75	23.15	24.50	38.86	35.35	129.69	89.00
1992	88.72	88.52	19.13	17.48	24.03	23.50	24.50	39.40	30.88	117.40	88.73
1993	116.30	115.26	20.99	18.44	23.83	23.50	25.12	39.40	30.90	142.18	91.79
1994	136.76	131.91	22.93	NA	25.70	23.50	27.61	39.40	32.24	169.00	102.33
1995	142.34	143.17	25.32	NA	25.70	24.88	29.98	39.40	34.47	NA	126.32
1996	137.28	136.07	23.94	NA	25.81	25.00	31.16	NA	35.90	NA	122.29
1997	133.38	139.40	18.12	NA	25.67	NA	32.00	NA	28.60	NA	108.20
1998[1]	110.10	118.76	15.57	NA	25.50	NA	33.23	NA	24.12	NA	109.36

[1] Preliminary. [2] 10 gauge; thru 1992,list prices;1993 to date, market prices. [3] Specialties scrap. [4] *Consumer buying prices.*
NA = Not available. *Source: American Metal Market (AMM)*

Salient Statistics of Steel in the United States In Thousands of Net Tons

Year	Pig Iron Production	Producer Price Index for Steel Mill Products (1982=100)	Raw Steel Production: By Type of Furnace: Basic Oxygen	Open Hearth	Electric[2]	Stainless	Carbon	Alloy	Total	Net Shipments Steel Mill Products	Total Steel Products: Exports	Imports
1990	54,750	112.1	58,471	3,496	36,939	2,037	86,590	10,279	98,606	84,981	5,001	19,401
1991	48,637	109.5	52,714	1,408	33,774	1,878	77,879	8,139	87,896	78,846	7,112	17,743
1992	52,224	106.4	57,642	-----	35,308	1,993	82,458	8,498	92,949	82,241	5,016	19,033
1993	53,082	108.2	59,353	-----	38,524	1,956	86,865	9,056	97,877	89,022	4,727	21,796
1994	54,426	113.4	61,028	-----	39,551	2,022	89,535	9,022	100,579	95,084	4,852	32,705
1995	56,097	120.1	62,523	-----	42,407	2,265	92,656	10,009	104,930	97,494	8,157	27,270
1996	54,485	115.7	60,433	-----	44,876	2,061	93,649	9,599	105,309	100,878	6,168	32,115
1997	54,679	116.4	61,053	-----	47,508	2,382	95,933	10,246	108,561	105,858	7,369	34,389
1998	53,164	113.8	59,686	-----	49,067	2,214	97,054	9,484	108,752	102,420	5,520	41,520
1999[1]	51,115	105.4	57,722	-----	49,515	2,412	96,653	8,171	107,237	105,103	5,426	35,731

[1] Preliminary. [2] Includes crucible steels. *Sources: American Iron & Steel Institute (AISI); U.S. Geological Survey (USGS)*

Production of Steel Ingots, Rate of Capability Utilization[1] in the United States In Percent

Year	Jan.	Feb.	Mar.	Apr.	May	June	July	Aug.	Sept.	Oct.	Nov.	Dec.	Average
1990	83.1	85.1	85.7	85.2	85.7	84.5	82.0	85.5	84.6	85.1	83.8	75.0	84.0
1991	74.6	73.1	71.7	72.5	70.0	71.7	74.8	75.2	78.5	78.0	78.0	74.4	74.2
1992	80.5	82.4	83.5	85.3	83.5	82.1	78.9	78.7	78.3	80.9	80.4	77.7	82.2
1993	84.8	89.0	87.0	87.4	88.3	87.5	86.9	86.2	87.7	90.2	86.3	85.9	89.1
1994	87.7	92.2	91.3	91.4	91.2	88.7	87.1	87.7	90.0	92.0	92.6	94.3	93.0
1995	93.8	95.6	96.0	92.9	91.6	90.1	86.8	88.3	93.6	90.3	92.1	90.2	91.7
1996	92.2	92.6	93.8	90.5	89.7	91.3	86.6	87.1	87.7	88.0	87.0	87.9	89.5
1997	85.3	89.3	89.6	89.2	87.9	87.0	85.1	86.4	91.2	86.9	89.6	86.3	89.4
1998	90.0	95.2	93.1	92.5	89.1	86.1	83.0	86.4	83.0	81.0	74.4	74.8	85.7
1999[2]	77.2	79.5	81.7	81.8	81.7	79.7	79.4	82.8	82.3	88.2	89.1	88.5	82.7

[1] Based on tonnage capability to produce raw steel for a full order book. [2] Preliminary. *Sources: American Iron and Steel Institute (AISI); U.S. Geological Survey (USGS)*

Production of Steel Ingots in the United States In Thousands of Short Tons

Year	Jan.	Feb.	Mar.	Apr.	May	June	July	Aug.	Sept.	Oct.	Nov.	Dec.	Total
1990	8,241	7,624	8,505	8,209	8,529	8,142	8,101	8,452	8,094	8,424	8,021	7,422	98,906
1991	7,577	6,608	7,283	7,089	7,076	7,017	7,338	7,386	7,457	7,711	7,461	7,348	87,896
1992	7,754	7,432	8,043	7,875	7,968	7,584	7,542	7,526	7,249	7,742	7,449	7,438	92,949
1993	7,942	7,528	8,148	7,926	8,278	7,937	8,066	8,001	7,878	8,409	7,786	8,008	97,877
1994	8,003	7,598	8,323	8,180	8,437	7,941	7,996	8,053	7,993	8,477	8,256	8,684	100,579
1995	8,918	8,211	9,131	8,548	8,696	8,286	8,308	8,455	8,668	8,685	8,574	8,678	103,142
1996	8,981	8,438	9,136	8,588	8,798	8,661	8,585	8,627	8,407	8,702	8,276	8,689	104,356
1997	8,735	8,266	9,175	8,882	9,048	8,662	8,692	8,818	9,006	9,128	9,116	9,071	107,488
1998	9,510	9,087	9,839	9,524	9,483	8,863	8,832	9,194	8,548	8,681	7,710	8,013	107,643
1999[1]	8,422	7,837	8,854	8,643	8,914	8,413	8,619	8,993	8,650	9,574	9,357	9,604	105,882

[1] Preliminary. *Source: American Iron and Steel Institute (AISI)*

Shipments of Steel Products[1] by Market Classifications in the United States In Thousands of Net Tons

Year	Appliances Utensils & Cutlery	Automotive	Containers, Packaging & Shipping Materials	Construction Including Maint.	Contractors Products	Electrical Equipment	Export	Machinery, Industrial Equipment & Tools	Oil and Gas	Rail Transportaion	Steel for Converting & Processing[2]	Steel Service Center & Distributors	All Other[3]	Total Shipments
1990	1,540	11,100	4,474	9,245	2,870	2,453	2,487	2,388	1,892	1,080	9,441	21,111	14,900	84,981
1991	1,388	10,015	4,278	9,161	2,306	2,102	4,476	1,982	1,425	999	8,265	19,464	12,985	78,846
1992	1,503	11,092	3,974	9,536	2,694	2,136	2,650	1,951	1,454	1,052	9,226	21,328	13,645	82,241
1993	1,592	12,719	4,355	10,516	2,913	2,213	2,110	2,191	1,526	1,223	9,451	23,714	14,499	89,022
1994	1,736	14,753	4,495	10,935	3,348	2,299	1,710	2,427	1,703	1,248	10,502	24,153	15,775	95,084
1995	1,589	14,622	4,139	11,761	3,337	2,397	4,442	2,310	2,643	1,373	10,440	23,751	14,690	97,494
1996	1,713	14,665	4,101	15,561	[5]	2,401	2,328	2,410	3,254	1,400	10,245	27,124	15,676	100,878
1997	1,635	15,251	4,163	15,885	[5]	2,434	2,610	2,355	3,811	1,410	11,263	27,800	17,241	105,858
1998	1,729	15,842	3,829	15,289	[5]	2,255	2,556	2,147	2,649	1,657	9,975	27,751	16,741	102,420
1999[4]	1,712	15,639	3,768	14,685	[5]	2,260	2,292	1,547	1,544	876	7,599	21,439	31,742	105,103

[1] All grades including carbon, alloy and stainless steel. [2] Net total after deducting shipments to reporting companines for conversion or resale.
[3] Includes agricultural; bolts, nuts rivets & screws; forgings (other than automotive); shipbuilding & marine equipment; aircraft; mining, quarrying & lumbering; other domestic & commercial equipment machinery; ordnance & other direct military; and shipments of non-reporting companies.
[4] Preliminary. *Source: American Iron and Steel Institute (AISI)*

Net Shipments of Steel Products[1] in the United States In Thousands of Net Tons

Year	Cold Finished Bars	Rails & Acces-sories	Wire Drawn	Tin Mill Products	Plates (Cut & Coils)	Sheet & Strip Galv. (Hot Dipped)	Hot Rolled Bars	Pipe & Tubing	Structural Shapes & Steel Piling	Rein-forcing Bars	Hot Rolled Sheets	Cold Rolled Sheets	Carbon	Alloy	Stain-less
1990	1,486	519	918	4,031	7,945	7,878	6,655	4,652	5,670	5,305	13,388	13,199	78,818	4,647	1,516
1991	1,341	486	865	4,041	6,942	6,910	5,431	4,488	5,245	4,859	13,161	11,532	73,480	3,917	1,449
1992	1,458	562	900	3,927	7,102	8,199	5,806	4,198	5,081	4,781	13,361	12,692	76,625	4,101	1,514
1993	1,580	679	802	4,123	7,538	9,712	6,339	4,445	4,973	5,033	14,873	12,758	83,106	4,381	1,534
1994	1,786	631	788	4,137	8,556	10,943	7,088	4,966	5,942	4,929	15,654	13,016	88,505	4,859	1,720
1995	1,782	630	654	3,942	9,043	11,329	6,902	5,437	6,278	5,048	16,978	12,347	90,485	5,115	1,894
1996	1,685	722	652	4,108	8,672	11,456	6,999	5,895	6,140	5,762	17,466	14,089	93,019	5,948	1,912
1997	1,809	875	619	4,057	8,855	12,439	8,153	6,548	6,029	6,188	18,221	13,322	97,509	6,282	2,067
1998	1,780	938	725	3,714	8,864	13,481	8,189	5,409	5,595	5,909	15,715	13,185	94,536	5,847	2,037
1999[2]	1,775	646	611	3,771	8,200	14,870	8,078	4,772	5,995	6,183	17,740	13,874	97,873	5,104	2,126

[1] All grades, including carbon, alloy and stainless steel. [2] Preliminary. *Source: American Iron and Steel Institute (AISI)*

World Production of Pig Iron (Excludes Ferro-Alloys) In Thousands of Metric Tons

Year	Belgium	Brazil	China	France	Ger-many	India	Italy	Japan	Russia[4]	Ukraine[4]	United Kingdom	United States	World Total
1989	8,868	24,621	58,200	15,071	35,197	12,420	11,795	80,197	116,628	-----	12,638	50,977	561,762
1990	9,416	21,360	62,380	14,415	32,058	13,395	11,883	80,229	111,763	-----	12,277	50,058	549,000
1991	9,354	22,926	67,650	13,408	30,608	14,176	10,856	79,985	90,900	-----	11,883	44,510	528,000
1992	8,533	23,152	75,890	13,051	27,399	15,126	10,462	73,144	45,824	34,663	11,542	47,400	524,000
1993	8,178	23,982	87,390	12,679	26,970	15,674	11,066	73,738	40,871	26,999	11,534	48,200	531,000
1994	8,974	25,177	97,410	13,293	29,923	17,808	11,157	73,776	36,116	21,200	11,943	49,400	544,000
1995	9,199	25,090	105,293	12,860	29,828	18,626	11,684	74,905	39,762	20,000	12,238	50,900	564,000
1996	8,628	24,121	107,225	12,108	30,012	19,864	10,347	74,597	36,061	18,143	12,830	49,400	559,000
1997[1]	8,077	25,000	115,110	13,424	30,939	20,000	11,348	78,519	37,327	20,561	13,057	49,600	587,000
1998[2]	8,730	25,000	118,600	13,603	30,215	21,000	10,704	74,981	34,827	20,840	12,574	48,200	578,000

[1] Preliminary. [2] Estimate. [3] Formerly part of the U.S.S.R.; data not reported separately until 1992. *Source: U.S. Geological Survey (USGS)*

Production of Pig Iron (Excludes Ferro-Alloys) in the United States In Thousands of Short Tons

Year	Jan.	Feb.	Mar.	Apr.	May	June	July	Aug.	Sept.	Oct.	Nov.	Dec.	Total
1990	4,638	4,221	4,681	4,549	4,746	4,530	4,656	4,788	4,629	4,673	4,523	4,264	54,925
1991	4,077	3,470	4,047	3,830	3,885	3,830	4,179	4,121	4,175	4,251	4,300	4,338	48,503
1992	4,390	4,175	4,524	4,400	4,444	4,232	4,347	4,299	4,065	5,329	4,268	4,306	52,224
1993	4,503	4,503	4,454	4,328	4,555	4,351	4,522	4,504	4,367	4,652	4,218	4,514	53,103
1994	3,970	3,858	3,957	4,099	4,394	4,519	4,518	4,446	4,320	4,564	4,619	4,928	54,426
1995	4,820	4,453	4,916	4,568	4,674	4,499	4,576	4,688	4,727	4,687	4,738	4,762	56,115
1996	4,811	4,476	4,813	4,430	4,556	4,578	4,524	4,498	4,404	4,443	4,307	4,523	54,485
1997	4,489	4,243	4,713	4,440	4,690	4,452	4,420	4,443	4,605	4,662	4,717	4,861	54,680
1998	4,955	4,433	4,881	4,600	4,731	4,299	4,418	4,502	4,170	4,212	3,837	4,119	53,174
1999[1]	4,140	3,802	4,257	4,157	4,352	4,045	4,204	4,280	4,167	4,572	4,447	4,722	51,145

[1] Preliminary. *Source: American Iron and Steel Institute*

Salient Statistics of Ferrous Scrap and Pig Iron in the United States In Thousands of Metric Tons

	Consumption: Ferrous Scrap & Pig Iron Charged To												Stocks -- Dec. 31		
	Mfg. of Pig Iron & Steel Ingots & Castings			Iron Foundries & Misc. Users			Mfg. of Steel Castings	All Uses			Imports	Exports	Ferrous Scrap & Pig Iron at Consumers		
Year	Scrap	Pig Iron	Total	Scrap	Pig Iron	Total	(Scrap)	Ferrous Scrap	Pig Iron	Grand Total	of Scrap[2]	of Scrap[3]	Scrap	Pig Iron	Total Stocks
1989	52,733	50,210	102,943	13,270	892	14,162	1,894	67,897	51,122	119,019	1,016	11,149	4,293	246	4,539
1990	54,361	49,337	103,698	13,085	835	13,920	1,850	69,296	50,193	119,489	1,324	11,580	4,292	147	4,439
1991	48,778	44,095	92,873	11,126	656	11,782	1,609	61,513	44,765	106,278	1,073	9,502	4,072	190	4,262
1992	50,144	47,263	97,407	11,444	619	12,063	1,640	63,228	47,894	111,122	1,316	9,262	3,752	181	3,933
1993	53,084	48,092	101,176	12,658	676	13,334	1,900	68,000	48,777	116,777	1,390	9,805	3,725	220	3,945
1994	53,801	50,257	104,057	14,000	1,000	15,000	2,000	70,000	51,000	121,000	1,740	8,813	4,100	400	4,500
1995	56,000	51,000	107,000	13,000	1,100	14,100	2,000	72,000	52,000	124,000	2,090	10,400	4,200	620	4,820
1996	56,000	50,000	106,000	13,000	1,100	14,100	2,700	72,000	52,000	124,000	2,600	8,440	5,200	600	5,800
1997	58,000	51,000	109,000	13,000	1,200	14,200	1,800	73,000	52,000	125,000	2,870	8,930	5,500	510	6,010
1998[1]	58,000	49,000	107,000	13,000	1,200	14,200	2,000	73,000	50,000	123,000	3,060	5,570	5,200	560	5,760

[1] Preliminary. [2] Includes tinplate and terneplate. [3] Excludes used rails for rerolling and other uses and ships, boats, and other vessels for scrapping.
Source: U.S. Geological Survey (USGS)

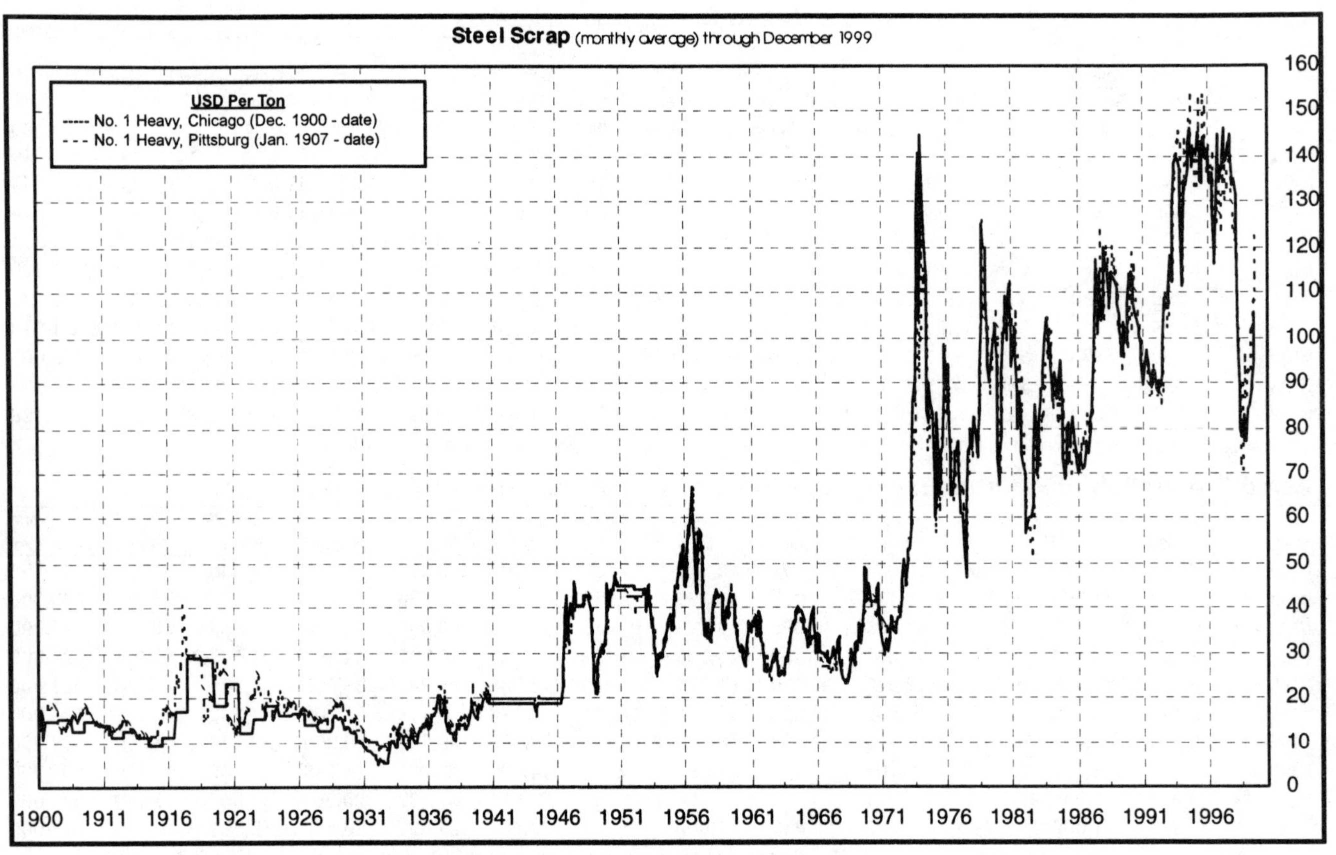

Consumption of Pig Iron in the U.S., by Type of Furnace or Equipment In Thousands of Metric Tons

Year	Open Hearth	Electric	Cupola	Basic Oxygen Process	Air & Other Furnace	Direct Casting	Total
1989	1,582	1,051	389	49,380	30	536	52,968
1990	2,072	982	332	47,307	19	387	51,099
1991	997	574	265	42,955	13	106	44,910
1992	-----	429	215	47,194	7	49	47,894
1993	-----	519	292	47,848	34	84	48,777
1994	-----	1,700	520	49,138	4	39	51,401
1995	-----	1,700	500	50,000	W	72	52,272
1996	-----	2,900	-----	45,000	-----	W	47,900
1997	-----	2,400	400	50,000	W	W	52,800
1998[1]	-----	2,900	W	42,000	W	W	44,900

[1] Preliminary. [2] Estimate. W = Withheld. *Source: U.S. Geological Survey (USGS)*

Wholesale Price of No. 1 Heavy Melting Steel Scrap in Chicago In Dollars Per Gross Ton

Year	Jan.	Feb.	Mar.	Apr.	May	June	July	Aug.	Sept.	Oct.	Nov.	Dec.	Average
1990	104.00	102.29	98.00	109.43	114.55	111.67	108.50	116.00	113.76	112.50	107.73	105.00	108.62
1991	104.76	100.74	98.00	97.80	93.18	87.50	87.74	94.14	98.50	97.50	91.97	90.50	95.19
1992	90.50	90.50	90.50	90.50	89.70	87.68	87.50	87.55	88.50	85.50	85.50	88.36	88.52
1993	98.34	109.50	109.50	106.50	106.50	111.27	118.50	114.18	113.50	125.88	131.50	138.00	115.26
1994	138.00	138.00	138.00	138.00	123.64	110.50	117.20	133.63	134.50	132.50	137.50	141.50	131.91
1995	152.05	147.50	140.20	141.50	144.50	141.64	141.50	149.76	144.90	141.50	136.50	136.50	143.17
1996	143.41	144.50	139.50	139.50	142.50	139.50	134.50	136.95	140.35	130.89	120.76	120.50	136.07
1997	131.14	143.50	139.70	132.59	136.50	136.50	143.50	146.50	139.60	139.63	142.50	142.50	139.51
1998	144.29	140.39	135.50	133.50	135.30	135.50	131.50	120.88	107.79	85.64	78.71	76.68	118.81
1999	89.66	101.50	90.89	90.50	100.00	104.32	100.98	105.95	106.50	106.50	113.40	120.17	102.53

Source: American Metal Market (AMM)

World Production of Iron Ore[3] In Thousands of Metric Tons (Gross Weight)

Year	Australia	Brazil	Canada	China	India	Maur-itania	Russia[4]	South Africa	Sweden	Ukraine[4]	United States	Vene-zuela	World Total
1989	105,810	157,900	40,509	171,850	53,418	12,110	241,348	29,958	21,763	-----	59,032	18,053	1,013,383
1990	110,508	152,300	34,855	168,300	53,700	11,590	236,000	30,291	19,877	-----	56,408	20,119	983,000
1991	117,134	151,500	39,307	176,070	56,880	10,246	199,000	29,075	19,328	-----	56,761	21,296	955,618
1992	112,101	146,447	33,167	197,600	54,870	8,202	82,100	28,226	19,277	75,700	55,593	18,070	924,993
1993	120,534	150,000	31,830	234,660	57,375	9,360	76,100	29,385	18,728	65,500	55,676	16,871	953,316
1994	128,493	177,331	37,703	240,200	60,473	11,440	73,300	30,489	19,663	51,300	58,454	18,318	991,858
1995	142,936	183,839	36,628	249,350	65,173	11,330	75,900	31,946	19,058	50,400	62,501	18,954	1,030,993
1996	147,100	174,157	36,030	249,550	66,657	11,400	69,600	30,830	20,273	47,600	62,083	18,412	1,017,824
1997[1]	157,766	185,128	37,277	268,000	69,400	11,700	70,800	33,225	21,893	53,000	62,971	18,359	1,072,254
1998[2]	153,456	195,310	38,875	210,000	75,000	11,400	72,343	32,948	20,930	50,659	62,931	19,932	1,020,935

[1] Preliminary. [2] Estimate. [3] Iron ore, iron ore concentrates and iron ore agglomerates. [4] Formerly part of the U.S.S.R.; data not reported separately until 1992. *Source: U.S. Geological Survey (USGS)*

Salient Statistics of Iron Ore[3] in the United States In Thousands of Metric Tons

Year	Net Import Reliance as a % of Apparent Con-sumption	Production: Total	Production: Lake Superior	Production: Other Regions	Ship-ments	Value Million $ (at Mine)	Average Value $ at Mine Per Ton	Stocks -- Dec. 31: Mines	Stocks -- Dec. 31: Con suming Plants	Stocks -- Dec. 31: Lake Erie Docks	Imports	Exports	Con-sumption	Value Million $ Imports
1989	22	59,032	56,981	2,052	58,299	1,939.9	33.27	4,575	15,730	2,171	19,596	5,365	80,447	522.3
1990	21	56,408	54,628	1,780	57,010	1,570.0	27.52	4,795	15,911	2,273	18,054	3,199	76,855	559.5
1991	11	56,761	55,636	1,124	56,775	1,900.0	33.40	4,850	17,612	2,981	13,335	4,045	66,366	436.8
1992	12	55,593	55,018	575	55,600	1,550.0	27.90	3,780	16,100	2,980	12,500	5,060	75,100	396.0
1993	14	55,661	54,814	848	56,300	1,380.0	24.50	2,500	16,500	2,290	14,100	5,060	76,800	419.0
1994	18	58,454	57,848	367	57,600	1,410.0	24.49	2,790	16,300	2,230	17,500	4,980	80,200	499.0
1995	14	62,501	62,026	427	61,100	1,730.0	28.32	4,240	17,100	2,140	17,600	5,270	83,100	491.0
1996	14	62,083	61,748	383	62,200	1,770.0	28.48	4,650	18,800	2,260	18,400	6,260	79,600	556.0
1997[1]	14	62,971	62,480	W	62,800	1,890.0	30.06	4,860	20,200	2,890	18,600	6,340	79,500	551.0
1998[2]	17	62,931			63,200	1,970.0	31.14	6,020	20,500	4,080	17,000	6,000	78,200	521.0

[1] Preliminary. [2] Estimate. [3] Usable iron ore exclusive of ore containing 5% or more manganese and includes byproduct ore. *Source: U.S. Geological Survey (USGS)*

U.S. Imports (for Consumption) of Iron Ore[2] In Thousands of Metric Tons

Year	Australia	Brazil	Canada	Chile	Maur-itania	Peru	Sweden	Vene-zuela	Total
1990	14	4,276	9,344	138	666	59	54	3,503	18,054
1991	-----	2,481	7,299	103	459	157	51	2,763	13,335
1992	163	2,442	6,834	107	280	70	64	2,540	12,504
1993	254	2,872	7,442	68	206	1	60	3,170	14,097
1994	675	3,610	10,073	134	124	2	45	2,778	17,466
1995	570	4,810	9,050	57	317	54	47	2,500	17,600
1996	511	5,170	9,800	164	275	43	48	2,140	18,400
1997	742	4,970	10,000	228	-----	252	149	2,090	18,600
1998	807	5,980	8,520	48	-----	126	276	1,000	17,000
1999[1]	525	3,686	4,183	-----	-----	40	254	262	9,257

[1] Preliminary. [2] Including agglomerates. *Source: U.S. Geological Survey (USGS)*

Total[1] Iron Ore Stocks in the United States, at End of Month In Thousands of Metric Tons

Year	Jan.	Feb.	Mar.	Apr.	May	June	July	Aug.	Sept.	Oct.	Nov.	Dec.
1990	22,088	21,986	20,958	20,609	20,501	21,019	21,863	22,110	22,268	22,027	22,042	22,978
1991	22,572	22,218	21,316	20,757	21,756	23,174	23,319	24,329	25,148	25,117	25,358	25,445
1992	24,527	23,162	20,922	20,550	21,501	22,492	23,046	21,721	22,735	23,190	23,433	22,856
1993	21,296	20,806	19,235	18,996	19,180	22,036	22,905	21,575	22,629	21,355	21,615	21,341
1994	19,013	17,816	15,950	14,880	15,251	16,592	17,864	18,931	20,554	20,760	21,552	21,339
1995	20,316	19,361	18,193	18,293	19,371	20,905	22,336	23,632	23,414	24,389	24,123	23,576
1996	22,277	20,744	19,779	20,104	23,426	21,822	22,445	23,663	24,116	24,866	25,465	25,701
1997	25,913	25,262	24,745	24,812	25,001	25,620	26,076	26,971	27,562	28,029	28,053	27,912
1998	27,977	26,317	24,039	25,251	25,576	26,197	27,605	29,037	30,301	30,095	30,199	30,725
1999[2]	29,631	28,463	28,614	28,292	29,151	29,021	28,857	27,840	26,506			

[1] All stocks at mines, furnace yards and at U.S. docks. [2] Preliminary. *Source: U.S. Geological Survey (USGS)*

Lard

Lard production is directly related to commercial hog production. As such, the largest producers of lard are also the largest producers of hogs. China is the world's largest producer with 40 percent of the market. The U.S. share is 7 percent. Other large producers of lard include Germany, Russia, Poland, Brazil and Spain.

The U.S.D.A. reported that U.S. beginning stocks of lard for the 1999/2000 (October-September) marketing year were 30 million pounds. Beginning stocks were some 26 percent less than a year earlier. At the start of the 1998/99 season, U.S. lard stocks were 40.4 million pounds.

U.S. production of lard in the 1999/00 season was forecast at 1.1 billion pounds, virtually the same as in 1998/99. Small amounts of lard are imported. In the 1999/00 season, U.S. lard imports are projected to be 2 million pounds, the same as in 1998/99. Total supply in 1999/00 was projected to be 1.13 billion pounds, down 1 percent from 1998/99.

In terms of usage, domestic use of lard was projected to be 980 million pounds, down 1 percent from the previous year. Exports of lard in the 1999/00 season were forecast at 122 million pounds, down 6 percent from the previous year. Total use of lard was projected to be 1.1 billion pounds, down 1 percent from 1998/99. Use of lard has been trending higher. Lard finds use in baking and frying fats as well as margarine. The emphasis on healthier diets which are much lower in fats could limit the use of lard in certain foods. Projected ending stocks of lard in the 1999/00 season were 30 million pounds, unchanged from stocks at the end of the 1998/99 season. Over the last five seasons, U.S. stocks of lard have averaged 29 million pounds.

World Production of Lard In Thousands of Metric Tons

Year	Brazil	Canada	China	France	Germany	Italy	Japan	Poland	Romania	Spain	United States	Former USSR	World Total
1990-1	158.6	75.6	1,605.6	137.3	476.3	187.6	87.0	288.3	129.0	169.7	415.0	762.8	5,586.2
1991-2	165.7	76.9	1,698.4	135.5	411.3	188.0	85.0	303.3	126.8	170.6	447.7	653.6	5,505.3
1992-3	175.5	77.0	1,767.6	142.9	418.2	192.1	85.8	283.6	119.6	185.8	445.0	534.1	5,487.7
1993-4	165.8	83.2	1,707.0	151.3	409.5	189.5	82.4	239.1	115.7	192.8	451.0	465.0	5,390.1
1994-5	181.6	86.3	1,931.8	153.2	404.8	191.3	83.8	267.9	106.9	196.7	471.2	414.1	5,640.7
1995-6	194.3	83.0	2,136.6	154.6	405.6	198.5	76.3	284.9	105.1	206.5	449.3	371.6	5,847.0
1996-7[1]	199.4	83.1	2,333.2	157.3	396.5	197.6	74.1	259.4	96.3	211.8	437.0	344.7	5,967.1
1997-8[2]	213.8	90.0	2,467.1	162.0	413.4	194.0	67.9	270.8	87.4	229.9	478.9	329.1	6,203.3
1998-9[3]	224.4	97.0	2,529.5	162.9	429.8	193.5	67.5	279.8	80.8	256.6	501.0	329.7	6,375.0

[1] Preliminary. [2] Estimate. [3] Forecast. *Source: The Oil World*

Supply and Distribution of Lard in the United States In Millions of Pounds

	Supply			Disappearance						
Year	Production	Stocks Oct. 1	Total Supply	Domestic	Baking & Frying Fats	Margarine[2]	Exports	Total Disappearance	Direct Use	Per Capita (Lbs.)
1991-2	1,016.3	24.1	1,042.9	884.8	299.0	39.0	131.0	1,015.7	423.7	3.3
1992-3	1,011.2	27.2	1,041.5	886.1	274.0	30.0	129.2	1,015.3	438.6	3.5
1993-4	1,014.7	26.2	1,043.6	890.4	251.0	39.0	118.8	1,009.2	573.0	3.4
1994-5	1,052.4	34.4	1,089.0	924.4	332.2	43.0	140.4	1,064.7	561.9	3.4
1995-6	1,012.6	24.3	1,038.8	921.8	295.9	33.0	94.3	1,016.1	593.0	3.5
1996-7	979.0	22.7	1,002.9	879.6	262.0	15.0	103.3	982.9	602.4	3.5
1997-8	1,064.7	19.9	1,086.7	924.6	285.0	17.0	121.8	1,046.4	623.3	3.4
1998-9[1]	1,106.0	40.4	1,148.4	992.6	254.7	15.0	135.0	1,127.6	NA	3.6
1999-00[2]	1,075.0	20.8	1,097.8	945.8	NA	NA	122.0	1,067.8	NA	NA

[1] Preliminary. [2] Forecast. [3] Includes edible tallow. NA = not avaliable. *Source: Economic Research Service, U.S. Department of Agriculture (ERS-USDA)*

Consumption of Lard (Edible and Inedible) in the United States In Millions of Pounds

Year	Jan.	Feb.	Mar.	Apr.	May	June	July	Aug.	Sept.	Oct.	Nov.	Dec.	Total
1991	-----	97.3	-----	-----	94.7	-----	-----	95.2	-----	-----	105.9	-----	393.1
1992	33.9	31.6	39.9	40.0	38.7	39.6	42.9	41.1	47.6	46.4	41.0	37.2	479.9
1993	40.1	34.4	45.9	36.8	38.2	38.8	32.6	38.4	41.8	44.0	43.0	40.3	474.3
1994	33.5	33.9	36.2	34.6	35.9	34.4	32.4	37.5	43.4	43.8	44.7	41.7	452.0
1995	37.5	34.7	41.2	36.2	42.2	44.4	34.9	35.9	35.9	40.1	38.9	36.8	458.7
1996	30.5	35.4	36.7	46.9	36.8	31.4	32.6	33.9	30.9	34.5	34.7	33.6	417.9
1997	26.5	30.5	31.0	36.5	39.9	36.2	36.1	35.0	37.4	39.0	41.5	40.4	429.8
1998	34.1	29.9	31.1	29.6	28.5	35.9	33.0	33.0	37.1	37.7	38.9	33.9	402.7
1999[1]	34.6	30.2	28.8	31.1	30.5	32.9	28.9	33.0	29.2	31.2	31.3	31.6	373.3

[1] Preliminary. *Source: Bureau of the Census, U.S. Department of Commerce*

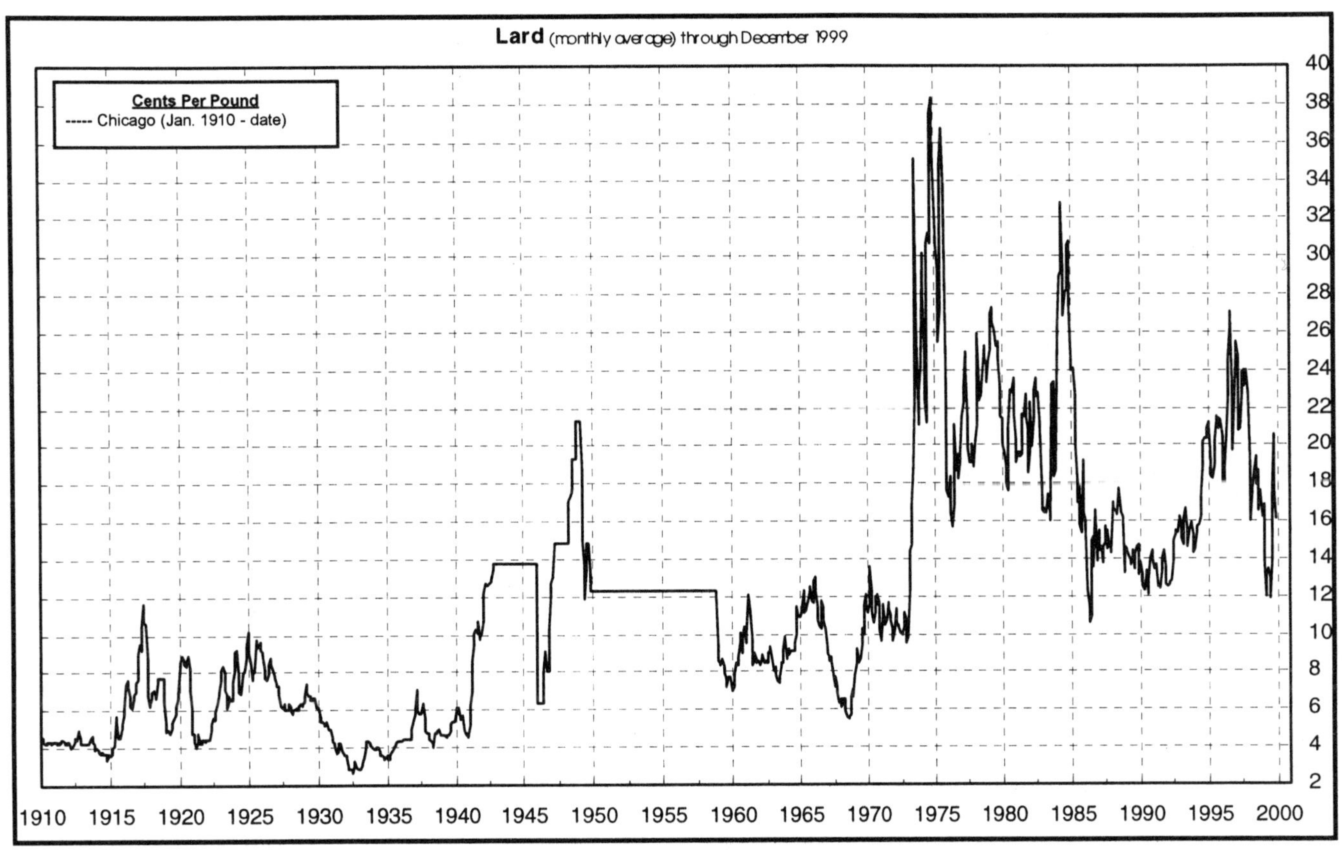

Average Wholesale Price of Lard, Loose, Tank Cars, in Chicago In Cents Per Pound

Year	Jan.	Feb.	Mar.	Apr.	May	June	July	Aug.	Sept.	Oct.	Nov.	Dec.	Average
1990	13.50	13.79	13.17	12.50	12.25	13.17	13.38	12.10	12.74	13.98	14.45	14.03	13.26
1991	13.50	13.50	13.54	13.63	12.50	12.49	12.44	13.41	13.96	14.42	13.60	12.64	13.30
1992	12.50	12.50	12.57	12.75	12.78	13.93	14.95	15.29	15.49	15.40	16.11	16.25	14.21
1993	15.83	15.03	14.70	16.15	16.67	15.50	14.64	15.42	15.50	15.93	15.26	14.31	15.41
1994	14.50	14.62	15.35	15.74	15.75	16.25	17.24	18.91	20.14	20.39	20.35	20.91	17.51
1995	21.21	21.13	19.25	18.34	18.25	19.02	20.25	21.30	21.48	20.90	21.38	21.35	20.32
1996	20.52	18.17	18.01	18.67	20.47	22.61	24.55	26.30	27.09	23.11	19.70	22.17	21.78
1997	24.93	25.47	24.69	20.82	20.94	22.68	23.83	23.95	23.14	23.41	23.97	22.85	23.39
1998	19.09	16.03	17.36	17.64	18.66	19.38	17.93	18.65	16.58	17.39	17.60	16.27	17.72
1999	16.89	13.91	11.98	13.12	13.43	12.98	11.87	13.89	17.44	20.55	17.74	16.12	14.99

Source: The Wall Street Journal

United States Cold Storage Holdings of all Lard[1], on First of Month In Millions of Pounds

Year	Jan.	Feb.	Mar.	Apr.	May	June	July	Aug.	Sept.	Oct.	Nov.	Dec.
1990	32.0	33.7	37.6	28.5	31.6	27.4	25.2	25.9	22.8	22.9	22.2	30.3
1991	-----	24.4	-----	-----	28.3	-----	-----	24.0	-----	-----	24.1	-----
1992	37.4	27.2	28.9	28.3	26.7	23.2	24.8	29.2	26.9	27.2	22.2	24.8
1993	22.7	25.9	27.2	24.0	22.8	25.8	31.1	27.4	23.6	26.2	24.6	30.1
1994	37.7	38.0	31.8	28.8	25.1	27.4	27.0	25.5	29.7	34.4	34.0	35.8
1995	40.6	50.3	46.4	43.0	36.8	27.1	25.8	22.1	30.2	24.3	19.9	21.6
1996	38.4	38.6	25.8	28.8	21.5	23.2	23.7	30.5	20.7	22.7	20.1	18.8
1997	18.9	16.3	18.5	19.2	18.9	18.7	23.0	23.2	21.5	19.9	21.3	19.7
1998	22.2	30.1	38.3	42.5	41.6	47.6	43.7	44.8	38.8	40.4	34.8	26.3
1999[2]	28.4	30.4	30.6	34.0	27.1	39.9	30.7	25.5	29.4	20.8	19.1	22.8

[1] Stocks in factories and warehouses (except that in hands of retailers). [2] Preliminary. *Source: Bureau of the Census, U.S. Department of Commerce*

Lead

Lead is used in the production of batteries, fuel tanks, ammunition, electrical equipment, cans and containers, and as solder for pipes and plumbing. Lead finds use as a covering for power and communication cables, but by far the largest use of lead is in lead-acid batteries. In the U.S., lead-acid batteries used about 88 percent of the lead that was consumed. Lead and compounds that contain lead are very toxic and there has been an effort to reduce the use of lead. For many products there are substitutes for lead including iron, tin, plastic and bismuth.

World mine production of lead in 1998 was estimated at 3.1 million tonnes, down 1 percent from 1997. The largest producer of lead in 1998 was Australia with 618,000 tonnes, an increase of 16 percent from the previous year. U.S. production of lead from mines in 1998 was estimated at 493,000 tonnes, up 7 percent from the previous year. Other large producers of lead include Peru, Canada, Mexico and Sweden. World refinery production of lead in 1998 was 5.88 million tonnes, up 1 percent from 1997.

U.S. mine production of lead in 1998 was estimated at 481,000 tonnes of recoverable lead. That represented an increase of 7 percent from 1997. In terms of refined primary lead production, U.S. production in 1998 was estimated at 338,000 tonnes, down 2 percent from 1997. Secondary lead production (lead content) in 1998 was 1.12 million tonnes, up almost 2 percent from 1997.

U.S. mine production of lead in June 1999 was 42,600 tonnes. In the January-June 1999 period, mine production was 258,000 tonnes, up 2 percent from the same period in 1998. U.S. reported production of secondary lead by smelters and refineries in July 1999 was 78,800 tonnes, down 11 percent from June. In the January-June 1999 period, production was 599,000 tonnes, down 4 percent from a year ago. For all of 1998, secondary refinery production was 1.08 million tonnes. Lead recovered from copper-base scrap in July 1999 was 1,250 tonnes, the same as in June. In the fist seven months of 1999, lead recovered was 8,750 tonnes, the same as a year ago. For all of 1998, the total was 15,000 tonnes. Total secondary lead production in July 1999 was 81,300 tonnes, down 11 percent from June. In the first seven months of 1999, production from secondary sources was 618,000 tonnes, down 4 percent from a year ago.

U.S. imports for consumption of ore and concentrates in January-June 1999 were 2,490 tonnes. Imports in June 1999 were 544 tonnes. Imports of refined lead metal in the January-June 1999 period were 132,000 tonnes while in June they were 26,200 tonnes. For all of 1998 refined lead metal imports were 267,000 tonnes.

U.S. reported consumption of lead in July 1999 was 123,000 tonnes, down 2 percent from the previous month. For the January-July 1999 period reported consumption was 871,000 tonnes and for all of 1998 it was 1.5 million tonnes. For the first half of 1999, U.S. exports of lead ore and concentrates were 10,300 tonnes, bullion exports were 31,200 tonnes, materials containing lead were 16,100 tonnes and lead scrap exports were 52,500 tonnes. Lead stocks held by consumers and secondary smelters in July 1999 were 63,700 tonnes.

World Smelter (Primary and Secondary) Production of Lead   In Thousands of Metric Tons

Year	Australia[3]	Belgium[4]	Canada[3]	China[2]	France	Germany	Italy	Japan	Mexico[3]	Spain	United Kingdom[3]	United States	World Total
1991	239.4	110.7	212.4	330.0	438.0	362.5	208.2	332.4	161.8	169.0	311.0	1,230	5,770
1992	232.0	116.3	252.9	365.0	284.1	354.3	186.3	330.2	177.0	120.0	346.8	1,220	5,230
1993	243.0	131.1	217.0	412.0	258.7	334.2	182.8	309.5	188.0	123.0	363.8	1,230	5,420
1994	237.0	123.5	251.6	467.9	260.5	331.7	205.9	292.2	171.0	140.0	352.5	1,280	5,360
1995	241.0	122.0	281.4	608.0	296.7	311.2	180.4	287.6	176.0	80.0	320.7	1,390	5,580
1996	228.0	125.0	309.4	706.0	302.8	238.1	209.8	287.4	160.0	86.0	345.6	1,400	5,590
1997[1]	238.0	110.8	271.4	707.0	302.3	329.2	211.6	296.8	178.0	74.9	391.0	1,450	5,820
1998[2]	205.0	120.0	265.0	733.0	306.0	335.0	248.0	302.0	170.0	87.0	350.0	1,450	5,880

[1] Preliminary. [2] Estimate. [3] Refinded & bullion. [4] Includes scrap. *Source: U.S. Geological Survey (USGS)*

Consumption of Lead in the United States, by Products   In Metric Tons

Year	Ammunition	Bearing Metals	Pipes, Traps & Bends[2]	Cable Covering	Calking Lead	Casting Metals	Other Metal Products[3]	Total Other Oxides[4]	Sheet Lead	Solder	Storage Battery: Grids, Post, etc.	Storage Battery: Oxides	Brass and Bronze	Total Consumption
1991	58,458	3,669	8,975	17,472	1,074	14,141	3,254	59,617	22,334	14,750	591,884	415,233	8,997	1,246,337
1992	64,845	4,785	11,652	15,992	1,045	17,111	3,024	63,225	21,006	13,518	629,147	373,185	9,175	1,236,571
1993	65,100	4,830	5,740	17,165	961	18,500	5,360	63,600	21,200	14,400	677,000	374,000	5,750	1,290,000
1994	62,400	5,560	3,370	16,000	764	18,900	5,330	62,700	21,500	12,200	797,000	425,000	6,320	1,450,000
1995	70,900	6,490	2,210	5,640	935	18,100	5,220	61,700	27,900	16,200	711,000	618,000	5,260	1,560,000
1996	52,100	4,350	1,810	W	767	18,900	5,220	62,100	19,400	9,020	635,000	706,000	5,460	1,540,000
1997	52,400	2,490	1,860	4,930	1,390	34,000	7,570	67,000	19,100	9,580	634,000	761,000	4,410	1,620,000
1998[1]	52,800	2,210	3,130	4,630	1,350	32,600	8,150	53,400	15,500	10,900	685,000	744,000	3,460	1,630,000

[1] Preliminary. [2] Including building. [3] Including terne metal, type metal, and lead consumerd in foil, collapsible tubes, annealing, plating, galvanizing and fishing weights. [4] Includes paints, glass and ceramic products, and other pigments and chemicals. W = Withheld proprietary data. *Source: U.S. Geological Survey (USGS)*

Salient Statistics of Lead in the United States   In Thousands of Metric Tons

Year	Net Import Reliance as a % of Apparent Consumption	Production of Refined Lead From: Domestic Ores[3]	Foreign Ores[3]	Total Primary	Total Value of Refined Million $	Secondary Lead Recovered: As Soft Lead	In Antimonial Lead	In Other Alloys	Total	Total Value of Secondary Million $	Stocks, Dec. 31: Primary	Consumer[4]	Average Price - Cents Per Pound: New York	London[5]
1989	8	379.0	17.4	396.5	343.9	438.0	418.6	34.7	891.3	773.3	15.6	82.4	39.35	30.63
1990	3	385.6	18.0	403.7	409.5	461.4	425.4	35.6	922.2	935.6	25.5	86.3	46.02	37.05
1991	6	323.9	21.9	345.7	255.2	421.9	426.9	35.8	884.6	652.9	9.1	71.7	33.48	25.30
1992	10	284.0	20.8	304.8	235.9	452.9	424.5	23.1	916.3	709.1	20.5	82.3	35.10	24.50
1993	15	310.7	24.9	335.6	234.4	444.0	417.0	17.0	893.0	625.0	14.3	80.5	31.74	18.42
1994	19	328.0	23.4	351.4	288.0	527.0	371.0	16.1	931.0	763.0	9.3	68.8	37.17	24.83
1995	17	374.0	W	374.0	348.0	584.0	400.0	19.2	1,020.0	951.0	14.2	79.4	42.28	28.08
1996	17	326.0	W	326.0	351.0	625.0	420.0	9.2	1,070.0	1,150.0	8.1	72.1	48.83	31.22
1997[1]	14	343.0	W	343.0	352.0	663.0	411.0	14.2	1,110.0	1,130.0	11.9	89.1	46.54	28.29
1998[2]	21	337.0	W	337.0	336.0	667.0	417.0	16.1	1,120.0	1,110.0	10.9	77.3	45.27	23.96

[1] Preliminary. [2] Estimate. [3] And base bullion. [4] Also at secondary smelters. [5] LME data in dollars per metric ton beginning July 1993.
W = Withheld Proprietary data. E = Net exporter. *Source: U.S. Geological Survey (USGS)*

United States Foreign Trade of Lead   In Thousands of Metric Tons

Year	Exports: Ore Concentrate	Unwrought Lead[3]	Wrought Lead[4]	Scrap	Ash & Residues	Imports for Consumption: Ores, Flue Dust or Fume & Mattes	Base Bullion	Pigs & Bars	Reclaimed Scrap, etc.	Value Million $	General Imports From: Ore, Flue Dust & Matte: Australia	Canada	Peru	Pigs & Bars: Canada	Mexico	Peru
1989	57.0	28.5	5.4	59.9	10.0	5.1	5.8	115.7	0.7	95.7	1.9	189.9	12.9	90.5	19.2	2.3
1990	56.6	57.2	6.8	75.0	13.0	10.7	2.7	90.6	0.3	91.2	1.2	124.3	7.1	70.7	25.0	1.0
1991	88.0	94.4	7.6	72.0	11.0	12.4	0.4	116.5	0.1	82.6	1.0	226.7	3.9	83.6	11.9	0.5
1992	72.3	64.3	5.3	63.2	2.1	5.3	0.2	190.7	0.2	120.6	-----	239.9	21.2	124.7	56.1	9.8
1993	41.8	51.4	7.1	54.1	1.7	0.5	-----	195.6	0.1	99.4	-----	55.7	13.6	130.8	40.3	18.3
1994	38.7	48.2	5.3	88.1	20.6	0.5	0.6	230.8	0.1	146.6	0.5	0.2	-----	159.0	31.9	25.6
1995	65.5	48.2	9.0	105.0	8.0	2.6	0.0	264.0	0.1	191.7	1.5	-----	0.1	182.0	54.3	22.1
1996	59.7	44.0	16.7	85.3	19.4	6.6	0.0	268.0	0.2	217.0	-----	4.4	-----	192.0	56.9	17.1
1997[1]	42.2	37.4	15.9	88.4	16.8	17.8	0.0	265.0	0.1	200.3	-----	0.8	3.4	186.0	70.4	6.4
1998[2]	72.4	24.1	15.4	99.2	9.0	32.7	0.5	267.0	[6]	191.9	2.4	6.5	18.5	181.0	63.6	11.4

[1] Preliminary. [2] Estimate. [3] And lead alloys. [4] Blocks, pigs, etc. [5] Formerly drosses & flue dust. [6] Less than 1/2 unit. NA = Not avaliable.
Source: U.S. Geological Survey (USGS)

Annual Mine Production of Recoverable Lead in the United States   In Metric Tons

Year	Total	Idaho	Missouri	Montana	Other States	Missouri's % of Total
1989	410,915	W	366,931	W	43,984	89%
1990	483,704	W	380,781	W	102,923	79%
1991	465,931	W	351,995	W	113,936	76%
1992	397,923	W	300,589	W	97,334	76%
1993	353,607	W	276,569	W	77,800	78%
1994	363,443	W	290,738	9,940	63,100	80%
1995	386,000	W	359,000	8,350	18,200	93%
1996	426,000	W	397,000	7,970	21,200	93%
1997[1]	448,000	W	412,000	9,230	26,600	92%
1998[2]	481,000	W	439,000	7,310	35,100	91%

[1] Preliminary. [2] Estimate. W = Withheld, included in Other States. NA = Not Avaliable. *Source: U.S. Geological Survey (USGS)*

Mine Production of Recoverable Lead in the United States   In Thousands of Metric Tons

Year	Jan.	Feb.	Mar.	Apr.	May	June	July	Aug.	Sept.	Oct.	Nov.	Dec.	Total
1990	42.4	39.0	39.9	37.4	40.8	38.8	42.3	47.2	37.9	43.0	38.5	36.6	483.7
1991	41.5	41.1	41.6	37.8	43.5	36.4	47.5	41.1	36.1	38.9	28.0	26.1	465.9
1992	36.0	34.0	34.0	31.2	31.5	32.4	33.8	32.5	32.5	33.3	30.8	31.7	392.7
1993	33.3	30.5	34.2	30.6	28.5	29.5	25.8	27.5	28.4	27.3	29.5	28.5	355.2
1994	27.6	28.8	33.0	31.3	32.4	29.1	29.4	30.4	31.2	28.0	31.7	29.9	363.4
1995	29.6	30.3	35.2	28.9	32.7	34.8	32.5	33.5	29.9	34.1	31.6	32.1	385.0
1996	36.9	36.4	35.6	35.9	37.5	33.8	35.6	34.1	26.9	35.2	33.6	35.7	426.0
1997	36.7	36.7	37.2	38.6	38.6	35.1	33.4	33.7	34.4	35.4	31.7	32.8	448.0
1998	37.4	35.4	37.8	37.3	35.7	34.7	34.3	35.6	36.1	40.3	37.8	39.2	449.0
1999[1]	40.1	42.1	44.4	43.1	41.7	42.6	47.2	43.6	41.5				515.1

[1] Preliminary. *Source: U.S. Geological Survey (USGS)*

LEAD

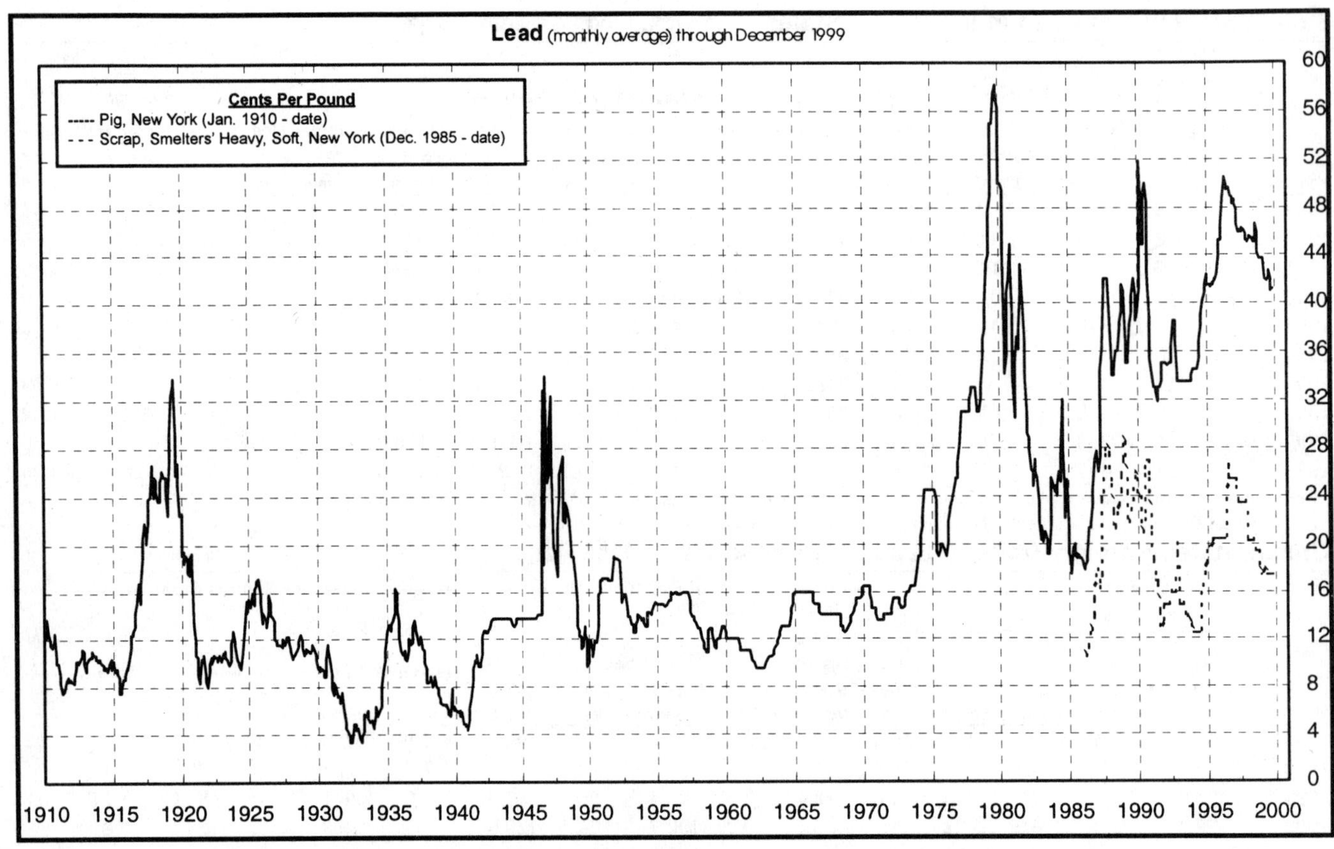

Average Price of Pig Lead, U.S. Primary Producers (Common Corroding)[1] In Cents Per Pound

Year	Jan.	Feb.	Mar.	Apr.	May	June	July	Aug.	Sept.	Oct.	Nov.	Dec.	Average
1990	39.73	41.74	54.45	48.10	45.00	45.14	50.62	51.00	49.08	44.52	41.33	37.03	45.65
1991	34.18	33.00	33.00	33.00	32.00	31.80	33.00	33.00	33.70	35.00	35.00	35.00	33.47
1992	35.00	35.00	35.00	35.00	35.00	35.00	36.91	40.00	40.00	36.64	32.63	32.00	35.68
1993	32.00	32.00	32.00	32.00	32.00	32.00	32.00	32.00	32.00	32.00	32.00	33.00	32.08
1994	34.00	34.00	34.00	34.00	34.00	35.73	37.70	38.00	40.00	42.00	43.70	44.00	37.59
1995	44.00	44.00	42.00	42.00	42.00	42.00	42.00	43.65	44.00	44.00	46.10	48.00	43.65
1996	48.00	49.50	50.96	52.00	52.00	52.00	50.29	49.18	50.00	50.00	50.00	50.00	50.33
1997	50.00	50.00	48.70	48.00	48.00	48.00	48.00	48.00	48.00	48.00	48.00	48.00	48.39
1998	48.00	48.00	48.00	48.00	48.00	48.00	48.00	48.00	48.00	48.00	45.47	45.00	47.54
1999	45.00	45.00	45.00	45.00	45.00	45.00	45.00	45.00	45.00	45.00	45.00	45.00	45.00

[1] New York Delivery. Source: American Metal Market (AMM)

Refiners Production[1] of Lead in the United States In Metric Tons

Year	Jan.	Feb.	Mar.	Apr.	May	June	July	Aug.	Sept.	Oct.	Nov.	Dec.	Total
1990	34,927	34,383	33,476	35,018	33,022	30,210	30,845	34,474	33,929	38,375	33,476	31,571	403,657
1991	30,763	30,863	33,771	30,248	27,031	22,371	27,973	28,204	29,411	29,846	26,428	28,813	345,714
1992	29,121	27,691	33,366	27,456	26,742	22,441	24,993	21,587	19,365	22,945	23,674	25,414	304,791
1993	29,627	26,693	30,197	27,578	29,814	28,253	16,734	22,817	32,725	31,220	27,953	31,312	335,014
1994	29,908	30,685	31,420	29,059	31,588	31,707	30,661	27,335	31,185	32,874	29,301	30,447	366,170
1995	32,100	29,100	32,600	32,300	32,600	28,300	31,000	29,300	30,600	34,200	30,100	31,500	374,000
1996	34,700	30,400	30,900	28,600	27,500	21,700	25,500	24,700	25,400	25,300	26,100	25,500	326,000
1997	28,800	28,500	31,900	30,400	30,800	28,700	25,900	28,000	21,600	30,500	29,000	28,700	343,000
1998	29,200	25,900	30,000	29,700	29,500	20,300	28,900	NA	NA	NA	NA	NA	337,000
1999[2]	NA	NA	NA	NA	NA	NA	NA	NA	NA				

[1] Represents refined lead produced from domestic ores by primary smelters plus small amounts of secondary material passing through these smelters. Includes GSA metal purchased for remelt. [2] Preliminary. *Source: U.S. Geological Survey (USGS)*

Total Stocks of Lead[1] in the United States at Refiners, at End of Month In Metric Tons

Year	Jan.	Feb.	Mar.	Apr.	May	June	July	Aug.	Sept.	Oct.	Nov.	Dec.
1990	14,697	18,325	16,420	21,138	19,323	19,596	20,775	19,958	20,593	23,769	22,771	25,492
1991	24,177	24,333	26,990	21,261	17,474	16,195	15,362	9,072	6,608	4,091	4,491	9,089
1992	9,774	15,785	21,682	25,220	28,940	26,490	26,634	22,347	17,736	14,971	14,796	20,543
1993	28,069	33,338	34,058	34,306	35,775	32,162	22,753	14,797	15,086	14,408	13,456	14,289
1994	11,964	12,633	12,048	11,445	11,598	10,251	12,368	9,256	8,897	10,659	9,060	9,271
1995	8,200	9,750	11,500	14,500	16,700	16,200	21,300	14,000	12,800	9,820	9,830	14,200
1996	15,000	15,000	15,000	15,000	15,000	19,600	19,900	14,200	12,200	7,060	7,830	8,160
1997	8,460	11,800	21,400	19,900	15,000	10,900	6,530	7,790	5,370	7,310	8,710	11,900
1998	13,000	15,900	18,700	20,900	11,400	11,400	13,700	NA	NA	NA	NA	10,900
1999[2]	NA	NA	NA	NA	NA	NA	NA	NA	NA			

[1] Primary refineries. [2] Preliminary. *Source: U.S. Geological Survey (USGS)*

Total[1] Lead Consumption in the United States In Thousands of Metric Tons

Year	Jan.	Feb.	Mar.	Apr.	May	June	July	Aug.	Sept.	Oct.	Nov.	Dec.	Total
1990	104.1	106.7	111.9	101.1	106.2	103.2	97.7	112.4	104.6	109.0	104.3	97.3	1,275
1991	101.3	105.3	101.2	101.3	98.4	92.4	90.8	101.9	102.7	106.9	102.4	92.7	1,246
1992	102.5	99.3	108.3	98.5	96.0	103.5	94.8	104.8	106.6	105.4	98.2	92.9	1,215
1993	108.9	107.5	112.3	104.6	109.2	113.8	106.8	112.6	117.1	113.2	109.3	102.2	1,357
1994	107.0	115.2	112.8	111.6	113.5	115.2	114.3	115.5	115.9	121.2	118.7	113.0	1,384
1995	119.0	119.0	119.0	109.0	110.0	113.0	115.0	105.0	115.0	116.0	118.0	116.0	1,370
1996	107.0	100.0	106.0	111.0	113.0	106.0	104.0	146.0	140.0	147.0	163.0	143.0	1,530
1997	139.0	138.0	138.0	140.0	137.0	141.0	116.0	119.0	122.0	123.0	117.0	117.0	1,600
1998	116.0	115.0	119.0	128.0	127.0	129.0	128.0	128.0	129.0	129.0	134.0	125.0	1,550
1999[2]	128.0	129.0	130.0	127.0	128.0	130.0	137.0	136.0	141.0	136.0			1,586

[1] Represents total consumption of primary & secondary lead as metal, in chemicals, or in alloys. [2] Preliminary. *Source: U.S. Geological Survey (USGS)*

Lead Recovered from Scrap in the United States In Thousands of Metric Tons (Lead Content)

Year	Jan.	Feb.	Mar.	Apr.	May	June	July	Aug.	Sept.	Oct.	Nov.	Dec.	Total
1990	68.7	69.6	73.0	69.4	66.9	67.9	67.0	71.8	71.0	77.5	72.3	77.3	923.0
1991	79.0	74.4	71.0	72.0	72.0	70.7	69.8	70.0	72.3	74.6	70.7	75.9	883.7
1992	76.1	71.5	66.5	71.0	73.3	72.3	71.1	77.7	77.5	79.6	76.9	74.3	888.5
1993	71.1	76.8	71.7	80.2	78.9	72.5	70.3	76.6	76.3	77.0	77.9	79.3	903.6
1994	74.0	76.0	84.2	81.7	81.1	79.0	78.9	79.8	78.4	76.4	81.0	80.4	949.0
1995	82.5	80.8	84.4	72.8	73.7	72.5	79.9	71.5	82.3	80.0	82.3	82.1	945.0
1996	75.7	76.2	84.2	83.7	84.7	80.7	81.2	89.0	92.1	98.8	97.3	93.2	1,100.0
1997	88.0	89.8	91.7	86.0	88.2	85.7	86.7	94.7	97.3	96.2	95.2	91.7	1,110.0
1998	95.0	92.0	92.6	94.1	92.5	89.7	89.3	95.7	94.4	95.0	95.1	90.7	1,110.0
1999[1]	89.5	89.1	88.9	91.0	90.2	91.1	81.3	91.9	91.6				1,072.8

[1] Preliminary. *Source: U.S. Geological Survey (USGS)*

Domestic Shipments[1] of Lead in the United States, by Refiners In Thousands of Short Tons

Year	Jan.	Feb.	Mar.	Apr.	May	June	July	Aug.	Sept.	Oct.	Nov.	Dec.	Total
1988	33.5	29.5	39.2	33.0	41.4	44.7	32.0	34.7	33.7	43.0	38.5	35.5	438.7
1989	29.3	28.5	32.2	35.7	45.1	36.4	32.8	41.5	40.0	44.2	40.2	31.1	437.1
1990	39.3	33.9	39.1	33.5	38.4	32.9	32.6	38.9	36.6	38.9	37.9	31.7	433.7
1991	35.4	33.8	34.3	39.8	33.9	26.0	31.8	37.9	35.1	35.7	28.7	26.7	399.2
1992	31.3	23.9	30.4	26.3	25.6	27.2	27.3	28.7	26.3	28.5	26.3	21.7	323.5
1993	24.6	23.6	32.5	30.0	31.3	35.1	28.9	34.0	35.5	35.5	31.7	33.5	376.2
1994	35.9	32.8	35.2	32.7	34.7	36.7	31.6	33.4	34.8	34.3	34.0	33.3	409.3
1995	36.5	30.3	35.1	31.1	33.7	31.9	28.6	40.3	34.9	40.9	33.2	29.8	406.4
1996	37.2	32.4	29.5	30.2	29.4	26.7	27.7	33.5	30.1	33.5	28.1	27.6	366.0
1997[2]	31.5	27.8	24.7	35.2	39.2	36.1	33.4	29.4	26.4	31.5	30.4	28.1	377.8

[1] Includes GSA metal. [2] Preliminary. *Source: American Metal Market (AMM)*

Lumber & Plywood

The U.S. economy continued strong in 1999, though by yearend interest rates were starting to rise. It was likely that as the year 2000 progressed, the Federal Reserve would increase rates further to slow the economy and head off any increase in the rate of inflation. Eventually this will result in a slower rate of economic growth. But, as 1999 ended, the higher interest rates had done little to slow the economy.

The key sector for lumber is the housing sector and higher interest rates could be expected to slow the rate of housing construction. Housing starts in August 1999 were running at a seasonally adjusted annual rate of 1.676 million units, about unchanged from July 1999, but 4 percent more than in August 1998. Housing starts in the first eight months of 1999 were 5 percent higher than a year earlier. Building permits were also stronger. In line with the increases in housing starts has been the increase in U.S. softwood lumber production.

U.S. softwood production in July 1999 was 3.1 billion board feet, down 7 percent from June 1999 and up over 1 percent from the year before. Total shipments of softwood lumber in July 1999 were 3.1 billion board feet which was down 8 percent from the previous month and 7 percent less than a year ago. Looking at production regions, July 1999 production in the Southern Pine Region was 1.44 billion board feet with shipments of 1.46 billion board feet. Production in the West Coast Region in July 1999 was 726 million board feet with Inland Region production of 648 million board feet. The California Redwood Region saw production of 107 million board feet. Other softwood production in July 1999 was 183 million board feet.

Maple flooring production in July 1999 was 1.91 million square feet with shipments of 2.46 million square feet. Oak flooring shipments in July 1999 were 34 million board feet. Production of structural panels in July 1999 was 2.5 million square feet which was up slightly from June 1999 but down 2 percent from the year before. Shipments of structural panels in July 1999 were 2.48 million square feet.

Softwood lumber production in the January-July 1999 period was 21.7 billion board feet, up 7 percent from the same period in 1998. Southern Pine Region production in the first seven months of 1999 was 10 billion board feet, up 7 percent from the year before. Shipments in the period were 10.1 billion board feet, up 9 percent from the same period of 1998. West Coast Region production in the first seven months of 1999 was 5.1 billion board feet, up 12 percent from the like period of 1998. Shipments in the period were 5.1 billion board feet, up 10 percent from 1998. Inland Region softwood production was 4.5 billion board feet, up 5 percent from the year before while shipments were 4.5 billion board feet, up 6 percent respectively. California Redwood Region softwood production was 759 million board feet, down 9 percent from the same period in 1998 while shipments were 777 million board feet, down 9 percent from the first seven months of 1998. Other softwood production was 1.28 billion board feet, up 7 percent from 1998 while shipments were 1.28 billion board feet, up 8 percent from 1998. Total softwood shipments in the January-July 1999 period were 21.7 billion board feet, up 8 percent from the year before.

Maple flooring production in the January-July 1999 period was 13.8 million square feet, down 2 percent from the year before. Maple flooring shipments in the period were 14.2 million square feet, up 3 percent from the year before. Shipments of oak flooring in the January-July 1999 period were 300.3 million square feet, up 23 percent from the year before. Structural panel production in the first seven months of 1999 was 17.2 billion square feet, up 2 percent from 1998. Shipments in the period were 17 billion square feet, down less than 1 percent from 1998. Particle board shipments in the first seven of 1999 were 2.9 billion square feet, up 4 percent from 1998.

U.S. imports of softwood lumber in July 1999 were 1.71 billion board feet, up 5 percent from June 1999. In the first seven months of 1999, softwood lumber imports were 11.1 billion board feet or some 2 percent more than in 1998. Imports of softwood lumber from Canada in July 1999 were 1.62 billion board feet or 6 percent more than in June 1999. For January-July 1999, softwood lumber imports from Canada were 10.6 billion board feet, up 1 percent from 1998. Softwood log imports in July 1999 were 17.3 million board feet which was down 29 percent from June 1999. In the first seven months of 1999, softwood log imports were 128 million board feet or some 61 percent higher than the year before. Hardwood lumber imports in July 1999 were almost 60 million board feet, up 1 percent from the previous year.

Futures Markets

Lumber futures and options are traded on the Chicago Mercantile Exchange (CME).

U.S. Housing Starts: Seasonally Adjusted Annual Rate In Thousands of Units

Year	Jan.	Feb.	Mar.	Apr.	May	June	July	Aug.	Sept.	Oct.	Nov.	Dec.	Average
1990	1,551	1,437	1,289	1,248	1,212	1,177	1,171	1,115	1,110	1,014	1,145	969	1,203
1991	798	965	921	1,001	996	1,036	1,063	1,049	1,015	1,079	1,103	1,079	1,009
1992	1,176	1,250	1,297	1,099	1,214	1,145	1,139	1,226	1,186	1,244	1,214	1,227	1,201
1993	1,210	1,210	1,083	1,258	1,260	1,280	1,254	1,300	1,343	1,392	1,376	1,533	1,292
1994	1,272	1,337	1,564	1,465	1,526	1,409	1,439	1,450	1,474	1,450	1,511	1,455	1,446
1995	1,383	1,325	1,246	1,278	1,309	1,294	1,464	1,404	1,378	1,382	1,451	1,404	1,360
1996	1,444	1,520	1,429	1,522	1,476	1,488	1,492	1,515	1,470	1,407	1,486	1,353	1,461
1997	1,394	1,547	1,477	1,480	1,404	1,502	1,461	1,383	1,501	1,529	1,523	1,540	1,776
1998	1,527	1,644	1,583	1,542	1,541	1,626	1,719	1,615	1,576	1,698	1,654	1,750	1,623
1999[1]	1,820	1,752	1,746	1,577	1,668	1,607	1,680	1,672	1,626	1,637	1,598	1,712	1,675

[1] Preliminary. Total Privately owned. Source: American Forest & Paper Association (AF&PA)

World Production of Industrial Roundwood by Selected Countries In Thousands of Cubic Meters

Year	Austria	Canada	Czech Repulic[3]	Finland	France	Germany	Japan	Poland	Russia[4]	Spain	Sweden	Turkey	United States
1990	14,160	173,897	16,398	40,196	34,913	40,934	29,300	15,549	305,300	13,790	49,071	5,960	430,200
1991	12,535	159,039	13,770	31,616	33,754	29,823	27,938	14,334	275,300	12,988	47,600	5,502	388,310
1992	9,255	165,436	8,820	35,279	32,596	29,159	26,934	15,720	164,000	11,624	49,720	8,458	403,100
1993	9,107	169,770	9,706	37,758	29,563	29,357	25,570	15,940	136,030	11,419	50,200	9,408	401,520
1994	11,101	177,346	11,172	44,319	32,442	36,018	24,456	16,711	83,650	12,990	52,100	9,211	410,781
1995	10,746	183,113	11,716	45,799	33,561	36,914	22,897	17,677	83,050	12,997	59,800	10,745	408,948
1996[1]	11,212	183,113	11,882	42,178	30,643	34,538	22,897	18,853	73,005	12,433	52,500	10,229	406,625
1997[2]	11,302	NA	12,881	46,862	NA	NA	NA	19,855	63,190	NA	56,400	9,773	416,092

[1] Preliminary. [2] Estimate. [3] Formerly part of Czechoslovakia; data not reported separately until 1992. [4] Formerly part of the U.S.S.R.; data not reported separately until 1992. NA = Not available. *Source: Food and Agriculture Organization of the United Nations (FAO-UN)*

Lumber Production and Consumption in the United States In Millions of Board Feet

	Production						Domestic Consumption								
	Softwood						Softwood								
Year	California Redwood	Inland Region	Southern Pine	West Coast	Total	Total Hardwood	Inland Region	Southern Pine	West Coast	Softwood Imports	Total	U.S. Hardwood	Hardwood Imports	Total Lumber
1991	1,657	9,510	12,507	7,908	33,161	11,633	9,302	12,147	6,454	11,742	42,225	10,278	226	52,730
1992	1,571	9,263	14,106	7,948	34,526	11,639	9,107	13,893	6,709	13,381	45,737	10,853	276	56,866
1993	1,354	8,312	14,392	7,319	32,947	11,914	8,129	14,020	6,043	15,260	45,810	10,556	335	56,702
1994	1,474	8,097	15,010	7,902	34,107	12,311	7,856	14,618	6,833	16,380	48,104	11,127	394	59,625
1995	1,305	7,015	14,708	7,452	32,233	12,434	6,956	14,384	6,530	17,396	47,749	11,372	380	59,501
1996	1,371	7,079	15,262	7,745	33,266	NA	7,073	15,112	6,821	18,214	49,883	NA	NA	NA
1997	1,511	7,383	16,113	7,772	34,667	NA	7,180	15,993	7,012	18,002	50,863	NA	NA	NA
1998[1]	1,391	7,298	16,151	7,797	34,677	NA	7,256	15,788	7,502	18,686	52,209	NA	NA	NA
I	340	1,822	3,849	1,917	8,423	NA	1,761	3,702	1,781	4,368	12,287	NA	NA	NA
II	349	1,818	4,140	1,944	8,766	NA	1,824	3,995	1,935	4,785	13,314	NA	NA	NA
III	388	1,841	4,129	2,047	8,931	NA	1,837	4,103	1,924	4,851	13,521	NA	NA	NA
IV	314	1,817	4,033	1,889	8,557	NA	1,834	3,988	1,862	4,682	13,087	NA	NA	NA
1999[1] I	316	1,915	4,055	2,087	8,896	NA	1,880	3,875	1,896	4,270	12,624	NA	NA	NA
II	336	1,926	4,510	2,289	9,628	NA	1,938	4,597	2,220	5,080	14,629	NA	NA	NA
III	331	1,984	4,113	2,174	9,140	NA	1,928	4,026	2,074	5,003	13,783	NA	NA	NA

[1] Preliminary. *Source: American Forest & Paper Association (AFPA)*

Stocks (Gross) of Softwood Lumber in the United States, on First of Month In Millions of Board Feet

Year	Jan.	Feb.	Mar.	Apr.	May	June	July	Aug.	Sept.	Oct.	Nov.	Dec.
1990	4,898	5,022	5,022	5,020	4,961	5,043	4,831	4,783	4,752	4,810	4,834	4,809
1991	4,734	4,925	4,949	4,946	4,849	4,600	4,699	4,684	4,793	4,786	4,741	4,710
1992	4,616	4,603	4,567	4,608	4,730	4,731	4,678	4,606	4,418	4,419	4,365	4,263
1993	4,669	4,217	4,166	4,239	4,490	4,618	4,599	4,526	4,418	4,445	4,282	4,298
1994	4,207	4,512	4,656	4,816	4,883	4,649	4,738	4,432	4,349	4,539	4,235	4,294
1995	4,403	4,336	4,344	4,653	4,352	4,663	4,508	4,323	4,342	4,359	4,361	4,335
1996	4,293	4,435	4,459	4,357	4,251	4,153	4,156	4,038	3,918	3,965	3,939	3,906
1997	3,973	4,019	4,113	4,067	3,963	4,017	3,915	3,871	3,875	3,927	3,925	3,865
1998	3,884	3,970	4,048	4,062	4,158	4,084	NA	NA	NA	NA	NA	NA
1999[1]	3,519	3,595	3,688	3,726	3,698	3,581	3,512	3,485	3,533	3,491	3,562	3,536

[1] Preliminary. NA = Not available. *Source: American Forest & Paper Association (AFPA)*

Lumber (Softwood)[2] Production in the United States In Millions of Board Feet

Year	Jan.	Feb.	Mar.	Apr.	May	June	July	Aug.	Sept.	Oct.	Nov.	Dec.	Total
1990	4,160	3,862	4,300	4,121	4,084	3,944	3,976	4,060	3,602	4,015	3,412	2,914	46,450
1991	3,534	3,410	3,661	3,958	3,837	3,762	3,664	3,808	3,682	3,933	3,473	3,254	43,976
1992	3,836	3,628	4,121	3,862	3,632	3,911	3,882	3,746	3,736	4,048	3,617	3,425	45,444
1993	3,545	3,596	3,954	3,809	3,555	3,787	3,685	3,930	3,824	4,103	3,883	3,576	45,247
1994	3,839	3,662	4,097	3,735	3,972	4,113	3,785	4,124	4,135	4,145	3,636	3,851	47,094
1995	4,084	3,577	3,931	3,675	3,805	3,897	3,641	3,866	3,757	4,105	3,549	3,297	45,184
1996	2,600	2,606	2,757	2,903	2,833	2,819	2,942	3,077	2,858	3,179	2,758	2,424	33,756
1997	3,012	2,791	2,866	3,149	2,890	3,027	3,097	2,889	2,905	3,094	2,536	2,487	34,743
1998	2,767	2,760	2,928	3,084	2,647	3,051	3,079	2,930	2,953	3,167	2,667	2,754	34,787
1999[1]	2,783	2,921	3,190	3,227	3,071	3,318	3,115	3,054	2,992	3,096	2,917		36,746

[1] Preliminary. [2] Data prior to 1996 are Softwood and Hardwood. *Source: American Forest & Paper Association (AFPA)*

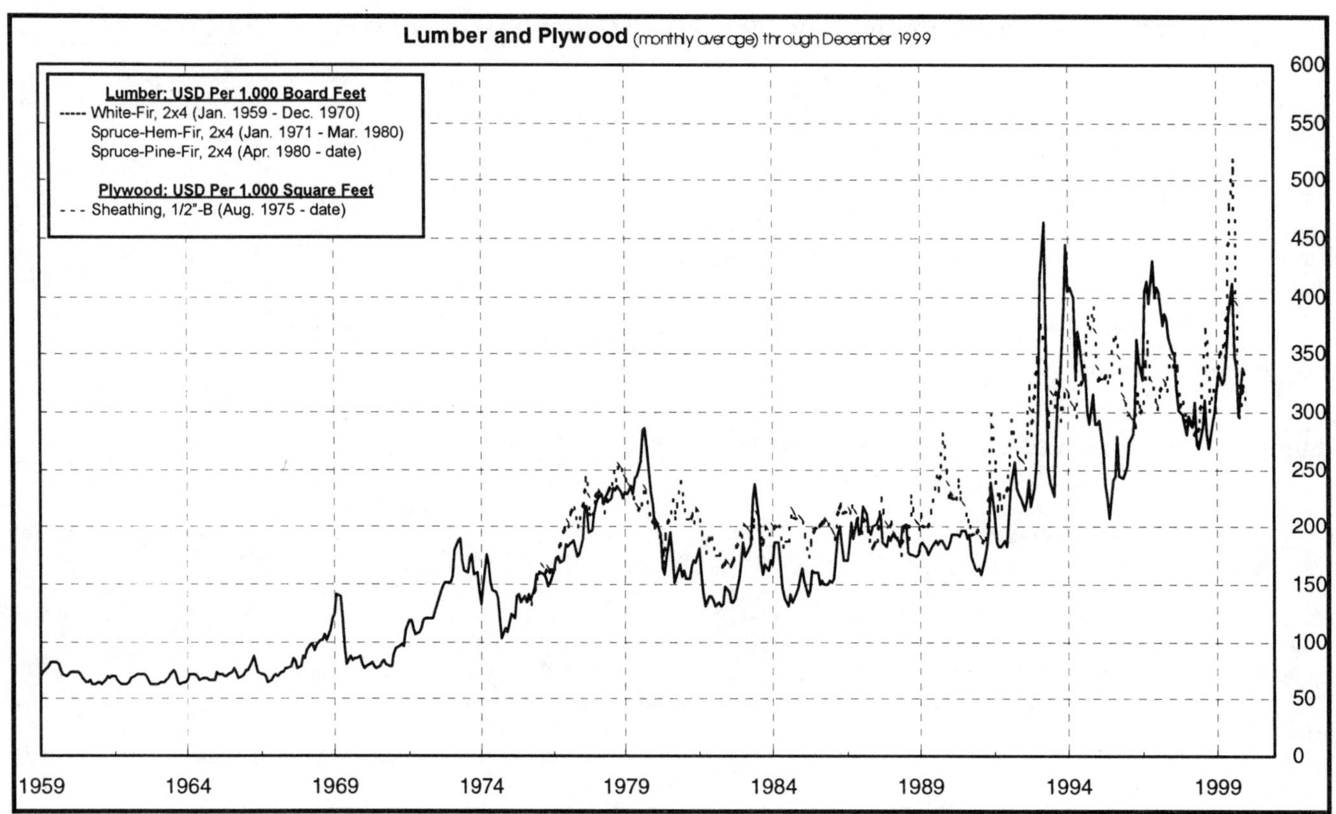

Lumber (Softwood)[2] Shipments in the United States In Millions of Board Feet

Year	Jan.	Feb.	Mar.	Apr.	May	June	July	Aug.	Sept.	Oct.	Nov.	Dec.	Total
1990	4,035	3,870	4,317	4,173	3,952	4,176	3,912	3,987	3,453	3,890	3,357	2,873	47,773
1991	3,240	3,301	3,617	4,037	4,028	3,764	3,412	3,926	3,676	4,012	3,477	3,370	44,559
1992	3,912	3,693	4,078	3,682	3,565	3,936	3,884	3,878	3,692	4,147	3,745	3,491	45,703
1993	3,575	3,649	3,852	3,563	3,402	3,759	3,721	3,997	3,724	4,211	3,798	3,617	44,868
1994	3,576	3,663	3,912	3,761	4,192	4,091	4,039	4,163	3,914	4,321	3,603	3,696	46,931
1995	3,971	3,584	3,855	3,831	3,765	4,026	3,826	3,870	3,760	4,055	3,478	3,367	45,388
1996	2,460	2,581	2,863	3,002	2,934	2,813	3,058	3,196	2,813	3,206	2,792	2,353	34,071
1997	2,966	2,697	2,890	3,253	2,834	3,126	3,139	2,885	2,852	3,096	2,598	2,461	34,797
1998	2,685	2,685	2,863	3,019	2,684	3,175	3,132	2,963	2,948	3,205	2,703	2,865	34,927
1999[1]	2,689	2,829	3,177	3,227	3,071	3,383	3,141	3,004	3,037	3,021	2,944		36,571

[1] Preliminary. [2] Data prior to 1996 are Softwood and Hardwood. *Source: American Forest & Paper Association (AFPA)*

Imports and Exports of Lumber in the United States, by Type In Millions of Board Feet

	Imports[2]								Exports[2]						
	Software								Softwood						
Year	Cedar	Douglas Fir	Hemlock	Pine	Spruce	Total	Total Hardwood	Total Lumber	Douglas Fir	Hemlock	Ponderosa/ White Pine	Southern Pine	Total	Total Hardwood	Total Lumber
1990	652.8	375.4	362.4	87.6	3,535.7	12,148.2	255.4	12,429.4	818.5	549.4	215.2	374.7	2,970.4	877.7	3,900.0
1991	700.6	354.1	287.8	55.7	2,248.3	11,741.5	226.2	11,998.2	798.1	497.7	222.9	396.0	2,863.2	934.3	3,858.9
1992	666.4	355.3	300.0	91.4	2,410.5	13,380.5	276.4	13,681.9	735.0	396.7	308.7	440.5	2,650.7	977.2	3,687.1
1993	615.3	327.6	354.9	84.6	3,104.1	15,259.9	335.0	15,625.4	664.9	340.4	273.3	339.6	2,376.4	1,008.9	3,468.9
1994	702.6	336.2	399.2	97.2	2,948.5	16,380.3	394.4	16,787.1	591.9	283.2	157.2	356.7	2,186.6	1,040.9	3,333.4
1995	768.0	395.4	258.1	97.1	2,827.7	17,395.3	379.7	17,786.9	637.9	227.0	106.7	334.6	1,987.5	1,100.5	3,192.5
1996	726.6	264.4	257.1	133.4	1,988.8	18,213.5	396.8	18,640.6	685.4	194.9	96.6	314.5	1,935.3	1,141.0	3,173.4
1997	586.1	263.9	249.8	314.2	1,040.4	18,014.3	464.5	18,505.9	435.8	104.6	122.1	299.3	1,820.0	1,281.4	3,189.0
1998	514.0	417.1	267.8	363.4	848.6	18,685.7	589.4	19,306.1	251.8	39.0	112.9	279.4	1,264.9	1,118.6	2,601.1
1999[1] I	131.8	87.0	68.7	91.7	191.1	4,269.6	177.2	4,449.0	70.1	8.5	26.5	74.9	344.8	296.4	711.5
II	157.3	104.1	72.1	113.1	209.6	5,080.2	165.2	5,248.8	64.7	15.8	31.9	83.0	366.5	322.1	746.3
III	149.9	124.8	64.8	118.6	205.1	5,003.1	184.0	5,192.9	52.2	15.4	51.4	87.9	379.5	307.7	713.4

[1] Preliminary. [2] Includes sawed timber, board planks & scantlings, flooring, box shook and railroad ties.
Source: American Forest & Paper Association (AFPA)

Average Open Interest of Random Lumber[1] Futures in Chicago In Contracts

Year	Jan.	Feb.	Mar.	Apr.	May	June	July	Aug.	Sept.	Oct.	Nov.	Dec.
1990	6,078	6,061	4,991	4,957	4,538	4,359	3,570	3,028	2,881	3,105	2,632	2,001
1991	1,922	2,003	2,023	2,354	2,076	2,601	2,571	2,181	2,276	2,480	2,206	1,606
1992	1,969	2,651	2,743	2,467	1,900	1,774	1,338	1,369	1,507	1,441	1,745	2,155
1993	2,194	2,432	2,163	2,055	2,302	2,658	2,254	2,141	2,011	2,080	2,140	2,721
1994	2,571	2,814	2,638	2,563	1,936	1,838	1,705	1,854	2,102	2,169	1,702	1,967
1995	1,757	1,923	2,142	2,509	2,742	3,252	2,896	2,918	2,809	3,039	2,626	2,940
1996	3,378	4,040	3,752	4,395	5,666	4,972	3,280	5,243	4,743	4,797	4,341	3,691
1997	3,745	3,211	3,048	3,337	2,895	3,137	2,767	3,119	3,267	4,006	3,606	4,068
1998	4,249	3,332	3,394	4,102	4,353	4,773	4,048	4,081	3,466	4,295	3,434	3,893
1999	4,864	5,497	4,698	4,456	4,927	6,404	6,262	4,882	3,456	3,703	2,962	2,868

[1] July 1995 thru March 1996, Lumber and Random Lumber. *Source: Chicago Mercantile Exchange (CME)*

Volume of Trading of Random Lumber[1] Futures in Chicago In Contracts

Year	Jan.	Feb.	Mar.	Apr.	May	June	July	Aug.	Sept.	Oct.	Nov.	Dec.	Total
1990	27,416	21,914	20,948	18,362	19,053	16,084	16,465	13,446	8,914	11,839	15,794	11,749	201,984
1991	10,535	13,460	10,326	11,309	15,135	19,029	19,350	14,912	12,214	14,054	10,295	9,902	160,521
1992	17,073	16,778	17,557	13,713	14,059	13,807	12,177	13,043	12,127	11,261	11,514	17,425	170,534
1993	14,915	15,080	14,808	14,661	14,241	15,308	13,287	13,358	12,400	13,248	18,150	18,728	178,184
1994	16,837	15,204	17,323	17,380	14,996	14,348	11,542	13,327	14,856	13,032	10,997	13,121	172,963
1995	12,150	12,909	15,088	12,139	14,536	20,126	13,766	16,919	15,718	18,981	15,551	14,803	182,686
1996	22,954	19,960	20,956	27,094	28,271	26,100	19,302	27,792	31,982	32,042	25,236	22,525	304,214
1997	28,561	20,946	21,071	24,624	18,248	24,797	20,308	18,503	21,736	24,416	15,131	21,977	260,318
1998	19,556	20,339	20,881	24,673	20,519	24,112	21,763	20,453	19,412	19,578	22,002	16,559	249,847
1999	25,962	22,184	28,151	22,618	23,835	30,410	30,791	25,683	24,177	18,125	20,802	15,118	287,856

[1] July 1995 thru March 1996, Lumber and Random Lumber. *Source: Chicago Mercantile Exchange (CME)*

LUMBER & PLYWOOD

Production of Plywood by Selected Countries In Thousands of Cubic Meters

Year	Austria	Canada	Finland	France	Germany	Italy	Japan	Poland	Romania	Russia	Spain	Sweden	United States
1993	150	1,824	621	460	416	415	5,263	133	100	1,042	200	73	17,093
1994	150	1,834	700	594	397	427	4,865	124	97	890	210	85	17,380
1995	150	1,831	778	559	498	418	4,421	115	83	939	210	108	17,140
1996	150	1,814	869	537	512	402	4,421	109	83	972	210	119	16,975
1997	150	1,828	987	576	392	414	NA	118	81	968	125	113	15,987
1998[1]	150	1,750	1,000	500	370	390	NA	140	70	1,180	125	112	15,178
1999[2]	150	1,750	1,000	500	370	400	NA	150	70	1,300	125	120	14,824

[1] Preliminary. [2] Estimate. NA = Not available. *Source: Food and Agricultural Organization of the United Nations (FAO-UN)*

Imports of Plywood by Selected Countries In Thousands of Cubic Meters

Year	Austria	Belgium	Canada	Denmark	France	Germany	Italy	Japan	Netherlands	Sweden	Switzerland	United Kingdom	United States
1993	77	436	288	152	263	865	241	4,087	612	98	118	1,157	1,630
1994	104	267	288	171	234	1,003	257	4,045	560	126	144	1,202	1,547
1995	116	146	353	188	260	1,177	323	4,394	552	112	136	1,127	1,791
1996	115	215	424	167	256	975	295	5,314	522	135	129	1,132	1,930
1997	120	313	428	196	310	1,083	312	5,326	484	184	138	947	1,973
1998[1]	120	250	120	200	323	1,100	330	NA	485	165	130	950	1,760
1999[2]	120	250	100	200	323	1,150	320	NA	485	140	130	950	1,801

[1] Preliminary. [2] Estimate. NA = Not available. *Source: Food and Agricultural Organization of the United Nations (FAO-UN)*

Exports of Plywood by Selected Countries In Thousands of Cubic Meters

Year	Austria	Baltic States	Belgium	Canada	Finland	France	Germany	Italy	Netherlands	Poland	Russia	Spain	United States
1993	129	90	87	416	542	194	110	104	99	41	464	60	1,562
1994	158	143	134	511	627	193	131	108	102	66	568	67	1,346
1995	130	138	88	818	668	183	149	96	72	60	670	48	1,395
1996	150	187	88	870	794	214	135	117	64	53	612	77	1,384
1997	166	198	101	859	861	223	135	125	50	90	615	69	1,624
1998[1]	170	NA	90	400	900	216	150	100	50	80	730	40	1,602
1999[2]	170	NA	90	400	900	216	150	100	50	85	750	40	1,697

[1] Preliminary. [2] Estimate. NA = Not available. *Source: Food and Agricultural Organization of the United Nations (FAO-UN)*

Selected World Prices of Plywood

Year	Jan.	Feb.	Mar.	Apr.	May	June	July	Aug.	Sept.	Oct.	Nov.	Dec.	Average
Southeast Asia, Lauan, Wholesale Price, Spot Tokyo In U.S. Cents Per Sheet[1]													
1995	551.01	599.11	656.48	665.11	635.41	627.00	562.66	560.56	527.43	526.55	539.65	540.20	582.60
1996	529.12	548.59	529.22	521.11	535.48	523.62	521.39	538.27	528.50	525.09	526.22	518.62	528.77
1997	500.31	479.63	489.39	485.57	511.91	524.85	512.10	500.68	480.05	454.68	438.61	424.25	483.50
1998	409.19	413.35	387.32	371.74	363.05	349.38	348.29	324.83	349.59	380.46	390.58	417.38	375.43
1999	441.27	420.34	418.38	434.22	426.27	430.68							428.53
Canada, Export Unit Value, F.O.B. In Canadian Dollar Per Cubic Meter													
1992	426.14	409.62	373.22	396.94	387.59	395.95	354.61	373.58	385.20	395.29	410.59	353.95	388.56
1993	392.59	396.65	393.73	424.19	515.51	448.76	408.39	435.72	505.58	517.58	494.52	476.08	450.78
1994	442.04	574.74	553.92	553.81	542.95	458.48	472.29	510.01	526.42	454.20	462.90	499.71	504.29
1995	473.77	480.78											477.28
Finland, Export Unit Value, F.O.B. In Markka Per Cubic Meter													
1995	3,681	3,809	3,751	3,897	3,752	3,769	3,771	3,543	3,430	3,370	3,268	2,923	3,579
1996	3,084	2,548	3,129	3,296	3,075	3,225	3,070	3,003	3,245	3,036	3,264	2,900	3,060
1997	3,021	2,943	3,032	3,157	3,174	3,336	3,220	3,222	3,321	3,408	3,465	3,563	3,235
1998	3,488	3,565	3,573	3,774	3,567	3,698	3,542	3,374	3,486	3,474	3,426	3,022	3,505
United Kingdom, Import Unit Value, C.I.F. In Pound Sterling Per Cubic Meter													
1995	232.68	239.77	257.68	264.72	229.18	268.11	256.09	241.61	263.31	285.36	275.38	282.68	258.05
1996	238.86	249.65	224.40	273.23	256.16	275.38	269.36	247.83	253.37	261.66	260.77	293.42	258.67
1997	235.57	234.39	340.66	378.17	274.27	256.75	248.45	276.09	268.64	277.69	270.27	294.06	262.92
1998	188.51	229.59	230.75	237.89	215.24	207.63	209.45	204.69	200.66	206.68	206.01		212.46

[1] Sheet measurement = 1.2cm X 90.0cm X 1.80m. *Source: Food and Agricultural Organization of the United Nations (FAO-UN)*

Magnesium

Magnesium is one of the most abundant elements found in the Earth's crust and the third most plentiful element found in seawater. Magnesium metal can be recovered from the ocean and is found in minerals such as dolomite, magnesite, olivine and brucite.

Although demand for magnesium in the U.S. continued to increase, the largest U.S. producer closed its Texas plant in 1998. As a result, domestic production of magnesium was replaced by imports. Among the countries that supply magnesium to the U.S. are Canada, China, Russia and Israel. Other countries are looking at new ways to produce magnesium or new products from which to extract it. New facilities in Canada are looking at using asbestos tailings as a material from which to extract magnesium while in Australia a facility is proposed to use magnesite as a raw material. In the U.S., aluminum alloying remained the largest end use for magnesium though there was strong growth in diecasting, as automobile manufacturers were using more magnesium components in vehicles.

World primary production of magnesium in 1998 was estimated at 389,000 metric tonnes, down 1 percent from 1997. The largest producer of magnesium is the U.S. with 1998 production estimated at 106,000 tonnes, down 6 percent from the previous year. The next largest producer is China with output in 1998 of 95,000 tonnes. Other large producers include Canada, Russia and Norway.

The U.S. Geological Survey reported that U.S. production of primary magnesium in 1998 was 106,000 tonnes, down 15 percent from 1997. Production of secondary magnesium in 1998 was estimated at 76,400 tonnes, down 2 percent from the previous year. U.S. imports of magnesium metal in May 1999 were 1,870 tonnes, up nearly 9 percent from the previous month. In the January-May 1999 period, imports of magnesium metal were 12,000 tonnes while for all of 1998 they were 26,500 tonnes. Imports of magnesium waste and scrap in May 1999 were 508 tonnes, down 15 percent from April. In the first five months of 1999, imports of waste and scrap were 2,550 tonnes while for all of 1998 they were 5,720 tonnes. Imports of alloys (magnesium content) in May 1999 were 3,870 tonnes, down 7 percent from April. In the January-May period, alloy imports were 20,900 tonnes while for all of 1998 they were 49,600 tonnes. Imports of sheet, tubing, ribbons, wire, powder and other magnesium materials (magnesium content) in May 1999 were 17 tonnes. In the first five months of 1999 they were 148 tonnes, and for all of 1998 imports were 756 tonnes.

U.S. exports of magnesium metal in May 1999 were 520 tonnes while in January-May 1999 exports were 2,320 tonnes. Exports of waste and scrap in May 1999 were 1,600 tonnes and in January-May 1999 they were 6,880 tonnes. Alloy exports in May were 294 tonnes and in January-May 1999 they were 1,130 tonnes.

World Production of Magnesium (Primary and Secondary) In Metric Tons

	Primary Production								Secondary Production				
Year	Brazil	Canada	China	France	Norway	Russia[4]	United States	World Total	Japan	United Kingdom	United States	Former USSR	World Total
1989	6,200	7,000	3,500	14,600	49,827	91,000	152,066	344,447	20,270	1,000	51,200	8,000	81,970
1990	8,700	25,300	5,900	14,000	48,222	88,000	139,333	354,000	23,308	900	54,808	7,500	88,100
1991	7,800	35,512	8,600	14,050	44,322	80,000	131,288	342,000	17,158	800	50,543	7,000	77,100
1992	7,300	25,800	10,600	13,660	30,404	40,000	137,000	295,000	12,978	800	57,000	6,500	78,900
1993	9,700	23,000	11,800	10,982	27,300	30,000	132,000	269,000	13,215	1,000	58,900	6,000	80,700
1994	9,700	28,900	24,000	12,280	27,635	35,400	128,000	282,000	19,009	1,000	62,100	5,000	88,700
1995	9,700	48,100	93,600	14,450	28,000	37,500	142,000	395,000	11,767	1,000	65,100	6,000	85,500
1996	9,000	54,000	73,100	14,000	28,000	35,000	133,000	368,000	21,243	1,000	70,200	6,000	100,000
1997[1]	9,000	57,700	75,990	13,740	28,000	39,500	125,000	378,000	22,797	1,000	80,200	NA	103,000
1998[2]	9,000	77,109	67,000	14,000	28,000	41,500	106,000	369,000	20,000	1,000	76,400	NA	99,000

[1] Preliminary [2] Estimate. [3] Formerly part of the U.S.S.R.; data not reported separately until 1992. W = Withheld proprietary data.
Source: U.S. Geological Survey (USGS)

Salient Statistics of Magnesium in the United States In Metric Tons

	Production								Domestic Consumption of Primary Magnesium					
		Secondary												
Year	Primary (Ingot)	New Scrap	Old Scrap	Total	Total Exports[3]	Imports for Consumption	Stocks Dec. 31[4]	$ Price Per Pound[5]	Castings (Structural Products)	Wrought (Structural Products)	Total (Structural Products)	Aluminum Alloys	Other Uses[6]	Total
1989	152,066	23,229	27,971	51,200	56,631	12,289	26,000	1.63	7,455	9,653	17,108	53,821	34,297	88,118
1990	139,333	23,424	31,384	54,808	51,834	26,755	26,000	1.43-1.63	9,078	10,944	20,022	45,060	31,026	76,086
1991	131,288	23,059	27,484	50,543	55,160	31,863	27,000	1.43	8,857	8,802	17,659	45,809	28,404	74,213
1992	136,947	26,191	30,854	57,045	51,951	11,844	13,000	1.46-1.53	10,223	8,843	19,066	41,003	33,758	74,761
1993	132,144	28,313	30,577	58,890	38,815	37,248	26,000	1.43-1.46	12,543	9,870	22,413	46,498	32,202	78,700
1994	128,000	32,500	29,600	62,100	45,200	29,100	20,030	1.63	15,676	7,690	23,366	61,100	27,900	89,000
1995	142,000	35,400	29,800	65,100	38,300	34,800	21,193	1.93-2.25	15,231	8,510	23,741	60,200	25,100	85,300
1996	133,000	41,100	30,100	71,200	40,500	46,600	25,000	1.70-1.80	16,400	8,080	24,480	52,300	25,500	77,800
1997[1]	125,000	47,000	30,500	80,200	40,500	65,100	23,000	1.60-1.70	20,643	6,840	27,400	50,000	23,000	73,000
1998[2]	106,000	44,600	31,800	80,000	35,400	82,500	27,000	1.52-1.62	25,290	7,100	32,400	49,900	20,900	70,800

[1] Preliminary. [2] Estimate. [3] Metal & alloys in crude form & scrap. [4] Estimate of Industry Stocks, metal. [5] Magnesium ingots (99.8%), f.o.b. Valasco, Texas. [6] Distributive or sacrificial purposes. W = Withheld proprietary data. *Source: U.S. Geological Survey (USGS)*

Manganese

Manganese is primarily used in the steel industry as an alloy. Manganese increases the metal's hardness so virtually all steel contains some manganese. Manganese is essential in iron and steel production because of its sulfur-fixing, deoxidizing and alloying properties. Steelmaking accounts for most of the demand for manganese, though it finds use in aluminum alloys and is used in oxide form in dry cell batteries. Manganese finds use in plant fertilizers and animal feeds. Manganese ore, when converted to a metallic alloy with iron, forms the compound ferromanganese.

World mine production of manganese in 1998 was estimated at 7.4 million metric tonnes, a decline of 4 percent from 1997. The major producer of manganese in 1998 was China with production estimated at 1.4 million tonnes, unchanged from 1997. The next largest producer was South Africa with 1998 production estimated at 1.35 million tonnes, an increase of 2 percent from 1997. The third largest producer was the Ukraine with output of 920,000 tonnes, 11 percent less than in 1997. Other large producers include Gabon, Australia and Brazil. World reserves of manganese are estimated at 680 million tonnes. The largest reserves are in South Africa where they are estimated to be 370 million tonnes.

U.S. imports for consumption of manganese totaled 477,000 tonnes in the January-July 1999 period. Of the total, manganese ore and dioxide totaled 207,000 tonnes while ferroalloy and metal imports totaled 270,000 tonnes. In July 1999, imports were 96,900 tonnes with ore and dioxide imports of 67,200 tonnes, while ferroalloy and metal imports were 29,700 tonnes. U.S. imports of silicomanganese in July 1999 were 23,400 tonnes with 15,700 tonnes of manganese content. The suppliers were Australia and South Africa.

U.S. imports of ferromanganese in July 1999 were 16,700 tonnes with manganese content of 13,200 tonnes. The major suppliers were South Africa, Australia, South Korea and Japan. In the January-July 1999 period, imports of ferromanganese were 195,000 tonnes with manganese content of 153,000 tonnes. U.S. imports of manganese ore in July 1999 were 403,000 tonnes with 193,000 tonnes of manganese content. The major suppliers were Gabon and Morocco.

In August 1999, U.S. reported consumption of manganese ore containing 35 percent or more manganese, exclusive of that at iron and steel plants, was 40,000 tonnes, up slightly from the previous month. In the first eight months of the year, consumption was 300,000 tonnes. Industry stocks of manganese ore at the end of August 1999 were 164,000 tonnes, this represented a decrease of 4 percent from the stocks at the end of July which totaled 170,000 tonnes.

World Production of Manganese Ore In Thousands of Metric Tons (Gross Weight)

Year	Australia[2] 37-53[4]	Brazil 30-50	China 30	Gabon 50-53	Georgia[5] 29-30	Ghana 30-50	Hungary[3] 30-33	India 10-54	Mexico 27-50	Morocco 50-53	South Africa 30-48+	Ukraine[5] 29-30	World Total
1989	2,124	1,904	3,200	2,592	-----	297	84	1,334	394	32	4,884	9,141	26,260
1990	1,920	2,300	4,080	2,423	-----	247	60	1,385	451	49	4,402	8,500	26,108
1991	1,412	2,000	5,150	1,620	-----	320	30	1,401	254	59	3,146	7,240	22,900
1992	1,251	1,703	5,300	1,556	500	276	18	1,810	407	44	2,464	5,819	21,800
1993	2,092	1,837	5,860	1,290	300	295	59	1,655	363	43	2,507	3,800	20,500
1994	1,920	2,199	3,570	1,436	150	270	55	1,632	307	31	2,851	2,979	18,000
1995	2,177	2,398	6,900	1,930	100	217	-----	1,764	472	-----	3,199	3,200	23,300
1996	2,109	2,506	7,600	1,980	97	448	-----	1,797	485	-----	3,240	3,070	24,300
1997	2,136	2,124	3,700	1,900	-----	437	-----	1,800	534	-----	3,121	3,040	19,800
1998[1]	1,500	2,100	4,000	2,092	-----	450	-----	1,600	510	-----	3,044	2,226	18,700

[1] Preliminary. [2] Metallurgical Ore. [3] Concentrate. [4] Ranges of percentage of manganese. [5] Formerly part of the U.S.S.R.; data not reported separately until 1992. *Source: U.S. Geological Survey (USGS)*

Salient Statistics of Manganese in the United States In Thousands of Metric Tons (Gross Weight)

Year	Net Import Reliance as a % of Apparent Consumption	Manganese Ore (35% or More Manganese): Imports for Consumption	Manganese Ore: Exports	Manganese Ore: Consumption	Manganese Ore: Stocks, Dec. 31[3]	Ferromanganese: Imports for Consumption	Ferromanganese: Exports	Ferromanganese: Consumption	Avg. Price Mn. Metallurgical Ore $ Lg. Ton Unit[4]	Silicomanganese: Exports	Silicomanganese: Imports
1989	100	580	52	559	470	432	8	399	2.76	6.5	281.5
1990	100	307	70	497	379	380	7	413	3.78	1.8	224.5
1991	100	234	66	473	275	320	15	346	3.72	2.9	258.3
1992	100	247	13	438	276	304	13	339	3.25	9.2	257.2
1993	100	232	16	389	302	347	18	341	2.60	9.4	316.0
1994	100	331	15	449	269	336	11	347	2.40	6.8	273.0
1995	100	394	15	486	309	310	11	348	2.40	7.8	305.0
1996	100	478	32	478	319	374	10	326	2.55	5.3	323.0
1997[1]	100	355	84	510	275	304	12	337	2.44	5.4	306.0
1998[2]	100	332	8	499	196	339	14	355	2.40	6.7	346.0

[1] Preliminary. [2] Estimate. [3] Including bonded warehouses; excludes Gov't stocks; also excludes small tonnages of dealers' stocks. [4] 46-48% Mn, C.I.F. U.S. Ports. *Source: U.S. Geological Survey (USGS)*

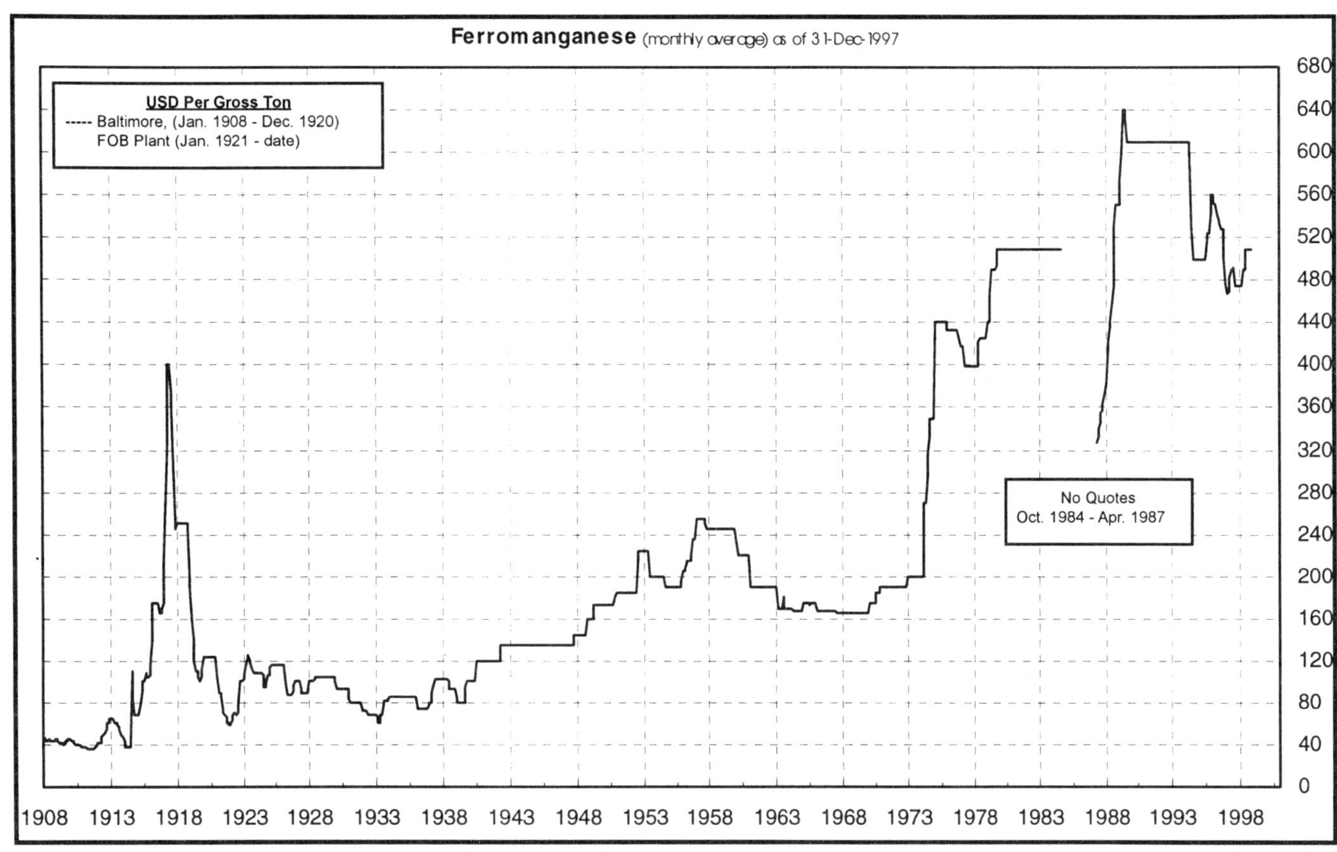

Imports[3] of Manganese Ore (20% or More Mn) in the United States In Metric Tons (Mn Content)

Year	Australia	Brazil	Gabon	Mexico	Morocco	South Africa	Total	Customs Value Thous. $
1989	54,828	84,626	99,463	8,916	18	19,612	270,786	43,794
1990	32,544	20,662	67,828	2,732	18	9,958	148,944	40,054
1991	16,485	2,583	79,997	4,673	44	-----	117,255	40,332
1992	25,519	15,541	75,354	3,930	56	-----	120,400	29,967
1993	30,171	5,573	66,659	7,317	43	6,006	115,770	24,927
1994	23,200	4,530	112,000	13,700	56	7,780	161,000	29,800
1995	31,600	7,080	104,000	23,600	37	13,100	187,000	33,300
1996	48,900	5,640	140,000	16,100	9	20,800	231,000	42,400
1997[1]	16,400	9,100	99,400	30,100	37	-----	156,000	30,800
1998[2]	18,700	12,100	94,900	14,600	-----	13,800	158,000	27,800

[1] Preliminary. [2] Estimate. [3] Imports for consumption. [4] Manganese content of 35% or more thru 1988. *Source: U.S. Geological Survey (USGS)*

Average Price of Ferromanganese[1] (High Carbon - F.O.B. Plant) In Dollars Per Gross Ton -- Carloads

Year	Jan.	Feb.	Mar.	Apr.	May	June	July	Aug.	Sept.	Oct.	Nov.	Dec.	Average
1989	550.00	550.50	573.75	597.50	640.00	640.00	640.00	634.00	610.00	610.00	610.00	610.00	605.48
1990	610.00	610.00	610.00	610.00	610.00	610.00	610.00	610.00	610.00	610.00	610.00	610.00	610.00
1991	610.00	610.00	610.00	610.00	610.00	610.00	610.00	610.00	610.00	610.00	610.00	610.00	610.00
1992	610.00	610.00	610.00	610.00	610.00	610.00	610.00	610.00	610.00	610.00	610.00	610.00	610.00
1993	610.00	610.00	610.00	610.00	610.00	610.00	610.00	610.00	610.00	610.00	610.00	610.00	610.00
1994	610.00	610.00	610.00	610.00	610.00	527.50	500.00	500.00	500.00	500.00	500.00	500.00	548.13
1995	500.00	500.00	500.00	500.00	500.00	500.00	500.00	518.75	525.00	525.00	542.50	560.00	514.27
1996	560.00	552.50	550.00	550.00	541.00	535.00	533.13	527.50	527.50	527.50	501.25	477.50	531.91
1997	477.50	467.50	470.00	482.50	490.00	490.00	490.00	492.50	475.00	475.00	475.00	475.00	480.00
1998	175.00	175.00	175.00	190.00	190.00	510.00	510.00	510.00	510.00	510.00	510.00	510.00	497.92

[1] Domestic standard. *Source: American Metal Market (AMM)*

Meats

U.S. commercial red meat production, consisting of the combined total of beef, veal, lamb and pork output, during the first ten months of 1999 was 38.4 billion pounds vs. 37.5 billion in the like 1998 period, suggesting a record high output when the full year totals are available. Red meat will account for about 55 percent of total U.S. meat production in 1999, a slightly smaller percentage than seen in prior years. Poultry accounts for the balance; the combined ten month total of 68 billion pounds compares with 65.6 billion in the year earlier period.

1999 beef production of 22.1 billion pounds compares with 21.6 billion in 1998. Pork production of 15.9 billion pounds in 1999 compares with 15.5 billion the previous year. Forecasts for total 1999 and 2000 beef output are 26.2 billion pounds and 24.9 billion, respectively; for pork the forecasts are 19.2 billion and 18.6 billion. Significantly, only poultry production is expected to increase in 2000, to a record high 31.2 billion pounds from 29.7 billion in 1999. U.S. veal and lamb production is insignificant.

Worldwide, China is the largest red meat producer with 45 million metric tonnes, of which 37.5 million tonnes is pork. In 1999, China accounted for one-third of the world meat output total with the U.S. second at 50 percent of China's output. The slide in red meat production in the former U.S.S.R. still shows little sign of abating, with only 3.5 million tonnes in 1999 vs. almost 4 million in 1998.

U.S. per capita beef consumption (retail weight) in 1999 of 68.7 pounds compares with 68.1 in 1998, and a forecast of 65.4 pounds in 2000. U.S. per capita pork usage of 53.5 pounds compares with 52.6 in 1998, and 51.6 pounds forecast for 2000. The relative gain in pork use partially reflects the aggressive industry advertising campaign associating pork as a white, and not a red meat, while the beef industry's advertising focuses on the ease (timewise) of preparing beef for dinner. For both meats, however, consumer preferences have shifted to foods containing less fat which has benefited poultry at red meat's expense. Per capita retail broiler and turkey consumption totaled a record large 95.7 pounds in 1999 and is forecast at 99.7 pounds in 2000.

Choice steer market prices (basis Nebraska) averaged about $64.91/cwt. in 1999 vs. $61.48 in 1998; forecasts for 2000 are from $66.00 to $72.00. Midwest hog barrow prices of around $32.42/cwt. in 1999 compare with $34.72 in 1998 and estimates for 2000 of $34-37.00/cwt.

U.S. red meat imports in 1999 are forecast to be 3.6 billion pounds comparing with 3.2 billion in 1999, and forecasts of 3.7 billion pounds in 2000 with beef imports accounting for about 80 percent of the totals. U.S. red meat exports, 65 percent of which are beef, totaled 3.7 billion pounds in 1999 vs. 3.4 billion in 1998, and a forecast of 3.5 billion pounds in 2000.

World Total Meat Production[4] In Thousands of Metric Tons

Year	Argentina	Australia	Brazil	Canada	China[5]	France	Germany	Italy	Mexico	Russia[6]	United Kingdom	United States	World Total
1991	2,735	2,704	5,513	2,022	27,238	3,963	5,552	2,608	2,535	7,526	2,389	17,956	121,244
1992	2,602	2,810	5,620	2,107	29,406	3,997	4,994	2,648	2,626	6,748	2,297	18,589	116,309
1993	2,630	2,780	5,795	2,052	32,254	3,901	4,796	2,642	2,718	6,260	2,236	18,488	115,852
1994	2,682	2,807	7,030	2,132	36,968	3,868	5,092	2,618	2,852	5,659	2,323	19,361	124,693
1995	2,668	2,644	7,530	2,204	42,653	3,941	5,053	2,602	2,942	4,860	2,359	19,811	129,482
1996	2,636	2,650	7,750	2,226	37,537	3,973	5,161	2,668	2,832	4,487	2,088	19,634	124,230
1997	3,033	2,914	7,590	2,332	40,895	4,046	5,053	2,626	2,875	4,086	2,183	19,667	127,881
1998	2,648	2,986	7,803	2,529	42,880	4,030	5,222	2,595	2,852	3,775	2,298	20,541	131,400
1999[1]	2,850	2,900	8,066	2,735	43,601	4,053	5,254	2,596	2,820	3,549	2,235	20,873	132,783
2000[2]	2,808	2,885	8,371	2,798	45,015	4,057	5,249	2,596	2,845	3,354	2,168	19,992	133,138

[1] Preliminary. [2] Forecast. [3] Includes beef, veal, pork, sheep and goat meat. [4] Predominately pork production. [5] Formerly part of the U.S.S.R.; data not reported separately until 1990. *Source: Foreign Agricultural Service, U.S. Department of Agriculture (FAS-USDA)*

Production and Consumption of Red Meats in The United States (Carcass Weight)

	Beef			Veal			Lamb & Mutton			Pork (Excluding Lard)			All Meats		
	Commercial Production	Consumption Total	Consumption Per Capita	Commercial Production	Consumption Total	Consumption Per Capita	Commercial Production	Consumption Total	Consumption Per Capita	Commercial Production	Consumption Total	Consumption Per Capita	Commercial Production	Consumption Total	Consumption Per Capita
Year	Million Pounds	Million Pounds	Lbs.[4]	Million Pounds	Million Pounds	Lbs.[4]	Million Pounds	Million Pounds	Lbs.[4]	Million Pounds	Million Pounds	Lbs.[4]	Million Pounds	Million Pounds	Lbs.[4]
1990	22,634	24,114	96.2	327	316	1.3	358	397	1.6	15,300	16,030	64.1	38,608	40,782	163.2
1991	22,800	24,261	95.4	306	296	1.2	358	397	1.6	15,948	16,399	64.9	39,402	41,214	163.1
1992	22,968	24,261	95.0	310	299	1.2	343	388	1.5	17,185	17,475	68.4	40,795	42,437	166.1
1993	22,942	24,006	93.0	267	286	1.1	329	381	1.5	17,030	17,419	67.5	40,568	42,092	163.1
1994	24,278	25,124	96.4	283	290	1.2	304	345	1.3	17,658	17,829	68.4	42,523	43,588	167.3
1995	25,115	25,534	97.0	308	319	1.2	264	338	1.1	17,085	16,826	63.3	42,772	43,017	162.6
1996	25,419	25,863	97.4	378	378	1.4	268	334	1.1	17,117	16,795	63.3	43,182	43,370	163.2
1997[1]	25,384	25,609	95.9	334	333	1.2	260	333	1.1	17,274	16,821	61.4	43,252	43,096	159.6
1998[2]	25,653	26,303	93.3	262	265	1.0	251	359	1.0	19,011	18,308	65.3	45,177	45,235	160.6
1999[3]	26,315	26,912		234	233		238	343		19,373	18,984		46,160	46,472	

[1] Preliminary. [2] Estimate. [3] Forecast. [4] Carcass weight. *Source: Economic Research Service, U.S. Department of Agriculture (ERS-USDA)*

Total Red Meat Imports (Carcass Weight Equivalent) of Principal Countries In Thousands of Metric Tons

Year	Canada	France	Germany	Hong Kong	Italy	Japan	Rep. of Korea	Nether-lands	Russia	Singa-pore	United Kingdom	United States	Total
1991	232	1,035	1,240	306	1,106	1,206	201	181	740	140	896	1,463	6,509
1992	237	1,027	1,338	265	1,231	1,388	187	208	292	147	885	1,424	5,733
1993	292	1,010	1,319	280	1,139	1,480	134	207	227	150	889	1,449	6,118
1994	313	39	190	298	77	1,628	191	35	880	28	217	1,434	6,529
1995	283	39	150	223	37	1,840	239	25	1,084	28	294	1,284	6,475
1996	276	45	143	202	62	1,904	240	31	1,059	41	276	1,253	6,486
1997	311	52	133	238	65	1,719	276	56	1,155	37	283	1,388	6,803
1998	303	58	94	313	57	1,733	173	32	895	28	239	1,568	6,674
1999[1]	295	50	99	273	60	1,842	304	40	885	27	218	1,696	7,023
2000[2]	315	46	84	288	60	1,855	370	30	885	26	217	1,783	7,204

[1] Preliminary. [2] Forecast. *Source: Foreign Agricultural Service, U.S. Department of Agriculture (FAS-USDA)*

Total Red Meat Exports (Carcass Weight Equivalent) of Principal Countries In Thousands of Metric Tons

Year	Argentina	Australia	Brazil	Canada	China	Denmark	France	India	Ireland	Nether-lands	New Zealand	United States	World Total
1991	402	1,391	290	375	494	1,007	757	151	529	1,438	845	669	8,040
1992	301	1,510	470	453	195	1,657	864	110	643	1,491	884	789	7,484
1993	283	1,469	425	494	315	1,272	917	120	672	1,470	858	779	7,290
1994	379	1,495	417	521	256	550	352	138	347	133	934	984	8,138
1995	522	1,374	320	576	328	399	302	152	367	136	864	1,186	8,165
1996	472	1,291	330	658	279	387	291	162	305	195	985	1,294	8,444
1997	438	1,465	354	776	209	531	281	171	271	202	999	1,446	8,996
1998	292	1,612	449	848	239	490	224	193	308	180	949	1,545	8,943
1999[1]	341	1,574	562	1,015	146	530	271	228	326	120	820	1,646	8,932
2000[2]	351	1,587	605	1,090	151	501	311	260	342	175	855	1,574	9,253

[1] Preliminary. [2] Forecast. *Source: Foreign Agricultural Service, U.S. Department of Agriculture (FAS-USDA)*

United States Meat Imports by Type of Product In Metric Tons

	Beef and Veal			Lamb, Mutton and Goat,	Pork							
Year	Fresh, Chilled & Frozen	Canned, Including Sausage	Other Pre-pared or Preserved	Except Canned	Fresh and Frozen	Canned[2]	Other Pre-pared or Preserved	Sausage, All Types	Mixed Sausage	Other Meats[3]	Variety Meats, Fresh or Frozen	Total
1988	703,415	67,109	10,124	19,239	281,965	143,356	10,214	2,906	2,732	17,449	8,905	1,253,995
1989	638,999	56,302	13,842	20,917	226,172	118,598	10,328	2,656	2,620	23,581	11,102	1,105,045
1990	694,163	57,636	10,939	19,056	233,536	31,539	13,375	3,421	1,874	18,560	11,423	1,100,710
1991	709,997	60,511	12,929	19,100	215,935	82,339	16,948	2,144	1,533	22,979	18,266	1,162,681
1992	728,922	64,303	10,641	23,853	185,671	61,005	16,553	2,453	1,674	19,225	20,059	1,134,359
1993	720,079	59,786	14,560	24,468	207,653	75,440	17,689	2,695	1,368	18,679	25,298	1,167,714
1994	714,450	61,575	13,335	23,277	209,026	75,443	17,577	2,237	1,900	18,724	27,407	1,164,951
1995	641,918	52,012	13,528	29,919	194,387	61,904	15,571	2,553	1,935	19,550	27,728	1,061,005
1996	640,678	52,800	13,549	32,988	183,298	55,247	14,088	2,368	1,636	16,284	32,464	1,045,400
1997[1]	641,918	51,007	12,018	37,856	190,450	56,353	13,381	2,423	1,605	19,965	44,156	1,253,143

[1] Preliminary. [2] Includes canned hams, shoulders and bacon; not specified elsewhere. [3] Mostly mixed lucheon meats.
Source: Foreign Agricultural Service, U.S. Department of Agriculture (FAS-USDA)

United States Meat Exports by Type of Product In Metric Tons

	Beef and Veal			Pork								
							Other Pork Prepared or Preserved					
Year	Fresh, Chilled & Frozen	Prepared and Preserved	Lamb and Mutton, Fresh or Frozen	Fresh, Chilled & Frozen	Hams & Shoul-ders, Cured	Bacon	Not Canned	Canned	Sausage, Bologna & Frank-furters	Variety Meats, Fresh, Chilled & Frozen	Other Meats[2]	Total
1988	214,530	14,083	619	54,598	2,138	1,045	4,924	268	8,439	302,087	75,084	677,815
1989	373,110	8,810	2,076	79,318	6,101	3,788	2,204	1,395	11,968	245,235	78,550	812,555
1990	339,925	7,783	2,490	66,756	5,567	4,518	4,310	1,036	14,208	226,623	70,558	743,774
1991	395,697	10,251	3,790	76,193	4,702	5,443	6,133	1,278	24,025	280,721	61,440	869,673
1992	436,455	12,064	3,278	116,496	8,181	7,396	5,812	2,352	22,796	303,295	57,154	975,279
1993	411,003	14,464	3,605	129,240	5,208	7,092	4,579	2,350	34,198	338,689	45,905	996,333
1994	517,507	13,545	3,766	149,318	8,477	12,076	4,470	2,973	46,925	373,662	34,734	1,167,453
1995	581,731	13,653	2,509	228,164	12,074	13,830	6,263	3,564	56,829	449,599	34,118	1,402,334
1996	596,891	14,565	2,475	267,419	9,733	15,838	7,541	5,343	92,476	469,320	42,172	1,523,773
1997[1]	676,490	15,210	2,548	286,210	9,024	12,346	9,233	7,693	104,568	424,483	58,540	1,606,345

[1] Preliminary. [2] Includes sausage ingredients, cured (excluding canned);meat and meat products canned; and baby food, canned.
Source: Foreign Agricultural Service, U.S. Department of Agriculture (FAS-USDA)

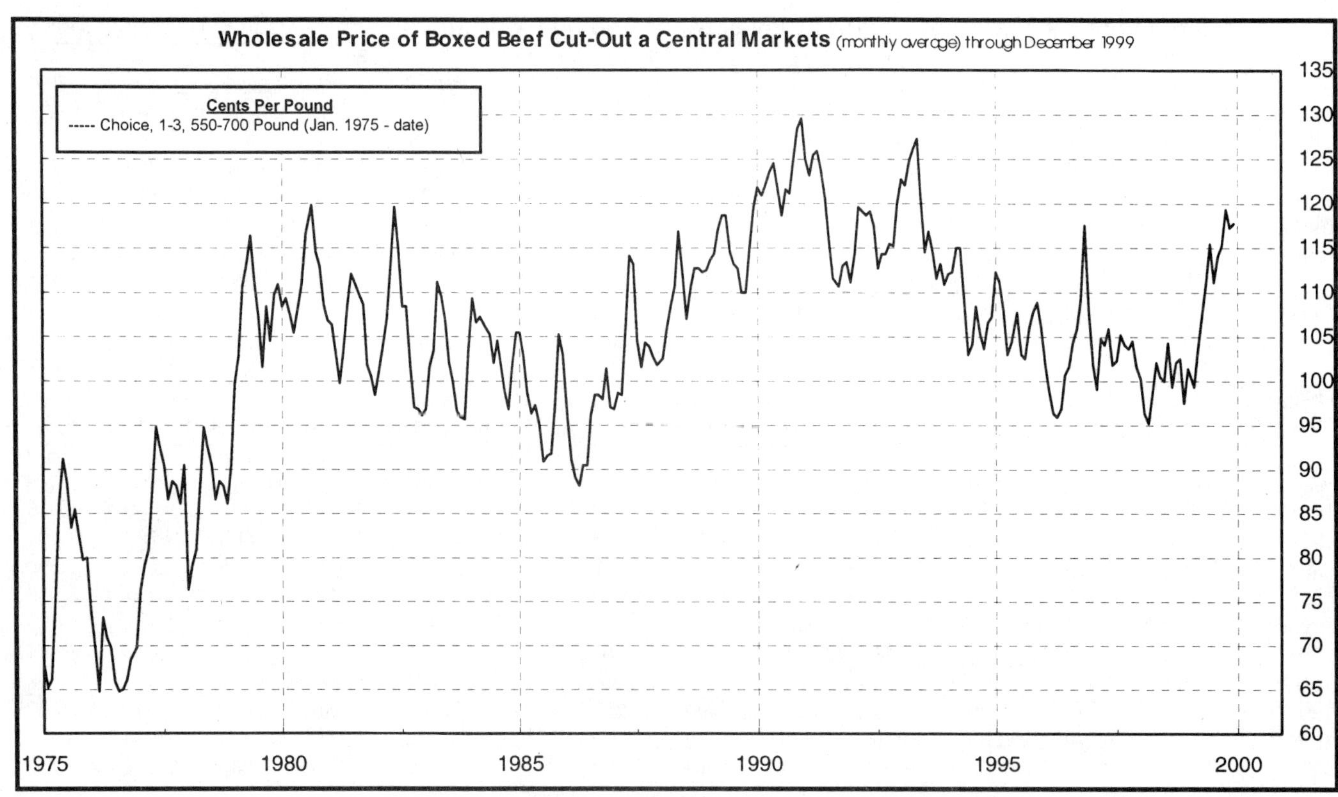

Exports and Imports of Meats in the United States (Carcass Weight Equivalent)[4] In Millions of Pounds

	Exports				Imports			
Year	Beef and Veal	Lamb and Mutton	Pork[4]	All Meat	Beef and Veal	Lamb and Mutton	Pork[4]	All Meat
1990	1,006	6	238	1,250	2,356	41	898	3,295
1991	1,188	10	290	1,488	2,406	41	775	3,223
1992	1,324	8	420	1,752	2,440	50	645	3,135
1993	1,275	8	446	1,730	2,401	53	740	3,194
1994	1,611	9	549	2,169	2,369	49	743	3,161
1995	1,821	6	787	2,614	2,103	64	664	2,831
1996	1,877	6	970	2,853	2,073	73	618	2,764
1997[1]	2,136	5	1,044	3,185	2,343	83	633	3,059
1998[2]	2,158	5	1,232	3,395	2,611	107	695	3,413
1999[3]	2,340	5	1,355	3,700	2,705	113	700	3,518

[1] Preliminary. [2] Estimate. [3] Forecast. [4] Includes meat content of minor meats and of mixed products. *Source: Economic Research Service, U.S. Department of Agriculture (FAS-USDA)*

Average Wholesale Prices of Meats in the United States In Cents Per Pound

Year	Composite Retail Price of Beef, Choice, Grade 3	Composite Retail Price of Pork[3]	Wholesale Value[4] Beef	Wholesale Value[4] Pork	Net Farm Value of Pork[5]	Cow Beef Canner & Cutter, Central US	Boxed Beef Cut-out, Choice 1-3, Central US, 550-700 Lbs.	Pork Carcass Cut-out, US No. 2	Lamb Carcass, Choice-Prime, East Coast, 55-65 Lbs.	Pork Loins, Central US, 14-18 Lbs.	Skinned Ham, Central US, 20-26 Lbs.[6]	Pork Bellies, Central US, 12-14 Lbs.
1991	288.30	211.90	182.50	108.90	78.40	99.42	118.31	67.02	117.33	108.39	75.68	47.79
1992	284.60	198.00	179.60	98.90	67.80	93.85	116.73	58.37	131.66	101.41	67.42	30.39
1993	293.40	197.60	182.50	102.90	72.50	95.43	118.74	62.19	143.97	107.47	67.85	41.62
1994	282.90	198.10	166.70	98.90	62.90	84.39	108.47	57.29	147.62	101.50	58.12	40.00
1995	284.30	194.80	163.90	98.80	66.70	68.22	106.68	59.98	163.45	107.74	58.56	43.04
1996	280.20	220.90	158.10	117.20	84.60	58.18	103.09	72.39	177.58	118.49	72.41	69.97
1997	279.53	231.54	-----	-----	-----	64.30	103.26	70.87	178.99	108.06	62.75	71.41
1998[1]	277.12	239.18	-----	-----	-----	61.33	99.82	52.80	156.75	99.75	44.75	51.94
1999[2]	286.49	241.02	-----	-----	-----	66.52	111.06	53.42	170.29	100.47	45.28	57.11

[1] Preliminary. [2] Estimate. [3] Sold as retail cuts (ham, bacon, loin, etc.). [4] Quantity equivalent to 1 pound of retail cuts. [5] Portion of gross farm value minus farm by-product allowance. [6] Prior to 1995, 17-20 pounds. *Source: Economic Research Service, U.S. Department of Agriculture (ERS-USDA)*

Average Wholesale Price of Boxed Beef Cut-Out[1], Choice, at Central Markets In Cents Per Pound

Year	Jan.	Feb.	Mar.	Apr.	May	June	July	Aug.	Sept.	Oct.	Nov.	Dec.	Average
1990	121.75	120.97	122.10	123.62	124.56	121.53	118.54	121.52	121.18	124.96	128.32	129.48	123.21
1991	125.04	123.24	125.45	125.96	123.76	120.61	115.82	111.54	110.61	113.04	113.43	111.18	118.31
1992	114.38	119.65	119.14	118.66	119.18	117.53	112.79	114.36	114.40	115.51	115.26	119.95	116.73
1993	122.69	122.13	124.80	126.12	127.19	120.52	114.48	116.73	114.65	111.52	113.26	110.83	118.74
1994	112.11	112.23	115.03	114.98	108.85	102.92	104.19	108.38	105.49	103.63	106.66	107.22	108.47
1995	112.17	111.12	107.87	103.03	104.21	107.65	103.03	102.55	105.82	107.77	108.88	106.08	106.68
1996	101.71	98.86	96.36	96.01	96.90	100.70	101.53	104.43	105.93	109.10	117.53	108.03	103.09
1997	101.90	98.98	104.87	104.17	105.97	101.83	102.38	105.14	104.06	103.72	104.63	101.50	103.26
1998	100.26	96.27	95.34	98.32	102.09	100.38	99.96	104.28	99.28	102.08	102.61	97.49	99.86
1999[2]	101.37	99.37	103.62	107.55	110.89	115.39	111.14	114.00	115.13	119.21	117.25	117.75	111.06

[1] Choice 1-3, 550-700 pounds. [2] Preliminary. *Source: Economic Research Service, U.S. Department of Agriculture (ERS-USDA)*

Production (Commercial) of All Red Meats in the United States In Millions of Pounds (Carcass Weight)

Year	Jan.	Feb.	Mar.	Apr.	May	June	July	Aug.	Sept.	Oct.	Nov.	Dec.	Total
1990	3,354	2,972	3,259	3,049	3,320	3,175	3,100	3,431	3,096	3,499	3,273	3,080	38,608
1991	3,430	2,954	3,081	3,285	3,291	3,059	3,253	3,425	3,308	3,708	3,324	3,284	39,402
1992	3,623	3,090	3,376	3,259	3,237	3,423	3,441	3,406	3,560	3,656	3,289	3,434	40,794
1993	3,304	3,012	3,396	3,299	3,212	3,481	3,342	3,504	3,516	3,499	3,449	3,554	40,568
1994	3,366	3,126	3,591	3,382	3,431	3,615	3,361	3,756	3,720	3,795	3,666	3,714	42,523
1995	3,560	3,210	3,751	3,304	3,758	3,798	3,424	3,860	3,697	3,795	3,748	3,553	43,458
1996	3,823	3,519	3,512	3,690	3,767	3,439	3,585	3,707	3,396	3,827	3,435	3,432	43,132
1997	3,735	3,278	3,444	3,592	3,571	3,492	3,657	3,619	3,665	4,005	3,453	3,715	43,226
1998	3,836	3,476	3,726	3,701	3,582	3,732	3,781	3,770	3,827	4,033	3,725	3,945	45,134
1999[1]	3,833	3,535	4,016	3,824	3,604	3,940	3,781	3,913	3,933	4,002	3,895	3,944	46,220

[1] Preliminary. *Source: Economic Research Service, U.S. Department of Agriculture (ERS-USDA)*

Cold Storage Holdings of All[1] Meats in the United States, at End of Month In Millions of Pounds

Year	Jan.	Feb.	Mar.	Apr.	May	June	July	Aug.	Sept.	Oct.	Nov.	Dec.
1990	564.7	609.6	637.5	653.0	632.8	591.6	565.9	507.4	507.5	536.7	536.7	536.4
1991	566.2	588.6	606.2	597.7	640.1	614.1	589.7	593.2	592.8	594.7	650.2	644.9
1992	707.9	690.5	725.4	706.8	692.2	665.3	646.0	595.6	613.4	637.8	626.6	615.1
1993	649.4	654.6	652.9	692.0	671.0	660.8	664.2	650.7	671.7	702.4	720.3	726.7
1994	807.7	800.5	842.5	858.0	837.5	822.6	816.2	771.9	788.5	822.7	827.5	802.0
1995	838.7	833.8	834.0	852.7	831.2	820.8	803.6	733.4	711.3	732.3	757.0	749.7
1996	779.5	781.6	729.3	748.6	716.2	687.9	642.7	657.4	678.4	655.5	627.1	621.3
1997	655.9	669.9	719.5	752.5	719.7	742.9	726.3	731.5	728.2	739.1	741.0	722.4
1998	802.8	825.8	816.3	849.3	814.3	771.0	747.2	728.2	738.8	794.9	794.1	821.0
1999[2]	833.0	863.1	883.5	936.4	901.2	843.9	810.4	834.9	746.3	780.3	750.5	748.3

[1] Includes beef and veal, mutton and lamb, pork and products, rendered pork fat, and miscellaneous meats. Excludes lard. [2] Preliminary.
Source: Economic Research Service, U.S. Department of Agriculture (ERS-USDA)

Cold Storage Holdings of Frozen Beef in the United States, on First of Month In Millions of Pounds

Year	Jan. 1	Feb. 1	Mar. 1	Apr. 1	May 1	June 1	July 1	Aug. 1	Sept. 1	Oct. 1	Nov. 1	Dec. 1
1990	251.7	259.8	267.6	304.3	293.3	270.4	256.5	265.4	240.5	243.0	267.4	277.2
1991	300.4	298.9	271.3	276.9	265.6	234.7	247.1	273.2	259.4	276.7	298.2	306.3
1992	315.9	329.1	298.9	313.7	302.1	303.5	299.4	294.1	288.9	275.2	291.2	275.9
1993	272.8	286.4	279.9	293.9	276.7	262.1	271.7	285.3	307.5	326.8	344.4	376.3
1994	401.0	430.2	414.4	423.2	399.5	367.9	379.4	388.9	377.2	406.8	410.6	419.5
1995	411.2	420.3	407.7	385.4	392.2	359.1	352.3	359.3	344.9	347.7	381.6	381.4
1996	389.6	367.9	362.6	347.3	335.6	307.4	306.7	291.1	305.2	312.2	295.9	288.1
1997	284.9	290.3	260.8	290.4	285.4	278.7	305.6	302.8	324.6	349.1	351.6	378.2
1998	350.2	331.1	331.0	330.0	335.5	310.2	316.5	303.0	306.7	323.1	358.2	328.3
1999[1]	296.4	301.3	300.3	309.4	317.0	306.7	292.8	292.3	377.9	294.4	322.5	301.7

[1] Preliminary. *Source: Economic Research Service, U.S. Department of Agriculture (ERS-USDA)*

Mercury

As has been the case since late 1990, nearly all U.S. mercury production in 1998 was of secondary origin, derived from recycled mercury containing devices. No domestic mine produced mercury as its primary product. Strict U.S. and foreign environmental policies, and the advancement of new technology continue to adversely affect both primary and secondary mercury production and usage, and the restrictions are expected to tighten further. Both U.S. primary mercury production and usage have declined since the early 1970's. The trend of the past several years has been to substitute for mercury rather than develop large-scale recycling programs. And, on a global basis, secondary mercury now accounts for a large part of supply.

Mercury is the only common metal that is liquid at room temperatures. It is also highly toxic, and in some respects a greater contaminant than lead because mercury can exist in vapor form. Ironically, despite the global efforts to confine mercury, it is now believed that airborne mercury (called methylmercury and formed from the mercury discharged into the air from industrial plants) is as much as three to six times greater than it was in pre-industrial times. In the U.S., prime virgin mercury is produced as a by-product of gold mining operations from fewer than ten mines in California, Nevada and Utah. The recovery is required to prevent environmental contamination.

World production of mercury is limited to four main countries and a half dozen marginal producers. World production in 1998 of 2,320 metric tonnes compares with 2470 tonnes in 1997. (One ton equals 29+ flasks of 76 pounds each.) Kyrgyzstan's 1998 production of 620 tonnes compares with 610 tonnes in 1997, most of which was exported to China. Algeria produced 370 tonnes in both 1998 and 1997. World mercury resources are estimated at nearly 600,000 tonnes which is viewed as sufficient to last at least a century or more, based on declining usage rates.

Mercury is a recoverable metal. U.S. secondary production totaled 400 tonnes in 1998 vs. 389 tonnes in 1997. E.P.A. restrictions banning landfill disposal and/or transport of mercury-containing wastes has encouraged more efficient recovery methods, especially from fluorescent lamps. The U.S. government has a mercury stockpile of about 4435 tonnes, authorized for disposal but with tight restrictions as to how much, if any, can be sold each year. Reportedly, the goal is to reduce the inventory to zero, but the timeframe is uncertain.

U.S. industrial consumption of refined mercury totaled 400 tonnes in 1998 vs. 346 tonnes in 1997. In the mid-1980's, battery production alone consumed 30,000 tonnes. Chlorine and caustic soda manufacture is now the largest domestic use for mercury. Substitutes for mercury include lithium and composite ceramic materials.

U.S. foreign trade in mercury is small. Imports of 200 tonnes in 1998 compare with 164 tonnes in 1997 while exports were 150 tonnes and 134 tonnes, respectively.

Mercury is usually sold in 34.5 kilogram flasks. The average free market price in 1998 of $139.84/flask compares with $159.52 in 1997.

World Mine Production of Mercury In Metric Tons (1 tonne = 29.008216 flasks)

Year	Algeria	China	Finland	Kyrgyz-stan[3]	Mexico	Spain	Tajik-istan[3]	Turkey	Ukraine[3]	United States	World Total
1990	637	1,000	141	-----	735	425	-----	60	800	562	4,100
1991	431	760	74	-----	340	100	-----	25	750	58	2,540
1992	476	580	75	350	21	36	100	5	100	64	1,960
1993	459	520	98	1,000	12	64	80	-----	50	W	2,390
1994	414	470	83	379	12	393	55	-----	50	W	1,960
1995	292	780	90	380	15	1,497	50	-----	40	W	3,250
1996	368	510	88	584	15	862	45	-----	30	W	2,580
1997[1]	370	830	90	610	15	413	40	-----	25	W	2,470
1998[2]	370	600	80	620	15	500	35	-----	20	W	2,320

[1] Preliminary. [2] Estimate. [3] Formerly part of the U.S.S.R.; data not reported separately until 1992. W = Withheld to avoid disclosing company proprietary data. *Source: U.S. Geological Survey (USGS)*

Salient Statistics of Mercury in the United States In Metric Tons

Year	Priducing Mines	Secondary Production: Industrial	Secondary Production: Govern-ment[3]	Secondary Production: NDS[4] Shipments	Consumer & Dealer Stocks, Dec. 31	Industrial Demand	Exports	Imports
1990	9	108	193	52	197	720	311	15
1991	8	165	215	103	313	554	786	56
1992	9	176	103	267	436	621	977	92
1993	9	350	-----	543	384	558	389	40
1994	7	466	-----	86	469	483	316	129
1995	8	534	-----	-----	321	436	179	377
1996	6	446	-----	-----	446	372	45	340
1997[1]	5	389	-----	-----	203	346	134	164
1998[2]	NA	NA	-----	-----	NA	NA	63	128

[1] Preliminary. [2] Estimate. [3] Secondary mercury shipped from the Department of Energy. [4] National Defense Stockpile. NA = Not available.
Source: U.S. Geological Survey (USGS)

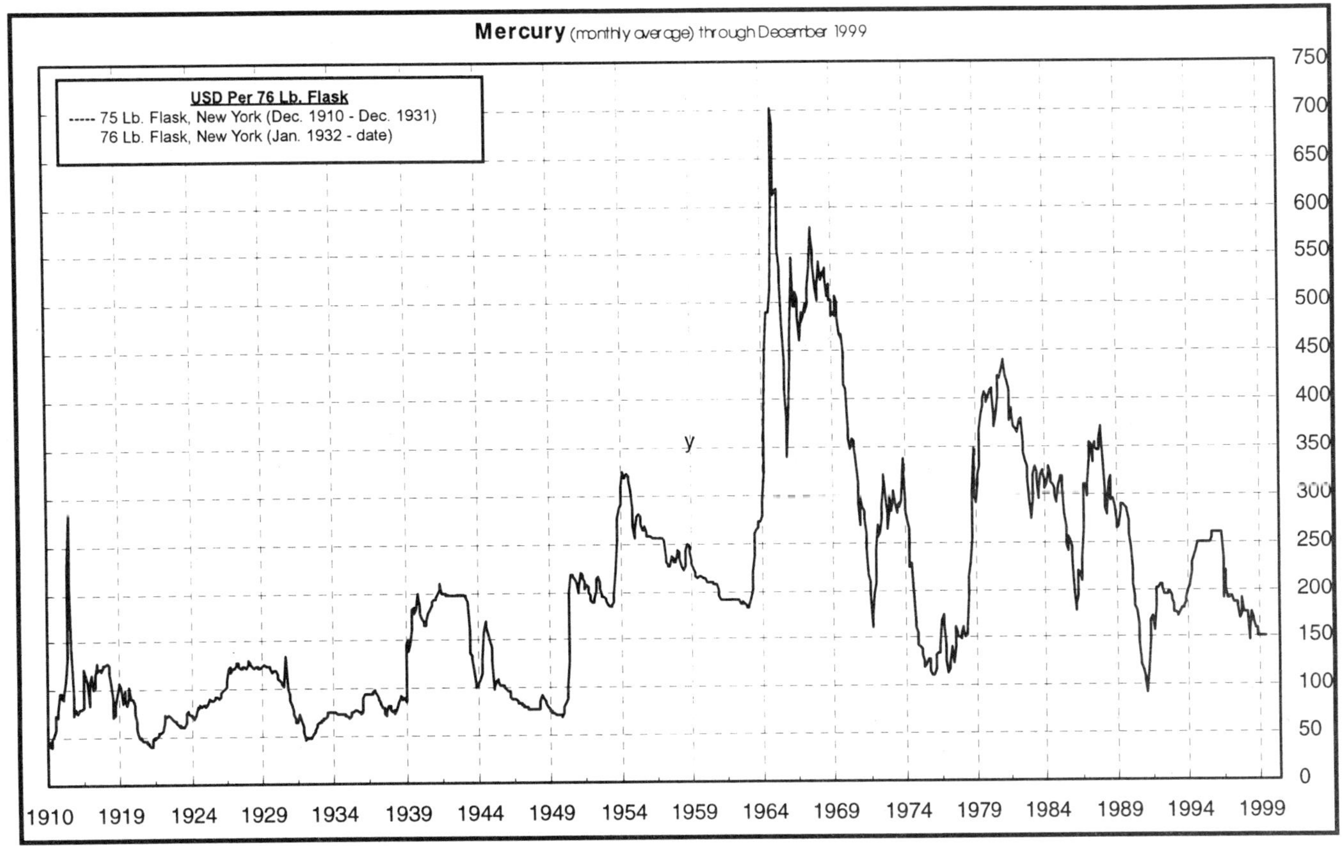

Average Price of Mercury in New York In Dollars Per Flask of 76 Pounds (34.5 Kilograms)

Year	Jan.	Feb.	Mar.	Apr.	May	June	July	Aug.	Sept.	Oct.	Nov.	Dec.	Average
1990	292.50	292.50	287.84	285.00	285.00	285.00	281.45	262.50	259.34	235.54	198.75	182.50	262.33
1991	181.55	169.08	150.36	140.68	129.77	119.75	110.36	102.50	98.00	94.02	127.50	150.12	131.14
1992	162.86	177.24	180.00	180.00	190.63	202.50	202.50	203.45	207.50	207.50	207.50	207.50	194.10
1993	207.50	207.50	207.50	207.50	207.50	201.30	191.00	191.00	185.00	185.00	181.00	175.00	195.57
1994	175.00	175.00	179.78	180.00	180.95	186.64	196.50	200.00	203.10	205.00	217.50	230.71	194.18
1995	235.00	240.00	241.30	250.00	250.00	250.00	250.00	250.00	250.00	250.00	250.00	250.00	247.19
1996	250.00	250.00	261.67	268.33	265.00	265.00	265.00	265.00	265.00	265.00	262.63	235.48	259.84
1997	233.98	232.76	228.88	228.64	220.00	199.05	200.00	198.10	190.83	198.83	191.47	187.00	209.13
1998	187.00	187.00	187.00	187.00	187.00	181.55	175.00	175.00	175.00	175.00	175.00	175.00	180.55
1999	175.00	152.63	150.00	150.00	150.00	150.00	150.00	150.00	150.00	150.00	150.00	150.00	152.30

Source: American Metal Market (AMM)

Mercury Consumed in the United States In Metric Tons

Year	Batteries[3]	Chlorine & Caustic Soda	Catalysts, Misc.	Dental Equip.	Electrical Lighting[3]	General Lab Use	Measuring Contraol Instrument	Paints	Wiring Devices & Switches[3]	Other Uses	Total
1988	448	354	86	53	31	26	77	197	176	55	1,503
1989	250	379	40	39	31	18	87	192	141	32	1,212
1990	106	247	29	44	33	32	108	14	70	38	720
1991	18	184	26	41	39	30	90	6	71	49	554
1992	13	209	20	42	55	28	80	-----	82	92	621
1993	10	180	18	35	38	26	65	-----	83	103	558
1994	6	135	25	24	27	24	53	-----	79	110	483
1995	-----	154	-----	32	30	-----	43	-----	84	93	436
1996[1]	-----	136	-----	31	29	-----	41	-----	49	86	372
1997[2]	-----	160	-----	40	29	-----	24	-----	57	36	346

[1] Preliminary. [2] Estimate. W = Withheld proprietary data. *Source: U.S. Geological Survey (USGS)*

Milk

U.S. production in 1999 of a record high 73.5 million metric tonnes compares with 70.9 million in 1998, the world's largest production. The U.S. 1999 milk-cow inventory at 9.1 million head was marginally lower than 1998. Despite the milk-cow inventory decline production rose because of an increase in milk-per-cow production. Estimates for 2000 suggest a further gain in milk production as favorable milk-feed price relationships sustain the expansion pattern that began in late 1998. The annual average of milk-cows in the twenty key producing states in 1999 of 7,745,000 head compares with 7,708,000 in 1998, and nearly 7.9 million in the mid-1990's.

As of the summer of 1998, U.S. Basic Formula Price (BFP) milk price was averaging about $15.00 per cwt. vs. the 1998 average of $14.20. The wholesale all-milk average price in 1998 of $15.43 per cwt. compares with $13.34 in 1997. Retail prices generally show more variance than wholesale values largely due to differences in transportation and marketing costs. The retail fluid milk price index for 1998 was at 101.3 (December '97=100) and averaged about 103 by late summer 1999.

Politics is deeply involved with U.S. milk prices. At issue most of the time is a convoluted Federal milk-pricing system devised in 1937 to insure that fresh milk was available in all parts of the country, with the minimum price that farmers can charge for milk fixed monthly by the U.S.D.A. In 1937 the country was divided into 31 regions with the set price higher the farther the regions are from Wisconsin, effectively making retail prices in the East higher than in the Midwest. Dairy technology and improved refrigeration have made the old system obsolete, but serious attempts to change the law have generally failed. However, in 1996 the Secretary of Agricultural received some powers to develop a more market-oriented system by 1999; yet at yearend very little progress in changing the pricing method had taken root.

The milk industry continues to aggressively advertise milk as a beverage in an effort to bolster U.S. fluid milk consumption which has been largely static for some time. U.S. fluid milk usage in 1999 of 26.8 million tonnes is about unchanged from 1996. It is believed that more than half of U.S. adults over age 35 have eliminated milk from their diets. Moreover, consumer milk patterns have changed with plain whole milk sales slipping in the 1990's, while over the same period low-fat and skim milk sales increased. About 87 percent of domestic milk output is produced in 22 states, led by California and Wisconsin. Seasonally, milk production is highest during the April-June quarter, during which 42 billion pounds were produced in 1999 vs. 40.8 billion a year earlier.

The world's 1999 milk production of almost 387 million metric tonnes compares with 384 million in 1998. Russia is the second largest producer with less than half of the U.S. output, but the country's production of 31 million tonnes compares with nearly 43 million in 1995. In Europe, France and Germany each produce about 26 million tonnes. The world's milk-cow inventory of 128 million head in 1999 compares with almost 130 million in 1998.

Futures Markets

BFP milk, nonfat dry milk and raw milk futures and options are traded on the CSCE division of the New York Board of Trade (NYBOT). Fluid milk futures and options are traded on the Chicago Mercantile Exchange (CME).

World Fluid Milk Production (Cow's Milk) In Thousands of Metric Tons

Year	Brazil	France	Germany	India	Italy	Netherlands	New Zealand	Poland	Russia	Ukraine	United Kingdom	United States	World Total
1993	16,250	25,049	28,080	30,600	10,400	10,953	8,735	12,650	46,300	18,377	14,645	68,303	377,633
1994	16,700	25,322	27,866	31,000	10,365	10,964	9,719	11,822	42,800	18,138	14,920	69,701	378,408
1995	18,375	25,413	28,621	32,500	10,500	11,294	9,684	11,420	39,300	17,181	14,700	70,440	380,729
1996	19,480	25,083	28,776	33,500	10,800	11,013	10,405	11,690	35,800	16,000	14,640	69,857	379,843
1997	20,600	24,893	28,702	34,500	10,818	10,922	11,500	11,980	34,100	13,650	14,857	70,802	380,786
1998	21,630	24,793	28,500	35,500	10,736	11,000	11,640	12,500	33,000	13,800	14,446	71,415	383,685
1999[1]	22,062	24,700	28,300	36,000	10,870	11,000	11,070	11,880	31,500	12,500	14,400	73,550	384,935
2000[2]	22,500	24,500	28,300	36,500	10,870	10,500	12,020	12,500	30,700	11,600	14,350	74,550	387,240

[1] Preliminary. [2] Forecast. *Source: Foreign Agricultural Service, U.S. Department of Agriculture (FAS-USDA)*

Milk-Feed Price Ratio[1] in the United States In Pounds

Year	Jan.	Feb.	Mar.	Apr.	May	June	July	Aug.	Sept.	Oct.	Nov.	Dec.	Average
1992	3.04	2.86	2.77	2.79	2.68	2.81	3.06	3.20	3.22	3.23	3.23	3.13	3.00
1993	2.96	2.87	2.77	2.79	2.81	2.91	2.78	2.70	2.80	2.79	2.77	2.65	2.80
1994	2.62	2.51	2.51	2.50	2.36	2.44	2.61	2.74	2.81	2.92	2.96	2.81	2.65
1995	2.73	2.75	2.73	2.60	2.53	2.46	2.39	2.50	2.55	2.60	2.69	2.55	2.59
1996	2.57	2.44	2.30	2.16	2.07	2.18	2.21	2.30	2.65	2.94	2.85	2.70	2.45
1997	2.42	2.36	2.26	2.16	2.16	2.11	2.25	2.35	2.44	2.63	2.73	2.80	2.39
1998	2.77	2.75	2.73	2.70	2.71	2.89	3.00	3.61	4.02	4.20	4.23	4.32	3.33
1999[2]	4.09	3.70	3.59	2.97	2.92	3.17	3.58	3.87	4.17	4.06	3.84	3.25	3.60

[1] Pounds of 16% protein mixed dairy feed equal in value to one pound of whole milk. [2] Preliminary. *Source: Economic Research Service, U.S. Department of Agriculture (ERS-USDA)*

Salient Statistics of Milk in the United States In Millions of Pounds

Year	Number of Milk Cows on Farms[3] (Thousands)	Supply: Production: Per Cow[4] (Pounds)	Supply: Production: Total[4]	Supply: Beginning Stocks[5]	Supply: Imports	Supply: Total Supply	Utilization: Exports[5]	Utilization: Domestic: Fed to Calves	Utilization: Domestic: Humans	Utilization: Total Use	Average Farm Price Received Per Cwt.: All Milk, Wholesale	Average Farm Price Received Per Cwt.: Milk Eligible for Fluid Market	Average Farm Price Received Per Cwt.: Milk, Manufacturing Grade	Per Capita Consumption[6] (Fluid Milk in Lbs.)
1992	9,688	15,570	150,582	15,840	2,520	169,246	7,569	1,436	144,519	155,032	13.15	13.19	11.91	231
1993	9,581	15,722	150,636	14,214	2,806	167,602	7,894	1,408	148,178	158,032	12.84	12.88	11.80	226
1994	9,494	16,179	153,602	9,570	2,880	166,072	5,555	1,305	152,791	160,312	13.01	13.02	11.85	226
1995	9,466	16,405	155,292	5,760	2,936	163,988		1,230			12.74	12.78	11.78	223
1996	9,372	16,433	154,006	4,168	2,911	161,085		1,190			14.88	14.95	13.38	224
1997[1]	9,252	16,871	156,091	4,714	2,697	163,502		1,166			13.34	13.38	12.18	221
1998[2]	9,158	17,191	157,441	5,274	4,736	167,451					14.37	14.41	12.76	222

[1] Preliminary. [2] Estimate. [3] Average number on farms during year including dry cows, excluding heifers not yet fresh. [4] Excludes milk sucked by calves. [5] Government and commercial. [6] Product pounds of commercial sales and on farm consumption. *Source: Economic Research Service, U.S. Department of Agriculture (ERS-USDA)*

Utilization of Milk in the United States In Millions of Pounds (Milk Equivalent)

Year	Butter from Whey Cream	Creamery Butter[2]	Cheese[3]	Cottage Cheese (Creamed)	Canned Milk[4]	Bulk Condensed Whole Milk: Unsweetened	Bulk Condensed Whole Milk: Sweetened	Dry Whole Milk Products	Ice Cream[5]	Other Frozen Dairy Products	Other Manufactured Products[6]	Used on Farms: Farm-Churned Butter	Used on Farms: Total
1992	4,150	30,478	49,458	592	1,872	417	301	1,227	2,367	11,825	188	455	1,892
1993	4,500	29,493	49,871	557	1,178	244	324	1,130	1,995	12,063	199	428	1,836
1994	4,592	29,127	51,143	524	1,184	205	277	1,227	2,083	13,182	216	394	1,700
1995	4,735	28,388	52,589	494	1,049	203	254	1,262	2,053	13,041	252	346	1,576
1996	4,911	26,187	53,937	461	1,013	242	266	983	2,058	13,190	217	301	1,489
1997[1]	4,939	25,714	35,000	NA	1,208	227	276	898	2,116	13,740	686	263	1,429

[1] Preliminary. [2] Excludes whey butter. [3] American and other. [4] Includes evaporated and sweetened condensed. [5] Milk equivalent of butter and condensed milk used in ice cream. [6] Whole milk equivalent of dry cream, malted milk powder, part-skim milk, dry or concentrated ice cream mix, dehydrated butterfat and other miscellaneous products using milkfat. *Source: National Agricultural Statistics Service, U.S. Department of Agriculture (NASS-USDA)*

Milk Production[1] in the United States In Millions of Pounds

Year	Jan.	Feb.	Mar.	Apr.	May	June	July	Aug.	Sept.	Oct.	Nov.	Dec.	Total
1993	10,728	9,908	11,060	10,927	11,410	12,957	12,894	12,492	11,978	12,272	11,872	12,427	150,582
1994	12,721	11,662	13,209	13,118	13,719	13,079	13,020	12,837	12,360	12,732	12,330	12,871	153,664
1995	13,147	12,142	13,640	13,343	13,875	13,302	13,152	12,793	12,381	12,716	12,297	12,804	155,423
1996	13,085	12,431	13,537	13,230	13,576	12,832	12,809	12,624	12,241	12,714	12,324	12,928	154,331
1997	13,126	12,141	13,694	13,406	13,902	13,375	13,319	13,059	12,427	12,814	12,362	12,977	156,602
1998	13,282	12,188	13,694	13,510	14,015	13,296	13,162	12,942	12,415	12,956	12,611	13,370	157,441
1999[2]	13,628	12,607	14,270	13,938	14,458	13,633	13,444	13,357	12,970	13,412	13,140	13,854	162,711

[1] Excludes milk sucked by calves. [2] Preliminary. *Source: Economic Research Service, U.S. Department of Agriculture (ERS-USDA)*

Average Price Received by U.S. Farmers for All Milk (Sold to Plants) In Dollars Per Hundred Pounds (Cwt.)

Year	Jan.	Feb.	Mar.	Apr.	May	June	July	Aug.	Sept.	Oct.	Nov.	Dec.	Average
1993	12.50	12.20	12.20	12.60	12.00	13.00	12.80	12.40	12.80	13.10	13.60	13.50	12.80
1994	13.60	13.40	13.50	13.40	12.80	12.60	12.20	12.40	12.80	13.00	13.10	12.80	12.97
1995	12.60	12.60	12.70	12.30	12.30	12.10	12.00	12.40	12.80	13.40	14.00	13.90	12.76
1996	14.00	13.80	13.70	13.90	14.30	14.80	15.40	15.90	16.50	16.40	15.20	14.30	14.85
1997	13.40	13.50	13.50	13.20	12.70	12.20	12.10	12.70	13.10	14.10	14.70	14.80	13.33
1998	14.70	14.70	14.40	14.00	13.30	14.10	14.20	15.50	16.70	17.70	17.80	18.00	15.43
1999[1]	17.40	15.50	15.00	12.60	12.80	13.10	13.70	15.00	15.80	15.00	14.30	12.20	14.37

[1] Preliminary. *Source: Economic Research Service, U.S. Department of Agriculture (ERS-USDA)*

Average Farm Price of Milk Eligible for Fluid Market In Dollars Per Hundred Pounds (Cwt.)

Year	Jan.	Feb.	Mar.	Apr.	May	June	July	Aug.	Sept.	Oct.	Nov.	Dec.	Average
1993	12.60	12.30	12.20	12.70	13.00	13.10	12.80	12.50	12.80	13.10	13.60	13.60	12.86
1994	13.60	13.50	13.50	13.50	12.90	12.70	12.20	12.50	12.80	13.10	13.10	12.90	13.03
1995	12.70	12.60	12.60	12.30	12.30	12.20	12.10	12.50	12.80	13.40	14.00	14.00	12.79
1996	14.00	13.90	13.70	13.90	14.30	14.90	15.50	16.00	16.60	16.40	15.30	14.40	14.91
1997	13.40	13.50	13.60	13.20	12.80	12.30	12.20	12.80	13.10	14.10	14.70	14.80	13.38
1998	14.70	14.80	14.50	14.00	13.30	14.10	14.20	15.50	16.80	17.80	17.80	18.10	15.47
1999[1]	17.50	15.60	15.10	12.60	12.80	13.10	13.80	15.00	15.80	15.00	14.40	12.20	14.41

[1] Preliminary. *Source: Economic Research Service, U.S. Department of Agriculture (ERS-USDA)*

Molasses

Molasses is a heavy, viscous fluid produced as a by-product of raw sugar refining. About 50 gallons of molasses are produced for each ton of raw sugar refined. Molasses contains 33 percent sucrose. U.S. supplies of molasses are about three million metric tonnes per year. Of this total, a third comes from mainland sugar mills, a quarter from beet sugar refiners and smaller amounts from Hawaiian cane and cane refiners. Beet molasses is used primarily as a livestock feed and a yeast by the pharmaceutical industry.

To a large extent, production of molasses is related to the refinement of sugar. Some countries produce and export raw sugar, while others produce and refine sugar leading to a production of molasses. An example is Thailand which produces both raw and white sugars for export.

The world sugar market in 1999/2000 is characterized by a surplus of sugar. Production continues to exceed consumption leading to an increased availability of molasses. The world's largest sugar producers are Brazil, India, the European Union, China, Thailand, Australia and Cuba. In December 1999, the U.S.D.A. forecast U.S. sugar production at 8.75 million short tons, up 4 percent from the 1998-99 season.

As of late December 1999, U.S. prices for sugarcane molasses were steady. Large quantities of domestic molasses continued to pressure the market. In addition to large supplies of molasses, supplies of other feed ingredients were large keeping pressure on prices. One area of improvement has been in Asia where demand had lagged because of the economic downturn. That situation appears to be improving.

In late December 1999, cane blackstrap molasses in New Orleans was priced at $32.50-$35.00 per short ton compared to $37.50 a year ago. Cane blackstrap molasses in Houston, Texas was priced at $37.50 per ton, while the price in Savannah, Georgia was $57.00. In Stockton, California molasses was priced at $60.00 per ton.

World Production of Sugarcane, by Selected Countries In Thousands of Metric Tons

Crop Year	Australia	Brazil	China	Cuba	India	Indonesia	Mexico	Pakistan	Philippines	South Africa	Thailand	United States	World Total
1990-1	25,140	75,000	57,620	67,500	135,494	28,074	36,000	22,604	18,600	18,083	40,563	24,018	707,497
1991-2	21,306	87,000	67,898	62,000	148,814	28,100	35,300	24,796	22,816	20,078	47,505	26,272	753,303
1992-3	29,400	90,000	73,011	47,150	123,985	32,000	39,700	27,276	23,850	12,955	34,711	26,264	719,671
1993-4	31,951	91,000	63,549	46,000	116,638	33,000	34,100	34,182	22,753	11,244	37,569	26,680	706,433
1994-5	34,860	110,000	60,300	39,000	159,593	30,545	40,134	34,193	18,415	15,683	50,459	25,485	783,373
1995-6	37,378	93,000	65,417	45,500	184,708	30,000	42,300	28,151	22,774	16,750	57,693	25,835	842,937
1996-7[1]	39,878	101,000	68,500	45,000	147,858	28,600	42,000	25,580	23,500	22,512	59,000	24,055	845,645
1997-8[2]	40,878	105,000	69,400	45,500	137,184	29,000		31,600			60,000		

[1] Preliminary. [2] Estimate. *Source: Economic Research Service, U.S. Department of Agriculture (ERS-USDA)*

World Production of Sugarbeet, by Selected Countries In Thousands of Metric Tons

Year	Belgium-Luxembourg	China	France	Germany	Italy	Poland	Russia	Spain	Turkey	Ukraine	United Kingdom	United States	World Total
1990-1	6,857	14,525	25,520	30,366	11,600	16,721	31,091	7,358	13,986	44,265	8,000	24,959	303,149
1991-2	6,043	16,289	24,403	25,926	11,400	11,412	24,280	6,679	15,474	36,168	7,672	25,485	277,368
1992-3	6,174	15,069	26,491	27,177	14,762	11,052	25,548	7,234	15,563	28,783	9,180	26,438	274,751
1993-4	6,120	11,938	25,514	28,606	10,510	15,621	25,468	8,622	15,463	33,717	8,988	23,813	272,746
1994-5	5,729	12,406	23,943	24,211	11,905	11,630	13,945	8,100	12,757	28,138	8,360	29,024	247,798
1995-6	6,291	13,984	25,121	26,049	12,932	13,309	19,110	7,450	10,989	28,000	8,360	25,460	257,984
1996-7[1]	6,100	13,900	24,400	27,000	11,150	17,460	16,500	7,700	14,383	25,500	8,432	24,104	254,335
1997-8[2]	6,000	14,000	24,500	26,500	12,500	14,000	17,000	6,800	15,100	25,400	8,400	26,134	256,393

[1] Preliminary. [2] Estimate. *Source: Economic Research Service, U.S. Department of Agriculture (ERS-USDA)*

U.S. Annual Average Prices of Molasses, by Types (F.O.B. Tank Car or Truck) In Dollars Per Short Ton[2]

	Blackstrap							Beet Molasses	
Year	New Orleans	South Florida	Baltimore	Upper Mississippi	Savannah	California Ports[3]	Houston	Montana, Wyoming & Nebraska	Red River Valley[4]
1992	61.27	68.36	80.41	92.95	76.70	78.43	63.75	67.81	57.50
1993	55.48	62.36	76.03	89.26	70.00	74.24	57.12	72.63	64.44
1994	65.53	72.23	85.94	91.97	79.23	83.31	69.86	-----	-----
1995	72.00	79.92	86.30	99.11	87.48	90.30	76.37	-----	-----
1996	74.88	83.07	91.27	104.71	92.55	97.11	79.41	-----	-----
1997	58.14	68.00	76.84	90.69	77.51	83.38	62.13	-----	-----
1998	46.35	59.92	63.37	78.00	68.75	69.30	48.85	-----	-----
1999[1]	33.77	49.15	51.06	65.50	56.63	58.32	36.30	-----	-----

[1] Preliminary. [2] To convert dollars per short ton to cents per gallon divide by 171. [3] Los Angeles and Stockton. [4] North Dakota and Minnesota.
Source: Agricultural Marketing Service, U.S. Department of Agriculture (AMS-USDA)

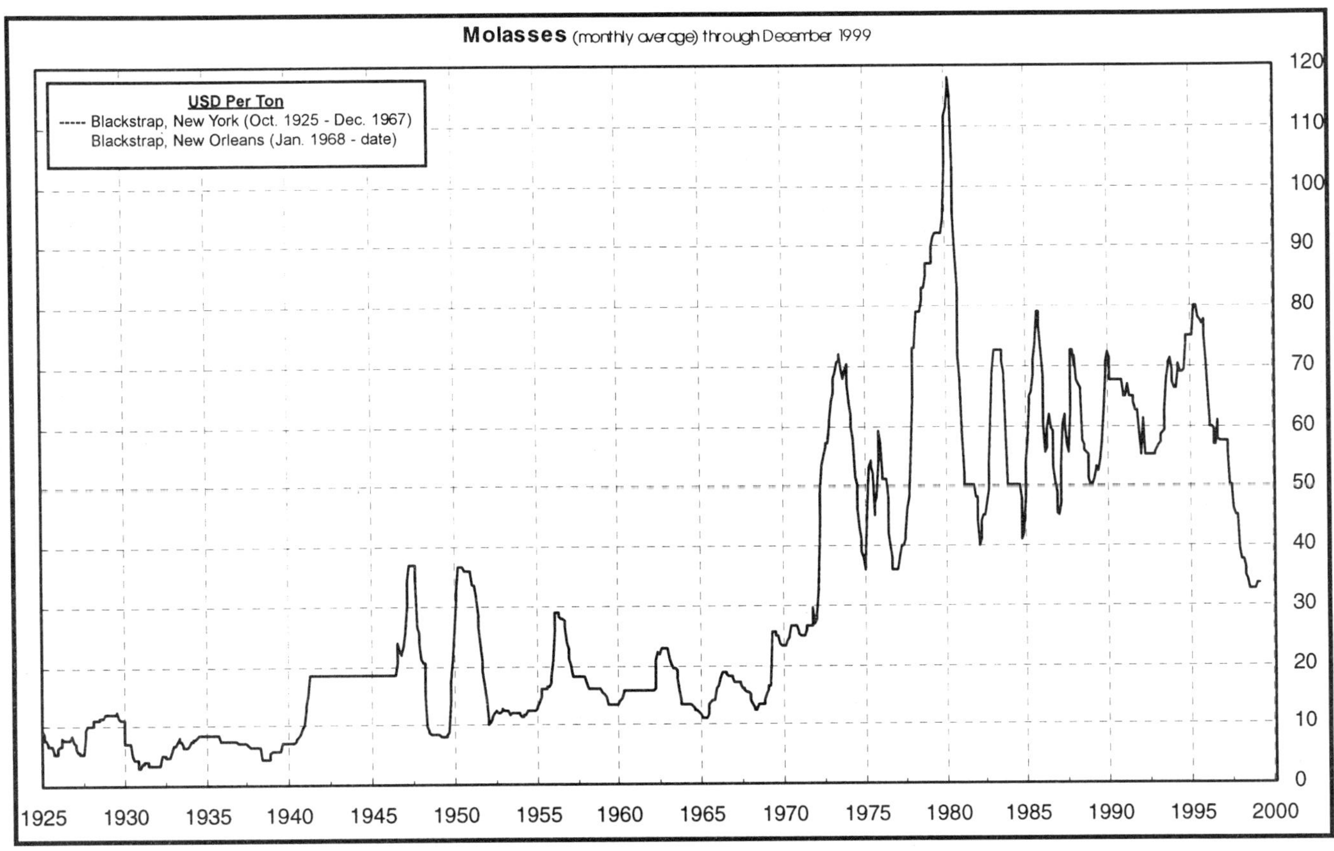

Salient Statistics of Molasses[3] in the United States In Metric Tons

	Production						Inedible Imports From						Production of Edible
		Mainland				In Shipments						Total	Molasses
		Mainland	Refiners Black-		Puerto	From	Total		Dominican		Mainland	U.S.	(1,000
Year	Hawaii	Hills[4]	strap	Beet	Rico	Hawaii	Imports	Brazil	Republic	Mexico	Exports[5]	Supply	Gallons)
1989	218,009	808,355	122,786	974,179	34,864	169,270	926,870	107,109	147,235	75,634	293,535	2,707,925	1,990
1990	228,968	741,749	105,124	948,820	24,959	214,045	1,078,924	70,986	145,543	88,401	212,263	2,876,399	1,405
1991	188,252	807,652	126,000	1,165,962	27,882	184,337	1,258,637	10,342	137,271	235,244	242,635	3,299,953	1,825
1992	182,849	782,566	123,000	950,312	25,097	183,657	1,115,863	0	127,500	117,722	282,098	2,873,300	1,460
1993	187,915	831,661	113,000	692,465	22,802	190,371	1,040,858	0	163,180	47,596	255,907	2,612,448	1,480
1994	180,884	824,453	114,000	1,200,000	18,531	151,172	1,556,640	0	121,320	197,753	277,098	3,459,167	1,500
1995	146,000	886,826	114,000	1,040,000	16,156	146,000	1,048,726	0	132,983	172,177	274,868	2,960,684	1,500
1996[1]	-----	NA	NA	NA	-----	NA	NA	-----	-----	-----	NA	NA	0
1997[2]	-----	900,000	100,000	1,200,000	-----	100,000	1,583,755	-----	-----	-----	300,000	3,583,755	0

[1] Preliminary. [2] Estimate. [3] Feed and industrial molasses. [4] Includes high-test molasses from frozen cane. [5] Excluding exports from Hawaii and Puerto Rico. NA = Not available. *Source: Agricultural Marketing Service, U.S. Department of Agriculture (AMS-USDA)*

Wholesale Price of Blackstrap Molasses (Cane) at New Orleans In Dollars Per Short Ton

Year	Jan.	Feb.	Mar.	Apr.	May	June	July	Aug.	Sept.	Oct.	Nov.	Dec.	Average
1990	52.75	53.13	52.50	54.25	57.19	57.50	62.75	68.75	70.63	72.25	71.25	67.50	61.70
1991	67.50	67.50	67.50	67.50	67.50	67.50	67.50	67.50	65.25	65.00	65.00	65.00	67.02
1992	65.00	65.00	65.00	65.00	63.75	62.50	62.50	62.50	58.75	55.31	55.00	55.00	61.27
1993	55.00	55.00	55.00	55.00	55.00	55.00	55.00	55.25	55.31	56.25	56.75	57.19	55.48
1994	57.75	57.50	59.38	62.50	68.00	70.00	70.63	71.25	69.38	67.50	66.25	66.25	65.53
1995	69.00	70.31	68.75	68.75	68.75	69.38	74.25	75.00	75.00	75.00	75.00	75.00	72.00
1996	80.00	80.00	80.00	78.00	77.50	77.50	77.50	77.50	75.00	70.00	65.63	60.75	74.88
1997	60.00	60.00	59.00	56.56	56.88	60.31	57.50	57.50	57.50	57.50	57.50	57.50	58.14
1998	57.50	55.63	51.00	50.00	50.00	46.00	45.00	45.00	45.00	37.50	37.50	37.50	46.35
1999[1]	37.50	36.25	35.00	34.38	32.50	32.50	32.50	32.50	32.50	32.50	33.75	33.75	33.80

[1] Preliminary. *Source: Agricultural Marketing Service, U.S. Department of Agriculture (AMS-USDA)*

Molybdenum

Molybdenum is a silver-gray metal used principally as an alloying agent in cast irons, steels and superalloys. It is used to enhance strength, toughness and wear resistance. In the form of molybdic acid or ferromolybdenum it is combined with or added to chromium, manganese, nickel, tungsten and other alloy metals. Molybdenum finds significant usage as a refractory metal in chemical applications.

World mine production of molybdenum in 1998 was estimated by the U.S. Geological Survey at 136,000 metric tonnes, down 3 percent from 1997. The major producer of molybdenum was the U.S. with 1998 production estimated at 53,500 tonnes. Other major producers include China, Chile, Russia and Canada. World reserves of molybdenum are estimated at 5.5 million tonnes in the U.S. and 12 million tonnes in the world. Molybdenum occurs both as the principal metal sulfide in large low-grade porphyry molybdenum deposits and as a subsidiary metal sulfide in low-grade porphyry copper deposits.

U.S. production of molybdenum concentrate in the first seven months of 1999 was 28,700 tonnes. For all of 1998, production was 53,500 tonnes. Domestic shipments of molybdenum, including molybdic oxides, metal powder, ammonium molybdate, sodium molybdate and others were 22,600 tonnes in the January-July 1999 period. For all of 1998, domestic shipments were 34,300 tonnes. U.S. reported production of molybdenum products in January-July 1999 was 24,900 tonnes while production for all of 1998 was 57,200 tonnes. U.S. internal consumption of molybdenum products in the first seven months of 1999 was 12,100 tonnes. For all of 1998, consumption was 23,400 tonnes.

U.S. reported consumption in July 1999 of molybdenum steel materials was 796,000 kilograms. Of this total, molybdic oxides comprised 531,000 kilograms while ferromolybdenum was 253,000 kilograms. Consumption of molybdenum superalloys in July 1999 was 182,000 kilograms. Molybdenum mill products made from metal powder saw consumption of 175,000 kilograms while molybdenum catalysts saw consumption of 77,300 kilograms. Consumption of molybdenum lubricants was 25,200 kilograms. Consumer stocks of molybdenum materials on July 31, 1999 were 1.74 million kilograms. Of the total, stocks of molybdic oxides were 571,000 kilograms with ferromolybdenum stocks 329,000 kilograms. Molybdenum scrap stocks were 15,500 kilograms.

U.S. exports of molybdenum ores and concentrates in the first half of 1999 were 13.3 million kilograms. For all of 1998, exports were 42 million kilograms. The major markets for molybdenum ore and concentrates are the Netherlands, Belgium, the United Kingdom, Chile, Canada, Sweden and China.

World Mine Production of Molybdenum In Metric Tons (Contained Molybdenum)

Year	Bulgaria	Canada[3]	Chile	China	Iran	Kazakhstan[4]	Mexico	Mongolia	Peru	Russia[4]	United States	Uzbekisten[4]	World Total
1989	190	14,073	16,550	15,700	785	-----	4,189	1,580	3,177	17,000	63,105	-----	136,494
1990	150	11,994	13,830	15,700	542	-----	2,000	1,578	2,510	17,000	61,611	-----	127,028
1991	120	11,329	14,434	13,200	395	-----	1,716	1,716	3,031	16,000	53,364	-----	115,000
1992	120	9,405	14,500	19,200	1,320	700	1,458	1,610	3,220	10,800	49,700	700	114,000
1993	120	9,700	14,899	18,300	700	600	1,705	2,050	2,980	10,300	36,800	700	99,200
1994	100	10,250	16,028	21,400	670	100	2,610	2,066	2,765	4,000	46,800	500	108,000
1995	400	9,113	17,889	33,000	560	75	3,883	1,822	3,411	3,000	60,900	400	136,000
1996	400	8,789	17,415	29,600	560	100	4,210	2,201	3,711	2,000	54,900	500	126,000
1997[1]	-----	7,612	21,339	33,300	600	100	4,842	1,992	3,835	2,000	60,900	500	139,000
1998[2]	-----	7,991	25,298	30,000	600	100	5,949	2,000	4,344	2,000	53,300	500	135,000

[1] Preliminary. [2] Estimate. [3] Shipments. [4] Formerly part of the U.S.S.R.; data not reported separately until 1992.
Source: U.S. Geological Survey (USGS)

Salient Statistics of Molybdenum in the United States In Metric Tons (Contained Molybdenum)

	Concentrate							Primary Products[4]: Net Production				Primary Products[4]: Shipments			
		Shipments													
Year	Production	Total (Includes Exports)	Value Million $	For Exports	Consumption	Imports For Consumption	Stocks, Dec. 31[3]	Grand Total	Molybolic Oxide[5]	Molybolic Metal Powder	Price Average Value $ / Kg.[6]	To Domestic Destinations	Oxide for Exports (Groos Weight)	Consumption	Producer Stocks, Dec. 31
1989	63,105	61,733	421.4	51,231	41,877	238	6,969	16,545	16,545	W	8.05	18,277	1,391	17,204	6,675
1990	61,611	61,580	346.3	41,380	35,455	478	7,672	15,727	15,727	W	7.39	17,983	787	18,060	5,919
1991	53,364	53,607	249.9	22,424	32,998	161	5,291	20,782	18,739	2,043	5.27	19,105	1,571	16,901	9,422
1992	49,700	43,100	189.9	33,439	15,200	831	11,900	13,880	11,916	1,964	4.85	17,300	557	17,200	7,480
1993	36,800	39,200	165.1	28,280	13,800	3,400	11,200	11,989	10,697	1,292	5.13	16,000	1,042	17,700	6,150
1994	46,800	46,000	284.0	14,568	17,200	2,280	5,510	16,000	14,900	1,070	4.60	21,400	2,240	19,100	3,940
1995	60,900	61,700	651.0	18,600	25,500	5,570	5,390	22,900	20,900	1,970	17.50	24,000	2,840	19,900	4,820
1996	54,900	57,900	456.0	19,700	24,500	5,480	2,470	24,100	20,400	1,970	8.30	24,100	1,790	20,900	5,780
1997[1]	60,900	59,100	406.0	20,000	24,300	6,330	3,660	25,900	22,700	2,000	9.46	25,900	1,240	20,000	6,500
1998[2]	53,300	50,500	200.0		35,900	6,570	6,270	38,000	31,600	2,270	8.50	38,000	1,100	19,000	7,780

[1] Preliminary. [2] Estimate. [3] At mines & at plants making molybdenum products. [4] Comprises ferromolybdenum, molybdic oxide, & molybdenum salts & metal. [5] Includes molybdic oxide briquets, molybdic acid, molybdenum trioxide, all other. [6] U.S. producer price per kilogram of molybdenum oxide contained in technical-grade molybdic oxide. W = Withheld proprietary data. *Source: U.S. Geological Survey (USGS)*

Nickel

Nickel is used in the production of stainless steel and other corrosion-resistant alloys. About a fifth of the nickel produced in the U.S. is used in plating to provide hard, tarnish-resistant, polishable surfaces. Nickel is used in coins to replace silver, in rechargeable batteries and in electronic circuity. Nickel-based alloys are used in wire, bars, sheets and in tubular forms. Elemental nickel is used to make nickel-base corrosion resistant alloys. Nickel plating techniques, like electroless coating or single-slurry coating, are employed in such applications as turbine blades, helicopter rotors, extrusion dies and rolled steel strip.

World mine production of nickel in 1998 was estimated at 1.17 million metric tonnes, a 4 percent increase from 1997. The world's largest producer of nickel was Russia with 1998 mine production of 265,000 tonnes, an increase of 2 percent from the previous year. The next largest producer was Canada with output of 225,000 tonnes, up 17 percent from the previous year. Other large producers include Australia, New Caledonia, Cuba, China and Indonesia. The reserve land base of nickel is estimated at 140 million tonnes. Of the total, about 60 percent is in laterites and 40 percent in sulfide deposits. There are extensive deep-sea resources of nickel also.

U.S. reported consumption of nickel in July 1999 was 9,180 tonnes. In the January-July 1999 period, U.S. consumption of nickel was 63,200 tonnes. This was some 3 percent more than in the same period of 1998. Consumption of nickel cathodes, pellets, briquets and powder in the first seven months of 1999 was 7,550 tonnes. For all of 1998, consumption was 81,400 tonnes. Consumption of ferronickel in January-July 1999 was 1,160 tonnes and for all of 1998 it was 13,700 tonnes.

U.S. ending stocks of nickel at the end of July 1999 were 3,980 tonnes. Stocks of cathodes, pellets, briquets and powder were 3,550 tonnes while stocks of ferronickel were 170 tonnes. Stocks of nickel oxide-sinter, salts and other forms of nickel were 261 tonnes.

U.S. consumption of purchased secondary nickel scrap in January-July 1999 was 35,200 tonnes (nickel content). This was 1 percent less than in 1998. Consumption of ferrous scrap in the first seven months of 1999 was 28,800 tonnes, down 3 percent from the year before. Consumption of nonferrous scrap was 6,470 tonnes, up 10 percent from 1998. For all of 1998, nickel scrap consumption was 56,900 tonnes. U.S. stocks of ferrous scrap in July 1999 were 2,620 tonnes, down 48 percent from the year before. Stocks of nonferrous scrap in July 1999 were 174 tonnes, down 6 percent from the year before. Total U.S. stocks of nickel scrap in July 1999 were down 46 percent from July 1998.

Futures Markets

Nickel is traded on the London Metals Exchange.

World Mine Production of Nickel In Metric Tons (Contained Nickel)

Year	Australia[3]	Botswana	Brazil	Canada	China	Dominican Republic	Greece	Indonesia	New Caledonia	Phillippines	Russia	South Africa	World Total
1989	67,041	23,700	18,826	200,899	34,250	31,264	16,097	62,987	96,200	15,380	280,000	28,900	984,078
1990	67,000	23,200	24,100	196,225	33,000	28,700	18,500	68,308	85,100	15,818	280,000	29,000	974,000
1991	69,000	23,500	26,400	192,259	31,000	29,062	19,300	71,681	114,492	13,658	245,000	27,700	991,000
1992	57,683	23,000	29,372	186,384	32,800	42,641	17,000	77,600	113,000	13,022	280,000	28,400	1,010,000
1993	64,717	23,000	32,154	188,080	30,700	37,423	12,940	65,757	97,092	7,663	244,000	29,868	926,000
1994	78,962	19,041	32,663	149,886	36,900	45,588	18,821	81,175	97,323	9,895	240,000	30,751	929,000
1995	98,467	18,672	25,469	180,984	41,800	44,051	19,947	88,183	121,457	15,075	251,000	29,803	1,030,000
1996	113,134	24,200	25,600	183,059	43,000	45,000	20,000	90,000	142,200	14,700	230,000	33,613	1,080,000
1997[1]	120,000	22,600	27,200	182,000	41,000	47,000	18,000	76,000	157,000	15,000	230,000	31,800	1,080,000
1998[2]	145,000	21,300	31,500	225,000	40,000	32,000	12,900	76,400	137,000	17,000	265,000	34,700	1,170,000

[1] Preliminary. [2] Estimate. [3] Content of nickel sulfate and concentrates. *Source: U.S. Geological Survey (USGS)*

Salient Statistics of Nickel in the United States In Metric Tons (Contained Nickel)

Year	Net Import Reliance as a % of Apparent Consumption	Production: Plant[4]	Production: Secondary[5]	Nickel Consumed[1], By Uses: Alloy Sheets	Cast Irons	Copper Base Alloys	Electroplating Anodes	Nickel Alloys	Stainless & Heat Resisting Steels	Super Alloys	Chemicals	Apparent Consumption	Stocks, Dec. 31: At Consumers' Plants	Stocks, Dec. 31: At Producer Plants	Primary & Secondary Nickel: Exports	Primary & Secondary Nickel: Imports	Avg. Price LME[6] $/Lb.
1989	71	347	52,131	6,094	2,318	9,928	21,604	18,757	68,866	10,956	1,164	157,103	16,562	6,326	31,460	137,017	6.04
1990	69	3,701	57,367	7,007	2,646	7,594	15,550	16,315	96,120	15,713	1,500	170,042	13,971	8,065	37,057	145,600	4.02
1991	67	7,065	53,521	5,536	1,185	6,938	15,474	16,882	84,292	13,787	1,363	156,663	15,940	11,794	36,902	138,210	3.70
1992	59	8,960	55,871	4,988	1,202	6,313	16,538	15,946	83,460	10,872	51	159,373	17,480	10,140	33,860	128,510	3.18
1993	63	4,880	54,702	4,940	805	6,078	16,611	17,004	87,300	10,783	1,170	158,000	14,430	15,700	33,180	132,710	2.40
1994	64	-----	58,590	5,930	499	7,940	15,500	20,500	88,700	11,700	2,670	164,000	11,000	10,200	41,920	133,070	2.88
1995	60	8,290	64,600	9,570	491	8,510	15,600	21,800	103,000	14,100	5,210	181,000	12,300	12,700	51,550	156,930	3.73
1996	59	15,100	59,200	6,240	563	7,300	16,200	19,700	94,000	12,600	5,310	183,000	12,900	11,200	46,700	150,060	3.40
1997[2]	56	16,100		7,500	W	W	14,100	W	42,400	11,700	W		14,200	11,500	56,500	158,000	3.14
1998[3]	65	4,290															

[1] Exclusive of scrap. [2] Preliminary. [3] Estimate. [4] Smelter & refinery. [5] From purchased scrap (ferrous & nonferrous). W = Withheld proprietary data. NA = Not avaliable. *Source: U.S. Geological Survey (USGS)*

Oats

Oat prices, basis Chicago futures, traversed a narrow range beginning in the second half of 1998 and continuing throughout 1999. The sideways pattern generally traded in a range bounded by $1.00 per bushel on the downside and $1.20 per bushel on the upside.

Within both the U.S. and the worldwide feed grain complex oat production is the smallest of all crops. The U.S. 1999/2000 crop (June to May) of a record low 148 million bushels compares with 166 million in 1998/99. The U.S. harvested oat acreage in 1999/00 of 2.5 million acres is the smallest on record. In the 1980's acreage averaged about 12 million acres. Average yield, however, has increased over the years, averaging 63 bushels per acre for the 1999 crop vs. 62 bushels in 1998. The Dakotas are generally the largest producing states with Wisconsin and Minnesota close by. Imports, primarily from Canada, help compliment U.S. supplies and are forecast at 100 million bushels in 1999/00 vs. 108 million in 1998/99.

U.S. oat 1999/00 carry-in stocks, as of June 1, 1999, of 81 million bushels compare with 74 million a year earlier. The total supply for 1999/00 of 329 million bushels compares with 348 million in 1998/99. Disappearance was estimated at 263 million bushels vs. 266 million, respectively. Feed and residual use was forecast at 165 million bushels in 1999/00 vs. 170 million in 1998/99; feed/seed/industrial use was placed at 96 million, about unchanged from 1998/99. U.S. oat exports of about 2 million bushels are insignificant. Carryover stocks on May 31, 2000 are forecast at a near record low 66 million bushels. The average farm price for 1999/00 was forecast at $1.00-1.10 per bushel vs. $1.10 in 1998/99 and $1.96 in 1996/97, the highest farm price of the 1990's.

World oats production in the mid 1980's totaled about 50 million metric tonnes, for 1999/00 the total was less than 25 million as less acreage continues to be allocated to oats. In 1999/00 world acreage of 14.2 million hectares compares with 15.4 million in 1998/99 with an average yield 1.74 tons per hectare vs. 1.67, respectively. Russia is one of the largest producers, but their 1999/00 crop of 4.5 million tonnes compares with 9.4 million in 1997/98. Russian oat production is now only a fraction of what it was in the mid-1980's. Among the few major producers only Canada, the world's largest producer, has shown any real growth in production during the 1990's; a record high 5.9 million tonnes were produced in 1998/99 and 5.3 million in 1999/00.

Most of the world's oat production is consumed domestically and world trade is small. In 1999/00 exports were put at 2.2 million tonnes vs. 2.0 million in 1998/99 with Canada accounting for 1.3 million and 1.1 million, respectively. Importing nations are more numerous, but the U.S. is the consistent leader with a 1.75 million tonne forecast for 1999/00 vs. 1.6 million in 1998/99.

Futures Markets

Oat futures and options are traded on the Chicago Board of trade (CBOT) and the Winnipeg Commodity Exchange (WCE). Oats futures are traded on the Mid-America Commodity Exchange (MidAm).

World Production of Oats In Thousands of Metric Tons

Year	Argentina	Australia	Canada	China	France	Germany	Italy	Poland	Sweden	Turkey	United States	Ex-USSR	World Total
1990-1	434	1,530	2,692	685	830	2,104	298	2,119	1,584	270	5,189	15,081	39,042
1991-2	400	1,690	1,794	650	740	1,867	359	1,873	1,426	280	3,534	12,342	32,785
1992-3	450	1,937	2,823	640	700	1,314	333	1,229	807	280	4,298	13,974	33,587
1993-4	440	1,652	3,550	640	710	1,730	370	1,500	1,295	280	2,994	14,422	35,162
1994-5	350	920	3,640	600	680	1,660	360	1,240	990	300	3,320	13,850	33,160
1995-6	350	1,880	2,860	640	620	1,420	300	1,500	950	280	2,350	10,690	28,830
1996-7	310	1,700	4,360	600	620	1,610	350	1,580	1,200	250	2,250	10,030	30,590
1997-8[1]	510	1,630	3,490	400	560	1,600	310	1,630	1,280	280	2,430	11,230	30,900
1998-9[2]	390	1,880	3,960	650	660	1,280	380	1,460	1,140	310	2,410	6,120	26,050
1999-00[3]	380	1,500	3,640	600	560	1,350	370	1,500	1,200	250	2,120	6,050	24,830

[1] Preliminary. [2] Estimate. [3] Forecast. *Source: Foreign Agricultural Service, U.S. Department of Agriculture (FAS-USDA)*

Official Oats Crop Production Reports in the United States In Thousands of Bushels

Year	July 1	Aug. 1	Sept. 1	Oct. 1	Dec. 1	Final	Year	July 1	Aug. 1	Sept. 1	Oct. 1	Dec. 1	Final
1988	-----	206,330	206,330	210,766	-----	217,375	1994	248,151	247,753	247,753	229,717	-----	229,008
1989	387,593	380,690	380,690	370,693	-----	373,587	1995	181,508	186,167	186,167	-----	-----	162,027
1990	374,457	365,337	365,337	358,288	-----	357,654	1996	154,968	157,663	-----	-----	-----	153,245
1991	280,016	259,666	259,666	242,526	-----	243,851	1997	182,672	187,127	-----	-----	-----	167,246
1992	256,381	276,381	-----	-----	-----	294,229	1998	183,201	177,211	-----	-----	-----	165,981
1993	262,860	249,830	249,830	208,138	-----	206,770	1999	-----	162,096	-----	-----	-----	146,218

Source: National Agricultural Statistics Service, U.S. Department of Agriculture (NASS-USDA)

Oat Stocks in the United States In Thousands of Bushels

	On Farms				Off Farms				Total Stocks			
Year	Mar. 1	June 1	Sept. 1	Dec. 1	Mar. 1	June 1	Sept. 1	Dec. 1	Mar. 1	June 1	Sept. 1	Dec. 1
1990	140,000	82,850	234,700	194,700	74,749	74,062	117,009	99,398	214,749	156,912	351,709	294,098
1991	138,600	92,400	173,600	148,100	90,659	78,831	110,487	96,508	229,259	171,231	284,087	244,608
1992	98,150	61,000	199,900	161,200	76,735	66,721	94,717	81,292	174,885	127,721	294,617	242,492
1993	110,250	66,130	161,000	124,200	64,875	47,063	58,004	69,517	175,125	113,193	219,004	193,717
1994	85,050	53,940	144,300	113,400	61,502	51,583	75,551	78,664	146,552	105,523	219,851	192,064
1995	78,400	46,750	107,200	87,200	70,575	53,848	72,967	65,804	148,975	100,598	180,167	153,004
1996	57,350	32,600	93,400	80,650	55,268	33,708	38,716	45,218	112,618	66,308	132,116	125,868
1997	56,200	33,100	107,950	83,200	39,362	33,576	48,972	61,051	95,562	66,676	156,922	144,251
1998	58,800	34,500	110,300	81,500	52,418	39,498	51,502	61,835	111,218	73,998	161,802	143,335
1999[1]	61,700	40,700	97,300	82,100	50,850	40,678	51,151	53,973	112,550	81,378	148,451	136,073

[1] Preliminary. *Source: National Agricultural Statistics Service, U.S. Department of Agriculture (NASS-USDA)*

Supply and Utilizationof Oats in the United States In Millions of Bushels

Year	Acreage Planted	Acreage Harvested	Yield Per Acre	Production	Imports	Total Supply	Feed & Residual	Food, Alcohol & Industrial	Seed	Exports	Total Use	Ending Stocks	Farm Price	Findley Loan Rate	Target Price
	1,000 acres		(Bushels)	In Millions of Bushels									Dollars Per Bushel		
1990-1	10,423	5,947	60.1	357.7	63.4	578.0	311.7	75.3	19.1	.6	406.7	171.2	1.14	.81	1.45
1991-2	8,653	4,816	50.6	243.9	74.8	489.4	265.8	76.6	17.8	1.9	362.1	127.7	1.21	.83	1.45
1992-3	7,943	4,496	65.4	294.2	55.0	476.9	262.8	77.4	17.8	5.7	363.7	113.2	1.32	.88	1.45
1993-4	7,937	3,803	54.4	206.7	106.8	426.7	224.9	78.3	15.0	3.0	321.2	105.5	1.36	.88	1.45
1994-5	6,637	4,008	57.1	228.8	93.2	427.6	233.4	79.2	13.4	1.0	327.0	100.6	1.22	.97	1.45
1995-6	6,225	2,952	54.6	161.1	80.5	342.2	181.9	80.0	12.0	2.1	275.9	66.3	1.67	.97	1.45
1996-7	4,638	2,655	57.7	153.2	97.5	317.1	153.3	81.4	13.1	2.5	250.4	66.7	1.96	1.03	-----
1997-8	5,068	2,813	59.5	167.2	98.4	332.3	161.4	82.2	12.6	2.1	258.3	74.0	1.60	1.11	-----
1998-9[1]	4,892	2,755	60.2	166.0	108.0	348.0	170.0	82.8	12.2	1.7	266.0	81.0	1.10	1.11	-----
1999-00[2]	4,670	2,453	59.6	146.2	100.0	328.0	150.0			2.0	248.0	80.0	1.05-1.15	1.13	-----

[1] Preliminary. [2] Forecast. *Source: Economic Research Service, U.S. Department of Agriculture (ERS-USDA)*

Production of Oats in the United States, by States In Thousands of Bushels

Year	Illinois	Iowa	Michigan	Minnesota	Nebraska	New York	North Dakota	Ohio	Pennsylvania	South Dakota	Texas	Wisconsin	Total
1990	11,560	40,800	13,050	48,180	13,440	8,235	16,100	2,280	15,840	53,200	9,225	47,570	357,654
1991	6,600	21,250	5,400	22,800	11,880	5,000	10,200	1,292	8,400	38,500	7,200	26,500	243,851
1992	7,930	25,125	8,400	35,000	15,400	7,700	37,400	12,070	13,735	42,900	5,720	34,410	294,229
1993	4,590	9,000	7,150	23,750	6,880	6,510	37,100	9,000	10,000	26,520	7,420	24,150	206,770
1994	5,490	26,660	6,270	24,750	7,500	7,040	33,550	6,720	8,480	31,360	5,200	25,380	229,008
1995	5,360	14,625	5,130	18,000	4,500	5,310	21,600	6,900	9,440	11,500	5,040	18,700	162,027
1996	4,620	12,920	3,600	15,120	7,455	3,850	19,000	5,130	7,560	21,600	3,400	17,400	153,245
1997	5,550	16,790	4,880	17,400	5,850	5,850	18,700	6,660	8,990	14,850	6,760	20,160	167,246
1998	3,920	10,915	4,800	19,530	5,320	6,510	25,200	6,500	8,480	20,100	6,890	18,300	165,981
1999[1]	4,260	11,375	4,875	17,700	4,650	4,760	16,830	7,000	7,975	12,800	4,840	18,600	146,218

[1] Preliminary. *Source: National Agricultural Statistics Service, U.S. Department of Agriculture (NASS-USDA)*

Average Cash Price of No. 2 Heavy White Oats in Toledo In Dollars Per Bushel

Year	June	July	Aug.	Sept.	Oct.	Nov.	Dec.	Jan.	Feb.	Mar.	Apr.	May	Average
1990-1	1.33	1.19	1.14	1.09	1.11	1.10	1.15	1.12	1.12	1.22	1.22	1.26	1.17
1991-2	1.14	1.24	1.29	1.28	1.31	1.30	1.34	1.41	1.58	1.61	1.48	1.50	1.37
1992-3	1.46	1.47	1.46	1.58	1.54	1.58	1.55	1.54	1.49	1.43	1.53	1.50	1.51
1993-4	1.42	1.50	1.49	1.43	1.41	1.38	1.37	1.43	1.40	1.37	1.37	1.25	1.40
1994-5	1.35	1.26	1.26	1.32	1.35	1.28	1.27	1.34	1.45	1.43	1.48	1.59	1.37
1995-6	1.65	1.76	1.83	1.90	1.76	1.91	2.21	2.14	2.06	2.17	2.32	2.05	1.98
1996-7	NQ	2.45	2.34	2.19	2.02	1.96	1.96	1.99	2.16	2.26	2.12	2.08	2.14
1997-8	2.12	1.79	1.84	1.80	1.77	NQ	NQ	NQ	NQ	NQ	NQ	NQ	1.86
1998-9	NQ	NQ	NQ	NQ	NQ	NQ	NQ	NQ	NQ	NQ	NQ	NQ	NQ
1999-00[1]	NQ	NQ	NQ	NQ	NQ	NQ	NQ	NQ					

[1] Preliminary. NQ = No quotes. *Source: Economic Research Service, U.S. Department of Agriculture (ERS-USDA)*

OATS

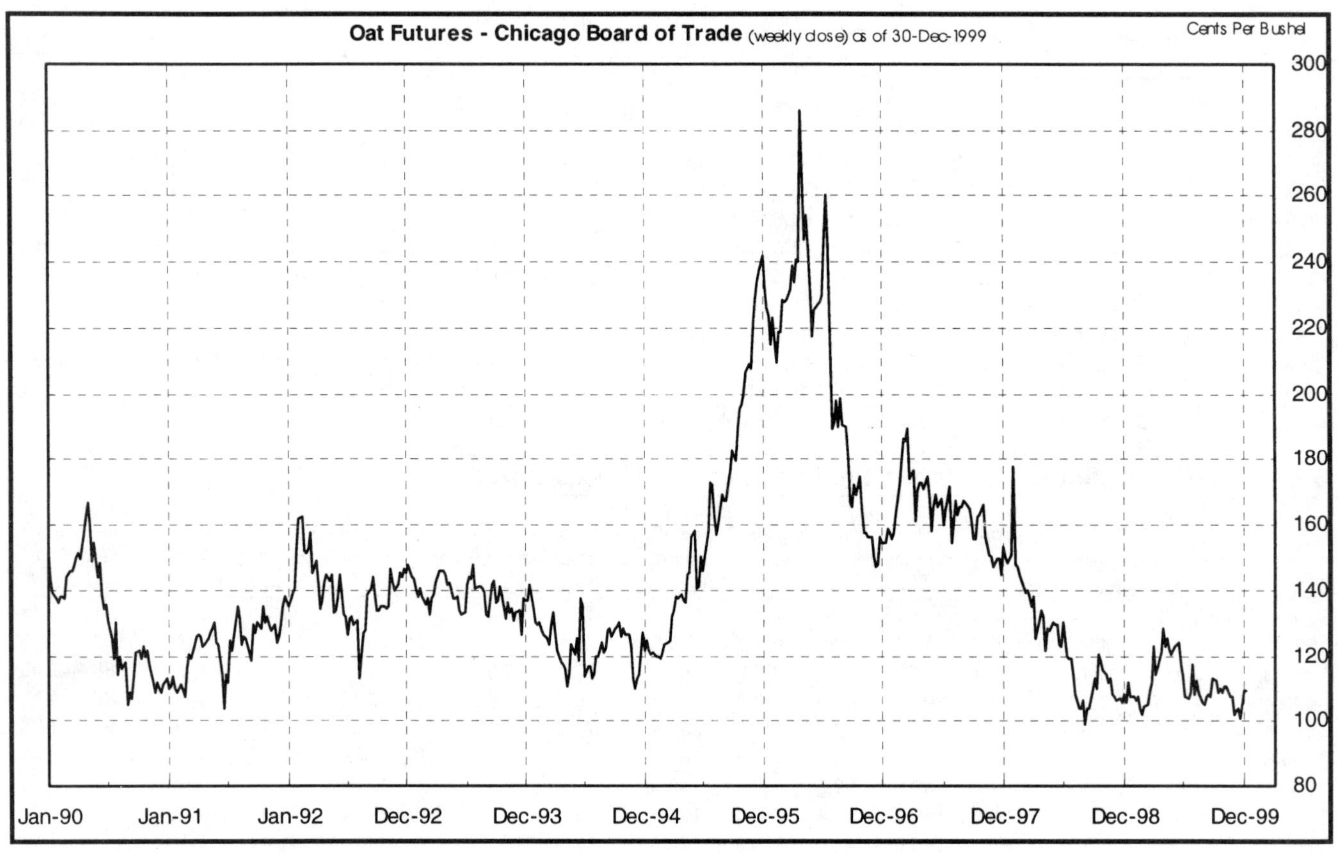

Volume of Trading in Oats Futures in Chicago In Contracts

Year	Jan.	Feb.	Mar.	Apr.	May	June	July	Aug.	Sept.	Oct.	Nov.	Dec.	Total
1990	24,660	31,740	33,880	45,140	54,000	46,360	32,040	49,600	25,200	27,800	47,380	15,560	433,360
1991	20,040	30,280	30,320	42,720	20,580	44,940	37,100	41,060	17,860	20,300	34,560	15,200	354,960
1992	31,020	84,020	42,260	47,060	42,020	54,540	22,200	40,160	25,100	16,580	35,220	19,400	459,580
1993	20,480	26,500	26,060	63,140	33,420	43,120	33,300	32,080	26,880	40,780	72,320	37,260	455,340
1994	47,980	57,060	39,800	53,820	34,300	69,760	20,760	39,340	28,840	24,900	56,940	19,680	493,180
1995	13,512	37,014	29,490	45,536	34,116	107,082	29,862	45,677	31,676	38,641	52,321	47,005	511,932
1996	61,451	52,079	34,608	77,395	47,161	34,498	38,960	33,316	30,801	37,579	37,856	16,154	501,858
1997	34,238	51,608	39,607	41,988	27,028	29,632	25,473	26,486	21,241	42,630	38,187	19,214	397,332
1998	21,150	51,247	25,551	65,381	23,490	55,376	29,870	42,156	27,131	31,426	51,172	18,924	442,874
1999	23,747	35,706	43,671	44,974	22,399	40,722	35,812	27,928	17,893	16,155	42,029	20,370	371,406

Source: Chicago Board of Trade (CBT)

Average Open Interest of Oats in Chicago In Contracts

Year	Jan.	Feb.	Mar.	Apr.	May	June	July	Aug.	Sept.	Oct.	Nov.	Dec.
1990	11,227	11,809	11,355	12,243	12,513	10,891	10,743	12,112	12,965	14,804	15,115	11,758
1991	11,890	12,832	13,895	15,620	14,223	13,091	11,117	10,894	10,368	11,560	11,257	9,355
1992	9,555	15,499	15,359	15,052	15,329	14,773	12,759	11,100	9,869	9,178	8,781	7,287
1993	7,398	7,739	7,655	11,579	13,357	12,020	10,894	11,381	11,171	14,116	20,057	20,547
1994	21,193	20,137	20,194	19,882	18,312	14,575	11,710	13,923	14,743	16,266	15,354	13,376
1995	13,133	13,231	13,000	15,426	16,054	13,611	11,019	11,348	11,012	11,970	12,542	13,003
1996	13,253	14,095	14,231	14,497	13,897	11,697	11,336	11,803	11,457	11,918	11,150	8,550
1997	8,088	9,650	12,649	11,024	9,830	9,395	8,131	8,606	8,618	10,953	11,816	10,964
1998	12,782	15,368	16,553	17,748	17,441	16,437	14,255	15,052	14,771	16,263	18,466	17,048
1999	17,126	17,019	16,677	15,398	13,491	12,704	11,927	11,669	9,801	10,637	12,754	12,342

Source: Chicago Board of Trade (CBT)

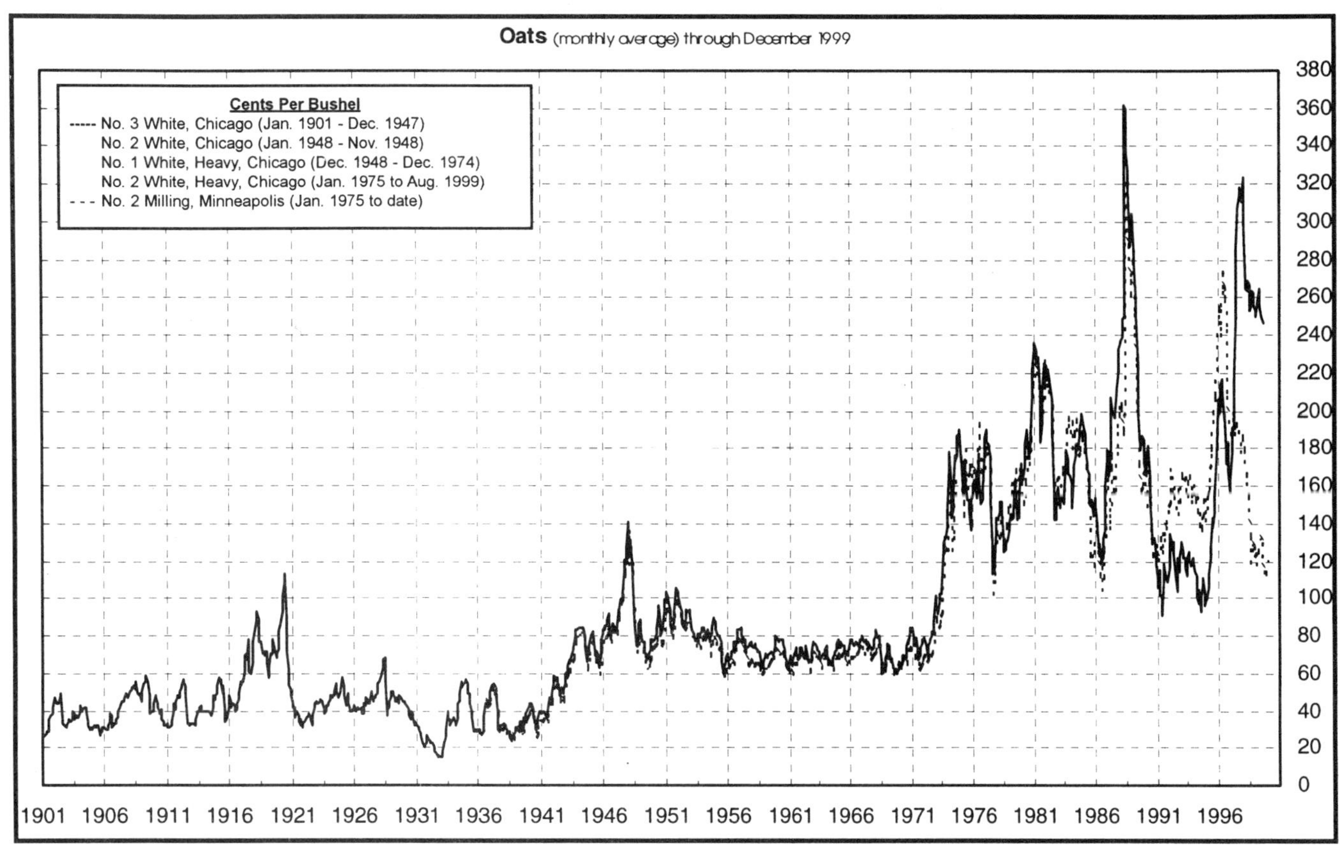

Average Cash Price of No. 2 Heavy White Oats in Minneapolis In Dollars Per Bushel

Year	June	July	Aug.	Sept.	Oct.	Nov.	Dec.	Jan.	Feb.	Mar.	Apr.	May	Average
1990-1	1.52	1.37	1.25	1.23	1.29	1.30	1.24	1.22	1.18	1.27	1.32	1.36	1.30
1991-2	1.25	1.33	1.38	1.35	1.41	1.42	1.49	1.50	1.68	1.66	1.57	1.59	1.47
1992-3	1.55	1.49	1.45	1.58	1.52	1.59	1.63	1.66	1.63	1.63	1.66	1.57	1.58
1993-4	1.54	1.63	1.63	1.66	1.56	1.51	1.56	1.57	1.52	1.55	1.46	1.37	1.55
1994-5	1.47	1.36	1.44	1.44	1.44	1.41	NQ	1.46	1.42	1.54	1.62	1.76	1.36
1995-6	1.73	1.92	1.96	2.04	2.11	2.63	2.50	2.40	2.31	2.47	2.56	2.68	2.28
1996-7	2.11	2.48	2.36	2.08	2.06	1.87	1.86	1.89	1.94	1.99	1.88	1.81	2.03
1997-8	1.89	1.76	1.80	1.78	1.75	1.65	1.71	1.68	1.59	1.65	1.54	1.58	1.70
1998-9	1.52	1.42	1.21	1.30	1.29	1.32	1.31	1.33	1.26	1.35	1.36	1.39	1.34
1999-00[1]	1.34	1.25	1.20	1.17	1.20								1.23

[1] Preliminary. NQ = No quote. *Source: Economic Research Service, U.S. Department of Agriculture (ERS-USDA)*

Average Price Received by U.S. Farmers for Oats In Dollars Per Bushel

Year	June	July	Aug.	Sept.	Oct.	Nov.	Dec.	Jan.	Feb.	Mar.	Apr.	May	Average
1990-1	1.33	1.15	1.06	1.09	1.14	1.16	1.17	1.13	1.13	1.16	1.16	1.16	1.14
1991-2	1.08	1.08	1.09	1.12	1.21	1.25	1.25	1.31	1.44	1.44	1.46	1.43	1.21
1992-3	1.38	1.32	1.23	1.28	1.31	1.35	1.36	1.42	1.42	1.43	1.45	1.51	1.32
1993-4	1.43	1.36	1.32	1.31	1.33	1.39	1.42	1.42	1.42	1.39	1.32	1.49	1.36
1994-5	1.31	1.20	1.16	1.18	1.21	1.18	1.18	1.22	1.22	1.33	1.36	1.41	1.22
1995-6	1.38	1.52	1.48	1.43	1.50	1.72	1.91	1.93	1.96	2.04	2.13	2.48	1.46
1996-7	2.17	2.13	2.00	1.83	1.84	1.85	1.72	1.83	1.81	1.91	1.87	1.86	1.96
1997-8	1.81	1.68	1.57	1.47	1.62	1.66	1.57	1.60	1.60	1.64	1.61	1.53	1.61
1998-9	1.39	1.19	1.02	1.07	1.09	1.10	1.19	1.20	1.20	1.21	1.18	1.31	1.18
1999-00[1]	1.22	1.08	.97	1.08	1.07	1.11	1.17	1.18					1.11

[1] Preliminary. *Source: National Agricultural Statistics Service, U.S. Department of Agriculture (NASS-USDA)*

Olive Oil

Olive oil production tends to be cyclical in that large crops are followed by small crops in a two year biennial cycle. That in turn leads to cyclicality in world production. As an example of this, the newsletter Oil World reported that world production of olive oil in the 1993/94 season was 1.88 million metric tonnes. Production in 1994/95 recovered to 1.96 million tonnes, an increase of 4 percent. In 1995/96, production declined on a cyclical basis to 1.6 million tonnes, down 19 percent from the year before. The 1996/97 season saw a very large increase in world production to 2.85 million tonnes. This was a cyclical rebound from the small 1995/96 crop of 1.6 million tonnes. That huge increase in production marked a high in olive oil production and may have exhausted the trees. Since then production has been declining.

Oil World reported that production of olive oil in the 1999/2000 season would decline to 2.2 million tonnes. After the production peak in 1996-97, world olive oil production fell in each succeeding season. Oil World noted that one reason for the decline in production was the drought in Spain, the world's largest producer. Offsetting the smaller world crop are large stocks of olive oil. Olive oil stocks in the European Union are at record levels of close to a million tonnes. Dry weather in Turkey and North Africa should also lead to production declines. The major producers of olive oil are Spain, the European Union, Greece, Turkey, Tunisia and Syria.

In other developments in the olive oil market, Syria had a drought which reduced production. The 1999 crop was about cut in half. Another country adversely impacted by dry weather was Turkey which could see a production decline of 70 percent. A country that had good weather was Tunisia which has emerged as a large producer. The 1999/00 crop was expected to exceed the 1998/99 crop slightly. Despite the cyclical changes in production, world stocks of olive oil have been trending higher and this will work to offset the production declines.

World Production of Olive Oil (Pressed Oil) In Thousands of Metric Tons

Year	Algeria	Argentina	Greece	Italy	Jordan	Libya	Morocco	Portugal	Spain	Syria	Tunisia	Turkey	World Total
1992-3	26.5	10.5	339.0	469.8	15.5	6.0	43.0	26.9	673.9	95.0	133.0	65.0	1,974.0
1993-4	21.0	8.5	275.0	451.5	9.5	8.0	45.5	36.1	593.2	71.0	251.0	55.0	1,875.2
1994-5	14.0	10.0	389.8	464.4	15.0	6.5	50.0	36.2	547.0	101.5	106.5	181.5	1,963.6
1995-6	23.0	11.5	362.0	540.0	15.5	4.0	40.0	48.6	320.0	84.0	64.5	45.5	1,598.4
1996-7	46.0	12.0	469.8	317.0	25.5	10.0	121.0	48.8	1,027.5	138.0	288.5	222.0	2,771.6
1997-8[1]	6.5	8.0	375.0	538.0	14.0	6.0	70.0	42.0	1,077.0	70.0	93.0	40.0	2,372.2
1998-9[2]	39.5	6.5	473.0	397.0	21.5	8.0	65.0	36.0	786.4	115.0	215.0	170.0	2,370.7
1999-00[3]	25.0	6.5	350.0	620.0	7.0	7.0	40.0	40.0	545.9	80.0	200.0	70.0	2,029.4

[1] Preliminary. [2] Estimate. [3] Forecast. *Source: The Oil World*

World Imports and Exports of Olive Oil (Pressed Oil) In Thousands of Metric Tons

	Imports							Exports					
Year	Australia	Brazil	Italy	Japan	Spain	United States	World Total	Greece	Italy	Spain	Tunisia	Turkey	World Total
1992-3	17.3	17.3	75.9	5.0	16.8	123.2	373.3	14.1	112.7	64.9	134.4	8.7	379.6
1993-4	15.5	18.2	85.8	6.2	46.3	123.9	399.2	8.6	118.2	58.2	166.2	8.7	402.4
1994-5	18.0	23.2	122.6	8.3	68.0	127.6	458.2	9.1	111.4	56.6	141.4	53.2	437.5
1995-6	16.7	18.8	47.0	16.1	26.4	113.6	313.9	7.8	98.0	54.4	33.1	28.9	306.8
1996-7	19.0	26.5	108.1	24.3	35.2	148.1	458.9	10.7	136.8	72.0	98.4	46.7	463.0
1997-8[1]	18.0	29.0	89.0	36.0	28.0	161.0	463.0	15.0	140.0	82.0	111.0	42.0	463.0
1998-9[2]	24.0	20.0	146.0	28.0	61.0	170.0	560.0	20.0	154.0	69.0	156.0	78.0	562.0
1999-00[3]	25.0	24.0	109.0	28.0	35.0	167.0	505.0	15.0	177.0	83.0	130.0	31.0	505.0

[1] Preliminary. [2] Estimate. [3] Forecast. *Source: The Oil World*

World Consumption and Ending Stocksof Olive Oil (Pressed Oil) In Thousands of Metric Tons

	Consumption							Ending Stocks					
Year	Brazil	Morocco	Syria	Tunisia	Turkey	United States	World Total	Greece	Italy	Spain	Syria	Turkey	World Total
1992-3	17.3	48.6	77.9	65.4	55.3	113.5	2,068.4	70.5	204.2	235.1	27.0	30.0	735.3
1993-4	18.2	53.5	82.0	66.8	63.4	119.9	2,016.3	32.0	224.4	189.3	19.0	14.0	667.3
1994-5	23.2	46.7	93.4	42.1	71.4	120.8	2,055.6	45.6	133.9	223.0	28.0	71.0	596.0
1995-6	18.8	32.9	93.8	32.4	64.7	110.5	1,881.1	30.9	81.4	88.4	12.0	23.0	320.4
1996-7	26.5	57.2	96.5	94.1	83.3	130.9	2,254.7	115.0	44.0	265.0	50.0	115.0	833.3
1997-8[1]	29.0	61.0	101.0	73.0	83.0	155.0	2,364.0	116.0	173.0	545.0	25.0	35.0	1,038.0
1998-9[2]	20.0	58.0	102.0	83.0	91.0	161.0	2,440.0	102.3	163.0	490.0	49.0	55.0	1,164.0
1999-00[3]	24.0	56.0	104.0	84.0	87.0	162.0	2,476.0				33.0	14.0	885.0

[1] Preliminary. [2] Estimate. [3] Forecast. *Source: The Oil World*

Onions

The U.S.D.A. forecast fresh onion production in 1999 at 5.8 billion pounds, an increase of 2 percent from 1998. Over the last five years, U.S. production of fresh onions has averaged 5.72 billion pounds. Imports of fresh onions in 1999 were forecast at 615 million pounds, an increase of almost 3 percent from 1998. Over the last five years, fresh onion imports have averaged 580 million pounds each year. Season beginning stocks of onions in 1999 were 1.01 billion pounds, down 5 percent from a year ago. The total supply of onions in 1999 was 7.43 billion pounds, up 1 percent from 1998.

In terms of utilization, U.S. exports of onions in 1999 were forecast to be 655 million pounds, an increase of 4 percent from 1998. Exports set a high in 1993 when 817 million pounds were shipped. Over the last five seasons, exports of fresh onions have averaged 627 million pounds. Shrink and loss accounted for 690 million pounds, up 2 percent from the previous year. Domestic use of fresh onions in 1999 was forecast at 5.05 billion pounds, less than 1 percent more than in 1998. Projected ending stocks of fresh onions were 1.03 billion pounds, almost 2 percent more than in 1998.

Per capita use of fresh onions in trending higher. Per capita use in 1999 was estimated at 18.6 pounds, the same rate of use as the year before. In 1997, per capita use was 17.9 pounds. In 1990, per capita use of fresh onions was 15.1 pounds while in 1980 it was 11.4 pounds. In 1975, per capita use was 10.5 pounds.

Salient Statistics of Onions in the United States

Crop Year	Harvested Acres	Yield Per Acre	Production 1,000 Cwt.	Price Per Cwt.	Farm Value $1,000	Jan. 1 Pack Frozen	Annual Pack Frozen	Imports Canned	Exports (Fresh)	Imports (Fresh)	Per Capita[3] Utilization -- Lbs., Farm Weight -- All	Fresh
						In Millions of Pounds						
1994	160,350	396	63,531	9.87	626,778	36.1	241.3	4.2	802.1	544.7	18.1	17.1
1995	164,000	391	64,182	11.10	633,692	51.2	246.8	4.0	662.1	483.7	19.3	18.0
1996	166,210	386	64,106	10.50	604,789	48.8	259.5	3.6	586.3	625.2	18.6	18.7
1997	165,910	414	68,769	12.60	769,974	40.8	230.1	3.8	600.9	576.0	20.0	19.1
1998[1]	166,340	397	66,024	13.85	826,141	42.2	235.0	3.5	628.8	598.5	19.7	18.6
1999[2]	169,200	422	71,379	11.00	703,854	40.3			655.0	615.0	19.6	18.6

[1] Preliminary. [2] Forecast. [3] Includes fresh and processing. *Source: Economic Research Service, U.S. Department of Agriculture (ERS-USDA)*

Production of Onions in the United States In Thousands of Hundredweight (Cwt.)

	Spring				Summer										
Year	Arizona	California	Texas	Total (All)	California	Colorado	Idaho	Michigan	Minnesota	New Mexico	New York	Oregon (Malheur)	Texas	Total (All)	Grand Total
1994	688	2,948	4,704	10,297	12,710	6,125	5,547	2,178	312	3,318	3,844	7,378	837	53,324	63,531
1995	672	3,300	3,763	10,110	12,658	6,141	5,481	1,856	125	4,095	4,032	7,134	870	54,072	64,182
1996	760	2,736	4,030	9,290	13,330	5,200	5,590	1,798	114	3,266	2,736	7,080	924	52,079	61,369
1997	746	3,204	1,661	9,087	13,772	5,355	5,658	1,568	180	-----	3,660	7,440	-----	58,120	68,769
1998	1,175	4,050	2,907	10,356	14,388	6,080	4,640	1,092	150	-----	3,750	6,120	-----	55,668	66,024
1999[1]	1,635	3,197	3,900	11,487	12,470	5,220	5,293	1,200	136	-----	3,313	7,482	-----	53,824	65,311

[1] Preliminary. *Source: Agricultural Statistics Board, U.S. Department of Agiculture (ASB-USDA)*

Cold Storage Stocks of Frozen Onions in the United States, on First of Month In Thousands of Pounds

Year	Jan.	Feb.	Mar.	Apr.	May	June	July	Aug.	Sept.	Oct.	Nov.	Dec.
1994	27,349	25,740	21,630	20,530	20,156	21,067	21,877	30,794	35,832	38,571	42,691	41,044
1995	37,472	36,240	35,402	33,906	30,071	30,790	31,309	32,175	32,081	33,594	36,360	34,877
1996	35,354	35,819	31,784	32,782	27,670	29,200	27,511	27,536	27,659	30,288	27,889	32,261
1997	30,481	29,255	32,227	31,811	29,693	28,061	29,314	28,520	27,336	26,908	29,831	30,513
1998	31,187	28,724	27,710	24,428	23,443	22,787	22,179	21,468	18,755	24,553	27,070	25,965
1999[1]	24,596	24,665	27,280	27,972	33,113	35,809	35,605	33,171	31,675	31,338	35,573	41,677

[1] Preliminary. *Source: National Agricultural Statistics Service, U.S. Department of Agriculture (NASS-USDA)*

F.O.B. Price Received by Growers for Onions in the United States In Dollars Per Hundred Pounds (Cwt.)

Year	Jan.	Feb.	Mar.	Apr.	May	June	July	Aug.	Sept.	Oct.	Nov.	Dec.	Season Average
1994	31.40	33.90	18.80	10.80	8.64	8.49	12.30	9.54	9.32	10.60	12.20	12.70	10.80
1995	13.50	17.50	17.90	20.00	14.60	10.50	13.70	9.67	10.00	9.89	9.52	10.00	11.10
1996	10.70	10.10	8.11	8.86	9.54	11.10	12.10	12.60	12.70	11.50	10.40	10.20	10.50
1997	9.75	7.87	8.09	14.90	13.30	16.50	14.20	13.60	10.20	9.19	9.86	10.90	12.60
1998	11.40	13.50	17.10	17.80	17.70	14.90	19.10	14.30	12.80	12.70	14.00	15.90	13.80
1999[1]	16.70	13.80	11.20	16.90	17.80	17.60	17.10	15.40	12.30	8.92	8.30	7.88	

[1] Preliminary. *Source: Economic Research Service, U.S. Department of Agriculture (ERS-USDA)*

Oranges and Orange Juice

The world's largest producers of oranges and frozen concentrated orange juice (FCOJ) are Brazil and the United States. Brazilian production is mostly in Sao Paulo, Brazil, where about 95 percent of the citrus trees are grown. Brazil is the largest producer of oranges and FCOJ, having passed Florida several years ago. The domestic market in Brazil generally prefers fresh oranges which are then squeezed for juice. Oranges that are processed for FCOJ are usually destined for export markets in the U.S., Europe and Asia.

In the U.S., oranges for processing are growing for the most part in Florida. California, Texas and Arizona also grow oranges. The industry in Florida has been there for many years. Production has had several changes over the years. A series of freezes in the 1980's led to the destruction of trees in the northern part of the state. The groves were shifted to the southern part of the state with the development of more sophisticated irrigation systems. An important development has been the increase in the number of trees grown on each acre. This increased density of the groves, along with the fact that they are located more to the south, means that there is much less chance that a freeze will damage the crop.

For U.S. oranges, the most important report of each year is the October crop production report from the U.S.D.A. This is the first report of the season and as such provides the initial idea on how large the crop will be. For the 1999/2000 season, the U.S.D.A. in October estimated Florida production at 211 million boxes. This was some 14 percent more than the 1998/99 crop of 185.7 million boxes, but well below the 1997/98 record crop of 244 million boxes. The California crop was forecast at 67 million boxes, up 76 percent from last year's weather damaged crop. The U.S. orange crop was forecast at 280.5 million boxes. In the U.S.D.A.'s December crop production report, the Florida crop estimate was increased to 214 million boxes. The early midseason Navel crop was estimated at 124 million boxes while the Valencia crop was forecast at 90 million boxes. The FCOJ yield was forecast to be 1.60 gallons per box.

The Brazilian crop is always difficult to forecast. The U.S.D.A. agricultural attache reported that the 1999/00 (July-June) crop was expected to be 440 million boxes with FCOJ production of 1.27 million tonnes. The Sao Paulo area was expected to contribute 295 million boxes for processing. By mid-December 1999, the Brazilian Association of Citrus Exporters had reported that cumulative production of FCOJ was 1.04 million tonnes or some 7 percent less than that in the same period of 1998/99. The inventory was almost 784,000 tonnes, down 5 percent from the year before.

Futures Markets

Frozen concentrated orange juice futures and options are traded on the NYCE Division of the New York Board of Trade (NYBOT).

World Production of Oranges In Thousands of Metric Tons

Year	Argentina	Australia	Brazil	Egypt	Greece	Italy	Mexico	Morocco	South Africa	Spain	Turkey	United States	World Total
1988-9	620	544	14,150	1,199	770	2,170	2,000	994	629	2,216	740	8,272	35,835
1989-90	750	458	12,036	1,397	932	2,067	1,900	775	697	2,400	740	7,083	33,361
1990-1	600	485	12,362	1,574	819	1,760	2,300	1,103	648	2,590	735	7,222	33,938
1991-2	640	595	14,974	1,694	820	1,842	2,100	780	680	2,651	830	8,175	38,193
1992-3	660	578	14,484	1,771	1,042	2,111	2,913	874	712	2,926	820	10,074	41,582
1993-4	746	651	13,710	1,324	854	2,100	3,174	916	739	2,509	840	9,462	39,595
1994-5	712	416	16,520	1,513	865	1,710	3,500	657	770	2,644	920	10,641	43,539
1995-6[1]	703	589	16,973	1,360	838	1,770	2,600	870	850	2,440	880	10,454	43,066
1996-7[2]	841	557	18,972	1,613	946	2,100	3,500	774	970	2,145	800	11,598	47,780
1997-8[3]	770	369	15,014	1,370	960	2,000	3,700	1,120	970	2,614	750	12,829	45,684

[1] Preliminary. [2] Estimate. [3] Forecast. NA = Not available. *Source: Foreign Agricultural Service, U.S. Department of Agriculture (FAS-USDA)*

Salient Statistics of Oranges & Orange Juice in the United States

	---- Production[4] ----					------ Florida Crop Processed ------				-------- Frozen Concentrated Orange Juice - Florida --------				Brazilian U.S. Imports of Frozen Concentrated OJ		
															----- Exports -----	
Year	California	Florida	Total U.S.	Farm Price $ Per Box	Farm Value Million $	Frozen Concentrates	Chilled Products	Total Processed	Yield Per Box Gallons[5]	Carry-in	Pack	Total Supply	Total Season Movement	Pack	Total	U.S.
	----- Million Boxes -----					------------- Million Boxes -------------				---------------- In Millions of Gallons (42 Deg. Brix) ----------------						
1989-90	71.4	110.2	184.5	7.96	1,465.1	70.1	33.5	110.2	1.2	46.3	184.7	231.0	191.1	362.0	330.7	132.4
1990-1	25.6	151.6	179.0	8.70	1,584.7	100.4	38.2	151.6	1.5	40.0	221.2	261.2	229.2	294.8	284.5	87.7
1991-2	67.4	139.8	209.6	7.43	1,545.2	90.6	37.0	139.8	1.6	31.8	211.7	243.5	212.6	274.1	279.3	107.8
1992-3	66.8	186.6	255.8	5.77	1,489.9	128.3	47.2	186.6	1.6	31.0	292.0	322.9	269.4	394.8	418.2	103.1
1993-4	63.6	174.4	240.5	6.37	1,541.3	111.7	51.0	174.4	1.6	53.5	261.7	315.2	256.6	388.2	387.5	102.0
1994-5	56.0	205.5	263.6	6.08	1,624.1	144.7	54.8	199.8	1.5	58.6	274.2	332.8	290.4	356.9	370.7	96.5
1995-6	58.0	203.3	263.9	6.85	1,821.6	132.9	64.5	197.7	1.5	42.4	284.5	326.9	285.7	-----	360.8	65.9
1996-7[1]	64.0	226.2	293.0	6.16	1,836.7	153.8	65.7	220.4	1.6	41.2	301.7	342.9	273.9	-----	398.3	67.5
1997-8[2]	69.0	244.0	315.5	6.13	1,965.4	160.9	74.8	236.6	1.6	69.7	298.8	368.4	263.8			
1998-9[3]	38.0	185.7	226.3	7.85	1,807.4	97.2	80.1	177.9	1.6							

[1] Preliminary. [2] Estimate. [3] Forecast. [4] Fruit ripened on trees, but destroyed prior to picking not included. [5] *42 deg. Brix equivalent.*
Source: Economic Research Service, U.S. Department of Agriculture (ERS-USDA); Florida Department of Citrus

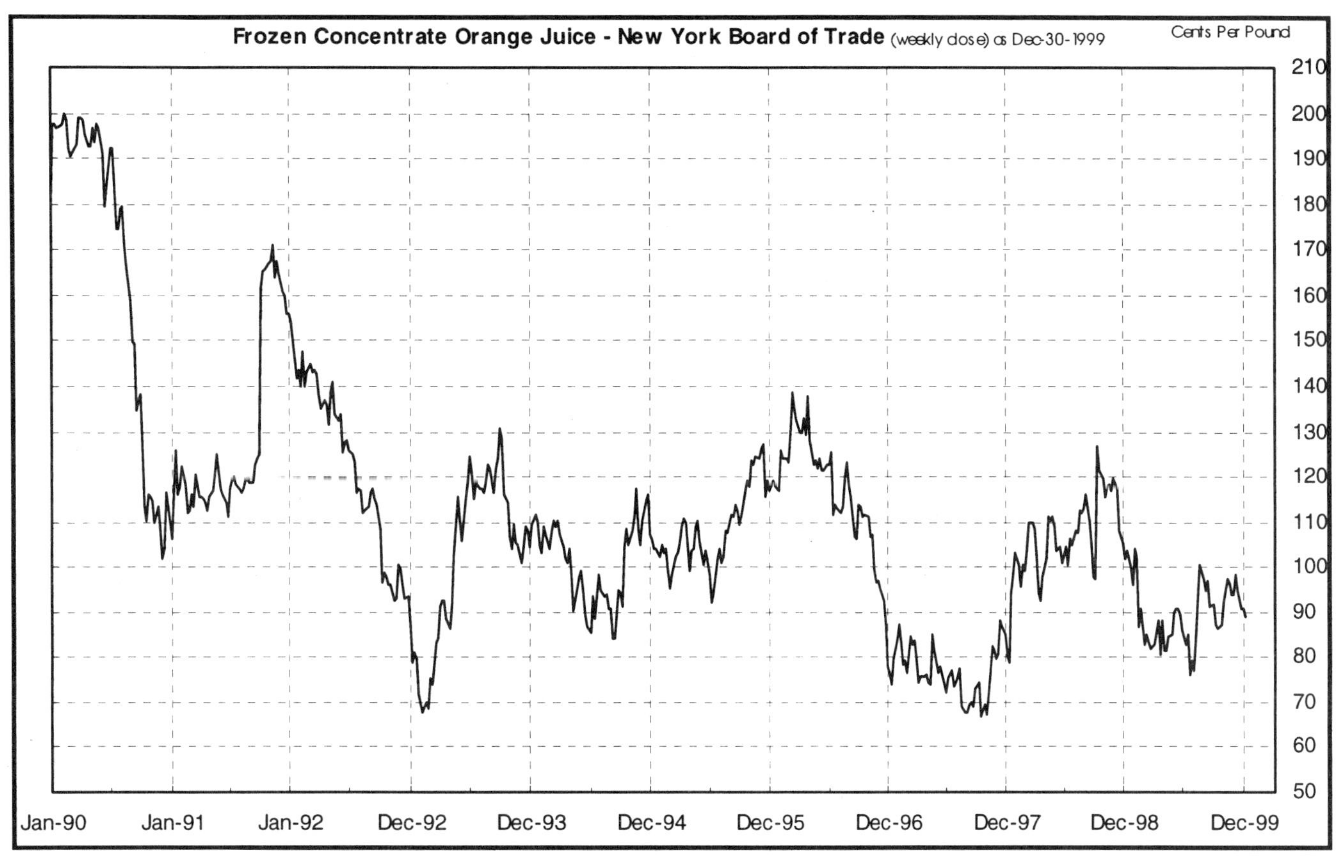

Average Open Interest of Frozen Concentrated Orange Juice Futures in New York In Contracts

Year	Jan.	Feb.	Mar.	Apr.	May	June	July	Aug.	Sept.	Oct.	Nov.	Dec.
1990	9,667	11,067	11,877	11,952	10,528	10,229	9,413	7,485	6,867	5,939	5,802	6,983
1991	6,773	6,457	5,739	6,255	5,762	6,338	5,653	6,556	9,854	11,924	9,877	9,101
1992	9,095	10,033	9,872	11,309	10,791	9,776	10,109	12,132	11,910	14,224	16,669	17,455
1993	17,733	18,199	19,030	20,210	18,525	19,267	20,000	18,899	18,287	18,825	18,422	20,367
1994	17,544	18,137	19,073	21,607	21,450	23,530	24,829	21,874	22,739	23,385	26,859	26,413
1995	27,439	25,885	26,407	30,172	27,057	26,844	23,537	17,881	20,918	22,460	26,303	24,202
1996	22,943	21,670	25,232	23,788	21,724	20,934	20,159	19,834	18,029	18,000	22,513	26,405
1997	29,171	26,929	26,331	28,955	29,868	33,639	31,799	34,339	36,057	40,365	41,811	46,169
1998	38,885	37,893	36,843	33,146	35,749	32,608	25,503	26,394	28,017	26,506	21,984	24,562
1999	25,917	28,965	28,707	31,199	26,669	28,362	28,087	30,021	28,922	27,498	26,892	25,886

Source: New York Board of Trade (NYBOT)

Volume of Trading of Frozen Concentrated Orange Juice Futures in New York In Contracts

Year	Jan.	Feb.	Mar.	Apr.	May	June	July	Aug.	Sept.	Oct.	Nov.	Dec.	Total
1990	53,133	32,035	31,676	28,025	23,656	45,028	21,302	24,029	13,131	21,793	16,473	30,739	342,574
1991	35,037	28,221	17,298	17,116	17,991	20,956	14,905	20,187	26,412	42,016	23,228	24,171	287,076
1992	30,508	28,177	21,371	31,725	21,253	22,473	21,877	27,208	26,912	29,604	33,133	44,979	339,230
1993	43,634	46,067	58,298	52,554	53,566	60,330	49,415	52,381	56,838	63,808	44,167	58,073	640,131
1994	46,166	51,123	43,075	55,955	48,236	60,110	37,069	55,711	52,209	73,155	54,978	76,037	653,824
1995	50,875	66,370	51,292	78,288	32,607	80,165	41,357	67,528	38,781	64,904	45,688	71,077	688,932
1996	59,666	82,057	46,272	65,752	62,247	44,827	40,884	58,346	44,239	40,680	39,291	70,676	654,937
1997	84,982	89,875	66,340	82,772	62,890	78,690	47,242	118,286	55,081	108,413	100,941	134,349	1,029,861
1998	96,020	81,554	66,235	101,651	70,909	79,319	48,844	85,544	81,187	98,639	29,541	75,171	914,614
1999	64,149	92,868	40,027	92,522	49,180	78,627	48,177	99,531	49,323	71,914	42,532	68,734	797,584

Source: New York Board of Trade (NYBOT)

ORANGES AND ORANGE JUICE

Cold Storage Stocks of Orange Juice Concentrate in the U.S., on First of Month In Millions of Pounds

Year	Jan.	Feb.	Mar.	Apr.	May	June	July	Aug.	Sept.	Oct.	Nov.	Dec.
1990	749.6	926.6	1,046.5	1,119.2	980.9	1,148.2	1,074.8	1,008.1	901.4	797.1	802.0	871.3
1991	1,031.6	1,195.8	1,199.5	1,236.9	1,363.2	1,304.7	1,110.6	1,007.5	876.9	765.2	617.3	655.4
1992	828.4	1,130.7	1,150.0	1,102.9	1,269.3	1,294.8	1,143.8	978.0	874.9	741.9	665.5	638.0
1993	892.9	1,135.9	1,282.8	1,297.5	1,440.9	1,462.3	1,351.8	1,147.0	1,029.6	875.7	813.3	890.9
1994	955.5	1,248.9	1,429.0	1,273.8	1,499.6	1,615.2	1,521.8	1,449.1	1,257.5	1,119.6	1,026.1	1,055.9
1995	1,353.1	1,704.0	1,685.1	1,773.3	1,864.6	1,833.8	1,631.6	1,424.1	1,233.7	1,038.3	830.3	897.7
1996	1,050.6	1,295.4	1,353.0	1,322.3	1,443.9	1,596.9	1,535.0	1,423.6	1,238.6	965.6	732.7	691.0
1997	1,069.4	1,522.6	1,677.6	1,752.9	1,993.4	2,176.0	1,977.7	1,761.8	1,571.8	1,287.8	1,140.9	1,214.4
1998	1,503.4	1,945.9	2,029.7	2,025.0	2,487.0	2,627.5	2,457.7	2,249.0	2,025.1	1,803.9	1,470.7	1,540.2
1999[1]	1,791.9	1,999.4	2,222.9	2,191.3	2,535.9	2,152.2	2,001.5	1,823.0	1,618.5	1,443.4	1,182.0	1,102.7

[1] Preliminary. *Source: Agricultural Statistics Board, U.S. Department of Agriculture (ASB-USDA)*

Retail and Nonretail Sales of Orange Juice in the United States In Millions of SSE Gallons

Year	Retail Sales	% Change[2]	Nonretail Sales	% Change[2]	Apparent Consumption	% Change[2]	Per Capita Consumption	% Change[2]
1987-8	667	-4.9%	432	12.2%	1,229	-1.1%	5.0	-2.0%
1988-9	690	3.4%	401	-7.2%	1,238	.7%	5.0	0
1989-90	628	-9.0%	317	-20.9%	1,079	-12.8%	4.3	-14.0%
1990-1	701	11.6%	296	-6.6%	1,146	6.2%	4.5	4.7%
1991-2	689	-1.7%	268	-9.5%	1,112	-3.0%	4.3	-4.4%
1992-3	748	8.6%	371	38.4%	1,328	19.4%	5.1	18.6%
1993-4	740	-1.1%	-----	-----	1,368	3.0%	5.2	2.0%
1994-5	740	0	-----	-----	1,355	-1.0%	5.1	-1.9%
1995-6[1]	718	-2.9%	-----	-----	1,363	.6%	4.9	-3.9%
1996-7[1]	700	-2.5%	-----	-----	1,320	-3.1%	NA	NA

[1] Estimate. [2] Percentage change from previous period. *Source: Florida Department of Citrus*

Producer Price Index of Frozen Orange Juice Concentrate 1982 = 100

Year	Jan.	Feb.	Mar.	Apr.	May	June	July	Aug.	Sept.	Oct.	Nov.	Dec.	Average
1990	137.6	162.4	162.8	159.9	159.7	160.0	160.4	160.8	150.9	147.2	120.9	117.8	150.0
1991	114.4	114.4	111.7	111.7	111.0	111.0	111.0	107.2	107.4	116.0	127.3	131.5	114.6
1992	135.1	134.7	134.7	134.3	126.2	118.5	115.5	114.5	112.5	106.5	104.2	98.8	119.6
1993	91.6	88.8	88.2	89.0	89.3	97.5	104.5	104.5	104.7	104.7	107.9	107.9	98.2
1994	107.9	104.8	104.2	104.2	102.7	101.2	100.2	100.1	99.9	99.8	100.7	100.5	102.2
1995	107.4	105.4	107.6	107.6	109.1	109.1	109.1	105.3	101.0	101.6	106.1	107.3	106.4
1996	109.4	112.5	117.2	119.5	119.5	119.5	115.3	113.6	113.6	112.8	112.8	108.8	114.5
1997	106.9	106.9	106.0	107.6	107.7	107.3	105.3	105.8	102.7	101.4	95.0	94.2	103.9
1998	94.9	101.2	104.1	103.2	108.8	109.1	109.5	109.6	109.5	110.2	119.1	121.2	108.4
1999[1]	119.7	118.6	118.0	115.5	113.3	113.2	112.5	111.3	112.4	112.7	113.1	112.3	114.4

[1] Preliminary. *Source: Bureau of Labor Statistics, U.S. Department of Labor (BLS)*

Average Price of Oranges (Equivalent On-Tree) Received by Growers in the U.S. In Dollars Per Box

Year	Jan.	Feb.	Mar.	Apr.	May	June	July	Aug.	Sept.	Oct.	Nov.	Dec.	Average
1990	5.92	5.82	6.00	6.47	6.97	6.61	5.74	4.38	4.48	5.04	5.78	5.76	5.75
1991	5.64	6.28	6.94	7.09	7.95	19.43	17.40	18.45	21.39	9.87	6.27	5.79	11.04
1992	5.90	6.02	5.81	6.14	6.16	4.26	1.85	1.02	1.05	2.43	4.10	3.67	4.03
1993	3.37	3.21	3.41	4.00	4.03	4.09	5.02	7.25	11.85	11.40	6.15	4.00	5.65
1994	3.76	3.90	4.66	4.83	5.04	4.94	4.08	4.24	3.44	2.92	3.44	3.43	4.06
1995	3.43	3.59	4.22	4.61	4.90	5.63	7.44	7.30	7.26	7.90	3.57	3.55	5.28
1996	3.97	4.39	5.20	6.11	6.63	6.72	6.97	8.15	13.70	10.94	4.30	3.91	6.75
1997	3.97	3.98	4.46	4.94	5.15	5.11	6.64	7.03	7.15	3.90	2.41	2.81	4.80
1998	3.15	3.73	5.14	5.79	5.86	6.70	6.71	5.37	6.03	6.38	5.37	4.99	5.44
1999[1]	4.98	5.60	6.02	5.82	6.46	8.78	10.10	11.48	7.98	10.25	4.33	3.41	7.10

[1] Preliminary. *Source: Economic Research Service, U.S. Department of Agriculture (ERS-USDA)*

Palm Oil

Palm oil is the world's second largest vegetable oil crop, but first in foreign trade. Palm oil is a tropical oil, but competes directly with other cooking oils such as soybean and sunflower oils that are grown in more temperate climates. Almost all of the world's production comes from Malaysia and Indonesia. However, it's expected that Indonesia's output will overtake Malaysia in ten years or less, assuming no fresh currency crises develop that hamper the anticipated new investment in palm oil plantations.

Palm oil production in 1999/2000 (October/September) is forecast to be a record 20.6 million metric tonnes vs. 19.2 million in 1998/99. Two-thirds of the world's production is exported. Estimated consumption of a record 20.2 million tonnes in 1999/00 compares with 18.4 million in 1998/99 and annual usage of 11.5 million tonnes early in the 1990's. Palm oil exports go mostly to Europe, the world's largest importer of crude vegetable oils. World palm oil stocks are estimated to be 2.69 million tonnes at yearend 1999/00 (September) vs. 2.48 million a year earlier.

Malaysia's 1999/00 production is forecast at a record large 10.2 million tonnes vs. 9.8 million in 1998/99. Assuming the crop forecasts are realized, Malaysia's 1999/00 exports are estimated to be a record 8.7 million tonnes vs. 8.1 million in 1998/99. Carryover stocks, however, have been increasing in recent years and are expected to total a record 1.3 million tonnes at yearend 1999/00 vs. 1.2 million a year earlier. Indonesia's estimated 1999/00 crop of 6.4 million tonnes compares with 5.8 million in 1998/99. Palm kernel oil production is likewise concentrated in Southeast Asia; the 1999/00 world crop of 6.1 million tonnes compares with 5.8 million in 1998/99.

World palm oil prices traversed a wide range during the 1990's with a low of $318 per metric tonne in 1990/91 to a high of $651/mt in 1994/95, basis Malaysia, FOB. The 1998/99 average of $482/mt compares with $601/mt in 1997/98. Contributing to the firm prices is the strong growth in consumption. China's estimated 1999/00 consumption of 1.6 million tonnes compares with 1.25 million in 1998/99.

Futures Markets

Crude Palm Oil and crude Palm Kernel Oil are traded on the Kuala Lumpur Commodity Exchange (KLCE).

World Palm Oil Statistics In Thousands of Metric Tons

Crop Year	Production: Colombia	Production: Indonesia	Production: Ivory Coast	Production: Malaysia	Production: Nigeria	Production: Thailand	Production: World Total	Imports: China	Imports: Pakistan	Imports: World Total	Exports: Indonesia	Exports: Malaysia	Exports: World Total
1993-4	348	3,630	305	7,103	640	311	13,793	1,653	1,080	10,346	1,965	6,737	10,391
1994-5	391	4,144	282	7,771	661	346	15,073	1,786	1,215	10,674	1,904	6,728	10,573
1995-6	393	4,587	277	8,264	667	369	16,152	1,178	1,166	10,558	2,082	6,896	10,582
1996-7	440	5,078	250	9,000	678	386	17,487	1,851	1,020	11,729	2,419	7,794	11,875
1997-8[1]	437	5,086	266	8,509	688	363	16,967	1,490	1,210	11,831	2,416	7,847	11,689
1998-9[2]	460	5,841	270	9,759	713	389	19,102	1,419	1,050	12,471	2,760	8,482	12,645
1999-00[3]	487	6,300	274	10,532	735	427	20,526	1,640	1,090	13,786	3,230	9,325	14,018

[1] Preliminary. [2] Estimate. [3] Forecast. *Source: The Oil World*

Supply and Distribution of Palm Oil in the United States In Thousands of Metric Tons

Year Beginning Oct. 1	Stocks Oct. 1	Imports	Total Supply	Consumption: Edible Products	Consumption: Inedible Products	Consumption: Total End Products	Total Disappearance	Exports	Prices: U.S. Import Value[4]	Prices: Malaysia, F.O.B., RBD	Prices: Palm Kernal Oil, Malaysia, C.I.F. Rotterdam
				In Millions of Pounds					U.S. $ Per Metric Ton		
1994-5	16.4	98.7	115.1	38.1	113.6	151.7	101.8	5.9	538	647	680
1995-6	7.4	106.9	114.3	6.7	103.9	110.6	91.1	9.2	511	545	729
1996-7	14.0	146.4	160.4	-----	91.8	91.8	134.8	4.2	432	544	680
1997-8[1]	21.4	163.0	184.4	-----	93.8	93.8	155.0	4.4	464	640	653
1998-9[2]	29.0	181.0	210.0	-----	72.4	72.4	173.0	4.1	-----	514	725
1999-00[3]	34.0	205.0	239.0	-----	77.9	77.9	202.0	-----	-----	371	

[1] Preliminary. [2] Estimate. [3] Forecast. [4] Market value in the foreign country, excluding import duties, ocean freight and marine insurance.
Sources: The Oil World; Economic Research Service, U.S. Department of Agriculture (ERS-USDA)

Average Wholesale Palm Oil Prices, CIF, Bulk, U.S. Ports In Cents Per Pound

Year	Jan.	Feb.	Mar.	Apr.	May	June	July	Aug.	Sept.	Oct.	Nov.	Dec.	Average
1993	23.18	23.09	22.99	22.26	21.95	21.01	20.31	19.84	19.43	18.83	19.74	21.90	21.21
1994	21.91	21.67	21.72	23.08	26.27	28.94	27.44	30.18	32.15	31.93	34.95	36.83	28.09
1995	34.26	33.82	36.18	35.56	32.80	33.06	33.68	32.59	30.86	31.45	31.96	30.00	33.02
1996	27.08	26.52	26.33	27.52	28.57	25.43	24.78	24.46	27.24	26.13	26.95	27.45	26.54
1997	28.68	29.25	28.00	28.18	28.93	27.25	26.17	25.55	25.37	27.33	27.28	25.05	27.25
1998	29.30	29.59	30.53	32.10	31.11	31.42	32.33	33.14	33.14	33.06	33.30	34.00	31.92
1999[1]	31.06	28.58	25.52	25.52	24.50	21.30	18.15	18.70	21.00				23.81

[1] Preliminary. *Source: Economic Research Service, U.S. Department of Agriculture (ERS-USDA)*

Paper

The United States is by far the world's largest producer of paper and paperboard. Production in recent years has exceeded 85 million metric tonnes annually. The next largest producer is Japan where production has been about 28 million tonnes per year. Canada follows with output of about 18 million tonnes. While the U.S., Japan and Canada remain the largest producers, there are other significant producers including the Scandinavian countries. German production of paper and paperboard has been in excess of 14 million tonnes. Finland's production has exceeded 10 million tonnes while Sweden produces in excess of 9 million tonnes.

In newsprint production, by far the largest producer is Canada. Production of newsprint has averaged 9.5 million tonnes per year. The United States is the next largest producer averaging about 6.4 million tonnes per year or about 67 percent of Canadian production. Japan is the third largest producer of newsprint with 1998 production of about 3.2 million tonnes. Sweden in 1998 produced almost 2.5 million tonnes of newsprint followed by Germany with close to 1.8 million tonnes. South Korea produced just over 1.5 million tonnes while Finland's production in 1998 was almost 1.5 million tonnes. Other significant producers include Russia, France, China, Australia and India.

Production of Paper and Paperboard by Selected Countries In Thousands of Metric Tons

Year	Austria	Canada	Finland	France	Germany	Italy	Japan	Netherlands	Russia	Spain	Sweden	United Kingdom	United States
1992	3252	16,585	9,147	7,690	13,214	6,040	28,324	2,835	5,765	3,449	8,378	5,151	75,161
1993	3300	17,528	9,990	7,975	13,034	6,019	27,764	2,855	4,459	3,348	8,781	5,406	77,167
1994	3603	18,349	10,909	8,701	14,457	6,705	28,527	3,011	3,412	3,503	9,284	5,829	80,948
1995	3599	18,713	10,942	8,619	14,827	6,810	59,664	2,967	4,073	3,684	9,159	6,093	85,526
1996	3653	17,472	10,441	8,566	14,733	6,954	30,014	2,987	3,224	3,684	9,018	6,188	81,971
1997[1]	3816	17,976	12,148		15,953	7,533		3,159	3,332		9,779	6,455	86,274

[1] Preliminary. *Source: Food and Agriculture Organization of the United Nations (FAO-UN)*

Production of Newsprint by Selected Countries (Monthly Average) In Thousands of Metric Tons

Year	Australia	Brazil	Canada	China	Finland	France	Germany	India	Japan	Rep. of Korea	Russia	Sweden	United States
1993	34.8	23.0	761.0	52.4	118.7	66.8	108.5	23.9	243.1	61.9	70.4	193.8	534.9
1994	33.5	22.0	776.8	60.1	120.5	70.3	124.9	22.9	247.7	72.8	86.5	201.3	582.0
1995	37.4	24.6	768.8	72.1	118.8	74.2	143.8	26.3	258.2	79.0	121.4	195.5	529.3
1996	36.5	23.1	751.3	79.6	110.6	65.2	131.0	24.8	261.7	108.7	103.8	190.2	525.3
1997	34.0	22.1	767.1	68.7	122.5	65.3	134.8	23.3	266.0	132.7	99.8	200.9	545.3
1998[1]	33.9	22.6	718.6	70.8	123.6	75.7	148.0	28.8	272.0	128.1		206.9	
1999[2]	32.5	20.5		90.9	124.4			29.1	273.9			208.3	

[1] Preliminary. [2] Estimate. *Source: United Nations*

Index Price of Paperboard 1982 = 100

Year	Jan.	Feb.	Mar.	Apr.	May	June	July	Aug.	Sept.	Oct.	Nov.	Dec.	Average
1993	133.0	131.6	131.3	130.6	129.9	128.9	128.6	128.0	128.0	129.7	130.2	130.5	130.0
1994	130.2	130.1	131.1	133.4	133.1	133.5	137.8	143.5	146.9	153.6	156.0	156.7	140.5
1995	165.3	171.2	172.3	183.8	188.2	188.4	189.9	190.6	190.3	188.8	185.7	182.2	183.1
1996	175.7	172.6	166.6	161.8	154.0	150.6	148.0	145.5	145.6	146.6	146.9	147.6	155.1
1997	147.1	144.2	139.7	137.2	136.8	137.5	137.8	143.8	148.4	150.1	154.4	156.1	144.4
1998	155.9	156.1	156.0	155.2	154.2	153.7	152.2	150.9	149.0	146.9	144.7	143.6	151.6
1999[1]	142.2	142.3	146.4	148.1	149.3	149.5	154.5	158.6	161.0	162.7	162.3	162.4	153.3

[1] Preliminary. *Source: Bureau of Labor Statistics, U.S. Department of Commerce (BLS) (0914)*

Index Price of Wood Pulp, Bleached Suphate Softwood 1982 = 100

Year	Jan.	Feb.	Mar.	Apr.	May	June	July	Aug.	Sept.	Oct.	Nov.	Dec.	Average
1993	121.6	118.1	112.7	112.3	112.7	112.7	110.7	108.9	108.6	107.1	105.5	104.0	111.2
1994	106.7	106.9	109.6	113.5	113.4	118.0	119.4	124.3	130.3	137.1	141.4	142.2	121.9
1995	150.9	153.0	187.5	193.0	202.4	215.2	217.8	223.3	218.8	223.3	217.0	212.7	201.2
1996	195.0	175.4	155.5	123.5	111.1	120.1	126.9	129.0	129.4	130.3	129.3	131.5	138.1
1997	129.6	125.9	123.9	119.0	121.8	123.9	130.9	134.4	135.7	135.7	136.8	136.2	129.5
1998	132.0	131.3	127.8	118.7	118.0	122.8	125.7	122.8	117.2	113.7	111.9	111.4	121.1
1999[1]	103.2	102.6	102.4	100.8	101.1	102.3	112.5	115.6	117.9	117.1	121.2	126.5	110.3

[1] Preliminary. *Source: Bureau of Labor Statistics, U.S. Department of Commerce (BLS) (0911-0211)*

Index Price of Shipping Sack Paper[2] 1982 = 100

Year	Jan.	Feb.	Mar.	Apr.	May	June	July	Aug.	Sept.	Oct.	Nov.	Dec.	Average
1993	155.7	155.7	155.7	155.7	151.8	151.8	151.8	151.8	151.8	151.8	152.5	152.5	153.2
1994	151.3	150.9	154.3	154.5	159.3	163.9	169.9	170.3	176.6	178.2	184.9	185.5	166.6
1995	190.4	204.5	209.5	212.0	221.5	224.2	224.2	224.2	224.0	223.4	212.8	207.3	214.8
1996	205.2	202.2	201.5	194.7	194.3	193.1	189.9	185.7	183.0	183.0	185.8	185.8	192.0
1997	185.8	186.4	186.7	186.5	184.3	184.1	183.9	188.1	182.0	188.5	196.9	197.6	187.6
1998	197.1	197.2	197.2	197.2	196.3	196.3	194.4	194.4	194.4	194.4	194.4	194.4	195.6
1999[1]	194.4	194.4	194.4	199.7	201.7	203.2	203.2	207.8	208.4	208.0	208.4	208.4	202.7

[1] Preliminary. [2] Unbleached kraft. *Source: Bureau of Labor Statistics, U.S. Department of Commerce (BLS) (0913-0307)*

Producer Price Index of Standard Newsprint 1982 = 100

Year	Jan.	Feb.	Mar.	Apr.	May	June	July	Aug.	Sept.	Oct.	Nov.	Dec.	Average
1993	110.4	111.2	114.1	113.9	113.0	113.1	112.7	112.6	111.3	111.2	111.0	111.0	112.1
1994	109.9	109.5	110.7	110.6	112.2	113.8	116.9	116.9	121.7	123.8	126.8	127.3	116.7
1995	135.8	134.6	140.1	147.4	152.3	164.8	166.1	166.1	174.5	186.2	186.2	186.2	161.8
1996	186.2	186.2	185.2	182.7	173.5	164.4	157.4	148.7	145.7	133.1	127.3	123.1	159.5
1997	121.1	120.9	123.1	128.6	135.9	137.2	138.6	139.4	139.4	139.4	141.3	141.8	133.9
1998	142.2	142.5	141.8	142.3	140.0	140.3	143.4	143.1	144.6	147.6	147.6	145.0	143.4
1999[1]	143.0	135.9	128.1	125.0	117.8	117.7	110.3	111.7	111.4				122.3

[1] Preliminary. *Source: Bureau of Labor Statistics, U.S. Department of Commerce (BLS) (0913-02)*

Index Price of Coated Printing Paper, No. 3 1982 = 100

Year	Jan.	Feb.	Mar.	Apr.	May	June	July	Aug.	Sept.	Oct.	Nov.	Dec.	Average
1993	123.4	123.3	123.3	123.4	123.4	123.3	123.0	123.0	123.2	122.9	122.9	122.9	123.2
1994	122.0	122.1	121.8	122.2	121.6	121.6	121.6	125.2	130.7	131.7	132.9	136.3	125.8
1995	139.5	145.8	150.2	153.1	147.7	152.0	159.3	159.3	160.4	160.3	160.3	160.3	154.0
1996	160.2	159.7	159.4	159.2	155.6	153.5	153.0	152.5	152.2	151.8	151.9	152.9	155.2
1997	152.7	153.1	152.9	153.2	153.2	154.6	154.5	154.5	153.2	153.3	153.2	153.3	153.5
1998	153.8	154.7	154.2	154.2	154.1	154.0	154.0	153.8	151.9	151.5	151.5	151.9	153.3
1999[1]	151.1	150.8	149.4	149.4	152.4	152.0							150.9

[1] Preliminary. *Source: Bureau of Labor Statistics, U.S. Department of Commerce (BLS) (0913-0113)*

International Paper Prices--Export Unit Value

Year	Jan.	Feb.	Mar.	Apr.	May	June	July	Aug.	Sept.	Oct.	Nov.	Dec.	Average
NEWSPRINT - Finland In Markka Per Metric Ton													
1995	2,563	2,589	2,577	2,614	2,598	2,667	3,037	3,122	3,172	3,187	3,214	3,191	2,885
1996	3,320	3,412	3,438	3,463	3,442	3,362	3,265	3,110	3,010	3,709	2,899	2,841	3,207
1997	2,741	2,662	2,669	2,667	2,701	2,602	2,642	2,709	2,736	2,697	2,706	2,755	2,694
1998	2,852	2,843	2,858	2,896	2,890	2,839	2,858	2,870	2,847	2,809	2,755	2,748	2,838
PRINTING AND WRITING - Finland In Markka Per Metric Ton													
1995	3,816	3,897	3,905	4,066	4,165	4,284	4,473	4,416	4,439	4,555	4,569	4,400	4,235
1996	4,556	4,555	4,503	4,374	4,265	4,069	3,871	3,743	3,644	3,644	3,667	3,654	4,027
1997	3,620	3,579	3,648	3,651	3,698	3,656	3,620	3,649	3,725	3,738	3,799	3,803	3,687
1998	4,029	4,068	4,097	4,155	4,104	4,070	4,060	4,042	4,003	3,951	3,884	3,841	4,029

Source: Food and Agricultural Organization of the United Nations (FAO-UN)

International Paper Prices--Import Unit Value

Year	Jan.	Feb.	Mar.	Apr.	May	June	July	Aug.	Sept.	Oct.	Nov.	Dec.	Average
NEWSPRINT - United Kingdom In British Pounds Per Metric Ton													
1995	344	353	348	363	376	384	428	465	470	473	469	241	393
1996	498	534	529	514	518	513	504	476	461	412	435	427	485
1997	439	400	394	380	372	380	200	385	374	368	373	377	370
1998	379	367	367	370	357	361	360	357	364	360	359		364
PRINTING AND WRITING - United Kingdom In British Pounds Per Metric Ton													
1995	613	571	611	617	643	619	670	698	718	713	675	684	653
1996	709	776	683	639	661	635	607	919	664	631	629	684	686
1997	606	561	580	561	554	530	555	549	594	559	602	565	568
1998	535	540	540	530	550	516	514	494	532	511	513		525

Source: Food and Agricultural Organization of the United Nations (FAO-UN)

Peanuts and Peanut Oil

World raw peanut (groundnut) production in 1999/2000 trailed initial forecasts, but still proved the third highest crop on record. Production of 27.8 million metric tonnes compares with the record high 1998/99 crop of 28.9 million tonnes. On a shelled basis the totals would be about 25 percent lower. Peanuts are the world's fourth largest oilseed crop, generally just topping sunflowerseed production. While world acreage devoted to major oilseeds has generally increased, the area devoted to peanuts has changed little throughout the 1990's. Currently there are 21 million hectares devoted to peanut production globally.

China produced a record large 12.3 million tonnes in 1999/00 vs. 11.9 million in 1998/99. India's crop of 6 million tonnes compares with 7.4 million, respectively. The two countries together produce nearly two-thirds of the world's crop, with the U.S. a distant third at 1.73 million tonnes in 1999/00. India's peanut acreage is nearly twice that of China, but India's average yield is about a third of China's yield.

Foreign trade and world carryover in peanuts is small as most peanut crops are consumed locally. World imports during 1999/00 of 1.5 million tonnes were marginally higher than in 1998/99.

The world's peanut crush is among the smallest of the major oilseeds at 13.5 million tonnes in 1999/00, about a tenth of the soybean crush. More of the world's peanut crop is allocated to meal production than oil, as meal production totaled 5.4 million tonnes in 1999/00 vs. 5.8 million in 1998/99, totals about equal to consumption in both years. Peanut oil production in 1999/00 of 4.2 million tonnes compares with 4.4 million in 1998/99. Foreign trade in meal and oil is small and carryover stocks are generally insignificant.

The average world peanut oilseed prices in 1998/99 (October/September) of $847 per metric tonne, basis Rotterdam, compares with $1055 in 1997/98 and a ten-year average of $997 per tonne. Rotterdam meal prices in 1998/99 averaged $104 per metric tonne vs. $134 in 1997/98 and the ten-year average of $161; oil prices of $801 per tonne compare with $964 and $739, respectively. In the U.S., the average price for peanut meal, basis southeast mills FOB during 1998/99 of $110 per tonne compares with $231 in 1997/98; peanut oil prices averaged $876 and $1065, respectively.

In the U.S., the 1999/00 crop (October/September) of 3.85 billion pounds compares with 3.96 billion in 1998/99. U.S. peanut production is largely concentrated in the Southeastern states. Peanuts are also grown in the Southern plains states where irrigation is often needed and production costs run higher. The average yield for the 1999 crop was put at 2,660 pounds per acre vs. 2,702 a year earlier. The acreage harvested of 1.44 million acres compares with 1.47 million, respectively.

Georgia is the largest producing state with at least a third of total production (1.4 billion pounds in 1999) followed by Texas (with the largest gains in production in recent years), North Carolina and Alabama. Total supplies in 1999/00 of 5.3 billion pounds compares with 5.0 billion in 1998/99, and include an estimated October 1, 1999 carry-in of 1.3 billion pounds vs. 848 million a year earlier. U.S. peanut imports are generally small, 165 million pounds in 1999/00. Imports, however, have seen wide swings at times, from 401 million pounds in 1980 to 2 million pounds in the early 1990's.

Total U.S. peanut disappearance in 1999/00 of 4.0 billion pounds compares with 3.7 billion in 1998/99. The crush was forecast at 700 million pounds vs. 460 million, and exports at 800 million pounds vs. 650 million, respectively. The October 1, 2000 carry-in is forecast as unchanged at 1.3 billion pounds. U.S. peanut exports go mostly to Canada followed by the Netherlands and U.K. As a direct food, 2.2 billion pounds were forecast for 1999/00 vs. 2.1 billion in 1998/99. Peanut use as a direct foodstuff has slipped during the past decade. Contributing to the decline is reduced demand for peanut butter, a drop in snack peanut consumption and little growth in peanut based candies.

Futures Market

Peanut futures are traded on the Beijing Commodity Exchange (BCE).

World Production of Peanuts (in the Shell) In Thousands of Metric Tons

Year	Argentina	Burma	China	India	Indonesia	Nigeria	Senegal	South Africa	Sudan	Thailand	United States	Zaire	World Total
1990-1	574	440	6,368	7,514	860	250	703	112	325	162	1,634	380	22,206
1991-2	400	440	6,300	7,065	890	220	724	114	400	160	2,235	380	22,138
1992-3	210	433	5,953	8,854	913	250	579	172	390	162	1,943	380	23,082
1993-4	209	389	8,420	7,760	865	250	620	190	390	165	1,539	380	23,996
1994-5	280	445	9,682	8,255	880	250	720	105	390	165	1,927	380	26,278
1995-6	460	500	10,200	7,400	1,060	1,580	830	190	370	150	1,570	580	28,400
1996-7	300	590	10,140	9,020	990	330	650	140	370	150	1,660	570	28,530
1997-8	630	560	9,650	7,580	990	350	510	100	370	150	1,610	570	26,630
1998-9[1]	340	560	11,890	7,450	990	380	550	150	370	160	1,800	570	28,870
1999-00[2]	320	560	12,300	6,000	990	400	600	150	370	160	1,760	570	27,820

[1] Preliminary. [2] Estimate. *Source: Foreign Agricultural Service, U.S. Department of Agriculture (FAS-USDA)*

Salient Statistics of Peanuts in the United States

Crop Year	Agreage Planted (1,000 Acres)	Acreage Harvested for Nuts (1,000 Acres)	Average Yield Per Acre In Lbs.	Production 1,000 Lbs.	Season Farm Price Cents/Lb.	Farm Value Million Dollars	Exports Unshelled	Exports Shelled	Imports Unshelled	Imports Shelled
							Thousand Pounds (Year Beginning August 1)			
1986-7	1,564.7	1,535.2	2,408	3,700,745	29.2	1,073.3	75,687	441,954	328	1,598
1987-8	1,567.4	1,547.4	2,337	3,619,440	28.0	1,021.9	76,345	407,557	880	1,949
1988-9	1,657.4	1,628.4	2,445	3,980,917	27.9	1,115.2	105,746	437,867	650	2,094
1989-90	1,665.2	1,644.7	2,426	3,989,995	28.0	1,116.5	126,682	577,807	55	1,477
1990-1	1,840.0	1,809.5	1,991	3,602,770	34.7	1,257.2	250,851	401,149	6,429	20,571
1991-2	2,039.2	2,015.7	2,444	4,926,570	28.3	1,392.0	997,000	630,000	5,000	27,000
1992-3	1,686.6	1,669.1	2,567	4,284,416	30.0	1,285.4	951,000	611,250	2,000	2,000
1993-4	1,733.5	1,689.8	2,008	3,392,415	30.4	1,030.9	555,000	352,500	2,000	1,420
1994-5	1,641.0	1,618.5	2,624	4,247,455	28.9	1,229.0	878,000	583,142	74,000	55,385
1995-6	1,537.5	1,517.0	2,282	3,461,475	29.3	1,013.3	824,000	564,021	153,000	108,303
1996-7	1,401.5	1,380.0	2,653	3,661,205	28.1	1,029.8	666,000	440,438	127,000	95,041
1997-8	1,434.0	1,413.8	2,503	3,539,380	28.3	1,001.6	681,000	455,264	141,000	101,792
1998-9[1]	1,521.0	1,467.0	2,702	3,963,440	28.0	1,109.6	561,000	-----	155,000	-----
1999-00[2]	1,533.0	1,427.5	2,711	3,870,200	27.9	1,066.0	800,000	-----	165,000	-----

[1] Preliminary. [2] Estimate. *Source: Economic Research Service, U.S. Department of Agriculture (ERS-USDA)*

Supply and Disposition of Peanuts (Farmer's Stock Basis) & Support Program in the United States

Crop Year	Supply: Production	Supply: Imports	Supply: Stocks Aug. 1	Supply: Total	Disposition: Exports	Disposition: Crushed fior Oil	Disposition: Seed, Loss & Residual	Disposition: Food	Disposition: Total Disappearance	Gov't Support: Support Price	Gov't Support: Additional	Amount Put Under Support: Quantity Mil. Lbs.	Amount Put Under Support: % of Production
	In Millions of Pounds									Cents per Lb.			
1986-7	3,697	2	845	4,544	663	514	291	2,073	3,541	30.37	7.5	290	7.8
1987-8	3,616	2	1,003	4,621	618	560	539	2,071	3,788	30.41	7.5	700	19.3
1988-9	3,981	2	833	4,816	688	814	217	2,254	3,974	30.76	7.5	540	13.6
1989-90	3,990	2	843	4,835	989	624	211	2,312	4,136	30.79	7.5	401	10.0
1990-1	3,604	27	701	4,331	652	689	288	2,020	3,649	31.57	7.5	576	16.0
1991-2	4,927	5	683	5,615	997	1,103	254	2,207	4,561	32.14	7.5	1,070	21.7
1992-3	4,284	2	1,055	5,341	951	891	227	2,122	3,991	33.75	6.6	436	10.2
1993-4	3,392	2	1,350	4,744	553	670	372	2,088	3,683	33.75	6.6	324	9.6
1994-5	4,247	74	1,061	5,382	878	982	316	2,009	4,184	33.92	6.6	820	19.3
1995-6	3,461	153	1,198	4,812	824	999	238	1,993	4,054	33.92	6.6	818	24.0
1996-7	3,661	127	758	4,546	666	692	363	2,029	3,750	30.50	6.6	320	8.7
1997-8	3,539	141	795	4,475	681	544	303	2,099	3,627	30.50	6.6	417	11.8
1998-9[1]	3,963	155	848	4,966	561	460	374	2,137	3,532	30.50	6.6	-----	-----
1999-00[2]	3,821	165	1,436	5,422	800	700	322	2,160	3,982	30.50	6.6	-----	-----

[1] Preliminary. [2] Estimate. *Source: Economic Research Service, U.S. Department of Agriculture (ERS-USDA)*

Production of Peanuts (Harvested for Nuts) in the United States, by States In Thousands of Pounds

Year	Alabama	Florida	Georgia	New Mexico	North Carolina	Oklahoma	South Carolina	Texas	Virgina	Total
1986	494,940	233,160	1,632,575	28,700	440,440	184,500	25,530	385,000	275,900	3,700,745
1987	465,300	215,800	1,575,000	29,760	392,200	222,750	31,200	441,000	243,000	3,616,010
1988	561,680	228,600	1,801,550	30,552	419,985	225,040	32,110	417,500	263,900	3,980,917
1989	537,750	214,890	1,849,500	43,680	370,120	210,700	32,500	484,700	246,155	3,989,995
1990	386,560	233,120	1,347,500	50,000	475,600	235,320	30,105	534,650	309,915	3,602,770
1991	638,485	279,660	2,228,550	51,075	461,700	243,800	33,600	682,500	307,200	4,926,570
1992	591,180	202,510	1,820,465	58,236	406,980	236,180	32,500	680,150	256,215	4,284,416
1993	473,220	194,880	1,383,545	56,680	299,585	233,580	24,500	550,175	176,250	3,392,415
1994	446,220	207,480	1,862,630	51,660	485,465	261,000	36,250	605,570	291,180	4,247,455
1995	483,360	193,590	1,414,880	43,000	347,040	201,880	30,800	540,000	206,925	3,461,475
1996	449,805	236,160	1,433,770	37,950	367,500	195,210	32,550	689,000	219,260	3,661,205
1997	372,490	228,060	1,333,830	46,710	329,640	184,800	30,450	822,150	191,250	3,539,380
1998	432,415	233,100	1,511,655	62,040	397,155	159,750	28,175	917,900	221,250	3,963,440
1999[1]	471,500	263,200	1,419,600	58,800	291,550	197,600	26,450	924,000	217,500	3,870,200

[1] Preliminary. *Source: Agricultural Statistics Board, U.S. Department of Agriculture (ASB-USDA)*

PEANUTS AND PEANUT OIL

Supply and Reported Uses of Shelled Peanuts and Products in the United States In Thousands of Pounds

Crop Year Beginning Aug. 1	Shelled Peanuts --- Stocks, Aug. 1 --- Edible	Oil Stock[2]	Shelled Peanuts ------ Production ------ Edible	Oil Stock[2]	Reported Used (Shelled Peanuts -- Raw Basis) --- Edible Grades Used In --- Candy[3]	Snacks[4]	Sandwich Spread	Butter[5]	Other Products	Total	Shelled Peanuts Crushed[6]	Crude Oil Pro-duction	Cake & Meal Pro-duction
1990-1	455,586	15,194	1,836,052	330,102	305,324	355,258	-----	742,384	37,888	1,440,854	517,712	213,112	299,820
1991-2	386,155	65,950	2,538,398	616,170	327,617	346,255	-----	886,367	34,173	1,594,412	828,986	356,276	459,457
1992-3	871,207	57,829	2,376,782	533,641	328,324	352,775	-----	797,910	24,981	1,503,990	669,942	285,904	377,301
1993-4	679,639	42,054	1,748,734	425,710	362,418	348,867	-----	727,006	36,301	1,474,592	503,674	212,216	292,093
1994-5	752,814	57,188	1,741,824	511,635	349,630	301,548	-----	709,823	36,854	1,397,855	738,221	314,189	415,394
1995-6	370,431	58,188	1,253,451	491,818	350,663	277,089	-----	728,076	32,015	1,387,843	751,281	320,909	420,919
1996-7	498,954	126,318	1,692,581	305,674	360,846	290,102	-----	727,531	33,825	1,412,304	520,413	220,877	294,590
1997-8	509,476	41,000	1,694,016	290,882	351,017	306,908	-----	760,230	35,471	1,453,626	409,249	175,853	228,276
1998-9[1]	788,877	16,454	2,186,629	286,060	380,176	346,221	-----	742,180	22,131	1,490,708	345,911	145,254	192,425

[1] Preliminary. [2] Includes straight run oil stock peanuts. [3] Includes peanut butter made by manufacturers for own use in candy. [4] Formerly titled Salted Peanuts. [5] Includes peanut butter made by manufacturers for own use in cookies and sandwiches, but excludes peanut butter used in candy. [6] All crushings regardless of grade. *Source: National Agricultural Statistics Service, U.S. Department of Agriculture (NASS-USDA)*

Shelled Peanuts (Raw Basis) Used in Primary Products, by Type In Thousands of Pounds

Year	Virginia Candy[2]	Virginia Snack Peanuts	Virginia Peanut Butter[3]	Virginia Total	Runner Candy[2]	Runner Snack Peanuts	Runner Peanut Butter[3]	Runner Total	Spanish Candy[2]	Spanish Snack Peanuts	Spanish Peanut Butter[3]	Spanish Total
1990-1	26,043	142,113	101,069	286,242	259,995	189,254	580,691	1,049,423	19,286	23,841	60,624	105,189
1991-2	51,312	142,514	89,045	297,570	244,815	180,609	759,747	1,203,233	31,490	23,132	37,575	93,609
1992-3	49,223	124,875	92,355	275,895	259,498	203,732	674,962	1,152,775	19,603	24,168	30,593	75,320
1993-4	44,889	99,381	63,270	222,641	298,325	227,286	365,047	1,179,396	19,204	22,200	28,689	72,555
1994-5	26,857	97,389	51,354	190,916	302,697	185,377	644,711	1,152,110	20,076	18,782	13,758	54,829
1995-6	25,176	93,041	71,310	203,183	304,285	169,142	634,350	1,123,719	21,202	14,906	22,416	60,941
1996-7	24,158	91,882	64,274	193,166	318,924	176,851	634,387	1,149,347	17,764	21,369	28,870	69,791
1997-8	48,428	80,309	59,228	182,100	302,791	206,718	676,839	1,206,946	19,798	19,581	24,163	64,580
1998-9[1]	36,178	95,888	57,864	193,422	321,838	234,412	668,179	1,242,148	22,160	15,921	16,137	55,138

[1] Preliminary. [2] Includes peanut butter made by manufacturers for own use in candy. [3] Includes peanut butter made by manufacturers for own use in cookies and sandwiches, but excludes peanut butter used in candy. *Source: National Agricultural Statistics Service, U.S. Department of Agriculture (NASS-USDA)*

Production, Consumption, Stocks and Foreign Trade of Peanut Oil in the U.S. In Millions of Pounds

Crop Year Beginning Aug. 1	Production Crude	Production Refined	Consumption In Refining	Consumption In End Products	Stocks Dec. 31 Crude	Stocks Dec. 31 Refined	Imports for Con-sumption	Exports
1991-2	261.5	125.6	132.3	141.0	27.5	3.1	1.0	151.0
1992-3	285.9	181.1	188.4	182.1	46.2	5.3	0	59.0
1993-4	212.2	155.2	163.7	149.1	6.5	3.9	11.0	61.0
1994-5	319.9	120.0	126.1	118.9	5.0	2.8	5.0	21.5
1995-6	329.0	125.7	129.9	126.0	19.9	2.8	3.2	47.8
1996-7	233.9	133.5	138.9	138.4	85.6	2.8	5.0	13.0
1997-8	144.3	104.0	111.6	121.6	42.6	3.0	5.0	35.0
1998-9[1]	172.9	118.3	123.7	180.1	47.2	3.8		
1999-00[2]	208.8	173.3	278.2	242.4	19.7	1.7		

[1] Preliminary. [2] Forecast. NA = Not available. *Source: Bureau of the Census, U.S. Department of Commerce*

Production of Crude Peanut Oil in the United States In Millions of Pounds

Year	Jan.	Feb.	Mar.	Apr.	May	June	July	Aug.	Sept.	Oct.	Nov.	Dec.	Total
1990	11.1	15.8	14.2	22.2	24.9	24.1	14.0	8.5	2.1	14.4	12.5	15.9	179.7
1991	-----	70.8	-----	-----	71.1	-----	-----	59.5	-----	-----	60.1	-----	261.5
1992	28.0	26.8	42.5	40.9	39.8	40.6	37.3	31.3	35.1	24.2	19.2	15.6	381.3
1993	16.9	17.0	24.1	28.8	23.3	29.0	25.6	22.5	3.6	8.6	16.4	14.6	230.4
1994	18.1	18.3	21.2	18.7	25.6	15.4	21.7	16.8	17.2	11.9	18.4	24.2	227.5
1995	27.9	28.6	42.7	36.9	39.2	29.2	26.9	26.3	17.4	13.2	19.5	24.3	332.0
1996	29.2	31.9	36.8	36.8	36.7	33.3	31.4	31.5	27.1	21.1	20.6	21.8	358.2
1997	19.9	16.1	18.8	17.9	13.3	15.9	9.9	12.1	6.1	12.2	11.6	14.0	167.7
1998	16.4	14.5	14.3	13.0	10.8	10.0	9.5	6.3	5.8	6.9	13.6	13.9	134.9
1999[1]	16.2	18.2	15.8	18.2	16.4	20.7	20.8	17.8	16.3	13.5	16.9	22.5	213.4

[1] Preliminary. NA = Not available. *Source: Bureau of the Census, U.S. Department of Commerce*

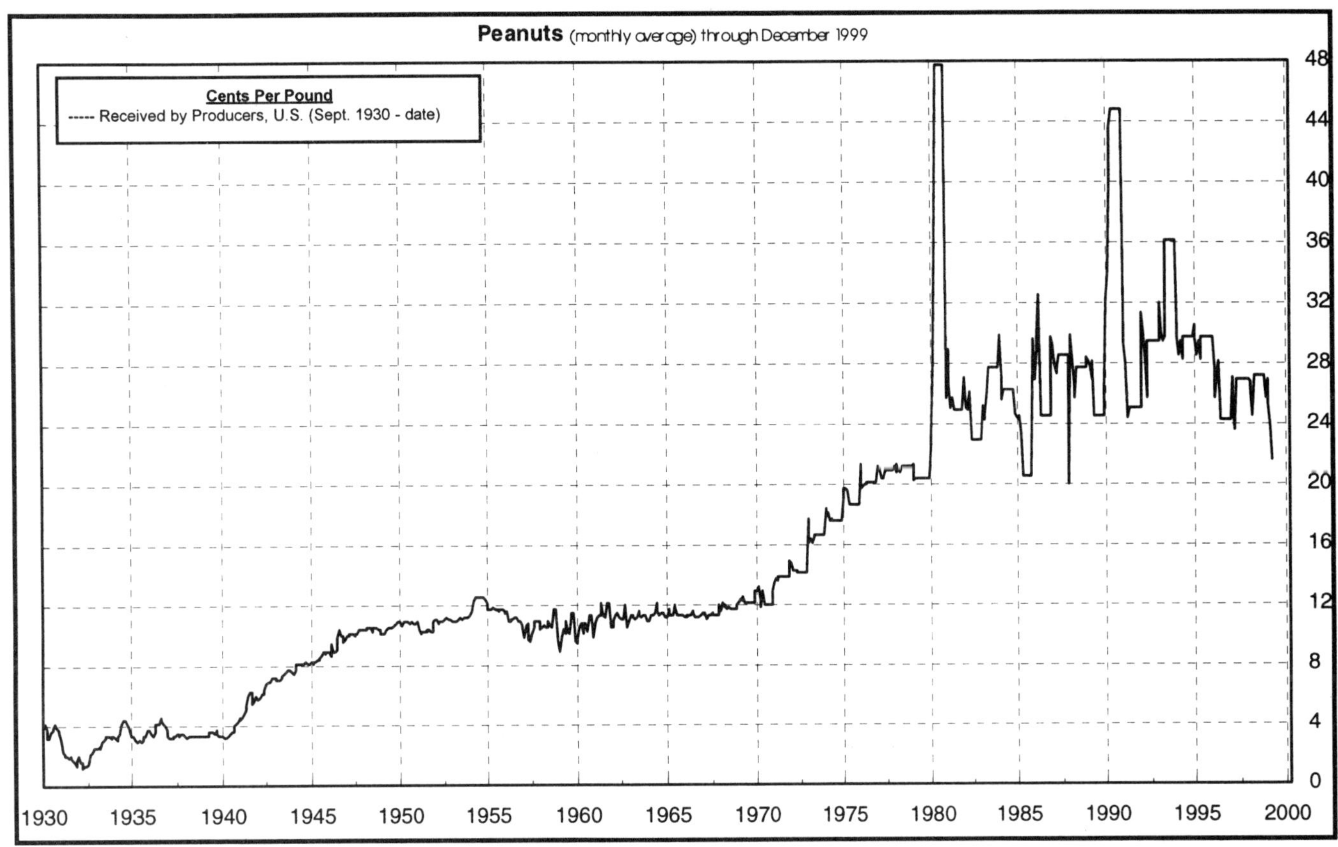

Average Price Received by Producers for Peanuts (in the Shell) in the U.S. In Cents Per Pound

Year	Aug.	Sept.	Oct.	Nov.	Dec.	Jan.	Feb.	Mar.	Apr.	May	June	July	Average[1]
1990-1	26.5	32.2	34.0	40.1	43.6	44.8	NQ	NQ	NQ	NQ	NQ	NQ	34.7
1991-2	30.4	29.3	28.1	24.4	25.1	NQ	NQ	NQ	NQ	NQ	NQ	NQ	28.3
1992-3	NQ	31.3	29.9	28.2	25.7	29.5	NQ	NQ	NQ	NQ	NQ	NQ	30.0
1993-4	NQ	32.0	30.0	29.5	29.7	36.1	NQ	NQ	NQ	NQ	NQ	NQ	30.4
1994-5	NQ	30.6	28.6	25.9	25.8	25.7	NQ	NQ	NQ	NQ	NQ	NQ	27.9
1995-6	30.6	29.7	28.6	29.5	28.3	29.8	NQ	NQ	NQ	NQ	NQ	NQ	29.4
1996-7	NQ	27.6	25.8	27.1	28.1	24.3	NQ	NQ	NQ	NQ	NQ	NQ	26.6
1997-8	23.3	27.1	25.4	25.0	30.7	24.7	NQ	NQ	NQ	NQ	NQ	NQ	26.0
1998-9	NQ	26.8	26.3	24.6	27.2	NQ	NQ	NQ	NQ	NQ	NQ	NQ	26.2
1999-00[2]	25.7	27.0	25.4	23.9	21.6	13.3							22.8

[1] Weighted average by sales. [2] Preliminary. NQ = No quote. *Source: National Agricultural Statistics Service, U.S. Department of Agriculture (NASS-USDA)*

Average Price of Domestic Crude Peanut Oil (in Tanks) F.O.B. Southeast Mills In Cents Per Pound

Year	Oct.	Nov.	Dec.	Jan.	Feb.	Mar.	Apr.	May	June	July	Aug.	Sept.	Average
1990-1	48.13	44.20	43.00	41.00	42.83	47.60	46.75	43.33	42.25	41.50	35.33	30.66	42.22
1991-2	34.33	27.67	23.50	23.50	23.63	23.17	25.00	27.88	25.60	26.19	23.88	22.00	25.53
1992-3	23.63	25.58	30.30	30.88	27.17	26.00	27.50	30.00	30.20	33.00	39.50	35.93	29.97
1993-4	40.20	43.33	43.17	46.10	46.12	44.50	43.40	44.25	43.75	44.00	45.00	43.10	43.91
1994-5	46.00	50.88	53.80	50.25	41.83	41.00	41.25	40.25	39.00	39.13	41.50	41.30	43.85
1995-6	42.50	41.63	39.20	37.25	36.00	36.60	39.25	42.80	43.00	43.00	42.60	40.80	40.39
1996-7	41.50	39.20	40.75	43.50	43.88	44.75	45.00	46.20	47.88	48.06	48.00	47.25	44.66
1997-8	49.63	51.00	51.25	51.60	51.00	51.00	50.00	47.20	45.50	44.00	43.75	43.88	48.32
1998-9	45.40	45.00	44.25	44.00	39.75	34.75	35.20	35.00	37.75	39.00	38.75	38.00	39.74
1999-00[1]	40.40	41.00	35.40	33.00									37.45

[1] Preliminary. *Source: Agricultural Marketing Service, U.S. Department of Agriculture (AMS-USDA)*

Pepper

Pepper prices increased in the January-October 1999 period. The price of black pepper (Malabar-Lampong-Brazilian) in January 1999 was reported to be $2.23 per pound. By May 1999, the price had increased 13 percent to $2.53 per pound. By October 1999, the price had risen another 6 percent to $2.68 per pound. When compared to the year before, the price of black pepper in January 1999 was some 12 percent higher than in January 1998. In May 1999, the price was 4 percent less than a year ago, while in October it was up 10 percent from 1998. The price of black pepper in October 1999 was some 136 percent higher than the price recorded in October 1995.

The price of white pepper (Muntok) did not increase over the same period. In January 1999, the New York spot price was $3.61 per pound, an increase of almost 4 percent from the year before. In May 1999, white pepper prices were $3.53 per pound, down 10 percent from the year before. In October 1999, white pepper prices were $3.23 per pound, down 5 percent from the year before. Overall, black pepper prices in the first 10 months of 1999 increased 20 percent while white pepper prices declined 11 percent.

The International Pepper Community (IPC) estimated that global pepper production in the year 2000 would be 217,164 metric tonnes, up over 2 percent from the 1999 pepper crop of 212,200 tonnes. The largest producer of pepper is India with a market share of about 25 percent. For the year 2000, the IPC estimated that India's crop would be 56,000 tonnes. India's stocks at the beginning of the season were estimated at 10,000 tonnes. Domestic consumption in India was estimated at 30,000 tonnes while projected exports were 36,000 tonnes. India's 2000 season crop was expected to be almost 30 percent less than in 1999 because of poor weather.

The next largest producer is Indonesia with the IPC projecting the 2000 season crop at 45,500 tonnes. Heavy rains in Sumatra appear to have damaged the crop in late 1999. As such it is possible that production will be less than expected. Domestic consumption in Indonesia is almost 13,000 tonnes with exports projected to be 32,000 tonnes.

Vietnam has emerged as a large pepper producer. The IPC forecast Vietnam's crop in year 2000 at 36,000 tonnes with exports of 34,000 tonnes. Other large producers and exporters include Brazil, Malaysia, China and Sri Lanka.

The IPC reported that U.S. imports of black pepper in the January-September 1999 period were 33,766 tonnes, up 54 percent from the same period in 1998. India was the largest supplier of black pepper to the U.S. followed by Indonesia, Malaysia and Brazil.

World Exports of Pepper (Black and White) and Prices in the United States In Metric Tons

	Exports (In Metric Tons)								New York Spot Prices (Cents Per Pound)				
									Indonesian			Indian	
Year	Brazil	India	Indonesia	Madagascar	Malaysia	Mexico	Sri Lanka	Vietnam	Lampong Black	Muntok White	Brazilian Black	Malabar Black	Tellicherry[2]
1989	27,717	25,120	42,138	1,417	26,260	2,388	1,576	7,551	138.2	146.2	136.2	135.9	174.8
1990	28,014	34,429	47,675	1,222	27,706	2,663	2,609	1,288	99.1	90.3	97.1	97.1	139.1
1991	47,553	18,735	49,667	1,844	25,458	1,861	2,058	16,252	71.1	70.1	67.1	67.1	117.8
1992	26,277	22,684	62,136	1,948	22,919	3,636	2,143	22,347	56.1	70.8	54.7	54.7	86.1
1993	26,254	47,677	27,684	2,001	16,737	2,430	5,032	20,138	62.5	114.6	62.3	62.3	84.0
1994	22,231	36,536	36,036	2,066	23,275	2,615	1,850	16,000	95.3	151.9	95.0	95.0	110.7
1995	22,158	25,270	57,781	1,274	14,869	3,085	2,082	17,900	116.8	182.3	116.8	116.8	150.9
1996	24,178	47,211	36,849	1,570	28,124	4,200	2,612	25,300	114.8	178.9	114.8	114.8	140.0
1997[1]	13,962	40,000	33,386	894	29,000	4,210	3,485	23,000	206.7	304.6	206.7	206.7	225.8
1998[1]									239.5	356.5	239.5	239.5	286.6

[1] Preliminary. [2] Extra bold. *Source: Foreign Agricultural Service, U.S. Department of Agriculture (FAS-USDA)*

United States Imports of Unground Pepper from Specified Countries In Metric Tons

	Black Pepper							White Pepper					
Year	Brazil	India	Indonesia	Malaysia	Singapore	Sri Lanka	Total	Brazil	China	Indonesia	Malaysia	Singapore	Total
1989	11,038	1,272	11,016	6,732	324	375	31,819	37	38	5,272	63	90	5,549
1990	8,778	6,679	8,444	6,768	457	644	32,980	17	15	5,506	24	86	5,721
1991	15,069	2,308	11,330	8,154	391	396	38,860	2	7	4,938	37	96	5,174
1992	6,601	9,892	20,768	2,073	52	310	40,590	51	2	5,089	29	261	5,544
1993	4,580	21,985	7,666	209	-----	539	35,969	322	114	4,304	137	363	5,481
1994	8,215	21,097	11,877	829	90	386	43,011	312	756	3,974	228	302	6,102
1995	3,165	10,836	19,630	268	30	327	34,465	414	280	4,037	164	211	5,266
1996	4,267	18,350	17,213	1,084	101	411	41,602	519	54	4,370	150	391	5,765
1997	4,328	23,404	13,610	2,203	678	285	45,319	75	522	3,755	199	750	5,751
1998[1]	5,806	15,540	13,045	9,014	185	578	3,658	32	108	4,571	195	203	5,393

[1] Preliminary. *Source: Foreign Agricultural Service, U.S. Department of Agriculture (FAS-USDA)*

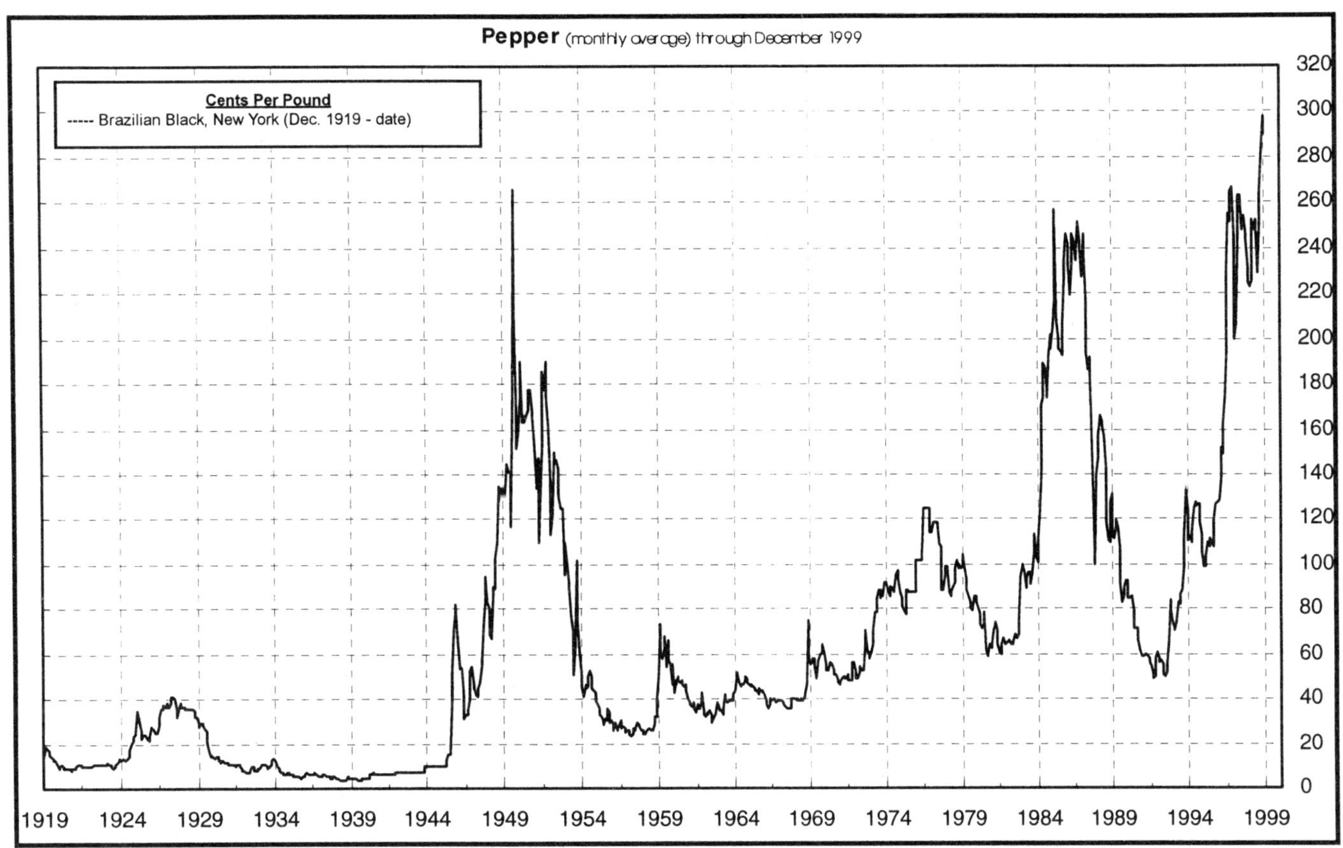

Average Black Pepper in New York (Brazilian) In Cents Per Pound

Year	Jan.	Feb.	Mar.	Apr.	May	June	July	Aug.	Sept.	Oct.	Nov.	Dec.	Average
1990	107.0	110.8	115.4	115.0	106.0	91.0	82.3	85.8	88.5	92.3	89.6	81.8	97.1
1991	79.0	78.5	78.6	74.5	66.8	70.0	68.8	61.6	59.5	56.8	55.8	55.0	67.1
1992	55.6	54.5	56.0	55.3	54.0	54.0	50.8	49.0	50.0	57.8	61.0	58.0	54.7
1993	56.0	56.5	54.3	51.2	50.0	51.5	55.8	64.8	84.0	79.0	74.2	70.8	62.3
1994	69.3	74.3	82.0	82.8	82.0	86.5	87.8	97.8	112.2	131.5	123.5	110.4	95.0
1995	111.0	110.0	114.2	124.8	127.3	126.0	127.0	126.3	118.2	113.5	104.8	99.0	116.8
1996	99.3	103.3	109.2	108.3	111.2	109.5	108.0	119.8	126.5	127.5	127.6	128.0	114.8
1997	138.6	151.8	149.0	161.8	173.4	193.8	229.5	255.0	251.3	264.8	266.3	245.0	206.7
1998	199.4	205.5	243.8	262.8	262.8	247.5	253.0	253.8	246.3	243.0	231.3	225.0	239.5
1999	222.5	225.8	252.5	248.0	252.5	250.0	229.0	249.3	263.8	282.0	297.5	290.0	255.2

Source: Foreign Agricultural Service, U.S. Department of Agriculture (FAS-USDA)

Average White Pepper in New York (Indonesian)[1] In Cents Per Pound

Year	Jan.	Feb.	Mar.	Apr.	May	June	July	Aug.	Sept.	Oct.	Nov.	Dec.	Average
1990	102.3	100.5	99.2	95.5	93.8	82.8	80.0	88.2	91.5	88.0	83.2	78.0	90.3
1991	77.0	72.5	71.4	70.0	67.4	66.0	66.3	63.2	67.0	70.8	78.6	71.5	70.1
1992	70.0	70.0	70.0	70.0	68.0	65.0	64.2	65.0	72.7	79.2	78.5	77.4	70.8
1993	79.0	89.0	85.3	84.0	81.3	87.3	97.0	121.5	181.3	172.6	154.7	142.4	114.6
1994	144.5	139.5	141.3	140.8	137.0	143.3	143.4	156.3	159.2	167.5	176.5	173.0	151.9
1995	179.5	175.8	168.0	181.3	195.0	184.2	187.5	190.8	191.0	182.0	178.5	174.2	182.3
1996	174.5	177.5	181.6	179.5	172.6	164.8	154.0	169.6	181.5	193.5	191.8	205.8	178.9
1997	256.0	264.5	255.0	250.0	241.0	248.8	280.3	324.0	332.5	362.0	433.8	407.5	304.6
1998	348.0	346.3	362.5	390.0	393.0	358.8	354.0	356.3	348.8	340.0	340.0	340.0	356.5
1999	361.3	355.0	365.0	355.0	352.5	335.0	310.0	313.8	325.0	327.0	316.3	305.0	335.1

[1] Muntok White. *Source: Foreign Agricultural Service, U.S. Department of Agriculture (FAS-USDA)*

Petroleum

Energy prices moved higher during 1999. At the end of 1998, prices for crude oil were around $10.00 per barrel. By the end of 1999, prices were approaching $30.00 per barrel. There were two reasons for the price rally. One was that the Organization of Oil Exporting Countries (OPEC) met and agreed on production cutbacks. That, along with increased demand for crude oil, managed to reduce inventories of oil which had pushed prices so low in 1998. While OPEC has had similar agreements in the past which were aimed at having member countries reduce output, the current agreement appears to have more participation. In the past, when oil prices moved higher, OPEC members tended to unilaterally increase production which, in effect, negated the agreement. With the current production cutback it looks like members are holding to their export quotas. A key question for the energy market in the year 2000 is whether OPEC will be able to continue with the current agreement and even extend it further, or whether member compliance will begin to slip allowing more oil onto the market.

The U.S. Energy Information Administration reported that U.S. domestic field production of petroleum in August 1999 was 8.17 million barrels per day. This was up 1 percent from the previous month and 2 percent less than a year earlier. In the January-August 1999 period, field production of petroleum averaged 8.11 million barrels per day, some 5 percent less than in the comparable period of 1998, and 6 percent less than the like period of 1997. For all of 1998, field production of petroleum was 8.39 million barrels per day. U.S. field production of petroleum has been trending lower for many years. In 1973, production averaged almost 11 million barrels per day. By 1990, that average had dropped to 8.99 million barrels per day.

U.S. production of natural gas plant liquids in August 1999 averaged 1.77 million barrels per day. That was down 6 percent from the previous month, but 3 percent more than a year earlier. In the first eight months of 1999, production averaged 1.77 million barrels per day. That represented a decline of 1 percent from the same period of 1998 and 3 percent less than in the like period of 1997. For all of 1998, natural gas plant liquid production averaged 1.76 million barrels per day.

U.S. imports of petroleum products (not including crude oil) in August 1999 were 1.87 million barrels per day. That was a decline of 8 percent from the previous month but about 1 percent more than a year earlier. In the January-August 1999 period, petroleum product imports averaged 1.97 million barrels per day, down 1 percent from the same period in 1998, and some 4 percent less than in the like period of 1997. For all of 1998, imports averaged 2 million barrels per day. U.S. imports of crude oil in August 1999 were 8.79 million barrels per day, down 5 percent from the previous month and 4 percent less than a year earlier. In the January-August 1999 period, U.S. imports of crude oil averaged 8.75 million barrels per day. That was about the same import level as in 1998, but almost 8 percent more than in the comparable period of 1997. U.S. imports of crude oil have been trending higher over time. In 1985, imports averaged 3.20 million barrels per day. For all of 1998, imports averaged 8.71 million barrels per day.

U.S. exports of petroleum products (not including crude oil) in August 1999 averaged 876,000 barrels per day. In the January-August 1999 period they averaged 782,000 barrels per day. For all of 1998, exports averaged 835,000 barrels per day. The U.S. exports small amounts of crude oil. In the January-August 1999 period, exports averaged 136,000 barrels per day. For 1998, exports averaged 110,000 barrels per day.

Field production of crude oil in Alaska in August 1999 averaged 1 million barrels per day. For the January-August 1999 period, production averaged 1.06 million barrels per day. This was down 10 percent from the same period in 1998, and 18 percent less than the like period in 1997. Production of crude oil in Alaska has been trending lower. In 1988 production peaked at 2.02 million barrels per day. For all of 1998, Alaskan crude oil production averaged 1.18 million barrels per day.

Futures Markets

Futures and options on light sweet crude oil are traded on the New York Mercantile Exchange (NYMEX). Other energy products traded there include heating oil, unleaded gasoline, propane and natural gas. London's International Petroleum Exchange (IPE) trades Brent crude oil futures and options. The IPE also trades gasoil, natural gas and fuel oil. The Singapore International Monetary Exchange Ltd. (SIMEX) trades Brent crude oil futures.

World Production of Crude Petroleum In Thousands of Barrels Per Day

Year	Canada	China	Indo-nesia	Iran	Kuwait	Mexico	Nigeria	Russia[3]	Saudi Arabia	United Kingdom	United States	Vene-zuela	World Total
1990	1,553	2,774	1,462	3,088	1,175	2,553	1,810	10,975	6,410	1,820	7,355	2,137	60,566
1991	1,548	2,835	1,592	3,312	190	2,680	1,892	9,992	8,115	1,797	7,417	2,375	60,207
1992	1,605	2,845	1,504	3,429	1,058	2,669	1,943	7,632	8,332	1,825	7,171	2,371	60,213
1993	1,679	2,890	1,511	3,540	1,852	2,673	1,960	6,730	8,198	1,915	6,847	2,450	60,236
1994	1,746	2,939	1,510	3,618	2,025	2,685	1,931	6,135	8,120	2,375	6,662	2,588	60,991
1995	1,805	2,990	1,503	3,643	2,057	2,618	1,993	5,995	8,231	2,489	6,560	2,750	62,335
1996	1,837	3,131	1,547	3,686	2,062	2,855	2,188	5,850	8,218	2,568	6,465	3,053	63,711
1997	1,893	3,200	1,546	3,664	2,083	3,023	2,317	5,884	8,562	2,517	6,452	3,315	66,420
1998[1]	1,981	3,198	1,518	3,634	2,085	3,070	2,153	5,938	8,389	2,616	6,252	3,167	66,874
1999[2]	1,890	3,193	1,506	3,569	1,895	2,917	2,137	6,065	7,831	2,687	5,944	2,830	65,680

Includes lease condensate. [1] Preliminary. [2] Estimate. [3] Formerly part of the U.S.S.R.; data not reported separately until 1992.

Source: Energy Information Administration, U.S. Department of Energy (EIA-DOE)

Refiner Sales Prices of Petroleum Products for Resale (Excluding Taxes) In Cents Per Gallon

Year	Jan.	Feb.	Mar.	Apr.	May	June	July	Aug.	Sept.	Oct.	Nov.	Dec.	Average
						Residual Fuel Oil (Sulfur 1% or less)							
1993	36.8	35.5	39.1	38.4	34.8	33.7	32.7	31.6	31.9	32.1	30.7	27.5	33.7
1994	33.8	39.3	30.0	29.4	31.7	35.8	37.8	37.1	32.6	32.6	35.7	36.9	34.5
1995	39.1	37.1	38.3	36.8	40.4	39.9	36.8	35.5	36.4	35.3	36.6	44.7	38.3
1996	49.9	42.8	47.1	48.3	45.0	40.4	41.4	42.0	42.8	47.9	49.1	51.4	45.7
1997	46.2	43.7	39.6	37.6	36.6	39.4	38.5	39.4	40.1	44.6	46.5	38.7	41.5
1998	35.2	30.7	29.4	32.9	31.9	29.3	30.7	26.9	29.9	31.0	27.3	24.0	29.9
1999[1]	27.6	21.9	27.2	30.7	34.9	34.8	38.2	44.5	48.1	47.8			35.6
						No. 2 Fuel Oil							
1993	54.4	56.9	59.0	57.5	56.9	55.0	51.0	51.0	54.8	58.1	53.1	45.1	54.4
1994	50.7	54.2	49.7	48.9	49.0	49.8	50.9	51.4	50.1	50.8	51.0	49.5	50.6
1995	49.4	49.1	48.1	50.4	52.4	49.3	48.1	51.0	52.0	50.5	53.4	57.3	51.1
1996	56.8	58.9	62.8	67.5	61.1	53.7	57.1	62.1	68.7	72.7	71.4	71.2	63.9
1997	69.8	64.5	57.7	58.6	58.8	54.5	53.8	55.3	54.3	59.0	58.4	53.4	58.9
1998	48.9	47.7	44.9	44.9	43.4	39.9	38.8	36.9	41.8	41.2	38.9	34.6	42.2
1999[1]	36.3	33.0	39.7	44.5	43.7	44.2	51.4	56.3	60.9	61.2			47.1
						No. 2 Diesel Fuel							
1993	54.9	57.4	60.0	59.8	59.6	57.2	53.2	53.2	58.9	65.8	58.9	46.8	57.0
1994	49.1	52.8	52.9	52.3	51.7	52.2	53.7	54.1	54.2	55.2	55.1	50.8	52.9
1995	50.1	50.6	51.2	54.8	55.9	52.6	51.4	54.2	55.7	54.6	56.3	57.6	53.8
1996	56.2	57.9	61.9	70.1	67.0	59.1	60.0	64.9	71.7	75.4	73.2	71.0	65.9
1997	69.9	67.8	62.5	61.7	60.7	56.5	55.8	58.9	57.8	61.7	61.5	55.0	60.6
1998	49.6	48.3	45.8	48.2	47.0	43.6	42.6	41.4	45.6	45.5	41.4	35.6	44.4
1999[1]	36.5	35.5	43.6	48.7	47.8	50.3	56.6	61.4	65.0	65.1			51.1
						Kerosine-Type Jet Fuel							
1993	57.7	60.4	60.3	59.8	60.1	58.5	55.1	55.1	56.6	60.5	58.7	51.0	57.7
1994	52.6	56.0	52.4	50.8	50.6	51.5	53.8	54.4	54.0	54.4	56.3	53.1	53.4
1995	52.3	52.1	50.1	52.6	54.7	53.1	51.3	53.1	55.2	54.1	56.3	58.6	53.9
1996	60.3	57.2	59.6	65.3	62.2	57.5	59.6	64.5	71.6	73.6	72.2	73.0	64.6
1997	73.5	71.4	61.8	60.5	59.4	58.1	56.8	59.4	58.8	61.3	61.3	55.6	61.2
1998	53.4	50.2	45.7	46.6	46.9	43.5	43.8	42.9	44.6	45.8	43.1	36.5	45.0
1999[1]	36.9	35.0	39.3	46.9	47.2	49.3	53.6	59.0	62.5	63.5			49.3
						Propane (Consumer Grade)							
1993	40.2	36.7	38.2	36.2	34.0	33.8	33.3	33.3	34.1	34.7	33.6	30.9	35.1
1994	32.3	34.0	31.8	30.5	30.4	29.9	29.8	31.0	31.7	33.5	35.0	35.8	32.5
1995	35.6	34.5	34.3	33.0	33.2	32.6	32.1	33.2	33.8	34.4	34.7	37.9	34.4
1996	41.6	44.1	41.1	37.8	36.2	36.2	36.9	38.9	45.3	51.1	58.0	67.7	46.1
1997	59.9	44.7	41.3	37.7	36.9	36.4	35.9	37.5	39.5	41.1	39.6	37.5	41.6
1998	35.4	33.1	31.2	30.3	29.3	26.6	25.7	25.7	26.3	27.6	27.7	25.7	28.8
1999[1]	26.5	26.2	26.9	28.6	29.0	29.6	34.6	38.3	41.5	43.7			32.5

[1] Preliminary. *Source: Energy Information Administration, U.S. Department of Energy (EIA-DOE)*

Supply and Disposition of Crude Oil in the United States In Thousands of Barrels Per Day

	Supply						Stock		Disposition		Ending Stocks		
	Field Production		Imports			Unaccounted for Crude Oil	Withdrawal[3]						
Yearly Average	Total Domestic	Alaskan	Total	SPR[2]	Other		SPR[2]	Other	Refinery Inputs	Exports	Total	SPR[2]	Other Primary
	In Thousands of Barrels Per Day										In Millions of Barrels		
1990	7,355	1,773	5,894	27	5,867	258	16	-51	13,409	109	908	586	323
1991	7,417	1,798	5,782	0	5,782	195	-47	5	13,301	116	893	569	325
1992	7,171	1,714	6,083	10	6,073	258	17	-18	13,411	89	893	575	318
1993	6,847	1,582	6,787	15	6,772	168	34	47	13,613	98	922	587	335
1994	6,662	1,559	7,063	12	7,051	266	13	5	13,866	99	929	592	337
1995	6,560	1,484	7,230	0	7,230	193	0	-93	13,973	95	895	592	303
1996	6,465	1,393	7,508	0	7,508	215	-71	-53	14,195	110	850	566	284
1997	6,452	1,296	8,225	0	8,225	145	-7	57	14,662	108	868	563	305
1998	6,252	1,175	8,706	0	8,706	115	22	52	14,889	110	895	571	324
1999[1]	5,938	1,051	8,585	4	8,581	302	-11	-93	14,816	116	858	568	291

[1] Preliminary. [2] Strategic Petroleum Reserve. [3] A negative number indicates a decrease in stocks and a positive number indicates an increase.

Note: Crude oil includes lease condensate. Stocks of Alaskan crude oil in transit were included beginning in January 1981.

Source: Energy Information Administration, U.S. Department of Energy (EIA-DOE)

PETROLEUM

Crude Petroleum Refinery Operations Ratio[1] in the United States In Percent of Capacity

Year	Jan.	Feb.	Mar.	Apr.	May	June	July	Aug.	Sept.	Oct.	Nov.	Dec.	Average
1990	88.0	88.0	84.0	85.0	87.0	89.0	93.0	91.0	91.0	84.0	84.0	83.0	87.3
1991	83.0	84.0	83.0	85.0	87.0	90.0	89.0	89.0	88.0	83.0	84.0	87.0	86.0
1992	83.0	81.0	85.0	86.0	89.0	92.0	92.0	89.0	91.0	89.0	90.0	88.0	87.9
1993	87.0	87.0	89.0	91.0	93.0	95.0	95.0	93.0	93.0	92.0	92.0	91.0	91.5
1994	89.8	88.7	87.6	92.4	95.4	95.8	95.5	96.4	94.4	89.8	92.7	92.6	92.6
1995	89.6	87.9	86.7	90.5	94.0	95.6	94.0	94.0	95.6	90.5	92.1	93.3	92.0
1996	90.6	89.1	90.6	93.7	94.4	95.4	93.9	95.0	95.5	94.6	94.7	94.3	93.5
1997	89.3	87.3	90.7	92.6	97.3	97.7	97.1	98.6	99.7	96.7	95.6	97.2	95.0
1998	93.3	91.3	94.4	96.4	97.1	98.9	99.2	99.8	95.0	89.7	94.7	95.1	95.4
1999[2]	91.4	91.0	91.0	94.2	93.7	93.4	94.8	95.4	94.1	91.1	92.0		92.9

[1] Based on the ration of the daily average crude runs to stills to the rated capacity of refineries per day. [2] Preliminary.
Source: Energy Information Administration, U.S. Department of Energy (EIA-DOE)

Crude Oil Refinery Inputs in the United States In Thousands of Barrels Per Day

Year	Jan.	Feb.	Mar.	Apr.	May	June	July	Aug.	Sept.	Oct.	Nov.	Dec.	Average
1990	13,491	13,487	12,876	13,051	13,386	13,689	14,212	14,142	14,104	12,825	12,953	12,708	13,409
1991	12,735	13,046	12,839	13,042	13,539	13,918	13,703	13,800	13,694	12,896	12,929	13,465	13,301
1992	12,923	12,486	13,083	13,260	13,679	14,059	13,953	13,426	13,714	13,584	13,547	13,194	13,411
1993	12,938	12,865	13,200	13,538	13,829	14,129	14,136	13,844	13,841	13,729	13,686	13,571	13,613
1994	13,286	13,130	12,985	13,809	14,272	14,351	14,344	14,491	14,234	13,529	13,968	13,951	13,866
1995	13,604	13,365	13,480	13,817	14,303	14,553	14,403	14,276	14,402	13,598	13,833	14,011	13,973
1996	13,708	13,529	13,755	14,263	14,401	14,535	14,319	14,423	14,483	14,276	14,276	14,194	14,181
1997	13,632	13,425	14,047	14,283	15,083	15,139	14,958	15,217	15,297	14,790	14,654	14,898	14,626
1998	14,313	14,034	14,590	14,961	15,104	15,368	15,496	15,660	14,854	14,001	14,769	14,832	14,837
1999[1]	14,483	14,430	14,495	15,039	14,946	14,943	15,232	15,280	15,107	14,590	14,704	14,522	14,816

[1] Preliminary. *Source: Energy Information Administration, U.S. Department of Energy (EIA-DOE)*

Production of Major Refined Petroleum Products in Continental United States In Millions of Barrels

			Fuel Oil					Natural		Liquified Gasses		
		Aviation				Jet	Kero-	Gas Plant	Lubri-		at	at
Year	Asphalt	Gasoline	Distillate	Residual	Gasoline	Fuel	sene	Liquids	cants	Total	L.P.G.[2]	L.P.G.[3]
1990	164.0	8.5	1,067.5	346.6	2,650	555.6	15.5	598.3	59.7	638.4	456.2	182.2
1991	156.8	8.0	1,081.0	341.1	2,554	525.0	14.0	639.2	57.0	683.1	487.5	195.6
1992	153.0	7.9	1,088.4	326.1	2,591	512.0	14.8	668.0	57.5	721.9	499.7	222.2
1993	165.6	7.9	1,139.7	303.9	2,644	518.8	17.5	631.2	58.4	849.4	633.5	215.9
1994	164.8	7.9	1,169.7	301.4	2,621	528.4	21.1	630.2	62.1	734.2	511.1	223.2
1995	170.4	7.8	1,151.7	287.6	2,722	516.8	19.2	643.2	63.7	759.9	521.1	238.8
1996	167.8	7.3	1,213.6	265.5	2,769	554.5	22.8	669.8	63.3	789.1	546.7	242.5
1997	177.0	7.2	1,238.0	258.3	2,826	567.3	23.9	663.3	65.9	799.4	547.3	252.2
1998	179.7	7.3	1,248.6	278.0	2,865	554.6	28.6	639.9	67.2	771.2	526.3	244.9
1999[1]	181.9	7.1	1,249.9	278.0	2,881	556.8	27.8	642.2	67.3	775.2	529.3	245.9

[1] Preliminary. [2] Gas processing plants. [3] Refineries. *Source: Energy Information Administration, U.S. Department of Energy (EIA-DOE)*

Stocks of Petroleum and Products in the United States on January 1 In Millions of Barrels

			Refined Products											
	Crude	Strategic			Aviation	Fuel Oil		Finished	Jet	Kero-	Liduified	Lubri-	Motor Gasoline	
Year	Petroleum	Reserve	Total	Asphalt	Gasoline	Distillate	Residual	Gasoline	Fuel	sene	Gases[2]	cants	Total	Finished[3]
1990	921.1	579.9	508.3	20.6	2.1	105.7	43.8	179.1	40.9	5.1	80.2	13.8	213	177
1991	908.4	585.7	566.8	18.7	1.7	132.2	48.6	182.4	52.1	5.6	97.9	12.4	220	181
1992	893.1	568.5	576.7	22.3	1.6	143.5	49.9	183.3	48.8	5.8	92.3	12.3	219	182
1993	892.9	574.7	549.1	17.7	1.6	140.6	42.6	179.1	43.1	5.7	88.7	13.3	216	178
1994	922.5	587.1	465.8	19.1	1.8	140.9	44.2	185.7	40.4	4.1	106.6	11.8	226	187
1995	928.9	591.7	468.0	18.6	2.3	145.2	41.9	175.9	46.8	8.0	108.0	11.5	215	176
1996	895.0	591.6	401.2	26.3	2.2	106.3	34.8	162.8	38.4	4.0	99.2	11.7	206	161
1997	868.1	565.8	452.6	22.3	1.7	139.0	40.4	166.1	43.9	7.3	89.5	13.2	203	157
1998	868.1	563.4	451.6	22.1	1.7	138.4	40.5	166.4	44.0	7.3	95.2	12.9	166	166
1999[1]	894.9	571.4	479.2	21.4	1.8	156.1	44.9	171.2	44.7	6.9	115.1	13.2	172	172

[1] Preliminary. [2] Includes ethane & ethylene at plants and refineries. [3] Includes oxygenated. *Source: Energy Information Administration, U.S. Department of Energy (EIA-DOE)*

Stocks of Crude Petroleum in the United States, on First of Month In Millions of Barrels

Year	Jan.	Feb.	Mar.	Apr.	May	June	July	Aug.	Sept.	Oct.	Nov.	Dec.
1990	921.1	932.9	924.0	955.9	953.1	968.7	970.9	966.2	959.2	932.7	935.7	924.7
1991	908.4	905.3	912.8	905.3	907.2	924.3	915.3	910.6	913.8	909.1	910.7	912.0
1992	893.1	909.7	914.8	907.1	916.5	912.0	894.6	902.2	898.3	893.5	906.2	899.4
1993	892.9	902.0	908.1	914.7	930.4	935.0	935.1	935.2	919.6	906.4	916.5	924.1
1994	922.5	925.3	922.6	932.6	930.6	922.7	919.6	924.2	920.2	927.0	934.9	938.0
1995	922.2	920.8	931.0	929.4	924.1	919.6	907.3	899.5	897.5	902.8	910.6	894.9
1996	894.9	894.7	892.9	888.8	889.7	889.7	898.9	891.3	890.8	875.8	881.5	869.1
1997	849.7	865.9	862.1	877.6	883.9	890.5	885.3	873.0	864.2	866.6	879.3	886.9
1998	868.1	884.3	885.7	899.8	914.6	916.1	896.4	902.6	893.5	873.0	897.4	906.2
1999[1]	894.4	896.6	897.4	908.0	902.3	914.8	902.8	906.0	889.1	878.0	875.7	866.2

[1] Preliminary. *Source: Energy Information Administration; U.S. Department of Energy (EIA-DOE)*

Production of Crude Petroleum in the United States In Thousands of Barrels Per Day

Year	Jan.	Feb.	Mar.	Apr.	May	June	July	Aug.	Sept.	Oct.	Nov.	Dec.	Average
1990	7,546	7,497	7,433	7,407	7,328	7,106	7,173	7,287	7,224	7,542	7,387	7,338	7,355
1991	7,500	7,637	7,546	7,509	7,409	7,320	7,347	7,316	7,368	7,437	7,328	7,299	7,417
1992	7,361	7,389	7,348	7,293	7,169	7,167	7,131	6,922	7,030	7,126	7,024	7,103	7,171
1993	6,961	6,943	6,974	6,881	6,847	6,795	6,688	6,758	6,712	6,839	6,912	6,858	6,847
1994	6,817	6,770	6,746	6,612	6,688	6,611	6,501	6,544	6,609	6,658	6,628	6,760	6,662
1995	6,682	6,794	6,600	6,604	6,629	6,579	6,449	6,447	6,416	6,421	6,585	6,530	6,560
1996	6,495	6,577	6,571	6,444	6,394	6,458	6,338	6,360	6,482	6,481	6,476	6,506	6,465
1997	6,402	6,514	6,452	6,441	6,474	6,442	6,409	6,347	6,486	6,467	6,459	6,531	6,452
1998	6,515	6,449	6,399	6,483	6,363	6,252	6,193	6,193	5,918	6,152	6,072	5,938	6,243
1999[1]	5,954	5,984	6,048	5,977	5,985	5,880	5,873	5,912	5,820	5,878	5,895	6,051	5,938

[1] Preliminary. *Source: Energy Information Administration, U.S. Department of Energy (EIA-DOE)*

U.S. Foreign Trade of Petroleum and Products In Thousands of Barrels Per Day

	Exports		Imports						Exports		Imports				
Year	Total[2]	Petroleum Products	Crude	Petroleum Products	Distillate Fuel Oil	Residual Fuel Oil	Net Imports[3]	Year	Total[2]	Petroleum Products	Crude	Petroleum Products	Distillate Fuel Oil	Residual Fuel Oil	Net Imports[3]
1980	544	258	5,263	1,646	142	939	6,365	1990	857	748	5,894	2,123	278	504	7,161
1981	595	367	4,396	1,599	173	800	5,401	1991	1,001	885	5,782	1,844	205	453	6,626
1982	815	579	3,488	1,325	93	776	4,298	1992	950	861	6,083	1,805	216	375	6,938
1983	739	575	3,329	1,722	174	699	4,312	1993	1,003	904	6,787	1,833	184	373	7,618
1984	722	541	3,426	2,011	272	681	4,715	1994	942	843	7,063	1,933	203	314	8,054
1985	781	577	3,201	1,866	200	510	4,286	1995	949	855	7,230	1,605	193	187	7,886
1986	785	631	4,178	2,045	247	669	5,439	1996	981	871	7,508	1,971	230	248	8,498
1987	764	613	4,674	2,004	255	565	5,914	1997	1,003	896	8,225	1,936	228	194	9,158
1988	815	661	5,107	2,295	302	644	6,587	1998	945	835	8,706	2,002	210	275	9,764
1989	859	717	5,843	2,217	306	629	7,202	1999[1]	918	802	8,585	1,958	215	235	9,626

[1] Preliminary. [2] Includes crude oil. [3] Equals imports minus exports. *Source: Energy Information Administration, U.S. Department of Energy (EIA-DOE)*

Domestic First Purchase Price of Crude Petroleum at Wells[1] In Dollars Per Barrel

Year	Jan.	Feb.	Mar.	Apr.	May	June	July	Aug.	Sept.	Oct.	Nov.	Dec.	Average
1990	18.49	18.16	16.57	14.52	13.82	12.79	14.03	21.87	28.46	30.86	27.53	22.63	20.03
1991	19.60	16.28	15.13	16.16	16.44	15.58	16.36	16.60	16.71	17.72	17.12	14.68	16.54
1992	13.99	14.04	14.12	15.36	16.38	17.96	17.80	17.07	17.20	17.16	16.00	14.94	15.99
1993	14.70	15.53	15.94	16.15	16.03	15.06	13.83	13.75	13.39	13.72	12.45	10.38	14.25
1994	10.49	10.71	10.94	12.31	14.02	14.93	15.34	14.50	13.62	13.84	14.14	13.43	13.19
1995	14.00	14.69	14.68	15.84	15.85	15.02	14.01	14.13	14.49	13.68	14.03	15.02	14.62
1996	15.43	15.54	17.63	19.58	17.94	16.94	17.63	18.29	19.93	21.09	20.20	21.34	18.46
1997	21.76	19.38	17.85	16.64	17.24	15.90	15.91	16.21	16.44	17.68	16.84	15.06	17.24
1998	13.48	12.16	11.53	11.64	11.49	10.00	10.46	10.18	11.28	11.32	9.65	8.05	10.88
1999[2]	8.59	8.58	10.75	12.84	13.84	14.34	16.13	17.58	20.10	19.63			14.24

[1] Buyers posted prices. [2] Preliminary. *Source: Energy Information Administration, U.S. Department of Energy (EIA-DOE)*

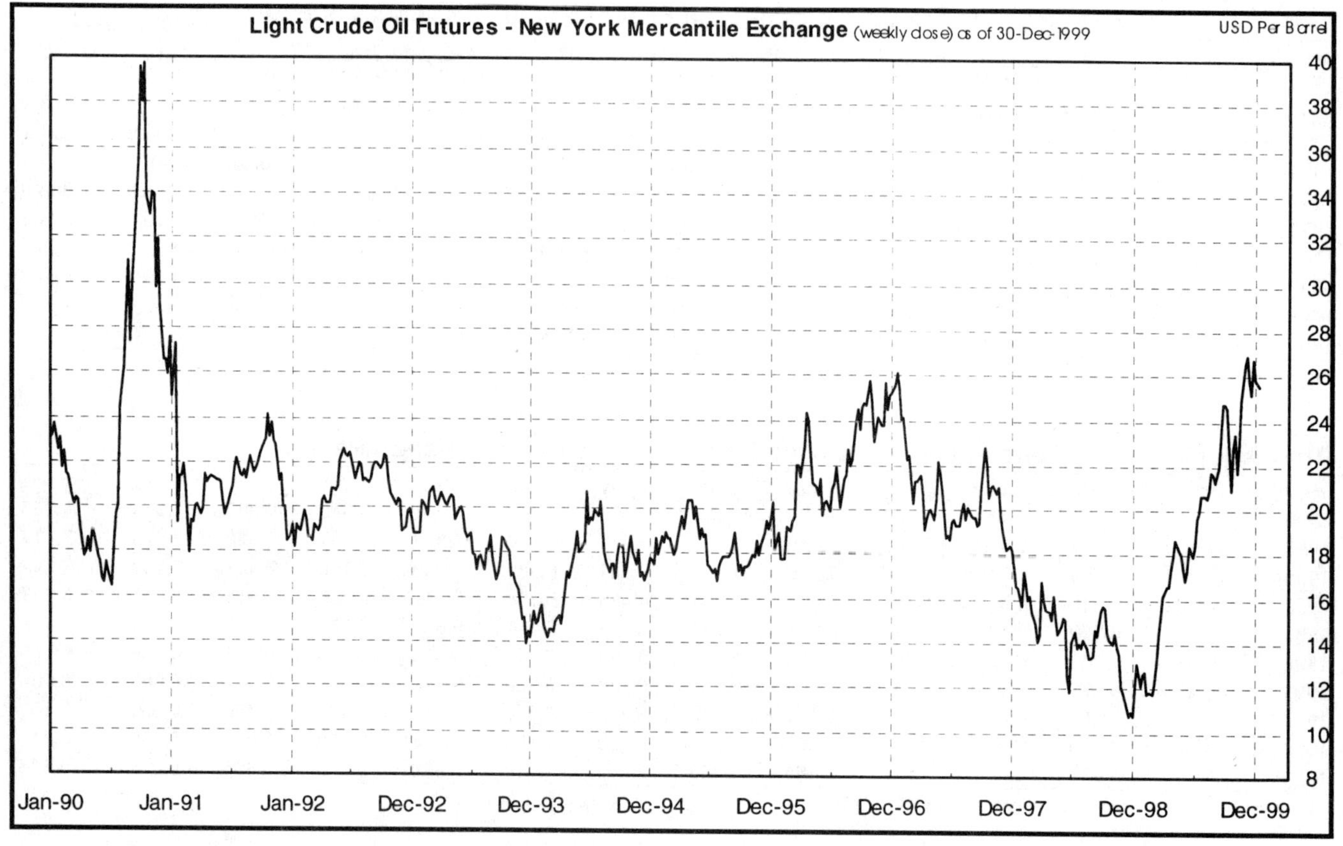

Volume of Trading of Crude Oil Futures in New York In Thousands of Contracts

Year	Jan.	Feb.	Mar.	Apr.	May	June	July	Aug.	Sept.	Oct.	Nov.	Dec.	Total
1990	2,153.4	1,780.8	1,785.3	1,803.0	1,944.9	1,831.7	2,045.3	2,719.0	2,072.9	2,436.9	1,768.7	1,301.8	23,643.4
1991	1,996.9	1,477.5	1,605.3	1,884.5	1,740.6	1,410.7	1,674.8	1,597.9	1,543.0	2,063.7	2,051.1	1,959.8	21,005.9
1992	2,096.6	1,629.9	1,619.8	1,888.6	1,884.7	2,005.7	1,796.3	1,530.9	1,540.7	1,796.8	1,542.1	1,777.5	21,109.6
1993	2,138.9	1,783.6	1,812.7	1,531.4	1,641.5	2,018.5	2,616.2	2,200.3	2,679.5	1,945.2	2,378.4	2,122.4	24,868.6
1994	2,295.6	1,933.0	2,227.7	2,381.7	2,602.3	2,575.8	2,186.5	2,543.6	1,897.5	2,194.5	2,195.9	1,778.2	26,812.3
1995	2,133.5	1,657.3	2,289.8	2,220.1	2,408.9	2,172.4	1,749.3	1,793.8	1,968.0	1,834.6	1,739.1	1,647.2	23,614.0
1996	2,260.1	1,928.3	2,399.3	2,489.9	2,161.3	1,601.7	1,732.1	1,657.0	1,912.6	2,098.0	1,643.1	1,604.3	23,487.8
1997	1,949.9	1,973.7	2,086.6	2,033.7	2,134.9	2,098.6	2,221.4	2,053.7	2,027.5	2,574.0	1,770.2	1,847.2	24,771.4
1998	2,468.3	2,208.3	2,902.8	2,451.1	2,603.6	3,079.5	2,375.0	2,066.7	2,617.8	2,592.4	2,552.9	2,577.3	30,495.6
1999	2,533.6	2,326.0	3,767.7	3,166.8	3,037.9	3,306.8	3,471.3	3,354.8	3,388.4	3,571.2	3,465.1	2,470.4	37,860.1

Source: New York Mercantile Exchange (NYMEX)

Average Open Interest of Crude Oil Futures in New York In Contracts

Year	Jan.	Feb.	Mar.	Apr.	May	June	July	Aug.	Sept.	Oct.	Nov.	Dec.
1990	273,193	300,069	287,013	287,538	278,600	285,384	275,771	262,746	266,313	269,167	242,500	232,405
1991	249,759	272,396	285,417	303,942	286,159	277,587	278,704	267,186	264,223	298,434	292,889	284,453
1992	310,763	331,050	316,544	340,315	335,545	364,155	331,972	316,066	314,446	301,381	308,467	330,134
1993	352,316	369,180	385,768	381,954	384,309	396,832	423,041	428,418	404,172	397,121	404,046	427,756
1994	427,705	438,929	424,462	410,974	427,071	414,257	409,251	396,657	395,194	413,206	388,932	391,151
1995	373,798	379,329	353,805	364,929	350,826	346,051	357,718	343,636	342,360	334,170	329,786	348,954
1996	389,935	400,236	427,306	460,841	424,994	376,164	367,405	364,458	395,358	410,387	385,415	368,331
1997	365,522	384,737	408,751	409,719	401,663	397,245	411,292	424,529	405,389	419,821	404,597	424,333
1998	424,810	445,167	468,438	463,961	450,611	467,998	476,516	486,499	486,047	481,657	487,175	501,591
1999	501,655	524,677	581,072	611,727	594,032	582,057	601,211	584,961	622,257	595,743	564,488	531,566

Source: New York Mercantile Exchange (NYMEX)

Plastics

Plastics are one of the most used materials in the U.S. for industrial and commercial purposes. The most important developments in the plastics industry have occurred since 1910. The period of 1930-40 saw the initial commercial development of the major thermoplastics used today. These include polyvinyl chloride, low density polyethylene, polystyrene and polymethyl methacrylate. World War II brought plastics into great demand as substitutes for material that was in short supply, such as natural rubber. In the U.S., the production of synthetic rubbers led to the development of more plastic materials. New materials that have been developed are competing with older plastics and other materials like wood. The demand for plastics has continued to increase.

U.S. plastic resin sales in 1998 were 85.5 billion pounds, dry weight basis, up 3 percent from the previous year. Of the total, plastic resin sales for the packaging industry in 1998 were 22.4 billion pounds, up almost 3 percent from the previous year. The building and construction industry used 18.1 billion pounds of plastic resin in 1998, an increase of 6 percent from the previous year. Consumer and institutional markets took 11.3 billion pounds, an increase of 7 percent from the previous year. The transportation market used 4.3 billion pounds of plastic resins in 1998, an increase of 5 percent from 1997. The furniture and furnishings market used 4 billion pounds of plastic resins in 1998, an increase of 7 percent from the previous year. The electrical and electronic market took 3.2 billion pounds of plastic resin, close to unchanged from 1997. Other markets for plastic resins are adhesives/inks/coatings and industrial machinery. Exports of plastic resins in 1998 were 9 billion pounds, down 7 percent from 1997.

Of the plastic resin sales in 1998, 76.4 billion pounds were thermoplastics. In terms of the major markets, packaging took 22.3 billion pounds of thermoplastics or 29 percent of the total. The building and construction market took 12.1 billion pounds of thermoplastics or 16 percent of the total used. The consumer and institutional products market took 11 billion pounds or 14 percent of the total. Use of thermoplastics in the transportation market in 1998 was 3.6 billion pounds while furniture and furnishings used 3.3 billion pounds.

The remaining 9.2 billion pounds of plastic resins used in 1998 are in the form of thermosets. By far the largest user was the building and construction industry which used 6 billion pounds in 1998 or 66 percent of the total. The transportation market used 708 million pounds in 1998 while furniture and furnishings took almost 305 million pounds of thermosets in 1998. The adhesives/inks and coatings market used 280 million pounds. The electrical and electronic market consumed 279 million pounds of thermosets while the industrial and machinery market used 223 million pounds.

Plastics Production by Resin in the United States — In Millions of Pounds

	Thermosets				Thermoplastics										
Year	Polyester Unsaturated	Phenlic	Epoxy	Total Thermosets	Thermoplastic Polyester	Polyvinyl Chloride	Polystyrene	Polypropylene	Nylon	Low Density Polyethylene[1]	High Density Polyethylene	Total Thermoplastics	Total Selected Plastics	Other Plastics	Total Plastics
1989	1,319	2,879	510	6,407	1,630	8,478	5,104	7,238	569	9,695	8,102	42,189	48,596	9,933	58,529
1990	1,221	2,946	499	6,364	1,879	9,096	5,021	8,310	558	11,148	8,337	45,646	52,010	9,950	61,960
1991	1,075	2,658	497	5,909	2,115	9,164	4,954	8,330	576	11,582	9,213	47,146	53,055	9,731	62,786
1992	1,175	2,923	457	6,335	2,413	9,989	5,096	8,421	668	11,917	9,808	49,751	56,086	10,285	66,371
1993	1,264	3,078	512	6,868	2,549	10,257	5,382	8,628	768	12,067	9,941	51,159	58,027	10,777	68,854
1994	1,468	3,229	601	7,513	3,196	11,712	5,848	9,539	943	12,600	11,117	56,794	64,307	11,664	75,971
1995	1,577	3,204	632	7,519	3,785	12,295	5,656	10,890	1,020	12,886	11,211	59,331	66,850	11,834	78,684
1996	1,557	3,476	662	8,129	4,031	13,220	6,065	11,991	1,103	14,145	12,373	64,526	72,655	11,640	84,295
1997	1,621	3,734	654	8,647	4,260	14,084	6,380	13,320	1,222	14,579	12,557	67,872	76,519	12,287	88,806
1998	1,713	3,940	630	9,163	4,423	14,502	6,237	13,825	1,285	14,805	12,924	69,555	78,718	12,967	91,685

[1] Includes LDPE and LLDPE. *Source: The Society of the Plastics Industry, Inc. (SPI)*

Total Resin Sales and Captive Use by Important Markets — In Millions of Pounds (Dry Weight Basis)

Year	Adhesive, Inks & Coatings	Building & Construction	Consumer & Industrial	Electrical & Electronics	Exports	Furniture & Furnishings	Industrial & Machinery	Packaging	Transportation	Other	Total
1989	1,211	11,096	6,217	3,145	[1]	2,285	475	14,711	2,547	10,911	52,598
1990	1,373	11,803	5,861	3,165	[1]	2,190	636	16,568	2,504	11,811	55,910
1991	1,391	10,650	5,689	2,896	7,418	2,255	587	16,723	2,328	6,616	56,553
1992	1,723	11,876	6,093	2,766	6,950	2,559	617	18,284	2,817	6,877	60,562
1993	1,572	12,885	6,015	2,981	6,632	2,759	768	19,569	3,221	7,234	63,636
1994	1,789	14,715	9,266	3,325	6,889	3,118	836	19,551	3,795	7,515	70,799
1995	1,795	14,321	9,054	2,966	7,742	3,198	818	19,334	3,916	8,050	71,194
1996	1,833	16,199	9,804	3,137	8,722	3,477	980	21,271	3,964	9,361	78,748
1997	2,019	17,117	10,649	3,150	9,667	3,721	950	21,767	4,102	9,573	82,715
1998	2,038	18,120	11,335	3,160	9,020	3,995	949	22,403	4,296	10,214	85,530

[1] Included in other. *Source: The Society of the Plastics Industry, Inc. (SPI)*

PLASTICS

Average Producer Price Index of Plastic Resins and Materials (066) in the United States (1982 = 100)

Year	Jan.	Feb.	Mar.	Apr.	May	June	July	Aug.	Sept.	Oct.	Nov.	Dec.	Average
1993	118.3	118.0	117.6	117.1	116.3	116.9	116.9	117.6	117.4	116.9	116.2	116.2	117.1
1994	115.0	114.7	114.5	116.5	117.7	119.1	119.6	121.5	126.3	131.9	134.1	138.1	122.4
1995	142.5	144.1	145.9	148.5	149.0	148.9	147.0	144.8	142.7	139.2	135.8	132.2	143.4
1996	129.9	128.4	128.4	127.7	130.6	132.1	133.2	135.2	137.9	138.0	138.0	137.7	133.1
1997	137.0	137.5	138.7	138.9	139.1	139.6	139.3	137.4	136.0	135.9	134.6	133.9	137.3
1998	134.0	132.2	131.0	130.7	128.8	126.8	125.0	123.7	119.6	118.6	117.1	115.9	125.3
1999[1]	115.9	115.8	117.3	118.6	122.1	123.1	127.9	130.0	133.8	134.1	134.2	135.9	125.7

[1] Preliminary. *Source: Bureau of Labor Statistics, U.S. Department of Commerce (BLS)*

Average Producer Price Index of Thermoplastic Resins (0662) in the United States (1982 = 100)

Year	Jan.	Feb.	Mar.	Apr.	May	June	July	Aug.	Sept.	Oct.	Nov.	Dec.	Average
1993	117.5	117.1	116.3	115.8	114.8	115.4	115.5	116.4	116.4	116.4	115.5	114.6	116.0
1994	113.0	112.7	112.5	115.0	116.2	117.9	118.4	120.1	125.4	131.6	133.9	138.4	121.3
1995	143.1	145.0	147.1	150.3	151.0	151.2	148.7	146.2	143.7	139.6	135.5	131.1	144.4
1996	128.4	126.7	126.8	125.9	129.4	131.1	132.5	134.8	137.8	137.9	137.9	137.6	132.2
1997	136.7	137.3	138.6	138.8	139.0	139.7	139.3	137.0	135.5	135.3	133.8	133.0	137.0
1998	133.0	130.7	129.5	129.2	127.0	124.7	122.5	121.0	116.4	115.3	113.7	112.2	122.9
1999[1]	112.3	112.5	114.4	116.1	120.4	121.6	127.5	129.9	134.5	134.8	134.9	137.1	124.7

[1] Preliminary. *Source: Bureau of Labor Statistics, U.S. Department of Commerce (BLS)*

Average Producer Price Index of PE Resin, Low, Film & Sheeting (0662-0301) in the United States

Year	Jan.	Feb.	Mar.	Apr.	May	June	July	Aug.	Sept.	Oct.	Nov.	Dec.	Average
1993	NA	151.4	145.6	141.8	135.5	137.1	132.2	136.6	129.2	128.4	127.6	127.4	135.7
1994	121.6	119.4	119.3	120.8	127.6	134.5	136.3	140.8	146.6	155.4	172.8	182.2	139.8
1995	188.5	196.0	202.0	210.6	215.4	211.1	205.7	194.4	185.0	173.4	167.5	157.4	192.3
1996	146.4	139.9	137.6	139.5	147.6	158.8	166.0	165.3	190.1	195.2	195.9	196.6	164.9
1997	191.8	189.0	189.7	193.8	196.8	199.4	197.9	201.0	190.2	185.1	182.5	177.2	191.2
1998	181.3	181.0	168.7	NA	159.1	162.9	158.0	152.8	NA	NA	NA	NA	166.3
1999[1]	NA	NA	NA	NA	NA	NA	NA	NA	NA	NA	NA	NA	NA

1982=100. [1] Preliminary. NA = Not available. *Source: Bureau of Labor Statistics, U.S. Department of Commerce (BLS)*

Average Producer Price Index of Styrene Plastics Materials (0662-06) in the United States (1982 = 100)

Year	Jan.	Feb.	Mar.	Apr.	May	June	July	Aug.	Sept.	Oct.	Nov.	Dec.	Average
1993	110.7	110.5	110.0	110.4	111.0	111.3	111.2	111.1	110.6	109.1	106.5	106.4	109.9
1994	105.8	104.1	104.1	108.1	108.3	109.2	110.4	110.6	116.0	123.3	125.3	126.2	112.6
1995	129.0	127.0	132.5	134.7	135.9	137.5	135.1	133.2	132.1	130.1	127.9	126.1	131.8
1996	125.7	123.5	125.0	118.3	120.1	122.7	123.4	123.3	123.6	122.8	122.0	120.9	122.6
1997	120.6	123.1	123.0	121.6	121.6	121.6	122.7	117.7	118.0	116.5	113.5	113.7	119.5
1998	113.3	113.9	115.5	114.9	114.1	112.8	111.3	111.2	107.6	107.9	107.1	106.3	111.3
1999[1]	103.5	102.4	103.5	104.7	103.0	102.3	103.1	101.5	101.4	99.8	99.2	100.1	102.0

[1] Preliminary. *Source: Bureau of Labor Statistics, U.S. Department of Commerce (BLS)*

Average Producer Price Index of Thermosetting Resins (0663) in the United States (1982 = 100)

Year	Jan.	Feb.	Mar.	Apr.	May	June	July	Aug.	Sept.	Oct.	Nov.	Dec.	Average
1993	126.1	126.5	127.4	127.5	127.8	128.0	127.7	127.7	127.9	127.8	127.8	128.3	127.5
1994	128.2	128.1	128.1	127.8	128.7	129.1	129.7	132.1	134.9	137.7	140.1	141.5	132.2
1995	144.3	145.1	145.4	145.2	144.7	143.5	144.0	143.5	142.9	142.3	142.4	142.1	143.8
1996	141.8	141.9	141.2	141.3	141.4	141.2	140.6	141.5	141.7	142.0	142.0	142.2	141.6
1997	142.1	142.3	142.7	143.1	143.2	143.0	142.8	142.9	143.0	143.1	142.9	142.9	142.8
1998	143.6	144.0	143.2	142.9	142.6	142.7	142.5	142.2	141.2	140.9	140.1	140.3	142.2
1999[1]	139.9	138.1	137.7	137.4	136.9	136.5	136.2	136.5	136.5	136.9	136.9	136.2	137.1

[1] Preliminary. *Source: Bureau of Labor Statistics, U.S. Department of Commerce (BLS)*

Average Producer Price Index of Phenolic & Tar Acid Resins (0663-02) in the United States (1982 = 100)

Year	Jan.	Feb.	Mar.	Apr.	May	June	July	Aug.	Sept.	Oct.	Nov.	Dec.	Average
1993	128.5	130.3	130.5	131.4	133.7	134.1	133.9	132.8	133.1	132.1	132.0	132.9	132.1
1994	133.0	130.9	129.7	131.3	134.1	135.9	139.2	143.7	147.2	154.7	161.0	161.5	141.9
1995	164.6	166.4	165.1	162.5	158.6	153.5	152.0	148.5	147.7	146.2	143.2	142.6	154.2
1996	142.7	142.6	141.9	142.2	143.1	143.4	143.2	147.2	148.7	149.1	149.8	150.5	145.4
1997	150.5	151.2	150.9	152.7	152.9	152.6	151.9	152.7	153.1	152.5	151.9	151.8	152.0
1998	153.1	154.9	153.0	151.0	148.7	148.8	148.5	149.0	142.8	141.7	140.6	138.6	147.6
1999[1]	NA	NA	NA	NA	NA	NA	NA	NA	NA	NA	NA	NA	NA

[1] Preliminary. *Source: Bureau of Labor Statistics, U.S. Department of Commerce (BLS)*

Platinum-Group Metals

Precious metals prices moved higher in 1999 for a number of reasons. In late September, the gold market staged a very strong rally as a number of central banks indicated they would limit sales of their gold stocks. With gold in the lead, other metals rallied. Platinum is a precious metal used in jewelry and when gold prices change, platinum prices change in the same direction. Not only does platinum find use and value as a precious metal, it is also an industrial metal with uses in the automotive industry. Palladium is more of an industrial metal finding uses primarily in pollution-control devices. Palladium prices rallied in 1999 and into 2000 as Russia shipments of the metal were slow. Other platinum group metals include rhodium, ruthenium, iridium and osmium.

The U.S. Geological Survey reported that U.S. mine production of platinum in 1998 was 3,500 kilograms, up 34 percent from 1997. U.S. mine production of palladium in 1998 was estimated to be 10,500 kilograms, up 25 percent from the previous year. In 1998, the U.S. had only one active platinum-group metals mine located in Montana. Small amounts of platinum-group metals are recovered as by-products of copper refining by two companies in the United States.

Most platinum-group metals are consumed by the automotive industry. The metals are used as oxidation catalysts in air pollution abatement devices that remove odors, vapors or carbon monoxide. There are chemical uses for platinum-group metals in processes such as hydrogenation and isomerization. Platinum alloys are used in jewelry. Platinum is finding more industrial uses in electronics and in the glass industry. Demand in the glass industry comes from the need for high quality glass for liquid crystal displays and cathode ray tubes. In the computer industry, data storage disks are often coated with platinum alloys.

Iridium is used in process catalysts. There has also been use of iridium in some autocatalysts. Iridium and ruthenium are used in the production of polyvinyl chloride. Rhodium is used in the automotive industry in pollution control devices. To some extent palladium has replaced rhodium but it is expected that more rhodium will be used with palladium in the future. Palladium is a metal that is much in demand. It finds use in the automotive industry in the production of pollution control devices. There continue to be ever lower standards for allowable levels of pollution and as the standards are lowered, the amount of palladium needed to build such devices increases. Some devices that used platinum-rhodium have been replaced by palladium only devices.

World mine production of platinum in 1998 was estimated to be 155,000 kilograms, up very slightly from 1997. The largest producer of platinum was South Africa with 125,000 kilograms, unchanged from 1997. The next largest producer was Russia with 17,500 kilograms, unchanged from 1997. Production by Canada was 7,300 kilograms, down 3 percent from the previous year. World mine production of palladium in 1998 was estimated at 125,000 kilograms, up 5 percent from the previous year. South Africa was the largest palladium producer with mine output of 57,300 kilograms in 1998, up 7 percent from 1997. Russian production was 47,000 kilograms, unchanged from the previous year. Canada, in 1998, produced 4,800 kilograms of palladium. World reserves of platinum-group metals are estimated to be 71 million kilograms. The largest reserves are in South Africa. World supplies of platinum-group metals are expected to increase as countries outside of South Africa expand production. These countries include the U.S., Canada and Zimbabwe.

U.S. imports of refined platinum in 1998 were 97,200 kilograms. By far the largest supplier of refined platinum was South Africa with 54,000 kilograms. The next largest supplier was the United Kingdom followed by Russia, Germany and Australia. Other suppliers included Switzerland, Belgium and Canada. U.S. imports of refined palladium in 1998 were estimated at 176,000 kilograms. The largest supplier was Russia with 93,400 kilograms, followed by South Africa with 24,000 kilograms. Other major suppliers of palladium to the U.S. were the U.K., Japan, Germany and Canada. Imports of refined rhodium in 1998 were 13,400 kilograms. South Africa supplied about half of these imports with 6,440 kilograms. Other suppliers of rhodium included Russia, the U.K., France and Germany. Imports of iridium in 1998 were 2,060 kilograms. The major suppliers were the U.K., South Africa and Russia. Imports of ruthenium were 9,330 kilograms with South Africa supplying 6,380 kilograms. Other suppliers included the U.K., Russia and Germany.

In May 1999, U.S. imports of platinum sponge were 5,860 kilograms (metal content). In the January-May 1999 period, platinum sponge imports were 26,000 kilograms. Imports of other platinum products in May 1999 were 2,440 kilograms while for all of 1999 they were 9,170 kilograms. Imports of platinum waste and scrap in May 1999 were 849 kilograms while for all of 1999 imports were 2,560 kilograms.

Imports of unwrought palladium in May 1999 were 5,050 kilograms. The major suppliers were Belgium and South Africa. In the January-May 1999 period, unwrought palladium imports were 89,300 kilograms. Imports of other palladium products in May 1999 were 3,520 kilograms with most supplied by Russia. In the first five months of 1999 imports totaled 9,720 kilograms. Imports of unwrought and other forms of iridium in May 1999 were 427 kilograms. For all of 1999 imports were 974 kilograms. The major supplier was South Africa. Imports of unwrought osmium in January-May 1999 totaled 5 kilograms. Imports of unwrought ruthenium in May 1999 were 1,010 kilograms, supplied by South Africa and Germany. In the January-May 1999 period, unwrought ruthenium imports were 3,680 kilograms. Imports of rhodium in May 1999 were 779 kilograms. The major supplier was the U.K. followed by South Africa. For the January-May 1999 period, imports of rhodium totaled 5,310 kilograms.

Futures Markets

Platinum and palladium futures and options are traded on the New York Mercantile Exchange (NYMEX). In Japan platinum and palladium futures are listed on the Tokyo Commodity Exchange (TOCOM).

PLATINUM-GROUP METALS

World Mine Production of Platinum In Kilograms

Year	Australia	Canada	Colombia[3]	Finland	Japan	Russia[4]	Serbia/ Montenegro[5]	South Africa	United States	Zimbabwe	World Total
1990	100	5,040	1,320	60	1,430	31,000	21	87,800	1,810	21	129,000
1991	100	4,680	1,600	60	988	30,000	22	88,900	1,500	19	128,000
1992	100	4,800	1,956	60	629	28,000	19	94,900	1,650	9	132,000
1993	100	5,000	1,722	60	661	20,000	10	109,000	2,050	4	139,000
1994	100	6,000	1,084	60	691	15,000	10	114,000	1,960	7	139,000
1995	100	9,320	973	60	730	18,000	10	102,000	1,590	7	133,000
1996	100	8,080	669	60	816	17,000	10	105,000	1,840	100	134,000
1997[1]	100	7,550	500	60	693	17,000	10	115,000	2,610	245	144,000
1998[2]	100	7,570	430	60	650	17,000	10	117,000	3,240	300	146,000

[1] Preliminary. [2] Estimate. [3] Placer platinum. [4] Formerly part of the U.S.S.R.; data not reported separately until 1992. [5] Formerly part of Yugoslavia; data not reported separately until 1992. *Source: U.S. Geological Survey (USGS)*

World Mine Production of Palladium and Other Group Metals In Kilograms

	Palladium										Other Group Metals		
Year	Australia	Canada	Finland	Japan	Russia[3]	Serbia/ Montenegro[4]	South Africa	United States	Zimbabwe	World Total	Russia[3]	South Africa	World Total
1990	400	5,270	100	1,050	84,000	130	38,300	5,930	31	135,000	10,000	15,800	27,200
1991	400	6,440	100	1,050	82,000	155	38,000	5,200	30	133,000	9,500	16,000	26,100
1992	400	5,800	100	986	70,000	130	41,000	5,440	19	124,000	6,000	17,000	24,300
1993	400	6,000	100	1,183	50,000	72	48,000	6,780	11	113,000	4,000	19,000	24,400
1994	400	7,000	100	1,277	40,000	50	47,800	6,440	17	103,000	3,000	22,100	27,100
1995	400	5,950	100	2,174	48,000	50	51,000	5,260	17	113,000	3,600	18,900	23,300
1996	400	5,160	100	2,180	47,000	50	52,600	6,100	120	11,400	3,500	19,400	23,600
1997[1]	400	4,810	180	1,900	47,000	50	56,300	8,430	345	119,000	3,500	13,700	17,900
1998[2]	400	4,810	180	1,900	47,000	50	57,300	10,600	400	123,000	3,500	13,700	17,900

[1] Preliminary. [2] Estimate. [3] Formerly part of the U.S.S.R.; data not reported separately until 1992. [4] Formerly part of Yugoslavia; data not reported separately until 1992. *Source: U.S. Geological Survey (USGS)*

Platinum-Group Metals Sold to Consuming Industries in the United States In Kilograms

	Automotive		Chemical		Electrical		Dental & Medical		Jewelry & Decorative		Petroleum		All Platinum-Group Metals			
Year	Platinum	Other[3]	Platinum	Other[3]	Platinum	Other[3]	Platinum	Other[3]	Platinum	Other[3]	Platinum	Other[3]	Platinum	Palladium	Other[3]	Total
1990	20,967	5,990	2,080	2,574	3,907	19,791	687	6,287	431	387	3,274	1,488	36,055	35,116	6,316	77,487
1991	18,643	5,338	861	1,749	3,910	14,428	598	4,918	626	500	3,163	181	31,112	25,747	5,738	62,597
1992	20,503	5,860	1,716	2,297	2,922	15,738	640	5,386	881	1,417	1,036	790	31,095	28,935	6,816	66,846
1993	19,446	10,124	2,364	3,121	2,125	12,699	687	5,562	1,024	1,422	1,204	709	29,879	26,840	8,544	65,063
1994	21,756	11,413	3,104	1,889	2,790	7,961	902	5,092	1,345	824	1,581	422	34,044	21,509	7,387	62,940
1995	27,990	12,440	2,022	2,395	4,510	18,225	778	6,158	1,337	1,431	3,421	871	43,524	45,188	-----	88,712
1996	28,550	19,282	2,115	2,457	4,541	17,665	778	6,285	1,493	1,493	3,514	902	44,489	45,157	-----	89,646
1997[1]	28,923	20,402	2,239	2,426	4,945	19,997	840	6,376	2,115	1,617	3,390	871	46,184	50,227	-----	96,411
1998[2]	29,483	26,528	2,301	2,488	5,194	20,215	902	6,376	2,333	1,617	3,390	809	47,396	61,827	-----	109,223

[1] Preliminary. [2] Estimate. [3] Includes Palladium, iridium, osmium, rhodium, and ruthenium. *Sources: U.S. Geological Survey (USGS); American Metal Market (AMM)*

Salient Statistics of Platinum and Allied Metals[3] in the United States In Kilograms

	Net Import Reliance as a % of Apparent Con-	Mine Production		Refinery Pro- duction (Secon-		Refiner, Importer & Dealer Stocks as of Dec. 31				Imports for Consumption		Exports		Apparent Con-
Year	sumption	Platinum	Palladium	dary)	Total Refined	Platinum	Palladium	Other[4]	Total	Refined	Total	Refined	Total	sumption
1990	88	1,810	5,930	71,248	71,312	13,421	14,425	2,478	30,324	120,631	125,354	20,148	55,044	117,043
1991	90	1,730	6,050	72,349	72,564	10,349	12,263	1,701	24,313	121,741	125,661	27,401	39,624	111,798
1992	87	1,650	5,440	64,309	64,309	14,187	10,641	2,118	26,946	129,419	132,006	31,060	57,830	109,469
1993	89	2,050	6,780	65,792	65,792	10,263	8,324	176	18,763	148,790	153,165	43,798	78,486	123,273
1994	91	1,960	6,440	63,000	63,000	10,304	9,345	123	19,772	167,681	170,907	46,259	88,561	127,000
1995	-----	1,590	5,260	-----	-----	-----	-----	-----	-----	214,143	220,613	41,825	50,575	-----
1996	84	1,840	6,100	-----	-----	-----	-----	-----	-----	248,860	255,880	39,709	48,836	-----
1997[1]	84	2,610	8,430	-----	-----	-----	-----	-----	-----	253,114	258,424	67,656	81,249	-----
1998[2]	94	3,240	10,600	-----	-----	-----	-----	-----	-----	297,961	303,351	52,715	73,162	-----

[1] Preliminary. [2] Estimate. [3] Includes platinum, palladium, iridium, osmium, rhodium, and ruthenium. [4] Includes iridium, osmium, rhodium, and ruthenium. W = Withheld proprietary data. *Source: U.S. Geological Survey (USGS)*

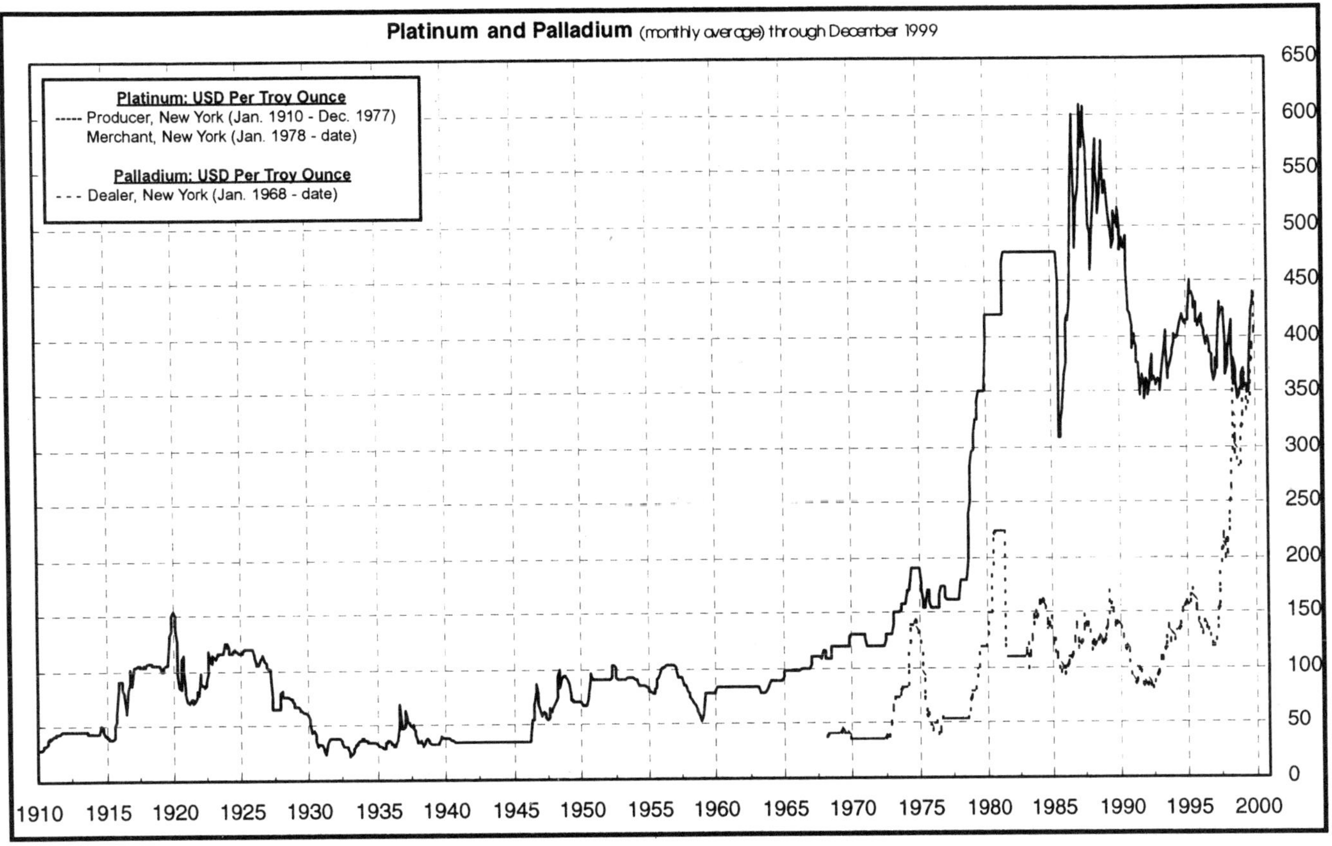

Average Merchant's Price of Platinum in the United States In Dollars Per Troy Ounce

Year	Jan.	Feb.	Mar.	Apr.	May	June	July	Aug.	Sept.	Oct.	Nov.	Dec.	Average
1990	949.93	517.34	500.32	478.33	485.89	486.60	476.93	492.02	463.87	423.78	424.12	446.94	474.26
1991	408.92	385.53	403.12	398.16	373.06	374.25	375.38	351.68	348.01	362.52	364.01	356.65	375.11
1992	341.88	362.97	356.84	347.73	354.75	368.17	378.89	360.20	361.60	359.75	355.81	361.98	359.21
1993	359.99	361.53	349.31	365.98	385.50	384.54	401.10	394.69	365.29	369.19	376.98	383.85	374.75
1994	390.30	393.95	398.29	400.38	395.41	401.42	408.25	411.91	415.93	421.11	415.73	408.83	405.13
1995	414.27	415.22	415.37	446.24	439.02	436.58	435.21	425.61	430.31	414.49	413.55	410.17	424.67
1996	416.59	421.45	412.39	405.71	402.86	393.18	392.00	400.97	391.43	385.53	383.92	372.80	398.24
1997	360.13	362.35	382.82	371.18	385.20	427.12	410.25	423.48	424.00	428.59	397.03	369.50	395.14
1998	373.45	390.56	396.18	413.14	392.00	357.38	378.20	372.24	361.56	347.27	349.29	352.35	373.64
1999[1]	353.93	364.24	370.14	357.27	355.65	355.73	349.29	350.06	370.71	421.19	433.52	439.55	376.77

[1] Preliminary. *Source: American Metal Market (AMM)*

Average Dealer[1] Price of Palladium in the United States In Dollars Per Troy Ounce

Year	Jan.	Feb.	Mar.	Apr.	May	June	July	Aug.	Sept.	Oct.	Nov.	Dec.	Average
1990	135.80	136.63	131.25	128.18	120.08	117.40	116.60	116.17	106.62	96.12	94.84	90.93	115.89
1991	86.61	85.11	86.44	95.25	96.61	97.39	95.57	84.55	82.49	81.87	85.96	82.72	88.38
1992	82.96	86.04	84.50	83.71	82.90	80.98	86.49	86.04	90.67	95.07	95.01	104.88	88.27
1993	110.39	112.57	106.22	113.79	119.94	125.36	139.74	137.37	121.95	130.04	123.62	125.60	122.22
1994	124.40	130.92	132.43	133.22	135.76	137.03	145.28	151.83	152.99	154.90	158.10	153.80	142.56
1995	156.67	157.53	161.18	170.91	160.87	158.59	156.27	138.81	143.76	137.36	135.57	132.37	150.83
1996	131.59	142.10	140.67	138.05	134.36	132.95	134.55	128.82	123.10	119.39	119.30	119.90	130.40
1997	124.73	141.26	139.55	143.73	173.38	209.47	195.73	221.57	200.38	214.21	217.05	202.64	181.98
1998	229.70	239.68	265.73	326.67	360.55	291.50	310.82	290.62	288.81	283.45	284.00	306.05	289.80
1999[2]	328.58	356.16	357.70	364.52	333.25	341.73	338.90	344.95	367.43	391.95	405.57	430.62	363.45

[1] Based on wholesale quantities, prompt delivery. [2] Preliminary. *Source: U.S. Geological Survey (USGS)*

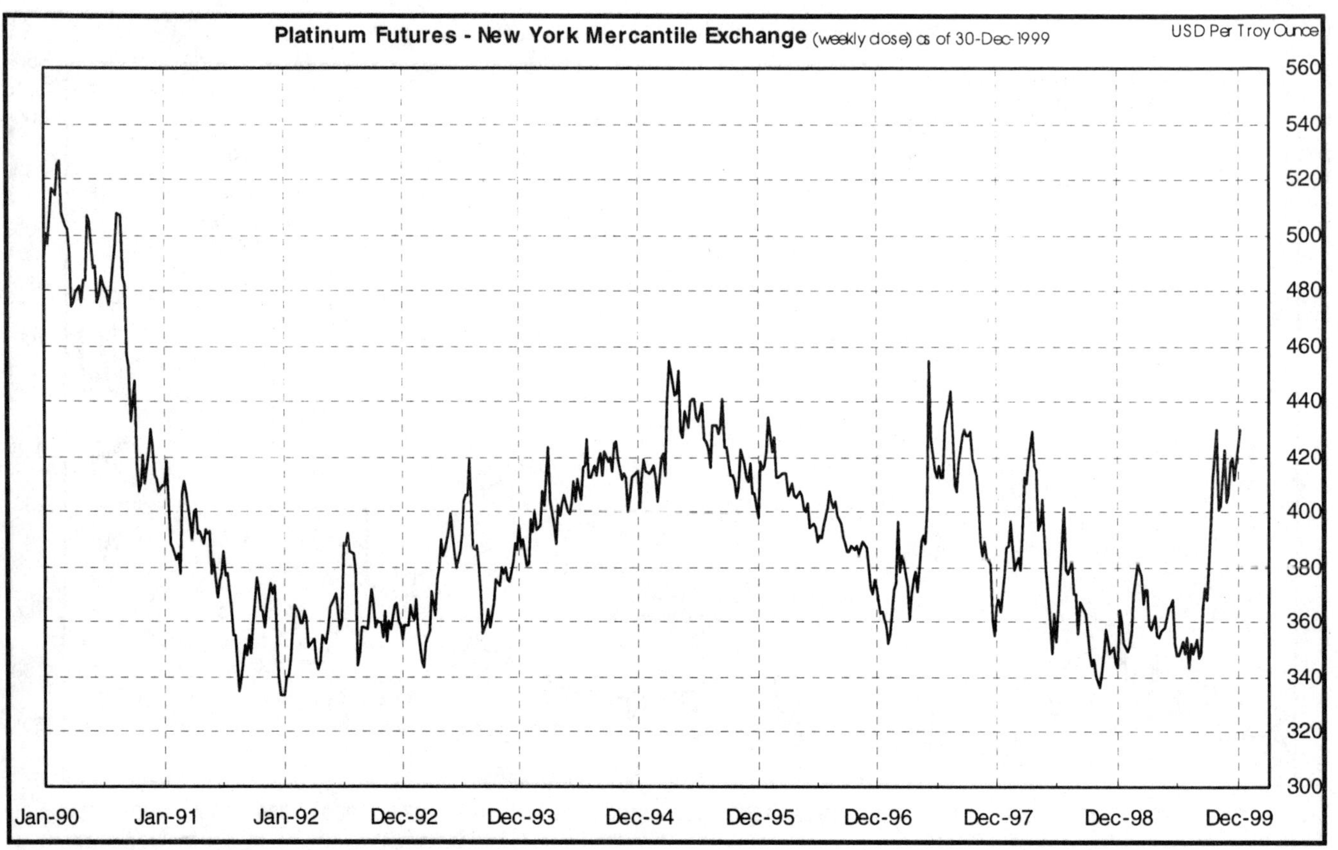

Volume of Trading of Platinum Futures in New York In Contracts

Year	Jan.	Feb.	Mar.	Apr.	May	June	July	Aug.	Sept.	Oct.	Nov.	Dec.	Total
1990	85,600	80,900	81,300	55,300	65,200	70,100	52,700	73,800	77,205	67,977	50,095	60,693	817,100
1991	50,807	42,327	72,663	42,995	51,059	55,650	40,589	45,742	55,812	44,867	41,870	60,265	598,600
1992	47,875	38,332	54,104	29,294	37,660	81,984	60,973	50,632	51,797	28,500	42,300	53,800	577,300
1993	29,400	55,555	61,425	50,603	65,778	72,535	59,751	56,399	58,552	36,965	43,998	60,269	651,222
1994	48,259	65,297	94,426	62,600	65,140	88,300	84,182	75,409	92,439	60,878	77,264	81,611	895,805
1995	61,400	38,594	131,294	69,892	60,382	75,353	53,422	62,451	98,837	55,919	56,339	82,810	846,693
1996	80,545	70,260	86,258	54,151	47,929	88,806	53,312	53,654	90,140	47,116	41,970	88,327	802,468
1997	60,515	83,325	86,242	57,719	67,000	72,481	37,836	36,391	62,462	46,188	28,913	58,625	698,597
1998	38,198	35,538	65,871	36,169	36,208	47,464	35,223	27,505	58,302	44,381	42,658	60,752	528,629
1999	37,700	53,698	68,350	36,900	26,507	75,444	57,536	36,115	102,196	30,637	32,176	40,009	597,268

Source: New York Mercantile Exchange (NYMEX)

Average Open Interest of Platinum Futures in New York In Contracts

Year	Jan.	Feb.	Mar.	Apr.	May	June	July	Aug.	Sept.	Oct.	Nov.	Dec.
1990	19,510	17,970	15,888	15,915	16,688	15,652	15,496	17,254	18,494	17,472	16,313	16,994
1991	15,497	16,043	16,083	14,334	15,779	18,273	17,503	19,214	18,611	15,933	13,579	14,533
1992	15,464	14,231	14,272	14,130	15,353	19,070	20,402	18,444	17,574	14,079	13,532	14,282
1993	11,889	14,315	12,990	15,490	19,641	17,919	20,931	18,892	16,883	15,690	16,658	19,633
1994	18,779	19,655	21,673	22,834	21,880	22,835	24,804	25,049	24,245	24,159	26,287	26,661
1995	23,285	23,058	23,470	23,657	20,984	21,533	20,801	25,288	23,489	24,498	22,137	21,534
1996	23,130	21,535	23,156	25,081	26,343	27,720	25,861	25,455	28,511	28,305	27,423	29,143
1997	25,890	26,092	22,364	16,568	18,933	18,440	13,280	14,180	13,639	13,466	12,396	13,501
1998	10,791	10,932	13,220	13,559	12,048	11,471	10,607	9,733	11,950	14,601	15,709	13,289
1999	12,311	14,481	16,493	11,471	12,256	12,435	14,703	13,776	15,014	14,892	13,401	12,016

Source: New York Mercantile Exchange (NYMEX)

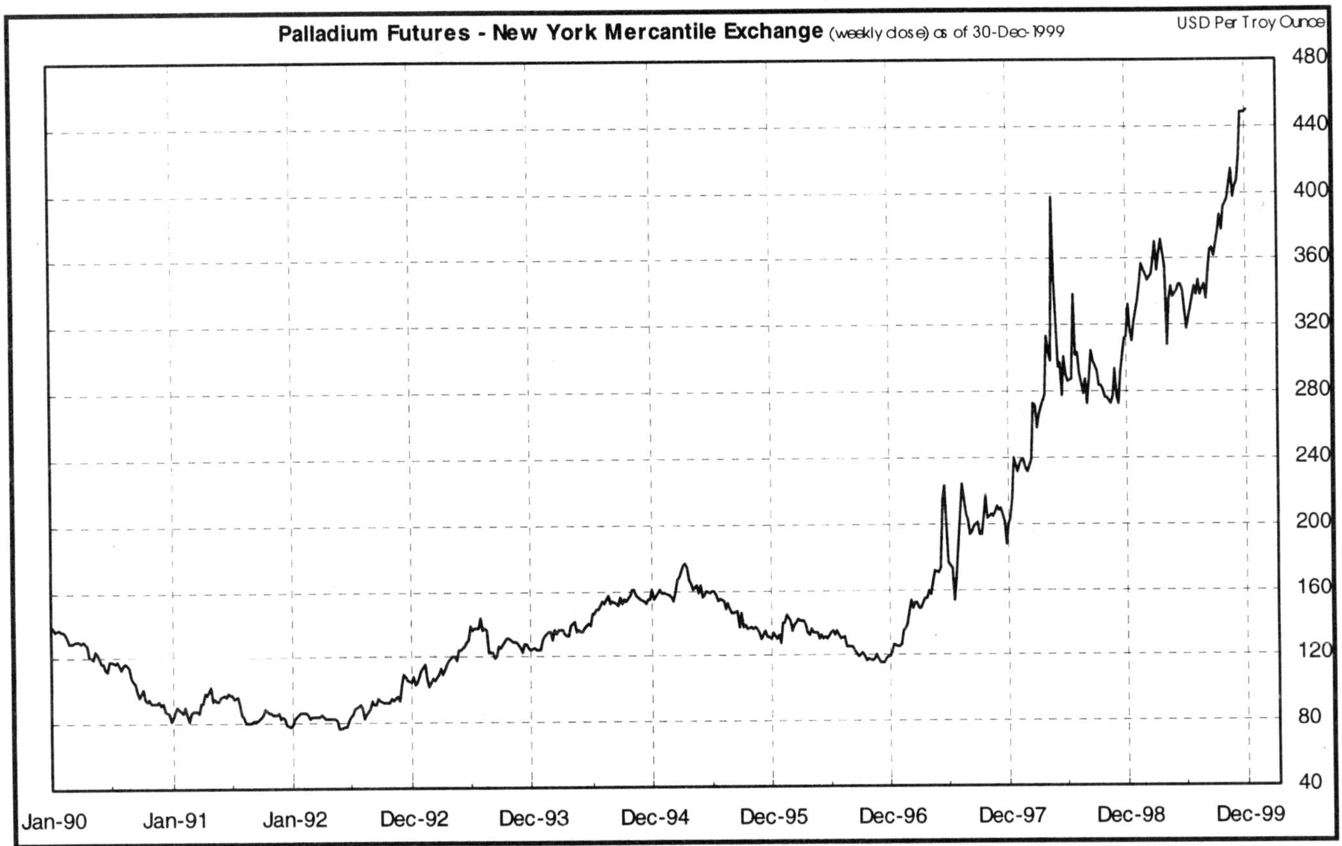

Volume of Trading of Palladium Futures in New York In Contracts

Year	Jan.	Feb.	Mar.	Apr.	May	June	July	Aug.	Sept.	Oct.	Nov.	Dec.	Total
1990	4,893	19,026	6,930	5,355	13,104	5,670	4,452	11,130	5,407	7,150	9,592	3,178	95,887
1991	5,017	10,542	5,380	7,245	10,521	4,447	5,230	10,114	2,914	5,668	8,150	2,971	78,199
1992	7,217	7,323	3,429	2,833	8,011	2,881	4,965	6,752	5,066	5,359	6,461	7,912	68,209
1993	7,708	14,461	8,057	10,034	12,190	7,368	7,043	13,356	6,977	9,220	12,477	4,790	113,681
1994	8,250	14,953	6,067	6,676	15,481	6,514	9,024	21,741	15,690	9,603	21,384	8,390	143,773
1995	10,684	17,092	21,001	12,775	17,413	9,615	11,816	18,948	9,754	9,320	16,662	11,633	166,713
1996	13,725	33,519	11,931	16,416	27,467	8,989	9,896	23,740	10,721	8,149	28,870	12,187	205,610
1997	13,908	43,160	22,796	21,604	36,422	17,647	18,097	18,751	8,331	13,094	13,143	11,763	238,716
1998	11,506	17,786	18,678	14,042	17,942	7,370	4,241	8,737	6,214	4,962	12,839	6,933	131,250
1999	3,092	11,614	4,082	7,097	8,890	3,411	5,053	6,868	5,826	3,722	10,670	5,069	75,394

Source: New York Mercantile Exchange (NYMEX)

Average Open Interest of Palladium Futures in New York In Contracts

Year	Jan.	Feb.	Mar.	Apr.	May	June	July	Aug.	Sept.	Oct.	Nov.	Dec.
1990	6,296	6,350	5,276	5,359	5,476	5,361	5,493	5,717	5,165	5,100	5,316	4,565
1991	4,658	4,559	4,319	4,686	4,559	4,302	4,454	4,429	4,429	4,384	4,337	4,042
1992	3,984	4,071	4,101	4,206	4,137	3,852	3,762	3,362	3,041	2,982	2,901	3,246
1993	3,718	4,213	4,365	4,897	5,312	4,513	4,655	5,080	4,360	4,495	4,472	4,484
1994	4,626	4,995	4,672	4,303	5,116	4,530	5,807	6,851	6,625	6,511	7,726	6,917
1995	7,484	7,579	7,102	7,231	6,519	6,413	6,739	6,852	5,950	6,120	6,486	6,090
1996	6,365	7,539	6,682	7,099	8,713	8,143	7,977	8,805	8,129	7,971	8,227	7,727
1997	8,291	10,946	10,528	9,759	9,947	7,072	5,538	4,973	3,822	4,282	4,291	4,030
1998	4,062	4,873	5,220	5,369	4,371	4,219	4,166	3,488	2,959	3,048	2,938	2,700
1999	2,846	3,234	2,957	3,015	2,796	2,756	2,822	2,495	2,754	3,209	3,300	3,045

Source: New York Mercantile Exchange (NYMEX)

Pork Bellies

Pork bellies, more commonly known as bacon, are obtained from the underside of a hog. A hog has two bellies, generally weighing about 8-18 pounds, depending on the hog's commercial slaughter weight. Slaughter weights now average about 255 pounds per head, equal to a dressed weight of about 190 pounds. Bellies account for about 12 percent of a hog's live weight, but represent a somewhat larger percentage of the total cutout value of the realized pork products. Frozen bellies deliverable against futures generally weigh between 12-14 pounds.

There are definitive seasonalities for pork bellies. Bellies are storable and the movement into cold storage builds early in the calendar year, peaking about midyear. Net withdrawals from storage then carry stocks to a low usually around October. The cycle then starts again. Retail bacon demand also follows an established trend, peaking in the summer when consumer preference shifts to lighter foods and tapering off to a low during the winter months. While demand patterns would suggest the highest prices in the summer and the lowest in the winter, just the opposite is not unusual. Such contra-seasonal price moves can be partially attributed to supply logistics, notably, the availability of frozen storage stocks deliverable against futures at exchange (CME) approved warehouses. When stocks prove either too large or too small the underlying demand variables for bacon can be relegated to the backburner as a market making variable. The fact that no contract months are traded between August and the following February adds to the price distortion that may occur in frozen belly futures, as seen in 1999.

Belly prices (cash and futures) are sensitive to the inventory in cold storage. Also important are the weekly reports of net movement in and out of storage which afford some insight to demand, although a better measure is the weekly quantity of bellies being sliced into bacon. Higher prices tend to encourage placing more supply into storage by discouraging retail bacon demand. Bacon is not a necessary foodstuff, but demand can be buoyed by favorable consumer disposable income. On the flip side, however, dietary standards have changed dramatically in recent years that do not favor the consumption of bacon, a food known to contain high levels of fat and salt.

Wholesale frozen pork belly prices, basis nearby Chicago futures, fell in mid-1999 to about $0.35 per pound, the lowest price since 1994 and about $0.25 cents below year earlier levels. Prices then recovered sharply, pushing into the mid $0.70 range by November, partly in response to the large number of hogs killed in North Carolina from Hurricane Floyd. Retail bacon prices started to climb in the fall, reaching $2.58/lb., about unchanged from a year earlier, but up about 8 cents per pound from midyear. The strong U.S. economy also buoyed demand and helped maintain a firm undertone to retail prices.

U.S. foreign trade in bacon as a processed product is small. Imports are largely from Denmark and exports go to Eastern Europe.

Futures Markets

Frozen pork belly futures and options are traded on the Chicago Mercantile Exchange (CME). Futures are also listed on the CME in fresh pork bellies, but there is little to no volume in that contract at this time.

Average Retail Price of Bacon, Sliced In Dollars Per Pound

Year	Jan.	Feb.	Mar.	Apr.	May	June	July	Aug.	Sept.	Oct.	Nov.	Dec.	Average
1990	1.97	2.01	1.99	1.98	2.04	2.15	2.21	2.24	2.18	2.21	2.24	2.28	2.13
1991	2.26	2.30	2.32	2.27	2.31	2.31	2.31	2.22	2.16	2.12	2.07	1.99	2.22
1992	1.96	1.95	1.92	1.92	1.90	1.93	1.95	1.94	1.93	1.89	1.85	1.86	1.92
1993	1.87	1.84	1.80	1.89	1.91	1.95	2.00	1.95	1.98	1.99	2.01	2.02	1.93
1994	2.04	2.02	2.02	2.06	1.99	1.99	2.00	1.99	1.97	1.97	1.92	1.89	1.99
1995	1.93	1.93	1.91	1.89	1.92	1.90	1.91	1.97	2.04	2.12	2.16	2.17	1.99
1996	2.14	2.20	2.20	2.24	2.35	2.49	2.54	2.68	2.81	2.72	2.66	2.64	2.47
1997	2.66	2.65	2.66	2.66	2.63	2.69	2.72	2.76	2.75	2.73	2.67	2.61	2.68
1998	2.64	2.62	2.54	2.44	2.44	2.46	2.52	2.51	2.58	2.57	2.62	2.58	2.54
1999[1]	2.52	2.52	2.51	2.45	2.47	2.50	2.50	2.54	2.58	2.57	2.66		2.53

[1] Preliminary. *Source: Economic Research Service, U.S. Department of Agriculture (ERS-USDA)*

Frozen Pork Belly Storage Stocks in the United States, on First of Month In Thousands of Pounds

Year	Jan.	Feb.	Mar.	Apr.	May	June	July	Aug.	Sept.	Oct.	Nov.	Dec.
1990	85,026	77,255	85,789	96,945	102,899	105,482	87,983	55,859	23,352	4,785	5,506	24,044
1991	46,998	48,750	54,529	68,094	80,382	79,936	72,032	45,915	29,832	15,944	25,558	48,311
1992	71,318	76,894	75,925	85,095	96,653	92,677	78,646	54,544	26,854	21,973	26,044	49,970
1993	70,576	65,280	65,919	66,064	79,430	77,903	70,251	46,630	20,811	10,964	14,345	33,563
1994	53,168	55,999	54,921	63,099	72,230	79,018	73,583	57,747	30,636	18,260	22,656	40,725
1995	61,073	62,776	64,228	78,975	78,539	77,919	67,607	47,055	17,435	6,255	13,478	37,092
1996	47,587	46,498	46,381	47,655	57,174	63,522	56,767	28,533	18,996	12,702	16,206	30,943
1997	37,930	38,030	44,277	54,767	54,015	55,274	52,274	33,657	18,346	11,148	14,408	25,365
1998	44,763	55,249	55,368	54,441	58,600	59,462	52,010	31,433	14,786	9,452	16,440	41,711
1999[1]	72,657	82,605	92,496	106,194	109,521	108,257	93,383	69,675	34,814	19,273	22,489	26,170

[1] Preliminary. *Source: National Agricultural Statistics Service, U.S. Department of Agriculture (NASS-USDA)*

Weekly Pork Belly Storage Movement

1998 Week Ending		In	Out	On Hand	Net Movement	1999 Week Ending		In	Out	On Hand	Net Movement
		Stocks[1] In Thousands of Pounds						Stocks[1] In Thousands of Pounds			
Jan.	3	4,946	119	25,190	4,827	Jan.	2	3,167	117	38,129	3,050
	10	3,255	83	28,362	3,172		9	2,620	785	39,964	1,835
	17	2,154	245	30,271	1,909		16	1,248	302	40,910	946
	24	1,541	230	31,582	1,311		23	1,452	415	41,947	1,037
	31	66	854	30,794	-788		30	1,245	226	42,966	1,019
Feb.	7	282	1,021	30,055	-739	Feb.	6	1,083	211	43,838	872
	14	706	663	30,098	43		13	511	200	44,149	311
	21	613	612	30,099	1		20	2,633	85	46,697	2,548
	28	734	404	30,429	330		27	2,687	160	49,224	2,527
Mar.	7	1,048	534	30,943	514	Mar.	6	2,336	128	51,432	2,208
	14	748	701	30,806	47		13	1,121	122	52,432	999
	21	719	369	31,156	350		20	2,067	124	54,375	1,944
	28	286	1,101	30,341	-815		27	1,260	148	55,487	1,112
Apr.	4	98	1,250	29,189	-1,152	Apr.	3	1,143	874	55,756	269
	11	897	989	27,488	-92		10	1,151	39	56,868	1,112
	18	1,757	2,132	28,476	-375		17	968	49	57,787	919
	25	3,197	1,108	30,565	2,089		24	382	208	57,961	174
May	2	1,193	169	31,589	1,024	May	1	1,169	311	58,819	858
	9	1,232	291	32,530	941		8	626	459	58,986	167
	16	301	239	32,592	62		15	330	293	59,023	37
	23	965	286	33,271	679		22	445	1,084	58,384	-639
	30	274	874	32,671	-600		29	325	667	58,042	-342
June	6	10	1,315	31,366	-1,305	June	5	163	1,335	56,870	-1,172
	13	49	2,061	29,354	-2,012		12	85	1,527	55,420	-1,442
	20	725	1,352	28,727	-627		19	0	2,706	52,722	-2,706
	27	92	1,658	27,161	-1,566		26	126	2,110	50,738	-1,984
July	4	181	2,580	24,762	-2,399	July	3	83	2,739	48,083	-2,656
	11	15	3,632	21,145	-3,617		10	244	1,788	46,539	-1,544
	18	0	2,604	18,541	-2,604		17	353	3,568	43,324	-3,215
	25	50	2,836	15,755	-2,786		24	52	2,717	40,659	-2,665
Aug.	1	0	2,630	13,125	-2,630		31	48	5,391	34,845	-5,343
	8	40	2,299	10,866	-2,259	Aug.	7	66	4,468	30,443	-4,402
	15	43	2,693	8,216	-2,650		14	0	4,163	26,280	-4,163
	22	48	2,546	5,718	-2,498		21	44	3,208	23,116	-3,164
	29	230	936	5,012	-706		28	165	3,411	19,870	-3,246
Sept.	5	841	816	5,037	25	Sept.	4	15	2,855	17,030	-2,840
	12	417	1,313	4,141	-896		11	7	2,080	14,957	-2,073
	19	0	788	3,352	-788		18	212	2,591	12,578	-2,379
	26	368	648	3,072	-280		25	301	1,832	11,047	-1,531
Oct.	3	452	472	3,052	-20	Oct.	2	14	1,215	9,846	-1,201
	10	379	226	3,205	153		9	108	1,209	8,745	1,101
	17	805	124	3,886	681		16	72	1,333	7,484	-1,261
	24	627	209	4,304	418		23	110	231	7,363	-121
	31	1,846	195	5,955	1,651		30	33	66	7,330	-33
Nov.	7	2,392	203	8,144	2,189	Nov.	6	88	93	7,325	-5
	14	3,613	163	11,594	3,450		13	592	440	7,477	152
	21	2,901	126	14,369	2,775		20	532	684	7,325	-152
	28	4,992	92	19,269	4,900		27	543	91	7,778	452
Dec.	5	1,946	22	21,193	1,924	Dec.	4	885	210	8,452	675
	12	1,981	17	23,157	1,964		11	1,226	98	9,580	1,128
	19	5,005	0	35,079	5,005		18	1,273	231	10,622	1,042
	26	0	0	35,079	0		25	2,851	216	13,257	2,635

[1] 57 Chicago and Outside Combined Chicago Mercantile Exchange approved warehouses. *Source: Chicago Mercantile Exchange (CME)*

PORK BELLIES

Average Open Interest of Pork Belly Futures in Chicago In Contracts

Year	Jan.	Feb.	Mar.	Apr.	May	June	July	Aug.	Sept.	Oct.	Nov.	Dec.
1990	12,885	12,114	13,017	15,338	14,513	13,038	11,146	6,104	6,059	7,851	11,419	12,589
1991	11,777	10,187	9,776	11,509	10,436	10,111	7,356	6,176	7,532	10,813	13,173	12,844
1992	12,521	12,195	11,901	12,345	12,497	13,598	12,623	7,149	6,540	7,033	9,251	10,953
1993	10,623	9,244	8,283	8,626	10,096	11,092	9,031	5,427	4,644	7,241	8,701	9,121
1994	11,053	10,426	9,375	9,894	8,092	8,248	7,836	7,841	8,398	10,072	10,141	10,216
1995	10,294	9,080	7,809	7,367	8,017	7,036	5,666	4,271	6,246	7,007	7,103	7,282
1996	7,094	8,028	10,521	10,753	10,018	8,136	6,432	6,296	6,056	6,395	6,050	6,480
1997	7,504	7,930	7,260	7,165	8,950	7,203	5,905	4,791	5,242	7,520	8,302	9,009
1998	9,187	9,145	9,082	7,825	6,786	5,406	4,185	3,493	2,933	3,841	4,987	7,085
1999	7,217	6,192	4,623	5,113	6,030	6,638	5,002	2,415	2,320	3,206	4,011	4,868

Source: Chicago Mercantile Exchange (CME)

Volume of Trading of Pork Belly Futures in Chicago In Contracts

Year	Jan.	Feb.	Mar.	Apr.	May	June	July	Aug.	Sept.	Oct.	Nov.	Dec.	Total
1990	109,036	100,813	129,476	133,946	165,880	143,663	122,187	74,653	53,428	76,549	112,752	80,746	1,303,129
1991	106,078	89,975	88,056	111,195	119,773	96,273	74,255	59,176	65,604	80,707	63,331	50,773	1,005,196
1992	80,697	79,700	67,470	57,565	73,137	73,081	78,588	54,663	39,839	64,248	60,724	54,440	784,152
1993	77,380	62,871	63,988	62,403	62,400	70,124	65,496	42,613	37,992	47,780	60,163	49,099	698,799
1994	60,316	67,250	58,183	53,839	56,575	58,424	50,450	47,626	38,375	45,525	49,280	47,803	633,646
1995	62,994	54,330	59,324	43,501	49,453	53,571	45,869	36,623	31,112	35,444	47,061	42,631	561,913
1996	48,563	56,623	61,669	61,703	61,868	55,337	55,121	45,399	39,182	48,973	42,709	35,502	612,649
1997	60,761	53,604	56,750	76,072	62,190	54,043	55,043	36,153	31,154	44,277	31,663	33,609	595,319
1998	41,894	50,105	47,249	61,910	36,058	48,913	41,133	33,832	24,006	30,538	30,093	35,521	481,252
1999	39,925	36,293	33,322	31,558	31,321	45,030	36,513	23,536	16,544	20,392	28,920	24,955	368,309

Source: Chicago Mercantile Exchange (CME)

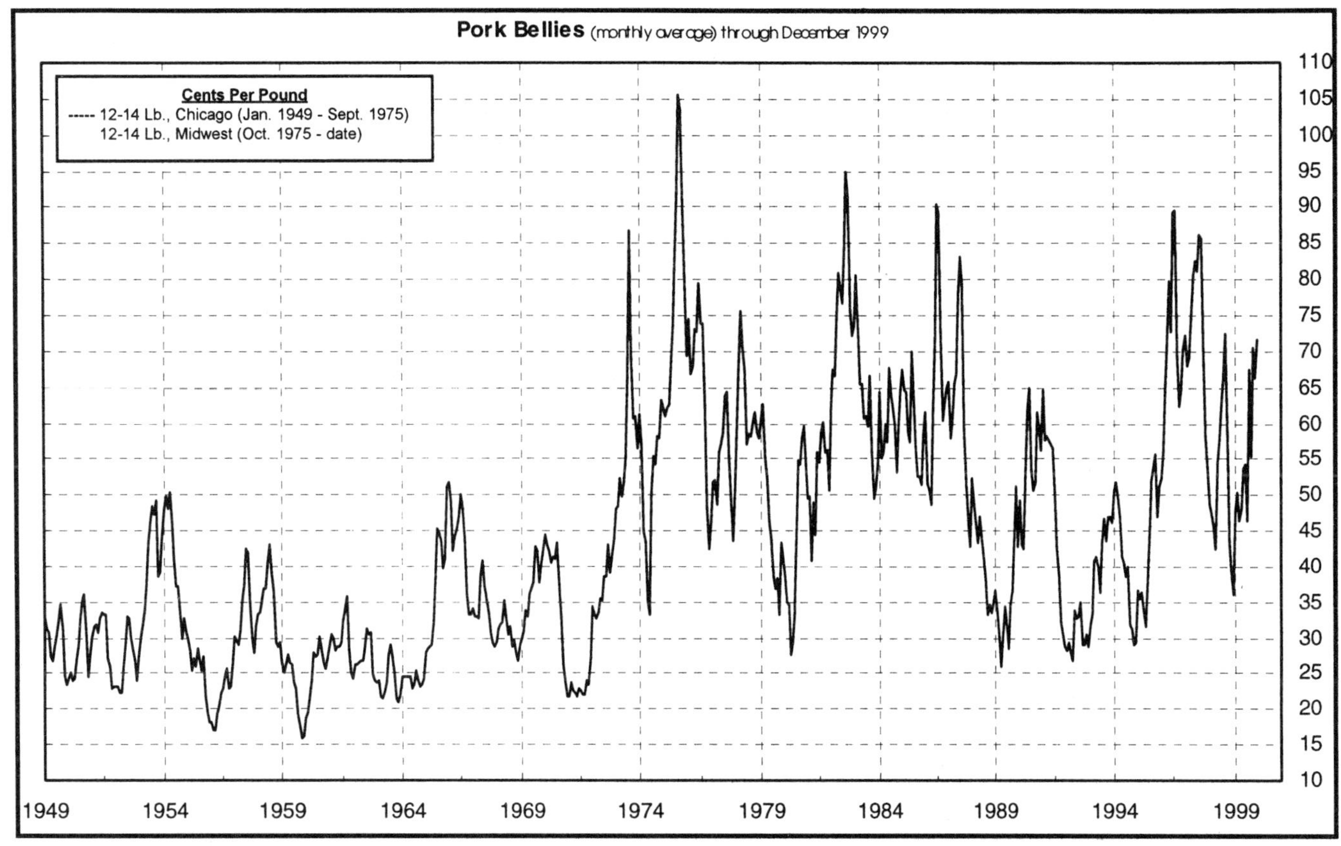

Average Price of Pork Bellies (12-14 Pounds) Midwest In Cents Per Pound

Year	Jan.	Feb.	Mar.	Apr.	May	June	July	Aug.	Sept.	Oct.	Nov.	Dec.	Average
1990	48.65	42.53	42.60	52.60	61.48	65.15	53.18	51.08	51.31	59.83	60.57	56.58	53.80
1991	64.11	57.20	58.52	57.25	57.50	56.48	50.40	42.01	38.97	32.26	30.04	28.79	47.79
1992	28.05	29.44	28.01	26.93	34.09	32.78	32.77	35.13	29.09	29.13	30.48	28.80	30.39
1993	31.97	33.22	41.28	41.19	39.86	36.24	44.51	46.68	43.82	47.25	47.21	46.21	41.62
1994	50.63	51.66	49.68	46.84	41.40	40.39	38.64	39.60	31.50	31.33	29.09	29.29	40.00
1995	36.03	35.80	36.30	33.83	31.70	37.94	43.10	52.42	54.43	56.20	47.28	51.45	43.04
1996	52.33	56.33	64.50	69.86	79.50	72.64	89.49	88.40	68.12	63.07	65.27	70.07	69.97
1997	72.04	68.42	59.05	80.54	82.58	80.68	86.70	85.43	72.25	57.97	53.77	47.52	70.58
1998	43.00	45.89	42.28	54.65	57.87	63.10	68.46	72.99	57.49	42.05	39.13	36.31	51.94
1999[1]	48.80	50.76	46.51	49.23	53.76	53.41	47.78	67.29	57.87	70.83	67.81	71.25	57.11

[1] Preliminary. *Source: Economic Research Service, U.S. Department of Agriculture (ERS-USDA)*

Average Price of Pork Loins (12-14 lbs.)[2] Central, U.S. In Cents Per Pound

Year	Jan.	Feb.	Mar.	Apr.	May	June	July	Aug.	Sept.	Oct.	Nov.	Dec.	Average
1990	101.36	107.75	117.26	120.68	136.06	125.62	144.14	119.56	121.64	113.71	98.94	103.50	117.52
1991	107.67	109.13	110.33	104.81	120.48	123.49	121.73	117.54	105.85	100.87	88.63	90.19	108.39
1992	96.89	99.13	94.10	98.65	108.94	113.94	108.22	111.18	102.98	96.98	89.64	96.22	101.41
1993	98.22	100.05	100.61	107.61	111.16	122.28	113.40	116.73	116.74	111.85	98.68	92.33	107.47
1994	103.90	110.75	100.45	101.89	103.99	103.84	109.79	112.86	105.34	95.65	80.00	89.50	101.50
1995	96.94	102.20	95.30	93.33	103.50	118.81	124.65	127.98	117.63	108.23	93.94	110.39	107.74
1996	110.00	116.43	120.49	119.70	131.61	115.73	126.16	118.18	112.28	115.40	115.39	120.45	118.49
1997	112.50	109.50	106.58	117.16	125.68	116.28	122.53	119.28	112.07	99.68	85.99	79.44	108.89
1998	76.50	103.03	104.56	102.51	130.64	113.13	106.51	105.90	97.23	99.63	79.90	72.49	99.34
1999[1]	105.82	92.35	83.47	99.35	107.44	97.62	105.72	111.55	104.99	98.98	94.64	103.75	100.47

[1] Preliminary. *Source: Economic Research Service, U.S. Department of Agriculture (ERS-USDA)*

Potatoes

Potatoes are the largest vegetable crop grown in the U.S. with 1998 production of 476 million hundredweight vs. the previous year's 467 million and the record large 1996 crop of 499 million. Although 1998 planted acreage increased to 1.42 million acres from 1.38 in 1997, the acreage increase was somewhat offset by a slight decline in average yield to 343 hundredweight per acre from 345 cwt. the previous year. Both yield and acreage, however, trailed the 1996 record crop.

The value of the 1998 potato crop of $2.6 billion was marginally higher than the 1997 crop's value, but the average price per hundredweight of $5.56 compares with $5.64 for the 1997 crop.

Total 1998 consumption (sales) also trailed the 1996 record of 452 million cwt., but at 435 million cwt. consumption was larger than the 1997 total of 429 million. Nonsales, consisting of seed use, shrinkage and loss, in 1998 of 41 million cwt. compares with 38 million in 1997 and 47 million in 1996. Total domestic foodstock usage of 282 million cwt. in 1998 compares with 268 million in 1997 and the record large 284 million in 1996; included in the totals were 143 million cwt. allocated to frozen french fry production vs. 132 million in 1997, and tablestock usage of 124 million cwt. vs. 132 million, respectively. For a time, in the mid-1990's, there was concern that the U.S. consumer's affinity for deep-fried processed potatoes may have peaked, but the rebound in 1998 from 1997 seems to suggest otherwise. Perhaps more surprising was the further slippage in fresh potato usage.

Potatoes are grown in all fifty states. The crop, however, is divided into four, but not necessarily distinct, seasonal groups based on harvest time. The fall crop, consisting of about two dozen states, accounts for 85-90 percent of total production and is usually harvested from September through November. The winter crop is the smallest and harvested only in Florida and California from January into March. The spring and summer crops tend to be fairly close in size. The seasonal disparities reflect major differences in planted acreage and realized yield which is consistently higher in the states that grow fall potato crops. The marketing season follows the harvest, but the movement of the fall crop can extend into the following July with supplies drawn from storage. The inventoried fall crop can serve as a supply buffer in the event the spring and summer crops are short. However, large fall stocks can also prove a depressant on prices should earlier crops prove large. Generally about one-third of farm marketings occur during September and October.

Idaho is the nation's largest potato producer with a 1998 fall crop of 138 million hundredweight vs. 140 million in 1997 and the record large 143 million cwt. in 1996. Washington's crop, a distant second, of 93 million cwt. compares with 88 million and 95 million, respectively. As usual, Washington's average yield was the nation's highest, 565 cwt. per acre in 1998 compared to Idaho's average of 338 cwt. per acre. Maine's crop, once the largest producing state, totaled only 18 million cwt. in 1998 vs. 19 million in 1997 and 21 million in 1996. Maine's production decline largely reflects the fact that nearly 80 different kinds of potatoes are grown in the state, whereas in Idaho production is focused on one type of baking potato, the Russet Burbank, which has enhanced marketing consistency and consumer preference.

About 55 percent of the 1998 crop was processed, either into frozen products or as a direct consumer food like potato chips. Frozen french fries account for about 20 percent of the nation's total potato usage, with chips accounting for almost 10 percent (50 million cwt. in 1998) and dehydrated potatoes another 10 percent (56 million cwt.). Generally about 1 percent, or 4.4 million cwt. in 1998, of the total crop is used for seed. Also a factor is the 1998 total of 35 million cwt. considered lost, mostly due to shrinkage.

Foreign trade in U.S. potatoes is small: Japan imports processed potatoes, mostly french fries, while Canada exports fresh potatoes, which are used mostly for seed.

Futures Markets

Potato futures and options are traded on the London International Financial Futures and Options Exchange (LIFFE). Potato futures and options are listed on the NYCE Division of the New York Board of Trade (NYBOT) but volume is virtually nonexistent.

Salient Statistics of Potatoes in the United States

				Farm Disposition									-- Foreign Trade[5] --			
					---- Used Where Grown ----				---- Value of ----			(Fresh)		Consumption[5]	
	------ Acreage ------		Yield Per Harvested	Total Pro-	Seed	Shrinkage		Farm	Pro-		Stocks on	Domestic		Per Capita	
Crop	Planted	Harvested	Acre	duction	& Feed	& Loss	Sold[2]	Price	duction[3]	Sales	Jan. 1	Exports	Imports	--- In Pounds ---	
Year	---- 1,000 Acres ----		Cwt.	--------- In Thousands of Cwt. ---------				$/Cwt.	---- Million $ ----		1,000 Cwt.	-- Millions of Lbs.--		Fresh	Total
1990	1,400	1,371	293	402,110	5,949	28,329	367,832	6.08	2,409	2,240	194,460	327,333	482,903	46.8	124.1
1991	1,408	1,374	304	417,622	5,995	32,429	379,198	4.96	2,043	1,880	211,005	341,682	437,349	50.4	135.5
1992	1,339	1,315	323	425,367	5,925	33,807	385,637	5.52	2,336	2,129	215,990	537,939	273,515	48.6	130.7
1993	1,385	1,317	326	428,693	5,931	30,152	392,610	6.17	2,637	2,424	217,300	539,345	541,382	49.3	134.9
1994	1,416	1,380	339	467,054	5,878	37,166	424,010	5.58	2,590	2,367	238,560	655,026	405,899	50.3	140.2
1995	1,398	1,372	323	443,606	5,745	29,530	408,331	6.77	2,992	2,762	223,550	583,938	458,926	49.5	138.4
1996	1,455	1,426	350	499,254	6,221	41,222	451,190	4.91	2,425	2,220	261,320	564,010	690,768	50.0	145.4
1997	1,384	1,354	345	467,091	5,475	32,183	429,433	5.64	2,623	2,421	246,550	670,270	512,321	48.5	142.0
1998	1,417	1,388	343	475,771	5,766	35,454	434,551	5.56	2,633	2,416	246,230	650,917	737,223	50.8	145.1
1999[1]	1,383	1,349	357	481,482				5.84	2,783		238,160			48.7	144.7

[1] Preliminary. [2] For all purposes, including food, seed processing & livestock feed. [3] Farm weight basis, excluding canned and frozen potatoes.

Source: Economic Research Service, U.S. Department of Agriculture (ERS-USDA)

Cold Storage Stocks of All Frozen Potatoes in the United States, on First of Month In Millions of Pounds

Year	Jan.	Feb.	Mar.	Apr.	May	June	July	Aug.	Sept.	Oct.	Nov.	Dec.
1990	917.3	932.7	995.6	1,041.2	1,059.0	1,061.3	977.6	769.3	688.1	852.5	995.6	999.5
1991	975.8	993.3	988.9	1,041.5	1,052.3	1,167.2	1,216.5	935.5	880.1	985.5	1,148.0	1,037.2
1992	980.8	996.5	1,036.3	1,082.7	1,077.6	1,137.3	1,131.4	966.4	948.7	949.1	1,067.1	1,038.7
1993	963.2	971.2	1,028.2	1,046.6	912.7	979.5	989.8	932.8	902.8	1,019.5	1,184.7	1,130.7
1994	1,006.4	1,019.9	1,057.1	1,054.4	1,050.5	1,118.9	1,099.9	979.8	1,028.2	1,108.7	1,189.0	1,163.5
1995	1,096.6	1,156.0	1,179.9	1,169.0	1,138.0	1,125.4	1,116.5	992.4	992.6	1,145.3	1,225.6	1,174.5
1996	1,123.7	1,147.2	1,172.5	1,164.6	1,112.1	1,076.4	1,059.7	907.1	957.8	1,124.9	1,225.2	1,146.3
1997	1,098.4	1,111.5	1,180.1	1,177.1	1,195.8	1,213.3	1,271.4	1,214.3	1,130.8	1,270.0	1,354.7	1,313.5
1998	1,163.5	1,147.2	1,235.7	1,278.3	1,225.1	1,282.8	1,316.5	1,234.7	1,204.5	1,266.8	1,341.0	1,290.5
1999[1]	1,151.3	1,219.7	1,272.9	1,278.8	1,236.2	1,255.5	1,234.1	1,142.3	1,169.8	1,235.5	1,307.8	1,254.5

[1] Preliminary. *Source: Agricultural Statistics Board, U.S. Department of Agriculture (ASB-USDA)*

Potato Crop Production Estimates, Stocks and Disappearance in the United States In Millions of Cwt.

	Crop Production Estimates						Total Storage Stocks[2]					Fall Crop				
	Total Crop			Fall Crop			Following Year					1,000 Cwt.				
Year	Oct. 1	Nov. 1	Dec. 1	Oct. 1	Nov. 1	Dec. 1	Jan. 1	Feb. 1	Mar. 1	Apr. 1	May 1	Production	Disappearance (Sold)	Dec. 1 Stocks	Average Price $/Cwt.	Value of Sales $ 1,000
1990	-----	393.2	-----	-----	371.7	225.5	194.5	162.9	134.5	101.2	63.0	344,200	320,033	225,500	5.42	1,734,476
1991	-----	417.6	-----	-----	379.5	242.1	211.0	178.5	145.8	108.9	69.1	363,541	334,893	242,070	4.16	1,393,749
1992	-----	425.4	-----	-----	372.4	246.8	216.0	184.6	152.8	115.8	75.0	368,516	341,209	246,820	5.17	1,762,984
1993	-----	428.7	-----	-----	372.4	249.4	217.3	185.5	153.4	115.2	72.9	376,954	353,052	249,710	5.65	1,981,017
1994	-----	467.9	-----	-----	412.4	273.3	238.6	202.5	169.6	129.8	87.6	410,839	380,818	272,290	5.06	1,914,311
1995	-----	444.8	-----	-----	402.4	256.7	223.6	189.4	156.0	115.9	75.9	394,785	370,679	256,710	6.43	2,372,983
1996	-----	491.5	-----	-----	447.9	295.1	261.3	226.1	189.2	147.6	103.2	443,704	408,247	295,100	4.35	1,772,037
1997	-----	459.4	-----	-----	417.5	278.8	246.6	212.6	175.9	134.2	92.8	423,190	387,089	278,830	5.20	2,011,004
1998	-----	471.0	-----	-----	429.0	280.9	246.2	209.6	173.7	131.2	87.9	432,737	392,922	280,910	5.07	1,994,030
1999[1]	-----	481.5	-----	-----	435.6	274.4	238.2	205.8				429,847		274,370		

[1] Preliminary. [2] Held by growers and local dealers in the fall producing areas. *Source: Agricultural Statistics Board, U.S. Department of Agriculture*

Production of Potatoes by Seasonal Groups in the United States In Thousands of Cwt.

	Winter	Spring			Summer			Fall								
Year	Total	California	Florida	Total	New Mexico	Virginia	Total	Colorado	Idaho	Maine	Minnesota	North Dakota	Oregon	Washington	Wisconsin	Total
1990	2,343	8,438	8,714	24,163	3,400	1,980	23,097	22,750	119,070	20,520	14,280	16,675	23,450	67,980	23,075	352,507
1991	2,609	8,284	6,600	20,636	3,450	1,485	22,647	23,800	122,175	18,170	17,160	30,030	22,170	75,435	23,275	371,730
1992	2,998	7,238	7,750	21,535	952	1,980	21,309	22,110	127,050	24,300	16,080	27,690	21,075	69,300	25,160	379,525
1993	2,552	7,508	6,068	19,654	1,290	1,760	14,922	25,270	126,192	19,890	14,780	21,090	23,103	88,500	22,588	385,935
1994	2,372	7,790	8,588	22,646	1,088	1,425	17,381	25,795	138,801	18,375	20,035	28,200	27,514	88,920	25,740	419,645
1995	2,473	6,230	7,830	20,193	1,344	2,040	17,931	23,808	132,657	17,160	20,790	25,410	24,788	80,850	26,000	403,009
1996	3,273	7,538	7,765	22,417	1,404	1,463	19,176	29,175	142,800	21,175	24,600	28,820	30,124	94,990	33,150	454,388
1997	3,431	8,073	7,150	22,299	1,248	1,268	18,171	24,993	140,314	19,080	20,440	22,000	27,319	88,160	30,175	423,190
1998	2,980	6,198	7,358	21,121	962	1,380	18,933	25,360	138,000	18,060	21,170	28,670	26,229	93,225	30,895	432,737
1999[1]	4,070	7,600	8,820	25,327	1,247	1,050	19,154	25,762	133,330	17,813	18,020	26,400	28,020	95,200	34,000	429,847

[1] Preliminary. *Source: Agricultural Statistics Board, U.S. Department of Agriculture (ASB-USDA)*

Production of Potatoes by Seasonal Groups in the United States In Thousands of Cwt.

	Winter	Spring			Summer			Fall								
Year	Total	California	Florida	Total	New Mexico	Virginia	Total	Colorado	Idaho	Maine	Minnesota	North Dakota	Oregon	Washington	Wisconsin	Total
1990	2,343	8,438	8,714	24,163	3,400	1,980	23,097	22,750	119,070	20,520	14,280	16,675	23,450	67,980	23,075	352,507
1991	2,609	8,284	6,600	20,636	3,450	1,485	22,647	23,800	122,175	18,170	17,160	30,030	22,170	75,435	23,275	371,730
1992	2,998	7,238	7,750	21,535	952	1,980	21,309	22,110	127,050	24,300	16,080	27,690	21,075	69,300	25,160	379,525
1993	2,552	7,508	6,068	19,654	1,290	1,760	14,922	25,270	126,192	19,890	14,780	21,090	23,103	88,500	22,588	385,935
1994	2,372	7,790	8,588	22,646	1,088	1,425	17,381	25,795	138,801	18,375	20,035	28,200	27,514	88,920	25,740	419,645
1995	2,473	6,230	7,830	20,193	1,344	2,040	17,931	23,808	132,657	17,160	20,790	25,410	24,788	80,850	26,000	403,009
1996	3,273	7,538	7,765	22,417	1,404	1,463	19,176	29,175	142,800	21,175	24,600	28,820	30,124	94,990	33,150	454,388
1997	3,431	8,073	7,150	22,299	1,248	1,268	18,171	24,993	140,314	19,080	20,440	22,000	27,319	88,160	30,175	423,190
1998	2,980	6,198	7,358	21,121	962	1,380	18,933	25,360	138,000	18,060	21,170	28,670	26,229	93,225	30,895	432,737
1999[1]	4,070	7,600	8,820	25,327	1,247	1,050	19,154	25,762	133,330	17,813	18,020	26,400	28,020	95,200	34,000	429,847

[1] Preliminary. *Source: Agricultural Statistics Board, U.S. Department of Agriculture (ASB-USDA)*

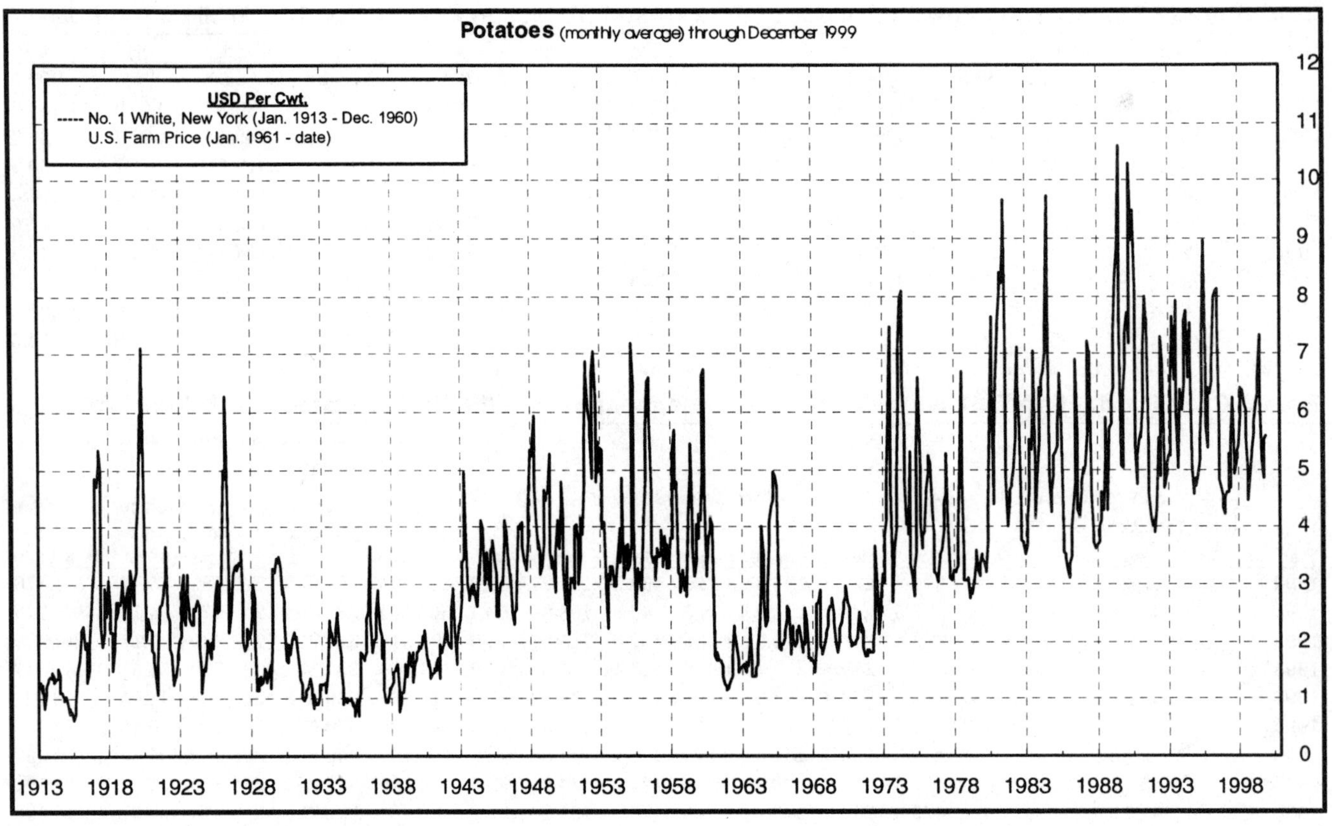

Per Capita Utilization of Potatoes in the United States In Pounds (Farm Weight)

Year	Total	Fresh	Processing: Freezing	Chips & Shoe-string	Dehy-drating	Canning	Total
1990	124.1	46.8	46.5	16.4	12.6	1.8	77.3
1991	134.5	50.4	51.2	17.3	13.9	1.7	84.1
1992	130.7	48.6	50.2	17.2	12.9	1.8	82.1
1993	134.9	49.3	52.9	17.5	13.5	1.7	85.6
1994	140.2	50.3	57.4	17.0	13.7	1.8	89.9
1995	138.4	49.5	56.9	16.6	13.4	2.0	88.9
1996	145.4	50.0	60.4	16.5	16.7	1.8	95.4
1997	142.0	48.5	59.7	16.0	16.0	1.8	93.5
1998[1]	145.1	50.8	60.7	15.0	16.8	1.8	94.3
1999[2]	144.7	48.7	61.5	15.7	17.0	1.8	96.0

[1] Preliminary. [2] Forecast. *Source: Agricultural Statistics Board, U.S. Department of Agriculture (ASB-USDA)*

Average Price Received by Farmers for Potatoes in the United States In Dollars Per Cwt.

Year	Jan.	Feb.	Mar.	Apr.	May	June	July	Aug.	Sept.	Oct.	Nov.	Dec.	Season Average
1990	7.36	7.71	9.17	10.30	9.32	8.96	9.50	8.09	5.36	4.73	5.24	5.46	6.08
1991	5.66	5.53	6.15	7.03	7.98	7.51	7.95	5.39	4.51	4.06	3.99	4.29	4.96
1992	4.07	4.08	4.64	5.16	4.43	4.71	7.00	6.64	4.89	4.55	4.90	5.06	5.52
1993	5.15	5.29	6.06	7.19	7.18	6.45	7.61	6.05	5.12	4.96	6.40	6.12	6.17
1994	6.02	6.43	7.67	6.69	6.59	6.67	7.50	6.28	5.04	4.58	4.75	4.87	5.58
1995	4.88	4.90	5.39	5.54	5.77	6.97	8.66	6.69	5.76	6.30	6.42	6.29	6.77
1996	6.65	6.92	7.51	7.83	8.09	8.14	8.02	5.59	4.93	4.76	4.43	4.32	4.91
1997	4.23	4.50	4.60	4.61	5.26	4.66	5.52	6.26	5.09	4.93	5.13	5.29	5.64
1998	5.40	5.94	6.41	6.27	6.39	6.13	6.03	5.55	4.97	4.47	4.86	5.30	5.24
1999[1]	5.32	5.61	5.81	6.14	6.30	6.58	7.34	6.33	5.15	4.84	5.51	5.58	

[1] Preliminary. *Source: Agricultural Statistics Board, U.S. Department of Agriculture (ASB-USDA)*

Potatoes Processed[1] in the United States, Eight States In Thousands of Cwt.

States	Storage Season	to Dec. 1	to Jan. 1	to Feb. 1	to Mar. 1	to Apr. 1	to May 1	to June 1	Entire Season
Idaho and	1990-1	24,780	31,100	37,550	44,220	51,030	58,660	-----	78,500
Oregon-	1991-2	22,980	28,910	35,700	42,840	50,260	57,290	-----	78,690
Malheur	1992-3	22,180	29,080	35,710	42,800	50,090	57,090	-----	80,570
Co	1993-4	24,090	30,540	37,150	44,720	53,070	61,440	-----	85,780
	1994-5	26,620	34,230	42,330	49,890	57,990	66,680	-----	90,300
	1995-6	27,310	35,040	43,260	51,530	59,060	66,690	-----	89,250
	1996-7	31,060	38,210	45,420	54,640	62,570	70,720	-----	96,970
	1997-8	26,880	33,950	41,050	49,470	57,620	65,750	-----	91,450
	1998-9	27,510	34,700	42,670	51,210	60,040	68,550	76,410	92,860
	1999-00	27,970	34,490	40,790					
Maine[2]	1990-1	2,105	2,690	3,420	3,900	4,460	5,120	-----	6,750
	1991-2	2,015	2,450	3,050	3,350	3,900	4,445	-----	5,210
	1992-3	1,195	1,630	2,205	2,720	3,390	4,020	-----	5,055
	1993-4	1,350	1,720	2,210	2,505	2,890	3,275	-----	4,555
	1994-5	1,505	1,840	2,265	2,540	2,985	3,330	-----	4,770
	1995-6	1,455	1,850	2,430	2,850	3,435	3,965	-----	5,725
	1996-7	1,790	2,115	2,820	3,280	3,820	4,420	-----	6,495
	1997-8	1,250	1,720	2,265	2,735	3,355	3,900	-----	5,870
	1998-9	1,430	1,935	2,530	2,985	3,595	4,180	4,705	5,945
	1999-00	1,375	1,670	2,310					
Wash. &	1990-1	24,780	29,830	35,170	39,950	45,600	50,780	-----	61,450
Oregon-	1991-2	26,345	30,570	35,320	41,320	47,120	52,605	-----	65,210
Other	1992-3	26,840	31,550	35,950	41,670	46,530	51,630	-----	63,510
	1993-4	28,260	33,350	39,010	45,020	51,290	57,180	-----	70,690
	1994-5	28,670	33,480	39,120	46,070	52,940	59,540	-----	76,780
	1995-6	30,000	35,170	39,460	45,280	51,730	57,360	-----	70,250
	1996-7	31,670	36,660	41,700	48,740	55,570	62,320	-----	80,970
	1997-8	28,580	33,990	38,690	46,400	53,720	59,780	-----	76,930
	1998-9	33,630	38,890	45,650	53,290	60,930	67,180	74,190	83,730
	1999-00	33,440	39,620	45,500					
Other	1990-1	6,585	8,605	10,405	12,425	14,635	17,010	-----	24,005
States[3]	1991-2	7,515	9,350	11,580	13,585	15,685	17,935	-----	24,990
	1992-3	7,140	9,220	11,265	13,305	15,550	17,555	-----	25,070
	1993-4	7,605	9,515	11,605	13,720	16,080	18,705	-----	25,690
	1994-5	9,725	13,110	15,630	18,260	21,115	24,060	-----	32,260
	1995-6	12,650	15,630	18,815	21,985	25,510	28,610	-----	33,580
	1996-7	13,720	17,000	20,645	24,085	27,650	30,830	-----	43,100
	1997-8	11,645	13,960	17,115	19,905	23,515	26,365	-----	37,842
	1998-9	11,615	14,550	18,150	20,900	24,710	27,855	31,635	37,662
	1999-00	11,785	14,495	17,295					
Total	1990-1	58,250	72,225	86,545	100,495	115,725	131,570	-----	170,705
	1991-2	58,855	71,280	85,650	101,095	116,965	132,275	-----	174,100
	1992-3	57,355	71,480	85,130	100,495	115,560	130,295	-----	174,205
	1993-4	61,305	75,125	89,975	105,965	123,330	140,600	-----	186,715
	1994-5	66,520	82,660	99,345	116,760	135,030	153,610	-----	204,110
	1995-6	71,415	87,690	103,965	121,645	139,735	156,625	-----	198,805
	1996-7	78,240	93,985	110,585	130,745	149,610	168,290	-----	227,535
	1997-8	68,355	83,620	99,120	118,510	138,210	155,795	-----	212,092
	1998-9	74,185	90,075	109,000	128,385	149,275	167,765	186,940	220,197
	1999-00	74,570	90,275	105,895					

[1] Total quantity received and used for processing regardless of the state in which the potatoes were produced. Excludes quantities used for potato chips in Maine, Michigan, Minnesota, North Dakota or Wisconsin. [2] Includes Maine grown potatoes only. [3] Michigan, Minnesota, North Dakota and Wisconsin. *Source: National Agricultural Statistics Service, U.S. Department of Agriculture (NASS-USDA)*

Rayon and Other Synthetic Fibers

World Cellulosic Fiber Production In Thousands of Metric Tons

Year	Austria	Brazil	China	Czech Republic	Finland	Germany	India	Japan	Taiwan	United Kingdom	United States	Ex-USSR	World Total
1990	135.0	54.5	214.3	55.0	63.8	199.1	216.7	275.8	147.9	71.0	229.2	544.0	2,757
1991	120.0	53.0	242.0	33.5	47.4	118.0	215.4	266.4	149.1	63.0	220.7	401.7	2,433
1992	128.3	54.2	249.1	39.3	56.0	139.9	219.9	254.4	139.3	65.0	224.5	292.3	2,327
1993	131.2	56.7	276.2	41.0	56.5	125.1	238.9	244.4	130.8	67.2	244.5	258.3	2,089
1994	134.3	58.6	336.0	33.7	58.5	138.1	239.7	218.9	149.3	67.0	225.0	189.8	2,308
1995	139.4	53.1	435.0	35.0	57.5	143.5	262.1	212.7	139.6	67.1	226.0	188.4	2,423
1996	145.0	34.4	432.0	31.4	49.8	143.6	251.9	198.2	144.7	62.3	213.1	127.3	2,270
1997	145.0	36.5	450.0	27.3	62.0	155.0	242.4	184.1	148.4	70.0	208.1	401.2	2,314
1998[1]	-----	35.4	450.2	26.9	-----	-----	264.4	164.5	142.6	-----	165.5	-----	2,185
1999[2]	-----	51.4	580.0	51.2	-----	-----	371.1	265.5	163.9	-----	213.7	-----	3,146

[1] Preliminary. [2] Producing capacity. *Source: Fiber Economics Bureau, Inc. (FEB)*

World Noncellulosic Fiber Production (Except Olefin) In Thousands of Metric Tons

Year	Brazil	China	West Germany	India	Italy/ Malta	Japan	Rep. of Korea	Mexico	Spain	Taiwan[3]	United States[4]	Ex-USSR	World Total
1990	207.8	1,342.8	777.0	436.6	578.3	1,425.0	1,269.7	366.8	255.0	1,621.5	2,886.0	893.5	14,894
1991	219.1	1,488.9	797.0	439.6	564.6	1,429.8	1,365.2	395.3	241.1	1,841.4	2,902.9	804.8	15,273
1992	220.2	1,733.7	817.3	530.5	589.9	1,448.8	1,451.4	425.3	257.0	2,042.6	2,980.6	744.8	16,161
1993	233.3	1,871.9	758.8	608.9	551.6	1,365.1	1,592.0	406.5	240.3	2,121.0	3,039.0	669.8	16,585
1994	243.2	2,119.0	807.6	681.1	599.9	1,394.0	1,825.0	484.4	273.6	2,301.5	3,250.3	658.1	17,939
1995	227.4	2,283.7	771.3	738.0	551.3	1,400.0	1,858.2	516.6	252.3	2,410.5	3,238.9	636.1	18,377
1996	229.4	2,729.6	-----	916.4	-----	1,399.0	2,025.2	563.3	-----	2,561.0	3,284.1	1,359.8	19,907
1997	256.3	3,332.5	-----	1,240.7	-----	1,433.6	2,403.3	594.1	-----	2,932.4	3,420.0	-----	22,152
1998[1]	264.2	3,840.5	-----	1,357.0	-----	1,363.6	2,446.0	558.3	-----	3,112.4	3,301.1	-----	22,741
1999[2]	336.4	4,814.0	-----	1,800.6	-----	1,803.2	2,998.5	755.0	-----	3,750.5	3,997.9	-----	29,292

[1] Preliminary. [2] Producing capacity. [3] Beginning 1995; data for S. Korea and Taiwan. [4] Beginning 1995; data for USA and Canada.
Source: Fiber Economics Bureau, Inc. (FEB)

World Production of Synthetic Fibers In Thousands of Metric Tons

	Noncellulosic Fiber Production (Except Olefin)							Glass Fiber Production							
	By Fibers				World Total										
Year	Acrylic & Mod-acrylic	Nylon & Aramid	Polyester	Other Fibers[3]	Yarn & Monofil-aments	Staple, Tow & Fiberfill	Total	Europe	Japan	Other Americas	United States	Total	China	Ex-USSR	Cigarette Tow Pro-duction
1990	2,320	3,738	8,678	158	7,035	7,859	14,894	445	371	60	675	1,631	75	120	464
1991	2,385	3,605	9,116	167	7,241	8,032	15,273	441	293	75	650	1,561	65	133	480
1992	2,365	3,723	9,916	155	7,971	8,188	16,159	442	307	83	700	1,652	75	84	475
1993	2,314	3,684	10,411	178	8,399	8,188	16,587	508	312	86	794	1,865	77	69	482
1994	2,543	3,706	11,468	222	9,087	8,852	17,939	545	313	87	959	2,235	78	54	536
1995	2,446	3,740	11,945	247	9,684	8,693	18,377	567	318	96	981	2,308	85	55	550
1996	2,583	3,858	13,184	282	10,685	9,222	19,907	585	316	94	996	2,387	98	54	584
1997	2,722	3,983	15,162	285	11,993	10,159	22,152	610	328	100	1,032	2,456	75	55	582
1998[1]	2,658	3,837	15,952	294	12,419	10,322	22,741	640	310	90	1,100	2,490	45	50	553
1999[2]	3,240	5,326	20,279	446	16,318	12,974	29,292	780	390	100	1,220	2,945	65	-----	-----

[1] Preliminary. [2] Producing capacity. [3] Alginate, azion, spandex, saran, etc. *Source: Fiber Economics Bureau, Inc. (FEB)*

Artificial (Cellulosic) Fiber Distribution in the United States In Millions of Pounds

	Yarn & Monofilament					Staple & Tow					
	Producers' Shipments					Producers' Shipments					
Year	Domestic	Exports	Total	Imports	Domestic Con-sumption	Domestic	Exports	Total	Imports	Domestic Con-sumption	Glass Fiber Ship-ments
1990	172.7	34.0	206.7	24.2	196.9	291.7	12.5	304.2	111.6	403.3	1,519.1
1991	179.9	32.3	212.2	30.8	210.7	255.5	8.1	263.6	92.0	347.5	1,488.5
1992	182.9	35.1	218.0	32.1	215.0	260.7	6.9	267.6	85.6	346.3	1,629.7
1993	196.5	31.5	228.0	40.4	236.9	273.6	10.3	283.9	89.5	363.1	1,780.6
1994	190.3	32.9	223.2	32.9	223.2	252.3	30.7	283.0	65.7	318.0	2,114.0
1995	169.3	41.5	210.8	34.0	203.3	259.8	28.7	288.5	40.8	300.6	2,163.0
1996	169.0	49.6	218.6	39.3	208.3	225.3	20.0	245.3	35.3	260.6	2,196.0
1997	145.9	41.2	187.1	42.9	188.8	205.3	60.1	265.4	51.6	256.9	2,275.0
1998[1]	111.2	32.7	143.9	38.1	149.3	184.4	31.4	215.8	47.4	231.8	2,275.0

[1] Preliminary. *Source: Fiber Economice Bureau, Inc. (FEB)*

Man-Made Fiber Production in the United States In Millions of Pounds

	Artificial (Cellulosic) Fibers – Rayon & Acetate			Synthetic (Noncellulosic) Fibers												
				Yarn & Monofilament				Staple & Tow							
Year	Filament Yarn & Monofilament	Staple & Tow	Total Cellulosic	Nylon	Polyester	Olefin	Total Yarn	Nylon	Polyester	Acrylic & Modacrylic	Olefin	Total Staple	Total Noncellulosic	Total Manufactured Fibers	Total Glass Fiber
1990	206	299	505	1,671	1,107	1,417	4,194	990	2,090	505	406	3,991	8,185	8,690	1,824
1991	213	273	486	1,667	1,208	1,408	4,282	869	2,202	454	459	3,984	8,266	8,752	1,818
1992	220	275	495	1,651	1,270	1,528	4,449	904	2,308	439	474	4,125	8,573	9,068	1,953
1993	227	278	505	1,700	1,284	1,659	4,643	959	2,274	433	483	4,149	8,791	9,296	2,061
1994	225	273	498	1,805	1,492	1,870	5,167	935	2,366	442	549	4,292	9,459	9,957	2,159
1995	208	290	498	1,829	1,597	1,907	5,333	874	2,290	432	521	4,117	9,450	9,948	2,282
1996	219	245	464	1,920	1,560	1,957	5,437	875	2,259	478	465	4,078	9,515	9,979	2,326
1997	187	266	453	2,005	1,642	2,058	5,704	793	2,454	440	629	4,317	10,012	10,465	2,408
1998[1]	144	216	360	2,060	1,536	2,181	5,776	804	2,319	355	701	4,179	9,955	10,314	2,454
1999[2]	117	199	316	2,035	1,592	2,213	5,840	796	2,280	329	750	4,155	9,995	10,311	2,259

[1] Preliminary. [2] Estimate. *Source: Fiber Economics Bureau, Inc. (FEB)*

Domestic Distribution of Synethic (Noncellulosic) Fibers in the United States In Millions of Pounds

	Yarn & Monofilament								Staple & Tow								
	Producers' Shipments – Domestic								Producers' Shipments – Domestic								
Year	Nylon	Polyester	Olefin	Total	Exports	Total	Imports	Domestic Consumption	Nylon	Polyester	Acrylic & Modacrylic	Olefin	Total	Exports	Total	Imports	Domestic Consumption
1990	1,537.5	1,046.2	1,404.9	3,988.6	265.1	4,253.7	154.7	4,143.3	950.2	2,015.4	352.2	387.9	3,705.7	278.9	3,984.6	209.8	3,915.5
1991	1,493.9	1,114.0	1,380.6	3,988.5	246.9	4,235.4	174.8	4,163.3	835.0	2,127.9	319.2	437.5	3,719.6	277.8	3,997.4	263.1	3,982.7
1992	1,570.1	1,229.6	1,496.1	4,295.8	194.8	4,490.6	209.3	4,505.1	891.7	2,202.1	322.3	441.0	3,857.1	267.2	4,124.3	397.7	4,255.0
1993	1,612.7	1,228.4	1,631.5	4,472.6	174.6	4,647.2	295.8	4,768.4	907.9	2,157.8	333.0	468.2	3,866.9	297.1	4,164.0	509.0	4,375.9
1994	1,700.0	1,402.8	1,838.2	4,941.0	204.9	5,145.9	377.7	5,318.7	911.7	2,221.3	319.6	489.0	3,941.6	390.9	4,332.5	622.9	4,564.5
1995	1,741.4	1,439.8	1,870.3	5,051.5	259.0	5,310.5	393.6	5,445.1	828.5	2,100.4	266.1	458.0	3,653.0	398.7	4,051.7	624.9	4,277.9
1996	1,801.2	1,428.7	1,954.4	5,183.1	250.7	5,434.6	482.0	5,665.9	843.8	2,015.8	287.9	614.1	3,761.6	465.1	4,226.7	607.7	4,369.3
1997	1,877.1	1,530.3	2,049.2	5,456.6	238.5	5,695.1	589.0	6,045.6	757.2	2,249.7	288.6	629.3	3,924.8	391.9	4,316.7	672.8	4,597.6
1998[1]	1,930.9	1,427.0	2,154.9	5,512.8	226.8	5,739.6	637.3	6,150.1	766.2	2,105.0	267.3	638.4	3,776.9	352.3	4,129.2	777.4	4,554.3

[1] Preliminary. *Source: Fiber Economice Bureau, Inc. (FEB)*

Mill Consumption of Fiber & Products and Per Capita Consumption in the U.S. In Millions of Pounds

	Cellulosic Fibers				Noncellulosic Fibers								Per Capita[4] Mill Consumption (Lbs.)				
Year	Yarn & Monofilament	Staple & Tow	Net Waste	Total Cellulosic	Noncellulosic	Net Waste	Total Noncellulosic	Total Manufactured Fibers[2]	Cotton	Wool	Other Fibers[3]	Grand Total	Man-made Fibers[2]	Cotton	Wool	Other Fibers[3]	Total All Fibers
1990	196.9	403.3	-1.3	598.9	8,058.8	179.3	8,238.1	8,837.0	4,036.5	153.0	75.1	13,102.6	39.3	23.2	1.1	2.6	66.3
1991	210.7	347.5	-1.7	556.5	8,146.0	158.7	8,304.7	8,861.2	4,347.5	172.6	77.6	13,459.9	39.1	24.6	1.2	2.5	67.4
1992	215.0	346.3	-3.6	557.7	8,760.1	181.1	8,941.2	9,498.9	4,714.7	171.5	75.7	14,461.8	41.5	27.6	1.2	2.5	72.9
1993	236.9	363.1	-5.6	594.4	9,144.3	189.8	9,334.1	9,928.5	4,921.9	179.5	73.0	15,103.9	43.2	29.2	1.3	2.7	76.4
1994	223.2	318.0	-21.4	519.8	9,883.2	102.4	9,985.6	10,505.5	5,191.6	171.9	53.8	15,923.8	44.5	30.2	1.4	2.7	78.8
1995	203.3	300.6	-22.7	481.2	9,722.5	76.3	9,798.8	10,280.0	5,199.9	161.8	64.6	15,707.8	43.6	30.2	1.4	2.5	77.7
1996	208.2	260.7	-12.8	456.1	9,909.5	99.8	10,009.3	10,465.4	5,191.9	164.4	44.9	15,993.3	44.5	29.6	1.4	1.8	77.2
1997	188.8	256.9	-18.4	427.3	10,562.8	100.4	10,663.2	11,170.9	5,419.5	164.3	42.1	16,797.7	46.9	32.5	1.3	2.0	82.8
1998[1]	149.3	231.8	-18.5	362.6	10,562.3	162.1	10,724.4	11,229.1	5,227.6	123.6	43.8	16,624.9	48.1	34.5	1.3	1.9	85.7

[1] Preliminary. [2] Excludes Glass Fiber. [3] Includes silk, linen, jute and sisal & others. [4] Mill consumption plus inports less exports of semimanufactured and unmanufactured products. *Source: Fiber Economics Bureau, Inc. (FEB)*

Producer Price Index of Grey Synthetic Broadwovens (1982 = 100)

Year	Jan.	Feb.	Mar.	Apr.	May	June	July	Aug.	Sept.	Oct.	Nov.	Dec.	Average
1989	114.3	112.0	112.2	112.2	112.1	113.1	114.7	115.0	115.0	115.8	115.9	115.3	114.0
1990	115.6	115.7	115.6	115.7	115.5	115.6	115.7	115.2	115.3	115.6	115.8	116.1	115.6
1991	115.7	114.7	114.4	114.1	114.3	113.9	114.8	116.4	116.5	116.5	116.8	118.2	115.5
1992	119.0	119.9	120.3	120.9	121.8	122.0	122.6	122.0	121.7	120.8	119.4	119.9	120.9
1993	119.6	119.1	119.1	119.2	117.1	118.4	118.0	118.0	116.9	117.3	115.2	114.5	117.7
1994	113.5	112.8	112.9	113.2	113.2	113.3	113.1	113.3	114.1	111.8	112.9	113.8	113.2
1995	114.8	116.8	116.7	116.3	116.6	117.1	115.4	114.8	116.9	116.4	114.7	116.2	116.1
1996	114.3	114.1	116.9	117.9	116.8	115.7	116.1	117.1	116.9	117.2	116.6	117.0	116.4
1997	117.9	118.3	118.3	117.9	118.4	119.0	118.8	118.5	119.4	118.7	117.6	119.6	118.5
1998[1]	120.1	120.4	119.7	120.2	119.8	119.7	118.0	118.1	116.7	114.2	115.1	115.0	118.1

[1] Preliminary. *Source: Bureau of Labor Statistics, U.S. Department of Commerce (BLS) (0337-03)*

Rice

International trading in rice, the world's second most popular foodstock after wheat, is small as most rice is consumed where it is produced. Still, global milled rice trade in calendar 2000 at 23.3 million metric tonnes will be second to the record high 27.4 million tonnes in 1998 as increased demand from the Middle East and Latin America offset weaker trade in Asia. U.S. exports of an estimated 3 million tonnes will not differ very much from 1998/99, leaving the U.S. among the top exporters.

Asia accounts for most of the world's exports with Thailand leading the way at 5.7 million tonnes in 2000, unchanged from 1999 and compared with the record high of 6.4 million tonnes in 1998. Importing countries are numerous but only three nations are expected to import one million tonnes or more in 2000. Indonesia is consistently the largest importer with 3 million tonnes forecast for 2000, slightly under 1999 but well under the 6 million tons imported in 1998. On a regional basis, the Middle East tends to be the largest importer.

For U.S. rice exports the Western Hemisphere is the primary destination and is higher priced than Asian rice. Low quality rice, an extremely price sensitive sector dominated by Asian sellers, constitutes a major portion of total imports. International prices, notably Asian, have been under pressure in the late 1990's primarily because of currency factors. U.S. prices, however, have held fairly steady reflecting, in part, a slow marketing pace by producers.

The longer term down trend in world stocks appears to have bottomed reflecting higher exports and consumption. Carryover 1999/2000 stocks of 50.9 million metric tonnes are higher than initially expected and compare with 52 million a year earlier. China holds almost half the total with India second at about 20 percent.

World rough rice production in 1999/00 of a record high 584 million tonnes (393 million, milled) compares with 582 million (388 million, milled) in 1998/99. World consumption of a record high 395 million tonnes (milled) compares with 389 million in 1998/99. China is the largest producer and consumer with about a third of each of the world's total; India is second.

Estimated U.S. rice production in 1999/00 (August-July) of a record large 212 million cwt. (9.6 million tons rough) compares with 188 million cwt. in 1998/99. Domestic usage was put at 113 million cwt. in 1999/00 vs. 121 million in 1998/99, and exports at 195 million cwt. vs. 205 million cwt., respectively.

The U.S. average farm price in 1999/00 was forecast at \$5.75-\$6.25 per cwt. vs. \$8.83 in 1998/99.

Futures Markets

Rough rice futures and options are traded on the Chicago Board of Trade (CBOT).

World Rice Supply and Distribution[4] In Thousands of Metric Tons

	Exports			Imports					Utilization			Ending Stocks		
Year	U.S.	Non-U.S.	Total	Brazil	Iran	Saudi Arabia	Unaccounted	Total	China	India	Total	China	India	Total
1995-6	2,624	17,083	19,707	786	1,344	814	1,776	19,707	130,000	79,203	371,363	21,732	11,000	50,465
1996-7	2,292	16,514	18,806	845	973	660	1,624	18,806	132,134	80,707	379,556	25,556	9,500	51,306
1997-8[1]	3,165	24,105	27,270	1,457	500	775	1,275	27,270	135,850	78,252	383,265	26,723	10,500	54,923
1998-9[2]	2,750	22,479	25,229	850	1,000	750	1,972	25,229	136,750	81,160	389,207	26,539	12,000	58,672
1999-00[3]	3,000	20,086	23,086	1,000	1,200	800	2,325	23,086	138,000	82,550	396,677	27,089	12,500	59,414

[1] Preliminary. [2] Estimate. [3] Forecast. [4] Production is on a rough basis; all other data are reported on a milled basis.
Source: Foreign Agricultural Service, U.S. Department of Agriculture (FAS-USDA)

World Production of Rough Rice In Thousands of Metric Tons

Year	Bangladesh	Brazil	Burma	China	India	Indonesia	Japan	Rep. of Korea	Pakistan	Philippines	Thailand	Vietnam	World Total
1995-6	26,533	10,026	17,000	185,214	119,442	51,100	13,435	6,386	5,951	11,174	21,800	26,792	551,310
1996-7	28,326	9,504	15,517	195,100	121,980	49,360	12,930	7,123	6,461	11,177	20,700	27,277	563,740
1997-8[1]	28,296	8,551	15,345	200,700	123,822	49,237	12,532	7,365	6,500	9,982	23,500	28,930	574,323
1998-9[2]	28,653	11,450	16,034	198,714	129,013	50,791	11,201	6,892	7,012	10,268	23,000	30,467	584,038
1999-00[3]	29,478	10,294	16,466	201,429	126,763	50,791	11,470	7,085	7,201	11,923	24,015	30,455	590,645

[1] Preliminary. [2] Estimate. [3] Forecast. *Source: Foreign Agricultural Service, U.S. Department of Agriculture (FAS-USDA)*

World Exports of Rice (Milled Basis) In Thousands of Metric Tons

Year	Argentina	Australia	Burma	China	European Union	Guyana	India	Pakistan	Thailand	Uruguay	Vietnam	United States	World Total
1995	327	519	645	32	323	201	4,179	1,592	5,891	451	2,315	3,073	20,891
1996	365	562	265	265	318	262	3,549	1,677	5,281	597	3,040	2,624	19,707
1997	530	641	15	938	372	286	1,954	1,982	5,216	640	3,327	2,292	18,806
1998[1]	589	542	94	3,734	346	250	4,491	1,800	6,367	639	3,776	3,165	27,270
1999[2]	650	661	75	2,708	350	300	2,400	1,850	6,679	725	4,638	2,750	25,229
2000[3]	550	500	100	2,850	350	310	1,500	2,000	5,500	700	4,000	3,000	23,086

[1] Preliminary. [2] Estimate. [3] Forecast. *Source: Foreign Agricultural Service, U.S. Department of Agriculture (FAS-USDA)*

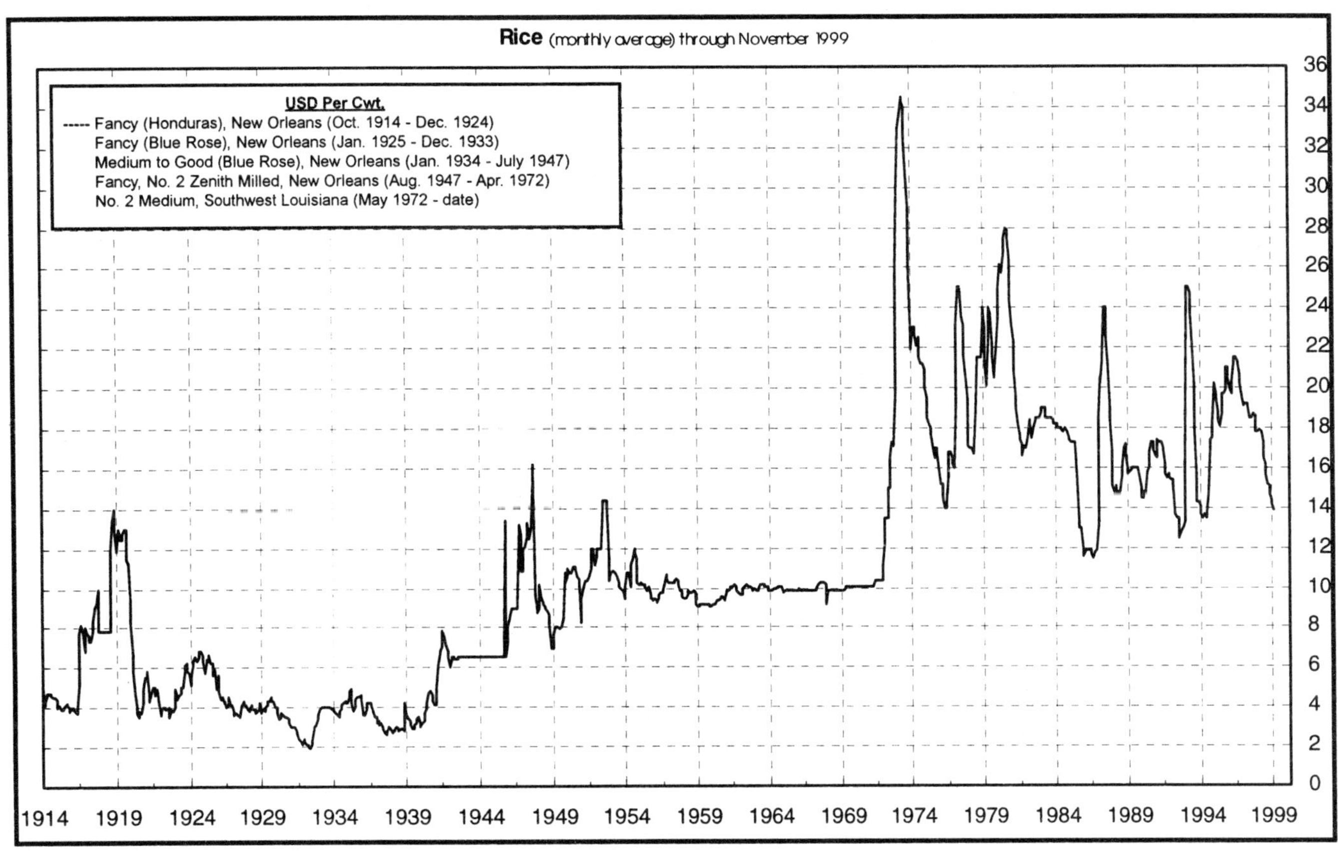

Average Wholesale Price of Rice No. 2 (Medium)[1] Southwest Louisiana In Dollars Per Cwt. Bagged

Year	Aug.	Sept.	Oct.	Nov.	Dec.	Jan.	Feb.	Mar.	Apr.	May	June	July	Average
1990-1	14.75	13.90	13.50	13.50	13.50	14.90	14.90	15.05	16.05	16.15	16.50	16.35	14.90
1991-2	15.85	16.00	16.00	16.00	16.00	16.00	15.90	15.50	15.50	15.15	14.50	14.50	15.60
1992-3	14.50	14.00	14.50	14.15	13.40	13.40	13.00	12.80	12.40	11.94	12.00	12.00	13.15
1993-4	12.25	12.45	15.65	21.95	24.00	24.00	23.88	23.80	24.00	23.70	22.00	20.00	20.65
1994-5	18.30	15.88	15.00	15.00	14.00	13.80	14.16	14.38	14.38	14.70	14.75	14.55	14.91
1995-6	15.44	17.50	20.25	20.13	20.00	20.00	19.88	19.25	19.13	19.38	19.40	19.50	19.15
1996-7	19.50	19.50	19.25	19.25	19.00	18.81	19.19	19.25	19.25	19.25	18.40	19.00	19.14
1997-8	18.25	18.35	18.63	19.00	19.00	19.00	19.00	18.20	18.00	18.13	18.50	18.50	18.55
1998-9	18.35	18.75	19.00	19.00	20.00	20.00	20.00	20.00	20.00	20.00	20.00	20.00	19.59
1999-00[2]	18.60	17.50	14.88	14.75									16.43

[1] U.S. No. 2 -- broken not to exceed 4%. [2] Preliminary. *Source: Economic Research Service, U.S. Department of Agriculture (ERS-USDA)*

Average Price Received by Farmers for Rice (Rough) in the United States In Dollars Per Cwt.

Year	Aug.	Sept.	Oct.	Nov.	Dec.	Jan.	Feb.	Mar.	Apr.	May	June	July	Average[2]
1990-1	6.66	6.21	6.02	6.29	6.13	6.39	6.75	7.07	7.43	7.44	7.43	7.21	6.68
1991-2	7.16	7.67	7.65	7.84	7.98	7.84	7.97	7.78	7.46	7.18	6.97	6.99	7.58
1992-3	6.60	6.41	6.40	6.42	6.39	6.36	6.06	5.64	5.52	5.24	5.02	4.92	5.89
1993-4	5.19	5.21	6.10	8.06	8.91	8.98	10.10	10.20	9.93	10.00	8.88	7.80	7.98
1994-5	6.87	6.89	6.47	6.53	6.56	6.78	6.71	6.64	6.70	6.75	7.03	7.17	6.78
1995-6	7.64	7.95	8.77	9.12	9.36	9.33	9.10	9.31	9.34	9.69	9.74	9.68	9.15
1996-7	10.10	10.00	9.66	9.41	9.82	9.95	10.10	10.20	10.30	10.20	9.90	10.00	9.96
1997-8	9.94	9.92	10.00	9.82	9.77	9.57	9.75	9.67	9.40	9.38	9.58	9.58	9.70
1998-9	8.95	9.35	9.25	8.98	9.06	9.05	8.97	8.86	8.54	8.16	8.20	8.15	8.83
1999-00[1]	7.62	6.88	6.23	6.11	6.19	6.27							6.80

[1] Preliminary. [2] Weighted average by sales. *Source: Economic Research Service, U.S. Department of Agriculture (ERS-USDA)*

Salient Statistics of Rice, Rough & Milled (Rough Equivalent) in the United States In Millions of Cwt.

Crop Year Beginning Aug. 1	Supply: Stocks Aug. 1	Supply: Production	Supply: Imports	Supply: Total Supply	Disappearance: Domestic: Food	Domestic: Brewers	Domestic: Seed	Domestic: Total	Residual	Exports	Total Disappearance	CCC Stocks July 31	Government Support Program: Put Under Price Support	Loan Rate ($ Per Cwt.): Rough[3]: Long	Rough[3]: Medium	Rough[3]: All Classes	Milled Long
1994-5	25.8	197.8	7.5	231.1	74.0	14.5	3.9	92.4	8.2	99.3	199.8	.1	131.2	6.64	6.13	6.50	10.72
1995-6	31.3	173.9	7.7	212.8	78.0	15.6	3.5	97.1	8.5	82.2	187.8	0	100.9	6.68	6.12	6.50	10.69
1996-7	25.0	171.6	10.5	207.1	81.0	15.8	3.9	100.7	2.0	77.2	179.9	0	68.9	6.68	6.17	6.50	10.77
1997-8	27.2	183.0	9.2	219.4	84.2	16.0	4.1	104.3	.2	86.9	191.5	0	67.6	6.67	6.14	6.50	10.69
1998-9[1]	27.9	188.1	10.5	226.5	87.3	16.0	4.4	107.7	11.4	85.3	204.4	0	80.2	6.67	6.14	6.50	10.71
1999-00[2]	22.1	210.5	10.8	243.3	90.1	16.0	4.1	110.2	6.5	86.0	202.7	0	107.6	6.67	6.12	6.50	10.66

[1] Preliminary. [2] Forecast. [3] Loan rate for each class of rice is the sum of the whole kernels' loan rate weighted by its milling yield (average 56%) and the broken kernels' loan rate weighted by its milling yield (average 12%). Source: Economic Research Service, U.S. Department of Agriculture (ERS)

Acreage, Yield, Production and Prices of Rice in the United States

Crop Year	Acreage Harvested (1,000 Acres): Southern States	Acreage: California	Acreage: United States	Yield Per Harvested Acre (In Lbs.): California	Yield: United States	Production 1,000 Cwt.: Southern States	Production: California	Production: United States	Value of Production $1,000	Wholesale Prices ($ Per Cwt.): Arkansas[2]	Wholesale Prices: Houston[3]	Milled Rice, Average C.I.F. at Rotterdam ($ Per Metric Ton): U.S. No. 2[4]	Thai "A"[5]	Thai "B"[5]
1994-5	2,831	485	3,316	8,500	5,964	156,555	41,224	197,779	1,336,570	14.47	14.70	325	412	331
1995-6	2,628	465	3,093	7,600	5,621	138,519	35,352	173,871	1,587,236	19.10	19.15	404	-----	407
1996-7	2,304	500	2,804	7,490	6,120	134,140	37,459	171,599	1,690,270	19.02	20.95	428	-----	380
1997-8	2,587	516	3,103	8,250	5,897	140,446	42,546	182,992	1,756,136	18.14	19.61	417	-----	345
1998-9	2,839	478	3,317	6,840	5,669	155,353	32,698	188,051	1,686,580	19.01	18.05	368	-----	333
1999-00[1]	3,023	548	3,571	7,000	5,929	173,354	38,360	211,714	1,257,071			303	-----	284

[1] Preliminary. [2] F.O.B. mills, Arkansas, medium. [3] Houston, Texas (long grain). [4] Milled, 4%, container, FAS. [5] SWR, 100%, bulk. NA = Not available. *Source: Economic Research Service, U.S. Department of Agriculture (ERS-USDA)*

U.S. Exports of Milled Rice, by Country of Destination In Thousands of Metric Tons

Year Beginning October	Canada	Haiti	Iran	Ivory Coast	Jamaica	Mexico	Netherlands	Peru	Saudi Arabia	South Africa	Switzerland	United Kingdom	Total
1991-2	143.7	116.9	11.6	73.4	46.3	157.0	67.7	43.6	179.6	136.6	94.2	59.8	2,279
1992-3	146.0	152.9	184.3	107.3	39.4	241.5	120.9	61.6	223.5	122.1	71.2	72.2	2,710
1993-4	141.3	57.2	60.4	34.2	53.8	234.0	92.8	47.0	180.5	110.9	64.8	82.4	2,433
1994-5	160.0	210.2	240.6	92.0	88.5	309.6	170.3	81.8	176.1	106.1	91.2	58.7	3,763
1995-6	172.1	149.6	24.5	61.3	63.1	359.1	113.9	97.8	141.5	169.9	80.3	85.4	2,826
1996-7[1]	162.9	178.7	-----	35.6	27.4	381.3	54.0	35.1	150.9	108.5	64.2	101.0	2,560

[1] Preliminary. *Source: Economic Research Service, U.S. Department of Agriculture (ERS-USDA)*

U.S. Rice Exports by Export Program In Thousands of Metric Tons

Fiscal Year	PL 480	Section 416	CCC Credit Programs[2]	CCC African Relief Exports	EEP[3]	Export Programs[4]	Exports Outside Specified Export Programs	Total U.S. Rice Exports	% Export Programs as a Share of Total Exports
1994	222	0	155	0	46	433	2,001	2,434	18
1995	196	0	321	0	113	644	3,119	3,763	17
1996	182	0	215	0	23	432	2,390	2,822	15
1997	116	0	90	0	0	220	2,340	2,560	9
1998	184	0	520	0	0	715	2,595	3,310	22
1999[1]	536	0	198	0	0	782	2,294	3,076	25

[1] Preliminary. [2] May not completely reflect exports made under these programs. [3] Sales not shipments. [4] adjusted for estimated overlap between CCC export credit and EEP shipments. *Source: Economice Research Service, U.S. Department of Agriculture (ERS-USDA)*

Production of Rice (Rough) in the United States, by Type and Variety In Thousands of Cwt.

Year	Long Grain	Medium Grain	Short Grain	Total	Year	Long Grain	Medium Grain	Short Grain	Total
1990	107,806	47,328	954	156,088	1995	121,730	51,241	900	173,871
1991	109,137	47,567	753	157,457	1996	113,629	56,901	1,069	171,599
1992	128,015	50,633	1,010	179,658	1997	124,485	57,091	1,416	182,992
1993	103,064	51,873	1,173	156,110	1998	141,624	44,453	1,974	188,051
1994	133,445	63,390	944	197,779	1999[1]	154,134	52,000	4,324	210,458

[1] Preliminary. *Source: National Agricultural Statistics Service, U.S. Department of Agriculture (NASS-USDA)*

Rubber

According to the International Rubber Study Group, world production of natural rubber in 1998 was 6.66 million metric tonnes. That represented an increase of 4 percent from 1997. Estates production of natural rubber in 1998 was 1.76 million tonnes, up 1 percent from the previous year. Smallholdings production of rubber was 4.9 million tonnes, up 6 percent from 1997. In the January-April 1999 period, world production of natural rubber was 2.16 million tonnes. Estates production of rubber in the same period was 600,000 tonnes and Smallholdings production was 1.56 million tonnes.

World consumption of natural rubber in 1998 was 6.60 million tonnes, an increase of 2 percent from 1997. In the January-April 1999 period, consumption of natural rubber was 2.17 million tonnes. Producer stocks of natural rubber at the end of April 1999 were 800,000 tonnes, some 82 percent more than the year before. Consumer's reported stocks of rubber at the end of April 1999 were 427,000 tonnes, up 6 percent from the year before. Consumer total stocks of rubber in April 1999 were 750,000 tonnes, up 6 percent from the year before. Stocks afloat in April 1999 were 300,000 tonnes compared to 620,000 the year before. World stocks of natural rubber in April 1999 were 1.85 million tonnes, up almost 5 percent from the year before.

World production of synthetic rubber in 1998 was 9.9 million tonnes, a decline of 2 percent from 1997. Production of synthetic rubber in the January-April 1999 period was 3.35 million tonnes. Global consumption of synthetic rubber in 1998 was 9.89 million tonnes, down 1 percent from 1997. In the first four months of 1999, world consumption of synthetic rubber was 3.36 million tonnes.

Reported world stocks of synthetic rubber at the end of April 1999 were 1.11 million tonnes. At the end of April 1998, stocks were 1.08 million tonnes. Russian Federation stocks of synthetic rubber in April 1999 were 110,000 tonnes. A year earlier stocks were 190,000 tonnes. China's stocks of synthetic rubber at the end of April 1999 were 870,000 tonnes, up 6 percent from the year before. Stocks afloat were 270,000 tonnes, up 4 percent from the year before. World stocks of synthetic rubber in April 1999 were 2.45 million tonnes, up 1 percent from the year before.

U.S. consumption of natural and synthetic rubber in 1998 was 3.51 million tonnes, up 4 percent from 1997. In the first four months of 1999, U.S. consumption of natural and synthetic rubber was 1.17 million tonnes. China's consumption of natural and synthetic rubber in 1998 was 1.84 million tonnes, down 4 percent from the year before. Japan's consumption in 1998 was 1.82 million tonnes, down 3 percent from 1997. Russian Federation consumption of rubber in 1998 was 425,000 tonnes, down 7 percent from the year before. Other large users of rubber are Germany, France and Brazil.

U.S. reported stocks of natural rubber held by consumers in April 1999 were 60,000 tonnes, down 1 percent from the year before. The U.S. stockpile of natural rubber held by the Defense Logistics Agency in April 1999 was 70,300 tonnes. U.S. reported stocks of synthetic rubber in April 1999 were 410,000 tonnes, up 6 percent from the year before.

The major producers of natural rubber are Thailand, Indonesia and Malaysia. Thailand's production of natural rubber in 1998 was 2.21 million tonnes, up almost 9 percent from the previous year. Production of natural rubber in Malaysia in 1998 was 885,700 tonnes, down 9 percent from 1997. Indonesia's production of natural rubber in 1998 was 1.74 million tonnes, up 16 percent from 1997. Other producers of natural rubber include Sri Lanka, Vietnam, China, India and the Ivory Coast.

The largest exporters of natural rubber are also the largest producers. Thailand's net exports of natural rubber in 1998 were 1.84 million tonnes, about unchanged from 1997. Indonesia's exports were 1.64 million tonnes, up 17 percent from 1997. Malaysia's exports were 424,900 tonnes, down 28 percent from the previous year. Other large exporters include Vietnam, Sri Lanka and Liberia.

Futures Markets

Natural Rubber and Rubber Index futures are traded on the Osaka Mercantile Exchange (OME). Rubber futures are traded on the Singapore Commodity Exchange (SCE) and the Tokyo Commodity Exchange (ToCom).

U.S. Imports of Natural Rubber (Includes Latex & Guayule) In Thousands of Metric Tons

Year	Jan.	Feb.	Mar.	Apr.	May	June	July	Aug.	Sept.	Oct.	Nov.	Dec.	Total
1990	72.3	58.6	81.9	63.1	89.5	77.7	60.4	61.0	83.0	55.7	81.7	75.7	820.1
1991	59.9	54.1	69.5	90.9	59.6	56.7	53.4	52.4	65.5	74.4	71.3	68.9	776.2
1992	77.5	75.2	84.7	64.7	79.0	73.8	80.5	77.2	73.9	81.3	68.1	77.5	913.4
1993	95.3	79.9	93.9	86.3	74.1	81.2	83.6	77.8	69.2	73.4	86.0	86.9	987.6
1994	87.5	74.7	102.6	78.9	88.3	77.8	66.7	85.0	78.8	89.3	70.0	76.0	975.6
1995	81.7	86.9	102.3	90.2	94.1	93.4	78.0	81.0	81.5	89.2	79.1	68.7	1,026.1
1996	105.4	86.1	82.2	90.6	65.1	70.4	79.0	81.0	82.1	113.6	73.5	85.0	1,014.0
1997	94.2	92.0	93.9	88.2	93.0	65.1	76.8	90.1	87.5	86.8	87.6	89.0	1,044.2
1998	104.4	76.6	102.8	81.0	98.0	92.9	96.4	100.8	123.2	104.8	84.5	111.4	1,176.8
1999[1]	91.8	90.7	93.4	101.6	84.8	80.0	76.6	112.2	88.7				1,093.1

[1] Preliminary. *Source: International Rubber Study Group (IRSG)*

RUBBER

World Production[1] of Rubber In Thousands of Metric Tons

	Natural								Synthetic				
Year	China	India	Indo-nesia	Malaysia	Sri Lanka	Thailand	Vietnam	World Total	Ger-many	Japan	United States	Russia[3]	World Total
1989	242.8	288.6	1,256.0	1,415.6	110.7	1,178.9	85.0	5,150	507.6	1,352.7	2,261.4	2,358.0	10,150
1990	264.2	323.5	1,262.0	1,291.0	113.1	1,275.3	103.0	5,080	524.5	1,425.8	2,114.5	2,277.0	9,890
1991	296.4	360.2	1,284.0	1,255.7	103.9	1,341.2	87.0	5,160	504.4	1,377.3	2,050.0	2,125.3	9,290
1992	309.3	383.0	1,387.0	1,173.2	106.1	1,531.0	114.0	5,440	544.7	1,389.9	2,300.0	1,610.5	9,300
1993	326.1	428.1	1,300.5	1,074.3	104.2	1,553.4	117.0	5,310	569.7	1,309.8	2,180.0	1,102.5	8,600
1994	374.0	464.0	1,358.5	1,100.6	105.3	1,717.9	149.0	5,710	621.6	1,349.0	2,390.0	631.9	8,880
1995	424.0	499.6	1,454.5	1,089.3	105.7	1,804.8	159.0	6,040	480.0	1,497.6	2,530.0	836.9	9,490
1996	430.0	540.1	1,527.0	1,082.5	112.5	1,970.4	189.0	6,360	548.1	1,519.9	2,486.0	775.1	9,770
1997	444.0	580.3	1,504.8	971.1	105.8	2,032.7	201.0	6,380	555.1	1,591.5	2,589.0	724.9	10,090
1998[2]	450.0	591.1	1,714.0	885.7	95.7	2,215.9	219.0	6,710	619.0	1,520.1	2,610.0	621.0	9,990

[1] Including rubber in the form of latex. [2] Preliminary. [3] Formerly part of the U.S.S.R., data reported separately until 1992.
Source: International Rubber Study Group (IRSG)

World Consumption of Natural and Synthetic Rubber In Thousands of Metric Tons

	Natural							Synthetic					
Year	Brazil	France	Ger-many	Japan	United Kingdom	United States	World Total	France	Ger-many	Japan	United Kingdom	United States	World Total
1989	124.3	184.0	221.1	657.0	132.5	866.9	5,190	358.0	476.0	1,103.0	240.0	2,051.0	10,070
1990	124.1	179.0	208.7	677.0	136.0	807.5	5,210	351.0	511.0	1,133.0	223.0	1,820.8	9,660
1991	122.8	183.0	210.7	689.5	119.0	755.8	5,060	342.0	502.0	1,118.5	201.0	1,768.1	9,220
1992	123.4	179.0	212.8	685.4	124.5	910.2	5,320	365.4	506.0	1,080.6	231.0	1,959.6	9,360
1993	131.7	168.5	174.9	631.0	119.0	966.7	5,430	314.7	488.0	1,022.0	211.0	2,001.0	8,630
1994	144.7	179.8	186.4	639.8	135.0	1,001.7	5,680	400.1	512.2	1,026.2	220.0	2,117.6	8,820
1995	155.2	176.0	211.7	692.0	118.0	1,003.9	5,980	430.2	426.4	1,085.0	226.0	2,172.0	9,250
1996	155.0	182.2	193.0	714.5	111.0	1,001.7	6,140	436.1	478.0	1,124.5	230.0	2,186.6	9,580
1997	160.0	192.3	212.0	713.0	119.0	1,044.1	6,500	416.2	501.0	1,163.0	235.0	2,322.7	10,000
1998[1]	160.0	223.0	247.0	707.3	139.0	1,157.4	6,590	451.4	569.0	1,115.7	181.0	2,354.4	9,880

[1] Preliminary. *Source: International Rubber Study Group (IRSG)*

World Stocks[1] of Natural & Synthetic Rubber (by Countries) on January 1 In Thousands of Metric Tons

		In Producing Countries							In Consuming Countries (Reported Stocks)				
Year	Total Synthetic	Africa	Indo-nesia	Malaysia	Sri Lanka	Thai-land	Vietnam	Total Natural	Brazil	India	Japan	United States	Total
1990	1,011	26.9	110	248.3	27.0	53.7	8.0	510	16.0	78.4	105.6	92.0	292
1991	980	18.2	110	190.3	29.8	83.7	11.0	490	11.9	92.9	91.6	94.3	291
1992	963	18.4	110	196.1	17.3	89.3	9.0	500	6.0	106.0	92.7	109.4	443
1993	1,004	19.6	110	187.2	16.0	89.0	12.0	560	17.0	90.9	82.9	108.0	442
1994	949	21.6	110	159.2	17.2	115.6	12.0	570	25.0	96.4	85.4	71.3	410
1995	915	17.0	110	187.0	16.5	96.5	15.0	480	17.0	94.1	72.9	45.2	363
1996	988	21.0	110	175.6	17.0	113.0	17.0	480	13.0	127.4	77.1	67.1	414
1997	1,057	20.4	70	190.3	17.6	147.7	20.0	490	16.0	123.4	86.8	79.3	430
1998	1,070	25.3	40	209.5	17.9	159.4	22.0	500	14.0	157.0	87.2	57.2	386
1999[1]	1,118	28.3	30	234.2	18.6	209.5	24.0	730	36.0	194.0	58.0	70.4	429

[1] Preliminary. *Source: International Rubber Study Group (IRSG)*

Net Exports of Natural Rubber from Producing Areas In Thousands of Metric Tons

Year	Cam-bodia	Guat-emala[4]	Indo-nesia	Liberia	Malaysia	Nigeria	Sri Lanka	Thai-land	Vietnam	Other Africa[2]	Other Asia[3]	World Total
1989	32.0	11.0	1,151.8	106.0	1,364.8	101.3	86.0	1,100.6	57.7	115.0	38.2	4,170
1990	28.0	13.4	1,077.3	19.0	1,185.6	81.2	86.7	1,150.8	75.9	118.0	37.6	3,940
1991	21.0	14.3	1,220.0	32.0	1,041.2	63.0	76.4	1,231.9	62.9	126.0	44.0	3,890
1992	20.0	15.7	1,268.1	30.0	939.1	70.4	78.6	1,412.9	80.9	135.0	25.9	4,010
1993	21.0	16.9	1,214.3	45.0	769.8	79.7	69.6	1,396.8	82.5	136.0	32.6	3,870
1994	32.0	22.3	1,244.8	10.0	782.1	49.6	69.1	1,605.0	106.6	145.0	28.9	4,200
1995	30.0	23.2	1,323.8	13.0	777.5	99.2	68.2	1,635.5	116.7	140.0	31.1	4,290
1996	31.0	29.2	1,434.3	30.0	709.8	48.8	72.1	1,763.0	141.0	167.0	41.0	4,490
1997	32.0	28.3	1,403.8	67.2	586.8	53.0	61.4	1,837.1	151.0	183.0	39.8	4,450
1998[1]	33.0	32.6	1,641.2	75.0	424.9	74.0	41.4	1,839.4	165.0	191.0	41.8	4,560

[1] Preliminary. [2] Includes Cameroon, Cote d'Ivoire, Gabon, Ghana and Zaire. [3] Includes Myanmar, Papua New Guinea and the Philippines.
Source: International Rubber Study Group (IRSG)

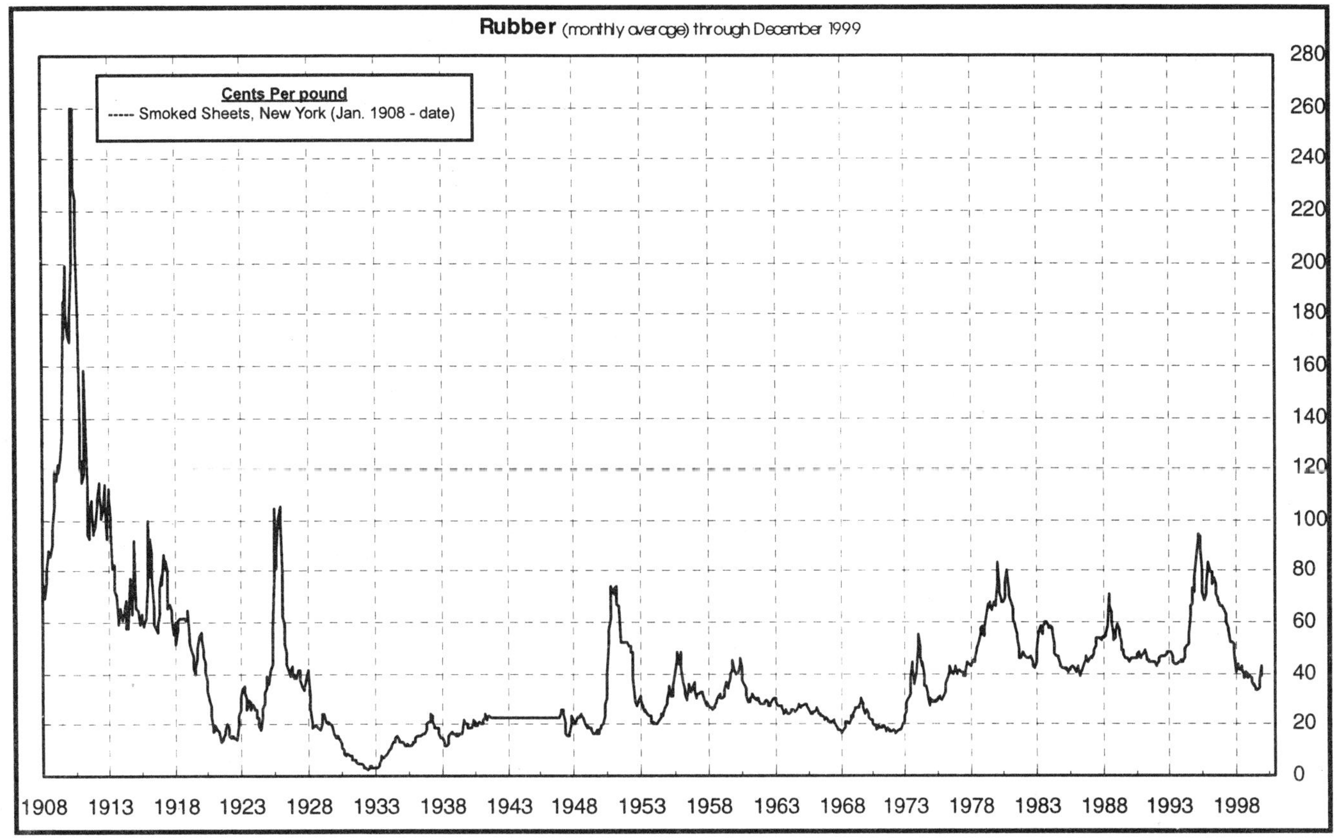

Average Spot Crude Rubber Prices (Smoked Sheets1) in New York In Cents Per Pound

Year	Jan.	Feb.	Mar.	Apr.	May	June	July	Aug.	Sept.	Oct.	Nov.	Dec.	Average
1990	44.72	45.75	45.92	45.64	45.80	46.00	45.80	47.46	48.43	46.50	46.23	47.03	46.27
1991	47.47	48.92	48.09	45.92	45.17	45.26	44.59	44.45	44.25	44.52	44.75	44.16	45.63
1992	43.11	43.95	44.50	45.86	46.41	46.57	46.78	47.05	46.86	47.83	48.00	48.03	46.25
1993	48.51	48.30	46.41	44.15	43.78	43.78	43.30	43.85	44.54	44.23	44.90	44.70	45.04
1994	44.92	46.11	49.62	50.83	51.43	55.13	62.49	66.35	67.15	73.51	71.76	77.35	59.72
1995	85.68	92.61	94.15	93.43	89.50	80.57	72.13	68.54	70.70	73.59	83.19	83.39	82.29
1996	80.25	79.90	79.76	75.08	76.99	75.10	71.03	69.13	68.75	66.32	66.32	66.14	72.90
1997	65.06	64.76	63.53	59.97	57.71	57.30	51.96	52.45	51.89	51.36	47.99	40.53	55.38
1998	40.21	43.96	41.70	41.23	42.65	41.28	40.03	38.58	38.62	40.26	39.96	38.20	40.56
1999	38.99	38.58	36.34	34.98	35.75	34.64	33.60	33.63	34.45	37.58	42.57	38.88	36.67

[1] No. 1, ribbed, plantation rubber. *Source: The Wall Street Journal*

Natural Rubber Prices in London In British Pounds Per Metric Ton

Year	Jan.	Feb.	Mar.	Apr.	May	June	July	Aug.	Sept.	Oct.	Nov.	Dec.	Average
Buyers' Price RSS 1 (CIF)													
1996	1,063.1	1,066.1	1,057.3	990.8	1,025.1	999.6	912.0	881.2	880.5	829.8	803.3	800.3	942.4
1997	777.6	783.6	800.9	731.3	715.1	699.6	605.9	604.1	592.5	573.9	525.9	461.4	654.3
1998	464.6	516.9	470.7	473.3	487.0	461.5	473.8	456.6	469.3	490.2	487.7	464.6	476.1
1999	495.8	463.3	430.0	4,144.0	442.4	435.7	410.2	404.5	419.9	455.4	509.8	484.7	758.0
Buyers' Prices RSS 3 (CIF)													
1996	1,057.3	1,058.6	1,049.9	981.4	1,015.5	984.6	895.2	863.0	862.0	814.7	790.7	782.1	929.6
1997	762.2	769.4	788.7	721.3	708.9	696.9	588.7	592.1	575.8	553.0	490.1	411.4	636.5
1998	416.0	500.3	445.5	465.6	480.7	451.0	466.3	439.1	454.3	478.0	467.1	430.0	457.6
1999	466.4	451.6	417.9	394.0	418.8	425.3	391.1	384.8	398.6	439.0	489.5	453.3	427.5
Sellers' Prices SMR 20 (CIF)													
1996	1,059.5	1,019.4	1,006.3	915.0	894.0	838.1	821.0	830.6	844.4	814.5	778.8	777.5	883.3
1997	767.5	769.4	765.0	697.5	663.1	653.8	597.0	600.0	580.6	567.5	530.0	468.3	640.7
1998	477.5	539.4	485.0	487.0	495.0	438.8	417.0	396.3	403.0	416.9	409.4	401.0	445.6
1999	414.4	411.9	380.5	375.0	396.9	393.5	373.8	388.8	417.0	453.1	518.8	480.0	417.0

Source: International Rubber Study Group (IRSG)

Consumption of Natural Rubber in the United States — In Thousands of Metric Tons

Year	Jan.	Feb.	Mar.	Apr.	May	June	July	Aug.	Sept.	Oct.	Nov.	Dec.	Total
1990	62.6	57.3	79.0	65.2	87.4	73.9	57.4	74.1	78.8	59.8	75.6	69.8	807.5
1991	60.0	60.0	65.0	65.0	65.0	60.0	55.0	55.0	65.0	70.0	65.0	66.0	755.8
1992	83.4	63.3	85.9	66.9	80.6	78.6	82.6	79.5	70.2	84.6	64.4	70.2	910.2
1993	96.3	76.0	93.4	93.4	67.9	76.8	77.3	84.9	72.0	73.6	82.9	72.2	966.7
1994	92.8	84.9	93.1	82.7	89.6	84.6	76.2	87.8	74.8	90.1	66.4	78.7	1,001.7
1995	70.5	75.8	98.4	90.3	92.2	93.3	85.0	82.7	83.1	89.9	81.4	61.3	1,003.9
1996	102.5	85.8	81.2	87.9	65.6	76.7	81.9	88.1	83.3	108.4	72.1	68.2	1,001.7
1997	94.2	92.0	93.9	88.2	93.0	65.1	76.8	90.1	87.5	86.8	87.5	89.0	1,044.1
1998	104.4	76.6	102.7	81.0	98.0	92.9	96.4	91.7	119.1	104.8	78.4	111.4	1,157.4
1999[1]	90.0	90.0	90.0	86.0	86.0	86.0	90.0	90.0	89.0				1,062.7

[1] Preliminary. *Source: International Rubber Study Group (IRSG)*

Stocks of Natural Rubber in the United States, on First of Month — In Thousands of Metric Tons

Year	Jan.	Feb.	Mar.	Apr.	May	June	July	Aug.	Sept.	Oct.	Nov.	Dec.
1990	92.0	100.2	100.2	101.6	97.1	97.3	99.8	101.6	87.2	90.3	84.7	89.6
1991	94.3	94.0	88.0	93.0	119.0	113.0	110.0	108.0	106.0	106.0	110.0	117.0
1992	109.4	103.6	112.7	110.4	107.5	105.9	101.1	99.0	96.7	100.3	97.0	100.7
1993	108.0	49.4	53.3	53.7	46.7	52.9	57.3	63.6	56.5	53.7	53.4	56.5
1994	71.3	65.9	55.7	65.2	61.4	60.0	53.2	43.8	41.0	45.0	44.2	47.8
1995	45.2	56.4	67.5	71.4	71.2	72.6	73.0	66.0	64.4	62.8	62.1	59.8
1996	67.1	70.0	70.3	71.2	73.9	73.4	67.1	64.2	57.2	56.0	61.1	62.4
1997	79.3	74.2	74.2	76.9	77.5	62.2	55.2	53.6	52.1	51.2	52.4	55.2
1998	57.2	61.2	65.5	63.5	60.9	66.7	53.6	57.9	54.7	58.3	58.9	66.5
1999[1]	70.4	70.3	70.3	70.3	70.3	70.3	70.3	70.3	70.3	70.3		

[1] Preliminary. *Source: International Rubber Study Group (IRSG)*

Stocks of Synthetic Rubber in the United States, on First of Month — In Thousands of Metric Tons

Year	Jan.	Feb.	Mar.	Apr.	May	June	July	Aug.	Sept.	Oct.	Nov.	Dec.
1990	404.0	393.5	392.5	385.8	406.8	397.5	395.0	414.9	420.8	419.6	405.0	393.9
1991	403.7	406.0	403.0	404.0	402.0	388.0	394.0	385.0	356.0	334.0	330.0	325.0
1992	403.7	386.0	381.2	383.9	393.2	389.2	372.8	382.7	382.1	375.1	378.6	401.1
1993	406.9	345.9	345.7	346.0	340.5	351.8	342.1	341.6	333.6	326.4	319.9	321.4
1994	331.1	313.3	313.3	307.9	306.0	314.2	302.5	323.2	318.5	304.6	299.4	299.5
1995	305.4	307.4	302.8	293.5	319.4	315.6	325.9	349.2	355.7	354.6	347.0	351.5
1996	366.2	355.3	342.0	354.8	365.4	360.0	367.0	377.3	366.0	362.8	354.1	370.6
1997	400.5	400.4	408.4	412.7	411.9	403.5	393.1	376.9	378.4	364.4	365.2	377.7
1998	377.7	382.2	375.7	379.5	387.5	402.8	394.6	406.8	394.2	398.7	395.7	396.5
1999[1]	409.3	402.0	402.0	408.0	401.0	422.0	418.0	422.0	425.0	407.0		

[1] Preliminary. *Source: International Rubber Study Group (IRSG)*

Production of Synthetic Rubber in the United States — In Thousands of Metric Tons

Year	Jan.	Feb.	Mar.	Apr.	May	June	July	Aug.	Sept.	Oct.	Nov.	Dec.	Total
1990	173.5	180.1	182.5	187.8	174.6	172.0	171.9	180.9	180.4	190.3	167.4	153.1	2,115
1991	168.0	163.0	184.0	174.0	173.0	159.0	154.0	133.0	159.0	159.0	173.0	164.0	2,050
1992	180.0	190.0	200.0	210.0	200.0	190.0	190.0	200.0	210.0	200.0	195.0	175.0	2,300
1993	120.0	160.0	220.0	190.0	200.0	180.0	190.0	180.0	180.0	180.0	190.0	180.0	2,180
1994	180.0	180.0	210.0	200.0	210.0	200.0	200.0	210.0	190.0	210.0	200.0	200.0	2,390
1995	220.0	200.0	210.0	210.0	240.0	220.0	210.0	230.0	210.0	200.0	200.0	190.0	2,530
1996	200.0	190.0	220.0	210.0	200.0	210.0	200.0	210.0	200.0	210.0	220.0	216.0	2,486
1997	220.0	200.0	220.0	230.0	220.0	200.0	220.0	220.0	230.0	210.0	210.0	203.0	2,589
1998	230.0	200.0	230.0	220.0	240.0	210.0	220.0	210.0	230.0	210.0	200.0	210.0	2,610
1999[1]	200.0	181.0	209.0	195.0	205.0	190.0	199.0	192.0	180.0				2,335

[1] Preliminary. *Source: International Rubber Study Group (IRSG)*

Consumption of Synthetic Rubber in the United States In Thousands of Metric Tons

Year	Jan.	Feb.	Mar.	Apr.	May	June	July	Aug.	Sept.	Oct.	Nov.	Dec.	Total
1990	159.6	158.7	161.6	144.1	161.5	151.6	137.1	149.5	155.6	175.3	147.1	119.1	1,821
1991	145.0	140.0	160.0	150.0	160.0	135.0	140.0	140.0	160.0	140.0	150.0	149.0	1,768
1992	167.8	159.5	174.7	158.9	162.6	184.2	154.5	177.7	180.2	171.5	155.1	148.2	1,960
1993	161.3	154.4	189.4	172.8	164.5	173.6	166.0	173.9	162.0	169.4	162.3	151.4	2,001
1994	177.7	160.8	191.8	173.0	173.5	187.5	164.9	187.1	176.0	178.8	175.7	170.8	2,118
1995	188.6	182.2	194.3	179.1	212.7	188.7	160.0	190.7	182.4	178.1	169.7	145.5	2,172
1996	188.0	173.7	186.9	176.8	184.9	178.5	177.0	197.3	182.9	201.0	177.8	165.5	2,187
1997	191.7	181.4	190.0	187.9	192.2	187.7	205.9	208.0	204.2	203.0	181.9	188.8	2,323
1998	196.5	192.5	214.8	194.4	199.8	201.4	192.0	204.5	202.2	200.3	181.2	174.8	2,354
1999[1]	166.0	166.0	192.0	178.0	170.0	180.0	181.0	167.0	186.0				2,115

[1] Preliminary. *Source: International Rubber Study Group (IRSG)*

U.S. Exports of Synthetic Rubber In Thousands of Metric Tons

Year	Jan.	Feb.	Mar.	Apr.	May	June	July	Aug.	Sept.	Oct.	Nov.	Dec.	Total
1990	45.6	39.0	50.2	42.6	42.7	41.0	37.4	43.1	42.0	50.8	50.3	39.0	523.7
1991	43.8	46.1	44.0	45.2	47.9	40.4	42.8	43.2	43.1	46.3	47.3	42.2	532.3
1992	52.3	55.1	51.3	59.1	58.2	51.6	46.5	52.8	58.0	51.4	48.1	39.7	624.1
1993	47.1	34.1	57.7	47.4	52.4	46.9	46.9	43.8	48.8	46.6	49.0	41.9	562.6
1994	48.8	46.4	55.4	57.0	52.4	49.6	50.2	62.8	60.7	59.9	56.9	55.0	655.1
1995	54.9	51.6	62.7	55.6	58.6	58.6	50.0	54.9	53.0	60.4	53.9	52.6	666.8
1996	61.1	57.7	64.0	68.0	48.2	66.8	62.3	57.1	63.9	65.2	58.6	58.6	731.5
1997	63.1	58.2	57.5	74.2	66.9	61.6	64.1	70.0	65.6	65.6	63.0	58.7	768.5
1998	61.1	60.8	62.8	59.8	66.9	61.8	60.1	64.4	63.7	62.3	59.2	59.2	742.1
1999[1]	57.6	63.3	65.0	70.5	64.7	66.0	61.5	68.2	65.1	79.0			793.1

[1] Preliminary. *Source: International Rubber Study Group (IRSG)*

Production of Tyres (Car and Truck) in the United States In Thousands of Units

Year	First Quarter	Second Quarter	Third Quarter	Fourth Quarter	Total	Year	First Quarter	Second Quarter	Third Quarter	Fourth Quarter	Total
1981	47,853	46,042	45,658	42,209	181,762	1990	55,915	53,856	51,163	49,729	210,663
1982	47,304	45,602	42,656	42,938	178,500	1991	51,296	52,796	49,183	51,115	202,391
1983	45,859	47,451	45,370	47,353	186,923	1992	57,890	57,319	57,554	57,487	230,250
1984	53,369	53,588	50,957	51,463	209,375	1993	61,809	60,752	57,702	57,184	237,447
1985	54,460	49,385	46,468	46,610	196,923	1994	63,586	63,331	57,018	59,442	243,696
1986	49,240	45,687	46,855	48,507	190,289	1995	63,800	63,800	63,800	63,754	255,521
1987	51,205	50,210	49,723	51,839	202,978	1996	64,000	64,000	64,000	63,700	255,723
1988	54,677	52,986	51,195	52,493	211,351	1997	-----	-----	-----	-----	264,020
1989	56,716	56,626	50,086	49,444	212,870	1998[1]	-----	-----	-----	-----	270,905

[1] Preliminary. [2] Estimate. *Source: International Rubber Study Group IRSG)*

U.S. Foreign Trade of Tyres (Car and Truck) In Thousands of Units

	Imports					Exports				
Year	First Quarter	Second Quarter	Third Quarter	Fourth Quarter	Total	First Quarter	Second Quarter	Third Quarter	Fourth Quarter	Total
1990	13,713	13,564	11,951	11,633	50,861	5,453	5,532	6,031	6,730	23,746
1991	12,011	13,008	11,320	10,158	46,497	6,407	6,388	6,623	6,342	25,760
1992	10,760	12,496	11,850	12,285	47,391	6,243	6,475	7,125	6,646	26,489
1993	11,519	13,045	12,688	13,036	50,288	7,266	6,930	7,163	7,133	28,492
1994	13,809	15,352	14,906	14,774	58,841	7,444	8,035	7,945	8,678	32,102
1995	14,883	14,977	13,762	12,718	56,340	8,438	8,502	8,478	9,174	34,592
1996	13,163	13,864	12,543	13,186	52,756	8,244	10,013	8,672	9,401	36,330
1997	13,359	14,487	15,314	16,064	59,224	9,466	11,386	10,456	11,085	42,393
1998[1]	17,046	17,728	18,016	19,346	72,136	12,840	10,678	10,018	10,372	43,908
1999[2]	19,471				77,884	9,874				39,496

[1] Preliminary. [2] Estimate. *Source: International Rubber Study Group (IRSG)*

Rye

The protracted slippage in U.S. rye production may have run its course in the late 1990's. During the 1980's, annual production averaged more than 20 million bushels and has since been almost halved. Rye is now a minor U.S. crop, leaving the U.S. as a net importer of rye, at times importing almost half of domestic production. The major producing states in 1999 were the Dakotas, Oklahoma and Georgia. Those three states accounted for more than half of 1998/99 production (June/May) of 11.8 million bushels vs. the 1997/98 record low of 8.1 million bushels. Production in 1999/2000 is forecast at 11.5 million bushels. Although average yield appears to have steadied in recent years, the area planted to rye continues low with only 160,000 hectares allocated in 1999/00, slightly under 1998/99.

In the U.S., rye is used as an animal feed and as an ingredient in bread and some whiskeys. About a third of the total supply is used as a feedstuff, an equal quantity as a foodstuff, and the balance as seed and for whisky. U.S. rye exports are minimal, generally about a million metric tonnes. Carryover stocks are also small; 19,000 tonnes at the end of 1997/98, with 1999/00 carryover forecast at 50,000 tonnes. The contraction in U.S. supply/demand reflects a seemingly deep-rooted lack of interest towards the grain by producers and consumers alike.

On a world basis, the slippage is also evident. For a time in the mid-1990's, production appeared to have stabilized in the 20-25 million metric tonne range vs. a mid-1980's average of more than 30 million tonnes ten years earlier. World production in 1999/00 of 19.8 million tonnes compares with 20.3 million in 1998/99. Average yield in 1999/00 was forecast unchanged from 1998/99, but acreage was estimated to have slipped to 10.06 million hectares from 10.35 million the year before.

Eastern Europe is the major producing area with more than half of the world's crop. Individually, Poland now appears to be the world's largest producer with 5.2 million tonnes in 1999/00 vs. 5.7 million in 1998/99, followed by Germany with 4.3 million tonnes and 4.8 million, respectively. Canada, whose output is not much larger than that of the U.S. but realizes a higher average yield, exports most of its crop to the U.S., about 75,000 tonnes in 1999/00 vs. 40,000 in 1998/99.

World trade in 1999/00 (October/September), of almost 1.8 million metric tonnes, was slightly under 1998/99, but well above the paltry 731,000 tonnes in 1997/98. Importing nations show wide year-to-year variance. China's 1999/00 imports of 500,000 tonnes is unchanged from 1998/99, but compares with only 11,000 tonnes in 1996/97. South Korea's 1999/00 imports of 200,000 tonnes compares with only 4,000 in 1997/98 and 928,000 in 1995/96. The largest exporter is the European Union with 1.5 million tonnes in 1999/00, unchanged from a year earlier but triple the 1997/98 total of 500,000 tonnes. Russia's exports the past few years have averaged about 50,000 tonnes.

World Production of Rye   In Thousands of Metric Tons

Year	Austria	Canada	Czech Republic[5]	Denmark	France	Germany	Poland	Russia[4]	Spain	Turkey	Ukraine[4]	United States	World Total
1990-1	396	599	736	545	240	3,988	6,044	-----	267	240	21,193	258	36,861
1991-2	350	339	484	395	210	3,324	5,899	-----	242	240	14,061	248	27,359
1992-3	278	265	255	308	205	2,422	3,981	13,890	230	240	1,160	304	28,656
1993-4	290	320	300	323	190	2,984	5,000	9,150	300	230	1,180	263	26,090
1994-5	320	400	280	380	180	3,450	5,300	6,000	220	250	940	290	21,890
1995-6	310	310	260	500	200	4,520	6,290	4,100	170	260	1,210	260	21,890
1996-7	150	310	200	340	230	4,210	5,650	5,900	300	250	1,100	230	22,230
1997-8[1]	210	320	260	450	210	4,580	5,300	7,500	230	240	1,350	210	24,400
1998-9[2]	240	400	260	540	220	4,770	5,660	3,300	230	240	1,140	310	20,320
1999-00[3]	230	390	200	240	190	4,320	5,200	4,500	230	250	1,200	280	19,780

[1] Preliminary. [2] Estimate. [3] Forecast. [4] Formerly part of the U.S.S.R.; data not reported separately until 1992. [5] Formerly part of Czechoslovakia; data not reported separately until 1992. *Source: Foreign Agricultural Service, U.S. Department of Agriculture (FAS-USDA)*

Production of Rye in the United States   In Thousands of Bushels

Year	Georgia	Kansas	Michigan	Minnesota	Nebraska	North Dakota	Oklahoma	Pennsylvania	South Carolina	South Dakota	Texas	Wisconsin	Total
1990	1,320	130	580	868	750	780	420	496	594	1,870	140	465	10,176
1991	1,300	115	360	648	1,000	992	665	297	630	1,152	228	435	9,761
1992	1,560	130	496	720	1,040	1,496	798	720	675	1,666	280	330	11,952
1993	1,380	693	420	667	500	1,050	660	340	380	1,600	363	260	10,340
1994	1,890	325	442	810	546	700	945	320	600	1,485	435	875	11,341
1995	1,155	400	544	609	480	726	810	330	440	1,650	380	480	10,064
1996	1,820	150	351	480	323	528	975	216	520	1,476	190	384	8,936
1997	1,430	300	450	400	240	513	1,080	400	250	728	330	432	8,132
1998	1,050	375	420	837	288	2,562	1,540	495	400	1,400	400	360	12,161
1999[1]	1,050	300	756	775	360	1,517	1,045	600	500	1,012	450	384	10,993

[1] Preliminary. *Source: Agricultural Statistics Board, U.S. Department of Agriculture (ASB-USDA)*

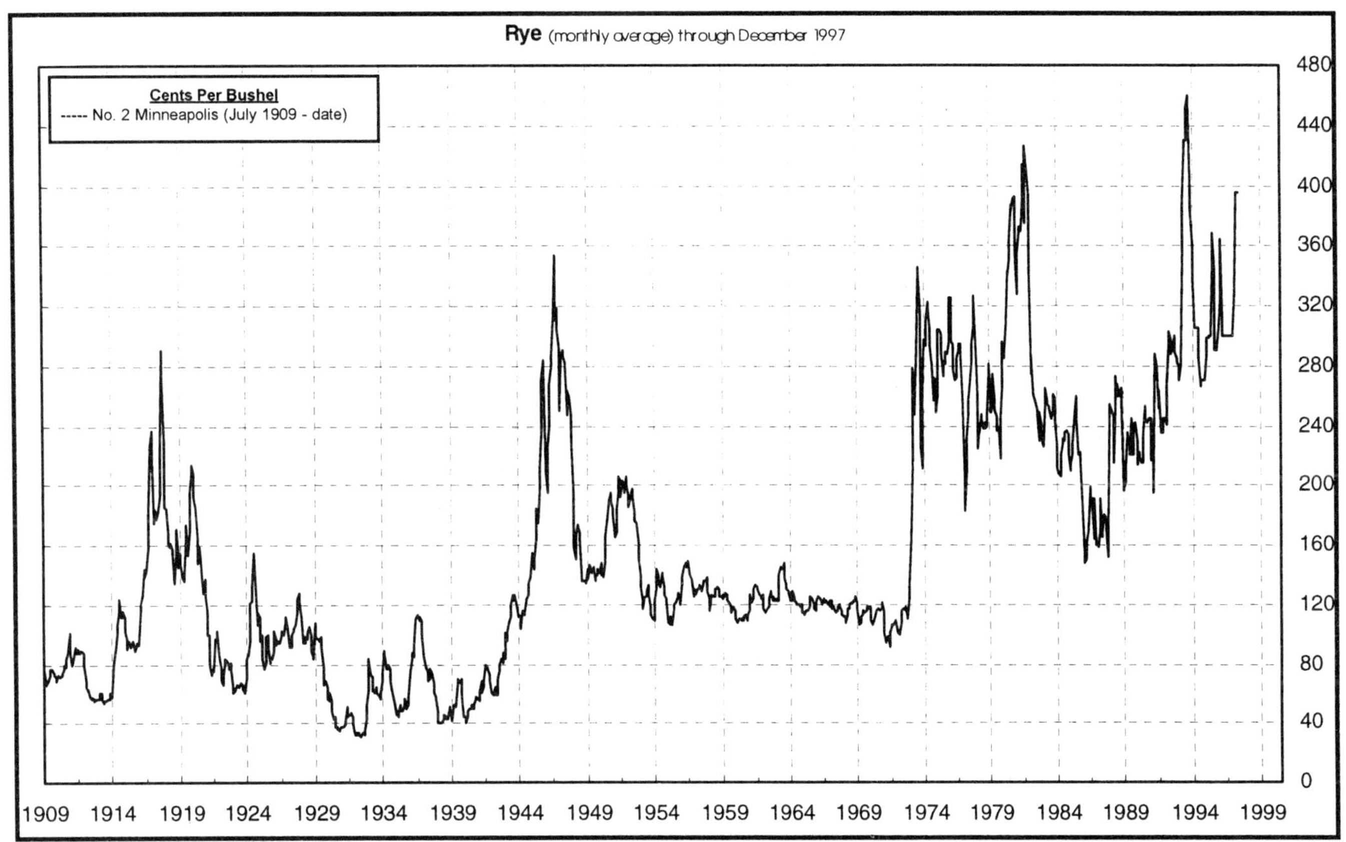

Salient Statistics of Rye in the United States In Thousands of Bushels

Crop Year Beginning June 1	Supply				Disappearance: Domestic Use							Acreage		Yield Per Harvested Acre
	Stocks June 1	Pro-duction	Imports	Total Supply	Food	Industry	Seed	Feed & Residual	Total	Exports	Total Disap-pearance	Planted	Harvested for Grain	Bushels
												1,000 Acres		
1990-1	5,642	10,176	3,895	19,713	3,500	2,000	3,000	7,670	16,170	213	16,383	1,625	375	27.1
1991-2	3,327	9,761	4,542	17,630	3,500	2,000	3,000	7,528	16,028	53	16,081	1,671	396	24.6
1992-3	1,523	11,952	3,099	16,100	3,400	2,000	3,000	6,084	14,484	14	14,498	1,582	406	29.4
1993-4	1,555	10,340	4,607	16,502	3,500	2,000	3,000	7,015	15,515	16	15,531	1,493	381	27.1
1994-5	971	11,341	4,386	16,698	3,300	2,000	3,000	6,912	15,212	35	15,247	1,613	407	27.9
1995-6	1,451	10,064	3,760	15,275	3,300	2,000	3,000	6,036	14,336	41	14,377	1,602	385	26.1
1996-7	898	8,936	4,327	14,161	3,433	2,000	3,000	4,942	13,375	32	13,407	1,457	345	25.9
1997-8[1]	754	8,132	5,562	14,448	3,500	3,000	2,000	5,104	13,604	80	13,684	1,400	316	25.7
1998-9[2]	800	12,161	4,000	16,961	3,500	3,000	3,000	6,300	15,800	100	15,800	1,566	418	29.1
1999-00[3]		10,993										1,582	383	28.7

[1] Preliminary. [2] Estimate. [3] Forecast *Source: Economic Research Service, U.S. Department of Agriculture (ERS-USDA)*

Average Price of Cash Rye No. 2 in Minneapolis In Cents Per Bushel

Year	July	Aug.	Sept.	Oct.	Nov.	Dec.	Jan.	Feb.	Mar.	Apr.	May	June	Average
1990-1	215	222	220	220	190	245	252	243	242	242	245	245	232
1991-2	216	238	195	288	288	279	251	263	235	235	235	245	247
1992-3	245	241	267	295	303	298	288	290	300	289	285	282	282
1993-4	280	270	280	354	387	427	430	430	452	460	400	383	372
1994-5	360	336	305	305	305	305	285	267	270	270	270	270	296
1995-6	287	298	299	300	300	350	368	346	290	290	290	304	310
1996-7	325	364	314	300	300	300	300	300	300	300	300	300	309
1997-8	300	327	395	395	395	395	NQ	NQ	NQ	NQ	NQ	NQ	382
1998-9	NQ	NQ	NQ	NQ	NQ	NQ	NQ	NQ	NQ	NQ	NQ	NQ	NQ
1999-00[1]	NQ	NQ	NQ	NQ	NQ	NQ	NQ	NQ					

Source: Agricultural Marketing Service, U.S. Department of Agriculture (AMS-USDA)

Salt

Salt, or sodium chloride, is a basic commodity with many uses. Salt is added to food to enhance flavor and to remove ice in winter. Salt is used in the manufacture of caustic soda and as a feedstock for chlorine. Salt is produced by a number of methods including solar evaporation, vacuum pan, mined as salt rock or taken from the ocean as brine. There are no economic substitutes or alternates for salt. Calcium chloride and calcium magnesium acetate, hydrochloric acid and potassium chloride can be substituted for salt in deicing, certain chemical processes and food flavoring at a higher cost.

The U.S. Geological Survey reported that U.S. salt production in 1998 was 42.1 million metric tonnes, up 2 percent from 1997. There were 28 companies operating 68 salt plants in 12 states. The estimated percentage of salt sold or used, by type, was salt in brine, 51 percent; rock salt, 31 percent; vacuum pan, 9 percent and solar salt 9 percent.

Reported consumption of salt in 1998 was 49.2 million tonnes, down 1 percent from 1997. The chemical industry consumed about 45 percent of total salt sales, with salt brine representing about 88 percent of the type of salt used for feedstock. In the chemical industry, the main consuming sectors were chlorine and caustic soda manufacturing. Salt used in highway deicing accounted for 30 percent of U.S. use.

U.S. salt imports for consumption in 1998 were 9.3 million tonnes, up almost 2 percent from 1997. The major import sources were Canada, Chile and Mexico. Exports were 800 tonnes in 1998, up 7 percent from 1997. Net imports of salt as a percentage of consumption in 1998 were 17 percent. Producer stocks of salt at the end of 1998 were 1.4 million tonnes.

World production of salt in 1998 was estimated at 200 million tonnes. The U.S. was by far the largest producer. The next largest producer was China with 1998 output of 30 million tonnes. Other large producers include Germany, Canada and Australia.

World Production of All Salt   In Thousands of Metric Tons

Year	Australia	Canada	China	France	Germany	India	Italy	Mexico	Poland	Spain	United Kingdom	United States	World Total
1991	7,791	11,993	24,100	6,500	14,870	9,503	3,954	7,533	3,840	4,070	6,828	36,400	191,000
1992	7,693	11,171	28,100	6,116	12,709	9,503	3,821	7,395	3,887	3,610	6,101	36,100	183,000
1993	7,737	10,900	29,500	6,980	12,688	9,503	3,730	7,490	3,817	3,410	6,790	39,300	187,000
1994	7,685	11,700	29,746	7,536	13,099	9,503	3,953	7,458	4,074	4,932	7,000	40,100	192,000
1995	8,148	10,957	29,780	7,539	15,224	9,503	3,552	7,670	4,214	4,776	6,650	42,200	196,000
1996	7,905	12,248	29,035	7,863	15,907	9,503	3,541	8,508	4,163	4,000	6,610	42,300	197,000
1997[1]	8,749	13,264	30,830	7,085	15,787	9,500	3,510	7,933	3,968	4,000	6,600	41,500	199,000
1998[2]	8,879	13,320	30,830	7,000	15,700	9,500	3,600	8,412	3,900	3,500	6,600	41,300	186,000

[1] Preliminary. [2] Estimate. *Source: U.S. Geological Survey (USGS)*

Salient Statistics of the Salt Industry in the United States   In Thousands of Metric Tons

Year	Net Import Reliance as a % of Apparent Consumption	Average Value FOB Mine Vacuum & Open Pan $ Per Ton	Production: Total	Production: Open & Vacuum Pan	Production: Solar	Production: Rock	Production: Brine	Sold or Used Producers: Open & Vacuum Pan	Sold or Used Producers: Rock Salt	Sold or Used Producers: Brine	Sold or Used Producers: Total Salt	Sold or Used Producers: Value[3] Million $	Imports for Consumption	Exports: Total	Exports: To Canada	Apparent Consumption
1991	11	114.75	36,316	3,654	2,813	11,188	18,660	3,623	11,064	18,640	35,902	801.5	6,188	1,777	1,288	40,313
1992	11	113.20	36,016	3,811	3,221	11,411	17,574	3,763	10,910	34,784	34,784	802.6	5,394	992	718	39,186
1993	12	111.97	39,200	3,864	2,960	14,253	18,100	3,850	13,401	18,100	38,200	904.0	5,868	688	499	43,400
1994	18	115.35	40,100	3,960	3,020	15,100	18,000	3,930	14,900	18,000	39,700	990.0	9,630	742	573	48,600
1995	14	118.63	42,100	3,950	3,540	14,000	20,600	3,920	13,000	20,500	40,800	1,000.0	7,090	670	558	47,200
1996	19	120.54	42,200	3,920	3,270	13,500	21,500	3,900	14,500	21,500	42,900	1,060.0	10,600	869	710	52,600
1997[1]	17	119.61	41,400	3,980	3,170	12,900	21,400	3,990	12,200	21,400	40,600	993.0	9,160	748	624	49,000
1998[2]	17	114.93	41,200	4,040	3,190	12,900	21,100	4,040	12,700	21,100	40,800	986.0	8,770	731	533	48,800

[1] Preliminary. [2] Estimate. [3] Values are f.o.b. mine or refinery & do not include cost of cooperage or containers. *Source: U.S. Geological Survey*

Salt Sold or Used by Producers in the U.S. by Classes & Consumers or Uses   In Thousands of Metric Tons

Year	Chemical[2]	Tanning Leather	Textile & Dyeing	Meat Packers	Canning	Baking	Agricultural Distribution	Feed Dealers	Feed Manufacturers	Rubber	Oil	Paper & Pulp	Metal Processing	Water Treatment	Grocery Stores	Water Conditioning Distrib.	Ice Control and/or Stabilization
1991	20,014	76	232	370	255	142	546	1,097	335	138	554	237	293	432	897	889	9,360
1992	18,538	67	271	389	252	161	553	1,020	392	34	1,208	230	217	435	849	899	7,814
1993	19,273	67	313	418	322	152	808	1,120	476	37	1,220	110	216	419	823	527	13,600
1994	18,400	82	304	410	342	157	842	1,070	478	33	1,290	150	239	440	934	505	16,400
1995	21,100	74	290	410	332	155	726	1,040	407	67	2,420	152	236	413	847	563	12,900
1996	22,400	83	288	407	336	169	661	1,150	403	71	2,430	122	199	534	855	719	17,700
1997	22,400	78	273	416	334	167	307	1,110	683	68	2,440	107	177	471	800	624	15,000
1998[1]	22,000	93	250	440	275	219	362	1,190	536	68	2,320	115	170	531	807	598	9,490

[1] Preliminary. [2] Chloralkali producers and other chemical. *Source: U.S. Geological Survey (USGS)*

Sheep & Lambs

The steady contraction in U.S. sheep inventory persists. The mid-1999 total of all sheep and lambs of 9 million head compares with 9.4 million in mid-1998 and the peak inventory of 56 million head in 1942. Of the 1999 total, the breeding sheep inventory declined to 5.35 million head vs. 5.57 million in 1998. The 1999 lamb crop of 4.75 million head compares with 5.01 million in 1998. The largest sheep producing states include Texas, South Dakota, and Wyoming. Commercial 1999 U.S. lamb production (through October) of 197 million pounds compares with 206 million in the like 1998 period. The U.S. is a net importer of lamb, almost all from Australia and New Zealand, totaling 58.5 million pounds through the first eight months of 1999 vs. 49.7 million in the like 1998 period. However, the U.S. imports live sheep from Canada. Per capita, retail weight disappearance of lamb in the U.S. totals about one pound.

Choice wholesale lamb prices, in late 1999, near $67.00 per hundredweight compare with the mid-$70.00/cwt. a year earlier, basis San Angelo, Texas. East Coast prices of $153.00/cwt. compare with over $160.00/cwt., respectively.

Although demand for sheep meat is low in the U.S., foreign demand is higher, especially in those countries with large sheep herds utilized for wool production from which there is a derived demand for meat. Thus, the price of wool is a key factor in determining the availability of sheep meat. World sheep numbers increased during the late 1990's due largely to gains in China and India.

World Sheep and Goat Numbers in Specified Countries on January 1 In Thousands of Head

Year	Argentina	Australia	China	India	Kazak-hstan	New Zealand	Romania	Russia	South Africa	Spain	Turkey	United Kingdom	World Total
1991	27,552	173,982	210,021	160,207	35,700	57,852	14,062	58,200	37,585	24,037	45,000	30,147	962,853
1992	25,706	161,073	206,210	161,084	34,556	55,162	13,879	55,255	36,076	24,625	44,700	28,932	931,903
1993	24,500	140,542	207,329	162,155	34,420	52,568	12,079	51,368	35,770	24,615	44,600	29,493	900,400
1994	23,500	120,900	217,314	169,569	34,208	50,298	12,276	43,700	33,800	23,872	44,000	29,333	881,258
1995	21,626	121,100	240,528	171,626	25,132	50,135	12,119	34,500	33,385	23,058	43,000	29,484	874,912
1996	17,956	121,200	230,000	173,519	19,600	48,816	11,086	28,336	35,145	21,322	42,400	28,797	894,331
1997	17,295	120,228	237,283	175,976	13,742	47,394	10,317	23,519	35,830	23,981	41,100	28,256	842,501
1998	15,232	119,579	255,560	178,462	10,896	46,970	9,747	20,697	36,821	24,857	39,500	30,118	855,673
1999[1]	13,953	117,800	280,000	180,130	9,556	46,150	9,167	18,213	34,910	23,751	37,300	31,080	869,181
2000[2]	13,800	116,900	310,000	180,885	9,000	46,460	8,700	18,213	35,000	23,490	34,400	30,505	894,087

[1] Preliminary. [2] Forecast. *Source: Foreign Agricultural Service, U.S. Department of Agriculture (FAS-USDA)*

Salient Statistics of Sheep & Lambs in the United States (Average Live Weight) In Thousands of Head

	-- Inventory, Jan. 1 --				--- Marketings[3] ---		---------- Slaughter ----------					Production (Live Weight)	Farm Value -------- Jan. 1 --------	
Year	Without New Crop Lambs	With New Crop Lambs	Lamb Crop	Total Supply	Sheep	Lambs	Farm	Commercial	Total[4]	Net Exports	Total Disappearance	Mil. Lbs.	All Million $	$ Per Head
1991	11,174	11,930	7,651	19,581	1,719	7,187	92	5,721	5,813	787	7,818	796.1	732.6	65.6
1992	10,797	11,507	7,225	18,732	1,923	7,007	87	5,496	5,585	770	7,595	746.0	660.7	61.2
1993	10,201	10,906	6,379	17,285	1,952	6,752	74	5,182	5,268	750	7,180	688.6	714.2	70.6
1994	9,836	9,714	5,897	15,611	1,536	6,384	76	4,938	5,008	760	6,742	630.0	681.4	69.9
1995	8,989	8,886	5,606	14,492	990	6,228	69	4,560	4,628	680	5,807	599.4	663.4	74.7
1996	8,465	8,461	5,282	13,743	1,024	6,023	65	4,184	4,249	264	5,488	565.7	732.2	86.5
1997	8,024	8,024	5,356	13,380	1,011	5,709	62	3,907	3,969		5,946	591.3	761.7	96.0
1998[1]	7,825	7,825	5,007	12,832			57	3,804	3,861				797.8	102.0
1999[2]	7,215	7,215	4,719	11,934				3,698					640.4	88.0

[1] Preliminary. [2] Estimate. [3] Excludes interfarm sales. [4] Includes all commercial and farm. Source: Economic Research Service, U.S. Department of Agriculture (ERS-USDA)

Sheep and Lambs[3] on Farms in the United States on January 1 In Thousands of Head

Year	California	Colorado	Idaho	Iowa	Minnesota	Montana	New Mexico	Ohio	South Dakota	Texas	Utah	Wyoming	Total
1992	995	710	273	345	293	658	445	215	602	2,140	488	870	10,749
1993	995	685	250	320	245	554	405	190	591	2,000	490	885	10,500
1994	1,120	647	266	267	231	534	340	198	550	1,895	442	813	9,742
1995	1,060	545	270	294	190	490	315	162	530	1,700	445	790	8,886
1996	1,000	535	273	345	185	465	265	153	500	1,650	395	680	8,461
1997	960	575	285	285	180	432	235	130	450	1,400	375	720	7,937
1998	800	575	285	265	165	415	290	135	420	1,530	420	710	7,825
1999[1]	810	440	265	260	175	380	275	125	420	1,350	400	630	7,215
2000[2]	800	440	275	256	165	370	290	134	420	1,200	400	570	7,026

[1] Preliminary. [2] Estimate. [3] Includes sheep & lambs on feed for market and stock sheep & lambs. Source: Economic Research Service, U.S. Department of Agriculture (ERS-USDA)

SHEEP & LAMBS

Average Wholesale Price of Slaughter Lambs (Choice) at San Angelo Texas In Dollars Per Cwt.

Year	Jan.	Feb.	Mar.	Apr.	May	June	July	Aug.	Sept.	Oct.	Nov.	Dec.	Average
1991	47.63	45.81	54.88	55.50	57.70	55.75	55.50	54.31	53.25	51.20	52.08	54.92	53.21
1992	58.56	57.69	66.55	74.63	68.88	64.50	58.17	52.38	53.61	52.81	56.93	67.25	61.00
1993	69.88	73.38	75.50	71.25	62.50	57.75	57.00	58.97	66.08	63.75	65.69	68.44	65.85
1994	56.67	62.31	61.19	51.25	60.94	66.92	75.33	79.50	76.08	69.96	73.60	67.50	66.77
1995	65.38	75.08	73.75	68.58	77.20	81.63	83.70	87.00	80.00	75.50	72.00	70.50	75.86
1996	74.44	85.63	84.07	83.10	86.17	97.50	92.67	83.75	84.40	82.58	80.00	88.88	85.27
1997	94.63	100.81	97.50	95.50	83.17	83.25	78.94	90.25	85.45	82.75	80.33	83.52	88.01
1998	74.38	74.31	71.50	63.00	73.00	91.21	82.21	82.05	69.50	67.20	63.33	71.44	73.59
1999[1]	69.31	67.88	68.54	70.50	82.70	81.06	77.29	81.17	77.00	74.81	78.00	83.29	75.96

[1] Preliminary. *Source: Economic Research Service, U.S. Department of Agriculture (ERS-USDA)*

Federally Inspected Slaughter of Sheep & Lambs in the United States In Thousands of Head

Year	Jan.	Feb.	Mar.	Apr.	May	June	July	Aug.	Sept.	Oct.	Nov.	Dec.	Total
1991	495	449	546	436	442	388	431	438	456	501	449	471	5,502
1992	468	422	481	503	374	419	427	400	470	452	413	460	5,289
1993	380	384	476	461	396	462	394	413	410	391	403	430	5,000
1994	383	409	515	402	418	377	302	382	384	381	393	411	4,756
1995	373	363	456	420	355	347	296	355	344	356	364	358	4,388
1996	352	353	403	374	313	271	313	315	313	365	324	336	4,032
1997	294	317	386	321	308	293	295	288	310	324	299	337	3,771
1998	301	300	377	367	270	283	269	263	295	312	290	344	3,671
1999[1]	260	291	411	295	260	259	253	283	294	293	317	341	3,557

[1] Preliminary. *Source: Economic Research Service, U.S. Department of Agriculture (ERS-USDA)*

Cold Storage Holdings of Lamb and Mutton in the U.S., on First of Month In Thousands of Pounds

Year	Jan.	Feb.	Mar.	Apr.	May	June	July	Aug.	Sept.	Oct.	Nov.	Dec.
1991	8,414	9,438	9,829	8,070	7,277	8,436	8,002	6,917	6,130	5,287	5,739	6,659
1992	6,296	7,255	6,670	8,455	8,580	9,870	10,968	11,711	9,314	8,751	8,520	8,406
1993	7,864	6,343	6,620	6,661	11,064	11,181	13,152	13,495	12,241	12,615	11,843	10,161
1994	8,372	9,198	9,507	11,194	11,505	11,368	12,124	12,026	11,016	9,261	8,946	8,796
1995	10,913	11,621	10,825	12,679	14,934	13,992	12,306	10,679	10,240	7,412	7,503	7,846
1996	7,606	9,794	13,017	12,247	13,649	12,187	13,726	13,164	14,645	11,249	10,494	9,788
1997	8,899	9,473	9,862	11,163	13,027	15,220	16,594	18,535	19,383	16,119	16,894	16,534
1998	13,741	13,920	15,284	16,226	16,306	16,666	16,040	16,188	14,530	12,253	12,558	11,914
1999[1]	11,721	10,452	12,134	12,374	13,146	12,313	12,459	11,975	12,240	9,815	9,158	9,446

[1] Preliminary. *Source: Economic Research Service, U.S. Department of Agriculture (ERS-USDA)*

Average Price Received by Farmers for Sheep in the United States In Dollars Per Cwt.

Year	Jan.	Feb.	Mar.	Apr.	May	June	July	Aug.	Sept.	Oct.	Nov.	Dec.	Average
1991	23.50	19.90	21.50	21.30	18.30	21.00	20.30	19.20	18.90	18.20	19.80	22.60	20.38
1992	28.10	29.80	31.60	28.30	23.10	22.60	24.00	25.80	25.00	25.30	25.50	33.20	26.86
1993	33.10	35.20	36.10	27.30	29.10	28.90	29.00	28.50	25.80	24.60	25.70	30.30	29.47
1994	35.10	37.00	34.30	29.60	29.30	33.60	30.10	29.40	27.90	27.30	30.50	34.70	31.57
1995	32.80	37.50	31.90	29.50	27.90	28.30	28.60	27.00	26.00	24.50	23.80	26.00	28.65
1996	34.40	33.80	34.00	27.30	25.30	26.60	30.50	29.10	30.20	28.80	29.80	34.20	30.33
1997	41.80	41.30	42.50	37.50	34.00	36.60	39.40	38.40	33.90	35.80	38.90	37.70	38.15
1998	42.00	39.60	41.00	34.40	30.30	30.20	29.40	28.30	26.80	26.10	26.40	30.10	32.05
1999[1]	32.40	30.20	32.70	31.80	31.50	28.90	32.00	29.20	29.20	26.40	30.20	33.40	30.66

[1] Preliminary. *Source: Economic Research Service, U.S. Department of Agriculture (ERS-USDA)*

Average Price Received by Farmers for Lambs in the United States In Dollars Per Cwt.

Year	Jan.	Feb.	Mar.	Apr.	May	June	July	Aug.	Sept.	Oct.	Nov.	Dec.	Average
1991	48.00	45.80	51.10	54.80	57.60	55.30	57.70	53.40	51.80	51.70	50.70	52.00	52.49
1992	53.50	55.20	63.40	69.30	68.80	65.60	62.20	55.90	56.70	55.40	58.20	65.20	60.78
1993	67.30	72.70	76.00	68.10	61.50	55.70	53.90	59.20	64.50	64.50	65.80	66.00	64.60
1994	60.60	59.40	58.60	54.50	54.50	63.00	72.80	75.50	71.20	68.00	70.60	69.10	64.82
1995	67.50	70.40	74.80	74.60	80.40	85.70	85.70	85.60	82.70	77.60	77.10	76.50	78.22
1996	76.10	84.30	86.60	85.90	90.30	100.70	98.30	89.10	88.50	87.00	84.60	88.20	88.30
1997	94.60	99.80	99.70	96.40	90.80	86.50	81.10	92.70	90.20	87.20	83.10	83.90	90.50
1998	78.40	75.00	70.10	66.00	63.00	88.90	81.30	80.10	71.80	67.60	62.60	64.70	72.46
1999[1]	68.20	67.20	67.40	67.40	82.80	81.30	77.00	68.90	75.30	72.60	76.30	77.60	73.50

[1] Preliminary. *Source: Economic Research Service, U.S. Department of Agriculture (ERS-USDA)*

Silk

Silk is the cloth and thread made from silkworms. The fiber used in commercial silk production is produced primarily by the mulberry silkworm. Silk is produced in a number of countries where the requirement is primarily a favorable climate and adequate labor. A primary requirement of silk production is an adequate number of mulberry trees. The mulberry leaf-feeding silkworm thrives on mulberry leaves. The silkworm spins a cocoon made of silk fiber which is then collected for a process called reeling. Reeling is the bringing together of two or more cocoons to form them into one continuous strand of silk.

World production of raw silk has seen little trend. Between 1992 and 1995, production averaged 110,750 metric tonnes. In 1996 and 1997 it averaged 83,500 tonnes. By far the world's largest producer of silk is China which in 1997 produced an estimated crop of 51,000 tonnes or 61 percent of the world total. The next largest producer is India with 19 percent of the market. Other significant producers of silk include North Korea, Japan, Brazil and Uzbekistan.

The world's largest exporter of silk is China. Reports from China in 1999 indicate that the government would like to see the Chinese silk industry reduce its surplus capacity to process silk and become more competitive internationally. While China produces and exports most of the world's silk, it has a large amount of excess capacity in terms of the number of spindles devoted to silk production.

One country that is trying to increase its share of the silk market is Uzbekistan. Officials in Uzbekistan indicated that for 1999, the silk harvest would be 750 tonnes of raw silk. That would represent an increase of 36 percent from the previous year. Uzbekistan will produce 12 million meters of silk fabrics in 1999, up from 8.8 million in 1998. Uzbekistan officials indicate that the country plans to expand its silk industry. The forecast is that by the year 2000, raw silk production will be 1,300 tonnes. Before the U.S.S.R. broke apart, Uzbekistan was the country's largest silk producer. In 1991, production of raw silk was estimated to be 2,418 tonnes with silk fabric production of 79 million meters.

World Production of Raw Silk In Metric Tons

Year	Brazil	China	India	Iran	Japan	North Korea	South Korea	Kyrgyzstan[3]	Thailand	Turkmenistan[3]	Uzbekistan[3]	Viet Nam	World Total
1988	1,900	42,041	10,255	900	6,862	3,800	1,355	-----	1,250	-----	4,300	420	73,866
1989	1,697	50,244	10,500	537	6,078	4,000	1,400	-----	1,250	-----	3,900	400	80,745
1990	1,693	55,003	11,000	537	6,000	4,200	971	-----	1,250	-----	4,094	500	85,987
1991	2,077	60,002	14,000	537	5,527	4,400	837	-----	1,300	-----	4,100	500	93,880
1992	2,296	70,302	15,000	537	5,085	4,500	870	1,200	1,300	600	2,200	500	105,220
1993	2,450	76,801	14,168	480	4,254	4,600	683	1,000	1,500	500	2,000	550	109,790
1994	2,450	84,001	14,500	600	2,400	4,700	700	1,000	1,600	500	2,000	600	115,796
1995	2,450	80,001	15,000	600	2,400	4,700	700	1,000	1,600	500	2,000	650	112,350
1996[1]	2,000	51,000	16,000	1,000	3,000	5,000	-----	1,000	1,000	1,000	2,000	1,000	84,000
1997[2]	2,000	51,000	16,000	1,000	3,000	5,000	-----	1,000	1,000	1,000	2,000	1,000	83,000

[1] Preliminary. [2] Estimate. [3] Formerly part of the U.S.S.R.; data not reported separately until 1992. *Source: Food and Agricultural Organization of the United Nations (FAO-UN)*

World Trade of Silk by Selected Countries In Metric Tons

	Imports							Exports					
Year	France	Hong Kong	India	Italy	Japan	South Korea	World Total	Brazil	China	Hong Kong	Japan	North Korea	World Total
1987	770	6,652	2,100	7,339	8,342	5,582	35,864	648	18,368	7,778	794	1,200	34,886
1988	771	7,489	1,411	8,094	10,259	4,851	39,216	670	20,168	8,553	442	1,200	37,276
1989	1,012	6,362	1,400	7,740	8,512	3,763	35,968	534	19,314	6,748	417	1,100	39,064
1990	796	3,928	1,647	4,775	7,111	3,204	27,322	1,064	13,066	4,102	380	1,200	27,977
1991	579	4,347	2,100	5,297	6,933	3,519	29,623	2,052	15,178	4,186	405	900	29,188
1992	693	4,400	2,843	4,337	5,137	3,627	28,239	1,552	13,474	4,358	701	800	26,433
1993	1,001	5,475	4,977	5,634	5,982	4,494	36,086	1,495	15,652	7,204	904	1,200	35,634
1994	1,047	6,165	5,750	9,235	5,772	4,128	44,136	1,739	21,004	6,149	1,265	1,400	41,998
1995	663	4,775	4,276	5,612	4,331	3,513	37,135	966	16,788	5,176	925	1,000	35,671
1996[1]	675	3,978	4,773	4,400	6,098	3,737	NA	1,071	15,791	4,165	946	1,000	NA

[1] Preliminary. *Source: Food and Agricultural Organization of the United Nations (FAO-UN)*

Silver

After holding in a sideways pattern for much of 1999, silver prices staged a strong rally in the second half of September, 1999. Prices increased nearly a dollar an ounce before moving back down to levels seen earlier in the year. The reason for the rally appeared to be developments in the gold market which saw an agreement to limit sales of gold stocks by central banks. After having been under strong selling pressure, gold prices reacted to the news by staging a strong rally though much of the gains were later given back. The rally in silver appeared to be more in sympathy with other precious metals, which moved higher, than with any change in the underlying fundamentals in the silver market.

The U.S. Geological Survey reported that U.S. mine production of recoverable silver in 1998 was 2,060 metric tonnes. This was down 4 percent from the 1997 output of 2,150 tonnes. U.S. mine production of silver has increased. In 1994 production was 1,490 tonnes. In 1998, silver was produced at 76 mines in sixteen states. The largest producer was Nevada followed by Alaska, Arizona and Idaho. Precious metal ores accounted for about one-half of domestic silver production while the other half saw silver recovered as a by-product from the processing of copper, lead and zinc ores.

About 1,700 tonnes were recovered from old and new scrap. There were 22 principal refiners of commercial-grade silver with an estimated output of 3,600 tonnes. About 30 fabricators accounted for more than 90 percent of the silver used in arts and industry. Silver is used primarily for industrial purposes in photographic materials, electrical products, catalysts, brazing alloys, dental products and bearings. Other aesthetic uses for silver are in jewelry, tableware and coins. U.S. apparent consumption of silver in 1998 was 5,240 tonnes, up 5 percent from the year before. At the end of 1998, stocks of silver at the Treasury Department were 400 tonnes, down 17 percent from the year before. The Government continues to dispose of silver held in the National Defense Stockpile. Most of it has been used in the production of commemorative coins. In the sixteen year period between 1982 and the end of September 1999, the Government reduced the amount of silver in the stockpile from 4,300 tonnes to about 1,100 tonnes.

World mine production of silver in 1998 was estimated at 16,200 tonnes, down 1 percent from 1997. The U.S. is a major producer of silver. Mexico's 1998 mine production was estimated at 2,700 tonnes, about the same as in 1997. Production by Peru in 1998 was estimated at 1,900 tonnes, down 9 percent from the year before. Other major producers include Canada and Australia. World reserves are estimated at 33,000 tonnes. About two-thirds of the world's silver resources are in copper, lead and zinc deposits. Remaining resources are in vein deposits where silver is the most valuable component.

U.S. mine production of silver in June 1999 was 170,000 kilograms, up 7 percent from May 1999 but 8 percent less than a year earlier. In the January-June 1999 period, mine production of silver was 983,000 kilograms, up 14 percent from the previous month. In the first six months of 1999, Nevada silver production was 298,000 kilograms, while for all of 1998 it was 670,000 kilograms. Idaho production of silver in June 1999 was 33,400 kilograms, the same as the previous month. For the first half of 1999, production was 201,000 kilograms, while for all of 1998 it was 447,000 kilograms. Arizona silver production in June 1999 was 16,800 kilograms, the same as the previous month. For the first half of 1999, Arizona production was 97,700 kilograms, and for all of 1998 it was 211,000 kilograms.

U.S. imports of silver bullion in May 1999 were 206,000 kilograms. In the January-May 1999 period imports were 1.19 million kilograms while for all of 1998 they were 2.8 million kilograms. The major suppliers were Canada, Mexico and Peru. Imports of silver metal powder in May 1999 were 16,100 kilograms. In the January-May 1999 period metal powder imports were 53,000 kilograms, while for all of 1998 they were 129,000 kilograms. Silver waste and scrap (gross weight) imports in May 1999 were 352,000 kilograms. In the January-May 1999 period imports totaled 861,000 kilograms, while for all of 1998 they were 1.8 million kilograms. The major suppliers were the Netherlands, Canada and Germany.

Futures Markets

Silver futures are traded on the Tokyo Commodity Exchange (TOCOM), the Chicago Board of Trade (CBOT), the Mid America Commodity Exchange (MidAm) and the New York Mercantile Exchange, COMEX division (COMEX). Options are traded on the European Options Exchange (EOE-Optiebeurs), the CBOT and the COMEX.

World Mine Production of Silver In Thousands of Kilograms In Metric Tons

Year	Australia	Bolivia	Canada[3]	Chile	China	Kazak-hstan[4]	Rep. of Korea	Mexico	Peru	Poland	Sweden	United States	World Total[2]
1989	1,075	267	1,371	545	125	2,500	239	2,400	1,840	1,003	228	2,008	16,425
1990	1,173	311	1,501	655	130	2,500	238	2,425	1,930	832	243	2,121	16,600
1991	1,180	376	1,339	678	150	2,200	265	2,295	1,927	899	239	1,860	15,600
1992	1,218	282	1,220	1,029	800	500	333	2,098	1,614	798	210	1,800	14,900
1993	1,092	333	896	970	840	500	215	2,136	1,671	767	255	1,640	14,100
1994	1,045	352	768	983	810	506	257	2,215	1,768	1,064	276	1,490	14,000
1995	939	425	1,285	1,041	910	489	299	2,324	1,929	1,001	268	1,560	14,800
1996	1,013	384	1,309	1,047	1,140	468	254	2,528	1,970	935	272	1,570	14,900
1997[1]	1,106	387	1,224	1,091	1,300	565	268	2,679	1,998	1,000	280	2,180	16,000
1998[2]	1,469	380	1,179	1,340	1,400	470	270	2,686	1,934	1,000	275	2,060	16,400

[1] Preliminary. [2] Estimate. [3] Shipments. [4] Formerly part of the U.S.S.R.; data not reported separately until 1992.

Source: U.S. Geological Survey (USGS)

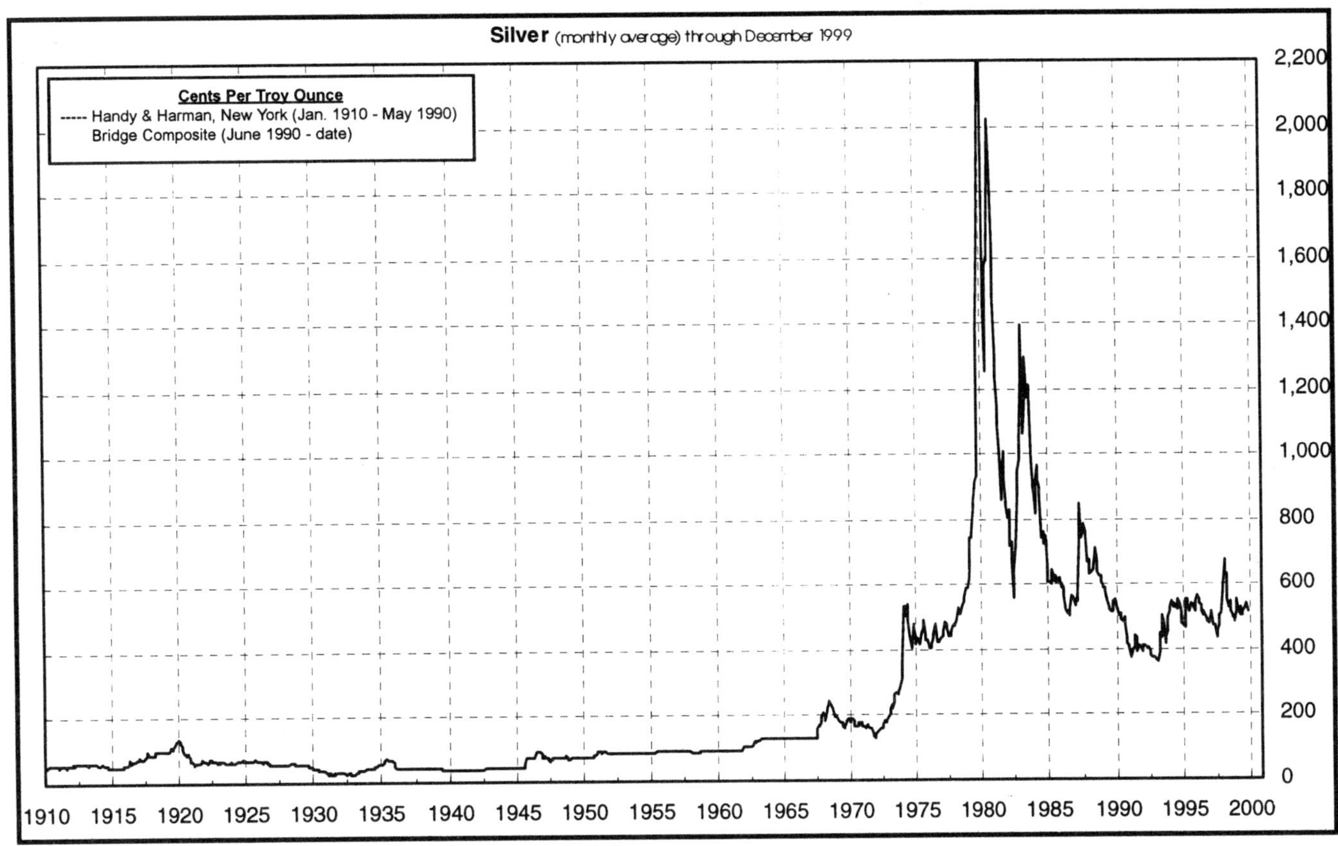

Average Price of Silver in New York (Handy & Harman) In Cents Per Troy Ounce (.999 Fine)

Year	Jan.	Feb.	Mar.	Apr.	May	June	July	Aug.	Sept.	Oct.	Nov.	Dec.	Average
1990	524.30	527.84	505.82	504.58	507.39	490.60	485.90	498.15	479.03	436.59	416.90	406.84	482.00
1991	402.82	372.34	396.90	397.07	404.07	438.85	430.38	393.80	403.60	410.22	406.05	390.90	403.92
1992	412.08	413.71	410.36	403.00	406.83	405.64	394.89	379.67	376.33	373.66	376.32	370.98	393.62
1993	367.93	364.39	364.80	396.36	445.02	437.50	503.74	480.61	417.19	433.45	450.25	496.83	429.84
1994	513.14	527.24	545.11	530.87	543.64	539.34	528.65	519.54	552.88	544.10	519.60	476.88	528.42
1995	476.36	469.53	464.83	552.42	555.25	535.27	517.58	539.59	540.78	534.48	529.30	514.75	519.18
1996	547.03	562.75	551.38	540.14	536.02	513.58	502.95	500.98	510.50	492.76	482.76	479.23	518.34
1997	476.39	508.76	519.88	476.41	475.80	474.60	435.96	451.36	472.69	501.15	506.00	571.53	489.21
1998	584.58	672.61	617.18	628.86	558.65	526.05	546.82	516.45	502.67	500.18	498.39	488.71	553.43
1999	516.21	554.55	519.85	509.21	529.83	507.73	522.81	525.25	527.86	541.67	519.20	521.95	524.68

Source: American Metal Market (AMM)

Average Price of Silver in London (Spot Fix) In Pence Per Troy Ounce (.999 Fine)

Year	Jan.	Feb.	Mar.	Apr.	May	June	July	Aug.	Sept.	Oct.	Nov.	Dec.	Average
1989	337.32	335.09	346.81	341.28	333.69	340.21	322.29	324.61	326.77	323.99	348.64	348.92	335.80
1990	317.67	311.77	312.45	309.08	302.29	287.85	269.56	263.50	255.45	225.76	212.45	210.97	273.23
1991	209.50	190.10	216.00	227.61	234.43	266.86	263.97	235.06	234.22	238.90	229.09	228.03	231.15
1992	227.68	233.21	238.36	230.72	225.02	219.32	206.74	197.03	203.89	226.06	246.94	240.01	224.58
1993	240.39	254.41	249.55	256.16	287.61	289.42	335.27	324.64	276.85	285.48	306.07	332.78	286.55
1994	344.48	354.77	364.74	358.95	360.86	353.28	341.86	336.67	353.15	339.73	326.64	306.49	345.14
1995	302.80	300.36	290.35	341.95	248.74	336.31	323.80	343.72	348.99	340.29	339.90	336.05	329.44
1996	359.20	367.64	362.03	392.85	354.25	334.68	325.81	330.93	322.98	310.78	290.51	289.77	336.79
1997	287.63	311.95	323.99	293.08	291.43	289.16	272.73	280.36	295.67	308.69	300.76	348.90	300.36
1998	359.62	416.55	375.76	378.77	339.42	319.05	331.87	317.74	297.40	295.41	298.72	291.77	335.17

Source: American Metal Market (AMM)

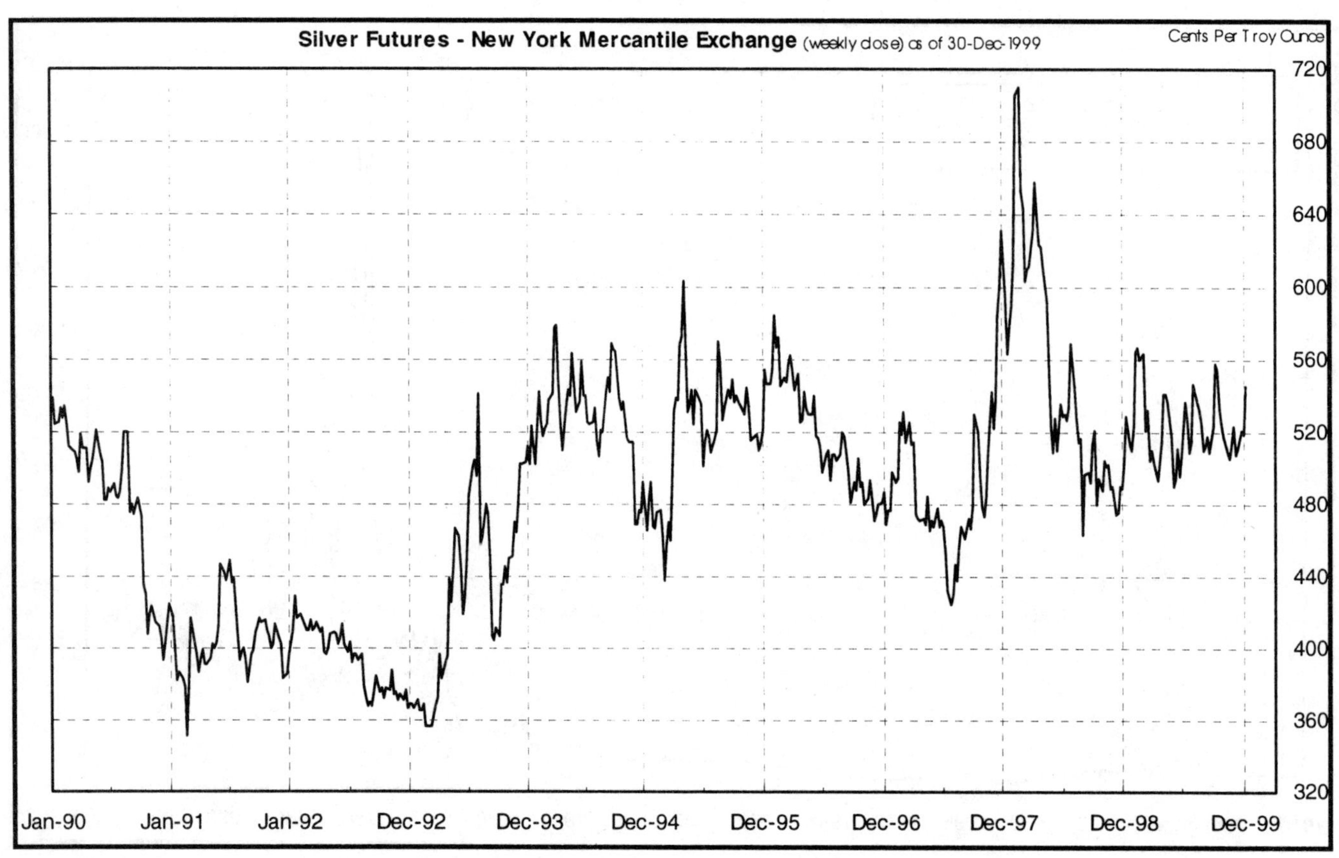

Average Open Interest of Silver Futures in New York (COMEX) In Contracts

Year	Jan.	Feb.	Mar.	Apr.	May	June	July	Aug.	Sept.	Oct.	Nov.	Dec.
1990	94,397	93,713	96,182	96,701	95,784	103,575	99,098	99,668	92,436	91,093	84,181	80,364
1991	91,685	101,352	99,564	99,791	94,921	105,646	97,554	95,536	87,079	90,791	89,765	91,390
1992	97,179	93,352	88,445	96,427	87,355	84,002	80,879	81,695	74,265	72,090	77,633	72,296
1993	80,155	86,241	87,127	100,985	105,931	102,539	107,537	109,427	93,891	93,316	101,576	110,029
1994	112,584	116,652	112,745	119,314	121,296	126,255	122,138	118,081	113,261	117,224	126,666	134,099
1995	132,158	139,806	132,317	129,063	112,723	108,941	101,842	111,251	95,433	101,763	105,453	95,551
1996	99,316	107,667	92,186	101,011	99,529	110,247	105,627	103,618	93,448	95,809	93,238	83,879
1997	91,385	94,539	90,531	97,434	87,510	90,145	96,777	89,250	79,344	100,464	96,695	93,761
1998	95,717	108,284	91,730	83,045	79,451	91,563	78,353	82,530	74,848	74,451	76,440	78,716
1999	77,946	97,593	82,435	82,824	78,745	78,942	78,150	86,601	77,489	86,577	80,563	70,275

Source: New York Mercantile Exchange (NYMEX), COMEX Division

Volume of Trading of Silver Futures in New York (COMEX) In Contracts

Year	Jan.	Feb.	Mar.	Apr.	May	June	July	Aug.	Sept.	Oct.	Nov.	Dec.	Total
1990	343,175	413,287	210,193	364,055	328,804	433,848	242,288	524,815	201,273	308,449	323,664	219,758	3,913,609
1991	309,841	420,092	446,491	395,957	255,548	547,495	344,683	320,639	268,660	252,983	349,698	242,617	4,154,704
1992	408,179	320,226	229,010	322,364	184,825	295,358	197,946	266,347	173,165	125,537	355,728	127,654	3,016,339
1993	167,201	315,916	242,974	476,554	433,460	523,961	503,935	531,772	428,366	338,189	520,591	373,005	4,855,924
1994	489,055	555,136	484,134	585,058	516,396	729,414	339,298	535,722	377,540	455,049	589,220	348,323	5,994,345
1995	390,453	501,454	541,807	592,620	500,522	476,481	280,651	655,854	344,182	272,362	447,095	179,755	5,183,236
1996	415,801	583,767	368,175	547,629	334,973	549,631	296,905	460,686	316,366	321,781	415,441	259,653	4,870,808
1997	401,995	530,514	360,871	493,999	280,536	472,306	340,245	425,471	335,400	430,397	488,024	333,762	4,893,520
1998	352,688	550,800	368,127	360,130	310,130	393,971	278,774	367,257	283,475	280,066	319,216	229,982	4,094,616
1999	315,165	550,271	355,559	424,822	274,002	373,662	288,480	422,653	328,907	318,256	344,289	161,434	4,157,500

Source: New York Mercantile Exchange (NYMEX), COMEX division

Mine Production of Recoverable Silver in the United States In Metric Tons

Year	Arizona	Idaho	Montana	Nevada	Total	Year	Arizona	Idaho	Montana	Nevada	Total
1987	114	NA	185	379	1,241	1993	157	190	125	713	1,610
1988	152	340	192	608	1,661	1994	183	158	71	602	1,390
1989	171	439	194	625	2,007	1995	220	182	76	766	1,640
1990	173	442	220	646	2,125	1996	189	234	11	596	1,570
1991	148	337	222	578	1,848	1997	190	341	W	878	2,180
1992	153	255	195	586	1,740	1998[1]	211	447	W	670	2,060

[1] Preliminary. NA = Not available. *Source: U.S. Geological Survey (USGS)*

Consumption of Silver in the United States, by End Use In Millions of Troy Ounces

Year	Brazing Alloy & Solders	Catalysts	Batteries[2]	Mirrors	Electrical Contacts-Conductors	Photo-graphic Materials[3]	Silver-plate	Jewerly[4]	Sterling Ware	Total Net Industrial Con-sumption	Coinage	Total Con-sumption
1988	NA	2.6	2.5	1.1	23.0	62.5	2.6	2.9	3.5	117.5	7.9	125.4
1989	NA	2.8	2.8	1.1	23.5	65.2	2.7	2.4	3.4	126.0	6.8	132.8
1990	2.8	3.0	3.0	1.2	23.3	67.0	2.8	2.0	3.5	118.2	9.4	131.0
1991	5.6	3.3	3.1	1.1	23.5	65.0	2.8	2.0	3.5	112.3	10.8	130.6
1992	6.5	3.8	3.1	1.2	25.8	63.5	2.9	3.0	3.9	114.5	8.4	131.3
1993	7.2	4.0	3.3	1.3	28.6	64.0	3.0	3.3	4.0	117.4	8.2	135.6
1994	7.7	-----	16.9	-----	31.6	67.8	-----	12.0	-----	136.3	8.7	145.0
1995	8.0	-----	17.9	-----	36.0	70.3	-----	12.5	-----	144.9	8.1	152.9
1996	8.2	-----	18.2	-----	36.3	74.4	-----	12.4	-----	150.2	6.1	156.3
1997[1]	8.4	-----	-----	-----	41.9	79.0	-----	12.5	-----	161.5	5.5	167.0

[1] Preliminary. [2] Beginning 1994, includes Batteries, Catalysts, and Mirrors. [3] Beginning 1994, includes Photographic Materials and Silverplate. [4] Beginning 1994, includes Jewelry and Sterlingware. *Source: The Silver Institute*

Commodity Exchange, Inc. (COMEX) Warehouse of Stocks of Silver In Thousands of Troy Ounces

Year	Jan. 1	Feb. 1	Mar. 1	Apr. 1	May 1	June 1	July 1	Aug. 1	Sept. 1	Oct. 1	Nov. 1	Dec. 1
1990	240,796	243,421	252,104	253,773	255,421	251,626	253,326	255,814	260,184	258,614	257,685	265,339
1991	266,206	263,832	257,851	263,563	263,686	266,087	276,961	270,804	269,661	265,874	262,835	270,734
1992	271,692	278,990	270,449	262,239	267,003	267,818	271,259	273,743	278,575	278,526	280,712	275,156
1993	272,824	273,629	271,856	265,580	270,800	273,947	277,228	278,745	276,819	275,370	277,666	263,138
1994	251,685	250,730	239,374	240,187	233,950	236,459	246,291	249,417	255,198	259,634	265,710	258,618
1995	260,708	264,045	235,114	211,028	189,668	184,570	181,269	175,764	156,544	156,529	156,110	156,932
1996	159,695	143,426	151,336	139,059	141,789	150,141	168,079	155,441	151,283	141,673	129,911	148,451
1997	204,051	195,450	193,381	191,676	189,498	201,682	184,691	169,079	164,296	138,775	133,470	128,252
1998	110,437	103,778	89,458	86,926	89,715	89,628	85,911	79,136	78,681	73,142	74,260	76,818
1999	76,301	75,017	78,135	79,664	79,415	76,976	73,973	77,592	80,126	79,388	78,738	78,416

Source: New York Mercantile Exchange (NYMEX), COMEX Division

Production[2] of Refined Silver in the United States, from All Sources In Metric Tons

Year	Jan.	Feb.	Mar.	Apr.	May	June	July	Aug.	Sept.	Oct.	Nov.	Dec.	Total
1990	278	244	221	271	267	274	256	241	237	249	303	252	3,093
1991	273	209	229	228	285	236	220	254	263	259	250	268	2,973
1992	414	388	396	375	408	295	366	350	323	393	331	364	4,403
1993	359	406	374	357	315	266	293	275	292	293	261	303	3,794
1994	278	327	319	307	209	371	239	288	273	254	297	281	3,443
1995	279	273	340	281	381	355	331	404	364	340	384	351	4,083
1996	373	299	332	321	327	316	354	314	333	344	304	403	4,020
1997	343	262	296	331	250	326	292	344	331	281	340	382	3,778
1998	338	486	426	372	377	374	394	324	463	443	469	447	4,860
1999[1]	423	418	440	355	366	395	405						4,803

[1] Preliminary. [2] Through 1991; output of commercial bars .999 fine, including U.S. Mint purchases of crude. Production is from both foreign and domestic silver. Beginning 1992; U.S. mine production of recoverable silver plus imports of refined silver. *Source: U.S. Geological Survey (USGS)*

SILVER

U.S. Exports of Refined Silver to Selected Countries In Thousands of Troy Ounces

Year	Canada	France	Germany	Hong Kong	Japan	Singapore	South Korea	Switzerland	United Arab Emirates	United Kingdom	Uruguay	Other Countries	World Total
1988	1,073	157	480	20	6,030	[2]	166	70	[2]	4,894	[2]	1,379	14,269
1989	2,597	61	519	3	5,997	2	588	88	[2]	3,722	[2]	251	13,828
1990	2,586	64	749	[2]	16,568	1,005	298	74	[2]	2,060	152	108	23,664
1991	736	22	350	755	6,519	1,593	2,823	8	3,462	8,628	259	73	25,318
1992	2,177	44	140	497	4,554	2,126	[2]	70	6,922	10,856	671	47	29,274
1993	4,910	[2]	34	1,002	3,414	2,500	1,492	38	4,403	3,673	530	44	22,673
1994	3,138	[2]	8	456	10,385	16	2,701	14	4,823	4,212	1,489	14	27,889
1995	1,665	431	[2]	[2]	5,819	2,209	2,932	1,177	10,288	63,980	939	5	90,462
1996	489	[2]	2	646	4,662	3,601	383	2,413	15,850	35,366	624	40	93,346
1997[1]	903	[2]	2	797	6,044	[2]	547	5,305	16,751	62,694	402	17	96,037

[1] Preliminary. [2] Included in other countries, if any. *Source: American Bureau of Metal Statistics, Inc. (ABMS)*

U.S. Imports of Silver From Selected Countries In Thousands of Troy Ounces

Year	Canada	Mexico	Other Countries	Total	Canada	Chile	Mexico	Peru	Uruguay	Other Countries	Total
1988	288	1,511	4,352	6,151	31,361	211	37,471	11	[2]	3,609	72,663
1989	56	129	40	225	37,203	724	53,262	2,761	1,958	2,521	98,429
1990	12	189	2	203	33,518	1,671	40,204	8,141	2,265	942	86,741
1991	42	277	29	348	25,389	6,640	34,448	13,748	[2]	973	81,198
1992	646	126	42	814	24,937	2,002	40,230	16,841	400	2	85,572
1993	299	836	12	1,147	28,622	1,058	27,241	12,709	[2]	28	70,189
1994	369	3,805	97	4,271	28,678	1,923	22,135	12,663	[2]	32	66,141
1995	312	6,269	244	6,825	27,640	4,694	29,200	13,732	[2]	78	84,446
1996	189	3,890	[2]	4,079	30,640	2,424	[2]	9,002	[2]	28	89,034
1997[1]	177	8,938	[2]	9,253	35,687	1,511	31,958	8,970	[2]	180	78,126

[1] Preliminary. [2] Included in other countries, if any. *Source: American Bureau of Metal Statistics, Inc. (ABMS)*

World Silver Consumption[1] In Millions of Troy Ounces

	Industrial Uses										Coinage							
Year	Canada	France	Germany	India	Italy	Japan	Mexico	United Kingdom	United States	World Total	Austria	Canada	France	Germany	Mexico	United States	World Total	Grand Total
1988	11.0	21.3	44.0	22.4	38.0	100.4	7.1	22.8	117.5	580.6	.6	1.1	2.2	3.2	2.0	7.9	17.8	598.5
1989	12.0	22.1	46.7	25.6	43.2	100.8	7.2	24.6	126.0	612.0	.4	3.3	2.2	3.2	1.7	6.8	18.5	630.5
1990	4.6	24.1	51.7	46.8	51.4	106.9	12.9	24.6	121.6	684.6	.5	1.9	2.1	2.6	1.2	9.4	32.1	716.7
1991	3.8	26.0	52.2	44.8	56.5	108.8	13.5	25.0	119.8	677.8	.6	.9	2.3	5.7	1.6	10.8	29.2	707.0
1992	1.5	28.5	49.2	58.1	61.0	104.9	14.2	26.3	122.9	681.2	.5	.8	2.1	5.6	8.7	8.4	33.4	714.6
1993	1.6	27.7	45.6	109.9	57.3	105.5	14.9	27.7	127.4	740.3	.5	1.2	2.1	2.8	17.1	8.2	40.6	780.9
1994	1.6	26.9	45.7	91.8	52.9	108.4	14.6	30.4	136.3	721.1	.5	1.5	1.0	7.1	13.0	8.7	43.0	764.1
1995	2.0	29.7	43.6	98.7	51.0	112.7	16.9	31.6	144.8	750.4	.6	.7	1.1	2.4	.6	8.1	23.8	774.2
1996	2.0	26.6	41.0	128.4	53.1	112.1	20.3	33.8	150.2	791.7	.4	.7	.3	4.6	.5	6.1	22.3	814.0
1997[2]	2.1	28.0	42.3	131.0	57.9	120.0	23.3	34.9	161.5	836.0	.3	.7	.3	3.7	.4	5.5	27.4	863.4

[1] Non-communist areas only. [2] Preliminary. *Source: The Silver Institute*

Soybean Meal

Soybean meal prices, basis Chicago futures, drifted during much of 1999 as they did in 1998, in both years pivoting around the $140.00 per ton area. Into mid-1999, a bearish bias persisted that carried to the $125.00 area; Prices then recovered, but the move lacked conviction and stalled near $160.00.

The world supply and demand situation for soybean meal showed persistent growth through the 1990's, and the pace is likely to quicken in the decade ahead due to the expansion in global poultry numbers. Soybean meal, a high protein feed used in formulating livestock and poultry rations, is obtained from the processing (crushing) of soybeans and is the world's top protein meal with about 60 percent of total production. Cottonseed and rapeseed meal account for a combined total of about 20 percent. The U.S. is the largest producer of soybean meal followed by Brazil and Argentina.

World soybean meal production in the mid-1990's averaged about 88 million metric tonnes. In 1999/2000, a record 106 million metric tonnes were produced, of which the U.S. produced a record large 35.1 million tonnes. Brazil's production proved larger than expected, reaching a record 16.3 million tonnes, however, Argentina's production at 14 million tonnes in 1999/00 was marginally under the previous year's 14.3 million. Part of the growth in meal production has been indirectly derived from the strong worldwide demand for vegetable oils, but the primary reason is that more countries have increasing livestock numbers and a burgeoning need for high protein feed; a fact that is underscored by the sharp expansion in the world's soybean meal trade. Significantly, many of the recent gains in foreign trade have come from developing nations in both Latin America and Asia.

World meal consumption in 1999/00 of a record large 105.9 million tonnes compares with 104.5 million in 1998/99. The U.S. is the largest single consumer using about 28 million tonnes, but the European Union and Asia run a close second each using 26 million tonnes in 1999/00. Asia's use was particularly strong during the past decade reflecting the growth in the region's poultry production. China's 1999/00 consumption of 10.5 million tonnes compares with an annual average of less than 10 million prior to 1996/97, but the current year's use lags the record 12.8 million tonnes in 1997/98.

China's imports have dropped, totaling 1.3 million tonnes in 1999/00 vs. 1.45 in 1998/99 and a record large 4.2 million in 1997/98. Still, earlier in the 1990's, China was a net exporter of soybean meal. France, in 1999/00, was the largest single importer with 4 million tonnes, nearly 10 percent of the world total.

Exports are dominated by Argentina and Brazil with a combined 24 million tonnes in 1999/00 out of a 40 million tonne total. World carryover at the end of the 1999/00 season is forecast at 3.9 million tonnes, marginally lower than a year earlier. As usual, Argentina and Brazil account for at least a third of the carryover.

U.S. soybean meal production (October-September) in 1999/00 of a record 38.7 million (short) tons compares with 37.9 million in 1998/99. Total 1999/00 supplies of 39 million tons compares with 38.2 million in 1998/99, including a small carry-in at the start of each crop year. Total supplies in the early 1990's averaged near 30 million tons. Domestic usage climbed steadily in the 1990's and is expected to total a record high 31 million tons in 1999/00 vs. 30.6 million in 1998/99, due primarily to increases in poultry production. It now appears that poultry demand controls the U.S. soybean crush, not demand for soybean oil. Cattle accounts for a minor amount of soybean meal usage, hogs slightly more.

U.S. soybean meal exports in 1999/00 were forecast at 7.8 million metric tonnes vs. 7.3 million in 1998/99 and a record large 9.3 million in 1997/98; the decline from the latter reflecting smaller demand from China and increased competition from Brazil and Argentina.

U.S. soybean meal prices, basis 48 percent protein, Decatur, Illinois, were expected to average between $145-$170.00 per short ton in 1999/00 vs. $138.50 in 1998/99.

Futures Markets

Soybean meal futures and options are traded on the Chicago Board of Trade. A smaller futures contract is traded on the Mid-America Commodity Exchange.

World Supply and Distribution of Soybean Meal In Thousands of Metric Tons

Year Beginning Oct. 1	Production					Exports			Imports		Consumption			Ending Stocks		
	Brazil	China	EC-12	United States	Total	Brazil	United States	Total	France	Total	EC-12	United States	Total	Brazil	United States	Total
1990-1	11,160	3,280	9,950	25,700	69,660	8,200	4,960	26,840	3,430	27,020	20,190	20,810	70,170	860	260	3,650
1991-2	11,740	2,750	10,530	27,060	73,200	8,780	6,300	28,620	3,550	28,250	21,170	20,870	73,360	520	210	3,140
1992-3	12,170	3,630	10,980	27,550	76,450	8,170	5,650	27,550	3,500	27,870	22,240	22,000	76,150	600	190	3,760
1993-4	14,500	6,160	9,850	27,680	81,280	10,310	4,860	29,950	3,800	29,470	22,680	22,940	80,920	940	140	3,970
1994-5	15,870	6,960	11,490	30,180	87,430	10,450	6,090	30,920	3,790	31,430	24,380	24,080	87,470	980	200	4,440
1995-6	17,040	6,050	10,910	29,510	88,970	11,940	5,450	33,810	3,340	32,590	22,650	24,140	87,920	970	190	4,310
1996-7	15,720	6,950	11,620	31,040	91,660	10,660	6,350	33,980	3,270	34,170	22,050	24,780	92,420	840	190	3,770
1997-8	15,730	8,580	12,100	34,630	100,160	9,620	8,460	37,050	3,900	37,180	23,890	26,210	100,340	940	200	3,720
1998-9[1]	16,600	9,450	12,140	34,290	105,870	10,300	6,460	39,130	3,900	38,480	26,230	27,820	104,540	840	300	4,400
1999-00[2]	16,510	9,600	11,920	34,510	106,210	9,740	6,350	38,730	4,060	37,850	26,150	28,260	106,010	800	250	3,720

[1] Preliminary. [2] Forecast. *Source: Foreign Agricultural Service, U.S. Department of Agriculture (FAS-USDA)*

SOYBEAN MEAL

Average Open Interest of Soybean Meal Futures in Chicago In Contracts

Year	Jan.	Feb.	Mar.	Apr.	May	June	July	Aug.	Sept.	Oct.	Nov.	Dec.
1990	60,010	71,773	74,762	76,897	77,307	69,658	63,824	62,033	58,915	68,888	76,899	70,901
1991	62,172	60,017	56,179	59,107	49,973	57,068	55,629	54,342	67,765	68,627	68,263	71,900
1992	67,575	56,453	55,370	59,528	57,204	60,519	66,315	66,861	66,648	72,403	73,255	72,881
1993	63,178	70,384	64,550	66,121	78,386	74,191	91,435	73,770	75,267	77,065	83,802	85,039
1994	87,612	91,142	82,193	89,453	85,553	81,721	84,461	82,691	85,508	94,483	101,030	98,717
1995	97,661	101,253	101,846	99,898	90,237	86,090	83,712	74,233	79,450	85,290	103,824	110,193
1996	95,903	90,010	87,468	101,204	91,453	88,641	77,961	80,727	93,373	88,969	90,007	84,399
1997	86,204	97,618	107,763	111,413	113,848	110,780	114,372	108,923	111,447	118,409	125,201	116,760
1998	114,243	122,979	131,390	137,251	136,212	136,216	126,108	139,239	140,904	141,426	134,095	122,788
1999	123,041	130,473	121,435	112,155	104,176	108,133	116,463	121,202	120,461	112,312	117,522	104,245

Source: Chicago Board of Trade (CBT)

Volume of Trading of Soybean Meal Futures in Chicago In Contracts

Year	Jan.	Feb.	Mar.	Apr.	May	June	July	Aug.	Sept.	Oct.	Nov.	Dec.	Total[1]
1990	308,579	276,395	400,206	428,351	421,021	398,333	460,165	436,320	401,620	476,265	448,686	448,530	4,904.5
1991	323,403	281,772	310,004	429,281	296,782	412,475	484,290	463,616	394,712	410,790	351,607	339,555	4,498.3
1992	368,714	290,492	312,556	312,187	388,097	380,975	425,995	333,639	327,556	320,176	327,854	357,156	4,145.4
1993	295,555	273,673	346,607	323,253	356,757	518,212	575,510	460,550	402,399	315,643	469,343	380,593	4,718.1
1994	405,590	339,834	330,694	380,736	467,223	456,279	384,508	354,372	366,263	317,438	370,377	420,500	4,593.8
1995	283,623	307,477	404,387	410,860	532,694	479,589	610,833	491,775	481,949	449,009	523,440	625,606	5,601.2
1996	496,414	442,937	435,764	655,984	439,212	442,370	507,240	490,349	425,850	581,126	491,917	452,139	5,861.3
1997	479,001	481,841	509,515	576,564	581,886	569,760	579,748	452,188	531,299	589,542	561,133	512,471	6,424.9
1998	458,519	454,310	449,806	592,614	499,468	749,765	675,104	536,650	504,088	553,224	521,231	559,067	6,553.8
1999	420,240	509,348	476,104	477,102	390,527	646,806	710,110	597,026	568,859	511,503	572,194	447,078	6,326.9

[1] In thousands of contracts. *Source: Chicago Board of Trade (CBT)*

Supply and Distribution of Soybean Meal in the United States In Thousands of Short Tons

Year Beginning Oct. 1	Supply: For Stocks Oct. 1	Supply: Production	Supply: Total Supply	Distribution: Domestic	Distribution: Exports	Distribution: Total	$ Per Ton Decatur 48% Protein Solvent	$ Per Metric Ton: Decatur 44% Protein Solvent	$ Per Metric Ton: Brazil FOB 45-46% Protein	$ Per Metric Ton: Rotterdam CIF
1990-1	318	28,325	28,688	22,934	5,469	28,403	181.40	187	178	198
1991-2	285	29,831	30,183	23,008	6,945	29,953	189.20	194	184	203
1992-3	230	30,364	30,687	24,251	6,232	30,483	193.75	201	185	207
1993-4	204	30,514	30,788	25,282	5,356	30,638	192.86	199	182	202
1994-5	150	33,269	33,483	26,542	6,717	33,260	162.55	167	172	184
1995-6	223	32,527	32,826	26,611	6,002	32,613	236.00	248	256	256
1996-7	212	34,211	34,525	27,321	6,994	34,316	270.90	286	289	278
1997-8[1]	210	38,176	38,442	28,894	9,330	38,224	185.54	193	201	197
1998-9[2]	218	37,793	38,109	30,662	7,117	37,779	138.50	145	150	150
1999-00[3]	330	38,120	38,500	31,150	7,100	38,250	140-165	162	177	173

[1] Preliminary. [2] Estimate. [3] Forecast. *Source: Economic Research Service, U.S. Department of Agriculture (ERS-USDA)*

U.S. Exports of Soybean Cake & Meal by Country of Destination In Thousands of Metric Tons

Year	Algeria	Australia	Canada	Dominican Republic	Italy	Japan	Mexico	Netherlands	Philippines	Russia[2]	Spain	Venezuela	Total
1989	389.1	7.7	569.2	66.2	188.6	10.8	269.5	269.0	59.1	1,417.9	44.2	283.8	4,712
1990	373.5	28.2	555.5	130.5	146.4	20.8	253.0	229.7	200.7	1,568.4	19.6	332.2	4,826
1991	323.5	99.4	651.2	142.6	33.5	24.1	303.6	339.8	150.4	2,271.0	5.5	405.9	5,536
1992	237.8	75.9	582.5	146.7	93.4	167.2	454.4	420.0	434.8	765.1	92.3	473.8	6,236
1993	266.1	90.6	646.7	200.8	91.5	208.7	187.8	580.8	295.7	697.1	203.8	425.0	5,536
1994	248.3	247.0	706.3	209.2	27.1	76.9	367.5	465.6	257.9	159.5	92.6	258.9	4,825
1995	216.7	190.2	798.7	219.2	70.2	246.7	340.0	751.6	593.4	11.1	127.7	181.4	5,890
1996	203.4	156.2	687.3	260.7	85.9	225.5	292.2	453.5	423.2	5.1	51.8	274.9	5,860
1997	250.8	134.1	651.6	261.1	284.1	263.0	142.1	451.2	483.1	8.3	329.1	336.7	6,994
1998[1]	263.2	135.5	774.7	221.2	217.6	265.7	127.8	274.6	758.7	-----	296.2	446.2	8,035

[1] Preliminary. [2] Formerly part of the U.S.S.R.; data not reported separately until 1992. *Source: The Oil World*

Production of Soybean Cake & Meal[2] in the United States In Thousands of Short Tons

Year	Oct.	Nov.	Dec.	Jan.	Feb.	Mar.	Apr.	May	June	July	Aug.	Sept.	Total	Yield in lbs.
1990-1	2,508.8	2,513.2	2,431.5	-----	7,082.0	-----	-----	6,640.8	-----	-----	7,148.9	-----	28,325	47.47
1991-2	-----	7,920.4	-----	2,665.5	2,393.8	2,544.4	2,411.3	2,262.5	2,372.4	2,434.2	2,429.0	2,397.3	29,831	47.51
1992-3	2,698.1	2,697.3	2,763.4	2,781.2	2,430.4	2,691.3	2,519.1	2,536.3	2,373.0	2,324.1	2,188.3	2,361.8	30,364	47.54
1993-4	2,707.1	2,714.8	2,696.7	2,632.3	2,458.1	2,696.3	2,510.0	2,446.4	2,330.7	2,398.0	2,406.6	2,517.1	30,514	47.62
1994-5	2,812.5	2,903.5	3,027.8	3,007.5	2,755.0	3,048.5	2,829.8	2,697.9	2,492.1	2,565.4	2,589.8	2,535.8	33,269	47.33
1995-6	2,893.2	2,948.9	2,972.3	2,945.2	2,652.1	2,757.5	2,683.1	2,534.6	2,566.2	2,656.3	2,513.4	2,404.1	32,527	47.69
1996-7	2,992.8	3,151.8	3,263.8	3,251.7	2,966.8	3,089.1	2,709.1	2,618.1	2,573.2	2,517.4	2,465.2	2,611.0	34,211	47.36
1997-8	3,344.0	3,390.6	3,624.2	3,596.0	3,278.9	3,478.1	3,172.1	2,956.2	2,794.7	2,941.0	2,665.0	2,930.0	38,171	47.41
1998-9	3,365.1	3,368.4	3,422.4	3,213.9	3,027.3	3,302.2	3,043.7	3,024.0	2,843.6	3,011.5	3,003.0	3,167.4	37,793	47.25
1999-00[1]	3,572.9	3,399.9											41,837	

[1] Preliminary. [2] At oil mills; including millfeed and lecithin. *Sources: Economic Research Service, U.S. Department of Agriculture (ERS-USDA)*

Stocks (at Oil Mills)[2] of Soybean Cake & Meal in the U.S., on First of Month In Thousands of Short Tons

Year	Oct.	Nov.	Dec.	Jan.	Feb.	Mar.	Apr.	May	June	July	Aug.	Sept.
1990-1	318.3	290.9	313.6	-----	455.8	-----	-----	527.8	-----	-----	425.0	-----
1991-2	-----	285.0	-----	281.0	258.3	291.3	315.6	310.4	310.2	274.7	260.5	209.9
1992-3	230.0	307.9	411.3	360.8	440.0	420.5	336.9	268.5	328.4	257.3	386.1	353.8
1993-4	204.4	375.1	282.3	290.1	230.0	283.1	277.3	333.0	325.2	254.3	267.5	144.9
1994-5	149.6	240.9	231.6	241.1	197.7	227.1	173.1	382.7	337.6	222.6	252.0	203.8
1995-6	223.4	196.9	241.3	394.8	302.2	229.9	369.3	382.1	306.8	406.2	298.8	218.3
1996-7	212.4	200.2	291.8	254.4	263.0	198.5	322.6	280.1	256.5	317.3	303.2	257.4
1997-8	206.6	218.2	412.2	262.0	269.3	280.7	238.0	210.4	290.2	193.1	205.3	187.2
1998-9	218.1	271.9	352.3	313.9	380.5	436.4	341.0	316.0	447.7	284.2	394.8	279.4
1999-00[1]	330.2	467.6										

[1] Preliminary. [2] Including millfeed and lecithin. *Source: Economic Research Service, U.S. Department of Agriculture (ERS-USDA)*

SOYBEAN MEAL

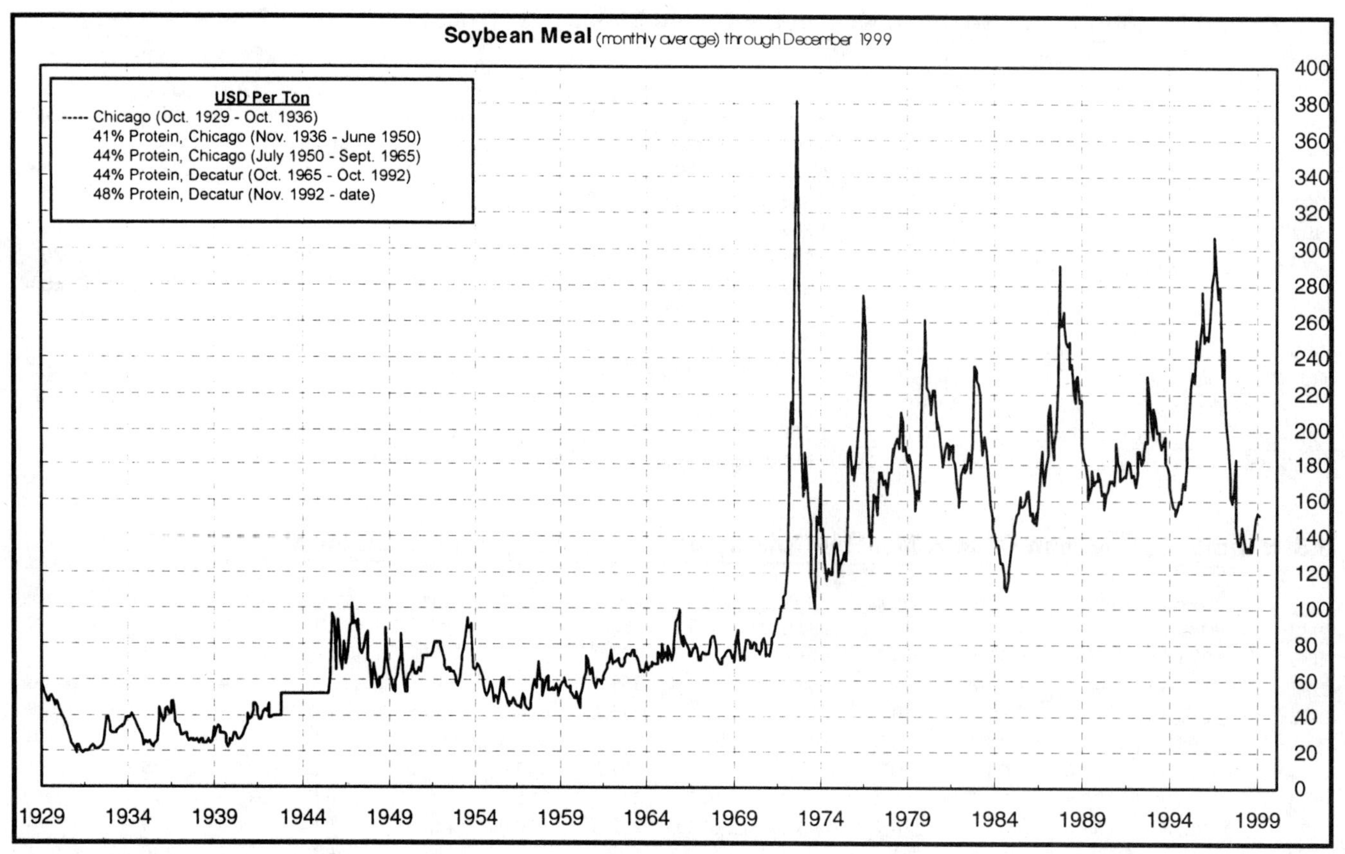

Average Price of Soybean Meal (44% Solvent) in Decatur Illinois In Dollars Per Short Ton -- Bulk

Year	Oct.	Nov.	Dec.	Jan.	Feb.	Mar.	Apr.	May	June	July	Aug.	Sept.	Average
1989-90	191.60	183.40	179.40	172.30	161.90	165.10	165.40	176.20	169.10	171.30	172.40	176.90	173.75
1990-1	172.50	163.80	164.80	153.70	163.50	165.75	171.50	171.00	171.10	169.70	177.60	191.90	169.74
1991-2	183.00	178.00	170.70	172.70	174.30	174.20	174.80	182.75	181.70	173.90	174.40	175.10	176.30
1992-3	168.60	170.90	176.40	175.60	167.50	172.40	175.60	181.70	181.30	217.60	206.90	186.50	181.75
1993-4	180.60	195.70	192.50	185.90	184.40	182.00	176.40	191.10	183.00	168.10	165.60	162.50	180.65
1994-5	156.40	150.90	145.40	145.10	149.40	145.70	151.00	148.10	149.10	160.10	157.50	171.75	152.54
1995-6	183.40	194.10	213.60	220.50	216.70	215.70	237.90	232.30	227.90	242.30	251.10	265.50	225.08
1996-7	238.00	242.70	240.90	240.70	253.60	270.40	277.70	296.00	275.90	261.49	261.60	265.70	260.39
1997-8	216.00	231.60	214.90	193.10	182.10	165.30	152.75	150.30	157.80	173.30	135.70	126.90	174.98
1998-9	129.40	139.30	139.60	139.70	133.70	133.20	135.50	133.20	137.40	134.58	140.34	150.23	137.18

Source: Economic Research Service, U.S. Department of Agriculture (ERS-USDA)

Average Price of Soybean Meal (48% Solvent) in Decatur Illinois In Dollars Per Short Ton -- Bulk

Year	Oct.	Nov.	Dec.	Jan.	Feb.	Mar.	Apr.	May	June	July	Aug.	Sept.	Average
1990-1	185.40	174.25	175.90	167.00	174.50	177.60	182.50	182.10	183.25	181.00	188.75	204.25	181.40
1991-2	196.30	190.25	183.10	184.00	185.40	185.90	187.20	195.25	203.90	186.25	186.00	187.00	189.20
1992-3	180.60	181.90	187.60	188.75	179.90	183.60	187.40	193.25	193.10	229.90	219.10	199.90	193.75
1993-4	194.50	209.40	206.00	198.30	198.40	195.40	188.90	193.75	195.50	181.10	178.60	174.50	192.86
1994-5	168.50	161.00	156.90	156.40	151.30	156.90	161.90	159.10	160.40	170.45	166.70	180.99	162.55
1995-6	193.90	204.10	223.60	232.00	228.30	226.57	249.30	244.30	238.80	252.50	261.20	276.40	235.90
1996-7	248.50	251.50	250.60	249.20	262.40	280.50	288.60	306.40	287.90	273.60	273.30	278.30	270.90
1997-8	229.30	245.30	222.50	202.85	192.75	174.20	162.50	160.00	168.55	183.40	146.25	135.80	185.28
1998-9	135.70	144.45	146.40	138.80	132.30	133.00	134.50	133.20	139.10	132.70	141.70	150.65	138.54
1999-00	153.57	154.70	154.00	163.41									156.42

Source: Economic Research Service, U.S. Department of Agriculture (ERS-USDA)

Soybean Oil

Throughout the 1990's, the world supply and demand situation for soybean oil showed a continuous progression of new record highs. World production in 1999/2000 of a record 24 million metric tonnes compares with the previous year's 23.9 million. The U.S., the world's largest soybean oil producer, generally accounts for about a third of total production. Brazil, the world's second largest producer, typically accounts for about 16 percent of the world total. Of the important edible vegetable oils, soybean oil is the world's largest with about 28 percent of the edible oil market in 1999/00, followed by palm oil and rapeseed oil. World usage of soybean oil in 1999/00 of a record 23.9 million tonnes equals consumption in 1998/99. The U.S. is the largest consumer with China a distant second. World carryover stocks at the end of 1999/00 were estimated at 2.3 million tonnes, unchanged from a year earlier. Nearly a third of the total carryover is in the U.S.

Global soybean oil exports in 1999/00 were estimated at 7.1 million tonnes vs. the previous year's record high 7.5 million tonnes. Argentina is the largest exporter with nearly 3 million tonnes in 1999/00. Importing nations are numerous with China now the largest single importer, 1.2 million tonnes in 1999/00, up slightly from 1998/99.

The U.S. soybean oil crop year begins October 1. The oil content of U.S. soybeans correlates directly with temperatures and sunshine during the pod-filling stages. Production in 1999/00 of a record high 18.3 billion pounds was a shade over the 1998/99 total. During the first half of the 1990's production averaged about 14 billion pounds. Carry-in stocks on October 1, 1999 were estimated at 1.6 billion pounds vs. 1.4 billion a year earlier. The U.S. supply for 1999/00 of a record high 20 billion pounds compares with 19.6 billion in 1998/99. Disappearance in 1999/00 of 17.9 billion pounds compares with 18 billion in 1998/99. Soybean oil stocks were forecast to build during 1999/00, lifting the yearend carryover to about 2.1 billion pounds vs. the record high 2.2 billion carryover on October 1, 1992.

Domestic soybean oil usage in 1999/00 is forecast at a record high 15.9 billion pounds vs. 15.6 billion in 1998/99 as domestic prices should prove competitive to other fats and oils. However, export pricing was not as favorable. U.S. exports of 2 billion pounds compare with 2.4 billion in 1998/99 and the decade's record high of nearly 2.7 billion in 1994/95.

Crude soybean oil prices (basis Decatur) in 1998/99 averaged $436.00 per metric tonne vs. $569.00 in 1998/98.

Futures Markets

Soybean oil futures and options are traded on the Chicago Board of Trade.

World Supply and Demand of Soybean Oil In Thousands of Metric Tons

Year	Production				Exports			Imports		Consumption					Stocks[3]	
Beginning Oct. 1	Brazil	EC-12	United States	Total	Brazil	United States	Total	India	Total	Brazil	EC-12	India	United States	Total	United States	Total
1990-1	2,679	2,230	6,082	15,917	686	356	3,034	24	3,036	2,157	1,656	372	5,515	15,853	810	2,055
1991-2	2,815	2,337	6,507	16,851	658	748	3,558	100	3,487	2,167	1,703	442	5,554	16,366	1,016	2,470
1992-3	2,910	2,540	6,250	17,220	690	640	4,210	40	3,900	2,280	2,000	560	5,920	17,230	710	2,010
1993-4	3,470	2,240	6,330	18,250	1,350	690	4,850	40	4,740	2,320	1,850	710	5,870	18,400	500	1,720
1994-5	3,800	2,580	7,080	19,740	1,490	1,220	5,920	60	6,130	2,470	1,920	560	5,860	19,460	520	2,210
1995-6	4,030	2,470	6,910	20,150	1,600	450	5,280	60	5,290	2,530	1,950	770	6,110	19,730	910	2,640
1996-7	3,720	2,630	7,150	20,660	1,290	920	6,040	50	6,940	2,600	1,800	710	6,470	20,650	690	2,550
1997-8	3,740	2,760	8,230	22,830	1,180	1,400	6,990	240	6,800	2,730	1,600	1,100	6,920	22,540	630	2,660
1998-9[1]	3,930	2,700	8,200	24,260	1,500	1,080	7,910	830	7,790	2,730	1,710	1,800	7,100	24,490	690	2,300
1999-00[2]	3,910	2,620	8,200	24,170	1,300	750	7,370	750	7,400	2,800	1,650	1,580	7,210	24,130	970	2,370

[1] Preliminary. [2] Forecast. [3] End of season. *Source: Foreign Agricultural Service, U.S. Department of Agriculture (FAS-USDA)*

Supply and Distribution of Soybean Oil in the United States In Millions of Pounds

					Domestic Disappearance									
						Food					Non-Food			
Year Beginning Oct. 1	Production	Imports	Stocks Oct. 1	Exports	Total Domestic	Shortening	Margarine	Cooking & Salad Oils	Other Edible	Total Food	Paint & Varnish	Resins & Plastics	Total Non-Food	Total Disappearance
1990-1	13,408	17	1,305	780	12,164	4,090	1,811	4,693	130	10,722	49	106	295	12,944
1991-2	14,345	1	1,786	1,648	12,245	4,091	1,911	4,961	148	11,112	46	98	301	13,893
1992-3	13,778	10	2,239	1,419	13,054	4,465	1,970	4,717	254	11,505	38	95	296	14,473
1993-4	13,951	68	1,555	1,529	12,942	4,773	1,840	4,999	221	11,832	46	115	304	14,471
1994-5	15,613	17	1,103	2,680	12,916	4,714	1,693	5,546	222	12,175	49	124	287	15,597
1995-6	15,240	95	1,137	992	13,465	4,702	1,699	5,317	159	11,877	48	119	297	14,457
1996-7	15,752	53	2,015	2,037	14,264	4,578	1,667	6,119	68	12,432	51	132	333	16,300
1997-8	18,143	60	1,520	3,077	15,264	4,688	1,623	6,188	78	12,576	49	128	490	18,341
1998-9[1]	18,081	83	1,382	2,374	15,653	4,842	1,590	6,191	120	12,743	37	117	576	18,027
1999-00[2]	18,080	80	1,520	1,650	15,900						46	94	575	17,550

[1] Preliminary . [2] Forecast. *Source: Economic Research Service, U.S. Department of Agriculture (ERS-USDA)*

SOYBEAN OIL

Stocks of Crude Soybean Oil in the United States, at End of Month In Millions of Pounds

Crop Year	Oct.	Nov.	Dec.	Jan.	Feb.	Mar.	Apr.	May	June	July	Aug.	Sept.
1994-5	850.8	811.4	826.6	880.6	876.7	838.3	860.5	893.9	885.9	906.3	895.3	905.7
1995-6	990.4	908.9	1,154.3	1,237.4	1,264.2	1,366.6	1,490.1	1,531.7	1,672.4	1,951.4	1,874.3	1,799.3
1996-7	1,796.5	1,711.6	1,805.1	1,928.5	1,982.6	1,938.2	1,929.9	1,919.4	1,917.8	1,760.3	1,492.8	1,321.1
1997-8	1,307.0	1,303.6	1,439.8	1,518.8	1,459.1	1,498.6	1,533.3	1,577.6	1,451.7	1,535.9	1,240.1	1,167.4
1998-9	1,195.0	1,142.0	1,041.1	1,066.2	1,209.5	1,318.6	1,462.0	1,499.5	1,411.8	1,441.8	1,417.8	1,316.1
1999-00[1]	1,378.3	1,422.9	1,516.5	1,741.8								

[1] Preliminary. *Source: Bureau of the Census, U.S. Department of Commerce*

Stocks of Refined Soybean Oil in the United States, at End of Month In Millions of Pounds

Crop Year	Oct.	Nov.	Dec.	Jan.	Feb.	Mar.	Apr.	May	June	July	Aug.	Sept.
1994-5	204.7	215.5	231.7	236.2	252.1	221.3	229.1	236.5	225.8	235.7	204.7	231.0
1995-6	205.5	223.1	254.6	275.2	257.2	287.0	257.3	227.2	216.1	205.1	217.1	216.1
1996-7	196.4	186.8	222.0	243.8	220.6	233.1	233.9	223.9	220.1	217.8	207.1	199.0
1997-8	218.6	221.9	239.8	269.1	252.1	264.0	324.3	279.4	260.9	243.2	213.0	215.0
1998-9	221.7	264.4	246.5	246.7	296.1	289.0	254.2	267.8	235.6	229.4	213.0	203.4
1999-00[1]	238.1	240.7	250.0	262.2								

[1] Preliminary. *Source: Bureau of the Census, U.S. Department of Commerce*

U.S. Exports of Soybean Oil[1], by Country of Destination In Metric Tons

Year Beginning Oct. 1	Canada	Ecuador	Ethiopia	Haiti	India	Mexico	Morocco	Pakistan	Panama	Peru	Turkey	Venezuela	Total
1988-9	5,364	30,930	8,960	2,846	28,127	17,730	80,023	453,067	6,695	5,778	0	29,055	753,576
1989-90	5,443	26,314	22,858	1,688	16,391	4,435	77,985	309,502	3,174	5,206	0	8,198	613,902
1990-1	3,790	20,832	14,948	4,946	13,544	11,087	73,255	66,209	8,123	6,566	16,460	0	353,959
1991-2	11,153	528	19,619	4,737	67,577	23,383	127,602	250	11,143	32,696	81,976	13	747,465
1992-3	28,585	17	8,272	6,753	49,452	44,194	57,995	-----	641	36,340	58,436	0	643,796
1993-4	4,401	0	24,509	1,747	46,846	18,499	31,563	72,204	248	24,081	34,920	26	693,697
1994-5	24,886	12,698	8,391	49,793	28,949	58,623	29,053	25,500	13,342	8,692	5,750	2,016	1,215,804
1995-6	43,912	1,155	4,546	15,041	20,841	46,643	-----	-----	9,512	35,999	1,960	1,877	449,876
1996-7[2]	60,318	6,587	19,492	36,436	26,675	81,901	46,682	-----	3,623	37,726	6,952	517	923,871

[1] Crude & Refined oil combined as such. [2] Preliminary. *Source: Economic Research Service, U.S. Department of Agriculture (ERS-USDA)*

Production of Crude Soybean Oil in the United States In Millions of Pounds

Year	Oct.	Nov.	Dec.	Jan.	Feb.	Mar.	Apr.	May	June	July	Aug.	Sept.	Total
1991-2	-----	3,772	-----	1,270	1,147	1,228	1,167	1,096	1,152	1,177	1,179	1,158	14,345
1992-3	1,238	1,200	1,239	1,247	1,102	1,216	1,148	1,152	1,083	1,070	1,006	1,078	13,778
1993-4	1,241	1,228	1,218	1,192	1,122	1,231	1,155	1,123	1,070	1,099	1,104	1,168	13,951
1994-5	1,328	1,342	1,403	1,400	1,289	1,419	1,333	1,275	1,183	1,205	1,228	1,208	15,613
1995-6	1,354	1,360	1,382	1,360	1,236	1,292	1,259	1,197	1,221	1,263	1,171	1,139	15,234
1996-7	1,401	1,430	1,473	1,474	1,348	1,413	1,254	1,216	1,196	1,176	1,141	1,231	15,752
1997-8	1,591	1,580	1,689	1,685	1,558	1,655	1,526	1,418	1,337	1,409	1,285	1,410	18,143
1998-9	1,598	1,598	1,611	1,528	1,439	1,587	1,453	1,451	1,383	1,452	1,453	1,529	18,081
1999-00[1]	1,688	1,597	1,600										19,537

[1] Preliminary. *Source: Economic Research Service, U.S. Department of Agriculture (ERS-USDA)*

Production of Refined Soybean Oil in the United States In Millions of Pounds

Year	Oct.	Nov.	Dec.	Jan.	Feb.	Mar.	Apr.	May	June	July	Aug.	Sept.	Total
1991-2	-----	2,918.1	-----	933.8	876.7	1,041.3	973.1	993.3	977.9	979.2	997.6	1,040.7	11,732
1992-3	1,095.6	999.4	951.0	960.1	935.4	1,054.9	1,039.7	950.6	1,042.8	978.2	1,066.7	1,109.7	12,184
1993-4	1,094.3	1,053.5	1,030.8	960.1	945.5	1,056.6	1,018.5	1,012.0	1,017.3	968.0	1,107.2	1,044.6	12,308
1994-5	1,123.0	1,079.2	1,060.6	1,002.5	968.2	1,063.6	1,010.4	1,077.0	993.5	940.9	1,076.8	1,039.8	12,435
1995-6	1,119.2	1,088.8	1,018.5	979.9	934.3	1,042.6	997.3	1,009.3	962.8	971.9	1,115.8	1,058.7	12,299
1996-7	1,111.7	1,064.1	1,025.7	969.8	931.5	1,057.1	1,023.7	1,026.2	984.8	1,019.1	1,094.3	1,072.5	12,381
1997-8	1,173.9	1,156.3	1,110.1	1,092.6	1,047.4	1,148.2	1,094.8	1,140.7	1,053.1	1,083.9	1,173.4	1,114.5	13,389
1998-9	1,200.6	1,108.8	1,042.2	1,016.7	976.7	1,138.2	1,073.2	1,087.7	1,060.7	1,058.6	1,122.6	1,116.2	13,002
1999-00[1]	1,201.1	1,195.2	1,150.4	1,056.9									13,811

[1] Preliminary. *Source: Bureau of the Census, U.S. Department of Commerce*

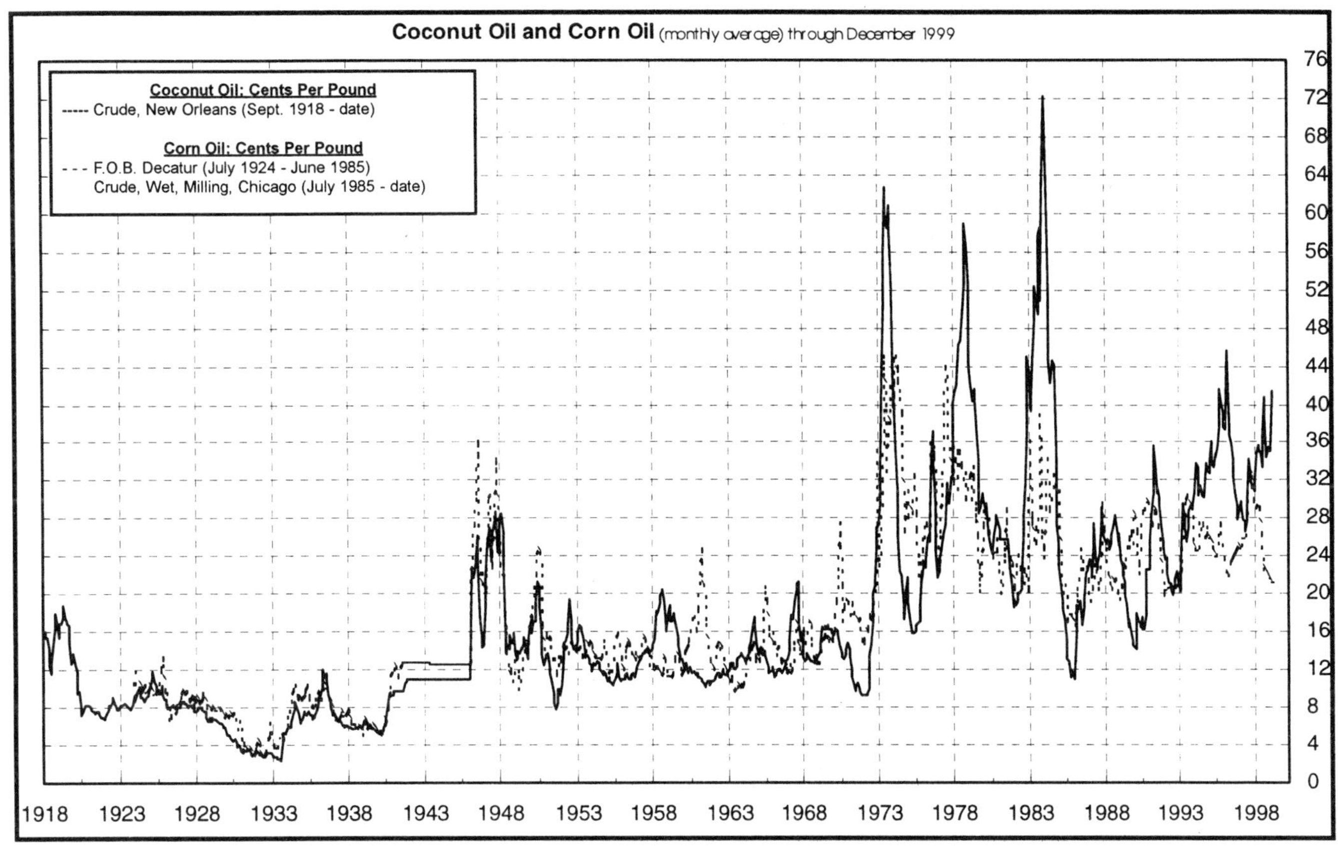

Consumption of Soybean Oil in End Products in the United States In Millions of Pounds

Year	Jan.	Feb.	Mar.	Apr.	May	June	July	Aug.	Sept.	Oct.	Nov.	Dec.	Total
1990	901.3	815.7	952.0	893.6	950.9	927.8	866.0	905.4	895.7	984.1	912.9	878.0	10,883
1991	-----	2,690.3	-----	-----	2,831.8	-----	-----	2,837.7	-----	-----	2,907.8	-----	11,268
1992	880.4	867.0	1,010.1	947.9	956.7	962.1	935.5	932.4	1,019.8	1,061.7	951.8	946.1	11,472
1993	934.5	942.2	1,092.6	1,044.6	981.2	1,036.0	1,019.3	1,097.3	1,103.3	1,123.6	1,092.1	1,029.2	12,496
1994	924.5	939.1	1,084.7	1,040.6	1,001.4	1,023.8	974.9	1,119.2	1,075.4	1,123.3	1,103.4	1,063.8	12,474
1995	991.1	950.0	1,093.8	1,006.2	1,077.3	1,020.8	948.7	1,046.1	1,042.3	1,092.0	1,067.7	1,002.6	12,339
1996	964.9	927.4	1,026.4	999.8	1,020.6	946.2	959.9	1,123.3	1,042.8	1,137.1	1,080.9	1,093.1	12,322
1997	1,086.0	979.7	1,104.9	1,060.4	1,034.1	995.2	991.4	1,126.1	1,067.8	1,128.5	1,100.0	1,087.8	12,762
1998	1,045.8	1,020.2	1,129.7	1,066.5	1,101.6	1,070.1	1,062.2	1,123.4	1,122.0	1,231.5	1,150.2	1,057.0	13,180
1999[1]	1,031.5	979.0	1,156.1	1,087.7	1,091.9	1,079.5	1,082.9	1,185.0	1,185.7	1,183.0	1,199.3	1,135.6	13,397

[1] Preliminary. *Source: Bureau of the Census, U.S. Department of Commerce*

U.S. Exports of Soybean Oil (Crude and Refined) In Millions of Pounds

Year	Jan.	Feb.	Mar.	Apr.	May	June	July	Aug.	Sept.	Oct.	Nov.	Dec.	Total
1990	95.4	136.2	164.4	33.0	112.0	161.9	122.6	82.8	132.9	85.4	43.9	12.1	1,183
1991	-----	71.8	-----	-----	132.3	-----	-----	434.8	-----	-----	336.1	-----	975
1992	140.0	171.9	134.6	155.4	69.1	129.1	163.7	205.2	142.5	169.5	113.2	91.6	1,686
1993	146.8	188.0	143.3	61.1	154.8	75.4	59.9	116.0	99.7	190.4	88.6	200.2	1,524
1994	120.4	144.6	94.4	46.1	111.6	36.1	57.7	184.6	254.0	154.8	303.2	305.9	1,813
1995	217.4	367.6	564.2	236.2	90.8	160.4	91.0	109.4	79.4	69.3	205.4	95.9	2,287
1996	189.1	97.0	68.0	75.3	63.9	16.1	27.1	28.0	56.7	121.0	303.8	213.3	1,259
1997	190.7	239.2	301.1	84.9	28.9	44.9	144.1	212.9	152.1	217.2	424.0	199.7	2,240
1998	449.4	387.6	268.6	191.1	148.1	204.7	161.8	316.0	108.9	189.6	343.5	376.7	3,146
1999[1]	246.1	231.1	130.8	230.8	91.3	135.0	111.7	91.2	196.2	209.1	114.9		1,951

[1] Preliminary. *Source: Economic Research Service, U.S. Department of Agriculture (ERS-USDA)*

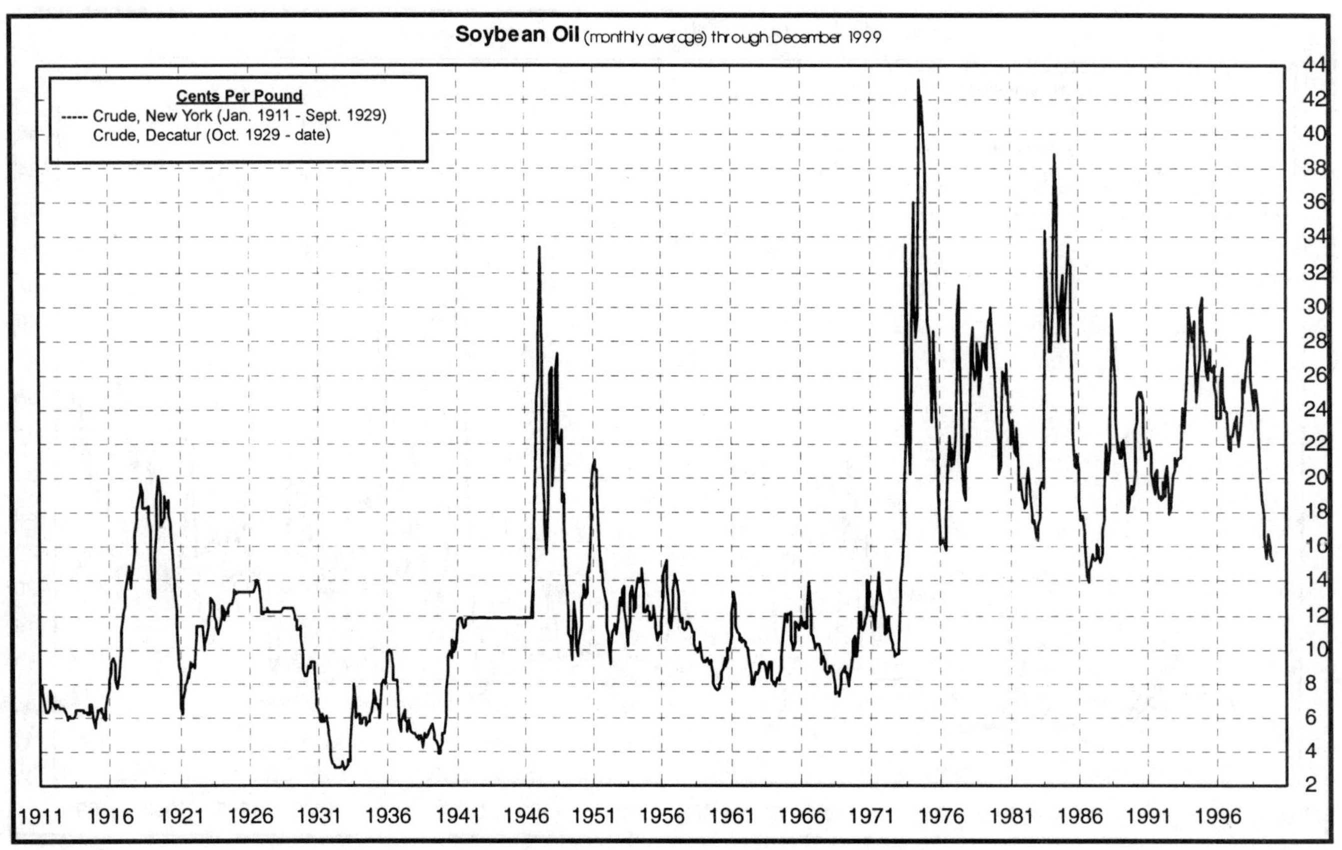

Stocks of Soybean Oil (Crude & Refined) at Factories and Warehouses in the U.S. In Millions of Pounds

Year	Oct. 1	Nov. 1	Dec. 1	Jan. 1	Feb. 1	Mar. 1	Apr. 1	May 1	June 1	July 1	Aug. 1	Sept. 1
1990-1	1,305.0	1,216.0	1,320.0	-----	1,463.8	-----	-----	1,874.6	-----	-----	1,853.1	-----
1991-2	-----	1,786.3	-----	2,217.0	2,159.0	2,402.0	2,400.0	2,423.0	2,433.0	2,426.5	2,421.0	2,363.0
1992-3	2,239.4	2,076.4	2,110.8	2,280.1	2,410.1	2,336.8	2,246.1	2,297.9	2,240.8	2,174.0	2,060.7	1,719.8
1993-4	1,554.8	1,452.7	1,399.6	1,406.9	1,414.6	1,400.9	1,402.2	1,553.3	1,566.8	1,553.8	1,570.9	1,339.4
1994-5	1,103.1	1,055.5	1,026.9	1,055.2	1,116.8	1,128.8	1,059.5	1,089.6	1,130.4	1,111.6	1,142.0	1,100.0
1995-6	1,136.7	1,195.9	1,132.0	1,408.9	1,512.6	1,521.5	1,653.5	1,747.4	1,758.9	1,888.5	2,156.5	2,091.4
1996-7	2,015.4	1,992.9	1,898.4	2,027.1	2,172.3	2,203.2	2,171.3	2,163.8	2,143.2	2,137.9	1,978.1	1,699.9
1997-8	1,520.2	1,525.6	1,525.5	1,679.6	1,787.9	1,711.2	1,762.6	1,857.6	1,857.0	1,712.6	1,779.1	1,453.2
1998-9	1,382.4	1,416.8	1,406.5	1,312.9	1,505.6	1,607.6	1,716.2	1,640.5	1,767.3	1,647.4	1,671.2	1,630.8
1999-00[1]	1,519.6	1,616.4	1,663.6									

[1] Preliminary. *Source: Economic Research Service, U.S. Department of Agriculture (ERS-USDA)*

Average Price of Crude Domestic Soybean Oil (in Tank Cars) F.O.B. Decatur In Cents Per Pound

Year	Oct.	Nov.	Dec.	Jan.	Feb.	Mar.	Apr.	May	June	July	Aug.	Sept.	Average
1990-1	22.59	21.05	21.55	21.56	21.66	22.21	21.50	20.23	19.65	19.05	20.23	20.46	21.00
1991-2	19.57	18.78	18.99	18.77	18.88	19.74	19.00	20.15	20.71	18.82	17.87	18.28	19.10
1992-3	18.36	20.10	20.52	21.23	20.72	21.00	21.24	21.15	21.30	24.13	23.47	23.61	21.40
1993-4	22.98	25.37	28.09	29.91	28.84	29.03	27.94	29.10	27.60	24.53	24.51	26.11	27.00
1994-5	27.06	29.84	30.61	29.01	28.15	28.33	27.16	26.00	26.78	27.60	26.56	26.26	27.51
1995-6	26.56	25.41	24.76	23.69	23.65	23.60	25.82	26.50	24.95	24.10	23.99	23.92	24.70
1996-7	21.95	21.80	21.60	22.45	22.41	23.29	23.17	23.68	22.97	21.89	22.06	22.88	22.50
1997-8	24.31	25.73	25.08	25.09	26.51	27.09	28.10	28.28	25.83	24.88	23.99	25.13	25.84
1998-9	25.20	25.20	24.00	22.90	20.00	19.50	18.80	17.85	16.50	15.30	16.50	16.80	19.88
1999-00[1]	16.08	15.63	15.33	15.56									15.65

[1] Preliminary. *Source: Economic Research Service, U.S. Department of Agriculture (ERS-USDA)*

Average Open Interest of Soybean Oil Futures in Chicago In Contracts

Year	Jan.	Feb.	Mar.	Apr.	May	June	July	Aug.	Sept.	Oct.	Nov.	Dec.
1990	73,368	80,842	87,615	92,845	103,116	103,747	88,763	81,310	73,841	78,548	86,786	75,995
1991	72,987	71,607	76,800	70,361	70,954	73,870	73,864	70,058	66,128	61,227	69,657	63,901
1992	68,619	73,919	75,508	68,749	65,084	71,507	64,450	72,569	70,228	65,243	76,168	76,908
1993	73,683	68,887	66,803	68,598	65,814	73,892	83,730	72,746	64,927	62,348	80,136	94,990
1994	97,198	99,640	100,334	98,659	97,595	83,165	93,994	88,196	81,735	86,901	108,327	114,928
1995	101,171	103,856	97,715	87,300	76,175	75,171	81,650	77,064	70,410	71,652	85,241	84,138
1996	87,214	85,611	87,859	95,954	95,422	86,366	81,440	80,090	83,211	98,514	97,496	86,119
1997	89,112	89,348	102,388	101,191	101,544	104,433	105,346	95,282	94,521	107,471	119,877	106,406
1998	105,798	121,657	142,100	160,004	159,248	139,934	117,487	112,177	115,879	115,260	110,386	104,738
1999	115,407	131,875	136,967	133,404	131,993	147,749	157,999	147,279	146,238	155,755	163,438	145,396

Source: *Chicago Board of Trade (CBT)*

Volume of Trading of Soybean Oil Futures in Chicago In Contracts

Year	Jan.	Feb.	Mar.	Apr.	May	June	July	Aug.	Sept.	Oct.	Nov.	Dec.	Total[1]
1990	294,121	397,052	413,924	447,663	488,779	441,516	462,294	405,583	319,184	344,068	370,224	273,894	4,658.3
1991	330,215	259,353	354,973	342,117	264,569	322,897	433,757	399,802	303,184	340,553	297,865	369,259	4,018.5
1992	344,204	293,729	399,754	255,848	381,807	352,349	413,086	298,001	425,859	346,755	365,760	405,526	4,282.7
1993	341,366	267,022	378,389	306,092	261,620	434,704	513,329	444,559	449,338	302,084	465,173	448,553	4,612.2
1994	442,026	401,580	366,007	391,175	442,419	378,177	397,483	357,896	415,407	476,936	516,724	477,358	5,063.2
1995	424,387	363,695	464,413	355,884	457,682	418,182	377,355	330,507	303,893	317,201	431,711	366,426	4,611.3
1996	354,602	355,220	375,237	443,408	376,716	423,089	512,563	449,014	425,850	414,018	396,233	454,327	4,980.3
1997	473,290	381,921	503,998	445,848	389,741	439,626	442,846	375,122	417,970	413,722	489,541	511,369	5,285.0
1998	443,562	556,982	497,887	673,091	624,518	648,098	629,642	491,155	558,032	383,844	450,073	540,379	6,498.3
1999	367,303	555,097	520,622	463,236	350,850	489,184	516,205	552,198	523,376	395,243	497,090	433,491	5,663.9

[1] In thousands of contracts. Source: *Chicago Board of Trade (CBT)*

Soybeans

U.S. soybean prices began a price slide in mid-1997 that persisted throughout 1998 and well into 1999, cutting the value of a bushel of soybeans by over 50 percent during the decline. Prices reached a low of $4.015 per bushel, basis nearby Chicago futures, on July 9, 1999, a price level that soybean futures had not seen since early 1973. Although futures recovered to over $5.00 per bushel in late summer, the rally lacked momentum and towards yearend futures were again trading below $5.00 per bushel. The entrenched weakness reflected both near record 1999/00 world supplies and ending carryover stocks.

The 1999/2000 world production total of 153.9 million metric tonnes trailed initial forecasts by about 1.1 million tonnes, as well as the 1997/98 record large world crop of 158 million tonnes. Still, production proved well above the growth trend of the early 1990's when production averaged less than 120 million tonnes. Although the 1999/00 U.S. crop proved to be smaller than expected, a near record large 2.7 billion bushels (73.4 million metric tonnes) were still realized. The U.S. produces nearly half of the world's soybeans, with Brazil, the second largest producer, about a third. Soybean production is expanding is a number of countries, but both the U.S. ranking and Brazil's runner-up slots are well entrenched.

A key question continues to focus on China, who during the past few years has vied with Argentina as the world's third largest producer. In 1999/00, China produced 14 million tonnes and Argentina 18 million; both forecasts were under the record large 1997/98 crops of 15 million and 19 million, respectively. The odds would seem to favor stronger growth in China in line with their expanding poultry flocks and the derived need for high protein soybean meal. However, as China's economy becomes more market sensitive growers may switch to higher priced crops as happened in the mid-1990's when soybean acreage was moved into corn and cotton production. It is possible that China's soybean acreage has temporarily peaked at around 8 million hectare, suggesting that further production gains will be dependent on realizing higher average yields, estimated at 1.79 tons per hectare in 1999/00.

Brazil's soybean crop is sown about the time the U.S. crop has been harvested. Brazilian 1999/00 production was forecast at 30.5 million tonnes in 1999/00 vs. 31 million in 1998/99. Percentagewise, Argentina's soybean production shows the fastest year-to-year gain in the 1990's. However, unlike Brazil, Argentine soybean farmers have significantly lower production costs and a better transportation structure. Brazil soybean acreage is nearly double Argentina's, 12.5 million hectare vs. 7.5 million in 1999/00, respectively. The 1999/00 yield per acre in both countries is about the same, 2.44 tons per hectare in Brazil vs. 2.40 tons in Argentina, although generally Argentina's soybean yield is higher. Brazil's crop year runs from February to January, Argentina's is from April to March.

World soybean trade in 1999/00 of a record large 41 million tonnes compares with 1998/99's 40 million. The U.S. now accounts for almost 60 percent of world exports, 24 million tonnes in 1999/00 vs. 22.1 million in 1998/99. This percentage has fallen since the early 1990's. Brazil's exports, however, more than doubled in the decade, totaling 9.4 million tonnes in 1999/00 vs. 9 million in 1998/99 and about 3.5 million in the mid-1990's.

Importing nations are more numerous, the biggest are generally the European Union at 16.1 million tonnes in 1999/00 with Germany taking 4.8 million, and Japan with 4.6 million tonnes. The ending 1999/00 world soybean carryover of a lower than expected 22 million tonnes compares with the year earlier 23.8 million. Generally the U.S., Brazil and Argentina account for most of the world's carryover stocks.

U.S. farmers harvested a record large 72.8 million acres of soybeans in 1999 vs. 70.4 million in 1998. The average yield of 37 bushels per acre was lower than expected and compares with 38.9 bushels in 1998. Iowa is the largest producing state, with Illinois a close second followed by Minnesota and Indiana.

The U.S. soybean crop year begins September 1. Carryover stocks on August 31, 1999, of a near record large 348 million bushels, lifted total 1999/00 supplies to 3.1 billion bushels vs. 2.9 billion in 1998/99. Total disappearance in 1999/00 was put at 2.7 billion bushels, of which at least 1.6 billion will be crushed, 900 million exported, and about 154 million allocated to seed and residual. Carryover as of August 31, 2000 is forecast at a record large 385 million bushels. Projected carryover as a percentage of usage in 1999/00 was forecast at about 14 percent, twice that of 1997/98.

U.S. soybean exports have seen a strong shift in regional demand during the past two years. The traditional European market has come to represent a smaller share of U.S. exports, while Asia and Mexico have increased their importance to U.S. exporters. Asia's share is expected to increase due to the area's improved economies and the shift away from importing meal and choosing instead to process soybeans. Historically, when a more positive soybean usage outlook takes hold it's apt to show in early calendar year prices. Demand bull years in soybeans generally show counterseasonal strength in January and February, however, if total usage holds neutral, and/or weakens, then futures prices tend to witness what is referred to as the "February break." If the latter develops, it's not unusual for prices to penetrate the harvest lows of the previous October-December quarter.

The U.S.D.A.'s average price received by farmers in 1999/00 was forecast at $4.75 to $5.25 per bushel vs. $5.02 in 1998/99. The highest farm price during the past decade was $7.35 in 1996/97, and the previous low, prior to 1998/99, had been $5.56 in 1992/93.

Futures Markets

Soybean futures are traded on the Bolsa de Mercadorias & Futuros (BM&F), the Mercado a Termino de Buenos Aires (MAT), the Dalian Commodity Exchange in China, the Tokyo Grain Exchange (TGE), the Chicago Board of Trade (CBOT), and the Mid-America Commodity Exchange (MidAm). Options are traded on the MAT, the TGE, the CBOT and the MidAm.

World Production of Soybeans In Thousands of Metric Tons

Crop Year[4]	Argen-tina	Bolivia	Brazil	Canada	China	India	Indo-nesia	Mexico	Para-guay	Thai-land	United States	Ex-USSR	World Total
1990-1	11,470	233	15,757	1,262	11,008	2,419	1,487	575	1,402	530	52,417	884	104,209
1991-2	11,315	384	19,456	1,460	9,713	2,492	1,555	725	1,315	436	54,065	830	108,050
1992-3	11,240	278	22,710	1,455	10,304	3,106	1,870	573	1,794	480	59,612	650	117,647
1993-4	12,200	491	24,963	1,851	14,600	3,700	1,709	497	1,796	513	50,919	572	116,952
1994-5	12,500	710	25,900	2,251	16,000	3,150	1,565	523	2,200	528	68,440	465	137,680
1995-6	12,430	887	24,150	2,293	13,500	4,350	1,689	190	2,400	386	59,170	321	124,890
1996-7	10,800	862	27,327	2,170	13,220	4,060	1,517	56	2,771	488	64,781	324	132,081
1997-8[1]	19,500	1,038	32,500	2,738	14,730	5,150	1,357	177	2,856	366	73,180	325	158,070
1998-9[2]	19,900	900	31,000	2,737	15,000	5,700	1,306	132	3,304	376	74,600	350	158,930
1999-00[3]	19,500		30,500		14,000						71,930		153,250

[1] Preliminary. [2] Estimate. [3] Forecast. [4] Spilt year includes Northern Hemisphere crops harvested in the late months of the first year shown combined with Southern Hemisphere crops harvested in the early months of the following year. *Sources: Oil World; Foreign Agricultural Service, U.S. Department of Agriculture (FAS-USDA)*

World Crushings and EndingStocks of Soybeans In Thousands of Metric Tons

	Crushings										Ending Stocks		
Year	Argen-tina	Brazil	China	Germany	India	Japan	Mexico	Nether-lands	United States	World Total	Brazil	United States	World Total
1990-1	6,985	14,197	4,075	2,656	2,095	3,364	1,990	3,276	32,498	87,675	4,970	8,960	20,550
1991-2	7,759	14,941	3,175	2,822	2,054	3,550	2,380	3,580	34,180	91,529	4,390	7,580	18,380
1992-3	8,520	15,550	4,390	3,107	2,754	3,785	2,480	3,642	34,731	96,131	6,070	7,960	20,210
1993-4	8,761	18,439	7,135	2,873	3,197	3,667	2,540	3,673	34,921	101,951	5,460	5,690	17,340
1994-5	8,693	20,189	7,825	3,437	2,643	3,708	2,250	3,991	38,283	110,252	7,200	9,110	23,690
1995-6	10,255	21,703	7,215	3,202	3,700	3,685	2,505	3,900	37,095	111,702	5,800	4,990	17,510
1996-7	11,046	20,022	8,695	3,550	3,410	3,772	2,930	3,996	39,350	117,005	4,000	3,590	13,460
1997-8[1]	12,930	19,900	10,730	3,816	4,420	3,720	3,600	4,108	43,460	125,960	6,500	5,440	21,600
1998-9[2]	17,510	21,010	11,850	3,955	4,950	3,680	3,720	4,115	43,260	133,960	6,000	9,480	24,010
1999-00[3]	17,800	20,900	12,000			3,620	3,790		43,550	134,210	4,800	9,390	20,930

[1] Preliminary. [2] Estimate. [3] Forecast. *Sources: Oil World; Foreign Agricultural Service, U.S. Department of Agriculture (FAS-USDA)*

World Imports and Exports of Soybeans In Thousands of Metric Tons

	Imports							Exports					
Year	China	Germany	Japan	Mexico	Nether-lands	Taiwan	World Total	Argen-tina	Brazil	Canada	Paraguay	United States	World Total
1990-1	1	2,862	4,375	1,604	3,941	2,236	25,799	4,468	2,478	203	1,011	15,236	24,867
1991-2	7	3,025	4,672	2,092	4,220	2,329	28,720	3,213	3,872	232	832	19,335	28,722
1992-3	210	3,274	4,866	1,908	4,233	2,491	29,700	2,397	4,041	298	1,430	20,788	29,823
1993-4	48	2,722	4,851	2,225	4,176	2,685	28,501	3,074	5,432	414	1,190	16,416	28,582
1994-5	155	3,272	4,837	2,006	4,544	2,810	33,053	2,503	3,572	528	1,458	23,807	33,190
1995-6	795	3,302	4,777	2,398	4,142	2,798	31,575	2,078	3,482	595	1,729	22,604	31,499
1996-7	2,350	3,384	5,043	2,983	4,538	2,632	36,315	484	8,425	437	1,686	24,418	36,290
1997-8[1]	2,940	3,410	4,870	3,480	5,000	2,390	38,980	3,230	8,750	738	2,390	23,760	40,480
1998-9[2]	3,850	3,750	4,650	3,600	5,030	2,150	39,610	3,230	8,900	850	2,400	21,810	38,500
1999-00[3]	4,800	3,740	4,700	3,700	4,950	2,200	41,890	3,500	9,300		2,000	24,220	41,290

[1] Preliminary. [2] Estimate. [3] Forecast. *Sources: Oil World; Foreign Agricultural Service, U.S. Department of Agriculture (FAS-USDA)*

Supply and Distribution of Soybeans in the United States In Millions of Bushels

Crop Year Beginning Sept. 1	Supply: Stocks, Sept. 1: Farms	Supply: Stocks, Sept. 1: Mills, Elevators[3]	Supply: Stocks, Sept. 1: Total	Supply: Pro-duction	Supply: Total Supply	Distribution: Crushings	Distribution: Exports	Distribution: Seed, Feed & Residual	Distribution: Total Distri-bution
1990-1	86.0	153.1	239.1	1,925.9	2,168.6	1,187.3	557.3	94.9	1,839.5
1991-2	118.4	210.6	329.0	1,986.5	2,319.0	1,253.5	683.9	103.1	2,040.6
1992-3	105.0	173.4	278.4	2,190.4	2,470.8	1,279.0	769.6	130.0	2,178.6
1993-4	125.0	167.3	292.3	1,869.7	2,168.4	1,275.6	589.1	95.6	1,959.3
1994-5	59.1	150.0	209.1	2,514.9	2,729.5	1,405.2	838.1	151.4	2,394.7
1995-6	105.1	229.7	334.8	2,174.3	2,513.5	1,369.5	851.2	109.3	2,330.1
1996-7	59.5	123.9	183.5	2,380.3	2,572.6	1,437.0	881.8	123.0	2,440.8
1997-8	43.6	88.2	131.8	2,688.8	2,825.6	1,597.0	870.4	158.4	2,625.8
1998-9[1]	84.3	115.5	199.8	2,741.0	2,944.0	1,590.0	801.0	205.0	2,596.0
1999-00[2]	145.0	203.0	348.0	2,643.0	2,994.0	1,600.0	890.0	159.0	2,649.0

[1] Preliminary. [2] Estimate. [3] Also warehouses. *Source: Economic Research Service, U.S. Department of Agriculture (ERS-USDA)*

SOYBEANS

Salient Statistics & Official Crop Production Reports of Soybeans in the U.S. In Millions of Bushels

Year	Planted	Acreage Harvested	Yield Per Acre	Farm Price	Farm Value (Million	Yield	Yield of	Crop Production Reports In Thousands of Bushels					
	---- 1,000 Acres ----		(Bu.)	($ / Bu.)	Dollars)	of Oil	Meal	Aug. 1	Sept. 1	Oct. 1	Nov. 1	Dec. 1	Final
1990-1	57,795	56,512	34.1	5.74	11,042	11.23	47.47	1,836,017	1,834,602	1,823,462	1,903,832	-----	1,925,947
1991-2	59,180	58,011	34.2	5.58	11,092	11.42	47.51	1,868,825	1,816,825	1,933,570	1,961,840	-----	1,986,539
1992-3	59,180	58,233	37.6	5.56	12,168	10.84	47.54	2,079,487	-----	-----	-----	-----	2,190,354
1993-4	60,135	57,347	32.6	6.40	11,950	10.87	47.62	1,902,023	1,909,188	1,890,808	1,833,788	-----	1,870,958
1994-5	61,670	60,859	41.4	5.48	13,756	11.08	47.33	2,282,367	2,316,077	2,458,087	2,522,527	-----	2,516,694
1995-6	62,575	61,624	35.3	6.72	14,737	11.15	47.69	2,245,901	2,284,551	2,190,661	2,182,991	-----	2,176,814
1996-7	64,205	63,409	37.6	7.35	17,440	10.91	47.36	2,299,675	2,269,505	2,346,220	2,402,610	-----	2,380,274
1997-8	70,005	69,110	38.9	6.47	17,373	11.25	47.41	2,744,451	2,745,891	2,721,843	2,736,115	-----	2,688,750
1998-9[1]	72,025	70,441	38.9	4.93	13,494	11.30	47.25	2,824,744	2,908,604	2,768,919	2,762,609	-----	2,741,014
1999-00[2]	73,780	72,476	36.5	4.75	12,451	11.26	47.58	2,869,519	2,778,392	2,696,272	2,672,972	-----	2,642,908

[1] Preliminary. [2] Forecast. *Source: National Agricultural Statistics Service, U.S. Department of Agriculture (NASS-USDA)*

Stocks of Soybeans in the United States In Thousands of Bushels

Year	On Farms				Off Farms[1]				Total Stocks			
	Mar. 1	Jun. 1	Sept. 1	Dec. 1	Mar. 1	Jun. 1	Sept. 1	Dec. 1	Mar. 1	Jun. 1	Sept. 1	Dec. 1
1990	535,800	255,300	86,000	754,000	519,705	340,614	153,139	929,963	1,055,505	595,914	239,139	1,683,963
1991	555,500	336,500	118,400	810,000	634,619	387,022	210,642	968,957	1,190,119	723,522	329,042	1,778,957
1992	505,000	279,000	105,000	876,100	672,343	416,671	173,437	959,885	1,177,343	695,671	278,437	1,835,985
1993	576,900	319,800	124,970	697,400	638,667	363,613	167,314	876,220	1,215,567	683,413	292,284	1,573,620
1994	425,700	195,000	59,080	985,800	595,917	360,260	150,037	1,116,156	1,021,617	555,260	209,117	2,101,956
1995	635,300	348,800	105,130	861,500	734,898	443,072	229,684	971,929	1,370,198	791,872	334,814	1,833,429
1996	512,000	234,100	59,523	935,100	678,356	388,701	123,935	889,984	1,190,356	622,801	183,458	1,825,084
1997	514,000	216,000	43,600	1,048,000	541,912	283,890	88,233	951,417	1,055,912	499,890	131,833	1,999,417
1998	637,000	318,000	84,300	1,187,000	565,922	275,654	115,499	999,440	1,202,922	593,654	199,799	2,186,440
1999	815,000	458,000	145,000	1,150,000	642,338	390,573	203,482	1,032,192	1,457,338	848,573	348,482	2,182,192

[1] Includes stocks at mills, elevators, warehouses, terminals and processors. NA = Not avaliable. *Source: National Agricultural Statistics Service, U.S. Department of Agriculture (NASS-USDA)*

Commercial Stocks of Soybeans in the United States, on First of Month In Millions of Bushels

Year	Jan.	Feb.	Mar.	Apr.	May	June	July	Aug.	Sept.	Oct.	Nov.	Dec.
1990	65.8	62.1	57.8	53.2	56.2	54.4	48.1	41.4	26.1	24.1	89.7	90.7
1991	90.2	78.1	70.5	56.2	43.5	35.5	33.3	25.5	25.3	29.7	80.6	84.0
1992	76.0	75.9	67.1	67.8	58.5	57.2	51.7	32.1	18.6	59.0	75.1	79.9
1993	71.5	63.5	54.5	48.5	44.0	32.1	26.6	24.4	15.8	9.6	52.3	60.2
1994	62.6	65.3	54.4	46.3	40.7	34.7	29.9	24.3	19.8	11.5	68.1	83.4
1995	80.7	72.5	67.8	63.5	51.8	50.8	44.3	35.7	33.6	23.0	60.8	61.7
1996	57.2	57.2	59.2	54.7	56.2	44.9	36.9	32.7	12.0	5.3	55.2	50.6
1997	32.6	28.8	22.9	26.0	29.2	24.7	14.3	12.8	6.3	4.5	50.2	49.4
1998	35.3	31.2	22.9	18.4	14.5	14.2	10.2	9.7	8.7	18.6	43.5	40.6
1999	39.1	31.5	29.0	28.7	25.0	18.9	16.1	17.3	14.1	19.5	46.9	42.3

Source: Livestock Division, U.S. Department of Agriculture (LD-USDA)

Stocks of Soybeans at Mills in the United States, on First of Month In Millions of Bushels

Year	Jan.	Feb.	Mar.	Apr.	May	June	July	Aug.	Sept.	Oct.	Nov.	Dec.
1990-1	45.2	34.5	130.1	130.7	-----	106.5	-----	-----	78.5	-----	-----	61.2
1991-2	-----	-----	67.0	-----	126.9	121.4	109.6	94.7	79.8	73.5	65.7	56.2
1992-3	43.8	46.3	132.3	137.4	119.1	111.2	97.2	90.1	83.6	67.7	67.1	55.3
1993-4	42.0	28.0	108.6	114.9	120.9	126.1	118.5	119.7	98.7	97.8	90.0	63.5
1994-5	47.9	46.8	114.1	124.3	108.0	114.7	114.3	112.6	94.1	81.2	69.1	55.1
1995-6	52.8	54.2	125.6	129.1	120.0	123.3	121.9	110.6	104.2	92.5	70.4	57.4
1996-7	40.7	23.4	101.1	117.4	106.0	112.6	122.2	104.9	89.2	78.2	64.0	43.6
1997-8	28.3	37.0	126.4	124.3	110.3	98.7	93.4	72.0	56.9	41.0	42.5	44.1
1998-9	32.8	66.5	175.0	154.3	131.0	109.6	102.5	93.7	80.5	56.9	55.5	48.1
1999-00[1]	41.7	70.8	162.9	144.7								

[1] Preliminary. *Source: Economic Research Service, U.S. Department of Agriculture (ERS-USDA)*

Production of Soybeans for Beans in the United States, by State In Millions of Bushels

Year	Arkan-sas	Illinois	Indiana	Iowa	Ken-tucky	Mich-igan	Minn-esota	Miss-issippi	Mis-souri	Neb-raska	Ohio	Tenn-essee	Total
1990	90.5	354.9	171.4	327.9	39.0	43.3	179.4	39.9	124.5	81.4	135.7	33.8	1,925.9
1991	89.6	341.3	171.6	349.5	36.7	52.8	195.3	46.8	135.1	82.4	135.7	31.5	1,986.5
1992	104.3	405.5	194.4	359.5	42.2	47.5	172.8	59.5	161.5	103.3	147.2	33.3	2,190.4
1993	92.3	387.0	223.1	257.3	38.0	54.7	115.0	42.9	118.8	90.0	156.2	32.2	1,871.0
1994	115.6	429.1	215.3	442.9	42.4	57.0	224.0	57.0	173.3	134.4	173.6	38.3	2,516.7
1995	88.4	378.3	196.7	407.4	41.4	59.6	234.9	37.8	132.8	101.0	153.1	34.6	2,176.8
1996	112.0	398.9	203.7	415.8	44.8	46.7	224.2	54.3	149.9	135.5	157.2	38.5	2,380.3
1997	109.8	427.9	230.6	478.4	42.1	71.6	255.5	64.2	174.6	143.8	191.0	40.8	2,688.8
1998	85.0	464.2	231.0	496.8	36.0	73.7	285.6	48.0	170.0	165.0	193.2	35.1	2,741.0
1999[1]	93.8	443.1	216.5	478.4	24.2	77.6	282.9	44.7	147.1	180.6	162.0	21.4	2,642.9

[1] Preliminary. *Source: Agricultural Statistics Board, U.S. Department of Agriculture (ASB-USDA)*

United States Exports of Soybeans In Millions of Bushels

Year	Sept.	Oct.	Nov.	Dec.	Jan.	Feb.	Mar.	Apr.	May	June	July	Aug.	Total
1990-1	27.9	29.8	62.8	55.8	-----	190.1	-----	-----	117.7	-----	73.9	-----	557.9
1991-2	26.8	-----	235.6	-----	73.8	90.6	63.3	56.6	28.3	27.3	42.6	39.2	683.9
1992-3	50.1	98.0	84.2	73.6	89.1	104.7	79.7	48.7	34.6	39.4	42.7	24.6	769.5
1993-4	30.1	73.6	72.4	73.9	71.0	67.8	53.6	34.8	27.5	26.7	17.1	40.7	589.1
1994-5	42.3	99.9	78.5	104.2	89.3	91.4	83.1	80.7	45.2	35.5	41.2	46.7	838.1
1995-6	70.7	77.4	65.5	89.6	106.2	82.9	93.5	52.9	42.1	51.8	46.0	52.6	851.2
1996-7	41.6	95.7	152.4	121.7	106.0	105.4	66.9	58.2	40.8	32.3	23.2	37.5	881.8
1997-8	42.6	170.3	152.4	120.5	91.1	94.8	55.9	36.3	27.7	23.2	29.0	26.6	870.4
1998-9	27.9	135.4	105.2	91.9	84.3	66.9	71.4	52.5	37.9	35.9	36.8	55.2	801.5
1999-00[1]	70.5	107.0	120.3										1,191.4

[1] Preliminary. *Source: Economic Research Service, U.S. Department of Agriculture (ERS-USDA)*

Spread Between Value of Products and Soybean Price in the United States In Cents Per Bushel

Year	Sept.	Oct.	Nov.	Dec.	Jan.	Feb.	Mar.	Apr.	May	June	July	Aug.	Average
1990-1	99	77	58	64	63	73	79	75	72	74	91	99	77
1991-2	118	120	94	82	74	74	75	78	87	104	80	83	89
1992-3	98	93	87	93	94	77	77	79	82	84	120	97	90
1993-4	95	108	105	92	93	99	88	85	89	88	94	118	96
1994-5	146	167	143	137	130	109	114	109	86	102	87	90	118
1995-6	88	107	82	88	82	77	79	94	73	76	77	71	82
1996-7	109	117	126	115	94	95	86	80	107	96	123	151	108
1997-8	207	127	140	112	80	76	55	56	56	55	77	68	92
1998-9	74	68	50	56	51	49	60	51	49	53	63	59	57
1999-00	64	76	79	79									75

Source: Economic Research Service, U.S. Department of Agriculture (ERS-USDA)

Soybean Crushed (Factory Consumption) in the United States In Milions of Bushels

Year	Sept.	Oct.	Nov.	Dec.	Jan.	Feb.	Mar.	Apr.	May	June	July	Aug.	Total
1990-1	92.1	106.1	106.0	102.7	-----	297.9	-----	-----	280.1	-----	202.5	-----	1,187
1991-2	98.9	-----	333.3	-----	112.0	100.8	107.2	101.6	95.2	100.0	102.3	102.3	1,254
1992-3	101.2	113.9	113.1	116.2	116.8	102.2	113.0	105.9	106.5	99.9	98.0	92.2	1,279
1993-4	98.4	113.7	114.4	114.1	110.7	103.3	113.3	105.6	103.0	97.2	101.0	101.0	1,276
1994-5	105.9	119.3	122.5	128.5	127.3	116.5	128.1	119.4	114.2	105.6	108.4	109.5	1,405
1995-6	107.4	120.6	123.4	125.1	122.8	111.2	115.5	112.1	106.3	107.5	111.9	105.7	1,370
1996-7	100.9	127.0	133.1	138.1	137.3	125.1	130.1	114.8	110.7	108.9	106.1	103.8	1,436
1997-8	110.8	142.2	142.8	153.1	151.9	138.2	147.0	133.9	123.9	117.5	123.8	111.9	1,597
1998-9	123.9	142.4	143.0	144.6	136.4	127.6	140.0	128.4	128.0	121.1	127.3	126.9	1,590
1999-00[1]	133.8	150.2	142.8	143.0									1,709

One Bushel = 60 Pounds. [1] Preliminary. *Source: Economic Research Service, U.S. Department of Agriculture (ERS-USDA)*

SOYBEANS

Average Open Interest of Soybean Futures in Chicago In Contracts

Year	Jan.	Feb.	Mar.	Apr.	May	June	July	Aug.	Sept.	Oct.	Nov.	Dec.
1990	95,718	99,367	111,395	123,005	131,173	118,009	96,789	91,706	97,929	119,841	125,136	123,552
1991	109,311	110,421	110,318	106,995	102,369	103,362	91,449	86,132	98,050	114,206	112,407	112,782
1992	114,871	118,317	132,639	121,171	121,398	137,896	116,208	106,830	104,115	125,734	118,877	114,261
1993	121,726	126,682	126,681	138,155	137,821	142,721	199,681	183,422	163,647	159,641	161,170	168,694
1994	177,648	167,217	156,059	147,569	145,798	150,203	132,010	121,126	126,947	147,198	137,187	136,351
1995	138,345	138,794	137,843	138,624	133,533	143,119	143,671	135,584	144,409	167,200	174,775	194,021
1996	198,731	199,150	192,927	207,284	191,989	179,548	180,817	182,324	196,361	178,872	155,937	152,966
1997	157,728	176,242	189,352	188,617	186,792	159,720	141,658	133,732	150,606	172,098	148,760	150,201
1998	135,340	142,778	147,900	152,732	143,994	149,563	133,532	140,236	158,627	163,759	143,814	146,463
1999	152,757	166,003	162,690	166,565	164,777	163,663	157,432	134,104	146,087	174,583	164,306	153,693

Source: Chicago Board of Trade (CBT)

Volume of Trading of Soybean Futures in Chicago In Thousands of Contracts

Year	Jan.	Feb.	Mar.	Apr.	May	June	July	Aug.	Sept.	Oct.	Nov.	Dec.	Total
1990	655.6	534.6	826.6	884.4	1,126.0	1,041.8	1,037.6	905.6	642.8	1,132.0	859.8	655.0	13,577
1991	745.0	620.8	715.4	808.0	684.4	776.2	992.4	943.2	662.4	876.2	571.2	619.0	8,974
1992	804.4	738.4	688.0	558.8	873.8	1,054.6	933.2	630.8	572.2	867.4	613.2	665.4	9,000
1993	683.4	624.6	675.8	761.2	778.0	1,287.0	1,643.2	1,180.0	925.0	962.2	1,188.0	941.4	11,649
1994	1,134.6	898.5	922.0	919.3	1,158.4	1,197.0	892.4	688.4	622.6	857.0	825.8	633.2	10,749
1995	614.0	572.0	799.6	698.3	949.4	1,050.8	1,196.7	817.0	800.2	1,127.8	840.4	1,145.4	10,612
1996	1,302.6	1,122.9	1,009.4	1,683.2	1,149.3	989.5	1,295.9	989.8	1,050.2	1,002.7	1,695.6	940.1	14,231
1997	1,119.8	1,254.2	1,405.9	1,585.5	1,391.1	1,355.6	1,217.4	835.0	852.3	1,505.8	1,010.7	1,006.6	14,540
1998	875.7	971.2	935.9	1,116.2	973.6	1,378.8	1,286.3	884.5	864.4	1,264.6	867.0	1,012.9	12,431
1999	871.1	1,025.3	1,440.1	963.5	823.6	1,149.5	1,502.5	1,669.8	903.0	1,158.6	839.4	872.3	12,482

Source: Chicago Board of Trade

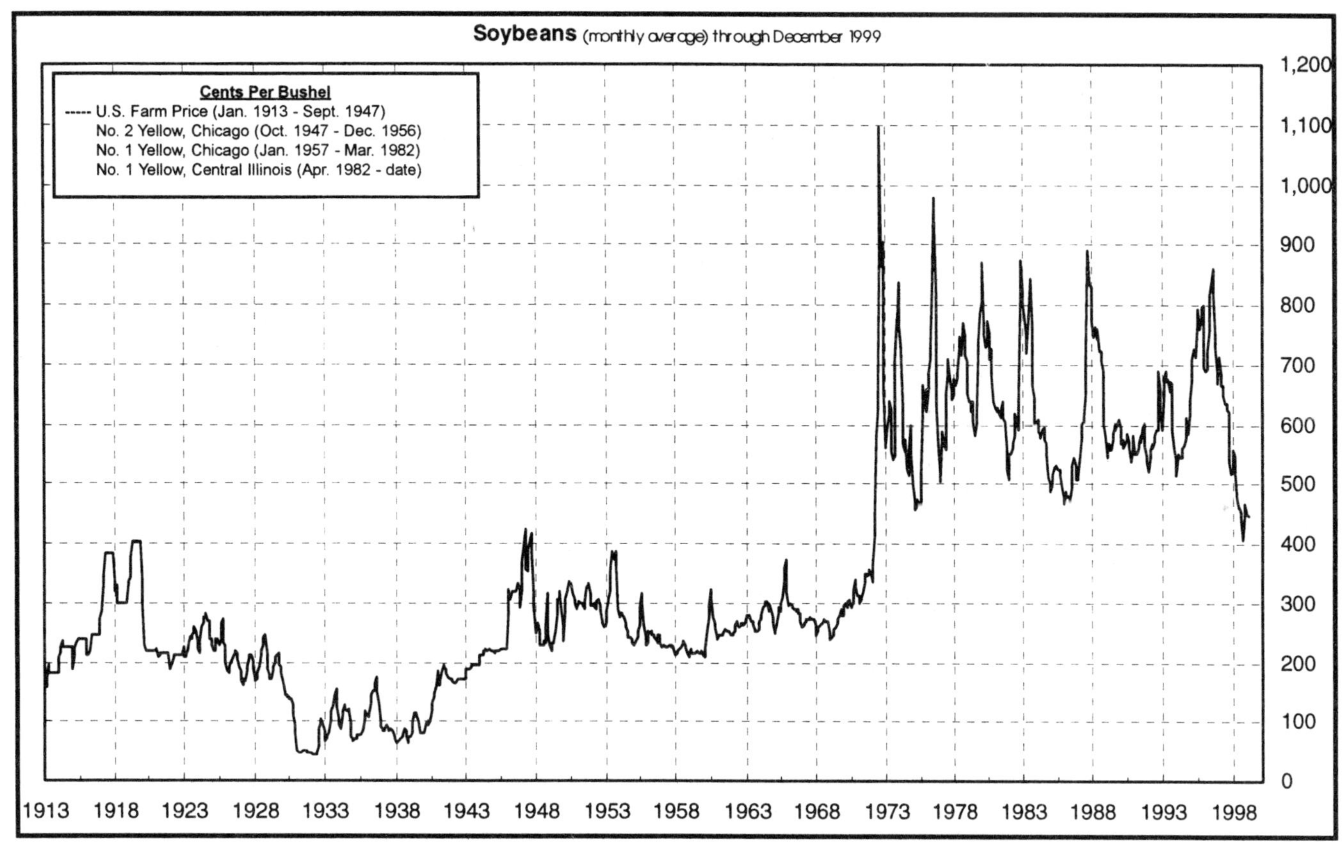

Average Cash Price of No. 1 Yellow Soybeans at Illinois Processor In Cents Per Bushel

Year	Sept.	Oct.	Nov.	Dec.	Jan.	Feb.	Mar.	Apr.	May	June	July	Aug.	Average
1990-1	628	614	587	591	576	585	592	601	589	583	554	578	590
1991-2	598	568	571	568	577	581	593	585	609	619	580	564	584
1992-3	554	535	560	572	582	575	587	597	607	606	689	679	595
1993-4	643	606	664	694	701	686	692	670	689	685	603	576	659
1994-5	557	531	566	567	558	560	574	578	580	577	623	602	573
1995-6	632	656	686	717	737	730	726	791	808	778	795	816	739
1996-7	820	711	704	708	737	769	833	854	878	837	769	741	780
1997-8	703	684	727	699	679	680	662	649	649	640	642	556	664
1998-9	533	536	572	558	532	490	475	480	468	462	425	465	522
1999-00[1]	485	470	464	460									470

[1] Preliminary. *Source: Economic Research Service, U.S. Department of Agriculture (ERS-USDA)*

Average Price Received by Farmers for Soybeans in the United States In Cents Per Bushel

Year	Sept.	Oct.	Nov.	Dec.	Jan.	Feb.	Mar.	Apr.	May	June	July	Aug.	Average
1990-1	599	588	578	572	571	565	576	577	567	556	536	566	574
1991-2	564	548	548	545	554	559	567	566	587	594	559	540	558
1992-3	536	526	536	546	558	556	565	573	581	590	656	656	556
1993-4	621	601	632	664	672	671	673	657	677	672	592	558	640
1994-5	547	530	536	541	547	540	551	555	556	568	590	583	548
1995-6	598	615	640	676	677	701	700	743	769	741	762	782	672
1996-7	779	694	690	691	713	738	797	823	840	816	752	725	735
1997-8	672	650	685	671	669	657	640	626	626	616	614	543	639
1998-9	525	518	540	537	532	480	461	463	450	444	419	439	484
1999-00[1]	457	447	445	444	459								450

[1] Preliminary. *Source: Economic Research Service, U.S. Department of Agriculture (ERS-USDA)*

Stock Index Futures, U.S.

1999 proved a record year for U.S. equity markets. All the major stock indices reached new highs, but the emphasis focused on the high-tech companies traded on the NASDAQ with its composite index up 85.6 percent, a record gain as was the closing 1999 value of 4,069, with a 1000 point advance in the October-December quarter alone. The NASDAQ 100 index doubled, closing the year at 3,707.83. The bellwether price weighted Dow-Jones Industrial Index, which in 1999 was modified to include some NASDAQ stocks, gained 25.22 percent; closing 1999 at a record high 11,497.12. The market capitalization weighted S&P 500 index gained 19.53 percent, to a record 1469.25; the Wilshire 5000 rose 20.63 percent; the Russell 2000 was up 22.05 percent; the Value Line "A", however, lost 1.4 percent.

Significantly, nearly 60 percent of the stocks traded on the New York Stock Exchange closed 1999 below year earlier levels as the sharp disparity between the gains in the NASDAQ and losses in the Value Line underscored. Trading volume set records: on the New York Stock Exchange 204 billion shares vs. 170 billion in 1998, while the Nasdaq's volume topped 264 billion shares vs. 198 billion in 1998.

As has been the case in the second half of the 1990's, market volatility was the rule rather than the exception, partially reflecting burgeoning computer driven day-trading that tends to feed upon itself. In mid-1999, the Dow Jones 30 industrial index fell from a then record high of nearly 11,400 to 10,000 by mid-October. The recovery that followed carried to yearend. Ironically, the markets' yearend strength came despite a tightening monetary policy by the Federal Reserve which in years past would have normally triggered price weakness. Obviously, the historical parameters that used to determine equity values have apparently been relegated to the backburner. The emphasis in 1999 focused on companies that were in someway connected to the Internet; the phrase "dot com" became a household term and the key to unprecedented stock market valuations.

The U.S. economy grew robustly in 1999 as the gross domestic product grew at a 5 percent annual rate. Unemployment was at its lowest level since the 1970's with benign consumer level inflation, two economic variables that theoretically should not happen at the same time. Moreover, the Federal Government's budget surplus tempered the Treasury's borrowing needs.

Mainstream America continued to view stocks as the best investment, accepting volatility as part of the game and pouring billions into stocks during 1999, with much of the capital allocated to pension programs. Throughout the year consumer confidence remained strong as evidenced by record vehicle sales. At yearend there was concern that equities during 2000 could not repeat the strength of the past year; then again, like feelings prevailed at the end of each of the past few years and the equity markets proved otherwise. On balance, the bullish momentum had deep root at yearend 1999, which appeared capable of supporting new highs for the major stock indices in 2000.

Futures Markets

The Chicago Mercantile Exchange (CME) IOM division trades index futures and options on the S&P 500, the S&P Midcap 400, the NASDAQ 100 and the Russell 2000. The Chicago Board of Trade (CBOT) lists futures and options on the Dow-Jones 30 industrial stock average. New York Stock Exchange Composite index futures and options are traded on the NYFE Division of the New York Board of Trade (NYBOT). The Kansas City Board of Trade (KCBT) lists futures and options on the Value Line Index.

Dow Jones Industrial Average (30 Stocks)

Year	Jan.	Feb.	Mar.	Apr.	May	June	July	Aug.	Sept.	Oct.	Nov.	Dec.	Average
1990	2,679.2	2,614.2	2,700.1	2,708.4	2,793.8	2,894.8	2,934.2	2,681.9	2,550.7	2,460.5	2,518.6	2,610.9	2,679.0
1991	2,587.6	2,863.0	2,920.1	2,925.5	2,928.4	2,968.1	2,978.2	3,006.1	3,010.4	3,019.7	2,986.1	2,958.6	2,929.3
1992	3,227.1	3,257.3	3,247.4	3,294.1	3,376.8	3,337.8	3,329.4	3,307.4	3,293.9	3,198.7	3,238.5	3,303.1	3,284.3
1993	3,277.7	3,367.3	3,440.7	3,423.6	3,478.2	3,513.8	3,529.4	3,597.0	3,592.3	3,625.8	3,674.7	3,744.1	3,522.1
1994	3,868.4	3,905.6	3,817.0	3,661.5	3,708.0	3,737.6	3,718.3	3,797.5	3,880.6	3,868.1	3,792.5	3,770.3	3,793.8
1995	3,872.5	3,953.7	4,062.8	4,230.7	4,391.6	4,510.8	4,684.8	4,639.3	4,746.8	4,760.5	4,935.8	5,136.1	4,493.8
1996	5,179.4	5,518.7	5,612.2	5,579.9	5,616.7	5,671.5	5,496.3	5,685.5	5,804.0	5,995.1	6,318.4	6,435.9	5,742.8
1997	6,707.0	6,917.5	6,901.1	6,657.5	7,242.4	7,599.6	7,990.7	7,948.4	7,866.6	7,875.8	7,677.4	7,909.8	7,441.1
1998	7,808.4	8,323.6	8,709.5	9,037.4	9,080.1	8,873.0	9,097.1	8,478.5	7,909.8	8,164.3	9,005.8	9,018.7	8,625.5
1999	9,345.9	9,323.0	9,753.6	10,443.5	10,853.9	10,704.0	11,052.2	10,935.5	10,714.0	10,396.9	10,809.8	11,246.4	10,464.9

Average. *Source: New York Stock Exchange (NYSE)*

Dow Jones Transportation Average (20 Stocks)

Year	Jan.	Feb.	Mar.	Apr.	May	June	July	Aug.	Sept.	Oct.	Nov.	Dec.	Average
1990	1,139.8	1,083.4	1,160.3	1,164.8	1,163.1	1,181.9	1,150.0	951.1	881.3	850.8	848.1	908.5	1,040.3
1991	962.2	1,110.4	1,113.5	1,138.8	1,167.6	1,205.2	1,204.7	1,204.7	1,182.3	1,241.5	1,237.1	1,233.3	1,166.8
1992	1,378.7	1,412.2	1,409.0	1,356.9	1,380.4	1,333.3	1,303.1	1,254.6	1,275.2	1,286.1	1,375.9	1,430.2	1,349.6
1993	1,488.1	1,533.2	1,541.6	1,619.7	1,583.4	1,533.9	1,553.7	1,631.6	1,623.9	1,660.5	1,732.6	1,763.2	1,605.5
1994	1,812.1	1,810.4	1,719.9	1,614.7	1,602.2	1,619.2	1,596.2	1,602.8	1,553.7	1,485.8	1,473.7	1,415.3	1,608.8
1995	1,515.8	1,547.2	1,584.6	1,648.9	1,646.2	1,699.3	1,852.1	1,883.9	1,961.4	1,922.9	2,008.3	2,029.5	1,775.0
1996	1,932.7	2,030.0	2,136.0	2,180.0	2,229.1	2,213.4	2,053.1	2,060.4	2,050.8	2,100.1	2,224.3	2,273.9	2,123.7
1997	2,295.0	2,341.4	2,427.8	2,464.0	2,635.1	2,711.4	2,858.0	2,925.8	3,086.0	3,239.9	3,155.7	3,233.5	2,781.1
1998	3,275.8	3,456.8	3,521.5	3,586.5	3,401.9	3,373.2	3,459.3	3,021.1	2,763.0	2,647.8	2,953.4	3,027.6	3,207.3
1999	3,172.0	3,188.3	3,296.4	3,477.7	3,628.2	3,396.1	3,423.7	3,207.0	3,006.2	2,928.7	2,988.7	2,902.1	3,217.9

Average. *Source: New York Stock Exchange (NYSE)*

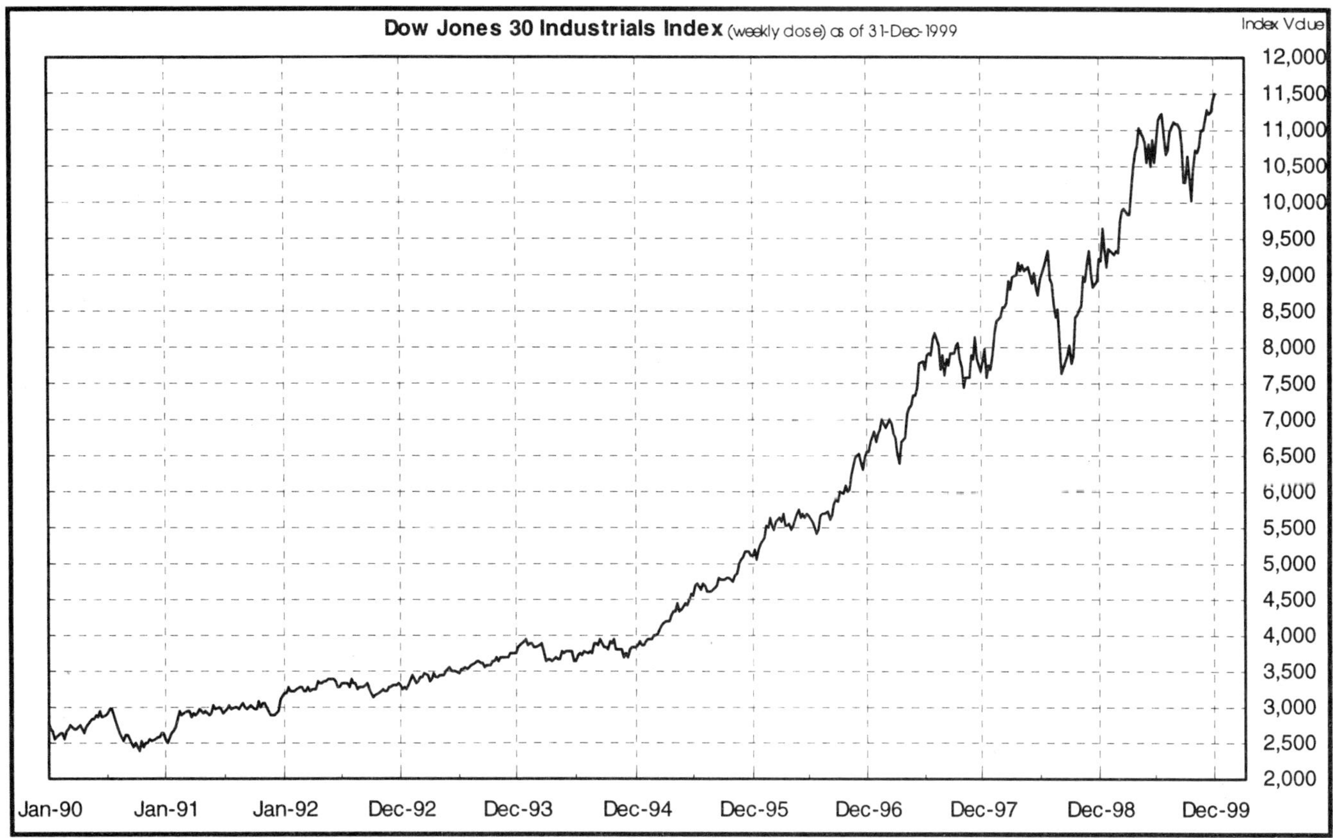

Dow Jones Public Utilities Average (15 Stocks)

Year	Jan.	Feb.	Mar.	Apr.	May	June	July	Aug.	Sept.	Oct.	Nov.	Dec.	Average
1989	188.9	186.6	182.8	188.0	196.3	206.7	215.5	218.1	216.0	215.7	221.0	232.1	205.6
1990	223.2	221.2	217.0	210.7	212.4	211.2	205.0	201.2	199.8	207.2	210.3	210.6	210.8
1991	205.3	213.7	213.2	214.4	211.2	204.6	199.6	204.4	208.0	213.6	216.7	219.3	210.3
1992	215.7	206.8	204.4	206.1	213.2	212.5	219.1	220.2	220.0	217.2	217.7	220.2	214.4
1993	222.0	234.2	240.0	242.1	237.8	241.5	246.5	252.0	253.0	243.1	227.1	227.1	238.9
1994	222.3	215.6	207.0	196.5	185.5	182.9	181.8	188.9	179.6	179.9	177.7	181.0	191.6
1995	186.9	194.0	187.9	192.7	197.6	204.5	202.5	202.8	207.2	216.4	215.3	221.4	202.4
1996	228.4	228.6	216.3	209.5	211.2	210.0	212.8	214.8	217.2	222.3	234.0	232.1	219.8
1997	235.8	230.5	223.7	213.8	222.1	223.5	232.0	231.9	238.9	242.9	249.2	263.9	234.0
1998	265.6	267.9	279.0	285.4	281.2	291.1	289.3	279.4	289.1	307.0	308.1	309.0	287.7

Average. *Source: New York Stock Exchange (NYSE)*

Standard & Poor's 500 Composite Price Index

Year	Jan.	Feb.	Mar.	Apr.	May	June	July	Aug.	Sept.	Oct.	Nov.	Dec.	Average
1990	340.0	330.5	338.5	338.2	350.3	360.4	360.0	330.8	315.4	307.1	315.3	328.8	334.6
1991	325.5	362.3	372.3	379.7	378.0	378.3	380.2	389.4	387.2	386.9	385.9	388.5	376.2
1992	416.1	412.6	407.4	407.4	414.8	408.3	415.1	417.9	418.5	412.5	422.8	435.6	415.7
1993	435.2	441.7	450.2	443.1	445.3	448.1	447.3	454.1	459.2	463.9	462.9	466.0	451.4
1994	473.0	471.6	463.8	447.2	451.0	454.8	451.4	464.2	467.0	463.8	461.0	455.2	460.3
1995	465.3	481.9	493.2	507.9	523.8	539.4	557.4	559.1	578.8	582.9	595.5	614.6	541.6
1996	614.4	649.5	647.1	547.2	661.2	668.5	644.1	662.7	674.9	701.5	735.7	743.3	662.5
1997	766.1	798.4	792.2	763.9	833.1	876.3	925.3	927.7	937.0	951.2	938.9	962.4	872.7
1998	963.4	1,023.7	1,076.8	1,112.2	1,108.4	1,108.4	1,156.6	1,074.6	1,020.7	1,032.5	1,144.5	1,190.0	1,084.3
1999	1,248.7	1,246.6	1,281.7	1,334.8	1,332.1	1,322.6	1,381.0	1,327.5	1,318.2	1,300.0	1,391.0	1,428.7	1,326.1

Average. *Source: Index and Option Market (IOM), division of the Chicago Mercantile Exchange (CME)*

STOCK INDEX FUTURES, U.S.

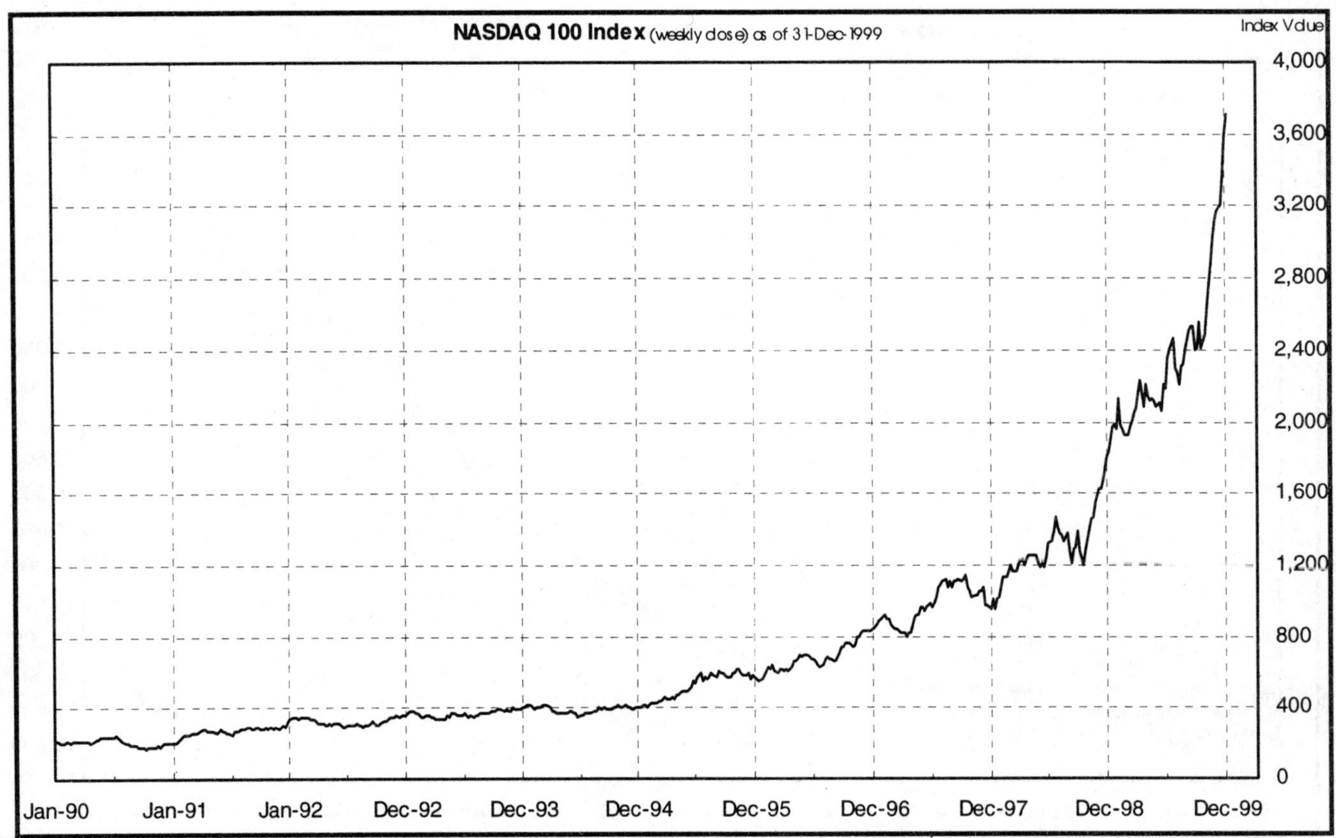

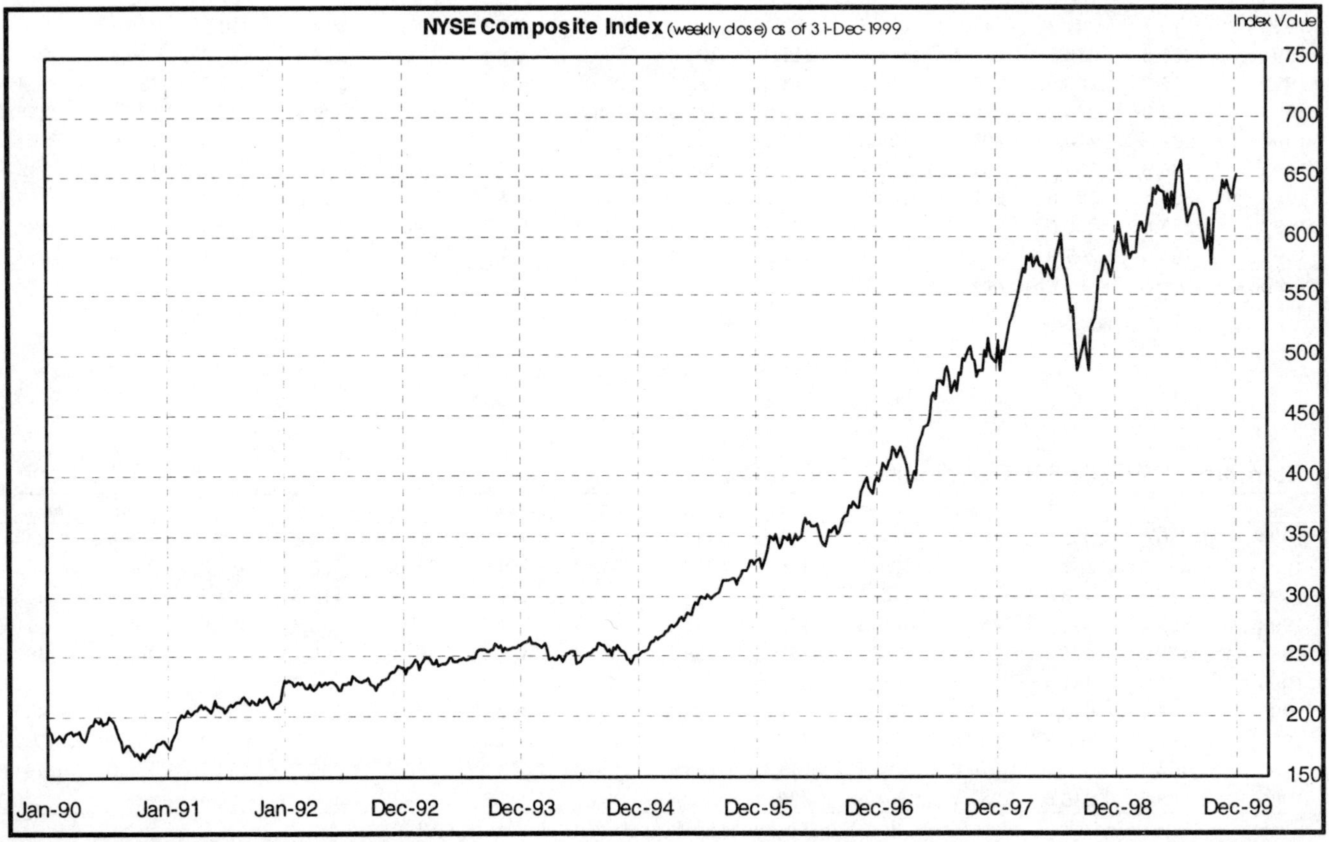

NYSE Composite Index (weekly close) as of 31-Dec-1999

Index Value

750
700
650
600
550
500
450
400
350
300
250
200
150

Jan-90 Jan-91 Jan-92 Dec-92 Dec-93 Dec-94 Dec-95 Dec-96 Dec-97 Dec-98 Dec-99

S&P 500 Index (weekly close) as of 31-Dec-1999
Index Value
1,600
1,500
1,400
1,300
1,200
1,100
1,000
900
800
700
600
500
400
300
200
Jan-90
Jan-91
Jan-92
Dec-92
Dec-93
Dec-94
Dec-95
Dec-96
Dec-97
Dec-98
Dec-99

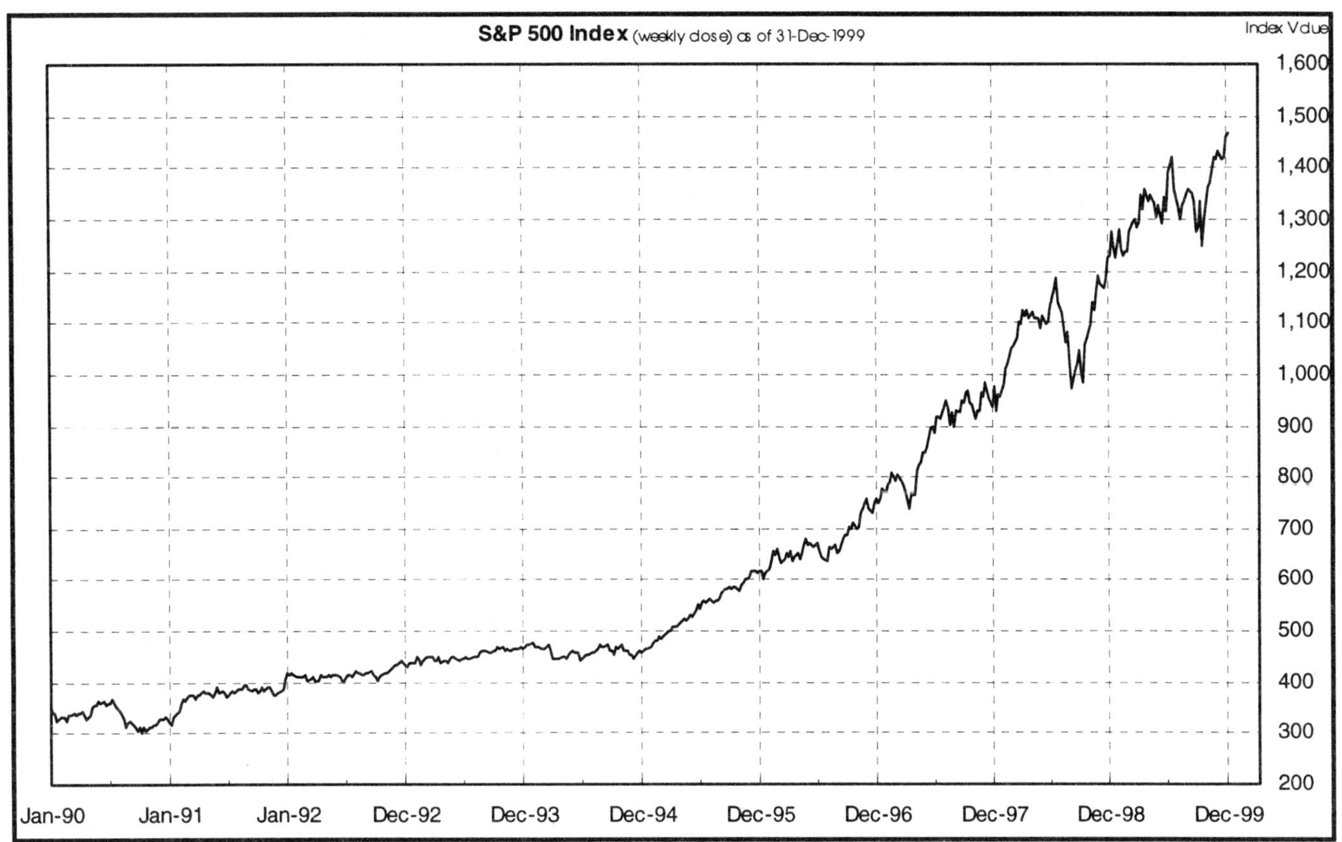

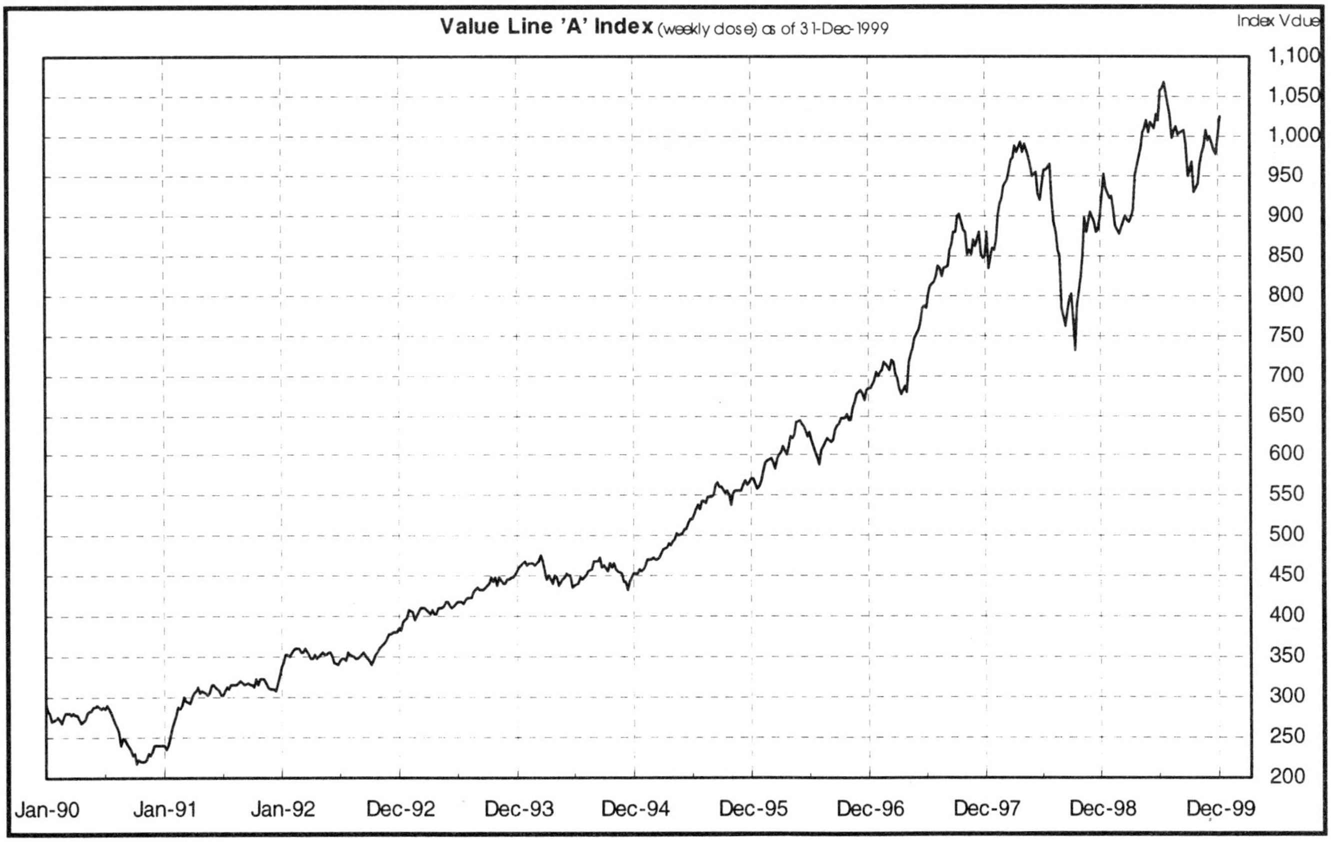

Value Line 'A' Index (weekly close) as of 31-Dec-1999
Index Value
1,100
1,050
1,000
950
900
850
800
750
700
650
600
550
500
450
400
350
300
250
200
Jan-90
Jan-91
Jan-92
Dec-92
Dec-93
Dec-94
Dec-95
Dec-96
Dec-97
Dec-98
Dec-99

STOCK INDEX FUTURES, U.S.

Composite Index of Leading Indicators (1992 = 100)

Year	Jan.	Feb.	Mar.	Apr.	May	June	July	Aug.	Sept.	Oct.	Nov.	Dec.	Average
1991	97.8	98.1	98.5	98.8	99.1	99.3	99.8	99.5	99.5	99.5	99.4	99.1	99.0
1992	99.4	99.7	99.9	99.9	100.0	99.9	99.9	99.9	99.9	100.1	100.4	101.0	100.0
1993	100.7	100.7	100.1	100.4	100.2	100.3	100.1	100.3	100.4	100.5	100.8	101.2	100.5
1994	101.2	101.0	101.5	101.4	101.4	101.4	101.2	101.5	101.4	101.5	101.6	101.6	101.4
1995	101.5	101.1	100.7	100.6	100.4	100.5	100.7	101.0	101.1	100.9	100.9	101.2	100.9
1996	100.5	101.4	101.6	101.8	102.1	102.3	102.3	102.4	102.5	102.5	102.5	102.6	102.0
1997	102.8	103.3	103.4	103.3	103.6	103.6	103.9	104.0	104.3	104.4	104.7	104.6	103.8
1998	104.8	105.2	105.4	105.4	105.4	105.2	105.6	105.6	105.6	105.7	106.2	106.4	105.5
1999[1]	106.9	107.1	107.2	107.1	107.4	107.7	108.0	108.0	107.9	108.0	108.3		107.6

[1] Preliminary. *Source: Bureau of Economic Analysis, U.S. Department of Commerce (BEA)*

Civilian Unemployment Rate

Year	Jan.	Feb.	Mar.	Apr.	May	June	July	Aug.	Sept.	Oct.	Nov.	Dec.	Average
1991	6.4	6.6	6.8	6.7	6.9	6.9	6.8	6.9	6.9	7.0	7.0	7.3	6.9
1992	7.3	7.4	7.4	7.4	7.6	7.8	7.7	7.6	7.6	7.3	7.4	7.4	7.5
1993	7.3	7.1	7.0	7.1	7.1	7.0	6.9	6.8	6.7	6.8	6.6	6.5	6.9
1994	6.7	6.6	6.5	6.4	6.0	6.1	6.1	6.1	5.9	5.8	5.6	5.4	6.1
1995	5.6	5.5	5.4	5.7	5.6	5.6	5.7	5.7	5.7	5.5	5.6	5.6	5.6
1996	5.7	5.5	5.5	5.5	5.5	5.3	5.4	5.2	5.2	5.2	5.3	5.3	5.4
1997	5.4	5.3	5.2	4.9	4.8	5.0	4.9	4.9	4.9	4.8	4.6	4.7	5.0
1998	4.6	4.6	4.7	4.3	4.4	4.5	4.5	4.5	4.5	4.5	4.4	4.3	4.5
1999[1]	4.3	4.4	4.2	4.3	4.2	4.3	4.3	4.2	4.2	4.1	4.1	4.1	4.2

[1] Preliminary. *Source: Bureau of Economic Analysis, U.S. Department of Commerce (BEA)*

Capacity Utilization Rates (Total Industry) In Percent

Year	Jan.	Feb.	Mar.	Apr.	May	June	July	Aug.	Sept.	Oct.	Nov.	Dec.	Average
1991	79.6	78.9	78.1	78.2	78.7	79.5	79.5	79.5	80.1	79.9	79.7	79.1	79.2
1992	79.0	79.4	79.9	80.4	80.6	80.2	80.6	80.2	80.5	81.0	81.3	81.2	80.4
1993	81.4	81.7	81.6	81.7	81.2	81.2	81.3	81.0	81.7	81.8	82.1	82.5	81.6
1994	82.6	82.8	83.2	83.3	83.7	83.9	84.1	83.9	83.8	84.1	84.4	84.9	83.9
1995	84.9	84.5	84.3	83.9	83.7	83.6	83.4	83.8	83.9	83.3	83.2	83.0	83.4
1996	82.4	83.2	82.6	83.1	83.2	83.5	83.2	83.2	83.1	83.0	82.5	82.5	82.4
1997	82.4	82.6	82.5	82.6	82.4	82.3	82.6	82.8	82.7	83.4	83.4	83.4	82.9
1998	83.0	82.6	82.6	82.6	82.6	81.5	81.1	82.0	81.3	81.5	80.9	80.6	81.9
1999[1]	80.4	80.4	80.5	80.4	80.5	80.5	80.7	80.7	80.6	81.0	81.0		80.6

[1] Preliminary. *Source: Bureau of Economic Analysis, U.S. Department of Commerce (BEA)*

Manufacturers New Orders, Durable Goods In Billions of Constant Dollars

Year	Jan.	Feb.	Mar.	Apr.	May	June	July	Aug.	Sept.	Oct.	Nov.	Dec.	Average
1991	119.26	120.00	112.54	117.55	120.64	116.85	132.82	125.62	122.36	123.66	124.96	116.97	121.10
1992	122.15	122.14	124.63	127.60	125.65	128.77	125.51	123.79	125.86	128.69	125.49	135.19	126.29
1993	129.56	133.47	128.50	130.20	126.93	131.29	128.27	128.99	130.31	133.01	135.60	136.82	131.08
1994	142.23	138.88	140.91	141.21	142.61	146.15	142.60	145.92	146.93	145.72	149.89	152.88	144.66
1995	153.42	151.82	151.72	146.32	149.74	148.21	147.45	152.12	156.78	154.37	154.09	158.89	154.10
1996	158.86	155.10	157.67	156.01	162.59	162.67	168.25	162.76	170.45	170.59	169.34	166.02	163.48
1997	171.73	174.80	170.02	173.13	177.05	176.93	175.82	181.08	181.15	181.33	189.71	181.44	177.03
1998	184.33	183.87	184.17	187.35	181.58	182.22	186.22	190.39	193.18	189.33	190.21	197.11	187.50
1999[1]	203.68	196.01	201.79	197.14	199.11	199.62	208.14	210.62	207.81	206.35	209.07		203.58

[1] Preliminary. *Source: Bureau of Economic Analysis, U.S. Department of Commerce (BEA)*

Change in Manufacturing and Trade Inventories In Billions of Dollars

Year	Jan.	Feb.	Mar.	Apr.	May	June	July	Aug.	Sept.	Oct.	Nov.	Dec.	Average
1991	60.8	-24.8	-99.2	-25.7	-50.0	-32.7	-10.5	-1.1	37.2	16.2	8.8	47.3	-6.1
1992	-60.6	-0.3	13.8	28.3	-22.3	53.6	28.4	21.4	-8.4	4.6	11.8	23.9	7.9
1993	34.9	31.8	66.7	43.7	12.9	25.6	7.3	39.0	34.8	27.2	63.2	1.6	32.4
1994	15.3	45.1	-8.1	42.1	114.2	56.3	60.8	98.6	60.3	71.8	65.3	64.5	57.2
1995	127.4	78.5	100.6	97.6	54.4	48.1	42.9	50.6	51.4	61.8	24.1	-39.7	58.5
1996	66.2	14.2	-27.7	61.5	-8.4	80.3	123.6	-272.1	90.6	143.4	86.1	72.0	19.9
1997	107.0	103.4	76.3	56.2	25.2	76.8	20.9	19.1	91.5	55.2	43.1	28.2	47.1
1998	27.8	86.1	85.7	38.5	5.5	11.4	-91.6	47.9	67.6	25.1	48.7	-5.4	34.7
1999[1]	2.0	37.2	63.7	24.4	39.0	40.9	41.7	41.5	57.2	28.9			37.7

[1] Preliminary. *Source: Bureau of Economic Analysis, U.S. Department of Commerce (BEA)*

Comparison of International Stock Price Indexes (1990 = 100)

Year	Jan.	Feb.	Mar.	Apr.	May	June	July	Aug.	Sept.	Oct.	Nov.	Dec.	Average
United States													
1994	144.8	140.4	134.0	135.5	137.2	133.5	137.7	142.9	139.1	142.0	136.4	138.1	138.5
1995	141.4	146.5	150.5	154.7	160.3	163.7	168.9	168.9	175.7	174.8	182.0	185.1	164.4
1996	191.2	192.5	194.0	196.6	201.1	201.6	192.4	196.0	206.6	212.0	227.6	222.7	202.9
1997	236.3	237.7	227.6	240.9	255.0	266.1	286.8	270.4	284.7	274.9	287.2	291.7	263.3
1998	294.7	315.4	331.2	334.2	327.9	340.8	336.9	287.7	305.7	330.2	349.8	369.5	327.0
1999[1]	384.6	372.2	386.7	401.3	391.3	412.6	399.4	396.9	385.6	409.7	417.5		396.2
Canada													
1994	133.1	129.3	126.6	124.7	126.5	117.7	122.2	127.1	127.3	125.4	119.7	123.2	125.2
1995	117.4	120.6	126.1	125.1	130.0	132.3	134.9	132.0	132.4	130.3	136.2	137.8	129.6
1996	145.2	144.2	145.3	150.4	153.4	147.4	144.1	150.3	154.7	163.7	175.9	173.2	154.0
1997	178.6	180.0	171.0	174.7	186.6	188.2	201.0	193.3	205.8	200.0	190.4	195.8	188.8
1998	195.8	207.3	220.9	224.0	221.9	215.3	202.6	161.7	164.0	181.5	185.4	189.6	197.5
1999[1]	196.7	184.5	192.9	205.0	200.0	204.9	207.0	203.8	203.4	212.1	220.0		202.8
France													
1994	128.4	123.1	114.6	119.2	111.7	104.1	114.2	113.8	103.4	104.9	108.7	103.5	112.5
1995	98.9	97.8	102.3	105.6	107.2	102.3	105.6	103.6	98.4	99.8	100.6	103.0	102.1
1996	111.2	109.5	112.5	118.1	116.1	116.9	109.8	108.4	117.4	117.8	127.4	127.4	116.0
1997	138.5	143.5	146.2	145.2	142.2	157.3	169.2	152.4	165.5	150.7	157.3	165.0	152.8
1998	174.5	188.3	213.3	213.5	222.4	231.3	229.8	200.9	176.0	193.8	211.5	216.9	206.0
1999[1]	233.9	225.2	231.0	242.4	239.4	249.6	241.1	252.5	252.6	269.0	293.9		248.2
Germany[2]													
1994	115.1	110.7	112.3	117.8	109.7	106.4	111.5	114.5	105.2	107.7	105.9	108.3	110.4
1995	103.8	108.2	98.6	103.5	106.6	106.6	112.8	113.7	111.4	109.3	111.9	114.0	108.4
1996	123.7	123.2	123.3	123.0	124.4	126.3	122.1	125.6	130.4	130.6	139.0	139.7	153.2
1997	147.0	157.8	167.8	167.1	172.2	183.8	209.6	184.1	195.3	177.8	186.0	196.3	221.4
1998	204.9	217.5	234.9	302.0	329.3	348.7	347.3	285.8	264.6	276.2	297.0	295.8	299.1
1999[1]	305.1	290.4	288.8	318.9	299.8	318.0	301.6	311.6	304.5	326.7	348.6		310.4
Italy													
1994	103.1	102.5	112.6	124.5	113.8	107.4	110.5	107.5	105.8	98.9	97.4	98.5	106.9
1995	102.8	97.5	93.3	99.8	98.8	94.9	98.8	99.0	96.1	90.5	86.1	91.8	95.8
1996	96.5	94.5	90.4	102.4	104.1	102.4	93.4	93.2	99.0	94.0	102.4	103.7	98.0
1997	119.8	115.4	115.3	119.5	117.9	130.0	144.5	136.6	155.0	144.6	149.4	164.0	134.3
1998	184.0	194.3	239.3	220.9	236.1	222.1	240.5	208.1	184.6	194.1	223.7	231.5	214.9
1999[1]	231.7	234.1	245.4	245.9	237.1	237.5	221.5	230.4	231.0	226.5	241.3		234.8
Japan													
1994	70.2	69.4	66.3	68.4	72.8	71.6	70.9	71.6	67.9	69.3	66.2	68.4	69.4
1995	64.7	59.2	56.0	58.3	53.6	50.4	57.9	62.9	62.1	61.2	65.0	68.9	60.0
1996	72.2	69.8	74.3	76.5	76.2	78.2	71.8	70.0	74.8	71.0	72.9	67.2	72.9
1997	63.6	64.4	62.5	66.4	69.6	71.5	70.5	63.2	62.1	57.1	57.7	52.9	63.5
1998	57.7	58.4	57.3	54.3	54.4	54.9	56.8	48.9	46.5	47.1	51.6	48.0	53.0
1999[1]	50.3	49.8	54.9	57.9	55.9	60.8	62.0	60.5	61.1	62.2	64.4		58.2
United Kingdom													
1994	161.3	154.8	144.3	146.0	138.7	135.2	142.8	150.3	139.6	141.9	141.2	140.5	144.7
1995	136.8	137.4	142.1	145.8	150.8	150.0	157.3	158.8	160.2	160.2	165.2	166.6	152.6
1996	170.2	170.0	170.3	176.9	174.2	171.5	169.6	177.0	179.7	180.8	183.4	186.0	175.8
1997	192.8	194.7	194.0	197.3	203.3	201.8	212.0	210.3	226.8	211.9	211.4	222.7	206.6
1998	234.3	247.9	257.0	257.6	258.9	253.4	252.6	225.5	216.6	231.4	242.7	247.0	243.7
1999[1]	249.0	261.0	267.4	279.8	266.9	272.2	270.2	271.5	261.1	268.3	285.2		268.4

[1] Preliminary. [2] Federal Republic of Germany. Not Seasonally Adjusted. *Source: Economic and Statistics Administration, U.S. Department of Commerce (ESA)*

Corporate Profits After Tax -- Quarterly In Billions of Dollars

Year	First Quarter	Second Quarter	Third Quarter	Fourth Quarter	Average	Year	First Quarter	Second Quarter	Third Quarter	Fourth Quarter	Average
1988	201.0	217.1	220.3	231.0	217.4	1994	312.1	342.5	361.6	377.7	348.5
1989	219.3	206.7	196.9	204.4	206.8	1995	401.0	405.9	411.8	418.8	409.4
1990	221.7	232.2	233.9	237.1	231.2	1996	438.7	450.0	447.5	454.0	454.1
1991	240.7	236.4	238.6	247.6	240.8	1997	467.2	475.3	504.7	487.1	488.3
1992	267.2	275.2	240.4	270.6	263.4	1998	479.2	481.8	477.3	472.5	477.7
1993	282.5	296.1	298.4	324.0	300.3	1999[1]	501.9	510.7	598.6		537.1

[1] Preliminary. *Source: Bureau of Economic Analysis, U.S. Department of Commerce (BEA)*

STOCK INDEX FUTURES, U.S.

Productivity: Index of Output per Hour, All Persons, Nonfarm Business -- Quarterly (1992 = 100)

Year	First Quarter	Second Quarter	Third Quarter	Fourth Quarter	Average	Year	First Quarter	Second Quarter	Third Quarter	Fourth Quarter	Average
1988	94.9	95.0	95.4	95.9	95.3	1994	100.2	100.5	101.0	101.2	100.7
1989	95.5	95.7	96.0	96.1	95.8	1995	100.5	100.9	101.3	101.1	100.7
1990	96.4	96.7	96.4	95.5	96.3	1996	101.5	101.7	102.0	102.4	103.7
1991	96.1	96.8	97.4	97.6	97.0	1997	103.4	104.0	105.6	105.9	107.2
1992	99.3	99.9	99.7	101.1	100.0	1998	106.6	106.6	107.3	111.5	110.2
1993	100.1	99.7	100.1	100.8	100.2	1999[1]	112.2	112.4	113.8		112.8

[1] Preliminary. *Source: Bureau of Economic Analysis, U.S. Department of Commerce (BEA)*

Consumer Confidence, The Conference Board (1985 = 100)

Year	Jan.	Feb.	Mar.	Apr.	May	June	July	Aug.	Sept.	Oct.	Nov.	Dec.	Average
1991	55.1	59.4	81.1	79.4	76.4	78.0	77.7	76.1	72.9	60.1	52.7	52.5	68.5
1992	50.2	47.3	56.5	65.1	71.9	72.6	61.2	59.0	57.3	54.6	65.6	78.1	61.6
1993	76.7	68.5	63.2	67.6	61.9	58.6	59.2	59.3	63.8	60.5	71.9	79.8	65.9
1994	82.6	79.9	86.7	92.1	88.9	92.5	91.3	90.4	89.5	89.1	100.4	103.4	90.6
1995	101.4	99.4	100.2	104.6	102.0	94.6	101.4	102.4	97.3	96.3	101.6	99.2	100.0
1996	88.4	98.0	98.4	104.8	103.5	100.1	107.0	112.0	111.8	107.3	109.5	114.2	104.6
1997	118.7	118.9	118.5	118.5	127.9	129.9	126.3	127.6	130.2	123.4	128.1	136.2	125.4
1998	128.3	137.4	133.8	137.2	136.3	138.2	137.2	133.1	126.4	119.3	126.4	126.7	131.7
1999[1]	128.9	133.1	134.0	135.5	137.7	139.0	136.2	136.0	134.2	130.5	137.0		134.7

[1] Preliminary. *Source: The Conference Board (TCB) Copyrighted.*

Average Open Interest of NYSE Composite Stock Index Futures in New York In Contracts

Year	Jan.	Feb.	Mar.	Apr.	May	June	July	Aug.	Sept.	Oct.	Nov.	Dec.
1991	4,736	5,720	5,264	5,488	6,190	6,010	5,056	5,997	5,869	5,512	6,438	6,195
1992	5,216	5,290	5,469	4,575	4,867	5,858	6,491	7,049	6,647	6,034	6,430	5,890
1993	5,033	5,083	4,113	3,613	4,222	4,340	3,714	4,178	3,997	4,315	4,721	4,539
1994	4,653	4,471	4,823	3,720	3,839	3,969	3,903	3,982	4,142	4,494	4,244	4,617
1995	3,695	4,159	4,113	3,476	3,396	3,254	3,205	3,029	2,966	2,683	3,125	3,403
1996	3,644	4,139	3,245	2,822	2,839	2,547	2,492	2,526	2,759	2,798	2,649	3,050
1997	3,126	3,232	3,194	2,801	3,154	2,744	2,316	2,823	2,780	2,384	3,005	4,354
1998	4,803	5,216	5,252	4,754	4,888	5,990	10,154	12,249	10,574	8,554	7,977	9,806
1999	8,299	8,661	5,457	4,050	4,169	3,849	3,418	3,882	3,729	3,958	4,455	4,260

Source: New York Futures Exchange (NYFE)

Average Open Interest of Mini-Value Line Stock Index Futures in Kansas City In Contracts

Year	Jan.	Feb.	Mar.	Apr.	May	June	July	Aug.	Sept.	Oct.	Nov.	Dec.
1991	196	221	249	225	214	236	212	277	324	256	293	321
1992	276	277	279	304	375	543	485	592	477	355	425	398
1993	330	393	382	375	497	449	387	455	413	359	519	534
1994	432	501	530	566	648	593	575	583	573	1,111	1,041	845
1995	678	792	951	1,108	1,132	972	839	1,042	966	980	1,193	1,138
1996	1,238	1,580	1,949	1,804	1,669	1,576	1,611	1,813	1,818	1,466	1,641	1,958
1997	1,459	1,354	1,338	1,448	1,326	1,686	2,160	2,523	1,980	1,477	1,213	1,675
1998	1,739	1,442	1,433	1,498	1,549	1,390	697	839	667	696	914	780
1999	746	738	699	725	900	967	514	503	380	314	300	282

Source: Kansas City Board of Trade (KCBT)

Average Open Interest of S & P 500 Stock Index Futures in Chicago In Contracts

Year	Jan.	Feb.	Mar.	Apr.	May	June	July	Aug.	Sept.	Oct.	Nov.	Dec.
1991	296,224	337,606	317,988	296,212	314,206	309,696	285,330	304,134	303,218	288,558	307,796	290,648
1992	294,868	286,026	283,884	273,982	283,514	299,924	306,070	327,226	336,526	340,130	356,684	359,884
1993	329,228	347,382	357,878	348,554	365,792	380,106	364,378	382,622	416,780	390,218	402,748	392,350
1994	376,450	391,648	420,130	401,636	438,218	599,134	434,056	455,742	475,868	461,188	487,162	502,740
1995	427,004	442,628	445,584	420,104	443,296	453,364	420,024	422,608	417,812	402,794	441,780	447,528
1996	406,400	428,058	419,688	368,620	399,070	407,914	369,248	382,266	413,944	374,726	416,102	448,382
1997	393,086	396,528	417,542	377,100	392,034	417,006	372,274	392,812	423,449	391,922	402,044	417,717
1998	394,410	408,851	417,721	365,746	371,732	412,739	370,410	385,820	434,838	405,395	421,928	435,907
1999	399,093	406,516	410,164	38,140	391,035	400,503	372,454	385,808	408,175	394,315	408,751	416,424

Source: Index and Option Market (IOM), division of the Chicago Mercantile Exchange (CME)

Average Open Interest of S & P 400 Midcap Stock Index Futures in Chicago In Contracts

Year	Jan.	Feb.	Mar.	Apr.	May	June	July	Aug.	Sept.	Oct.	Nov.	Dec.
1992	-----	2,776	3,060	3,017	3,712	4,476	4,073	4,350	4,762	4,355	5,778	6,883
1993	7,197	9,048	9,095	8,759	8,640	9,336	8,731	10,183	10,728	12,955	13,343	13,261
1994	13,183	11,999	12,748	10,801	10,829	11,902	11,970	12,369	15,002	13,702	13,896	14,494
1995	13,787	13,355	11,130	9,275	9,329	9,929	11,198	11,708	13,107	11,702	12,341	12,863
1996	11,088	10,474	11,375	8,700	9,254	10,403	9,763	10,867	11,168	9,641	10,596	11,107
1997	11,215	11,825	11,258	9,721	10,807	10,877	11,292	12,346	13,505	11,595	11,874	13,329
1998	12,688	13,319	14,363	14,130	13,352	13,940	12,964	13,589	14,893	16,645	16,768	17,569
1999	16,191	16,309	14,573	12,154	12,705	14,422	14,263	13,496	13,182	12,699	13,933	14,902

Source: Index and Option Market (IOM), division of the Chicago Mercantile Exchange (CME)

Average Open Interest of NASDAQ 100 Index Futures in Chicago In Contracts

Year	Jan.	Feb.	Mar.	Apr.	May	June	July	Aug.	Sept.	Oct.	Nov.	Dec.
1996	-----		-----	1,364	3,336	6,182	5,977	4,737	7,957	10,999	10,465	8,897
1997	6,610	7,064	8,073	7,627	7,587	8,270	6,346	8,255	8,444	6,235	8,831	8,210
1998	6,918	8,184	9,314	7,652	8,833	11,128	9,991	9,507	9,233	8,187	9,176	10,838
1999	10,669	14,766	19,786	21,286	23,028	26,938	21,646	22,764	21,807	19,946	23,429	27,875

Source: Index and Option Market (IOM), division of the Chicago Mercantile Exchange (CME)

Average Open Interest of Dow Jones Industrials Index Futures in Chicago In Contracts

Year	Jan.	Feb.	Mar.	Apr.	May	June	July	Aug.	Sept.	Oct.	Nov.	Dec.
1997	-----	-----	-----	-----	-----	-----	-----	-----	-----	5,249	11,542	15,952
1998	14,853	15,558	14,421	13,846	14,464	16,226	15,707	17,586	18,569	17,416	17,795	17,597
1999	16,794	19,401	19,807	20,492	25,890	22,198	21,556	25,333	23,976	24,846	22,341	17,299

Source: Chicago Board of Trade (CBT)

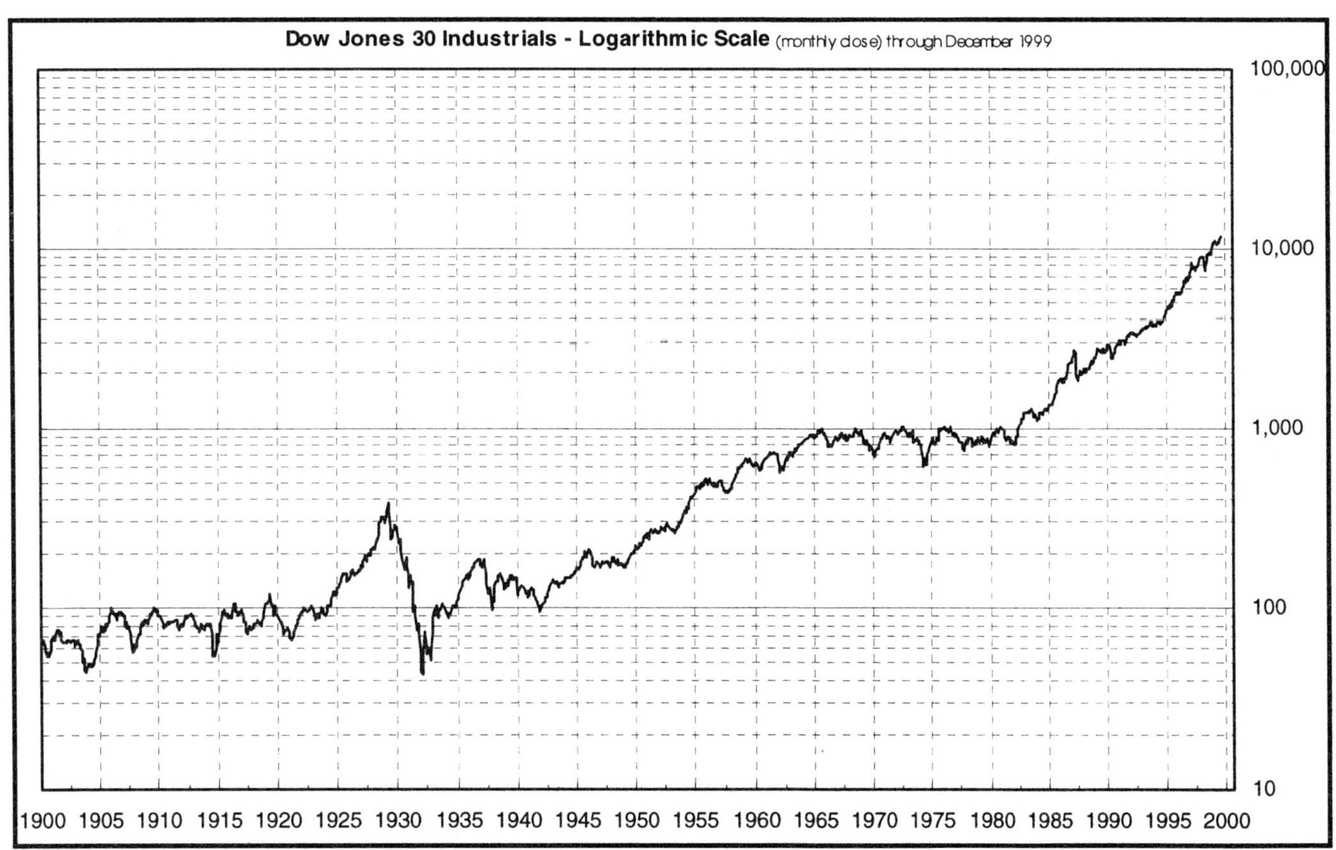

Stock Index Futures, Worldwide

The world's equity markets generally moved higher in 1999, although with sharp variations among the 61 major indexes tracked worldwide; a large number relative to the handful of indices that existed at the start of the 1990's.

Percentagewise, the Cyprus market had the largest gain in 1999, 584 percent, but the country's stock exchange only had 41 companies listed. Conversely, Columbia's Bogota Bolls Index fell about 25.5 percent during 1999. Aside from the percentile swings, of probably greater importance was the astonishing growth in Internet trading which caused a number of exchanges to merge. The odds are that the year 2000 will see further consolidation and/or electronic link-ups, such as plans to promote NASDAQ cross-trading of U.S. and Japanese stocks.

Despite the growth in world equity markets, the U.S. remains dominant: In late 1999, the New York Stock Exchange had a market capitalization of nearly $11 trillion, the NASDAQ and Tokyo markets $4.5 trillion each, followed by Osaka and London markets at $2.8 trillion each, Paris at $1 trillion and Switzerland at about $700 billion.

As usual, the world economic setting was sharply divided, but unlike in 1997 and 1998 when the Asian economies were in turmoil, euphoria seemed to dominate Asia in 1999, which seemed to view itself as the cradle of information technology and Internet related services. In Hong Kong, the benchmark Hang Seng Index rose 52 percent, its best performance in six years. South Korea's index gained 100 percent, the best performance of any Asian market although China's gain was a close second. Taiwan's equity market rose 50 percent despite a devastating earthquake in September. In Japan, whose economy remained somewhat shaky with unemployment around 4.5 percent despite fiscal and monetary priming, the Nikkei 225 Index strengthened from less than 14,000 in early 1999 to a yearend close near 19,000. Russia's RTS index, which fell 85 percent in 1998, rebounded more than 200 percent in 1999 to rate as the third best performance worldwide; on December 31 the index gained 16.8 percent following the resignation of President Yeltsin, its highest level since mid-1998. Turkey's index gained 221 percent despite a devastating earthquake, its impact was offset by the country's growing ties to the European Union. In South America, Argentina's equity market gained 33 percent; Brazil was up 62 percent. Mexico's Bolsa index gained 87 percent. The latter gains were in sharp contrast to the percentage losses seen in 1998 and reflected a pronounced change in sentiment towards many of the world's economies from the uncertainties that prevailed in 1998. On balance, foreign stock markets outperformed the U.S. equity indices in 1999, on a whole rising about 29 percent vs. 21 percent in the U.S., with the increase paced by the rebound in emerging markets.

In Europe, the unexpected weakness in the 11-nation Euro currency against the U.S. Dollar checked some of the markets' strength when measured against the dollar, although they did better when calculated in their local currencies. Germany's Dax gained 18 percent against the dollar, but nearly 40 percent when measured against the D-Mark; for France the gains were about 28 percent and 50 percent (against the Franc), respectively. The U.K. market was up about 13 percent in dollar terms, and almost 20 percent against the pound. However, it wasn't until the fourth quarter that European markets pushed higher. In Western Europe, equity markets surged in late December, paced by Germany's DAX index which reached a record high following the Government's proposal to allow German banks to sell their huge industrial shareholdings without paying a tax on the profits; if approved it would likely unleash tens of billions of dollars into Germany's economy, the expectation of which carried the Dow-Jones Stoxx 50, which is made up of 50 large European companies, to a record high. The best performer in Europe in 1999, as it was in 1998, was Finland whose equity market again more than doubled, due largely to the strength in telecommunication companies.

Perhaps the biggest surprise among the world markets in 1999 was Japan, where stocks rose about 60 percent in dollar terms and about 46 percent against the yen. From its historic high in late 1989 the Japanese stock market plunged about 58 percent in dollar terms to its late 1998 low. Even with the 1999 rally, Japan's equity market was still 16 percent below its 1989 peak. Still, Japanese investors began scrambling back into equities in 1999 as the government worked to buoy the banking system and the first signs of economic recovery appeared. The rush of mutual fund mangers and institutional investors, who had ignored Japan's market for years, was one of the more important bullish market variables in 1999. However, as in Europe and the U.S., much of the rally in the Japanese market came on the back of technology based companies.

Cyclically, the U.S. economy's expansionary phase has persisted for an unprecedented eight-plus years and appears likely to carry into 2000 although at a somewhat slower growth rate. The flow of capital into U.S. equities, much of it emanating from pension programs, shows little sign of slowing. While the U.S. equity markets would seem ripe for the long awaited pause, the public's bias was still solidly positive at yearend 1999. On a global basis, real economic growth in 2000 is forecast to reach 3.5 percent vs. earlier estimates of 2.9 percent. The revised forecast reflects further expansion in the Japanese and South Korean economy's, a modest upturn in Europe of 2.5 to 3 percent, and the resiliency of the U.S. economy, all of which appear likely to push the world's equity market indices to new highs in 2000.

Futures Markets

Futures and option trading on stock indices expanded rapidly in the 1990's, taking their place alongside debt instruments futures and options as the most successful exchange traded contracts. Because of this, nearly every global futures exchange lists a variety of stock index contracts, primarily on those indices based on their domestic stock markets. The lists of stock indices traded worldwide has grown too large for this space, but a listing is available in the worldwide futures exchange volume tables in the front section of this Yearbook.

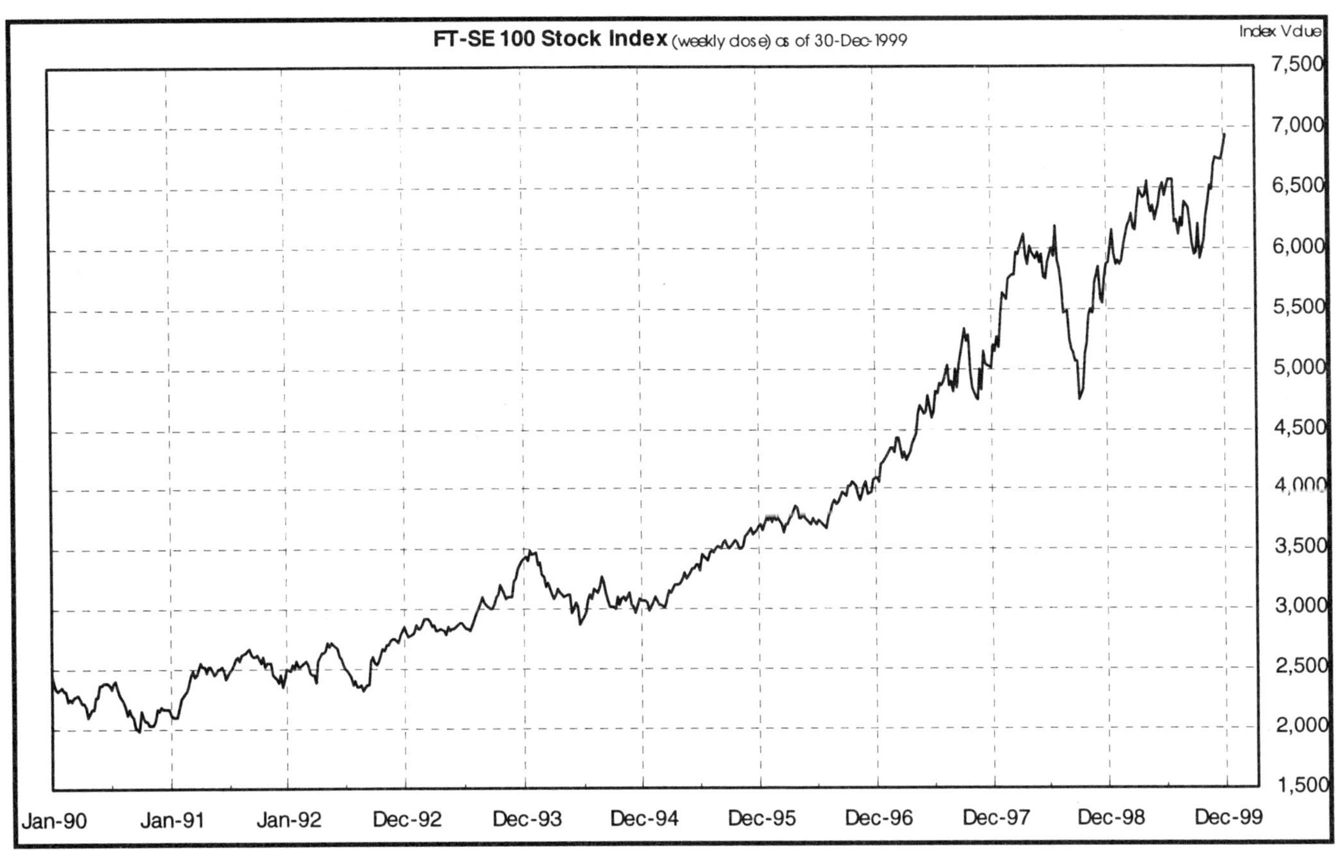
FT-SE 100 Stock Index (weekly close) as of 30-Dec-1999
Index Value
7,500
7,000
6,500
6,000
5,500
5,000
4,500
4,000
3,500
3,000
2,500
2,000
1,500
Jan-90
Jan-91
Jan-92
Dec-92
Dec-93
Dec-94
Dec-95
Dec-96
Dec-97
Dec-98
Dec-99

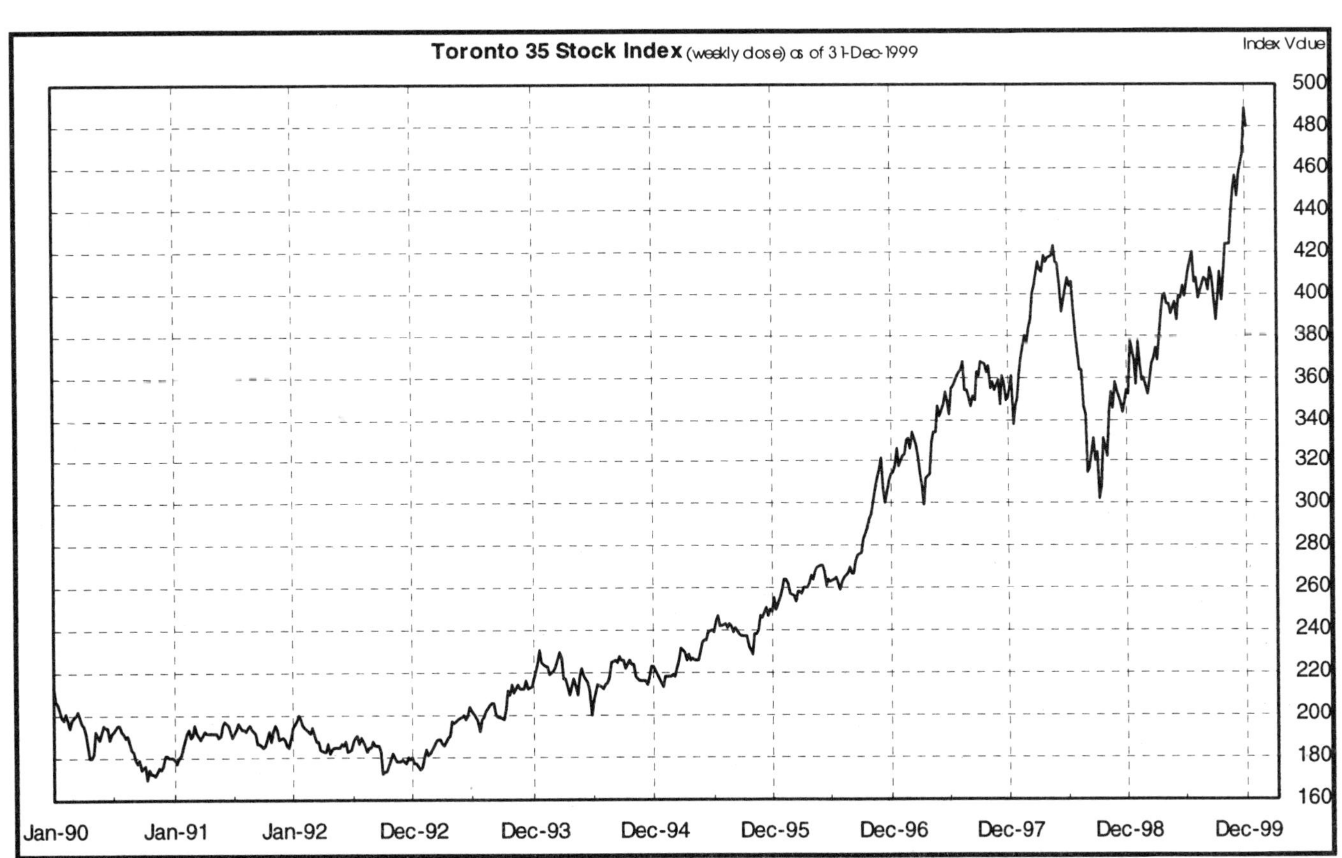
Toronto 35 Stock Index (weekly close) as of 31-Dec-1999
Index Value
500
480
460
440
420
400
380
360
340
320
300
280
260
240
220
200
180
160
Jan-90
Jan-91
Jan-92
Dec-92
Dec-93
Dec-94
Dec-95
Dec-96
Dec-97
Dec-98
Dec-99

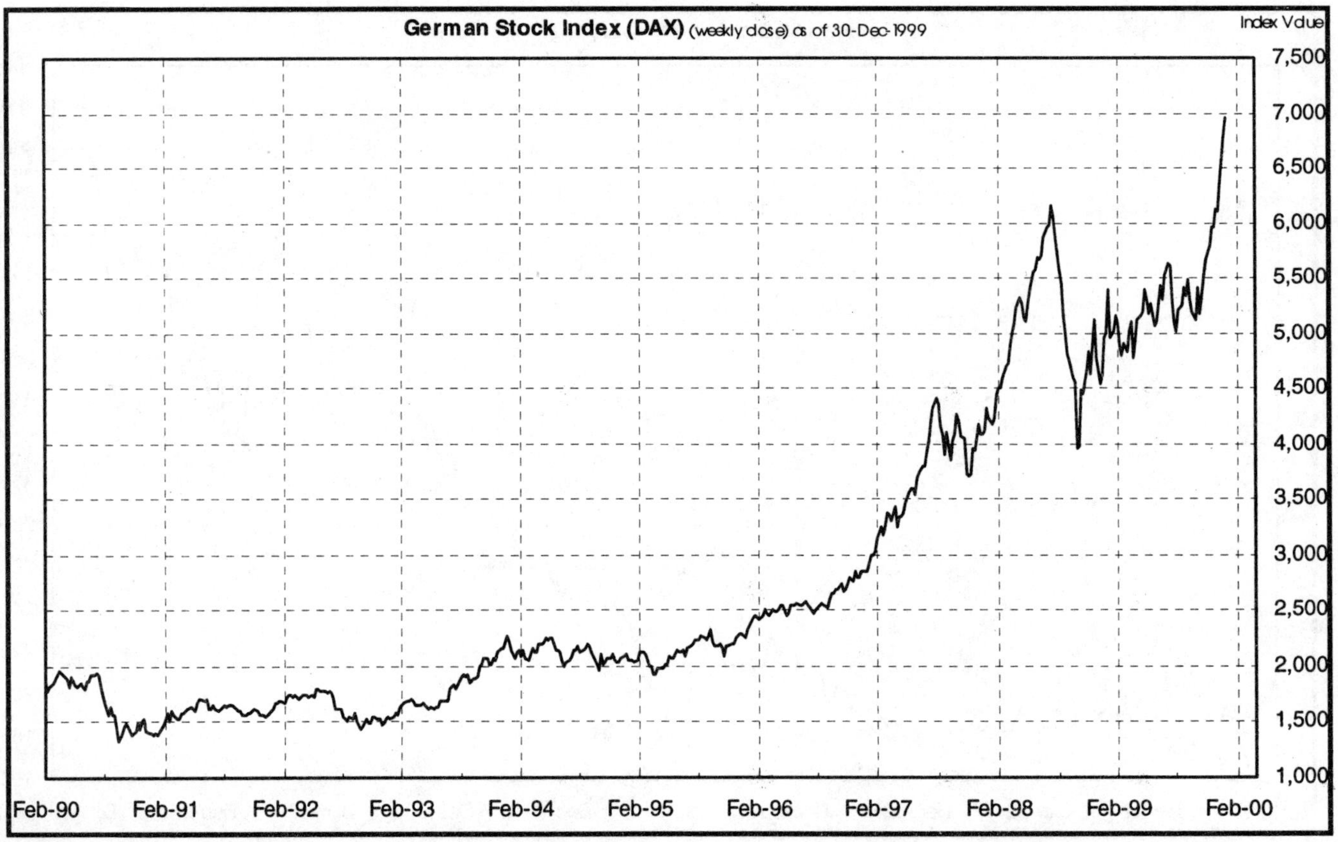

German Stock Index (DAX) (weekly close) as of 30-Dec-1999

Index Value

7,500
7,000
6,500
6,000
5,500
5,000
4,500
4,000
3,500
3,000
2,500
2,000
1,500
1,000

Feb-90 Feb-91 Feb-92 Feb-93 Feb-94 Feb-95 Feb-96 Feb-97 Feb-98 Feb-99 Feb-00

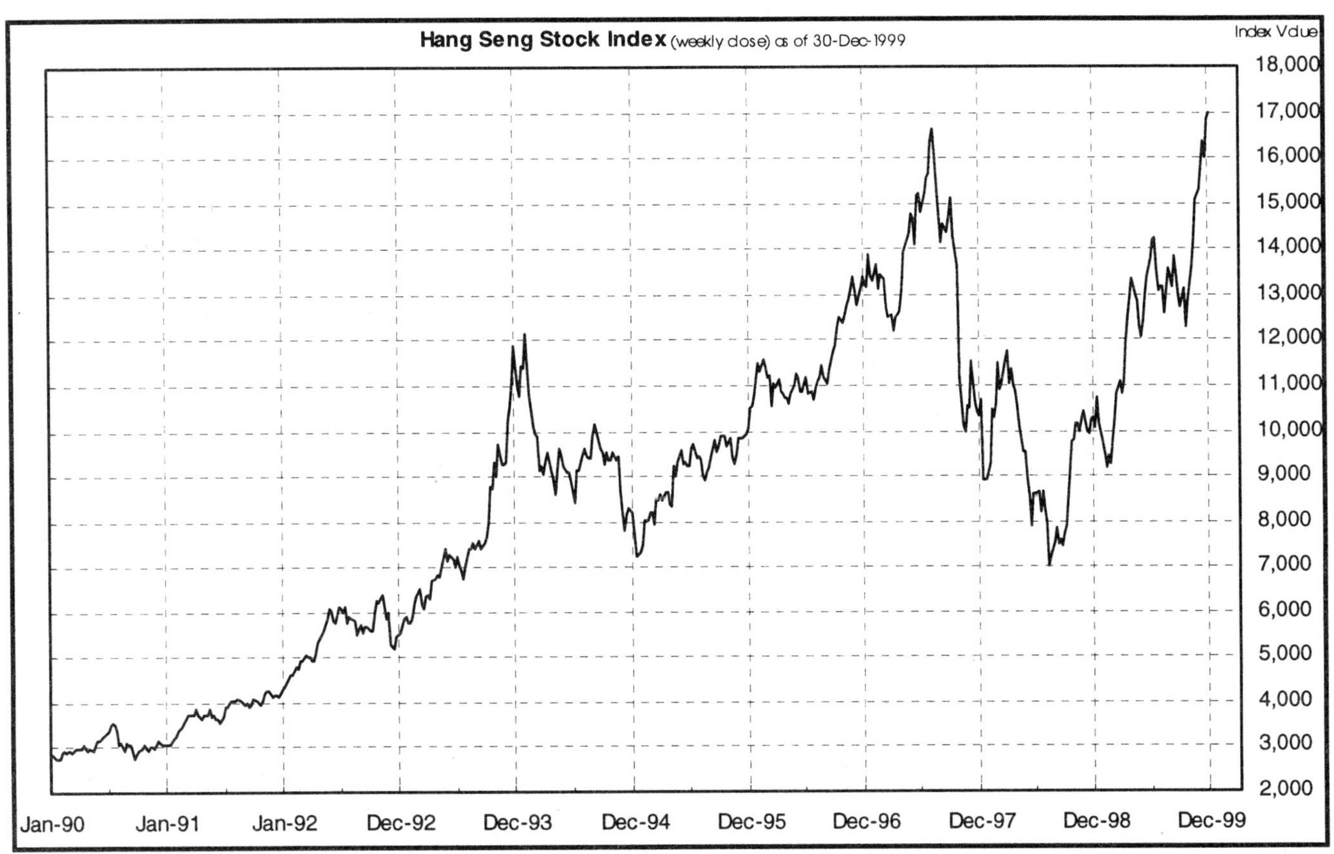
Hang Seng Stock Index (weekly close) as of 30-Dec-1999
Index Value
18,000
17,000
16,000
15,000
14,000
13,000
12,000
11,000
10,000
9,000
8,000
7,000
6,000
5,000
4,000
3,000
2,000
Jan-90
Jan-91
Jan-92
Dec-92
Dec-93
Dec-94
Dec-95
Dec-96
Dec-97
Dec-98
Dec-99

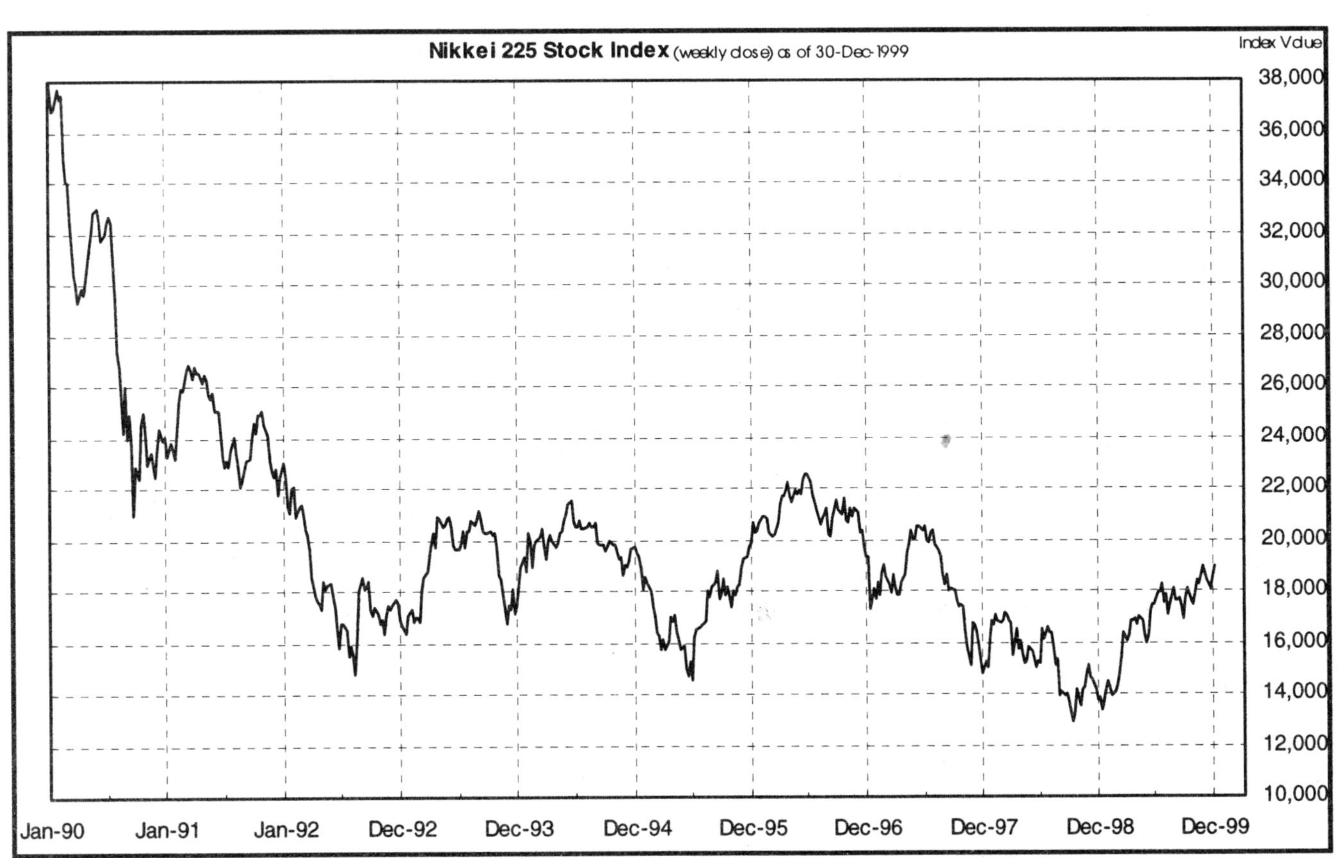
Nikkei 225 Stock Index (weekly close) as of 30-Dec-1999
Index Value
38,000
36,000
34,000
32,000
30,000
28,000
26,000
24,000
22,000
20,000
18,000
16,000
14,000
12,000
10,000
Jan-90
Jan-91
Jan-92
Dec-92
Dec-93
Dec-94
Dec-95
Dec-96
Dec-97
Dec-98
Dec-99

Sugar

A salient feature of the world sugar market is increasing stocks. World production of sugar has been increasing for several years and as production exceeds consumption over time, stocks of sugar increase. Stocks of sugar have gotten progressively larger and larger. This, in turn, has put pressure on prices which remain at historically low levels. For 1999-2000 (September-August), the fundamental outlook in sugar is likely to remain one in which production increases and stocks increase. The trade has mixed opinions about the coming 2000-01 season. There is some opinion that the fundamentals will start to improve as the low prices cause producers to switch to other crops. Others in the trade are of the opinion that not much will change simply because producers are not very responsive to prices. At low price levels, producers do not switch much acreage to other crops. Beet sugar is an annual crop that is planted every year and if there is some price responsiveness it would be seen in beet sugar plantings. Sugar cane is a perennial crop and its production is not likely to change much due to prices. One factor that could change the amount of sugar produced is the weather.

World production of sugar in 1999-00 has been variously estimated at between 132 and 136 million metric tonnes (raw value). World production has been trending higher and with that stocks have increased. Brazil remains the dominant producer of sugar and the largest exporter. Much of the increase in world production over the last ten years can be attributed to increased Brazilian production. Production in the 1999-00 season is likely to approach 18-20 million tonnes. The larger Center-South crop was excellent while the smaller North-Northeast cane crop was damaged by dry weather. Sugar exports were on a record pace late in the shipping season. The situation in Brazil is always complicated by the fact that a lot of sugar cane in Brazil is turned into alcohol which is used for fuel. If the supply of alcohol increases and alcohol prices decline, more sugar cane will be processed into sugar. Current low prices for sugar are leading some in the trade to conclude that Brazilian producers will move more of the 2000-01 crop into alcohol production. If that occurs to a significant degree it could have a major impact on the market because of Brazil's dominant position as an exporter of sugar.

If Brazil does produce less sugar in the 2000-01 season, which for Brazil starts in May, then a number of other countries could be in a position to expand production. One notable example is Cuba. In the 1998-99 season, Cuba produced 3.8 million tonnes of sugar which was up from the very low production of 3.3 million tonnes in 1997-98. In the 1999-00 season, it appears that Cuba will produce close to 4.1 million tonnes. Much of the increase in Brazilian production in the last few years came at the expense of declining Cuban production. If Brazil were to reduce production in the 2000-01 season, Cuba would likely increase production and exports. Another country that has increased sugar production is Thailand with output in the 1999-00 season expected to top 6 million tonnes, almost 20 percent more than in 1998-99. Next to Brazil, India is the largest single country producer of sugar. For the 1999-00 season, sugar production was estimated at between 16 and 18 million tonnes. It is expected in the trade that the 2000-01 season will see India produce less sugar. Australia is a larger producer and exporter of sugar. The 1999-00 crop was estimated at 5 to 6 million tonnes with exports expected to be about 75 percent of production.

The U.S.D.A. in the December 1999 Crop Production report forecast U.S. sugar production in 1999-00 (October-September) at 8.7 million short tons, up 4 percent from the previous year. Beet sugar production was estimated at 4.7 million tons, up 5 percent from 1998-99, while cane sugar production was 4.1 million tons or 3 percent more than the previous year. Sugar cane acreage harvested in 1999 was 931,400 acres, up 5 percent from the previous year. Florida harvested acreage was 445,000, up 4 percent from the year before, while Louisiana harvested acreage was 425,000 acres, up 6 percent. The U.S. yield of sugar cane per acre was 37.1 tons compared to 36.9 tons in 1998.

The U.S.D.A. forecast that in the 1999-00 season, U.S. imports of sugar would be 1.8 million tons, down slightly from 1998-99. Domestic food use of sugar was estimated at 10 million tonnes, up 2 percent from 1998-99. Ending stocks of sugar were projected to be 1.8 million tons, some 7 percent more than the year before. The projected ending stocks to use ratio was .168 compared to .16 the year before.

World consumption of sugar has been increasing at an annual rate of between 1 percent and 2 percent per year. In the 1997-98 season there were a number of economic crises in Asia as well as Russia. There had been a lot of concern in the trade that sugar consumption would decline but it now appears there was not much change in usage. This may have been due to the already very low price which had encouraged additional use despite the economic turmoil. In the Asian countries, expanding populations along with increasing incomes has led to increasing usage of sugar. Much of the increase in world sugar consumption over the last few years has been in lesser developed countries in Asia. As those economies recover more fully in 2000-01, sugar consumption is expected to increase further. One country which remains a question mark is Russia. While a large user of sugar, economic uncertainties could mean that consumption will not expand very much in 2000-01.

Futures Markets

Sugar futures are traded on the Bolsa de Mercadorias & Futuros (BM&F), Chubu Commodity Exchange (C-COM), Kansai Commodities Exchange (KANEX), the Tokyo Grain Exchange (TGE), the London International Financial Futures and Options Exchange (LIFFE), and the CSCE Division of the New York Board of Trade (NYBOT). Options are traded on the KANEX, the TGE, the LIFFE, and the NYBOT.

World Production, Supply & Stocks/Consumption Ratio of Sugar In 1000's of Metric Tons (Raw Value)

Marketing Year	Beginning Stocks	Production	Imports	Total Supply	Exports	Domestic Consumption	Ending Stocks	Stocks/ Consumption Percentage
1990-1	19,458	113,458	32,538	165,391	32,538	111,926	20,927	18.8
1991-2	21,011	116,527	30,831	168,369	30,831	114,029	23,509	20.7
1992-3	23,509	112,099	28,937	164,545	28,937	114,037	21,571	18.9
1993-4	21,570	109,731	29,565	160,866	29,565	112,054	19,247	17.2
1994-5	19,247	116,124	30,288	165,659	30,288	112,873	22,498	19.9
1995-6	22,498	122,300	34,138	178,936	34,138	118,465	26,333	22.2
1996-7	26,333	122,911	35,806	185,050	35,806	123,045	26,199	21.3
1997-8	26,199	125,207	34,799	186,205	34,799	125,071	26,335	21.1
1998-9[1]	26,335	130,462	35,566	192,363	35,566	125,760	31,037	24.7
1999-00[2]	31,037	133,882	36,729	201,648	36,729	130,541	34,378	26.3

[1] Preliminary. [2] Forecast. *Source: Foreign Agricultural Service, U.S. Department of Agriculture (FAS-USDA)*

World Production of Sugar (Centrifugal Sugar-Raw Value) In Thousands of Metric Tons

Year	Australia	Brazil	China	Cuba	France	Germany	India	Indonesia	Mexico	Thailand	United States	Ukraine	World Total
1990-1	3,606	7,900	6,765	7,620	4,736	4,675	13,707	2,120	3,900	3,954	6,330	5,369	113,458
1991-2	3,192	9,200	8,492	7,030	4,413	4,250	15,249	2,250	3,500	5,062	6,627	4,178	116,527
1992-3	4,367	9,800	8,300	4,280	4,723	4,401	12,447	2,300	4,330	3,750	7,111	3,965	112,099
1993-4	4,412	9,930	6,505	4,000	4,725	4,736	11,704	2,480	3,780	3,975	6,945	4,188	109,731
1994-5	5,196	12,500	6,299	3,300	4,363	3,991	16,410	2,450	4,556	5,448	7,191	3,600	116,124
1995-6	5,049	13,700	6,686	4,450	4,564	4,159	18,225	2,090	4,660	6,223	6,686	3,800	122,300
1996-7	5,659	14,650	7,789	4,200	4,594	4,558	14,616	2,094	4,835	6,013	6,536	2,935	122,911
1997-8	5,567	15,700	8,631	3,200	-----	-----	14,592	2,190	5,490	4,245	7,276	2,032	125,207
1998-9[1]	4,871	18,300	8,969	3,780	-----	-----	17,361	1,490	4,985	5,386	7,597	2,000	130,462
1999-00[2]	5,367	19,200	9,173	4,100	-----	-----	18,400	1,600	5,200	5,770	8,078	1,800	133,882

[1] Preliminary. [2] Forecast. *Source: Foreign Agricultural Service, U.S. Department of Agriculture (FAS-USDA)*

World Stocks of Centrifugal Sugar at Beginning of Marketing Year In Thousands of Metric Tons (Raw Value)

Year	Australia	Brazil	China	Cuba	France	Germany	India	Iran	Mexico	Philippines	United Kingdom	United States	World Total
1990-1	256	1,164	1,350	475	434	330	2,376	220	750	308	300	1,111	19,395
1991-2	189	757	1,350	500	689	428	3,563	275	1,505	242	228	1,371	21,011
1992-3	163	950	2,002	500	589	340	5,245	300	910	515	281	1,340	23,509
1993-4	125	880	1,508	130	701	358	3,502	400	1,040	679	416	1,546	21,570
1994-5	125	455	1,168	170	784	511	2,776	400	575	412	450	1,213	19,247
1995-6	152	710	3,215	400	437	271	5,990	270	601	100	453	1,126	22,498
1996-7	101	510	2,684	400	684	331	8,455	300	714	511	457	1,354	26,333
1997-8	228	860	2,784	300	-----	-----	6,979	480	634	345	-----	1,350	26,199
1998-9[1]	253	560	2,515	290	-----	-----	5,850	590	759	183	-----	1,523	26,335
1999-00[2]	371	1,010	2,495	155	-----	-----	7,330	365	844	460	-----	1,487	31,037

[1] Preliminary. [2] Forecast. *Source: Foreign Agricultural Service, U.S. Department of Agriculture (FAS-USDA)*

Average Wholesale Price of Refined Beet Sugar[1]--Midwest Market In Cents Per Pound

Year	Jan.	Feb.	Mar.	Apr.	May	June	July	Aug.	Sept.	Oct.	Nov.	Dec.	Average
1990	30.50	30.50	30.50	30.50	30.50	30.50	30.50	30.50	30.50	29.13	28.60	27.38	29.97
1991	26.88	26.50	26.50	26.13	26.00	25.75	25.50	25.50	25.00	24.94	24.60	24.50	25.65
1992	25.40	26.50	26.50	26.50	26.40	26.00	25.00	25.00	25.00	24.90	24.13	23.90	25.44
1993	23.25	23.00	23.00	23.50	23.50	23.50	25.50	27.75	27.50	27.50	27.25	26.50	25.15
1994	25.75	25.50	25.50	24.50	24.75	25.25	25.00	25.00	24.70	25.00	25.38	26.50	25.15
1995	25.50	25.50	25.50	25.50	25.13	25.10	24.75	24.75	25.50	25.75	28.13	28.85	25.83
1996	28.69	29.00	29.50	29.50	29.70	29.50	29.50	29.00	29.00	29.00	29.00	29.00	29.20
1997	29.00	29.00	28.13	28.00	28.00	27.50	27.00	26.65	26.38	24.90	25.00	25.50	27.09
1998	25.50	25.50	25.50	25.50	26.00	26.00	26.00	26.00	26.50	26.90	27.00	27.00	26.12
1999[2]	27.20	27.13	27.00	27.00	27.00	27.00	27.00	27.00	27.00	26.00	26.00	25.20	26.71

[1] These are f.o.b. basis prices in bulk, not delivered prices. [2] Preliminary. Source: Economic Research Service, U.S. Department of Agriculture (ERS)

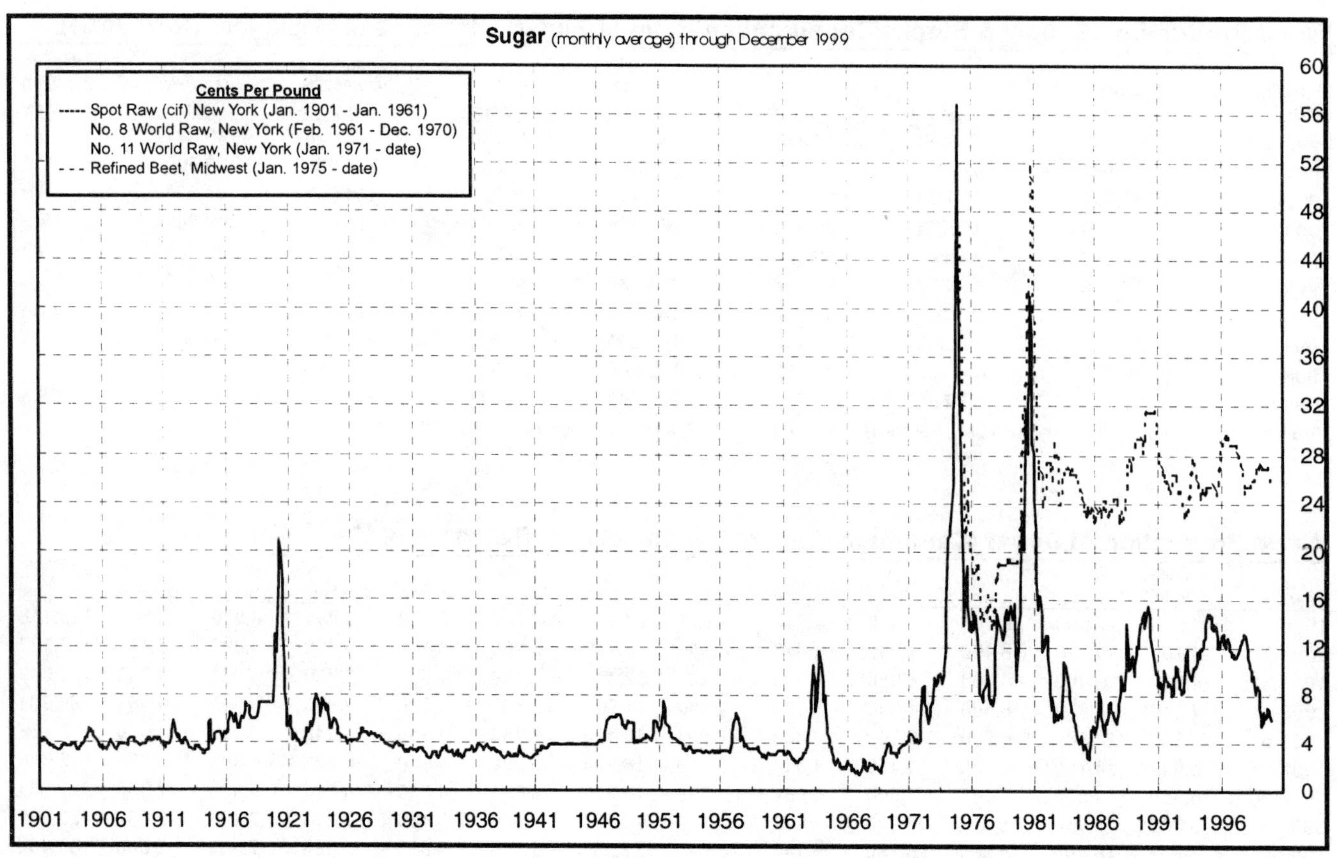

Average Price of World Raw Sugar[1] In Cents Per Pound

Year	Jan.	Feb.	Mar.	Apr.	May	June	July	Aug.	Sept.	Oct.	Nov.	Dec.	Average
1990	14.38	14.63	15.39	15.24	14.62	12.99	11.92	10.92	11.00	9.77	10.00	9.72	12.55
1991	8.88	8.57	9.22	8.55	7.88	9.37	10.26	9.45	9.39	9.10	8.79	9.03	9.04
1992	8.43	8.06	8.22	9.53	9.62	10.52	10.30	9.78	9.28	8.66	8.54	8.15	9.09
1993	8.27	8.61	10.75	11.30	11.87	10.35	9.60	9.30	9.52	10.27	10.10	10.47	10.03
1994	10.29	10.80	11.71	11.10	11.79	12.04	11.73	12.05	12.62	12.75	13.88	14.76	12.13
1995	14.87	14.43	14.58	13.63	13.49	13.99	13.46	13.75	12.72	11.94	11.96	12.40	13.44
1996	12.57	12.97	13.07	12.43	11.94	12.54	12.83	12.33	11.87	11.65	11.29	11.38	12.24
1997	11.13	11.06	11.17	11.50	11.54	12.02	12.13	12.54	12.65	12.86	13.19	12.90	12.06
1998	11.71	11.06	10.66	10.27	10.17	9.33	9.70	9.50	8.21	8.24	8.73	8.59	9.68
1999[2]	8.40	7.05	6.11	5.44	5.83	6.67	6.11	6.39	6.98	6.90	6.54	6.00	6.54

[1] Contract No. 11, f.o.b. stowed Caribbean port, including Brazil, bulk spot price. [2] Preliminary. *Source: Economic Research Service, U.S. Department of Agriculture (ERS-USDA)*

Average Price of Raw Sugar in New York (C.I.F., Duty/Free Paid, Contract #12/#14) In Cents Per Pound

Year	Jan.	Feb.	Mar.	Apr.	May	June	July	Aug.	Sept.	Oct.	Nov.	Dec.	Average
1990	23.11	22.93	23.58	23.81	23.58	23.33	23.42	23.27	23.23	23.29	23.15	22.47	23.26
1991	21.86	21.42	21.46	21.23	21.29	21.42	21.25	21.83	22.06	21.76	21.75	21.50	21.57
1992	21.38	21.56	21.36	21.38	21.04	20.92	21.10	21.34	21.55	21.61	21.39	21.11	21.31
1993	20.76	21.16	21.56	21.76	21.36	21.42	21.89	21.85	21.97	21.80	21.87	22.00	21.62
1994	22.00	21.95	21.95	22.08	22.18	22.44	22.72	21.84	21.78	21.58	21.57	22.35	22.04
1995	22.65	22.69	22.46	22.76	23.10	23.09	24.47	23.18	23.21	22.67	22.60	22.63	22.96
1996	22.39	22.68	22.57	22.71	22.62	22.48	21.80	22.51	22.38	22.37	22.12	22.14	22.40
1997	21.88	22.07	21.81	21.79	21.70	21.62	22.04	22.21	22.30	22.27	21.90	21.93	21.96
1998	21.85	21.79	21.74	22.14	22.31	22.42	22.66	22.19	21.92	21.67	21.83	22.19	22.06
1999[1]	22.41	22.38	22.55	22.57	22.65	22.61	22.61	21.24	20.10	19.50	17.45	17.87	21.16

[1] Preliminary. *Source: Economic Research Service, U.S. Department of Agriculture (ERS-USDA)*

Centrifugal Sugar (Raw Value) Imported into Selected Countries In Thousands of Metric Tons

Year	Algeria	Canada	China	France	Iran	Rep. of Korea	Malaysia	Morocco	Nigeria	Russia	United Kingdom	United States	World Total
1990-1	990	1,109	1,055	343	875	1,233	900	350	480	3,580	1,143	2,619	32,538
1991-2	980	961	1,230	398	825	1,258	921	380	560	3,850	1,442	2,071	30,831
1992-3	980	1,095	506	487	780	1,233	900	408	430	3,500	1,352	1,827	28,937
1993-4	990	1,219	1,469	156	950	1,258	958	417	510	3,150	1,363	1,604	29,565
1994-5	990	1,020	4,110	361	800	1,345	1,030	455	490	2,700	1,261	1,664	30,288
1995-6	1,000	1,174	1,775	523	940	1,411	1,120	477	542	3,200	1,361	2,536	34,138
1996-7	910	1,057	1,014	553	1,350	1,497	1,166	513	555	3,600	1,260	2,517	25,806
1997-8[1]	925	1,061	420	-----	1,200	1,424	1,065	586	660	4,210	-----	1,962	34,799
1998-9[2]	940	1,110	577	-----	900	1,450	1,220	502	700	5,400	-----	1,637	35,566
1999-00[3]	960	1,110	510	-----	1,500	1,480	1,280	450	750	3,800	-----	1,560	36,729

[1] Preliminary. [2] Estimate. [3] Forecast. *Source: Foreign Agricultural Service, U.S. Department of Agriculture (FAS-USDA)*

Centrifugal Sugar (Raw Value) Exported From Selected Countries In Thousands of Metric Tons

Year	Australia	Brazil	Cuba	Dominican Republic	France	Germany	Mauritius	Mexico	South Africa	Swaziland	Thailand	United Kingdom	Total
1990-1	2,819	1,300	6,800	328	2,751	1,857	621	285	757	469	2,741	255	32,538
1991-2	2,345	1,607	6,100	344	2,682	1,557	590	50	969	474	3,657	368	30,831
1992-3	3,476	2,425	3,800	327	2,822	1,607	621	0	123	409	2,332	300	28,937
1993-4	3,663	2,861	3,300	346	2,636	1,785	590	0	27	395	2,718	410	29,565
1994-5	4,321	4,300	2,600	295	3,004	1,417	508	235	369	296	3,809	263	30,288
1995-6	4,242	5,800	3,800	325	2,735	1,180	560	587	399	307	4,537	327	34,138
1996-7	4,564	5,800	3,600	364	2,730	1,430	593	750	1,056	293	4,194	388	35,806
1997-8[1]	4,554	7,200	2,500	270	-----	-----	644	1,135	1,160	272	2,490	-----	34,799
1998-9[2]	3,760	8,750	3,200	190	-----	-----	590	500	1,436	300	3,200	-----	35,566
1999-00[3]	4,200	9,700	3,000	190	-----	-----	340	900	1,325	250	3,400	-----	36,729

[1] Preliminary. [2] Estimate. [3] Forecast. *Source: Foreign Agricultural Service, U.S. Department of Agriculture (FAS-USDA)*

Supply and Utilization of Sugar (Cane and Beet) in the United States In 1,000's of Short Tons (Raw Value)

	Supply								Utilization						
	Production			Offshore Receipts									Domestic Disappearance		
Year	Cane	Beet	Total	Foreign	Territories	Total	Beginning Stocks	Total Supply	Total Use	Exports	Net Changes in Invisible Stocks	Refining Loss Adjustment	In Polyhydric Alcohol[4]	Total	Per Capita
1991-2	3,461	3,845	7,306	2,194	0	2,194	1,524	11,024	9,547	554	-13	0	11	8,907	64.4
1992-3	3,446	4,392	7,838	2,039	0	2,039	1,477	11,354	9,650	405	48	0	15	9,034	65.8
1993-4	3,565	4,090	7,655	1,772	0	1,772	1,704	11,131	9,794	454	7	0	15	9,175	66.1
1994-5	3,434	4,493	7,927	1,853	0	1,853	1,337	11,117	9,876	502	37	0	10	9,239	65.5
1995-6	3,454	3,916	7,370	2,777	0	2,777	1,241	11,388	9,896	385	-43	0	13	9,441	66.5
1996-7	3,191	4,013	7,205	2,774	0	2,774	1,492	11,471	9,983	211	30	0	21	9,564	67.2
1997-8[1]	3,631	4,389	8,020	2,163	0	2,163	1,488	11,671	9,992	179	-2	0	20	9,672	67.2
1998-9[2]	3,951	4,423	8,374	1,820	0	1,820	1,679	11,873	10,234	230	-62	0	25	9,872	68.7
1999-00[3]	4,025	4,725	8,750	1,795	0	1,795	1,639	12,184	10,500	250	0	0	22	10,053	69.9

[1] Preliminary. [2] Estimate. [3] Forecast. [4] Includes feed use. *Source: Economic Research Service, U.S. Department of Agriculture (ERS-USDA)*

Sugar Cane for Sugar & Seed and Production of Cane Sugar and Molasses in the United States

			Production					Farm Value		Sugar Production				
										Raw Value			Molasses Made	
Year	Acreage Harvested 1,000 Acres	Yield of Cane Per Harvested Acre Net Tons	for Sugar	for Seed	Total	Sugar Yield Per Acre Short Tons	Farm Price $ Per Ton	of Cane Used for Sugar	of Cane Used for Sugar & Seed	Total 1,000 Tons	Per Ton of Cane in Lbs.	Refined Basis 1,000 Tons	Edible	Total[3]
			1,000 Tons					1,000 Dollars					1,000 Gallons	
1991	884.7	33.6	28,960	1,292	30,252	3.95	29.0	840,194	876,479	3,430	237	3,206	1,825	181,668
1992	906.4	32.7	28,873	1,490	30,363	3.79	28.1	811,350	852,235	3,373	234	3,152	1,460	194,247
1993	923.9	32.8	29,652	1,449	31,101	3.82	28.5	846,132	886,285	3,482	235	3,255	1,480	198,167
1994	936.8	33.0	29,405	1,524	30,929	3.96	29.2	857,438	900,827	3,595	-----	3,308	-----	193,628
1995	932.3	33.0	29,155	1,641	30,796	3.90	29.5	859,604	906,956	3,489	-----	-----	-----	195,429
1996	888.9	33.1	27,687	1,777	29,464	-----	28.3	784,113	833,297	-----	-----	-----	-----	-----
1997	914.0	34.7	30,003	1,706	31,709	-----	28.1	842,840	890,257	-----	-----	-----	-----	-----
1998[1]	947.1	36.6	32,743	1,964	34,707	-----	27.3	999,969	1,060,842	-----	-----	-----	-----	-----
1999[2]	991.2	36.0	33,923	1,798	35,721	-----	-----	-----	-----	-----	-----	-----	-----	-----

[1] Preliminary. [2] Estimate. [3] Excludes edible molasses. *Source: Economic Research Service, U.S. Department of Agriculture (ERS-USDA)*

SUGAR

U.S. Sugar Beets, Beet Sugar, Pulp & Molasses Produced from Beets and Raw Sugar Spot Prices

Year of Harvest	Acreage: Planted (1,000 Acres)	Acreage: Harvested (1,000 Acres)	Yield Per Harvested Acre Ton	Production 1,000 Tons	Sugar Yield Per Acre Sh. Tons	Price[3] Dollars	Farm Value $1,000	Sugar Production: Equivalent Raw Value[4] (1,000 Short Tons)	Sugar Production: Refined Basis (1,000 Short Tons)	Raw Sugar Prices: World[5] Refined #5 (In Cents Per Pound)	Raw Sugar Prices: CSCE #11 World (In Cents Per Pound)	Raw Sugar Prices: CSCE N.Y. Duty Paid (In Cents Per Pound)	Wholesale List Price HFCS (42%) Midwest
1990	1,400	1,377	20.0	27,513	2.79	43.00	1,182,221	3,842	3,591	17.32	12.55	23.26	19.69
1991	1,427	1,387	20.3	28,203	2.68	38.50	1,085,728	3,729	3,485	13.41	9.04	21.57	20.93
1992	1,437	1,412	20.6	29,143	3.10	41.10	1,206,480	4,386	4,099	12.39	9.09	21.31	20.70
1993	1,438	1,409	18.6	26,249	2.87	39.00	1,023,687	4,047	3,792	12.79	10.03	21.62	18.83
1994	1,476	1,443	22.1	31,853	3.17	38.80	1,234,470	4,578	4,090	15.66	12.13	22.04	20.17
1995	1,445	1,420	19.8	28,065	2.78	38.10	1,070,663	3,944	-----	17.99	13.44	22.96	15.63
1996	1,368	1,323	20.2	26,680	3.06	45.40	1,211,001	3,900	-----	16.64	12.24	22.40	14.46
1997	1,459	1,428	20.9	29,886	3.00	38.80	1,160,029	-----	-----	14.33	12.06	21.96	10.70
1998[1]	1,498	1,451	22.4	32,499	-----	36.40	1,181,494	-----	-----	11.59	9.68	22.06	10.58
1999[2]	1,563	1,527	21.8	33,319	-----	-----	-----	-----	-----	9.55	6.54	21.16	11.71

[1] Preliminary. [2] Estimate. [3] Includes support payments, but excludes Government sugar beet payments. [4] Refined sugar multiplied by factor of 1.07. [5] F.O.B. Europe. *Source: Economic Research Service, U.S. Department of Agriculture (ERS-USDA)*

Sugar Deliveries and Stocks in the United States In Thousands of Short Tons (Raw Value)

Year	Quota Allocation	Actual Imports	Deliveries by Primary Distributors: Cane Sugar Refineries	Deliveries: Beet Sugar Factories	Deliveries: Importers of Direct Consumption Sugar	Deliveries: Mainland Cane Sugar Mills[3]	Deliveries: Total Deliveries	Total Domestic Consumption	Stocks, Jan. 1: Cane Sugar Refineries[4]	Stocks: Beet Sugar Factories	Stocks: CCC	Stocks: Refiners' Raw	Stocks: Mainland Cane Mills	Stocks: Total
1990	2,314.9	2,242.8	4,998	3,570	39	8	8,615	9,375	155	1,412	0	381	899	2,947
1991	1,526.7	1,477.0	4,786	3,713	30	11	8,540	9,499	168	1,327	0	371	812	2,729
1992	3,958.4	3,926.6	4,808	3,966	52	11	8,936	9,638	194	1,336	0	619	890	3,039
1993	[5]	[5]	4,781	4,087	52	15	9,064	9,577	183	1,640	0	507	895	3,225
1994	[5]	[5]	4,929	4,170	78	12	9,321	9,813	218	1,696	0	438	1,160	3,512
1995	2,413.2	2,308.0	4,808	4,486	44	15	9,451	9,337	192	1,600	6	448	906	3,139
1996	2,339.1	-----	5,539	3,923	33	14	9,619	9,496	195	1,383	0	334	996	2,908
1997	-----	-----	5,553	3,997	27	-----	9,755	9,578	196	1,520	0	323	1,156	3,195
1998[1]	-----	-----	5,347	4,313	24	-----	9,851	9,684	212	1,535	0	322	1,308	3,377
1999[2]	-----	-----	-----	-----	-----	-----	-----	-----	255	1,499	0	332	1,337	3,423

[1] Preliminary. [2] Estimate. [3] Sugar for direct consumption only. [4] Refined. [5] Combined with 1992. *Source: Economic Research Service, U.S. Department of Agriculture (ERS-USDA)*

Sugar, Refined--Deliveries to End User in the United States In Thousands of Short Tons

Year	Bakery & Cereal Products	Beverages	Confectionery[2]	Hotels, Restaurant & Institutions	Ice Cream & Dairy Products	Canned, Bottled & Frozen Foods	All Other Food Uses	Retail Grocers[3]	Wholesale Grocers[4]	Non-food Uses	Non-industrial Uses	Industrial Uses	Total Deliveries
1989	1,532	215	1,187	106	426	342	637	1,026	2,051	126	3,259	4,465	7,730
1990	1,608	228	1,279	108	462	332	642	1,077	2,130	109	3,391	4,660	8,051
1991	1,632	204	1,277	100	439	331	623	1,182	2,079	88	3,469	4,594	8,063
1992	1,719	164	1,246	101	429	315	649	1,230	2,104	69	3,668	4,591	8,259
1993	1,785	158	1,292	108	424	336	725	1,235	2,075	85	3,589	4,805	8,394
1994	1,952	156	1,313	93	453	322	704	1,269	2,039	77	3,598	4,977	8,575
1995	1,905	169	1,372	103	452	279	863	1,236	2,173	64	3,701	5,103	8,804
1996	1,993	196	1,335	80	445	318	849	1,263	2,241	66	3,759	5,202	8,962
1997	2,161	158	1,350	78	436	308	793	1,281	2,283	66	3,828	5,272	9,100
1998[1]	2,301	165	1,336	79	438	331	907	1,230	2,223	76	3,761	5,556	9,317

[1] Preliminary. [2] And related products. [3] Chain stores, supermarkets. [4] Jobbers, sugar dealers. *Source: Economic Research Service, U.S. Department of Agriculture (ERS-USDA)*

Deliveries[1] of All Sugar by Primary Distributors in the U.S., by Quarters In Thousands of Short Tons

Year	First Quarter	Second Quarter	Third Quarter	Fourth Quarter	Total	Year	First Quarter	Second Quarter	Third Quarter	Fourth Quarter	Total
1988	1,951	1,983	2,147	2,107	8,188	1994	2,121	2,265	2,532	2,260	9,177
1989	1,923	2,051	2,181	2,185	8,340	1995	2,105	2,311	2,542	2,379	9,337
1990	1,837	1,911	2,154	2,149	8,051	1996	2,191	2,355	2,519	2,445	9,496
1991	1,878	1,955	2,173	2,057	8,063	1997	2,143	2,401	2,591	2,443	9,578
1992	1,985	2,178	2,390	2,273	8,826	1998	2,233	2,428	2,565	2,458	9,684
1993	2,039	2,172	2,432	2,277	8,920	1999[2]	2,118	2,399	2,508		9,367

Raw Value. [1] Includes for domestic consumption and for export. [2] Preliminary. *Source: Economic Research Service, U.S. Department of Agriculture (ERS-USDA)*

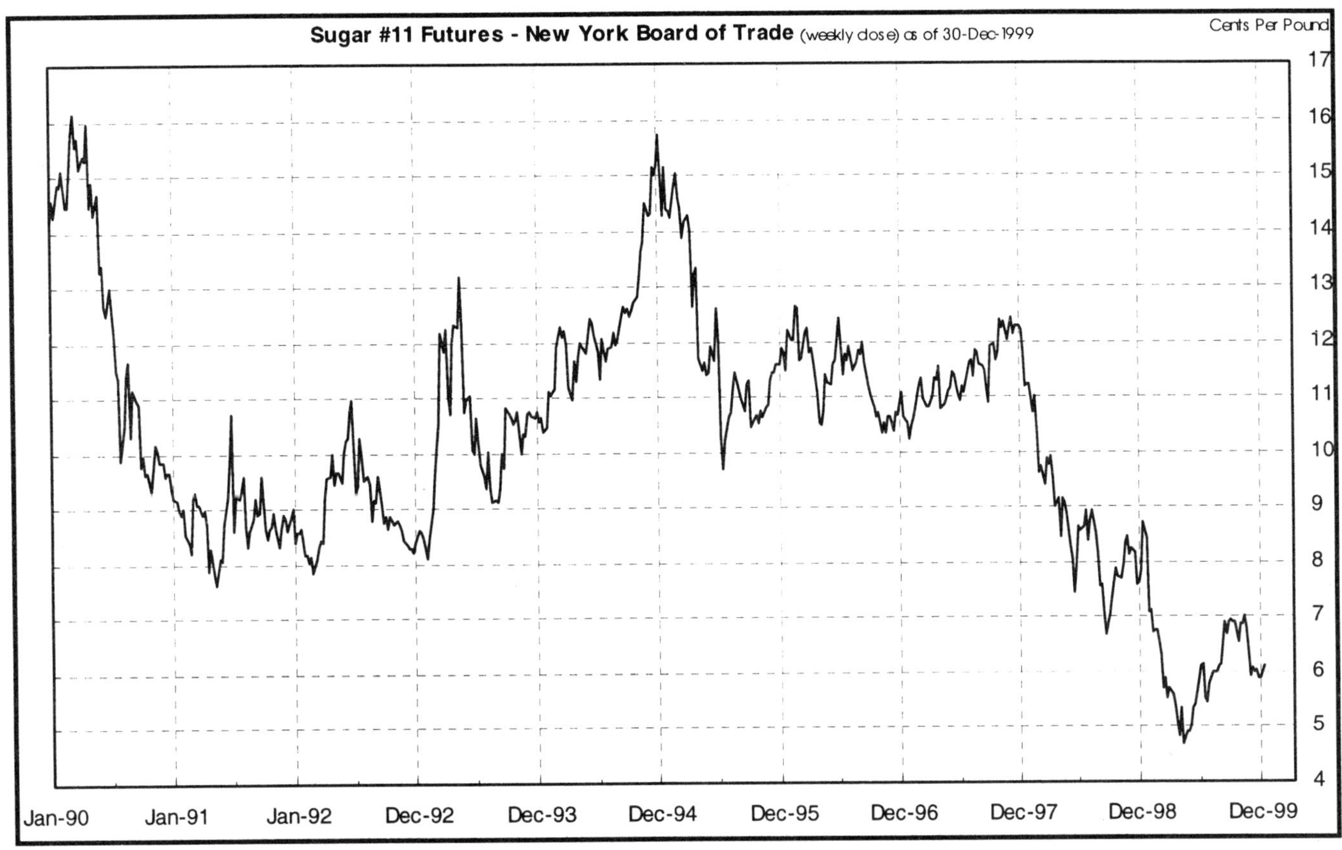

Average Open Interest of World Sugar No. 11 Futures in New York In Contracts

Year	Jan.	Feb.	Mar.	Apr.	May	June	July	Aug.	Sept.	Oct.	Nov.	Dec.
1990	164,235	160,509	163,155	168,962	170,351	161,320	133,208	121,665	112,065	109,986	110,047	108,939
1991	124,637	129,361	114,432	115,704	110,142	105,607	106,406	107,852	102,546	91,649	90,976	93,827
1992	96,255	105,166	93,774	109,137	95,101	106,310	96,038	87,089	77,740	69,023	74,292	93,039
1993	91,426	105,147	123,023	115,400	112,085	101,843	94,296	94,932	91,312	92,832	96,246	99,592
1994	108,936	123,148	137,582	115,060	117,030	126,843	106,749	118,057	141,361	140,011	171,843	191,801
1995	186,893	167,451	149,027	152,600	127,978	121,877	114,027	119,787	114,069	119,561	140,008	157,779
1996	156,047	159,563	150,093	142,773	137,897	148,447	144,527	153,845	153,202	144,830	150,866	150,573
1997	155,156	147,198	143,623	166,143	150,480	175,139	165,884	197,331	187,477	158,065	200,486	201,922
1998	206,100	212,072	183,472	182,770	171,555	186,978	149,536	152,754	155,076	138,762	139,896	148,983
1999	165,717	176,465	168,624	188,324	196,864	177,265	142,416	151,621	189,605	161,759	167,549	175,125

Source: New York Board of Trade (NYBOT)

Volume of Trading of World Sugar No. 11 Futures in New York In Contracts

Year	Jan.	Feb.	Mar.	Apr.	May	June	July	Aug.	Sept.	Oct.	Nov.	Dec.	Total
1990	519,886	523,591	588,021	505,492	598,320	532,937	384,116	441,608	448,195	372,925	303,065	206,645	5,424,801
1991	313,915	510,163	388,672	477,954	286,120	534,639	309,836	352,351	366,007	240,812	253,201	234,876	4,268,546
1992	376,704	395,793	255,501	583,535	246,360	454,854	264,528	275,677	334,962	163,263	168,470	147,844	3,667,481
1993	330,474	481,506	507,370	518,292	415,283	390,261	255,581	307,181	368,194	222,082	272,579	217,142	4,285,945
1994	289,593	486,222	360,787	472,388	407,343	443,002	252,012	349,079	471,899	316,330	484,943	387,620	4,719,218
1995	591,861	489,274	472,519	478,757	352,000	485,131	298,756	402,358	360,086	246,584	278,906	254,850	4,711,082
1996	550,780	544,514	341,940	526,255	384,302	496,745	279,707	290,732	562,082	264,290	203,921	306,584	4,751,852
1997	436,935	493,199	268,343	618,176	308,563	575,264	400,150	427,082	580,551	440,208	323,286	413,214	5,284,971
1998	601,378	688,036	431,818	551,628	364,203	686,997	294,354	370,179	527,270	303,951	358,096	346,201	5,524,111
1999	683,891	543,477	452,485	688,181	361,895	762,271	346,534	408,289	657,572	344,434	405,495	256,775	5,911,299

Source: New York Board of Trade (NYBOT)

Sulfur

Elemental sulfur is used in the synthesis of sulfur compounds. It finds use in the construction industry where it is added to concrete to aide corrosion resistance and added to asphalt in highway construction. The U.S. Geological Survey reported that in 1998, elemental sulfur and by-product sulfuric acid were produced at 149 operations in 30 states, Puerto Rico and the U.S. Virgin Islands. Elemental sulfur production in the U.S. was 9.7 million metric tonnes with Texas and Louisiana accounting for half of the domestic output. Elemental sulfur was produced by one company in two mines in two states, using the Frasch mining method.

World sulfur production in 1998 was 54 million tonnes, up 1 percent from 1997. The U.S. was the largest producer with output of 11.3 million tonnes of all forms of sulfur, down 6 percent from 1997. Canada was the next largest producer in 1998 with 10.2 million tonnes. Other large producers included China, Russia, Japan and Saudi Arabia. The world reserve base of sulfur is estimated at 3.5 billion tonnes.

U.S. production of sulfur from petroleum and natural gas (including Frasch) in August 1999 was 820,000 tonnes. In the January-August 1999 period, production was 6.58 million tonnes, while for all of 1998 it was 10.1 million tonnes. Production from petroleum in the first eight months of 1999 was 3.95 million tonnes, while production from natural gas was 2.63 million tonnes.

U.S. imports of sulfur in the January-July 1999 period were 1.58 million tonnes. Imports from Canada were 978,000 tonnes while imports from Mexico were 326,000 tonnes. In 1998, U.S. imports of sulfur were 2.27 million tonnes.

U.S. consumption of sulfur in July 1999 was 1.1 million tonnes. Of the total, 826,000 tonnes was from domestic sources and 230,000 tonnes was imported. In the January-July 1999 period, consumption was 6.86 million tonnes with 5.28 million tonnes from domestic sources and 1.58 million tonnes imported. For all of 1998, U.S. consumption of sulfur was 11.9 million tonnes.

World Production of Sulfur (All Forms) In Thousands of Metric Tons

Year	Canada	China	France	Germany	Iraq	Japan	Mexico	Poland	Russia[3]	Saudi Arabia	Spain	United States	World Total
1991	7,130	5,910	1,200	1,282	300	2,626	2,094	4,104	8,100	2,000	905	10,820	54,600
1992	7,487	5,900	1,150	1,160	350	2,745	2,300	3,134	3,500	2,370	885	10,700	50,700
1993	8,430	6,360	1,260	1,260	450	2,922	906	2,120	3,720	2,400	768	11,100	51,600
1994	8,850	7,020	1,180	1,005	475	2,900	1,177	2,325	3,650	1,630	694	11,500	53,400
1995	9,010	7,030	1,170	1,110	475	3,000	1,241	2,591	3,840	1,650	786	11,800	54,800
1996	9,116	7,260	1,090	1,110	475	3,080	1,280	1,916	3,800	1,750	943	11,800	55,700
1997[1]	9,081	7,640	1,060	1,160	450	3,320	1,340	1,962	3,750	2,000	967	12,000	58,300
1998[2]	9,250	6,150	1,050	1,180	450	3,400	1,390	1,570	4,480	2,000	993	11,600	57,800

[1] Preliminary. [2] Estimate. [3] Formerly part of the U.S.S.R.; data not reported separately until 1992. *Source: U.S. Geological Survey (USGS)*

Salient Statistics of Sulfur in the United States In Thousands of Metric Tons (Sulfur Content)

	Production of													
	Elemental Sulfur											Sales Value of Shipments F.O.B. Mine/Plant		
	Native - Sulfur[3] -	Recovered										$ Per Metric Ton		
Year	Frasch	Petroleum & Coke	Natural Gas	Total	By-product Sulfuric Acid	Other Sulfuric Acid Compounds	Production (All Forms)	Imports Sulfuric Acid[4]	Exports Sulfuric Acid[4]	Producer Stocks Dec. 31[5]	Apparent Consumption (All Forms)	Frasch	Recovered	Average
1991	2,869	4,243	2,402	6,645	1,302	4	10,820	3,020	149	1,194	13,500	87.05	64.17	71.45
1992	2,320	4,524	2,524	7,048	1,292	3	10,700	2,725	139	809	13,400	58.15	44.47	48.14
1993	1,900	4,820	2,905	7,725	1,430	3	11,100	2,440	145	1,382	12,600	51.60	25.06	31.86
1994	2,960	4,930	2,240	7,160	1,380	0	11,500	2,130	140	1,160	13,100	W	W	30.08
1995	3,150	5,040	2,210	7,250	1,400	0	11,800	1,920	170	583	14,300	W	W	44.46
1996	2,900	5,370	2,100	7,480	1,430	0	11,800	2,070	117	646	13,600	W	W	34.11
1997[1]	2,820	5,230	2,420	7,650	1,550	0	12,000	2,010	118	761	13,900	W	W	36.06
1998[2]	1,800	6,060	2,160	8,220	1,610	0	11,600	2,040	155	283	14,100	W	W	29.14

[1] Preliminary. [2] Estimate. [3] Or sulfur ore; Withheld included in natural gas. [4] Basis 100% H2SO4, sulfur equivalent. [5] Frasch & recovered.
[6] Data 1996 to date includes Frasch. W = Withheld proprietary data. *Source: U.S. Geological Survey (USGS)*

Sulfur Consumption & Foreign Trade of the United States In Thousands of Metric Tons (Sulfur Content)

	Consumption			Sulfuric Acid Sold or Used, by End Use[2]						Foreign Trade					
										Exports			Imports		
Year	Native Sulfur Frasch	Recovered Sulfur	Total Elemental Form	Total Sulfuric Acid	Pulpmills & Paper Product	Inorganic Chemicals[3]	Synthetic Rubber & Plastic	Phosphatic Fertilizers	Petroleum Refining[4]	Frasch	Recovered	Value 1,000 $	Frasch	Recovered	Value 1,000 $
1991	3,931	7,694	11,625	12,842	279	901	272	8,311	383	448	748	119,713	1,259	1,760	241,749
1992	3,083	8,368	11,451	12,340	296	617	278	8,300	385	362	604	69,662	845	1,877	129,894
1993	1,331	9,046	10,377	11,886	304	549	259	7,906	388	246	656	39,726	100	2,070	49,800
1994	W	11,100	11,100	11,300	295	448	256	8,040	236	-----	899	48,400	-----	1,650	62,000
1995	W	12,300	12,300	11,500	319	170	245	8,200	479	-----	906	66,200	-----	2,510	143,000
1996	W	11,500	11,500	10,900	343	152	270	7,380	525	-----	855	51,700	-----	1,960	70,200
1997	W	11,800	11,800	10,700	334	232	85	7,000	610	-----	703	36,000	-----	2,060	64,900
1998[1]	W	11,900	11,900	10,500	134	174	69	7,530	632	-----	889	35,400	-----	2,270	58,400

[1] Preliminary. [2] Sulfur equivalent. [3] Including inorganic pigments, paints & allied products, and other inorganic chemicals & products.
[4] Including other petroleum and coal products. W = Withheld proprietary data. NA = Not available. *Source: U.S. Geological Survey (USGS)*

Sunflowerseed, Meal and Oil

World sunflowerseed production in 1999/2000 ranked fifth among the world's major oilseed crops. However, unlike soybeans for which most of the crop is crushed for meal, sunflowerseed has nearly equal amounts of meal and oil produced. The U.S. produces only about 6 percent of global sunflowerseed production, but has a larger role in world trade.

World production in 1999/00 of a record large 26.8 million metric tonnes compares with 25.9 million in 1998/99. Argentina is the largest producer with 6.4 million tonnes in 1999/00 vs. the previous year's record of 6.8 million tonnes. The Russian Federation (FSU-12) remains the largest producer with 6.7 million tonnes in 1999/00 vs. 5.5 million in 1998/99.

The world sunflowerseed crush for 1999/00 is forecast at 24.1 million tonnes, some 500,000 tonnes above initial forecasts. Sunflowerseed is the third largest oilseed in foreign trade; 1999/00 exports of 4.5 million tonnes about equaled 1998/99. World stocks generally average about one million tonnes. Sunflower meal production in 1999/00 of 11 million tonnes compares with 10.4 million in 1998/99; sunflower oil production of 9.6 million tonnes compares with 9.1 million, respectively.

The acreage planted to sunflowerseed production in the U.S. tends to show an irregular year-to-year pattern as does average yield. However, the record acreage planted for the 1999/00 crop was only marginally higher than 1998/99's acreage. Average yield during the two crop years averaged 1404 pounds per acre in 1999/00 versus 1510 in 1998/99. Production (September/August) in 1999/00 of 2.3 million metric tonnes compares with 2.4 million in 1998/99. The Dakotas, notably North, are the largest producing states with about two-thirds of total U.S. production.

U.S. sunflower meal production in 1999/00 (October/September) of 540,000 tonnes compares with 608,000 in 1998/99. Total disappearance in both crop years about equaled supply and left carryover unchanged at about 5,000 tonnes. Sunflower oil production of 454,000 tonnes compares with 510,000 in 1998/99. However, unlike meal, most U.S. sunflower oil production is exported: 363,000 tonnes in 1999/00 vs. 333,000 tonnes in 1998/99. The U.S. also exports sunflower seed, about 358,000 tonnes in 1999/00 vs. 249,000 in 1998/99.

The 1999/00 U.S. sunflower oil price was forecast at $374.00-430.00 per metric tonne vs. $446.00 in 1998/99, basis average crude Minneapolis. The sunflower meal price was forecast to range from $69.00-97.00 per metric tonne vs. $72.00/ton, basis 28 percent protein. Abroad, the 1998/99 average sunflowerseed oil price of $560.00/metric tonne compares with $730.00/tonne in 1997/98, basis Rotterdam; for protein meal the Rotterdam average of $76.00 per metric tonne compares with $103.00, respectively.

World Production of Sunflowerseed In Thousands of Metric Tons

Crop Year	Argentina	Bulgaria	China	France	Hungary	India	Romania	South Africa	Spain	Turkey	United States	Ex-USSR	World Total
1990-1	4,027	389	1,339	2,413	684	889	556	628	1,312	860	1,032	6,559	23,010
1991-2	3,880	434	1,422	2,570	813	1,194	612	589	1,026	650	1,639	5,643	22,733
1992-3	3,100	595	1,473	2,110	765	1,185	774	250	1,343	950	1,181	5,734	21,642
1993-4	4,010	442	1,340	1,643	702	1,400	696	362	1,309	815	1,167	5,230	21,390
1994-5	5,900	602	1,367	2,053	664	1,204	764	352	979	740	2,194	4,516	23,927
1995-6	5,556	650	1,269	1,993	785	1,324	933	755	588	790	1,819	7,405	26,171
1996-7	5,450	530	1,420	1,996	905	1,315	1,096	560	1,178	670	1,614	5,289	24,612
1997-8	5,680	505	1,176	1,995	545	1,160	869	585	1,373	672	1,668	5,412	23,891
1998-9[1]	6,970	515	1,440	1,713	714	950	1,073	1,070	1,097	650	2,392	5,752	26,986
1999-00[2]	6,000	650	1,400	1,851	836	850	1,100	600	569	700	2,288	6,722	26,381

[1] Preliminary. [2] Forecast. Source: *The Oil World*

World Imports and Exports of Sunflowerseed In Thousands of Metric Tons

Crop Year	Imports: France	Germany	Netherlands	Spain	Turkey	World Total	Exports: Argentina	France	Hungary	Ex-USSR	United States	Uraguay	World Total
1990-1	6.4	55.4	97.9	30.2	27.9	886	368.6	0.3	83.9	211.7	106.5	0.9	894
1991-2	7.8	90.0	127.7	66.8	102.6	1,227	292.8	0.4	113.5	354.9	127.5	24.5	1,239
1992-3	19.5	87.0	219.2	96.8	54.9	1,169	198.4	4.7	147.5	353.3	90.0	10.6	1,158
1993-4	212.9	261.7	358.6	167.7	59.7	1,963	582.9	2.2	299.5	719.1	76.6	14.0	1,961
1994-5	97.0	226.2	459.1	462.0	294.9	2,484	840.7	84.2	271.4	592.9	334.5	43.7	2,516
1995-6	284.6	290.4	503.7	612.3	463.6	3,286	585.1	29.3	283.9	1,829.3	194.6	41.4	3,310
1996-7	337.9	405.6	496.4	295.9	532.3	3,305	65.4	78.1	212.3	2,378.3	117.4	70.9	3,245
1997-8	207.9	278.1	452.0	312.4	532.1	3,001	504.0	64.0	104.0	1,717.0	265.0	35.0	2,995
1998-9[1]	365.0	370.0	500.0	460.0	584.0	3,617	938.0	42.0	150.0	1,722.0	227.0	94.0	3,621
1999-00[2]	-----	-----	-----	-----	575.0	3,417	550.0	-----	-----	1,420.0	330.0	55.0	3,416

[1] Preliminary. [2] Forecast. Source: *The Oil World*

SUNFLOWERSEED, MEAL AND OIL

Sunflowerseed Statistics in the United States In Thousands of Metric Tons

Crop Year Beginning Sept. 1	Harvested Acres 1,000	Harvested Yield Per Cwt.	Farm Price $ Per Metric Ton	Value of Production Million $	Supply: Stocks, Sept. 1	Supply: Production	Supply: Imports	Supply: Total	Disappearance: Crush	Disappearance: Exports	Disappearance: Non-oil Use & Seed	Disappearance: Total
1990-1	1,851	12.29	240	245.8	25	1,031	40	1,096	593	121	295	1,011
1991-2	2,673	13.52	192	316.8	85	1,639	75	1,799	952	163	422	1,537
1992-3	2,043	12.55	215	254.3	262	1,163	47	1,472	923	118	363	1,404
1993-4	2,486	10.35	284	332.0	69	1,167	25	1,261	661	99	429	1,189
1994-5	3,430	14.10	236	512.8	71	2,194	42	2,306	1,313	287	604	2,203
1995-6	3,368	11.90	254	457.6	103	1,819	21	1,943	915	224	598	1,737
1996-7	2,479	14.36	258	414.8	205	1,614	18	1,837	844	149	648	1,641
1997-8	2,792	13.17	256	426.8	196	1,668	29	1,933	1,061	189	591	1,841
1998-9[1]	3,492	15.10	231	537.0	92	2,392	34	2,518	1,178	256	853	2,287
1999-00[2]	3,441	12.62	165	353.5	231	1,969	31	2,231	1,041	234	847	2,122

[1] Preliminary. [2] Forecast. *Source: Economic Research Service, U.S. Department of Agriculture (ERS-USDA)*

World Production of Sunflowerseed Oil and Meal In Thousands of Metric Tons

Year	Oil: Argentina	Oil: France	Oil: Spain	Oil: Turkey	Oil: Ex-USSR	Oil: World Total	Meal: Argentina	Meal: France	Meal: Spain	Meal: Turkey	Meal: United States	Meal: Ex-USSR	Meal: World Total
1990-1	1,543	516	467	401	2,181	8,171	1,621	752	542	447	293	2,223	9,884
1991-2	1,430	609	432	348	1,874	8,239	1,516	788	502	388	498	1,900	10,013
1992-3	1,247	538	426	394	1,908	7,745	1,319	727	500	439	439	1,903	9,440
1993-4	1,255	479	444	372	1,656	7,330	1,297	632	543	415	336	1,652	8,779
1994-5	1,831	587	516	400	1,416	8,277	1,948	770	610	446	679	1,419	9,942
1995-6	1,999	633	505	495	1,741	8,947	2,104	789	587	552	466	1,753	10,558
1996-7	2,159	689	562	503	1,184	9,146	2,260	838	653	561	456	1,189	10,864
1997-8	2,166	543	621	520	1,263	8,588	2,300	697	721	581	507	1,311	10,244
1998-9[1]	2,352	591	620	514	1,415	9,208	2,424	742	721	574	624	1,434	10,867
1999-00[2]	2,260	-----	-----	527	1,785	9,491	2,383	-----	-----	591	639	1,816	11,166

[1] Preliminary. [2] Forecast. *Source: The Oil World*

Sunflower Oil Statistics in the United States In Thousands of Metric Tons

Crop Year Beginning Oct. 1	Supply: Stocks, Oct. 1	Supply: Production	Supply: Total[3]	Disappearance: Exports	Disappearance: Domestic	Disappearance: Total	Minneapolis, Crude $ Per Metric Ton
1990-1	17	243	260	163	76	239	520
1991-2	21	413	438	214	179	393	476
1992-3	45	331	376	266	85	351	558
1993-4	25	263	292	204	58	262	683
1994-5	29	528	558	444	78	521	622
1995-6	37	390	428	285	76	361	560
1996-7	67	381	458	322	94	416	497
1997-8	42	435	481	370	84	454	608
1998-9[1]	27	515	544	363	126	489	446
1999-00[2]	55	435	494	340	113	453	369-413

[1] Preliminary. [2] Forecast. [3] Includes imports. *Source: Economic Research Service, U.S. Department of Agriculture (ERS-USDA)*

Sunflower Meal Statistics in the United States In Thousands of Metric Tons

Crop Year Beginning Oct. 1	Supply: Stocks, Oct. 1	Supply: Production	Supply: Total[3]	Disappearance: Exports	Disappearance: Domestic	Disappearance: Total	28% Protein $ Per Metric Ton
1990-1	5	293	298	5	288	293	97
1991-2	5	498	510	53	451	503	85
1992-3	6	440	451	48	401	449	98
1993-4	2	327	331	37	291	328	104
1994-5	5	653	660	89	566	653	72
1995-6	5	458	463	25	433	458	136
1996-7	5	440	445	21	419	440	122
1997-8	5	494	499	13	482	495	90
1998-9[1]	5	617	622	41	576	617	72
1999-00[2]	5	517	522	18	499	517	72-94

[1] Preliminary. [2] Forecast. [3] Includes imports. *Source: Economic Research Service, U.S. Department of Agriculture (ERS-USDA)*

Tall Oil

Tall oil is the major by-product of the kraft or sulfate processing of pinewood. Tall oil is obtained by chemically treating the cooking liquor used in pulp operations in paper manufacturing. After lumber is pulped, the resulting liquor concentrate is skimmed. These skimmings are then acidified to produce crude tall oil.

Crude tall oil contains 40-50 percent fatty acids such as oleic and linoleic acids; 5-10 percent sterols, alcohols and other neutral components. When distilled the resins and fatty acids are used in alkyd and synthetic resins, lubricants, adhesives, soaps and detergents, linoleum, flotation and waterproofing agents, paints, varnishes and drying oils.

Current data on tall oil production in the U.S. is difficult to obtain because there are limited production facilities. In the monthly Census Bureau reports on fats and oils production in the U.S., the data on tall oil production is withheld to avoid disclosing data for individual operations. U.S. annual production of crude tall oil between 1991-92 (October-September) and 1998-99 averaged 1.36 billion pounds.

The Census Bureau does report current estimates of consumption of tall oil (inedible). In August 1999, consumption of tall oil was estimated at 113 million pounds compared to 119.1 million pounds in July 1999 and 114.8 million pounds in August 1998. Tall oil consumption in September 1999 was estimated to be 103.9 million pounds, down 9 percent from the month before. In September 1998, tall oil consumption was 120.3 million pounds. The Census Bureau reported that tall oil consumption in October 1999 was 108.4 million pounds, up 4 percent from the previous month. In October 1998, consumption was 111.6 million pounds.

Consumption of Tall Oil in Inedible Products in the United States In Millions of Pounds

Year	Jan.	Feb.	Mar.	Apr.	May	June	July	Aug.	Sept.	Oct.	Nov.	Dec.	Total
1992	77.8	7.5	73.2	67.6	77.8	74.8	71.5	78.4	77.1	78.9	63.8	69.2	884
1993	68.6	64.8	73.1	68.1	76.3	68.8	79.0	78.1	78.0	75.4	78.4	83.2	892
1994	117.4	98.8	124.0	118.4	115.0	118.8	106.8	114.9	119.8	113.7	101.9	113.0	1,363
1995	99.8	93.6	96.9	95.8	87.3	96.5	93.1	102.3	89.4	91.6	100.5	88.9	1,136
1996	93.1	103.4	89.2	104.1	100.5	96.6	85.4	100.7	94.9	111.5	101.4	98.8	1,180
1997	111.5	89.0	91.0	99.5	97.0	105.8	103.7	94.4	84.7	87.2	87.3	88.4	1,139
1998	86.7	114.4	113.2	120.0	108.0	101.8	117.2	114.8	120.3	111.6	119.0	121.0	1,348
1999[1]	99.4	115.1	111.0	114.0	99.9	109.2	119.1	113.0	103.9	108.4	106.4	102.2	1,302

[1] Preliminary. *Source: Bureau of the Census, U.S. Department of Commerce*

Production of Crude Tall Oil in the United States In Millions of Pounds

Year	Oct.	Nov.	Dec.	Jan.	Feb.	Mar.	Apr.	May	June	July	Aug.	Sept.	Total
1992-3	120.2	114.7	122.7	119.4	128.4	142.1	131.8	120.0	126.6	117.0	104.3	117.3	1,347.2
1993-4	107.5	120.7	124.6	127.0	115.4	148.1	131.0	119.1	109.1	108.7	110.8	117.4	1,322.0
1994-5	111.1	114.5	115.1	108.3	108.1	123.0	111.1	116.5	118.2	116.4	119.2	102.9	1,261.6
1995-6	109.8	105.2	105.2	115.5	123.3	126.9	108.9	120.3	120.3	120.5	124.9	112.9	1,281.0
1996-7	119.2	113.9	114.5	119.9	125.1	125.1	118.5	116.6	116.4	135.0	132.9	130.8	1,337.2
1997-8	122.7	115.4	135.4	137.7	126.6	127.5	132.3	131.2	131.1	132.0	120.2	121.1	1,540.6
1998-9	118.4	113.4	119.3	118.0	115.2	134.6	121.0	103.8	100.7	103.2	103.5	113.6	1,364.8
1999-00[1]	93.8	101.6	107.8	101.3									1,213.5

[1] Preliminary. *Source: Bureau of the Census, U.S. Department of Commerce*

Stocks of Crude Tall Oil in the United States, on First of Month In Millions of Pounds

Year	Jan.	Feb.	Mar.	Apr.	May	June	July	Aug.	Sept.	Oct.	Nov.	Dec.
1992-3	173.3	167.5	143.7	137.8	162.5	170.8	184.7	187.3	165.3	179.2	173.1	149.9
1993-4	132.8	124.0	113.0	103.7	109.5	109.7	118.2	124.4	112.6	105.3	101.1	97.5
1994-5	86.3	82.7	94.1	104.1	107.6	117.2	123.4	132.1	118.1	132.3	134.7	135.0
1995-6	120.9	117.5	112.9	100.7	105.7	120.3	146.0	131.8	127.0	130.5	138.7	147.3
1996-7	172.3	192.1	167.4	182.4	173.0	196.0	200.8	220.6	187.3	237.5	248.5	242.2
1997-8	208.6	187.9	209.7	202.1	202.8	219.4	256.8	254.1	239.1	259.1	278.4	245.2
1998-9	268.7	219.8	200.3	197.5	164.8	156.9	163.3	177.5	183.0	180.7	183.6	152.7
1999-00[1]	146.8	130.9	135.3	121.5	131.8							

[1] Preliminary. *Source: Bureau of the Census, U.S. Department of Commerce*

Stocks of Refined Tall Oil in the United States, on First of Month In Millions of Pounds

Year	Jan.	Feb.	Mar.	Apr.	May	June	July	Aug.	Sept.	Oct.	Nov.	Dec.
1992-3	17.4	18.1	13.8	14.1	14.0	12.6	13.7	9.4	7.7	7.3	7.5	7.2
1993-4	7.0	7.5	8.5	10.7	13.7	13.5	13.5	12.0	10.2	9.7	11.6	10.9
1994-5	12.0	14.4	16.3	13.5	15.4	14.1	11.7	10.8	10.2	10.0	9.9	8.9
1995-6	10.1	11.6	7.9	6.0	7.9	9.7	8.5	10.4	8.5	6.0	6.1	7.2
1996-7	8.3	7.0	7.5	8.9	6.5	26.5	17.4	31.7	20.9	32.0	13.2	16.6
1997-8	32.3	25.6	34.9	21.4	30.4	17.0	14.2	13.0	13.1	15.1	14.7	15.3
1998-9	15.1	14.9	17.0	12.5	14.8	9.9	7.2	7.6	7.2	7.3	6.3	7.0
1999-00[1]	7.5	7.0	8.5	9.1	9.9							

[1] Preliminary. *Source: Bureau of the Census, U.S. Department of Commerce*

Tallow and Greases

Production of tallow and greases is related to the number of cattle produced. World production of tallow and greases (edible and inedible) has averaged about 8 million tonnes in the last several years. In late 1999, the world export supply of tallow and greases got much tighter which resulted in a steep increase in prices. There are substitutes for tallow and grease and users were likely to respond to the price increases in tallow by using substitutes such as palm stearin. The major suppliers of tallow and grease to the world market are the U.S., Canada, Australia and New Zealand. Other large producers of tallow and greases are Brazil and Russia.

The U.S.D.A. estimated that at the beginning of the 1999/2000 (October-September) season, U.S. stocks of edible tallow were 45 million pounds, down 2 percent from the previous year. U.S. production of edible tallow in 1999/00 was estimated at 1.63 billion pounds, some 3 percent less than the season before. Over the last five years, U.S. edible tallow production has averaged 1.56 billion pounds per season.

Imports of tallow in 1999/00 were expected to be 5 million pounds, up from 2 million pounds a year ago. The total supply of tallow for the 1999/00 marketing year was 1.68 billion pounds, down 3 percent from the previous year.

Tallow finds widespread use in the baking and cooking industries. Edible tallow usage in the U.S. in 1999/00 was estimated at 1.43 billion pounds, up 4 percent from a year ago. Over the last five years, U.S. consumption of edible tallow has averaged 1.33 billion pounds.

The U.S. is also an important exporter of edible tallow. Exports in 1999/00 were forecast to be 205 million pounds, down 32 percent from a year ago. Over the last five years, edible tallow exports have averaged 230 million pounds. Total use of edible tallow in 1999/00 was forecast to be 1.64 billion pounds, down 3 percent from the previous year. Ending stocks of tallow in the U.S. in September 2000 were projected to be 40 million pounds.

The U.S. Census Bureau reported that in October 1999 production of edible tallow was 149 million pounds, an increase of 1 percent from September. A year earlier, edible tallow production was 125 million pounds. Inedible tallow and grease production in October 1999 was 583 million pounds, down 1 percent from the previous month. In October 1998, production was 573 million pounds.

The Census Bureau reported that consumption of edible tallow in October 1999 was 27 million pounds, up 13 percent from the previous month. A year earlier production was 24 million pounds. Consumption of inedible tallow in October 1999 was 313 million pounds, down 10 percent from the previous month. In October 1998, consumption was 312 million pounds.

World Production of Tallow and Greases (Edible and Inedible) In Thousands of Metric Tons

Year	Argentina	Australia	Brazil	Canada	France	Germany	Rep. of Korea	Netherlands	New Zealand	Russia	United Kingdom	United States	World Total
1990	285	530	340	193	185	270	85	150	132	108	230	3,180	6,538
1991	268	472	336	212	275	197	121	150	134	106	225	3,309	6,679
1992	260	526	429	209	240	178	115	163	145	477	212	3,650	8,183
1993	250	446	435	213	206	167	120	159	135	437	215	3,851	8,207
1994	250	446	435	213	206	167	120	159	135	437	215	3,851	8,207
1995	248	423	462	217	220	166	118	158	147	377	230	3,756	8,312
1996	240	397	467	242	220	168	198	161	155	400	165	3,581	8,184
1997	265	456	460	250	220	167	209	190	161	340	160	3,467	8,025
1998[1]	230	466	467	260	220	166	225	170	150	340	170	3,694	8,293
1999[2]	235	448	478	248	210	167	225	169	149	340	185	3,651	8,283

[1] Preliminary. [2] Forecast. *Source: Foreign Agricultural Service, U.S. Department of Agriculture (FAS-USDA)*

Salient Statistics of Tallow and Greases (Inedible) in the United States In Millions of Pounds

Year	Supply: Production	Supply: Stocks, Jan. 1	Supply: Total	Exports	Consumption: Soap	Consumption: Feed	Consumption: Total	Wholesale Prices, Cents/Lb.: Edible, (Loose) Chicago	Wholesale Prices, Cents/Lb.: Inedible, No. 1 Chicago
1990	5,217	374	6,097	2,267	402	2,000	3,061	14.6	13.7
1991	5,759	357	6,116	1,936	392	1,748	2,949	14.3	13.3
1992	5,768	349	6,117	2,276	334	1,954	3,050	15.5	14.4
1993	6,621	309	6,930	2,117	300	1,995	3,018	16.2	14.9
1994	6,364	320	6,684	3,039	301	2,183	3,246	18.4	17.4
1995	6,481	350	6,831	2,486	264	2,071	2,334	21.4	19.2
1996	6,242	373	6,615	1,807	245	2,389	2,634	22.0	20.1
1997	6,249	266	6,515	775	245	2,401	2,646	23.5	20.8
1998[1]	6,644	339	6,983	1,041	228	2,533	2,761	19.1	17.5
1999[2]	7,079	437	7,516	867	229	2,847	3,076	15.3	13.0

[1] Preliminary. [2] Estimate. *Sources: Economic Research Service, U.S. Department of Agriculture (ERS-USDA); Bureau of the Census, U.S. Department of Commerce*

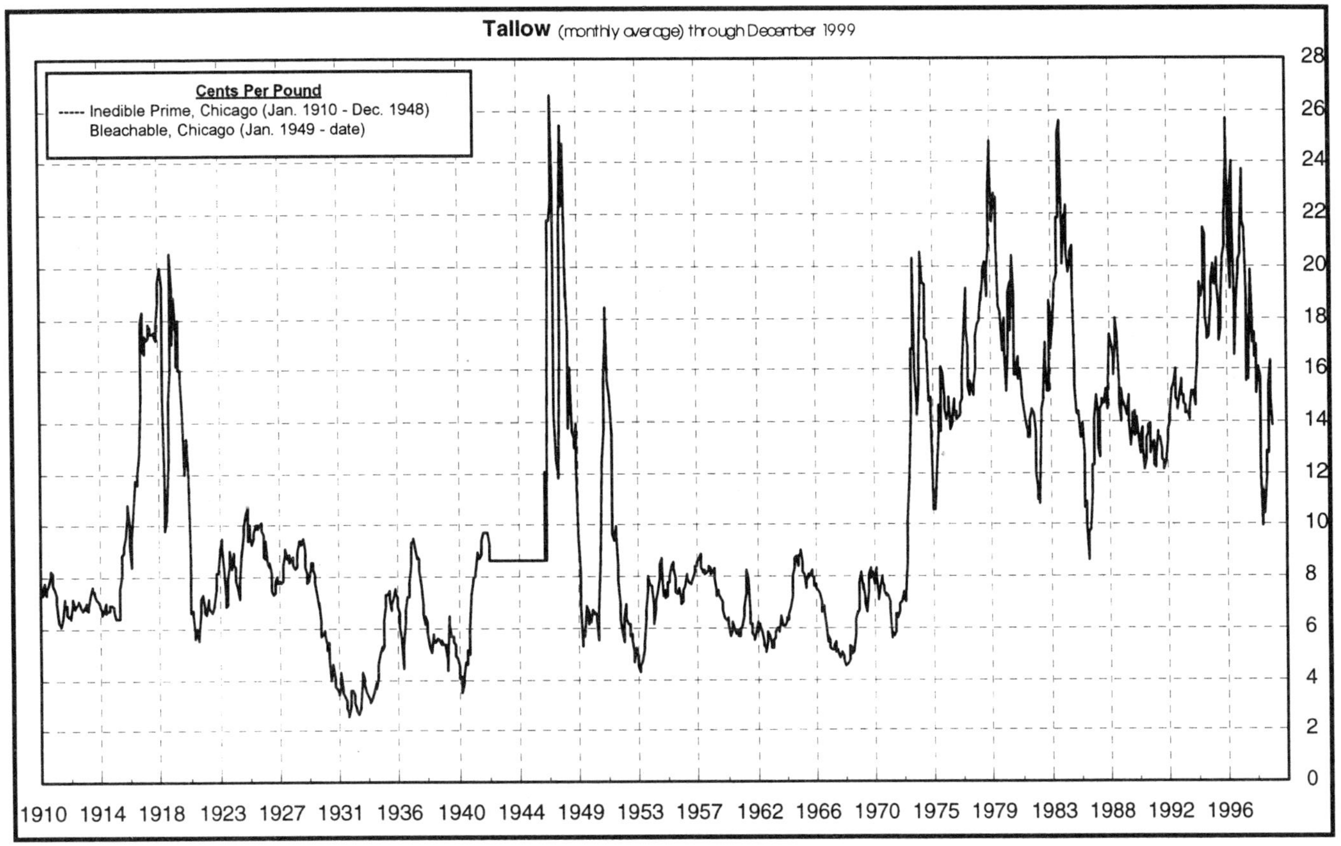

Supply and Disappearance of Edible Tallow in the United States In Millions of Pounds, Rendered Basis

	Supply			Disappearance					
Year	Stocks Jan. 1	Production	Total	Domestic	Exports	Total	Diret Use	Baking or Frying Fats	Per Capita (Lbs.)
1989	48	1,167	1,215	965	202	1,167	68	752	3.4
1990	38	1,207	1,251	963	252	1,214	154	637	3.2
1991	37	1,251	1,299	975	285	1,261	367	460	3.3
1992	39	1,527	1,571	1,205	333	1,538	610	427	4.1
1993	33	1,425	1,470	1,127	310	1,437	412	404	3.8
1994	33	1,510	1,606	1,275	295	1,570	639	405	4.0
1995	36	1,536	1,590	1,268	279	1,548	533	374	4.1
1996	43	1,520	1,568	1,317	218	1,535	602	320	4.2
1997[1]	33	1,416	1,455	1,223	185	1,408	585	312	3.6
1998[2]	47	1,537	1,586	1,301	215	1,547	868	259	3.2

[1] Preliminary. [2] Forecast. *Sources: Economic Research Service, U.S. Department of Agriculture (ERS-USDA); Bureau of the Census, U.S. Department of Commerce*

Wholesale Price of Tallow, Inedible, No. 1 Packers (Prime), Delivered, Chicago In Cents Per Pound

Year	Jan.	Feb.	Mar.	Apr.	May	June	July	Aug.	Sept.	Oct.	Nov.	Dec.	Average
1990	14.87	14.50	14.47	13.77	13.66	NA	13.50	10.12	12.00	13.42	14.09	14.75	13.56
1991	13.88	14.28	14.43	14.80	13.02	12.36	12.96	14.00	13.50	13.68	13.08	12.50	13.54
1992	12.25	12.63	12.68	13.25	13.75	13.98	14.75	15.42	15.25	15.94	16.75	16.13	14.40
1993	15.36	14.70	15.24	16.15	15.41	14.51	14.36	14.53	14.66	14.62	14.69	14.63	14.91
1994	15.00	15.00	15.22	15.19	15.25	15.63	16.67	18.64	19.50	19.78	20.38	22.48	17.40
1995	21.75	18.86	18.00	17.75	17.50	17.89	19.61	19.81	19.53	19.46	19.75	20.08	19.17
1996	19.45	17.00	17.03	17.54	19.37	19.50	20.98	22.40	25.98	21.05	19.65	21.63	20.13
1997	23.40	22.88	19.35	17.39	18.09	19.64	19.65	20.10	20.88	22.13	22.88	22.60	20.75
1998	18.20	16.88	17.58	17.70	20.35	19.63	17.31	17.57	16.69	16.98	16.90	16.70	17.71
1999[1]	16.30	12.53	11.18	11.38	10.40	11.49	11.50	11.69	14.38	16.37	14.95	13.88	13.00

[1] Preliminary. *Sources: Economic Research Service, U.S. Department of Agriculture (ERS-USDA)*

Tea

Tea is produced in a number of countries around the world. It is usually grown on plantations. The tea plant is an evergreen shrub which can grow 15-30 feet tall in its natural state, though on a plantation it is kept to a height of about five feet. It thrives in tropical climates with plenty of rain. It does well at higher altitudes though it can be grown at sea level. Most commercial production of tea takes place near the equator.

Tea is usually classified into three classes. The first is black tea or fermented tea; second is green tea or unfermented tea; and the third is oolong tea or semifermented. All of these teas are differentiated in processing, the tea leaves used are all the same. Black tea is made by taking tea leaves and fermenting them under damp clothes, then drying the leaves until they are black. The fermentation reduces astringency and changes flavor. Green tea is steamed in a boiler with fermentation before drying the leaves. Oolong teas are partially fermented. After drying teas are graded with orange pekoe being the highest quality.

World production of tea in 1997 was estimated by the Food and Agricultural Organization of the United Nations at 2.73 million metric tonnes. That represented an increase of about 1 percent from the previous year. World production of tea has been trending slowly higher. In 1988 production was estimated at 2.49 million tonnes. Five years later that figure had climbed to 2.65 million tonnes. The world's largest producer of tea is India. Production in 1997 was 785,000 tonnes or 29 percent of the world total. India produces mostly black tea and has been putting more emphasis on producing higher quality tea. Despite its large production, India is not the largest exporter of tea. Kenya, Sri Lanka and China all export more tea. India's tea exports in 1999 declined in the January-October period to 146 million kilograms, down 15 percent from the same period in 1998. The reason for the decline was in part a reduction in demand by Russia, one of the major importers of tea.

China is the next largest producer of tea. Production in 1997 was estimated to be 633,000 tonnes. China has also been trying to improve the quality of its tea. Green tea is produced for the domestic market while black tea is exported. The world's third largest tea producing country is Sri Lanka. Production in 1999 was estimated at just over 285,000 tonnes according to Sri Lanka tea industry officials. That would be just above the 1998 production record of 285,000 tonnes.

Tea production is also increasing in Africa. The largest African tea producer is Kenya. Officials in Kenya indicated that in the January-September 1999 period, tea production was 173,000 tonnes, down 20 percent from the same period in 1998. The decline was blamed in part on cold weather.

The U.S. is a major importer of tea, most of which is black tea. U.S. per capita consumption of tea is just over nine gallons. The U.S. exports small amounts of tea. The U.S. Department of Commerce reported that in October 1999, exports were 102 tonnes while in September 1999 exports were 62 tonnes.

World Tea Production, in Major Producing Countries — In Thousands of Metric Tons

Year	Argentina	Bangladesh	China	India	Indonesia	Iran	Japan	Kenya	Malawi	Sri Lanka	Turkey	Ex-USSR[2]	World Total
1988	44.0	43.6	545.0	700.0	133.8	55.6	89.8	164.0	40.2	228.2	166.4	118.0	2,490
1989	48.0	39.1	535.0	688.1	141.4	46.0	90.5	180.6	39.5	208.0	141.6	119.2	2,444
1990	50.0	45.9	540.0	720.3	145.2	44.0	89.9	197.0	39.1	234.1	126.7	123.2	2,528
1991	40.0	45.2	542.0	741.7	133.4	45.0	87.9	203.6	40.5	241.6	135.3	110.0	2,541
1992	43.0	46.0	580.0	704.0	163.0	55.0	92.0	188.0	28.0	179.0	144.0	57.0	2,439
1993	55.0	55.0	621.0	758.0	165.0	57.0	92.0	211.0	39.0	232.0	117.0	81.0	2,643
1994	50.0	51.0	613.0	744.0	136.0	56.0	86.0	209.0	35.0	242.0	134.0	66.0	2,615
1995	47.0	52.0	609.0	753.0	154.0	54.0	85.0	245.0	34.0	246.0	103.0	44.0	2,613
1996	47.0	48.0	617.0	780.0	159.0	62.0	89.0	257.0	37.0	258.0	115.0	38.0	2,701
1997[1]	48.0	53.0	633.0	785.0	162.0	62.0	91.0	221.0	38.0	277.0	121.0	38.0	2,734

[1] Preliminary. [2] Mostly Georgia and Azerbaijan. *Sources: Foreign Agricultural Service, U.S. Department of Agriculture (FAS-USDA); Food and Agriculture Organization of the United Nations (FAO-UN)*

World Tea Exports from Producing Countries — In Metric Tons

Year	Argentina	Bangladesh	Brazil	China	India	Indonesia	Kenya	Malawi	P. New Guinea	Sri Lanka	Vietnam	Zimbabwe	World Total
1988	34,258	26,187	9,686	198,289	200,956	92,687	138,201	36,961	5,834	219,710	14,800	14,190	1,039,313
1989	43,335	23,426	9,400	204,584	211,622	114,709	163,188	39,891	5,439	203,763	15,016	12,768	1,121,251
1990	45,966	26,970	7,976	195,471	209,085	110,964	169,586	43,039	5,375	215,251	24,698	11,507	1,141,026
1991	36,029	26,860	7,347	190,188	215,144	110,207	175,625	41,185	3,747	212,017	7,953	11,304	1,206,282
1992	36,530	24,990	8,211	180,834	166,359	121,243	172,053	37,056	5,638	181,259	12,967	6,088	1,130,355
1993	44,258	29,620	8,335	206,659	153,159	123,925	199,379	35,264	6,441	134,742	21,200	8,065	1,193,144
1994	43,355	29,040	8,377	184,071	150,874	84,916	176,962	38,670	3,400	115,097	23,500	9,688	1,078,460
1995	41,175	26,445	7,252	169,788	158,333	79,227	258,564	32,600	4,200	178,005	18,800	9,156	1,179,705
1996[1]	35,042	26,600	3,891	173,145	138,360	101,532	260,819	36,700	7,510	218,714	20,800	11,540	1,238,537
1997[2]	56,806	24,300	3,404	205,381	203,000	66,843	199,224	20,000	7,510	267,726	10,000	13,057	1,291,700

[1] Preliminary. [2] Estimate. *Source: Food and Agriculture Organization of the United Nations (FAO-UN)*

Tin

Tin is used in the manufacture of coatings for steel containers used to preserve foods and beverages. It finds use in solder alloys, electroplating, ceramics and in plastic. The U.S. Geological Survey estimated that the major uses for tin were: cans and containers, 30 percent; electrical, 20 percent; construction, 10 percent; transportation, 10 percent; other, 30 percent. In the U.S. there is no mine production of tin. Outside of imports, tin is produced by recycling old and new scrap. In the U.S., this was done at seven detinning plants and 110 secondary nonferrous metal processing plants. In 1998, U.S. production of secondary tin from old scrap was 7,900 metric tonnes, an increase of 1 percent from 1997. Production of tin from new scrap in 1998 was 4,500 tonnes, about the same as in 1997.

World mine production of tin in 1998 was estimated at 216,000 tonnes, an increase of 2 percent from the previous year. The largest producer of tin is China with 1998 production estimated at 67,000 tonnes, an increase of 3 percent from 1997. The next largest producer is Indonesia with 1998 production estimated at 48,000 tonnes, an increase of 2 percent from the previous year. The third largest producer is Peru with 1998 output estimated at 29,000 tonnes, up almost 4 percent from 1997. Mine production of tin in Brazil was 20,000 tonnes, up over 5 percent from 1997. Bolivia is another large producer with mine output of 16,000 tonnes, a 7 percent increase from 1997. Other large producers include Russia, Australia, Malaysia and Portugal. The world reserve base of tin is estimated at 12 million tonnes. The largest reserves are in China with 3.4 million tonnes and Brazil with an estimated 2.5 million tonnes. The world tin industry's major research and development laboratory, based in the United Kingdom, reported progress in several areas of tin research. One was the development of a tin foil capsule to replace lead foil capsules on wine bottles. Another was a noncyanide-based electrolyte that contains a coating of tin and zinc which could replace cadmium as an environmentally acceptable anticorrosion coating on steel.

U.S. consumption of primary tin in August 1999 was 3,510 tonnes, an increase of 3 percent from the previous month. In the January-August period, consumption was 27,200 tonnes while for all of 1998 it was 37,100 tonnes. Consumption of secondary tin in August 1999 was 886 tonnes, up 5 percent from the previous month. In the first eight months of 1999, consumption was 6,780 tonnes while for all of 1998 it was 8,620 tonnes.

U.S. tin imports in July 1999 were 3,740 tonnes, a decline of 16 percent from June. In the January-July 1998 period, tin metal imports were 25,400 tonnes, and for all of 1998 they were 44,000 tonnes. The suppliers of tin metal in 1999 were led by China with 7,290 tonnes or 29 percent of the total. The next largest supplier was Peru with 5,660 tonnes or 22 percent of the total. Indonesia supplied 4,680 tonnes or 18 percent of the total. Other large suppliers included Chile, Brazil and Bolivia.

U.S. imports of other tin products in July 1999 were 815 tonnes, down 1 percent from the month before. In the January-July 1999 period, imports were 5,300 tonnes while for all of 1998 they were 8,560 tonnes. In 1999, imports of tin alloys totaled 1,920 tonnes while waste and scrap totaled 1,690 tonnes. Tin bars and rods totaled 515 tonnes while plates, sheets and strip were 24 tonnes. Miscellaneous tin product imports totaled 1,160 tonnes. U.S. exports of tin metal in July 1999 were 537 tonnes, down 2 percent from the prior month. For the first seven months of 1999, tin metal exports were 3,660 tonnes while for all of 1998 they were 5,020 tonnes.

U.S. production of tinplate in August 1999 was 172,000 tonnes, gross weight, with a tin content of 830 tonnes. There were 4.8 kilograms of tin per metric tonne of plate. In July, tinplate production was 154,000 tonnes with a tin content of 748 tonnes. There were 4.9 kilograms of tin per tonne of plate. For all of 1998, tinplate production was 1.7 million tonnes with tin content of 8,900 tonnes. There were 5.2 kilograms of tin per tonne of plate.

Disposals of tin from the Defense Logistics Agency stockpile continued in 1999. In August, disposals were 220 tonnes, the same as in July. In 1998, August disposals were 250 tonnes. In the first eight months of 1999, disposals totaled 515 tonnes. For all of 1998, disposals totaled 1,900 tonnes.

Futures Markets

Tin futures and options are traded on the London Metals Exchange (LME).

World Mine Production of Tin In Metric Tons (Contained Tin)

Year	Australia	Bolivia	Brazil	China	Indonesia	Malaysia	Nigeria	Peru	Portugal	Russia[3]	Thailand	United Kingdom	World Total
1989	7,709	15,849	50,232	40,000	31,263	32,034	217	5,082	63	16,000	14,922	3,846	232,857
1990	7,377	17,249	39,149	42,000	30,200	28,468	192	5,134	4,780	15,000	14,635	3,400	221,000
1991	5,708	16,830	29,253	42,100	30,061	20,710	217	6,558	8,333	13,500	14,937	2,326	201,000
1992	6,609	16,516	27,000	43,800	29,400	14,339	415	10,044	6,560	15,160	11,484	2,044	191,000
1993	8,057	18,634	26,500	49,100	29,000	10,384	200	14,310	5,334	13,100	6,363	2,232	190,000
1994	7,495	16,169	16,619	54,100	30,610	6,458	278	20,275	4,332	10,460	3,926	1,922	178,000
1995	8,656	14,419	17,317	61,900	38,378	6,402	357	22,331	4,627	9,000	2,201	1,973	193,000
1996	8,828	14,802	19,617	69,600	38,500	5,175	139	27,004	4,800	8,000	1,457	2,103	206,000
1997[1]	10,169	12,898	18,291	67,500	47,000	5,065	150	27,952	4,000	7,500	756	2,396	210,000
1998[2]	10,204	11,305	18,300	79,000	40,000	5,756	200	25,747	4,000	4,500	700	376	206,000

[1] Preliminary. [2] Estimate. [3] Formerly part of the U.S.S.R.; data reported separately until 1992. *Source: U.S. Geological Survey (USGS)*

World Smelter Production of Primary Tin   In Metric Tons

Year	Australia	Bolivia	Brazil	China	Indo-nesia	Japan	Malaysia	Mexico	Russia[2]	South Africa	Spain	Thailand	World Total
1989	424	9,448	44,240	29,500	29,916	808	50,874	4,752	18,000	1,306	1,767	14,571	221,569
1990	312	12,567	37,580	35,000	30,389	816	49,067	5,004	16,000	1,140	600	15,512	246,000
1991	340	14,663	25,776	36,400	30,415	716	42,722	2,262	13,000	1,042	600	11,255	205,000
1992	240	14,393	27,000	39,600	31,915	821	45,598	2,590	15,200	592	600	10,679	194,000
1993	222	14,541	26,900	52,100	30,415	804	40,079	1,640	13,400	452	500	8,099	215,000
1994	315	15,285	20,400	67,800	31,100	706	37,990	768	11,500	43	500	7,759	216,000
1995	570	17,709	16,787	67,700	38,628	630	39,433	770	9,500	-----	500	8,243	223,000
1996	460	16,733	18,361	71,500	39,000	524	38,051	1,234	9,000	-----	150	10,981	228,000
1997	605	16,853	17,525	67,700	40,000	507	38,400	1,188	6,700	-----	150	12,028	231,000
1998[1]	655	11,102	17,500	78,800	35,000	500	27,900	1,200	3,000	-----	150	12,000	225,000

[1] Preliminary. [2] Formerly part of the U.S.S.R.; data not separately until 1992. *Source: U.S. Geological Survey (USGS)*

United States Foreign Trade of Tin   In Metric Tons

		Imports for Consumption											
		Concentrates[2] (Ore)			Unwrought Tin Metal								
Year	Exports (Metal)	Total All Ore	Bolivia	Peru	Total All Metal	Bolivia	Brazil	China	Indo-nesia	Malaysia	Singa-pore	Thailand	United Kingdom
1989	904	216	-----	149	33,988	4,795	10,572	4,793	5,162	2,392	456	180	391
1990	658	-----	-----	-----	33,810	8,472	6,535	4,339	4,695	3,873	40	60	227
1991	970	1	1	-----	29,102	8,912	4,489	5,281	4,425	1,751	100	-----	344
1992	1,890	-----	-----	-----	27,314	4,623	8,167	5,389	3,854	2,799	320	427	-----
1993	2,600	-----	-----	-----	33,682	8,027	11,366	4,202	5,678	846	220	-----	6
1994	2,560	-----	-----	-----	32,400	7,260	9,990	3,230	6,620	1,390	142	-----	666
1995	2,790	-----	-----	-----	33,200	6,630	8,070	5,610	7,230	3,810	40	-----	97
1996	3,670	-----	-----	-----	30,200	6,290	9,460	2,760	7,550	965	120	-----	243
1997	4,660	57	-----	-----	40,600	6,680	8,610	4,710	7,610	1,640	120	600	20
1998[1]	5,020	-----	-----	-----	44,000	5,160	4,710	9,870	7,880	1,870	822	540	790

[1] Preliminary. [2] Tin content. *Source: U.S. Geological Survey (USGS)*

Consumption (Total) of Tin (Pig) in the United States   In Metric Tons

Year	Jan.	Feb.	Mar.	Apr.	May	June	July	Aug.	Sept.	Oct.	Nov.	Dec.	Total
1990	4,000	4,000	4,200	4,100	4,200	4,100	4,100	4,300	4,100	4,100	4,200	3,900	44,363
1991	4,100	3,900	4,100	4,300	4,100	4,200	3,900	4,100	4,000	4,300	4,100	4,000	49,000
1992	3,800	3,800	3,800	3,800	3,700	3,800	3,800	3,500	3,600	3,600	3,400	3,300	45,090
1993	3,400	3,500	3,600	3,600	3,500	3,600	3,500	3,600	3,500	3,500	3,500	3,400	47,107
1994	3,500	3,700	3,700	3,600	3,600	3,700	3,500	3,400	2,500	3,600	3,600	3,400	42,700
1995	3,500	3,600	3,680	3,726	3,877	3,833	3,544	3,895	3,825	3,823	3,735	3,770	44,808
1996	3,862	3,938	3,940	3,878	3,894	3,976	3,926	3,996	3,687	3,779	3,908	3,730	48,800
1997	4,953	4,025	4,023	4,067	3,999	4,079	3,936	3,912	4,050	4,098	3,964	4,250	44,350
1998	4,410	4,493	4,445	4,508	4,388	4,483	4,273	4,300	4,404	4,402	4,348	4,268	52,722
1999[1]	4,660	4,667	4,790	4,790	4,760	4,700	4,254	4,396	4,340	4,316	4,275	4,227	54,175

[1] Preliminary. *Source: U.S. Geological Survey (USGS)*

Tin Stocks (Pig-Industrial) in the United States, on First of Month   In Metric Tons

Year	Jan.	Feb.	Mar.	Apr.	May	June	July	Aug.	Sept.	Oct.	Nov.	Dec.
1990	6,072	5,975	5,824	6,401	4,959	3,298	3,792	3,592	3,836	4,762	4,819	4,829
1991	6,337	6,677	6,688	6,177	5,993	5,991	6,348	6,739	6,544	8,544	6,616	6,347
1992	3,024	3,022	3,369	2,844	2,877	2,901	2,651	3,111	3,321	3,454	3,654	3,178
1993	3,221	3,572	4,450	4,483	3,898	3,609	4,648	4,652	4,561	3,709	3,262	3,535
1994	3,651	4,635	3,775	3,967	3,471	3,470	3,825	3,027	2,891	2,980	2,844	2,908
1995	2,741	3,931	3,850	2,780	3,000	3,080	3,210	3,910	3,800	3,880	4,380	4,290
1996	4,580	6,000	5,200	4,390	4,880	5,590	5,760	5,640	4,790	4,580	4,810	6,810
1997	4,670	5,100	5,610	5,600	5,070	5,270	5,180	5,650	5,590	5,420	5,290	5,590
1998	6,100	5,570	5,390	5,840	6,170	5,940	5,830	5,580	6,660	6,270	5,880	5,710
1999[1]	5,620	8,120	7,770	7,760	7,760	7,510	7,750	7,560	7,870	7,790	8,390	8,800

[1] Preliminary. *Source: U.S. Geological Survey (USGS)*

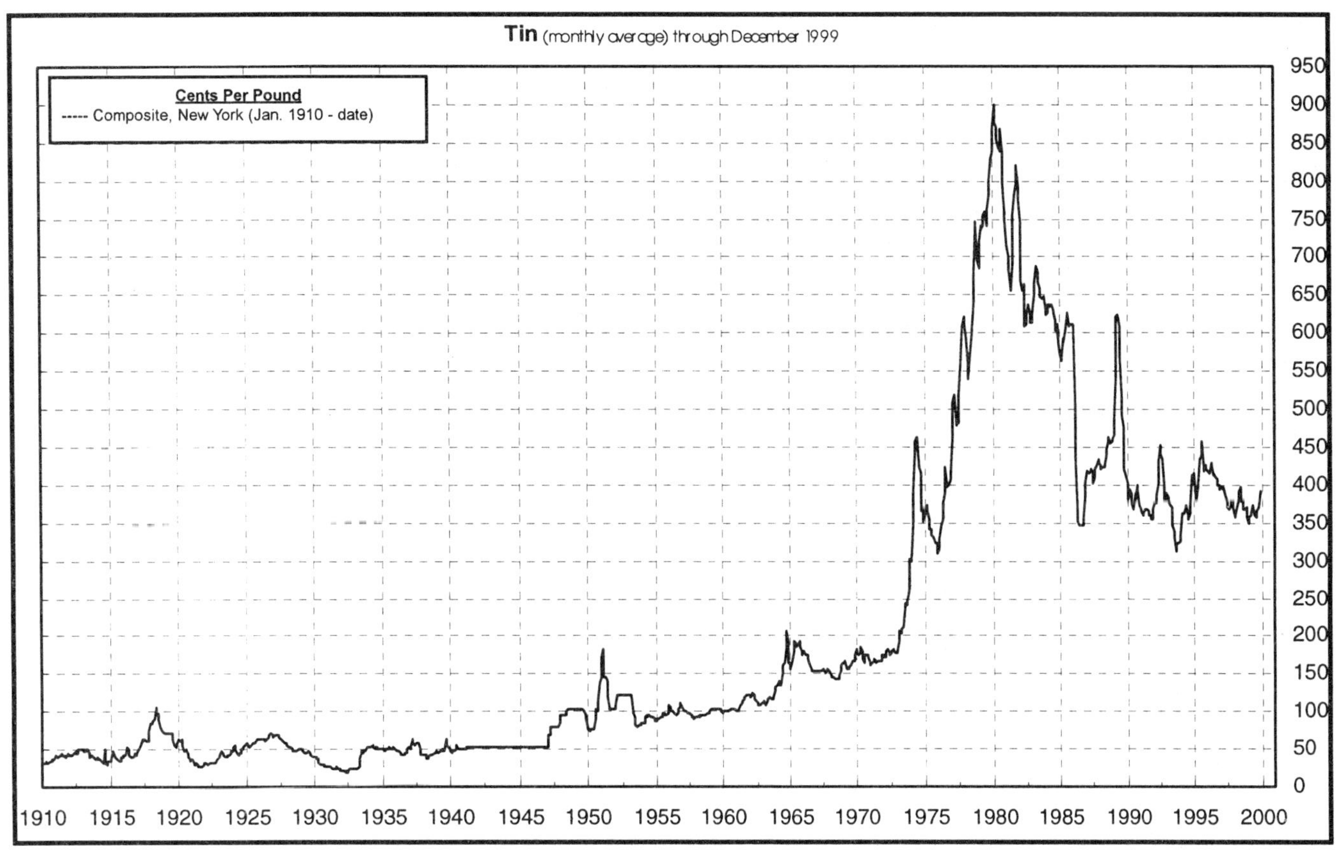

Average Price of Ex-Dock Tin in New York[1] In Cents Per Pound

Year	Jan.	Feb.	Mar.	Apr.	May	June	July	Aug.	Sept.	Oct.	Nov.	Dec.	Average
1990	317.89	296.28	302.41	308.97	307.02	295.86	288.09	287.48	279.20	296.11	292.27	261.82	294.45
1991	269.97	268.00	264.51	265.78	271.78	272.30	270.55	269.02	265.86	264.50	262.26	262.05	267.22
1992	261.30	267.79	267.52	277.20	290.05	313.07	331.10	322.19	315.66	291.60	268.54	271.76	289.82
1993	280.40	280.91	277.43	275.67	269.62	255.35	252.31	230.17	213.22	220.02	224.88	236.90	251.41
1994	249.55	267.55	261.20	258.49	264.18	264.45	254.83	249.18	255.10	262.46	293.72	284.99	263.81
1995	374.77	260.25	266.45	288.00	283.62	314.33	316.06	331.64	304.12	297.77	304.47	300.28	303.48
1996	299.55	297.45	296.68	308.49	306.71	296.20	298.47	291.30	292.13	285.11	285.87	280.61	294.88
1997	281.91	281.34	281.51	274.36	274.19	267.31	261.03	259.85	262.56	266.77	268.39	262.61	270.15
1998	249.39	252.65	262.36	271.65	280.71	284.27	284.27	270.98	260.79	259.17	261.82	251.55	265.80
1999	244.46	251.04	255.13	256.97	269.42	253.64	251.09	254.56	256.38	260.70	278.24	274.51	258.85

Source: American Metal Market (AMM)

Average Price of Tin (Straights) in New York In Cents Per Pound

Year	Jan.	Feb.	Mar.	Apr.	May	June	July	Aug.	Sept.	Oct.	Nov.	Dec.	Average
1990	403.31	380.61	387.60	394.20	389.34	376.17	367.19	390.25	380.34	399.32	394.50	372.81	386.30
1991	368.22	364.86	360.89	362.04	368.33	368.95	367.07	365.06	361.19	358.63	355.35	354.27	362.91
1992	367.89	375.70	375.25	386.88	402.70	431.63	453.05	441.89	434.02	398.27	380.41	380.89	402.38
1993	390.01	384.48	378.36	374.06	369.82	347.55	339.79	330.63	310.94	322.67	322.26	326.72	349.77
1994	334.38	362.81	361.86	363.65	371.63	372.59	360.45	353.85	362.48	371.82	411.63	401.31	369.04
1995	415.05	379.08	378.61	395.99	399.17	433.75	438.04	458.66	423.71	417.23	425.41	419.75	415.37
1996	418.68	415.65	414.71	429.34	427.24	413.65	416.63	409.12	407.79	400.25	400.65	394.46	412.35
1997	396.18	395.50	395.64	386.52	386.58	377.83	369.97	369.01	372.45	377.39	378.00	371.35	381.37
1998	356.97	359.76	370.96	381.99	392.16	397.36	377.72	380.02	368.89	366.87	370.49	357.69	373.41
1999	348.77	356.50	361.11	363.01	372.62	359.05	359.96	357.35	366.06	370.68	392.04	288.77	357.99

Source: Wall Street Journal (WSJ)

Tin Plate Production & Tin Recovered in the United States In Metric Tons

	----- Tin Content of Tinplate Produced -----												
		-------- Tinplate (All Forms) --------			---------- Tin Recovered from Scrap by Form of Recovery ----------								
Year	Tinplate Waste ---- Gross Weight ----		Tin Content (Tonne)	Tin Per Tonne of Plate (Kilograms)	Tin Metal	Bronze & Brass	Solder	Type Metal	Babbitt	Anti-monial Lead	Chemical Com-pounds	Misc.[2]	Grand Total
1985	146,041	2,215,042	9,321	4.2	1,302	8,045	3,565	122	88	791	186	10	14,109
1986	120,186	2,068,246	8,660	4.2	1,134	7,996	3,676	197	66	891	W	17	13,977
1987	141,842	2,302,173	10,357	4.5	1,353	10,245	3,765	66	77	623	W	30	16,159
1988	149,054	2,375,809	11,582	4.9	578	9,939	3,619	70	112	902	W	29	15,249
1989	153,542	2,263,769	11,764	5.2	569	10,305	3,225	46	116	952	W	W	15,213
1990	156,419	2,467,205	11,750	4.8	186	13,312	2,876	46	28	739	W	4	17,187
1991	166,647	2,468,769	11,482	4.7	234	11,719	W	44	24	928	W	2,705	12,949
1992	195,760	1,620,007	9,821	6.1	137	12,761	W	47	78	704	W	181	13,727
1993	196,874	1,625,132	9,945	6.0	112	10,670	W	43	51	796	W	W	11,672
1994	188,921	1,528,303	9,396	6.1	NA	NA	NA	NA	NA	NA	NA	NA	NA
1995	205,000	1,660,000	9,600	5.8	W	11,200	W	39	W	335	W	W	11,600
1996	181,100	1,551,000	9,617	6.2	W	11,400	W	37	34	171	W	W	11,600
1997	157,000	2,010,000	9,300	4.6	W	12,200	W	W	W	149	W	W	12,300
1998[1]	W	1,700,000	8,900	5.2	NA	NA	NA	NA	NA	NA	NA	NA	NA

[1] Preliminary. [2] Includes foil, terne metal, cable lead, and items indicated by symbol W. W = Withheld Proprietary data.
Source: U.S. Geological Survey (USGS)

Consumption of Primary and Secondary Tin in the United States In Metric Tons

			---------- Net Receipts ----------							
Year	Net Import Reliance as a % of Apparent Consumption	Industry Stocks Jan. 1[2]	Primary	Secondary	Scrap	Total	Available Supply	Stocks Dec. 31 (Total Available Less Total Processed)	Total Processed	Consumed in Manu-facturing Products
1985	72	8,430	38,006	8,904	7,471	54,381	62,811	13,928	48,883	48,669
1986	74	9,336	35,475	11,636	6,346	53,457	62,793	18,915	43,878	43,524
1987	74	9,876	38,401	11,707	6,635	56,743	66,619	21,887	44,731	44,219
1988	78	10,217	39,421	12,472	6,707	58,600	68,817	23,586	46,232	45,602
1989	77	9,242	37,760	10,901	8,168	56,829	66,071	19,184	46,887	46,463
1990	71	13,551	38,473	9,501	6,534	54,508	68,059	22,578	45,481	45,165
1991	74	12,502	36,126	1,622	8,370	46,118	58,620	13,540	45,080	44,805
1992	80	12,038	34,327	2,279	8,412	45,018	57,056	11,669	45,387	45,120
1993	84	8,556	37,700	3,280	8,768	49,700	58,300	11,566	46,700	46,600
1994	83	9,540	35,400	4,210	4,940	44,500	54,100	11,600	42,500	42,200
1995	84	8,480	39,400	5,020	6,240	50,600	59,100	13,000	46,100	46,000
1996	83	9,300	39,200	2,750	6,140	48,100	57,300	12,500	44,900	44,700
1997	85	9,180	39,000	2,360	6,010	47,300	56,500	11,900	44,600	44,400
1998[1]	NA	9,390	40,000	2,490	6,240	48,700	58,100	12,300	45,800	45,700

[1] Preliminary. [2] Includes tin in transit in the U.S. *Source: U.S. Geological Survey (USGS)*

Consumption of Tin in the United States, by Finished Products In Metric Tons (Contained Tin)

											------- Total -------		
Year	Tinplate[2]	Solder	Babbitt	Bronze & Brass	Tinning	Chem-icals[3]	Tin Powder	Bar Tin & Anodes	White Metal	Other	Total	Primary	Secondary
1985	9,321	18,621	1,488	4,330	1,511	W	976	466	937	12,100	48,669	36,524	12,145
1986	8,660	15,810	1,324	3,502	1,437	W	1,002	449	1,134	10,204	43,522	33,324	10,198
1987	10,357	15,240	1,060	3,559	1,398	W	W	703	1,175	10,704	44,219	35,620	8,599
1988	11,582	15,288	926	3,934	1,406	W	W	557	1,131	10,777	45,601	37,529	8,072
1989	11,764	16,370	794	3,693	1,505	W	711	619	1,074	9,926	46,456	36,603	9,853
1990	11,750	16,443	763	3,166	1,707	6,275	563	603	1,045	2,850	45,165	36,770	8,395
1991	11,482	16,296	941	2,896	1,465	6,564	539	436	868	3,318	44,805	35,138	9,667
1992	9,821	18,461	916	2,916	1,275	6,301	573	919	974	2,964	45,090	34,983	10,137
1993	9,650	19,000	823	3,093	1,249	6,446	608	946	789	3,927	46,600	34,600	11,900
1994	9,480	15,100	831	3,080	1,230	5,740	625	1,190	992	3,990	42,200	33,700	8,530
1995	9,670	17,700	871	2,830	1,110	7,060	W	1,200	965	4,550	46,000	35,200	10,800
1996	9,340	15,600	851	2,760	2,050	7,520	573	1,150	1,340	3,230	44,700	36,500	8,180
1997	9,350	15,900	909	3,160	1,210	8,170	W	684	754	3,980	44,400	36,200	8,250
1998[1]	8,900	16,900	1,020	3,610	1,100	8,170	W	704	778	4,260	45,700	37,100	8,620

[1] Preliminary. [2] Includes small quantity of secondary pig tin and tin acquired in chemicals. [3] Including tin oxide. W = Withheld proprietary data.
Source: U.S. Geological Survey (USGS)

Titanium

Titanium has unique properties including a density that is one-half that of steel, excellent strength and immunity to corrosion. These properties make titanium an ideal construction material for engines and air frames. Pure titanium metal is called "sponge" because of its porous cellular form. Titanium sponge is processed to form an ingot which is then processed by mills to make plate sheet tubing. Due to its unique properties of being lightweight with high strength, titanium has a growing number of uses. New uses in recent years include golf clubs and bicycles. In the automotive industry, titanium materials add strength and reduce weight which increases energy efficiency. Other uses of titanium are in pollution control devices, chemical processing, desalination plants and in tubing for power plants and oil refineries.

The U.S. Geological Survey reported that titanium sponge metal was produced by two firms in the United States. Ingot was made by the tow sponge producers as well as nine other firms. About 30 firms consume ingot to produce forged components, mill products and castings. In 1998, an estimated 65 percent of the titanium metal used was in aerospace applications. The remaining titanium was used in chemical processes, power generation, marine, ordnance, medical and other nonaerospace applications. Titanium dioxide pigment has uses in paint, varnishes, paper, plastics, ceramics, printing ink and floor coverings.

U.S. production of titanium sponge metal in the second quarter of 1999 was withheld by the U.S. Geological Survey to avoid disclosing company proprietary data. Production of titanium ingot in second quarter 1999 was 10,500 tonnes, an increase of 8 percent from the first quarter. For the first half of 1999, titanium ingot production was 20,200 tonnes while for all of 1998 it was 52,500 tonnes. Production of titanium mill products in second quarter 1999 was 6,150 tonnes, about the same as in the first quarter. For the first half of 1999, mill product production was 12,300 tonnes while for all of 1998 it was 33,400 tonnes.

U.S. consumption of titanium sponge in the second quarter of 1999 was 4,040 tonnes, down 16 percent from the first quarter. First half 1999 consumption was 8,840 tonnes, while 1998 consumption was 28,200 tonnes. Consumption of titanium scrap in second quarter 1999 was 5,240 tonnes, down 6 percent from first quarter. In first half 1999, scrap consumption was 10,800 tonnes while for all of 1998 it was 28,600 tonnes. Titanium ingot consumption in second quarter 1999 was 9,760 tonnes, 1 percent lower than in the first quarter. First half 1999 ingot consumption was 19,700 tonnes, while for all of 1998 it was 43,000 tonnes.

Average Prices of Titanium in the United States

Year	Ilmenite F.O.B. Australian Ports	Slag, 85% TiO2 F.O.B. Richards Bay, South Africa	Rutile Large Lots Bulk, F.O.B. U.S. East Coast	Rutile Bagged F.O.B. Australian Ports	Average Price of Grade A Titanium Sponge, F.O.B. Shipping Point	Titanium Metal Sponge	Titanium Dioxide Pigments, F.O.B. U.S. Plants	
	Dollars Per Metric Ton				Dollars Per Pound			
1989	67-75	275-300	540-550	553-632	5.11	4.80-5.30	1.01-1.02	1.04-1.05
1990	69-77	285-310	550-580	693-770	5.31	4.75	.99	1.01
1991	68-76	295-325	606-650	515-545	5.25	4.75	.99	.99
1992	58-62	310	510-520	380-414	3.96	3.50-4.00	.99	.92-.95
1993	61-64	330	NA	370-400	3.75	3.50-4.00	.99	.92-.95
1994	74-80	334	410-430	450-480	3.96	3.75-4.25	.94-.96	.92-.94
1995	81-85	349	550-650	650-800	4.06	4.25-4.50	.92-.96	.99-1.03
1996	82-92	353	525-600	700-800	-----	4.25-4.50	1.06-1.08	1.08-1.10
1997[1]	68-81	391	500-550	650-710	-----	4.25-4.50	1.01-1.03	1.04-1.06
1998[2]	72-77	386	470-530	570-620	-----	4.25-4.50	.96-.98	.97-.99

[1] Preliminary. [2] Estimate. NA = Not available. *Source: U.S. Geological Survey (USGS)*

Salient Statistics of Titanium in the United States In Metric Tons

Year	Titanium Dioxide Pigment: Production	Titanium Dioxide Pigment: Imports[3]	Titanium Dioxide Pigment: Apparent Consumption	Ilmenite: Imports[3]	Ilmenite: Consumption	Titanium Slag: Imports[3]	Titanium Slag: Consumption	Rutile[4]: Imports[3]	Rutile[4]: Consumption	Exports of Titaniu Products: Ores & Concentrates	Exports: Scrap	Exports: Dioxide & Pigments	Exports: Ingots, Billets, Etc.
1989	1,006,581	166,346	947,259	411,751	659,584	386,146	414,830	264,895	366,143	19,832	5,474	212,197	2,702
1990	978,659	147,592	925,447	345,907	688,948	373,623	390,537	274,605	369,454	18,765	5,487	202,288	2,371
1991	991,976	166,094	935,829	213,886	738,089	408,302	341,379	240,120	368,643	26,912	4,568	211,854	1,700
1992	1,137,038	169,260	999,930	294,585	684,882	537,118	539,323	317,399	460,969	34,665	2,770	270,422	1,455
1993	1,161,561	171,939	1,028,311	301,000	693,940	476,000	545,809	371,481	464,825	15,202	3,893	261,000	1,511
1994	1,250,000	176,000	1,090,000	808,000	W	472,000	583,000	332,000	510,000	19,000	4,120	313,000	1,559
1995	1,250,000	183,000	1,080,000	861,000	1,410,000	388,000	582,000	318,000	480,000	32,300	3,420	306,000	2,560
1996	1,230,000	167,000	1,070,000	939,000	1,400,000	421,000	NA	324,000	398,000	15,500	3,410	292,000	3,130
1997[1]	1,340,000	194,000	1,130,000	952,000	1,520,000	NA	NA	336,000	489,000	23,800	5,500	362,000	3,860
1998[2]	1,330,000	200,000	1,150,000	1,010,000	1,300,000	NA	NA	387,000	421,000	59,700	7,010	356,000	3,780

[1] Preliminary. [2] Estimate. [3] For consumption. [4] Natural and synthetic. [5] 1994 to date includes Slag. W = Withheld proprietary data.
Source: U.S. Geological Survey (USGS)

TITANIUM

World Produciton of Titanium Illmenite Concentrates In Thousands of Metric Tons

Year	Australia[2]	Brazil	China	India	Malaysia	Norway	Sierra Leone	Sri Lanka	Thailand	Ukraine[3]	World Total	-- Titaniferous Slag[4] -- Canada	South Africa
1985	1,433	76.4	140.0	143.0	314.7	735.8	-----	114.9	1.00	445	4,737	845	435
1986	1,252	75.5	140.0	140.0	414.9	803.6	-----	129.9	13.50	450	4,705	850	435
1987	1,509	169.3	140.0	140.0	509.2	852.3	5.6	128.5	27.10	455	3,937	925	650
1988	1,622	142.2	150.0	229.7	486.3	898.0	42.1	74.3	18.30	460	4,033	1,025	400
1989	1,714	144.2	150.0	240.7	533.7	929.8	62.3	101.4	16.99	460	4,353	1,040	725
1990	1,621	114.1	150.0	280.0	530.2	814.5	54.6	66.4	10.67	430	4,072	1,046	840
1991	1,381	69.1	150.0	311.5	336.3	625.0	60.4	60.9	17.08	400	3,360	701	808
1992	1,806	76.6	150.0	300.0	337.7	708.0	60.3	33.3	2.97	450	3,920	753	884
1993	1,804	90.6	155.0	320.0	279.0	713.0	62.9	76.9	20.82	450	3,990	653	892
1994	1,817	97.4	155.0	300.0	116.7	826.4	47.4	60.4	1.68	530	3,970	764	744
1995	2,011	102.1	160.0	300.0	151.7	833.2	-----	49.7	.03	359	4,010	815	990
1996	2,061	98.0	165.0	300.0	244.6	746.6	-----	62.8	-----	250	4,010	825	1,000
1997	2,265	97.2	170.0	300.0	167.5	750.0	-----	19.0	-----	250	4,070	850	1,100
1998[1]	2,407	97.5	175.0	300.0	126.0	590.0	-----	20.0	-----	250	4,650	950	1,100

[1] Preliminary. [2] Includes leucoxene. [3] Formerly part of the U.S.S.R.; data not reported separately until 1992. [4] Approximately 10% of total production is ilmenite. Beginning in 1988, 25% of Norway's ilmenite production was used to produce slag containing 75% TiO2. NA = Not available.
Source: U.S. Geological Survey (USGS)

World Production of Titanium Rutile Concentrates In Metric Tons

Year	Australia	Brazil	India	Sierre Leone	South Africa	Sri Lanka	Thailand	Ukraine[2]	World Total
1985	211,615	713	6,800	80,611	55,000	8,558	110	10,000	373,407
1986	215,774	495	7,000	97,100	55,000	8,443	48	10,000	393,860
1987	246,263	324	7,000	113,300	55,000	7,200	92	10,000	439,179
1988	230,637	1,514	5,000	126,358	55,000	5,255	128	10,000	433,892
1989	243,000	2,613	9,931	128,198	60,000	5,589	150	10,000	459,331
1990	245,000	1,814	11,000	144,284	64,056	5,460	NA	9,500	481,114
1991	201,000	1,094	13,635	154,800	77,000	3,085	76	9,000	460,000
1992	183,000	1,798	10,000	148,990	84,000	2,741	281	60,000	491,000
1993	186,000	1,744	13,900	152,000	85,000	2,643	87	60,000	501,000
1994	233,000	1,911	14,000	137,000	78,000	2,410	49	80,000	545,000
1995	195,000	1,985	14,000	-----	90,000	2,697	-----	112,000	416,000
1996	180,000	2,018	15,000	-----	115,000	3,532	-----	50,000	366,000
1997	235,000	1,742	14,000	-----	123,000	2,970	-----	50,000	427,000
1998[1]	237,000	1,750	14,000	-----	120,000	3,000	-----	50,000	426,000

[1] Preliminary. [2] Formerly part of the U.S.S.R.; data not reported separately until 1992. NA = Not available.
Source: U.S. Geological Survey (USGS)

World Production of Titanium Sponge Metal & U.S. Consumption of Titanium Concentrates

	Production of Titanium (In Metric Tons) -- Sponge Metal[2]						-- U.S. Consumption of Titanium Concentrates, by Products (In Metric Tons) -- Ilmenite (TiO_2 Content)			Rutile (TiO_2 Content)			
Year	China	Japan	Russia[3]	United Kingdom	United States	Total	Pigments	Misc.	Total	Welding Rod Coatings	Pigments	Misc.	Total
1985	1,814	15,366	42,638	1,361	21,099	82,555	430,522	5,751	436,273	4,428	217,631	37,843	259,902
1986	1,814	16,330	43,546	1,361	15,876	78,926	463,643	1,501	465,144	6,956	221,518	52,199	280,673
1987	1,814	10,074	44,453	1,361	17,849	75,298	420,099	1,648	421,747	3,781	246,448	51,309	301,538
1988	2,000	16,500	46,000	1,500	24,000	88,000	429,736	590	430,326	3,737	262,998	64,641	331,376
1989	2,000	21,000	46,000	1,500	25,225	95,725	419,329	414	419,743	3,603	271,208	71,178	345,989
1990	2,000	25,630	47,000	1,500	24,679	101,000	445,502	726	446,228	4,047	271,637	71,373	347,057
1991	2,000	18,945	20,000	2,000	13,366	56,000	476,145	495	476,640	6,931	286,741	42,200	335,872
1992	2,000	14,554	20,000	2,000	W	38,554	425,876	647	426,523	W	405,875	32,553	438,428
1993	2,000	14,400	20,000	1,000	27,938	37,000	434,097	451	434,548	W	405,784	30,223	436,007
1994	2,000	14,400	12,000	-----	29,510	33,000	W	637	W	W	460,000	18,500	478,500
1995	2,000	16,000	12,000	-----	W	35,000	1,010,000	[4]	1,010,000	W	417,000	22,300	439,300
1996	2,000	21,100	18,000	-----	W	51,000	1,010,000	[4]	1,010,000	W	341,000	24,200	365,000
1997	2,000	24,100	20,000	-----	W	58,000	1,410,000	[4]	1,410,000	W	406,000	27,600	434,000
1998[1]	-----	-----	-----	-----	-----	-----	1,290,000	14,000	1,300,000	W	384,000	37,300	421,000

[1] Preliminary. [2] Unconsolidated metal in various forms. [3] Formerly part of the U.S.S.R.; data not reported separately until 1993. [4] Included in Pigments. NA = Not available. W = Withheld proprietary data. *Source: U.S. Geological Survey (USGS)*

Tobacco

The U.S.D.A. reported that U.S. cigarette consumption in 1998 declined by 3 percent from 1997 to 465 million pieces. Taxable removals in 1998 were 457.9 billion pieces, down 3 percent from 1997. Total U.S. consumption of cigarettes in 1999 was estimated at 425 billion pieces, down 9 percent from the previous season. U.S. cigarette consumption has been trending lower for several years. Per capita cigarette consumption has also been declining. Per capita consumption of cigarettes by those 16 years and older in 1999 was estimated at 2,056 pieces. This was down 8 percent from 1998. In 1990, per capita cigarette consumption by those 16 years and older was 2,737 pieces. Per capita consumption of cigarettes by those 18 years and older in 1999 was estimated at 2,136 pieces, down 8 percent from 1998. In terms of actual tobacco consumption, 1999 per capita use of tobacco for cigarettes was 3.6 pounds.

Cigarette consumption continues to decline because of changes in social acceptance as well as higher prices. Wholesale cigarette prices increased five times in 1998. Between July 1998 and July 1999, retail prices for cigarettes increased over 30 percent. The increase of 45 cents per pack in November 1998 was the largest in history. In part, the increase in cigarette prices could reflect the effects of litigation against the tobacco industry which is still continuing.

On the state level, both New Hampshire and Maryland increased their cigarette taxes in 1998. The Federal excise tax was unchanged at 24 cents per pack through 1999. In January 2000, the Federal excise tax will increase by 10 cents to 34 cents a pack. Another increase of 5 cents per pack will take effect in January 2002.

In September 1999, the United States Attorney General filed a wide-ranging civil suit against the largest tobacco companies. The suit seeks to recover expenses paid by the Federal Government for treating smoking-related illnesses paid by Medicare to military veterans and Federal employees.

In 1999, per capita use of snuff by those 18 years and older was estimated to be 0.32 pounds, the same as in 1997. Per capita use of snuff has been trending slightly higher over time. Per capita consumption by males 18 years and older of large cigars and cigarillos in 1999 was 39, up 3 percent from the previous year. Cigar consumption has been trending higher. Per capita consumption of smoking tobacco in 1999 was 0.12 pounds, unchanged from 1998. Per capita consumption of chewing tobacco in 1999 was estimated at 0.64 pounds, unchanged from 1998. Consumption of smoking tobacco and chewing tobacco has been trending lower.

U.S. tobacco production in 1999 was estimated to be 1.31 billion pounds, down 11 percent from 1998. If realized, the 1999 crop would be the smallest since 1995. Harvested acreage was estimated at 661,000 acres, down 8 percent from 1998. Tobacco yield per acre was estimated at 1,984 pounds per acre, down 4 percent from the previous year.

The 1999 flue-cured tobacco crop was estimated in September 1999 at about 700 million pounds. Growers carried over 48.2 million pounds of the 1998 crop. There was damage to the crop from Hurricane Floyd, though most of the damage appeared to be to barns and warehouses. The crop also suffered from hot, dry weather. The 1999 burley tobacco crop was estimated by the U.S.D.A. at 536.1 million pounds, down almost 9 percent from 1998. Planted acreage declined and yields were lower due to the dry conditions. Southern Maryland tobacco is a light air-cured tobacco that is used almost entirely for cigarette production. The 1999 crop was estimated at 13.7 million pounds, down 11 percent from 1998. Acreage harvested fell 3 percent to 9,500 acres, while yields fell 8 percent to 1,445 pounds per acre. Cigar tobacco production in the 1999/2000 season was expected to be 15.6 million pounds, down 22 percent from 1998/99.

U.S. manufactured tobacco exports in January-July 1999 were 134,111 metric tonnes. This was up slightly from the previous year. The leading U.S. tobacco leaf export markets in 1999 were the European Union, Japan, the Russian Federation, Turkey, Malaysia, Korea and Thailand. Flue-cured tobacco exports in January-July 1999 were 57,268 tonnes, down 7 percent from a year earlier. The major markets are the European Union, Japan, Korea, Malaysia and Turkey. Burley tobacco exports in the first seven months of 1999 were 41,202 tonnes, down 11 percent from 1998. The leading export markets for burley tobacco are the European Union, Japan, Thailand and Turkey. U.S. cigarette exports in January-July 1999 were 92.4 billion pieces, down 24 percent from the previous year. The leading export markets are Japan, the European Union, Saudi Arabia, Cyprus, Lebanon, Israel, Singapore and Hong Kong. U.S. exports of bulk smoking tobacco in the January-July 1999 period were 36,091 tonnes. That was down 6 percent from the previous year.

World Production of Leaf Tobacco In Metric Tons

Year	Brazil	Canada	China	Greece	India	Indonesia	Italy	Japan	Pakistan	Turkey	United States	Zimbabwe	World Total
1989	462,000	75,573	2,830,353	197,316	492,800	146,914	197,316	74,397	71,089	269,517	620,152	135,205	7,110,889
1990	435,000	63,057	2,627,500	134,368	564,400	158,865	214,846	80,542	68,040	295,599	737,710	139,803	7,106,502
1991	422,000	78,704	3,030,700	165,650	555,900	164,850	193,296	69,897	80,806	239,405	754,949	178,107	7,262,539
1992	577,000	71,775	3,499,000	196,500	584,400	145,420	150,784	79,366	107,980	331,786	780,944	211,394	8,160,788
1993	608,000	86,094	3,451,000	148,000	580,600	152,800	135,698	67,430	105,966	338,068	731,914	235,286	8,261,069
1994	442,000	71,500	2,238,000	135,400	528,000	160,000	131,010	79,503	100,351	187,733	717,990	177,816	6,391,977
1995	398,000	79,287	2,317,700	131,875	587,100	171,400	124,492	78,212	80,917	204,900	575,380	209,042	6,376,704
1996	439,000	65,320	3,076,000	131,000	562,750	177,000	130,590	66,031	80,760	229,400	688,258	207,767	6,962,473
1997[1]	576,600	71,110	3,390,000	132,450	623,700	184,300	131,410	68,504	86,279	296,000	810,154	192,107	7,769,543
1998[2]	442,500	69,300	2,524,500	132,000	635,000	175,631	132,000	67,100	90,450	266,500	696,116	212,050	6,676,850

[1] Preliminary. [2] Estimate. *Source: Foreign Agricultural Service, U.S. Department of Agriculture (FAS-USDA)*

Production and Consumption of Tobacco Products in the United States

Year	Cigarettes	Cigars[3]	Chewing Tobacco: Plug	Twist	Loose-leaf	Total	Smoking Tobacco	Snuff[4]	Consumption[5] of Per Capita[6]: Cigarettes	Cigars[3]	Cigarettes	Cigars[3]	Smoking Tobacco	Chewing Tobacco	Total Products
	- Billions -	- Millions -	In Millions of Pounds						Number		In Pounds				
1990	709.7	1,896	7.4	1.3	64.3	72.9	16.4	53.1	2,834	26.4	4.89	.43	.20	.80	5.62
1991	694.5	1,740	6.7	1.2	64.3	72.2	15.7	54.3	2,727	25.1	4.83	.41	.18	.80	5.54
1992	718.5	1,741	5.9	1.2	61.6	68.7	14.9	57.5	2,647	24.5	4.62	.40	.18	.75	5.30
1993	661.0	1,795	5.3	1.1	58.0	64.4	13.7	59.1	2,543	23.4	4.70	.38	.17	.70	5.39
1994	725.5	1,942	4.6	1.1	56.8	62.5	13.5	15.1	2,524	25.3	4.23	.41	.16	.67	4.90
1995	746.5	2,058	4.1	1.1	57.7	62.9	12.2	60.2	2,505	27.5	4.22	.45	.13	.67	4.70
1996	755.4	2,413	3.9	1.1	56.0	61.1	12.0	61.5	2,482	32.7	4.20	.54	.12	.64	4.70
1997	719.6	2,324	3.5	1.0	53.7	58.1	11.5	64.3	2,423	36.9	4.10	.53	.12	.64	4.55
1998[1]	679.7	2,751	3.0	1.0	49.2	53.3	11.7	65.5	2,320	37.8	3.90	.53	.12	.64	4.49
1999[2]	635.0	2,800	2.7	0.9	47.1	50.7	15.5	66.8	2,136	39.0	3.60	.53	.12	.64	4.19

[1] Preliminary. [2] Estimate. [3] Large cigars and cigarillos. [4] Includes loose-leaf. [5] Consumption of tax-paid tobacco products. Unstemmed processing weight. [6] 18 years and older. *Source: Economic Research Service, U.S. Department of Agriculture (ERS)*

Production of Tobacco in the United States, by States In Thousands of Pounds

Year	Florida	Georgia	Indiana	Kentucky	Maryland	North Carolina	Ohio	Pennsylvania	South Carolina	Tennessee	Virginia	Wisconsin	Total
1990	19,044	103,845	15,050	442,253	9,656	639,639	18,915	19,780	109,905	112,218	110,269	13,346	1,626,380
1991	15,312	80,600	18,920	479,794	12,900	634,655	22,776	20,765	111,180	121,524	116,849	15,191	1,664,372
1992	19,575	100,980	18,900	524,378	11,931	609,873	21,840	20,840	112,320	146,556	111,459	13,100	1,721,671
1993	18,673	96,320	17,415	455,080	12,255	608,415	18,900	18,260	110,760	139,423	99,544	6,643	1,613,319
1994	16,575	80,660	15,265	453,687	12,750	599,853	18,360	18,360	108,100	132,289	106,092	5,866	1,582,896
1995	17,676	84,000	13,601	328,581	11,475	484,599	15,015	15,685	105,000	92,907	81,269	6,220	1,268,538
1996	20,100	113,620	14,972	395,542	10,000	585,542	12,640	16,817	117,810	109,888	103,543	5,162	1,518,704
1997	19,053	89,225	18,690	497,928	12,000	731,199	22,230	17,020	126,360	114,292	117,576	5,690	1,787,399
1998	17,102	90,200	17,000	443,628	9,100	551,730	17,934	15,720	92,250	111,100	95,898	4,230	1,479,867
1999[1]	15,300	64,020	11,700	404,863	9,100	449,620	17,052	11,170	78,000	110,569	87,185	2,790	1,275,438

[1] Preliminary. *Source: Agricultural Statistics Board, U.S. Department of Agriculture (ASB-USDA)*

Salient Statistics of Tobacco in the United States

Year	Acres Harvested 1,000 Acres	Yield Per Acre Pounds	Production Million Pounds	Farm Price Cents/Lb.	Farm Value Million $	Tobacco (July - June) Exports[2]	Imports[3]	U.S. Exports of Cigarettes	Cigars & Cheroots	All Tobacco	Smoking Tobacco	Stocks of Tobacco[5] Various Types: All Tobacco	Fire Cured[6]	Cigar Filler[7]	Maryland
						- Million Pounds -		Millions		In Millions of Pounds					
1990	732.3	2,218	1,625	173.8	2,827	487.4	415.0	164,301	72	493	58.0	2,401	70.2	26.9	19.3
1991	763.4	2,179	1,664	177.3	2,951	511.0	502.2	179,200	70	499	63.2	2,232	66.7	25.6	12.1
1992	784.4	2,195	1,722	177.7	3,059	528.8	881.0	205,600	76	574	59.1	2,280	61.6	26.7	9.4
1993	746.4	2,161	1,613	175.3	2,830	529.7	706.1	195,476	67	458	62.5	2,412	64.0	26.7	7.5
1994	671.1	2,359	1,583	177.4	2,779	442.1	537.5	220,200	75	434	77.0	2,588	69.7	24.1	8.4
1995	663.1	1,913	1,269	182.0	2,305	432.6	623.3	231,100	78	462	91.8	2,541	80.5	20.5	11.7
1996	733.1	2,072	1,519	188.2	2,854	533.1	717.2	243,900	84	486	110.4	2,225	80.2	17.9	15.0
1997	836.2	2,137	1,787	180.2	3,217	450.1	565.8	217,000	136	487	118.2	2,031	83.3	13.2	18.7
1998	717.6	2,062	1,480	182.8	2,701	461.9	529.6	201,300	158	467	142.5	2,250	84.8	13.0	20.6
1999[1]	644.3	1,980	1,275	183.0	2,328	266.8	385.3	150,000	149	474	132.3	2,298	86.7	11.4	26.0

[1] Preliminary. [2] Domestic. [3] For consumption. [4] In bulk. [5] Flue-cured and cigar wrapper, year beginning July 1; for all other types, October 1. [6] Kentucky-Tennessee types 22-23. [7] Types 41-46. *Source: Economic Research Service, U.S. Department of Agriculture (ERS-USDA)*

Tobacco Production in the United States, by Types In Thousands of Pounds (Farm-Sale Weight)

Year	11-14	21	22	23	31	32	35-36	37	41	41-61	51	54	55	61
1990	939,234	2,762	22,931	9,285	597,927	16,316	7,491	102	13,120	30,278	1,160	9,328	4,018	2,652
1991	911,887	3,563	20,620	8,704	658,181	19,920	8,776	156	13,735	32,587	1,433	9,799	5,392	2,228
1992	906,025	2,567	23,736	10,486	719,552	18,771	10,332	124	14,000	30,098	1,484	8,460	4,640	1,514
1993	886,908	1,872	26,985	12,060	633,838	18,335	11,123	104	12,180	22,094	1,694	4,690	1,953	1,577
1994	869,920	2,403	31,723	14,205	612,398	19,770	11,797	124	11,340	20,680	1,808	4,180	1,686	1,666
1995	746,616	1,540	26,609	11,041	436,343	17,935	8,488	79	9,225	19,887	2,441	4,513	1,707	2,001
1996	908,345	1,738	29,461	13,029	520,483	16,545	8,550	112	10,272	20,441	2,901	3,610	1,552	2,106
1997	1,047,438	1,968	27,952	12,342	648,633	18,240	8,196	119	10,780	22,511	3,637	4,194	1,496	2,404
1998	812,797	2,340	25,922	11,573	582,336	15,370	9,663	122	9,450	19,744	3,633	3,270	960	2,431
1999[1]	653,620	2,475	23,515	10,484	544,202	14,350	10,613	160	5,920	16,019	4,370	2,068	722	2,939

[1] Preliminary. *Source: Agricultural Statistics Board, U.S. Department of Agriculture (ASB-USDA)*

U.S. Exports of Unmanufactured Tobacco In Millions of Pounds (Declared Weight)

Year	Australia	Belgium-Luxem.	Denmark	France	Germany	Italy	Japan	Netherlands	Sweden	Switzerland	Thailand	United Kingdom	Total
1990	8.3	12.4	15.1	5.7	75.9	19.3	106.5	45.3	9.5	13.3	22.2	20.5	492.5
1991	7.7	11.0	14.8	6.5	82.8	19.9	83.1	42.8	8.3	14.8	19.5	18.9	499.3
1992	6.9	21.4	15.6	4.2	93.3	19.0	131.0	49.9	8.8	7.5	16.9	24.3	574.4
1993	5.7	12.8	15.5	4.3	52.1	7.3	124.7	38.1	8.1	6.1	17.8	20.8	458.0
1994	6.4	12.3	14.9	3.1	54.1	11.3	126.2	30.9	7.3	6.0	19.0	14.7	433.9
1995	4.8	17.9	14.6	3.9	70.7	14.8	106.9	39.2	3.0	14.4	19.0	14.2	461.8
1996	5.6	40.1	15.1	3.2	60.3	17.5	88.7	40.4	37.4	14.9	15.9	34.4	490.1
1997	4.2	39.1	15.5	7.0	72.2	18.3	80.5	30.2	5.3	11.4	21.6	18.2	488.3
1998	3.7	23.6	14.7	5.7	75.3	11.3	72.4	37.5	2.6	10.1	12.1	15.4	412.9
1999[1]	2.9	17.1	12.9	3.4	58.4	12.0	54.3	60.6	3.4	13.4	5.9	8.4	358.6

[1] Preliminary. *Source: Economic Research Service, U.S. Department of Agriculture (ERS-USDA)*

U.S. Salient Statistics for Flue-Cured Tobacco (Types 11-14) in the United States In Millions of Pounds

Crop Year	Acres Harvested 1,000	Yield Per Acre Pounds	Marketings	Stocks July 1	Total Supply	Exports	Domestic Disappearance	Total Disappearance	Farm Price Cents/Lb.	Placed Under Gov't Loan Million Lb.	Price Support Level Cents/Lb.	Loan Stocks Nov. 30	Loan Stocks Uncommitted
1990-1	416.9	2,253	920	1,308	2,228	403	609	1,012	167.3	74.4	148.8	226.4	223.8
1991-2	402.6	2,265	883	1,216	2,098	403	471	875	172.3	49.9	152.8	153.7	174.5
1992-3	401.5	2,257	901	1,224	2,125	420	509	929	172.6	81.8	156.0	223.6	129.0
1993-4	400.1	2,217	892	1,196	2,087	359	433	792	168.1	204.9	157.7	330.5	317.5
1994-5	359.5	2,420	807	1,295	2,102	346	569	915	169.8	97.7	158.3	298.5	396.5
1995-6	386.2	1,933	854	1,187	2,041	345	531	875	179.4	12.0	159.7	157.6	62.3
1996-7	422.2	2,151	897	1,166	2,064	391	555	947	183.4	1.8	160.1	181.0	.0
1997-8	458.3	2,285	1,014	1,117	2,130	334	541	877	172.0	195.5	162.1		.0
1998-9[1]	368.8	2,204	815	1,253	2,068	341	492	834	175.5	82.4	162.8		
1999-00[2]	306.0	2,153	645	1,234	1,879	325	450	775	173.6				

[1] Preliminary. [2] Estimate. *Source: Economic Research Service, U.S. Department of Agriculture (ERS-USDA)*

Salient Statistics for Burley Tobacco (Type 31) in the United States In Millions of Pounds

Crop Year	Acres Harvested 1,000	Yield Per Acre Pounds	Marketings	Stocks Oct. 1	Total Supply	Exports	Domestic Disappearance	Total Disappearance	Farm Price Cents/Lb.	Gross Sales[3]	Price Support Level Cents/Lb.	Loan Stocks Nov. 30	Loan Stocks Uncommitted
1990-1	270.6	2,204	592	847	1,439	199	475	674	175.3	467.8	155.8	226.4	52.0
1991-2	312.0	2,110	657	765	1,422	209	407	616	178.8	501.5	158.4	62.3	32.8
1992-3	332.7	2,163	700	807	1,507	183	385	568	181.5	502.4	164.9	131.2	71.7
1993-4	299.7	2,115	627	939	1,566	152	399	552	181.6	492.4	168.3	178.8	141.9
1994-5	266.3	2,300	568	1,014	1,582	155	468	623	184.1	455.7	171.4	345.2	380.8
1995-6	234.2	1,863	483	959	1,441	165	386	551	185.5	341.6	172.5	212.5	50.8
1996-7	268.3	1,940	516	890	1,407	192	446	656	192.2	422.6	173.7	216.8	27.1
1997-8	335.0	1,934	628	751	1,379	189	379	548	188.5	337.9	176.0		24.1
1998-9[1]	307.0	1,896	590	832	1,422	190	349	520	190.3	431.6	177.8		
1999-00[2]	306.0	1,750	545	901	1,447	190	320	470		356.6			

[1] Preliminary. [2] Estimate. [3] Before Christmas holidays. *Source: Economic Research Service, U.S. Department of Agriculture (ERS-USDA)*

Exports of Tobacco from the United States (Quantity and Value) In Metric Tons

	Unmanufactured							
Year	Flue-Cured	Value 1,000 USD	Burley	Value 1,000 USD	Total	Value 1,000 USD	Manufactured	Value 1,000 USD
1990	131,155	883,155	50,262	349,561	223,413	1,441,116	NA	5,038,830
1991	115,481	776,654	61,852	441,223	226,463	1,427,630	NA	4,574,086
1992	146,100	983,478	64,481	483,743	260,526	1,650,559	58,115	4,509,395
1993	111,636	752,646	51,892	389,964	207,747	1,306,067	49,669	4,253,286
1994	107,411	749,305	49,859	380,993	196,792	1,302,744	63,837	5,367,220
1995	123,040	866,208	47,129	365,206	209,481	1,399,863	77,135	5,221,487
1996	112,797	786,473	52,202	380,012	222,316	1,390,311	83,383	5,238,340
1997	116,457	832,381	56,803	454,849	221,510	1,553,314	85,734	4,956,392
1998[1]	90,800	644,797	49,322	402,475	187,287	1,302,615	-----	4,517,500
1999[2]	69,436	488,868	46,190	377,799	162,607	1,107,471	-----	3,232,862

[1] Preliminary. [2] Forecast. NA = Not available. *Source: Foreign Agricultural Service, U.S. Department of Agriculture (FAS-USDA)*

Tung Oil

Tung oil is a yellow drying oil produced from the seeds of the tung tree. It finds use as an industrial lubricant and drying agent. The tung tree is found mainly in China which produces about 75 percent of the world supply. Other producers include Argentina and Paraguay. Tung oil is poisonous, containing glycerol esters of unsaturated acids, and is the most powerful drying agent known. It is used as a substitute for linseed oil in paints, varnishes, and linoleum, and as a waterproofing agent. While production of tung oil is concentrated in a few countries, consumption occurs in many industrialized countries. Among the largest importers of tung oil are South Korea, Japan, the U.S. and Taiwan. Tung oil prices have shown a lot of variability. In 1993, the average price of tung oil (imported, drums) f.o.b. New York was $1.19 per pound. That was well above the 1991 average price of 63 cents per pound. By 1995 the average price had fallen back to 60 cents. In 1997 and 1998 the price had once again risen above $1.00 per pound.

The U.S. Department of Commerce reported that consumption of tung oil in inedible products in the U.S. in 1998 was 14.3 million pounds, down 26 percent from the 1997 total of 19.4 million pounds. Consumption reached a recent high in 1996 when the U.S. used 21.6 million pounds. U.S. stocks of tung oil at factories and warehouses in December 1998 were 2.27 million pounds, down 2 percent from a year earlier.

World Tung Oil Trade In Metric Tons

	Imports								Exports				
Year	Germany	Hong Kong	Japan	Netherlands	South Korea	Taiwan	United States	World Total	Argentina	China	Hong Kong	Paraguay	World Total
1992	1,036	8,509	13,326	782	3,722	6,676	4,996	43,827	5,808	20,867	8,174	4,221	40,253
1993	777	5,222	6,549	1,427	3,490	3,595	4,270	30,834	2,497	16,990	6,004	2,295	30,074
1994	957	7,843	8,628	1,729	4,594	7,454	5,401	44,140	2,415	30,582	6,476	4,603	46,901
1995	842	3,671	8,429	2,174	7,200	5,777	4,427	39,220	4,319	25,620	3,838	4,587	40,079
1996	873	1,247	3,619	1,253	7,317	4,244	3,944	28,621	2,427	18,205	1,266	3,156	27,435
1997[1]	756	1,404	6,807	1,123	6,700	5,931	6,264	35,777	3,976	25,260	991	3,000	36,411
1998[2]	653	1,101	3,813	944	6,000	5,730	3,880	29,538	2,205	21,115	552	2,000	28,797

[1] Preliminary. [2] Estimate. *Source: The Oil World*

Consumption of Tung Oil in Inedible Products in the United States In Thousands of Pounds

Year	Jan.	Feb.	Mar.	Apr.	May	June	July	Aug.	Sept.	Oct.	Nov.	Dec.	Total
1993	958	966	693	1,041	833	1,022	867	1,427	1,354	860	585	593	11,199
1994	608	592	635	1,408	1,558	840	861	910	480	392	660	382	9,326
1995	427	503	976	1,389	1,437	1,387	1,886	2,830	2,549	2,645	2,455	2,126	20,610
1996	1,724	1,427	1,730	1,750	1,498	1,813	2,214	2,024	1,431	2,045	1,908	2,081	21,645
1997	934	1,922	2,720	2,170	1,335	2,034	2,618	1,262	1,267	1,099	857	1,157	19,375
1998	935	1,146	1,342	1,103	1,536	1,255	1,248	1,172	1,214	1,216	1,037	1,112	14,316
1999[1]	862	797	967	1,071	2,137	1,140	1,519	1,043	1,012	933	962	937	13,380

[1] Preliminary. *Source: Bureau of the Census, U.S. Department of Commerce*

Stocks of Tung Oil at Factories & Warehouses in the U.S., on First of Month In Thousands of Pounds

Year	Jan.	Feb.	Mar.	Apr.	May	June	July	Aug.	Sept.	Oct.	Nov.	Dec.
1993	3,122	2,038	2,390	2,120	2,966	1,773	866	815	1,596	1,217	1,635	1,752
1994	1,551	2,053	1,507	2,049	2,091	2,591	2,148	1,562	820	2,455	1,712	1,909
1995	1,764	1,490	1,055	3,193	2,554	2,551	2,369	2,116	2,038	2,361	2,210	2,048
1996	2,013	1,635	2,232	3,018	2,386	2,532	2,641	2,381	2,670	2,525	2,459	2,834
1997	2,373	2,754	3,417	2,808	2,134	2,230	2,230	1,561	2,525	2,535	2,311	2,326
1998	2,484	3,116	4,548	3,949	3,357	3,300	2,435	2,409	3,578	2,523	2,501	2,272
1999[1]	2,010	3,427	5,427	3,740	3,078	2,788	2,710	2,346	2,047	1,959	1,359	1,002

[1] Preliminary. *Source: Bureau of the Census, U.S. Department of Commerce*

Average Price of Tung Oil (Imported, Drums) F.O.B. in New York In Cents Per Pound

Year	Jan.	Feb.	Mar.	Apr.	May	June	July	Aug.	Sept.	Oct.	Nov.	Dec.	Average
1993	130.00	130.00	130.00	130.00	117.00	130.00	130.00	130.00	107.50	100.00	94.75	93.00	118.52
1994	93.00	79.25	78.00	78.00	78.00	78.00	78.00	78.00	78.00	74.40	60.00	60.00	76.05
1995	60.00	60.00	60.00	60.00	60.00	60.00	60.00	60.00	60.00	60.00	60.00	60.00	60.00
1996	60.00	60.00	64.00	64.00	64.00	64.00	64.00	64.00	64.00	64.00	64.00	64.00	63.33
1997	74.00	92.00	92.00	103.00	103.00	103.00	103.00	108.00	110.00	110.00	110.00	110.00	101.50
1998	110.00	110.00	110.00	110.00	100.00	100.00	100.00	100.00	100.00	100.00	100.00	100.00	103.33
1999[1]	100.00	100.00	100.00	100.00	100.00	74.00	74.00	74.00	74.00				88.44

[1] Preliminary. *Source: Economic Research Service, U.S. Department of Agriculture (ERS-USDA)*

Tungsten

Tungsten has unique high-temperature properties making it a material that has a wide range of industrial uses. It has a high melting point, high density, good corrosion resistance, and excellent wear-resistance and cutting properties. Most tungsten is used to produce tungsten carbide which is used in the production of cemented carbides. Cemented carbides, or hardmetals, are wear-resistant materials used in mining, metalworking and construction. Tungsten is used to make dies, bearings, superalloys for turbine blades as well as armor-piercing military projectiles. Tungsten metal wires, electrodes and contacts are used in electrical, heating, welding and lighting applications. Tungsten is employed in chemical processes as a catalyst, inorganic pigment and high-temperature lubricant.

World production of tungsten in 1998 was estimated to be 33,500 metric tonnes, the same as in 1997. China is by far the largest producer of tungsten with 1998 production estimated at 25,500 tonnes, up 2 percent from 1997. Other large producers include Russia, Australia and Portugal. The world reserve base was estimated to be 3.2 million tonnes.

U.S. reported consumption of tungsten concentrate in 1998 was 3,210 tonnes. Consumption of tungsten scrap in the first seven months of 1999 was estimated at 1,190 tonnes while for all of 1998 it was 3,300 tonnes. Imports for consumption of tungsten concentrate for all of 1998 were 4,750 tonnes.

U.S. consumption of ammonium paratungstate in the January-July 1999 period was 5,250 tonnes. For all of 1998, consumption was 9,210 tonnes. Consumption of tungsten carbide powder in the first seven months of 1999 was 3,240 tonnes. Consumption of metal powder was 791 tonnes while ferrotungsten use was 301 tonnes.

World Concentrate Production of Tungsten   In Metric Tons (Contained Tungsten[3])

Year	Australia	Austria	Bolivia	Brazil	Burma	China	Kazakhstan[4]	Mongolia	Peru	Portugal	Rep. of Korea	Russia[4]	World Total
1992	159	1,490	851	205	531	25,000	200	260	543	1,126	247	10,000	42,900
1993	23	105	287	245	524	21,600	350	250	388	768	-----	8,000	34,300
1994	11	-----	462	196	544	27,000	122	-----	259	59	-----	4,000	34,000
1995	-----	738	655	98	531	27,400	249	34	728	875	-----	5,400	38,500
1996	-----	1,413	582	98	334	26,500	-----	17	332	776	-----	3,000	34,700
1997[1]	-----	1,400	513	51	272	25,000	-----	26	279	1,036	-----	3,000	33,200
1998[2]	-----	1,400	497	50	200	24,700	-----	36	76	831	-----	3,000	32,200

[1] Preliminary. [2] Estimate. [3] Conversion Factors: WO3 to W, multiply by 0.7931; 60% WO3 to W, multiply by 0.4758. [4] Formerly part of the U.S.S.R.; data not reported separately until 1992. *Source: U.S. Geological Survey (USGS)*

Salient Statistics of Tungsten in the United States   In Metric Tons (Contained Tungsten)

Year	Net Import Reliance as a % of Apparent Consumption	Total Consumption	Consumption of Tungsten Products by End Uses: Steel: Tool	Steel: Stainless & Heat Assisting	Steel: Alloy Steel[3]	Superalloys	Cutting & Wear Resistant Materials	Products Made from Metal Powder	Miscellaneous	Chemical and Ceramic	Exports	Imports for Consumption	Stocks at End of Year — Concentrates: Consumers	Producers
1992	86	4,310	407	52	66	25	4,211	1,309	828	W	38	2,477	702	44
1993	81	2,870	388	43	40	282	5,064	1,434	2	37	63	1,721	592	44
1994	95	3,630	529	20	19	300	5,920	1,200	W	108	44	2,960	756	44
1995	90	5,890	265	W	18	215	6,590	1,200	3,600	W	20	4,660	627	44
1996	89	5,260	434	107	177	371	5,960	687	0	97	72	4,190	569	44
1997[1]	84	6,590	361	151	277	366	6,280	828	0	123	40	4,850	658	44
1998[2]	78	3,210	[4]	532	219	333	6,640	1,270	0	97	50	4,800	658	44

[1] Preliminary. [2] Estimate. [3] Other than tool. [4] Included with stainless & heat assisting. W = Withheld proprietary data; included with Miscellaneous. *Source: U.S. Geological Survey*

Average Price of Tungsten at European Market (London)   In Dollars Per Metric Ton

Year	Jan.	Feb.	Mar.	Apr.	May	June	July	Aug.	Sept.	Oct.	Nov.	Dec.	Average
1994	29.94	29.94	37.71	35.38	35.38	37.09	38.10	38.10	42.03	45.36	47.63	49.56	38.85
1995	56.00	60.00	64.00	64.00	65.00	66.00	67.00	66.00	66.00	66.00	66.00	62.50	64.04
1996	56.00	54.00	56.00	57.00	57.00	57.00	53.50	50.00	50.00	47.50	45.00	48.00	52.58
1997	48.00	49.00	50.00	50.00	50.00	50.00	50.00	43.00	43.00	43.00	46.00	46.00	47.33
1998	46.00	46.00	46.00	46.00	46.00	46.00	45.00	43.00	43.00	43.00	43.00	43.00	40.00

65% WO3 Basis, C.I.F., combined wolframite and scheelite quotations; data thru 1970 are for 60% WO3. *Source: U.S. Geological Survey (USGS)*

Average Price of Tungsten at U.S. Ports (Including Duty)   In Dollars Per Short Ton

Year	Jan.	Feb.	Mar.	Apr.	May	June	July	Aug.	Sept.	Oct.	Nov.	Dec.	Average
1994	37.48	40.79	44.10	44.10	44.10	44.53	47.95	48.50	48.50	48.50	48.50	48.50	45.46
1995	44.00	44.00	44.00	44.00	55.00	65.00	65.00	62.50	60.00	60.00	60.00	60.00	55.29
1996	60.00	60.00	60.00	60.00	60.00	60.00	60.00	60.00	60.00	60.00	60.00	60.00	60.00
1997	60.00	60.00	60.00	60.00	60.00	60.00	60.00	60.00	60.00	55.00	50.00	50.00	57.92
1998	64.00	64.00	64.00	64.00	64.00	62.44	57.00	57.00	57.00	57.00	54.43	49.88	57.19

U.S. Spot Quotations, 65% WO3, Basis C.I.F. *Source: U.S. Geological Survey (USGS)*

Turkeys

U.S. federally inspected turkey production stabilized in the late 1990's following a period of steady annual gains early in the decade. Production totaled 5.3 billion pounds in 1999, unchanged from 1998, but down from a record high 5.5 billion pounds in 1997. Production in the first half of the 1990's averaged about 4.5 billion pounds. On the demand side, to help iron out the pronounced yearend holiday seasonality for whole birds, the industry has shifted a larger proportion of retail sales to prepackaged turkey parts. The additional processing required to cut up and package turkey cuts, such as breast and legs, has increased the supply of edible trimmings which processors sell in several forms, including mechanically deboned turkey (MDT). A strong market for the latter is exports. Also, as a relatively low-cost meat protein, MDT can be readily incorporated into sausage and other meat products.

U.S. per capita ready-to-cook retail weight turkey consumption reached a record high 18.5 pounds in 1996, but has since trailed expectations. 1999 usage slipped to 17.9 pounds vs. 18.1 pounds in 1998, and is forecast to dip to 17.8 pounds in 2000. The October-December period still accounts for more than a third of total domestic use followed by a sharp drop in the January-March period. Traditionally, November is the highest slaughter month with about 25 million birds in recent years. Prices follow a similar pattern; peaking generally in the fourth quarter and trending lower during the first quarter, basis 8-16 pound hens in New York. Heavier turkeys, 14-22 pounds, are classified as toms. However, with the industry's new marketing approach and changes in consumer food tastes, shifts in the traditional seasonalities may be taking root. An estimated 275 million turkeys were raised in the U.S. in 1999, down 4 percent from 285 million raised in 1998. Six states account for about two-thirds of the turkeys produced. North Carolina is generally the largest producer with pre-hurricane Floyd forecasts of 48.5 million birds. Minnesota ranked second with 43.5 million birds.

U.S. turkey exports have slipped in recent years, totaling 378 million pounds in 1999 vs. 446 million in 1998 and 606 million in 1997. Exports are forecast at 390 million in 2000. Mexico remains the largest importer with at least half the total followed by Hong Kong. Russian imports have proven sporadic, but on balance appear to be on the decline. The bulk of low priced turkey shipments to Russia were defined as "other prepared or preserved meat, meat offal, or blood of turkey."

Wholesale Eastern turkey prices in 1999 averaged 69.30 cents per pound vs. 62.20 cents in 1998 and forecasts of 66.00-72.00 cents in 2000.

Production and Consumption of Turkey Meat, by Selected Countries In Thousands of Metric Tons (RTC)

	Production							Consumption						
Year	Canada	France	Germany	Italy	United Kingdom	United States	World Total	Canada	France	Germany	Italy	United Kingdom	United States	World Total
1991	131	487	149	273	242	2,088	3,722	126	342	240	265	236	2,060	3,630
1992	132	558	159	269	246	2,167	3,892	129	354	272	268	228	2,072	3,732
1993	128	532	169	266	252	2,176	3,911	126	321	280	256	249	2,075	3,769
1994	133	568	180	269	266	2,239	4,041	128	324	177	245	271	2,110	3,755
1995	141	650	206	294	289	2,299	4,122	126	353	196	262	287	2,133	3,801
1996	146	671	217	315	293	2,450	4,362	123	352	220	277	298	2,225	4,021
1997	142	708	243	338	293	2,455	4,493	126	332	240	295	277	2,141	4,016
1998	139	725	256	361	268	2,366	4,460	130	360	250	302	276	2,214	4,119
1999[1]	140	715	265	343	280	2,366	4,482	134	340	260	280	267	2,220	4,114
2000[2]	144	700	270	365	295	2,419	4,579	134	332	264	300	262	2,219	4,139

[1] Preliminary. [2] Forecast. *Source: Foreign Agricultural Service, U.S. Department of Agriculture (FAS-USDA)*

Salient Statistics of Turkeys in the United States

			Liveweight			Ready-to-Cook Basis			Consumption		Production Costs		Wholesale -- Ready-to-Cook --	
Year	Poults Placed[3]	Number Raised[4]	Produced	Price	Value of Production	Production	Beginning Stocks	Exports	Total	Per Capita	Feed	Total	Production Costs	3-Region Weighted Average Price[5]
	In Thousands		Mil. Lbs.	Cents/Lb.	Million $	In Millions of Pounds				Lbs.	Liveweight Basis			
1989	290,678	261,394	5,467.6	40.9	2,235.1	4,136	250	41	4,109	16.6	26.70	40.40	66.80	65.75
1990	304,863	282,445	6,043.2	39.6	2,393.4	4,514	236	54	5,390	17.6	23.40	37.10	62.60	62.35
1991	308,083	284,910	6,114.6	38.5	2,353.0	4,603	306	122	4,523	17.9	22.72	36.42	61.83	60.79
1992	307,823	289,880	6,355.3	37.7	2,396.4	4,777	264	202	4,568	17.9	23.06	36.76	62.25	60.48
1993	308,871	287,650	6,432.6	39.0	2,509.1	4,798	272	244	4,577	17.7	22.20	35.86	61.12	62.83
1994	317,468	286,585	6,540.3	40.4	2,643.1	4,937	249	280	4,652	17.8	24.00	37.70	63.40	65.90
1995	320,882	292,356	6,761.3	41.0	2,769.4	5,069	254	348	4,705	17.9	21.90	35.60	60.80	66.20
1996	325,375	302,713	7,222.8	43.3	3,124.5	5,466	271	438	4,907	18.5	31.60	45.30	72.90	66.80
1997[1]	305,612	301,251	7,225.1	39.9	2,884.4	5,478	328	606	4,720	17.6	28.20	41.90	68.70	63.80
1998[2]	297,798	283,503	7,002.8	38.0	2,661.7	5,281	415	446	4,880	18.1	22.96	36.66	62.12	62.15

[1] Preliminary. [2] Estimate. [3] Poults placed for slaughter by hatcheries. [4] Turkeys place August 1-July 31. [5] Regions include central, eastern and western. Central region receives twice the weight of the other regions in calculating the average. *Source: Economic Research Service, U.S. Department of Agriculture (ERS-USDA)*

Turkey-Feed Price Ratio in the United States In Pounds[1]

Year	Jan.	Feb.	Mar.	Apr.	May	June	July	Aug.	Sept.	Oct.	Nov.	Dec.	Average
1990	5.9	5.7	6.1	5.9	6.0	6.2	6.4	6.7	7.0	7.6	7.7	6.7	6.5
1991	6.0	6.3	6.4	6.5	6.7	6.9	7.2	7.1	7.0	6.5	6.4	6.5	6.6
1992	6.0	5.8	6.0	6.0	6.0	6.1	6.5	6.8	6.7	7.1	7.2	7.1	6.4
1993	6.3	6.4	6.6	6.5	6.6	6.7	6.4	6.4	6.9	7.2	6.7	6.1	6.6
1994	5.4	5.4	5.5	5.8	5.9	6.0	7.0	7.3	7.3	7.8	8.0	7.3	6.6
1995	6.7	6.4	6.5	6.4	6.3	6.3	6.0	6.3	6.4	6.3	6.5	5.7	6.3
1996	5.3	5.2	5.1	4.7	4.6	4.9	4.9	4.8	5.3	6.1	6.4	6.2	5.3
1997	5.4	5.0	5.0	5.1	5.3	5.6	6.0	5.9	6.1	6.2	6.2	5.8	5.6
1998	5.4	5.2	5.3	5.7	5.8	6.1	6.5	7.6	8.1	8.3	8.3	7.7	6.7
1999[2]	6.5	7.1	7.5	7.8	8.3	8.8	9.7	9.5	9.6	10.0	10.0	9.2	8.7

[1] Pounds of feed equal in value to one pound of turkey, liveweight. [2] Preliminary. [3] New data series due to NASS switching to basing ration costs on raw ingredient prices (corn and soybeans) rather than commercial feed prices. *Source: Economic Research Service, U.S. Department of Agriculture (ERS-USDA)*

Average Price Received by Farmers for Turkeys in the United States (Liveweight) In Cents Per Pound

Year	Jan.	Feb.	Mar.	Apr.	May	June	July	Aug.	Sept.	Oct.	Nov.	Dec.	Average
1990	35.4	33.7	36.4	36.6	38.3	38.7	39.1	40.2	40.3	42.5	42.3	36.9	38.4
1991	33.6	35.1	37.0	37.6	38.3	38.7	39.1	40.1	40.2	37.0	37.0	38.1	37.7
1992	36.3	35.5	37.0	37.0	37.7	37.7	37.9	37.8	37.5	38.5	39.4	39.3	37.6
1993	35.6	35.7	37.6	37.6	37.7	37.6	38.7	39.6	41.1	43.2	42.7	40.8	39.0
1994	37.0	37.3	38.4	39.2	39.9	40.3	40.6	42.1	43.1	44.5	44.3	42.2	40.7
1995	39.3	37.2	38.3	38.3	38.4	39.3	39.6	41.9	43.6	45.2	47.3	44.0	41.0
1996	40.9	42.4	41.8	42.2	43.2	44.4	45.0	44.3	44.2	45.1	45.5	43.2	43.5
1997	38.6	36.4	37.8	39.7	41.3	41.6	41.1	41.0	41.1	41.0	41.9	38.7	40.0
1998	35.5	34.0	34.6	35.7	35.5	35.9	37.5	38.6	40.2	42.7	43.8	40.3	37.9
1999[1]	34.8	35.7	37.0	38.7	39.7	41.5	41.8	43.1	44.5	45.4	45.6	42.2	40.8

[1] Preliminary. *Source: Economic Research Service, U.S. Department of Agriculture (ERS-USDA)*

Average Wholesale Price of Turkeys[1] (Hens, 8-16 Lbs.) in New York In Cents Per Pound

Year	Jan.	Feb.	Mar.	Apr.	May	June	July	Aug.	Sept.	Oct.	Nov.	Dec.	Average
1990	55.55	55.16	58.86	59.62	61.27	62.88	63.37	66.57	68.99	76.15	73.70	56.05	63.18
1991	53.49	55.76	59.10	60.32	62.32	62.68	63.41	64.66	64.38	60.52	63.07	65.18	61.24
1992	58.74	55.00	58.77	60.00	60.03	59.46	57.02	57.80	61.02	63.92	65.57	65.14	60.21
1993	58.05	56.83	58.41	58.98	58.81	58.35	59.76	63.43	66.73	71.28	71.76	68.20	62.55
1994	60.09	59.32	60.98	61.58	63.14	64.61	65.26	66.39	68.98	73.13	74.01	70.35	65.65
1995	60.71	58.54	60.04	60.05	60.57	62.76	64.78	68.52	72.92	76.73	80.31	70.35	66.36
1996	64.60	64.65	65.07	64.82	65.39	65.85	65.66	64.94	64.16	69.09	73.58	70.05	66.49
1997	59.71	57.84	59.30	62.93	66.64	68.60	68.59	68.20	67.89	67.33	70.07	62.18	64.94
1998	55.65	54.04	55.49	55.49	58.68	58.14	58.68	63.17	65.65	71.52	72.95	69.00	61.54
1999[2]	57.67	58.84	61.69	63.02	65.55	68.89	71.62	73.57	76.28	79.30	78.99	72.39	68.98

[1] Ready-to-cook. [2] Preliminary. *Source: Economic Research Service, U.S. Department of Agriculture (ERS-USDA)*

Certified Federally Inspected Turkey Slaughter in the U.S. (RTC Weights) In Millions of Pounds

Year	Jan.	Feb.	Mar.	Apr.	May	June	July	Aug.	Sept.	Oct.	Nov.	Dec.	Total
1990	334.0	298.3	351.1	328.4	384.1	389.2	395.7	444.0	382.9	478.4	446.2	328.6	4,561
1991	365.6	322.0	329.7	375.8	398.2	380.7	402.2	421.8	404.8	482.0	419.2	349.9	4,652
1992	362.9	331.7	361.3	385.2	374.2	435.0	451.8	411.9	431.3	467.6	423.0	393.1	4,829
1993	354.1	322.7	382.9	391.9	378.7	446.7	419.3	426.9	436.0	451.4	461.8	375.3	4,848
1994	347.8	342.0	400.9	380.6	415.6	457.9	405.6	483.6	447.7	459.1	453.9	397.5	4,992
1995	386.3	368.9	433.1	369.6	441.4	478.4	409.1	447.3	419.5	480.2	463.0	394.4	5,091
1996	412.4	426.5	422.3	430.9	483.0	454.7	484.8	476.6	440.9	518.1	465.9	406.1	5,422
1997	439.7	389.5	399.6	448.8	465.8	481.4	488.8	453.0	457.6	510.0	450.6	457.9	5,443
1998	430.5	407.7	437.8	444.0	419.1	454.2	456.0	409.9	425.3	470.5	459.5	428.2	5,243
1999[1]	408.9	357.1	426.8	434.6	437.1	451.2	434.2	464.0	451.3	468.4	487.2	425.6	5,247

[1] Preliminary. *Source: Economic Research Service, U.S. Department of Agriculture (ERS-USDA)*

TURKEYS

Per Capita Consumption of Turkeys in the United States In Pounds

Year	First Quarter	Second Quarter	Third Quarter	Fourth Quarter	Total	Year	First Quarter	Second Quarter	Third Quarter	Fourth Quarter	Total
1989	3.2	3.2	4.2	6.0	16.6	1995	3.6	3.9	4.2	6.2	17.9
1990	3.5	3.6	4.2	6.2	17.6	1996	3.7	3.9	4.6	6.2	18.5
1991	3.7	4.0	4.1	6.4	18.0	1997	3.5	4.0	4.2	6.0	17.6
1992	3.4	3.8	4.2	6.5	18.0	1998	3.9	3.9	4.2	6.0	18.1
1993	3.5	3.7	3.9	6.5	17.7	1999[1]	3.8	3.8	4.4	5.9	18.0
1994	3.6	3.9	4.4	6.2	17.8	2000[2]	3.7	4.0	4.2		17.8

[1] Preliminary. [2] Estimate. *Source: Economic Research Service, U.S. Department of Agriculture (ERS-USDA)*

Storage Stocks of Turkeys (Frozen) in the United States on First of Month In Millions of Pounds

Year	Jan.	Feb.	Mar.	Apr.	May	June	July	Aug.	Sept.	Oct.	Nov.	Dec.
1990	235.9	268.4	276.3	317.9	354.9	405.6	481.3	541.7	593.1	623.6	625.1	338.4
1991	306.4	302.5	342.2	370.0	408.5	453.4	503.1	571.3	625.8	667.2	653.0	305.5
1992	264.1	325.5	354.1	392.3	430.2	486.8	580.1	662.1	684.2	734.4	714.7	320.5
1993	271.7	314.7	359.8	359.2	424.4	474.0	556.1	624.2	678.6	713.8	683.6	290.6
1994	249.1	279.8	304.8	346.5	399.1	461.4	539.2	588.1	623.4	648.6	636.2	280.7
1995	254.4	312.9	359.5	432.1	466.2	536.3	598.8	651.1	678.2	686.0	644.2	270.1
1996	271.3	339.2	423.1	445.4	514.5	587.4	679.7	718.2	723.2	721.0	658.3	347.8
1997	328.0	401.0	446.4	496.5	543.3	611.8	667.9	714.3	742.0	770.7	736.6	438.6
1998	415.1	497.6	512.7	527.0	579.7	614.1	656.5	701.8	706.8	699.5	658.7	310.4
1999[1]	304.3	363.8	375.6	374.9	455.4	494.3	556.1	599.0	580.3	596.4	494.5	252.3

[1] Preliminary. *Source: Economic Research Service, U.S. Department of Agriculture (ERS-USDA)*

Average Retail[2] Price of Turkeys (Whole frozen) in the United States In Cents Per Pound

Year	Jan.	Feb.	Mar.	Apr.	May	June	July	Aug.	Sept.	Oct.	Nov.	Dec.	Average
1990	65.20	64.60	67.30	69.40	70.10	70.10	68.70	73.60	76.60	81.90	82.30	66.40	71.35
1991	62.30	63.06	66.61	66.78	69.70	70.00	70.30	72.20	72.80	69.10	70.80	73.90	68.96
1992	67.90	65.80	68.10	68.70	69.24	69.04	65.70	68.10	69.60	72.30	74.00	74.90	69.45
1993	67.85	67.22	67.94	68.80	68.40	68.19	67.08	72.07	74.91	78.37	80.08	75.03	71.33
1994	70.27	69.39	70.55	70.93	72.01	72.58	72.77	74.75	77.32	79.89	83.33	77.34	74.26
1995	69.54	67.08	68.47	68.62	70.05	72.49	74.18	77.77	81.60	84.89	86.50	77.50	74.89
1996	103.50	104.70	106.90	101.40	104.30	104.10	104.40	108.60	106.50	107.40	98.10	102.00	104.33
1997	106.30	106.70	104.70	103.20	104.50	107.80	107.40	109.20	108.90	106.20	97.60	98.20	105.06
1998	103.40	100.10	99.60	97.20	95.70	99.10	100.80	102.40	105.20	102.50	93.40	95.40	99.57
1999[1]	96.90	100.10	98.40	93.60	97.50	100.50	103.10	103.40	101.80	102.50	96.40	97.60	99.32

[1] Preliminary. [2] Data prior to 1996 are prices to selected retailers. *Source: Economic Research Service, U.S. Department of Agriculture (ERS-USDA)*

Average Retail-to-Consumer Price Spread of Turkeys (Whole) in the United States In Cents Per Pound

Year	Jan.	Feb.	Mar.	Apr.	May	June	July	Aug.	Sept.	Oct.	Nov.	Dec.	Average
1990	33.7	33.7	32.1	27.7	29.8	29.7	32.1	27.8	26.7	23.7	8.8	29.6	28.0
1991	37.1	38.1	31.2	33.7	30.9	32.0	32.6	31.2	30.3	34.9	20.8	17.5	30.9
1992	28.2	29.2	27.0	29.4	29.6	29.5	33.3	32.5	31.4	27.2	15.4	18.1	27.6
1993	30.0	31.7	32.6	31.9	32.3	34.5	35.8	29.7	27.7	25.0	13.6	20.4	28.8
1994	27.5	29.7	28.1	25.1	27.1	28.8	28.7	27.6	27.1	25.5	13.9	20.3	25.8
1995	28.5	32.0	33.7	32.1	32.7	32.8	30.8	28.2	27.0	20.1	10.6	21.2	27.5
1996	30.4	30.7	33.6	28.0	29.3	28.0	27.9	32.1	30.3	28.9	18.0	26.6	28.7
1997	38.3	40.7	37.5	32.0	29.6	32.0	32.0	34.5	34.3	31.9	20.0	26.9	32.5
1998	38.8	37.2	35.2	31.2	29.4	30.7	29.6	29.0	29.3	21.3	10.3	19.0	28.4
1999[1]	29.9	32.7	28.6	21.3	22.5	22.6	23.2	21.9	18.5	17.6	12.0	19.6	22.5

[1] Preliminary. *Source: Economic Research Service, U.S. Department of Agriculture (ERS-USDA)*

Uranium

The U.S. Energy Information Administration reported that in 1998, U.S. uranium production was 4.7 million pounds (in the form of uranium concentrate) or 1,800 metric tonnes of uranium. This represented a decline of 16 percent from the 1997 level of 5.6 million pounds. U.S. production of uranium has been on a fairly steady decline for a number of years. In 1989, U.S. uranium production was 13.8 million pounds. Production declined sharply in 1993 to 3.1 million pounds.

U.S. mine production of uranium in 1998 was 4.8 million pounds which represented an increase of 2 percent from 1997. Mine production reached a recent low in 1992 when it fell to one million pounds, while in 1989 it was 9.7 million pounds. U.S. uranium reserves at the end of 1998 were 276 million pounds, a decline of 2 percent from the previous year. In 1998, there were 15 uranium mines operating in the United States. That was up from 14 mines in 1997, but well below the 1990 total of 39 mines. Of the 1998 total of 15 mines; 4 were underground mines, there were no open pit mines, 6 mines involved in-situ leaching while other sources, like mill tailings and mine water, totaled 5.

Total exploration and development expenditures in 1998 were $21.7 million, a decline of 29 percent from the previous year. Surface drilling (exploration and development) in the U.S. in 1998 was 4.6 million feet, down from 4.9 million in 1997. U.S. uranium companies held 825,000 acres for all exploration purposes at the end of 1998. In 1997 the total was 840,000 acres. There were 6,000 acres acquired in 1998.

Uranium purchases by U.S. brokers and traders in 1998 totaled 24.4 million pounds, up 24 percent from 1997. Uranium purchased by U.S. utilities in 1998 totaled 42.7 million pounds, up almost 2 percent from the previous year. Foreign purchases of uranium by U.S. suppliers and utilities were 43.7 million pounds, an increase of nearly 2 percent from 1997. Foreign sales of uranium by U.S. suppliers and utilities were 15.1 million pounds, down 11 percent from 1997.

Fuel assemblies loaded into U.S. commercial nuclear power reactors in 1998 totaled 38.3 million pounds, down 21 percent from 1997. U.S. utility inventories of uranium at the end of 1998 were 66.9 million pounds, up almost 2 percent from the previous year. U.S. utility and supplier inventories at the end of 1998 were 137.6 million pounds, up 30 percent from 1997.

In July 1999, U.S. nuclear power facilities generated 66.5 billion kilowatthours of electricity. In the January-July 1999 period, nuclear power plants generated 413.9 billion kilowatthours of electricity. The nuclear share of electric utility net generation was 22.1 percent. In July 1999, the U.S. had 104 operating nuclear power units. There were no new units on order or being constructed. There were no plants shut down in the first seven months of 1999.

World Production of Uranium Oxide (U_3O_8) Concentrate In Short Tons (Uranium Content)

Year	Australia	Canada	China	Czech Rep. & Slovakia	France	Gabon	Germany	Namibia	Niger	South Africa	United States	Ex-USSR	World Total
1989	4,752	14,855	1,039	2,989	4,183	1,157	4,961	4,000	3,874	3,810	6,919	18,849	75,264
1990	4,589	11,400	1,039	2,600	3,661	922	3,864	4,030	3,682	3,169	4,443	18,199	64,642
1991	4,909	10,609	1,039	2,340	3,204	882	1,569	3,185	3,853	2,248	3,975	13,650	53,458
1992	3,032	12,087	1,039	2,040	2,755	702	325	2,199	3,855	2,449	2,822	11,205	46,124
1993	2,949	11,990	1,300	911	2,220	769	195	2,168	3,786	2,261	2,587	10,491	43,027
1994	3,050	11,950	-----	-----	1,700	750	-----	2,500	3,800	2,250	1,950	-----	41,750
1995	4,900	13,600	-----	-----	1,250	800	-----	2,600	3,750	1,850	3,050	-----	43,050
1996	6,450	15,250	-----	-----	1,200	750	-----	3,150	4,300	2,200	3,150	-----	46,650
1997[1]	7,150	15,650	-----	-----	975	600	-----	3,800	5,100	1,450	2,900	-----	46,550
1998[2]	6,395	14,200	-----	-----	550	950	-----	3,585	4,750	1,260	2,450	-----	44,445

[1] Preliminary. [2] Estimate. *Source: American Bureau of Metal Statistics, Inc. (ABMS)*

Commercial and U.S. Government Stocks of Uranium, End of Year In Millions of Pounds U_3O_8 Equivalent

	Utility		Domestic Supplier			DOE Owned & USEC Held	
Year	Natural Uranium	Enriched Uranium[1]	Natural Uranium	Enriched Uranium[1]	Total Commercial Stocks	Natural Uranium	Enriched Uranium[1]
1991	70.9	27.1	18.7	2.0	118.7	46.8	36.7
1992	66.5	25.5	19.1	6.1	117.3	45.8	23.1
1993	57.9	23.3	19.1	5.4	105.7	52.4	26.9
1994	42.4	23.0	17.4	4.1	86.9	57.2	28.0
1995	41.2	17.5	13.2	.5	72.5	82.0	28.8
1996	42.2	23.9	13.0	1.0	80.0	83.2	25.3
1997	47.1	18.8	10.3	30.1	106.2	53.2	0
1998	42.3	24.6	34.8	35.9	137.6	24.5	0

[1] Includes amount reported as UF_6 at enrichment suppliers. DOE = Department of Energy USEC = U.S. Energy Commission

Source: Energy Information Administration, U.S. Department of Energy (EIA-DOE)

URANIUM

Reported Average Price Settlements for Purchases by U.S. Utilities and Domestic Suppliers — In $/Pound

Year of Delivery	Contract Price	Market Price[1]	Price & Cost Floor	Total	Contract & Market	Year of Delivery	Contract Price	Market Price[1]	Price & Cost Floor	Total	Contract & Market
	Averages of Reported Prices						Averages of Reported Prices				
1989	20.87	11.48	22.50	15.42	19.56	1994	10.68	9.76	20.03	10.57	10.63
1990	17.94	9.18	19.40	11.65	15.70	1995	10.58	10.19	17.86	12.05	10.79
1991	13.94	9.04	21.84	12.62	13.66	1996	13.40	13.66	16.13	14.91	13.72
1992	13.16	8.65	18.35	13.89	13.45	1997	13.33	11.20	14.52	12.11	13.13
1993	14.96	9.57	14.87	11.03	13.14	1998	12.53	9.33	13.50	10.31	12.37

[1] No floor. Note: Price excludes uranium delivered *under litigation settlements. Price is given in year-of-delivery dollars.*
Source: Energy Information Administration, U.S. Department of Energy (EIA-DOE)

Uranium Industry Statistics in the United States — In Millions of Pounds U_3O_8

Year	Production: Mine	Production: Concentrate	Concentrate Shipments	Employment – Person Years: Exploration	Mining	Milling	Processing	Total	Deliveries to U.S. Utilities[1]	Average Price Delivered Uranium $/Lb. U_3O_8	Imports	Avg. Price Delivered Uranium Imports $/Lb. U_3O_8	Exports
1989	9.7	13.837	14.808	86	659	367	471	1,583	18.4	19.56	13.7	16.75	2.1
1990	5.9	8.885	12.957	73	664	304	293	1,335	20.5	15.70	26.6	12.55	2.0
1991	5.2	7.952	8.437	52	411	191	361	1,016	26.8	13.66	23.1	15.55	3.5
1992	1.0	5.645	6.853	51	219	129	283	682	23.4	13.45	45.4	11.34	2.8
1993	2.0	3.063	3.374	36	133	65	145	871	15.5	13.14	41.9	10.53	3.0
1994	2.5	3.352	6.319	41	157	105	149	980	38.3	10.40	36.6	8.95	17.7
1995	3.5	6.000	5.500	27	226	121	161	1,107	43.4	11.25	41.3	10.20	9.8
1996	4.7	6.300	6.000	27	333	155	175	1,118	47.3	14.12	45.4	13.15	11.5
1997	4.7	5.600	5.800	30	413	175	175	1,097	42.0	12.88	43.0	11.81	17.0
1998	4.8	4.700	4.900	30	518	160	203	1,120	42.7	12.14	43.7	11.19	15.1

[1] From suppliers under domestic purchases. *Source: Energy Information Administration, U.S. Department of Energy (EIA-DOE)*

Month-End Uranium (U_3O_8) Transaction Values[1] — In Dollars Per Pound

Year	Jan.	Feb.	Mar.	Apr.	May	June	July	Aug.	Sept.	Oct.	Nov.	Dec.	Average
1989	12.25	12.00	11.25	11.00	10.75	10.45	9.95	9.80	9.80	9.65	9.55	9.40	10.49
1990	9.25	9.05	8.75	8.65	8.55	8.80	9.75	10.80	11.40	10.10	9.30	9.15	9.46
1991	9.40	9.45	9.35	9.30	9.30	9.20	9.15	8.95	8.70	8.35	7.45	7.50	8.84
1992	7.55	7.80	7.95	7.90	7.85	7.80	7.75	7.85	7.95	8.40	8.55	8.75	8.01
1993[2]	8.80	8.60	8.80	9.20	8.70	8.90	8.20	8.80	9.05	8.45	8.60	8.71	8.74
1994	8.58	8.45	8.25	8.25	8.23	8.25	8.23	8.15	8.13	8.10	8.13	8.25	8.25
1995	8.30	8.45	8.65	8.78	9.18	9.48	9.50	9.83	9.83	9.83	9.95	10.05	9.32
1996	10.20	10.48	10.93	11.70	13.03	13.25	14.93	15.18	15.40	15.53	15.48	15.38	13.45
1997	15.33	15.08	14.85	14.75	14.43	10.95	10.68	10.45	10.55	10.48	10.43	10.53	12.37
1998	10.63	10.63	10.60	10.05	10.00	9.80	9.80	9.73	9.55	9.35	9.25	9.05	9.87

[1] Transaction value is a weighed average price of recent natural uranium sales transactions, based on prices paid on transactions closed within the previous three-month period for which delivery is scheduled within one year of the transaction date; at least 10 transactions involving a sum total of at least 2 million pounds of U_3O_8 equivalent. [2] Beginning December 1993; data represents average of Unrestricted and Restricted.
Source: American Metal Market (AMM)

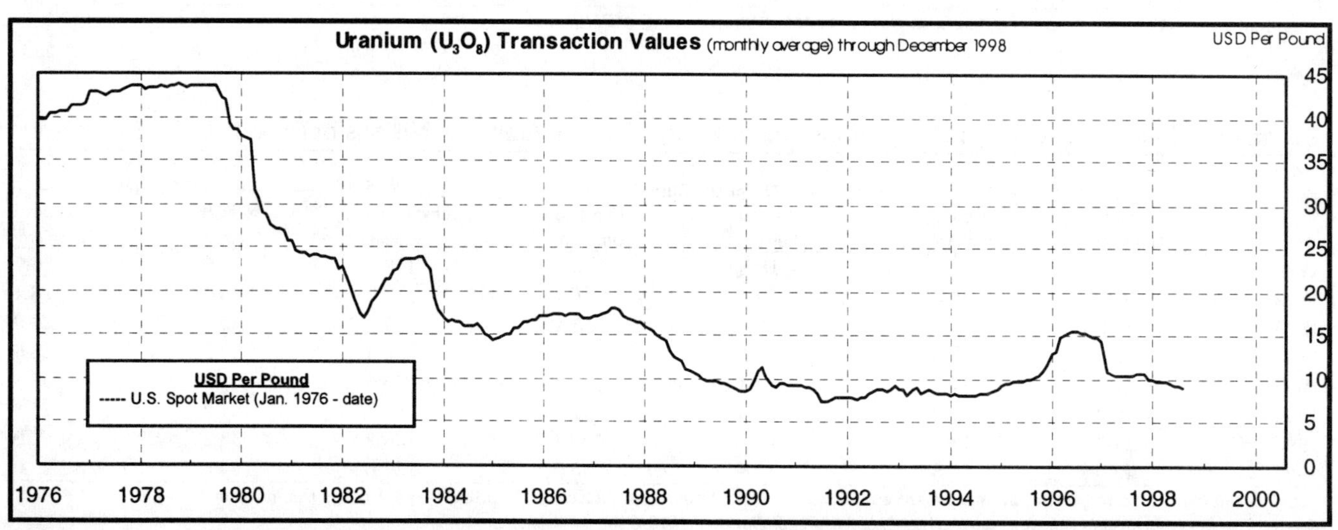

Vanadium

Vanadium is used in the production of carbon and alloy plates and steel, pipe steels and structural bars. Vanadium finds use as an oxidation catalyst and is used in tool production to provide strength and toughness. Ferrochromium is an iron alloy used in steel. Vanadium pentoxide is used in dyeing and painting applications. Vanadium is important in the production of aerospace titanium alloys and as a catalyst in the production of nucleic anhydride and sulfuric acid. There are some substitutes for vanadium in steels. Steels that contain other alloying elements can be substituted for steels containing vanadium. Among the metals than can to some degree be interchanged with vanadium are manganese, molybdenum, columbium, tungsten and titanium. In chemical processes, platinum and nickel are substitutes to some extent. There is no substitute for vanadium in aerospace titanium alloys.

Vanadium occurs in deposits of titaniferous magnetite, phosphate rock and in the uraniferous sandstone and siltstone. Vanadium is also found in bauxite materials. Vanadium is usually recovered as a by-product of other mining activities. Vanadium is recovered from vanadium-bearing ferrophosphorus slag, iron slag, petroleum residues and spent catalysts.

World mine production of vanadium in 1998 was about 35,000 metric tonnes, down 6 percent from 1997. The major producers of vanadium are South Africa, Russia and China.

U.S. consumption of ferrovanadium in August 1999 was 282,000 kilograms, contained vanadium, an increase of 4 percent from July. For all of 1998, U.S. consumption of ferrovanadium was 4.01 million kilograms. Consumption of other vanadium-containing products like vanadium metal and vanadium pentoxide in August 1999 was 38,400 kilograms, up 4 percent from July. For all of 1998, consumption was 387,000 kilograms. U.S. stocks of ferrovanadium in August 1999 were 288,000 kilograms compared to stocks at the end of 1998 of 302,000 kilograms. Total U.S. stocks of vanadium at the end of August 1999 were 310,000 kilograms.

U.S. imports for consumption of aluminum-vanadium master alloy in the January-July 1999 period were 1.11 million kilograms. Imports of vanadium metal, including waste and scrap, in the same period were 20,200 kilograms. U.S. imports of ferrovanadium in the first seven months of 1999 were 914,000 kilograms. Imports of vanadium pentoxide in the same period were 77,300 kilograms. Imports of vanadium slag in the period were 569,000 kilograms.

World Production of Vanadium In Metric Tons (Contained Vanadium)

	From Ores, Concentrates and Slag						From Petroleum Residues, Ash, Spent Catalysts			
			Republic of South Africa							
Year	China[3]	Russia[4]	Content of Pentoxide & Vanadate Products	Content of Vanadiferous Slag Products	Total	Total[5]	Japan[4]	United States[7]	Total	World Total
1989	4,500	9,600	7,270	11,300	18,567	32,967	868	2,389	3,257	36,224
1990	4,500	9,000	7,100	10,000	17,106	33,900	700	2,308	3,008	36,900
1991	4,500	8,500	6,500	8,460	14,962	31,700	404	2,250	2,650	34,300
1992	4,700	11,000	6,300	7,730	14,285	31,600	245	1,347	1,590	33,200
1993	5,000	12,800	6,650	8,400	15,051	33,900	252	2,867	3,120	37,000
1994	5,400	11,900	6,050	9,600	16,350	34,700	252	2,740	2,990	37,700
1995	13,700	11,000	6,500	9,000	16,297	42,100	245	1,990	2,240	44,400
1996	14,000	11,000	-----	-----	14,770	40,900	245	3,730	3,980	45,800
1997[1]	14,500	9,000	-----	-----	15,590	40,200	245	-----	-----	-----
1998[2]	14,700	9,000	-----	-----	17,000	41,800	245	-----	-----	-----

[1] Preliminary. [2] Estimate. [3] In vanadiferous slag product. [4] Formerly part of the U.S.S.R.: data not reported separately until 1992. [5] Excludes U.S. production. [6] In vanadium pentoxide product. [7] In vanadium pentoxide and ferrovanadium products. Source: U.S. Geological Survey(USGS)

Salient Statistics of Vanadium in the United States In Metric Tons (Contained Vanadium)

Year	Consumer & Producer Stocks, Dec. 31	Vanadium Consumption by Uses in the U.S.: Tool Steel	Cast Irons	High Strength, Low Alloy	Stainless & Heat Resisting	Superalloys	Carbon	Full Alloy	Total	Average $ Per Lb. V_2O_5	Exports: Vanadium Pentoxide, Anhydride	Oxides & Hydroxides	Ferrovanadium	Imports: Ores, Slag, Residues	Vanadium Pentoxide, Anhydride	Oxides & Hydroxides	Ferrovanadium
1989	1,736	420	18	1,225	96	38	1,103	898	4,646	6.17	1,171	1,080	399	4,210	133	106	527
1990	1,082	421	18	1,122	38	42	994	814	4,081	4.21	819	976	271	3,826	83	217	244
1991	935	242	15	919	37	14	919	739	3,293	2.85	700	1,110	94	882	133	110	420
1992	1,084	453	17	989	28	13	1,262	828	4,079	2.28	26	1,113	213	838	206	103	592
1993	900	373	21	981	33	13	1,413	789	3,973	1.45	126	895	219	1,454	70	19	1,630
1994	1,110	424	31	979	26	16	1,680	777	4,290	1.55	335	1,050	374	1,900	294	3	1,910
1995	1,100	443	40	1,070	32	20	1,870	833	4,640	4.63	229	1,010	340	2,530	547	36	1,950
1996	1,070	433	W	890	22	16	1,820	1,030	4,200	3.11	241	2,670	479	2,270	485	11	1,880
1997[1]	1,000	481	W	944	20	24	1,800	908	4,730	9.20	614	385	446	2,950	711	126	1,840
1998[2]	300	269	W	950	42	20	1,650	891	4,390	10.38	681	232	579	2,400	847	33	1,620

[1] Preliminary. [2] Estimate. [3] Less than 1/2 unit. W = Withheld proprietary data. *Source: U.S. Geological Survey (USGS)*

Vegetables

The U.S.D.A. forecast for U.S. production of fresh tomatoes in 1999 was 3.6 billion pounds. That would represent an increase of 15 percent from 1998. U.S. imports of fresh tomatoes in 1999 were estimated at 1.58 billion pounds, a decline of 16 percent from 1998. The total supply of fresh tomatoes was 5.18 billion pounds, an increase of 4 percent from 1998. In terms of utilization, U.S. exports of fresh tomatoes in 1999 were forecast at 340 million pounds, an increase of 19 percent from the previous year. Domestic use of fresh tomatoes was projected to be 4.84 billion pounds, an increase of almost 3 percent from 1998. U.S. per capita use of fresh tomatoes in 1999 was projected to be 17.7 pounds compared to 17.4 pounds in 1998. In 1990, per capita use was 15.5 pounds while in 1980 it was 12.8.

U.S. production of fresh onions in 1999 was forecast to be 5.8 billion pounds, an increase of over 2 percent from 1998. U.S. imports of fresh onions in 1999 were estimated at 615 million pounds, an increase of almost 3 percent from the previous season. With season beginning stocks of 1.01 billion pounds, the total supply of fresh onions in 1999 was projected to be 7.43 billion pounds, an increase of just over 1 percent from 1998. Exports of fresh onions were forecast at 655 million pounds, an increase of 4 percent from the previous year. Domestic use of fresh onions was projected to be 5.05 billion pounds. U.S. per capita use of fresh onions in 1999 was 18.6 pounds, the same as in 1998.

Production of fresh carrots in 1999 was estimated at 3.7 billion pounds, down 1 percent from 1998. Imports were estimated at 300 million pounds for a total supply of 4 billion pounds. In terms of use, exports of fresh carrots in 1999 were 250 million pounds, down 2 percent from the previous year. Domestic utilization was 3.75 billion pounds, up 2 percent from 1998. Per capita use of fresh carrots in 1999 was 13.8 pounds, up from 13.6 pounds the previous year.

Index of Prices Received by Growers for Commercial Vegetables[1] in the United States

Year	Jan.	Feb.	Mar.	Apr.	May	June	July	Aug.	Sept.	Oct.	Nov.	Dec.	Average
1994	116	113	93	88	97	104	98	94	105	117	124	164	109
1995	120	116	148	174	155	121	98	102	117	97	98	101	121
1996	94	111	147	122	103	116	99	116	102	109	112	96	111
1997	113	107	122	115	111	118	114	125	119	147	142	136	122
1998	120	112	120	147	126	105	119	111	111	132	113	112	119
1999[2]	107	115	116	128	122	111	101	105	104	97			111

Not seasonally adjusted. 1990-92=100. [1] Includes fresh and processing vegetables. [2] Preliminary. *Source: National Agricultural Statistics Service, U.S. Department of Agriculture (NASS-USDA)*

Index of Prices Received by Growers for Fresh Vegetables (0113-02) in the United States

Year	Jan.	Feb.	Mar.	Apr.	May	June	July	Aug.	Sept.	Oct.	Nov.	Dec.	Average
1994	146.3	99.3	96.1	91.4	91.2	94.9	104.8	95.7	107.1	113.8	128.1	244.7	117.8
1995	163.5	149.2	159.2	199.1	167.2	127.2	107.3	94.8	152.9	116.0	115.8	125.5	139.8
1996	133.9	119.4	202.5	155.6	108.2	96.6	108.8	97.2	91.3	106.0	131.5	99.3	120.9
1997	105.2	126.2	150.4	109.6	103.2	112.2	115.7	125.2	121.8	143.1	124.7	118.5	121.3
1998	133.1	136.6	148.2	162.9	123.2	106.5	153.7	114.9	135.0	161.9	131.2	148.1	137.9
1999[1]	131.9	93.1	117.4	144.4	111.3	125.8	103.4	113.7	117.5	100.0	100.9	151.6	117.6

Not seasonally adjusted. 1990-92=100. [1] Preliminary. *Source: National Agricultural Statistics Service, U.S. Department of Agriculture (NASS)*

Producer Price Index of Canned[1] Processed Vegetables (0244) in the United States 1982 = 100

Year	Jan.	Feb.	Mar.	Apr.	May	June	July	Aug.	Sept.	Oct.	Nov.	Dec.	Average
1994	113.1	115.1	116.8	116.5	117.9	118.0	118.9	118.1	116.0	116.0	114.0	112.4	116.1
1995	112.6	114.3	114.7	112.9	115.6	117.5	118.2	117.5	117.6	117.8	118.4	119.6	116.4
1996	120.4	119.8	120.4	120.4	120.8	121.0	122.6	122.1	121.9	121.8	121.9	121.8	121.2
1997	121.5	121.1	120.5	120.1	119.8	119.9	119.1	119.3	119.3	120.2	120.3	120.7	120.1
1998	121.2	121.9	121.8	121.8	121.9	121.9	122.0	122.0	120.0	119.6	120.0	120.0	121.2
1999[2]	120.6	120.6	120.9	120.9	121.0	121.0	120.8	120.9	120.7	120.7	121.6	121.4	120.9

Not seasonally adjusted. [1] Includes canned vegetables and juices, including hominy and mushrooms. [2] Preliminary. *Source: Bureau of Labor Statistics, U.S. Department of Labor (BLS)*

Producer Price Index of Frozen Processed Vegetables (0245) in the United States 1982 = 100

Year	Jan.	Feb.	Mar.	Apr.	May	June	July	Aug.	Sept.	Oct.	Nov.	Dec.	
1994	125.5	126.1	126.1	126.4	126.9	127.0	126.4	126.4	125.2	124.9	124.7	125.0	126.0
1995	125.1	124.7	124.9	125.1	124.3	123.6	123.2	123.6	124.4	124.6	123.7	124.0	124.3
1996	125.1	124.8	124.6	124.9	125.0	125.4	125.5	125.8	126.0	125.7	125.8	126.0	125.4
1997	125.9	125.7	125.6	125.6	125.7	125.7	126.9	125.6	125.7	126.6	125.5	125.3	125.8
1998	125.2	126.0	124.8	125.7	125.0	124.6	125.5	125.6	125.3	125.6	125.5	125.2	125.3
1999[1]	125.8	126.6	125.6	126.7	125.9	126.0	126.8	126.1	126.0	126.4	126.1	125.3	126.1

Not seasonally adjusted. [1] Preliminary. *Source: Bureau of Labor Statistics, U.S. Department of Labor (BLS)*

Per Capita Use of Selected Commercially Produced Fresh and Processing Vegetables in the U.S.

In Pounds, farm weight basis

Crop	1989	1990	1991	1992	1993	1994	1995	1996	1997	1998[9]	1999[10]
Asparagus, all	1.0	1.0	1.0	1.0	1.0	.9	1.0	.9	1.0	1.1	1.1
Fresh	.6	.6	.6	.6	.6	.6	.6	.6	.7	.8	.8
Canning	.3	.3	.3	.3	.3	.2	.3	.2	.2	.2	.2
Freezing	.1	.1	.1	.1	.1	.1	.1	.1	.1	.1	.1
Snap Beans, all	7.1	6.7	7.0	7.2	7.3	7.4	7.0	7.3	6.9	7.5	7.5
Fresh	1.2	1.1	1.1	1.5	1.5	1.6	1.7	1.5	1.4	1.7	1.8
Canning	3.9	3.7	4.1	4.0	4.0	3.8	3.6	3.9	3.7	3.8	3.7
Freezing	2.0	1.9	1.8	1.7	1.8	2.0	1.7	1.9	1.8	2.0	2.0
Broccoli, all[1]	6.0	5.6	5.4	5.8	5.7	6.8	7.0	7.2	7.4	7.7	8.1
Fresh	3.8	3.4	3.1	3.4	3.4	4.5	4.4	4.6	5.1	5.6	5.8
Freezing	2.2	2.2	2.3	2.4	2.3	2.3	2.6	2.6	2.3	2.1	2.3
Carrots, all[2]	11.5	11.9	11.2	12.3	14.8	17.1	15.6	17.2	18.5	18.0	18.0
Fresh	8.1	8.3	7.7	8.3	10.9	12.8	11.3	12.6	14.4	13.6	13.8
Canning	.9	1.3	1.1	1.7	1.1	1.5	1.7	1.7	1.5	1.5	1.5
Freezing	2.5	2.3	2.4	2.3	2.8	2.8	2.6	2.9	2.6	2.9	2.7
Cauliflower, All[1]	3.1	3.0	2.6	2.5	2.8	2.6	2.3	2.2	2.2	2.4	2.1
Fresh	2.3	2.2	2.0	1.8	2.1	2.0	1.7	1.7	1.8	1.6	1.6
Freezing	.8	.8	.6	.7	.7	.6	.6	.5	.4	.8	.5
Celery, fresh	7.5	7.2	6.8	7.4	7.3	7.4	6.9	6.4	6.1	6.2	6.3
Sweet Corn, all[3]	24.4	26.3	26.4	27.8	28.0	27.6	28.9	29.5	27.9	28.4	28.2
Fresh	6.5	6.7	5.9	6.9	7.0	8.2	7.9	8.5	8.4	9.0	8.8
Canning	9.5	11.0	11.1	11.9	11.2	10.2	10.5	10.5	9.3	9.4	9.1
Freezing	8.4	8.6	9.4	9.0	9.8	9.2	10.5	10.5	10.2	10.0	10.3
Cucumbers, all	10.0	9.7	9.7	9.6	9.7	10.2	10.8	10.1	11.8	11.1	10.7
Fresh	4.8	4.7	4.6	5.0	5.3	5.4	5.7	6.0	6.5	6.7	5.9
Pickles	5.2	5.0	5.1	4.6	4.4	4.8	5.1	4.1	5.3	4.4	4.8
Melons, all	26.5	24.6	23.4	25.4	24.7	25.7	26.4	29.3	28.8	28.2	29.6
Watermelon	13.6	13.3	12.8	14.8	14.3	15.2	15.4	16.8	15.8	14.5	15.5
Cantaloupe	10.4	9.2	8.7	8.5	8.7	8.5	9.1	10.4	10.7	11.3	11.5
Honeydew	2.5	2.1	1.9	2.1	1.7	2.0	1.9	2.1	2.3	2.4	2.6
Lettuce, Head	28.8	27.8	26.1	25.9	24.6	25.3	22.5	21.9	26.7	22.8	24.0
Onions, all	16.4	17.1	17.3	17.6	19.3	18.1	19.3	19.6	20.0	19.7	19.6
Fresh	14.8	15.1	15.7	16.2	17.3	17.1	18.0	18.7	19.1	18.6	18.6
Green peas, all[4]	3.7	4.2	4.2	4.1	3.5	3.7	3.7	3.4	3.6	3.4	3.6
Canning	1.7	2.0	1.9	2.1	1.6	1.5	1.6	1.5	1.5	1.5	1.5
Freezing	2.0	2.2	2.3	2.0	1.9	2.2	2.1	1.9	2.1	1.9	2.1
Tomatoes, all	86.2	90.9	92.8	89.2	92.8	93.5	92.7	91.9	91.0	93.0	93.0
Fresh	16.8	15.5	15.4	15.5	16.4	16.4	17.1	17.7	17.1	17.4	17.7
Canning	69.4	75.4	77.4	73.7	76.4	77.1	75.6	74.2	73.9	75.6	75.3
Subtotal, all[8]	263.7	268.1	268.2	272.5	280.1	285.1	280.8	285.9	291.7	289.9	293.7
Fresh	142.6	138.5	134.3	141.6	146.3	153.4	149.3	156.0	164.0	160.3	164.3
Canning	98.7	107.3	110.8	108.8	109.6	108.6	107.2	105.5	104.4	105.9	105.6
Freezing	20.8	20.3	21.5	20.7	22.2	22.1	23.0	23.5	22.4	22.6	22.8
Potatoes, all	127.1	124.1	134.5	130.8	134.8	140.2	138.3	145.4	142.1	145.1	144.7
Fresh	50.0	46.8	50.4	48.6	49.3	50.3	49.5	50.0	48.5	50.8	48.7
Processing	77.1	77.3	84.1	82.2	85.5	89.9	88.8	95.4	93.6	94.3	96.0
Sweetpotatoes, all	4.1	4.6	4.0	4.3	3.9	4.7	4.5	4.6	4.5	4.1	4.6
Total, all items	404.6	407.5	418.2	419.4	430.2	442.4	435.8	447.9	450.3	451.3	455.4

[1] All production for processing broccoli and cauliflower is for freezing. [2] Industry allocation suggests that 27 percent of processing carrot production is for canning and 73 percent is for freezing. [3] On-cob basis. [4] In-shell basis. [5] Includes artichokes, brussels sprouts, eggplant, endive/escarole, garlic, radishes, and spinach. [6] Includes beets, chile peppers (1980-94, all uses), and spinach. [7] Includes green lima beans, spinach, and miscellaneous freezing vegetables. [8] Fresh, canning, and freezing data do not add to the total because onions for dehydrating are included in the total.
[9] Preliminary. [10] Forecast. Source: Economic Research Service, U.S. Department of Agriculture (ERS-USDA)

Average Price Received by Growers for Broccoli in the United States In Dollars Per Cwt.

Year	Jan.	Feb.	Mar.	Apr.	May	June	July	Aug.	Sept.	Oct.	Nov.	Dec.	Season Average
1992	17.50	14.30	27.60	16.70	22.00	26.30	23.60	27.40	24.00	24.70	30.50	32.80	23.50
1993	32.60	28.10	28.60	23.70	22.30	26.80	24.50	20.00	36.60	22.40	24.20	30.00	26.60
1994	23.50	21.40	19.50	21.80	27.10	21.10	21.60	18.50	38.60	37.00	57.70	46.00	27.50
1995	24.70	34.30	54.40	34.00	26.50	27.30	19.50	31.30	27.70	23.60	20.80	26.90	29.30
1996	34.60	22.00	30.90	25.20	28.20	30.60	24.10	24.10	23.90	24.30	31.10	28.60	27.10
1997	36.80	27.80	25.90	24.20	23.10	30.30	27.50	23.30	31.20	40.70	27.00	30.20	29.10
1998	34.70	27.00	31.40	40.50	27.10	29.60	23.30	27.60	29.20	32.80	29.70	35.00	30.80
1999[1]	27.70	20.10	22.10	20.30	18.60	23.10	18.70	27.40	29.30	24.10			

[1] Preliminary. *Source: National Agricultural Statistics Service, U.S. Department of Agriculture (NASS-USDA)*

Average Price Received by Growers for Carrots in the United States In Dollars Per Cwt.

Year	Jan.	Feb.	Mar.	Apr.	May	June	July	Aug.	Sept.	Oct.	Nov.	Dec.	Season Average
1992	19.00	17.10	13.20	12.80	11.70	10.80	16.90	16.70	14.40	12.80	12.00	13.80	14.50
1993	18.00	13.20	11.20	12.70	11.20	10.20	9.04	10.10	9.98	10.30	11.00	10.90	11.90
1994	10.70	10.50	11.50	10.30	12.10	12.10	13.50	16.10	15.30	15.30	15.10	15.70	13.00
1995	19.20	16.90	18.70	19.40	19.20	15.20	15.00	16.10	16.10	15.30	15.50	13.00	16.80
1996	12.60	13.80	15.90	15.70	12.00	11.00	10.50	14.50	12.60	12.00	16.00	17.20	13.30
1997	15.00	14.80	13.50	12.60	12.60	12.60	12.60	13.20	12.70	12.00	12.50	16.80	13.10
1998	13.60	12.90	12.90	12.40	11.80	11.80	10.60	10.80	10.60	11.00	11.80	11.70	12.30
1999[1]	16.10	19.60	21.20	26.30	24.80	21.80	15.60	12.70	9.86	9.92			

[1] Preliminary. *Source: National Agricultural Statistics Service, U.S. Department of Agriculture (NASS-USDA)*

Average Price Received by Growers for Cauliflower in the United States In Dollars Per Cwt.

Year	Jan.	Feb.	Mar.	Apr.	May	June	July	Aug.	Sept.	Oct.	Nov.	Dec.	Season Average
1992	23.70	19.60	21.90	25.00	33.90	37.80	23.20	43.40	26.20	27.10	38.00	40.30	29.00
1993	34.30	29.10	24.70	44.90	26.90	37.00	28.30	29.30	38.70	27.40	21.60	30.90	31.20
1994	24.80	24.90	23.10	20.80	32.20	29.10	31.40	24.30	34.00	31.30	42.50	29.80	28.80
1995	31.40	31.50	53.90	68.40	47.70	37.60	26.70	34.20	25.40	21.10	22.60	33.20	34.70
1996	35.20	36.10	52.80	37.00	37.70	35.70	24.30	27.20	23.80	29.20	30.00	31.10	33.00
1997	29.60	33.80	32.60	27.70	20.70	31.20	38.90	23.40	34.60	46.90	27.60	28.90	31.20
1998	35.10	44.00	49.50	43.80	35.50	26.40	23.20	26.00	32.30	25.90	42.30	50.00	36.20
1999[1]	29.40	30.80	39.70	46.00	23.40	25.50	19.30	24.80	20.30	20.20			

[1] Preliminary. *Source: National Agricultural Statistics Service, U.S. Department of Agriculture (NASS-USDA)*

Average Price Received by Growers for Celery in the United States In Dollars Per Cwt.

Year	Jan.	Feb.	Mar.	Apr.	May	June	July	Aug.	Sept.	Oct.	Nov.	Dec.	Season Average
1992	8.81	7.74	10.40	15.10	15.80	12.10	11.30	14.50	15.90	13.00	12.40	15.60	12.30
1993	24.00	35.60	27.40	16.50	14.40	9.45	9.41	11.80	14.20	13.30	11.50	11.10	14.80
1994	11.40	8.85	7.78	8.34	13.50	8.92	12.40	14.90	12.60	12.00	13.90	25.50	12.50
1995	24.30	26.00	20.60	33.30	24.50	14.40	11.50	10.50	16.50	13.20	12.90	11.40	16.30
1996	7.90	8.50	12.20	11.60	8.90	11.50	11.50	10.30	11.60	9.79	12.40	13.40	10.60
1997	16.20	16.20	12.30	10.50	15.40	9.89	19.30	17.00	14.30	13.40	18.40	19.10	15.10
1998	11.20	11.40	16.40	13.80	15.40	12.40	10.60	10.40	10.60	10.40	11.90	14.00	12.20
1999[1]	9.51	8.47	8.35	10.20	12.80	18.30	14.00	10.80	11.60	9.46			

[1] Preliminary. *Source: National Agricultural Statistics Service, U.S. Department of Agriculture (NASS-USDA)*

Average Price Received by Growers for Sweet Corn in the United States In Dollars Per Cwt.

Year	Jan.	Feb.	Mar.	Apr.	May	June	July	Aug.	Sept.	Oct.	Nov.	Dec.	Season Average
1992	26.30	21.90	28.20	16.20	14.70	12.00	14.80	14.60	13.70	16.80	20.40	22.60	14.60
1993	23.30	39.20	25.20	23.50	20.60	17.70	18.50	16.80	14.70	22.10	16.60	24.30	17.80
1994	26.80	17.60	26.40	17.90	20.40	20.20	19.10	11.90	15.30	19.70	19.90	26.00	17.20
1995	25.00	44.70	27.80	16.60	24.50	18.80	18.60	17.10	18.50	20.70	24.00	23.30	18.20
1996	29.90	30.20	28.90	21.90	17.50	14.00	18.90	17.40	16.70	17.90	19.40	17.70	16.90
1997	29.00	25.80	33.90	26.00	21.20	17.00	18.40	18.10	16.90	15.30	18.90	19.90	17.70
1998	18.70	31.60	24.20	19.60	16.90	13.80	16.80	16.60	18.20	25.40	23.50	19.40	17.60
1999[1]	24.30	19.60	26.30	17.20	18.50	14.90	14.70	16.10	16.50	17.00			

[1] Preliminary. *Source: National Agricultural Statistics Service, U.S. Department of Agriculture (NASS-USDA)*

Average Price Received by Growers for Head Lettuce in the United States — In Dollars Per Cwt.

Year	Jan.	Feb.	Mar.	Apr.	May	June	July	Aug.	Sept.	Oct.	Nov.	Dec.	Season Average
1990	9.44	6.58	7.69	8.24	7.94	8.03	12.40	14.20	18.30	19.70	18.80	10.70	11.50
1991	10.20	6.63	10.40	9.00	23.10	9.51	6.70	8.32	11.30	10.80	21.40	9.66	11.40
1992	7.23	6.75	11.90	9.91	11.20	9.84	13.00	19.90	21.00	13.60	9.63	16.30	12.50
1993	10.80	18.70	14.30	37.80	12.60	11.50	18.80	14.90	16.80	12.20	10.50	8.28	16.00
1994	7.91	11.80	9.71	11.70	11.40	13.80	10.60	10.90	17.30	22.10	22.40	37.20	13.30
1995	13.40	9.32	27.00	48.20	47.00	15.60	12.60	15.20	25.60	13.30	11.50	16.10	23.50
1996	11.30	14.90	16.50	13.20	13.30	15.20	12.70	23.50	13.70	15.40	17.70	8.87	14.70
1997	14.90	9.58	13.50	15.60	10.40	14.90	17.10	22.80	22.30	34.80	29.90	21.30	17.30
1998	19.00	10.90	12.50	24.60	14.10	11.80	15.50	16.30	14.00	21.10	10.90	9.00	15.20
1999[1]	10.30	15.40	14.50	20.60	14.00	11.40	12.50	11.90	13.00	13.50			

[1] Preliminary. *Source: National Agricultural Statistics Service, U.S. Department of Agriculture (NASS-USDA)*

Average Price Received by Growers for Tomatoes in the United States — In Dollars Per Cwt.

Year	Jan.	Feb.	Mar.	Apr.	May	June	July	Aug.	Sept.	Oct.	Nov.	Dec.	Season Average
1990	116.00	97.60	32.30	14.60	22.30	23.30	26.80	26.00	24.80	31.50	30.90	29.70	27.40
1991	23.10	31.60	44.00	49.30	56.10	59.50	30.50	21.90	21.20	20.50	23.90	15.40	31.70
1992	40.50	76.00	80.70	32.40	16.70	21.90	28.30	23.50	29.30	60.10	39.10	34.30	35.80
1993	38.30	21.90	21.20	45.20	58.10	22.90	23.30	32.70	29.80	19.40	31.60	57.60	31.70
1994	41.50	19.30	24.50	16.50	20.60	31.30	26.90	30.60	22.70	28.50	31.20	37.40	27.40
1995	41.10	29.80	37.10	20.50	14.70	35.70	24.40	19.60	19.50	22.50	33.10	25.00	25.80
1996	18.40	40.00	81.70	50.50	24.40	24.20	26.00	22.10	23.40	28.30	29.70	30.40	28.00
1997	33.50	47.30	58.80	26.30	33.40	32.60	28.60	27.30	25.20	27.40	45.40	48.80	33.00
1998	26.40	44.00	34.00	37.20	36.50	17.80	40.60	25.50	28.60	44.90	43.60	47.70	35.00
1999[1]	39.90	35.20	24.80	23.40	25.30	33.70	25.40	22.70	26.90	19.90			

[1] Preliminary. *Source: National Agricultural Statistics Service, U.S. Department of Agriculture (NASS-USDA)*

Frozen Vegetables: January 1 and July 1 Cold Storage Holdings in the U.S. — In Thousands of Pounds

Crop	1995 July 1	1996 Jan. 1	1996 July 1	1997 Jan. 1	1997 July 1	1998 Jan. 1	1998 July 1	1999 Jan. 1	1999 July 1	2000[1] Jan. 1
Asparagus	15,493	9,689	14,001	8,353	12,276	6,908	11,766	6,162	15,712	12,076
Lima Beans	29,783	60,208	33,350	60,696	28,015	72,221	37,659	75,469	38,390	71,993
Snap Beans	87,436	224,297	80,224	202,648	95,868	230,661	91,266	213,400	82,525	186,390
Broccoli	110,075	136,850	150,883	120,972	108,411	112,311	108,673	113,752	189,160	157,375
Brussels sprouts	18,181	18,883	9,533	16,314	7,975	19,926	7,485	18,745	15,145	25,649
Carrots	176,054	307,645	177,248	283,770	162,153	300,070	163,176	256,623	162,569	307,197
Cauliflower	49,561	65,008	38,355	54,376	32,785	58,512	38,028	5,298	32,894	57,812
Corn, Sweet[2]	199,148	498,626	215,553	494,308	203,740	532,645	228,765	673,315	255,389	585,866
Mixed vegetables	59,414	60,492	67,031	54,208	50,755	45,744	79,375	53,020	46,699	51,537
Okra	43,367	39,954	23,902	28,576	18,711	52,230	63,950	46,567	51,951	39,837
Onions	42,810	48,761	38,342	40,790	37,817	42,218	33,598	40,348	49,002	58,262
Black-eyed peas	3,145	9,994	3,529	9,795	2,952	9,344	6,654	8,039	5,598	6,517
Green peas	219,669	281,349	163,293	224,134	137,615	219,533	230,233	277,858	226,888	276,154
Peas and carrots	9,034	10,401	8,340	6,731	6,840	5,760	7,154	10,285	10,062	11,314
Spinach	100,274	68,940	86,281	46,890	104,073	67,092	10,369	69,232	142,617	73,349
Squash	39,494	57,785	44,785	58,749	48,184	75,397	64,966	70,272	49,942	58,254
Southern greens	30,079	21,659	32,363	26,936	16,681	20,771	37,660	32,765	39,455	26,944
Other vegetables	189,124	319,519	235,880	314,640	253,158	285,670	251,391	301,595	243,759	272,866
Total	1,422,141	2,390,428	1,422,893	2,185,704	1,317,049	2,303,007	1,539,168	2,317,745	1,657,757	2,279,392
Potatoes	1,116,454	1,123,744	1,057,470	1,131,642	1,271,316	1,163,547	1,316,450	1,151,294	1,234,126	1,165,389
Grand total	2,538,595	3,514,172	2,480,363	3,317,346	2,588,365	3,466,554	2,855,618	3,469,039	2,891,883	3,444,781

[1] Preliminary. [2] Cut-basis with cob corn converted to cut-basis using a factor of 0.4706. *Source: National Agricultural Statistics Service, U.S. Department of Agriculture (NASS-USDA)*

Wheat

U.S. and world wheat prices showed little decisiveness during 1999, but on balance were generally on the defensive. This continued a downtrend that took hold in 1996, although at a much slower rate.

World wheat production in 1999/2000 of 578 million metric tonnes compares with 588 million in 1998/99 and the record high 1997/98 crop of 609 million tonnes. Production in the mid-1990's averaged about 540 million tonnes.

Global consumption in 1999/00 of 586 million tonnes compares with the record high 591 million in 1998/99. For the second consecutive season, a draw on carryover stocks will be necessary; the projected ending 1999/00 carryover of 128 million tonnes compares with 136 million a year earlier and the record high 139 million of two years ago. Still, carryover supplies appear adequate, certainly relative to the 106 million tonnes at yearend 1995/96, the lowest since the 1970's. The 1999/00 world stocks-to-usage ratio of about 21 percent compares with 23 percent a year earlier.

Since the late 1980's, China has been the world's largest single wheat producer with nearly 20 percent of total production, 117 million tonnes in 1999/00 vs. 116 million in 1998/99. China's wheat acreage appears to have stabilized near 29.5 million hectares, but average yield improved during the 1990's. China's 1999/00 domestic wheat usage was forecast at a record large 117 million tonnes, marginally higher than in 1998/99. Despite the moderate supply/demand imbalance, China's 1999/00 imports of only 1.5 million tonnes pale relative to numbers earlier in the 1990's when imports over 10 million tonnes were not unusual. China's carryover increased during the late 1990's, but the marketplace tends to view the government's official totals as suspect: the ending 1999/00 carryover of 27.1 million tonnes compares with 28.1 million a year earlier. What seems more certain is that China's import needs are very price sensitive and world prices can quickly strengthen on talk, real or otherwise, of Chinese buying which, in turn, brakes their interest.

The persistent decline during the 1990's in the former U.S.S.R.'s wheat production may have been finally stabilized. 1999/00 production totals were forecast in the key republics at: Russia, 31 million tonnes vs. 27 million in 1998/99; Kazakstan at 7.5 million vs. 4.7 million; and the Ukraine at 14 million vs. 15 million, respectively. The larger crops reflect some improvement in average yield amidst little change in acreage.

The Russian Federation was once the world's largest importer. Russia's 1999/00 imports of only 2.2 million tonnes compare with 14 million tonnes early in the 1990's, the drop reflecting a chronic lack of foreign exchange and credit. Consumption among the Russian republics has also fallen with Russia's use estimated at 33 million tonnes in 1999/00 vs. 35 million in 1998/99, and more than 50 million on average early in the 1990's. The Ukraine's 1999/00 usage of 12 million tonnes compares with the early 1990's average of more than 20 million.

The 1999/00 world wheat trade is forecast at a near record large 101.2 million tonnes vs. 100.2 million in 1998/99. Four countries generally account for about two-thirds of total exports: Argentina, Australia, Canada and the U.S., with the E.U. supplying much of the balance. The U.S., the single largest exporter, is forecast to ship 30.5 million tonnes in 1999/00 vs. 29 million in 1998/99. Canadian 1999/00 exports are forecast at 17.5 million tonnes vs. 14.5 million in 1998/99; and E.U. exports of 16 million tonnes are about unchanged. Australian exports have soared to 17.5 million tonnes in 1999/00 from a mid-1990's average of less than 10 million. Importing nations are scattered; among those taking at least 5 million tonnes in 1999/00 are Brazil, Egypt and Japan.

The U.S. 1999 wheat crop (June/May) of 2.31 billion bushels compares with 2.55 million in 1998/99, the decline reflecting an average yield of 42.7 bushels per acre vs. 43.2 and, more importantly, a drop in harvested acreage to 54.3 million acres from 59 million, respectively. Winter wheat accounts for more than half of U.S. production: 1.7 billion bushels in 1999/00 vs. 1.9 billion in 1998/99. Kansas is the largest producing state with 432 million bushels in 1999/00. North Dakota is the largest spring wheat and durum producing state. The 1999/00 durum wheat crop of 110 million bushels compares with 138 million in 1998/99. Other spring wheat production was put at 509 million bushels vs. 528 million, respectively.

The U.S. imports some wheat, mostly from Canada. Carry-in stocks as of June 1, 1999, of 946 million bushels, compare with 722 million a year earlier. The U.S. wheat supply for 1999/00 of 3.37 billion bushels is about unchanged from 1998/99. Total usage in 1999/00 of 2.38 billion bushels compares with 2.43 billion in 1998/99. Exports generally account for almost half the total disappearance. Food use takes about two-thirds of domestic usage; feed about 20 percent, and seed the balance. If the 1999/00 supply/demand estimates are realized, U.S. ending stocks on May 31, 2000, would rise to at least 986 million bushels, boosting the stock-to-use ratio to 41 percent vs. 39 percent a year earlier. This ratio is often used to forecast prices, the smaller it is the greater the likelihood for higher prices as the crop year progresses.

The 1999/00 average price received by farmers was forecast to range from $2.45 to $2.65 a bushel vs. $2.65 in 1998/99 and the 1990's high of $4.55 in 1995/96.

Futures Markets

Wheat futures and options are traded on the Mercado a Termino de Buenos Aires (MAT), Sydney Futures Exchange (SFE), London International Financial Futures and Options Exchange (LIFFE), the Chicago Board of Trade (CBOT), the Kansas City Board of Trade (KCBT), the Minneapolis Grain Exchange (MGE) and the Mid-America Commodity Exchange (MidAm). Feed wheat futures and options are traded on the Winnipeg Commodity Exchange (WCE), futures only on the Budapest Commodity Exchange. Milling wheat futures and options are traded on the Budapest Commodity Exchange, futures only on the ParisBourse SA.

World Production of Wheat In Thousands of Metric Tons

Year	Argentina	Australia	Canada	China	France	Germany	India	Pakistan	Russia	Turkey	United Kingdom	United States	World Total
1990-1	10,900	15,066	32,098	98,229	33,600	15,242	49,850	14,429	49,596	16,000	14,000	74,292	587,995
1991-2	9,880	10,557	31,946	96,000	34,594	16,610	55,134	14,565	38,900	16,500	14,400	53,891	542,132
1992-3	9,800	16,184	29,871	101,590	32,777	15,542	55,690	15,684	46,170	15,500	14,000	67,135	561,807
1993-4	9,700	16,479	27,232	106,390	29,630	15,767	57,210	16,157	43,500	16,500	12,890	65,220	559,316
1994-5	11,300	8,903	23,122	99,300	30,550	16,480	59,840	15,212	32,100	14,700	13,314	63,167	525,196
1995-6	8,600	16,504	25,037	102,215	30,860	17,760	65,470	17,002	30,100	15,500	14,310	59,404	538,547
1996-7	15,900	23,702	29,801	110,570	35,940	18,920	62,097	16,907	34,900	16,000	16,100	61,980	582,751
1997-8[1]	14,800	19,417	24,280	123,389	33,760	19,830	69,350	16,650	44,200	16,000	15,020	67,534	609,419
1998-9[2]	12,000	22,110	24,076	109,726	39,790	20,190	66,350	18,694	26,900	18,500	15,470	69,327	589,130
1999-00[3]	14,500	23,500	26,850	115,000	37,000	19,680	70,780	17,854	31,000	16,500	14,870	62,662	584,796

[1] Preliminary. [2] Estimate. [3] Forecast. *Source: Foreign Agricultural Service, U.S. Department of Agriculture (FAS-USDA)*

World Supply and Demand of Wheat In Millions of Metric Tons/Hectares

Crop Year	Area Harvested	Yield	Production	World Trade	Utilization Total	Ending Stocks	Stocks as a % of Utilization
1990-1	231.4	2.54	588.0	101.1	561.9	145.0	25.8
1991-2	222.5	2.44	542.9	111.2	555.5	132.5	23.8
1992-3	222.9	2.52	562.4	113.0	550.3	144.5	26.3
1993-4	222.0	2.52	558.8	101.7	561.6	141.7	25.2
1994-5	214.5	2.44	524.0	101.5	547.0	118.7	21.7
1995-6	219.2	2.46	538.5	99.5	549.3	107.9	19.6
1996-7	230.3	2.53	582.8	103.6	577.1	113.5	19.7
1997-8[1]	227.9	2.67	609.4	103.3	584.6	138.3	23.7
1998-9[2]	224.7	2.62	589.1	100.5	591.9	135.6	22.9
1999-00[3]	217.3	2.69	584.8	104.2	593.1	127.2	21.5

[1] Preliminary. [2] Estimate. [3] Forecast. *Source: Foreign Agricultural Service, U.S. Department of Agriculture (FAS-USDA)*

Salient Statistics of Wheat in the United States

Crop Year	Planting Intentions	Acreage Harvested: Winter	Spring	All	Average - All Yield Per Acre in Bushels	Value of Production $1,000	Foreign Trade[5]: Domestic Exports[2]	Imports[3]	Per Capita[4] Consumption: Flour	Cereal
	1,000 Acres						In Millions of Bushels		In Pounds	
1990-1	77,041	49,721	19,382	69,103	39.5	7,166,888	1,069.5	36.4	136.0	4.3
1991-2	69,881	39,506	18,297	57,803	34.3	5,954,912	1,282.3	40.7	137.0	4.5
1992-3	72,219	42,123	20,638	62,761	39.3	8,009,711	1,353.6	69.4	139.0	4.7
1993-4	72,168	43,811	18,901	62,712	38.2	7,647,527	1,227.8	108.9	143.0	5.0
1994-5	70,349	41,335	20,415	61,770	37.6	7,968,237	1,188.3	91.9	144.0	5.2
1995-6	69,132	40,972	19,973	60,945	35.8	9,787,213	1,241.1	67.9	142.0	5.4
1996-7	75,105	39,574	23,245	62,819	36.3	9,782,238	1,001.5	92.3	149.0	5.4
1997-8	70,412	41,340	21,500	62,840	39.5	8,286,741	1,040.4	94.9	150.0	5.4
1998-9	65,821	40,126	18,876	59,002	43.2	6,780,623	1,042.4	103.0	-----	-----
1999-00[1]	62,814	35,572	18,337	53,909	42.7	5,903,501	1,050.0	95.0	-----	-----

[1] Preliminary. [2] Includes flour milled from imported wheat. [3] Total wheat, flour & other products. [4] Civilian only. [5] Year beginning June.
Source: Economic Research Service, U.S. Department of Agriculture (ERS-USDA)

Supply and Distribution of Wheat in the United States In Millions of Bushels

Crop Year Beginning June 1	Supply: Stocks, June 1: On Farms	Mills, Elevators[3]	Totl Stocks	Production	Imports[4]	Total Supply	Domestic Disappearance: Food	Seed	Feed & Residual[5]	Total	Exports[4]	Total Disappearance
1990-1	212.5	324.0	536.5	2,729.8	36.4	3,302.6	789.8	92.9	482.4	1,365.1	1,069.5	2,434.5
1991-2	341.2	524.7	868.1	1,980.1	40.7	2,889.0	789.5	97.7	244.5	1,131.7	1,282.3	2,413.9
1992-3	144.6	327.2	475.0	2,466.8	70.0	3,011.8	834.8	99.1	193.6	1,127.5	1,353.6	2,481.2
1993-4	183.8	345.3	530.7	2,396.4	108.8	3,035.9	871.7	96.3	271.7	1,239.7	1,227.8	2,467.4
1994-5	175.3	393.2	568.5	2,321.0	91.9	2,981.4	853.0	89.0	344.5	1,286.6	1,188.3	2,474.8
1995-6	163.4	343.2	506.6	2,182.7	67.9	2,757.2	882.9	103.5	153.7	1,140.1	1,241.1	2,381.2
1996-7	74.6	301.4	376.0	2,277.4	92.3	2,745.7	890.8	102.3	307.6	1,300.7	1,001.4	2,302.1
1997-8	154.6	289.0	443.6	2,481.5	94.9	3,020.0	914.1	92.6	250.5	1,257.1	1,040.4	2,297.5
1998-9[1]	224.2	498.3	722.5	2,547.3	103.0	3,372.8	907.3	80.7	396.6	1,384.5	1,042.4	2,426.9
1999-00[2]	277.7	667.2	945.9	2,302.4	95.0	3,343.4	905.0	91.0	300.0	1,296.0	1,050.0	2,346.0

[1] Preliminary. [2] Estimate. [3] Also warehouses and all off-farm storage not otherwise designated, including flour mills. [4] Imports & exports are for wheat, including flour & other products in terms of wheat. [5] Mostly feed use. *Source: Economic Research Service, U.S. Department of Agriculture*

Stocks, Production and Exports of Wheat in the United States, by Class In Millions of Bushels

Year Beginning June 1	Hard Spring Stocks June 1	Hard Spring Production	Hard Spring Exports[3]	Durum[2] Stocks June 1	Durum[2] Production	Durum[2] Exports[3]	Hard Winter Stocks June 1	Hard Winter Production	Hard Winter Exports[3]	Soft Red Winter Stocks June 1	Soft Red Winter Production	Soft Red Winter Exports[3]	White Stocks June 1	White Production	White Exports[3]
1990-1	155	555	201	50	122	53	215	1,196	369	32	547	230	85	313	216
1991-2	279	431	380	62	104	45	360	901	559	80	325	105	87	219	193
1992-3	131	707	438	55	100	47	194	967	464	41	427	210	54	266	195
1993-4	171	512	266	49	71	54	204	1,066	486	43	401	173	64	347	249
1994-5	201	515	292	28	97	40	227	971	422	45	434	212	67	304	222
1995-6	193	475	230	26	102	39	194	825	384	37	456	250	57	325	238
1996-7	106	631	300	25	116	38	154	759	286	35	420	140	55	352	237
1997-8	166	491	240	31	88	57	143	1,098	358	45	472	180	59	332	205
1998-9	220	486	247	26	138	40	307	1,180	453	80	443	105	90	301	198
1999-00[1]	233	448	220	55	99	40	435	1,055	490	136	453	150	87	247	150

[1] Preliminary. [2] Includes Red Durum. [3] Includes four made from U.S. wheat & shipments to territories. *Source: Economic Research Service, U.S. Department of Agriculture (ERS-USDA)*

Seeded Acreage, Yield and Production of all Wheat in the United States

Year	Seeded Acreage -- 1,000 Acres: Winter	Other Spring	Durum	All	Yield Per Harvested Acre (Bushels): Winter	Other Spring	Durum	All	Production (1,000,000 Bushels): Winter	Other Spring	Durum	All
1990	56,748	16,723	3,570	77,041	40.7	36.7	34.9	39.5	2,024.2	583.1	122.4	2,729.8
1991	51,024	15,604	3,253	69,881	34.7	33.4	32.5	34.3	1,371.6	504.6	104.0	1,980.1
1992	50,922	18,750	2,547	72,219	38.2	41.8	39.7	39.3	1,609.3	757.6	99.9	2,466.8
1993	51,587	18,340	2,241	72,168	40.2	33.7	33.6	38.2	1,760.1	565.8	70.5	2,396.4
1994	49,197	18,329	2,823	70,349	40.2	31.8	35.6	37.6	1,661.9	562.3	96.7	2,321.0
1995	48,686	17,010	3,436	69,132	37.7	32.2	30.5	35.8	1,544.7	535.7	102.3	2,182.6
1996	51,445	20,030	3,630	75,105	37.1	35.1	32.6	36.3	1,469.6	691.7	116.1	2,277.4
1997	47,985	19,117	3,310	70,412	44.6	29.9	27.6	39.5	1,845.5	548.2	87.8	2,481.5
1998	46,449	15,567	3,805	65,821	46.9	34.9	37.0	43.2	1,880.7	528.5	138.1	2,547.3
1999[1]	43,431	15,348	4,035	62,814	47.8	34.1	27.8	42.7	1,700.0	503.1	99.3	2,302.4

[1] Preliminary. *Source: Economic Research Service, U.S. Department of Agriculture (ERS-USDA)*

Production of Winter Wheat in the United States, by State In Thousands of Bushels

Year	Colorado	Idaho	Illinois	Kansas	Missouri	Montana	Nebraska	Ohio	Oklahoma	Oregon	Texas	Washington	Total
1990	84,150	69,000	91,200	472,000	76,000	87,500	85,500	79,650	201,600	54,600	130,200	138,600	2,024,224
1991	71,300	49,000	44,800	363,000	48,000	76,000	67,200	52,920	135,000	41,600	84,000	40,600	1,371,617
1992	70,500	55,250	62,100	363,800	64,800	65,250	55,500	59,095	168,150	42,900	129,200	102,000	1,609,284
1993	94,350	67,150	68,200	388,500	53,200	102,900	73,500	52,520	156,600	61,060	118,400	162,500	1,760,143
1994	76,500	56,880	50,400	433,200	50,400	64,750	71,400	68,440	143,100	55,680	75,400	124,200	1,661,943
1995	102,600	58,520	68,110	286,000	47,970	54,800	86,100	73,810	109,200	57,750	75,600	133,300	1,544,653
1996	70,400	68,800	41,800	255,200	48,750	61,380	73,500	51,870	93,100	58,680	75,400	164,500	1,469,618
1997	86,400	68,800	66,490	501,400	58,320	55,100	70,300	68,670	169,600	53,790	118,900	141,900	1,845,528
1998	99,450	63,140	57,600	494,900	57,500	48,750	82,800	74,240	198,900	52,930	136,500	136,500	1,880,733
1999[1]	103,200	53,960	60,600	432,400	44,160	36,860	86,400	72,100	150,500	29,610	122,400	96,860	1,699,989

[1] Preliminary. *Source: Crop Reporting Board, U.S. Department of Agriculture (CRB-USDA)*

Official Winter Wheat Crop Production Reports in the United States In Thousands of Bushels

Crop Year	May 1	June 1	July 1	August 1	September 1	Current December	Final
1990-1	2,091,614	2,089,234	2,035,087	2,054,287	2,036,059	-----	2,030,874
1991-2	1,495,943	1,449,418	1,361,316	1,371,946	1,372,182	-----	1,372,617
1992-3	1,618,017	1,618,017	1,573,901	1,600,931	-----	-----	1,609,284
1993-4	1,807,657	1,824,062	1,821,345	1,788,005	1,788,005	-----	1,760,143
1994-5	1,657,938	1,674,563	1,658,426	1,670,436	1,670,436	-----	1,661,043
1995-6	1,638,211	1,608,396	1,529,950	1,552,230	1,552,230	-----	1,544,653
1996-7	1,363,851	1,369,861	1,484,836	1,494,716	-----	-----	1,477,058
1997-8	1,561,470	1,603,580	1,780,554	1,855,474	-----	-----	1,845,528
1998-9	1,706,784	1,743,294	1,898,719	1,914,359	-----	-----	1,880,733
1999-00[1]	1,614,799	1,611,559	1,673,222	1,688,582	-----	-----	1,699,989

[1] Preliminary. *Source: Crop Reporting Board, U.S. Department of Agriculture (CRB-USDA)*

Production of All Spring Wheat in the United States, by State In Thousands of Bushels

	Durum Wheat						Other Spring Wheat							
Year	Arizona	California	Montana	North Dakota	South Dakota	Total Durum	Idaho	Minnesota	Montana	North Dakota	Oregon	South Dakota	Washington	Total Other
1990	4,136	5,346	4,465	103,700	3,204	122,171	30,600	134,750	53,900	277,200	3,016	67,200	11,480	583,124
1991	3,705	3,360	5,907	88,350	1,675	103,957	32,660	64,170	81,600	212,350	2,300	49,000	58,000	504,565
1992	3,740	5,115	4,851	81,700	990	99,906	44,840	137,500	79,050	382,200	4,900	85,000	17,640	757,608
1993	4,500	3,800	3,534	57,970	432	70,476	43,200	69,750	99,900	274,350	3,900	54,540	15,080	565,821
1994	8,554	5,605	5,340	76,375	598	96,747	43,400	70,000	100,500	278,775	2,900	51,480	9,800	562,291
1995	8,514	6,800	7,950	77,760	896	102,280	44,800	70,400	133,000	221,400	5,928	33,600	20,470	535,658
1996	14,760	13,800	7,000	79,380	720	116,090	50,400	105,000	106,600	313,500	6,405	83,250	18,170	691,680
1997	8,010	13,680	7,540	57,860	513	87,783	45,030	75,200	118,900	210,000	6,600	63,000	23,220	548,155
1998	15,120	15,750	12,040	94,400	624	138,119	39,270	78,720	108,000	211,200	4,560	59,200	20,925	528,469
1999[1]	7,275	8,925	9,450	72,000	1,512	99,322	50,560	78,000	108,000	168,000	5,049	59,850	27,280	503,132

[1] Preliminary. *Source: Crop Reporting Board, U.S. Department of Agriculture (CRB-USDA)*

Grindings of Wheat by Mills in the United States In Millions of Bushels (60 Pounds Each)

Year	July	Aug.	Sept.	Oct.	Nov.	Dec.	Jan.	Feb.	Mar.	Apr.	May	June	Total
1990-1	62.3	73.2	65.7	74.9	73.9	64.3	66.7	65.2	63.2	67.6	69.9	60.9	807.8
1991-2	65.3	71.2	67.7	72.2	73.5	65.6	65.7	66.0	65.6	67.3	67.0	67.2	814.3
1992-3	70.0	77.3	71.9	77.9	71.9	65.5	68.1	70.0	76.2	72.0	69.6	67.9	858.2
1993-4	69.2	75.2	74.1	75.8	77.0	76.3	70.0	68.3	81.1	73.0	73.0	70.6	883.8
1994-5	68.9	78.7	76.3	77.9	75.9	71.1	69.0	65.2	76.9	66.6	74.7	71.9	873.1
1995-6	69.8	77.8	74.2	78.4	74.8	70.0	70.1	72.4	72.1	69.4	72.6	67.7	869.1
1996-7	73.6	77.4	75.1	82.7	73.7	71.3	69.6	66.9	70.3	73.2	72.5	72.2	878.6
1997-8	76.4	75.8	78.4	82.7	75.3	74.8	-----	215.5	-----	-----	216.6	-----	895.5
1998-9	-----	224.7	-----	-----	238.6	-----	-----	212.8	-----	-----	226.7	-----	902.8
1999-00[1]	-----	230.9	-----	-----	239.5	-----	-----		-----	-----		-----	940.8

[1] Preliminary. *Source: Bureau of the Census, U.S. Department of Commerce*

Wheat Stocks in the United States In Millions of Bushels

	On Farms				Off Farms				Total Stocks			
Year	Mar. 1	June 1	Sept. 1	Dec. 1	Mar. 1	June 1	Sept. 1	Dec. 1	Mar. 1	June 1	Sept. 1	Dec. 1
1990	376.0	212.5	1,000.0	763.2	567.1	324.0	1,409.5	1,144.8	943.1	536.5	2,409.5	1,909.5
1991	532.9	341.2	828.0	564.8	863.3	524.7	1,212.7	877.3	1,396.3	865.9	2,040.7	1,442.1
1992	275.6	144.6	979.4	672.0	611.7	327.2	1,128.2	918.5	887.2	471.9	2,107.6	1,590.5
1993	378.0	183.8	987.0	653.1	670.3	346.8	1,145.6	932.6	1,048.3	530.7	2,132.6	1,585.7
1994	363.2	175.3	859.8	575.6	664.8	393.2	1,209.7	920.6	1,028.0	568.5	2,069.5	1,491.1
1995	335.3	163.4	743.6	477.0	633.8	343.2	1,137.5	861.3	969.1	506.6	1,881.1	1,338.3
1996	220.6	74.6	824.5	584.2	602.9	301.4	899.7	634.7	823.5	376.0	1,724.2	1,218.8
1997	320.8	154.6	794.4	604.0	501.1	289.0	1,282.0	1,015.2	821.8	443.6	2,076.3	1,619.2
1998	399.9	224.2	885.7	680.2	766.6	498.3	1,499.6	1,215.5	1,166.6	722.5	2,385.3	1,895.7
1999[1]	471.2	277.7	888.1	648.8	979.2	668.2	1,557.0	1,230.2	1,450.4	945.9	2,445.0	1,879.0

[1] Preliminary. *Source: National Agricultural Statistics Service, U.S. Department of Agriculture (NASS-USDA)*

Wheat Supply and Distribution in Canada, Australia and Argentina In Millions of Metric Tons

	Canada (Year Beginning Aug. 1)					Australia (Year Beginning Oct. 1)					Argentina (Year Beginning Dec. 1)				
	Supply			Disappearance		Supply			Disappearance		Supply			Disappearance	
Crop Year	Stocks Aug. 1	New Crop	Total Supply	Domestic	Exports[3]	Stocks Oct. 1	New Crop	Total Supply	Domestic	Exports[3]	Stocks Dec. 1	New Crop	Total Supply	Domestic	Exports[3]
1990-1	6.4	32.1	38.5	6.6	21.7	3.0	15.1	18.1	3.5	11.8	0	10.9	10.9	4.5	5.6
1991-2	10.3	31.9	42.2	7.8	24.5	2.8	10.6	13.4	3.4	7.1	.8	9.9	10.7	4.6	5.8
1992-3	10.1	29.9	40.0	8.1	19.7	2.9	16.2	19.1	4.2	9.9	.3	9.8	10.1	4.3	5.9
1993-4	12.2	27.2	39.4	9.3	19.1	5.0	16.5	21.5	4.1	13.7	0	9.7	9.7	4.3	5.0
1994-5	11.1	23.1	34.2	7.8	20.9	3.7	8.9	12.7	3.9	6.3	.4	11.3	11.7	4.3	7.3
1995-6	5.7	25.0	30.7	7.8	16.3	2.4	16.5	18.9	4.2	13.3	.2	8.6	8.8	4.2	4.5
1996-7	6.7	29.8	36.5	8.2	19.5	1.5	23.7	25.2	3.6	19.2	.2	15.9	16.1	5.1	10.2
1997-8	9.0	24.3	33.3	7.3	20.1	2.4	19.4	21.8	5.2	15.3	.8	14.8	15.6	4.5	10.7
1998-9[1]	6.0	24.1	30.1	8.2	14.7	1.3	22.1	23.4	5.1	16.0	.4	12.0	12.4	3.9	8.2
1999-00[2]	7.4	26.9	34.3	8.5	18.5	2.4	23.5	25.9	5.1	18.5	.3	14.5	14.8	4.5	10.0

[1] Preliminary. [2] Forecast. [3] Including flour. *Source: Foreign Agricultural Service, U.S. Department of Agriculture (FAS-USDA)*

WHEAT

Quarterly Supply and Disappearance of Wheat in the United States In Millions of Bushels

Crop Year Beginning June 1	Supply: Beginning Stocks	Supply: Production	Supply: Imports[3]	Supply: Total Supply	Disappearance, Domestic Use: Food	Domestic Use: Seed	Domestic Use: Feed & Residual[7]	Domestic Use: Total	Exports[3]	Total Disappearance	Ending Stocks: Gov't Owned[4]	Ending Stocks: Privately Owned[5]	Ending Stocks: Total Stocks
1989-90	701.6	2,036.6	23.4	2,760.7	748.9	104.3	139.1	992.3	1,232.0	2,224.3	116.6	419.9	536.5
June-Aug.	701.6	2,036.6	5.9	2,744.1	190.7	1.7	264.9	457.3	368.7	826.0	167.9	1,750.1	1,918.0
Sept.-Nov.	1,918.0	-----	7.1	1,925.1	191.7	70.3	-87.8	174.2	328.6	502.8	154.5	1,268.0	1,422.5
Dec.-Feb.	1,423.0	-----	4.7	1,427.1	184.3	2.7	37.4	224.4	259.6	484.0	136.5	806.6	943.1
Mar.-May	943.1	-----	5.8	947.9	182.2	29.6	-75.4	136.4	275.1	411.5	116.6	419.9	536.5
1990-1	536.5	2,729.8	36.4	3,302.6	789.8	92.9	482.4	1,365.1	1,069.5	2,434.6	162.7	705.4	868.1
June-Aug.	536.5	2,729.8	8.0	3,274.2	194.1	1.7	399.7	595.5	267.7	863.2	104.6	2,306.5	2,411.1
Sept.-Nov.	2,409.5	-----	13.4	2,424.5	210.6	62.9	-38.3	235.2	279.4	514.6	129.9	1,780.0	1,909.9
Dec.-Feb.	1,908.0	-----	7.8	1,917.7	191.0	2.1	101.5	294.6	225.5	520.1	152.5	1,245.2	1,397.7
Mar.-May	1,396.0	-----	7.2	1,404.9	194.1	26.3	19.5	239.9	296.9	536.8	162.7	705.4	868.1
1991-2	868.1	1,980.1	40.7	2,889.0	789.5	97.2	244.5	1,131.2	1,282.3	2,413.5	152.0	323.0	475.0
June-Aug.	868.1	1,980.1	7.8	2,856.1	189.4	1.2	359.1	549.7	251.7	801.4	162.8	1,891.9	2,054.7
Sept.-Nov.	2,054.7	-----	7.3	2,062.0	213.0	62.2	-26.9	248.3	365.9	614.2	160.7	1,287.1	1,447.8
Dec.-Feb.	1,447.8	-----	10.7	1,458.5	192.9	2.4	-.5	194.8	371.7	566.5	156.9	735.1	892.0
Mar.-May	892.0	-----	14.9	906.9	194.2	31.9	-87.3	138.8	293.0	431.8	152.0	323.0	475.0
1992-3	475.0	2,466.8	70.0	3,011.8	834.3	99.1	194.2	1,127.6	1,353.6	2,481.2	150.0	380.7	530.7
June-Aug.	475.0	2,466.8	20.1	2,962.0	212.1	1.4	345.3	558.8	282.6	841.4	151.6	1,969.0	2,120.6
Sept.-Nov.	2,120.6	-----	16.4	2,137.0	218.8	63.4	-81.9	200.3	345.0	545.3	151.1	1,440.6	1,591.7
Dec.-Feb.	1,591.7	-----	17.4	1,609.1	196.7	2.6	5.2	204.5	356.3	560.8	150.4	897.9	1,048.3
Mar.-May	1,048.3	-----	16.1	1,064.4	206.7	31.7	-74.4	164.0	369.7	533.7	150.0	380.7	530.7
1993-4	530.7	2,396.4	108.8	3,035.9	871.7	96.3	271.7	1,239.7	1,227.8	2,467.4	150.3	418.2	568.5
June-Aug.	530.7	2,396.4	14.6	2,941.7	211.3	1.3	295.8	508.4	300.7	809.1	149.9	1,982.7	2,132.6
Sept.-Nov.	2,132.6	-----	30.1	2,162.7	225.3	60.9	-38.5	247.7	329.2	577.0	150.3	1,435.4	1,585.7
Dec.-Feb.	1,585.7	-----	26.9	1,612.6	211.0	2.3	39.0	252.3	332.3	584.6	150.4	877.6	1,028.0
Mar.-May	1,028.0	-----	37.2	1,065.2	224.1	31.8	-24.7	231.2	265.5	496.7	150.3	418.2	568.5
1994-5	568.5	2,321.0	92.0	2,981.4	852.5	89.2	344.9	1,286.6	1,188.3	2,474.9	142.1	364.5	506.6
June-Aug.	568.5	2,321.0	30.7	2,920.2	213.2	1.6	376.3	591.1	259.6	850.7	146.4	1,923.1	2,069.5
Sept.-Nov.	2,069.5	-----	21.4	2,090.9	229.3	61.1	-28.8	261.6	338.2	599.8	142.8	1,348.3	1,491.1
Dec.-Feb.	1,491.1	-----	17.7	1,508.8	201.5	2.2	25.6	229.3	310.4	539.7	142.3	826.8	969.1
Mar.-May	969.1	-----	22.2	991.2	208.5	24.3	-28.2	204.6	280.1	484.7	142.1	364.5	506.6
1995-6	506.6	2,182.6	67.9	2,757.1	882.9	104.1	153.0	1,139.9	1,241.1	2,381.1	118.2	257.8	376.0
June-Aug.	506.6	2,182.6	22.7	2,711.9	215.3	8.0	305.0	528.3	302.5	830.8	141.5	1,739.6	1,881.1
Sept.-Nov.	1,881.1	-----	16.3	1,897.4	232.2	64.9	-98.7	198.3	360.8	559.1	141.2	1,197.1	1,338.3
Dec.-Feb.	1,338.3	-----	11.8	1,350.0	215.8	3.0	13.3	232.1	294.5	526.6	137.5	686.0	823.5
Mar.-May	823.5	-----	17.2	840.7	219.6	28.2	-66.5	181.3	283.4	464.6	118.2	257.8	376.0
1996-7	376.0	2,277.0	92.4	2,753.5	891.4	103.1	314.0	1,308.5	1,001.4	2,309.9	93.0	350.6	443.6
June-Aug.	376.0	2,277.0	14.9	2,676.0	223.7	8.8	385.3	617.8	334.1	951.9	109.5	1,614.7	1,724.2
Sept.-Nov.	1,724.2	-----	20.7	1,744.9	233.8	60.4	-76.4	217.8	308.3	526.1	96.1	1,122.7	1,218.8
Dec.-Feb.	1,218.8	-----	27.1	1,245.9	213.1	1.8	29.9	244.8	179.3	424.1	95.3	726.5	821.8
Mar.-May	821.8	-----	29.7	851.6	220.8	32.1	-24.8	228.1	179.8	407.9	93.0	350.6	443.6
1997-8	443.6	2,481.0	96.0	3,020.0	917.0	93.0	248.0	1,258.0	1,040.0	2,298.0	93.0	581.2	722.0
June-Aug.	443.6	2,481.0	23.0	2,948.0	228.0	3.0	352.0	583.0	288.0	871.0	93.2	1,983.1	2,076.0
Sept.-Nov.	2,076.0	-----	23.0	2,099.0	239.0	59.0	-113.0	185.0	296.0	481.0	93.1	1,521.8	1,619.0
Dec.-Feb.	1,619.0	-----	24.0	1,643.0	220.0	2.0	-1.0	221.0	255.0	476.0			1,167.0
Mar.-May	1,167.0	-----	26.0	1,192.0	230.0	29.0	10.0	269.0	201.0	470.0			722.0
1998-9[1]	722.0	2,547.0	103.0	3,285.0	908.0	80.0	396.0	1,384.0	1,042.0	2,426.0			946.0
June-Aug.	722.0	2,547.0	24.0	3,294.0	226.0	1.0	425.0	652.0	257.0	909.0			2,385.0
Sept.-Nov.	2,385.0	-----	24.0	2,409.0	241.0	55.0	-74.0	222.0	292.0	514.0			1,896.0
Dec.-Feb.	1,896.0	-----	28.0	1,924.0	213.0	1.0	12.0	226.0	246.0	472.0			1,450.0
Mar.-May	1,450.0	-----	27.0	1,478.0	228.0	23.0	33.0	284.0	247.0	531.0			946.0
1999-00[2]	946.0	2,302.0	95.0	3,343.0	905.0	91.0	300.0	1,296.0	1,050.0	2,346.0			997.0
June-Aug.	946.0	2,302.0	31.0	3,279.0	224.0	6.0	279.0	509.0	325.0	834.0			2,445.0
Sept.-Nov.	2,445.0	-----	19.0	2,465.0	238.0	54.0	2.0	294.0	291.0	585.0			1,879.0

[1] Preliminary. [2] Forecast. [3] Imports & exports include flour and other products expressed in wheat equivalent. [4] Uncommitted, Government only. [5] Includes total loans. [6] Less than 50,000 bushels. [7] Includes alcoholic beverages. *Source: Economic Research Service, U.S. Department of Agriculture (ERS-USDA)*

Wheat Government Loan Program Data in the United States Loan Rates (Cents Per Bushel)

Crop Year Beginning June 1	Farm Loan Prices: National Average	Target Rate	Corn Belt (Soft Red Winter)	Central & Southern Plains (Hard Winter)	Northern Plains (Spring & Durum)	Pacific Northwest (White)	Placed Under Loan	% of Production	Acquired by CCC Under Program	Stocks Ending May 31: Total Stocks	Total CCC Stocks	Outstanding: CCC Loans	Outstanding: Farmer-Owned Reserve	"Free"
							In Millions of Bushels							
1991-2	204	400	209	200	204	214	143	7.2	1	475	152	20	50	273
1992-3	221	400	232	220	221	237	240	9.8	0.1	531	150	47	28	353
1993-4	245	400	251	243	245	269	258	14.7	0.3	569	150	0	6	413
1994-5	258	400	253	257	258	271	231	10.0	0	507	142	0	0	365
1995-6	258	400	254	258	258	276	114	5.2	0	376	118	13	0	258
1996-7	258	NA	253	257	258	271	194	8.1	0	444	93	72	0	351
1997-8[1]	258	NA	253	257	258	271	248		0	723	94	134	0	629
1998-9[2]	258	NA								946	128	100	0	818

[1] Preliminary. [2] Estimate. [3] The national average loan rate at the farm as a percentage of the parity-priced wheat at the beginning of the marketing year. [4] Beginning with the 1996-7 marketing year, target prices are no longer applicable. NA = Not avaliable. *Source: Agricultural Marketing Service, U.S. Department of Agriculture (AMS-USDA)*

Exports of Wheat (Only)[2] from the United States In Thousands of Bushels

Year	June	July	Aug.	Sept.	Oct.	Nov.	Dec.	Jan.	Feb.	Mar.	Apr.	May	Total
1991-2	59,167	79,319	97,794	94,991	124,155	136,385	112,771	132,413	115,126	103,024	116,850	59,764	1,231,759
1992-3	75,045	96,382	99,290	92,723	132,232	108,235	111,389	111,584	118,607	118,782	126,845	104,540	1,295,653
1993-4	85,874	103,836	100,516	104,732	100,618	112,667	121,900	109,389	87,250	96,873	71,575	82,838	1,178,068
1994-5	73,364	66,314	103,941	117,555	101,450	107,549	104,139	93,735	97,478	98,876	85,251	75,006	1,124,658
1995-6	78,355	88,649	119,797	131,424	117,679	105,535	99,175	96,085	91,876	108,800	90,373	78,303	1,206,051
1996-7	73,715	108,437	145,840	125,910	98,302	75,245	50,979	63,431	59,039	55,936	69,821	47,640	974,295
1997-8	65,654	92,465	123,141	119,029	89,331	79,528	80,906	97,090	68,972	63,914	64,623	68,359	1,013,012
1998-9	67,372	86,605	96,664	90,507	109,168	81,913	96,486	73,017	63,794	65,522	86,066	85,057	1,002,171
1999-00[1]	90,594	110,814	107,168	91,438	96,154	89,211							1,170,758

[1] Preliminary. [2] Grains. *Source: Economic Research Service, U.S. Department of Agriculture (ERS-USDA)*

United States Wheat and Wheat Flour Imports and Exports In Thousands of Bushels

Crop Year Beginning June 1	Imports: Wheat: Suitable for Milling	Wheat: Unfit for Human Consumption	Grain	Flour & Products[2]	Total	Exports: P.L. 480	Foreign Donations Sec. 416	Aid[3]	Total Concessional	CCC Export Credit	Export Exhancement Programs	Total U.S. Wheat Exports
			Wheat Equivalent			In Thousands of Metric Tons						
1990-1	25,540	NA	25,574	9,932	36,373	3,067	0	0	3,159	8,339	15,150	26,792
1991-2	30,924	NA	31,019	8,751	40,598	2,286	0	0	2,416	13,334	21,111	34,322
1992-3	56,859	NA	56,859	9,435	69,416	2,043	891	NA	4,001	8,538	21,806	36,081
1993-4	91,287	NA	91,287	11,086	108,860	2,801	0	NA	3,527	5,874	18,157	31,145
1994-5	70,561	NA	70,561	13,313	91,947	1,491	0	NA	1,948	4,202	18,073	32,088
1995-6	47,753	NA	47,753	13,493	67,933	1,530	0	NA	1,530	5,662	570	33,708
1996-7	71,727	NA	71,727	14,220	92,333	1,009	0	NA	1,155	4,844	0	24,526
1997-8[1]	73,245	NA	73,245	15,501	94,801	1,453	0	NA	1,727	4,550	0	25,791

[1] Preliminary. [2] Includes macaroni, semolina & similar products. [3] Shipment mostly under the Commodity Import Program, financed with foreign aid funds. NA = Not available. *Source: Economic Research Service, U.S. Department of Agriculture (ERS-USDA)*

Comparative Average Cash Wheat Prices In Dollars Per Bushel

Crop Year Beginning June 1	Received by U.S. Farmers	No. 2 Soft Red Winter, Chicago	No. 1 Hard Red Ordinary Protein, Kansas City	No. 2 Soft Red Winter, St. Louis	Minneapolis: No. 1 Dark Northern Spring 14%	Minneapolis: No. 1 Hard Amber Durum	No. 1 Soft White, Portland, Oregon	No. 2 Western White Pacific Northwest	No. 2 Soft White, Toledo	Export Prices[2] (U.S. $ Per Metric Ton): Australian Standard Wheat	Canada Vancouver No. 1 CWRS 13 1/2%	Argentina F.O.B. B.A.	U.S. Gulf No. 2 Hard Winter	Rotterdam C.I.F. U.S. No. 2 Hard Winter
1992-3	3.24	3.49	3.67	3.54	3.91	3.88	4.11	3.69	3.18	165	177	122	152	173
1993-4	3.26	3.22	3.60	3.23	5.02	5.76	3.53	3.12	3.16	154	192	131	141	200
1994-5	3.45	3.52	3.97	3.62	4.26	5.98	4.16	3.75	3.37	162	199	131	150	210
1995-6	4.55	4.83	5.49	4.82	5.72	7.03	5.27	4.74	4.41	198	204	178	177	221
1996-7	4.30	3.92	4.88	4.10	4.97	5.59	4.54	4.26	3.71	229	230	218	207	235
1997-8	3.38	3.29	3.71	3.43	4.31	5.47	3.78	3.41	3.12	192	181	157	160	166
1998-9	2.65	NA	3.08	2.40	3.83	4.06	3.02	NA	NA	167	167	120	126	132
1999-00[1]	2.55		2.85	2.35	3.63	4.21	3.09							

[1] Preliminary. [2] Calendar year. NA = Not available. *Source: Economic Research Service, U.S. Department of Agriculture (ERS-USDA)*

WHEAT

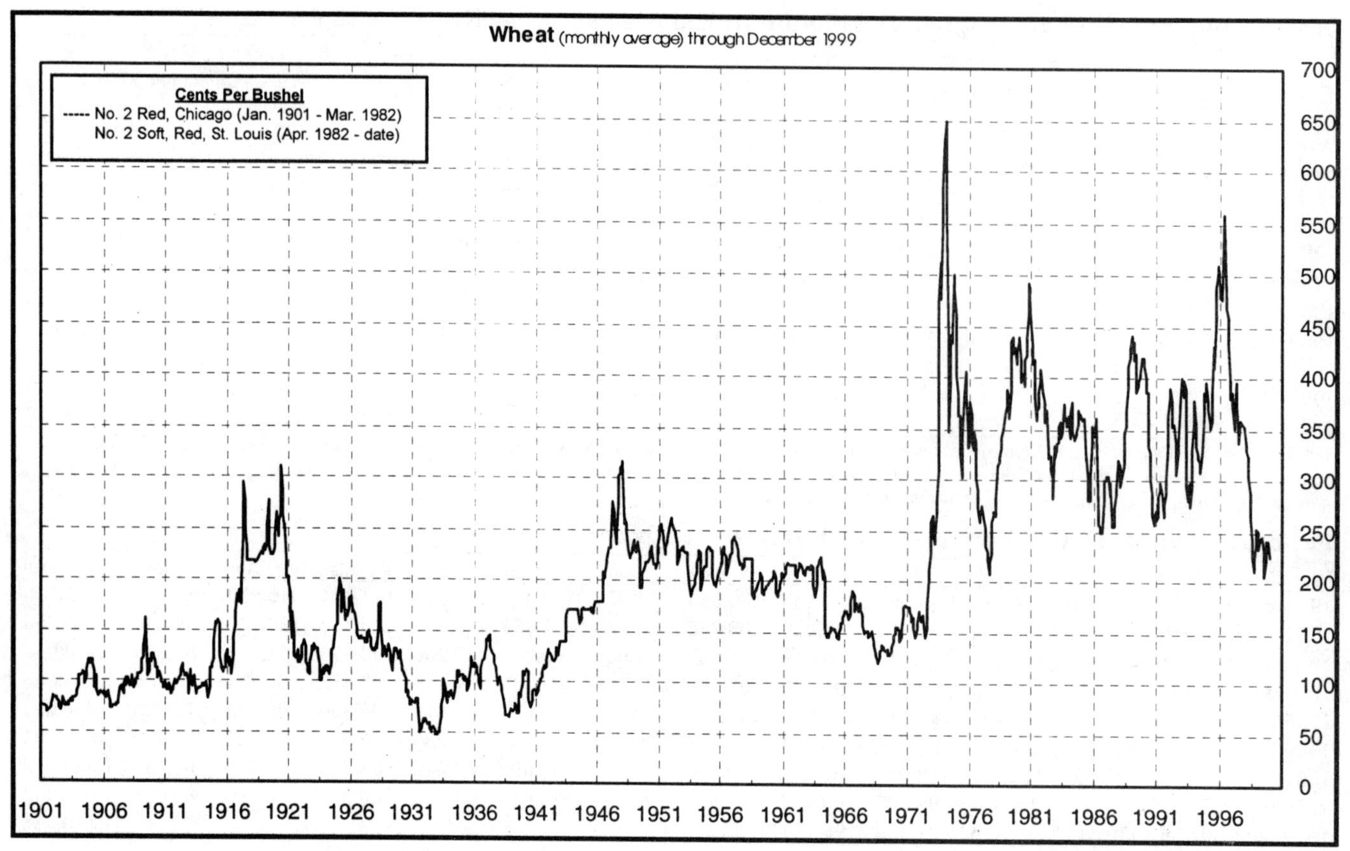

Average Price of No. 2 Soft Red Winter (30 Days) Wheat in Chicago In Dollars Per Bushel

Year	June	July	Aug.	Sept.	Oct.	Nov.	Dec.	Jan.	Feb.	Mar.	Apr.	May	Average
1989-90	3.87	3.92	3.94	3.93	4.07	4.07	4.13	4.03	3.92	3.61	3.83	3.71	3.92
1990-1	3.26	3.04	2.83	2.62	2.62	2.41	2.52	2.50	2.53	2.76	2.80	2.83	2.73
1991-2	2.86	2.79	2.97	3.24	3.50	3.57	3.79	4.12	4.15	3.71	3.53	3.68	3.49
1992-3	3.60	3.39	3.09	3.24	3.39	3.60	3.59	3.77	3.67	3.58	3.72	3.19	3.49
1993-4	2.82	3.03	3.12	2.99	3.02	3.29	3.53	3.67	3.48	3.28	3.19	3.15	3.22
1994-5	3.21	3.14	3.37	3.75	3.83	3.63	3.76	3.68	3.55	3.39	3.40	3.56	3.52
1995-6	3.91	4.41	4.28	4.53	4.72	4.85	5.04	4.92	5.10	4.99	5.65	5.57	4.83
1996-7	4.94	4.64	4.49	4.33	3.96	3.57	3.54	3.47	3.29	3.49	3.77	3.57	3.92
1997-8	3.38	3.30	3.52	3.49	3.51	3.44	3.31	3.27	3.26	3.25	2.91	2.87	3.29
1998-9[1]	2.72	2.51	2.39	2.32	2.56	2.58	2.49	2.46	2.28				2.48

[1] Preliminary. *Source: Economic Research Service, U.S. Department of Agriculture (ERS-USDA)*

Average Price[1] Received by Farmers for Wheat in the United States In Dollars Per Bushel

Year	June	July	Aug.	Sept.	Oct.	Nov.	Dec.	Jan.	Feb.	Mar.	Apr.	May	Average
1990-1	3.08	2.79	2.58	2.46	2.43	2.39	2.40	2.42	2.42	2.53	2.60	2.65	2.61
1991-2	2.55	2.50	2.63	2.80	3.07	3.25	3.44	3.54	3.78	3.72	3.65	3.64	3.00
1992-3	3.43	3.15	3.01	3.20	3.21	3.29	3.31	3.37	3.33	3.30	3.26	3.11	3.24
1993-4	2.84	2.85	2.96	3.10	3.25	3.47	3.63	3.58	3.60	3.70	3.56	3.43	3.26
1994-5	3.21	3.04	3.25	3.57	3.76	3.75	3.74	3.69	3.61	3.52	3.48	3.66	3.45
1995-6	3.84	4.10	4.26	4.53	4.72	4.81	4.88	4.83	4.98	5.07	5.32	5.73	4.55
1996-7	5.25	4.73	4.58	4.37	4.18	4.14	4.06	4.03	3.88	3.93	4.11	4.09	4.28
1997-8	3.52	3.23	3.56	3.67	3.55	3.50	3.45	3.33	3.27	3.32	3.15	3.06	3.38
1998-9	2.77	2.56	2.39	2.41	2.79	2.97	2.87	2.80	2.74	2.65	2.62	2.53	2.68
1999-00[2]	2.50	2.23	2.52	2.57	2.58	2.66	2.52	2.52					2.51

[1] Includes an allowance for unredeemed loans and purchases. [2] Preliminary. *Source: Economic Research Service, U.S. Department of Agriculture*

Average Price of No. 1 Hard Red Winter (Ordinary Protein) Wheat in Kansas City — In Dollars Per Bushel

Year	June	July	Aug.	Sept.	Oct.	Nov.	Dec.	Jan.	Feb.	Mar.	Apr.	May	Average
1990-1	3.60	3.11	2.89	2.82	2.81	2.78	2.78	2.71	2.77	2.94	2.98	3.04	2.94
1991-2	2.99	2.91	3.10	3.31	3.64	3.76	4.06	4.66	4.51	4.33	4.02	3.90	3.77
1992-3	3.91	3.52	3.27	3.56	3.60	3.78	3.81	3.97	3.75	3.74	3.59	3.51	3.67
1993-4	3.33	3.38	3.34	3.37	3.52	3.39	4.15	4.00	3.80	3.64	3.63	3.65	3.60
1994-5	3.60	3.48	3.70	4.05	4.31	4.24	4.27	4.06	3.98	3.87	3.86	4.22	3.97
1995-6	4.72	4.98	4.76	5.00	5.28	5.34	5.51	5.40	5.67	5.63	6.60	7.02	5.49
1996-7	6.12	5.34	5.01	4.70	4.76	4.78	4.70	4.61	4.52	4.58	4.78	4.61	4.88
1997-8	4.08	3.57	3.84	3.86	3.88	3.87	3.72	3.61	3.64	3.61	3.39	3.41	3.71
1998-9	3.16	3.02	2.74	2.81	3.30	3.42	3.31	3.27	3.05	3.02	2.94	2.89	3.08
1999-00[1]	2.93	2.68	2.85	2.92	2.80	2.89	2.81	2.90					2.85

[1] Preliminary. *Source: Economic Research Service, U.S. Department of Agriculture (ERS-USDA)*

Average Price of No. 1 Dark Northern Spring (14% Protein) Wheat in Minneapolis — In Dollars Per Bushel

Year	June	July	Aug.	Sept.	Oct.	Nov.	Dec.	Jan.	Feb.	Mar.	Apr.	May	Average
1990-1	3.96	3.56	3.05	2.84	2.85	2.80	2.82	2.83	2.85	3.00	3.07	3.10	3.06
1991-2	3.04	2.94	3.10	3.21	3.68	3.78	4.11	4.36	4.56	4.36	4.28	4.44	3.82
1992-3	4.42	4.04	3.65	3.79	3.85	3.94	3.88	4.05	3.87	3.87	3.80	3.71	3.91
1993-4	3.96	4.80	4.88	4.90	5.17	5.50	5.45	5.32	5.29	4.94	4.99	5.05	5.02
1994-5	4.20	4.14	4.00	4.27	4.40	4.41	4.37	4.21	4.09	4.11	4.30	4.61	4.26
1995-6	4.89	5.52	5.06	5.27	5.52	5.63	5.80	5.62	5.82	5.81	6.53	7.14	5.72
1996-7	6.73	6.04	5.29	4.63	4.69	4.64	4.51	4.62	4.45	4.62	4.78	4.58	4.97
1997-8	4.44	4.36	4.49	4.36	4.35	4.42	4.27	4.12	4.15	4.26	4.29	4.24	4.31
1998-9	4.01	3.89	3.58	3.53	4.03	4.15	3.97	3.92	3.78	3.79	3.65	3.61	3.83
1999-00[1]	3.73	3.68	3.58	3.55	3.70	3.78	3.64	3.37					3.63

[1] Preliminary. *Source: Economic Research Service, U.S. Department of Agriculture (ERS-USDA)*

Average Farm Prices of Winter Wheat in the United States — In Dollars Per Bushel

Year	June	July	Aug.	Sept.	Oct.	Nov.	Dec.	Jan.	Feb.	Mar.	Apr.	May	Average
1992-3	3.36	3.13	2.99	3.24	3.30	3.31	3.41	3.47	3.39	3.32	3.20	3.03	3.26
1993-4	2.72	2.76	2.83	2.88	3.00	3.21	3.43	3.41	3.36	3.26	3.24	3.17	3.11
1994-5	3.09	2.99	3.23	3.57	3.79	3.76	3.75	3.67	3.61	3.47	3.45	3.65	3.50
1995-6	3.77	4.05	4.22	4.47	4.70	4.78	4.88	4.80	5.01	5.06	5.39	5.81	4.75
1996-7	5.14	4.67	4.52	4.28	4.07	4.05	4.04	4.02	3.90	3.98	4.14	4.14	4.25
1997-8	3.42	3.16	3.39	3.47	3.42	3.31	3.25	3.16	3.16	3.15	2.94	2.90	3.23
1998-9	2.68	2.47	2.25	2.29	2.66	2.76	2.68	2.70	2.55	2.53	2.48	2.34	2.53
1999-00[1]	2.32	2.13	2.34	2.46	2.47	2.42	2.27	2.35					2.35

[1] Preliminary. *Source: National Agricultural Statistics Service, U.S. Department of Agriculture (NASS-USDA)*

Average Farm Prices of Durum Wheat in the United States — In Dollars Per Bushel

Year	June	July	Aug.	Sept.	Oct.	Nov.	Dec.	Jan.	Feb.	Mar.	Apr.	May	Average
1992-3	3.31	3.03	2.75	2.96	2.92	3.04	3.00	3.00	3.08	3.09	3.10	3.26	3.05
1993-4	3.18	3.26	3.43	3.92	4.23	4.91	4.92	4.97	5.36	5.71	5.70	4.93	4.54
1994-5	4.59	4.32	4.30	4.51	4.89	4.88	4.67	4.61	4.68	4.61	4.48	4.82	4.61
1995-6	5.20	5.29	5.33	5.87	5.80	5.78	5.75	5.66	5.72	5.73	5.63	5.62	5.62
1996-7	5.58	5.13	5.03	4.69	4.78	4.56	4.59	4.47	4.31	4.32	4.40	4.50	4.70
1997-8	4.21	4.61	5.23	5.35	5.09	5.25	5.17	5.02	4.71	4.68	4.45	4.29	4.84
1998-9	3.98	3.39	3.23	3.03	3.04	3.08	3.05	3.20	2.84	2.82	2.80	2.84	3.11
1999-00[1]	2.93	2.89	2.74	2.30	2.17	2.62	2.96	3.00					2.70

[1] Preliminary. *Source: National Agricultural Statistics Service, U.S. Department of Agriculture (NASS-USDA)*

Average Farm Prices of Other Spring Wheat in the United States — In Dollars Per Bushel

Year	June	July	Aug.	Sept.	Oct.	Nov.	Dec.	Jan.	Feb.	Mar.	Apr.	May	Average
1992-3	3.87	3.63	3.12	3.19	3.18	3.28	3.24	3.33	3.34	3.32	3.34	3.19	3.34
1993-4	3.21	3.50	3.51	3.37	3.50	3.67	3.75	3.69	3.68	3.64	3.68	3.63	3.57
1994-5	3.51	3.28	3.19	3.38	3.52	3.51	3.56	3.50	3.40	3.38	3.34	3.53	3.43
1995-6	3.78	4.26	4.19	4.27	4.45	4.61	4.72	4.66	4.81	4.88	5.21	5.67	4.63
1996-7	5.48	5.30	4.63	4.41	4.23	4.11	4.01	3.95	3.80	3.83	4.04	3.94	4.31
1997-8	3.74	3.66	3.75	3.64	3.49	3.55	3.51	3.45	3.34	3.42	3.41	3.31	3.52
1998-9	3.22	3.08	2.69	2.62	3.04	3.23	3.19	3.12	3.09	3.00	2.95	2.92	3.01
1999-00[1]	3.01	2.93	2.85	2.86	2.80	2.95	2.87	2.82					2.89

[1] Preliminary. *Source: National Agricultural Statistics Service, U.S. Department of Agriculture (NASS-USDA)*

Average Open Interest of Wheat Futures in Chicago In Contracts

Year	Jan.	Feb.	Mar.	Apr.	May	June	July	Aug.	Sept.	Oct.	Nov.	Dec.
1990	54,225	56,395	56,984	51,548	56,624	63,819	64,576	59,792	57,237	58,231	55,850	47,061
1991	48,597	51,520	55,922	53,668	53,030	58,997	54,946	52,283	55,220	61,257	57,679	51,845
1992	61,484	70,152	58,957	53,706	50,978	50,340	60,116	62,071	50,093	54,564	57,693	49,263
1993	50,329	47,858	44,885	48,354	51,353	55,829	58,705	64,335	58,603	61,496	62,877	50,523
1994	53,912	48,013	45,110	47,430	44,552	54,622	57,151	65,388	73,200	78,419	70,815	67,150
1995	66,715	67,768	55,973	55,612	67,875	90,208	101,351	90,800	91,505	103,987	102,475	99,422
1996	102,718	104,807	91,378	98,260	93,378	81,211	69,222	66,128	65,561	65,639	60,810	58,533
1997	63,388	71,304	76,747	85,516	84,721	83,675	92,815	105,320	104,587	108,480	101,089	90,386
1998	96,870	99,103	97,585	114,193	115,199	116,008	121,794	127,240	125,747	131,322	130,186	116,249
1999	119,096	131,961	118,503	117,905	111,541	117,074	120,397	129,747	128,403	135,884	140,798	124,208

Source: Chicago Board of Trade (CBT)

Volume of Trading of Wheat Futures in Chicago In Contracts

Year	Jan.	Feb.	Mar.	Apr.	May	June	July	Aug.	Sept.	Oct.	Nov.	Dec.	Total
1990	211,769	197,397	209,873	251,823	346,922	296,337	297,182	298,383	197,304	201,589	231,845	135,846	2,876,270
1991	198,340	182,158	291,762	268,560	234,880	391,134	286,097	271,625	187,232	300,628	271,927	262,501	3,146,844
1992	366,736	460,354	318,810	236,063	290,148	303,044	304,217	283,379	250,003	220,502	257,017	188,541	3,498,814
1993	246,125	237,936	277,632	217,898	173,607	268,206	366,414	266,893	202,308	256,329	310,464	195,817	3,019,629
1994	288,321	211,703	187,617	244,544	300,324	370,135	272,492	330,758	343,548	398,041	354,975	318,173	3,620,631
1995	353,603	302,950	316,330	279,099	345,455	598,762	507,876	527,716	436,145	472,794	454,352	359,985	4,955,067
1996	628,340	510,138	455,981	660,722	531,979	512,883	452,690	345,626	305,448	362,047	359,005	261,108	5,385,967
1997	312,680	373,411	368,547	567,099	422,935	469,158	470,992	493,225	401,277	405,978	432,621	340,722	5,058,645
1998	363,511	473,114	452,186	514,557	432,167	601,149	401,508	490,242	475,766	543,680	539,488	394,201	5,681,569
1999	426,524	597,448	710,375	559,211	444,696	674,580	523,516	665,897	536,014	437,689	613,633	380,442	6,570,025

Source: Chicago Board of Trade (CBT)

Commercial Stocks of Domestic Wheat[1] in the United States, on First of Month In Millions of Bushels

Year	July	Aug.	Sept.	Oct.	Nov.	Dec.	Jan.	Feb.	Mar.	Apr.	May	June
1990-1	121.8	212.7	289.7	290.2	284.6	264.8	243.7	237.7	-----	-----	174.5	174.5
1991-2	244.8	275.5	296.9	308.2	271.0	264.8	249.8	227.0	205.2	180.7	170.9	209.1
1992-3	269.6	290.5	202.5	228.2	231.9	202.7	185.5	169.5	153.3	132.6	112.9	87.0
1993-4	102.9	145.1	171.8	194.9	199.3	174.9	169.5	168.3	162.2	143.8	127.3	111.3
1994-5	145.7	203.9	243.0	269.7	268.6	238.2	199.5	181.0	162.5	150.2	108.7	91.8
1995-6	92.3	161.7	201.1	234.3	228.3	200.2	178.7	170.8	156.6	137.7	107.6	87.2
1996-7	86.3	112.9	128.0	145.3	117.2	94.9	89.0	80.4	77.0	75.6	68.1	64.6
1997-8	80.1	186.3	235.2	268.1	258.1	231.4	196.8	178.1	170.6	158.0	146.4	145.7
1998-9	209.8	265.0	314.9	325.6	307.3	291.3	272.9	265.7	256.8	251.5	236.7	218.3
1999-00	248.6	294.9	335.8	354.0	334.6	301.5	277.4	273.7	267.8	251.5	236.7	218.3

[1] Domestic wheat in storage in public and private elevators in 39 markets and wheat afloat in vessels or barges at lake and seaboard ports, the first Saturday of the month. *Source: Livestock Division, U.S. Department of Agriculture (LD-USDA)*

Stocks of Wheat Flour Held by Mills in the United States In Thousands of Sacks -- 100 Pounds

Year	Jan. 1	April 1	July 1	Oct. 1	Year	Jan. 1	April 1	July 1	Oct. 1
1988	5,858	4,508	4,822	5,303	1994	5,611	5,904	5,834	6,020
1989	4,800	4,423	5,116	5,489	1995	7,060	6,496	6,312	6,582
1990	5,207	5,072	5,818	7,980	1996	6,869	6,927	6,400	6,350
1991	8,051	5,474	8,115	6,336	1997	6,671	6,040	5,820	6,330
1992	5,660	5,210	5,841	5,864	1998	6,343	6,245	6,210	7,345
1993	5,487	4,863	6,197	5,882	1999[1]	7,544	5,808	5,570	4,085

[1] Preliminary. *Source: Bureau of the Census, U.S. Department of Commerce*

Average Producer Price Index of Wheat Flour (Spring) June 1983 = 100

Year	Jan.	Feb.	Mar.	Apr.	May	June	July	Aug.	Sept.	Oct.	Nov.	Dec.	Average
1990	109.4	109.0	106.9	108.8	107.9	106.0	99.7	93.4	92.0	91.2	89.4	89.8	100.3
1991	88.7	90.2	92.0	93.0	94.0	93.7	91.3	94.1	96.3	100.1	97.5	102.7	94.5
1992	109.7	116.4	111.5	110.3	109.2	111.0	104.9	99.6	104.1	104.4	104.7	103.5	107.4
1993	107.5	108.1	107.2	108.4	105.2	104.7	103.7	107.2	102.1	107.3	108.4	112.5	106.9
1994	111.8	110.5	108.9	107.9	109.4	106.4	100.8	101.2	109.1	112.0	110.9	111.4	108.4
1995	110.7	108.5	107.9	109.8	113.5	118.6	127.4	126.7	129.5	132.6	132.3	133.5	120.9
1996	130.4	138.0	136.6	137.6	160.1	146.8	138.0	127.0	121.5	125.7	121.7	121.4	133.7
1997	119.4	119.3	116.6	121.8	120.8	117.4	112.1	113.5	115.1	112.6	111.5	111.1	115.9
1998	106.8	108.1	111.5	110.1	109.9	106.4	105.5	101.8	100.9	106.6	107.8	104.8	106.7
1999[2]	104.8	102.7	105.0	100.5	102.2	102.7	100.7	103.5	101.4	99.9	101.4	96.8	101.8

[1] Standard patent. [2] Preliminary. *Source: Bureau of Labor Statistics, U.S. Department of Commerce (BLS) (0212-0301)*

World Wheat Flour Production (Monthly Average) In Thousands of Metric Tons

Year	Australia	France	Germany	Hungary	India	Japan	Kazakhstan	Rep. of Korea	Mexico	Poland	Russia	Turkey	United Kingdom
1990	114.9	442.7	218.1	102.4	394.3	387.7	163.5	134.7	209.4	150.6	-----	112.9	323.0
1991	112.7	464.8	341.1	97.7	398.0	389.8	167.8	130.4	207.3	128.6	-----	111.1	320.0
1992	113.9	465.2	327.0	106.9	400.0	389.0	161.0	129.4	223.3	167.1	-----	112.2	320.0
1993	116.3	480.6	336.4	75.0	399.4	399.3	155.3	129.5	214.0	113.4	449.5	122.1	331.0
1994	116.9	470.8	378.8	62.9	400.0	387.2	157.0	132.6	219.8	150.5	348.0	104.9	337.0
1995	112.6	473.1	382.3	84.0	400.0	389.3	131.0	139.9	210.7	156.9	274.6	119.7	341.0
1996	123.8	-----	394.2	75.1	400.0	389.6	105.5	141.2	215.9	108.5	309.7	119.3	353.5
1997	-----	-----	404.8	77.7	412.5	388.1	103.0	145.9	216.0	115.9	361.9	159.1	354.5
1998[1]	-----	-----	407.6	70.7	430.6	382.0	129.8	143.5	213.2	116.8	347.8	152.6	355.5
1999[2]	-----	-----	392.3	65.0	-----	375.2	66.7	148.7	189.8	123.0	360.0	-----	-----

[1] Preliminary. [2] Estimate. NA = Not available. *Source: United Nations (UN)*

WHEAT

Production of Wheat Flour in the United States   In Millions of Sacks (100 Pounds Each)

Year	July	Aug.	Sept.	Oct.	Nov.	Dec.	Jan.	Feb.	Mar.	Apr.	May	June	Total
1991-2	29.2	31.8	30.1	32.2	32.7	29.2	29.3	29.3	29.4	30.0	29.8	29.8	363.0
1992-3	31.1	34.2	31.9	34.6	32.2	29.2	30.6	31.3	34.1	32.0	31.0	30.3	382.4
1993-4	30.7	33.3	32.9	33.5	34.0	33.8	30.9	30.2	35.9	32.3	32.2	31.1	390.8
1994-5	30.5	34.9	34.2	35.0	33.7	31.7	30.9	29.4	34.5	29.9	33.5	32.3	390.4
1995-6	31.0	34.5	33.0	35.1	33.4	31.2	31.6	32.3	32.2	31.2	33.2	30.6	389.3
1996-7	33.9	35.6	34.6	37.5	33.1	32.0	31.3	30.0	31.8	33.1	32.6	32.5	397.9
1997-8	34.0	34.3	35.1	37.2	33.8	33.5	-----	96.0	-----	-----	96.2	-----	400.1
1998-9	-----	100.2	-----	-----	106.5	-----	-----	95.2	-----	-----	102.5	-----	404.4
1999-00[1]	-----	102.7	-----	-----	106.7	-----	-----		-----	-----		-----	418.7

[1] Preliminary.   *Source: Bureau of the Census, U.S. Department of Commerce*

United States Wheat Flour Exports (Grain Equivalent[2])   In Thousands of Bushels

Year	June	July	Aug.	Sept.	Oct.	Nov.	Dec.	Jan.	Feb.	Mar.	Apr.	May	Total
1991-2	5,582	5,362	4,207	3,743	1,179	2,222	3,140	2,549	5,549	4,630	3,771	4,579	46,513
1992-3	3,257	5,284	2,856	2,325	3,840	4,641	3,903	2,325	7,744	5,832	7,499	5,285	54,791
1993-4	4,408	3,793	1,811	3,642	3,840	3,416	3,170	5,838	4,390	6,099	4,198	3,368	47,973
1994-5	2,922	6,824	5,636	3,407	3,105	4,721	4,734	2,805	7,085	7,617	6,945	6,005	61,806
1995-6	2,822	5,018	7,520	2,249	2,080	1,221	3,458	808	2,537	1,230	2,415	1,830	33,188
1996-7	2,005	2,008	1,669	3,133	2,496	2,748	2,240	1,344	1,897	2,490	1,253	2,086	25,369
1997-8	1,731	2,849	1,621	3,101	2,518	1,631	3,118	1,403	2,723	1,280	1,257	925	24,157
1998-9	1,971	1,740	2,027	2,914	3,812	2,354	6,472	2,551	3,341	4,126	3,105	1,948	36,361
1999-00[1]	5,900	5,085	3,673	6,503	4,576	2,332							56,138

[1] Preliminary.   [2] Includes meal, groats and durum.   *Source: Economic Research Service, U.S. Department of Agriculture (ERS-USDA)*

Supply and Distribution of Wheat Flour in the United States

Year	Wheat Ground	Millfeed Production	Flour Production[2]	Flour & Product Imports	Total Supply	Exports: Flour	Exports: Products	Domestic Disappear-ance	Total Population July 1	Per Capita Disappear-ance
	- 1,000 Bu. -	- 1,000 Tons -	In 1,000 Cwt.						- Millions -	- Pounds -
1991	808,966	6,436	362,311	3,858	366,169	19,739	428	346,002	252.6	137
1992	833,339	6,707	370,829	4,749	375,578	20,382	599	354,597	255.4	138.8
1993	871,408	6,963	387,419	5,786	393,205	22,886	531	369,788	258.1	143.3
1994	884,707	7,186	392,519	8,425	400,944	23,884	715	376,345	260.7	144.4
1995	869,296	7,144	388,689	8,918	397,607	23,770	702	373,135	263.2	141.8
1996	878,070	7,042	397,776	8,574	406,350	10,825	707	394,818	265.5	148.7
1997	885,843	6,886	404,143	8,684	412,827	11,190	1,015	400,622	267.9	149.5
1998[1]	895,369	6,955	398,914	9,745	413,625	12,551	1,215	399,859	270.3	147.9
1999[1]	909,922	7,071	407,049							

[1] Preliminary.   [2] Commercial production of wheat flour, whole wheat, industrial and durum flour and farina reported by Bureau of Census.
Source: Economic Research Service, U.S. Department of Agriculture (ERS-USDA)

Wheat and Flour -- Price Relationships at Milling Centers in the United States   In Dollars

Crop Year (June-May)	At Kansas City: Cost of Wheat to Produce 100 lb. Flour[1]	At Kansas City: Wholesale Price of Bakery Flour 100 lb. Flour[2]	At Kansas City: Wholesale Price of By-Products Obtained 100 lb. Flour[3]	At Kansas City: Total Products Actual	At Kansas City: Total Products Over Cost of Wheat	At Minneapolis: Cost of Wheat to Produce 100 lb. Flour[1]	At Minneapolis: Wholesale Price of Bakery Flour 100 lb. Flour[2]	At Minneapolis: Wholesale Price of By-Products Obtained 100 lb. Flour[3]	At Minneapolis: Total Products Actual	At Minneapolis: Total Products Over Cost of Wheat
1990-1	6.86	7.78	1.29	9.07	2.21	6.98	7.73	1.21	8.94	1.96
1991-2	8.58	9.53	1.26	10.79	2.21	8.71	9.39	1.16	10.55	1.84
1992-3	8.53	9.65	1.28	10.93	2.40	8.91	10.12	1.15	11.27	2.37
1993-4	10.03	10.34	1.46	11.79	1.77	11.45	12.50	1.28	13.77	2.33
1994-5	9.25	10.50	1.21	11.71	2.46	9.71	11.01	1.04	12.05	2.34
1995-6	12.97	13.35	1.93	15.28	2.31	13.04	13.03	1.68	14.71	1.67
1996-7	11.22	11.89	1.92	13.81	2.60	11.32	11.68	1.87	13.54	2.22
1997-8	9.03	9.99	1.43	11.41	2.38	9.83	10.62	1.34	11.96	2.12
1998-9	8.03	9.15	1.11	10.26	2.24	8.88	9.91	1.03	10.93	2.05
June-Aug.	7.80	8.93	1.10	10.03	2.23	8.72	9.97	1.00	10.97	2.24
Sept.-Nov.	8.15	9.43	.94	10.37	2.22	9.05	10.03	.92	10.95	1.90
Dec.-Feb.	8.13	9.10	1.29	10.39	2.26	8.87	9.72	1.17	10.88	2.02

[1] Based on 73% extraction rate, cost of 2.28 bushels: At Kansas City, No. 1 hard winter 13% protein; and at Minneapolis, No. 1 dark northern spring, 14% protein.   [2] quoted as mid-month bakers' standard patent at Kansas City and spring standard patent at Minneapolis, bulk basis.   [3] Assumed 50-50 millfeed distribution between bran and shorts or middlings, bulk basis.   *Source: Agricultural Marketing Service, U.S. Department of Agriculture (AMS-USDA)*

Wool

World wool production declined steadily during the 1990's. The decline directly reflects the steady contraction in world sheep numbers, to less than 900 million head in 1999, from an average of over 1.1 billion head in the late 1980's. Except for China, the sheep flock has been contracting worldwide. In Australia, sheep numbers fell from over 160 million head in 1990 to less than 120 million in 1999 with a corresponding drop in wool production. However, demand has also fallen due to changing worldwide consumer attitudes which has an adverse effect on wool usage; casual dress codes that use more cotton and man-made fibers than wool are now widely acceptable.

New Zealand has seen its sheep herd drop to about 46 million head, the lowest since the 1960's, although the decline shows signs of having run its course. China's 1999 sheep inventory, in excess of 150 million head, is now the world's largest and probably almost double that of the early 1990's. On the other hand, Russia's sheep inventory in 1999 of less than 20 million head is estimated to have fallen at least 50 percent since the early 1990's.

The drop in U.S. sheep numbers is not much better, the 1999 inventory of 7 million head is about half the number on hand in the late 1980's. U.S. shorn wool production (tops and noils) is insignificant, about 18 million pounds in the first half of 1999, and lower than the like 1998 period. In the early 1980's, production averaged about 105 million pounds.

In line with the world's declining wool production and usage, foreign trade has also fallen. Australia remains the largest exporter followed by New Zealand, the two nations accounting for at least 75 percent of total world exports. Importing nations are numerous but China leads followed by Japan, the U.K., Italy and France.

U.S. raw wool imports (clean) through the first eight months of 1999 totaled 35 million pounds vs. 46 million in the year earlier period. Australian wool accounts for most of U.S. imports. The U.S. also imports a relatively small quantity of wool tops. However, the U.S. also exports wool with the January-July 1999 total of 3.4 million pounds comparing with 2.5 million a year earlier.

Global wool prices are based on origin and grade. South African wool tends to be much more expensive than Australian wool which, in turn, is moderately higher than New Zealand wool. U.S. clean wool prices (56's) were under pressure in 1999, the late summer price of $0.55/lb. compares with $0.82 a year earlier while U.S. 60's grade averaged $0.79/lb. in September 1999 vs. Australian 60's at $1.26. Australian 60's in the mid-1990's averaged near $3.00/lb.

Futures Markets

Wool futures are traded on the Sydney Futures Exchange (SFE). Wool Yarn futures are traded on the Osaka Mercantile Exchange (OME).

World Production of Wool In Metric Tons--Degreased

Year	Argentina	Australia	China	Kazak-hstan[3]	New Zealand	Pakistan	Romania	Russia[3]	South Africa	United Kingdom	United States	Uruguay	Total
1989	87,600	622,000	120,111	-----	302,800	34,800	20,900	284,400	46,500	52,765	21,665	60,000	2,011,693
1990	85,800	724,000	122,400	64,750	233,000	28,200	26,500	136,050	49,500	53,358	21,140	58,100	2,029,209
1991	75,400	699,000	123,000	62,640	227,000	28,900	19,196	122,700	51,000	51,055	20,830	56,500	1,953,339
1992	74,200	574,000	121,500	63,000	221,000	29,600	16,800	107,400	48,500	50,876	19,980	50,700	1,780,613
1993	58,000	557,000	122,000	56,800	193,000	30,300	15,600	95,000	45,000	48,329	18,520	49,410	1,688,806
1994	48,000	570,000	130,000	55,000	214,000	31,000	17,000	73,000	40,000	47,000	16,000	50,000	1,693,000
1995	44,000	475,000	141,000	35,000	214,000	32,000	16,000	56,000	35,000	48,000	15,000	46,000	1,512,000
1996[1]	39,000	447,000	152,000	25,000	199,000	32,000	16,000	46,000	38,000	46,000	14,000	43,000	1,449,000
1997[2]	39,000	447,000	153,000	25,000	200,000	33,000	13,000	42,000	38,000	46,000	14,000	48,000	1,450,000

[1] Preliminary. [2] Estimate. [3] Formerly part of the U.S.S.R.; data not reported separately until 1990. *Source: Food and Agriculture Organization of the United Nations (FAO-UN)*

Production of Wool Goods[1] in the United States In Millions of Yards

Year	First Quarter	Second Quarter	Third Quarter	Fourth Quarter	Total	Year	First Quarter	Second Quarter	Third Quarter	Fourth Quarter	Total
1990	38.0	38.7	32.6	31.4	140.7	1995	46.8	45.9	35.2	34.3	162.2
1991	38.0	48.7	41.4	41.5	169.6	1996	44.8	43.6	30.8	32.8	152.0
1992	45.7	47.2	43.9	39.5	176.3	1997	42.7	49.7	42.3	40.5	175.2
1993	48.4	48.9	43.9	42.8	184.0	1998	38.8	37.5	29.6	26.3	132.2
1994	49.1	51.1	39.4	39.0	178.6	1999[2]	25.0	26.9	17.4	14.4	83.7

[1] Woolen and worsted woven goods, except woven felts. [2] Preliminary. *Source: Bureau of the Census, U.S. Department of Commerce*

Consumption of Apparel Wool in the United States In Millions of Pounds--Clean Basis

Year	First Quarter	Second Quarter	Third Quarter	Fourth Quarter	Total	Year	First Quarter	Second Quarter	Third Quarter	Fourth Quarter	Total
1990	31.5	31.7	26.9	30.5	120.6	1995	36.3	35.5	29.4	28.1	129.3
1991	31.6	37.1	34.6	33.9	137.2	1996	39.1	36.2	27.4	26.8	129.5
1992	36.4	35.1	33.6	31.1	136.1	1997	33.1	33.8	30.6	32.8	130.4
1993	35.5	35.9	35.5	34.4	141.4	1998	29.3	29.6	21.9	17.5	98.4
1994	36.3	35.6	32.7	34.0	138.6	1999[2]	17.8	17.4	16.3	14.1	65.5

[1] Woolen and worsted woven goods, except woven felts. [2] Preliminary. *Source: Bureau of the Census, U.S. Department of Commerce*

Salient Statistics of Wool in the United States

Year	Sheep & Lambs Shorn[4]	Weight Per Fleece	Shorn Wool Production	Price Per Lb.	Value of Production	Support	Payment Rate	Raw Wool (Clean Content): Total Wool Production	Domestic Production	Exports Domestic Wool	Dutiable Imports for Consumption[3] 48's & Finer	Total New Supply[2]	Duty Free Imports (Not Finer than 46's)	Mill Consumption: Apparel	Mill Consumption: Carpet
	-1,000's-	-In Lbs.-	1,000 Lbs.	Lb.	1,000 $	--Cents Per Lb.--		In Thousands of Pounds							
1990	11,222	7.84	88,033	80.0	69,534	182	102.0	88,033	46,481	2,736	50,328	115,428	21,355	120,622	12,124
1991	11,009	7.97	87,740	55.0	47,178	188	133.0	87,740	46,327	3,867	68,242	128,868	18,166	137,187	14,352
1992	10,521	7.88	82,943	74.0	60,162	197	123.0	82,943	43,794	3,413	65,457	129,640	23,802	136,143	14,695
1993	9,976	7.77	77,535	51.0	39,077	204	153.0	77,535	40,938	2,529	76,001	138,286	21,876	141,380	15,431
1994	8,877	7.73	68,577	78.0	52,377	209	131.0	68,577	36,209	2,863	64,889	122,880	24,645	138,563	14,739
1995	8,138	7.80	63,513	104.0	64,277	212	108.0	63,513	33,535	6,042	63,781	116,313	25,039	129,299	12,667
1996	7,279	7.79	56,669	70.0	39,659	-----	-----	56,669	29,921	5,715	54,063	99,575	20,971	129,525	12,311
1997	7,032	7.70	53,889	84.0	45,172	-----	-----	53,889	28,630	4,732	51,484	100,344	24,295	130,386	13,576
1998[1]	6,400	7.70	49,200	60.0					26,100	1,700	45,760		23,121	98,373	16,331

[1] Preliminary. [2] Production minus exports plus imports; stocks not taken into consideration. [3] Apparel wool includes all dutiable wool; carpet wool includes all duty-free wool. [4] Includes sheep shorn at commercial feeding yards. *Source: Economic Research Service, U.S. Department of Agriculture (ERS-USDA)*

Shorn Wool Prices

Year	U.S. Farm Price Shorn Wool Greasy Basis[1]	Australian Offering Price, Clean[2]: Grade 70's Type 61	Grade 64's Type 63	Grade 64/70's Type 62	Grade 60/62's Type 64A	Grade 58's-56's 433-34	Market Indicator[3]	Graded Territory Shorn Wool, Clean Basis[4]: 64's Staple 2 3/4" & up	60's Staple 3" & up	58's Staple 3 1/4" & up	56's Staple 3 1/4" & up	54's Staple 3 1/2" & up
	-Cents/Lb.-	In Dollars Per Pound					-Cents/Kg.-	In Dollars Per Pound				
1990	80.0	4.76	3.60	4.03	2.87	2.46	870	2.56	1.66	1.45	1.30	1.18
1991	55.0	3.56	2.32	2.70	1.87	1.68	627	1.99	1.31	1.14	1.03	.93
1992	74.0	2.58	2.32	2.17	2.10	1.94	557	2.04	1.61	1.47	1.35	1.23
1993	51.0	2.08	1.70	1.84	1.49	1.44	488	1.37	1.13	1.05	.99	.94
1994	78.0	3.72	2.43	3.01	1.96	1.86	547	2.12	1.50	1.26	1.27	1.21
1995	104.0	3.22	2.81	3.01	2.49	2.33	888	2.49	1.93	1.77	1.63	1.53
1996	70.0	2.81	2.34	2.54	1.96	1.84	619	1.93	1.54	1.43	1.31	1.22
1997	84.0	3.56	2.57	2.90	2.06	1.95	615	2.38	1.78	1.64	1.43	1.14
1998	60.0	2.70	1.94	2.02	1.74	1.60	663	1.62	1.31	1.21	1.06	.94

[1] Annual weighted average. [2] F.O.B. Australian Wool Corporation South Carolina warehouse in bond. [3] Index of prices of all wool sold in Australia for the crop year July-June. [4] Wool principally produced in Texas and the Rocky Mountain States. *Source: Economic Research Service, U.S. Department of Agriculture (ERS-USDA)*

Average Wool Prices[1] --Australian-- 64's, Type 62, Duty Paid--U.S. Mills In Cents Per Pound

Year	Jan.	Feb.	Mar.	Apr.	May	June	July	Aug.	Sept.	Oct.	Nov.	Dec.	Average
1990	417	404	403	414	406	342	338	352	355	343	332	332	370
1991	334	335	209	221	271	286	NA	248	229	215	274	270	263
1992	259	270	277	264	268	246	NA	224	210	192	195	193	236
1993	186	176	170	158	179	169	167	154	153	171	175	176	170
1994	204	216	205	223	249	258	243	248	259	256	273	297	244
1995	281	297	302	302	307	308	292	284	266	236	242	237	280
1996	240	237	238	234	242	245	236	234	228	220	225	232	234
1997	234	261	254	261	279	287	NA	270	262	250	245	240	258
1998	218	225	247	205	214	179	NA	144	144	140	156	147	184
1999	158	150	157	156	150	149	152	148	139	139	143	137	148

[1] Raw, clean basis. NA = Not available. *Source: Economic Research Service, U.S. Department of Agriculture (ERS-USDA)*

Average Wool Prices --Domestic[1]-- Graded Territory, 64's, Staple 2 3/4 & Up--U.S. Mills In Cents Per Pound

Year	Jan.	Feb.	Mar.	Apr.	May	June	July	Aug.	Sept.	Oct.	Nov.	Dec.	Average
1990	294	287	287	284	275	257	242	235	235	235	225	220	256
1991	217	210	163	167	203	230	230	167	156	148	148	155	183
1992	163	203	195	196	199	218	210	188	210	193	168	168	193
1993	158	148	132	127	135	140	138	140	130	129	133	133	137
1994	140	150	170	201	226	230	230	235	250	238	238	252	213
1995	245	252	265	288	295	285	261	250	235	185	208	192	247
1996	188	192	197	197	195	192	192	192	192	192	190	190	192
1997	190	190	208	228	248	255	255	255	255	255	260	260	238
1998	236	195	195	188	177	170	170	150	115	115	115	115	162
1999	115	115	115	110	117	122	116	110	105	100	100	95	110

[1] Raw, shorn, clean basis. *Source: Economic Research Service, U.S. Department of Agriculture (ERS-USDA)*

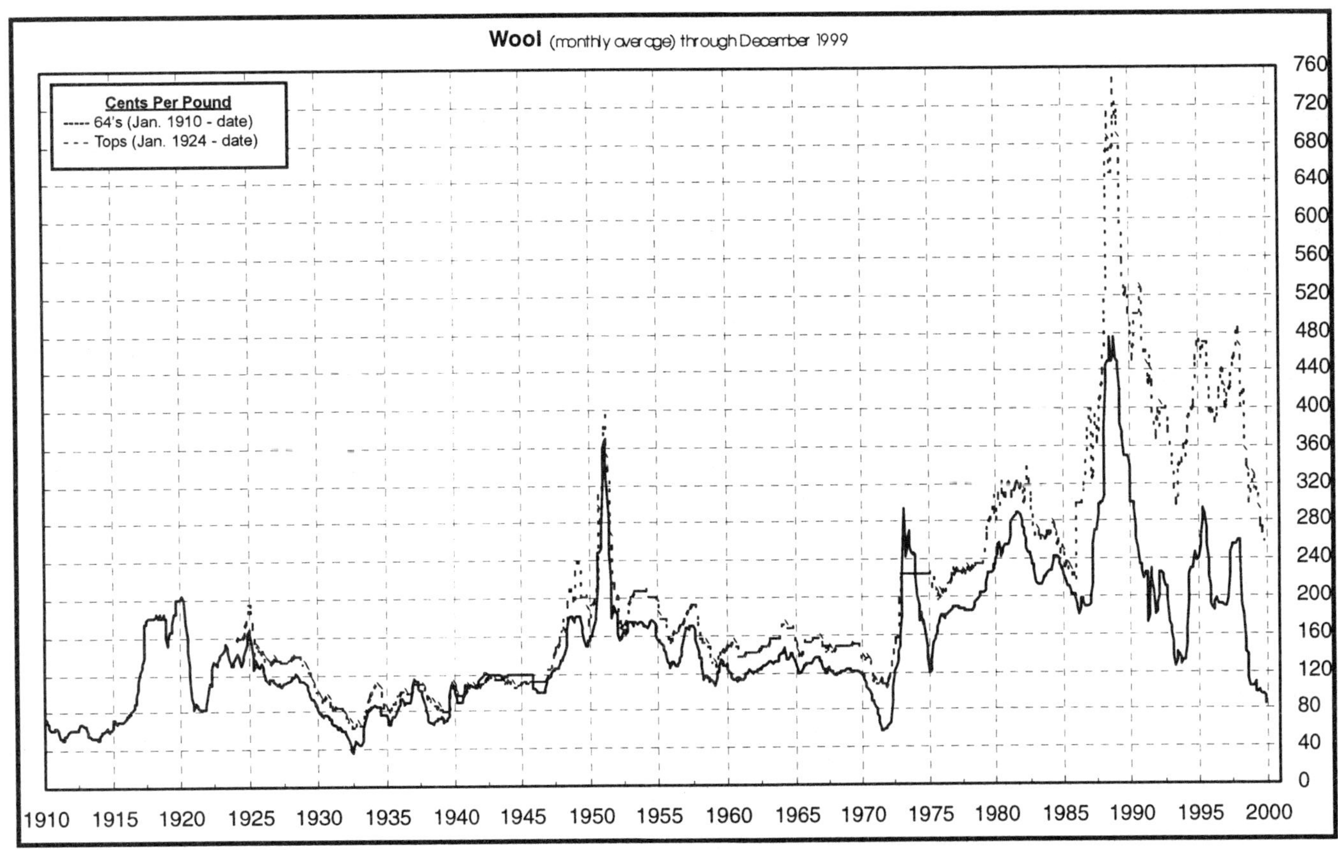

Wool: Mill Consumption, by Grades in the U.S., Scoured Basis In Millions of Pounds

	Apparel Class[1]							
	Woolen System			Worsted System				
Year	60's & Finer	Coarser Than 60's	Total	60's & Finer	Coarser Than 60's	Total	All Total	Carpet Wool[2]
1989	24,123	21,803	45,935	56,065	18,534	74,599	120,534	14,122
1990	26,173	24,941	51,114	50,630	18,878	69,508	120,622	12,124
1991	31,961	26,599	58,560	56,521	22,106	78,627	137,187	14,352
1992	33,878	25,600	59,478	58,495	18,170	76,665	136,143	14,695
1993	40,895	26,624	67,519	58,834	15,027	73,861	141,380	15,431
1994	35,960	26,038	61,998	59,599	16,966	76,565	138,563	14,739
1995	30,211	27,089	57,300	54,980	17,019	71,999	129,299	12,667
1996	42,141	27,575	69,716	46,057	13,752	59,809	129,525	12,311
1997[3]	49,038	21,303	70,341	48,153	11,892	60,045	130,386	13,576
1998[4]	31,258	15,079	46,337	15,079	36,957	52,036	98,373	16,331

[1] Domestic & duty-paid foreign. [2] Duty-free foreign. [3] Preliminary. [4] Estimate. *Source: Economic Research Service, U.S. Department of Agriculture (ERS-USDA)*

United States Imports[1] of Unmanufactured Wool (Clean Yield) In Millions of Pounds

Year	Jan.	Feb.	Mar.	Apr.	May	June	July	Aug.	Sept.	Oct.	Nov.	Dec.	Total
1990	7.3	9.2	4.7	8.2	5.0	4.8	3.4	5.5	5.0	6.9	7.5	4.2	71.7
1991	10.7	6.9	5.4	5.5	7.3	8.1	9.2	7.0	4.4	7.8	5.1	9.0	86.4
1992	10.2	8.1	7.3	10.6	8.8	6.2	6.9	5.0	3.9	5.5	9.1	7.8	89.4
1993	7.8	8.7	8.5	9.3	11.0	9.6	9.7	8.7	5.7	7.7	7.2	8.4	102.2
1994	10.0	7.7	7.7	12.7	7.5	7.7	6.9	6.5	4.1	5.7	8.1	7.0	91.7
1995	10.4	7.7	10.8	6.0	11.5	5.2	7.3	7.3	4.9	7.9	7.7	4.1	90.6
1996	9.6	9.1	8.8	5.6	7.0	5.9	5.3	6.6	3.1	4.6	4.6	5.1	75.3
1997	5.1	5.8	5.8	6.6	5.8	4.2	4.9	4.2	4.8	8.5	7.3	8.6	71.5
1998	8.8	5.4	5.4	7.2	5.9	5.5	5.7	4.4	3.3	7.3	4.9	4.3	68.0
1999[2]	6.2	3.5	3.9	4.6	3.5	3.0	3.7	3.1	2.6	3.8	2.8	2.5	43.1

[1] For consumption. [2] Preliminary. *Source: Economic Research Service, U.S. Department of Agriculture (ERS-USDA)*

Zinc

Zinc is utilized as a protective coating for other metals, such as iron and steel, in a process known as galvanizing. Zinc also finds use as an alloy with copper to make brass, and as an alloying compound with aluminum and magnesium.

The U.S. Geological Survey reported that, despite numerous mine closings, world mine production of zinc increased by nearly 5 percent from 1997 to 7.8 million metric tonnes in 1998. The major producer of zinc was China with 1998 production estimated at 1.25 million tonnes, an increase of 4 percent from 1997. The next two largest producers were Australia and Canada. Mine production by Australia, in 1998, was estimated to be 1.1 million tonnes, an increase of 4 percent from 1997. Production by Canada was also estimated to be 1.1 million tonnes, an increase of nearly 4 percent from the previous year. Other major producers of mined zinc are Peru, the United States and Mexico.

The world reserve base of zinc was estimated to be 440 million tonnes. Australia has the largest reserve base, currently estimated at 90 million tonnes. The U.S. reserve base is also large at 80 million tonnes, as is China's base. Other countries with large reserve bases include Canada, Peru and Mexico.

U.S. production of mine zinc in July 1999 was 67,000 tonnes (zinc content of concentrate). In the January-July 1999 period mine production was 459,000 tonnes, while for all of 1998 it was 755,000 tonnes. Mine production of zinc (recoverable zinc) in July 1999 was 63,000 tonnes. In the first seven months of 1999 it was 435,000 tonnes, while for all of 1998 it was 722,000 tonnes. Smelter production of zinc (refined) in July 1999 was 30,100 tonnes. In the January-July 1999 period it was 210,000 tonnes, and for all of 1998 it was 380,000 tonnes. Ending stocks of refined zinc at the end of July 1999 were 9,380 tonnes. U.S. production of zinc oxide in July was 8,660 tonnes. For the first seven months of 1999 it was 77,700 tonnes, and for all 1998 it was 153,000 tonnes. Ending stocks of zinc oxide in July 1999 were 3,310 tonnes.

U.S. apparent consumption of refined zinc in July 1999 was 120,000 tonnes, down 2 percent from June. In the January-July 1999 period refined zinc consumption was 803,000 tonnes, while in 1998 it totaled 1.29 million tonnes. Of the 1999 total, galvanizing took 55 percent, brass and bronze took 15 percent, zinc-base alloy took 19 percent, and other uses like zinc powder, anodes and chemicals took about 11 percent.

Zinc oxide shipments in July 1999 were 8,600 tonnes, down 4 percent from the month before. Shipments in May were 11,900 tonnes. In the January-July 1999 period zinc oxide shipments were 79,500 tonnes, while for all of 1998 they were 153,000 tonnes. Shipments to the rubber industry in 1999 were 50,700 tonnes, while the chemical industry took 17,400 tonnes. Shipments to the ceramics industry were 4,280 tonnes, while paints took 3,470 tonnes.

U.S. reported consumption of refined zinc in July was 38,100 tonnes, down 16 percent from the previous month. In the first seven months of 1999, reported refined zinc consumption was 289,000 tonnes, while for all of 1998 it was 647,000 tonnes. Zinc ore consumption in July 1999 was 85 tonnes, and for the first seven months of 1999 it was 595 tonnes. For 1998, zinc ore consumption was 1,020 tonnes. Zinc-base scrap (zinc content) consumption in July was 18,800 tonnes, the same as in June, while for 1999 it totaled 131,000 tonnes. For all of 1998 it totaled 225,000 tonnes. Copper-base scrap (zinc content) consumption in July was 16,700 tonnes, the same as in June, and for 1999 it totaled 117,000 tonnes. For all of 1998 the total was 200,000 tonnes. Aluminum-base and magnesium-base scrap (zinc content) consumption in July was 103 tonnes, and for 1999 totaled 720 tonnes. For all of 1998 the total was 1,240 tonnes.

U.S. imports for consumption of refined (slab) zinc in the first seven months of 1999 were 490,000 tonnes. For all of 1998 they were 879,000 tonnes. Imports of zinc oxide in 1999 totaled 32,600 tonnes, and for all of 1998 were 58,900 tonnes. Zinc ore and concentrate imports in 1999 totaled 38,300 tonnes, and for 1998 were 46,300 tonnes.

Futures Markets

Zinc futures and options are traded on the London Metals Exchange (LME).

Salient Statistics of Zinc in the United States In Metric Tons

Year	Slab Zinc Production: Primary	Slab Zinc Production: Secondary	Mine Production (Recovered)	Imports for Consumption: Slab Zinc	Imports for Consumption: Ore (Zinc Content)	Exports: Slab Zinc	Exports: Ore (Zinc Content)	Consumption: Slab Zinc	Consumption: Consumed as Ore	Consumption: All Classes[3]	Net Import Reliance as a % of Consumption	High-Grade, Price -Cents/Lb.-
1989	260,305	97,904	275,883	711,554	40,974	5,532	78,877	1,060,000	2,107	1,311,000	61	82.02
1990	262,704	95,708	515,355	631,742	46,684	1,238	220,446	992,000	2,178	1,240,000	41	74.59
1991	253,276	124,078	517,804	549,137	45,419	1,253	381,416	931,000	2,098	1,160,000	24	52.77
1992	272,000	128,000	523,430	644,482	44,523	565	307,114	1,050,000	2,400	1,290,000	33	58.38
1993	240,000	141,000	488,374	723,563	33,093	1,410	311,278	1,120,000	2,200	1,340,000	36	46.15
1994	216,600	139,000	570,000	793,000	27,374	6,310	389,000	1,180,000	2,400	1,400,000	35	49.26
1995	232,000	131,000	614,000	856,000	10,300	3,080	424,000	1,230,000	2,400	1,460,000	35	55.83
1996	226,000	140,000	600,000	827,000	15,100	1,970	425,000	1,210,000	1,400	1,450,000	33	51.11
1997[1]	226,000	141,000	605,000	876,000	49,600	3,630	461,000	1,240,000	-----	1,480,000	35	64.56
1998[2]	234,000	134,000	722,000	879,000	46,300	2,330	552,000	1,290,000	-----	1,580,000	35	51.43

[1] Preliminary. [2] Estimate. [3] Based on apparent consumption of slab zinc plus zinc content of ores and concentrates and secondary materials used to make zinc dust and chemicals. *Source: U.S. Geological Survey (USGS)*

World Smelter Production of Zinc[3] In Thousands of Metric Tons

Year	Australia	Belgium	Canada	France	Germany	Italy	Japan	Kazak-hstan[4]	Mexico	Poland	Spain	United States	World Total
1989	296.5	306.0	669.7	265.8	372.0	259.5	714.7	977.0	193.3	163.7	246.4	358.2	7,245
1990	308.5	356.5	591.8	263.1	350.3	264.4	731.6	890.0	199.3	132.2	252.7	358.4	7,178
1991	326.5	384.2	660.6	299.6	345.7	263.8	778.7	800.0	189.1	126.0	262.2	376.0	7,310
1992	333.0	310.6	671.7	318.7	383.1	252.6	780.6	260.0	151.6	134.6	351.9	399.0	7,260
1993	321.0	299.6	659.9	310.0	380.9	182.0	744.6	263.0	209.9	149.1	341.6	382.0	7,360
1994	328.0	306.2	691.0	306.0	359.9	203.6	713.0	172.4	209.2	154.4	294.7	356.0	7,330
1995	325.0	301.1	720.3	300.0	322.5	180.4	711.1	169.2	222.7	162.7	358.0	363.0	7,440
1996	331.0	234.4	715.6	324.3	327.0	269.0	642.3	190.0	221.7	163.1	360.8	366.0	7,580
1997[1]	317.0	244.0	703.8	346.0	251.7	227.7	650.2	170.0	231.4	165.0	364.2	367.0	7,850
1998[2]	322.0	250.0	743.2	321.0	334.0	235.0	652.8	241.0	230.0	165.0	370.0	368.0	8,230

[1] Preliminary. [2] Estimate. [3] Secondary metal included. [4] Formerly part of the U.S.S.R.; data not reported separately until 1992.
Source: U.S. Geological Survey (USGS)

Consumption (Reported) of Slab Zinc in the United States, by Industries and Grades In Metric Tons

		By Industries					By Grades			
Year	Total	Galvanizers	Brass Products	Zinc-Base Alloy[3]	Zinc Oxide	Other	Special High Grade	High Grade	Remelt and Other	Prime Western
1989	887,203	444,603	95,798	189,690	70,417	84,147	458,020	120,433	94,340	214,410
1990	801,969	388,421	104,276	171,771	67,532	69,969	445,427	92,424	78,265	210,373
1991	764,038	364,629	97,952	169,883	64,035	67,539	421,316	91,468	57,786	189,930
1992	814,228	396,480	112,990	165,598	71,224	67,936	414,661	119,660	56,185	223,723
1993	1,035,000	532,400	139,500	222,000	63,448	141,100	403,696	116,500	71,202	182,309
1994	859,000	395,000	107,000	196,000	68,300	92,400	486,000	112,000	68,400	192,000
1995	1,240,000	390,000	91,500	194,000	70,900	90,800	135,000	98,200	54,400	251,000
1996	788,000	398,000	87,400	142,000	[4]	161,000	385,000	111,000	54,000	238,000
1997[1]	672,000	347,000	76,800	107,000	[4]	141,000	319,000	88,700	57,200	207,000
1998[2]	647,000	320,000	60,300	122,000	[4]	145,000	331,000	728,000	51,700	192,000

[1] Preliminary. [2] Estimated. [3] Die casters. [4] Included in other. *Source: U.S. Geological Survey (USGS)*

United States Foreign Trade of Zinc In Metric Tons

	Imports for Consumption							Zinc Ore & Manufactures Exported						
								Blocks, Pigs, Anodes, etc.		Wrought & Alloys				
Year	Ores[1]	Blocks, Pigs, Slabs	Sheets, Plates, Other	Waste & Scrap	Dross, Ashes, Fume	Dust, Powder & Flakes	Total Value $1,000	Un-wrought	Un-wrought Alloys	Sheets, Plates & Strips	Angles, Bars, Rods, etc.	Waste & Scrap	Dust (Blue Powder)	Zinc Ore & Con-centrates
1989	40,974	711,554	3,066	9,367	9,031	7,253	1,241,659	5,532	2,423	16,515	2,653	108,086	8,137	78,877
1990	46,684	631,742	929	31,720	6,411	8,834	1,049,940	1,238	4,566	11,881	3,731	109,316	8,701	220,446
1991	45,419	549,137	539	31,596	6,483	15,424	687,879	1,253	4,224	10,385	6,151	96,314	5,737	381,416
1992	44,523	644,482	171	31,176	11,813	17,051	910,289	5,886	NA	NA	NA	82,088	5,889	307,114
1993	33,093	723,563	135	38,079	11,862	16,218	799,999	8,765	NA	NA	NA	46,385	6,727	311,278
1994	27,374	793,482	475	51,676	12,152	11,954	878,100	13,220	NA	NA	NA	58,297	6,603	389,488
1995	10,300	856,000	332	42,300	10,900	11,700	1,018,620	NA	NA	NA	NA	55,900	8,840	424,000
1996	15,100	827,000	16,900	31,900	14,500	10,300	1,001,800	NA	NA	NA	NA	45,500	11,100	425,000
1997[2]	49,600	876,000	19,200	29,600	-----	11,700	1,340,390	NA	NA	NA	NA	46,100	9,980	461,000
1998[3]	46,300	879,000	16,900	29,200	-----	17,600	1,096,960	NA	NA	NA	NA	35,000	5,530	552,000

[1] Zinc content. [2] Preliminary. [3] Estimate. NA = Not available. *Source: U.S. Geological Survey (USGS)*

Mine Production of Recoverable Zinc in the United States In Thousands of Metric Tons

Year	Jan.	Feb.	Mar.	Apr.	May	June	July	Aug.	Sept.	Oct.	Nov.	Dec.	Total
1990	26.9	24.8	26.4	26.2	27.9	45.6	50.7	57.1	44.7	42.7	40.4	43.6	515.4
1991	45.5	41.9	43.8	45.5	49.4	36.9	43.0	47.4	49.5	39.0	33.4	38.0	517.8
1992	41.5	48.8	47.7	40.3	40.7	40.4	46.2	49.1	47.6	36.2	40.4	42.2	520.1
1993	48.0	42.5	46.4	39.5	43.0	40.7	33.5	32.1	35.9	41.8	41.4	43.4	488.3
1994	43.2	40.2	48.4	44.0	47.9	47.1	52.5	47.1	50.1	41.6	46.0	48.0	557.0
1995	49.8	48.1	52.8	45.6	54.5	50.0	50.2	55.0	48.1	52.0	47.8	48.1	601.0
1996	52.4	48.9	49.7	45.5	50.7	49.9	53.7	48.1	46.8	43.4	43.1	42.6	600.0
1997	46.2	45.7	45.8	47.9	49.7	45.3	45.9	49.8	53.0	47.6	44.2	48.4	574.0
1998	50.1	48.3	56.5	56.2	56.7	55.0	59.5	57.2	60.1	55.7	62.0	61.9	722.0
1999[1]	61.4	57.6	63.0	67.0	61.7	62.8	68.2	72.1	60.8	67.8	62.0	63.0	767.4

[1] Preliminary. *Source: U.S. Geological Survey (USGS)*

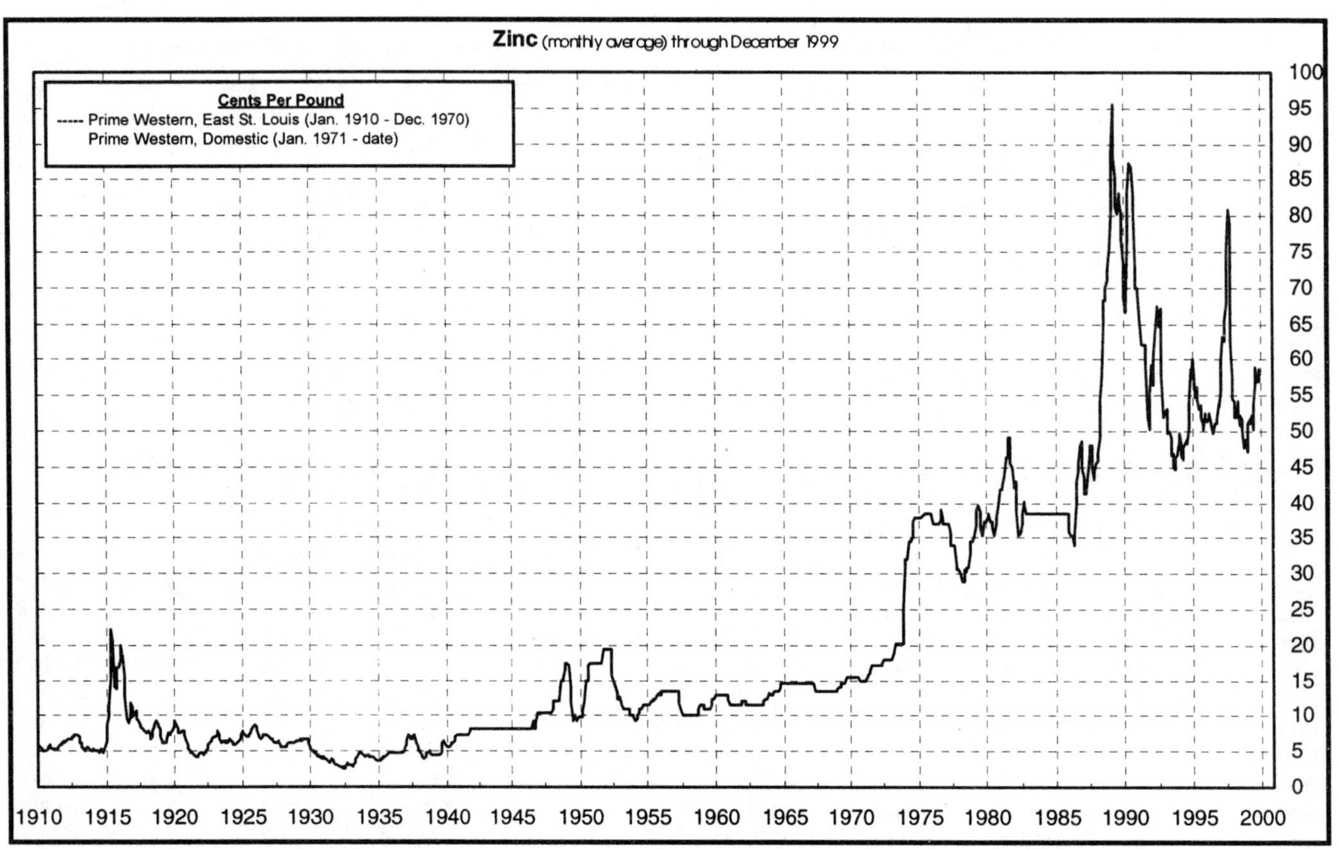

Consumption of Slab Zinc by Fabricators in the United States In Thousands of Metric Tons

Year	Jan.	Feb.	Mar.	Apr.	May	June	July	Aug.	Sept.	Oct.	Nov.	Dec.	Average
1990	82.4	79.2	88.0	74.0	79.4	91.0	102.8	100.0	73.0	86.0	73.0	67.1	826.5
1991	80.0	69.0	65.9	67.8	68.3	68.8	73.6	78.0	79.3	85.9	84.2	82.0	764.0
1992	93.8	77.2	85.0	89.9	76.0	76.9	47.2	53.8	52.2	53.5	50.3	47.6	814.2
1993	50.9	49.2	55.8	59.2	60.8	55.7	44.6	49.1	47.0	52.7	50.9	51.0	774.0
1994	50.8	53.7	55.7	58.5	58.7	52.7	48.0	53.2	53.6	53.9	52.5	45.0	623.0
1995	51.3	57.8	56.3	57.9	53.4	58.0	44.0	44.0	58.8	57.0	56.0	54.5	838.0
1996	56.3	55.6	59.3	55.7	56.3	55.9	48.9	48.1	54.4	56.4	54.2	53.1	788.0
1997	47.2	43.1	48.6	50.1	48.1	45.3	45.1	45.5	50.9	49.6	44.3	46.2	588.0
1998	46.3	45.2	47.4	44.8	45.4	49.0	46.0	45.0	45.9	45.9	40.5	43.9	647.0
1999[1]	40.5	45.4	43.8	40.3	42.5	47.1	37.8	40.1	42.0	42.8	41.1	39.8	503.2

[1] Preliminary. *Source: U.S. Geological Survey (USGS)*

Average Price of Zinc, Prime Western Slab (Delivered U.S. Basis) In Cents Per Pound

Year	Jan.	Feb.	Mar.	Apr.	May	June	July	Aug.	Sept.	Oct.	Nov.	Dec.	Total
1990	71.33	66.47	77.37	83.12	87.38	87.38	86.54	82.45	81.00	72.30	70.00	70.00	77.95
1991	70.00	64.53	62.00	62.00	62.00	62.00	62.00	NQ	NQ	50.44	54.85	59.22	60.90
1992	57.62	56.40	60.19	64.12	66.83	67.29	64.57	66.47	67.12	57.84	52.16	52.71	61.11
1993	52.70	53.18	49.72	50.07	49.27	46.75	46.90	45.08	44.54	46.21	46.54	48.69	48.30
1994	49.64	48.29	46.70	46.16	47.66	48.42	48.81	48.26	50.55	53.81	58.64	57.41	50.36
1995	60.11	55.44	54.84	56.08	54.61	53.08	53.75	52.00	50.77	50.42	52.52	51.60	53.77
1996	51.35	51.86	52.66	51.03	50.76	49.75	49.86	51.22	51.11	51.76	53.81	53.78	51.58
1997	55.64	59.82	63.28	62.62	65.65	67.78	75.29	80.89	78.96	62.55	57.83	54.45	65.40
1998	51.86	54.24	51.98	54.31	52.77	50.78	52.23	51.64	50.29	47.63	48.74	48.44	51.24
1999	47.29	51.11	51.68	51.07	52.20	50.35	53.73	56.45	59.12	57.07	56.91	58.75	53.81

NQ = No Quote. *Source: American Metal Market (AMM)*